S0-ABD-523

CRITICAL SURVEY OF

Long Fiction

Fourth Edition

CRITICAL SURVEY OF

Long Fiction

Fourth Edition

Volume 4

Hamlin Garland—Aldous Huxley

Editor

Carl Rollyson

Baruch College, City University of New York

SALEM PRESS

Pasadena, California Hackensack, New Jersey

Cover photo: Maxim Gorki (The Granger Collection, New York)

Some of the essays in this work, which have been updated, originally appeared in the following Salem Press publications: *Critical Survey of Long Fiction, English Language Series* (1983), *Critical Survey of Long Fiction, Foreign Language Series* (1984), *Critical Survey of Long Fiction, Supplement* (1987), *Critical Survey of Long Fiction, English Language Series, Revised Edition* (1991; preceding volumes edited by Frank N. Magill), *Critical Survey of Long Fiction, Second Revised Edition* (2000; edited by Carl Rollyson).

∞ The paper used in these volumes conforms to the American National Standard for Permanence of Paper for Printed Library Materials, Z39.48-1992 (R1997).

Library of Congress Cataloging-in-Publication Data

Critical survey of long fiction / editor, Carl Rollyson. — 4th ed.
p. cm.
Includes bibliographical references and index.
ISBN 978-1-58765-535-7 (set : alk. paper) — ISBN 978-1-58765-536-4 (vol. 1 : alk. paper) — ISBN 978-1-58765-537-1 (vol. 2 : alk. paper) — ISBN 978-1-58765-538-8 (vol. 3 : alk. paper) — ISBN 978-1-58765-539-5 (vol. 4 : alk. paper) — ISBN 978-1-58765-540-1 (vol. 5 : alk. paper) — ISBN 978-1-58765-541-8 (vol. 6 : alk. paper) — ISBN 978-1-58765-542-5 (vol. 7 : alk. paper) — ISBN 978-1-58765-543-2 (vol. 8 : alk. paper) — ISBN 978-1-58765-544-9 (vol. 9 : alk. paper) — ISBN 978-1-58765-545-6 (vol. 10 : alk. paper)
1. Fiction—History and criticism. 2. Fiction—Bio-bibliography—Dictionaries. 3. Authors—Biography—Dictionaries. I. Rollyson, Carl E. (Carl Edmund)
PN3451.C75 2010
809.3—dc22

2009044410

First Printing

PRINTED IN CANADA

CONTENTS

COMPLETE LIST OF CONTENTS

Volume 1

Volume 2

Volume 3

Volume 4

Volume 5

Volume 6

Volume 7

Volume 8

Volume 9

Volume 10

PRONUNCIATION KEY

Foreign and unusual or ambiguous English-language names of profiled authors may be unfamiliar to some users of the *Critical Survey of Long Fiction*. To help readers pronounce such names correctly, phonetic spellings using the character symbols listed below appear in parentheses immediately after the first mention of the author's name in the narrative text. Stressed syllables are indicated in capital letters, and syllables are separated by hyphens.

VOWEL SOUNDS

Symbol	*Spelled (Pronounced)*
a	answer (AN-suhr), laugh (laf), sample (SAM-puhl), that (that)
ah	father (FAH-thur), hospital (HAHS-pih-tuhl)
aw	awful (AW-fuhl), caught (kawt)
ay	blaze (blayz), fade (fayd), waiter (WAYT-ur), weigh (way)
eh	bed (behd), head (hehd), said (sehd)
ee	believe (bee-LEEV), cedar (SEE-dur), leader (LEED-ur), liter (LEE-tur)
ew	boot (bewt), lose (lewz)
i	buy (bi), height (hit), lie (li), surprise (sur-PRIZ)
ih	bitter (BIH-tur), pill (pihl)
o	cotton (KO-tuhn), hot (hot)
oh	below (bee-LOH), coat (koht), note (noht), wholesome (HOHL-suhm)
oo	good (good), look (look)
ow	couch (kowch), how (how)
oy	boy (boy), coin (koyn)
uh	about (uh-BOWT), butter (BUH-tuhr), enough (ee-NUHF), other (UH-thur)

CONSONANT SOUNDS

Symbol	*Spelled (Pronounced)*
ch	beach (beech), chimp (chihmp)
g	beg (behg), disguise (dihs-GIZ), get (geht)
j	digit (DIH-juht), edge (ehj), jet (jeht)
k	cat (kat), kitten (KIH-tuhn), hex (hehks)
s	cellar (SEHL-ur), save (sayv), scent (sehnt)
sh	champagne (sham-PAYN), issue (IH-shew), shop (shop)
ur	birth (burth), disturb (dihs-TURB), earth (urth), letter (LEH-tur)
y	useful (YEWS-fuhl), young (yuhng)
z	business (BIHZ-nehs), zest (zehst)
zh	vision (VIH-zhuhn)

CRITICAL SURVEY OF

Long Fiction

Fourth Edition

HAMLIN GARLAND

Born: West Salem, Wisconsin; September 14, 1860
Died: Hollywood, California; March 4, 1940
Also known as: Hannibal Hamlin Garland

PRINCIPAL LONG FICTION

Jason Edwards: An Average Man, 1892
A Little Norsk, 1892
A Member of the Third House, 1892
A Spoil of Office, 1892
Rose of Dutcher's Coolly, 1895
The Spirit of Sweetwater, 1898 (reissued as *Witch's Gold*, 1906)
Boy Life on the Prairie, 1899
The Eagle's Heart, 1900
Her Mountain Lover, 1901
The Captain of the Gray-Horse Troop, 1902
Hesper, 1903
The Light of the Star, 1904
The Tyranny of the Dark, 1905
The Long Trail, 1907
Money Magic, 1907 (reissued as *Mart Haney's Mate*, 1922)
The Moccasin Ranch, 1909
Cavanagh, Forest Ranger, 1910
Victor Ollnee's Discipline, 1911
The Forester's Daughter, 1914

OTHER LITERARY FORMS

Hamlin Garland published in nearly every literary form—short story, biography, autobiography, essay, drama, and poetry. Several of his short stories, such as "Under the Lion's Paw," "A Soldier's Return," and "A Branch Road," were much anthologized. His autobiographical quartet, *A Son of the Middle Border* (1917), *A Daughter of the Middle Border* (1921), *Trail-Makers of the Middle Border* (1926), and *Back-Trailers from the Middle Border* (1928), is a valuable recounting of life during the latter part of the nineteenth century through the early twentieth century. Garland also wrote about psychic phenomena in such books as *Forty Years of Psychic Research: A Plain Narrative of Fact* (1936).

ACHIEVEMENTS

Hamlin Garland was a pioneer in moving American literature from Romanticism to realism. His early works of frontier life on the Middle Border (the midwestern prairie states of Wisconsin, Iowa, Minnesota, and Nebraska, as well as the Dakotas) made his reputation, and even today he is best known for his strongly regional, unpretentious pictures of the brutalizing life on the farms and in the isolated communities of the monotonous prairie lands.

Even though his reception as a writer did not afford him the financial rewards he sought, Garland was an active participant in the literary scene in Chicago and New York. He traveled widely in the United States and made the obligatory trip to Europe. He counted among his friends and acquaintances such literary giants as William Dean Howells, Mark Twain, George Bernard Shaw, and Rudyard Kipling, and others such as Bliss Carmen, Kate Wiggins, George Washington Cable, and Frank Norris (whom he regarded as a promising young writer).

While Garland published stories in magazines such as *The Arena*, *Circle*, and *Century*, he augmented his income by lecturing, often at the University of Chicago. He was instrumental in organizing and perpetuating literary clubs and organizations such as the National Institute of Arts and Letters, the MacDowell Club, The Players, and the Cliff Dwellers Club. When his fiction-writing skills began to abate in his late middle age, Garland wrote plays, articles about psychic phenomena in magazines such as *Everybody's*, and his memoirs. The popular reception of his autobiographical quartet on the Middle Border region revived his confidence in his writing ability, and he won the Pulitzer Prize for the second of the quartet, *A Daughter of the Middle Border*.

Though Garland wrote several novels after his critically noteworthy Middle Border novel *Rose of Dutcher's Coolly*, they were mostly set in the Far West and dealt with cowboys, American Indians, and rangers; compared to his earlier work, they can be considered strictly commercial potboilers.

Primarily a gifted short-story writer, Garland had difficulty sustaining a narrative for the length of a novel.

With the exception of *Rose of Dutcher's Coolly*, Garland is to be remembered more for what he accomplished as a writer of short stories and autobiography than for what he produced as a novelist. He was elected to the board of directors of the American Academy of Arts and Letters in 1918 and, in 1922, he won the Pulitzer Prize for biography and autobiography.

Biography

Hamlin Garland's early years were spent on an Iowa farm. As soon as he was big enough to walk behind a plow, he spent long hours helping to plow the acres of land on his father's farm. After twelve years of springs, summers, and early falls working at the ceaseless toil of farming, Garland came to realize that education was the way out of a life of farm drudgery. He attended and graduated from Cedar Valley Seminary. He next held a land claim in North Dakota for a year but mortgaged it to finance a trip to Boston, where he intended to enroll at Boston University. Once in Boston, he was unable to attend the university but continued his education by reading voraciously in the Boston Public Library. He also began to write at that time.

Hamlin Garland. (Library of Congress)

Garland's instincts for reform were ignited in Boston, where he joined the Anti-Poverty Society and, introduced to the work of Henry George, came to believe that the single tax theory was a solution to many contemporary social problems. He eventually returned to North Dakota and began to see some of his stories, sketches, and propagandistic novels published. By 1894, he had formulated in a series of essays his theory of realism, which he called "veritism."

Garland married Zulime Taft in 1899, and the couple had two daughters (in 1904 and 1907). He continued to write, but by 1898, he had begun to feel that he had exhausted "the field in which [he] found *Main-Travelled Roads* and *Rose of Dutcher's Coolly*." He believed that he had "lost perspective" on the life and characters of the Middle Border and had found new "creative strength" in the Colorado Hills, where he visited frequently.

By 1911, Garland believed that he had "done many things but nothing which now seems important." His various literary and cultural activities seemed to him to have been "time killers, diversions [adding] nothing to [his] reputation." At age fifty-two, he knew he had "but a slender and uncertain income." His home was mortgaged, his ranch unproductive, his health not particularly good, and he had "no confident expectation of increasing [his] fortune."

Then, after rejections from six editors, Garland finally sold *Son of the Middle Border* to *Collier's* magazine. His reputation was firmly established by 1918 with his election to the board of directors of the American Academy of Arts and Letters and then later with winning the Pulitzer Prize. In 1930, he built a home in the Laughlin Park area of Los Angeles, probably to be near his two married daughters. He died in 1940 of a cerebral hemorrhage.

Analysis

Hamlin Garland's theory of literature, detailed in his book *Crumbling Idols: Twelve Essays on Art* (1894), grew out of two concepts formulated early in his writing career: "that truth has a higher quality than beauty, and that to spread the reign of justice should everywhere be the design and intent of the artist." This theory of veritism obligated him to write stories early in his career that he said were "not always pleasant, but . . . [were] generally true, and always provoke thought."

Garland wrote about "truth" that, for the most part, he had himself experienced. The "justice" he sought to perpetuate was simplified by a reformer's zeal. As a result, he produced a series of didactic early novels that often retell his life experiences in thin disguise. Later on, when he began to view writing as a business, churning out books and shorter pieces that were intentionally commercial, he wrote a series of safely inoffensive novels that were more romantic than realistic and that are consequently of little importance today.

A Spoil of Office

In his first novel, *A Spoil of Office*, Garland set out to write propaganda, or social protest. In it, he achieved greater continuity of plot than in many subsequent books, he included fewer digressions, and he realized his indisputable though not lofty aim. *A Spoil of Office* is one of his better novels.

It is the story of a hired man, Bradley Talcott, who, inspired by political activist Ida Wilbur, decides to make something of himself, to become more than he is. He goes back to school, then on to law school, and becomes in succession a lawyer, an Iowa state legislator, and ultimately a Congressman in Washington, D.C. He falls in love with and marries Ida, and together they work in the crusade for equal rights for everyone.

Garland showed in *A Spoil of Office* that corruption and inequality prevail in the legislative process. Prejudiced against the moneyed classes, Garland laid much of the injustice against the poor and average folk at the door of the well-to-do: Brad implies that the financially poorer legislators are the more honorable ones; that while living in a hovel is no more a guarantee of honesty than living in a brownstone is a "sure sign of a robber," it is a "tolerably safe inference."

Garland's own experiences and interests are reflected in Brad's fondness for oratory and Ida's alliances with various reform movements and organizations (the Grange, women's rights, the Farmers Alliance). In his youth, Garland had entertained the notion of an oratorical career; his reform activities under the influence of Benjamin O. Flowers, editor of the radical magazine *The Arena*, are well documented.

A Little Norsk

The "truth" of prairie living, its harshness and its prejudices, is seen in Garland's short novel of realistic incident, *A Little Norsk*. The story is about a Norwegian girl, Flaxen, adopted and reared by two bachelors. She grows up, well-loved by her adopted "father" and "uncle." When the two men find their paternal feelings changing to more romantic love, they wisely send her off to school. Flaxen, called so because of her blond hair, meets and marries an irresponsible young man and they soon have a child. The young man, hounded by gambling debts, flees them and his family; a drowning accident removes him permanently from Flaxen's life. She moves back with the older, fatherly bachelor, taking her baby daughter with her. The novel ends with the strong implication that she will marry the younger bachelor.

In spite of a contrived plot, the novel is a realistic portrayal of the harshness of life on the prairie. Garland describes the blizzard that kills Flaxen's parents, conveying the terror that uncontrollable natural phenomena brought to the hapless prairie settlers. Although often romanticized for the benefit of those who had never experienced it, a blizzard on the isolated prairie was the harbinger of possible death. When a death occurs, as it does in *A Little Norsk*, there is the gruesome prospect of the dead bodies being attacked by hungry mice and even wolves—a prospect that Garland does not fail to dramatize.

Garland shows how Scandinavian women were treated by "native-born" American men when Flaxen occasionally encounters the village men who wink at her and pinch her. The two bachelors are aware that "the treatment that the Scandinavians' women git from the Yankees" is not nearly as respectful as that which Yankee women can expect. Ironically, Garland himself was probably guilty of such prejudices, because many of his fictional and autobiographical works reveal a condescending, patronizing attitude toward blacks, a disregard for hired hands (unless they are main characters, such as Brad Talcott), and an apparent dislike for immigrants such as Germans, Scandinavians, and Jews. (In *Rose of Dutcher's Coolly*, a character says of another, "he's a Jew, but he's not too much of a Jew.") *A Little Norsk* thus documents both the harsh physical realities and the purely human harshness and prejudice of prairie life.

Rose of Dutcher's Coolly

Garland's most sustained novel is *Rose of Dutcher's Coolly*. At the time of its publication in 1895, it was a most daring book, primarily because it treats rather openly the sexual misdemeanors of adolescents. To a modern reader, however, Garland's treatment of this subject will appear markedly restrained and even genteel, hardly in keeping with his resolve to tell the truth without evasion or prettification.

Rose, a motherless child, spends her infancy and early childhood with her father on their farm. She grows up hearing and seeing things that many children are never confronted with: the "mysterious processes of generation and birth" with a "terrifying power to stir and develop passions prematurely"; obscene words among the farm hands; "vulgar cackling of old women"; courtship, birth, and death. She goes to her father with all her questions and he, with sometimes blundering answers, manages to keep her from becoming too curious too soon. When the time comes in her teenage years when she can no longer hold her feelings in check, she, like other youngsters, experiments with sex. She tells her father, and he, by appealing to her love for him and his wish that she be a good girl, staves off further episodes.

Rose is interested in reading and writing, and Doctor Thatcher, who visits her school, is so impressed by her that he promises to try to help her get into a college-preparatory school. Though her father is reluctant, she is finally allowed to go. Once there, she—now a beautiful young woman—has many suitors but is not interested in them beyond friendship. She wishes for a life of intellectual activity and creative writing. Finishing the seminary, she goes to Chicago, again with her father's reluctant approval. There she meets and falls in love with Mason. After overcoming his disinclination to marry, Mason finally proposes to Rose.

Rose of Dutcher's Coolly has been called Garland's best novel. He dared to speak frankly about natural, common occurrences in a sincere, sensible way. This blunt approach was perhaps what shocked his first readers; apparently they were unprepared to face in print those things about which they hardly talked and never in mixed company. Libraries ruled out the book, calling it "unsafe reading." Yet, even with these realistic elements, the book does not live up to its promise because Garland, as usual, romanticizes his "beautiful" heroine. Rose is nevertheless, a heroine fit to share the stage with Stephen Crane's Maggie and Theodore Dreiser's Sister Carrie.

The Captain of the Gray-Horse Troop

One of Garland's most successful novels is a romanticized story of the Far West, *The Captain of the Gray-Horse Troop*. Captain George Curtis, surveying the mountainous land he has come to love, sums up the novel's plot elements when he says to his sister Jennie, "Yes, it's all here, Jennie . . . the wild country, the Indian, the gallant scout, and the tender maiden." Add the noble captain and the villainous ranchers, and the mix that makes the story is complete.

Unlike Garland's earlier novels set in the Middle Border, *The Captain of the Gray-Horse Troop* is realistic primarily in the sense that it deals with a genuine problem (the encroachment on Native American lands and rights by avaricious Caucasians). Intentionally or not, it also reveals the whites' attitude of superiority in regard to the American Indian. Curtis is a good and honorable man, yet he can say, having learned of a barbaric execution of an Indian, "It's a little difficult to eliminate violence from an inferior race when such cruelty is manifested in those we call their teachers." Earlier he remarks of the Indians that "these people have no inner resources. They lop down when their accustomed props are removed. They come from defective stock."

This "superiority" is reflected elsewhere throughout the novel: in the unintentionally ironic comment describing "a range of hills which separate the white man's country from the Tetong reservation," and in comments such as "A Mexican can't cook no more'n an Injun." Yet Garland has Captain Curtis, unaware of his own prejudice, remark about another character who is blatantly anti-Native American that she is "well-schooled in race hatred." Written in the stilted style more reminiscent of the genteel tradition than of the veritism Garland espoused in his earlier years, *The Captain of the Gray-Horse Troop* truthfully depicts relations between American Indians and Caucasians in the nineteenth century. Interestingly enough, all the white characters, even those who, like Curtis, want to help the Indians and thwart their persecutors, seem to believe that the Indians are at best very low on the social scale.

The significance of this novel today may well lie not in the story of one white man's attempt to secure justice for the oppressed Indians but rather in its revelation of the bigoted attitudes of whites toward nonwhites. In its time, the book sold very well, going into several editions. It ultimately sold nearly 100,000 copies, Garland's largest sale. (Thirty years after publication it was still selling.) It received better reviews than Garland had hoped for, even from critics who had condemned his earlier books.

Apparently it was the success of this book (which had been considered during the height of its popularity for a motion-picture production) that convinced Garland that his earlier Middle Border stories would never bring him financial success. It is not difficult to understand why the remainder of his novels were like *The Captain of the Gray-Horse Troop*, though less successful.

Garland's subsequent literary output offers little that is memorable. His reputation in American literature rests primarily on his work as a short-story writer and autobiographer. An early realist, he also had a naturalistic bent. His earlier works, up to and including *Rose of Dutcher's Coolly*, show that individuals are controlled by the "outer constraints of environment and circumstance" as well as by the "inner constraints of instinct and passion." Garland uses local color not to caricature or make fun of his characters but to make his work more realistic and true to nature. The social elements he includes help to provide the significance he felt all literature must have to survive. The impressionistic tendencies seen in certain very subjective descriptions indicate a concern for "individualism as the coloring element of a literature." His minor lapses into romantic sentimentality and genteel restraint (typified by his habit of referring to "legs" as "limbs") are in themselves evidence of this same individualism; his restraint demonstrates his personal reluctance to be unnecessarily graphic in describing certain aspects of life. Still he was forthright in delineating most of his subjects. Garland's early novels are, for the most part, fine examples of his veritistic theory.

American literature is indebted to Garland for the stronger realism and the wealth of social history he contributed. It is not difficult to applaud Garland's early novels. He set out to show truth in time, place, people, and incident. He sought to bring social significance to his work. He succeeded in several novels before succumbing to commercialism and the desire or need to be not only a good writer but also a financially successful one.

Jane L. Ball

Other major works

SHORT FICTION: *Main-Travelled Roads: Six Mississippi Valley Stories*, 1891; *Prairie Folks*, 1893; *Wayside Courtships*, 1897; *Other Main-Travelled Roads*, 1910; *They of the High Trails*, 1916; *The Book of the American Indian*, 1923.

PLAY: *Under the Wheel: A Modern Play in Six Scenes*, pb. 1890.

POETRY: *Prairie Songs*, 1893.

NONFICTION: *Crumbling Idols: Twelve Essays on Art*, 1894; *Ulysses S. Grant: His Life and Character*, 1898; *Out-of-Door Americans*, 1901; *A Son of the Middle Border*, 1917; *A Daughter of the Middle Border*, 1921; *Trail-Makers of the Middle Border*, 1926; *The Westward March of American Settlement*, 1927; *Back-Trailers from the Middle Border*, 1928; *Roadside Meetings*, 1930; *Companions on the Trail: A Literary Chronicle*, 1931; *My Friendly Contemporaries: A Literary Log*, 1932; *Afternoon Neighbors*, 1934; *Joys of the Trail*, 1935; *Forty Years of Psychic Research: A Plain Narrative of Fact*, 1936; *Selected Letters of Hamlin Garland*, 1998 (Keith Newlin and Joseph B. McCullough, editors).

Bibliography

Foote, Stephanie. "The Region of the Repressed and the Return of the Region: Hamlin Garland and Harold Frederic." In *Regional Fictions: Culture and Identity in Nineteenth-Century American Literature*. Madison: University of Wisconsin Press, 2001. Garland is among several novelists whom Foote defines as a "regionalist." She argues that Americans' conceptions of local identity originated with Garland and other regional fiction writers of the late nineteenth and early twentieth centuries.

Joseph, Philip. "The Artist Meets the Literary Community: Hamlin Garland, Sarah Orne Jewett, and the

Writing of 1890's Regionalism." In *American Literary Regionalism in a Global Age*. Baton Rouge: Louisiana State University Press, 2007. Joseph analyzes works of literary regionalism, including Garland's novel *A Spoil of Office* and some of his short stories and nonfiction, to determine if these works remain relevant in the modern global world. He concludes that Garland and other regionalists share a belief that local communities can benefit from global contact.

Kaye, Frances. "Hamlin Garland's Feminism." In *Women and Western Literature*, edited by Helen Winter Stauffer and Susan Rosowski. Troy, N.Y.: Whitston, 1982. Kaye discusses Garland's feminism, identifying him as the only male author of note at the end of the nineteenth century who spoke in favor of women's rights, including suffrage and equality in marriage.

McCullough, Joseph. *Hamlin Garland*. Boston: Twayne, 1978. This study follows Garland through his literary career, dividing it into phases, with major attention to the first phase of his reform activities and the midwestern stories. Includes a primary bibliography and a select, annotated secondary bibliography.

Nagel, James, ed. *Critical Essays on Hamlin Garland*. Boston: G. K. Hall, 1982. Nagel's introduction surveys the critical responses to Garland's work. This volume is especially rich in reviews of Garland's books, and it also includes twenty-six biographical and critical essays.

Newlin, Keith. *Hamlin Garland: A Life*. Lincoln: University of Nebraska Press, 2008. Newlin's biography of Garland, the first to be published in more than forty years, is based in part on previously unavailable letters, manuscripts, and family memoirs. Discusses Garland's contributions to literature and places Garland's work within the artistic context of its time. Includes notes, an index, a list of Garland's works, and illustrations.

Petty, Leslie. "Expanding the Vision of Feminist Activism: Frances E. W. Harper's *Iola Leroy* and Hamlin Garland's *A Spoil of Office*." In *Romancing the Vote: Feminist Activism in American Fiction, 1870-1920*. Athens: University of Georgia Press, 2006. Petty analyzes Garland's book and several other novels about politically active women and discusses how these books influenced the women's rights movement of the late nineteenth and early twentieth centuries.

Pizer, Donald. *Hamlin Garland's Early Work and Career*. Berkeley: University of California Press, 1960. Pizer treats in careful detail Garland's intellectual and artistic development during the first phase of his literary and reformist career, from 1884 to 1895. He discusses Garland's development of his creed, his literary output, and reform activities in society, theater, politics, and the arts. Includes a detailed bibliography of Garland's publications during these years.

Silet, Charles, Robert Welch, and Richard Boudreau, eds. *The Critical Reception of Hamlin Garland, 1891-1978*. Troy, N.Y.: Whitston, 1985. This illustrated volume contains thirty-three essays that illustrate the development of Garland's literary reputation from 1891 to 1978. The introduction emphasizes the difficulty critics have had trying to determine the quality of Garland's art.

Taylor, Walter Fuller. *The Economic Novel in America*. 3d ed. New York: Octagon Books, 1973. Taylor examines Garland's work in the context of fiction that reflects economic issues and trends. He sees in Garland's literary career a reflection of the fall of pre-American Civil War agrarian democracy with the halting of the advance of the frontier and the decline of populism.

GEORGE GARRETT

Born: Orlando, Florida; June 11, 1929
Died: Charlottesville, Virginia; May 25, 2008
Also known as: George Palmer Garrett, Jr.

Principal long fiction

The Finished Man, 1959
Which Ones Are the Enemy?, 1961
Do, Lord, Remember Me, 1965
Death of the Fox, 1971
The Succession, 1983
Poison Pen, 1986
Entered from the Sun, 1990
The King of Babylon Shall Not Come Against You, 1996
Double Vision, 2004

Other literary forms

In addition to his novels, George Garrett published several volumes of poems and collections of short stories. He also wrote plays, screenplays, and a biography of James Jones, and he edited or coedited many books about literature.

Achievements

George Garrett served as poetry editor of the *Transatlantic Review*, coeditor of *The Hollins Critic*, and contributing editor to *Contempora* and *Film Journal*. He received a fellowship in poetry from the *Sewanee Review*, the Prix de Rome from the American Academy of Arts and Letters, a Ford Foundation grant, a Guggenheim grant, a grant from the National Endowment for the Arts, and an award in literature from the Academy and Institute for the Arts. In 2005, the Fellowship of Southern Writers presented Garrett with the Cleanth Brooks Medal for Lifetime Achievement.

Biography

George Palmer Garrett, Jr., was born in Orlando, Florida, in 1929, the son of George Palmer and Rosalie Roomer Garrett. He attended Sewanee Military Academy and the Hill School before entering Princeton University in 1947, from which he graduated with a B.A. degree in 1952, the year in which he also married Susan Parrish Jackson. The couple would have three children: William, George, and Alice. Garrett served in the U.S. Army before returning to Princeton for his master's degree in 1956. In 1985, he was awarded a Ph.D. in literature from his alma mater. Garrett taught writing and literature and served as writer-in-residence at Wesleyan University, Rice University, the University of Virginia, Princeton, Hollins College, the University of South Carolina, and the University of Michigan.

Garrett's death on May 25, 2008, was followed by an outpouring of tributes to his work from critics and fellow writers. Most praised two features of his long career: his constant and successful experimentations in the form and content of his fiction and his trenchant and sophisticated literary criticism. It is likely that a full assessment of his literary career—now in its nascent stages—will concentrate on these two elements of his work.

Analysis

George Garrett's career as a novelist was divided into two stages, with distinct changes in style, subject material, and characterization coming at the beginning of his monumental Elizabethan trilogy. His early novels are essentially traditional American novels of the mid-twentieth century. They explore American life—mostly life in the South—with a mixture of smiling humor and serious concern about contemporary social issues. The characters of Garrett's early novels are people caught up in social and political troubles that threaten their senses of identity and self-worth. In these early novels, the press of a corrupting world intrudes on deeply principled characters who sometimes buckle or break under the onslaught. Garrett's *Do, Lord, Remember Me* is a transitional novel. It retains his established technique of blending humorous and serious themes in a straightforward narrative line, but it points a new direction in its narrative voice. The story is told from the points of view of several of the novel's characters. Garrett had been experimenting with this device in his three previous volumes of short stories, and he carried the technique to full flower in his Elizabethan trilogy of novels: *Death of the Fox*, *The Succession*, and *Entered from the Sun*.

The Finished Man

Garrett's first novel, *The Finished Man*, published in 1959, is a southern political novel in the tradition of Robert Penn Warren's *All the King's Men* (1946). The central character, Mike Royle, is a man embroiled in the sins and deceits of a political system that is fearfully inhumane and racist, a system that is a travesty of Jeffersonian democracy. Royle works in the reelection campaign of an unprincipled senator whose cynical opportunism brings about his ultimate downfall. Also, Royle is witness to the failure of his father, a highly moral, charitable judge who is betrayed by his own vision and by the corrupt politics around him. Royle hopes to learn about society and himself using these two failed lives as object lessons. What Royle actually learns is that the complexities of human motives are most often undiscoverable and that evil often seems to have a life and body of its own. At the end of the novel, Royle attempts to discover meaning through an inspection of the lives of his forebears. Here Garrett touches on that American version of Shintoism that is a mainstay of the southern novel. Much of *The Finished Man* is told through periodic flashbacks that enliven the psychological portraits of the main characters.

Do, Lord, Remember Me

Do, Lord, Remember Me tells the story of evangelist Red Smalley and his perverse entourage of friends and lovers as they tour the American South with their revival show, fleecing the rubes and causing noisy trouble. Garrett succinctly catalogs the misbehavior on the tent-revival trail—the dramatically phony faith healings, the sexual escapades of the brothers and sisters of the mad faith, and the sleazy magic tricks designed to bilk the naïve believers. Red Smalley is no comic stereotype preacher, however; he is a complex man pulled in opposite directions and pulled apart. He wants to be a true man of God, but he loves being a charlatan and a drunk. He believes his own propaganda from the makeshift pulpit, but he cannot bring himself to live the Faith that he prescribes for others. The members of Smalley's revival crew, an ungodly collection of misfits, are similarly conflicted. They want to be what they cannot be, what they will not allow themselves to be.

This complex novel is told from several narrative points of view, with all of the main characters telling their own versions of the novel's tumultuous events and interrelationships. Like Smalley, the other narrators are troubled by one overriding realization. They all are trying to escape the inescapable truth that forms the core of the novel: Human beings are inherently evil, and the institutions that they create and support are shot through with that evil.

In many ways *Do, Lord, Remember Me* is a testing ground for the large fictional techniques that pervade Garrett's Elizabethan cycle. The novel's choric narrative technique, the use of interior monologues, and the employment of various typography devices are expanded and supplemented in the three Elizabethan novels.

Garrett's first assumption about historical fiction was that a given historical period or event or character is locked in time; it has a definable beginning, middle, and end. Nevertheless, inside that static frame, he believed, the novelist may create a limitless theater for the individual and collective human imagination. In his essay "Dreaming with Adam: Notes on Imaginary History," Garrett defines this imagination about which he was writing: "The subject is the larger imagination, the possibility of imagining lives and spirits of other human beings, living and dead, without assaulting their essential and, anyway, ineffable mystery, to dream again in recapitulation the dream of Adam, knowing, as he did not until he awoke that it is true."

Death of the Fox

Death of the Fox, the first novel in Garrett's Elizabethan cycle, centers on the final days of the adventurer Sir Walter Ralegh as he contemplates his beheading. Ralegh was a poet, explorer, courtier, and politician, and one of Queen Elizabeth's favorites. Ralegh's flamboyant personality dominates the novel. His story is told by Ralegh himself, James I, Henry Velverton, and others. These multiple narrations are blends of memory and imagination, so that interior monologues are bonded into recollections of historical events, people, and the familiar objects of everyday life. This blend allows the narration to travel back and forth in time and space, creating a fictional mosaic that finally combines into a portrait of the life and death of Ralegh. As Garrett portrays him, Ralegh is the embodiment of the spirit of the English Renaissance. He is a man who strives for moral and spiritual autonomy yet one who is swept into the intrigues of a complex political system that he cannot understand or control.

Garrett's encyclopedic knowledge of the Elizabethan and Jacobean periods brings forth many fascinating details of Ralegh's times. In the novel are discussions of types of English beer, theaters, common utensils, clothing, foods, manners, ships, household pests, illnesses, and other incidentals of daily life. The cataloging of ordinary objects and concerns fastens the novel into a concrete reality that serves as the foundation for the actions and imaginings of the characters. Garrett's concentration on exact details of daily life illustrates a major theme in all of his fiction. He consistently turned to topical subjects to serve as kelson and ballast for his writing.

The Succession

A dozen years after the appearance of *Death of the Fox*, Garrett published *The Succession*, a big novel that chronicles the last days of Queen Elizabeth and the succession of King James I to the throne of England. As in earlier novels, Garrett uses the multiple-narrator technique. Separate parts of the novel are told through the letters of Elizabeth and James, by a courtier, a priest, an actor who was involved in Essex's rebellion, and others of low and high caste.

As the novel begins, Elizabeth, now an old and dying woman, is contemplating her successor. She has kept James of Scotland dangling—and thereby has kept the armies of Scotland at bay. She has put down rebellion and imminent civil war with her intelligence and political cunning. On her deathbed, however, she is pondering larger issues. She concerns herself with the mysteries of mortality and immortality. The novel travels from idea to idea, from London to Scotland's castles and back, shuttling through time, as the narrators tell of their lives and their aspirations. As the novel ends, one of the speakers, a drunken plowman, shivering in the cold of a December night in 1602, says that he is "fearful of nothing, not past or future." Speaking into the dark, he wishes his dying queen a good night. Garrett's narrative voices create here what he referred to as "simultaneity." He wrote, "I was trying to deal in different ways with a variety of characters, some of whom really don't cause large things to happen in history but are a part of the whole picture."

Poison Pen

In 1986, Garrett interrupted the Elizabethan cycle with the publication of the stinging satirical novel *Poison Pen*. This work is composed mostly of letters written by a failed academic, John Towne, who gives false names as signatures to his poison-pen letters. (This same John Towne is a character in Garrett's manuscript novel "Life with Kim Novak Is Hell," which was in progress for decades but never published.) Another level of fictional complexity is added: Towne's letters are collected and annotated by yet another failed academic, Lee Holmes, the "oldest Assistant Professor" at "Nameless College," a man who is desperate to publish something—just anything.

The bitter letters are addressed to various public figures and celebrities—actor Brooke Shields, model Cheryl Tiegs, politician Barry Goldwater, and a dozen others. Now and then, author Garrett intrudes with direct commentary, most notably when he accuses a noted editor and writer of plagiarism and in a long autobiographical letter to model Christie Brinkley in which Garrett declares that he is the leading candidate for the "Tomb of the Unknown American Writer."

In praising the satirical bite of *Poison Pen*, Thomas Fleming, writing for the *National Review*, compared the novel to Alexander Pope's *The Dunciad* (1728-1743): "Like Pope Garrett is merciless on the pretensions of intellectual life . . . and like Pope, too, he combines a reactionary social vision with a relentless contempt for dullness."

Entered from the Sun

Entered from the Sun, the third and concluding volume in Garrett's Elizabethan cycle, investigates the unsolved mystery of the death of famous poet and playwright Christopher Marlowe, who was killed in a pub brawl in 1593. In this novel, the fictional characters Joseph Hunnyman, an actor, and Captain Barfoot, a war-scarred soldier, are hired by unnamed people to uncover the intrigues behind Marlowe's murder. Hunnyman and Barfoot are joined by two other narrators, the beautiful widow Alysoun and an unsuccessful playwright, Cartwright.

The rare genius Marlowe was an enigmatic character in practically all ways. He may have been an outlawed Papist; he may have been a militant anti-Catholic, an atheist; and he may have been spying for Queen Elizabeth—or her enemies. In the course of the novel, Garrett shows that the Elizabethan Age is one of dramatic political intrigue, a time, as he puts it, when "half the people in England are spying on the other half." The narrators point out time and again that much of Elizabethan life is a life of illusion. Actor Hunnyman proposes, for example, that the drama of pretense, violence, and bombast sounding from the London stage serves as microcosm for English society at large. At the novel's end, the mystery is not solved; instead, it is deepened by the crosscurrents of illusion.

In his "Author's Farewell" at the conclusion of *Entered from the Sun*, Garrett expresses his feelings about the trilogy: "I hope that I shall always be able, for as long as I live, to go back to the Elizabethans for delight and instruction. I hope that I will not cease to visit that age and my old friends and enemies who live there. It seems that I could not even if I wanted to."

The King of Babylon Shall Not Come Against You

In 1996 Garrett published *The King of Babylon Shall Not Come Against You*, a novel that partly fulfills his ambition to "measure the impact of Martin Luther King's assassination on a Florida town." The town is Paradise Springs in central Florida, once a backwater farming community, now a town being transformed by commercial and real estate development. The novel's central character, a journalist named Bill Tone, returns to his hometown hoping to write a true-crime book about three murders that occurred there in 1968 during the week of the King assassination. The novel is told by several narrators, including Tone, who tells of the town's past (in sections titled "Then and There") and of the town's present (in sections titled "Here and Now"). Diverse characters—librarians, a real estate developer, a successful black lawyer, a poet, a newspaper editor, an English professor, and Tone himself—tell their parts of what becomes a murder mystery. They also comment on the life, career, and death of Martin Luther King, Jr.

Garrett's experiments in tone and voice here create unity, a unity that is described in typical Garrett playfulness by Bill Tone's advice to the poet who is struggling with the organization of his novel about King. Tone tells the poet, "Why not put King at the center and then tell the story from all three points of view—the assassin, the advisers, the disciple?" In this work Garrett returns to the setting of his first novel, *The Finished Man*, published almost four decades before. The straightforward narration of the earlier novel, however, is replaced here by diverse voices and shifting time elements.

Double Vision

Garrett's last novel, *Double Vision*, revisits some of the narrative devices of his 1986 novel *Poison Pen*. In *Double Vision*, a character named George Garrett, himself a writer and literary critic, is asked to review a biography of the novelist Peter Taylor, who in real life was author George Garrett's friend and neighbor in Charlottesville, Virginia. Garrett the author then invents literary surrogates for Garrett and Taylor the characters. Taylor becomes the fictional character Aubrey Carver, and Garrett becomes the fictional character Frank Toomer. Thus the author creates two sets of doubles in *Double Vision*. Carver is at the end of his life and has completed his last work, a novel set at the time of the 1893 World's Fair in Chicago, and Toomer is writing a fictional account of the life of the Elizabethan poet and playwright Robert Greene. Echoes from the past abound here: Garrett had planned to write what he called "an American Trilogy," one volume of which was to be set at the Chicago Fair in 1893. Also, Toomer's Robert Greene links to Garrett's fascination with the Elizabethan period.

Double Vision offers an intense look at the literary life as experienced by the characters, both real and imagined, who have devoted their careers to writing. In particular, the novel focuses on Garrett's examination of the state of American letters in the preceding fifty years. The characters discuss the notions of literary fame and obscurity, literary jealousies, and the torturous uncertainties of the American publishing industry. The satiric edge that is constant in Garrett's work reappears in *Double Vision*, taking as its frequent target the sorrows of the writer in American universities.

In a larger way, *Double Vision* is a meditation on aging and death. The physical life and the imaginative life in this novel are not separate entities but are frequently conjoined so that they become reflective of each other. Toomer and Carver are old men who have reached the summing up. In her review of *Double Vision*, novelist

Kelly Cherry writes that the novel is "the work of a writer at the height of his powers."

Charles Israel

Other major works

SHORT FICTION: *King of the Mountain*, 1958; *In the Briar Patch*, 1961; *Cold Ground Was My Bed Last Night*, 1964; *A Wreath for Garibaldi, and Other Stories*, 1969; *The Magic Striptease*, 1973; *An Evening Performance: New and Selected Stories*, 1985; *The Old Army Game: A Novel and Stories*, 1994; *A Story Goes with It*, 2004; *Empty Bed Blues*, 2006.

PLAYS: *Garden Spot, U.S.A.*, pr. 1962; *Sir Slob and the Princess: A Play for Children*, pb. 1962; *Enchanted Ground*, pb. 1981.

POETRY: *The Reverend Ghost*, 1957; *The Sleeping Gypsy, and Other Poems*, 1958; *Abraham's Knife, and Other Poems*, 1961; *For a Bitter Season: New and Selected Poems*, 1967; *Welcome to the Medicine Show: Postcards, Flashcards, Snapshots*, 1978; *Luck's Shining Child*, 1981; *The Collected Poems of George Garrett*, 1984; *Days of Our Lives Lie in Fragments: New and Old Poems, 1957-1997*, 1998.

SCREENPLAYS: *The Young Lovers*, 1964; *The Playground*, 1965; *Frankenstein Meets the Space Monster*, 1966 (with R. H. W. Dillard and John Rodenbeck).

NONFICTION: *James Jones*, 1984; *Understanding Mary Lee Settle*, 1988; *My Silk Purse and Yours: The Publishing Scene and American Literary Art*, 1992; *The Sorrows of Fat City: A Selection of Literary Essays and Reviews*, 1992; *Going to See the Elephant: Pieces of a Writing Life*, 2002 (Jeb Livingood, editor); *Southern Excursions: Views on Southern Letters in My Time*, 2003 (James Conrad McKinley, editor).

EDITED TEXTS: *New Writing from Virginia*, 1963; *The Girl in the Black Raincoat*, 1966; *Man and the Movies*, 1967 (with W. R. Robinson); *New Writing in South Carolina*, 1971 (with William Peden); *The Sounder Few: Essays from "The Hollins Critic,"* 1971 (with R. H. W. Dillard and John Moore); *Film Scripts One, Two, Three, and Four*, 1971-1972 (with O. B. Hardison, Jr., and Jane Gelfman); *Craft So Hard to Learn*, 1972 (with John Graham); *The Writer's Voice*, 1973 (with Graham); *The Botteghe Oscure Reader*, 1974 (with Katherine Garrison Biddle); *Intro 5*, 1974 (with Walton Beacham); *Intro 6: Life as We Know It*, 1974; *Intro 7: All of Us and None of You*, 1975; *Intro 8: The Liar's Craft*, 1977; *Intro 9: Close to Home*, 1979 (with Michael Mewshaw); *Elvis in Oz: New Stories and Poems from the Hollins Creative Writing Program*, 1992 (with Mary Flinn); *The Wedding Cake in the Middle of the Road: Twenty-three Variations on a Theme*, 1992 (with Susan Stamberg); *That's What I Like (About the South), and Other New Southern Stories for the Nineties*, 1993 (with Paul Ruffin); *The Yellow Shoe: Selected Poems, 1964-1999*, 1999.

MISCELLANEOUS: *Whistling in the Dark: True Stories and Other Fables*, 1992; *Bad Man Blues: A Portable George Garrett*, 1998.

Bibliography

Betts, Richard. "'To Dream of Kings': George Garrett's *The Succession*." *Mississippi Quarterly* 45 (Winter, 1991). Argues that Garrett's Elizabethan fiction has been unjustly overlooked by critics.

Clabough, Casey. *The Art of the Magic Striptease: The Literary Layers of George Garrett*. Gainesville: University Press of Florida, 2008. In-depth examination of Garrett's fiction draws on the author's private papers in discussing his experiments with genre and form. Includes an interview with Garrett as well as a previously unpublished short story.

Dillard, R. H. W. *Understanding George Garrett*. Columbia: University of South Carolina Press, 1988. First major critical work on Garrett contains individual chapters on *The Finished Man*, *Which Ones Are the Enemy?*, *Do, Lord, Remember Me*, and *Poison Pen*, as well as the historical novels. Supplemented with a bibliography.

Garrett, George. "Going to See the Elephant: Why We Write Stories." In *Bad Man Blues: A Portable George Garrett*. Dallas: Southern Methodist University Press, 1998. The author discusses growing up in a large family of storytellers and addresses the deeper motivation of storytelling, suggesting that the duty of the storyteller is like that of Pygmies hunting an elephant and then telling the story of the hunt.

Horvath, Brooke, and Irving Malin, eds. *George Garrett: The Elizabethan Trilogy*. Huntsville: Texas Review Press, 1998. Collection of essays focuses on a number of historical figures as they relate to Garrett's work, including Sir Walter Ralegh and Christopher Marlowe. Includes bibliography and index.

Mewshaw, Michael. "George Garrett and the Sweet Science of Fiction." *Sewanee Review* 110 (Summer, 2002): 267-273. Presents Mewshaw's recollections of Garrett as a teacher and mentor.

Robinson, W. R. "Imagining the Individual: George Garrett's *Death of the Fox.*" *Hollins Critic* 8 (1971): 1-12. Explores the mixture of fact and creation that is inherent in fiction and the historical novel in particular, with extensive quotations from Garrett on the subject. Argues that the quality of Garrett's work surpasses that of conventional historical fiction.

Rozett, Martha Tuck. "Constructing a World: How Postmodern Historical Fiction Reimagines the Past." *Clio* 25 (Winter, 1996): 145-164. Examines the experimental techniques used by authors of postmodern historical fiction. Includes discussion of Garrett's Elizabethan trilogy.

Spears, Monroe K. "George Garrett and the Historical Novel." *The Virginia Quarterly Review* 61, no. 2 (Spring, 1985): 262-276. Considers how closely *The Succession* and *Death of the Fox* correspond to the traditional definition of the historical novel.

Wier, Allen. "Skin and Bones: George Garrett's Living Spirits." In *Bad Man Blues: A Portable George Garrett*, by George Garrett. Dallas: Southern Methodist University Press, 1998. Introduction to collection of Garrett's work addresses the author's interest in the relationship between fact and fiction and the relationship between the present and the past. Comments on Garrett's experimentation with ways of telling stories.

ELIZABETH GASKELL

Born: Chelsea, London, England; September 29, 1810
Died: Holybourne, England; November 12, 1865
Also known as: Elizabeth Cleghorn Stevenson; Mrs. Gaskell; Cotton Mather Mills, Esq.

Principal long fiction

Mary Barton: A Tale of Manchester Life, 1848
Cranford, 1851-1853 (serial), 1853 (book)
Ruth, 1853
North and South, 1854-1855 (serial), 1855 (book)
A Dark Night's Work, 1863
Sylvia's Lovers, 1863
Cousin Phillis, 1863-1864 (serial), 1864 (book)
Wives and Daughters: An Every-Day Story, 1864-1866 (serial), 1866 (book)

Other literary forms

The novels of Elizabeth Gaskell (GAS-kehl) appeared in serial form in journals such as *Household Words* and *All the Year Round*, edited by Charles Dickens, and the *Cornhill Magazine*, edited by William Makepeace Thackeray. During the years of novel writing, she also published travel sketches, essays, and short stories. Her collections of stories that appeared in serial as well as hardcover form were *Lizzie Leigh, and Other Tales* (1855); *Round the Sofa* (1859), containing also the separate tales inset in "My Lady Ludlow"; *Right at Last, and Other Tales* (1860); *Lois the Witch, and Other Tales* (1861); and *Cousin Phillis, and Other Tales* (1865). Sketches of Manchester life appeared as *Life in Manchester* (1847) under the pseudonym Cotton Mather Mills, Esq. Gaskell's biography of Charlotte Brontë, still regarded as a standard source, appeared in 1857. The standard edition of Gaskell's work is the Knutsford edition (1906), which includes both fiction and nonfiction. *The Letters of Mrs. Gaskell* (1966) was edited by Arthur Pollard and J. A. V. Chapple.

Achievements

The reputation of Elizabeth Gaskell sank in the modernist reaction to Victorian literature in the post-World

War I period, and she was relegated to the status of a second or third-rate novelist, markedly inferior to Dickens, Thackeray, George Eliot, George Meredith, and Anthony Trollope, and even placed below Charles Kingsley and Wilkie Collins. With the reassessment of Victorian writers that has gone on since World War II, her reputation has risen, and the concerns of the feminist movement beginning in the 1970's led to such a revaluation that the scholar Patricia M. Spacks refers to her as "seriously underrated" in the twentieth century. Other women's movement writers, including Elaine Showalter, Jenni Calder, and Ellen Moers, have praised Gaskell for detailing faithfully in her fiction the relation between women and marriage, the struggle for self-achievement, and the intermixture of women's careers and public history. The sense in her work of women of all classes as victims of economic and social restrictions has caused scholars to study her work and life more closely. She has been elevated to the ranks of the major Victorian novelists.

BIOGRAPHY

Elizabeth Gaskell's life was divided between the industrial Midlands of the north and London and rural Hampshire in the south of England, as was that of her heroine, Margaret Hale, in *North and South*. Her mother's family, the Hollands, substantial landowners, were established near Knutsford, Cheshire, which became the "Cranford" of her best-known work. Gaskell was born Elizabeth Cleghorn Stevenson on September 29, 1810, in Chelsea, then just outside London, where the family had settled after a period in Scotland. Because of her mother's death, Gaskell was taken to Knutsford, where she spent the next thirteen years in the care of her aunt, Hannah Lumb. The years at Knutsford were very happy ones, and her affection for the town is indicated by the tales in *Cranford* about its inhabitants. Her brother, John, twelve years older, went into the merchant navy but disappeared on a voyage to the Far East in 1823, an event marked in Gaskell's fiction by various lost and recovered brothers.

Gaskell's father remarried, having two more children, and at age fourteen Gaskell was sent to Avonbank School in Stratford, which was kept by the Byerley sisters, her stepmother's aunts. It was a progressive school by Victorian standards of feminine education, serving Unitarian and other liberal religious groups. She left school at age seventeen to tend her paralyzed father, the relationship between the two having been somewhat strained in the preceding years. From 1827 until his death in 1829, she faithfully nursed him, her dedication to the task bringing forth a grateful testimony from her stepmother. The experience furnished the basis for Margaret Hale's nursing of her critically ill mother.

The experience of Margaret Hale in the fashionable home of her London relations appears to parallel the months spent by Gaskell with her uncle, Swinton Holland, a banker, and her cousin, Henry Holland, a London physician. Following the fashion for educated and leisured Victorian women, she visited various places during the next few years: in and out of Knutsford (like her narrator, Mary Smith, in *Cranford*), two winters in Newcastle with a minister, William Turner (the model for the kindly Unitarian minister, Thurstan Benson, in *Ruth*), and his daughter, Anne, a visit to Manchester to Anne's sister, Mary, and a winter in Edinburgh with the intellectual and artistic company there. At Manchester, she met William Gaskell, assistant minister of Cross Street Unitarian Chapel, and their warm relationship eventuated in marriage at Knutsford in August, 1832. At her various residences in Manchester, to whose busy industrial life and brusque manners she had to adjust, Gaskell became the mother of four daughters and a son: Marianne, Margaret Emily, Florence, Julia, and William, whose death at the age of ten months caused her great sorrow and resulted in the writing of an idealized portrait of a boy, found in her novel *Ruth*.

Gaskell's husband, who became senior minister in 1854, had a solid reputation as a public speaker, a teacher of English history and literature, an editor of church publications, and a preacher. Despite the uncomfortable weather and atmosphere of Manchester, it was a gathering place for well-educated Unitarians and other non-Anglicans, Cross Street Chapel being a center of lively discussion and numbering many self-made mill owners among its members. It was also true, however, that class divisions between the mill owners and their workers were strongly evident to Gaskell, whose character, Margaret Hale, wonders why two groups so dependent on each other regard their interests as opposed.

To understand Gaskell's preoccupation with social problems in her fiction, one must note her constant involvement in social welfare with Sunday and weekday schools for children of workers, her visits to working-class homes in the course of parish duties, and her concern for victims of the social system such as unwed mothers. The depression of 1839 to 1840, the Chartist movement aimed at gaining more political power for workers, the Factory Act of 1832 opposed by industrialists and widely evaded in its purpose of restricting hours of labor for women and children—all these conditions provided Gaskell with subject matter.

Gaskell's immediate impulse to write came from grief over her son's death, a decision that her husband hoped to channel constructively by encouraging her in her efforts. Her first attempt at a diary and further encouragement from publisher friends resulted in sketches about *Life in Manchester*, but this was a prelude to her first success as a novelist, *Mary Barton*. This novel presented the sufferings of the workers during labor unrest, the resistance of the mill-owners, the failure of parliament to respond to labor grievances, and the need for reconciliation. The book was praised by Friedrich Engels and Karl Marx and condemned as unfair by the wealthy parishioners of Cross Street Chapel, a denouncement that led Gaskell to present what she considered an account more favorable to the industrialists in *North and South*.

Elizabeth Gaskell. (Library of Congress)

The acclaim and damnation of *Mary Barton* made Gaskell rather visible among British intellectuals such as Thomas Carlyle, the social critic; Walter Savage Landor, the poet; Benjamin Jowett, the classicist; John Ruskin, the reformer of industrial ugliness; Charles Kingsley, author of *Alton Locke* (1850) and *Yeast* (1851) and a founder of Christian socialism; Antony Cooper, earl of Shaftesbury, the prime mover of legislative reform in mid-Victorian England; and Dickens. Thus, Gaskell joined the reforming group bent on altering the unsatisfactory living and working conditions among the laboring class in Britain.

Gaskell's friendship with Dickens inspired her to produce a story about an unmarried mother, "Lizzie Leigh," for Dickens's journal *Household Words* and created a writer-editor relationship that lasted more than a dozen years. Having become interested in the fate of the "fallen woman," she used, as the basis for her novel *Ruth* (first serialized and then published in 1853), the actual case of a sixteen-year-old female dressmaking apprentice who had been seduced, abandoned, and then imprisoned for theft in trying to keep herself alive. In the novel, a similar young girl is saved from a parallel disgrace by the intervention of a kindly minister and his sister and brought back to respectability and social usefulness by their tender concern. The presentation of Ruth's case, mild by modern standards, became almost instantly controversial, various prudish fathers refused to allow their wives and daughters to read it, and even Gaskell kept the book from her own daughters. Gaskell had already interested herself in promoting emigration by unwed mothers to the colonies as a practical way of restoring their reputations and building new futures; the book was an outcome of her own concern, though Ruth is rehabilitated within the community rather than leaving it and must still suffer unfair stigmatization, precisely the kind that the novel itself received.

While visiting another reformer, James Kay-Shuttleworth, who promoted educational advancements for workers, Gaskell met Charlotte Brontë, who had recently risen to prominence with *Jane Eyre* (1847); a strong friendship developed from this meeting and continued until Brontë's death in 1855. In fact, the riot of the workingmen against their employer in *North and South* has similarities to a scene in Brontë's *Shirley*, which appeared six years before Gaskell's novel.

While *Ruth* was exciting controversy, *Cranford*, the work that for a long time overshadowed Gaskell's reputation as a social critic, created a nostalgic and melancholic mood. Yet even in this novel, Gaskell expresses a concern for lives that are close to poverty, genteel survivors of once lively and secure families. To please Dickens, in 1863 Gaskell added one more story to the collection for *All the Year Round*, his second magazine. Gaskell had by then established the parameters of her work: the creation of moving depictions of life under an industrializing social order; the alertness to social injustice; the longings for a more rural, innocent, and organic world of natural feelings and associations; and the melancholy strain of hopes unrealized because of social or financial constraints.

In *North and South*, completed two years after *Cranford*, Gaskell made a determined effort to present the mill-owner, Thornton, as a man with integrity, initiative, and humanitarian concern for his workers, a sort of Samuel Greg who weathers the financial crisis both with the support of his wife, Margaret Hale, newly rich, and that of his workers, drawn to him by his philanthropy. Northern energy, brusque efficiency, and the rough democracy of industrialists sprung from the humble origins of their own workers are set against the arduous toil and isolation of southern farm laborers and the class consciousness of southern workers, town dwellers, and professional people.

In the same year, Gaskell drew on memories of Avonbank School for stories, which she inset in a frame story narrated by an aristocrat, Lady Ludlow. These appeared as "My Lady Ludlow," later added to and published as *Round the Sofa*. During these years, Gaskell also wrote various sketches, such as "Cumberland Sheep Shearers" with its Wordsworthian setting of rough toil among natural beauties, and Christmas stories, some with ghostly apparitions in the style of Dickens's own stories, which appeared in *Household Words*. Dickens's *Hard Times* (1854) provoked some anxiety in Gaskell since it dealt in part with union agitation and industrial unrest, as did *North and South*. What strained the relationship with Dickens, however, was the leisurely description and extended characterization in *North and South* together with difficulties of episodic compression for weekly publication in his journal. Though Dickens eventually came to appreciate the virtues of *North and South*, the editorial struggle over it induced Gaskell to look for publication elsewhere in more prestigious journals run on a monthly basis.

Upon the death of Charlotte Brontë in March, 1855, Gaskell undertook to write the authorized biography, using Brontë's words where possible but interpreting the facts somewhat freely. The biography, published in March, 1857, led to a continuing friendship with her new publisher, George Smith, Jr., whose firm, Smith, Elder, and Company, had been Brontë's publisher. Smith's support proved most helpful when questions of libelous statements in the biography necessitated apologies and vexatious changes in the third edition. Despite the partisanship evident in certain passages, the feeling for its subject and the general fairness in its presentation make it a good study of a writer by another writer.

Gaskell's work from 1858 to 1863 was uneven. She desired sales apparently to pay for increasing amounts of travel with her daughters, expenses of weddings for two of them, and new property. In Rome, in 1857, a new friend and major correspondent appeared, an American, Charles Eliot Norton, future president of Harvard University, who probably gave her information on Puritan New England to add to her lore of witchcraft and demonism on which she drew for the stories found in *Lois the Witch, and Other Tales*. A trip to Heidelberg, Germany, provided legendary matter for *Right at Last, and Other Tales*. At this time, there was much interest in Great Britain in folklore materials and romantic wonders derived from ghostly and spiritual legends, and Gaskell, among others, was willing to fictionalize this type of literature.

Writing in another contrary strain, Gaskell employed rural settings in her next two novels, *Sylvia's Lovers* and *Cousin Phillis*; the novel or novella following these two was *A Dark Night's Work*, intended to capture part of the market for intriguing mystery and suspense stories. As *Cousin Phillis* was winding up its serial publication in August, 1864, Gaskell started what some critics consider her major work, *Wives and Daughters*, an exploration of the role of women in Victorian intellectual and social life. The work was never completed. Gaskell's unceasing activity, including essays for the *Sunday School Magazine*, was taking its physical toll. She had already had fainting spells. Hoping to retire to Holybourne, Hampshire, which she had used a decade earlier as Margaret Hale's beloved home community, she had purchased a home there as a surprise for her husband. While spending a trial weekend with family and guests there, she suffered a sudden and fatal stroke on November 12, 1865. She was buried at Brook Street Chapel, Knutsford, where her husband was also buried in June, 1884.

Analysis

Despite her own creativity, which certainly had the support of her husband, Elizabeth Gaskell, when questioned by a young writer, insisted that a woman's first duty was to husband and family. Friends recollected her carrying out her early career while conducting household activities. Later, however, she often went traveling alone or with her daughters but—except for jaunts to a beloved vacation spot near Manchester—never with her husband. The traveling periods gave her isolation for writing, suggesting that her own practice ran counter to her advice.

Enid L. Duthie has found in Gaskell's fiction a strong interest in natural scenery, in country customs, crafts, and tales; a sympathy for conservative small towns, yet equally a concern for working men and women; a desire for practical knowledge to enhance living; a focus on the family as the stable social unit where affections are close but able, on occasion, to extend to others in need; and an insistence that violence is futile, the human condition precarious, faith necessary. John McVeagh sees Gaskell as insisting that absolute judgments become meaningless when related to concrete human situations requiring compromise. In Gaskell's treatment of the laboring element, Calder sees her as avoiding the duality of other portrayers of working-class families—sympathetic yet condescending—and refers to Gaskell as one of the few major Victorian writers showing marriage from a woman's viewpoint and not simply as an escape, a bid for social status, or a profitable contract.

Gaskell has been praised for her concrete presentation of social milieus, in the spirit of seventeenth century Dutch genre painters, and her gift for recording the relationship between work and home and between husbands and wives is a special one. Spacks refers to a "steady integrity of observation" and "penetrating accuracy," especially as Gaskell draws, tacitly, the analogy between the plight of women in their dependence and that of workers in relation to their employers.

Gaskell's dilemma for a feminist such as Showalter lies in Victorian expectations of feminine domesticity and marriage as an end to intellectual creativity. Gaskell herself surmounted the problem, but her characters find it a difficult challenge. Spacks points out that Margaret Hale, Gaskell's greatest heroine, from *North and South*, tries to mediate between an impoverished working class that really does respect its own labor and an enlightened upper-class self-interest that enjoys emotional and cultural richness. In the end, however, Margaret must inherit property as a defense for her own introspective feeling and the diminution of her former social vitality. It is her way of surviving in a materialistic world.

Mary Barton

The titular heroine of *Mary Barton* has a true lover, Jem Wilson, and a potential seducer, Henry Carson, son of a textile mill owner. The love interest is established as the background for a social problem that Gaskell treats with historical accuracy. John Barton, Mary's father, aware of the sufferings of his fellow mill workers during a lockout by the employers, is enraged by the death of the wife of his friend, Davenport, while the masters enjoy leisure, modernize their mills, and keep up profits by using scabs and decreasing wages when they reopen. Barton is hopeful that the workers will find redress for their grievances from a sympathetic parliament, to which the unionists will present the Chartist Petition. The charter is rejected, however, and the embittered workers are further incensed by Henry Carson's casual caricature of the striking workers, which he passes around at a meeting of employers.

Carson is selected as the target of assassination, Barton being chosen to murder him. Jem is accused of the murder, and Mary faces a conflict, since she can clear

Jem only by exposing her father. Though Jem's acquittal makes this step unnecessary, the other workers shun him (a situation Gaskell borrowed from the true story of a former convict ostracized by those in the workplace), and he and Mary are forced to emigrate. Her father, still publicly innocent, confesses, somewhat implausibly, to Carson, Sr., and gains forgiveness. The solution to class conflict comes through mutual goodwill, recognition of wrongdoing, and restitution.

RUTH

The heroine of *Ruth*, which takes issue with Victorian hostility toward the unmarried mother, is seduced among the romantic clouds and mountains of Wales. The idyllic moment turns to desperation when she is abandoned by her lover, Bellingham. A kindly, crippled Unitarian minister, Thurstan Benson, and his sister, Faith, take Ruth into their home and community, modeled on Knutsford, and deceive people about her condition to protect her reputation. The lie is the price of social respectability. Ruth's discreet conduct from this point on gains her admittance to the mill-owning Bradshaw family as companion to their daughter, Jemima.

The electoral reforms of 1832 give Bellingham a chance to stand for political office, his reappearance in Ruth's life leading to a renewal of his interest in her and a new temptation for her to forgo her independence by accepting an offer of marriage. Her pride in her child, Leonard, makes Ruth reject Bellingham. Unfortunately, Bradshaw learns the truth about Ruth, and his self-righteous indignation leads him to repel Ruth and denounce his friend, Thurstan. Denied the opportunity for further cultural development in the Bradshaw family, Ruth must turn to nursing to establish her social usefulness. As a visiting nurse, her conscientious assistance during a typhoid epidemic brings the praise of the community.

Critics have said that Gaskell, having made her point that unmarried mothers should be treated humanely so that their talents can be made productive, should have ended her novel. Unfortunately, three-volume publication, extended serialization, and a tendency toward melodrama fostered by Dickens, led Gaskell to have Bradshaw's son forge a signature on some stocks entrusted to him by Thurstan. Bradshaw denounces his son, comes back ignominiously to the chapel worship he has furiously abandoned, and eventually breaks down and is reconciled to Thurstan, having repented of his harshness toward Ruth. Ruth, however, is not permitted to live since Gaskell apparently felt that her rehabilitation was not enough to gain sympathy. Wearied by constant care of the sick, Ruth falls sick while somewhat improbably tending her former lover, Bellingham. She dies possessing an aura of sanctity, and perhaps it was this martyrdom that Victorian critics found too much to accept.

NORTH AND SOUTH

In *North and South*, the protagonist Margaret Hale must adjust to life in industrial Darkshire (Derbyshire) after living in rural Hampshire, and, through her perceptions, Margaret guides the reader to a major issue: the way in which a money-oriented competitive society challenges a more leisured, socially stratified one. The abrasive confrontations of Margaret and John Thornton, a mill-owner being tutored in classics by Margaret's father, define the mutual incomprehension of North and South in England. Thornton wants to have a "wise despotism" over his workers; Margaret contends for understanding based on common destiny in the mills. The question of authority is raised in another dimension in the Hale family's personal travail over the enforced exile of Margaret's brother, Frederick, because of charges, unwarranted, of inciting the crew of his naval vessel to mutiny.

Through friendship with Bessy Higgins, a mill girl dying of a disease fostered by textile manufacturing, Margaret, the central consciousness of the novel, is able to observe the sufferings of the working class during a strike caused by union efforts to prevent wage cuts, which the mill-owners justify because of American competition. The owners themselves, while cooperating in opposition to workers, fight one another for economic survival, according to Thornton, who sees an analogy with the theory of survival of the fittest. Though Margaret can see the closeness of working men and women in their common suffering, a riot, instigated without union approval by Nicholas Boucher, a weak agitator, against Irish scab labor, seriously compromises the position of the union in terms of its own self-discipline. The issue is posed whether coercive tactics to enlist worker support of unions can be justified when a weak leader can jeopardize legitimate demands. Margaret terminates the riot, in fact, by heroically intervening between Thornton and the rioters. She quite literally mediates between the two sides.

The difficulty of reconciliation is made evident, however, when Bessy's father, Nicholas Higgins, a unionist, argues that Christian forbearance will not answer the industrialists, though he admits that workers and employers might compromise if they could understand one another. The blacklisting of Nicholas by other employers leads to Margaret's intervention, encouraging Thornton to rehire him, his own persistence equally helping to regain a job. Thornton realizes that employer responsibility must be broadened. The turmoil of the riot, in which Margaret must confront social disruption, has its counterpart in her own turmoil over the approaching death of her mother and the secret reappearance of her brother to be with their mother. Unfortunately, Frederick's departure from town involves a scuffle with a drunken informer that later requires that Margaret lie to protect Frederick. This lie, like that in *Ruth*, produces its painful outcome when Thornton, who has observed the scuffle, thinks that she is lying to protect a lover, thus causing further altercations. Margaret realizes, however, that her moral condemnation of manufacturers has been too harsh. Indeed, to an Oxford don, an old family friend who comes to her mother's funeral, she suggests that it would be well if intellectuals associated with manufacturers.

Margaret's opinions about the South as a preferable society also undergo change. She counsels Nicholas that his going to the South, when he is blacklisted, would lead to deadening toil, no real companionship, and intellectual decay because of the rural isolation. Visiting Helstone, her old home, Margaret encounters an old native superstition when a live cat is boiled to avert a curse. A meeting with her former lover, Lennox, confirms that Thornton is the more vital man. A fortunate inheritance from the Oxford don, Mr. Bell, enables Margaret to save Thornton, who is faced with mounting debts because of competition. He, too, has faced a moral dilemma: whether it is right to borrow money to keep himself afloat knowing that the lenders are at a strong risk. Thornton wishes to start again, seeking an opportunity for social interchange with his workers beyond the cash nexus. Margaret, now an heiress, helps Thornton stay afloat and marries him. Higgins, providentially having witnessed the scuffle, knows who Frederick really is. Thus, North and South are united, and Thornton becomes a philanthropist.

Wives and Daughters

In *Wives and Daughters*, Gaskell explores the question of the middle-class woman seeking to define herself and her goals in an atmosphere uncongenial to intellectual independence. Molly Gibson, whose mother has died, must cope in her teens with the remarriage of her father, who has sought a wife as much to guide Molly as out of real love. Her father's new wife, Hyacinthe Kirkpatrick, is the epitome of the parasitical woman, a former governess previously married out of necessity and then forced back into supporting herself and her daughter, Cynthia, upon her husband's death. She has become a companion to the newly aristocratic Cumnor family, but, wanting comfort, she can achieve it only by marrying Gibson. Molly receives her moral education, in part, by seeing through her stepmother's artificial pretenses. Cynthia, shuffled off while her mother has pursued Gibson, comes to reside in the household and establishes a close friendship with Molly despite her moral skepticism and social opportunism. Thus, the daughters are contrasted, not in black and white, but as possible responses to the dependence of women.

Cynthia's mother tries to marry her to Osborne Hamley, eldest son of an old family, not knowing that he is already married, and that the child of the marriage has been kept secret for some time. The event has caused Hamley to fail in attaining his degree, and he returns home to mope, thus arousing the antagonism of his father, to whom he cannot acknowledge his liaison. Hamley finally dies, causing Mrs. Kirkpatrick to shift her sights for Cynthia to the second son, Roger. Molly meanwhile has naïvely pledged herself at sixteen to the odious Preston, a situation from which she is rescued by the more forthright Cynthia, who is in love with Roger but also the object of the affections of Walter Henderson, Gaskell's ideal of the practical, creative scientist, a new social type. Cynthia, socially ambitious, realizes that the Hamley family enjoys ancient honor but is materially threatened, and she transfers her affections to a superficial, weak, but socially prominent young man.

Molly is left to marry Roger, but the problem remains as to whether she can forge for herself a free life with her husband's support. The lifestyles of the two older women, Lady Harriet Cumnor and Mrs. Hamley, provide alternatives for her development. Lady Harriet is a realist about feminine hypocrisy as the price of dependence and wishes to challenge it, but Mrs. Hamley, despite her efforts to mother Molly, is emotionally sterile. Her death leaves Squire Hamley bereft and helplessly alienated from his infant grandson. The other, older men in the novel fare no better; Mr. Gibson suppresses his feelings about his wife to the point of emotional numbness, Lord Cumnor takes refuge in foolish snobbery, and even the younger Osborne painfully learns the price of romantic impulsiveness.

The novel's probing analysis of the dilemma of femininity in a world guided by material values and restricted social consciousness, a world in which men too are caught by the inhibitions of social position and frozen into immobility, gives it peculiar power. It is an indication of what Gaskell could have accomplished if she had lived longer, and it shows her continuing effort to link broader social issues to very specific circumstances with careful attention to detail.

Roger E. Wiehe

Other major works

SHORT FICTION: *The Moorland Cottage*, 1850; *Lizzie Leigh, and Other Tales*, 1855; *The Manchester Marriage*, 1858; *Round the Sofa*, 1859; *Right at Last, and Other Tales*, 1860; *Lois the Witch, and Other Tales*, 1861; *The Cage at Cranford*, 1863; *Cousin Phillis, and Other Tales*, 1865.

NONFICTION: *Life in Manchester*, 1847 (as Cotton Mather Mills, Esq.); *The Life of Charlotte Brontë*, 1857; *The Letters of Mrs. Gaskell*, 1966 (Arthur Pollard and J. A. V. Chapple, editors); *Further Letters of Mrs. Gaskell*, 2000 (Chapple and Alan Shelston, editors).

MISCELLANEOUS: *The Works of Elizabeth Gaskell*, 2005-2006 (10 vols.; Joanne Shattock, editor).

Bibliography

Bonaparte, Felicia. *The Gypsy-Bachelor of Manchester: The Life of Mrs. Gaskell's Demon*. Charlottesville: University Press of Virginia, 1992. A sensitive reading of the life and fiction of Gaskell, and an innovative study treating the writer's life, letters, and works as a single "poetic text."

Craik, Wendy A. *Elizabeth Gaskell and the English Provincial Novel*. New York: Harper & Row, 1975. A major rehabilitation of Gaskell as an important novelist, comparing her with her contemporaries. Sets her long fiction within the provincial novel tradition and demonstrates how she expanded the possibilities and universality of that tradition. Includes a short bibliography and chronology of major nineteenth century provincial novels.

Duthie, Enid. *The Themes of Elizabeth Gaskell*. 1980. Reprint. London: Macmillan, 1990. Duthie draws upon Gaskell's work and letters to reconstruct her imaginative world and the themes central to it. Includes a select bibliography and an index.

Foster, Shirley. *Elizabeth Gaskell: A Literary Life*. New York: Palgrave, 2002. This accessible introduction to the author relies on the best available biographies. It offers interesting comparisons of Gaskell's novels with others of the period and emphasizes women's issues as addressed by Gaskell.

Gerin, Winifred. *Elizabeth Gaskell: A Biography*. 1976. Paperback ed. New York: Oxford University Press, 1990. The first biography able to make use of the publication in 1966 of *The Letters of Mrs. Gaskell*, and still one of the best. Select bibliography and an index.

Hughes, Linda K., and Michael Lund. *Victorian Publishing and Mrs. Gaskell's Work*. Charlottesville: University Press of Virginia, 1999. Places Gaskell's writing in the context of the Victorian era, describing how she negotiated her way through the publishing world by producing work that defied the conventions of her times but also was commercially successful.

Nash, Julie. *Servants and Paternalism in the Works of Maria Edgeworth and Elizabeth Gaskell*. Burlington, Vt.: Ashgate, 2007. Examines the servants in Gaskell's stories and novels, including *Cranford*, *Mary Barton*, and *North and South*, to show how her nostalgia for a traditional ruling class conflicted with her interest in radical new ideas about social equality.

Spencer, Jane. *Elizabeth Gaskell*. New York: St. Martin's Press, 1993. Chapters on Gaskell's career, her biography of Charlotte Brontë, and the novels *Mary*

Barton, Cranford, North and South, Sylvia's Lovers, and *Wives and Daughters*. Includes notes and a bibliography.

Stoneman, Patsy. *Elizabeth Gaskell*. 2d ed. New York: Manchester University Press, 2006. This feminist reading claims that previous accounts of Gaskell and her work are seriously flawed and that the interaction of class and gender must be made central in any interpretation of her work. Select bibliography and an index.

Uglow, Jenny. *Elizabeth Gaskell: A Habit of Stories*. New York: Farrar, Straus and Giroux, 1993. A major critical biography, exploring both Gaskell's life and her work. Uglow pays close attention to primary source material, especially letters, providing a definitive biography. Includes illustrations and notes.

WILLIAM H. GASS

Born: Fargo, North Dakota; July 30, 1924
Also known as: William Howard Gass

Principal long fiction

Omensetter's Luck, 1966
Willie Masters' Lonesome Wife, 1968
The Tunnel, 1995
The Cartesian Sonata, and Other Novellas, 1998

Other literary forms

Chiefly a writer of novels, William H. Gass is also the author of a book of short stories titled *In the Heart of the Heart of the Country, and Other Stories* (1968) and four volumes of essays about literature. In the chief of these, the collections *Fiction and the Figures of Life* (1970) and *The World Within the Word: Essays* (1978), Gass illuminates his own work as a writer of fiction. He prefers novels, as his essay "Imaginary Borges and His Books" suggests, that render fictional worlds that are highly contrived metaphors for the real world. He values the kind of verbal experimentation, and the implications about human consciousness that lie behind it, characteristic of the fiction of Jorge Luis Borges, Gertrude Stein, and Robert Coover. Ultimately, Gass sees the fictional text as less a reflection of objective reality than an artifact created out of the consciousness of the author.

Achievements

Although William H. Gass is a highly individual writer, one whose work does not reflect the influence of his contemporaries, his fiction shares with work by authors such as John Barth, Donald Barthelme, and Thomas Pynchon an emphasis on the text as verbal construct. As his *On Being Blue: A Philosophical Inquiry* (1976) indicates, Gass believes that the words used to talk about a thing reveal the essence of the thing being talked about. His prose itself is highly rhythmic and reflexive, filled with images and allusions. The novels Gass has written are as much meditations on the art of writing fiction as narratives about their title characters. His essays, often published in literary journals before their appearance in book form, are cogent statements of Gass's own thematic and technical preoccupations. They influence both other writers and general readers, not only in the way they read Gass's work but also in the way they read the fiction of his contemporaries. In recognition of his contributions to literature, in 1998 Gass was honored with a star on the St. Louis Walk of Fame.

Biography

While born in Fargo, North Dakota, on July 30, 1924, William Howard Gass was reared in Warren, Ohio. He attended Kenyon College and Ohio Wesleyan, served in the U.S. Navy during World War II, and returned to receive a degree from Kenyon in 1947. Gass came into contact with John Crowe Ransom there, but his chief interest as a student was philosophy. He went on to do graduate work at Cornell University, and after writing his dissertation "A Philosophical Investigation of Metaphor," he received his doctorate in 1954. He taught at a number of colleges, beginning to publish fiction while teaching philosophy at Purdue University. Beginning in 1969, Gass was at Washington University in St. Louis, Missouri, first as distinguished university professor in humanities, then, beginning in 1990, as director of the International Writers Center. He received grants from the Rockefeller and Guggenheim foundations.

In addition to his magnum opus, *The Tunnel* in 1995, Gass published his fourth collection of literary and philosophical essays, *Finding a Form*, in 1996 and a collection of novellas, *The Cartesian Sonata, and Other Novellas*, in 1998. In the essays, he censures the Pulitzer Prize in fiction, the minimalists for lacking depth, and multicultural critics for ignoring the importance of form. In the stories, he continues to fly in the face of late twentieth century realism with stories that explore fictional figures caught in the web of language and thought.

Analysis

Examination of the stories collected in *In the Heart of the Heart of the Country, and Other Stories* reveals the degree to which Gass's fiction reflects his emphasis as a critic on creation of an autonomous verbal construction. In the title story of the volume, for example, he uses recurring images, syntactic patterns, and subject matter to depict a rural community as perceived by a poet who has come to a small Indiana town to recover from a failed love affair. "In the Midwest, around the lower Lakes," the first-person narrator comments,

> the sky in the winter is heavy and close, and it is a rare day, a day to remark on, when the sky lifts and allows the heart up. I am keeping count, and as I write this page, it is eleven days since I have seen the sun.

As is typical of all of Gass's work, the first-person narrator of the story "In the Heart of the Heart of the Country" controls the development of the tale's narrative structure. It is his story, and Gass works through the narrator to reveal its meaning. The narrator's eye for detail is sharp: Nevertheless, he interprets it in terms of his own isolation and despair. "Lost in the corn rows, I remember feeling just another stalk, and thus this country takes me over in the way I occupy myself when I am well . . . completely—to the edge of both my house and body." This metaphor is central to the point of the story, for Gass demonstrates that his protagonist so fuses the data of his sensory experience and his subjective response to it that the two cannot be separated.

Omensetter's Luck

In this respect, this protagonist is typical of characters in Gass's longer fiction. In the novels, however, the narrative strategy is more complex than in the stories. Gass uses four different narrators in *Omensetter's Luck*, circling about the meaning of the life of Brackett Omensetter without ever entering into his consciousness. According to Henry Pimber, Omensetter's friend and landlord, he

> was a wide and happy man. . . . He knew the earth. He put his hands in water. He smelled the clean fir smell. He listened to the bees. And he laughed his deep, loud, wide and happy laugh whenever he could—which was often, long, and joyfully.

William H. Gass. (Joyce Ravid/Knopf)

To the citizens of Gilean, a town on the Ohio River to which he comes around 1890, Omensetter is a mythic figure who is magically in touch with the natural world. That perception precipitates the emotional responses they have to him. It also precipitates a series of human tragedies.

Israbestis Tott, the first narrator Gass uses in *Omensetter's Luck*, functions like the narrator of "In the Heart of the Heart of the Country," in that he chronicles the history of a town. "Imagine growing up in a world," Tott comments at the start of the book, "where only generals and geniuses, empires and companies, had histories, not your own town or grandfather, house . . . none of the things you'd loved." Tott comes at the conflict at the center of Omensetter's story indirectly, not needing to explain to himself as he muses about the past that actually took place. He speaks from the perspective of old age. His Gilean is that of the reader's present, and he refers to Omensetter's life from the perspective of a survivor of the central action of the novel, which took place before the end of the nineteenth century.

Gass's use of Tott as his initial focus, and the placement of the action of the first section of *Omensetter's Luck* at an auction of the property of the late Lucy Pimber, enables him to suggest that the lack of vitality in Gilean derives from the community's inability to accept Omensetter. One of the items at auction is the cradle Omensetter and his wife used for their infant son Amos, and Tott wonders why Mrs. Pimber had it. She never had any children of her own. Her husband, Henry, the character Gass uses to narrate the second section of the novel, is ambivalent about Omensetter's strength and vitality. Both drawn to him and jealous of him, Pimber commits suicide by hanging himself from a tree deep in the woods. This death is the central element in the plot of the novel. Unsure of what has happened to Henry Pimber, the townspeople search for his body and speculate about the role Omensetter has played in his death.

Pimber is convinced that Omensetter is lucky beyond all deserving. On the rainy day on which he brings his family and household goods to Gilean in an open wagon, Omensetter miraculously escapes the rain. The house he rents from Pimber is subject to flooding, but the Ohio River avoids it while Omensetter's family lives there. Even when a fox falls into the well at the house, he is inclined to let nature take its course in confidence that things will work out. Angered by this attitude, Pimber shoots the fox in the well and wounds himself with a refracted shotgun pellet. Neither Dr. Orcutt's drugs nor Reverend Furber's prayers seem to affect the lockjaw Pimber develops, but Omensetter's beet poultice does the trick. The experience becomes fraught with spiritual significance for Pimber. "It lay somewhere in the chance of being new . . . of living lucky, and of losing Henry Pimber." He sees Omensetter as a sign, as a secret indication of how he himself should live; unable to see that Omensetter is no more than a man, like himself, Pimber hangs himself in despair about ever becoming the kind of person he believes Omensetter to be.

While Henry Pimber sees Omensetter as emblematic of positive elements, the Reverend Jethro Furber, the third of Gass's narrators in *Omensetter's Luck*, sees him as the embodiment of moral evil. Furber is the most difficult to understand of the men Gass uses to narrate the story. His account comes so entirely from within his own consciousness that only the previous evidence of Tott and Pimber serves to put it in perspective. Furber sees Omensetter as a threat to his moral authority. Having coerced him into attending church one Sunday morning, Furber finds himself unable to preach effectively. Speaking to Matthew Watson, the blacksmith in Gilean, he suggests that Omensetter is an agent of Satan. "Listen Matthew, he was in the young corn walking and I said leave us Omensetter, leave us all. Oh I accursed him. I did. Yes, I said, you are of the dark ways, Omensetter, leave us all." When Henry Pimber disappears and foul play is suggested, Furber encourages the townspeople to suspect Omensetter of killing his landlord.

Obsessed by the sight of Omensetter and his pregnant wife, Lucy, bathing in a stream, Furber makes of the scene an icon of his own lust. He is gored by sexual fantasies, conceding to himself that there is more pleasure in dirty words than real experience, yet the unconstrained relationship of Brackett and Lucy Omensetter excites his jealousy. He titillates himself with words, those drawn from scripture as well as those describing sexual acts, and eventually produces a blasphemous mixture of elements suggesting a parallel between Omensetter, his wife, Lucy, and Furber himself and Adam, Eve, and Satan:

> Now there was in heaven, as you know, an angel, prince among them, Prince of Darkness. And he felt his wife drawn painfully from him, out of his holy body, fully half of himself, and given a place of dazzling splendor. How he hated it, and suffered his loss loudly.

Furber sees himself simultaneously as Adam and Satan; he both displaces Omensetter as the husband of Lucy/Eve and reveals the guilt he feels at this idea. Furber imagines that the sex act reunites the parts that God separated, reintegrating the masculine and feminine halves of his own personality, and he thereby suggests the roots of his own jealousy of Omensetter.

Gass provides the last chapters of *Omensetter's Luck* with an anonymous third-person narrator, one who stays largely outside the consciousness of Furber. The action of the plot develops with absolute clarity at this point. Omensetter comes to the minister with the news that he has located Pimber's body deep in the snowy winter forest. He knows that Furber is trying to persuade others that he murdered Pimber, and he needs to clear his name. "A friend. I've spent my life spreading lies about you," Furber tells Omensetter tauntingly. Yet he does tell the search party the truth when they find Pimber's corpse. By this time, Furber is caught up in his own dark spiritual vision. "God was coming true, coming slowly to light like a message in lemon. And, what was the message? in yet another lingo? Truth is the father of lies; nothing survives; only the wicked can afford to be wise." Since his arrival in Gilean, Furber had tended a shady, walled garden attached to his church. With the graves of his predecessors in its four corners, the garden is an emblem straight from the fiction of Nathaniel Hawthorne or Herman Melville. Furber's dark vision has the same traditional literary source, but the people of Gilean see his words only as the ramblings of a madman. The Reverend Furber spends his final years in a mental institution.

Omensetter himself does not handle well the roles in which the people of Gilean have cast him. He is essentially a careless, happy man who is not deeply reflective about life. Cast as the embodiment of natural good by Henry Pimber and spiritual evil by Jethro Furber, he himself is unsure of his identity. For Omensetter, his arrival in Gilean was filled with the promise of a new life: "The trees were bare, I remember, and as we came down the hill we could see the tracks of the wagons glistening. You could see what your life would be." He is eager to prove that this promise was not a lie, and so he gambles on the life of his sick son, Amos, to see if the luck imputed to him by others will hold. "The infant lingered on alive, an outcome altogether outside science, Doctor Orcutt said, and Israbestis swore that Omensetter's luck would be a legend on the river—quite a while, he claimed—perhaps forever." Omensetter and his family leave Gilean, however, suggesting that his self-confidence has been permanently shaken by his experiences. With them, Gass suggests, goes all hope for vitality in the community.

Willie Masters' Lonesome Wife

In a fundamental sense, Omensetter, Furber, Pimber, and Tott are aspects of a single personality. They are the voices of human impulses competing for control. The multiple narrators of *Willie Masters' Lonesome Wife* are less clearly fragments of a single character, but they are equally strong symbol-making voices. Divided into four sections, each printed on paper of a different color, this novella is more overtly an experiment in narrative construction than *Omensetter's Luck*. It has little coherent plot at all, but there is plenty of action.

The central character of *Willie Masters' Lonesome Wife* is Barbara Master, Willie Masters's wife, a lonesome woman who consoles herself with sexual encounters: "Well, I'm busty, passive, hairy, and will serve," she comments in the first, and blue-colored, section of the book. "Departure is my name. I travel, dream. I feel sometimes as if I *were* imagination (that spider goddess and thread-spinning muse)—imagination imagining itself imagine." While engaged in sexual intercourse with a bald man named Gelvin, Busty Babs—as her father called her—thinks about differences in the ways men and women think about sexuality. This is a topic to which Gass has returned time and again in his fiction; it fuels the speculations of the narrator of "In the Heart of the Heart of the Country" and the nearly pornographic fantasies of Furber in *Omensetter's Luck*.

Barbara Masters is a former stripper who danced professionally in a blue light. This explains, in part, the blue paper on which her thoughts are printed. She allows her mind to wander while Gelvin works out his fantasies on her body, and she imagines herself the author of a Russian play—printed in Gass's text on yellow paper to suggest its lurid nature—about a Russian named Ivan and his wife. Barbara casts herself in the role of the wife. The subject of the play is Ivan's reaction to evidence of his wife's infidelity, but the play soon gets overwhelmed by the footnotes providing a running commentary at the foot of each yellow page. The notes get longer, they are at times addressed to the reader of *Willie Masters' Lonesome Wife*, and eventually they swallow up the play. The text and notes do not match up, so the reader must choose whether to read the pages as printed or to work actively to construct a more coherent text.

Gass refers openly to the proposition that the reader is a collaborator in the section of *Willie Masters' Lonesome Wife* that is printed on red paper. The narrator here, perhaps still Barbara Masters, remarks,

> The muddy circle you see just before you and below you represents the ring left on a leaf of the manuscript by my coffee cup. Represents, I say, because, as you must surely realize, this book is many removes from anything I've set pen, hand, or cup to.

Like the play on yellow pages, this section contains simultaneous narratives. There is a dialogue about poetry and sexuality among characters named Leonora, Carlos, Angela, and Philippe; there is a running commentary on the art of writing—containing references to works by Henry David Thoreau, Henry James, and Thomas Hardy; and there is an interior monologue composed of random memories, supposedly events in the life of the narrator. In one sense, this technique re-creates the effect of a single human mind thinking simultaneously about several different subjects. In another, it is simply an elaborate parody of the method Gass uses in *Omensetter's Luck*. In a fictional text such as this one, all interpretations of significance are equally valid (or invalid), and there is ultimately nothing but a subjective reaction to be made out of the materials.

Gass addresses this fact in the final pages of the red section of the book. "You've been had," says the narrator, "haven't you, jocko? you sad sour stew-face sonofabitch. Really, did you read this far?" As Gass has made clear in his essays about literature, the essential nature of a literary text is the fact that it is made up of words. In the fourth section of *Willie Masters' Lonesome Wife*, printed on white paper and without the typographical variation to be found in the other sections of the book, the narrator identifies herself as a verbal construct:

> I am that lady language chose to make her playhouse of, and if you do not like me, if you find me dewlapped, scabby, wrinkled, old (and I've admitted as many pages as my age), well sir, I'm not like you, a loud rude noise and fart upon the town.

She is a new incarnation of the most traditional of muses, just as Willie Masters is a mask for the author William Gass himself.

The Tunnel

After twenty-five years of work, Gass published his long-awaited novel *The Tunnel* in 1995. The central figure and nonstop voice of the book is William Frederick Kohler, a history professor at a midwestern university, who studied in Germany during the 1930's and was a consultant during the Nuremberg Trials. Trying to write a simple, self-congratulatory preface to his magnum opus, *Guilt and Innocence in Hitler's Germany*, he writes about his own life instead. The result is *The Tunnel*, a sprawling personal exploration filled with bitterness, hatred, lies, self-pity, and self-indulgence.

In *The Tunnel*, everything that has happened to Kohler, everyone that he has encountered, is converted into the stuff of his mind. Kohler's mind is not one that many would find hospitable; rather, it is the closed-in, claustrophobic world of the narrow-minded bigot. Long passages reveal his resentment of his unforgiving, hard-fisted father and his self-pitying, alcoholic mother, as well as his loathing for his fat, slothful wife, his contempt for his nondescript adolescent sons, and his scorn for his pedantic colleagues and his superficial lovers.

However, it is not this rambling referential subject matter that makes *The Tunnel* Gass's most ambitious effort, but rather the highly polished prose, wonderfully sustained for more than six hundred pages, and the philosophical exploration of the relationship between historical fascism and domestic solipsism. Gass continually breaks up the naïve realist illusion that the subject of a novel—the territory it depicts—is identical to its maplike pattern or language. Filled with references to the great works of history, philosophy, and literature that Kohler both honors and debunks, the work seems on the surface to be a rambling free association; it is actually such a carefully controlled aesthetic pattern that readers cannot for a moment lose sight of the fact that it is language they are experiencing, not physical life.

The Tunnel is a narcissistic novel in which the only real person is the narrator; all others are merely grist for his mental mill. What it means to be human, the novel suggests, is to confront the hard truth that the self is the only consciousness one can grasp. Kohler knows that if one does not become pure subjective consciousness one runs the risk of being transformed into the consciousness of someone else. *The Tunnel* is an escape route out of the prison of the self as well as a gold mine in which the way to the treasure is the treasure. It is the entrance to the womb, the removal of all human restraints, and the reduction of the self to its most elemental.

Robert C. Petersen
Updated by Charles E. May

Other major works

SHORT FICTION: *In the Heart of the Heart of the Country, and Other Stories*, 1968; *The First Winter of My Married Life*, 1979.

NONFICTION: *Fiction and the Figures of Life*, 1970; *On Being Blue: A Philosophical Inquiry*, 1976; *The World Within the Word: Essays*, 1978; *The Habitations of the Word: Essays*, 1985; *Finding a Form*, 1996; *Reading Rilke: Reflections on the Problems of Translation*, 1999; *Three Essays: Reflections on the American Century*, 2000 (with Naomi Lebowitz and Gerald Early); *Tests of Time: Essays*, 2002; *Conversations with William H. Gass*, 2003 (Theodore G. Ammon, editor); *A Temple of Texts: Essays*, 2006; *Vanishing America: The End of Main Street*, 2008 (with Michael Eastman).

EDITED TEXTS: *The Writer in Politics*, 1996 (with Lorin Cuoco); *Literary St. Louis: A Guide*, 2000 (with Cuoco); *The Writer and Religion*, 2000 (with Cuoco).

Bibliography

Ammon, Theodore G., ed. *Conversations with William H. Gass*. Jackson: University Press of Mississippi, 2003. A collection of interviews with Gass, in which the author discusses his ideas about writing and the philosophical ideas of others who have influenced his work. Includes a debate with John Gardner, in which the two writers express their differences about the art of fiction writing.

Bradbury, Malcolm. *The Modern American Novel*. New York: Oxford University Press, 1983. Places Gass in the company of postmodern writers of the 1960's and 1970's. In discussing Gass's fiction and critical writing, Bradbury notes Gass's background in philosophy and that he is conscious of the "discrepancy between language and reality."

Gass, William. "An Interview with William Gass." Interview by Lorna H. Dormke. *Mississippi Review* 10, no. 3 (1987): 53-67. An extensive interview with Gass.

Hix, H. L. *Understanding William H. Gass*. Columbia: University of South Carolina Press, 2002. Hix examines similarities between Gass's fiction and nonfiction works and explores the ethical, metaphysical, and psychological themes in his four novels and other writings. Includes notes, a bibliography, and an index.

Holloway, Watson L. *William Gass*. Boston: Twayne, 1990. A good critical study of Gass's fiction, including the novels. Includes a bibliography and an index.

Hove, Thomas B. "William H. Gass." In *Postmodernism: The Key Figures*, edited by Hans Bertens and Joseph Natoli. Malden, Mass.: Blackwell, 2002. This examination of postmodernism includes not only the movement's key authors but also its screenwriters, directors, actors, visual artists, and philosophers. The essay on Gass summarizes his work, and the book itself places him within a larger cultural context. Includes a bibliography.

Kaufmann, Michael. "The Textual Body of William Gass's *Willie Masters' Lonesome Wife*." In *Textual Bodies: Modernism, Postmodernism, and Print*. Lewisburg, Pa.: Bucknell University Press, 1994. Kaufmann studies works by Gass, William Faulkner, Gertrude Stein, and James Joyce, focusing on the writers' experiments with typography and the physical form of the text. In analyzing Gass's novel, he argues that the voice of the work is not the voice of the protagonist, Willie Masters's wife, but the voice of the text itself.

Kellman, Steven G., and Irving Malin, eds. *Into "The Tunnel": Readings of Gass's Novel*. Newark: University of Delaware Press, 1998. Kellman focuses on the psychological element in Gass's novel *The Tunnel*. Includes a bibliography and an index.

Saltzman, Arthur. *The Fiction of William Gass: The Consolation of Language*. Carbondale: Southern Illinois University Press, 1986. Saltzman's book includes seven chapters on various aspects of Gass's fiction; the last chapter contains an interesting interview with Gass. Analysis includes discussion of the published novels *Omensetter's Luck* and *Willie Masters' Lonesome Wife* as well as *The Tunnel*, which Gass was then in the process of writing.

Stone, Robert. "The Reason for Stories: Toward a Moral Fiction." *Harper's*, June, 1988. Discusses Gass's argument about the estrangement of art and moral goodness in his essay "Goodness Knows Nothing of Beauty." Claims that Gass does not practice the ideas expressed in his essay, which are at odds with the imperatives of writing. Contends that to be independent of morality, fiction would have to be composed of something other than language, for the laws of language and art impose choices that are unavoidably moral.

JEAN GENET

Born: Paris, France; December 19, 1910
Died: Paris, France; April 15, 1986

Principal long fiction

Notre-Dame des Fleurs, 1944, 1951 (*Our Lady of the Flowers*, 1949)
Miracle de la rose, 1946, 1951 (*Miracle of the Rose*, 1966)
Pompes funèbres, 1947, 1953 (*Funeral Rites*, 1968)
Querelle de Brest, 1947, 1953 (*Querelle of Brest*, 1966)

Other literary forms

Jean Genet opened his literary career with a small group of highly personal lyric poems, beginning with "Le Condamné à mort" ("The Man Condemned to Death"). His poems are collected in *Poèmes* (1948) as well as in the later collections *Treasures of the Night* (1980) and *The Complete Poems* (2001).

Genet published several plays, including *Les Bonnes* (pr. 1947, revised pr., pb. 1954; *The Maids*, 1954), *Haute Surveillance* (pr., pb. 1949, definitive edition pb. 1963; *Deathwatch*, 1954), *Le Balcon* (pb. 1956, revised pb. 1962; *The Balcony*, 1957), *Les Nègres: Clownerie* (pb. 1958; *The Blacks: A Clown Show*, 1960), and *Les Paravents* (pr., pb. 1961; *The Screens*, 1962). A so-called autobiography, *Journal du voleur* (1948, 1949; *The Thief's Journal*, 1954), contains probably more allegory than fact, but it remains an important source of information on the early years of Genet's life. Genet's nonfiction includes essays on the philosophy of art, such as "L'Atelier d'Alberto Giacometti" ("Giacometti's Studio") of 1957 and "Le Funambule" ("The Funambulists") of 1958, and essays dealing with dramatic theory, of which the most important by far is the "Lettre à Pauvert sur les bonnes," an open letter to the publisher Jean-Jacques Pauvert written in 1954 including letters to Roger Blin (collected as *Lettres à Roger Blin*, 1966; *Letters to Roger Blin*, 1969) and various prefaces to his own plays. Genet also wrote a series of sociopolitical broadsheets, beginning with "L'Enfant criminel" ("The Child-Criminal") of 1949 and leading to a sequence of pamphlets in defense of the Black Panthers (perhaps epitomized in his "May-Day Speech" of 1968) and of the Palestinian liberation movement.

Achievements

In any attempt to assess Jean Genet's achievement as a novelist, it is essential to separate his qualities as a writer from what might be termed the "sociological" aspect of his subject matter. Though the two interact, in the critical period between 1945 and 1965 it was the nonliterary import of his work that predominated. Genet's name came to be synonymous with the growing demand of the post-World War II generation to read what it wanted to read and to learn the truth about the less palatable aspects of the human condition, regardless of what a paternalistic censorship might decide was good for it.

In this attempt to break through the barriers of what now seems like an antiquated obscurantism but what until the late twentieth century was a powerful and deeply rooted social attitude, Genet did not stand alone. In this respect, he trod in the footsteps of James Joyce and D. H. Lawrence, of Marcel Proust and Jean Cocteau; among his contemporaries, Norman Mailer, Henry Miller, and Vladimir Nabokov were inspired by similar aims. The battle over Lawrence's *Lady Chatterley's Lover* (1928) was fought and won in 1961; behind the writers stood a small group of publishers (Grove Press in New York, Gallimard in Paris, Rowohlt-Verlag in Hamburg, Anthony Blond in London) who were prepared to fight their cases through the courts. In comparison with many of his contemporaries, Genet had one distinct advantage: He wrote in French. French censorship allowed greater latitude to "clandestine" publications (usually in the form of "limited editions," available to subscribers only) than did that of other countries. This same censorship turned a blind eye to books that, although published in France, were in languages other than French (hence the fact that Genet's earliest translator, Bernard Frechtman, lived and worked in Paris). The French magistrates presiding at censorship trials had always at the back of their minds the specter of that guffaw of disbelieving ridicule that still echoes over their predecessors, who, within the space of half a dozen years, had condemned as "immoral" both Gustave Flaubert's *Madame Bovary* (1857) and Charles Baudelaire's *Les Fleurs du mal* (1857, 1861, 1868).

As a result, Genet, who never once resorted to anonymity or sought to disguise who or what he was, was able to appear in print with material whose publication would have been inconceivable at that time in other societies or under other conditions. It was at this point that the quality, both of his writing and of his thought, became significant, for it won over to his cause a group of eminent figures who would scarcely have bothered to

Jean Genet. (Library of Congress)

jeopardize their own reputations by championing a mere "pornographer." Thus, in 1950, when the prestigious firm Gallimard decided to risk publishing Genet's four novels (expurgated remarkably lightly) together with a selection of the early poems, the editors were able to call upon Jean-Paul Sartre, the leading intellectual of his generation, to write an introduction. This introduction, moreover, which appeared in 1952, constitutes what is one of the most significant treatises on ethics written in the twentieth century: *Saint-Genet: Comédien et martyr* (*Saint Genet: Actor and Martyr*, 1963).

French literature from the eighteenth century onward can boast of a long tradition of writers—from Jean-Jacques Rousseau and the Marquis de Sade, by way of Guillaume Apollinaire, to Jean Paulhan, Georges Bataille, and Monique Wittig—who have used the "pornographic" novel (that is, the novel whose principal material resides in the detailed description of extreme and violent forms of sexual experience) not merely to titillate the reader's imagination but for positive and serious purposes of their own. These purposes vary: The intention may be one of self-analysis or of "confession," it may be a concern with the absolutes of realism, or it may be a matter of denouncing the hypocrisies and the false assumptions by which the majority of "right-thinking people" choose to live. Mystics have been fascinated by the "surreal" quality of erotic experience, but so have anthropologists. The violence of sexual intensity constitutes one of the most readily accessible means of intuiting a dimension of irrational transcendentality; progressively, as European thought has moved toward a climate of materialist rationalism, the attraction of the irrational has grown more powerful. It is perhaps Genet's most significant achievement, in this quasi-sociological domain, to have brought for the first time into the full light of intellectual consciousness the role that "inadmissible" dimensions of experience may play in humankind's objective assessment of itself. To describe this, in Freudian terms, merely as "beneath the ego lies the id" is to bury it under the colorless abstractions of a Viennese-based scientific observer trained by Jean-Martin Charcot. Genet, in the characters of Divine and Mignon, of Bulkaen and Harcamone, of Jean Decarnin and of the Brothers Querelle, clothes these aspects of the human psyche in flesh and blood, illuminates them with the brilliant and torturous recall of his own experiences, and gives them an unforgettable reality.

Biography

The career of Jean Genet has often been compared to that of his late-medieval predecessor, the thief and poet François Villon. That Genet was a thief is undeniable; the interest lies in how he was transformed into a poet.

The solid facts concerning Genet's early life are few, because, for reasons that are both literary and personal, he took great pains to transmute them into his "legend." Born on December 19, 1910, in a public maternity ward on the Rue d'Assas in Paris, the child of a prostitute and an unknown father, Genet was adopted by the Assistance Publique (the national foundling society) and, as soon as he could crawl, was sent off to foster parents in the hill country of Le Morvan, between Dijon and Nevers. There, growing up with a classic sense of insecurity, he took to petty thieving and, by the age of ten, was branded irrevocably as a thief. Many years later, probably under the influence of Sartre's philosophy of existential choice, he attributed to this critical period of his life a positive significance: His "self" was what he was for "others"; because, for others, he was a "thief," a thief was what he must necessarily be. How much of this persona is fact and how much is legend is impossible to determine. At all events, by his early teens, Genet found himself confined to a reformatory for juvenile criminals at Mettray, a few miles north of Tours; there, he was subjected to all the most brutal forms of assault and seduction common to establishments of that type. How and when he was released, or escaped, is unknown, as is most of his career during the next ten years or more. He appears, on one hand, to have developed as a classic layabout—a male prostitute, a skilled pickpocket, a semiskilled shoplifter, and a remarkably unskilled burglar (burglary, considered as an exercise in poetic ecstasy, would not lead to the best results). His vagabond existence took him to Spain and then to North Africa, where he developed a feeling of kinship with the Arab victims of colonization that was later to emerge in *The Screens*. On the other hand, and less ostentatiously, he pursued a career as an assiduous autodidact who, on an occasion when he was arrested for stealing a volume of poems by Paul Verlaine, was more concerned with the quality of the poetry than with the commercial value of the book itself.

These two strains—criminality and poetry—would seem to have run together in not uncomfortable harness for a dozen years or more. According to one source, when Genet was sixteen, he worked as guide and companion to a blind poet, René de Buxeuil, from whom he learned at least the rudiments of French prosody, if not also the principles of Charles Maurras's fascism. Some years later, in 1936 or 1937, he deserted from the Bataillons d'Afrique (the notorious "Bat' d'Af"—the punitive division of the French army in North Africa), after having struck an officer and stolen his suitcases, illegally crossing frontiers in Central Europe and running a racket involving fake or clandestine currency. Yet, in the same period, he taught French literature to the daughter of a leading gynecologist in Brno, Moravia, writing her long letters in which explications of Arthur Rimbaud's "Le Bâteau ivre" (1883, "The Drunken Boat") alternate with laments for the fall of Léon Blum's Front Populaire in June, 1937. His next arrest, in or about 1938, was, according to some authorities, for stealing a car; according to others, it was for forging documents to save republican refugees from the Spanish Civil War.

Which crime led him to the prison at Fresnes in 1942 is again unknown. What is certain is that it was during this period of detention that Genet wrote his first published poem, "The Man Condemned to Death," and also drafted his first novel, *Our Lady of the Flowers*—according to the legend, on stolen brown paper; when the first draft was discovered and confiscated by a warder, Genet simply began all over again.

During this period there was a visitor to the prison at Fresnes named Olga Barbezat. Her husband, Marc Barbezat, owned a small press, L'Arbalàte, in Lyons, and his friends included Jean Cocteau, while she herself had for some years been acquainted with Simone de Beauvoir. Genet's manuscripts began to circulate, and it was Cocteau who first acclaimed them as works of genius. When Genet had been released and arrested yet again (the "volume of Verlaine" thievery), Cocteau himself appeared among the witnesses in court for the defense, declaring publicly that he considered Genet to be "the greatest writer in France." The outcome is again unknown, but Genet nevertheless continued his dual career as a brilliant writer and an incompetent burglar. Between 1942 and 1946, he appears to have written all four of his novels, as well as *The Thief's Journal* and the plays *Deathwatch* and *The Maids*. *Our Lady of the Flowers* was published in September, 1944, and the other novels appeared in rapid succession over the next four years. Genet's name was becoming known; in 1948, however, he was arrested again, and on that occasion was sentenced to "perpetual preventive detention."

The circumstances of this final appearance of Genet-as-criminal are, as usual, obscure. According to his supporters, he had quixotically taken upon himself the crimes of one of his lovers, Jean de Carnin (the Jean Decarnin of *Funeral Rites*), who had died heroically fighting the Germans during the liberation of Paris some three years earlier. At all events, Genet had powerful backers. On July 16, 1948, the influential newspaper *Combat* addressed an open letter (signed by Sartre, Cocteau, and the literary editors of the paper, Maurice Nadeau and Maurice Saillet) to the president of the Republic, "imploring his clemency on behalf of a very great poet." The president, Vincent Auriol, was convinced, and a free pardon was granted. From that point on, Genet was merely a writer. "I don't steal the way I used to," he told an interviewer from *Playboy* (April, 1964) nearly two decades later. "But I continue to steal, in the sense that I continue to be dishonest with regard to society, which pretends that I am not."

Genet's later work, apart from the three plays *The Balcony, The Blacks*, and *The Screens*, all written during the 1950's, is comparatively slight; he never repeated the great outburst of creativity that took hold of him between 1942 and 1948. His later works include a scattering of film scripts and critical essays in the 1960's, and a series of short but searingly controversial articles in defense of the Black Panthers and of the Palestinian terrorists. It is as though, having employed literature to effect his own escape from degradation, he then had little further use for it. In the main, until his death in 1986, he seemed content simply to be alive.

Analysis

The elements out of which Jean Genet contrived his vision of that haunting and monstrous "other" world, which lies carefully concealed beneath the controlled and rational surface of everydayness, all belong to previously accredited literary traditions; nevertheless, the balance, and consequently the overall impact, is new. The components can be analyzed as follows.

The confession: Both *Our Lady of the Flowers* and *Miracle of the Rose*, at least as much as *The Thief's Journal*, are basically autobiographical and, in their original (perhaps subconscious) intention, would seem to have been inspired by a desire to *escape*—to escape from the intolerable degradations of existence as a petty criminal, convict, and male prostitute by externalizing these experiences through the rigorous and formal disciplines of prose and poetry, by projecting the self through words into the minds of others, thus making acceptable to them that which, without their connivance and acknowledgment, could not be acceptable to *him*. In one memorable phrase, Genet describes his pilgrimage through literature as "une marche vers l'homme": a progress toward virility—or, perhaps, simply away from dehumanization.

The "normalization" of homosexuality: To the nineteenth century mind, the homosexual was the ultimate social and moral outlaw, the criminal for whom there could exist no forgiveness. Progressively, the second half of the twentieth century saw the weakening of these strictures: The homosexual, in emotional relationships, could be as "normal" as the heterosexual lover, perhaps even more so; because of previous persecution, the homosexual became almost a "hero of the time." If this attitude is not the most original feature of Genet's work, it nevertheless constitutes a powerful motivation: the concern to portray his own emotions as something as intense and as moving as those of "normal" human beings.

The existential of the self: The intellectual relationship between Sartre and Genet is complex and awaits analysis. What is clear is that if Genet was not only influenced by Sartre's *L'Être et le néant*, 1943 (*Being and Nothingness*, 1956) but also, according to his own confession, reduced for years to silence by the devastating accuracy of Sartre's psychophilosophical analysis of Genet's creative processes in *Saint Genet: Actor and Martyr*, Sartre, likewise, at least in *Le Diable et le Bon Dieu* (pr. 1951; *The Devil and the Good Lord*, 1953), acknowledges his debt to Genet. Genet, in fact, takes the Sartrean ontology toward conclusions that Sartre himself hardly dared to explore. If the essence of the self is a void (*un néant*), then it can only "be," either what it *thinks* itself to be (according to Sartre) or what others think it to be (according to Genet). In either case, it can *know* itself to be what it is only in terms of the effectiveness of its actions (Sartre) or by looking at itself in the mirror (Genet). Yet, if a man (a negative) looks at himself and sees his reflection (a positive) in the mirror, then that which is perceived (the inanimate-positive image) is more "real" than the perceiver (the animate-negative). The image is thus more "real" than the subject, the fake more "authentic" than the genuine. For Genet, "to be" (this is also a Beckettian theme) is "to be perceived"—especially in the mirror. Hence, Genet's fiction is pervaded by the image of the mirror and of the double—from the early ballet *'Adame miroir* to the last of the novels, *Querelle of Brest*, in which the identical twin brothers, Querelle and Robert, constitute an identity only by their absolute reflection of each other.

The reversal of moral values: If the fake is more authentic than the genuine, then, in moral terms also, the evil is more authentic than the good. Genet, brought up as a Catholic believer and profoundly influenced by another Christian believer, Fyodor Dostoevski, argues as follows: Christ stated that the Kingdom of Heaven is for the humble; no man can *will* himself to be humble, any more than he can will himself to be a saint, without a degree of hypocrisy that destroys both humility and sanctity (this is, in fact, the theme of the play *Deathwatch*). Humility, the supreme virtue of the true Christian, can be achieved only involuntarily: One can be truly humble only by being *humiliated*. Consequently, the most truly meritorious acts are those that result in a total rejection or humiliation by the community—for example, murder or treason. The murderer, therefore, or the traitor (or, on a lesser level, the sneak thief) comes closer to achieving "sanctity" than the parson or the social worker. This argument is well summed up in Lawrence's vitriolic parody.

And the Dostoyevsky lot:
'Let me sin my way to Jesus!'—
And so they sinned themselves off the face of the earth.

Divine of *Our Lady of the Flowers* would agree wholeheartedly.

The attack on the establishment: Genet's existential-Dostoevskian reversal of accepted moral values is basically a rationalization of his rejection of *all* values accepted by the French establishment of his time. That does not mean, in any political sense, that he is a "revolutionary," because "the revolution" (as in *The Balcony*) implies the acceptance of a code of values as rigid as, and perhaps even more intolerant than, those that it claims to replace. In political terms, Genet is an anarchist in the most literal sense: The conformism of the Left is as repugnant to him as the conformism of the Right. Jews, blacks, criminals, Algerians, pimps, prostitutes—these are "his" people, the social outcasts, the "submerged tenth," as unwelcome to one regime as to another. From this point of view, *Funeral Rites*, while one of the weakest of Genet's novels, is at the same time one of his most significant. Ostensibly, its hero is one Jean Decarnin, a stalwart of the Resistance, Genet's lover. Yet no sooner is Decarnin dead than Genet embarks on a paean to all that is Nazi, for Adolf Hitler and for the jackbooted SS battalions that had trampled over the fair land of France. If the new establishment is to be the victorious Resistance, then Genet is as emphatic in his rejection of it as he had been in his rejection of the *grande bourgeoisie* that had preceded it. Michel Leiris once argued that the so-called committed writer can justify his calling only if, like a bullfighter, he *genuinely* exposes himself to danger. Genet accepted the challenge, in a way that Leiris himself, for all of his intelligence, seems scarcely to have envisaged. If Genet rejected the bourgeoisie, it was not so much by writing as by *being* that which no establishment can accept. Therefore, with deliberate delight, Genet, even when he was an acknowledged poet, continued to be an inefficient burglar: the last of his protests against a society that stole "in a different way."

One of the most intriguing features of the Parisian underworld of criminals, pimps, and prostitutes is its tradition of bestowing on this unlovely riffraff the most elaborate and frequently the most haunting of poetic nicknames. It is as though the highest form of human aspiration stood guard over the most debased of its activities. This is the paradox that Genet, with his passion for masks and symbols, for those moments of "mystic" revelation in which an object is perceived simultaneously to be itself and not itself, takes as the starting point of his first and, in the opinion of many critics, his best novel. The "magical" name Our Lady of the Flowers (which is also the designation of Filippo Brunelleschi's noble Florence cathedral) conceals beneath its high sonorities the sordid reality of a moronic adolescent thug, one Adrien Baillon, a former butcher boy and author of a particularly brutal and senseless murder; "Darling" (Mignon-les-Petits-Pieds) turns out to be a stereotypical muscleman, pimp, and shoplifter; and "Divine," the hero (or rather, the heroine, for that is how "she" would prefer it), is a cross-dressing male streetwalker, as are "her" companions of the sidewalk, "Mimosa II" (René Hirsch), "First-Communion" (Antoine Berthollet), and "Lady-Apple" ("Pomme d'Api," or Eugène Marceau), among others: "A host, a long litany of beings who *are* the bright explosion of their names." Half or more of these names have religious connotations, notably that of Divine herself, for surely the most beautiful of masks is that of the Son of God, even if it serves to hide a Dantesque inferno.

Our Lady of the Flowers

There is no conventional "plot" to *Our Lady of the Flowers*, any more than there is to its successor, *Miracle of the Rose*. Because both of Genet's first two novels are, in part at least, autobiographical (the actual process of writing them was, for their author, a means of liberation, of escape from anonymous degradation, sexual abjection, and possible madness), their structure is as complex as life itself. How Louis Culafroy *became* Divine, how Divine *became* Genet-in-prison, is not told; few things interest Genet less than a coherent narrative in time. The episodes are superimposed on one another, absorbed into one another, so that the beginning is the funeral of Divine and the end is the death of Divine, and both are interwoven with the voice of Genet, who "is" Divine and who is dead and yet alive. The central figure is always Divine, who, in "her" precious dialect of a painted and decaying transvestite, pursues the unending *via dolorosa* laid down for her by her quest for the Absolute.

Divine's most terrifying characteristic is her purity, for hers is a demoniac chastity, born where good and evil meet, the purity of that hell that lies beyond Hell and that consequently drags all those who cannot follow her as far down into the depths as she herself has plunged, toward death and perdition. Her lovers are caught, one by one, in the toils of her "sanctity" and annihilated. Even Our Lady, the "sublime" adolescent strangler, becomes possessed (almost in the biblical sense) with the spirit, or rather with the gestures, of Divine, and confesses to his crime, gratuitously and needlessly—needlessly, in terms of everyday values, but *necessarily* in the context of Divine's world, where the figure has no reality without the image, nor the criminal without his punishment, and where damnation is essential to justify the ways of God to man. Confession is not repentance but defiance without repentance. If God is infinitely high above man exactly to the extent that man is infinitely far below God, then the supreme exaltation and glorification of God lies in *willing* the opposite of God, which is evil, and, with evil, its punishment. Then, and then only, are the two halves joined and the cycle completed.

In place of plot, then, *Our Lady of the Flowers* interweaves variations on a theme; this theme is the relationship between God and his most ignominious creation, man. The vision of God, for that contemporary mystic Genet, owes much to Dostoevski, something to village-church Catholicism, and most of all to post-Freudian anthropology. From Dostoevski comes Genet's obsession with the figure of the *humiliated* Christ—the Christ who, through His humiliation, bears away the sins of the world—and of the saint who achieves his sanctity through his very degradation. From village Catholicism (albeit oddly distorted) come the cherubim and the archangels, the crude plaster statuettes of the Blessèd Virgin working fake miracles. From the anthropologists comes the notion of transgression: the sophisticated equivalent of the taboo. What transforms Genet's antiheroes from subjects of psychiatric case histories, or instances in a criminologist's notebook, into symbols of a metaphysical reality is the fact that they violate not laws, but taboos.

Hence, in *Our Lady of the Flowers*, Genet is interested in crime and in criminals only insofar as they perpetrate a sacrilege, that is, insofar as they violate the laws, not of society, but of that "Other Dimension," which is God. In one of his allegories, or "parables," Genet sees himself thwarting God. Here lies the key to Genet's attitudes and, furthermore, to the significance of Divine and Darling and Our Lady. They are at death grips with God, because God offers them sanctity and salvation on *his* terms. They are tempted, but they will not be bullied. They are human beings, and they have one inalienable right: to be what they are. God would take away from them this right, so they defy God. If they are destined for sanctity, they are resolved to achieve it in their own way, not God's. They will plunge headfirst into the mire; their abjection is their dignity; their degradation is their ultimate authenticity. God has sided with society; therefore, God has betrayed them. Not for that, however, will they renounce God's kingdom, but they will get there by diving headforemost into the ditch, which reflects the stars—the mirror image of Heaven.

Miracle of the Rose

Genet's second novel, *Miracle of the Rose*, contains at least as much, if not more, autobiographical material than the first. In *Our Lady of the Flowers*, both Divine and the child, Culafroy, are semimythical figures, all immediate reality being concealed beneath a golden mask of signs and symbols. In *Miracle of the Rose*, by contrast, Genet speaks in his own name. The "I" who endures (and endows with "magic") the sordid and stultifying brutality of the great prison-fortress of Fontevrault—now redeemed from that function and restored to its former status as a minor château of the Loire Valley—is the same "I" who earlier had been subjected to the vicious cruelty of the reformatory at Mettray, a few miles to the northeast. In neither novel is the material, in any usual sense, "romanticized." The misery and horror, the nightmarish ugliness of the life that Genet describes, is never glossed over. On the contrary, it is portrayed lingeringly in all of its nauseating detail, and the ingenious sadism by which a vengeful society deliberately sets out to reduce its victims to a level considerably below that of animals is, if anything, exaggerated. The signs and the symbols are still present and still serve to transmute prison latrines and punishment blocks into miracles and roses, but the symbolism is rather more self-conscious and therefore more self-revealing. In consequence, the reality underlying these symbols is not concealed as much as it is heightened, given a spiritual or aesthetic significance without ever losing sight of its grim and ugly materiality.

The Central Prison (Lan Centrale) of Fontevrault is an isolated community cut off from the rest of the world, cruel, intense, superstitious, hierarchical, and ascetic—not very different from the medieval abbey, with its dependent monasteries and convents, that had originally occupied the same site. The convicts of the present are simultaneously the monks and lay brothers of the long-dead past, an identification that destroys the intervening barrier of time, thus giving the whole prison a dreamlike and "sacred" quality that Genet discreetly emphasizes by setting the time of his own arrival there late on Christmas Eve: "The prison lived like a cathedral at midnight. . . . We belonged to the Middle Ages." Thus Genet establishes the basic structure of *Miracle of the Rose*, which consists in eliminating the "profane" dimension of time by superimposing different fragments of experience in time, identifying them and allowing them to interpenetrate so that the reality that survives is outside time altogether.

Undoubtedly, *Miracle of the Rose* owes something to Proust's *À la recherche du temps perdu* (1913-1927; *Remembrance of Things Past*, 1922-1931); it is understandable that Genet, comparing his own childhood with that of the wealthy, spoiled hypochondriacal young Marcel, must have felt a definite sense of alienation. *Miracle of the Rose*, however, differs from the Proustian narrative in its superimposition of a third plane of experience over and above Proust's levels of time past and time present.

That plane is the plane of the sacred, of existence that is still technically *in* life but, in fact, outside life, space, and time alike—the level of experience that is symbolized by Harcamone. Harcamone, from the mystic solitude of his condemned cell, is already "beyond life"; he lives a "dead life," experiencing the "heartbreaking sweetness of being out of the world before death." Harcamone has, in fact, through his transgression and later through his condemnation, attained that level of sanctity, isolation, and total detachment from profane reality to which Divine aspired yet failed to reach—the level at which all miracles are possible. Genet and his convict-lovers, Bulkaen and Divers, exist simultaneously on two planes, in time and space; Harcamone, on three. Consequently, it is Harcamone who dominates the rest—and not only dominates but, being himself a symbol, gives meaning to all the other symbols that compose the worlds of Fontevrault and of Mettray.

As in *Our Lady of the Flowers*, there is no plot in *Miracle of the Rose*. It is a closely woven, glittering tapestry of memories and of symbols. It is not, however, a Symbolist novel; it is, rather, a novel wherein the obsessions of memory fuse into the totality of a significant experience through the multiplicity of symbols with which they are illuminated. Frogs become princes while still remaining frogs. Murderers are changed into roses (Genet, incidentally, dislikes flowers) while still remaining murderers. Harcamone, the murderer, is the Rose of Death, yet the warden he killed was known as Bois de Rose, recalling the rosewood used for coffins. The rose is head and heart; cut off from its stem, it falls as heavily to the ground as the head beneath the knife of the guillotine; it is mourning, it is mystery, it is passion. It is beauty that symbolizes its mirror-opposite, evil and ugliness; it is paradox, blossoming simultaneously in the profane and sacred worlds. It is the Head of Christ and the Crown of Thorns. It is the Miracle and the symbol of the Miracle; it is profanation, transgression, and ultimately—in Genet's special sense—sanctity.

Once Genet began to outgrow his basically autobiographical inspiration, his novels became less impressive; after *Miracle of the Rose*, it was the drama that was destined to become his true medium of expression. *Funeral Rites*, although it contains many interesting ideas in embryo, is the weakest of his full-length published works. Its technique is uncertain: Deprived of the electrifying impulse given by the memory of his own humiliations, Genet descends to the level of the commonplace novelist struggling with the exigencies of a conventional plot.

Querelle of Brest

By contrast, *Querelle of Brest* is the most technically sophisticated of Genet's novels. It is less lyric, less subjective, less poetic, and perhaps less haunting than *Our Lady of the Flowers*; on the other hand, it has a far more substantial structure, it develops its themes with a persistence in logic (or antilogic) that was missing from the earlier works; it creates a whole new range of characters, symbols, and images to replace the purely personal obsessions of *Our Lady of the Flowers*; finally, in the character of Madame Lysiane, it introduces for the first time a woman who plays an essential part in the development of the plot.

From the outset, Genet's metaphysic was based on the symbol of the mirror. The self had reality only as observed by the other (as image and reflection), but this dual self could be granted authenticity only if apprehended simultaneously by a third source of awareness. Claire and Solange in *The Maids* are reflections of each other; their "reality" depends on Madame, whose consciousness alone can embrace both. In *Querelle of Brest*, this theme of the double is worked out in greater complexity and is pushed toward its inevitable and logical conclusion. What previously was a mirror image is now literally incarnated in the double (Georges Querelle and his identical-twin brother Robert), while the "observers" are equally duplicated (Madame Lysiane and Lieutenant Seblon). To complicate the pattern, both Georges Querelle and Lieutenant Seblon—respectively a seaman and an officer in the French navy—are "doubled" by being both "themselves as they are" and the image or reflection of themselves presented to the world by the uniforms they wear. The double, with all its intricacies of significance in Genet's aesthetic, is the central theme of *Querelle of Brest*.

Genet, to begin, presents a double murder. In the everlasting fogs and granite-veiling mists of the traditional French naval base of Brest, Querelle murders Vic, his messmate, who was his accomplice in smuggling opium past the watchful eyes of the customs officers; perhaps in the same instant, Gil Turko, a young stonemason employed as a construction worker in the dockyard, goaded beyond endurance by the taunting contempt of Théo, a middle-aged fellow construction worker, fills himself with brandy to fire his courage and slashes his enemy's throat with the butt end of a broken bottle. From this moment onward, the two alien destinies begin to coincide—with this difference: Whereas Gil, terrified and hiding from the police in the ruined shell of the ancient galley slaves' prison by the Vieux Port, is the victim, Querelle is the master of his fate, or at least as near master as any mortal can hope to be. Querelle sees in Gil his own reflection, his imitator, his young apprentice who might one day grow up to be the equivalent of himself. He takes care of Gil, feeds him, argues with him, encourages him, secretly exploits him, and finally, for good measure, betrays him to the police. The relationship between Georges Querelle and Gil Turko is, however, only the central relationship in a series of doubles; not only is Georges Querelle doubled by his twin brother Robert, but Madame Lysiane, who loves Robert, also loves Querelle and at most times is unable to distinguish between them. Mario, the Chief of Police in Brest, finds his double in Norbert ("Nono"), the proprietor of the most favored brothel in the dock area, La Féria, and the husband of Madame Lysiane. Even in the absence of character pairs there are mirrors: the great wall mirrors of La Féria, against which a man can lean, propping himself against his own reflection so that he "appears to be propped up against himself."

The arguments of *Querelle of Brest*, both moral and metaphysical, are ingenious, intricate, and awkwardly paradoxical; as usual, they owe much to Dostoevski and something to the Marquis de Sade. Thomas De Quincey, writing "On Murder Considered as One of the Fine Arts," might have learned something from Querelle, just as Querelle might have learned something from Oscar Wilde's "Pen, Pencil, and Poison." The outstanding achievement of the novel, however, lies in the way in which structure, plot, argument, and symbols are integrated, forming an imaginative pattern in which every element serves to reinforce the others. The symbol of Querelle's dangerous virility is the granitic, the vertical. Querelle, on the other hand, is flexible and smiling. His symbol is transferred outside himself: It is the ramparts of Brest where he murders Vic; it is the dockyard wall over which the packet of opium must be passed; it is the walls of La Rochelle in Querelle's childhood memories. In the place of roses and angels, Genet is now using a much more abstract, sophisticated, and, in the end, powerful type of symbol. There is a geometrical precision, both of imagery and of argument, in *Querelle of Brest*, which contrasts significantly with the comparative formlessness, the viscosity, and the self-indulgent subjectivity of *Our Lady of the Flowers* or of *Miracle of the Rose*.

In his autobiographical *The Thief's Journal*, Genet refers at one point to his "decision to write pornographic books." As a statement, this is categorical; in any context (not only in that of the 1940's), Genet's novels are unquestionably and deliberately pornographic. There are passages that, even now, are difficult to read without a sickening feeling of disgust: The animality of man is unspeakable, so why speak of it?

In earlier generations, Puritans spoke with similar disgust of the "beastliness" of human appetites. The only difference, compared with Genet, is that they spoke in generalities, allegories, or abstractions. When John Milton's Comus appeared (in *Comus*, 1634), it was in the company of a "rout of monsters, headed like sundry sorts of beasts, but otherwise like men and women, their apparel glistening." The rest of *Comus*, however, is pure poetry; the "rout of monsters" is forgotten. Genet parades before us a similar rout of monsters, but he does not forget about them. Nor, in the last analysis, is he less puritanical than Milton. The exquisite ecstasy of disgust with human sexuality is something that he has known from personal experience; if he chooses to speak of it, it is at least with an authority greater than Milton's. Pushed to its ultimate indignities, pornography becomes puritanism, and puritanical pornography is instinct with poetry. Every word that Genet uses is selected with rigorous and elaborate precision. Divine and her transvestite companions are "the bright explosion [*l'éclaté*] of their names." *L'éclaté* is a rare and precious seventeenth century word, not listed in modern dictionaries, dragged by Genet out of its antique obscurity because it alone possessed the jewel-like precision of the poetic nuance he wished to convey. Genet's pornography is poetry of the highest, most rigorous, and most uncompromising order.

Richard N. Coe

Other major works

PLAYS: *Les Bonnes*, pr. 1947 (revised pr., pb. 1954; *The Maids*, 1954); *Haute Surveillance*, pr., pb. 1949 (definitive edition pb. 1963; *Deathwatch*, 1954); *Le Balcon*, pb. 1956 (in English; pr. 1960 in French; revised pb. 1962; *The Balcony*, 1957); *Les Nègres: Clownerie*, pb. 1958 (*The Blacks: A Clown Show*, 1960); *Les Paravents*, pr., pb. 1961 (*The Screens*, 1962); *Splendid's*, pb. 1993 (wr. 1948; English translation, 1995).

POETRY: *Poèmes*, 1948; *Treasures of the Night: The Collected Poems of Jean Genet*, 1980; *The Complete Poems*, 2001.

NONFICTION: *Journal du voleur*, 1948, 1949 (*The Thief's Journal*, 1954); *Lettres à Roger Blin*, 1966 (*Letters to Roger Blin*, 1969); *L'Ennemi déclaré: Texts et entretiens*, 1991 (*The Declared Enemy: Texts and Interviews*, 2004); *Lettres au petit Franz, 1943-1944*, 2000.

MISCELLANEOUS: *Œuvres complètes*, 1951-1991 (6 volumes).

Bibliography

Coe, Richard N. *The Vision of Jean Genet*. London: Peter Owen, 1968. Examines Genet's "ideas, his art, his imagery and his dreams . . . as he has chosen to give them to us in his [work]." Approaches Genet's works through the theme of solitude.

Gaitet, Pascale. *Queens and Revolutionaries: New Readings of Jean Genet*. Newark: University of Delaware Press, 2003. Uses feminist theory and gender theory to reevaluate Genet's work, exploring his representations of cross-dressing, homosexuality, and sexuality. Also reexamines the political nature of Genet's work, contradicting Jean-Paul Sartre's argument (in the work cited below) that these writings were nonpolitical.

Jones, David Andrew. *Blurring Categories of Identity in Contemporary French Literature: Jean Genet's Subversive Discourse*. Lewiston, N.Y.: Edwin Mellen Press, 2007. Analyzes how Genet's work destroys "binary oppositions," integrating opposing character traits, such as homosexuality and heterosexuality, blackness and whiteness, and masculinity and femininity. Also discusses Genet's use of language, interpreting it from the perspectives of deconstructionism, feminist theory, queer theory, and postcolonialism. Useful for advanced students or readers with a prior knowledge of Genet's works.

Knapp, Bettina L. *Jean Genet*. Rev. ed. Boston: Twayne, 1989. Excellent revision of a valuable introductory study presents chapters on Genet's life and on his individual novels. Includes chronology and annotated bibliography.

Read, Barbara, and Ian Birchall, eds. *Flowers and Revolution: A Collection of Writings on Jean Genet*. London: Middlesex University Press, 1997. Collection of essays provides discussion of many aspects of Genet's works, including analysis of how they challenged conventional ways of understanding society and personal experience and how they influenced twentieth century writers and pop-culture figures such as David Bowie and Patti Smith. Includes bibliographical references and index.

Reed, Jeremy. *Jean Genet: Born to Lose*. London: Creation Books, 2005. Brief biography recounts the details of Genet's life, including information on his novels, criminal activities, sexual relationships, friendships, and obsession with death. Includes illustrations.

Sartre, Jean-Paul. *Saint Genet: Actor and Martyr*. New York: George Braziller, 1963. Sartre was one of the earliest champions of Genet's work, and this book, which made of Genet a kind of dark saint of modernism, remains the classic biography of the author.

Thody, Philip. *Jean Genet: A Study of His Novels and Plays*. New York: Stein & Day, 1968. Explores both Genet's biography and his major themes (evil, homosexuality, sainthood, and language) and then presents in-depth discussions of his novels. Includes bibliography.

White, Edmund. *Genet*. New York: Alfred A. Knopf, 1993. Novelist and critic White has contributed a worthy successor to Sartre's influential biography. White is more scholarly than Sartre, but he writes clearly and with flair. Provides very detailed notes and an extremely thorough chronology.

KAYE GIBBONS

Born: Nash County, North Carolina; May 5, 1960
Also known as: Bertha Kaye Batts

Principal long fiction

Ellen Foster, 1987
A Virtuous Woman, 1989
A Cure for Dreams, 1991
Charms for the Easy Life, 1993
Sights Unseen, 1995
On the Occasion of My Last Afternoon, 1998
Divining Women, 2004
The Life All Around Me by Ellen Foster, 2006

Other literary forms

Kaye Gibbons is known almost exclusively for her novels. She has published two works of nonfiction, *How I Became a Writer: My Mother, Literature, and a Life Split Neatly into Two Halves—A Nonfiction Piece* (1988) and *Frost and Flower: My Life with Manic Depression So Far* (1995).

Achievements

Kaye Gibbons is an award-winning writer. Her first novel, *Ellen Foster*, won the Sue Kaufman Prize for First Fiction from the American Academy of Arts and Letters in 1988 and a special citation from the Ernest Hemingway Foundation. For her second novel, *A Virtuous Woman*, she was awarded a National Endowment for the Arts Fellowship. In 1991, she received the Nelson Algren Heartland Award for Fiction given by the *Chicago Tribune*. For her next novel, *A Cure for Dreams*, she won a PEN/Revson Foundation Fellowship and a Sir Walter Raleigh Award from the North Carolina Literary and Historical Association. Also in 1991, she was named a Chevalier of the Order of Arts and Letters, France. *Ellen Foster* was made into a television movie and broadcast in 1997, and that same year the novel was selected, along with *A Virtuous Woman*, for Oprah's Book Club.

Biography

Kaye Gibbons was born Bertha Kaye Batts on May 5, 1960, in a rural Nash County, North Carolina, community known locally as Bend of the River, near the town of Rocky Mount. Her father, Charles Batts, was a tobacco farmer, and her mother was Alice Batts. Gibbons has a brother, thirteen years her senior, and a sister, nine years older.

In addition to the hardship of poverty, Gibbons also endured a childhood made tragic by her mother's manic depression (bipolar disorder) and her father's abuse and alcoholism. Her mother committed suicide by taking an overdose of sleeping pills in 1970; she was only forty-seven years old. Gibbons lived with her father for a short while until he died as a result of his drinking. After living with several relatives, she finally moved in with her older brother in Rocky Mount once he married. She attended public schools, beginning college at North Carolina State on a Veterans Administration scholarship, then transferring to the University of North Carolina at Chapel Hill, where she majored in English but did not graduate.

Hospitalized for her own bipolar disorder in Raleigh, North Carolina, Gibbons continued to attend classes. During this time she also met her first husband, Michael Gibbons, whom she married on May 12, 1984. They had three daughters: Mary, born in 1985; Leslie, born in 1987; and Louise, born in 1989. In the summer of 1985, Gibbons took a course in southern literature with the renowned teacher and critic Louis Rubin. After reading widely in the literature of the region, she began a manuscript that was eventually published by Rubin's firm, Algonquin Books of Chapel Hill. Gibbons and her first husband were divorced in the early 1990's, and in 1993 she married Frank P. Ward, a Raleigh attorney. They were divorced in 2002.

Analysis

Kaye Gibbons's novels are celebrated primarily for the original and authentic voices of her female protagonists and for the strength and endurance of all her women characters. More broadly, as a southerner herself who sets her stories in the South she knows, she works in the strong American tradition of regionalism. In fact, in 2000 she wrote the introduction to an edition of *The*

Awakening, and Selected Short Stories (1899) by Kate Chopin, a pioneering regionalist who set her fiction in New Orleans and its environs, a world she had come to call home. Gibbons's own works evoke a powerful sense of place, a grasp of the paradox of society's rigidity and transience, women characters who find themselves restricted by present circumstances and often manage to endure or overcome these in courageous ways, a mastery of the colloquial voice, a gift for rendering conversation, and a southerner's understanding of the profound importance of both history and, in particular, story.

Gibbons must be placed within the continuing tradition of great southern writers extending most famously from William Faulkner through a group of acclaimed women writers including Eudora Welty, Flannery O'Connor, Carson McCullers, Alice Walker, Lee Smith, and Jill McCorkle, to name a few. As with Faulkner and so many of the women writers who are her predecessors and contemporaries, Gibbons's work is full of humor; unlike Faulkner in his tragic sense of southern history, her work is optimistic, that is, ultimately comic in the truest sense of the word. In addition, as a postmodern southern writer, her work is assertively feminist, and in its evocations of place and character, she demonstrates the oppression upon which the myth of a white, patriarchal South rested. She replaces that world with one in which those who suffered or would have suffered in the past can claim some measure of autonomy and power.

Gibbons's work almost exclusively features first-person narrators, almost all female, in varying stages of life, from eleven-year-old Ellen Foster to the elderly widow Emma Garnet of *A Virtuous Woman*. As these characters tell their own stories, they often shift back and forth in time, weaving memory into their recounting of the present. Given the richness of her character development, sometimes over significant expanses of time, and given the complexity of her narrative technique, Gibbons writes with surprising economy.

A critically celebrated writer, if Gibbons can be faulted it is for her male characters, who are often stereotypes, lack depth and development, and too evil, and in one case, too good to be believed.

ELLEN FOSTER

Gibbons's first novel, published when she was only twenty-six years old, is still her most popular. It also is her most autobiographical. Sometimes classified as young adult fiction, *Ellen Foster* is widely taught and often compared to Mark Twain's *Adventures of Huckleberry Finn* (1884), J. D. Salinger's *The Catcher in the Rye* (1951), and Harper Lee's *To Kill a Mockingbird* (1960) as an important American coming-of-age tale.

Eleven-year-old Ellen Foster narrates her own story, that of a traumatic year in her life in which she faces the critical illness of and death by suicide of her mother, the neglect and abuse of her alcoholic father, the painful experience of being shifted from one unwelcoming family member to another, the happier experiences of her brief time with her friend Starletta's family, of living with her art teacher and her husband, and of her seeking out and finally finding the foster mother after whom she names herself—the joyful, secure place from which she tells the story of her recent past.

Her first-person voice is highly individual. Gibbons achieves this in part through a preponderance of brief simple and compound sentences, sparse punctuation,

Kaye Gibbons. (John Rosenthal)

and a plain but specific and concrete vocabulary. Ellen's idiom is southern when it is not so unique as to be beyond classification. She is an exceptionally bright child, too.

As this is a maturation tale, the reader is privy to Ellen's blind spots and thus keenly aware of her growth by the end of the novel. Certainly, she learns painful lessons about social class. Her mother has married beneath her class to grave consequences. When Ellen is abused by her grandmother, the abuse is justified because the old woman seeks to eliminate any semblance of her father in her by working her like a field hand. Eventually, however, though Ellen recognizes injustice in such stratifications, she is happy to have found her way safely into the middle class. Her beloved Starletta and her family are sources of an even more significant lesson: Ellen gradually sheds her racism as she endures hardships of her own. In fact, the last line of the novel is dedicated to this transformation.

Ultimately, Ellen's achievement is her initiative, cleverness, and courage in saving herself, perhaps even inventing herself, in the presence of the female models she knows best, in the self-destruction of her mother, in the callousness of her aunts, and in the bitter death-in-life of her grandmother. This is a woman's story, but one that defies all the old paradigms. Ellen is helped along the way, but her rescue is her own.

Charms for the Easy Life

After experimenting with multiple first-person narrators in the two novels that followed *Ellen Foster*, Gibbons returned to the single narrator in *Charms for the Easy Life*. Gibbons's interest in individual voices and history convene here as she studies Works Progress Administration interviews collected during the Great Depression. In the book's preface, she cites Studs Terkel as a source of inspiration, especially his *The Good War: An Oral History of World War II* (1984). Unlike Ellen Foster, though, Margaret is more educated and confident, but shy. Her sophisticated voice is reflected in correct grammar, longer and more complex sentences, and fewer of the comic colloquialisms that enliven that younger narrator's voice.

Charms for the Easy Life is the story of three women, Charlie Kate—the grandmother; Sophia—her daughter; and the narrator, Margaret, Sophia's daughter. Set mostly between the mid-1930's in the thick of the Great Depression and the early 1940's and World War II, this novel is much more specific than earlier works in the details of its setting. The historical milieu, the story's context, is richly evoked. While the novel is still set in the South, readers see life in the cities, from impoverished Beale Street in Memphis, Tennessee, to the affluent reaches of Raleigh, North Carolina. Margaret also supplies much detail about the folklores of an earlier, more rural South, especially as they relate to healing.

As in Gibbons's earlier novels, marriage, especially disastrous marriage, features large here, though this novel has been criticized for its fairy tale ending. Both Sophia and Margaret make happy love matches with worthy men as the story closes, but there are still many challenges along the way. More important, however, is the theme of self-determination for women. Charlie Kate begins as a rural midwife, but through experience and reading becomes a figure easily mistaken for a doctor, recognized for her compassion and expertise. Despite a brief return to the husband who abandoned her, she lives most of her life happily single, devoted to Margaret and her future, increasingly skilled and respected for her work. Also important is Charlie Kate's ability to end the career of a male doctor who has managed to accrue wealth and property despite his carelessness and incompetence. Sophia, Charlie Kate's daughter, is the most conventional woman of the three. She is an avid reader, but lonely without a husband. She finds love with a worthy man at last and needs nothing else. Margaret is set by the end of the novel, ready to begin her education to become the doctor her grandmother never became and set to marry a supportive and loving husband.

As in the earlier novels, both race and class are significant issues in *Charms for the Easy Life*. The three women travel up from the intolerance and ignorance of the working-class South (though never abandoning what is best there, especially its folkways) into the light of the tolerance and educated enlightenment of the upper middle class. The South of the Depression is still plagued by racism, though these women prove themselves to be color blind, cutting down and reviving a lynched man and ministering to the needs of African American women in Memphis and other places. The "charm" for the "easy life" is a gift to Charlie Kate from the man she and her husband cut down from the tree. As the charm and the title suggest, life is never strictly easy for these women, but they each end up with a life that must seem charmed to all who know them.

On the Occasion of My Last Afternoon

Narrated by Emma Garnet Tate Lowell at the end of her life at the beginning of the twentieth century, *On the Occasion of My Last Afternoon* is a historical novel, set around the time of the American Civil War, primarily in Virginia and North Carolina. Again, Gibbons uses a first-person narrator who recounts the story of her and her family's life through memory.

Emma and her servant, Clarice, are strong women characters (and Emma's sister, Maurine, becomes strong through the novel), and Gibbons once again presents a father figure who, abused himself, is domineering and cruel; he also is a great lover of books and learning, and completely identifies with the Old South. Two other male figures are rendered here more completely than usual for Gibbons—Emma's brother, Whatley, and her husband, Quincy. The men range along a spectrum of characteristics. Whatley is educated like his father and is kind but ineffectual. Quincy is loving, supportive, educated, and strong, making him almost too good to be true. However, Quincy, as an enlightened northerner, plays a significant role because he validates Emma's own defiance of her father's South.

The Civil War setting allows Gibbons to deal with the theme of race at more length than in any of her other books. Emma is an abolitionist in her sympathies, in part because she witnesses her father's brutal killing of a slave on the plantation. Clarice, a free black, is a sustaining figure in a household with a kind but weak mother, yet her experiences in both Virginia and North Carolina suggest the inferior status of African Americans in the Civil War South. Once Emma moves to the city of Raleigh and the war progresses, Gibbons's story focuses mainly on the suffering of the slaves of that city and those of Emma's own household.

The Life All Around Me by Ellen Foster

The Life All Around Me by Ellen Foster, a sequel to *Ellen Foster*, is narrated by a now-fifteen-year-old Ellen. It begins with her unconventional letter to Harvard University as she tries to gain early admission. The style of the novel reflects Ellen's growing maturity and intellect. She no longer expresses herself in the simple and compound sentences of the earlier novel, evident in how the page appears—no longer abounding in white space. She now narrates her story in complex sentences using a plethora of introductory elements, almost self-consciously as if to reflect all she has read and studied. The effect of this complexity and a much more sophisticated vocabulary, mixed with her still characteristic colloquialisms, makes for rich comedy in the novel's style.

Ellen herself lives out two significant themes evident in Gibbons's fiction: courtship and an offer of marriage, and the prospect of marrying "down," that is, below her class and sophistication. In this novel, she is courted by her friend Stuart, the kind but relatively ignorant son of a man who makes a living burning castoff tires. She manages to extricate herself from this situation in her continuing journey toward self-determination. She goes to a camp for the gifted at Johns Hopkins University, and the novel ends with a response from the president of Harvard suggesting that when she is ready, she will be admitted there.

Ellen's longtime friend Starletta, and Starletta's mother, have now become such integrated and enduring parts of Ellen's life, and the life of Laura, her foster mother, that the novel suggests some progress is made in race relations in the South. Starletta, though, is still a somewhat silent companion, more a ball of fierce energy spinning in and out of Ellen's life.

Susie Paul

Other major works

NONFICTION: *How I Became a Writer: My Mother, Literature, and a Life Split Neatly into Two Halves—A Nonfiction Piece*, 1988; *Frost and Flower: My Life with Manic Depression So Far*, 1995.

Bibliography

DeMarr, Mary Jean. *Kaye Gibbons: A Critical Companion*. Westport, Conn.: Greenwood Press, 2003. A thorough study of Gibbons's work (to 1998) through the lens of feminist, Marxist, and cultural theory. A chapter is dedicated to each novel and includes analyses of persistent themes, issues of genre, style, and narrative technique.

Groover, Kristina K. "Re-visioning the Wilderness: *Adventures of Huckleberry Finn* and *Ellen Foster*."

Southern Quarterly 30, nos. 2/3 (Winter/Spring, 1992): 187-197. A study of the theme of the female quest in *Ellen Foster*, comparing that quest to the journeys of Huck Finn in Mark Twain's novel.

Guinn, Matthew. *After Southern Modernism: Fiction of the Contemporary South*. Jackson: University Press of Mississippi, 2000. In the chapter "Mediation, Interpolation: Bobbie Ann Mason and Kaye Gibbons," Guinn argues that Gibbons "modif[ies] the male paradigm," and is too easily linked as a "traditionalist" to Eudora Welty, negating the more subversive elements of her portrayal of the South. He discusses *Ellen Foster, Charms for the Easy Life*, and *On the Occasion of My Last Afternoon* at some length.

Snodgrass, Mary Ellen. *Kaye Gibbons: A Literary Companion*. Jefferson, N.C.: McFarland, 2007. A thorough study of Gibbons's work that lays out the characters, plots, dates, allusions, literary motifs, and themes of her novels for new readers. An appendix features a time line of historical events in the novels that correspond to actual events in the history of the South.

WILLIAM GIBSON

Born: Conway, South Carolina; March 17, 1948
Also known as: William Ford Gibson

Principal long fiction

Neuromancer, 1984
Count Zero, 1986
Mona Lisa Overdrive, 1988
The Difference Engine, 1990 (with Bruce Sterling)
Virtual Light, 1993
Idoru, 1996
All Tomorrow's Parties, 1999
Pattern Recognition, 2003
Spook Country, 2007

Other literary forms

William Gibson first established his reputation as the central figure in the cyberpunk movement with a sequence of short stories, some written in collaboration with other presumed members of the movement, including John Shirley, Bruce Sterling, and Michael Swanwick. Gibson has also written several screenplays; the first to be commercially produced was *Johnny Mnemonic* (1995). He has also published journalistic articles on cyberpunk and has written about the genre's key themes. He cowrote two episodes of the television series *The X-Files* with Tom Maddox (1998 and 2000).

Achievements

William Gibson became one of very few modern authors to be considered more visionary prophet than literary artist. His novel *Neuromancer*, which won the Hugo, Nebula, and Philip K. Dick awards, became the handbook of an odd kind of social movement, representing the perverse dreams and ambitions of a large number of alienated adolescents. The novel's success achieved mythical proportions, its relevance seeming so great that it became the most extensively studied science-fiction text in the history of the genre. The role of cultural guru was one for which Gibson was somewhat ill fitted, but inevitably relished. He took good care in his subsequent fiction to represent and extrapolate contemporary social trends that caught his attention and warranted intelligent comment.

Neuromancer helped to rejuvenate generic science fiction, which had been weakened by a loss of faith in the mythical future of the space age. The space age had provided science fiction with a frontier for exploration. By the mid-1980's, the belief that there was attainable extraterrestrial "real estate" in the future had faded to absurd optimism or utter desperation. Then, Gibson revealed that outer space was not, after all, the final frontier, and that there was a new frontier waiting, on the desktop rather than the doorstep. When asked what and where cyberspace was, he became accustomed to answering, "It's where your money is."

The rejuvenation of science fiction was brief—reality caught up with imagination so quickly that Bruce Sterling famously declared that cyberpunk was dead even before the term had been coined. However, the rejuvenation brought about by *Neuromancer* was spectacular, and it left an indelible imprint on contemporary images of the future.

William Gibson. (Karen Moskowitz)

Biography

William Gibson was born in Conway, South Carolina, on March 17, 1948. He moved to a small town in Virginia at the age of eight following the death of his father. His mother died while he was in his teens. He was expelled from the boarding school in Tucson, Arizona, to which he had been sent for smoking marijuana. He went to Canada in 1968—to avoid the military draft, according to most sources (some sources allege that he had actually been rejected by the draft board). He subsequently traveled through Europe and the Near East, but moved to Vancouver, Canada, following his marriage to Deborah Thompson in 1972.

Thompson began studying for a master's degree at the University of British Columbia (UBC), inspiring Gibson to complete his own education. He graduated from UBC with a bachelor's degree in English in 1977. He began writing around this time as well, producing "Fragments of a Hologram Rose" (1977) as part of a science-fiction course. Four years elapsed before he published "The Gernsback Continuum" (1981), which was followed by the model text for what was eventually labeled "cyberpunk" fiction, "Johnny Mnemonic" (1981).

Analysis

William Gibson had little knowledge of or interest in science when he began writing science fiction, but he was keenly interested in the counterculture (including protests against the Vietnam War) that opposed dominant trends in American politics. Significantly, he also was interested in the potential impact of new communications technologies on its associated subcultures. He not only recognized the possibilities but also relished the thought that the rapid development of information networks facilitated by computer technology would become a metaphorical frontier. He believed that within this frontier's shifting margins, nonconformists could flourish and then carry forward a subversive crusade against the would-be monopolists of the military-industrial complex and its political puppets.

In actual space—most of which has decayed into a postindustrial wasteland—such nonconformists are permanently on the run, and there is no hope for them to live a rewarding life, even if they were able to settle. In cyberspace, cyber outlaws are potential heroes, and they feel a sense of belonging, which they do not receive in the actual world.

This hypothetical way of life, formed by *Neuromancer*, exerted a magnetic romantic attraction on countless young science-fiction readers who knew that the world to which they were condemned would be irreparably changed by computer technology. Readers found that they could steal a march on their elders by mastering intricacies that were difficult and alien to persons—including their elders—educated in a "predigital" era.

Although *Neuromancer*'s literary style was cleverly polished, and its artfully designed narrative magnificently forceful, the novel became a modern literary classic by virtue of its status as a cyberculture handbook. The book helped spawn hordes of dedicated nonconformists, who were not only employable but much in demand because of their skills in making computers do things that were beyond the capabilities of more orthodox thinkers.

In reality, most cyberpunk hopefuls "went native," using their skills' economic rewards to escape the threat of abandonment in the urban wasteland—but Gibson did not. As a writer, he kept the faith, and even though his work became steadily more naturalistic, with the "futures" featured in his work retreating toward and ultimately merging with the dynamic present, he maintained his commitment to heroes on the margins of society. In his personal life, Gibson was reasonably settled and content—the blog he began in 2003 makes this clear—but because he was a writer and, thus, by some definition, socially marginalized, he was allowed to live the cyberpunk dream to some degree in spite of his admittedly limited computer skills. *Neuromancer*, famously, was composed on a manual typewriter.

Neuromancer

Neuromancer was the archetype of cyberpunk fiction. The central character of the novel, the fallen hero Case, is an outlaw whose ability to "jack into" computers gives him the freedom to roam the virtual wide-open plains of cyberspace, armed and dangerous in ways that are infeasible in real space, and far more "glamorous."

Blacklisted after betraying his former employers, Case is given one last chance to hit the big time as a "cowboy" hacker by jacking into networked computers. Once jacked in he steers his projected personality through a landscape in which masses of data seem solid, although its most promising pastures are hidden behind forbidding walls of ice (Intrusion Countermeasures Electronics).

Case's redemption mission, suitably complicated by the involvement of other "viewpoint" characters, enables him to be present when the new universe acquires its own godlike resident consciousness in the form of an ambitious artificial intelligence (AI) named Wintermute. The AI declares that the computer network is now called the Matrix—another term that acquired totemic significance in the burgeoning cyberculture.

Count Zero *and* Mona Lisa Overdrive

The two sequels to *Neuromancer*, *Mona Lisa Overdrive* and *Count Zero*, similarly alternate viewpoint characters to construct elaborate multithreaded narratives, but *Neuromancer* had used up the climactic bonanza. *Count Zero* attempts to recomplicate *Neuromancer*'s climax by instituting a conflict between numerous godlike AI's inhabiting the Matrix. In *Mona Lisa Overdrive*, the third novel in Gibson's so-called Sprawl series, Case has retired and settled down to comfortable domesticity with his four children.

The sequels' adventures, in effect, seem understated. The novels appear brilliantly polished, yet they also look like compilations of hectic footnotes. Their true merit lies in their details.

The Difference Engine

The Difference Engine is a "steampunk" novel set in an alternative history in which Victorian England has undergone a sweeping technological revolution because of the development of Charles Babbage's mechanical computer. The novel testifies, even more clearly than in the dark cynicism of Gibson's futuristic thrillers, to the deep skepticism with which Gibson regarded the potentials of such technology. This skepticism had to be forgiven by worshipful would-be pioneers of cyberculture, but it was welcomed and admired by celebrants of postmodernism.

The Bridge trilogy

Virtual Light is the first book of Gibson's Bridge trilogy, so called because the San Francisco-Oakland Bay Bridge in California serves as a central location in all three novels. The bridge, following a severe earthquake, becomes the site of an eccentric countercultural ghetto.

The protagonist of *Virtual Light*, Chevette Washington, a bike messenger, steals a pair of glasses from a man at a party. The glasses, it turns out, provide a window into a virtual world containing a valuable secret, thus occasioning a hectic pursuit to recover the glasses from Chevette.

Idoru is set in the same near-future milieu, but mostly in Tokyo. One of *Idoru*'s central characters, Colin Laney, has a marginally supernatural talent that allows him to sense "nodal points" in floods of data that seem inchoate to normal perception. He obtained this supersensory ability after being doused with a chemical substance repeatedly during his childhood. Colin can also see into the future, but not without consequences.

In *All Tomorrow's Parties*, the chemical substance that gave Colin his heightened perception also makes him very sick. He ends up back in San Francisco, in pursuit of the source of the "big change" he envisions.

In the Bridge trilogy, cyberspace is no longer a trackless wilderness open to anyone who can melt or crack its walls of ice; it is much more thoroughly compartmentalized and privatized—an infinite series of fenced-in microcosms rather than an essentially boundless macrocosm. Although the Enclosures Act that has facilitated this fencing-in has by no means excluded the possibility of intrusion, the invaders whose threat engenders the greatest paranoia are not the would-be outlaws but the would-be regulators. The big players in the moneyworld are no longer imperfectly guarded and isolated fortresses; they are the secure Establishment. It is the outlaws and anarchists who are now compelled to build themselves "hidey-holes" and surround them with walls that, hopefully, cannot be breached.

Whereas *Idoru* and *All Tomorrow's Parties* develop technothriller story arcs that are similar to *Virtual Light*, their real brilliance is in the intricately detailed cultural and technological décor that they gradually accumulate for the reader.

Pattern Recognition

Pattern Recognition, the first novel in Gibson's third sequence, moves the action back to the threshold of the present. The book's heroine, Cayce Pollard—the first name is a deliberate echo—is a neurotic market researcher; like Colin in *Idoru*, she has a quasi-psychic talent, this time for trend-spotting. She is hired to hunt down the source of mysterious video clips that have built up a cult following on the Internet—a quest that inevitably involves her in the usual routine of threats and pursuits.

Spook Country

Spook Country is a multithreaded thriller in which various characters—many of them involved with the production and promotion of "locative art"—pursue an obscure object of desire whose relevance is somehow connected with "geospatial technologies." Rock music, Santeria, and international money-laundering are key features in the typically intricate background of the novel, which embodies the notion that "cyberspace has [now] colonized our everyday life" and that the process still has a long way to go.

Brian Stableford

Other major works

short fiction: "Fragments of a Hologram Rose," 1977; "The Gernsback Continuum," 1981; "Johnny Mnemonic," 1981; "Burning Chrome," 1982; *Burning Chrome*, 1986.

screenplay: *Johnny Mnemonic*, 1995 (adaptation of his short story).

teleplays: *Kill Switch*, 1998 (*X-Files* episode; with Tom Maddox); *First Person Shooter*, 2000 (*X-Files* episode; with Maddox).

miscellaneous: *Agrippa: A Book of the Dead*, 1992 (multimedia; with Dennis Ashbaugh); *No Maps for These Territories*, 2000 (documentary).

Bibliography

Bukataman, Scott. *Terminal Identity: The Virtual Subject of Post-Modern Science Fiction*. Durham, N.C.: Duke University Press, 1993. An early analysis of postmodern science fiction, in which Gibson's work assumes a central role.

Burrows, Roger. "Cyberpunk as Social Theory: William Gibson and the Sociological Imagination." In *Imagining Cities*, edited by Sallie Westwood and John Williams. New York: Routledge, 1997. Approaches Gibson's work from an unusual, but highly relevant, angle, concentrating on his representations of future city life.

Cavallero, Dani. *Cyberpunk and Cyberculture: Science Fiction and the Work of William Gibson*. London: Athlone, 2000. A retrospective study of the cyberpunk phenomenon, with Gibson as its center.

Conte, Joseph. "The Virtual Reader: Cybernetics and Technocracy in William Gibson and Bruce Sterling's *The Difference Engine*." In *The Holodeck in the Garden: Science and Technology in Contemporary American Fiction*, edited by Peter Freese and Charles B. Harris. Normal, Ill.: Dalkey Archive Press, 2004.

A useful analysis of the least studied of Gibson's works.

Foster, Thomas. *The Souls of Cyberpunk: Posthumanism as Vernacular Theory*. Minneapolis: University of Minnesota Press, 2005. An account of the movement's legacy, especially in terms of its colonization of other media. Chapter 2 includes a useful, close reading of *Neuromancer*.

Heuser, Sabine. *Virtual Geographies: Cyberpunk at the Intersection of the Postmodern and Science Fiction*. New York: Rodopi, 2003. A reflective survey that focuses primarily on the works of Gibson, Pat Cadigan, and Neal Stephenson, analyzing the history of the cyberpunk movement as well as the fiction.

Hollinger, Veronica. "Stories About the Future: From Patterns of Expectation to *Pattern Recognition*." *Science Fiction Studies* 33, no. 3 (2006): 452-473. The most sophisticated of three articles in a special section devoted to *Pattern Recognition*. The other articles are by Christopher Palmer and Neil Easterbrook.

McCaffery, Larry, ed. *Storming the Reality Studio: A Casebook of Cyberpunk and Postmodern Science Fiction*. Durham, N.C.: Duke University Press, 1991. A definitive showcase anthology, more influential in the academic community (and more wide-ranging) than Bruce Sterling's definitive cyberpunk anthology *Mirrorshades* (1986). Includes articles on Gibson's work and an interview with Gibson by the editor.

Olsen, Lance. *William Gibson*. Mercer Island, Wash.: Starmont House, 1992. An overview of Gibson's early work, locating it within the conventional contexts of cyberpunk and postmodernism.

Rapatzikou, Tatiani G. *Gothic Motifs in the Fiction of William Gibson*. New York: Rodopi, 2004. An unusual but productive approach to Gibson's work, in which the author finds abundant neo-Gothic imagery.

Slusser, George E., with Tom A. Shippey, eds. *Fiction 2000: Cyberpunk and the Future of Narrative*. Athens: University of Georgia Press, 1992. A key collection of early responses to the academicization of cyberpunk; the items most tightly focused on Gibson are the essays by Paul Alkon, Istvan Csisery-Ronay, Jr., John Huntington, and Carol McGuirk.

ANDRÉ GIDE

Born: Paris, France; November 22, 1869
Died: Paris, France; February 19, 1951
Also known as: André-Paul-Guillaume Gide

Principal long fiction

L'Immoraliste, 1902 (*The Immoralist*, 1930)
La Porte étroite, 1909 (*Strait Is the Gate*, 1924)
Les Caves du Vatican, 1914 (*The Vatican Swindle*, 1925; better known as *Lafcadio's Adventures*, 1927)
La Symphonie pastorale, 1919 (*The Pastoral Symphony*, 1931)
Les Faux-monnayeurs, 1925 (*The Counterfeiters*, 1927)
Thésée, 1946 (*Theseus*, 1950)

Other literary forms

André Gide (zheed) began his literary career with a number of prose works that defy conventional classification; among them are poetic works in prose, such as *Les Cahiers d'André Walter* (1891; *The Notebooks of André Walter*, 1968) and *Les Nourritures terrestres* (1897; *Fruits of the Earth*, 1949), and the stories *Paludes* (1895; *Marshlands*, 1953) and *Le Prométhée mal enchaîné* (1899; *Prometheus Misbound*, 1953). Although closely related to his development as a novelist, such works are perhaps best described as lyric essays discussing the nature and limits of human freedom. Gide is known also for his *Journal* (1939-1950, 1954; *The Journals of André Gide, 1889-1949*, 1947-1951); several autobiographical volumes, including *Si le grain ne meurt* (1926; *If It Die . . .*, 1935) and *Et nunc manet in te* (1947,

1951; *Madeleine*, 1952); and the travelogues *Voyage au Congo* (1927; *Travels in the Congo*, 1929) and *Retour de l'U.R.S.S.* (1936; *Return from the U.S.S.R.*, 1937). As early as 1899, Gide also applied his talents to the writing of plays; the products of these efforts are rarely performed but were published in English in the collection *My Theater* (1952) one year after the author's death at the age of eighty-one.

Achievements

Despite the relatively small portion of his output that can be classified legitimately as prose fiction, André Gide ranks among the most internationally influential French novelists of his time. With the notable exception of Marcel Proust, Gide was the preeminent French novelist of the period between 1900 and 1950, even though he refused to apply the term "novel" to all but one of his extended prose narratives. Although his reputation declined somewhat during the two decades immediately following his death, he would later be regarded among the major figures, both as theoretician and as practitioner, in the history of modern prose fiction.

Belonging, along with Proust and the somewhat younger François Mauriac, to the last generation of French writers whose private means released them from the need to earn a living, Gide wrote at first to discover and define himself, initially supplying the costs of publication out of his own pocket. Influenced at the beginning of his career by the Decadent and Symbolist movements, Gide's work soon assumed a personal stamp and direction, acquiring universality even as the author sought primarily to find the best possible expression for his own particular concerns. *Fruits of the Earth*, a lyric meditation published in 1897, established Gide's promise as an original writer and a rising literary figure, although it was not until some twenty years later, during and after World War I, that the book would render its author famous (or infamous) for his inspiration (or corruption) of an entire generation of European youth. By that time, Gide's audacious speculations on the nature of freedom and identity had found expression also in the form of extended narratives for which the author adamantly denied the appellation "novel," preferring such recondite (and attention-getting) alternatives as *récit* (tale) or *sotie*, the latter a term for a satiric improvisation performed by French law students during the late Middle Ages.

Such early *récits* as *The Immoralist* and *Strait Is the Gate* established Gide as a master of psychological narrative; *Lafcadio's Adventures*, published in 1914 as a *sotie*, demonstrated Gide's mastery of social satire, with multiple narratives and viewpoints. In *The Pastoral Symphony*, published in 1919, perhaps the most widely read of Gide's prose narratives, he skillfully combined the psychological and satiric strains. It was not, however, until 1925 that Gide saw fit, with *The Counterfeiters*, to publish a book plainly labeled as a "novel" (*roman*). The result was one of the most widely read and influential novels of the decade—indeed, of the entire period between the two world wars and afterward, in view of its considerable effect on such later developments as the New Novel of the 1950's.

After *The Counterfeiters*, Gide wrote extensively in a variety of genres, although among his later major efforts only *Theseus* might reasonably be considered as extended fiction. Among the first (and oldest) of literary celebrities to be extensively photographed and interviewed, the otherwise reticent Gide spent his later years as an internationally famous literary figure. He received the Nobel Prize in Literature in 1947, not long after the publication of *Theseus*.

Perhaps correctly identified as a precursor of many significant developments in modern and postmodern fiction, Gide was among the first writers, along with Hermann Hesse, to explore the changing relationships between the individual and society, raising serious epistemological questions with regard to the nature of human identity. He is respected also as a master of prose style in his native language, having perfected a spare, neoclassical sentence that is almost instantly recognizable yet difficult to imitate.

Biography

André-Paul-Guillaume Gide was born in Paris on November 22, 1869, the only child of Paul Gide (a law professor) and the former Juliette Rondeaux. A shy, introspective boy, inevitably influenced by his parents' severe Protestantism, Gide soon perceived in himself an avid sexuality that would tend toward inversion; as early as the age of seven, he was expelled from school for masturbation and would remain haunted for life by a nagging guilt that he kept trying to neutralize through his various writings. The death of his father in 1880, at the age of forty-seven, added further complication to an already troubled childhood, and Gide would soon undergo treatment for a variety of nervous disorders. Around the age of thirteen, Gide developed a strong, lifelong attachment to his first cousin Madeleine Rondeaux, two years his senior, who became his wife soon after the death of his mother in 1895. Their marriage, although never consummated, was the dominant emotional relationship of Gide's life and ended only with Madeleine's death in 1938 at the age of seventy-one.

Even before his marriage, Gide had begun to emerge as a potential literary figure, thanks in part to a curious work that was written initially with Madeleine in mind. *The Notebooks of André Walter*, privately published in 1891 at the young author's expense, purports to be the diary of a young man, by then deceased, describing his love for one Emmanuèle, under which name Madeleine Rondeaux appears in thin disguise. Although the book failed to sell, it was disseminated within Parisian artistic circles, and Gide continued writing, producing such documents as the Symbolist parable *Le Traité du Narcisse* (1891; "Narcissus," in *The Return of the Prodigal Son*, 1953), the protonovel *Le Voyage d'Urien* (1893; *Urien's Voyage*, 1964), and the experimental *Paludes*, about a young man who is planning a novel to be called *Paludes*. In 1893, Gide at long last came to terms with his homosexuality during the course of a trip to North Africa, the details of which would receive chaste (but, for that time, explicit) fictional treatment in *The Immoralist*. Having for all practical purposes discontinued his formal education after belatedly passing the *baccalauréat* on his second attempt, in 1889, Gide nevertheless continued to develop as a self-taught intellectual, reading widely and participating fully in the vigorous cultural activity then centered in Paris. His first truly significant publication, *Fruits of the Earth*, begun as early as the trip to North Africa, was finished shortly after his marriage to Madeleine but was not published until 1897.

André Gide. (© The Nobel Foundation)

Gide's marriage, discussed at considerable length by numerous commentators as well as by Gide himself, remained a dominant feature of both his life and his work. There is little doubt that his love for Madeleine was as deep and intense as it was otherworldly, firmly rooted in the oddly protective emotion that had overwhelmed him when Madeleine was fifteen and he was two years younger. Like her fictional counterpart, Alissa, in *Strait Is the Gate*, Madeleine had recently discovered her own mother's marital infidelity and was quite undone by what she had learned; André, although little more than a child (and a disturbed child at that), instinctively sought to comfort his cousin. There was thus at the base of their affective relationship a denial of the physical that would never really change. Commentator Thomas Cordle, inspired in part by Denis de Rougemont's landmark essay *L'Amour et l'occident* (1939; *Love in the Western World*, 1983), sees in Gide's love for Madeleine a personification of heretical Catharist doctrine as perpetuated in the Tristan legend; in any case, the nature of Gide's love was such that the prospect of consummation might well have threatened to corrupt its "purity."

Madeleine, for her part, was surely not unaware of her cousin's sexual ambiguities by the time she consented to marry him, after several prior refusals; it is likely, too, that she shared his instinctive horror of the physical, although she appears at one time to have contemplated the possibility of pregnancy and childbirth. In either event, the union appears to have proceeded with relative mutual satisfaction until 1918, when Madeleine, bitter over Gide's apparent homosexual "elopement" with the future film director Marc Allégret, burned all the letters that André had written to her since their adolescence. Gide, claiming those letters to have been the only true record of his life and an irreplaceable personal treasure, decided that Madeleine's spiteful gesture had ruined his career; most of Gide's commentators agree that his career, although not in fact ruined, developed thereafter in a different direction from that it might otherwise have taken. The author's marriage, although not ruined either, remained seriously flawed for the remainder of Madeleine's life. Gide's only child, duly christened Catherine Gide, was born in 1923 to Elizabeth van Rysselberghe, daughter of Gide's close friends Théo and Maria van Rysselberghe. Although Gide claimed both Catherine and his eventual grandchildren, he left no written record of his feelings (if any) toward the mother of his only child.

In 1909, already famous as the author of *The Immoralist* and the well-circulated parable *Le Retour de l'enfant prodigue* (1907; *The Return of the Prodigal Son*, 1953), Gide assumed an active part in the founding of the influential periodical *La Nouvelle Revue française*, along with such other literary figures as Jean Schlumberger and Henri Ghéon. Soon thereafter, he began work (along with numerous other projects) on the controversial *Corydon* (English translation, 1950), a quasi-Socratic dialogue in defense of homosexuality that would be released privately in 1911, against the advice of Gide's closest friends, and eventually published commercially in 1924. In retrospect, it appears that Gide rather enjoyed controversy, having long (and vociferously) resisted the efforts of several fellow writers to bring him "back into the fold" of the Roman Catholic Church. Because Gide had been reared as a Protestant, there was in fact no question of bringing him "back," as he had never been there; his collected correspondence nevertheless contains a voluminous and vigorous exchange of letters, many of which appeared in print at the time, involving such noted literary contemporaries as the poet Francis Jammes and the playwright-poet Paul Claudel. Although Gide had abjured his Protestant faith, his writings continued to give evidence of a strong religious sensibility that Claudel and others thought might still be "salvageable." The story is told that Claudel, less than a week after Gide's death in 1951, received a telegram purportedly signed by Gide and claiming, "There is no Hell."

During the 1920's, Gide's penchant for controversy began to acquire political overtones as well, albeit in sporadic and idiosyncratic ways. Ordinarily among the least political of writers, virtually oblivious to the two world wars through which he lived and wrote, Gide nevertheless aroused considerable attention with two well-publicized (and recorded) voyages, the first to colonial Africa and the second, in the mid-1930's, to the Soviet Union. For all of his intelligence, Gide on both occasions appears to have been quite naïve in his expectations; in Chad and the Congo, for example, he was as surprised as he was appalled by the frequent (and flagrant) violation of human rights by the colonial "oppressors." Partly as a result of such observations, Gide in the 1930's began flirting openly with international communism and was duly courted by the Russians in return; he repeatedly refused, however, to become a Party member, and while touring the Soviet Union as a guest of the Soviet government, he became every bit as disillusioned with the Soviet experiment as he had been by French colonialism a decade earlier in Africa. Still cherishing an ideal of communism, Gide wrote bitterly of its "failure" in the Soviet Union.

Following his visit to the Soviet Union and the death of Madeleine Gide not long thereafter, Gide effectively retreated from the political scene. Much as he personally deplored the onset of another war and the subsequent collaborationist regime at Vichy, Gide found little place for the war in his writings, preferring instead the sort of inner reflection that had characterized his work from the start. From 1942 until the end of the war, he resided in North Africa, refusing offered passage to London even after North Africa was liberated. It was there, after all, that he had experienced his first great liberations both as person and as writer, and it was there that he would produce his last great *récit*, a reflection on the life and career of Theseus. Honored in 1947 with the Nobel Prize in Literature, Gide remained active with the writing of essays, memoirs, and translations until his death in February, 1951.

Analysis

Although André Gide's career as a published author spanned nearly sixty years, his position in literary history depends primarily on five prose narratives published in the first quarter of the twentieth century. As Gide's reputation rose to prominence, roughly between 1910 and 1920, critics and commentators were quick to discover the author's earlier writings and, in them, the clear annunciation of Gide's mature output. It is likely, however, that without the merited success of *The Immoralist, Strait Is the Gate, Lafcadio's Adventures, The Pastoral Symphony*, and *The Counterfeiters*, Gide's earliest writings might well have remained mere literary curiosities of the late Symbolist period. A notable exception might well be *Fruits of the Earth*, a transitional work, which in the years following World War I enjoyed a belated success quite unrelated to that of Gide's other writings. In any case, *The Immoralist* and its successors bear witness to a controlled, mature talent that has few peers in the subsequent history of French fiction.

With *The Immoralist*, a slim volume of deceptive simplicity, Gide reclaimed for the French tradition a strong foothold in the psychological novel. Skillful psychological narrative had been associated with France as early as the seventeenth century, thanks to Madame de La Fayette and her *La Princesse de Clèves* (1678; *The Princess of Clèves*, 1679), but had recently been pushed aside by the seemingly more urgent claims of realism and naturalism; it was not until the 1920's and early 1930's that the Belgian Georges Simenon, hailed and admired by Gide, would combine psychological narrative with the strongest legacies of naturalism. In the meantime, Gide further established his claim with *Strait Is the Gate*, another economical tale, which, although quite different, is in several respects a mirror image of *The Immoralist*. Particularly remarkable in both short novels is the emergence of Gide's mature style—a clear, concise form of expression far removed from his early verbosity yet not without certain affective mannerisms, particularly noticeable in his frequent inversion of adverb and verb; it is quite likely that the proverbial aspect of Gide's style derives at least in part from his frequent reading of the Bible.

Common to Gide's first two *récits* is his skillful use of a somewhat unreliable first-person narrator whose impressions are "corrected" by other narrative or correspondence that is used to frame the text. In both cases, however, Gide is careful not to point to a moral or to intrude himself as narrator within the working of the text. The canvas remains small, perhaps justifying Gide's use of the description *récit* in place of the more ambitious *roman:* In each tale, only two characters are singled out for close attention, with fewer than ten more appearing in the background. *The Immoralist* is the story of the process by which Michel, at once thoughtful and thoughtless, discovers himself, at the cost of his marriage and the life of his wife, Marceline; *Strait Is the Gate*, told mainly by the ineffectual Jérôme, presents the story of Alissa, whose renunciation and sacrifice seem hardly less selfish, in retrospect, than the deliberate indulgence of Michel in *The Immoralist*. More than once during his career, Gide pointed out that the two tales were in fact twins, having formed in his mind at the same time.

The Immoralist

Gide, in his earliest attempts at writing—intended mainly for himself, his school friends, and his cousin Madeleine—tried to discover and define the nature of a freedom that was felt but not yet experienced. Gide's initial voyage to Africa, in 1893, resulted in an awakening that was psychological and spiritual as well as sexual, inspiring the young would-be author to shake off the bonds imposed by his austere French Protestant upbringing. One of the first concepts to emerge in his quest was that of *disponibilité* (availability). As expressed primarily in *Fruits of the Earth*, Gide's idea of *disponibilité* holds that the individual should keep himself "available" to the full range of potential human experience, for only then can he discover all of himself and conduct himself in a truly sincere and authentic manner. Clearly, Gide as early as 1902 had perceived the possible dangers and advisable limits of such an attitude, for *The Immoralist* is at least in part a cautionary tale about personal freedom pushed thoughtlessly to its extreme. Still, the physical and spiritual flowering of the formerly frail and bookish Michel is not without a certain intentional appeal. Between extremes, Gide appears to be suggesting, even advocating, a self-liberation that stops short of incurring such disastrous consequences as the early death of one's wife. For the purposes of fiction, however, *The Immoralist* is extremely well structured and memorable, involving the decline and failure of Marceline's health in inverse proportion to that of her husband.

Like most of his work published both before and since, *The Immoralist* draws heavily upon the established data of Gide's life; here as elsewhere, however, it would be erroneous to see in the work of fiction a direct transposition of the author's experience. Michel's awakening under the hot sun of North Africa, complete with his sexual initiation by young Arabs, obviously owes much to Gide's own experience; Gide, however, initially discovered Africa before his marriage and not while on his honeymoon. Michel's most important discoveries, however, appear to be not sexual but psychological, as in the memorable scene of the Arab boy Moktir stealing Marceline's scissors. Michel, initially shocked, observes the theft with growing fascination and invents a false tale to tell his wife; only later does he learn from his mysterious friend Ménalque, who hands him the worn and battered scissors, that Moktir, in turn, was aware of being watched. Michel's growing sense of complicity in the reversal of conventional morality constitutes no small part of his newfound freedom; later, upon his return to France, he will conspire with poachers to steal from his own land. Throughout the tale, recounted mainly in the first person by Michel, Gide equates Michel's growing health and strength with his increasing fondness for the wild and elemental; later, when Marceline miscarries and falls ill, the erstwhile near-invalid Michel will prove strangely insensitive to her suffering, claiming that he "got well" all by himself and wondering why she cannot do the same. Still, Michel remains sufficiently attached to Marceline that he will dismiss his "experiment in liberation" as a failure when she ultimately dies.

In *The Immoralist*, as in his later narratives, Gide is particularly concerned to show the negative effects of conventional morality upon the individual; here, however, little mention is made of religion per se, and Gide's concerns are implied rather than directly stated. Clearly, the circumstances of Michel's comfortable bourgeois background are to be seen as stifling, confining, and detrimental to his health; it is not until he breaks away from the security of a precocious academic career (as an archaeologist) that Michel begins to "get well," discovering at the same time what Gide portrays as his authentic self. As in Gide's own case, however, the ties of love remain strong and are less easily dismissed than the constraints of traditional morality.

Strait Is the Gate

In *Strait Is the Gate*, conceived around the same time as *The Immoralist*, Gide presents what he sees as the other side of the same coin. Quite unlike Michel, yet with equal intransigence, Jérôme's cousin Alissa chooses the path of renunciation and self-abnegation, causing some early readers to see in *Strait Is the Gate* a religious or devotional work—indeed, a rebuttal of *The Immoralist*. As in the earlier work, however, ambiguities abound on every page, and it is soon clear that Alissa's "experiment" is hardly more successful or "exemplary" than that of her counterpart Michel; like Michel, indeed, she thoughtlessly contributes to needless human suffering.

Narrated mainly by the callow and ineffectual Jérôme, Alissa's first cousin and sometime fiancé, *Strait Is the Gate* exemplifies and partially satirizes what Cordle has identified as the Catharist dimension of Gide's thought and art. No doubt indebted to the author's life and marriage in certain details, including the age difference and Alissa's discovery of her mother's extramarital affairs, the portrayal of Alissa through Jérôme's love-struck eyes demonstrates a mastery of ironic technique that is all but lacking in *The Immoralist* and finds its strongest expression in *The Pastoral Symphony*. If Alissa indeed suffers from a variety of moral blindness in her adherence to Scripture at the expense of humanity, Jérôme, in turn, suffers from a literal-minded imperceptivity only partially explained by his scholarly training and plans. Perhaps most tellingly, he remains quite unaware of his sensual appeal to Alissa even as he records the effects of that attraction for his potential readers. The latent irony of *Strait Is the Gate* is further enhanced by the inclusion of Alissa's diaries, discovered only posthumously, recording not only her intense feelings toward Jérôme but also her "selfless," determined, and ultimately unsuccessful effort to "marry him off" to her sister Juliette.

Like the love of Gide and Madeleine, the emotion that binds Jérôme and Alissa is clearly "too good for this world," incapable in any case of satisfaction. Although some readers continue to feel that Alissa has given ample proof of sainthood, it is somewhat more likely that she, like Michel of *The Immoralist*, has pushed her inclination to extremes. The reader, although invited to share the excruciating pain of two passionate individuals so hopelessly unable to communicate, might also find occasion to question Alissa's taste in fastening her affections upon a creature as spineless as Jérôme. A stronger Jérôme would render the tale quite implausible, if not impossible, but his limitations spread outward to encompass *Strait Is the Gate* as well, perhaps adding an unintentional note of irony to the book's biblical title.

Lafcadio's Adventures

With *Lafcadio's Adventures*, Gide broadened his narrative canvas considerably, involving a large cast of frequently outrageous characters in a broad social satire that leaves few sacred cows unmilked. For the first time in his fiction, Gide gives evidence of a perceptive, pervasive sense of humor, which, with some effort and the wisdom of hindsight, has been detected by some critics between the lines of his earlier works. If here, as elsewhere, Gide's stated aim is to disturb the reader, he manages also to entertain, and lavishly so. In his lively evocation of a criminal scheme to extort funds from the faithful in order to "ransom" a Pope who has not in fact been kidnapped, Gide expresses his familiar concerns in a most unfamiliar way; if his main preoccupation remains with the individual, Gide nevertheless gains considerable appeal by placing those individuals against the background of society. Characteristically, however, Gide eschewed the description "novel" even for this effort, preferring the archaic (and exotic) term *sotie*, in part to underscore the *sottise* (stupidity) of most of the characters involved. His true novel, *The Counterfeiters*, moreover, was already in the planning stage, although not to be published until after *The Pastoral Symphony*.

In *Lafcadio's Adventures*, Gide at last gave free rein to the strong ironic bent that is little more than latent in his earlier efforts; in addition, he added a strong portion of humor that is generally lacking elsewhere in his work, with keen observation that often crosses over into broad caricature. Based presumably upon a true incident recorded in European newspapers during the 1890's, *Lafcadio's Adventures* is nevertheless peopled exclusively with characters that could have sprung only from Gide's increasingly active imagination. Even the names are strange, from the novelist Julius de Baraglioul and his brother-in-law Amédée Fleurissoire to Julius's illegitimate half brother Lafcadio Wluiki; there is also the prostitute Carola, whose surname, Venitequa, means "come here" in Latin. Believers and freethinkers alike are treated with irreverence, portrayed as "crustaceans" whose institutionalized beliefs have stunted and distorted what might have been their true personalities. Here, as in *The Counterfeiters*, Gide clearly adumbrates the same demand for authentic behavior that would later dominate the work of Jean-Paul Sartre; unlike Sartre, however, he is not quite ready to accept the implications of total human freedom. To be sure, he offers a tantalizing portrayal of freedom in the person of the nineteen-year-old Lafcadio, whose illegitimacy purportedly exempts him from the bondage of polite society, yet it is hard even for Gide to condone the now-famous *acte gratuit*, or unmotivated deed, in which Lafcadio, more or less from sheer boredom, pushes the unsuspecting Fleurissoire out the door of a moving train. As in *The Immoralist*, freedom still has its limits, and Lafcadio will find that he has thus murdered the brother of his own sister-in-law. By apparent chance, however, he will go unpunished.

Particularly effective in *Lafcadio's Adventures* is Gide's satiric portrayal of the bourgeois "crustaceans": Julius, unlike Gide, is among the most complacent (and presumably boring) of novelists; Anthime Armand-Dubois, a scientist cast in the mold of Gustave Flaubert's pharmacist Homais of *Madame Bovary* (1857; English translation, 1886), undergoes a sudden conversion to Catholicism that is no less hilarious for being totally sincere. Fleurissoire, the most amiable (if also the most apparently ridiculous) of the three, conserves his goodwill through a harrowing sequence of tortures, only to meet senseless death at the idle hands of Lafcadio; several of Gide's commentators argue with some justice that Fleurissoire may well be the true hero of the book, exhibiting the patience of Job when subjected to similar ordeals. In any event, the fundamental weakness of all three men is their gullibility, reflected in the book's resonant French title, *Les Caves du Vatican*; in French, the word *cave* can refer to the victim of a hoax, similar to the word "mark" in English.

Throughout *Lafcadio's Adventures*, Gide, despite a certain fascination, is careful not to side too closely with the hoaxers, led by the ubiquitous, many-visaged, truly protean Protos. After all, Gide suggests, such parasites can flourish only as long as they find willing victims, and who in his right mind would hand over money to ransom a captive Pope? Only a "crustacean," which further proves the need for increasingly authentic conduct of one's life. Paradoxically, even Lafcadio can exist as he does only in relation to the society he professes to despise; for all of his vaunted freedom, he functions only as the inverted mirror image of respectability, and were respectability to vanish he would vanish too—or change, as do the three "crustaceans" once they have been gulled.

The Pastoral Symphony

Serving clear notice of the author's ironic intentions as early as its title, *The Pastoral Symphony*, both broadens and deepens the *récit* as Gide had earlier conceived it, presenting the voice of a most unreliable narrator, who nevertheless is presented with sufficient skill not to strain the reader's credulity. Recalling the legend of Oedipus along with that of Pygmalion, *The Pastoral Symphony* presents the testimony of a Protestant pastor who hypocritically overlooks his own motivations as he ministers to the blind foundling Gertrude. Although the sustained images of sight and blindness are likely to appear too obvious in summary, they are extremely well-managed within the story itself, a minor masterpiece of "unreliable" first-person narrative. Here, as in *Strait Is the Gate*, and, later, in *The Counterfeiters*, Gide presents a scathing satire of the Protestant milieu from which he sprang, demonstrating the ill effects of that particular doctrine upon the human spirit. Toward the end of Gide's life, *The Pastoral Symphony* was successfully filmed, with Michéle Morgan in the role of Gertrude.

With *The Pastoral Symphony*, Gide returns to the *récit*, investing the form with deeper resonance and insight than are to be found in either *Strait Is the Gate* or *The Immoralist*. As heavily ironic as *Lafcadio's Adventures*, yet tightly controlled within the first-person narrative viewpoint, *The Pastoral Symphony* continues Gide's inquiry into the potentially negative effects, both psychological and social, of organized religion. Significantly, the narrator-protagonist is a Protestant minister, subspecies Calvinist, whose Swiss enclave is hemmed in on all sides by Roman Catholicism. In apparent reaction against Roman Catholic tradition, he has developed a strong personal faith and doctrine based primarily upon the Gospels. In time, however, he has allowed his faith to harden into a crustacean shell that protects him from true introspection as well as from outside influences; thus does he remain hypocritically blind to his true feelings toward Gertrude and insensitive to the needs of his own wife and family.

A dozen years earlier, in 1907, Gide had written the oft-reprinted *The Return of the Prodigal Son*, an extended parable or prose poem retelling the tale of the prodigal son. In Gide's version, the prodigal son returns only because he is hungry; although he decides to stay, he inspires his younger brother (a Gidean invention) to leave on the same kind of pagan pilgrimage from which the prodigal has just returned. Intended at least in part as an explanation to his Catholic friends of why he could not join their church, Gide's brief text is interpreted also by some commentators as a concise overview of Catholicism, Protestantism, Judaism, and Islam. It remains a remarkable text, foreshadowing many of the tensions that were later to animate the action of *The Pastoral Symphony*.

The pastor, like the prodigal son, instinctively recoils from the restrictions and prohibitions brought to Christianity by the epistles of Saint Paul, preferring instead the good news of love propounded by the Gospels. Unfortunately, he manages to misread the Gospels as shelter for his own hypocrisy, retreating into the shell of his faith when in fact it is his illicit love for Gertrude, and not his Calvinism, that is making his family uneasy. The conflict reaches crisis proportions when the pastor's son, Jacques, who has been preparing to follow his father into the ministry, finds himself simultaneously attracted to Gertrude and to the Roman Catholic Church; in several telling passages, the wily pastor attempts to dissuade his son from both attractions by berating his son with Protestant theology; he also attempts to forestall an operation that would restore young Gertrude's eyesight. Gertrude, meanwhile, has become increasingly sensitive to the tensions at work in the pastor's household and perceives, even before the successful operation, that she poses a threat to the pastor's marriage, even as she truly loves Jacques. Her de facto suicide, presented as a selfless gesture, occurs only after she and Jacques have both been baptized as Roman Catholics; thus does the pastor conclude that he has "lost" them both.

Given the time of its composition, a number of Gide's commentators have seen in *The Pastoral Symphony* an artistic transposition of the author's own homosexual affair with the young Marc Allégret (whom he later adopted) and his subsequent rupture with Madeleine after she burned his letters. To be sure, the pastor's marriage is portrayed as dry and loveless, based more on habit than on affection; at one point, the pastor observes that the only way he can please Amélie is to avoid displeasing her. Still, *The Pastoral Symphony* might also be seen as the least autobiographical of Gide's published novels, relating less to his life than to his sustained preoccupation with religion and its potential pitfalls. In *The Counterfeiters*, albeit on a larger canvas, he continued his inquiry into what he saw as the "inevitable" hypocrisy engendered by Protestant belief.

The Counterfeiters

Late in 1925, already in his middle fifties, Gide at last presented the "novel" that had long occupied his time and energy. Similar in scope to *Lafcadio's Adventures*, its satire softened somewhat by deeper reflection, *The Counterfeiters* proved well worth waiting for, assuring a receptive audience also for Gide's logbook, *Le Journal des "Faux-monnayeurs"* (1926; *Journal of "The Counterfeiters,"* 1951). Like that of *The Pastoral Symphony*, the title is intended to be understood on several levels; although a band of counterfeiters does, in fact, appear in the novel, the title applies also to nearly all of the adult characters presented in the book, who assume all manner of disguises in order to serve as role models for their understandably disoriented children. It is with the children and adolescents that Gide the novelist is primarily concerned, and they receive his mature sympathy: The adults have all "sold out," in one way or another, leaving the children to fend for themselves. Particularly biting is Gide's satiric portrayal of the Pension Azaïs-Vedel, a seedy Protestant boarding school whose pastor-proprietors, a father and son-in-law, have long since lost the attention and respect of their truly inquiring charges. Through the person of one Édouard, an aspiring novelist approaching middle age, Gide explores the various levels of truth and falsehood not only in life but also in the novel; Édouard, for his part, is planning a volume to be called *Les Faux-monnayeurs*, but one that doubtless will never be written. To his credit, however, Gide in *The Counterfeiters* managed to avoid most of the pitfalls that have awaited his followers in the dubious art of writing a novel about a novelist who is writing a novel. In so doing, moreover, he brought to full expression most of the themes and concerns that preoccupied or haunted him throughout his career. *The Counterfeiters* remains both Gide's masterwork and a landmark in the development of the modern novel.

Reared in the austere and defensive minority environment that was and is French Protestantism, Gide experienced Calvinist guilt at an early age and never really liberated himself from its pervasive clutches. Still, he knew too much, had seen too much, ever to return to the small fold. It is hardly surprising, therefore, that in his first and only "novel" Gide should equate Christianity with Protestantism of a most narrow and unappealing kind. Almost without exception, the troubled adolescents of *The Counterfeiters* are somehow involved with the Pension Azaïs-Vedel, a marginal Protestant boarding school whose precepts are more often honored in the breach than in the observance. Earlier in life, the writer Édouard, in his late thirties at the time of the novel, was both shocked and amazed by the ease with which his young charges shrugged off the solemn pronouncements of old Azaïs; it was not long, however, before Édouard, hired as a teacher, recognized the students' response as the only reasonable one. Like the pastor of *The Pastoral Symphony*, both Azaïs and his son-in-law Vedel are steeped in smug hypocrisy, having long since made their private, unrecognized concessions to the demands of human nature. The pupils therefore have little choice but to listen politely, then go and do as they please.

Armand Vedel, grandson of Azaïs, may well be the most potentially corrupt of all the adolescents surveyed in the novel; he is at all events the most jaded. Still seeking further corruption and "adventure," Armand refuses to consult a physician about his possible throat cancer—an affliction that symbolizes the state of his mind. His sisters, meanwhile, have fared hardly better: Rachel, the eldest, has never married and bears upon her shoulders the day-to-day administration of the school, including frequent financial shortfalls; her father, meanwhile, could not care less, blindly believing that "the Lord will provide." Her younger sister Laura, formerly in love with Édouard, who would not marry her although he returned her love, has abandoned her teacher-husband for an affair with the dissolute medical student Vincent Molinier, brother of two pension students who figure prominently in the novel. Now abandoned in turn by Vincent and carrying his child, Laura will eventually be invited to rejoin her husband with the promise of forgiveness. Ironically, however, it is Édouard whom she still loves.

Perhaps because of the multiplicity of characters and necessary subplots deemed appropriate to the "novel" as opposed to the more restricted *récit*, *The Counterfeiters* often appears confused in its organization, its disparate parts frequently linked by implausible coincidence or by cumbersome (and uncharacteristic) intervention on the part of the author. In order to allow the reader access to Édouard's unpublished journal, for example, Gide arranges for Édouard to have his suitcase stolen by the runaway Bernard Profitendieu, a friend of Édouard's nephew Olivier Molinier; the reader thus reads the journal, as it were, over the shoulder of Bernard, who is reading it himself and will act upon what he has learned. The journal, meanwhile, intersperses facts with frequent ruminations on the theory of the novel.

As in *Lafcadio's Adventures*, and as befits the title of his "novel," Gide in *The Counterfeiters* appears primarily concerned with the nature of authentic thought and behavior, making fun of middle-aged "crustaceans" or "counterfeiters," whose essence has retreated behind mere form. Édouard's brother-in-law Oscar Molinier, for example, is a veteran womanizer who believes his wife, Pauline, to be quite unaware of his philandering; when a packet of letters from his mistress disappears, he concludes that Pauline has discovered him at last. Pauline, no stranger to her husband's secret life, is even more appalled by the disappearance of the letters, correctly guessing that their youngest son, Georges, has stolen them to use as a form of blackmail. Édouard, Pauline's brother, is thus drawn into several levels of intrigue within the story, and it is his rather inept effort to make sense of his own observations that provides the backbone of the novel within a novel, while Gide himself remains in control. As in his earlier efforts, Gide proves especially skillful at unreliable first-person narration, for Édouard is in his own way every bit as much a counterfeiter as the rest of his contemporaries.

Throughout *The Counterfeiters*, partly because of a more liberal literary climate than obtained at the beginning of the twentieth century, Gide for the first time in his creative prose speaks freely of homosexual love and attraction, as well as of the autoeroticism that had plagued his own childhood and youth. Édouard, although apparently bisexual, is strongly attracted to boys and men, including his nephew Olivier, who, with Pauline's tacit permission, becomes Ëdouard's lover after Édouard saves Olivier from an attempted suicide. This sexual ambiguity in Édouard prevents him from providing Laura Douviers-Vedel with the love and affection that she both wants and needs. Nor is Édouard the only gay man in *The Counterfeiters*; several rungs below him on the moral level stands Count Robert de Passavant, also a writer, who openly seeks to corrupt the young (Olivier Molinier as well as Armand Vedel) and maintains a sporadic sybaritic relationship with the cold, frankly amoral Lilian, also known as Lady Griffith.

Bernard Profitendieu, whose flight from his home opens the action of the novel, remains a pivotal if minor figure throughout all that follows. The reason for his flight is that he has discovered his own illegitimacy, learning that his mother bore him out of wedlock. The discovery provides him with all the ammunition that he seems to need for revolt against the authoritarian figure of Judge Albéric Profitendieu, and for a while Bernard tests and tries to enjoy the "bastardly freedom" of the author's earlier creation Lafcadio (who, according to Gide, was initially supposed to appear in *The Counterfeiters* as well). In time, however, with the approach of true spiritual maturity (symbolized by a rather bizarre supernatural experience), Bernard will return to the Profitendieu household, having grown, developed, and learned more than most of the other characters.

In the person of the diabolic counterfeiter Strouvilhou, aided by his nephew Ghéridanisol and their occasional associate Robert de Passavant, Gide invests the shadowy underworld with an even more sinister presence than that of Protos in *Lafcadio's Adventures*.

Strouvilhou, himself a former student at the Pension Azaïs-Vedel, is less a confidence man than a true anarchist for whom crime serves merely as one possible means to the eventual end of total chaos. Not content with mere counterfeiting, he inspires his young victims to blackmail their parents and consciously engineers the gratuitous suicide of the troubled young Boris, who has enrolled in the pension to be near his grandfather, Édouard's longtime friend, the elderly musician La Pérouse. As in *Lafcadio's Adventures*, however, Gide takes pains to show that the criminal element, however motivated, can exist only at the expense of a polite society that is its complaisant, if less than willing, host. If the novelist Édouard emerges at the end of the novel with the grudging respect of author and reader alike, it is because he fares better than most at the difficult task of being honest with himself. Of all the characters, however, it is doubtless Bernard whose attitude most closely approaches the exemplary.

With the publication of his "novel," Gide likely concluded that his exploration of the novel form was complete. An early commentator, Albert Guérard, observed that Gide was in fact less a "novelist" than a traditional French "man of letters" who happened, occasionally, to write novels. Such an assertion appears to be borne out by subsequent developments in Gide's career; although unflaggingly active as a writer well into his eighties, Gide would return only once to the prose narrative form, and then to the *récit* that he had helped to perfect nearly half a century earlier. *Theseus*, which might be read as a philosophical tale or meditation in the manner of Voltaire, provides a fitting capstone to Gide's distinguished if sporadic career as a writer of narrative prose, restating his habitual concerns about human freedom with a wisdom that only age could provide. In all likelihood, however, *The Pastoral Symphony* and *The Counterfeiters* will continue to be regarded as his true masterpieces.

David B. Parsell

Other major works

SHORT FICTION: *Paludes*, 1895 (*Marshlands*, 1953); *Le Prométhée mal enchaîné*, 1899 (*Prometheus Misbound*, 1953).

PLAYS: *Philoctète*, pb. 1899 (*Philoctetes*, 1952); *Le Roi Candaule*, pr., pb. 1901 (*King Candaules*, 1952); *Bethsabé*, pb. 1903 (*Bathsheba*, 1952); *Saül*, pb. 1903 (English translation, 1952); *My Theater*, 1952.

NONFICTION: *Amyntas*, 1906 (English translation, 1958); *Corydon*, 1911, 1924 (English translation, 1950); *Le Journal des "Faux-monnayeurs,"* 1926 (*Journal of "The Counterfeiters,"* 1951); *Si le grain ne meurt*, 1926 (*If It Die . . .*, 1935); *Voyage au Congo*, 1927 (*Travels in the Congo*, 1929); *Retour de l'U.R.S.S.*, 1936 (*Return from the U.S.S.R.*, 1937); *Retouches à mon "Retour de l'U.R.S.S.,"* 1937 (*Afterthoughts on the U.S.S.R.*, 1938); *Journal*, 1939-1950, 1954 (*The Journals of André Gide, 1889-1949*, 1947-1951); *Et nunc manet in te*, 1947, 1951 (*Madeleine*, 1952); *Ainsi soit-il: Ou, Les Jeux sont faits*, 1952 (*So Be It: Or, The Chips Are Down*, 1959).

MISCELLANEOUS: *Les Cahiers d'André Walter*, 1891 (*The Notebooks of André Walter*, 1968); *Le Traité du Narcisse*, 1891 ("Narcissus," in *The Return of the Prodigal Son*, 1953); *Le Voyage d'Urien*, 1893 (*Urien's Voyage*, 1964); *Les Nourritures terrestres*, 1897 (*Fruits of the Earth*, 1949); *Le Retour de l'enfant prodigue*, 1907 (*The Return of the Prodigal Son*, 1953); *Les Nouvelles Nourritures*, 1935 (*New Fruits of the Earth*, 1949).

Bibliography

Bettinson, Christopher. *Gide: A Study*. London: Heinemann, 1977. Good introductory study provides a succinct biography in its first chapter, and subsequent chapters concentrate on the major novels. The final chapter addresses Gide's social and political activities and writings. Includes a short bibliography.

Brée, Germaine. *Gide*. New Brunswick, N.J.: Rutgers University Press, 1963. A study by one of the great scholars of modern French literature, with chapters discussing the Gide of fact and legend, the man of letters, and the major novels. Includes detailed notes and bibliography.

Cordle, Thomas. *André Gide*. 1969. Rev. ed. New York: Twayne, 1992. Provides a useful introduction to the author. Chapters include "The Gidean Personality," "Decadence and Symbolism," "Romantic Resurgence," and "Social Realism." Includes notes and bibliography.

Driskill, Richard T. *Madonnas and Maidens: Sexual Confusion in Lawrence and Gide*. New York: Peter Lang, 1999. Examines the issues of sexuality, Christianity, and psychology in *The Immoralist* and *Strait Is the Gate*. Argues that in these novels, Gide explores the destructive effects of narrowly defined gender roles on sensitive young women.

Fowlie, Wallace. *André Gide: His Life and Art*. New York: Macmillan, 1965. One of the enduring standard works on Gide, with chapters on his childhood and adolescence, his early career, his major novels, his journals and autobiography, his relationship to Catholicism, and his vocation as a writer.

Littlejohn, David, ed. *Gide: A Collection of Critical Essays*. Englewood Cliffs, N.J.: Prentice-Hall, 1970. Presents essays by distinguished critics on Gide's fiction, including Germaine Brée on *The Counterfeiters* and Jean-Paul Sartre on Gide's career. The introduction, chronology, and bibliography provide a comprehensive overview of his life and career.

Lucey, Michael. *Gide's Bent: Sexuality, Politics, Writing*. New York: Oxford University Press, 1995. Specialized study aimed at advanced students analyzes Gide's novels and other works from the 1920's and 1930's, the years when he was most involved in leftist politics and most open about his homosexuality, to examine how these works express Gide's political, sexual, and literary concerns.

_______. *Never Say I: Sexuality and the First Person in Colette, Gide, and Proust*. Durham, N.C.: Duke University Press, 2006. Examines Gide's novels and other works to describe how he created characters, narrative techniques, and points of view that enabled him to write "about, for, or as" someone who was attracted to persons of the same sex.

Sheridan, Alan. *André Gide: A Life in the Present*. Cambridge, Mass.: Harvard University Press, 1999. Comprehensive literary biography describes how Gide transformed his life into fiction. Includes analyses of all of Gide's works and their relationships to one another.

Walker, David H., ed. *André Gide*. New York: Longman, 1996. Presents a selection of criticism and interpretation of Gide's oeuvre, including pieces written during and after his lifetime. Each essay begins with an introduction that places the piece discussed in context. Includes bibliography and index.

NATALIA GINZBURG

Born: Palermo, Italy; July 14, 1916
Died: Rome, Italy; October 7, 1991
Also known as: Alessandra Tornimparte

Principal long fiction

La strada che va in città, 1942 (*The Road to the City*, 1949)
É stato cosí, 1947 (*The Dry Heart*, 1949)
Tutti i nostri ieri, 1952 (*A Light for Fools*, 1956; also known as *Dead Yesterdays* and *All Our Yesterdays*)
Valentino, 1957 (novellas; also includes *Sagittario* and *La madre*; partial translation as *"Valentino" and "Sagittarius": Two Novellas*, 1988)
Le voci della sera, 1961 (*Voices in the Evening*, 1963)
Lessico famigliare, 1963 (*Family Sayings*, 1967; also known as *The Things We Used to Say*)
Cinque romanzi brevi, 1964
Caro Michele, 1973 (*No Way*, 1974; also known as *Dear Michael*)
Famiglia, 1977 (*Family*, 1988)
La città e la casa, 1984 (*The City and the House*, 1987)

Other literary forms

Though Natalia Ginzburg is known primarily as a novelist and short-story writer, she was also a talented dramatist, essayist, and poet. She published two collections of plays, *Ti ho sposato per allegria, e altre commedie* (1967; I married you for the fun of it, and other comedies) and *Paese di mar, e altre commedie* (1973; sea town, and other comedies), some of which have been performed in London and New York. Her three volumes of essays and articles, *Le piccole virtù* (1962; *The Little Virtues*, 1985), *Mai devi domandarmi* (1970; *Never Must You Ask Me*, 1973), and *Vita immaginaria* (1974; imaginary life), range over a wide variety of subjects, including literary and film criticism. Her scholarly biography of the family of Italy's greatest novelist of the nineteenth century, *La famiglia Manzoni* (1983; *The Manzoni Family*, 1987), has won critical acclaim. Her poetry has been published in various newspapers and literary reviews.

Achievements

One of the best-known Italian female writers of the second half of the twentieth century, Natalia Ginzburg began her career by publishing short stories in *Solaria* and *Letteratura* in the mid-1930's. Her first short novel, *The Road to the City*, was published under the pseudonym Alessandra Tornimparte because of the anti-Jewish laws. Her narrative works of the 1940's and 1950's established her critical reputation and associated her with the brief but significant neorealist movement in Italian literature and film. In 1947, her second short novel, *The Dry Heart*, won the Tempo Prize. Her first long novel, *Dead Yesterdays*, was awarded the Veillon Prize in the year of its publication. In 1957, Ginzburg received the Viareggio Prize for the short novel *Valentino*.

Ginzburg's second long novel, *Family Sayings*, which received the prestigious Strega Prize in 1964, is generally considered one of her strongest works, together with the novel that preceded it, *Voices in the Evening*. Ginzburg's uncomplicated narrative style, with which she recounts stories that hover between fiction and nonfiction, has made hers one of the most distinctive voices in postwar Italian letters. One of her several plays, *L'inserzione* (pb. 1967; *The Advertisement*, 1969), was honored with the Marzotto International Prize of 1968.

Biography

Although Natalia Ginzburg was born in Palermo on July 14, 1916, she spent her childhood and adolescence in Turin, where her father was a professor of comparative anatomy. The daughter of a Catholic mother and a Jewish father (both nonpracticing), she acquired a sense of social isolation at an early age and was educated at home and in the schools of Turin. (She told the story of her family in *Family Sayings*.) In 1938, she married Leone Ginzburg, a professor of Russian literature and an active antifascist. From 1940 to 1943, the Ginzburgs, together with their three children, lived in compulsory political confinement in a remote district of the Abruzzi. After moving to Rome, Leone Ginzburg was arrested and imprisoned for the second time in November, 1943, and died in Rome at the Regina Coeli prison on February 5, 1944.

After the war, Natalia Ginzburg returned to Turin and worked there as a consultant for the Einaudi publishing firm. In 1950, she married Gabriele Baldini, a professor of English literature. When Baldini was named head of the Italian Institute of Culture in London, the family took up residence in that city, where they lived from 1959 to 1962, at which time they returned to the Italian capital. In 1968, her second husband died. Thereafter, she took up permanent residence in Rome, where she worked as a consultant for Einaudi in addition to her writing and her occasional contributions to Italian newspapers and magazines. She died in Rome in October, 1991.

Analysis

From her first short stories and novellas published in the 1930's and 1940's to her epistolary novels of the 1970's and 1980's, Natalia Ginzburg provides a female perspective on the Italian bourgeoisie during a period of widespread social change. Viewed in its entirety, her career shows a progression from the short story toward the more sustained form of the novel, with a developing interest in the theater. Her dominant themes, which can be related in part to her affinity to Cesare Pavese, revolve around the inevitability of human suffering and isolation, the impossibility of communication, the failure of love, the asymmetries in modern Italy between urban and rural existence, and the influence of the family on the individual human person.

Ginzburg's early novels, *The Road to the City* and *The Dry Heart*, both present first-person female narrators whose interior monologues focus on human emotions rather than external events. Relatively little happens in these early works, which are generally low-key in tone, straightforward in plot structure, and uncomplicated in lexicon and syntax. The elemental character of

Ginzburg's prose makes her work accessible to students whose knowledge of Italian may still be rudimentary. In fact, her clear and direct approach to writing has won for her high praise as a stylist. Her later novels depend more on dialogue than on description, and her talent for reproducing realistic speech patterns expresses itself with equal felicity in her writings for the theater.

With *Family Sayings*, which is generally considered to be her best novel, Ginzburg introduced a more openly autobiographical element into her work. A chronicle of the author's family life during fascism, the Resistance, and the immediate postwar period, *Family Sayings* testifies to the author's statement that memory provides the most important stimulus for her writing. Her interest in the family as a social unit is also manifest in her other works of the 1970's and 1980's and underlies such epistolary novels as *No Way* and *The City and the House*, as well as works as diverse as the novel *Family* and the scholarly biography *The Manzoni Family*.

The Road to the City recounts the experience of a sixteen-year-old-girl, Delia, whose boredom with her squalid peasant environment leads her into the trap for which she seems destined. Blinded by the glitter of city life (as personified in her older, more sophisticated sister), she allows herself to be seduced by a young law student named Giulio, for whom she feels only a superficial attraction. She becomes pregnant and marries Giulio while her cousin and true friend, Nino, dies from abuse of alcohol and frustration at being unable to establish a meaningful relationship with her. During the wedding ceremony, Delia realizes that she is marrying a man she does not love, but she fails to realize the underlying circumstances that have caused her to enter into a loveless marriage. This study in disillusionment contains the typical elements of Ginzburg's early work: Her narrator-protagonists are naïve and simple young women who find themselves attracted to the charms of city life but are ultimately disappointed by the role that society offers them.

The Dry Heart

Relying on similarly uncomplicated stylistic devices, *The Dry Heart* recounts a murder story from the perspective of a first-person female narrator, a young schoolteacher from the country whose life in the city is full of disappointments. Like Delia, she enters into a loveless marriage. Unable to draw her husband away from his mistress, the unnamed narrator-protagonist kills him, seemingly against her own will. The murder is related in the novel's opening paragraphs, and the bulk of the novel is made up almost entirely of a monologue in which the protagonist seeks to justify and to understand her own actions. The detached, isolated "I" that appears throughout the narrative mirrors the naïveté, passivity, and resignation of the main character. Brief units of dialogue are embedded in blocks of the narrator's monologue, which is almost completely bereft of commas. This singular punctuation helps create the monotonous, despairing tone of a novel that treats the inability of human beings to establish mutually satisfactory relationships. The failure of a marriage leads to murder and to the protagonist's own drift toward suicide.

Dead Yesterdays *and* Valentino

With *Dead Yesterdays*, Ginzburg's fiction took a significant step forward. Her first novel of a substantial length, this work seeks to add a historical dimension missing from her previous fiction. Composed while neorealism was enjoying its brief moment in the sun, *Dead Yesterdays* abandons the first-person narrative style of the early short novels in favor of the third person.

The novel centers on the sufferings of two Italian families during the reign of fascism, the war, and the Resistance; the book's plot structure is more developed than the author's previous work, and external events have a greater importance. Indeed, *Dead Yesterdays* seeks to tell the story of an entire generation. For the first time, Ginzburg's strange heroes become involved in the broader fabric of social reality. An unnamed industrial city in the North and a fictional village in the South constitute the settings. The main characters include Anna, the younger sister in the less wealthy of the two families; Concettina, her elder sister; and Cenzo Rena, an intellectual of the Left whose commitment to social problems furnishes Ginzburg's fiction with a successfully drawn portrait of an engagé figure. His decision to take the blame for the death of a German soldier is tantamount to suicide, but it saves the villagers from a brutal Nazi reprisal. His politically motivated self-sacrifice brings the novel to an end on a positive note.

The 1950's and the 1960's witnessed a fruitful development in Ginzburg's maturing narrative production. In

1951, she wrote *Valentino*, a novella published in 1957 together with *Sagittario* (Sagittarius) and *La madre* (the mother) in a single volume. These three novellas were awarded the Viareggio Prize of 1957 and further express Ginzburg's continuing preoccupation with the power of the family as a social unit.

Voices in the Evening

In the early 1960's, Ginzburg lived with her husband in London, where in the spring of 1961 she wrote *Voices in the Evening*. Set completely in Italy in an unnamed provincial town, *Voices in the Evening* chronicles the disintegration of an Italian middle-class family. Through a series of flashbacks (each one a portrait of a different member of the family), Ginzburg alternates dialogue with the narrator's monologue. Against a backdrop of fascism and the war and its aftermath, once again the coming-of-age of a young woman, Elsa, provides the focal point for Ginzburg's nostalgic narrative. Elsa's unhappy affair with Tommasino, a young man whose family background renders him incapable of giving love, is presented in the flat, unsentimental narrative style that has become Ginzburg's trademark.

Family Sayings

Family Sayings was awarded the Strega Prize in 1964 and is regarded by many critics as the author's major work. Having grown up in the antifascist atmosphere of Turin, Ginzburg manages to capture the feeling of an entire epoch in recounting the minimal details of her own family life. In *Family Sayings*, Ginzburg draws a portrait of the people who have mattered the most in her private world, many of whom, it should be noted, such as Leone Ginzburg, Filippo Turati, and Cesare Pavese, have also played a significant role in Italian culture and politics. Paradoxically, the openly autobiographical element of *Family Sayings*, the turning inward to mine her own private stock of memories, seems to have sharpened Ginzburg's abilities as an observer of social reality, abilities that she puts to good use in her three volumes of essays.

No Way *and* Family

In the epistolary novel *No Way*, one finds the themes that Ginzburg elaborates throughout the previous four decades, but here they are brought into the context of the social unrest of Italy in the 1970's: The unhappy marriage of a middle-class Roman couple has disastrous effects on their offspring. The exchange of letters between the novel's various characters revolves around Michele, the young protagonist, who moves to London, where he marries an alcoholic divorcée, and who later dies in Bruges at the hands of a group of neofascists. From a technical standpoint, the epistolary structure of the novel allows Ginzburg to experiment with multiple monologues and multiple points of view.

Family and *Borghesia*, the titles of the two novellas that make up the volume *Family*, indicate the twin themes that Ginzburg has pursued throughout her career. As in the novel that preceded this work, here she brings her focus on the Italian bourgeois family into the highly charged political atmosphere of Italy in the 1970's.

The City and the House

With *The City and the House*, Ginzburg returns to the epistolary form used a decade earlier in *No Way*. Her cast of letter-writing characters includes the protagonist Giuseppe, a middle-aged Italian who, in emigrating to New Jersey, cuts himself off from his friends and his roots. The letter as a technical device also fits well with Ginzburg's attempt to fashion a sparse, unadorned style intended to reproduce the rhythms of actual speech. Her focus on the common objects and conflicting emotions of daily life has led critics to compare her work with that of Anton Chekhov.

At the same time, as critic Allan Bullock has suggested (an intuition confirmed by the author herself), Ginzburg's use of dialogue beginning in the early 1960's owes a debt to a writer very different from Chekhov: the English novelist Ivy Compton-Burnett. Ginzburg's most accomplished novels, *Voices in the Evening* and *Family Sayings*, combine elements of autobiography, memory, and emotion within the broader context of historical events and social change. Ginzburg's gift for interweaving the private and the social, the personal and the historical in a simple, straightforward prose style may be her most significant contribution to Italian letters.

John P. Welle

Other major works

PLAYS: *Ti ho sposato per allegria e altre commedie*, pr. 1966; *L'inserzione*, pb. 1967 (*The Advertisement*, 1969; *Paese di mar, e altre commedie*, pb. 1973; *Teatro*, pb. 1990.

NONFICTION: *Le piccole virtù*, 1962 (*The Little Virtues*, 1985); *Mai devi domandarmi*, 1970 (*Never Must You Ask Me*, 1973); *Vita immaginaria*, 1974; *La famiglia Manzoni*, 1983 (biography; *The Manzoni Family*, 1987); *Serena Cruz: O, La vera giustizia*, 1990; *E difficile parlare di sé*, 1999 (Cesare Garboli and Lisa Ginzburg, editors; *It's Hard to Talk About Yourself*, 2003); *Non possiamo saperlo: Saggi, 1973-1990*, 2001 (Domenico Scarpa, editor); *A Place to Live, and Other Selected Essays of Natalia Ginzburg*, 2002 (Lynne Sharon Schwartz, editor).

MISCELLANEOUS: *Opere*, 1986-1987 (2 volumes).

Bibliography

Amoia, Alba della Fazia. "Natalia Ginzburg: The Ill-Tempered Family." In *Twentieth-Century Italian Women Writers: The Feminine Experience*. Carbondale: Southern Illinois University Press, 1996. Ginzburg is included in this feminist study of eleven Italian women whose writings are critical of women's role in Italian society and whose writings express women's unconscious desires.

Bullock, Allan. *Natalia Ginzburg: Human Relationships in a Changing World*. New York: Berg, 1991. Bullock examines all of Ginzburg's novels and her other works to point out the characteristics of Ginzburg's writing, including her comic yet pessimistic view of the human condition.

Jeannet, Angela M., and Giuliana Sanguinetti Katz, eds. *Natalia Ginzburg: A Voice of the Twentieth Century*. Buffalo, N.Y.: University of Toronto Press, 2000. A collection of essays, including pieces analyzing Ginzburg's epistolary novels and the novels *Voices in the Evening* and *Family Sayings*. Some of the other essays explore Ginzburg's literary style and her representation of gender, generation, and memory.

Manson, Christina Siggers. "Family Disintegration and Emigration in Natalia Ginzburg's Epistolary Novels *La Città e la Casa* and *Caro Michele*." In *Politics and Culture in Post-War Italy*, edited by Linda Risso and Monica Boria. Newcastle, England: Cambridge Scholars Press, 2006. Manson's analysis of Ginzburg's novels is included in a collection of essays examining postwar Italian culture, including literature, women's studies, film, history, and politics.

Nocentini, Claudia. "Racial Laws and Internment in Natalia Ginzburg's *La strada che va in citta* and *Tutti i nostri ieri*." In *The Italian Jewish Experience*, edited by Thomas P. DiNapoli. Stony Brook, N.Y.: Forum Italicum, 2000. Nocentini's analysis of Ginzburg's novels *The Road to the City* and *Dead Yesterdays* was originally presented at a 1998 conference on the history of Italian Jews held at the State University of New York at Stony Brook. This book contains all of the conference papers.

Picarazzi, Teresa L. *Maternal Desire: Natalia Ginzburg's Mothers, Daughters, and Sisters*. Madison, N.J.: Fairleigh Dickinson University Press, 2002. Picarazzi examines the narratives of the daughters, mothers, and sisters in Ginzburg's fiction to demonstrate how the writer created a distinctly feminine aesthetic.

Simborowski, Nicoletta. "Music and Memory in Natalia Ginzburg's *Lessico famigliare*." *Modern Language Review* 94, no. 3 (July, 1999): 680-690. Covers the debate over whether to classify *Family Sayings* as a romance or an autobiography. Examines the poetic aspects of the work and the musical metaphors applied to it.

_______. "Natalia Ginzburg's *Lessico famigliare*." In *Secrets and Puzzles: Silence and the Unsaid in Contemporary Italian Writing*. Oxford, England: Legenda, European Humanities Research Centre, 2003. Examines post-World War II works by Ginzburg and three other Italian writers, focusing on the issue of self-censorship. These writers were alive during the fascist era; although that era's censorship no longer existed after the war, Simborowski describes how these writers nevertheless chose to censor parts of their texts.

JEAN GIONO

Born: Manosque, France; March 30, 1895
Died: Manosque, France; October 8, 1970

Principal long fiction

Colline, 1929 (*Hill of Destiny*, 1929)
Un de Baumugnes, 1929 (*Lovers Are Never Losers*, 1931)
Naissance de l'"Odyssée," 1930
Regain, 1930 (*Harvest*, 1939; the three previous novels are known collectively as the Pan trilogy)
Le Grand Troupeau, 1931 (*To the Slaughterhouse*, 1969)
Jean le bleu, 1932 (*Blue Boy*, 1946)
Le Serpent d'étoiles, 1933 (*The Serpent of Stars*, 2004)
Le Chant du monde, 1934 (*The Song of the World*, 1937)
Que ma joie demeure, 1935 (*Joy of Man's Desiring*, 1940)
Batailles dans la montagne, 1937
Pour saluer Melville, 1943
Noé, 1947
Un Roi sans divertissement, 1947
Les Âmes fortes, 1949
Mort d'un personnage, 1949
Le Hussard sur le toit, 1951 (*The Hussar on the Roof*, 1953; also known as *The Horseman on the Roof*)
Les Grands Chemins, 1951
Le Moulin de Pologne, 1952 (*The Malediction*, 1955)
Le Bonheur fou, 1957 (*The Straw Man*, 1959)
Angélo, 1958 (English translation, 1960)
Deux cavaliers de l'orage, 1965 (*Two Riders of the Storm*, 1967)

Other literary forms

Jean Giono (ZHYAW-noh) is remembered chiefly for his novels. During the 1930's, however, he surfaced briefly as a social theorist with such volumes as *Les Vraies Richesses* (1936; true riches) and *Le Poids du ciel* (1938; the weight of the sky). He also wrote several performed plays, of which the most noteworthy is *La Femme du boulanger* (1942), expanded from an episode in his autobiographical novel *Blue Boy* and filmed by Marcel Pagnol in 1938.

Achievements

Championed early in his career by André Gide and other prominent writers of the time, Jean Giono is the preeminent "regional," or rural, French novelist of the twentieth century; his novels have been compared to those of Thomas Hardy in England and William Faulkner in the United States. In the mid-1930's, Giono acquired a considerable following as a "poet and prophet of the soil," emerging as leader of the agrarian Contadour movement that flourished during the years preceding World War II. Briefly imprisoned both in 1939 and in 1945 for the unshakable pacifist convictions he had developed during his years of service in World War I, Giono fell from favor as a writer, only to rebound spectacularly during the late 1940's and early 1950's with a new documentary style quite different from his earlier modes. In 1953, he received the Prix Monégasque, awarded by the prince of Monaco for the finest ensemble of works in the French language; the following year, he was elected to the prestigious Académie Goncourt.

Biography

Jean Giono was born in 1895 at Manosque, a rural village in southern France where, except for extended military service during World War I, he would spend his entire life. His father, a cobbler, and his mother, a launderer, had married when they were no longer young, and Jean was their only child. His childhood, recalled in *Blue Boy* and elsewhere, appears to have been a reasonably happy one, although lived close to the poverty line and in close touch with the forces of nature. In 1911, faced with the declining health of his father, Jean cut short his formal education to take a job in the local branch of a national bank; with time out for military service, he would remain with the bank until 1930, when he at last believed himself capable of earning a living from his writings; it was in that year that he bought the house in which he would spend the remaining forty years of his life, and in which he would receive visitors attracted from throughout the world by the increased success of his writings. In 1920, soon after the death of his father, he married Élise Maurin; the couple had two daughters, Aline in 1926 and Sylvie in 1934.

As early as 1931, with *To the Slaughterhouse*, Giono began to express in his writings the deep and obdurate pacifism that was the result of nearly five years of enlisted service during World War I. With the publication of his rural epics, notably *The Song of the World* and *Joy of Man's Desiring*, Giono's pacifism gradually fused with his glorification of rustic life to produce the phenomenon of Contadour, a back-to-the-soil movement that anticipated by some thirty years many similar communal experiments in the United States and Western Europe. According to critic and Giono expert Maxwell Smith, the Contadour experience arose more or less by accident when, in the fall of 1935, the number of youthful "pilgrims" to Giono's home in Manosque exceeded the Gionos' capacity for hospitality, and Élise suggested to her husband that he take some of their uninvited guests "for a walk." Knapsacks on backs, Giono and some three dozen of the faithful set off soon thereafter on an extended hike through areas that Giono especially loved or about which he had written. When, after several days, the leader happened to sprain his ankle near the tiny town of Contadour, the group decided that they had found what they had been seeking. Housed at first in a barn, the group later bought land for sheep farming and a permanent residence.

As Smith points out, the true function of the Contadour pilgrimages, several of which would occur annually until the onset of World War II, was to test the mettle and adaptability of disillusioned urbanites in search of an alternative lifestyle; in time, the Contadour movement became associated with that of the International Youth Hostels, which completed the task of "resettling" many former city dwellers throughout rural France. During the late 1930's, the Contadour movement published its own quarterly, *Cahiers*, and helped to inspire Giono's social essays of the same period.

With the outbreak of war in 1939, Giono came under severe public censure for his pacifist sentiments and activism and spent two months in prison at Marseilles, from which he was released upon the combined intervention of Gide and the Queen Mother of Belgium. Erroneously suspected of being a fascist sympathizer, Giono remained purely and simply a pacifist, who saw in all wars the denial and destruction of his strongest personal values. Returning to Manosque, he was again imprisoned at the end of the war, largely for his own protection against reprisals from the far Left, whose sympathizers had gained control of the region following cessation of hostilities; he was also censured and blacklisted for a time by the increasingly Left-leaning Comité National des Écrivains.

Between prison sentences, Giono appears to have spent most of his time and energy on the French translation of Herman Melville's *Moby Dick* (1851), a project begun in the mid-1930's with his longtime friend, Lucien

Jean Giono. (AP/Wide World Photos)

Jacques, and their British acquaintance, Joan Smith. Jacques, a writer, artist, and sometime editor, had helped to publish and publicize some of Giono's earliest writings; the two men were further bound by shared pacifist convictions resulting from service in the previous war, and Jacques had assumed an active part in the Contadour experiment. An unexpected side effect of the translation was the writing and publication of *Pour saluer Melville*, Giono's tribute, in the form of a novel to a writer he had long admired. Bordering closely upon a literary hoax, although intended in utter good faith, *Pour saluer Melville* inserts totally invented characters and incidents between the recorded lines of Melville's life—so convincingly, in fact, that at least one of Melville's descendants would accept the story as authentic.

Once cleared of suspicion after World War II, Giono, by then in his early fifties, returned to the literary scene in full vigor, but in a new and different mode that he himself called *chroniques* (chronicles). As different from his spare early style as from his rural epics of the 1930's, the *chroniques* won for him new admirers while disappointing certain older ones. Historical in context, drawing heavily upon the lives and exploits of Giono's paternal Italian ancestors, the *chroniques* are perhaps as epic in scope as *The Song of the World*, but with new attention paid to the delineation of character, sometimes at the expense of plot. The so-called Hussar cycle, inaugurated by *The Horseman on the Roof* in 1951, demonstrated Giono's eventual mastery of the new form and brought him honors that only a short time earlier might have been considered unthinkable. Although somewhat disillusioned by the failure of his social thought, dismissing the Contadour movement as a youthful mistake, Giono remained personally optimistic, vigorous, and active as a writer well into his seventies, continuing to welcome the visitors who came from far and wide to see him. Giono died at his home in Manosque in 1970.

Analysis

Almost without exception, Jean Giono's commentators trace the emergence of his early styles to his voracious reading of the Greek classics in translation, a program of self-education and entertainment begun in childhood, to be continued after-hours at the bank. While in school, Giono, like his contemporary Antoine de Saint-Exupéry (1900-1944), had performed poorly in French composition, showing little promise for his eventual career. As Henri Peyre has pointed out, however, Giono had the distinct advantage of acquiring the classics on his own, outside the classroom in a rustic Mediterranean environment not utterly different from that of ancient Greece; in all likelihood, the sights, sounds, and smells were much the same, as were humankind's perennial contact and struggle with the soil. Indeed, Giono's first attempt at long fiction, not published until subsequent works had made him a better risk for publishers, was *Naissance de l'"Odyssée,"* a vigorous, ironic work written "within the margins" of Homer's *Odyssey* (c. 725 B.C.E.).

Pan trilogy

Giono first rose to prominence in the late 1920's and early 1930's with the Pan trilogy, comprising *Hill of Destiny*, *Lovers Are Never Losers*, and *Harvest*. Giono, later to be succeeded by the Spanish-born dramatist Fernando Arrabal (b. 1932), evokes the spirit of Pan to symbolize the forces of nature, with which humankind often coexists in an uneasy truce. In *Hill of Destiny*, nature quite literally goes "on strike" against human "improvements" wrought upon the land; the elderly Janet is unjustly accused of witchcraft, having acquired the odd gift of communication with nature and having warned his fellow villagers to mend their ways before it is too late. *Lovers Are Never Losers*, by contrast, presents the lyric aspect of Pan, singing the lost-and-found love of Albin for Angèle through the voice of the old peasant Amédée. *Harvest*, later successfully filmed, unites humanity with nature in the marriage of the near-giant Panturle and the itinerant Arsule, who has saved him from drowning; love, although present, is here subordinated to the cycle of the seasons.

As Maxwell Smith observes, Giono in his Pan trilogy delighted readers with his seemingly effortless gift for striking, apt, and memorable metaphor, particularly in his descriptions of nature or of the forest fire in *Hill of Destiny*. In *Lovers Are Never Losers*, description is equally vivid, although style and vocabulary are pared down somewhat, to suit the speech patterns of the uneducated peasant narrator. The style of *Harvest* remains restrained if colorful, with seemingly authentic rustic speech. Only in the middle volume, *Lovers Are Never*

Losers, does Giono see fit to delineate or humanize his characters in a way that makes them memorable; in *Hill of Destiny* and *Harvest*, it is nature itself that dominates, often attaining the stature of a character through the author's vivid descriptions.

Lovers Are Never Losers

Perhaps the most successful of Giono's novels in his earliest mode, *Lovers Are Never Losers* combines his rare evocative power with a sure gift for storytelling. The narrative, although limited in voice and viewpoint to the uneducated old peasant Amédée, is both sensitive and credible in its portrayal of young Albin and his pining love for Angèle, who has been "carried away by a city slicker." Within the context of the tale, Baumugnes is a village whose Huguenot inhabitants, their tongues cut out by religious persecutors, learned to communicate with one another by playing the harmonica; understandably, their descendants, including the unfortunate Albin, have supposedly inherited an uncanny gift for playing that instrument, and Albin's talent stands him in good stead in the rescue of Angèle, long since abandoned by her lover and held captive on her father's farm. Unlikely though the story may sound in summary, *Lovers Are Never Losers* remains a remarkable and memorable narrative, as notable for the deftness of its characterizations as for the economy of its style. Only the city-bred seducer Louis seems closer to caricature than to character, but even that lapse can be seen as credible within the story's rural context.

In 1930, the year that he resigned from the bank and purchased his house, Giono managed also to publish his first-written novel, *Naissance de l'"Odyssée,"* which would enjoy an even larger printing eight years later, with another publisher. He also began for the first time to put himself into his books, with such semiautobiographical novels as *To the Slaughterhouse* and *Blue Boy*. His style in these volumes is increasingly confident and frankly lyric, tending toward exuberance; perhaps his most masterful scene, also a metaphor (as reflected in the original title *Le Grand Troupeau*), shows two old men stampeding sheep through a provincial village; the young shepherds who would normally have done the job have themselves been "stampeded"—to war. Giono's descriptions, worthy of the Greek poets whom he so admired, anticipate the "epic" style that would soon burst forth, full-blown, in *The Song of the World* and *Joy of Man's Desiring*. The style of the meandering, episodic *Blue Boy* is more restrained, although amply supplied with deft similes and metaphors. Representative of the book's tone and content is the doubt of old Franchesc Odripano, on hearing of the Wright brothers' flight, "that anything will really change."

With his epic novels of the middle 1930's, Giono began increasingly to assert the claims of the soil against, and above, those of modern technology. Indeed, the modern world is conspicuous primarily by its absence from his impassioned, vivid storytelling, set in modern times but showing man eternally involved with nature.

The Song of the World

In *The Song of the World*, the first, as well as the best-remembered and most durable, of his epic novels, Giono depicts the primordial, archetypal struggle between the peasants Antonio and Matelot, on one side, and the seemingly malevolent mountain tyrant Maudru, on the other; storms and the river, meanwhile, pose at least as powerful a threat to both sides as the opposing sides do to each other. Credible though the incidents may be, little effort is made toward verisimilitude; the author instead aspires to the monumental. Here, both humans and nature are writ large, with much of the action taking place at night, in the false shelter of ominous shadows. Giono's choice of title is seconded by Henri Peyre, who observes that Antonio, Matelot, and even the menacing Maudru are "epic heroes not because they accumulate feats in violent battle but because they are the very forces of nature embodied in simple, strong creatures; they echo the song of the world." Reduced to simple plot, the action of *The Song of the World* might well be seen as little more than a feud among peasants. In Giono's capable hands, however, the narrative assumes truly monumental as well as highly memorable proportions, enriched by the author's vivid, resonant vocabulary and a country dweller's homage to the cycle of the seasons.

Joy of Man's Desiring

Joy of Man's Desiring, despite a proliferation of unhappy characters, waxes so lyric in its paean to the rustic life as to have inspired in some critics an unflattering recollection of Jean-Jacques Rousseau and of Voltaire's observation that his notorious contemporary was inviting humankind "to walk upon all fours." Significantly, it was soon after the publication of *Joy of Man's Desiring* that the Contadour movement arose as if spontaneously, although Giono's novels had begun to attract a following as early as 1931, before his epic phase.

Batailles dans la montagne

Batailles dans la montagne, published between the two propaganda volumes *Les Vraies Richesses* and *Le Poids du ciel*, is perhaps the most effective of the three "epics" in portraying the human struggle with nature; a small mountain village is doubly threatened with destruction by flood, both from a melting glacier and from a river accidentally dammed by a landslide. Particularly memorable, and epic, is Giono's description of the hero Saint-Jean's anguished quest for dynamite to blow up the dam, in the course of which he is pitted against an enraged bull. Here as elsewhere, Giono excels in his deft, if verbose, evocation of nature, whose phenomena are as beautiful as they are terrifying.

Thanks in part to his enviable mastery of the French language and its vocabulary—a mastery exceeding that of many more sophisticated writers—Giono managed throughout most of his career to avoid accusations of false primitivism as well as of condescension to his characters or audience. Giono was, in fact, a true provincial, a committed son of the soil who was ready and more than willing to meet the rest of the world on its own terms; many another writer, transplanted urbanite as well as native rustic, has tried and failed to achieve the artistic position that Giono was to assume as if by birthright. Despite Giono's occasional vulnerability to charges of being a latter-day Rousseau, the integrity and vigor of his thought and prose protected him from the danger of becoming a literary counterpart to Grandma Moses or even Norman Rockwell. At worst, the social propaganda of his Contadour period reflects a certain shallowness; happily, however, such weaknesses are absent from the novels written around the same time.

Un Roi sans divertissement

In his postwar novels, collectively known as *chroniques*, Giono moved on to a new, quasi-documentary style of narrative exposition that he claimed to have developed contemporaneously with his epic novels, although the results would not be seen until the late 1940's. The first published novel in the new mode, which appeared in 1947, was *Un Roi sans divertissement*, seen by some observers as a glorified detective story. Consisting of first-person testimony from a variety of participants and witnesses, *Un Roi sans divertissement* deliberately leaves unresolved many of the ambiguities that would be reconciled in a more conventional mystery. Reviewers, although somewhat nonplussed by Giono's seemingly abrupt change of manner, found much to praise in his delineation of character, especially in the case of the protagonist, Langlois.

Noé

Noé, published later in the same year, appears to have been the author's favorite among his many novels and was reissued at his own request in 1961; described by Smith and others as a "novelist's novel," *Noé* builds upon the autobiographical foundation of the earlier *Blue Boy* to provide fresh insight into the author's art and craft as characters from his work in progress begin to appear in his mind, much in the manner of persons encountered in "real life." In style and content, however, *Noé* is closely related to the *chroniques*, with which it is usually classified.

Between 1949 and 1952, Giono added three major volumes to his series of *chroniques*. *Les Âmes fortes*, consisting entirely of conversation among three old ladies at a wake, reconstructs in often hair-raising, apparently realistic detail a curious tale of envy, fraud, and murder covering the preceding sixty years. *Les Grands Chemins*, likewise dealing with murder and fraud, has generally been deemed less successful. *The Malediction* recalls in grim detail the "family curse" hanging over the head of a certain Julie Coste. The novel was well received, but Giono, in the meantime, had attracted even more critical attention with *The Horseman on the Roof*, published in 1951 and inaugurating what would come to be known as his Hussar cycle.

The Straw Man *and* The Horseman on the Roof

A subgrouping of the *chroniques*, Giono's Hussar novels are set against the background of nineteenth century Europe, before the unification of Germany and Italy. Drawing heavily upon his own Italian origins, Giono presents in the Hussar cycle a colorful fresco of tribulation and adventure featuring the carbonaro Angelo Pardi, a character modeled, at least in part, on Giono's own paternal grandfather. In *The Horseman on the Roof*, Giono involves Angelo and other recurring characters in the cholera epidemic of 1838, portraying the human struggle against disease in a chronicle that has been favorably compared to Albert Camus's *La Peste* (1947; *The Plague*, 1948). *The Straw Man* shows Angelo cast as a scapegoat or "straw man" by conspirators during the Italian campaign against Austrian rule in 1848; dismissed by some commentators as an unsuccessful imitation of Stendhal's *La Chartreuse de Parme* (1839; *The Charterhouse of Parma*, 1895), *The Straw Man* was correctly recognized by others as a step in the direction of postmodern fiction; like Alain Robbe-Grillet, Michel Butor, and other New Novelists of the 1950's, Giono, in *The Straw Man*, was clearly experimenting with modes of perception and presentation in the novel, questioning established concepts of time and character even as he sought to present a rousing, well-told tale against a historical background.

Different though it may be from Giono's nature epics of the 1930's, the documentary style of the *chroniques*, including the Hussar cycle, remains strongly rooted in the soil. As in his earliest novels, the landscape in *The Horseman on the Roof* is never far removed from view, even as increasing attention is paid to the delineation and development of character. Although nature is cast in a relatively minor role, Giono's characters are still very much at the mercy of the elements—the cholera epidemic, for example, is similar to the floods, storms, and savage beasts that figure prominently in the earlier novels—which in turn help define both personality and behavior. In the view of some critics, *The Horseman on the Roof* is the finest of Giono's novels.

Set largely in Giono's hometown of Manosque as it must have been some sixty years before his birth, the novel takes its rather unusual title from the fact that Angelo Pardi, fleeing for his life after killing an Austrian spy in a duel, is eventually driven to the rooftops in his search for sanctuary; the people of Manosque, superstitious by nature and further maddened by the presence of the plague, wrongly suspect the fugitive Angelo of having poisoned the town's water supply. Told in a sober, matter-of-fact style somewhat different from Giono's earlier mode, *The Horseman on the Roof* excels also in its portrayal of humanity's inhumanity to humans, as Angelo witnesses innumerable scenes of brutality and violence from the relative sanctuary of his elevated hiding place. As in Camus's *The Plague*, however, the narrative is saved from gloominess by the exemplary behavior of the featured characters. The character of Angelo Pardi, together with that of the Marquise Pauline de Théus, reappeared throughout Giono's subsequent novels, although here they are perhaps at their most memorable. Significantly, it is *The Horseman on the Roof* that appears to have brought to Giono's work, at long last, the double honor of the Prix Monégasque and election to the Académie Goncourt.

Although Giono's reputation declined somewhat in the years following his death, he is still recognized for a singular talent of rare scope and evocative power, perhaps impossible to imitate. As a pacifist inalienably committed to the land and its values, he may also be seen as presaging by some thirty years the counterculture of the 1960's, which in turn exerted considerable influence upon later writers and others.

David B. Parsell

Other major works

SHORT FICTION: *Solitude de la pitié*, 1931 (*The Solitude of Compassion*, 2002).

PLAYS: *Lanceurs de graines*, pr. 1932; *Le Bout de la route*, pr. 1937; *La Femme du boulanger*, pr. 1942; *Théâtre*, 1943 (collection); *Voyage en calèche*, pb. 1946.

NONFICTION: *Les Vraies Richesses*, 1936; *Le Poids du ciel*, 1938; *Triomphe de la vie*, 1942; *Voyage en Italie*, 1953; *Notes sur l'affaire Dominici*, 1955; *Le Désastre de Pavie*, 1963 (*The Battle of Pavia*, 1966); *Correspondance, 1928-1963*, 2000 (Pierre Citron, editor).

TRANSLATION: *Moby Dick*, 1939, 1943 (with Lucien Jacques and Joan Smith; of Herman Melville's novel).

Bibliography

Badr, Ibrahim H. *Jean Giono: L'Esthétique de la violence*. New York: Peter Lang, 1998. An examination, in English, of violence in Giono's work, particularly the horror and psychological effects of war. Badr explains how Giono, a pacifist, used war and other forms of violence as literary motifs.

Ford, Edward. *Jean Giono's Hidden Reality*. Lewiston, N.Y.: Edwin Mellen Press, 2004. An analysis of Giono's writings, in which Ford argues that the quest for faith is a continual theme. Ford also defends the works Giono wrote during World War II, arguing that he did not collaborate with the Vichy government and the Nazis, as other critics have charged.

Golsan, Richard Joseph. "Jean Giono: Pacifism and the Place of the 'Poet.'" In *French Writers and the Politics of Complicity: Crises of Democracy in the 1940's and 1990's*. Baltimore: Johns Hopkins University Press, 2006. Golsan, who has written journal articles about Giono's collaboration with the Nazis during the German Occupation, discusses that complicity in this chapter of his book. Golsan argues that for Giono and two other French writers of the period, cooperation with the Nazis often arose from "nonpolitical" motives, such as sexual orientation, antimodern aesthetics, and distorted religious beliefs.

Goodrich, Norma L. *Giono: Master of Fictional Modes*. Princeton, N.J.: Princeton University Press, 1973. Chapters on Giono's major work, divided into studies of "modes," including "the apocalyptic," "the surrealist," "the symbolic," "the epic," "the tragic," and "the autobiographical." Includes a detailed bibliography and an index.

Peyre, Henri. *The Contemporary French Novel*. New York: Oxford University Press, 1955. Dated, yet contains one of the finest analyses of Giono's fiction by a distinguished literary critic.

Redfern, W. D. *Jean Giono: Le Hussard sur le toit*. Glasgow, Scotland: University of Glasgow French and German Publications, 1997. A brief introductory overview of *The Horseman on the Roof* for beginning students. Includes bibliographical references.

_______. *The Private World of Jean Giono*. Oxford, England: Basil Blackwell, 1967. Begins with a biographical note, introduction, and then chapters on Giono's uses of imagination, the inner life, the modern world, the apocalypse, a world of words, and a post-World War II world. Includes notes and a bibliography.

Smith, Maxwell A. *Jean Giono*. New York: Twayne, 1966. Smith devotes two chapters to Giono's family background, early childhood, and youth and follows with Giono's debut in literature and his major fiction. Provides a chronology, notes, and an annotated bibliography.

JOSÉ MARÍA GIRONELLA

Born: Darnius, Spain; December 31, 1917
Died: Arenys de Mar, near Barcelona, Spain; January 3, 2003
Also known as: José María Gironella Pous

Principal long fiction

Un hombre, 1946 (*Where the Soil Was Shallow*, 1957)
La marea, 1949
Los cipreses creen en Dios, 1953 (*The Cypresses Believe in God*, 1955)
Un millón de muertos, 1961 (*One Million Dead*, 1963)
Mujer, levántate y anda, 1962
Ha estallado la paz, 1966 (*Peace After War*, 1969)
Condenados a vivir, 1971
Los hombres lloran solas, 1986
La dud inquietante, 1988
A la sombra de Chopin, 1990
El corazón alberga muchas sombras, 1995
Se hace camino al andar, 1997
El apocalipsis, 2001
Por amor a la verdad, 2003

Other literary forms

The renown of José María Gironella (hee-roh-NEH-yah) springs from the series of panoramic novels that depict the Spanish Civil War, although the author published in a variety of literary forms. His first work in print was poetry (*Ha llegado el invierno y tú no estás aquí*, 1945), but he quickly abandoned the genre in favor of the novel. *Los fantasmas de mi cerebro* (1959; *Phantoms and Fugitives: Journeys to the Improbable*, 1964; includes translation of *Todos somos fugitivos*) is the documentation in a series of essays of a nervous breakdown. A partial collection of Gironella's short stories appears in *Phantoms and Fugitives*.

Gironella also produced travel books—*Personas, ideas, y mares* (1963; persons, ideas, and seas), *El Japón y su duende* (1964; Japan and her ghosts), and *En Asia se muere bajo las estrellas* (1968; in Asia you die under the stars)—along with essays that outline his personal vision in a wide variety of subjects, newspaper articles, literary analyses, criticism, biographical accounts, interviews, and meditations. *China, lágrima innumerable* (1965; China, countless tears) is an expanded essay accompanied by photographs. *Gritos del mar* (1967; shouts from the sea) collects in one volume various articles previously published in periodicals.

Achievements

José María Gironella has been labeled as a post-Spanish Civil War writer belonging to the realist tradition of nineteenth century literature, a fact that places him in Spain's Generation of '36. His novels represent a rupture in the trend toward introspection and intellectualization that existed prior to the Civil War. Gironella is a serious writer who identifies with the common person, desiring to convey through literature his own experiences in life. One is impressed by his sincerity and flexibility, his awe and optimism as he effects his personal ongoing search for knowledge and willingly shares it.

Gironella's major literary success has centered on his personal commitment to explain, through the historical novel, the reality and complexity of the Spanish Civil War (1936-1939); his epic novels *The Cypresses Believe in God* and *One Million Dead*—made both discrete and panoramic through the author's attempt to be objective—have become international best sellers.

Biography

José María Gironella—whose full name was José María Gironella Pous—spent his early life in the northeastern Spanish province of Gerona, the locale of his most successful literature. His childhood desire to enter the priesthood was abandoned primarily because his attitude toward the Catholic Church had failed to crystallize. He worked at various unskilled positions until the eve of the Spanish Civil War, at which time he was employed in the Arús Bank in Gerona. During the war, Gironella served on the side of the Nationalists with a battalion of ski soldiers in the Pyrenees mountains. At the conclusion of the conflict, he returned to Gerona. He had already begun to write, and now he nurtured this desire with a position as a newspaper reporter and contributor of articles to various journals.

In 1946, Gironella married his childhood sweetheart, Magda, and won the coveted Nadal Prize with the publication of his first novel. A year later, Gironella and his wife left Spain illegally and began several years of travel throughout Europe. During this time, he published his second novel, and, in 1951, he suffered a nervous breakdown. Gironella freely wrote about his illness while he sought relief at various clinics. The publication of *The Cypresses Believe in God* brought international recognition, and its sequel, *One Million Dead*, was also well received. These works assured for their creator a place in the literary history of Spain. The novelist returned to a residence in his native country, but until his death in 2003, he traveled extensively throughout the world while continuing to write.

Analysis

According to José María Gironella, the seed for his mammoth enterprise, to create in novel form an explanation of historical events in contemporary Spain, was planted December 30, 1937. Spain was in its second winter of civil war. Gironella was serving as a ski soldier in the Pyrenees along Spain's border with France when he was approached by a French girl from among the many skiers who frequented the area. Tearing a button from Gironella's uniform as a souvenir, the girl quickly darted away on her skis, but not before inquiring as to the ridiculousness of shooting one's brothers. This incident provoked in the young Spaniard a desire to explain to this girl and the entire world what was occurring in his country. Sixteen years later, with the publication of *The Cypresses Believe in God*, Gironella's effort became a reality. This first work of the series covers the pre-Civil War period, from April, 1931, to July, 1936, and won for its author Spain's national prize for literature in 1953. It is considered to be the author's masterpiece.

The Cypresses Believe in God

The Cypresses Believe in God is an ambitious epic written in the realistic tradition; it neither defends nor condemns but rather observes and records, with the attitude that the reader may reach his or her own conclusions relative to the events that are narrated. To afford continuity to the epic, the author has selected one family, the Alvears, and one location, the city of Gerona, in Catalonia, as representative of all Spanish families and places who contribute to the amalgam of the period that incubates the war. The Alvears are thus elevated to a symbolic stature, and Gerona as well becomes a microcosm of the entire country, one in which the reader can view the evolution of those forces that divided Spain into two uncompromising extremes.

Though it is a panoramic work, sociopolitical in intent, *The Cypresses Believe in God* is also the chronicle of a family. Matías Alvear, a Castilian and clerk at the local telegraph office, is married to Carmen Elgazu, a Basque. In the home, there is an atmosphere of mutual respect in spite of the native differences, which are reflected also in the contrasts among the three children. César, given to meditation and spiritual matters, enters the priesthood aided by the urging of his mother. Pilar is sheltered and obedient. Ignacio, a mirror of the author, is both an idealist and a skeptic. He is the protagonist who, like Spain itself, bears the burden of an inner struggle as he searches but continues to doubt during the course of the national conflict. The novel is primarily Ignacio's story, narrating his journey into adulthood and documenting the challenges and growth that are associated with the individual, the family, and the national scene as well.

Upon leaving the seminary, Ignacio determines to experience life as abundantly as possible. He acquires a position at a bank while continuing to work toward a degree in law. Through Ignacio and his association with various individuals, the reader is provided a tour of the culture and institutions of Gerona, the intellectual arguments and positions of all political parties, platforms, and events, in a variety of social environments. Ignacio's cousin, José, representing the voice of the Falange, schools the protagonist in anticlericalism and introduces him into politics. Together, they attend political meetings and discussions. David and Olga Pol allow Ignacio the perspective from the political Left, and they, in turn, instruct Ignacio in their ideology. They escort the protagonist to an overcrowded mental institution and discuss with him the need for social reform. These and other characters serve as representatives of the various social and political points of view.

The fictional episodes of the Alvear family and Ignacio's experiences are interwoven with the historical events surrounding the deterioration of the political crisis. The protagonist becomes romantically involved with the aristocrat Ana María, and while on vacation with his family, he quits school and later returns to the study of law. A schoolmate, Mateo Santos, a leader of the Falange, becomes a major character through his romantic involvement with Pilar. As the threat of war escalates, the Communists, reacting to the execution of a member of the party, set fire to the cypress forests around Gerona. This action is for Ignacio's brother, César, a signal of the potential for a godless Spain, as these stately trees symbolize a belief in the deity (hence the title of the novel). This act of violence brings the Falange into political prominence, and the atrocities escalate on both sides. Ignacio's political commitment remains nebulous, although he has developed feelings for Marta de Soria, a Falangist leader.

The protagonist passes part of his law examinations, but the political situation forces him to postpone the completion of his studies. His friend, Mateo Santos, who has been detained, is freed and goes into hiding. César is detained also and, despite Ignacio's belated attempt to save his brother, is executed for no good reason. This death, although fulfilling César's desire to achieve martyrdom, demonstrates the chaos that accompanies the violence of the period. The novel closes with César's execution, and the reader, who is not subjected to his moralizing, is nevertheless impressed that a senseless action has occurred.

The character of Ignacio is a combination of idealism and hope in conflict with doubt and skepticism. He represents a struggle between reason and emotion and is a symbol of two Spains, the struggle between the progressive and the traditional. Inasmuch as Gironella utilizes the protagonist to effect a composite view of the Spain of that period, the character has been assessed as a transparent window, without depth of character or personal convictions, through which one might view the opinions and intrigues that precipitated the war. Indeed, one of the principal shortcomings of the novel is the protagonist's failure to generate a strong personal commitment to anything. Yet the character is artfully drawn and does represent an active force in the novel.

Ignacio and his creator believe that the individual, through his or her own moral capabilities, will survive over the collective. Each Spaniard will develop a personal interpretation of the war based on his or her own experiences. It is this personal concept, directed toward the future in the hope of creating a more sensitive and searching national conscience, that distinguishes Gironella. In spite of the tragedy of the war, Gironella teaches that each side may retain its personal dignity and yet recognize the courage and honor of the other.

The epic nature of the novel is enhanced by the artistic integration of historical data with fiction. Thus, the sweeping proportions of *The Cypresses Believe in God* do not diminish the reality that the novel is about a family. For Gironella, the family is the basic unit of a successful society, and throughout this novel an accounting is made of each of the Alvears. The novel succeeds on both levels, yet the breadth of the work is extensive at the expense of depth. Historical, economic, and political intricacies, as well as family episodes of minor importance, could have been omitted.

One Million Dead

One Million Dead narrates the period from July 30, 1936, to April 1, 1939, and purports to provide a panoramic view of the war years. The author portrays the two factions simultaneously and attempts to be as impartial as possible. Gironella evinces a skill for meticulous documentation and verisimilitude, and, as for the preceding volume, he spent years collecting data, interviewing Spanish and foreign participants and witnesses, and searching archives for pertinent newspapers, photographs, and editorials. His personal participation in the conflict contributes to his insight. The title of this novel is intended to stand for the actual number of those who died in the conflict—slightly less than half a million—as well as those who, possessed by hate, destroyed their own souls.

In this novel, the Alvear family continues to occupy center stage, but the setting broadens to include all parts of Spain. The action begins in the cemetery where César has been killed. Ignacio discovers his brother's body and is haunted by the speculation that he might have been able to save him. The incident ignites a criticism of the war by the protagonist, who, with his family, is neutral as the struggle escalates. Ignacio's present sweetheart, Marta de Soria, a Falange activist, escapes to France. She has a short-lived relationship with an Italian soldier who, like many other characters in this volume, introduces an international thread to the fabric of the conflict. As the war proceeds, Ignacio finally enlists in the Nationalist armies as a medical aide. His travels take him to Barcelona and Madrid, where he works in a hospital for the wounded. He also experiences a journey into the Pyrenees, where he meets a group of Nationalist soldiers in a ski patrol. He is awed by the peace that he finds in these mountains. This and many other incidents in the novel reveal the author's autobiographical stamp on the action of the narrative.

Ignacio's mother adopts a homeless orphan whose parents had been killed at Guernica. As the war draws to a close, the various members of the family are drawn again to Gerona. Mateo de Soria also returns, as does his sister, Marta. Together, the family attends the first public mass to be held in Gerona's cathedral in three years. The novel concludes with a quiet scene in which General Francisco Franco, at work in his office in Nationalist headquarters, is informed by an aide that the war is officially over. Franco simply responds that it is good and, thanking the aide, returns to his work.

This novel is broader in scope than its predecessor. It narrates the war from the point of view of both factions, not simply from a military perspective; it includes sociological, religious, and political intrigues as well. The author remains apart and detached as he analyzes each occurrence without judging. This preference for the external and for objective distance does not serve Gironella well in his portrayal of the inner world of his characters. As a result, the vitality of some of the characters in *The Cypresses Believe in God* is fettered in the sequel. The author isolates himself from individuality, though he makes an effort to portray the distinctive souls of the provinces of Spain and to bless his characters with a unique and personal psychological depth. In each case, the author fails, a victim of his need to discover objectively and explain the significance of the Civil War.

Although *One Million Dead* does not accommodate the empathy that might unlock the interior world of its characters, it is a systematic, organized analysis of the war. *The Cypresses Believe in God* has been termed a novel with historical pretensions, whereas *One Million Dead* has been judged a historical work interlaced with fiction.

The fictional aspect of the novel is further weakened by the author's tendency to stereotype minor characters and to level certain judgments based on their political affiliations. Communists, for example, are generally portrayed as villains in contrast to the noble efforts of the Falangists. Although Gironella insists on impartiality in his portrayal of the historical and political aspect of his novels, there is a tendency to favor the Nationalist platform. His continual reminder of the strength of the family unit as the key to Spain's hope for the future is a constant reiteration of the Nationalist theme. The victorious Falange is spared severe criticism, although it has been argued that Gironella was required to tread with care to avoid possible censorship. As the novel concludes, General Franco is portrayed, without excessive praise or propaganda, as the hope of Spain's future.

Peace After War

Peace After War—a slow-paced and all-too-predictable sequel to *One Million Dead*—treats the period between 1939 and 1941. Its emphasis is on the reconstruction of Spain under Franco, and the author praises the reforms of the Nationalists while portraying an atmosphere of unity and pride. Reform and greater national liberty through changes instituted by the government are emphasized, while resentment against the regime is kept to a minimum. Gironella demonstrates complete acceptance of Franco's policy and places emphasis once again on the fictional aspects of the work. The Alvears are reunited. Ignacio graduates from the University of Barcelona and assumes a life given more to reflection than to action. His sweetheart, Marta de Soria, devotes her attention to politics, while Ignacio renews his affection for his first love, Ana María.

The marriage of Pilar to Mateo Santos assumes a more important position in this novel. Mateo displays a fanatical zeal to sacrifice his life, if necessary, in the fight against Communism. Pilar makes an unsuccessful attempt to dissuade him, but, unable to draw from herself the strength she requires, she withdraws to her family for moral support. Pilar's foil is her cousin, Paz, sensual, alienated from the family because of her leftist politics, but, unlike most of Gironella's protagonists, strong and motivated.

In addition to his Spanish Civil War cycle, Gironella published several other novels, but his reputation ultimately will rest on a single work, *The Cypresses Believe in God*. Although in many respects this novel has dated badly, it retains its historical value as a sweeping portrait of Spain during a crucial period in its history.

Alfred W. Jensen

Other major works

SHORT FICTION: *Todos somos fugitivos*, 1961 (English translation, 1964).

POETRY: *Ha llegado el invierno y tú no estás aquí*, 1945.

NONFICTION: *El novelista ante el mundo*, 1954; *Los fantasmas de mi cerebro*, 1959 (*Phantoms and Fugitives: Journeys to the Improbable*, 1964; includes translation of *Todos somos fugitivos*); *Personas, ideas, y mares*, 1963; *El Japón y su duende*, 1964; *China, lágrima innumerable*, 1965; *Gritos del mar*, 1967; *Conversaciones con don Juan de Borbon*, 1968; *En Asia se muere bajo las estrellas*, 1968; *Cien españoles y Dios*, 1969; *El Mediterraneo es un hombre disfrazado de mar*, 1974; *El escandola de Tierra Santa*, 1977; *Carta a mi padre muerto*, 1978; *Cita en el cementerio*, 1983; *Jerusalén de los Evangelios*, 1989; *Yo, Mahoma*, 1989; *Carta a mi madre muerta*, 1992; *Nuevos 100 españoles y Dios*, 1994.

Bibliography

Boyle, John F. "True Fiction." *Commonweal* 130, no. 12 (June 20, 2003). Boyle discusses *The Cypresses Believe in God*, praising the novel for its well-conceived story and its ability to give "shape, color, and substance in understanding the Spanish Civil War."

Longyear, R. M. "*The Cypresses Believe in God*." In *Masterplots: Eighteen Hundred One Plot Stories and Critical Evaluations of the World's Finest Literature*, edited by Frank N. Magill et al. Vol. 3. Pasadena, Calif.: Salem Press, 1996. Gironella's masterpiece, *The Cypresses Believe in God*, is reviewed in this collection of brief but comprehensive critical essays examining the best of world literature.

Schwartz, Ronald. *José María Gironella*. New York: Twayne, 1972. This volume, the only full-length study of Gironella in English, provides a comprehensive account of his achievements and works. Includes a bibliography.

Thomas, Gareth. *The Novel of the Spanish Civil War*. New York: Cambridge University Press, 1990. Gironella's trilogy receives a chapter, and the introductory chapters are valuable in providing a context. The citations from Gironella and his critics are all in the original Spanish or French.

GEORGE GISSING

Born: Wakefield, England; November 22, 1857
Died: St. Jean-Pied-de-Port, France; December 28, 1903
Also known as: George Robert Gissing

Principal long fiction

Workers in the Dawn, 1880
The Unclassed, 1884
Demos, 1886
Isabel Clarendon, 1886
Thyrza, 1887
A Life's Morning, 1888
The Nether World, 1889
The Emancipated, 1890
New Grub Street, 1891
Born in Exile, 1892
Denzil Quarrier, 1892
The Odd Women, 1893
In the Year of Jubilee, 1894
Eve's Ransom, 1895
The Paying Guest, 1895
Sleeping Fires, 1895
The Whirlpool, 1897
The Town Traveller, 1898
The Crown of Life, 1899
Our Friend the Charlatan, 1901
The Private Papers of Henry Ryecroft, 1903
Veranilda, 1904
Will Warburton, 1905

Other literary forms

Though George Gissing will be remembered primarily as a novelist, he tried his hand at a variety of literary projects. In the 1890's especially, he found it profitable to write short stories; these were generally published in periodicals, but one volume—*Human Odds and Ends* (1897)—was published during his lifetime. Many of his other short stories, some from his early contributions to Chicago newspapers, have since been collected: *The House of Cobwebs* (1906), *Sins of the Fathers* (1924), *A Victim of Circumstances* (1927), and *Brownie* (1931). Gissing also wrote essays for a number of periodicals. *Notes on Social Democracy* (1968, with an introduction by Jacob Korg), reprints three articles he wrote for the *Pall Mall Gazette* in 1880. *George Gissing: Essays and Fiction* (1970) prints nine prose works published for the first time. Late in his life, Gissing published *Charles Dickens: A Critical Study* (1898) and *By the Ionian Sea* (1901), his "notes of a ramble in southern Italy."

Achievements

During his lifetime, George Gissing achieved neither the fame nor the fortune that he would have liked. His reputation, though it grew steadily, especially in the 1890's, was always overshadowed by the powerhouse writers of the late Victorian era. Gissing was nevertheless seriously reviewed and often applauded by the critics for his objective treatment of social conditions in England. After his death, his reputation was eclipsed for many years, and it was only in the late twentieth century that Gissing began to receive the reevaluation needed to determine his place in English literary history. The renewed academic attention, manifested by numerous new editions of his novels, critical biographies, full-length studies of his novels, and several volumes of his correspondence, suggested that Gissing's niche would become more firmly established.

Biography

Born on November 22, 1857, in Wakefield, Yorkshire, George Robert Gissing was the eldest of five children of Thomas Waller and Margaret Bedford Gissing. Thomas Gissing was a chemist in Wakefield and something of a religious skeptic whose extensive library provided the young George with convenient access to a variety of reading material. The early years of financial security and familial harmony were disrupted when Thomas Gissing died in December, 1870. George, only thirteen, and his two brothers were sent to Lindow Grove School at Alderley Edge, Cheshire. There, the young Gissing's studious habits gained for him the first of many academic accolades. His performance on the Oxford local examination in 1872 was especially encouraging, but financial circumstances made it necessary for him to attend Owens College in Manchester, where he had won free tuition for three sessions and where he continued with his academic success.

Gissing was not, however, enjoying the same success in his personal life. Living a lonely and studious life in Manchester, he fell in love with a young prostitute named Marianne Helen Harrison, or Nell. With the zeal of the reformer, Gissing tried to save her from her profession and her penury, apparently not realizing at first that she was an alcoholic as well. Exhausting his own funds, the young Gissing stole miscellaneous property from his fellow students at Owens College. He was soon caught and the course of his life was radically altered, for he was forced to abandon all thoughts of an academic life. With the aid of friends, he sailed for the United States in the fall of 1876 and worked briefly as a high school teacher in Waltham, Massachusetts. Why he left Waltham, where he apparently enjoyed a reasonably good life, is not known, but in the spring of 1877 he moved to Chicago, where he tried to eke out an existence as a writer. Though he did publish his first work (a short story called "The Sins of the Fathers," in the *Chicago Tribune*, March 10, 1877), he was not well paid for his endeavors and left after only four months. He worked at odd jobs in New England and elsewhere, and then in the fall of 1877 he made his way back to England.

In London, Gissing lived in near poverty, working sporadically as a tutor and drafting his first novels. Nell came to live with him, and in October, 1879, they were married. Despite Gissing's noble intention to reform her apparently self-destructive character, the marriage was not successful. A vivid fictionalized account of the sordidness of their married life is given in *Workers in the Dawn*, Gissing's first published novel. He lived a turbulent life with Nell until he put her in a so-called invalids' home in January, 1882. Even after that, she gave him trouble, both financial and emotional, until she died in 1888.

The direction of Gissing's writings in the 1880's was influenced not only by his failed marriage but also by a number of other lifelong interests that were well established by the end of the decade: his friendship with the budding German writer Eduard Bertz, his reading of Auguste Comte, his unfailing compassion for the poverty of late Victorian England, his friendship with Frederic Harrison, who read his first novel and provided much-needed encouragement, and his friendship with Morley Roberts, who later became Gissing's first biographer with the thinly disguised *The Private Life of Henry Maitland* (1912). Not until 1886, with the publication of *Demos*, did Gissing gain moderate success with his writing. Buoyed by more favorable circumstances, especially the sense of freedom once Nell died, Gissing left for an extended tour of Europe in September, 1888. He also shifted the emphasis of his novels from the working class to the middle class, beginning in 1890 with *The Emancipated*.

The 1890's began auspiciously for Gissing's literary career, particularly with the publication of *New Grub Street* and *Born in Exile*. His personal life, however, was following a different course. On a trip to Italy in 1890, he noticed the first signs of the respiratory illness that would plague him the rest of his life. On February 25, 1891, he married Edith Underwood, a "work-girl," as he described her, with whom he was not in love. The marriage was a complete failure, despite the birth of two sons (Walter Leonard, born 1891, and Alfred Charles, born 1895). Gissing's literary success in the 1890's, as moderate as it was, was achieved in spite of his loveless marriage and domestic unrest. He persevered until September, 1897, when he permanently separated from his wife and went to Italy. In the summer of 1898, he met Gabrielle Fleury, a Frenchwoman who was the complete opposite of his two wives in her refined and cultured manner. Gissing was immediately attracted to her and would have legally married her had a divorce from Edith been possible. Instead, the two sanctified their relationship with each other in a private ceremony on May 7, 1899, in Rouen.

George Gissing. (Getty Images)

Living in France under the most favorable circumstances of his entire life, Gissing continued to write, and in 1903 he saw *The Private Papers of Henry Ryecroft*, his most popular work, go through three editions. His health, however, had been growing steadily worse, and his short-lived happiness came to an end when he died on December 28, 1903, of myocarditis at St. Jean-Pied-de-Port in France.

Analysis

In his personal life, George Gissing was a man of divided mind, and the biographical antitheses were paralleled by the literary and philosophical influences on his work. In private life, he gravitated toward Frederic Harrison's circle of intellectuals and sophisticated people; at the same time, he was drawn into marriages with psychologically, intellectually, and socially unsuitable women. He was attracted to a scholarly career as a historian, philosopher, and classicist, but he was also drawn to journalism, hackwork, and lectures to workingmen's associations with an emphasis on social reform. Like many writers at the end of the nineteenth century, he was caught between the sociological realists with reform instincts and the adherents of an aesthetic movement with their emphasis on the attainment of ideal beauty. His sensuousness conflicted with his intellectual idealism; his desire for popularity and material success with his austere integrity as an artist.

Gissing's career as a novelist, at least until the late twentieth century, has been assessed in the context of nineteenth century realism and naturalism. Certainly, the techniques employed in his novels, especially the early ones, owe much to the Victorian conventions that had become well established by the time of Gissing's first published novel. He was thoroughly acquainted with the work of Charles Dickens; his own novels are often sentimental, cautiously admonitory, and riddled with subplots. Gissing, however, never treated his subject matter as humorously as did Dickens in his early novels. Dickens's treatment of poverty, for example, is sometimes used for picturesque effects; Gissing saw poverty in a solemn manner, finding it both lamentable and execrable.

For other literary precedents, Gissing turned to the French and Russian writers, discovering in the French naturalists such as Émile Zola the pervasive effects of physical and social environments and finding in the Russian naturalistic psychologists the precise and complete analysis of character. Like Zola, he described the squalor of poverty, probed the psychology of sex (though with more reserve), and generally ended his novels in dismal defeat. Yet, unlike the naturalists, Gissing was not so much concerned with the particular details of the workshop, with conflicts between capital and labor, but with the whole atmosphere of poverty, especially the resultant loss of integrity on the part of those who struggle to rise beyond and above it.

To divide Gissing's career into neat stages is not an easy task. For the purposes of an overview, however, it is convenient to look at three large, if not always distinct, groups of his novels. In the 1880's, beginning with *Workers in the Dawn* and ending with *The Nether World*, Gissing was most often concerned with the lower class and social reform. In the first half of the 1890's, beginning with *The Emancipated*, Gissing turned to the middle class, examining the whole middle-class ethic and ranging his focal point from the tradesman to the "new woman." In the last half of the 1890's and until his death in 1903, Gissing's work was more varied, ranging from a historical romance to a travel book to reworkings of his early themes. In those last years, his works were not always successful, either commercially or critically, but that was the period of his most popular work, the semiautobiographical *The Private Papers of Henry Ryecroft*.

In an early and important reassessment of Gissing's career, Jacob Korg (in "Division of Purpose in George Gissing," *PMLA*, June, 1955) points out that the dichotomy between Gissing's artistic principles and his anger over Victorian England's social problems is evident in five of his novels published in the 1880's: *Workers in the Dawn*, *The Unclassed*, *Demos*, *Thyrza*, and *The Nether World*. In each of these novels, Gissing the reformer contends with Gissing the artist; in none of them is the tension resolved satisfactorily.

Workers in the Dawn

Most of the material Gissing used in *Workers in the Dawn* can be found repeatedly in the other novels of the 1880's, and most of that material springs from his own experiences. Clearly, his early marriage to a girl from the slums underlined his interest in social themes throughout his life. In the late 1870's and 1880's, he had also become enthusiastic about the radical party, read Comte, promoted positivist doctrines, and spoke at various radical-party meetings. Between 1879 and 1880, Gissing began writing *Workers in the Dawn*, a novel of avowed social protest in which he serves, as he says in a letter of June 8, 1880, as "a mouthpiece of the advanced Radical party." Equally obvious in the novel, however, is that Gissing is perturbed about placing art in service to political and moral dogma.

Arthur Goldring, the hero of the novel, is both a painter and a social reformer, but he is clearly upset with this duality in his life. Convinced that the aims of his two avocations are antithetical, he looks for consolation from Helen Norman, the woman he loves. Through the mouth of Helen, Gissing propounds the ideas that he had gleaned from Percy Bysshe Shelley's *A Defence of Poetry* (1840)—most specifically that art is the true legislator of the moral order. Gissing, however, found it difficult to practice what he held to be intellectually valid; thus, the early Gissing, like Goldring, constantly found difficulty in accepting the tenet that art should not attempt to teach morality directly.

The Unclassed

In *The Unclassed*, Gissing continued to struggle with the intricacies of the artist's world. The result was a novel in which the fall of the two artist figures is in one case oversimplified and in the other muddled. Confused and worried about his own failings, Gissing attempted to analyze the artistic temperament and the forces operating against such a temperament by segmenting the artist into Julian Casti and Osmond Waymark. Casti's story is Gissing's attempt to depict an artist undone by an overriding sense of moral obligation to a shrewish and possessive woman, Harriet Smales, a character with clear similarities to Gissing's own wife Nell. Not until the last chapter is the physically debilitated and intellectually frustrated Casti convinced that his moral obligation to Harriet is futile. He leaves for the Isle of Wight, where he quietly spends his last days plaintively talking of the epic he will never write.

The portrait of Waymark is Gissing's attempt to counterbalance the oversimplified Casti. Waymark is a more complex figure, and his role as an artist is more thoroughly scrutinized by Gissing. Waymark is thwarted in his pursuit of art by a variety of causes: his aborted social consciousness, his vaguely defined ideological tenets, his relationship with women, and his pecuniary predicament. By the end of the novel, after a plethora of complications, Waymark is neither a complete success nor a complete failure. His one published novel receives mediocre reviews, and Waymark himself shows little concern either for its intrinsic value or for its critical reception. By placing his artist-hero in the grips of consuming personal, political, and economic woes, Gissing tries to suggest that art cannot flourish with integrity or purity. The portrait of Waymark, however, is finally very muddled, for it is not clear to which forces Waymark the artist succumbs. Questions about the role of art in the political and moral order continued to dominate Gissing's thinking in much the same way throughout the 1880's, and he entered the 1890's very much in the middle of the two main currents of literary thought, drawn both to the didacticism of the realists and naturalists and to the ivory towers of the aesthetes.

In the 1890's, Gissing broadened the range of his novels and produced his best work. At the beginning of the decade, he published *The Emancipated*, the story of a young middle-class widow restricted by religious scruples until she finds release in art. In *Denzil Quarrier*, Gissing tried his hand at a political novel and produced one of his more popular works. In *Eve's Ransom*, a short novel that was first serialized, he focused on the pangs ofunrequited love. In *Born in Exile*, Gissing examined the life of one born in the lower classes who has the opportunity to rise to a higher socioeconomic level. In *The Odd Women*, Gissing focused his attention on early feminists, making a careful study of women who never marry but who must support themselves in a male-dominated society.

NEW GRUB STREET

The novel on which Gissing's reputation has most depended is *New Grub Street*, his full-length study of the artist's role in society. From Jasper Milvain to Whelpdale to Alfred Yule to Edwin Reardon to Harold Biffin, Gissing offers a finely graduated hierarchy of the late nineteenth century artist. He is particularly interested in characterizing the artist manqué and the forces that have contributed to his failure. Unlike the earlier novels, however, *New Grub Street* presents a wider-ranging understanding of the artist's dilemma. It is no longer a simple case of idealized social reform versus an even more idealized artistic purity. In keeping with his social interests of the early 1890's, Gissing sees the factors operating against the artist arising more from without than from within. He concentrates on two particularly potent forces that militate against the artist and ultimately ensure his downfall.

The first force is "the woman," and her influence on the artist is subtle, pervasive, and lasting. Often sensitive and frequently lonely, the nascent artists of Gissing's Grub Street are prime targets for the love of a good woman. She appeals particularly to the psychologically insecure artist, promising a lifetime of emotional stability. At the outset, she is a source of inspiration, yet time and disillusionment reveal more distressing realities. It is the age-old femme fatale who lures the artist away from his art into an emotionally draining existence, thwarting his inclination and energy for production. It is "the other woman" who instigates a complicated triangle with like results. It is the husband-hunting woman who tantalizes the frustrated artist with the attraction of domestic security, but soon she either stifles that inexplicable drive to write for the sake of writing or provides a marriage so socially disadvantageous that advancement is precluded.

Economics is the second, equally potent, force militating against the three failed artists (Reardon, Biffen, Yule) of *New Grub Street*. While the force of woman is chiefly felt on a psychological level, her destructive influence within the economic sphere is evident. After all, the necessity of supporting a wife and children increases the financial difficulties the artist must face. Monetary matters also prove a problem in and of themselves. An artist such as Biffen easily falls victim to the myth of so many struggling artists, convinced that poverty and hardship are essential in the experience of any would-be writer. In the portrait of Reardon, however, one quickly sees the artist at odds with real poverty, rarely an inspiration and usually a deterrent to his work.

Edwin Reardon is the novel's central character, and it is Reardon who is subjected to the greatest number of debilitating forces. When he is introduced, it is immediately clear that his marriage to Amy has entangled him in a finely woven web. At the outset, Reardon is thirty-two years old, has been married two years, and has a ten-month-old child. None of his decisions, artistic or otherwise, can be wholly unaffected by this domestic responsibility. Gissing makes his viewpoint clear in the very first scene with Reardon and Amy. In this scene, largely a heated discussion over Reardon's approach to writing, Amy chides her husband for not compromising his artistic integrity and forcibly reminds him that "art must be practised as a trade, at all events in our time. This is the age of trade." Thus, in this one early scene, the two powerful influences of woman and commerce come together, and there is little doubt that they will take a heavy toll on Reardon the artist. Reardon's failure as an artist, both aesthetically and materially, runs in direct proportion to the failure of his marriage and the decline of his economic status.

Obviously lending itself to autobiographical interpretation, the artist-novel is the means by which the real-life writer works out—or fails to work out—his own aesthetic and personal conflicts. *New Grub Street*, like Gissing's earlier novels, has its share of autobiographical elements, but the author's analysis of his emotional and intellectual condition is far more perceptive. He has gained tighter control on the raw materials of the artist's world, which are treated ambiguously in the early novels. The eleven years between *Workers in the Dawn* and *New Grub Street* were the training ground for an increased self-insight and a more encompassing, objective portraiture of the artist figure and the gray areas with which he must cope.

LATE NOVELS

The work Gissing wrote in the last half of the 1890's has not generally contributed to his critical reputation. Part of his later years he spent on a variety of projects that are not especially characteristic of his overall career. He worked on a historical novel that was never completed but was published posthumously as *Veranilda* in 1904. The novels that Gissing published in his last years are for the most part undistinguished and often are reworkings of his earlier themes. *The Whirlpool* is a study of marriage in the "whirlpool" of modern life. *The Crown of Life* is his paean to the perfect marriage, significantly begun shortly after he met Gabrielle Fleury in 1898.

In 1900, Gissing did most of the writing of *The Private Papers of Henry Ryecroft*, though it was not published until 1903. Pretending to be merely the book's editor, Gissing provides a short preface saying that he has come across the papers of his friend, Henry Ryecroft, and has ordered them in an arbitrary way. There are four main sections, each labeled with one of the seasons, beginning with spring and ending with winter. The book is a mixture of autobiography and reverie, providing the author a platform on which he can discuss sundry subjects. Thus, there are memories of childhood, of poverty in London, of peaceful trips to Italy. There are descriptive sketches of rural scenes in England. There are short essays on philosophical ideas and terse confessions of various preferences, ranging from food to countries. The book provides delightful if not exciting reading and gives a memorable portrait of the aging author who has retired to the calmness of Exeter to ruminate.

When Gissing died in 1903, he left behind an impressive corpus, but the reputation he had at the time of his death did not continue to grow. By some, he was criticized as being too ponderous and undramatic, inclined to publish an analytical study rather than a dramatized story. By others, he was accused of being melodramatic, relying too exclusively on the contrivances of the Victorian "triple-decker." In the second half of the twentieth century, however, especially during the last two decades, Gissing attracted more attention in academic circles. His seriousness as a novelist has slowly been recognized, both for his historic role in the heyday of English realism and for his integrity as an individual novelist.

David B. Eakin

OTHER MAJOR WORKS

SHORT FICTION: *Human Odds and Ends*, 1897; *The House of Cobwebs*, 1906; *Sins of the Fathers*, 1924; *A Victim of Circumstances*, 1927; *Brownie*, 1931.

NONFICTION: *Charles Dickens: A Critical Study*, 1898; *By the Ionian Sea*, 1901; *The Immortal Dickens*, 1925; *Letters of George Gissing to Members of His Family*, 1927; *George Gissing and H. G. Wells: Their Friendship and Correspondence*, 1961; *The Letters of George Gissing to Eduard Bertz*, 1961; *George Gissing's Commonplace Book*, 1962; *The Letters of George Gissing to Gabrielle Fleury*, 1964; *George Gissing: Essays and Fiction*, 1970; *The Diary of George Gissing, Novelist*, 1978; *Collected Works of George Gissing on Charles Dickens*, 2004-2005 (3 volumes; Pierre Coustillas, editor).

BIBLIOGRAPHY

Connelly, Mark. *Orwell and Gissing*. New York: Peter Lang, 1997. Compares Gissing's *New Grub Street* to George Orwell's *Keep the Aspidistra Flying* (1936).

Coustillas, Pierre, and Colin Partridge, eds. *Gissing: The Critical Heritage*. London: Routledge & Kegan Paul, 1972. A very important research tool for the study of Gissing, containing a large selection of reviews dating from his own time to the late 1960's.

Grylls, David. *The Paradox of Gissing*. London: Allen and Unwin, 1986. Maintains that paradox is the key to reading Gissing properly. Gissing was attracted to conflicting points of view on various topics, including women, social reform, poverty, and art; his novels express these contradictions, often by a sharp break in the middle. In *New Grub Street*, Gissing achieved an integration of diverse opinions.

Halperin, John. *Gissing: A Life in Books*. New York: Oxford University Press, 1982. A comprehensive work on the life of Gissing. Its dominant theme is that he wrote about his own life in his novels, and much of the book discusses Gissing's fiction from this point of view.

James, Simon J. *Unsettled Accounts: Money and Narrative in the Novels of George Gissing*. London: Anthem Press, 2003. Examines Gissing's preoccupation with money as reflected in *New Grub Street* and his other novels, placing his work within the context of nineteenth century economic theory and the work of other English novelists. James concludes that Gissing's work expresses an "unhappy accommodation with money's underwriting of human existence and culture."

Liggins, Emma. *George Gissing, the Working Woman, and Urban Culture*. Burlington, Vt.: Ashgate, 2006. Liggins examines *New Grub Street*, *The Nether World*, and other works by Gissing to analyze how they realistically depict London culture and changing class and gender identities, particularly for working women.

Michaux, Jean-Pierre, ed. *George Gissing: Critical Essays*. New York: Barnes & Noble Books, 1981. This valuable anthology provides a good selection of twentieth century critics' discussions of Gissing. Includes an influential essay by Q. D. Leavis, who praised Gissing's portrayal of the miseries of the Victorian world.

Postmus, Bouwe, ed. *A Garland for Gissing*. New York: Rodopi, 2001. Essays examine Gissing's representation of working women, women's inadequate education, and women's desire for independence. Other pieces discuss his depiction of working men, the problem of identity, and commercial culture.

Ryle, Martin, and Jenny Bourne Taylor, eds. *George Gissing: Voices of the Unclassed*. Burlington, Vt.: Ashgate, 2005. Collection of essays that analyze *New Grub Street*, Gissing's representation of working women, Gissing in the context of the "cultural politics of food," and Gissing's place in twentieth century English literature.

Selig, Robert L. *George Gissing*. Rev. ed. New York: Twayne, 1995. An excellent introductory biography, with chapters on Gissing's major works and his career as a man of letters. Includes a chronology, notes, and an annotated bibliography.

Sloan, John. *George Gissing: The Cultural Challenge*. New York: St. Martin's Press, 1989. Chapters on Gissing's "Hogarthian beginnings," his working-class novels, and his career from *The Emancipated* to *New Grub Street* and *The Odd Women*. Includes detailed notes and a bibliography.

ELLEN GLASGOW

Born: Richmond, Virginia; April 22, 1873
Died: Richmond, Virginia; November 21, 1945
Also known as: Ellen Anderson Gholson Glasgow

Principal long fiction

The Descendant, 1897
Phases of an Inferior Planet, 1898
The Voice of the People, 1900
The Battle-Ground, 1902
The Deliverance, 1904
The Wheel of Life, 1906
The Ancient Law, 1908
The Romance of a Plain Man, 1909
The Miller of Old Church, 1911
Virginia, 1913
Life and Gabriella, 1916
The Builders, 1919
One Man in His Time, 1922
Barren Ground, 1925
The Romantic Comedians, 1926
They Stooped to Folly, 1929
The Sheltered Life, 1932
Vein of Iron, 1935
In This Our Life, 1941

Other literary forms

In addition to nineteen novels, Ellen Glasgow (GLAS-goh) wrote a book of short stories, *The Shadowy Third, and Other Stories* (1923); a book of poems, *The Freeman, and Other Poems* (1902); a book on her views of fiction writing (concerned primarily with her own works), *A Certain Measure: An Interpretation of Prose Fiction* (1943); and an autobiography, *The Woman Within* (1954). She also wrote a number of articles on fiction for various periodicals and magazines. Her letters were published in 1958.

Achievements

Although Ellen Glasgow never felt that she had received the critical acclaim she deserved, or at least desired, she nevertheless played an important part in the development of southern letters. A significant figure in the so-called Southern Renaissance, she provided in her novels a new picture of the South, a region reluctantly ushered into the modern world. Against a sentimentalized view of the Old South, Glasgow advocated an acceptance of the inevitability of change.

Prior to 1925, Glasgow's critical reception was mixed—more positive than negative, but nothing that would mark her as a writer of the first rank. With *Barren Ground*, however, Glasgow's reputation began to grow with both critics and readers. That novel made the 1925 *Review of Reviews* list of twenty-five outstanding novels of the year. Represented also on the list for 1925 were Sinclair Lewis's *Arrowsmith*, Edith Wharton's *The Mother's Recompense*, Willa Cather's *The Professor's House*, and Sherwood Anderson's *Dark Laughter*. Glasgow's *The Sheltered Life* was a best seller and greatly enhanced her reputation. *Vein of Iron* and *In This Our Life*, which received the Pulitzer Prize in 1942, helped to ensure her position as a writer of major significance.

"The chief end of the novel, as indeed of all literature," Glasgow wrote, is "to increase our understanding of life and heighten our consciousness." To this end she directed her artistic skills, writing with care and precision, for, as she also said, "The true novel . . . is, like poetry, an act of birth, not a device or invention."

Biography

Born in Richmond, Virginia, in 1873, Ellen Glasgow came from a combination of stern Scotch-Irish pioneers on her father's side and Tidewater, Virginia, aristocratic stock on her mother's side. Francis Glasgow was an ironworks executive, an occupation well suited to his Puritan temperament and character. Ellen Glasgow had little positive to say about her father. Her mother was a cultivated, gracious, and humane woman. These divergent influences provided the crucible from which Glasgow's writings were to emerge.

The next to the youngest in a family of four sons and six daughters, Glasgow experienced a more or less lonely childhood, with Rebe, her younger sister, and Mammy Lizzie Jones, her black nurse, providing her only companionship. Because of fragile health and a nervous temperament that precluded adjustment to formal schooling, her isolation was increased, and most of her education came from her father's extensive library. As a child, Glasgow admired the novels of Charles Dickens, Henry Fielding, and Jane Austen. From Dickens, she gained reinforcement for her already strong aversion to cruelty, and from the latter two, she learned that only honest writing can endure. "Lesser" novelists, she felt, lacked "the creative passion and the courage to offend, which is the essential note of great fiction."

Glasgow grew up in that period following the American Civil War when, as she described it, the "prosperous and pleasure-loving" agrarians of the antebellum years were struggling for existence amid "the dark furies of Reconstruction." It was a conservative, even reactionary, time when, according to Glasgow, "being a rebel, even an intellectual one, was less exciting and more uncomfortable than it is nowadays." Rejecting the harsh Calvinism of her father and the bloodless social graces of Richmond society, she retreated even further into a life of the mind. Glasgow's growing sense of alienation and rebelliousness has been seen by critics as the wellspring of her literary vision.

By 1890, just one year after her hearing had begun to fade, Glasgow had produced some four hundred pages of a novel, *Sharp Realities* (unpublished). Putting that effort aside, she began writing *The Descendant* in 1891. Two years later, however, upon the death of her mother, with whom she had great affinity, she destroyed a good part of what she had written. Another two years passed before she returned to the novel and completed it. The following year, she made the first of numerous trips to Europe.

With the publication (anonymously) of *The Descendant* in 1897, Glasgow was launched on her prolific career, a career that saw novels appearing every two years or so. Writing became and remained her role in life, and she was ever mindful of the growth of her literary reputation, changing publishers when she felt it to her advantage and making sure that critics were fully aware of her books.

Presumably while on a trip to Europe in 1899, Glasgow fell in love with a married man, to whom she refers in her autobiography *The Woman Within* as Gerald B_____. A mystery man, Gerald B_____ was described by Glasgow as an older Wall Street man with a wife and children. There is some evidence, however, indicating that Gerald B_____ was a physician. Another serious love affair was with Henry Watkins Anderson, a Richmond lawyer. He and Glasgow met in 1915 and were engaged in 1917. In July of the next year, Glasgow attempted suicide when she learned that Anderson, who was working with the Red Cross in the Balkan States, was attracted to Queen Marie of Romania. This turbulent love affair between Glasgow and Anderson was tacitly broken about 1920. In two novels, *The Builders* and *One Man in His Time*, Glasgow incorporated aspects of her relationship with Anderson.

As Glasgow began receiving the critical recognition for which she longed, her health began to fail. A heart condition worsened, and she died on November 21, 1945, in Richmond.

Ellen Glasgow. (Library of Congress)

Analysis

Turning away from a romanticized view of her own Virginia, Ellen Glasgow became a part of the revolt against the elegiac tradition of southern letters. Although she rejected romance, she did not turn to realism; rather, she saw herself as a "verist": "The whole truth," she said, "must embrace the interior world as well as external appearances." In this sense, she strove for what she called "blood and irony"—blood because the South had grown thin and pale and was existing on borrowed ideas, copying rather than creating; and irony because it is the surest antidote to sentimental decay. Certain that life in the South was not as it had been pictured by previous writers, she produced a series of novels that recorded the social history of Virginia through three generations, picturing sympathetically the social and industrial revolutions that were transforming the romantic South.

A central theme in this record is that of change—change brought about by the conflict between the declining agrarian regime and the rising industrial system. Arguing that such change must be accepted and even welcomed, Glasgow observed

> For thirty years I have had a part in the American literary scene, either as a laborer in the vineyard or as a raven croaking on a bust of Pallas. In all these years I have found that the only permanent law in art, as in the social order, is the law of change.

In pursuing the theme of change, however, Glasgow was careful not to go to the extreme in her presentation of deterioration, feeling that "the literature that crawls too long in the mire will lose at last the power of standing erect." In this respect, her works, unlike those of William Faulkner or Erskine Caldwell, lack shocking or sensational detail and maintain an almost Victorian sense of decorum. For example, when Dorinda in *Barren Ground* goes to the city, she is first approached by a fascinating lady clad in black who wants her to enter into a disreputable house. She is then rescued by a kindly doctor who gives her money to go back to Virginia and establish a dairy farm.

This tendency toward propriety found in Glasgow's writing is explained in her plea to the novelist of the southern gothic school:

> All I ask him to do is to deal as honestly with living tissues as he now deals with decay, to remind himself that the colors of putrescence have no greater validity for our age, or for any age, than . . . the cardinal virtues.

The theme of change gives a mythic quality to Glasgow's work. It is that quality that Henry Canby refers to when he says that Glasgow sees her world as always a departing and a becoming. Her instrument for this cutting away is her sense for tender and ironic tragedy, a tragedy that is, in the words of Canby, "a tragedy of frustration—the waste of life through maladjustment of man to his environment and environment to its men."

Often, too, Glasgow's works picture nobility cramped by prejudice, or beauty gone wrong through an inability to adjust to the real, or a good philosophy without premises in existing experience. A good example of the latter theme can be found in the character of John Fincastle in *Vein of Iron*. A man of deep thought, he is considered "as a dangerous skeptic, or as a man of simple faith, who believed that God is essence, not energy, and that blessedness, or the life of the spirit, is the only reality." Fincastle is a part of the constant change in the world, but he himself does not fully realize the implications of the dynamic society in which he lives. He sees nothing of any potential value in the machine age and is unable to reconcile his own philosophy to the reality of the times.

Although all of Glasgow's works contain a note of pessimism, there is also present a note of optimism. More often than not, this hope comes after a protagonist's contact with city life. Dorinda, for example, returns to Pedlar's Mill after her stay in the city, to start a successful farm and gain revenge from Jason. Then, too, there is Ada in *Vein of Iron*, who, with her cynical husband, returns to the manse that was once her home and, strengthened by the recovery of "that lost certainty of a continuing tradition," looks forward to a new beginning.

Perhaps, when compared with Faulkner or Thomas Wolfe, the theme of change, as treated by Glasgow, may seem somewhat sentimental; there is, however, a refreshing and heartening chord in her work that lends credence to the idea that the world is not destined to be one great naturalistic garbage can, but may perhaps be fertile enough for an occasional bed of flowers. At any rate, as Glasgow phrased it, "the true revolution may end in a ditch or in the shambles, but it must begin in the stars."

VIRGINIA

In *Virginia*, her first acknowledged masterpiece, Glasgow focuses on the southern woman. "As an emblem," she writes of the southern woman in *The Deliverance*, "she followed closely the mid-Victorian ideal, and though her sort was found everywhere in the Western world, it was in Virginia that she seemed to attain her finest and latest flowering." It would follow, then, that if southern women attained their "finest and latest flowering" in Virginia, that also is where they would be most affected by the winds of social change that were sweeping over the South in the late nineteenth and early twentieth centuries. Bred and reared to tradition, they faced a new order that was both challenging and perplexing. While some held firmly to the pedestal on which they had been placed, others leaped from it and immersed themselves in the new world.

Virginia Pendleton, the heroine of *Virginia*, is, like her mother, the ideal southern woman, the image of propriety and gentility. "Whenever I attempt to recall the actual writing of Virginia," Glasgow writes in *A Certain Measure*,

> and to recapture the mold in which the book was conceived, I find myself moving again in an imaginary world which was then more real to me than the world which I inhabited. I could not separate Virginia from her background, because she was an integral part of it, and it shared her validity. What she was, that background and atmosphere had helped to make her, and she, in turn, had intensified the life of the picture.

In Dinwiddie, Virginia, during the 1800's, Virginia has been reared as "the perfect flower of the Victorian ideal" and "logical result of an inordinate sense of duty, the crowning achievement of the code of beautiful behavior and the Episcopal Church." She has been taught that duty, devotion, and sacrifice are the lot of women and that husband and family must come before all else.

Virginia, educated at Miss Priscilla Battle's finishing school, the Dinwiddie Academy for Young Ladies, is indeed "finished," at least as far as any real purpose in life is concerned. The basis of her education was simply that "the less a girl knew about life, the better prepared she would be to contend with it." Thinking him an excellent choice for a husband, she marries Oliver Treadwell, son of an industrialist, and, bearing him three children, settles down to family life. Oliver, like his father, who had dominated Oliver's mother, exercises this same control over Virginia. A would-be dramatist, Oliver is unsuccessful as a serious playwright, but he does receive some financial return by writing claptrap for the New York stage. Although Virginia has become middle-aged and worn, Oliver has maintained the look of youth. Finding no understanding from Virginia, who is not equipped to give him any, he deserts her for Margaret Oldcastle, an actor. Not knowing how to fight for her husband's love, Virginia is left with her two daughters, whose independence and aggressiveness she cannot understand, and her devoted son, Harry. The purpose in life for which she and so many other southern women had been prepared is gone. "Nothing but constancy was left to her," says Glasgow, "and constancy, when it has outlived its usefulness, is as barren as fortitude."

Virginia, in her minor tragedy, represents the ideal woman as victim of change, a change for which she has not been prepared and for which there is no effective antidote. One detects at least a small tear shed by Glasgow for the Virginias of the world. Once seen as ornaments of civilization and as restraints upon the more coarse natures of men, they now must replace self-sacrifice with an assertiveness that will be more in keeping with the changing social order. In that sense, Virginia points forward to *Barren Ground*.

BARREN GROUND

Barren Ground marks Glasgow's emergence not only from a period of despondency regarding her social life but also as a novelist who has moved without question from apprentice to master. Certainly her finest work to that time, *Barren Ground* was to Glasgow the best of all her novels. One of her country novels, it deals with that class of people often referred to as "poor whites." Glasgow herself refutes this appellation, preferring instead to call them "good people," a label that distinguishes them from the aristocratic "good families." Lineal descendants of the English yeoman farmer, good people were the ones who pushed the frontier westward. In this novel, they stand as a "buffer class between the opulent gentry and the hired labourers."

Dorinda Oakley, the heroine, is the offspring of a

union of opposites: her father, Joshua, a landless man whose industry and good nature do not compensate for his ineffectuality; and her mother, Eudora, the daughter of a Presbyterian minister, with a religious mania of her own. This background, says Glasgow, has kept Dorinda's heart "in arms against life." More important, however, she has also inherited a kinship with the earth. This kinship enables her to make something positive out of "barren ground."

Dorinda falls in love with Jason Greylock, a young doctor, seeing in him the promise of something more than the grinding poverty she has known. They plan to marry, but Jason cannot go against his father's wishes, and he marries Geneva Ellgood instead. Pregnant by Jason, Dorinda flees to New York, where, after being struck by a taxi, she loses the unborn baby. She works as a nurse for Dr. Faraday until she learns that her father is dying. She returns home with enough money borrowed from Faraday to start a dairy farm. Back on the land, she becomes a tough-minded spinster and makes a success of the farm. Although she marries Nathan Pedlar, a storekeeper, she remains the head of the family. After his death in a train wreck, she is again alone, but happy, rearing Nathan's child by a previous marriage and managing the farm. Jason, in the meantime, has lost his wife by suicide and is forced to sell his farm to Dorinda. Because he is ill and an alcoholic, she unwillingly provides him with food and shelter. After a few months, he dies, and once more she is alone. When a local farmer asks Dorinda to marry him, she responds, "I am thankful to have finished with all that."

A tragic figure of sorts, Dorinda sees herself trapped by fate, "a straw in the wind, a leaf on a stream." Even so, she is not content to be simply a passive victim of that fate. Unlike Jason, who through his inherited weakness, succumbs to the forces that beset him, Dorinda looks upon the land as a symbol of that fate against which she must struggle. Hardened by adversity and with a deep instinct for survival, she refuses to surrender.

Although Dorinda's life may be compared to barren ground because it has been emotionally unfulfilled, it nevertheless is a successful life in that she does master herself and in turn masters the land. Just as the broom sedge must be burned off the land, so must romantic emotions be purged from Dorinda's soul. In giving her life to the land, she, in a sense, gains it back—and is thus, ironically, both victim and victor.

The Romantic Comedians

Following *Barren Ground*, Glasgow turned to the novel of manners with *The Romantic Comedians*. The first of a trilogy—the subsequent works being *They Stooped to Folly* and *The Sheltered Life*—this novel has been regarded by some critics as Glasgow's finest. After *Barren Ground*, Glasgow comments, a novel "which for three years had steeped my mind in the tragic life, the comic spirit, always restless when it is confined, began struggling against the bars of its cage." Because she never before had turned her hand to comedy of manners, *The Romantic Comedians* was written in the nature of an experiment.

The novel exhibits a high spirit of comedy with tragic overtones. "Tragedy and comedy were blood brothers" in Glasgow's image-making faculty, she writes, "but they were at war with each other, and had steadily refused to be reconciled." In *The Romantic Comedians*, says Blair Rouse, "we see people and their actions as participants in the follies of the comic genre; but we see, too, that a very slight shift of emphasis may reveal a tragic mask upon the actors."

Judge Gamaliel Bland Honeywell, the protagonist, "is a collective portrait of several Virginians of an older school," says Glasgow, "who are still unafraid to call themselves gentlemen." Living in Queenborough (Richmond, Virginia), he seeks female companionship after his wife of thirty-six years dies. At age sixty-five, he is expected to marry a former sweetheart, Amanda Lightfoot. Disdaining such expected decorum, however, he falls in love with and marries Annabelle Upchurch, a young cousin of his wife. Annabelle marries him not so much for love but rather to heal the pain of being jilted by Angus Blount. As one might suspect in such a marriage, Annabelle is soon looking for greener pastures, finding them in Delaney Birdsong, with whom she goes to New York. Unable to win her back, the Judge, ill and disillusioned, believes that life holds nothing more for him. With the coming of spring, however, he looks upon his attractive young nurse and muses, "Spring is here, and I am feeling almost as young as I felt last year."

Judge Honeywell, like many of Glasgow's women, is of another tradition. More than age separates him from

Annabelle. While he is the target of some satiric jibes in the book and one finds it difficult to find much sincerity in him, he is, nevertheless, a victim of the same kind of romantic claptrap that dooms other Glasgow characters.

A refreshing book when contrasted with Glasgow's previous efforts, *The Romantic Comedians* displays the author's humanity as well as her humor. While she makes the reader laugh at the actions of the judge and the other characters of the novel, she never lets them become completely ridiculous. Whatever else the judge is, for example, he is a human being—and no one recognizes that more than Glasgow.

THE SHELTERED LIFE

In *The Sheltered Life*, the last novel of her trilogy on manners, Glasgow employs two points of view—that of youth and that of age, in this case a young girl and an old man, respectively. Against the background of a "shallow and aimless society of happiness hunters," she presents more characters of Queenborough as they are revealed through the mind and emotions of Jenny Blair and her grandfather, General David Archbald.

Glasgow intended General Archbald as the central character in the novel—a character who "represents the tragedy, wherever it appears, of the civilized man in a world that is not civilized." General Archbald sees before him a changing world, a world that is passing him by. Thus, he holds to the social traditions of the nineteenth century, which have provided little shelter for him. He was never a man for his time. A sensitive person who had wanted to be a poet, he was ridiculed in his earlier years. Poetry had been his one love in life; it was lost before it could be realized. He married his wife only because of an accidental, overnight sleigh ride that, in tradition-bound Queenborough, demanded marriage to save appearances. A compassionate man, he gives up his desire to marry again after his wife dies in order not to disrupt the lives of his son's widow and her daughter, Jenny.

Jenny, too, unknowingly is caught in the patterned existence of the Archbald heritage. A willful girl, she has been sheltered from the real world by culture and tradition and can see things only in terms of her own desires. At the age of eighteen, she falls in love with an older married man, George Birdsong. George's wife, Eva, eventually finds them in each other's arms. Jenny flees the scene, only to learn later that Eva has killed George.

Eva Birdsong is another perfect image of southern womanhood, beautiful and protected all her life. A celebrated belle prior to her marriage to George, she has striven to achieve a perfect marriage. Without children, she and George are thrown upon each other. Over the years, George has been a bit of a roué, seeking pleasure where he could find it. In the end, Eva is left with the realization that what women "value most is something that doesn't exist."

When Jenny realizes what she has done, she flies to the general's understanding and sheltering arms, crying, "Oh, Grandfather, I didn't mean anything. . . . I didn't mean anything in the world." Ironically enough, she is right: She did not mean anything.

The Sheltered Life is more a tragicomedy than simply a comedy of manners. It is also, perhaps, Glasgow's best work, the novel toward which its predecessors were pointed. Symbol, style, characterization, and rhythm all combine to make *The Sheltered Life* a poignant and penetrating illustration of the futility of clinging to a tradition that has lost its essential meaning.

Glasgow's goal in all of her writing is perhaps stated best in *A Certain Measure*, when she says in reference to her last novel, *In This Our Life*, that she was trying to show "the tragedy of a social system which lives, grows, and prospers by material standards alone." One can sense in such a statement a conservative regard for tradition; even though Glasgow and many of her characters struggled against a shallow romanticism, a yearning for a genuine tradition was never far from her own artistic vision. The land seems to be the single sustaining factor in all of Glasgow's novels—it was the land that gave rise to and nourished the so-called southern tradition and that provides the "living pulse of endurance" to so many of her characters.

Wilton Eckley

OTHER MAJOR WORKS

SHORT FICTION: *The Shadowy Third, and Other Stories*, 1923; *The Collected Stories of Ellen Glasgow*, 1963.

POETRY: *The Freeman, and Other Poems*, 1902.

NONFICTION: *A Certain Measure: An Interpretation of Prose Fiction*, 1943; *The Woman Within*, 1954; *Letters of Ellen Glasgow*, 1958; *Perfect Companionship:*

Ellen Glasgow's Selected Correspondence with Women, 2005 (Pamela R. Matthews, editor).

Bibliography

Goodman, Susan. *Ellen Glasgow*. Baltimore: Johns Hopkins University Press, 1998. A biography that demonstrates Glasgow's significance as a southern author at the end of the nineteenth century and beginning of the twentieth century. Goodman discusses the gap between Glasgow's reception by her contemporaries and her later reception.

McDowell, Frederick P. W. *Ellen Glasgow and the Ironic Art of Fiction*. Madison: University of Wisconsin Press, 1960. An interesting analysis of Glasgow's oeuvre, analyzing it primarily in terms of style, irony, and wit. Includes an extensive bibliography.

Matthews, Pamela R. *Ellen Glasgow and a Woman's Traditions*. Charlottesville: University Press of Virginia, 1994. Matthews uses feminist psychological theory to reevaluate Glasgow's work, discussing, among other topics, Glasgow's perception of herself as a female author. Includes bibliographical references and an index.

The Mississippi Quarterly 49, no 2 (Spring, 1996). A special issue on Glasgow includes essays on her novels *The Sheltered Life*, *The Romantic Comedians*, and *The Descendants*, as well as a discussion of her use of childbirth metaphors and the impact of her deafness upon her writing.

Nicolaisen, Peter. "Rural Poverty and the Heroics of Farming: Elizabeth Madox Roberts's *The Time of Man* and Ellen Glasgow's *Barren Ground*." In *Reading Southern Poverty Between the Wars, 1918-1939*, edited by Richard Godden and Martin Crawford. Athens: University of Georgia Press, 2006. Argues that many of the southern writers, social scientists, activists, and others who professed to be progressive actually upheld the traditional economic and social systems that maintained poverty. The essay on Glasgow analyzes *Barren Ground*.

Patterson, Martha H. "Mary Johnston, Ellen Glasgow, and the Evolutionary Logic of Progressive Reform." In *Beyond the Gibson Girl: Reimagining the American New Woman, 1895-1915*. Urbana: University of Illinois Press, 2005. At the end of the nineteenth and beginning of the twentieth century, an image emerged of the "New Woman," who was well-educated, progressive, and white. Patterson's book describes how Glasgow and other writers challenged this image by creating women characters who were African American, southern, and in other ways different from popular notions of womanhood.

Rouse, Blair. *Ellen Glasgow*. New York: Twayne, 1962. Presents facts, analyses, and interpretations of Glasgow's life; discusses the nature and purposes of her writing; and analyzes the scope of her work and her attainment as a literary artist. Rouse, a southerner, was one of the first contemporary critics to appreciate Glasgow. Includes an annotated bibliography.

Scura, Dorothy M., ed. *Ellen Glasgow: New Perspectives*. Knoxville: University of Tennessee Press, 1995. Detailed essays on Glasgow's major novels and themes, two essays on her autobiographies, and two essays on her poetry and short stories. Includes a helpful overview in the introduction, and a bibliography.

Taylor, Welford Dunaway, and George C. Longest, eds. *Regarding Ellen Glasgow: Essays for Contemporary Readers*. Richmond: Library of Virginia, 2001. This collection includes essays about some of the novels and examinations of Glasgow's work in the context of southern history, Calvinism, depictions of southern women, and feminism. Includes a chronology, a bibliography, and an index.

Wagner, Linda W. *Ellen Glasgow: Beyond Convention*. Austin: University of Texas Press, 1982. An excellent analysis of Glasgow's work, placing it in the context of her time and place, as well as in relation to later work by other American authors.

Weaks-Baxter, Mary. "Veins of Iron: Ellen Glasgow's Virginia Farmers." In *Reclaiming the American Farmer: The Reinvention of a Regional Mythology in Twentieth-Century Southern Writing*. Baton Rouge: Louisiana State University Press, 2006. Weaks-Baxter analyzes works by Glasgow and other southern authors in the years from 1900 until 1960, focusing on how their works replaced idealized descriptions of the plantation system with a new agrarian mythology that glorified the yeoman farmer.

RUMER GODDEN

Born: Eastbourne, Sussex, England; December 10, 1907
Died: Thornhill, Dumfriesshire, Scotland; November 8, 1998
Also known as: Margaret Rumer Godden

PRINCIPAL LONG FICTION

Chinese Puzzle, 1936
The Lady and the Unicorn, 1937
Black Narcissus, 1939
Gypsy, Gypsy, 1940
Breakfast with the Nikolides, 1942
A Fugue in Time, 1945 (also known as *Take Three Tenses: A Fugue in Time*)
The River, 1946
A Candle for St. Jude, 1948
A Breath of Air, 1950
Kingfishers Catch Fire, 1953
An Episode of Sparrows, 1955
The Greengage Summer, 1958
China Court: The Hours of a Country House, 1961
The Battle of the Villa Fiorita, 1963
In This House of Brede, 1969
The Peacock Spring: A Western Progress, 1975
Five for Sorrow, Ten for Joy, 1979
The Dark Horse, 1981
Thursday's Children, 1984
Coromandel Sea Change, 1990
Pippa Passes, 1994
Cromartie v. the God Shiva: Acting Through the Government of India, 1997

OTHER LITERARY FORMS

Rumer Godden published children's picture books and novels as well as adult nonfiction. She retold folktales in *The Old Woman Who Lived in a Vinegar Bottle* (1970). She drew on her interest in dogs, especially the Pekingese, in the children's book *Fu-Dog* (1989), and her interest in ballet, in the children's book *Listen to the Nightingale* (1992). Godden's children's fiction presents a serious exploration of human nature and motivations. Her first children's book, and the first of her doll stories, *The Doll's House* (1947), recounts how Charlotte and Emily Dane's doll-play rivalry results in the accidental incineration of the doll mother. *The Diddakoi* (1972) deliberately eschews a romantic portrayal of Roma (Gypsy) life to focus on the clash of cultures that forms the center of most of Godden's adult fiction. Writer Kingsley Amis, a Whitbread Prize judge, described *The Diddakoi* as "the sort of book children had to fight for to get it from adults."

The majority of Godden's nonfiction was written about India. The early autobiographical volume, *Two Under the Indian Sun* (1966), is a spare account of her childhood and was written with her sister Winsome Ruth, known as Jon Godden. Godden's personal memoirs, *A Time to Dance, No Time to Weep* (1987), recounting her life until 1945, and *A House with Four Rooms* (1989), covering her life from 1945 to 1977, include reproduced correspondence and family photographs.

ACHIEVEMENTS

Many of Rumer Godden's books sold well. Several were made into films, and many were chosen for entry in the *Reader's Digest Condensed Books* series. In 1991, *Coromandel Sea Change* received a Booker Prize nomination. Godden's children's novel, *The Diddakoi*, received the following awards: Children's Book of the Year Award, Whitbread Children's Book Award, and the Silver Pen (Dutch National Book Award).

BIOGRAPHY

Margaret Rumer Godden was born December 10, 1907, in Eastbourne, Sussex, England. She was known as Peggie until late in life. Although born in England, she grew up in India. From 1914, the family lived in the largest house in Narayanganj, East Bengal. Godden was the second of the four daughters of Arthur Leigh Godden, an agent for a Calcutta-based shipping company, and Katherine Norah Hingley Godden, descendant of a successful iron manufacturer. Godden and her youngest sister, Rose Mary (b. 1913), were born in Eastbourne, while their oldest sister, Jon (b. 1906), and their younger sister,

Nancy (b. 1910), were born in India. The girls enjoyed the lavish lifestyle of English expatriates known as Anglo-Indians. Godden's 1946 novel, *The River*, draws on her childhood memories of the time and place, from the house and gardens to the noise of the nearby jute factory.

Godden was five years old whe she and Jon were sent to England to attend school and live with their paternal relatives. As World War I began they returned to India, and they resumed their schooling after the war's end. At Moira House, Godden's English teacher, Mona Swann, encouraged her to write. Thirty years later, Godden's own two daughters were boarding students and studied with Swann.

In 1924, Godden's mother, with her four daughters, set out to tour the battlefields of France, but the mother became ill, and the group remained at Chateau Thierry on the Marne. Godden's 1958 coming-of-age novel, *The Greengage Summer* is based on the events of this summer. In 1925, Godden and Jon accompanied their mother to Narayanganj for the social season. After breaking off an engagement and working with her father in an agricultural college, Godden went back to London to train as a dance-school teacher.

Godden returned to India in 1929 and opened the Peggie Godden School of Dance, first in Darjeeling and then in Calcutta. She admitted English children, then opened classes to upper-caste Indians and eventually Eurasians, mixed-race children, and young women, one of whom became the actor Merle Oberon. Although the dancing school thrived, Godden's choice of profession and clientele alienated her from the Anglo-Indian society in which she had been raised. Her sister, Nancy, took over the dancing school when Godden married British stockbroker Laurence Sinclair Foster on March 9, 1934. Their son, David, died four days after birth. The next year their daughter, Jane, was born in London.

In 1936, Godden's first novel, *Chinese Puzzle*, was published to good reviews, but it did not sell well. The novel that followed, *The Lady and the Unicorn*, coincided with the birth the following year of Godden's second daughter, Paula, in 1938. The novel's subject matter, a Eurasian family's unhappy involvement with Anglo-Indians, further alienated Godden from Anglo-Indian society.

One month before Paula's birth, Godden finished the manuscript of *Black Narcissus*, published the following year to overwhelming success in the United States. By August, seventeen thousand copies of the book had been sold, making it the fourth best-selling book in the United States that month. The stage adaptation debuted in New York in 1942. Seven years later, the film version, starring Deborah Kerr and David Farrar, disappointed Godden because it lacked authentic settings and costumes. The book chronicles the trials of a group of Anglican nuns determined to establish a school and hospital in a former Indian general's palace, but the nuns are ultimately defeated by the exotic atmosphere.

As World War II intensified, Godden returned to Calcutta with her two daughters. Her husband was now deep in debt and part of the British regiment, and the couple's strained relationship is reflected in the unhappy marriage of the two main characters in *Breakfast with the Nikolides*. Godden and her daughters lived in Jinglam House amid the Darjeeling tea plantations. The diary she kept during this year, published as *Rungli-Rungliot (Thus Far and No Further)* in 1943, is a collection of descriptive essays and notes. For two years ending in 1944, she lived with her children in Dove House in remote Kashmir. She began an herb farm but ended the experiment when her cook tried to poison the family with a mixture of ground glass and drugs. This incident formed the center of her 1953 novel, *Kingfishers Catch Fire*, in which a servant poisons the household's food in a failed attempt to make a love potion by substituting ground glass for pearls.

Godden and her children returned to England in 1945. *The River* was published the following year. French filmmaker Jean Renoir began production of a film version of the novel three years later. Godden helped with the script as well as the two years of filming in India. She had been disappointed by *Enchantment*, the 1948 film version of *A Fugue in Time*, but she was pleased by the authenticity of *The River*. Renoir cast English and Indian amateur actors, including Nancy's son, Richard.

Also in 1948, Godden's divorce from Laurence Foster was finalized, and she began a relationship with James Haynes-Dixon, who became her husband one year later. In the 1950's, Godden and Haynes-Dixon relocated to London to be near Jane. Godden converted to Catholicism in 1957, one year after Jane converted. Godden helped establish The Company of Nine, a poetry reading group that gave public performances. By 1958, she had published five novels. Two of them, *An Episode of Sparrows* and *The Greengage Summer*, were made into films.

The 1960's was an even more prolific period for Godden; eleven of her novels were published. *The Battle of the Villa Fiorita*, a story about children who take matters into their own hands and bring their mother back from Italy, where she had fled with her lover, garnered large print advances for Godden as well as $100,000 for the film rights. In 1968, Godden and Haynes-Dixon moved into Lamb House, the former residence of Henry James. Godden coauthored two books with her older sister. The decade closed with the publication of *In This House of Brede*, the life of fictional Benedictine nuns that was researched primarily in the abbey of Stanbrook. Godden worked with scriptwriters to produce the 1975 television-movie version of the novel, and she shared the substantial profits from the film with the Stanbrook nuns.

In the 1970's, Godden published five of her twenty-six children's books. *The Diddakoi* was adapted for television as *Kizzy*. In 1993, she was made a officer of the Order of the British Empire. The following year, she returned to India with the British Broadcasting Corporation to make a documentary of her life; the film aired in 1995. Her final novel, *Cromartie v. the God Shiva*, was published in 1997. She died November 8, 1998, one month shy of her ninety-first birthday.

Analysis

The majority of Rumer Godden's work—fiction and nonfiction, adult and children's books—drew on her attachment to India as a child and young adult. From her position as an Anglo-Indian, she depicted both British and Indians empathetically and she tried to be objective. Although her thorough research allowed her to draw complex depictions of colonialism, postcolonialism, religious life, and family life, the popularity of Godden's work weakened its reception as serious literature.

Godden must be recognized for her inventive if not brilliant storytelling, as a writer whose plots become the vehicle for the psychological revelations of characters drawn from her unique life experiences and research. Godden's heroes are not quite heroes and her villains are not thoroughly dastardly. Their choices propel the twists of the plot and prove that they are very human. At the end of each story, readers are left with a sense of justice.

The Peacock Spring

The Peacock Spring is a coming-of-age story that delves deep into the psyche of the young female protagonist as well as the nature of love, even more so than in *The Greengage Summer*. Godden does not draw on a specific life experience, and her narrative is more explicit and even harsh as she describes the deceit, deception, and selfishness at the core of love. Sir Edward Gwithiam uses his daughters—Una and her sister Hal—to cover up his affair with their Eurasian "tutoress" who uses Sir Edward to escape her caste. Ravi, a young Brahman poet who is posing as a gardener to hide from the police, uses Una to feed his artistic and sexual ego and his medical-student friend Hem to take the blame for his misdeeds.

The rawness of the emotions is heightened by the realistic narration. Godden matter-of-factly describes the filth as well as the beauty of the streets and bazaars. The monkey man with his lewd monkey show becomes a metaphor for the characters' appetites. Sir Edward tries to keep Una from watching the show, but Una lives the truth of a character's insight. "We are all in leading-strings," she says, finally addressing her father, "Good night, Mr. Monkey Man," and finally seeing her lover as a vain peacock.

The differences between the British, Indian, and Eurasian worlds feeds the characters' appetites. Each desires the idealized and unattainable Other, whom their counterparts pretend to be. The tutor represses her upbringing, and the alcoholic mother for whom she steals the embassy's whisky lies about having attended the Sorbonne. Ravi cloaks his spoiled-child nature in his pose as a misunderstood artist. Only Una is who she claims to be, a naïve schoolgirl who falls in love with an ideal of a man and a country, and she pays the price in a loss of innocence and a miscarriage.

Coromandel Sea Change

Coromandel Sea Change and *Cromartie v. the God Shiva* were published six years apart, but in the afterword to the latter novel, Godden calls the two works "Siamese twins" that share characters, settings, and narration. Both consist of themes that are expected from a postcolonial fiction writer. Godden developed a type of Magical Realism in her presentation of the events of the plot, the descriptions of the characters, and the style of the narrative.

The "sea change" of the novel takes place in the characters who are vacationing during local elections at Patna Hall Hotel on the coast at Coromandel. British and Indian are each seduced by the "exoticism" of the other, and their reactions to their seductions determine their fate. Newlywed Mary Browne seeks and finds the "real" India in Auntie Sannie, the Eurasian hotelier, in her staff of lower-caste Indians, and in the well-educated, charismatic, dark-skinned political candidate Krishnan Bhanj, whom she meets one night in a secluded grove. Her blond-haired husband, Blaise St. John, is a budding diplomat who prefers British-run establishments and rebels against Aunt Sannie's practical rules for hotel guests, such as swimming with a guide to avoid treacherous ocean currents. In the end, Blaise drowns from carelessness or suicide because of what he assumes is his wife's betrayal of him with Krishnan, as well as his betrayal of her with the maid KuKu, who was entranced by his fair complexion. After Blaise's death, Mary seeks karmic atonement by going to Calcutta to work with the poor, while KuKu gives birth to a son who looks like a reincarnation of his father.

The ordinary becomes extraordinary and the extraordinary becomes everyday. The political campaign takes on the mysticism of a religious ceremony with crowds of adoring worshipers. Krishnan, made up to look like the god Krishna, is paraded through the streets on a float with Mary, who is made up to look like the goddess Radha; KuKu, too, is made up—to look like the goddess Lakshmi.

Godden's descriptions of even the most ordinary tasks or objects are as spare or as lush as the plot and its revelations require. Her evocative descriptions of hidden temples and elephant rides through the jungle do not mask the seamier side of life that has little to do with setting and a lot to do with human nature. One unscrupulous journalist, for example, takes advantage of the orphan boy Kanu as an informant as well as a sex object. Godden presents the narrative through multiple points of view, as if each piece were part of a collage in a kaleidoscope. The picture shifts and changes without evident transitions, nevertheless moving the plot forward.

Auntie Sannie stands over all as the watchful goddess who cannot prevent catastrophe, but who can pick up the pieces and mete out imperfect justice. She protects Kanu by banishing his abuser and attempts to unite Blaise's illegitimate son with his paternal grandparents.

Cromartie v. the God Shiva

Cromartie v. the God Shiva also takes place at Patna Hall and includes Auntie Sannie and her trusted staff. The hotel is a bit more down-at-the-heels, but the Britons who are regulars do not seem to mind. Michael Dean is sent by his law firm to investigate the theft and sale of an antiquity, a figure of the god Shiva, from Patna Hall. Michael's detective work mixes with his childhood memories as he interviews locals, shrewdly unravels the mystery, and falls in love with Artemis Knox, the British antiquities professor and thief.

Knox uses British and Indian people alike to accomplish the theft as part of a psychological game of revenge on her absent father. The Magical Realism is hinted at in the government initiating a court case on behalf of the god Shiva and in Godden's descriptions of the antiquity, temples, and banquets. The novel is shorter and more of a plot-driven whodunit than its predecessor. Godden's sense of justice is clear not only in Knox's suicidal high dive into the shark-infested sea but also in the sense the reader gets that the individual chooses whether or not the allure of India will be corrupting or uplifting.

Cecile Mazzucco-Than

Other major works

SHORT FICTION: *Mooltiki, and Other Stories and Poems of India*, 1957; *Swans and Turtles: Stories*, 1968 (also known as *Gone: A Thread of Stories*); *Mercy, Pity, Peace, and Love: Stories*, 1989 (with Jon Godden; also known as *Indian Dust*, 1989).

NONFICTION: *Rungli-Rungliot (Thus Far and No Further)*, 1943 (also known as *Rungli-Rungliot Means in Paharia, Thus Far and No Further* and *Thus Far and No Further*); *Bengal Journey: A Story of the Part Played by Women in the Province 1939-1945*, 1945; *Two Under the Indian Sun*, 1966 (autobiography; with Jon Godden);

Shiva's Pigeons: An Experience of India, 1972 (with Jon Godden); *The Butterfly Lions: The Story of the Pekingese in History, Legend, and Art*, 1977; *A Time to Dance, No Time to Weep*, 1987 (autobiography); *A House with Four Rooms*, 1989.

CHILDREN'S LITERATURE: *The Doll's House*, 1947; *In Noah's Ark*, 1949; *The Mousewife*, 1951; *Impunity Jane: The Story of a Pocket Doll*, 1954; *The Fairy Doll*, 1956; *The Story of Holly and Ivy*, 1958; *Candy Floss*, 1960; *Miss Happiness and Miss Flower*, 1961; *Little Plum*, 1963; *Home Is the Sailor*, 1964; *The Kitchen Madonna*, 1967; *Operation Sippacik*, 1969; *The Diddakoi*, 1972; *Mr. McFadden's Hallowe'en*, 1975; *The Rocking Horse Secret*, 1977; *A Kindle of Kittens*, 1978; *The Dragon of Og*, 1981; *The Valiant Chatti-Maker*, 1983; *Fu-Dog*, 1989; *Great Grandfather's House*, 1992; *Listen to the Nightingale*, 1992; *Premlata and the Festival of Lights*, 1996.

EDITED TEXTS: *Round the Day, Round the Year, the World Around: Poetry Programmes for Classroom or Library*, 1966 (with Margaret Bell); *A Letter to the World: Poems for Young People*, 1968 (by Emily Dickinson); *Mrs. Manders' Cookbook*, 1968 (by Olga Manders).

BIBLIOGRAPHY

Chisholm, Anne. *Rumer Godden: A Storyteller's Life*. New York: Greenwillow Books, 1998. The official biography of Godden. Chisholm was given access to Godden's papers, and she accompanied Godden to India in 1995. Includes interviews with Godden and key people in her life.

Dukes, Thomas. "Evoking the Significance: The Autobiographies of Rumer Godden." *Women's Studies* 20, no. 1 (1991): 15-36. Dukes describes the strong connection between Godden's fiction and her biography. He studies her use of narrative voice and the genre of the female bildungsroman to illustrate Godden's perception of life itself as story.

Lassner, Phyllis. *Colonial Strangers: Women Writing the End of the British Empire*. New Brunswick, N.J.: Rutgers University Press, 2004. Lassner, who argues that "no place has been found" for Godden "in the postcolonial canon," makes a place beside Muriel Spark, Elspeth Huxley, and others, who wrote from and about outposts of the British Empire, especially during World War II. Focuses on novels such as *Black Narcissus* and *Breakfast with the Nikolides* to show Godden's Anglo-India as an "oppressively walled garden" for her female protagonists.

Miller, Edmund. "Submission and Freedom: *Five for Sorrow, Ten for Joy*." *Renascence: Essays on Values in Literature* 54, no. 4 (Summer, 2002): 258-268. Miller points out the rarity of studies of Godden's works. He chooses one of her lesser known novels, one about religious life, to illustrate her narrative skill and her insight into the human psyche.

Rosenthal, Lynne M. *Rumer Godden Revisited*. Boston: Twayne, 1996. Rosenthal examines the figure of the child in Godden's fiction as a lightning rod for society's struggles, hopes, and fears. Analyses focus on *An Episode of Sparrows*, *The Greengage Summer*, *Pippa Passes*, *The Diddakoi*, *The Doll's House*, and *Thursday's Children*.

GAIL GODWIN

Born: Birmingham, Alabama; June 18, 1937
Also known as: Gail Kathleen Godwin

Principal long fiction

The Perfectionists, 1970
Glass People, 1972
The Odd Woman, 1974
Violet Clay, 1978
A Mother and Two Daughters, 1982
The Finishing School, 1985
A Southern Family, 1987
Father Melancholy's Daughter, 1991
The Good Husband, 1994
Evensong, 1999
Queen of the Underworld, 2006

Other literary forms

In addition to her novels, Gail Godwin has published two collections of short fiction: *Dream Children* (1976) and *Mr. Bedford and the Muses* (1983). Godwin is also a frequent reviewer of contemporary fiction for *The New York Times Book Review* and other publications. In 1985, she served as editor for *The Best American Short Stories*. Godwin has also achieved success as a librettist for composer Robert Starer's musical works, including *Remembering Felix*, recorded in 1987. In 2006, she published the first installment of a planned two-volume memoir, *The Making of a Writer: Journals, 1961-1963*.

Achievements

Gail Godwin has done much to broaden the scope of the contemporary woman's novel. While the struggles of women who seek both independent lives and productive connections to others are central to her work, she strives in her novels and short fiction to place those efforts within a larger context, especially within the framework of modern theories of art and psychology. In 1971-1972, Godwin was a fellow of the Center for Advanced Studies, University of Illinois at Urbana-Champaign. Her other awards include a grant from the National Endowment for the Arts in 1974, a Guggenheim Fellowship in 1975, and an Award in Literature from the American Institute and Academy of Arts and Letters in 1981. Her story "Amanuensis" was included in the *Prize Stories, 1980: O. Henry Awards* collection.

Biography

Gail Kathleen Godwin was born on June 18, 1937, and was reared by her mother and her widowed grandmother in Asheville, North Carolina. She attended Peace Junior College in Raleigh, North Carolina, and in 1959 graduated with a B.A. in journalism from the University of North Carolina at Chapel Hill (the alma mater of Asheville's other great native writer, Thomas Wolfe). After working as a reporter for the *Miami Herald*, she lived in London and worked with the United States Travel Service at the American embassy. After returning to the United States, she took an M.A. (1968) and a Ph.D. (1971) in English at the University of Iowa, where she later served on the faculty of the Writers' Workshop. She has taught English and creative writing at Vassar College and at Columbia University.

Godwin has been married twice, to *Miami Herald* photographer Douglas Kennedy and to British psychotherapist Ian Marshall. Her one-year marriage to Marshall is the basis for her first novel, *The Perfectionists*, as her early years with her mother and grandmother are the basis for parts of *Glass People* and *The Odd Woman*. Godwin has also used her relationships with her father and her stepfather in her fiction, especially in *Violet Clay* and *The Odd Woman*, respectively. Events in her novella *Evenings at Five*, published in 2003, closely resemble those in Godwin's own life surrounding the death of her longtime companion Robert Starer in 2001. Since 1976, she has resided in Woodstock, New York.

Analysis

Gail Godwin's novels (and her short fiction as well) all deal with several easily identifiable themes. First, and most often cited perhaps, is the theme of the modern woman, her dilemma in defining self and others in an era when the old frameworks and definitions have broken down, at least for the sort of women about whom Godwin writes. The conflict most often arises between the woman's work, usually an artistic pursuit of some kind, and her desire for security, love, and connection, most often through a relationship with a man. The theme of the woman struggling for identity thus divides into two separate thematic strands: her identity as artist and her identity as lover.

Another recurring theme in Godwin's work is, in many ways, the reverse of this quest for self-identity. Often, her characters long to penetrate the identities of the people around them; that is, they consciously seek to violate the human heart's sanctity, to use Nathaniel Hawthorne's description of such activity. Again, however, Godwin's perspective is definitively modern. These characters are all aware of the impossibility of coming to such knowledge in the almost mystical way that Hawthorne describes in the section of *The Scarlet Letter* (1850) titled "The Custom House," and they are also conscious of the questionable morality of such invasions. Therefore, they seek lesser but more concrete knowledge and understanding by prying, by scrutinizing the objects the others possess or the words they write or say, words that the seekers examine with total (or what they assume to be total) awareness of the ironies and ambiguities involved in both the saying and their interpretation.

These divergent pursuits are most easily forged into a manageable aesthetic form through an artist figure; the role of the artist in relation to self, other, and art itself is, finally, Godwin's most important theme. Her main characters tend to be so self-consciously "artists," even when they are lawyers or psychiatrists or unemployed, that they make life itself into an art, which is to say that they view their own lives as artists view the canvases or the sheets of paper before them.

What makes Godwin an interesting and important figure in the world of contemporary fiction is the narrative technique by which she manages to develop and retell this essentially unchanging story. One can trace the noticeable and impressive growth in Godwin herself as an artist by examining the structural and technical variations in her telling of her stories. In the earlier novels, the distance between narrator and protagonist is less clearly defined. The overblown and romanticized version of the character sometimes seems to be an accurate representation of the narrator's perspective as well. Beginning with *The Odd Woman*, however, and culminating in *A Southern Family*, Godwin makes that distance itself a matter of chief concern. Her narrators seem acutely aware of the responsibility involved in entering into the lives and souls of "others." The characters seem to move from being primarily concerned with personal happiness and security to doing true and constructive work that recognizes the dignity in whatever lives the artist consumes for the sake of the work and that acknowledges the limitations and fallibilities of the artist. These later characters, by having real and constructive work to do, manage to be less obsessed with their personal lives as objects of art; they also manage to find satisfaction in the art and the work itself, whether their personal lives are or are not so satisfying at any given moment.

Gail Godwin. (© Jerry Bauer)

The Perfectionists *and* Glass People

The protagonists of *The Perfectionists* and *Glass People*, Dane Empson and Francesca Bolt, are both self-absorbed and frustrated in their relationships with their spouses. They are also the last of Godwin's protagonists to be married and unemployed. Not only are they unemployed, but also neither of them shows any desire for doing constructive, creative work. When these novels are read in the context of Godwin's later work, the conclusion that their shared lack of ambition and motivation is crucial to their discontent is inevitable.

Dane Empson has been married to John Empson, a psychologist, for ten months when they go on vacation with John's illegitimate son, Robin, and one of John's female patients, Penelope MacMahon. Although Dane worked as a journalist prior to her marriage—in fact, she met John when she covered a meeting at which he was the speaker—she no longer pursues her career. Her primary concerns are her relationship with John, in which she has begun to lose interest, and her efforts to become a mother to his son. Thus, what Godwin does with this character, although it is done in a most unconventional way, is to have her confront the traditional roles and conflicts of the wife and mother. Dane fails in these roles, however, and she is most aware of that failure. She feels nothing, absolutely nothing, of the satisfaction and joy that the mythic versions of those roles provide.

The overt source of conflict in the story is Robin's total refusal to acknowledge Dane. He will not speak in her presence; he will not respond to her displays of affection; he will not compromise in any way in the small, daily struggles between parent and child. He does, however, make demands on Dane, in both practical and emotional matters. She is expected to feed, clothe, and entertain him. She is also expected to nurture and soothe him while his father is thinking and writing in his journal. Because Godwin sets up the child as a double for the father, a point that John frequently reinforces by comparing himself to the child, the narrator suggests that Dane's real problem is John's refusal to acknowledge her.

Dane is guilty of expecting her husband to provide her with an identity to be acknowledged. She surreptitiously searches through his journal entries for clues as to what he sees when he looks at her, what he thinks when he thinks of her. When she does rebel, venturing outside the prescribed role that she has accepted with apparent willingness, she takes up with another frustrated wife, Polly Heykoop, who devotes herself to spying on her husband with his lovers, photographing their sexual encounters and compiling a scrapbook of the photos to present to him in their old age.

Dane's act in defiance of this utter decadence of domestic life is to beat the child, almost to kill him, in order to reassert her personal identity. Symbolically, she is also beating John, who, in her imagination, responds to her confession by ruining it. He points out that the action she takes in order to feel a powerful and private emotion is of necessity shared with the child and, by extension, with him. Because she cannot deny the truth of that observation and because she has available to her no other means of self-expression, she remains as self-absorbed and frustrated as she is at the novel's beginning.

Dane's counterpart in *Glass People*, Francesca Bolt, is even less involved in life. Wife to a successful attorney and politician who requires absolutely nothing of her except that she be beautiful for him, Francesca has retreated from all human activity. She languishes in her bedroom, living for the alternate days when she tweezes the hairs from her legs one by one. At the instigation of Cameron, her husband, she undertakes a quest to discover a life for herself, a quest more dramatic and independent than that of Dane.

After a disappointing visit to her newly remarried and pregnant mother fails to allow Francesca to retreat into a former identity, she embarks on a series of adventures, each eventually as unsuccessful as her visit home. She has an affair, a one-weekend liaison with a man she meets in the airport, but she romanticizes the encounter into much more than it is. When he does not reappear, she bravely tries to follow the plan the two of them laid to free her from Cameron's worshipful but manipulative grasp. She rents a room in a cheap New York hotel and briefly takes a job as amanuensis to a bizarre woman named M. She even finds herself buoyed by the successful completion of the tasks she performs for her employer, the basic cleaning, shopping, and cooking chores she could not bring herself to do at home in California. After less than a week of being actively engaged in the world with nothing more than her own identity to define her, Francesca collapses in a complete and devastating illness. She fears that all the fluids within her will leave her body and she will disappear.

Cameron appears, however, a deus ex machina in the best romantic tradition—the heroic man come to save the fallen beauty. The problem, as Francesca knows, is that he will save her for his own purposes, and her identity will be defined by those purposes. Still, despite this awareness, she cannot resist the comfort and ease of his salvation. That she is pregnant with the child of her lover seems only to increase Cameron's worshipful desire to hold and control her. As she moves around their beautiful apartment, decorated and maintained by Cameron, and eats plentifully of the food he prepares for her, secure in the knowledge that her husband will never let her get fat, Francesca thinks of the power she holds and of the possibilities for manipulating her husband with that power. She is the last of Godwin's protagonists to accept this traditional sort of power struggle as the best solution for her life.

Narratively, the problem with these novels is a matter of point of view. Because both are dominated by the perspectives of the protagonists, who have so constrained their lives as to have no outside viewpoints against which to test their own (except those of their spouses, whom they can only undermine as valid reference points), Godwin finds herself telling her stories without a reliable observer. Even in *Glass People*, where brief passages are given over to Cameron's point of view, the reader already so distrusts Cameron, from having seen him through his wife's eyes, that the narrator cannot give his view much credence.

In each of these novels, the narrative voice, although it is a third-person voice, does not maintain enough distance between itself and the protagonist to convince the reader that the values of that character are not, in fact, the values being espoused by the novel. At the same time, however, the violent impotence of Dane Empson and the luxurious laziness of Francesca Bolt both carry a faintly distasteful flavor for most readers.

THE ODD WOMAN

The perspective of Jane Clifford, the protagonist of *The Odd Woman*, marks a significant step forward for Godwin as a storyteller. First, her perspective is a much broader one than that of either of her predecessors. Jane works as a teacher of literature, and her work as a graduate student writing her dissertation on George Eliot, in addition to her current work—grading the exams for her just-finished course in visionary literature and preparing to teach a course on women in literature—is an integral part of the narrative. Furthermore, Jane Clifford has a family, a background, that is richly developed and explored across several generations. Unlike Francesca's fruitless journey back home, Jane's similar trip, to her grandmother's funeral, produces extended encounters with her memories of the grandmother and of her mother, stepfather, sister, and brothers. In *Glass People*, Kate, mother of Francesca, spends most of her daughter's visit behind the closed door of her bedroom. Jane, in contrast, is involved in talks, reminiscences, and arguments that test her perspective constantly.

Jane also has friends, male and female, to whom she talks, in whom she confides. There is the male colleague with whom she trades confidences about sex and bathroom regularity; there is her old college friend Gerda, the editor of a feminist newspaper in Chicago; and there is Sonia Marx, her colleague at the university where she teaches and the woman who serves as the role model for what Jane wants to be—someone with a career, husband, and family, managing it all with every sign of ease and brilliance. Again, although Jane's point of view is the point of view of the novel, her constant encounters with these others broadens and modifies her view throughout.

Jane also has a lover, a married man, Gabriel Weeks, an art historian. In him, Jane finds an alternative to the cynical and jaded perspective she finds pervasive in the academic world. She gradually comes to realize, however, that the Gabriel she has found is a creature of her own making. She has imagined him and orchestrated their relationship in such a way as to provide herself with a view of the world that must come from within, must be made from oneself, if it is to have true value.

Here, Godwin begins to develop the ironic awareness of self as artist that is crucial to the success of her subject matter. Jane Clifford is painfully aware of her life as an object of art, with herself as the artist. She sees the scenes of her life as just that, scenes, and she manipulates both her own part and the parts of others. The problem is that such a life will never reach the state of natural grace and spontaneity that is Jane's primary goal.

Jane is thus more like Dane and Francesca than she would like to be. She does not find a way to overcome her frustrations with her need to rewrite the role she has been given or has voluntarily taken on. Unlike those predecessors, however, she does not capitulate. She takes actions that give her a chance for progress. She ends her affair; she takes an extension on her temporary appointment at the university, meaning that she will have productive work for another year; she confronts the demons of her past as represented by the family, Greta, and the actor who has been for half a century the archvillain of the family history.

Through these actions and confrontations, she learns that all truths may be artificial and self-imposed, but she also comes to believe in some purer, more absolute version of her own life that will be possible for her, if she acts to pursue it. Thus, despite Jane's own limitations, because Godwin equips her with such an acute sense of irony about herself as well as others, Jane is the first step toward a successful Godwin protagonist.

Violet Clay

The promise of a truly successful Godwin woman made with Jane is realized in the protagonist of *Violet Clay*, Godwin's first novel to employ the first-person point of view. Although it might seem that first-person narration would lead to even greater self-absorption, this does not happen. Using the same principles that made *The Odd Woman* such a step forward, Godwin generated a plot in *Violet Clay* with a death. Jane keeps her job and her lover through most of her story, however, whereas, in addition to losing her uncle—her only living relative—Violet Clay loses what Jane is able to keep. Violet is forced by these events of plot to confront the essentials of her character, to test the view of herself that she has created. While she probes into her uncle's past to make sense of his suicide, she learns much about herself as well and about how the artist manufactures both life and art, each feeding off the other. When she finally paints the painting that will set her on the road she has long aspired to travel, Violet uses some of the same material that her uncle failed to transform into the novel that he had struggled for decades to write.

Violet's success comes because she learns the limits of both life and art, partly through her uncle's example, his legacy to her, and partly through her own increasing ability to forget about "poor little me" and to enter into and learn from the struggles of those around her with compassion and respect. She learns that the artist must not and finally cannot both live and work successfully if she violates the integrity of the other, of the lives out of which her art and her own life are to be constructed.

A Mother and Two Daughters

If *Violet Clay* states an aesthetic credo, *A Mother and Two Daughters* puts that credo into action. In this novel, for the first time, Godwin is able to render a world of multiple viewpoints throughout the story; not coincidentally, it is her longest book to date as well as her most accomplished.

Nell Strickland and her two daughters, Lydia and Cate, are very different women. They, too, find themselves propelled into a plot generated by a death, in this case that of their husband and father. Each also finds herself continuing in the plot of her own life. Nell finds that she relishes the independence and privacy of her widowhood, and she also finds herself in love again before the novel concludes. Lydia, who is recently separated and eventually divorced from her husband and is mother to two teenage sons, returns to school, acquires a lover, and develops a career. Cate struggles with her own love life and the roller coaster of her career as a teacher of drama.

These women are the least self-conscious of all of Godwin's heroines, and their stories are the most straightforward and least manipulated among her works. Even so, the reader is always aware that each of the three women is shaping, in an increasingly conscious way, her life, constructing it so that it gives her the most satisfaction possible within the limitations of a "realistic" environment.

Each of these three women also engages in a sustained relationship with a man during the course of the story. For Nell, it is the traditional relationship of marriage, but in her second marriage she is a different woman from the one she was in her first because of the time she spends alone and the things she learns about herself during that time. She is able to bring about a merging of the independent self and the attached self. Lydia and Cate also reach such an integration of these strands of their lives, but for them, traditional marriage is not the form that integration takes. Lydia and her lover, Stanley, live in a hard-won but precarious balance, together but unmarried, separate but irrevocably joined. He thinks at the novel's end, "You can still be independent and mine, at the same time. You are these two things now."

Cate, always more independent and free-spirited than her sister or her mother, has an even more unusual arrangement. She has designed a job to suit her, packaging classes and traveling to the places people want to have them taught, a sort of academic entrepreneur. She has also reached a stability in her relationship with Roger Jernigan after years of tension about how their feelings for each other could be formed into a pattern acceptable to them both. They are good visitors to each other.

The possibilities for marriage are not closed off for either sister, but the necessity of marriage does not exert its terrifying influence over them either. As Godwin goes into and out of the consciousnesses of these women and sometimes briefly into the points of view of the people who make up their worlds, she approaches a compassionate and respectful omniscience that would be unthinkable for the narrators of her earlier works.

The Finishing School

In *The Finishing School*, the narrator is again a first-person voice, this time Justin Stokes, a forty-year-old actress remembering the summer she turned fourteen. Justin's preoccupations during that summer are typical of all of Godwin's characters' preoccupations. She has experienced loss: Her father and her beloved grandparents have died, and she, her mother, and her younger brother, Jem, have had to leave their Virginia home and move north to a newly created subdivision in Clove, New York. Justin develops a special relationship with an older woman, Ursula DeVane, who instructs her in the art of making one's life an artistic creation, lessons that feed into Justin's predisposition for the dramatic and her aspirations to the stage. Most important, however, Justin shares with the characters from Jane Clifford onward in Godwin's work a deep desire to come to terms with her own use of others' lives to construct her own, to make it what she needs it to be. In addition, Justin writes to thank Ursula for her contribution to the process of Justin's becoming the adult woman she wanted to be. Despite the fact that their relationship ended badly, Justin cannot overlook the crucial role that Ursula played in helping her through the most difficult summer of her childhood.

Godwin dedicates this sixth novel to "the Ursulas of this world, whoever they were—or weren't"; that dedication seems echoed by Justin's sentiments after she remembers and makes a story from her summer with Ursula. Justin says,

> I was able to be charmed and possessed by that woman. Such possessions are rare now. I mean by another person. The only thing I can rely on to possess me continually with that degree of ardor is my work. Most of the time I consider this a victory. Sometimes, however, it makes me a little sad. So here I am, in the middle of my own life. . . . And it has taken me this long to understand that I lose nothing by acknowledging her influence on me. . . . I know something of life's betrayals and stupidities myself. . . . I even know the necessity for making constant adjustments to your life story, so you can go on living in it. . . . But I also know something else that I didn't know then. As long as you can go on creating new roles for yourself, you are not vanquished.

A Southern Family

In many ways Godwin's seventh novel, *A Southern Family*, is the aesthetic fruit of a challenge similar to the one her fictional alter ego raises at the end of *The Finishing School*. In *A Southern Family* Godwin creates for herself a new role as author/narrator, using for the first time in her novels the narrative strategy of multiple limited perspectives. She also appears to be moving toward a new role for the "typical" Godwin woman within her fictional world. The Godwin woman in *A Southern Family* is Clare Campion, the author's first novel protagonist to share her profession. In fact, Clare is a writer whose career, as rendered in this fiction, closely parallels Godwin's own. The "new" role Godwin carves out for Clare is that of secondary, rather than primary, character; her challenge is thus to accept this new (and inevitably "lesser") status without losing the power to make art (stories) from her experience.

The plot of *A Southern Family* is generated by the death of Clare Campion's half brother Theo Quick in an incident that the police rule a murder-suicide. The story is presented from the perspectives of Clare, her best friend Julia Richardson, Clare's mother and her stepfather, her surviving half brother, Theo's ex-wife, and Sister Patrick, a beloved nun who has taught Clare and her brothers. (That Godwin's half brother Tommy Cole died in circumstances similar to those described in the novel further suggests the strongly autobiographical nature of *A Southern Family*.)

Perhaps the most significant achievement of the novel is Godwin's broadening of her narrative spectrum to include male characters, characters from a variety of social classes, and characters with varying degrees of connection to the central action. There is no pretense of the omniscience that marks *A Mother and Two Daughters* here; the narrative in each section of the book is strictly limited to one or sometimes two perspectives.

A Southern Family opens up new narrative directions and a new approach to her "typical" protagonist for Godwin, but the novel also provides a clear culmination of other strands that are woven throughout the body of her fiction. The title makes clear that this is a family story, a southern story—themes that have always been among the author's central concerns. The greater emphasis here on the family as a group, a unit, rather than on an individual's struggles reinforces the narrative decision Godwin makes.

A Southern Family also continues Godwin's exploration of people, particularly women, who tend to see their lives as performances, themselves as actors in a drama partly of their own making, partly a by-product of their environment and conditioning. Theo's action causes everyone in his family to reexamine his or her role in the Quick family drama, causes each individual whose consciousness the novel explores to evaluate the role he or she plays in the unfolding events before and after the momentary act that calls the foundations of family life into question. In addition to generating the story this novel tells, this profound examination of self-as-actor that takes place in *A Southern Family*, read with full knowledge of the work that precedes it, is, in a sense, a reexamination of the author's body of work as well.

Father Melancholy's Daughter

Father Melancholy's Daughter is a first-person narrative following Margaret Gower's search for self. The daughter of an Episcopal clergyman given to bouts of depression, Margaret finds herself becoming his primary caregiver at age six when her mother, Ruth, leaves with Madelyn Farley, an artist and teacher from her college days, and is killed in a car accident a short time later. The narrative switches from present to past as twenty-two-year-old Margaret seeks to understand her mother's leaving, her father's flaws, and her own spirituality and identity.

While the narrative centers on Margaret and her close relationship with her father, it also paints a portrait of small-town Romulus, Virginia, where the congregation of Margaret's father's church speculates on the reasons for Ruth's leaving. Margaret learns to play the role of her father's accomplice in dealing with the expectations of these secondary characters. Putting her father's needs before her own becomes second nature for Margaret; by the time she goes to college to major in English, she has become almost obsessed with her father's well-being. His sudden death from a stroke, near the novel's end, leaves her free to find her own direction. Surprisingly, Margaret chooses to travel to England with Madelyn Farley, the woman whom she has practically hated all her life, to see the spot where her mother died. As the narrative ends, Margaret is applying to colleges to seek a master of divinity degree, having finally come to terms with her needs as a woman and a full human being.

Father Melancholy's Daughter portrays Margaret Gower as a modern woman who can combine the nurturing of the traditional female life with the satisfaction of a traditional male career. She, like the typical Godwin heroine, is a smart, literate woman who takes responsibility for her own life. The novel is very much a novel of ideas, not just of character. Beneath its plot lie questions about despair, self-determination, and the honorable life, but the most important issue of the novel may be the importance of understanding the influence of parents. Margaret works consciously to understand the people her parents were, and then she can go forward to discover who she is and what her place in the human drama will be.

The Good Husband

The Good Husband returns to a multiple-perspective narrative structure, moving among the four major characters (two married couples) for its limited omniscient points of view. The central character of the four is Magda Danvers, an academic made famous by her one book on the visionary poets, *The Book of Hell*. Facing death from cancer, she imagines herself taking her "Final Examination" as her devoted younger husband, Francis Lake, attends to her every need. Less analytical than Magda,

Francis, who left seminary to marry her, is unable to engage in the introspection that Magda encourages until her death frees him of her towering intellect.

Balancing this unlikely couple as the novel's protagonists are Alice Henry, an editor who as a teenager lost her entire family in a car accident, and her husband Hugo Henry, a brooding southern novelist who must face not only his waning literary inspiration and his son's homosexuality but also the fact that his marriage to the much younger Alice is crumbling after their child dies at birth. These characters' lives become intertwined when Alice begins to visit the dying Magda, finding herself drawn to Magda's keen understanding and to the "good husband" Francis, who thrives on nurturing the love of his life. While *The Good Husband* continues Godwin's exploration of the difficulty the modern woman has in defining her self and her art, it broadens her scope by focusing equally on the male characters' relation to self, art, and other people. All the characters face conflict in balancing the public life with the private, and all show the human need for security and love as well as for self-understanding.

EVENSONG

In *Evensong*, a sequel to *Father Melancholy's Daughter*, Godwin continues to explore the questions of how people cope with tragedy and what lessons they learn from it. Margaret is now thirty-three years old and married to her father's former friend, Adrian Bonner. She is the newly appointed pastor at All Saints, considered the "classy" Episcopalian church in the resort town of High Balsam, nestled in the Great Smoky Mountains. The town is experiencing difficult economic times, and underlying the current worry is an old resentment toward the town's wealthy summer residents as the eve of the Third Millennium approaches with harbingers of more disasters. Margaret continues to earn the respect of the parishioners, having overcome their initial skepticism of a woman pastor. While her older husband struggles in his role as headmaster at a local boys' school, he deals with bouts of depression manifested as assertions of unworthiness.

Into this world of simmering tensions, those in the present and others from the past, come three people who exacerbate the tenuous balance and test Margaret's ability to cope as a pastor and wife. The first is a local woman, Grace Munger, a fiery evangelical fundamentalist with a grim past. She proposes a millennium birthday march for Jesus to heal the conflict between the locals and the summer people. Margaret declines, but Grace aggressively pursues her. Their confrontations provide some of the most riveting scenes woven into this theologically themed drama. The second character to arrive and stir up unrest in High Balsam is Tony, an octogenarian monk with dyed hair, a tattoo, and a prison record. He presents himself as a "monk on the move" and carries a dark secret. The third personality is Adrian's favorite student, Chase Zorn, a self-destructive orphan who joins the rectory household. Margaret and Adrian are forced to acknowledge and heal old wounds before their power destroys them and those they seek to help.

Godwin's heroines are clearly drawn, yet underneath their facades of calm determination they seek answers about themselves and their personal places in their world. This kind of search persists in *Evensong* and extends into an exploration of the spiritual milieu. Godwin first explored this theme in *A Southern Family* and continued in *Father Melancholy's Daughter*. In *Evensong*, Margaret struggles with the spiritual and domestic commitments she has chosen. Her weapons are a mixture of persistence and mysticism. The richly drawn details in the daily life of a minister, the graceful tone of the writing, and the insights into the characters constitute a new dimension in Godwin's depictions of strong women protagonists.

QUEEN OF THE UNDERWORLD

Queen of the Underworld is set in Miami, Florida, during a vibrant time for that city. It is 1959, and Cuban refugees, moneyed and educated, throng into the city to escape Fidel Castro's regime. Miami is on the brink of becoming the principal home and a gateway for this new group of immigrants. Into this maelstrom of cultural, ethnic, and linguistic conflicts comes the novel's smart and ambitious protagonist, Emma Gant.

The novel opens with Emma leaving her home in North Carolina after her graduation from the journalism program at the University of North Carolina at Chapel Hill. Her decision to accept a reporter's job on the *Miami Star* is based as much in her need to escape her ill-tempered stepfather as it is in her desire to join her married lover, Paul Nightingale, the owner of a Miami supper club. Emma settles into a room at the Julia Tuttle Hotel (the fictional hotel is named after Miami's real-life founder) and starts work at the paper. She nurtures her ambition to succeed as a journalist and avoid being thrown in with other women writers who produce "fluff" for the paper's society section or obituaries. She dreams of being a famous reporter—that is, until she wins a Pulitzer Prize for fiction.

Godwin's Emma approaches life with the same verve and single-mindedness as Jane Austen's heroine of the same name. Godwin's heroine, however, has the distinctly American flaw of too much self-absorption and not enough awareness of the characters she meets at the hotel or at the paper. Godwin weaves into this story a voluptuous and diverse cast of characters who engage the reader's attention. These individuals deal with their displacement in a foreign country by using the creative instincts of survivors. Among them are a diminutive German who creates and sells personalized perfume scents for high-profile buyers, a Cuban dentist on a secret mission of moving arms marked as "dental equipment," a Jewish mafioso, a young woman reporter with a "gleaming effect" whom Emma views as a direct threat to her job advancement, and Ginevra Brown, known as the Queen of the Underworld, a serial practitioner of suicide and former Miami madam once betrothed to a mobster. Slowly, Emma awakens to all the personalities and possible stories around her, but she misses the chance to tell the heroic story of the distinguished academic who fled Cuba with his memoir stitched into his wife's wedding dress. At last, by the end of the novel, Emma realizes that she must seek outside herself to understand what lies within.

Queen of the Underworld continues Godwin's examination of the modern woman's challenge to define herself and her art within a culture. In this work of fiction it is 1959, a little over a decade since the conclusion of World War II and the emergence of the Cold War—a time of conflicted feelings for women seeking to find answers to the questions of who they are and how they can be true to themselves in pursuing their art or their careers. Marriage's weighted importance to women during this time plays a peripheral part in this story. The fact that Emma is having an affair with a married man makes the reader aware of the issue.

Gail Godwin the author has grown in much the same direction as her characters and narrators. The movement has been in the life-affirming direction of compromise, recognition of others, acceptance of responsibility for the self, and productive creativity. The life that Godwin affirms is the well-made life, the one shaped out of the complexities and ambiguities of human experience. Godwin's novels speak clearly of the challenges involved in being a sensitive and thoughtful woman in today's world. They speak just as eloquently of what such a woman can make from those challenges.

Jane Hill; Rebecca G. Smith
Updated by Modrea Mitchell-Reichert

Other major works

SHORT FICTION: *Dream Children*, 1976; *Mr. Bedford and the Muses*, 1983; *Evenings at Five*, 2003.

PLAYS: *The Last Lover*, pr. 1975 (libretto; music by Robert Starer); *Journals of a Songmaker*, pr. 1976 (libretto; music by Starer); *Apollonia*, pr. 1979 (libretto; music by Starer); *Anna Margarita's Will*, pr. 1980 (libretto; music by Starer); *Remembering Felix*, pb. 1987 (libretto; music by Starer).

NONFICTION: *Heart: A Personal Journey Through Its Myths and Meanings*, 2001; *The Making of a Writer: Journals, 1961-1963*, 2006.

EDITED TEXT: *The Best American Short Stories 1985*, 1985.

Bibliography

Baker, John F. "Gail Godwin: A Leap of Faith in a New Novel." *Publishers Weekly*, February 15, 1999. Profile touches on how Godwin's writing has changed over the years, noting that her emphasis on conventional young women's searching to come to terms with themselves and their place in society has morphed into an exploration of the more spiritual side of those characters.

Cheney, Anne. "Gail Godwin and Her Novels." In *Southern Women Writers: The New Generation*, edited by Tonette Bond Inge. Tuscaloosa: University of Alabama Press, 1990. Presents a comprehensive overview of Godwin's career through *A Southern Family*. Emphasizes the autobiographical elements of the works, the contemporary love-hate relationship with the traditional South, and the evolving maturity of the author's vision.

Emerick, Ron. "Theo and the Road to Sainthood in Gail Godwin's *A Southern Family*." *Southern Literary Journal* 33, no. 2 (Spring, 2001): 134-145. In-depth examination of the spiritual elements in the novel shows the new direction Godwin takes with her characters in their search for answers through religion and spirituality to questions of who they want to be, their place as they want to define it, and possibly the meaning to their lives.

Godwin, Gail. "A Novelist and Her Journals." Interview by Elfrieda Abbe. *The Writer* 119, no. 5 (May, 2006): 18-23. Godwin discusses her use of journals since she was thirteen years old, describing how she culls through the pages to uncover the raw material of life experiences that leads her to shape her memorable characters and interesting stories.

Hill, Jane. *Gail Godwin*. New York: Twayne, 1992. Approaches Godwin's work through plot and character, with a focus on the novels. Acknowledges the regional and gender-related aspects of Godwin's work as a southern woman writer, but points out that Godwin's long fiction also connects with the larger tradition of the novel in the United States and Europe. One of the best studies of Godwin available for the general reader.

Shands, Kerstin W. "Four-Telling, Foretold: Storytelling in Gail Godwin's *The Good Husband*." *Southern Quarterly* 35 (Winter, 1997): 77-86. Explores the controlling metaphor of matrimony in the novel by examining alliances among and within the characters. Discusses the multiple fourfold patterns in the book as well as its complex blending of oppositions, such as death and birth, stasis and development, endings and beginnings.

Westerlund, Kerstin. *Escaping the Castle of Patriarchy: Patterns of Development in the Novels of Gail Godwin*. Stockholm: Almqvist & Wiksell International, 1990. Discusses Godwin's novels up to *A Southern Family* in terms of female development, which is linked to Godwin's treatment of male-female relationships. Includes a chapter on Godwin and American feminism.

Wimsatt, Mary Ann. "Gail Godwin, the South, and the Canons." *Southern Literary Journal* 27 (Spring, 1995): 86-95. Asserts that Godwin is excluded from the southern literary canon because of her best-seller status and her feminism, and argues for her inclusion in that canon based on her strong portrayals of characters' struggles with difficulties caused by family, race, and class in a changing South.

Xie, Lihong. *The Evolving Self in the Novels of Gail Godwin*. Baton Rouge: Louisiana State University Press, 1995. Argues that instead of accepting the postmodern deconstruction of the self, Godwin has constructed a concept of the self as evolving, finding itself not in essence but in process.

Zipp, Yvonne. "How Gail Godwin Became a Writer." *Christian Science Monitor*, February 7, 2006. Review of *Queen of the Underworld* weaves in commentary on Godwin's memoir *The Making of a Writer*, showing that the nonfiction work is the source of the novel's plot and its memorable characters. Illustrates how Godwin's life feeds her writing craft.

JOHANN WOLFGANG VON GOETHE

Born: Frankfurt am Main (now in Germany); August 28, 1749
Died: Weimar, Saxe-Weimar-Eisenbach (now in Germany); March 22, 1832

Principal long fiction

Die Leiden des jungen Werthers, 1774 (*The Sorrows of Young Werther*, 1779)
Wilhelm Meisters Lehrjahre, 1795-1796 (4 volumes; *Wilhelm Meister's Apprenticeship*, 1824)
Die Wahlverwandtschaften, 1809 (*Elective Affinities*, 1849)
Wilhelm Meisters Wanderjahre: Oder, Die Entsagenden, 1821 (revised 1829; 2 volumes; *Wilhelm Meister's Travels*, 1827)

Other literary forms

Johann Wolfgang von Goethe (GUR-tuh) was a master in every major literary genre. He published his first book of poetry, *Neue Lieder* (*New Poems*, 1853), in 1770. Most of his well-known poems appeared individually in journals and were later collected in the fourteen-volume *Works* (1848-1890). Collections of Goethe's poetry that were published separately include *Epigramme: Venedig 1790* (1796; *Venetian Epigrams*, 1853), *Römische Elegien* (1793; *Roman Elegies*, 1876), *Xenien* (1796, with Friedrich Schiller; *Epigrams*, 1853), *Balladen* (1798, with Schiller; *Ballads*, 1853), *Sonette* (1819; *Sonnets*, 1853), and *Westöstlicher Divan* (1819; *West-Eastern Divan*, 1877), the translations of which are to be found in *Works*. Many well-known poems appeared in his novels; others were published in his posthumous works.

Goethe's first play, *Die Laune des Verliebten* (*The Wayward Lover*, 1879), was written in 1767 and produced in 1779. Many tragedies, comedies, and operettas (or *Singspiele*) followed, the most famous of which are *Clavigo* (pr., pb. 1774; English translation, 1798, 1897), *Stella* (pr., pb. 1776; English translation, 1798), *Iphigenie auf Tauris* (pr. 1779; *Iphigenia in Tauris*, 1793), *Egmont* (pb. 1788; English translation, 1837), *Torquato Tasso* (pb. 1790; English translation, 1827), *Faust: Ein Fragment* (pb. 1790; *Faust: A Fragment*, 1980), *Die natürliche Tochter* (pr. 1803; *The Natural Daughter*, 1885), *Faust: Eine Tragödie* (pb. 1808; *The Tragedy of Faust*, 1823), and *Faust: Eine Tragödie, zweiter Teil* (pb. 1833; *The Tragedy of Faust, Part Two*, 1838).

Goethe also wrote a collection of short fiction, *Unterhaltungen deutscher Ausgewanderten* (1795; *Conversations of German Emigrants*, 1854), and a paradigm of the short prose form titled simply *Novelle* (1826; *Novel*, 1837). Other short stories appeared in his later novels, and he also wrote two verse epics, *Reinecke Fuchs* (1794; *Reynard the Fox*, 1855) and *Hermann und Dorothea* (1797; *Herman and Dorothea*, 1801); an autobiography, *Aus meinem Leben: Dichtung und Wahrheit* (1811-1814; *The Autobiography of Goethe*, 1824; better known as *Poetry and Truth from My Own Life*); and essays on literature, art, and science. His letters and diaries in dozens of volumes reveal insights into his life, work, and times.

Achievements

Johann Wolfgang von Goethe has been called the last Renaissance man. Not only was he a writer whose work in every literary genre was startlingly new and exemplary for later generations of writers, but he also took great interest in painting, music, botany, geology, physiology, optics, and government, and many of his ideas in these fields of endeavor were novel and seminal.

Goethe belongs to a select group of writers—including Homer, Dante, Leonardo da Vinci, Michelangelo, Miguel de Cervantes, and William Shakespeare—who were able to encompass all aspects of the human condition in their creativity. Goethe's work is universal; it reflects humankind's sufferings and joys, successes and failures. From his earliest work, Goethe had a concept of what he thought humans should be: active, striving individuals not afraid to make errors but dedicated to discovering their capabilities and to perfecting them to the best of their ability. His tragedy *Faust*, on which he worked for more than fifty years, can be viewed as a summation of his thought, and it belongs among the masterpieces of world literature.

The long-term influence of Goethe, like that of Shakespeare, can hardly be measured. Goethe has become a part of German and world culture. Every generation has poets, philosophers, artists, and general readers who look to him as a model, and the volumes that make up the Goethe bibliography attest that influence.

BIOGRAPHY

Johann Wolfgang von Goethe was born August 28, 1749, in Frankfurt am Main. His father, Johann Kaspar Goethe, was a well-to-do nonpracticing lawyer holding the title of imperial councilor. His learning and multifaceted interests were passed on to the young Goethe. The father was strict, often overbearing, and Goethe was never close to him. Goethe's mother, Katharina Elisabeth (née Textor), the daughter of the mayor, received more of his affection. In Frankfurt, Goethe first made contact with the theater through puppet plays and French troupes. He recorded these impressions vividly in his autobiography, *Poetry and Truth from My Own Life*. From 1765 to 1768, he attended the university in Leipzig, famous for its Enlightenment and Rococo writers, and studied law. There he also studied painting and had the first of his many famous love affairs (this one with Kätchen Schönkopf), which always resulted in beautiful poetry. His not atypical student life was interrupted by a lung hemorrhage, which compelled him to return to Frankfurt. Home again, and sickly, he came under the influence of the Pietist and mystic Susanna von Klettenberg, whose teachings can be found in "Bekenntnisse einer schönen Selle" ("Confessions of a Fair Saint"), which constitutes the sixth book of *Wilhelm Meister's Apprenticeship*.

Goethe returned to the university in 1770, this time to Strasbourg, where he received his degree in 1771. While in this French-German border city, he met Johann Gottfried Herder, the theologian and critic who, at that time, was singing the praises of Shakespeare, Ossian, primitive poetry, and the need for a German literature freed from French influence. Herder's great influence on Goethe is unmistakable and can be seen especially in Goethe's drama *Götz von Berlichingen mit der eisernen Hand* (pb. 1773; *Goetz of Berlichingen, with the Iron Hand*, 1799) and in a speech commemorating Shakespeare. This university period produced famous poems to Friederike Brion in *Sesenheimer Liederbuch* (1775-1789, 1854; *Sesenheim Songs*, 1853).

After receiving his degree, Goethe returned to Frankfurt and somewhat grudgingly set up a law practice. The years 1771 to 1775 mark Goethe's Sturm und Drang period, years of feverish literary activity. His best-known works from these years are the play *Goetz of Berlichingen, with the Iron Hand*, the novel *The Sorrows of Young Werther*, and his Sturm und Drang lyrics.

In 1775, Duke Karl August invited Goethe to Weimar, and, feeling the need to begin a new "epoch" in his life, Goethe decided to stay in the Thuringian city. Except for numerous trips, he spent the rest of his life in Weimar. This transitional period from the tempestuousness of the Sturm und Drang to the restraint of his classical period was marked by an intensive study of nature and the sciences and by numerous court activities. Goethe wrote many minor works in the following decade, and he started or continued several major works that for various reasons he left unfinished.

A need for a rebirth, a rejuvenation, drove Goethe to Italy, where he stayed from 1786 to 1788. There he experienced the "noble simplicity and quiet grandeur" (in the words of Adam Oeser and Johann Winckelmann) of Roman and Greek art and gained new impetus for his work, completing *Iphigenia in Tauris* and *Egmont*. He chronicled these travels in his *Italienische Reise* (1816, 1817; *Travels in Italy*, 1883), which makes up part of his autobiography. In the decade after his return to Weimar, he took up new scientific endeavors and wrote numerous works, including *Torquato Tasso*, *Venetian Epigrams*, *Roman Elegies*, and *Wilhelm Meister's Apprenticeship*.

The year 1794 marked the beginning of Goethe's friendship with Friedrich Schiller, which proved fruitful for both men. Their shared interests can be seen in *Epigrams*, a collection of satiric distiches, in *Ballads*, and in their insightful two-volume correspondence. The last thirty years of Goethe's life reveal an unflagging productivity. In addition to pursuing his increasing scientific interests, he wrote his autobiography, the novels *Elective Affinities* and *Wilhelm Meister's Travels*, and the lyric cycle *West-Eastern Divan*, and he succeeded in finishing his lifework, *Faust*. He died at the age of eighty-two on

March 22, 1832, and was buried in Weimar, next to Schiller.

Analysis

Johann Wolfgang von Goethe's first novel, *The Sorrows of Young Werther*, did for the German novel what his early play *Goetz of Berlichingen, with the Iron Hand* did for German drama—it revolutionized prose writing in German and rescued German literature from a deadening provincialism. The people and places in *The Sorrows of Young Werther* have been so well documented, to a great extent by Goethe himself in his autobiography, that the reader with biographical knowledge of Goethe has difficulty separating the author from the titular hero Werther. The autobiographical content of the novel has often led to one-sided interpretations that have ignored other important aspects of the work, yet the genesis of the story in Goethe's own experience is impossible to ignore.

Johann Wolfgang von Goethe. (Library of Congress)

After Goethe had finished his law studies in Strasbourg, he returned to his parental home in Frankfurt to pursue, somewhat halfheartedly, a law career. At the behest of his father, Goethe went in May, 1772, to Wetzlar, which still claimed fame as the seat of the Reichskammergericht (supreme court) of the Holy Roman Empire. At a ball in the small town (which becomes one of the central episodes in the novel), Goethe met Lotte Buff, who was unofficially engaged to Johann Christian Kestner, a secretary to the Hanoverian legation. Goethe often visited her at the home of her father, a widower with many children, and he, like Werther, eventually fell in love with her; but Goethe fell in love often and easily, and the intensity of his relationship with Buff has been overemphasized. Goethe's letters to her do not read like Werther's; the identification of Goethe with Werther should not be carried too far. This is not to say that Goethe's emotions for Buff were shallow—his hasty retreat from Wetzlar without even a farewell speaks against this—but Goethe was attracted to married or "taken" women, a not unimportant psychological phenomenon.

After leaving Wetzlar, Goethe visited Sophie von La Roche, a popular writer of sentimental novels, at Ehrenbreitenstein. There he fell in love with the author's daughter, Maximiliane, who, like Buff, was engaged to be married. This sensitive situation continued even after Maximiliane's marriage, until her husband, Brentano, put an end to it, nearly a year and a half after Goethe had left Wetzlar.

Shortly after Goethe left Wetzlar, Kestner, who carried on a correspondence with Goethe for many years, wrote to Goethe and described in great detail the suicide of a young man two years Goethe's senior, Karl Wilhelm Jerusalem, whom Goethe had met. Jerusalem had killed himself over unrequited love for a married woman. Although in his autobiography Goethe claims that the Jerusalem incident was the catalyst for *The Sorrows of Young Werther* (a catalyst that took nearly two years to bring about an effect), later scholarship would indicate that it was not until Goethe's affair with Maximiliane that he began to get the idea for the novel. By the time Goethe wrote *The Sorrows of Young Werther*, he was naturally no longer the same man he was two years earlier. He had essentially already left behind many of his Sturm und Drang traits, those rebellious Romantic characteristics that modern humans so fondly cherish in their struggles against society and technology. Like his contemporary Friedrich Maximilian Klinger, Goethe saw the dangers of Romantic excess, and *The Sorrows of Young Werther* can claim to be Goethe's reckoning with his not-too-distant past.

The Sorrows of Young Werther

The Sorrows of Young Werther begins (as does Jean-Jacques Rousseau's epistolary novel *Julie: Ou, La Nouvelle Héloïse*, 1761; *Eloise: Or, A Series of Original Letters*, 1761; better known as *The New Héloïse*) and ends (as does Samuel Richardson's epistolary novel *Pamela: Or, Virtue Rewarded*, 1740-1741) with comments by the editor, who has collected Werther's letters to provide "consolation" for those who have fallen like Werther. The first letter is dated May 4, 1771, and serves as exposition. Werther has been sent by his mother to find out about an inheritance. He has left behind "the poor Leonore," whom he has abandoned after being attracted to her sister. This often-overlooked fact reveals much about Werther's character and does not present Werther in a favorable light at the beginning of the novel.

Werther is an artist, or at least he claims to be, but he deludes himself. In his second letter (May 10), he writes: "I am so happy, dear friend, so completely immersed in the feeling of a tranquil existence that my art suffers from it. I couldn't draw now, not a line, and have never been a greater painter than at this moment." Werther allows himself to be overwhelmed by his feelings for nature, and he uses these feelings to rationalize his dilettantism.

Werther loses himself in nature, in reveries about an old love, in the patriarchal atmosphere of Homer, and essentially withdraws from society into himself. The letter of June 16, the longest in the novel, describes the ball where Werther meets Lotte. He has been warned that Lotte is engaged to Albert, but that is of little concern to him. His letter is replete with broken thoughts, effusions, and dashes that portray his inner turmoil, and the fact that this letter comes seventeen days after the previous one shows how enthralled he is with his "new" love. Werther imagines the idyllic scene at the end of Oliver Goldsmith's *The Vicar of Wakefield* (1766), a scene that for him must remain unrealized. Lotte serves as a new cathexis; Werther completely loses himself in thoughts of her and does not know "either that it's day or night." His search, his yearning for an idyllic, harmonious life, contrasts with his romantic longing for independence.

Werther often compares himself to a child and is very fond of children. He mentions his mother only briefly and his father not at all. He often longs for the innocence of childhood and subconsciously seems to wish that he could be among children for whom Lotte cuts the daily bread. His search for security, for protection, is very childlike, and he looks to Lotte as much for maternal as for sexual affection.

His passing comment about the local preacher's daughter ("I must say I found her not unpleasing"), who again is "taken," underlines his emotional instability. At times, however, Werther is capable of profound thoughts and of analyzing his own problems: "If we once have the power to pull ourselves together, our work will pass briskly through our hands, and we shall find a true pleasure in our activity" (July 1). "Activity" is a key word for Goethe and serves as a means of interpreting the novel. Wilhelm, the recipient of Werther's letters, and Werther's mother admonish him to find some kind of productive activity, which he only ridicules: "Am I not now active, and isn't it basically one and the same whether I count peas or lentils?" (July 20).

Later in the novel, Werther begins to read James Macpherson's skillful forgery *The Works of Ossian* (1765), in whose stormy and turbulent descriptions of nature he finds his own feelings mirrored. Goethe commented later (August 2, 1829) that Werther read Homer while sane and Ossian after he went mad. The changing style of Werther's letters reflects his inner turmoil. Absent now are the pithy statements; subjectivism has taken over. Again, his friend Wilhelm admonishes him "to get rid of the miserable feeling that must consume all of your powers," but Werther notes in his diary that there is no "appearance of improvement."

Werther's second-longest letter deals with his argument with Albert about suicide (August 12). Werther justifies it, while Albert ridicules it as a tool of a spineless man, and the reader has a presentiment. Only ten days later, Werther writes that he is incapable of doing anything: "I have no imaginative powers, no feeling for nature, and books make me sick." He hopes that a new position will cure him (another important theme in Goethe's works), but the first book closes with his statement, "I see no end to this misery but the grave."

The second book begins one month and ten days after the last letter of book 1 and more than five months after the first letter of the novel. Werther now has the position of secretary to an ambassador, a position that he cannot endure for long. The position does, however, bring about a kind of recovery that enables Werther to see his problem: "Nothing is more dangerous than solitude" (October 20). There are now longer intervals between the letters, in which he often vacillates between recognizing his problems and putting the blame on others for them: "And you are all to blame whose twaddle placed this yoke on me and who have prated so much about activity. Activity!" (December 24).

Three months after his arrival, Werther writes Lotte for the first time, and his vocabulary once again is marked by words such as "isolation," "loneliness," and "limitation." Goethe interjects the parallel story of a farmhand, whom Werther had met earlier, whose unrequited love will later lead to murder. Werther identifies so much with this man's fate that he later makes an attempt to save him. This and the parallel motif of a man who worked for Lotte's father, fell in love with Lotte, was driven from the household, and became insane as a result of his unrequited love skillfully mark Werther's decline.

On December 6, about nineteen months after the first letter of the novel, Werther's correspondence ends, and the editor tells how he gathered the material that covers Werther's last days. The editor's longer, analytical sentences contrast sharply with Werther's rhapsodic prose. Like Wilhelm, he speaks of Werther's inactivity—"He seemed to himself justified in his inactivity by all this"—but he also presents material (the very informed source is not given) that shows Lotte was not totally without blame, that she spurred Werther on somewhat until it was too late. When Werther, at the end of the novel, sends his servant to borrow Albert's pistols for a supposed trip, Lotte reacts in horror; she knows that Werther wants the pistols to shoot himself, yet she does nothing about it, because Werther had visited her against Albert's wishes and she now fears Albert's remonstrations.

The end of the novel is masterful in its succinct style: "At twelve noon he died. . . . At night toward eleven [the steward] had him buried at the spot Werther had chosen. The steward followed the body, and his sons, but Albert found it impossible. People feared for Lotte's life. Workmen carried him. No clergyman escorted him."

Goethe intended to depict in *The Sorrows of Young Werther* the problems of an excessively sensitive soul, showing how unbridled emotions and inactivity could lead to death. He drew from his own life, but he also saw many Werthers around him, as in the figure of the gifted contemporary poet and dramatist Jakob Michael Reinhold Lenz. The influence of the novel was great, but Goethe's intent was widely misunderstood. Young men with romantic hearts saw in the book a justification for excessive emotion and suicide, and they emulated Werther by dressing in the blue coat and yellow vest that he wears in the novel. "Werther fever" was on the rise, and there was even a spate of suicides à la Werther. For this and other reasons, Goethe revised the novel in 1787. Still, Werther became a model for Romantic writers throughout the world, and to this day, his story is the best known among Goethe's works.

Wilhelm Meister's Apprenticeship

Like most of Goethe's mature works, *Wilhelm Meister's Apprenticeship* had a long genesis. Goethe made first mention of this, his second novel, in an entry in his diary dated February 16, 1777, although he probably was working on the novel as early as 1776; it took him nearly twenty years to complete it. To be sure, he had finished a large portion of the novel by 1785, through book 6 and part of book 7, but work on the novel, as with the plays *Iphigenia in Tauris*, *Egmont*, and *Torquato Tasso*, was interrupted by his trip to Italy from 1786 to 1788. Not until his friendship with Friedrich Schiller, who supplied insightful criticism and suggestions, many of which Goethe adopted, did Goethe regain interest and finish the work. The novel Goethe published in 1795 and 1796 was essentially a thorough revision of the earlier version titled *Wilhelm Meisters Theatralische Sendung* (1911; *Wilhelm Meister's Theatrical Mission*, 1913), the manuscript of which was not discovered until 1910.

Wilhelm Meister's Theatrical Mission is a bildungsroman in both literal and figurative senses. The fragment opens with Wilhelm as a boy, and the interesting psychological development of the child, which closely follows Goethe's autobiography, is to a great extent sacrificed in *Wilhelm Meister's Apprenticeship*, which begins with Wilhelm as a young man about to leave the parental home (the few childhood scenes are told in retrospect). In *Wilhelm Meister's Apprenticeship*, the theater loses in importance: *Wilhelm Meister's Theatrical Mission* reflects the ambitions and concerns of a budding dramatist; *Wilhelm Meister's Apprenticeship*, Goethe's ideas on culture and human development. The former follows the pattern woven by Goethe in many of his early poems and dramas about the artist; the latter can no longer be termed "a portrait of the artist as a young man." The theater represents only one step on Wilhelm's path of self-development. The language of the former reads much like Goethe's Sturm und Drang prose and is quite different from the stylized, sculptured prose in the latter, which is characteristic of Goethe's prose style after his years in Italy. Many of the ideas and most of the characters, however, were transferred from the early fragment to the novel and merely reshaped to represent the thinking of the mature Goethe.

Thematically, *Wilhelm Meister's Apprenticeship* consists of five parts: home (book 1 and book 2, chapters 1 and 2), Wilhelm's travels as a businessman and his first theatrical encounter (book 2, chapter 3, to book 3, chapter 12), the theater of Serlo (book 3, chapter 13, to book 5, and book 7, chapter 8), "Confessions of a Fair Saint" (book 6), and the "Society of the Tower" episodes (book 7, chapters 1-7 and 9, and book 8). The linear construction enables the reader to follow the development of Wilhelm from a somewhat naïve, eager young man through his many trials and tribulations to his reception into the Society of the Tower, where he is given an indenture that will guide him in his journeyman years.

At the beginning of the novel, Wilhelm, like many young people, disdains his family's supposed avarice and bourgeois life and views the theater as a means of escape. His mother curses the day she gave him a puppet theater, for she believes his calling to the theater will ruin him physically and morally. Goethe's description of theater life mirrors quite accurately the circumstances and plight of theater groups in Germany in the 1760's and 1770's.

A series of coincidences and misunderstandings involving Wilhelm's lover, Marianne—an actor who, unbeknown to him, is pregnant—causes him to abandon her and resign himself to his father's business. Years pass; Wilhelm despairs over his ability as a writer, which he still believes to be his calling, burns his manuscripts, and seems to dedicate himself diligently to his father's merchant profession. Following the advice of his father and his friend Werner, Wilhelm sets out on a trip to collect some debts owed to his father. As soon as he hears of a theatrical troupe performing in the vicinity where his travels have taken him, the old flame smoldering inside flares up and he is consumed by the idea of the theater. He encounters a motley group of actors and takes up with them.

The two theater episodes help Wilhelm gain insights into himself. At first enthusiastic about pursuing his dream of belonging to an acting troupe, he dedicates body and soul to the theater, which he serves as actor, writer, and director. (These activities reflect Goethe's involvement as writer, actor, and, after 1791, director of the Weimar Theatre.) While at a castle with the troupe, Wilhelm is introduced to the theater of Shakespeare by Jarno, a mysterious figure and a member of the Society of the Tower whose function becomes clear only later. Shakespeare has a profound effect on Wilhelm, as he did on all the German dramatists of the 1770's; Wilhelm's conversations about Shakespeare and *Hamlet* (pr. c. 1600-1601) with Serlo, the director of a troupe in a large city of commerce (probably modeled on Hamburg), and with his sister Aurelie, and their subsequent successful performance of the play, form the nucleus of the fourth book. The sections on *Hamlet* do not, however, represent the thinking of the older Goethe, but rather the subjective sentimentality of the Sturm und Drang writers. Wilhelm's dissatisfaction with the members of the troupe and the bustle of the city causes him to reflect on the direction he has taken in his life; for the first time, he admires the order and activity of the world of commerce (book 4, chapter 20). Wilhelm still views the theater as a goal, however, writing to his friend Werner, "to develop myself exactly as I am, that was vaguely my wish and my intention from the days of my youth." The German word *(aus)bilden* (to develop, to educate, to cultivate), a variant of which is found in "bildungsroman," is a key word in the novel and appears more than one hundred times. At this point in the novel, Wilhelm knows he must develop himself, but he still falsely views the theater as an end and not as a means.

Toward the end of the fifth book, Wilhelm becomes more and more disillusioned with the theater, and his criticism of it culminates in the declaration in book 7, chapter 8: "I am leaving the theatre to join up with men whose association has to lead me in every sense to a pure and certain activity." The word "activity" (*Tätigkeit*), as in *The Sorrows of Young Werther*, is a key word in Goethe's novels, and it is toward an active, constructive life that Wilhelm must move.

The Society of the Tower makes up most of book 7 and all of book 8. Wilhelm discovers that many of the people who have crossed his path throughout the novel (Jarno, the Abbé, Natalie "the beautiful amazon," the Countess, Friedrich, and others) are connected with the society and have monitored and guided his development. Wilhelm is now initiated into the secrets of the society, and the Abbé says: "Your apprenticeship is over, nature has released you" (book 7, chapter 9). Wilhelm discovers that the boy Felix, who has been with him since his days with Serlo, is his son by Marianne, who died in childbirth. He also learns that Mignon and the harp player, those Romantic spirits whom he met while with the first acting troupe, are father and daughter from an incestuous affair. Symbolically, they must die, for they represent an aberrant side of life not compatible with Wilhelm's active, healthy endeavors. (Significantly, and ironically, German Romantic writers and musicians of the early nineteenth century were enraptured with the figures of Mignon and the harp player.)

Wilhelm falls in love with Natalie, who, like the other members of the Society of the Tower, will play a significant role in the continuation of the novel, *Wilhelm Meister's Travels*. Wilhelm's development, however, is not yet over; the society will direct him on his next journey, which he will make with his son Felix.

Wilhelm Meister's Apprenticeship is a milestone in the development of the novel as a genre. Not until Charles Dickens did a novelist again weave such an intricate plot. Goethe had literary debts to such writers as Samuel Richardson, Jean-Jacques Rousseau, and Oliver Goldsmith, but he paid them back with interest. His use of different genres within the novel—of letters, songs, and stories within the story—was to have a great influence on the next generation of novelists in England, France, and Russia. In Germany, Goethe made the novel into an art form, a form that, unlike poetry or drama, was able to encompass the breadth of the human condition.

Elective Affinities

Goethe's third novel, *Elective Affinities*, was first conceived as a novella to be placed in what was later to become his fourth novel, *Wilhelm Meister's Travels*, but the idea became so important to Goethe that he expanded the novella into a novel in what was for him a relatively short period of time; of his novels, only *The Sorrows of Young Werther* was written more quickly. Goethe himself said that *Elective Affinities* should be read three times to comprehend its ramifications, and in his diary, he noted that the idea behind the novel was to portray "social relationships and their conflicts in a symbolic way."

Elective Affinities differs from Goethe's other novels in that it focuses attention on a group of people rather than on an individual, as in *The Sorrows of Young Werther* and *Wilhelm Meister's Apprenticeship*. In *Elective Affinities*, Goethe, somewhat like his contemporary, Jane Austen, uses a small group of people as a microcosm to represent the problems of contemporary society.

Elective Affinities begins with what seems to be an idyll. Edward and Charlotte live on a large estate and are arranging it to their tastes. They are both in their second marriage. Having been lovers in their youth who were forced into marriages of convenience, they were able to marry after the deaths of their spouses. Soon, however, flaws begin to appear in the idyllic setting. Edward and Charlotte are designing a new house, a pleasure pavilion (*Lustgebäude*), and, as with most actions in the novel, this one is symbolic: The old house, representing their marriage, is no longer adequate, and the building of the new one is an unconscious admission that their marriage itself is no longer adequate to one or to both of them. Apart from *Faust*, *Elective Affinities* is Goethe's most symbolic work, and attention must be paid to every object—the plane trees, the church, water, the paths, headaches, and so on—for symbolic meaning blended into the novel in a masterful way.

The stagnation of the marriage becomes clear when Edward wants to invite his old friend, the Captain, who has fallen on hard times, to come live with them. Charlotte, who is by far more perceptive than Edward, fears this move. She knows that a third person will change their lives, but whereas she is completely happy and satisfied in her activity (*Tätigkeit*), Edward is a dilettante who needs the "active" Captain to stimulate him. The narrator, whose function in *Elective Affinities* is generally to analyze the characters and their relationships objectively rather than to admonish, as in *The Sorrows of Young Werther*, comments that before the arrival of the Captain, Edward and Charlotte had had less conversation than usual, because they had disagreed over the building of the park: "Thus daily Charlotte felt lonelier."

The Captain arrives, and Charlotte decides to have Ottilie, the orphaned daughter of an old friend, brought from the boarding school that she attends with Luciane, Charlotte's daughter from her first marriage; thus, the tragic constellation is complete. One day, the four of them are together when the Captain begins speaking of elective affinities, the tendency in chemistry for particles to break up and form new combinations. Edward, who misconstrues nearly everything, comments that these relationships become interesting only when they cause separations (*Scheidungen* in German, also meaning "divorces"), and he makes the analogy (quite unaware, consciously at least, of its implications) that Charlotte represents A, he himself B, the Captain C, and Ottilie D: When A and B break up, and C and D likewise, they form the new unions of AC and BD. Edward's casual talk disturbs Charlotte, who recognizes in it his subconscious yearning.

The new pairs are indeed gradually formed. Charlotte finds with the Captain new "activity" that she no longer shares with Edward, and Edward delights in being with Ottilie, with whom he shares a childlike nature. The names of the characters are themselves significant: Edward's real name, "Otto" (which is also the Captain's first name), "Charlotte," and "Ottilie" all have the same root, showing symbolically the close affinity among them. The action of the first part pinnacles in a scene of psychological adultery. Edward visits Charlotte's bedroom one night after "a strange mix-up took place in his soul," and during intercourse, he thinks of Ottilie while Charlotte thinks of the Captain. Upon waking, Edward has a presentiment and considers what he has done a crime. Thereafter the thought of Ottilie consumes him, just as Lotte's image consumed Werther.

Elective Affinities, like most of Goethe's later works, contains the theme of renunciation (*Entsagung*), and it could, in fact, justifiably carry the German subtitle of *Wilhelm Meister's Travels: Oder, Die Entsagenden* (or those who renounce). Charlotte learns to renounce the Captain; Edward does not renounce, nor does Ottilie at this point in the novel. The Captain leaves, and when Edward learns that Charlotte is pregnant, he flees to seek his end in a war of which he has no real understanding, just as he does not understand most things in his life.

The first half of the second part deals with how Charlotte and Ottilie lead their lives during the absence of Edward and the Captain. Ottilie, even though she still longs for Edward, matures, and this maturation process can be followed in her diary, excerpts from which occasionally break the narrative flow of the novel. At times, it is hard to believe that Ottilie, who had difficulties in school, can actually understand the pithy statements she copies into her diary. Readers of Goethe are inclined to view Ottilie as an authorial mouthpiece in these passages, just as the aphorisms in "Makarien's Archive," at the end of *Wilhelm Meister's Travels*, serve to represent Goethe's thinking. Ottilie's diary also prepares the reader for her renunciation of Edward and for her belief that it is wrong to break up the marriage of Edward and Charlotte. When the baby, which has Ottilie's eyes and the Captain's facial features, is born (conceived on the night of psychological adultery), Ottilie begins to sublimate her love for Edward into a pseudo-mother-love for the child.

In *Elective Affinities*, Goethe assimilates, as in his other novels, a variety of literary genres. Ottilie's diary has already been mentioned; particularly striking is the function of the novella, "The Strange Neighbor Children," which is integrated into the novel. The children in the novella parallel to a certain degree the characters in the novel, but the novella, based on events in the Captain's past, has a happy ending (despite the parallel symbols of water and drowning), unlike the novel.

One day, Ottilie takes the baby to the lake, where she is suddenly surprised by Edward. Edward has returned from the war ever more intent on having Ottilie. He has met with the Captain (who is now a major, perhaps through advancement in the same war in which Edward fought) and has convinced him, even though the Captain hesitated at first, that Charlotte and he should divorce and that the Major should marry Charlotte and raise the baby. Ottilie resists Edward's proposal that they marry, saying that Charlotte must decide their fate. In her confusion, she hurries, after parting from Edward, to a skiff, loses her balance, and drops the baby into the lake. By the time she retrieves it, it is dead.

Despite the tragic loss, Charlotte agrees to a divorce. Ottilie, however, has learned to "renounce." She resolves to be a teacher and to return to the boarding school, where she can be "active." Edward surprises her on her journey back to the school and gets her to return to the estate. During their brief meeting at an inn, however, Ottilie does not say a word; she refuses to express her love for Edward, realizing that the only escape for her is in death. Her maturation and new convictions become apparent when they return to the estate and she places Charlotte's and Edward's hands together. She continues not to speak and resolves to starve herself to death. Edward soon follows her in death, and the two are buried side by side.

Wilhelm Meister's Travels

Wilhelm Meister's Travels belongs to that group of Goethe's later works (in poetry, *West-Eastern Divan*, and in drama, *Faust*) that are characteristic of his *Altersstil* (mature style) and that are not easily accessible. Goethe himself recognized the difficulty of his last novel; he admitted (February 17, 1827) that it could not have been written earlier. In a conversation six years before this admission (June 8, 1821), he cited the problem readers would have with the novel: "Everything is really to be taken symbolically, and everywhere there is something else hidden behind it. Every solution to a problem is a new problem." The absence of plot; the interspersed novellas, poems, letters, aphorisms, dramatic dialogue, and technical discussions of various trades; and the often obscure wisdom of the aged Goethe make for difficult reading, but when the novel is read in the context of Goethe's later works and his worldview, its seemingly vague symbols become clearer.

Goethe formed the conception of *Wilhelm Meister's Travels* as soon as he finished its companion piece, *Wilhelm Meister's Apprenticeship*, but actual work on the novel did not begin until 1807, and it was not completed for more than twenty years. The novel fuses materials of two kinds: the novellas, written mostly between 1807 and 1818, which in style and content differ from the framework, and the framework itself, most of which was completed later. A first version appeared in 1821 and was then thoroughly revised for the second version in 1829. The novellas present vignettes of the human condition and the vicissitudes of human existence, and they are moralistic in that they reinforce the teachings implicit in the novel's framework; almost all of them deal with the problem of passion. The title of the novel itself is bipartite: *Wilhelm Meister's Travels* indicates a continuation, however loosely, of *Wilhelm Meister's Apprenticeship*; the subtitle, *Die Entsagenden* (those who renounce), mirrors the philosophy of the society that directs the protagonist.

The Society of the Tower has given Wilhelm rules that dictate his travels: He cannot stay longer than three days under one roof; when he leaves a place, he must travel at least one German mile (approximately five miles); and he cannot return to the same place for more than a year. The novel begins with Wilhelm and his son Felix journeying through the mountains. Goethe immediately introduces the symbolic figures of Joseph, a carpenter, and Maria, his wife, who live in an abandoned monastery and offer Wilhelm shelter. Goethe's ideas on religion are encapsulated in this segment, both symbolically (the ruins of the monastery and Joseph's work on it) and explicitly (in conversations between Wilhelm and Joseph). The theme of the family recurs throughout the novel, and this "first family" serves as a model.

Continuing on his wanderings, Wilhelm meets Montan, the Jarno of *Wilhelm Meister's Apprenticeship*. Like many of the characters in the novel, Montan/Jarno is one who has "renounced," and he later fulfills a utilitarian function in the new society; his métier is geology, hence his name. The characters in the novel who will later make up the society have professions that represent the vast and varied interests of Goethe: astronomy, weaving, geology, botany, and so on.

Wilhelm and Felix come to the house of the "Uncle" (*der Oheim*), where they meet Hersilie, with whom Felix falls in love. Felix's love for Hersilie depicts the impetuous and immature side of love. His handling of the situation parallels to a great extent Wilhelm's amorous adventures in *Wilhelm Meister's Apprenticeship* and is juxtaposed to the maturity of the now older and wiser Wilhelm. Wilhelm also meets at the Uncle's house Juliette and Leonardo. Leonardo has been away to educate himself, has overcome the many obstacles of impetuous youth, and is now returning to his Uncle's to take up new activities. The Uncle owns vast tracts of land in America, which Leonardo will inherit. The Society of the Tower also possesses large landholdings in America, and Leonardo plans to join them to found colonies in the new land for those people of the mountain regions whose skills are being replaced by the machines of the Industrial Revolution. (This utopian vision of America runs throughout German literature and would remain present in the novels of several young Austrian writers and German filmmakers in the late twentieth century.)

Wilhelm visits the castle of Aunt Makarie, whose nebulous figure seems to shed guiding light over the society's proceedings. Her pithy advice and aphorisms allow Goethe to express his wisdom on every subject of interest to him. Makarie is the example par excellence of one who has renounced. She is confined to a chair, but her wisdom and guidance are sought by everyone. Wilhelm then comes to the Pedagogical Province, where he leaves Felix to be educated while he continues his journey. The Pedagogical Province is a strict, almost totalitarian educational system (with overtones from Plato, Rousseau, and Johann Heinrich Pestalozzi) where young people are rigorously trained to serve a function in society. Every aspect of the student's life is dictated, and at first, Felix, again as a figure of youth whose passions must be controlled, is hesitant, but he does conform. The idea behind the Province is that man can attain the highest that he is capable of reaching. Some of the Province's pupils will emigrate to America with the Society of the Tower.

Wilhelm later comes to that mountainous region whose inhabitants are threatened by the Industrial Revolution. There he meets a group planning to emigrate to America, and he begins practicing the profession he has chosen in order to be a useful member of society, namely, that of a doctor. Book 3 contains long passages on technical aspects of spinning and weaving, the society's plans for colonies in America and in Europe, and finally a meeting of the immigrants at Markarie's castle. Here some of the principal characters from *Wilhelm Meister's Apprenticeship* come together; they now all have a useful profession, a function in the new society: Friedrich, because of his good memory, is a copyist; the frivolous Philine has become, somewhat incredulously, an expert, selfless seamstress; and the Abbé is a teacher.

The novel ends as it began, symbolically. As Wilhelm travels upriver to join Felix, who is now several years older, a horse with rider plunges into the river. It is Felix, who has recently visited Hersilie on a mission of love, was rejected, and was riding grief-stricken when his horse fell into the river. Wilhelm saves his son by opening a vein—he has now completed his education; several years before, a similar incident had occurred in Wilhelm's life, but he was untrained and had to watch a fisher-boy die. Wilhelm will now join Natalie and the Society of the Tower.

Wilhelm Meister's Travels is not a psychological study of humankind and society as is *Elective Affinities*; rather, it is a receptacle into which Goethe poured the wisdom gathered over a long life. It contains some of his most profound thoughts on humankind, society, literature, art, music, and the sciences. It also contains the vision of *Faust*: The central themes of activity and renunciation help define humankind's purpose on earth and the function of human beings in society—an unusual optimism for a writer in his eightieth year.

Kim Vivian

OTHER MAJOR WORKS

SHORT FICTION: *Unterhaltungen deutscher Ausgewanderten*, 1795 (*Conversations of German Emigrants*, 1854); *Novelle*, 1826 (*Novel*, 1837).

PLAYS: *Götz von Berlichingen mit der eisernen Hand*, pb. 1773 (*Goetz of Berlichingen, with the Iron Hand*, 1799); *Clavigo*, pr., pb. 1774 (English translation, 1798, 1897); *Götter, Helden und Wieland*, pb. 1774; *Erwin und Elmire*, pr., pb. 1775 (libretto; music by Duchess Anna Amalia of Saxe-Weimar); *Claudine von Villa Bella*, pb. 1776 (second version pb. 1788; libretto); *Die Geschwister*, pr. 1776; *Stella*, pr., pb. 1776 (second version pr. 1806; English translation, 1798); *Iphigenie auf Tauris*, pr. 1779 (second version pb. 1787; *Iphigenia in*

Tauris, 1793); *Die Laune des Verliebten*, pr. 1779 (wr. 1767; *The Wayward Lover*, 1879); *Jery und Bätely*, pr. 1780 (libretto); *Die Mitschuldigen*, pr. 1780 (wr. 1768; second version wr. 1769; *The Fellow-Culprits*, 1879); *Die Fischerin*, pr., pb. 1782 (libretto; music by Corona Schröter; *The Fisherwoman*, 1899); *Scherz, List und Rache*, pr. 1784 (libretto); *Der Triumph der Empfindsamkeit*, pb. 1787; *Egmont*, pb. 1788 (English translation, 1837); *Faust: Ein Fragment*, pb. 1790 (*Faust: A Fragment*, 1980); *Torquato Tasso*, pb. 1790 (English translation, 1827); *Der Gross-Cophta*, pr., pb. 1792; *Der Bürgergeneral*, pr., pb. 1793; *Was wir bringen*, pr., pb. 1802; *Die natürliche Tochter*, pr. 1803 (*The Natural Daughter*, 1885); *Faust: Eine Tragödie*, pb. 1808 (*The Tragedy of Faust*, 1823); *Pandora*, pb. 1808; *Des Epimenides Erwachen*, pb. 1814; *Faust: Eine Tragödie, zweiter Teil*, pb. 1833 (*The Tragedy of Faust, Part Two*, 1838); *Die Wette*, pb. 1837 (wr. 1812).

poetry: *Neue Lieder*, 1770 (*New Poems*, 1853); *Sesenheimer Liederbuch*, 1775-1789, 1854 (*Sesenheim Songs*, 1853); *Römische Elegien*, 1793 (*Roman Elegies*, 1876); *Reinecke Fuchs*, 1794 (*Reynard the Fox*, 1855); *Epigramme: Venedig 1790*, 1796 (*Venetian Epigrams*, 1853); *Xenien*, 1796 (with Friedrich Schiller; *Epigrams*, 1853); *Hermann und Dorothea*, 1797 (*Herman and Dorothea*, 1801); *Balladen*, 1798 (with Schiller; *Ballads*, 1853); *Neueste Gedichte*, 1800 (*Newest Poems*, 1853); *Gedichte*, 1812-1815 (2 volumes; *The Poems of Goethe*, 1853); *Sonette*, 1819 (*Sonnets*, 1853); *Westöstlicher Divan*, 1819 (*West-Eastern Divan*, 1877).

nonfiction: *Von deutscher Baukunst*, 1773 (*On German Architecture*, 1921); *Versuch die Metamorphose der Pflanzen zu erklären*, 1790 (*Essays on the Metamorphosis of Plants*, 1863); *Beyträge zur Optik*, 1791, 1792 (2 volumes); *Winckelmann und sein Jahrhundert*, 1805; *Zur Farbenlehre*, 1810 (*Theory of Colors*, 1840); *Aus meinem Leben: Dichtung und Wahrheit*, 1811-1814 (3 volumes; *The Autobiography of Goethe*, 1824; better known as *Poetry and Truth from My Own Life*); *Italienische Reise*, 1816, 1817 (2 volumes; *Travels in Italy*, 1883); *Zur Naturwissenschaft überhaupt, besonders zur Morphologie*, 1817, 1824 (2 volumes); *Die Belagerung von Mainz, 1793*, 1822 (*The Siege of Mainz in the Year 1793*, 1849); *Campagne in Frankreich, 1792*, 1822 (*Campaign in France in the Year 1792*, 1849); *Essays on Art*, 1845; *Goethe's Literary Essays*, 1921; *Goethe on Art*, 1980.

miscellaneous: *Works*, 1848-1890 (14 volumes); *Goethes Werke*, 1887-1919 (133 volumes).

Bibliography

Armstrong, John. *Love, Life, Goethe: Lessons of the Imagination from the Great German Poet*. New York: Farrar, Straus and Giroux, 2007. Clearly written, comprehensive volume enables readers to gain a better understanding of Goethe's work and the circumstances that inspired it. Discusses a wide range of Goethe's writings, including his lesser-known works, and also presents a close study of his personal life. Armstrong provides his own translations from German to English of several key passages in the works.

Atkins, Stuart. *Essays on Goethe*. Columbia, S.C.: Camden House, 1995. Collection of essays by a well-respected Goethe scholar addresses topics such as Goethe as an apprentice novelist, *The Sorrows of Young Werther*, and other aspects of the author's work.

Boyle, Nicholas. *The Poetry of Desire (1749-1790)*. Vol. 1 in *Goethe: The Poet and the Age*. New York: Oxford University Press, 1991.

_______. *Revolution and Renunciation (1790-1803)*. Vol. 2 in *Goethe: The Poet and the Age*. New York: Oxford University Press, 2000. Comprehensive two-volume critical biography provides analysis of Goethe's works as well as details of his life and personality. The second volume includes extensive discussion of the Wilhelm Meister novels.

Hutchinson, Peter, ed. *Landmarks in the German Novel*. New York: Peter Lang, 2007. Traces the development of the German novel from the eighteenth century until 1959 by analyzing thirteen milestone works, including separate essays discussing Goethe's *The Sorrows of Young Werther*, *Wilhelm Meister's Apprenticeship*, and *Elective Affinities*.

Kerry, Paul E. *Enlightenment Thought in the Writings of Goethe: A Contribution to the History of Ideas*. Rochester, N.Y.: Camden House, 2001. Analyzes Goethe's novels and other works to demonstrate how he was influenced by Voltaire, David Hume, and other Enlightenment philosophers and writers. Includes bibliography and index.

Lange, Victor, ed. *Goethe: A Collection of Critical Essays*. Englewood Cliffs, N.J.: Prentice-Hall, 1968. The essays collected in this informative volume emphasize Goethe's extraordinary poetic range as well as the pervasive consequences of scientific and social concerns in his life and work. The wide-ranging critical debate over the author's classical synthesis of private and collective responsibility is well represented. Includes a chronology of significant dates and a select bibliography.

Reed, T. J. *The Classical Centre: Goethe and Weimar, 1775-1832*. New York: Barnes & Noble Books, 1980. Asserts that Goethe's work came as a fulfillment of a need felt by a culture that lacked the essentials of a literary tradition. Focuses on Goethe's years in Weimar and emphasizes Goethe's position as the center of German literature and the primary creator of German classicism.

Remak, Henry H. H. *Structural Elements of the German Novella from Goethe to Thomas Mann*. New York: Peter Lang, 1996. Tests the three constituents of Goethe's famous definition of the novella against his own novellas. Discusses Goethe's seminal role in the development of the novella as the supreme literary achievement of Germany in the nineteenth century.

Sharpe, Lesley, ed. *The Cambridge Companion to Goethe*. New York: Cambridge University Press, 2002. Collection of commissioned essays analyzes Goethe's fiction and other works. Topics include Goethe and gender, philosophy, and religion as well as discussion of the critical reception of his works. Includes bibliography and index.

Swales, Martin, and Erika Swales. *Reading Goethe: A Critical Introduction to the Literary Work*. Rochester, N.Y.: Camden House, 2002. Comprehensive critical analysis of Goethe's literary output argues that the writer is an essential figure in German modernity. Chapter 3, "Narrative Fiction," focuses on Goethe's novels. Includes bibliography and index.

Wagner, Irmgard. *Goethe*. New York: Twayne, 1999. Excellent introduction to the author provides a chronological analysis of his novels and other works. Includes bibliographical references and index.

Williams, John R. *The Life of Goethe: A Critical Biography*. Malden, Mass.: Blackwell, 1998. Presents detailed examination of Goethe's major writings, including novels, lyric poems, and plays. Discusses Goethe's personal and literary reactions to historical events in Germany, his relationship with leading public figures of his day, and his influence on contemporary culture. Suggests that Goethe's creative work follows a distinct biographical profile. Includes an extensive bibliography.

NIKOLAI GOGOL

Born: Sorochintsy, Ukraine, Russian Empire (now in Ukraine); March 31, 1809
Died: Moscow, Russia; March 4, 1852
Also known as: Nikolai Vasilyevich Gogol

Principal long fiction

Myortvye dushi, 1842, 1855 (2 parts; *Dead Souls*, 1887)

Taras Bulba, 1842 (revision of his 1835 short story; English translation, 1886)

Other literary forms

Nikolai Gogol (GAW-guhl) authored many short stories, most of which are part of his "Ukrainian cycle" or his later "Petersburg cycle." He also wrote many plays, including *Revizor* (pr., pb. 1836; *The Inspector General*, 1890) and *Zhenit'ba* (pr., pb. 1842; *Marriage: A Quite Incredible Incident*, 1926), as well as a great deal of nonfiction, much of it collected in *Arabeski* (1835; *Arabesques*, 1982) and *Vybrannye mesta iz perepiski s druzyami* (1847; *Selected Passages from Correspon-*

dence with Friends, 1969). Gogol's *Polnoe sobranie sochinenii* (1940-1952; collected works), which includes unfinished works and drafts as well as his voluminous correspondence, fills fourteen volumes. All of Gogol's finished works, but not his drafts or correspondence, are available in English translation.

Achievements

Nikolai Gogol's first collection of short stories, *Vechera na khutore bliz Dikanki* (1831, 1832; *Evenings on a Farm near Dikanka*, 1926), made him famous, and his second collection, *Mirgorod* (1835; English translation, 1928), highlighted by the story "Taras Bulba," established his reputation as Russia's leading prose writer. While Gogol's early stories, set in the Ukraine, are for the most part conventionally Romantic, his later Petersburg cycle of short stories, among which "Zapiski sumasshedshego" ("Diary of a Madman") and "Shinel" ("The Overcoat") are two of the best known, marks the beginning of Russian critical realism. Gogol's comedic plays are classics and are as popular on the stage (and screen) today as they were in Gogol's lifetime.

Gogol's novel *Dead Souls* is rivaled only by Leo Tolstoy's *Voyna i mir* (1865-1869; *War and Peace*, 1886) as the greatest prose work of Russian literature. Russian prose fiction is routinely divided into two schools: the Pushkinian, which is objective, matter-of-fact, and sparing in its use of verbal devices; and the Gogolian, which is artful, ornamental, and exuberant in its use of ambiguity, irony, pathos, and a variety of figures and tropes usually associated with poetry. Tolstoy and Ivan Turgenev belong to the Pushkinian school; Fyodor Dostoevski, to the Gogolian. In his historical, critical, and moral essays, but especially in *Selected Passages from Correspondence with Friends*, Gogol established many of the principles of Russian conservative thought, anticipating the ideas of such writers as Dostoevski and Apollon Grigoryev.

Biography

Nikolai Vasilyevich Gogol, the son of a country squire, was born and educated in the Ukraine. Russian was to him a foreign language, which he mastered while attending secondary school in Nezhin, also in the Ukraine. After his graduation in 1828, Gogol went to St. Petersburg, where he joined the civil service. His first literary effort, "Hans Küchelgarten" (1829), a sentimental idyll in blank verse, was a failure, but his prose fiction immediately attracted attention. After the success of *Evenings on a Farm near Dikanka*, Gogol decided to devote himself entirely to his literary career. He briefly taught medieval history at St. Petersburg University (1834-1835) and thereafter lived the life of a freelance writer and journalist, frequently supported by wealthy patrons. The opening of his play *The Inspector General* at the Aleksandrinsky Theater in St. Petersburg on April 19, 1836, attended and applauded by Czar Nicholas I, was a huge success, but it also elicited vehement attacks by the reactionary press, enraged by Gogol's spirited satire of corruption and stupidity in the provincial administration, and Gogol decided to go abroad to escape the controversy.

From 1836 to 1848, Gogol lived abroad, mostly in Rome, returning to Russia for brief periods only. The year 1842 marked the high point of Gogol's career with the appearance of the first part of *Dead Souls* and the publication of a four-volume set of collected works, which contained some previously unpublished pieces, in particular the great short story "The Overcoat." After 1842, Gogol continued to work on part 2 of *Dead Souls*, but he was becoming increasingly preoccupied with questions of religion and morality. His book *Selected Passages from Correspondence with Friends*, actually a collection of essays in which Gogol defends traditional religious and moral values as well as the social status quo (including the institution of serfdom), caused a storm of protest, as liberals felt that it was flagrantly and evilly reactionary, while even many conservatives considered it to be unctuous and self-righteous.

Sorely hurt by the unfavorable reception of his book, Gogol almost entirely withdrew from literature. He returned to Russia for good in 1848 and spent the rest of his life in religious exercise and meditation. Shortly before his death, caused by excessive fasting and utter exhaustion, Gogol burned the final version of part 2 of *Dead Souls*. An earlier version was later discovered and published in 1855.

Analysis

The cover of the first edition of *Dead Souls*, designed by Nikolai Gogol himself, reads as follows: "*The Adven-*

tures of Chichikov or Dead Souls. A Poem by N. Gogol. 1842." "The Adventures of Chichikov" is in the smallest print, "Dead Souls" is more than twice that size, and "A Poem" is twice again the size of "Dead Souls." The word "or" is barely legible. The fact that "The Adventures of Chichikov" was inserted at the insistence of the censor, who felt that "Dead Souls" alone smacked of blasphemy, accounts for one-half of this typographical irregularity. The fact that "A Poem" (Russian *poema*, which usually designates an epic poem in verse) dominates the cover of a prose work that at first glance is anything but "poetic" also had its reasons, as will be seen.

Dead Souls

The plot structure of *Dead Souls* is simple. Chichikov, a middle-aged gentleman of decent appearance and pleasing manners, travels through the Russian provinces on what seems a mysterious quest: He buys up "dead souls," meaning serfs who have died since the last census but are still listed on the tax rolls until the next census. Along the way, he meets various types of Russian landowners: the sugary and insipid Manilov; the widow Korobochka, ignorant and superstitious but an efficient manager of her farm; the dashing Nozdryov, a braggart, liar, and cardsharp; the brutish but shrewd Sobakevich; and the sordid miser Plyushkin. Having returned to the nearby provincial capital to obtain legal title to his four-hundred-odd "souls," Chichikov soon comes under a cloud of suspicion and quickly leaves town. Only at this stage does the reader learn about Chichikov's past and the secret of the dead souls. A civil service official, Chichikov had twice reached the threshold of prosperity through cleverly devised depredations of the state treasury, but each time he had been foiled at the last moment. After his second fiasco, he had been allowed to resign with only a small sum saved from the clutches of his auditors. Undaunted, he had conceived yet another scheme: He would buy up a substantial number of "dead souls," mortgage them at the highest rate available, and disappear with the cash.

The plot of part 1 takes the story only this far. In what is extant of part 2, Chichikov is seen not only trying to buy more dead souls but also getting involved in other nefarious schemes. It also develops, however, that Chichikov is not happy with his sordid and insecure existence and that he dreams of an honest and virtuous life.

Nikolai Gogol. (Library of Congress)

He would be willing to mend his ways if he could only find a proper mentor who would give him the right start. There is reason to believe that Gogol planned to describe Chichikov's regeneration and return to the path of rightenousness in part 3. The whole plot thus follows the pattern of a picaresque novel, and many details of *Dead Souls* are, in fact, compatible with this genre, which was well established in Russian literature even before Gogol's day.

Actually, part 1 of *Dead Souls* is many things in addition to a picaresque novel: a humorous novel after the fashion of Charles Dickens's *Pickwick Papers* (1836-1837, serial; 1837, book), with which it was immediately compared by the critics; a social satire attacking the corruption and inefficiency of the imperial administration and the crudity and mental torpor of the landed gentry; a moral sermon in the form of grotesque character sketches; and, above all, an epic of Russia's abjection and hoped-for redemption. The characters of part 2, while copies, in a way, of those encountered in part 1, have redeeming traits and strike the reader as human beings rather than as caricatures. The landowner Tentetnikov, in particular, is clearly a prototype of Oblomov, the hero of Ivan Goncharov's immortal novel of that title (1859; English translation, 1915), and, altogether, part 2 of *Dead Souls* is a big step in the direction of the Russian realist novel of the 1850's and 1860's. The following observations apply to part 1, unless otherwise indicated.

The structure of *Dead Souls* is dominated by the road, as the work begins with a description of Chichikov's arrival at an inn of an unidentified provincial capital and ends with him back on the road, with several intervening episodes in which the hero is seen on his way to his next encounter with a potential purveyor of dead souls. Chichikov's tippling coachman, Selifan, and his three-horse carriage (*troika*) are often foregrounded in Gogol's narrative, and one of the three horses, the lazy and stubborn piebald, has become one of the best-known "characters" in all of Russian fiction. The celebrated *troika* passage concludes part 1. Vladimir Nabokov has written that critic Andrey Bely saw "the whole first volume of *Dead Souls* as a closed circle whirling on its axle and blurring the spokes, with the theme of the wheel cropping up at each new revolution on round Chichikov's part."

When Chichikov is not on the road, the narrative becomes a mirror, as each new character is reflected in Chichikov's mind with the assistance of the omniscient narrator's observations and elucidations. One contemporary critic said that reading *Dead Souls* was like walking down a hotel corridor, opening one door after another—and staring at another human monster each time.

The road and the mirror by no means exhaust Gogol's narrative attitudes. *Dead Souls* features some philosophical discussions on a variety of topics; many short narrative vignettes, such as when Chichikov dreamily imagines what some of his freshly acquired dead souls may have been like in life; an inserted novella, *The Tale of Captain Kopeikin*, told by the local postmaster, who suspects that Chichikov is in fact the legendary outlaw Captain Kopeikin; repeated apostrophes to the reader, discussing the work itself and the course to be taken in continuing it; and, last but not least, Gogol's much-debated lyric digressions. Altogether, while there is some dialogue in *Dead Souls*, the narrator's voice dominates throughout. In fact, the narrative may be described as the free flow of the narrator's stream of consciousness, drifting from observation to observation, image to image, and thought to thought. It is often propelled by purely verbal associations. A common instance of the latter is the so-called realized metaphor, such as when a vendor of hot mead, whose large red face is likened to a copper samovar, is referred to as "the samovar"; when Chichikov, threatened with bodily harm by an enraged Nozdryov and likened to a fortress under siege, suddenly becomes "the fortress"; or when the bearlike Sobakevich is casually identified as a "fair sized bear" in the role of landowner. It is also verbal legerdemain that eventually turns Sobakevich's whole estate into an extension of its owner: "Every object, every chair in Sobakevich's house seemed to proclaim: 'I, too, am Sobakevich!'"

Hyperbole is another device characteristic of Gogol's style. Throughout *Dead Souls*, grotesque distortions and exaggerations are presented as a matter of course—for example, when the scratching of the clerks' pens at the office where Chichikov seals his purchase of dead souls is likened to "the sound of several carts loaded with brushweed and driven through a forest piled with dead leaves a yard deep." Often the hyperbole is ironic, such as when the attire of local ladies is reported to be "of such fashionable pastel shades that one could not even give their names, to such a degree had the refinement of taste attained!"

A sure sign of the author's own point of view surfaces in frequent literary allusions and several passages in which Gogol digresses to discuss the theory of fiction—for example, the famous disquisition, introducing chapter 7, on the distinction between the writer who idealizes life and the writer who chooses to deal with real life. Gogol, who fancies himself to be a realist, wryly observes that "the judgment of his time does not recognize that much spiritual depth is required to throw light upon a picture taken from a despised stratum of life, and to exalt it into a pearl of creative art" but feels "destined by some wondrous power to go hand in hand with his heroes, to contemplate life in its entirety, life rushing past in all its enormity, amid laughter perceptible to the world and through tears that are unperceived by and unknown to it!" The phrases "to exalt it into a pearl of creative art" and "amid laughter perceptible to the world and through tears that are unperceived by and unknown to it" have become common Russian usage, along with many others in *Dead Souls*.

Dead Souls is studded with many outright digressions. It must be kept in mind, however, that the mid-nineteenth century novel was routinely used as a catchall for miscellaneous didactic, philosophical, critical, scholarly, and lyric pieces that were often only superficially, if at all, integrated into the texture of the larger work. Still, the number and nature of digressions in *Dead Souls* are exceptional even by the standards of a *roman feuilleton* of the 1840's. As described by Victor Erlich, two basic types of digressions are found in *Dead Souls:* "the lateral darts and the upward flights." The former are excursions into a great variety of aspects of Russian life, keenly observed, sharply focused, and always lively and colorful. For example, having observed that Sobakevich's head looks quite like a pumpkin, Gogol, in one of his many "Homeric similes," veers off into a village idyll about a peasant lad strumming a balalaika made from a pumpkin to win the heart of a "snowy-breasted and snowy-necked Maiden."

Gogol's upward flights are of a quite different order. They permit his imagination to escape the prosaic reality of Chichikov's experience and allow him to become a poet who takes a lofty view of Russia and its destiny. In several of these passages, Gogol's imagination becomes quite literally airborne. One of them, at the conclusion of chapter 5, begins with a lofty aerial panorama: "Even as an incomputable host of churches, of monasteries, with cupolas, bulbous domes, and crosses, is scattered all over holy and devout Russia, so does an incomputable multitude of tribes, generations, peoples swarm, flaunt their motley and scurry across the face of the earth." It ends in a rousing paean to "the Russian word which, like no other in the world, would burst out so, from out the very heart, which would seethe so and quiver and flutter so much like a living thing."

Early in chapter 11, Gogol produces another marvelous panoramic vision of Russia, apostrophized in the famous passage, "Russia, Russia! I behold thee—from my alien, beautiful, far-off vantage point I behold thee." (Gogol wrote most of *Dead Souls* while living in Italy.) The conclusion of this, the final chapter of part 1, then brings the most famous lines of prose in all of Russian literature, the *troika* passage in which a speeding three-horse carriage is elevated to a symbol of Russia's historical destiny. The intensity and plenitude of life and emotion in these and other airborne lyric passages stand in stark contrast to the drab world that is otherwise dominant in *Dead Souls*. These lyric digressions were challenged as incongruous and unnecessary even by some contemporary critics who, as do many critics today, failed to realize that Gogol's is a dual vision of manic-depressive intensity.

As a *poema* (epic poem), *Dead Souls* is a work that Gogol perceived as the poetic expression of an important religious-philosophical conception—that is, something on the order of Dante's *La divina commedia* (c. 1320; *The Divine Comedy*, 1802) or John Milton's *Paradise Lost* (1667, 1674). Incidentally, there is one rather inconsequential allusion to Dante in chapter 7, where one reads that a collegiate registrar "served our friends even as Virgil at one time had served Dante, and guided them to the Presence."

Immediately after the appearance of *Dead Souls*, critics were split into two camps: those who, like Konstantin Aksakov, greeted the work as the Russian national epic, found numerous Homeric traits in it, and perceived it as a true incarnation of the Russian spirit in all of its depth and plenitude, and those who, like Nikolai Alekseevich Polevoi and Osip Ivanovich Senkovsky, saw it as merely an entertaining, though rather banal and in places pretentious, humorous novel. The latter group—which included even the great critic Vissarion Belinsky, who otherwise felt that *Dead Souls* was a perfect quintessence of Russian life—found Gogol's attempts at philosophizing and solemn pathos merely pompous and false. There has never been agreement in this matter. Nevertheless, several passages in part 1, the whole drift of part 2, and a number of quite unequivocal statements made by Gogol in his correspondence (in *Selected Passages from Correspondence with Friends* and in his posthumous "Author's Confession") all suggest that Gogol did indeed perceive *Dead Souls* as a *Divine Comedy* of the Russian soul, with part 1 its *Inferno*, part 2 its *Purgatory*, and part 3 its *Paradise*.

How, then, is part 1 in fact an *Inferno*, a Russian Hell? It is set in a Hades of dead souls, of humans who lead a shadowy phantom existence bereft of any real meaning or direction. Thus, it must be understood that in the Romantic philosophy of Gogol's time, the "normal" existence of a European philistine was routinely called "illusory," "unreal," and even "ghostly," while the ideal quest of the artist or philosopher was considered "substantial," "real," and "truly alive." As Andrey Bely demonstrated most convincingly, all of part 1 is dominated by what he calls "the figure of fiction." Whatever is said or believed to be true is from beginning to end a fiction, as unreal as Chichikov's financial transactions. For example, when the good people of N. begin to suspect that something is wrong with Chichikov, some of them believe that he plans to abduct the Governor's daughter, others conjecture that he is really Captain Kopeikin, a highway robber of legendary fame, and some actually suspect that he is Napoleon escaped from his island exile, but nobody investigates his motive for buying dead souls. As Bely also demonstrated, even time and space in *Dead Souls* are fictitious: The text will not even allow one to determine the season of the year; Chichikov's itinerary, if methodically checked, is physically impossible; and so on. Behind the figure of fiction, there looms large the message that all earthly experience and wisdom are in fact illusory, as Gogol makes explicit in a philosophical digression found in chapter 10.

In this shadowy world of fiction there exist two kinds of dead souls. There are the dead serfs who are sold and mortgaged and who, in the process, acquire a real semblance of life. Mrs. Korobochka, as soon as she has understood that Chichikov is willing to pay her some money for her dead serfs, is afraid that he may underpay her and somewhat timidly suggests that "maybe I'll find some use for them in my own household." Sobakevich, who haggles about the price of each dead soul, insists on eloquently describing their skills and virtues, as though it really mattered. Chichikov himself firmly rejects an offer by the local authorities to provide him with a police escort for the souls he has purchased, asserting that "his peasants are all of eminently quiet disposition." The same night, however, when he returns home from a party thrown by the local police chief to honor the new owner of four hundred souls, he actually orders Selifan "to gather all the resettled peasants, so he can personally make a roll call of them." Selifan and Petrushka, Chichikov's lackey, barely manage to get their master to bed.

The humanitarian message behind all of this is obvious: How could a person who finds the buying and selling of dead souls "fantastic" and "absurd" have the effrontery to find the same business transactions involving living souls perfectly normal? This message applies not only to Russia in the age of serfdom (which ended only in 1861—that is, at about the same time formal slavery ended in the United States) but also to any situation in which human beings are reduced to their social or economic function.

The other dead souls are the landowners and government officials whom we meet in *Dead Souls*. As the critic Vasily Rozanov observed, the peculiar thing about Gogolian characters is that they have no souls; they have habits and appetities but no deeper human emotions or ideal strivings. This inevitably deprives them of their humanity and renders them two-dimensional personifications of their vices—caricatures. Sobakevich is a very shrewd talking bear. Nozdryov is so utterly worthless that he appears to be a mere appendage of his extraordinarily handsome, thick, and pitch-black sideburns, thinned out a bit from time to time, when their owner is caught cheating at cards and suffers a whisker pulling. Plyushkin's stony miserliness has deprived him of all feeling and has turned him, a rich landowner, into a beggar and an outcast of society. *Dead Souls* has many such caricatures, which have been likened to Brueghelian grotesque paintings. This analogy applies to the following passage in chapter 11, for example: "The clerks in the Treasury were especially distinguished for their unprepossessing and unsightly appearance. Some had faces for all the world like badly baked bread: one cheek would be all puffed out to one side, the chin slanting off to the other, the upper lip blown up into a big blister that, to top it all off, had burst."

As early as 1842, the critic Stepan Shevyrev suggested that *Dead Souls* represented a mad world, thus following an ancient literary and cultural tradition (which today is often referred to as that of the "carnival"). The massive absurdities, non sequiturs, and simply plain foolishness throughout the whole text could, for Gogol and for many of his readers, have only one message: That which poses for "real life" is in fact nothing but a ludicrous farce. The basic course of Gogol's imagination is that of a descent into a world of ridiculous, banal, and vile "nonbeing," from which it will from time to time rise to the heights of noble and inspired "being."

Taras Bulba

While *Dead Souls* is unquestionably Gogol's masterpiece, his only other work of long fiction, *Taras Bulba*, is not without interest. The 1835 version of this work is a historical novella; the 1842 version, almost twice as long and thus novel-sized, has many digressions and is at once more realistic and more gothic but also more patriotic, moralizing, and bigoted. The plot is essentially the same in both versions.

Taras Bulba is a Ukrainian Cossack leader, so proud of his two fine sons recently back from school in Kiev that he foments war against the hated Poles, so that Ostap and Andriy can prove their manhood in battle. The Cossacks are initially successful, and the Poles are driven back to the fortress city of Dubno. The Cossacks lay siege to it, and the city seems ready to fall when Andriy is lured to the city by a messenger from a beautiful Polish maiden with whom he had fallen in love as a student in Kiev. Blinded by her promises of love, Andriy turns traitor. The Cossacks' fortunes now take a turn for the worse. They are pressed hard by a Polish relief force. On the battlefield, Taras meets Andriy (now a Polish officer), orders him to dismount, and shoots him. The Cossacks, however, are defeated, and Ostap is taken prisoner. Old Taras makes his way to Warsaw, hoping to save him, but can only witness his son's execution. Having returned to the Ukraine, Taras becomes one of the leaders of yet another Cossack uprising against the king of Poland. When peace is made, Taras alone refuses to honor it. He continues to wreak havoc on the Poles all over the Ukraine but is finally captured by superior Polish forces. He dies at the stake, prophesying the coming of a Russian czar against whom no power on earth will stand.

There is little historical verity in *Taras Bulba*. Different details found in the text point to the fifteenth, sixteenth, and seventeenth centuries as the time of its action. It is thus an epic synthesis of the struggle of the Orthodox Ukraine to retain its independence from Catholic Poland. The battle scenes are patterned on those in the works of Vergil and Homer, and there are many conventional epic traits throughout, such as scores of brief scenes of single combat, catalogs of warriors' names, extended Homeric similes, orations, and, of course, the final solemn prophecy. Taras Bulba is a tragic hero who expiates his hubris with the loss of his sons and his own terrible death.

The earlier version of *Taras Bulba* serves mostly the glorification of the wild, carefree life at the Cossack army camp. In the later version, this truly inspired hymn to male freedom is obscured by a message of Russian nationalism, Orthodox bigotry, and nostalgia for a glorious past that never was. The novel features almost incessant baiting of Poles and Jews. Gogol's view of the war is a wholly unrealistic and romantic one: The reader is told of "the enchanting music of bullets and swords" and so on. From a literary viewpoint, *Taras Bulba* is a peculiar mixture of the historical novel in the manner of Sir Walter Scott and the gothic tale. The narrator stations himself above his hero, gently faulting him on some of his uncivilized traits, such as the excessive stock Taras puts in his drinking prowess or his maltreatment of his long-suffering wife. Rather often, however, the narrator descends to the manner of the folktale. His language swings wildly from coarse humor and naturalistic grotesque to solemn oratory and lyric digressions. Scenes of unspeakable atrocities are reported with relish, but some wonderful poems in prose are also presented, such as the well-known description of the Ukrainian steppe in the second chapter.

Altogether, *Taras Bulba* contains some brilliant writing but also some glaring faults. It immediately became a classic, and soon enough a school text, inasmuch as its jingoism met with the approval of the czar—and eventually of Soviet school administrators. Several film versions, Russian as well as Western, have been produced.

Although Gogol's production of fiction was quite small by nineteenth century standards, both his novels and his short stories have had extraordinary influence on the development of Russian prose—an influence that was still potent at the end of the twentieth century, as witnessed by the works of Andrei Sinyavsky and other writers of the Third Emigration.

Victor Terras

Other major works

SHORT FICTION: *Vechera na khutore bliz Dikanki*, 1831, 1832 (2 volumes; *Evenings on a Farm near Dikanka*, 1926); *Arabeski*, 1835 (*Arabesques*, 1982);

Mirgorod, 1835 (English translation, 1928); *The Complete Tales of Nikolai Gogol*, 1985 (2 volumes; Leonard J. Kent, editor).

PLAYS: *Revizor*, pr., pb. 1836 (*The Inspector General*, 1890); *Utro delovogo cheloveka*, pb. 1836 (revision of *Vladimir tretey stepeni*; *An Official's Morning*, 1926); *Igroki*, pb. 1842 (*The Gamblers*, 1926); *Lakeyskaya*, pb. 1842 (revision of *Vladimir tretey stepeni*; *The Servants' Hall*, 1926); *Otryvok*, pb. 1842 (revision of *Vladimir tretey stepeni*; *A Fragment*, 1926); *Tyazhba*, pb. 1842 (revision of *Vladimir tretey stepeni*; *The Lawsuit*, 1926); *Vladimir tretey stepeni*, pb. 1842 (wr. 1832); *Zhenit'ba*, pr., pb. 1842 (wr. 1835; *Marriage: A Quite Incredible Incident*, 1926); *The Government Inspector, and Other Plays*, 1926.

POETRY: *Hanz Kuechelgarten*, 1829.

NONFICTION: *Vybrannye mesta iz perepiski s druzyami*, 1847 (*Selected Passages from Correspondence with Friends*, 1969); *Letters of Nikolai Gogol*, 1967.

MISCELLANEOUS: *The Collected Works*, 1922-1927 (6 volumes); *Polnoe sobranie sochinenii*, 1940-1952 (14 volumes); *The Collected Tales and Plays of Nikolai Gogol*, 1964.

Bibliography

Bojanowska, Edyta M. *Nikolai Gogol: Between Ukrainian and Russian Nationalism.* Cambridge, Mass.: Harvard University Press, 2007. Analyzes Gogol's life and works in terms of his conflicted national identity. Gogol was born in Ukraine when it was a part of the Russian empire; Bojanowska describes how he was engaged with questions of Ukrainian nationalism and how his works presented a bleak and ironic portrayal of Russia and Russian themes.

Erlich, Victor. *Gogol.* New Haven, Conn.: Yale University Press, 1969. Provides an accessible and evenhanded discussion of Gogol for nonspecialists. Focuses on Gogol's oeuvre, dealing with much of the "myth" about the author, and supplies interesting background to the making of Gogol's works.

Fanger, Donald L. *The Creation of Nikolai Gogol.* Cambridge, Mass.: Belknap Press of Harvard University Press, 1979. Digs deeply into background material and includes discussion of Gogol's works both published and unpublished in an effort to reveal the genius of Gogol's creative power. Worthwhile in many respects, particularly for the wealth of details provided about Gogol's life and milieu. Includes endnotes and index.

Gippius, V. V. *Gogol.* Translated by Robert Maguire. Ann Arbor, Mich.: Ardis, 1981. Originally written in 1924, this famous monograph supplies not only the view of a fellow countryman but also a vast, informed, and intellectual analysis of both the literary tradition in which Gogol wrote and his innovation and contribution to that tradition. Vastly interesting and easily accessible. Includes notes and a detailed list of Gogol's works.

Luckyj, George Stephen Nestor. *The Anguish of Mykola Hohol a.k.a. Nikolai Gogol.* Toronto, Ont.: Canadian Scholars' Press, 1998. Explores Gogol's life and discusses how it affected his work. Includes bibliographical references and index.

Maguire, Robert A. *Exploring Gogol.* Stanford, Calif.: Stanford University Press, 1994. One of the most comprehensive studies of Gogol's ideas and entire writing career available in English. Includes chronology, detailed notes, and extensive bibliography.

_______, ed. *Gogol from the Twentieth Century: Eleven Essays.* Princeton, N.J.: Princeton University Press, 1974. Collection of essays represents some of the most famous and influential opinions on Gogol in the twentieth century. Following a lengthy introduction by the editor and translator, the contributors address and elucidate some of the most problematic aspects of Gogol's stylistics, thematics, and other compositional elements. Includes bibliography and index.

Setchkarev, Vsevolod. *Gogol: His Life and Works.* Translated by Robert Kramer. New York: New York University Press, 1965. Standard work on Gogol is still often recommended in undergraduate courses. Concentrates on both the biography and the works, seen individually and as an artistic system. Very straightforward and easily readable.

Spieker, Sven, ed. *Gogol: Exploring Absence—Negativity in Nineteenth Century Russian Literature.* Bloomington, Ind.: Slavica, 1999. Collection of essays focuses on the negativity in *Dead Souls* and Gogol's other works and in the works of other Russian writers. Includes bibliography and index.

Troyat, Henri. *Divided Soul*. Translated by Nancy Amphoux. Garden City, N.Y.: Doubleday, 1973. Provides perhaps the most information on Gogol's life available in English in a single volume. Demonstrates masterfully how Gogol's life and work are inextricably intertwined and does not neglect the important role that "God's will" played in Gogol's life, as the thread that lends the greatest cohesion to the diverse developments in his creative journey. Includes some interesting illustrations as well as bibliography, notes, and index.

Weiner, Adam. "The Evils of *Dead Souls*." In *By Authors Possessed: The Demonic Novel in Russia*. Evanston, Ill.: Northwestern University Press, 1998. Chapter focusing on *Dead Souls* is included in a wider analysis of nineteenth and twentieth century Russian "demonic novels," defined as novels in which the protagonists are incarnated with the evil presence of the Devil.

WILLIAM GOLDING

Born: St. Columb Minor, Cornwall, England; September 19, 1911

Died: Perranarworthal, Cornwall, England; June 19, 1993

Also known as: William Gerald Golding

Principal long fiction

Lord of the Flies, 1954
The Inheritors, 1955
Pincher Martin, 1956 (also known as *The Two Deaths of Christopher Martin*)
Free Fall, 1959
The Spire, 1964
The Pyramid, 1967
Darkness Visible, 1979
Rites of Passage, 1980 (with *Close Quarters* and *Fire down Below*, known as *A Sea Trilogy*)
The Paper Men, 1984
Close Quarters, 1987
Fire down Below, 1989
To the Ends of the Earth: A Sea Trilogy, 1991 (includes *Rites of Passage*, *Close Quarters*, and *Fire down Below*)
The Double Tongue, 1995

Other literary forms

William Golding's first and only book of poetry, titled simply *Poems*, was published in 1934. *Envoy Extraordinary*, a 1956 novella, was recast in 1958 in the form of a play, *The Brass Butterfly*; this work, set in Roman times, uses irony to examine the value of "modern" inventions. *Envoy Extraordinary* was published along with two other novellas, *The Scorpion God* and *Clonk Clonk*, in a 1971 collection bearing the title *The Scorpion God*.

Golding also produced nonfiction; his book reviews in *The Spectator* in the period 1960 to 1962 frequently took the form of personal essays. Many of his essays and autobiographical pieces were collected in *The Hot Gates, and Other Occasional Pieces* (1965). *A Moving Target* (1982) is another set of essays; *An Egyptian Journal* (1985) is a travelogue. Golding also gave numerous interviews explaining his work; these have appeared in a variety of journals and magazines.

Achievements

Sir William Golding is without doubt one of the major British novelists of the post-World War II era. He depicted in many different ways the anguish of modern humanity as it gropes for meaning and redemption in a world where the spiritual has been all but crushed by the material. His themes deal with guilt, responsibility, and salvation. He depicts the tension between individual fallenness and social advance, or, to put it differently, the cost of progress to the individual.

Golding's works portray a period in which the last vestiges of an optimistic belief in evolutionary progress collapsed under the threat of nuclear destruction. In creating these works, Golding moved the classic British novel tradition forward both in stylistic and formal technique and in the opening up of a new, contemporary social and theological dialectic.

Golding was a fellow of the Royal Society of Literature (elected in 1955), and in 1983 he received the Nobel Prize in Literature. He was awarded the James Tait Black Memorial Prize in 1979 for *Darkness Visible* and the Booker Prize in 1980 for *Rites of Passage*. He was knighted in 1989.

Biography

Born in the county of Cornwall in the southwest corner of England, the son of a rationalistic schoolmaster, William Gerald Golding had a relatively isolated childhood. Eventually his family moved to Marlborough, in Wiltshire, where his father was a science teacher. There Golding received his high school education while revisiting Cornwall frequently. He graduated from Brasenose College, Oxford, in science and literature. The choice of arts over science was made at the university, but scientific interests and approaches can be easily discerned in his literary work. Each of Golding's novels is, in a way, a new experiment set up to test a central hypothesis.

After the unsuccessful publication of a book of poetry in 1934, Golding moved to London and participated in fringe theater without achieving anything of significance. In 1939 he married Ann Brookfield and accepted a teaching post at Bishop Wordsworth's School, Salisbury, also in Wiltshire. Soon after the outbreak of World War II, he joined the Royal Navy; during his service, he saw extensive action against German warships, was adrift for three days in the English Channel, and participated in the Normandy landings.

After the war, he resumed teaching and tried writing novels. His first four were highly imitative and were met only with editorial refusals. He then decided to write as he wanted, not as he thought he ought to write. This shift in approach led to the immediate publication of *Lord of the Flies* in 1954, a work that became almost at once a landmark on the British literary scene. Golding was able to follow this achievement with three more novels in the space of only five years, by which time paperback versions were being issued on both sides of the Atlantic. In 1961 he retired from teaching, becoming for two years a book reviewer with *The Spectator*, one of the leading British weekly cultural reviews. In *The Paper Men*, Golding depicts a novelist whose first novel turned out to be a gold mine for him—an autobiographical echo, no doubt.

After the publication of *The Pyramid* in 1967, when Golding was fifty-six years old, there came rather a long silence, and many people assumed that he had brought his career to a close. With the publication of *Darkness Visible* twelve years later, however, a steady stream of new novels emerged, including a trilogy. This second phase also marked Golding's reception of various prizes, including the Nobel Prize in Literature, and his being knighted, a comparatively rare honor for a novelist in Britain.

Golding had one son and one daughter. He and his wife returned to Cornwall to live in 1984. Two years after his death in 1993, his nearly completed final novel *The Double Tongue* was published.

Analysis

William Golding, like his older British contemporary Graham Greene, is a theological novelist: That is to say, his main thematic material focuses on particular theological concerns, in particular sin and guilt, innocence and its loss, individual responsibility and the possibility of atonement for mistakes made, and the need for spiritual revelation. Unlike Greene, however, he does not write out of a particular Christian, or even religious, belief system; the dialectic he sets up is neither specifically Catholic (like Greene's) nor Protestant. In fact, Golding's dialectic is set up in specific literary terms, in that it is with other works of literature that he argues, rather than with theological or philosophical positions per se. The texts with which he argues do represent such positions or make certain cultural assumptions of such positions; however, it is through literary technique that he argues—paralleling, echoing, deconstructing—rather than through narratorial didacticism.

Golding's achievement is a literary tour de force. The British novel has never contained theological dialectic easily, except at a superficial level, let alone a depiction of transcendence. Golding accepted the nineteenth century novel tradition but modified it extensively. Each novel represented a fresh attempt for him to refashion the language and the central consciousness of that tradition.

William Golding. (© The Nobel Foundation)

Sometimes he pushed it beyond the limits of orthodox mimetic realism, and hence some of his novels have been called fables, allegories, or myths. In general, however, his central thrust is to restate the conflict between individuals and their society in contemporary terms and, in doing this, to question at a fundamental level many cultural assumptions and to point up the loss of moral and spiritual values in twentieth century Western civilization—an enterprise in which most nineteenth century novelists were similarly involved for their own time.

Lord of the Flies

Golding's first and most famous novel, *Lord of the Flies*, illustrates this thesis well. Although there is a whole tradition of island-castaway narratives, starting with one of the earliest novels in English literature, Daniel Defoe's *Robinson Crusoe* (1719), the text with which Golding clearly had in mind to argue was R. M. Ballantyne's *Coral Island* (1858), written almost exactly one hundred years before *Lord of the Flies*. The names of Ballantyne's three schoolboy heroes (Ralph, Jack, and Peterkin) are taken over, with Peterkin becoming Simon (the biblical reversion being significant), and in the novel Golding parodies various episodes in Ballantyne's book—for example, the pigsticking.

Ballantyne's yarn relied on the English public school ethos that boys educated within a British Christian discipline would survive anything and in fact would be able to control their environment—in miniature, the whole British imperialistic enterprise of the nineteenth century. Most desert-island narratives do make the assumption that Western men can control their environment, assuming that they are moral, purposeful, and religious. Golding subverts all these suppositions: Except for a very few among them, the abandoned schoolboys, significantly younger than Ballantyne's and more numerous (making a herd instinct possible), soon lose the veneer of the civilization they have acquired. Under Jack's leadership, they paint their faces, hunt pigs, and then start killing one another. They ritually murder Simon, the mystic, whose transcendental vision of the Lord of the Flies (a pig's head on a pole) is of the evil within. They also kill Piggy, the rationalist. The novel ends with the pack pursuing Ralph, the leader democratically elected at the beginning; the boys are prepared to burn the whole island to kill him.

Ironically, the final conflagration serves as a powerful signal for rescue (earlier watch fires having been pathetically inadequate), and, in a sudden reversal, an uncomprehending British naval officer lands on the beach, amazed at the mud-covered, dirty boys before him. Allegorically it might be thought that as this world ends in fire, a final divine intervention will come. Ironically, however, the adult world that the officer represents is also destroying itself as effectively, in a nuclear war. Salvation remains problematic and ambiguous.

What lifts *Lord of the Flies* away from simple allegory is not only the ambiguities but also the dense poetic texture of its language. The description of Simon's death is often quoted as brilliantly heightened prose—the beauty of the imagery standing in stark contrast to the brutality of his slaying—but almost any passage in the novel yields its own metaphorical textures and suggestive symbolism. Golding's rich narrative descriptions serve to point up the poverty of the boys' language, which can only dwell on basics—food, defecation, fears and night terrors, killings. Golding's depiction of the children is immediately convincing. The adult intervention (the dead airman, the naval officer) is perhaps not quite so, being too clearly fabular. In general, however, the power of the novel derives from the tensions set up between the book's novelistic realism and its fabular and allegorical qualities. The theological dialectic of humanity's fallenness (not only the boys') and the paper-thin veneer of civilization emerges inexorably out of this genre tension.

The Inheritors

The thinness of civilization forms the central thesis of Golding's second novel, *The Inheritors*. The immediate literary dialectic is set up with H. G. Wells's *The Outline of History: Being a Plain History of Life and Mankind* (1920), which propounds the typical social evolutionism common from the 1850's onward. At a more general level, Golding's novel might also be seen as an evolutionary version of John Milton's *Paradise Lost* (1667): Satan's temptation to Eve is a temptation to progress; the result is the Fall. Just as Adam and Eve degrade themselves with drunken behavior, so do Golding's Neanderthal protagonists, Lok and Fa, when they stumble over the remains of the cannibalistic "festivities" of *Homo sapiens*.

Golding subverts the Wellsian thesis that Neanderthals were totally inferior by depicting them as innocent, gentle, intuitive, playful, and loving. They stand in ironic contrast to the group of *Homo sapiens* who eventually annihilate them, except for a small baby whom they kidnap (again reversing a short story by Wells, in which it is Neanderthals who kidnap a human baby). The humans experience terror, lust, rage, drunkenness, and murder, and their religion is propitiatory only. By contrast, the Neanderthals have a taboo against killing anything, and their reverence for Oa, the earth mother, is gentle and numinous in quality.

As in *Lord of the Flies*, the conclusion is formed by an ironic reversal—the reader suddenly sees from the humans' perspective. The last line reads, "He could not see if the line of darkness had an ending." It is a question Golding is posing: Has the darkness of the human heart an end?

Golding's technique in *The Inheritors* is remarkable: He succeeds in convincing the reader that primitive consciousness could have looked like this. He creates language that conveys that consciousness, yet is articulate enough to engage one imaginatively so that one respects the Neanderthals. He explores the transition from intuition and pictorial thinking to analogous and metaphoric thought. The ironic treatment of *Homo sapiens* is done also through the limits of Neanderthal perceptions and consciousness. Unfortunately, humans, as fallen creatures, can supply all too easily the language for the evil that the Neanderthals lack.

Pincher Martin

Golding's third novel, *Pincher Martin* (first published in the United States as *The Two Deaths of Christopher Martin*), returns to the desert-island tradition. The immediate dialectic is perhaps with Robinson Crusoe, the sailor who single-handedly carves out an island home by the strength of his will aided by his faith. Pincher Martin is here the faithless antihero, although this is not immediately apparent. He, like Crusoe, appears to survive a wreck (Martin's destroyer is torpedoed during the war); he kicks off seaboots and swims to a lonely island-rock in the Atlantic. With tremendous strength of will, he appears to survive by eating raw shellfish, making rescue signals, forcing an enema into himself, and keeping sane and purposeful.

In the end, however, his sanity appears to disintegrate. Almost to the end it is quite possible to believe that Christopher Martin finally succumbs to madness and death only after a heroic, indeed Promethean, struggle against Fate and the elements. The last chapter, however, presents an even greater reversal than those in the first two novels, dispelling all of this as a false reading: Martin's drowned body is found washed up on a Scottish island; his seaboots are still on his feet. In other words, the episode on the rock never actually took place. The reading of *Pincher Martin* thus becomes deliberately problematic in a theological sense. The rock must be an illusion, an effort of the will indeed, but an effort after physical death. It is not that all of one's life flashes before one's eyes while one drowns, though that does happen with Martin's sordid memories of his lust, greed, and terror; it is more that the text is formed by Martin's ongoing dialectic with, or rather against, his destiny, which he sees as annihilation. An unnameable god is identified with the terror and darkness of the cellar of his childhood memories. His will, in its Promethean pride, is creating its own alternative. Theologically, this alternative can only be Purgatory or Hell, since it is clearly not heaven. Satan in *Paradise Lost* says, "Myself am Hell": Strictly, this is Martin's position, since he refuses the purgatorial possibilities in the final revelation of God, with his mouthless cry of "I shit on your heaven!" God, in his compassion, strikes Martin into annihilation with his "black lightning."

Free Fall

Golding's first three novels hardly suggested that he was writing from within any central tradition of the British novel. All three are highly original in plot, for all of their dialectic with existing texts, and in style and technique. In his next novel, *Free Fall*, Golding writes much more recognizably within the tradition of both the bildungsroman (the novel of character formation) and the *Künstlerroman* (the novel of artistic development). Sammy Mountjoy, a famous artist, is investigating his past life, but with the question in mind, "When did I lose my freedom?" The question is not in itself necessarily theological, but Sammy's search is conducted in specifically theological categories.

It has been suggested that the literary dialectic is with Albert Camus's *La Chute* (1956; *The Fall*, 1957), a novella published some three years earlier. Camus's existentialism sees no possibility of redemption or regeneration once the question has been answered; his protagonist uses the question, in fact, to gain power over others by exploiting their guilt, so the whole search would seem inauthentic. Golding sees such a search as vital: His position seems to be that no person is born in sin, or fallen, but inevitably at some stage, each person chooses knowingly to sin. At that moment the individual falls and loses the freedom to choose. The only possibility of redemption is to recognize that moment, to turn from it, and to cry out, "Help me!"

This is Sammy's cry when he is locked in a German prisoner-of-war camp and interrogated. His physical release from his cell is also a spiritual release, a moment of revelation described in Pentecostal terms of renewal and a new artistic vision. His moment of fall, which he discovers only near the end of the book (which is here culmination rather than reversal), was when he chose to seduce Beatrice (the name of Dante's beloved inspiration also), whatever the cost and despite a warning that "sooner or later the sacrifice is always regretted."

Other theological perspectives are introduced. Two of Sammy's teachers form an opposition: the rational, humanistic, likable Nick Shales and the religious, intense, but arrogant Miss Pringle. Sammy is caught in the middle, wanting to affirm the spiritual but drawn to the materialist. The dilemma goes back in the English novel to George Eliot. Though Golding cannot accept Eliot's moral agnosticism, he has to accept her inexorable moral law of cause and effect: Sammy's seduction of Beatrice has left her witless and insane. The scene in the prison cell is balanced by the scene in the mental institution. Redemption costs; the past remains. The fall may be arrested and even reversed, but only through self-knowledge and full confession.

The Spire

In *Free Fall*, Golding chose for the first time to use first-person narrative. Before that he had adopted a third-person narrative technique that stayed very close to the consciousness of the protagonists. In *The Spire*, Golding could be said to have perfected this latter technique. Events are seen not only through the eyes of Dean Jocelin but also in his language and thought processes. As in Henrik Ibsen's play *Bygmester Solness* (pb. 1892; *The Master Builder*, 1893), Golding's protagonist has an obsessive drive to construct a church tower, or rather a spire on a tower, for his cathedral lacks both. (Inevitably one takes the cathedral to be Salisbury, whose medieval history is almost identical, although it is not named.) Ibsen's play deals with the motivation for such an obsession, the price to be paid, and the spiritual conflicts. Golding, however, is not so much in a dialectic situation with the Ibsen play as using it as his base, agreeing with Ibsen when the latter talks of "the power of ideals to kill." At the end of the novel, the spire has been built in the face of tremendous technical difficulties, but Jocelin lies dying, the caretaker and his wife have been killed, the master builder, Roger, is a broken man, and the whole life of the cathedral has been disrupted.

Thus Golding raises the question of cost again: What is the cost of progress? Is it progress? The power of the book is that these questions can be answered in many different ways, and each way searches out new richness from the text. The patterning of moral and theological structures allows for almost endless combinations. The novel can also be read in terms of the cost of art—the permanence of art witnessing to humanity's spirituality and vision, as against the Freudian view of art as sublimation and neurotic outlet, the price of civilization.

By staying very close to Jocelin's consciousness, the reader perceives only slowly, as he does, that much of his motivation and drive is not quite as visionary and spiritual as he first thinks. Freudian symbolism and imagery increasingly suggest sexual sublimation, especially centered on Goody Pangall, whom he calls "his daughter in God." In fact, much later one learns that he received his appointment only because his aunt was the king's mistress for a while. Jocelin manipulates people more and more consciously to get the building done and chooses, perhaps unconsciously at first, to ignore the damage to people, especially the four people he regards as his "pillars" to the spire. Ironically, he too is a pillar, and he damages himself, physically, emotionally, and spiritually (he is almost unable to pray by the end, and has no confessor). Despite all the false motives, however, the novel suggests powerfully that there really has been a true vision that has been effected, even if marred by humanity's fallenness and "total depravity," every part affected by the fall.

The language of *The Spire* is the most poetic that Golding attempted. The density of imagery, recurring motifs, and symbolism both psychological and theological blend into marvelous rhythms of ecstasy and horror. The interweaving of inner monologue, dialogue, and narrative dissolves the traditional tight bounds of time and space of the novel form, to create an impassioned intensity where the theological dialectic takes place, not with another text, but within the levels of the moral, spiritual, and metaphoric consciousness of the text itself.

The Pyramid

After the verbal pyrotechnics of *The Spire*, Golding's next novel, *The Pyramid*, seems very flat, despite its title. It returns to *Free Fall* in its use of first-person narrative, to a modified form of its structure (flashbacks and memories to provide a personal pattern), and to contemporary social comedy, strongly echoing Anthony Trollope. The language is spare and unadorned, as perhaps befits the protagonist, Olly, who, unlike Sammy Mountjoy, has turned away from art and spirit to become *un homme moyen sensual*. His life has become a defense against love, but as a petit bourgeois he has been protected against Sammy's traumatic upbringing, and so one feels little sympathy for him. Theological and moral dialectic is muted, and the social commentary and comedy have been better done by other novelists, although a few critics have made out a case for a rather more complex structuring than is at first evident.

Darkness Visible

Perhaps the flatness of *The Pyramid* suggests that Golding had for the time being run out of impetus. He published only two novellas in the next twelve years, and then, quite unexpectedly, *Darkness Visible* appeared. In some ways this work echoes Charles Williams, the writer of a number of religious allegorical novels in the 1930's and 1940's. The reality of spiritual realms of light and darkness is made by Golding as explicitly as by Williams, especially in Matty, the "holy fool." Golding never quite steps into allegory, however, any more than he did in his first novel. His awareness of good and evil takes on a concreteness that owes much to Joseph Conrad. Much of the feel of the novel is Dickensian, if not its structure: The grotesque serves to demonstrate the "foolishness of the wise," as with Charles Dickens.

The book divides into three parts centering on Matty, orphaned and hideously burned in the bombing of London during the war. At times he keeps a journal and thus moves the narrative into the first person. The second part, by contrast, focuses on Sophy, the sophisticated twin daughter of a professional chess player (the rationalist), and overwhelmingly exposes the rootlessness and anomie of both contemporary youth culture and the post-1960's bourgeoisie (the children of Olly's generation). The third part concerns a bizarre kidnapping plot in which Matty and Sophy nearly meet as adversaries; this is the "darkness visible" (the title coming from the hell of *Paradise Lost*). The end remains ambiguous. Golding attempts a reversal again: The kidnap has been partially successful. Matty has not been able to protect the victims, nor Sophy to complete her scheme, but still children are kidnapped.

Central themes emerge: childhood and innocence corrupted; singleness of purpose, which can be either for good or for evil (contrast also Milton's single and double darkness in *Comus*, 1634); and the foolishness of the world's wisdom. "Entropy" is a key word, and Golding, much more strongly than hitherto, comments on the decline of Great Britain. Above all, however, Golding's role as a novelist of transcendence is reemphasized: Moments of revelation are the significant moments of knowledge. Unfortunately, revelation can come from dark powers as well as from those of the light. Ultimately, Golding's vision is Miltonic, as has been suggested. The theological dialectic is revealed as that between the children of light and the children of darkness.

A Sea Trilogy

When *Rites of Passage* followed *Darkness Visible* one year later, Golding had no intention of writing a trilogy (now generally called *A Sea Trilogy*). It was only later he realized that he had "left all those poor sods in the middle of the sea and needed to get them to Australia." The trilogy was well received, perhaps because the plot and themes are relatively straightforward and unambiguous, and the social comedy is more obvious than the theological dialectic. The trilogy fits well into the bildungsroman tradition of Dickens's *Great Expectations* (1860-1861, serial; 1861, book) in that it follows the education of a snob, Edmund Talbot, who, under the patronage of an aristocratic and influential godfather, is embarking on a political career by taking up an appointment in the new colony of New South Wales, Australia, in 1810. It is also enlivened by Golding's wide knowledge of sailing ships and life at sea; the trilogy is the fullest literary expression of this interest he allowed himself.

The narrative proceeds in a leisurely fashion in the first person as Edmund decides to keep a diary. In *Rites of Passage*, the plot focuses on the death of one of the passengers, a ridiculous young clergyman, the Reverend Robert James Colley. He is made the butt of everyone's fun, including that of the ordinary sailors. As the result of the shame of a joke, where he is made drunk and then engages in homosexual sex, he more or less wills himself to die. Captain Anderson covers up the incident—at which Edmund, for the first time, feels moral outrage and vows to expose the captain to his godfather when he can. The moral protest is vitiated, however, by Edmund's use of power and privilege.

In *Close Quarters*, Edmund's education continues. As conditions aboard ship deteriorate, he increases in stature, losing his aristocratic bearing and becoming willing to mix socially. His relationship with Summers, the most morally aware of the ship's lieutenants, is good for him in particular. He also shows himself sensitive: He weeps at a woman's song, he falls in love (as opposed to the lust in *Rites of Passage*), and he admires Colley's written style (Colley, too, has left behind a journal). He suffers physically and shows courage. His falling in love is delightfully described, quite unselfconsciously. He learns, too, the limits of his power: The elements control everything. The speed of the ship runs down as weeds grow on its underside, reintroducing the entropy motif of *Darkness Visible*. He cannot prevent suicide or death. As the novel proceeds, the "ship of fools" motif of late medieval literature becomes very strong. Edmund is no more and no less a fool than the others.

Fire Down Below closes the trilogy as the ship docks in Sidney Cove, and Edmund is reunited happily with the young lady he met. The ending seems to be social comedy, until one realizes that Summers's fear, that a fire lit belowdecks to forge a metal band around a broken mast is still smoldering, is proved true. The anchored ship bursts into flame, and Summers is killed, having just been given promotion, partly through Edmund's efforts. Despite this tragedy, the ending is Dickensian, for the voyage has turned into a quest for love for Edmund, and love has helped mark his way with moral landmarks. Edmund has learned much, although at the end he has still far to go. The ending is perhaps the most mellow of all Golding's endings: If Australia is not "the new Jerusalem," it is not hell either, and if Edmund lacks spirituality, he is yet more than *un homme moyen sensual*.

The Paper Men

The Paper Men is, like *Free Fall*, a *Künstlerroman*. The style is much more akin to that of twentieth century American confessional literature, especially Saul Bellow's. Golding's Wilfred Barclay could easily be a Henderson or a Herzog, with the same energetic, somewhat zany style, and with the themes of flight and pursuit in a frantic search for identity. Unusually for Golding, the novel seems to be repeating themes and structures, if not style, and perhaps for that reason has not made the same impact as his other novels. Wilfred's revelation of the transcendent in an ambiguous spiritual experience of Christ (or Pluto) marks the high point of the novel.

The Double Tongue

Golding's final novel, *The Double Tongue*, was still in its third draft at the time of his death. For the first time he uses a female first-person voice; also for the first time, he employs a classical Greek setting. Arieka is the prophetess, or "Pythia," of the renowned Delphic oracle, but during a period of its decline after the Roman occupation. She tells of her own calling, her first experience of the prophetic, and of the continuing marginalization of the oracle. The male presence is represented by Ionides, the high priest of Zeus and master in charge of the sacred complex of Delphi and its wider network. The only other full character is the slave-librarian, Perseus.

The style of the novel is sparer and more relaxed than that of Golding's earlier novels, with few characters and minimal plot. Its interest lies, as in *The Paper Men*, with the nature of epiphany and with whether the experience of transcendence actualizes anything of significance in an increasingly secular world. The political genius of Rome, and even the literary legacy of the Ancient Greek writers, seem much more powerful influences. The sacred is reduced almost to superstition: The questions posed to the oracle become more and more trivial.

Ionides, while institutionally having to acknowledge the sacred, behaves as if the human spirit is the ultimate source of the prophetic. Arieka, having been seized, or "raped," by Dionysos, the god of prophecy, knows the truth to be otherwise, but even she increasingly feels that her prophetic gift has ceased to be supernatural and has become a natural expression of her human wisdom. In a way, this concern with the prophetic can be traced back to Simon in *The Lord of the Flies*, and then to the form of the *Künstlerroman*. Unlike the latter, however, the context here is specifically sacred, and it would be a mistake to deconstruct the novel in terms of the nature of artistic inspiration. Nevertheless, the problematic nature of inspiration, whether divine or poetic, is as real to Golding in his last novel as in, say, *The Spire*.

The setting of a declining Greece continues the concern with entropy so powerfully expressed in *Darkness Visible*. Signs of cultural entropy include the growth of "copying" manuscripts rather than creating texts, the marginalization of the transcendent, and the *trahison des clercs*—Ionides is found to be plotting a pathetic revolt against Roman hegemony. Politics has undermined any integrity he had.

There would not appear to be a specific subtext with which Golding is arguing in *The Double Tongue*. The novel bears remarkable similarities to C. S. Lewis's final, and most literary, novel, *Till We Have Faces: A Myth Retold* (1956), also set in classical Greek times. In both, a female consciousness aware of its own physical ugliness yet possessing real power undergoes a spiritual journey with multifarious symbolic levels. Lewis's novel, however, ends with epiphany as closure; Golding's begins with it, and the rest of the novel seeks ambiguously to give it meaning. Golding's epiphany here is the god's laughter, at least that laughter of which Arieka is aware.

Although each Golding novel, with a few exceptions, is a new "raid on the inarticulate," certain thematic and technical features remain constant over the years. Golding's moral and didactic concerns consistently sought theological grounding out of which to construct a critique of the lostness and fallenness of humankind, and specifically of contemporary Western civilization, with its spiritual bankruptcy. In this quest there is a line of continuity back to George Eliot and Charles Dickens in the English novel tradition. In his affirmation of the primacy of the spiritual over the material, Golding echoes not only them but also, in different ways, Thomas Hardy and D. H. Lawrence. In his vision of the darkness of the human soul, unenlightened by any transcendent revelation, he follows Joseph Conrad.

Golding also sought, as did E. M. Forster and Lawrence, to find a style that would escape the materiality of prose and attain the revelatory transcendence of poetry. The result was usually dramatic, incarnational metaphors and motifs. The mode of Golding's novels is usually confessional, almost Augustinian at times, coming from a single consciousness, though often with a sudden reversal at the end to sustain an ambiguous dialectic.

There is in Golding no articulated framework of beliefs: Transcendence lies ultimately beyond the articulate. God is there, and revelation is not only possible but also necessary and salvific. The revelation remains ambiguous, fleeting, and numinous, however, rather than normative. In the end, this often means that Golding's social critique, of the moral entropy of Britain in particular, comes over more powerfully than the darkness that is the refusal of the terror of believing in God.

David Barratt

OTHER MAJOR WORKS

SHORT FICTION: *The Scorpion God: Three Short Novels*, 1971.

PLAYS: *The Brass Butterfly*, pr., pb. 1958.

POETRY: *Poems*, 1934.

RADIO PLAYS: *Miss Pulkinhorn*, 1960; *Break My Heart*, 1962.

NONFICTION: *The Hot Gates, and Other Occasional Pieces*, 1965; *A Moving Target*, 1982; *An Egyptian Journal*, 1985.

BIBLIOGRAPHY

Bloom, Harold, ed. *William Golding's "Lord of the Flies."* New ed. New York: Bloom's Literary Criticism, 2008. Collection of essays about the novel features contributions by many top Golding scholars. Some of the essays compare the book to Golding's novel *The Inheritors* and compare Golding's work to that of Aldous Huxley. Includes bibliography and index.

Dick, Bernard F. *William Golding*. Boston: Twayne, 1987. Provides an excellent introduction to Golding's life and works. Includes bibliography.

Dickson, L. L. *The Modern Allegories of William Golding*. Tampa: University of Southern Florida Press, 1990. Renewed theoretical interest in fantasy and allegory produced this reading of Golding's novels, which suggests a useful balance to earlier studies that focused on psychological realism.

Gindin, James. *William Golding*. New York: Macmillan, 1988. Offers comparisons of various pairings of Golding's novels, examines themes in Golding's work, and discusses the work's critical reception. Includes bibliography and index.

Kinkead-Weekes, Mark, and Ian Gregor. *William Golding: A Critical Study of the Novels*. 3d rev. ed. London: Faber & Faber, 2002. Third revised edition of one of the standard critical accounts of Golding features a biographical sketch by Golding's daughter, Judy Carver. Provides full analyses of all of Golding's novels, and two chapters discuss his work as a whole.

McCarron, Kevin. *The Coincidence of Opposites: William Golding's Later Fiction*. Sheffield, England: Sheffield Academic Press, 1995. Analyzes five of Golding's later works: *Darkness Visible*, *The Paper Men*, and the three novels of *A Sea Trilogy*. Includes bibliography.

_______. *William Golding*. 2d rev. ed. Tavistock, England: Northcote House/British Council, 2006. Part of a series of books aimed at students and general readers, this volume provides an introductory overview to Golding's life and works. Includes bibliography and index.

Page, Norman, ed. *William Golding: Novels, 1954-1967*. New York: Macmillan, 1985. This volume in the excellent Casebook series consists of an introductory survey, several general essays on Golding's earlier work, and eight pieces on specific novels through *The Pyramid*.

Redpath, Philip. *William Golding: A Structural Reading of His Fiction*. Totowa, N.J.: Barnes & Noble Books, 1986. Explores how Golding's novels create meaning, especially through their structure. Treats the works thematically rather than chronologically as in most studies. Offers suggestions for the future of Golding criticism.

Tiger, Virginia. *William Golding: The Unmoved Target*. New York: Marion Boyars, 2003. Examination of all of Golding's novels draws on Tiger's conversations and correspondence with the author to describe how the books explore themes of human destiny and vision.

OLIVER GOLDSMITH

Born: Pallas, County Longford(?), Ireland; November 10, 1728 or 1730
Died: London, England; April 4, 1774

Principal long fiction

The Citizen of the World, 1762 (collection of fictional letters first published in *The Public Ledger*, 1760-1761)
The Vicar of Wakefield, 1766

Other literary forms

Oliver Goldsmith contributed significantly to several literary genres. His works of poetry include *The Traveller: Or, A Prospect of Society* (1764) and *The Deserted Village* (1770), a classic elegiac poem of rural life. He wrote biographies as well, including *The Life of Richard Nash of Bath* (1762), which is especially valuable as a study in the social history of the period, *Life of Henry St. John, Lord Viscount Bolingbroke* (1770), and *Life of Thomas Parnell* (1770). Goldsmith developed principles of literary criticism in *An Enquiry into the Present State of Polite Learning in Europe* (1759), a history of literature in which he laments the decline of letters and morals in his own day. In addition to these publications and works of literary journalism that included humorous studies of London society, Goldsmith wrote two comic plays, *The Good-Natured Man* (pr., pb. 1768) and *She Stoops to Conquer: Or, The Mistakes of a Night* (pr., pb. 1773), a rollicking lampoon of the sentimental comedy then in vogue; *She Stoops to Conquer* is still performed today. In addition, Goldsmith published translations, histories, and even a natural history, *An History of the Earth, and Animated Nature* (1774), containing some quaint descriptions of animals.

Achievements

Oliver Goldsmith's contemporaries and posterity have been somewhat ambivalent about his literary stature, which is epitomized in English writer Samuel Johnson's estimation of him: "Goldsmith was a man who, whatever he wrote, did it better than any other man could do." Johnson demurred on Goldsmith's *The Vicar of Wakefield*, however, judging it "very faulty." There can be little dispute over critic A. Lytton Sells's judgment that Goldsmith's "versatility was the most remarkable of his gifts."

Although the novel *The Vicar of Wakefield* has usually been considered his best work, Goldsmith despised the novelist's art and regarded himself principally as a poet. His most famous poem is the reflective and melancholic *The Deserted Village*, a serious piece in heroic couplets; however, perhaps his real poetic gift was for humorous verse, such as *The Haunch of Venison: A Poetical Epistle to Lord Clare* (1776) and "Retaliation" (1774). Indeed, humor and wit are conspicuous in all his major works: There is the gentle irony of *The Vicar of Wakefield*, the comic portraits and satiric observations in *The Citizen of the World*, and the outright farce of *She Stoops to Conquer*.

Goldsmith was not a Romantic but a classicist by temperament, whose taste was molded by the Latin classics, the Augustan poetry of John Dryden and Alexander Pope, and seventeenth century French literature, and for whom the canons of criticism laid down by Nicolas Boileau-Despréaux and Voltaire were authoritative. Reflecting that background, Goldsmith's style is, in Johnson's words, "noble, elegant, and graceful."

Biography

Oliver Goldsmith was born of English stock to Ann Jones and the Reverend Charles Goldsmith, an Anglican curate. He first attended the village school of Lissoy and was taught by Thomas Byrne, a veteran of the War of the Spanish Succession. Byrne, a versifier who regaled his pupils with stories and legends of old Irish heroes, perhaps inspired Goldsmith with his love of poetry, imaginative romance, and adventure. In 1747, Goldsmith attended Patrick Hughes's school at Edgeworthstown, where he received a thorough grounding in the Latin classics. While there he probably first heard Turlogh O'Carolan, "the last of the bards," whose minstrelry left a lasting impression on him. In 1745, he entered Trinity College, Dublin, as a sizar, a position that required him to do menial work in exchange for room, board, and tuition. Goldsmith earned his B.A. degree in either 1749 or 1750. In 1752, he journeyed to Edinburgh, Scotland, to study medicine, and he continued to pursue his medical studies at the University of Leiden, in the Netherlands, in 1754. The next year he set out on a grand tour of the Continent. In February, 1756, he arrived in London, where he briefly taught in Dr. Milner's school for nonconformists and eked out a living doing hack writing.

A reversal of his fortunes occurred in 1759 with the publication of his first substantial work, *An Enquiry into the Present State of Polite Learning in Europe*. Goldsmith subsequently befriended such luminaries as the great critic and writer Johnson, the Scottish novelist Tobias Smollett, the actor David Garrick, the writer and statesman Sir Edmund Burke, and the aesthetician and portraitist Sir Joshua Reynolds. In 1763, they formed themselves into the famous Literary Club, which is memorialized in James Boswell's great biography of Johnson. Goldsmith died in 1774, possibly of Bright's disease exacerbated by worry over debts, and was buried in Temple Churchyard. Two years later, the Literary Club erected a monument to him in Poet's Corner of Westminster Abbey, for which Johnson wrote an inscription.

ANALYSIS

The themes that run through Oliver Goldsmith's long fiction are his philosophical inquiries into human nature, the problem of evil, the vying of the good and the bad within the human breast, and the conflict between "reason and appetite." His fiction addresses at its deepest level the perennial problem of theodicy, or why God allows the innocent to suffer so grievously. Lien Chi in *The Citizen of the World* exclaims, "Oh, for the reason of our creation; or why we were created to be thus unhappy!" Dr. Primrose in *The Vicar of Wakefield* ruminates, "When I reflect on the distribution of good and evil here below, I find that much has been given man to enjoy, yet still more to suffer." Both come to terms with the conundrum of evil practically, by resolving, in Lien Chi's words, "not to stand unmoved at distress, but endeavour to turn every disaster to our own advantage."

THE CITIZEN OF THE WORLD

The ninety-eight essays that make up *The Citizen of the World* were originally published as the "Chinese Letters" in various issues of *The Public Ledger* from January 24, 1760, to August 14, 1761. They were subsequently collected and published in book form in 1762. These essays purport to be letters from Lien Chi Altangi, a Mandarin philosopher from Peking who is visiting London, to his son Hingpo and to Fum Hoam, first president of the Ceremonial Academy of Peking. This work may be classified as long fiction because of the well-delineated characters it creates and the interwoven stories it relates.

The principal character is Lien Chi, a type made familiar in the eighteenth century by Montesquieu's *Lettres persanes* (1721; *Persian Letters*, 1722). Lien Chi represents the man who, through travel, has overcome provincialism and prejudice and has achieved a cosmopolitan outlook. More specifically, perhaps, he represents the sociable, sanguine, and rational side of Goldsmith, who himself had traveled extensively in Europe.

To reinforce the notion that these are the letters of a Chinese man, Goldsmith studs them with Chinese idioms and makes references throughout to Asian beliefs, manners, and customs. Lien Chi cites the philosopher Confucius, and he compares the enlightenment of the East with the ignorance and folly of the West. *The Citi-*

Oliver Goldsmith. (Library of Congress)

zen of the World capitalizes on the enthusiasm in eighteenth century England for anything Eastern—particularly Chinese—in the way of literature, fashion, design, and art, a vogue that Goldsmith satirizes through the bemused observations of Lien Chi.

Through the character of Lien Chi, a naïve but philosophically astute observer of the human scene, Goldsmith presents a full-blown satire of English society that is reminiscent of his compatriot Jonathan Swift's *Gulliver's Travels* (1726), but not so savage. In his letters, Lien Chi gives his impressions of the English, particularly of London society—their institutions, traditions, customs, habits, manners, foibles, and follies. He describes for readers a series of charming and funny pictures of London life in the eighteenth century, the literary equivalent of a William Hogarth painting. He shows readers coffeehouses, literary clubs, theaters, parks and pleasure gardens, churches, and private homes. Two scenes are particularly memorable: In one, Lien Chi describes a church service at St. Paul's Cathedral, where he mistakes the organ for an idol and its music for an oracle. In another scene, he attends a dinner for some clergy of the Church of England and is shocked to find that their sole topic of conversation is nothing more spiritual than the merits of the victuals they are intent on devouring. Aside from the entertainment and edification they afford, these letters are a document in social history, much like Samuel Pepys's diary.

While touring Westminster Abbey, Lien Chi meets and befriends the Man in Black, who represents the "melancholy man," a stock character of the Renaissance. He more particularly can be seen to represent Goldsmith's introverted and melancholy side. Through the Man in Black, Lien Chi meets Beau Tibbs, "an important little trifler" who is a rather shabby, snobbish, and pathetic fop who lives by flattering the rich and the famous. In a particularly comic scene, Lien Chi, the Man in Black, the pawnbroker's widow, Beau Tibbs, and his wife make a visit to Vauxhall Gardens. The Tibbses insist on having supper in "a genteel box" where they can both see and be seen. The pawnbroker's widow, the Man in Black's companion, heartily enjoys the meal, but Mrs. Tibbs detests it, comparing it unfavorably to a supper she and her husband lately had with a nobleman. Mrs. Tibbs is asked to sing but coyly declines; however, after repeated entreaties she obliges. During her song, an official announces that the waterworks are about to begin, which the widow is especially bent on seeing. Mrs. Tibbs, however, continues her song, oblivious to the discomfort she is causing, right through to the end of the waterworks. Goldsmith here anticipates Charles Dickens in his comic portrayal of character.

In addition to stories featuring the characters described above, *The Citizen of the World* includes Asian fables interspersed throughout, inspired no doubt by English translations of *The Arabian Nights' Entertainments* (fifteenth century). The *British Magazine* aptly described *The Citizen of the World* as "light, agreeable summer reading, partly original, partly borrowed." A. Lytton Sells regards the work as fundamentally a parody of the genre of satiric letters to which Montesquieu and Jean-Baptiste de Boyer had earlier contributed. It reveals Goldsmith at the top of his form as a humorist, satirist, and ironist.

The Vicar of Wakefield

The Vicar of Wakefield, Goldsmith's only true novel, was published in 1766. It is a first-person narrative set in eighteenth century Yorkshire. It is largely autobiographical, with Dr. Primrose modeled on Goldsmith's father and brother and George modeled on Goldsmith himself. Goldsmith likely intended the work to satirize the then-fashionable sentimental novel, particularly Laurence Sterne's *The Life and Opinions of Tristram Shandy, Gent.* (1759-1767). Its style and conventions, such as digressions, charming pastoral scenes, and mistaken identities, are those of the eighteenth century English novel.

Dr. Charles Primrose, the vicar, narrates the story of his family's misfortunes. In addition to his wife, there are six children, among whom George, Olivia, and Sophia figure most prominently in the story. The vicar loses most of his inherited wealth to an unscrupulous banker, necessitating the removal of him and his family to a humbler abode. Their new landlord is Squire Thornhill, a notorious rake, whose uncle is Sir William Thornhill, a legendary benefactor. The family is subsequently befriended by Mr. Burchell and cheated by Ephraim Jenkinson.

Olivia is abducted, and, after a search, her father finds her in an inn, where she informs him that the squire had arranged her abduction and married her, as he had other women, in a false ceremony. The squire visits and invites

Olivia to his wedding with Miss Wilmot, assuring Olivia that he will find her a suitable husband. Dr. Primrose is outraged, insisting that he would sanction only the squire's marriage to Olivia. He is subsequently informed of Olivia's death and of Sophia's abduction. Presently Mr. Burchell enters with Sophia, whom he has rescued from her abductor. It is now that Mr. Burchell reveals his true identity as Sir William Thornhill. Witnesses testify that the squire had falsely married Olivia and was complicit in Sophia's abduction. However, on the occasion of the squire's marriage to Olivia, the squire was tricked by Jenkinson with a real priest and marriage license. Jenkinson produces both the valid license and Olivia, having told Dr. Primrose that Olivia was dead in order to induce him to submit to the squire's terms and gain his release from prison.

The Vicar of Wakefield can be read on many levels. First, it is a charming idyll depicting the joys of country life. Second, it dramatizes the practical working-out of virtues such as benevolence and vices such as imprudence. Third, it severely tests seventeenth century German philosopher Gottfried Wilhelm Leibniz's dictum that we live in the best of all possible worlds where all things ultimately work for good. *The Vicar of Wakefield* is thus a philosophical romance, like Voltaire's *Candide: Ou, L'Optimisme* (1759; *Candide: Or, All for the Best*, 1759) and Johnson's *Rasselas, Prince of Abyssinia* (1759), that challenges the shallow optimism of the Enlightenment.

The *Vicar of Wakefield* has been criticized for its overly sentimentalized and idealized picture of English country life, its virtuous characters whose displays of courage in the face of adversity strain credulity, and its villains bereft of any redeeming virtue. Some commentators, however, see these apparent faults as integral to Goldsmith's ironic intention. E. A. Baker was the first to recognize that the work is ironic and comic. Robert Hopkins went further by claiming that Goldsmith intended Dr. Primrose "to satirise the complacency and materialism of a type of clergy."

Richard A. Spurgeon Hall

Other major works

PLAYS: *The Good-Natured Man*, pr., pb. 1768; *She Stoops to Conquer: Or, The Mistakes of a Night*, pr., pb. 1773.

POETRY: "An Elegy on the Glory of Her Sex: Mrs. Mary Blaize," 1759; "The Logicians Refuted," 1759; *The Traveller: Or, A Prospect of Society*, 1764; "Edwin and Angelina," 1765; "An Elegy on the Death of a Mad Dog," 1766; *The Deserted Village*, 1770; "Threnodia Augustalis," 1772; "Retaliation," 1774; *The Haunch of Venison: A Poetical Epistle to Lord Clare*, 1776; "The Captivity: An Oratoria," 1820 (wr. 1764).

NONFICTION: *The Bee*, 1759 (essays); *An Enquiry into the Present State of Polite Learning in Europe*, 1759; *The Life of Richard Nash of Bath*, 1762; *An History of England in a Series of Letters from a Nobleman to His Son*, 1764 (2 volumes); *Life of Henry St. John, Lord Viscount Bolingbroke*, 1770; *Life of Thomas Parnell*, 1770; *An History of the Earth, and Animated Nature*, 1774 (8 volumes; unfinished).

MISCELLANEOUS: *The Collected Works of Oliver Goldsmith*, 1966 (5 volumes; Arthur Friedman, editor).

Bibliography

Dixon, Peter. *Oliver Goldsmith Revisited.* Boston: Twayne, 1991. Informative introduction to the life and works of Goldsmith presents a discussion of *The Vicar of Wakefield* in chapter 4. Includes bibliography and index.

Donoghue, Frank. *The Fame Machine: Book Reviewing and Eighteenth-Century Literary Careers.* Stanford, Calif.: Stanford University Press, 1996. Examines the careers of Goldsmith and other authors to demonstrate how eighteenth century literary reviewers changed writers' and readers' perceptions of writers and their work.

Flint, Christopher. "'The Family Piece': Oliver Goldsmith and the Politics of the Everyday in Eighteenth-Century Domestic Portraiture." *Eighteenth-Century Studies* 29 (Winter, 1995/1996): 127-152. Argues that the family portrait in *The Vicar of Wakefield* is typical of family in eighteenth century culture, and claims that Goldsmith suggests that both the novel and portraiture are engaged in political acts of domestic regulation free of the corruption often associated with "politics."

Harkin, Maureen. "Goldsmith on Authorship in *The Vicar of Wakefield*." *Eighteenth Century Fiction* 14 (April-July, 2002): 325. Analysis of the novel focuses on what Harkin describes as Goldsmith's "uncertainties about what the character and possibilities of his age are, especially for the writer and literary intellectual."

Hopkins, Robert H. *The True Genius of Oliver Goldsmith*. Baltimore: Johns Hopkins University Press, 1969. Interprets Goldsmith's work, not taking the traditional view of the author as a sentimental humanist but examining him as a master of satire and irony. Devotes a chapter each to Goldsmith's crafts of persuasion, satire, and humor, and a chapter titled "Augustanisms and the Moral Basis for Goldsmith's Art" delineates the social, intellectual, and literary contexts in which Goldsmith wrote. Includes a detailed examination of *The Vicar of Wakefield*.

Lucy, Séan, ed. *Goldsmith: The Gentle Master*. Cork, Ireland: Cork University Press, 1984. Brief collection of essays provides interesting biographical material on Goldsmith as well as critical commentary on his works. An essay on *The Vicar of Wakefield* identifies elements of the Irish narrative tradition in the novel.

Quintana, Richard. *Oliver Goldsmith: A Georgian Study*. New York: Macmillan, 1967. Incorporates biography and criticism in a readable account of Goldsmith's colorful life and his development as a writer. Discusses Goldsmith's works in many literary genres in depth, with chapters on his fiction, poetry, drama, and essays. A lengthy appendix offers notes on Goldsmith's lesser writings, such as his biographical and historical works.

Rousseau, G. S., ed. *Goldsmith: The Critical Heritage*. London: Routledge & Kegan Paul, 1974. This collection of critical commentary on Goldsmith is organized by particular works, with an additional section on Goldsmith's life and his works in general. Includes commentary written only up to 1912, but pieces by Goldsmith's contemporaries, such as Sir Joshua Reynolds's sketch of Goldsmith's character, and by later critics, such as William Hazlitt and Washington Irving, offer interesting perspectives on Goldsmith's place in literary history.

Sells, A. Lytton. *Oliver Goldsmith: His Life and Works*. New York: Barnes & Noble Books, 1974. Presents biographical information as well as discussion of the author's works. Individual chapters focus on particular facets of Goldsmith's work (such as "The Critic," "The Journalist," "The Biographer"), whereas others provide more detailed analysis of his major works, including *The Vicar of Wakefield*.

Swarbrick, Andrew, ed. *The Art of Oliver Goldsmith*. New York: Barnes & Noble Books, 1984. Excellent collection of ten essays offers a wide-ranging survey of Goldsmith's works. Essays treat individual works as well as more general topics, such as the literary context in which Goldsmith wrote, the elements of classicism in his works, and his place in the Anglo-Irish literary tradition.

WITOLD GOMBROWICZ

Born: Małoszyce, Poland; August 4, 1904
Died: Vence, France; July 24, 1969
Also known as: Witold Marian Gombrowicz

Principal long fiction

Ferdydurke, 1937 (English translation, 1961)
Opetani, 1939 (unfinished; *Possessed: Or, The Secret of Myslotch*, 1980)
Trans-Atlantyk, 1953
Pornografia, 1960 (English translation, 1966)
Kosmos, 1965 (*Cosmos*, 1966)
Three Novels by Witold Gombrowicz, 1978 (includes *Ferdydurke*, *Pornografia*, and *Cosmos*)

Other literary forms

In addition to his four principal novels, Witold Gombrowicz (gawm-BRAW-veech) wrote three equally important plays and the monumental three-volume *Dziennik* (1957-1967; diary), which represents a unique blend of intimate diary, fiction, and literary or philosophical essay. His literary debut was a 1933 collection of short stories (reedited in an enlarged version in 1957); the genre of the short story, however, appears as marginal in his output. The same is true of literary criticism, which he cultivated most intensely in the 1930's, returning to it only occasionally in the later decades. Throughout his life, he was characteristically preoccupied with commenting upon and explaining his own work; in addition to *Dziennik*, such a self-explanatory purpose is served, more or less directly, by a book-length interview conducted by Dominique de Roux, *Rozmowy z Gombrowiczem* (conversations with Gombrowicz; actually, the writer's own confession published in guise of an interview, 1969; translated as *A Kind of Testament*, 1973) and by an autobiographical book, *Wspomnienia polskie: Wędrówki po Argentynie* (1977; *Polish Memories*, 2004).

ACHIEVEMENTS

The story of Witold Gombrowicz's literary career presents a striking contrast between his nearly lifelong isolation as a writer and the international fame enjoyed by his works after the 1960's. He is universally considered one of the major European novelists and playwrights of the twentieth century, a towering figure in modern Polish literature; his works have been translated into many foreign languages and have occasioned numerous critical analyses. All of this, however, including the coveted Formentor Prize in 1967, came only toward the end of his life, after the sixty-year-old Gombrowicz moved back to Europe from his Argentinian retreat, where he had spent twenty-four years, known only to a handful of his Argentinian admirers and to his enthusiasts in Poland.

The Polish reception of Gombrowicz appears as another paradox. Although his work, as that of an émigré writer, was steadfastly banned by the Communist regime (with the exception of a brief interval in 1957-1958), it was always known in Poland's intellectual circles thanks to the wide circulation of émigré editions. Oddly enough, after the writer's death, it became possible in Poland to stage his plays and publish critical monographs on his work, although his books were still banned until the fall of the Communist regime. This bizarre situation came about because Polish authorities apparently had political objections to certain passages of Gombrowicz's diary; the writer specified in his last will that his work not be reprinted in Poland unless in its entirety. In spite of the difficulties that Polish readers faced in obtaining copies of his books, Gombrowicz's reputation in his homeland grew as steadily as it did abroad; his work has exerted a particularly strong influence on the development of recent Polish fiction, drama, and criticism.

BIOGRAPHY

Witold Marian Gombrowicz's life falls into two main phases, separated by his decision in September, 1939, to stay in Argentina, where he was caught by the outbreak of World War II in Europe. He was born in 1904 into the family of a landed proprietor-turned-industrialist; in 1911, his family moved from a country manor in southern Poland to Warsaw. The most rebellious and whimsical child in his family, Gombrowicz nevertheless graduated from high school and, in 1922, acceding to his father's wish, began to study law at Warsaw University. After he graduated in 1927, he continued his studies in Paris but soon returned to Poland, where his unorthodox views made it impossible for him to find a job as a lawyer. In all probability, this professional failure hastened his decision to devote himself entirely to writing. In 1933, his first book, a collection of short stories under the provocative title *Pamiętnik z okresu dojrzewania* (a memoir written in puberty), was published to rather skeptical reviews that generally dismissed the book as "immature." Nevertheless, Gombrowicz quickly won recognition in the circles of young writers. By the mid-1930's, he was already enjoying a moderate fame as a colorful personality and fascinating *causeur* as well as an insightful literary critic. It was, however, his first novel, *Ferdydurke*, that became a genuine event of Polish literary life. Published in 1937, *Ferdydurke* provoked a heated critical debate on avant-garde tendencies in modern Polish prose.

Before the war, Gombrowicz managed to publish in magazines and journals three more short stories, his first play, *Iwona, księżniczka Burgunda* (pb. 1938; *Princess Iwona*, 1969), and an unfinished novel, *Possessed*, a gothic parody that was published pseudonymously as a newspaper series in 1939.

By a strange twist of fortune, only a few weeks before the German invasion of Poland, Gombrowicz took part in a trip of a group of young writers to Argentina. While in Buenos Aires, he learned about the outbreak of war and decided not to return. The first Argentinian years, while offering him inner freedom by cutting off all of his ties and obligations, were also extremely difficult, marked by isolation and financial hardship. To make his living, he took a poorly paid job as a clerk in a Polish bank in Buenos Aires. At the same time, he stubbornly continued his writing and after some time gained recognition—not so much among Polish émigrés, however, as among young Argentinian writers. He returned to the literary scene in 1953 with the novel *Trans-Atlantyk* and the play *Ślub* (revised 1957; *The Marriage*, 1969). Also in 1953, he began to publish fragments of his diary in the Institut Littéraire's monthly, *Kultura*.

The publication of *Trans-Atlantyk*, a novel dealing satirically with the notion of traditional Polish patriotism, was met with vitriolic attacks from the conservative segment of the émigré community. On the other hand, after 1957-1958, when four books by Gombrowicz had been published in Poland during the short-lived political "thaw," he became almost a cult object for many young writers and critics, who enthusiastically welcomed everything avant-garde and unorthodox after the years of Socialist Realist boredom.

Between 1957 and 1966, Gombrowicz published, through the Institut Littéraire, the rest of his most important books written in exile: two novels, *Pornografia* and *Cosmos*, and the diary in three volumes, the last of which also included his third play, *Operetka* (1966; *Operetta*, 1971). Meanwhile, in 1963, he received a grant from the Rockefeller Foundation and left for Europe. After some time spent in West Berlin (this stay as well as some of Gombrowicz's public statements made him a victim of vicious attacks in the official media in Poland), he moved to Paris and finally settled with his young French wife in the small town of Vence in southern France. The last years of his life were marked by his rapidly growing international fame as well as by his deteriorating health. He died in Vence in 1969, after a long struggle with illness.

Analysis

Seemingly nonsensical and capricious, Witold Gombrowicz's work is revealed, on a closer look, to be based on an amazingly consistent and complex philosophical system, as original as it is profound. Regardless of genre, the writer explores throughout his works the fundamental notions and antinomies that underlie his vision of the human world; in a sense, his novels are modern versions of the philosophical parable, although they are far from being didactic.

What can be called the basic existential experience of Gombrowicz is his awareness of human solitude and helplessness in confrontation with the powerful pressure of culture—if "culture" is understood in a Freudian sense, as a collective superego that stifles the authentic impulses of the human self. Accordingly, the chief antinomy of Gombrowicz's philosophical system is the omnipresent conflict between the solitary individual and the rest of the human world; the individual's natural need is to remain free, independent, spontaneous, unique, whereas the outside world crams the individual into the schematic frames of what is socially and culturally acceptable.

This conviction would appear as not particularly original (in fact, it would seem a mere continuation of the argument of Jean-Jacques Rousseau and the Romantics) were it not for the fact that Gombrowicz immediately counterpoises it with its exact opposite. He is equally aware that, contrary to his need to remain free and unique, the individual also feels constantly the fear of isolation and desires to affirm himself (or herself) through contacts with other people, through his reflection in the eyes of others. This contradiction is particularly dominant in the case of an artist or writer: He wishes to reveal his individual uniqueness to the audience, but to reach the latter and be understood, he has to resort to a "language" of approved convention, which, in turn, destroys his uniqueness. In other words, each manifestation of the artist's freedom-seeking self means his imprisonment in a rigid scheme of finished shapes—and thus, it means his death as an artist.

The situation of an artist, however, is considered by Gombrowicz as only one particularly dramatic version of a more universal paradox of human existence as such. In his view, every individual lives his or her life in constant suspension between two ideals: "Divinity" and "Youth." Divinity can be understood as fullness, completeness, perfection; Youth is synonymous with unfulfillment, spontaneity, freedom. In yet other terms, the opposition of Divinity versus Youth equals that of Form versus Chaos. The main characters in Gombrowicz's fiction (more often than not, fictional impersonations of himself and his own neurotic obsessions) are always torn between their striving for Form on one hand and Chaos on the other; or the plot consists of a clash between characters symbolizing Form and those symbolizing Chaos (significantly, the motif of a duel or fight is frequently used in crucial scenes).

This basic opposition takes on many specific shapes. The struggle between Form and Chaos may reveal itself, for example, in its sociological version, in which Aristocracy (or higher classes in general) represents the complete, perfect Form, while Peasantry (or lower classes in general) stands for spontaneous, chaotic Youth. It may also be illustrated by the inequality of civilizations—Western civilization is, in this respect, a symbol of Form, while the "second-rate," "immature" civilizations of countries such as Poland represent Chaos. Finally, the tension between the extremes of Form and Chaos can also be demonstrated on the level of individuals; here, the already shaped personality of an adult is another version of Form, while the still-developing personality of a child or teenager is a symbolic image of Chaos. It is evident that all possible embodiments of the opposition between Form and Chaos have a common denominator in the concept of inequality; each opposed pair can be interpreted as a case of Superiority confronted with Inferiority. According to Gombrowicz, the essence of human existence lies in the individual's striving all of his or her life for Superiority and Form but is not really attracted by these values, since their ultimate attainment would be tantamount to death. Therefore, the individual secretly desires Inferiority and Chaos, because only these extremes offer a chance of freedom. On the other hand, the ultimate attainment of this other goal would mean isolation, lack of communication, and impossibility of affirming one's self-image through its reflection in the eyes of others. In the final analysis, the conflict is insoluble.

It can be, however, partly overcome and contained, if not fully resolved, by artistic creativity. Gombrowicz, as noted above, views the artist as someone who experiences the existential antinomy in a particularly acute way, but the artist has, at the same time, a certain advantage that nobody else has. Even though he cannot avoid the use of Form—if he did, he would not be understood—he can at least be aware of the artificial nature of Form and, as a consequence, he can be free to play with it. To play with Form means, in practice, to use it consciously and to make it "visible" instead of concealing it. Accordingly, Gombrowicz's own works are filled with deliberately introduced literary conventions that the reader can recognize instantly—the conventions of the mystery novel, operetta, family chronicle, traditional oral tale, Shakespearean historical drama, or novel of the life of the upper classes. At the same time, the personality of the narrator is usually multilayered: He exists within the world presented by his narration, but he can also at any given moment rise above that reality and his own narration to comment on them, or rise even higher to comment on his own comment, and so forth; in other words, he plays not merely with the conventions of literary genres and styles but also with the very convention of literary discourse.

All of his ambiguity considered, the narrator's point of view in Gombrowicz's novels is, however, stable in one specific sense: As a rule, he represents the author, if not fully identifying himself with Gombrowicz (even to the point of assuming the latter's name). Likewise, the time of the novel's action is always, or at least seems to be, historically specified, and it usually coincides with various phases of Gombrowicz's own life. What is particularly meaningful is the place of the novel's action, usually a single and rather limited setting; the narration more often than not begins with the moment of the narrator's arrival in a certain place new to him, which he must then explore and comprehend. In the course of such exploration, the narrator is usually confronted with a problem that he is supposed to solve, and thus the next phases of action develop conspicuously along the lines of the traditional detective story or novel of adventure.

What seems to be particularly characteristic of Gombrowicz is that his narrator's relationship with the reality presented is twofold. On one hand, it is a reality that oppresses him, poses problems to solve, forces him to assume a certain stance or adopt a certain behavior. On the other hand, it is, simultaneously, the narrator himself who attempts to shape reality, to stage and direct events, to manipulate other characters, to impose some sense upon the world that surrounds him. Accordingly, two basic models of fictional plot coexist with each other in Gombrowicz's novels—the model of an investigation (in which reality appears to the narrator as a problem to solve) and the model of a stage setting (in which the narrator becomes an active manipulator of reality).

All of this is additionally complicated by the world presented in Gombrowicz's fiction: The world consists not only of facts, persons, objects, and their mutual relations but also words and their sounds and meanings. Words not only serve here as a means to tell the story but also assume, as it were, an independent existence. This particular aspect of Gombrowicz's artistic play has for its object the tension between the order of facts and the order of words, between the meaning of a related situation and the meaning of specific words or expressions in which the situation is related; one can never be sure whether the action will follow the former or the latter semantic line. Sometimes, for example, a word that is central to a specific situation is foregrounded by constant repetition and other stylistic devices to such an extent that it, so to speak, proliferates and begins to function as an independent Form imposed on the Chaos of reality.

Ferdydurke

This is particularly noticeable in Gombrowicz's first and most famous work of long fiction, *Ferdydurke*, which has been perhaps artistically surpassed by his later novels, yet still remains the most exemplary illustration of his philosophy, his vision of society, his idea of narration, and his use of language. The attacks against this novel from both the Right and the Left in the late 1930's seem, in a sense, understandable, since the novel ridicules all ideologies or, more generally, all socially sanctified attitudes, conventions, or Forms.

Ferdydurke falls into three sharply divided parts, each of which is preceded by a brief essay or parable. At the outset of the story, the reader meets the narrator (and, at the same time, the main character of the whole novel), a man in his thirties who, like Gombrowicz himself, has published his first book and has been massacred by the critics as an immature and irresponsible youngster. The narrator is torn between his desire to achieve maturity and social acceptance (that is, any Form) and his dislike for various specific Forms that have been imposed on him by others and that he cannot accept as his authentic self. What, actually, is his "authentic" Form? To find an answer, he embarks on writing another book. Here, however, something unexpected occurs: A certain Professor Pimko, an old-fashioned high school teacher, arrives and literally kidnaps the narrator to put him back in school, as if he were still a teenager.

The subsequent three parts of the novel put the narrator-turned-teenager into three different locales, each of which represents a different kind of petrified, inauthentic Form. After the school sequence, the narrator is placed by Pimko as a subtenant in the house of Mr. and Mrs. Youthful, a middle-aged couple imprisoned, as it were, within their own idea of what is "modern" and "progressive"; finally, he finds himself in a countryside manor where the conservative social distinctions between the upper class and the "boors" are still very much alive. In none of these three places—the school, the "modern" household, the traditional manor—can the narrator feel fully identified with the Form that prevails there, nor can he find an authentic Form of his own. Each of the three plots sooner or later develops into the narrator's attempts to manipulate the people who surround him, which in turn leads each time to a conflict culminating in a grotesque brawl and the narrator's escape. The conflict between Form and Chaos, shown simultaneously in its cultural, social, civilizational, generational, and sexual dimensions, cannot possibly be resolved—escape is the only solution. Even that, however, proves futile: In the final scene, the escaping narrator winds up in the company of his hosts' young daughter and thus unwillingly contributes to the triumph of yet another hollow Form—the romantic stereotype of lovers' elopement.

Trans-Atlantyk

In his subsequent novels, Gombrowicz continued to explore the fundamental problem of Form versus Chaos, illustrating it with even more intricate fictional plots. *Trans-Atlantyk*, a novel ostensibly based on the author's 1939 Argentinian defection, dissects Form in its specific version of patriotic stereotype, while the extreme of Chaos, Freedom, and Youth is identified with a refusal to conform to such a stereotype. There is, perhaps, no other work by Gombrowicz in which language, style, and literary convention would play such a crucial role: A twentieth century story is told here in the masterfully parodied style of an oral tale spoken by a seventeenth century old Polish nobleman.

Pornografia *and* Cosmos

In *Pornografia*, the relationship between Form and Chaos, Divinity and Youth, takes on the shape of a perverse story of a young couple whose love is "stage set" and "directed" by a pair of older men—all of this against the social and political background of Nazi-occupied Poland. Gombrowicz's last novel, *Cosmos*, is his most metaphysical, although, like everything he wrote, it also reveals his powerful *vis comica* and penchant for the grotesque. The central problem here is nothing less than the nature of external reality as reflected in human consciousness. Is meaning immanent, or is it merely imposed on reality by the human mind? Gombrowicz asks this question by structuring his novel once again on the model of an investigation and by means of parody referring in its style and construction to the conventions of the mystery story. Like the rest of Gombrowicz's work, *Cosmos* can be read as a mad piece of nonsensical tomfoolery—but it can also be read as a profound philosophical treatise on the most excruciating conflicts of human existence.

Stanisław Barańczak

Other major works

short fiction: *Pamiętnik z okresu dojrzewania*, 1933; *Bakakaj*, 1957 (includes *Pamiętnik z okresu dojrzewania* and other stories; *Bacacay*, 2004).

plays: *Iwona, księżniczka Burgunda*, pb. 1938 (revised 1958; *Princess Iwona*, 1969; best known as *Ivona, Princess of Burgundia*); *Ślub*, pb. 1948 (revised 1957; *The Marriage*, 1969); *Historia*, pb. 1975; *Operetka*, pb. 1966 (*Operetta*, 1971).

nonfiction: *Dziennik, 1953-1956*, 1957 (*Diary: Volume I*, 1988); *Dziennik, 1957-1961*, 1962 (*Diary: Volume II*, 1989); *Dziennik, 1961-1966*, 1967 (*Diary: Volume III*, 1993); *Sur Dante: Glose*, 1968; *Rozmowy z Gombrowiczem*, 1969 (*A Kind of Testament*, 1973); *Varia*, 1973; *Wspomnienia polskie: Wędrówki po Argentynie*, 1977 (*Polish Memories*, 2004); *Cours de philosophie en six heures un quart*, 1995 (*Philosophy in Six Lessons and a Quarter*, 1999).

miscellaneous: *Dzieła zebrane*, 1969-1977 (11 volumes).

Bibliography

Berressem, Hanjo. *Lines of Desire: Reading Gombrowicz's Fiction with Lacan*. Evanston, Ill.: Northwestern University Press, 1999. Berressem interprets Gombrowicz's novels from the perspective of contemporary literary theory and psychoanalysis, particularly the concepts of Jacques Lacan. Aimed at advanced students.

Giroud, Vincent. *The World of Witold Gombrowicz, 1904-1969*. New Haven, Conn.: Beinecke Rare Book and Manuscript Library, Yale University, 2004. This catalog, which contains photographs and information about Gombrowicz's life and works, accompanied the library's 2004 exhibition commemorating the centenary of the author's birth.

Gombrowicz, Witold. "Excerpts from *Diary*." In *Polish Writers on Writing*, edited by Adam Zagajewski. San Antonio, Tex.: Trinity University Press, 2007. An excerpt from Gombrowicz's diary is included in this English-language anthology of works in which Polish authors describe what it means to be a writer.

Longinovic, Tomislav. *Borderline Culture: The Politics of Identity in Four Twentieth-Century Slavic Novels*. Fayetteville: University of Arkansas Press, 1993. Longinovic's analysis of the treatment of identity in Slavic fiction includes the chapter "Modernity, Gender, and Identity in *Ferdydurke*." Includes notes, references, and an index.

Newton, Adam Zachary. "The Scandal of Human Countenance: Witold Gombrowicz and Bruno Schulz in Exile from the Country of Forms." In *Mapping the Ethical Turn: A Reader in Ethics, Culture, and Literary Theory*, edited by Todd F. Davis and Kenneth Womack. Charlottesville: University Press of Virginia, 2001. This discussion of Gombrowicz is included in a collection of essays that trace the connections between literary criticism and ethical thinking in selected works of literature. Aimed at advanced students.

Segel, Harold B. "Celebrating Witold Gombrowicz."

World Literature Today 79, no. 2 (May-August, 2005): 29-30. A brief overview of Gombrowicz's works that examines the themes of his novels and the narrative strategy of his writing, and also provides an analysis of *Ferdydurke*.

Thompson, Ewa M. *Witold Gombrowicz*. Boston: Twayne, 1979. A useful book featuring a biography, analysis of major works, and a good bibliography. One of the volumes in the Twayne World Authors series.

Ziarek, Ewa Plonowska, ed. *Gombrowicz's Grimaces: Modernism, Gender, Nationality*. Albany: State University of New York Press, 1998. A collection of essays, some of which explore physical and psychic aberrations in Gombrowicz's novels, his aesthetics, and his critical reception in the United States.

IVAN GONCHAROV

Born: Simbirsk, Russia; June 6, 1812
Died: St. Petersburg, Russia; September 15, 1891
Also known as: Ivan Alexandrovich Goncharov

Principal long fiction

Obyknovennaya istoriya, 1847 (*A Common Story*, 1890)
Oblomov, 1859 (English translation, 1915)
Obryv, 1869 (*The Precipice*, 1916)

Other literary forms

The early stories and poems of Ivan Goncharov (gon-chah-RAHF) were considered mediocre by the author himself as well as the public and have long been out of print. Goncharov's first significant piece was the sketch "Ivan Savich Podzhabrin," available in *Sobranie sochinenii* (1883, 1888, 1952; collected works). Still widely published and read is the travelogue *Fregat Pallada* (1858; *The Voyage of the Frigate Pallada*, 1965). During the final two decades of his life, Goncharov concentrated on critical essays, reminiscences, and polemical articles. "Mil'yon terzaniy" (1872), his analysis of Alexander Griboyedov's *Gore ot uma* (1825, 1831; English translation, 1857), and his autobiographical memoir "Luchshe pozdno, chem nikogda" (1879; better late than never) have limited circulation, even among literary specialists.

Achievements

Ivan Goncharov's novels mark the transition from Russian Romanticism to a much more realistic worldview. They appeared at a time when sociological criteria dominated analysis and when authors were expected to address the injustices of Russian life. The critic Nikolay Dobrolyubov derived the term *Oblomovism* from Goncharov's most famous novel, using it to denote the physical and mental sluggishness of Russia's backward country gentry. Thus, Goncharov is credited with exposing a harmful national type: the spendthrift serf-holding landowner who contributed nothing to the national economy and resisted progress for fear of destroying his carefree existence.

By presenting this type in his rather ordinary surroundings and endeavors, stripped of the Romantic aura with which Alexander Pushkin's classical and Mikhail Lermontov's Romantic verse had imbued him, Goncharov gained renown as a critical realist. While all three of his novels remain popular classics in his homeland, only *Oblomov* has found a wide readership and critical acclaim abroad. Emphasis on that work has caused modern Western scholars to value Goncharov as highly for his artful psychological portraits of stunted adults adrift in a changing world as for his sociological contribution.

Oblomov's "return to the womb" predates Sigmund Freud by several decades. On the artistic level, Goncharov far transcends the realistic label often applied to him. His talent for transforming an endlessly mundane provincial existence into a delicate poetic network of pre-Petrine Russian values set standards for the budding Russian novel; his stream-of-consciousness approach points ahead to James Joyce and Marcel Proust. Goncharov has firmly established a place for himself within the genre of the modern psychological novel.

Biography

Ivan Goncharov was born Ivan Alexandrovich Goncharov on June 18, 1812, in remote Simbirsk (now Ulyanovsk) on a country estate of the type featured in his novels. After losing his merchant father at age seven, he was reared in the old tradition by his strong-willed mother and her landowning companion. This heritage of easygoing manor life and progressive mercantile activity characterizes Goncharov's own outlook and that of his major fictional characters. Encouraged to follow in his father's footsteps, he languished for eight years in a school of commerce without graduating. From 1831 to 1834, he attended Moscow University, without taking an active part in the famous philosophical student circles of the time. Instead, he entered the literary world as a tutor in the culturally sophisticated Maikov family, using this experience to produce his first poems and stories.

Goncharov's rise to fame was slow, and he was trapped in a civil service career spanning more than thirty years, almost half of which was spent uneventfully as a translator in the finance ministry. Goncharov's private existence turned out to be equally monotonous. Although he was attracted to a number of women, his courtships were not successful, and he never married. The frustrations of his relationships with women are prominently mirrored in all three novels.

The success of his first novel, *A Common Story*, did not alleviate Goncharov's self-doubt, and he remained fettered to extraliterary activity. A worldwide sailing tour on behalf of the trade ministry in the 1850's yielded material for his travel sketches. The same period brought an appointment to the literary censorship board, a result of Czar Alexander II's relaxed attitude. Goncharov followed a middle-of-the-road philosophy in this post, often enraging progressive writers, whose harsh judgments of conservative ideals he would not accept. He secured his own literary fame with *Oblomov* but felt too insecure to devote himself exclusively to literature. After a brief try at editing the official newspaper *Severnaya pchela* in the 1860's, he returned to a censorial post in the influential Press Council. His civic duties earned for him the Order of Vladimir, third class, prior to retirement in 1868.

Ivan Goncharov.

Meanwhile, Goncharov's mental state had gradually deteriorated. Ivan Turgenev's literary success easily eclipsed that of Goncharov, and when Turgenev's *Dvoryanskoe gnezdo* (1859; *Liza: Or, "A Nest of Nobles,"* 1869; better known as *A Nest of Gentlefolk*, 1959) superseded *Oblomov* in critical acclaim, Goncharov accused his rival of plagiarism. Arbitration found Turgenev innocent, and the writers reconciled, but in private, the increasingly neurotic Goncharov continued the accusations, venting on Turgenev all the frustrations of his own unsatisfactory existence. Philosophically, Goncharov moved from a modestly progressive stance to a firm defense of the traditional values of the landed gentry. These sentiments found expression in *The Precipice*, in which moral regeneration is embedded in the unchanging order of provincial Russia.

Goncharov died on September 15, 1891, a stranger to the swiftly moving social currents of the latter part of the century. His later published works chronicle his artistic decline. A complete recluse, he burned his letters and manuscripts. He spent his final days not unlike his major hero, Oblomov, in a St. Petersburg flat, looked after by a kindly woman and her children.

Analysis

"My life began flickering out from the very first moment I became conscious of myself." Thus, Ilya Oblomov explains his arrested development to his successful business friend, Stolz, who is making a last try to rouse Oblomov from his fatal lethargy, and thus Goncharov points the reader to the cause of Oblomov's inertia: his childhood in a sleepy, backward manor house, attended by an army of serfs, every moment structured to reinforce an existence of indolently blissful inactivity, a paradise to which the adult strives all of his life to return. Oblomov's failure as a man and his search for a surrogate childhood in a simple St. Petersburg family fit perfectly the scheme of the psychological novel. From this perspective, the seemingly typical Russian landowner Oblomov becomes a universal figure, and the old-fashioned Russian village becomes merely background.

Such a perspective, however, has its drawbacks. If one considers *Oblomov* apart from Goncharov's other novels, as is often the case in the West, the wider artistic sweep of his fiction is neglected. Each of his novels gives expression to a different facet of the contradictions encountered by the Russian patriarchal order as it confronted sociopolitical reform. Goncharov's characters can be said to embody the two warring dominant philosophies of nineteenth century Russia: Slavophilism and Westernization. The author's own struggle between these two opposing forces is cast into sharp focus in the novels, as his progress-oriented mind gradually loses ground to his tradition-loving, Slavophile heart.

Neither Goncharov's personal dissatisfactions nor his conservative turn impair his stature as an accomplished novelist. The expert use of several literary devices contributes to this renown. There is, first of all, his power of observation, the ability to create such a lifelike image of an ordinary event through accumulation of detail that his scenes are compared to Flemish interiors. Authorial ambiguity also enriches the narrative. The first two novels conceptually demonstrate the advantages of a progressive economy and the futility of perpetuating serfdom, but Goncharov presents a dying way of life with such a wealth of attractive imagery that social indifference, indeed exploitation, infantilism, and stagnation, are turned into a languidly cozy, almost noble way of life, feeding on nostalgia and winning sympathy for its prejudices.

No less impressive is Goncharov's skill in suggesting the delusions of the regressive personality. Oblomov's insecure psyche reshapes his ordinary village into a harmless, safe refuge, smoothing craggy mountains into gentle hillocks, swift rivers into murmuring brooks, extremes of climate into eternally pleasant weather, passions into lethargy. Readers are scarcely aware that the descriptions are no longer objective, but the distortions of a frightened mind.

Finally, Goncharov excels in drawing exquisite female portraits; his women also symbolize the synthesis between the old and new. In *A Common Story*, Lizaveta is able to balance the contradictory forces that pull the male characters into adversary position; in *Oblomov*, Olga combines the best of old Russia, its cultural heritage, with an inquisitive mind and an active personality; in *The Precipice*, Vera eventually unites the positive features of her patriarchal upbringing with the progressive forces of a commercially enterprising spouse.

In his final novel, Goncharov's moralizing instincts undermine his mastery of style, as didactic elements intrude too explicitly. The author's own estrangement from the present and his nostalgia for a less complex existence color his perceptions. His slow-paced upbringing, his later insecurities, his realization that progress was necessary, his struggle between old and new, and his final withdrawal from society are the building blocks of all of his works. He delicately managed to balance these elements before yielding to his own preferences.

A Common Story

The unstinting praise of Russia's foremost social critic, Vissarion Belinsky, assured the success of *A Common Story* the moment it appeared in the literary journal *Sovremennik*. Ironically, the work was hailed as an exposé of the degenerate gentry class and a call for modernization. Critics and readers alike noted only the main character Alexander Aduev's final acceptance of St. Petersburg's progressive lifestyle, not his mentor-uncle's disillusionment with it. They also overlooked the author's cautious suggestion that the city's competitive utilitarianism was no more satisfying than the monotony of the backward village.

This misperception attests Goncharov's balancing skill. Alexander is lured from his peaceful, idyllic estate, lovingly presented in the fragrance of its lilacs, berries, bushes, and forests, by visions of cosmopolitan dazzle. Once he is taken in hand by a "new man," his coldly efficient, philistine uncle, Peter, one disappointment succeeds another. Like an early Oblomov, Alexander adjusts only superficially, never able to integrate his rustic values with St. Petersburg's diverse phenomena. Like a young Goncharov, Alexander blunders from one unsuccessful love affair to another. His literary endeavors, characterized by overblown sentimental clichés, are equally fruitless. Despite all efforts by Peter, he turns into a rather ridiculous figure, an out-of-place relic in the bustling city. Goncharov's ambiguous attitude, however, gives enough scope to elicit a measure of pity from the reader, to mark the young man's discomforts and his inability to cope.

Peter's young wife, Lizaveta, compassionately brings out Alexander's positive traits. When all attempts at acclimatization end in failure, he returns to his quiet country home and recovers his bearings. yet the lessons of the city are not lost. At a distance, its hectic multiplicity develops into a fair alternative to the boring idyll of the placid province. In the end, Alexander sets out for St. Petersburg once more, cured of his romantic expectations, determined to copy his uncle's career through realistic adaptation and lowered sights. His success is presented in the epilogue. He parallels Peter faithfully: fat and balding, engaged to a young heiress, adjusted, mature, eager for progressive endeavors.

While this conclusion heartened liberal critics, Goncharov's reservations are apparent in the incompletely dramatized and therefore unconvincing psychological transformation of Alexander. The artistically unmotivated ending causes a change of focus. The carefully developed juxtaposition of old versus new, village versus city, Slavophile versus Westernizer assumes the outline of a bildungsroman. Peter and Alexander represent two stages of identical development. Alexander's romantic striving mirrors Peter's own youthful immaturity, while Peter's rational, mature stage serves as a marker for Alexander's similar destiny. At the moment of Alexander's arrival at that stage, Peter's dry and joyless stance casts doubt on the wisdom of these very accomplishments, foreshadowing eventual disillusionment for his nephew. The general inattention to this downbeat element is a result of the shortage of bourgeois heroes in Russian literature.

The Romantic characters of Pushkin, Lermontov, and the early Turgenev are immobile, purposeless, and contemptuous of practical activity. Liberal critics had long called for a positively depicted, businesslike nobleman, and they accepted Alexander in his final guise enthusiastically as such. The careful reader is left questioning both men's aspirations and sharing Lizaveta's wistful awareness that St. Petersburg's progress is far from ideal. The alternative of seeking that ideal in Russia's past surfaces only in Goncharov's later works, although the absence of a critical stand against serfdom and landowner privileges already serves to modify the seeming victory of Westernization.

OBLOMOV

Turgenev's popular *A Nest of Gentlefolk* threatened to overshadow *Oblomov*, which was first printed in *Otechestvennye zapiski*, until critic Dobrolyubov's 1859 article "Chto takoyo Oblomovshchina?" ("What Is Oblomovism?") swiftly drew national attention to the work. Following Dobrolyubov's cue, most readers and succeeding generations saw in *Oblomov* the hero's inertia the psychological consequence of total dependence on serf labor. By lavishing endless pages on the harmful effects of Oblomovism and the virtues of Stolz, a Western-influenced business type, Goncharov seemed to strike a forceful blow at the roots of Russia's economic and social evils.

Oblomov appears as the epitome of the superfluous nobleman, the lazy, alienated dreamer who cannot adjust to change or find a place for himself in the present. Different embodiments of this type exist in Pushkin's Onegin, Lermontov's Pechorin, and Turgenev's Rudin. Oblomov differs from these characters in that he rejects even the search for an alternative, preferring instead the never-changing ways of his childhood Oblomovka. The location of this estate on the Asian border aptly suggests the Asian fatalism and circular philosophy that represent Oblomov's and, by extension, Russia's Eastern Tartar heritage. The hero's Asian dressing gown, serving as his security blanket and finally his shroud, is an equally fitting symbol.

The reader is initiated into all the details of Russian provincial backwardness through Oblomov's lengthy dream of his sleepy backwater. The dream, a thematic outline of the work and its centerpiece, had been published separately as a sort of overture as early as 1849. The finished novel shows the deadening effect of this "blessed spot" on those who cannot free themselves from the dependencies it fosters. Little Ilya was born a normal child, willing to experiment, to rough it, to develop. The atmosphere of Oblomovka snuffed out all of these inclinations. Tradition stipulates that a Russian gentleman sit, surrounded by hordes of serfs who attend to his every whim, that he eat and doze most of the day, phlegmatically observe the seasonal and ecclesiastical rituals, ignore any attempt at change, be it literacy or postal service, and hope that the waves of Peter the Great's Westernizing reforms never reach his quiet hamlet. Inevitably, they do reach Oblomovka, and the product of its upbringing must serve his term in St. Petersburg.

The innumerable ways in which the transplanted Oblomov manages to ignore the city's reality take up a good portion of the narrative. Each failure on the realistic plane is paralleled by a success on the imaginary level, which always features a happy Oblomov in a paradisiacal Oblomovka. Eventually, Oblomov gains a questionable victory. A motherly widow's shabby lodging transforms itself into a blissful surrogate of Oblomovka for the by-now infantile hero. He has returned to the womb and lives out a short but happy span, until mental stagnation and greedy overeating end his life.

Two people try their best to save Oblomov. First Stolz, the half-German entrepreneur, as lean as an English racehorse where Oblomov is fat and flabby, uses reason and intellectual appeal to convince Oblomov to change. Then Olga, already adapted to a modern intelligentsia but preserving a deep love for Russia's cultural past, lures him with promises of selfless love. Sexually aroused, Oblomov briefly responds to her, but when he finds that Olga also demands intellectual arousal, constant mental awareness, he takes flight. The equally dull-witted widow offers both maternal and mistress services without the necessity of mental effort.

Stolz and Olga, who eventually marry, represent the best of traditional Russia fused with the best of imported progressive behavior. Stolz is an improved version of Peter Aduev. The latter's negative traits and final pessimistic outlook have been replaced by Stolz's cheerfulness and compassion. Even here, however, the author's descriptive talents hover lovingly over the blubbery Oblomov—over his dreams, his reflections, his blunders—while Stolz comes across as artificial and wooden, the victim of uninspired portrayal. Olga, who loves and appreciates Oblomov's values, is a more credible figure, and it is she who embodies and carries into the future the reconciliation of the conflict. In some respects, she acts as Goncharov's mouthpiece. Her dissatisfactions, even with the faultless Stolz, echo the author's own inability to believe fully in the spiritual benefits of a forward-moving Russia.

Goncharov had no such reservations when it came to praising the charms of Oblomovka. Its oneness with nature renders each inhabitant a paragon of virtue. No passionate outbursts or personal animosities mar the peacefulness. Serfs are not slaves, but content to be reflections of their masters. Their sloth and their ample participation in all the feasting, indulged by benevolent owners, help to deplete Oblomovka's reserves. When this slothful behavior is transplanted to St. Petersburg in the person of Oblomov's loyal valet Zakhar, it loses much of its bucolic enchantment, yet the touching interdependence of master and servant redeems the ineptness. It was simply impossible for Goncharov to carry to its logical conclusion his commonsense understanding that radical Slavophilism would result in national stagnation and regression.

The Precipice

Goncharov's unwillingness to endow his progressive characters with the vitality necessary to make them convincing and interesting asserts itself more fully in his last major work, *The Precipice*. It appeared in *Vestnik Evropy* at a time when emancipation was a fact, when Alexander II's liberalism gave wide scope to social commentators, when literature closely echoed the zeitgeist of reform. Goncharov's liberal representative is the political exile Volokhov, who, like Turgenev's nihilist Bazarov, spreads unrest in a deeply conservative village. Volokhov's positive qualities are quickly neutralized by his seduction of a virtuous country woman, Vera, who naïvely tries to straighten him out. Vera is also a link to the other male principal, Raisky, a St. Petersburg intellectual, who has failed to find a purpose in life and returns to his country estate in search of a footing. It is easy to see in him yet another embodiment of Goncharov's favorite type: the neurotic male whose interests, convictions, and common sense pull him toward reform but whose temperament and deep-seated impulses chain him to the past. In each of these split personalities, Goncharov's own schism finds expression. As before, he reserves the best of his descriptive talents for the backwoods, symbolized by the figure of the grandmother. It is in this traditional setting that the abused Vera finds regeneration and mental recovery; it is the rural past that bequeaths stability, sanity, and direction for the future.

Goncharov had once again drawn an exquisite cameo of old Russia, once again contrasted the conflicting values of old and new, once again pictured an artistically masterful "homecoming." Despite the popularity of the somewhat meandering work, Goncharov's point of view drew heavy moral indignation. Liberal critics were quick to point out that Goncharov had come down on the side of rural conservatism, that he favored the Slavophiles. Obviously and painfully out of step with the tenor of the time, and psychologically unable and unwilling to recapture his artistic independence, Goncharov withdrew. His subsequent writings did not approach the stature of his novels.

Goncharov's significance in the development of the Russian novel and Russian intellectual history remains great. He brought to life the characters of old Russia, with a style peculiarly his own, at a time when that patriarchal order began to disintegrate. In his portraits of Slavophiles and Westernizers, he elaborated on the dominant conflict of midcentury Russia. He was the first Russian author to integrate psychological complexities successfully and expertly into his plots, and thereby he created universal types.

Margot K. Frank

Other major works

SHORT FICTION: "Ivan Savich Podzhabrin," 1848; "Slugi starogo veka," 1888.

NONFICTION: *Fregat Pallada*, 1858 (*The Voyage of the Frigate Pallada*, 1965); "Mil'yon terzaniy," 1872; "Luchshe pozdno, chem nikogda," 1879; "V universitete," 1887; "Na rodine," 1888; "Neobyknovennaya istoriya," 1924.

MISCELLANEOUS: *Sobranie sochinenii*, 1883, 1888, 1952 (8 volumes).

Bibliography

Diment, Galya. "The Two Faces of Ivan Goncharov: Autobiography and Duality in *Obyknovennaia Istorija*." *Slavic and East European Journal* 32 (Fall, 1988). Diment discusses Goncharov's use of autobiographical facts in his writings, focusing on his novel *A Common Story*.

_______, ed. *Goncharov's "Oblomov": A Critical Companion*. Evanston, Ill.: Northwestern University Press, American Association of Teachers of Slavic and East European Languages, 1998. Collection of essays analyzing various aspects of the novel, including its questions of heroism; themes of mistaken identities and "food, eating, and the search for communion"; and its Freudian perspectives.

Ehre, Milton. *Oblomov and His Creator: The Life and Art of Ivan Goncharov*. Princeton, N.J.: Princeton University Press, 1973. A literary biography and a deep analysis of Goncharov's works. An excellent starting point for research.

Frank, Joseph. "Being and Laziness." *The New Republic*, January 29, 2007. Frank, a professor of comparative literature and Slavic languages and literature at Stanford University, provides a detailed discussion of both Goncharov's life and the novel *Oblomov* in response to the publication of a new translation of the work.

Lyngstad, Alexandra, and Sverre Lyngstad. *Ivan Goncharov*. New York: Twayne, 1971. A psychological sketch of the author and a discussion of his literary works, including separate chapters analyzing *Oblomov* and "The Art of Goncharov." Includes notes, references, and an index.

Maguire, Robert A. "The City." In *The Cambridge Companion to the Classic Russian Novel*, edited by Malcolm V. Jones and Robin Feuer Miller. New York: Cambridge University Press, 1998. Maguire's essay about the theme of the city in *Oblomov* and novels by other authors places Goncharov's work within the broader context of the development of the Russian novel.

Platonov, Rachel S. "Remapping Arcadia: 'Pastoral Space' in Nineteenth-Century Russian Prose." *Modern Language Review* 102, no. 4 (October, 2007): 1105-1121. An examination of the role of space and spatiality in *Oblomov* and three other Russian prose pastorals. Platonov argues that Russian culture gives a particular significance to the notion of boundaries, which explains, in part, why Russian writers' depictions of pastoral paradises are "particularly prone to disintegration and self-destruction."

EDMOND DE GONCOURT AND JULES DE GONCOURT

Edmond de Goncourt

Born: Nancy, France; May 26, 1822
Died: Champrosay, France; July 16, 1896
Also known as: Edmond-Louis-Antoine de Goncourt

Jules de Goncourt

Born: Paris, France; December 17, 1830
Died: Auteuil, France; June 20, 1870
Also known as: Jules-Alfred Huot de Goncourt

Principal long fiction

En 18 . . . , 1851
Les Hommes de lettres, 1860 (better known as *Charles Demailly*, 1868)
Sœur Philomène, 1861 (*Sister Philomène*, 1890)
Renée Mauperin, 1864 (English translation, 1888)
Germinie Lacerteux, 1865 (English translation, 1887)
Manette Salomon, 1867
Madame Gervaisais, 1869
La Fille Élisa, 1877 (by Edmond de Goncourt; *Elisa: The Story of a Prostitute*, 1959)
Les Frères Zemganno, 1879 (by Edmond de Goncourt; *The Zemganno Brothers*, 1886)
La Faustin, 1882 (by Edmond de Goncourt; English translation, 1882)
Chérie, 1884 (by Edmond de Goncourt)

Other literary forms

Edmond and Jules de Goncourt (gohn-KOOR) began their writing careers with minutely detailed studies of the eighteenth century on such diverse subjects as the French Revolution, art, and women. They wrote several plays, although without achieving any great success on the stage. Their talent for documentation and observation can best be seen in their famous *Journal: Mémoires de la vie littéraire* (1887-1896, 1956-1959), which preserves an unparalleled view of social and literary life in nineteenth century France. After his brother's death, Edmond continued the *Journal* by himself and also published studies on Japanese art.

Achievements

The Goncourt brothers excelled at depicting the manners and morals of contemporary French society, both in their *Journal* and in their novels, which, at times, resemble sociological studies. They were among the first to describe realistically the unfortunate lives of the lower classes of society. The realism of the Goncourts was an important precursor of Émile Zola's naturalism.

As historians, the Goncourts produced studies of eighteenth century painting that are still read by students of art history. In their *Journal* is preserved an irreplaceable chronicle of their own period in French history. Their most concrete achievement was the establishment of the Goncourt Academy, whose members still award an annual prize for literary excellence.

Biography

Edmond-Louis-Antoine and Jules-Alfred Huot de Goncourt were the sons of a cavalry officer in Napoleon's Imperial army and the grandsons of Antoine Huot de Goncourt, deputy of the national assembly of 1789. They were, respectively, the eldest and the youngest child of Annette-Cécile Guérin and Marc-Pierre Huot de

Goncourt. Edmond was born in Nancy on May 26, 1822, but the family moved to Paris shortly thereafter. Jules was born in Paris on December 17, 1830. Their father died four years later, leaving the boys and their mother in modest financial circumstances that nevertheless permitted the boys to attend school until both had passed the *baccalauréat* examination. Edmond began to study law in 1841 but, for financial reasons, left his studies in 1847 to take a minor position in the treasury.

When the Goncourts' mother died in 1848, they inherited a limited income, but one that spared them the necessity of working for a living and allowed them to devote themselves to art. Jules had recently finished his studies, and, once their financial affairs were in order, the brothers decided to hike to southern France while considering what direction their lives should take. They both sketched and kept a diary of their travels, in which they tried to capture the landscape in words as it would appear in a painting. Later, they viewed this trip as the turning point at which they became men of letters instead of artists, but on their return to Paris, they both continued to paint while collaborating on several inconsequential one-act plays and contributing essays on art criticism to contemporary reviews.

During this period, the brothers also wrote their first novel, *En 18 . . .* , which suffered the misfortune of appearing on December 2, 1851, the very day of Napoleon III's coup d'état. (Fate was not kind to the Goncourts with their publication dates: *La Faustin* was issued on the morning of Léon Gambetta's downfall, and the seventh volume of the *Journal* on the day of Sadi Carnot's assassination.) The publisher of *En 18 . . .* refused to advertise it, for fear that the new regime would see in the title an allusion to Napoleon I's eighteenth of Brumaire (the French republican calendar's equivalent of November 9, 1799).

In 1851, the Goncourts' cousin, the comte de Villedeuil, decided to found a weekly review of literature and the arts and offered editorial positions to Edmond and Jules. The first issue of *L'Éclair* appeared in January, 1852, but soon gave way to *Le Paris*, a review intended for a broader audience and to which the brothers continued to make literary contributions. Through these periodicals, the Goncourts met many personalities in literary and artistic circles, such as Gavarni, Nadar, and Théodore de Banville. The brothers were arrested on one occasion for having quoted some slightly erotic verse in an article. They were eventually acquitted of the charge of committing "an outrage against public morality," but the shock hastened their departure from the world of journalism.

Between 1859 and 1870, the Goncourts published monographs on eighteenth century painters, which were later collected in a single volume, *L'Art au XVIIIe siècle* (1859-1875; *French Eighteenth Century Painters*, 1948). They also wrote on the social history of the eighteenth century, publishing works of a more intimate nature than the official political histories. At the same time, they kept their *Journal* faithfully, recording the lives of their circle of literary and artistic friends. The salon of Princess Mathilde Bonaparte figures prominently, for example, as well as their friendships with Gustave Flaubert, Zola, Guy de Maupassant, and Alphonse Daudet.

The two decades between 1850 and 1870 were marked by regular publications of novels and historical works and by a brief return to the theater in 1865, when their first major play, *Henriette Maréchal* (pr. 1865), was produced by the Comédie-Française. The opening night provoked a hostile demonstration by students from the Latin Quarter, not because of the play itself, which was rather conventional, but because of the Goncourts' anti-Republican sympathies and their friendship with Princess Mathilde. After several performances, the audiences became more calm, but then the Imperial censors decided to ban the play. It was Jules's theory that Empress Eugénie had acted out of dislike for Princess Mathilde. In any case, the play, caught between the Republican opposition and the Imperial regime, was withdrawn by the end of its first month.

In 1868, the brothers moved to the Paris suburb of Auteuil because of Jules's declining health. They managed to continue work on *Madame Gervaisais*, for which they had prepared during trips to Italy in 1856 and 1867. The novel was published in 1869, but the brothers were not pleased with it. Their melancholy deepened when their friend Charles-Augustin Sainte-Beuve, the influential critic, did not review the novel. During that summer, they traveled gloomily, until finally, in September, they focused all of their energy on writing a biography of Gavarni, who had died in 1866.

On January 19, 1870, Jules made his last entry in the *Journal*. He began to lose his ability to spell, to recognize objects, and finally, to speak. He died on June 20 at the age of thirty-nine. Thus came to an end the remarkably close professional and emotional partnership between Jules and Edmond de Goncourt.

In the summer of 1870, however, the Franco-Prussian War overwhelmed Edmond's private sorrow. He had continued making entries in the *Journal* in a desultory way, but he was now revitalized by a desire to chronicle first the illusion of victory and then the disintegration of defeat. By the time the Germans had laid siege to Paris, Edmond had taken on the responsibility of reporting the afflictions of war, the nightmarish reality beneath the collective self-deception of his compatriots. During the turmoil of the Commune, Edmond's house in Auteuil was bombarded, and he witnessed the death of Communards at the barricades. These events resulted in some of the best-written and most vivid accounts in the *Journal*.

The last decades of Edmond's life were entirely devoted to literature. He wrote new novels and saw early ones adapted to the stage. Literary friendships were cultivated during regular evenings in his *grenier* (attic). The perpetuation of the Goncourts' name was ensured through the establishment of the Goncourt Academy. Edmond's will of 1874 set up a board of directors that would award an annual prize for a promising new literary talent. The first directors were chosen by Edmond himself from among the best writers of the day who represented new directions in literature—and who would not become members of the French Academy. The directors began their work upon Edmond's death in 1896 and awarded their first prize in 1903.

Edmond de Goncourt. (Library of Congress)

Analysis

In the second half of the nineteenth century, intellectual analysis became the driving force behind the art of fiction in France. In reaction to Romanticism, the new generation produced the realism of Flaubert and of Edmond and Jules de Goncourt. Although no novel by the Goncourts can be compared to Flaubert's *Madame Bovary* (1857; English translation, 1886), the Goncourt brothers are credited with producing the precursors of the great works of naturalism by Zola. For these writers, the novel became a kind of critical commentary on human society and especially on the social structure of the Second Empire. The Goncourts tended to focus on the plight of a single individual, analyzing the hereditary and environmental factors that contribute to the particular conflict at the heart of each novel.

Charles Demailly

Charles Demailly, written nearly a decade after *En 18 . . .*, was the first of the Goncourts' novels to receive serious critical attention. The hero, Charles Demailly, is a journalist for a newspaper called *Le Scandale*. Attempting to keep his personal integrity intact, he isolates himself from his cronies and writes a serious novel. At the same time, he marries an actor, Marthe, who turns out to be stupid and cruel and who destroys him with the help of a colleague in journalism who is envious of Charles's literary success. Marthe's betrayal causes Charles to go mad, and he ends up in an asylum.

As might be expected, the novel was not favorably received by journalist critics at the time. As would nearly always be the case, the characters were closely modeled on acquaintances of the Goncourts, but in *Charles Demailly* the emphasis is on venal journalism; writers of quality are omitted. A typical flaw is the lack of a plot line to blend the disparate scenes.

SISTER PHILOMÈNE

It was the Goncourts' next novel that brought their first critical success. In *Sister Philomène*, the Goncourts left their own familiar world of arts and letters to write of a nursing sister who falls in love with an intern. To research the setting of their novel, the Goncourts spent several days in the hospital in Rouen, to which they gained entry through Flaubert, whose father was a doctor. The result was a novel in which life in a hospital—reactions of the patients, conversations among the interns, visits of the chief surgeon—creates an absorbing, somber atmosphere.

The publication of *Sister Philomène* coincided with the vogue for realism, and as a result it received praise as a study from life. The realist writers were heavily influenced by the work of Hippolyte Taine, who held that an individual can be explained by his or her race, his or her moment in history, and his or her milieu. Thus, the novel begins with a lengthy section showing how the girl, Marie Gaucher, is reared and how her temperament, social class, and upbringing cause her to become the nurse, Sister Philomène. The Goncourts were always fascinated by the interplay of illusion and reality in human lives, and here the theme appears in the portrait of the idealistic young nurse beginning to perceive the realities of her new profession.

The first scene in the hospital takes place at night, when the nurses make their rounds by candlelight. The play of darkness and light underscores Philomène's confusion between a romanticized view of her profession (bringing light and life to the suffering) and the inescapable realities of pain and death. This passage demonstrates the Goncourts' artistry in description, for unlike some extreme advocates of realism, they believed that flat documentation must be illuminated by a fine writing style and artistic effects. In time, their characteristic style became known as *écriture artiste* (artistic writing).

Philomène's beloved is a young doctor, Barnier, who conceals a sensitive soul beneath a gruff, even crude, exterior. He finds the ideal love he seeks in his relationship with Sister Philomène. This love contrasts with the disillusion he encounters when obliged to operate on a former mistress, Romaine. She had remained for him a symbol of youthful love but now appears in a "fallen" state, having been injured during an orgy. Nevertheless, when his surgical skill cannot save Romaine, Barnier is in anguish. In a moment of madness, he embraces Philomène with passion, then commits suicide out of guilt and despair.

Sister Philomène demonstrates that the Goncourts had learned how to manage the form of the novel, providing credible motivations for their characters against a realistic setting. They had also proved capable of leaving their own world to examine a strange, even disagreeable, milieu in a way that has been called prenaturalistic.

RENÉE MAUPERIN

For their next novel, the brothers wished to study an entire social class, that of the modern bourgeoisie during the Second Empire. The novel was to have analyzed that middle class held in contempt by artists and writers of the time for its love of money, lack of taste, and naïve belief in "progress." The initial plan was modified when the Goncourts became friends with Louis and Blanche Passy. Jules admired Blanche to the extent of wishing to make her the heroine of a novel, and thus *Renée Mauperin* became the story of an intelligent, lively girl at odds with the conventions of her bourgeois family.

Most of the novel is a study of the bourgeoisie, for which Renée serves as a foil and a victim. The premise is that Renée has been educated by her doting father to think for herself and to see through the dull pretensions of her social class. It is not surprising, then, that she refuses all offers of marriage to the shallow young men her despairing mother finds as suitors. The central situation of the novel, however, deals with Renée's social-climbing, eminently proper brother, Henri, and his machinations to marry the wealthy daughter of his mistress.

This situation violates Renée's sense of honor, especially when Henri gives up his family name, at the request of his future father-in-law, to take on a noble one. The new name is supposed to have been extinct, but a last survivor appears, having been notified by Renée. When the aristocrat kills the arriviste in a duel, Renée falls ill of a heart disease and dies.

The novel scores some points against the pretensions of conventional society, especially in the portraits of Renée's older brother and sister. Henri is clearly an unscrupulous, but superficially correct, young man. The implication of his social success is that he is a typical bourgeois type, ambitious for money and power. The sister, Madame Davarande, has accepted society's values entirely and without question. She spells her name in the aristocratic fashion, d'Avarande, and seeks moral guidance from a fashionable priest, who "makes God seem *chic*."

Renée's spiritual and physical drama, which dominates the final chapters of the novel, is considerably less engrossing. After her shock at having indirectly caused her brother's death, Renée is taken to the country, where her lively, impertinent personality fades with her health. Furthermore, her illness is not medically believable, but resembles a literary death from a broken heart. Even the psychological motivation is unsound, because her brother is portrayed as insufferably unworthy of her love. Even so, in her refusal to compromise with the social system, Renée deflates its shallow, vulgar pretensions and reveals the vacuous posing at its heart.

GERMINIE LACERTEUX

Germinie Lacerteux, generally considered to be the Goncourts' finest work, is a study of the class that serves the bourgeoisie. It is the story of a servant girl whose character and upbringing lead her to debauchery, theft, sickness, and death. The character Germinie is based on the Goncourts' own servant, Rose Malingre, who had been an ideal servant to them from the time of Jules's infancy. When she died, bills began to arrive from her creditors revealing a sordid double life. She had stolen from her employers to support her lover and had even given birth to a child, managing to conceal her pregnancy. When the infant died, she sank into a life of frantic sexual promiscuity and alcoholism. The pneumonia and pleurisy that ended her life were contracted while she stood all night in the rain watching the house where her lover entertained another woman. The Goncourts, who had tended her faithfully during her illness, were astounded, although part of Rose's success in deceiving them was no doubt the result of their aristocratic myopia with regard to the lower classes. For them, Rose was a beloved servant, but not quite a whole and authentic individual.

The preface to *Germinie Lacerteux* proclaims the desire of the authors to seek the truth in fiction. The novel they offer the public represents a serious social inquiry, undertaken with scientific methods of analysis and psychological investigation. In *Germinie Lacerteux*, the Goncourts showed themselves to be in the vanguard of the enthusiasm for science that marked the decades of positivism. In comparing the work of the novelist to scientific work, they directly anticipated naturalism.

The resounding call, in the preface, for the common people to have their own novel certainly laid down a principle for future novelists that led to a broadening social representation in the novel. *Germinie Lacerteux*, however, provides a voyeuristic tour of the lower classes for aristocratic and middle-class readers. In this work, the brothers depict the sordid byways of vice and pathology and thus serve as observers and collectors of what is ugly, morbid, and repulsive.

The intention of the Goncourts was not to show a debauched hypocrite masking her nature beneath a proper maid's exterior. They wished to make her degeneration the logical and inescapable outcome of her social background and individual temperament. Thus, the novel begins with an exposition of her early childhood, her peasant origins, the death of her parents, and the necessity of joining her sisters in Paris. Germinie is abused and raped in her first jobs and finally finds a tranquil home as maid to an elderly spinster, Mademoiselle de Varandeuil, who lives in genteel poverty.

To this point, Germinie has been the passive victim of society's exploitation, but now her own temperament (which, the misogynist brothers imply, is typically feminine) begins to emerge. "Like all women," she needs to confide, to love, and to have a child. Unfortunately, Germinie is a guileless innocent when it comes to judging human nature, and her first friend and lover, a mother and son, respectively, take ruthless advantage of the love that comes to obsess Germinie.

Germinie has a child and is briefly happy until the infant dies, whereupon her degradation accelerates under the impetus of her insatiable and uncontrollable desires. At the same time, however, she remains devoted to her mistress. Even as she steals to pay her lover, Germinie is tormented by the possibility that her secret life may be revealed to Mademoiselle de Varandeuil. In the end, Germinie suffers the death of Rose Malingre and is buried in an unmarked pauper's grave.

Manette Salomon *and* Madame Gervaisais

The Goncourts' next two novels both follow the pattern of isolation and disintegration established in *Renée Mauperin* and *Germinie Lacerteux*. *Manette Salomon* is the story of a brilliant artist, Coriolis, who takes as his mistress the beautiful, exotic model Manette Salomon. When Manette becomes a mother, the drive of her maternal instinct overwhelms and destroys the artist's fragile creative genius. The novel's anti-Semitism and misogyny make it unpalatable reading today, for Coriolis weakens progressively as Manette alienates his Gentile friends. In *Madame Gervaisais*, the last novel the brothers wrote together, it is the heroine's extreme religious mysticism that isolates her from all but her brutal, perverse confessor, Father Sibilla.

The Goncourts based *Madame Gervaisais* on the religious conversion of their aunt, Nephtalie Lebas de Gourmont, whose anticlerical husband considered her to have gone nearly mad after a visit to Rome. The purpose of the text was to demonstrate how the combination of milieu and character could lead to a religious crisis in even an educated woman; this premise was supported by the brothers' belief that all women have an emotional need for religion.

The novel was not well received, in part because Father Sibilla preaches a twisted philosophy that causes the heroine to renounce her own child. The psychological motivation of the heroine is unconvincing, and her extreme isolation results in a work bereft of action and dialogue. It is a disappointing end to the collaboration of the two brothers.

Elisa

After Jules's death, Edmond returned to fiction writing with a novel they had prepared together, *Elisa*, but that displays a heavily sociological style, no doubt attributable to the absence of Jules's lighter touch. This novel recalls *Germinie Lacerteux* in its depiction of the depths of society. In this case, the brothers also wished to expose the horrors of incarceration in a women's prison and especially of the "Auburn system," under which inmates were kept in total silence. Finally, they wished to be strictly faithful to social reality, believing that literary portrayals of prostitutes were often sentimentalized.

As had been the usual practice of the brothers, Edmond chose to focus on one individual rather than to paint a social panorama. The novel opens in the courtroom where Elisa is condemned to death for the murder of a soldier, after which the novel reverts to her childhood to show how heredity and environment formed the young girl. In those days, midwives were closely linked to prostitutes in the social system, so Elisa drifts easily from the home of her mother, exhausted by that profession, into a life of prostitution.

Being too lazy to learn any other kind of work, Elisa is made to bear part of the responsibility for her plight, but the focus begins to shift to demonstrate how a young prostitute is victimized by society. As Elisa drifts from one bordello to another, she gradually loses her individuality as well as control over her own destiny. Feeling helpless, she begins to hate all men, and at last, degraded and dehumanized, she stabs a young soldier to death. Although for the reader her act is perfectly well motivated, the jury can only condemn it as an unjustifiable murder. Elisa's sentence is commuted to life imprisonment, and in prison her mind disintegrates under the rule of silence. She dies, a victim of a hypocritical penal system and social injustice. The pattern of progressive isolation is entirely appropriate to the subject.

The Zemganno Brothers

Edmond's next novel was, in a sense, a tribute to his brother Jules. *The Zemganno Brothers* tells of two brothers, Gianni and Nello, who perform together in a traveling circus. Many of the biographical details are drawn from the Goncourts' own lives. The two acrobats seem almost to become one as they perform, until their act is sabotaged and the younger brother breaks his legs. They are forced to become violinists for the circus, an end nearly as tragic as death.

Aside from the psychological insights into the relationship between Edmond and Jules, *The Zemganno Brothers* gives full play to the theme of illusion and reality. The motif of the mask, both literal and figurative, intrigued Edmond profoundly, especially the notion that an illusion can reveal a truth. The circus world obviously provides an ideal setting for such a theme, and in the novel, Nello is perplexed when his circus persona seems to absorb the real man. *The Zemganno Brothers*, psychologically complex and sociologically accurate, deserves to be better known.

LA FAUSTIN *and* CHÉRIE

With his interest in worlds of illusion, it is no surprise that Edmond should have written *La Faustin*, the life of an actor. Based on the life of Rachel (the stage name of Élisa Félix), the inspired tragedian, *La Faustin* tells of a famous actor at the Comédie-Française whose greatest role is Phèdre. She does not achieve brilliance, however, until she experiences a great passion of her own. When this passion—her lover—dies, La Faustin cannot keep from imitating his agonized grimace, thus revealing that for her, the mask of the actor has become the only reality.

With his last work, *Chérie*, Edmond attempted to depict the life of fashionable society in a series of vignettes centered on a young girl, spoiled by her grandfather. Unwilling to conform to popular standards of fiction, Edmond failed to breathe life into a subject that had already been dealt with successfully by Zola. *Chérie* is, nevertheless, typical of even the best of the Goncourts' novels in its lack of plot in the traditional sense. Analysis and sociological documentation dominate their creations, revealing their pessimistic view of human nature and social institutions. In an age of positive belief in progress, they could see only a static reality beneath an optimistic illusion. For them, the only human progress was toward death.

It is this very obsession with reality, however, that makes the Goncourts' novels compelling documents of their age. Ultimately, their achievement in fiction lies in their search for the truth in all realms of society and in their insistence on being historians and sociologists as much as novelists.

Jan St. Martin

OTHER MAJOR WORKS

PLAYS: *Henriette Maréchal*, pr. 1865; *La Patrie en danger*, pb. 1873; *À bas le progrès*, pr. 1893.

NONFICTION: *Histoire de la société française pendant la Révolution*, 1854; *Histoire de la société française pendant le Directoire*, 1855; *Sophie Arnould*, 1857; *Histoire de Marie Antoinette*, 1858; *L'Art au XVIIIe siècle*, 1859-1875 (*French Eighteenth Century Painters*, 1948); *Les Maîtresses de Louis XV*, 1860 (*The Confidantes of a King: The Mistresses of Louis XV*, 1907); *La Femme au XVIIIe siècle*, 1862 (*The Woman of the Eighteenth Century*, 1927); *Gavarni*, 1869; *Journal: Mémoires de la vie littéraire*, 1887-1896, 1956-1959; *Outamaro*, 1891 (*Utamaro*, 2008); *Hokousai*, 1896; *The Goncourt Journals (1851-1870)*, 1937, 1958.

MISCELLANEOUS: *Œuvres complètes*, 1922-1937 (41 volumes).

BIBLIOGRAPHY

Ashley, Katherine. *Edmond de Goncourt and the Novel: Naturalism and Decadence*. New York: Rodopi, 2005. Ashley analyzes Edmond's four solo novels, arguing that in these books he deviated from the strict naturalistic style that characterized the novels he wrote with his brother, Jules. She places Edmond's work within the larger context of late nineteenth century fin de siècle literature.

Baldick, Robert. *The Goncourts*. New York: Hillary House, 1960. A brief but highly informative overview of the Goncourts' lives and works, focusing on the biographical background to *Charles Demailly* and the brothers' other novels.

Billy, André. *The Goncourt Brothers*. Translated by Margaret Shaw. New York: Horizon Press, 1960. Considered the standard biography of the Goncourts, Billy's book is more detailed and comprehensive than that of Robert Baldick.

Brookner, Anita. "The Brothers Goncourt: The Breakdown of Joy." In *Romanticism and Its Discontents*. New York: Farrar, Straus and Giroux, 2000. Brookner, a Man Booker Prize-winning novelist and art historian, examines nineteenth century French Romantic painting in the light of the era's literature, including the work of the Goncourt brothers.

Grant, Richard B. *The Goncourt Brothers*. New York: Twayne, 1972. A volume in the Twayne World Authors series that interweaves biographical information about the Goncourts with detailed analyses of the themes and styles of their novels.

Heil, Elissa. *The Conflicting Discourses of the Drawing-Room: Anthony Trollope and Edmond and Jules de Goncourt*. New York: Peter Lang, 1997. Heil focuses on the social discourses among characters in the Goncourts' *Renée Mauperin* and Anthony Trollope's *Barchester Towers*, analyzing how the authors use these conversations to depict gender differences and other aspects of nineteenth century bourgeois society.

Weir, David. "Decadence and Naturalism: The Goncourts' *Germinie Lacerteux*." In *Decadence and the Making of Modernism*. Amherst: University of Massachusetts Press, 1995. Weir analyzes novels by the Goncourts and other European authors to demonstrate how late nineteenth and early twentieth century decadence was a significant literary movement and an important link between romanticism and modernism.

N. V. M. GONZALEZ

Born: Romblon, Philippines; September 8, 1915
Died: Manila, Philippines; November 28, 1999
Also known as: Nestor Vicente Madali Gonzalez

Principal long fiction

The Winds of April, 1940
A Season of Grace, 1956
The Bamboo Dancers, 1959

Other literary forms

Although N. V. M. Gonzalez traveled widely and taught the craft of writing on several continents, his principal rapport was always with the farmers and fishermen of his homeland. For such folk, social change over the centuries has been minimal, and their daily lives are attached to unvarying natural cycles. In each of his collections of short stories, Gonzalez found a deceptively simple style appropriate to the tempo of frontier life and the peasant mind-set.

Many of his first stories in *Seven Hills Away* (1947) seem more like sketches, reproducing the quiet, sometimes desperate, static lifestyle of the Philippine *kainginero*. On the small islands of Romblon and Mindoro, south of Manila, the landless frontiersman regularly leaves the village barrio in search of land. The wilderness is his if he will clear it by slash-and-burn techniques; yet it can never be cultivated well enough, by these primitive means, to support a large population. The first and last stories in the collection establish an outward movement from a growing settlement by pioneers anxious to find one more uninhabited horizon. Even as the stress falls on small-scale self-reliance, however, the fulfillment of ancestral patterns in the process of pioneering becomes dramatically evident. The animistic minds of the *kaingineros* tell them that nature is unfriendly, but they meet each setback with a stoic lack of surprise and complaint. The style of these stories is stark.

In Gonzalez's next collection, *Children of the Ash-Covered Loam* (1954), the potential for melodrama and self-pity is further undercut by reliance on children and plain women as narrators or central characters. The women are long-suffering and resilient; their own bodies' rhythms have made them knowledgeable about the mysteries of nature. As for the children, they are experiencing at first hand the wonders of birth and death, the depletion of innocence, which slowly drains away, and the gentle pace of experience. Contrasted with the enduring virtues of these ordinary people is the sophisticated lack of feeling in Mrs. Bilbao, failed wife and mother, in "Where's My Baby Now?" Too busy with city social obligations, she neglects her family.

A more elaborate contrast controls the 1963 collection *Look, Stranger, on This Island Now* as the restless peasants' new horizon becomes the town of Buenavista, in Romblon, and later the commercial centers of the principal Philippine island, Luzon. Disconnected from nature, the townspeople suffer from loneliness and the tensions between their competing needs for companionship and privacy. At best, they achieve momentary consolations. Stories in the second half of the volume express the sense of exile among city dwellers who have left the rural lifestyle behind but who have no traditions to guide them in their new life. In *Mindoro and Beyond* (1979), the five stories added to sixteen selected from previous volumes still waver between these poles: integrity, sustained with difficulty among the peasant poor, and the insecurity and corruption that befall those who desert the land.

Very early in his career, Gonzalez wrote poetry. Although comparatively few and short, the poems appeared in prestigious publications such as *Poetry* magazine and the anthologies *Heart of the Island* (1947), *Philippine Writing: An Anthology* (1953), and *Returning a Borrowed Tongue* (1995).

ACHIEVEMENTS

The paradox of N. V. M. Gonzalez is that he gained an international reputation for himself at a variety of intellectual centers, while identifying constantly with the uneducated but folk-wise peasant in the Philippines. His humor is far more subtle than that of Carlos Bulosan, for example, and his social criticism, though very real, is never doctrinaire, never polemical. For the pure portrait of the Filipino as frontier farmer—the dream of every landless tenant during centuries of oppression from Spanish overlords and now from estate holders who are his own countrymen—readers turn to the deceptively simple fiction of Gonzalez. Recognition of the honesty of these peasant images made both the author and his work necessary guests in many lands.

A 1949 Rockefeller Fellowship led to publication of Gonzalez's stories in a number of distinguished American "little magazines": *Sewanee Review*, *Literature East and West*, *Hopkins Review*, *Pacific Spectator*, *Literary Review*, and *Short Story International*. Gonzalez's work also appeared in such anthologies as *Stories from Many Lands* (1955), *Mentor Book of Modern Asian Literature* (1969), *Asian PEN Anthology* (1966), and *Asian-American Authors* (1972), and, in translation, in anthologies in several countries.

Gonzalez's tight control of form, contrary to florid Malayan-Spanish traditions, his reliance on a narrative's ability to convey its own meaning without intrusion by the author, and especially his ability to find English constructions that, to the Filipino ear, retain resemblances to the native vernaculars of his characters: All these qualities have influenced numbers of younger writers, who occasionally refer to him as the Anton Chekhov or Ernest Hemingway of the Philippines. For his influence as a writer of fiction, as an essayist, and as a workshop director, he received the Republic Award of Merit (1954), the Republic Cultural Heritage Award (1960), and the Rizal Pro Patria Award (1961), thus fulfilling the earlier promise shown when, in 1940, his first novel won honorable mention in the Commonwealth Literary Awards contest, and, in 1941, his collection of stories, then called *Far Horizons*, shared first prize in the same annual contest.

BIOGRAPHY

Born in 1915 on one of the smaller mid-archipelago Philippine islands, Nestor Vicente Madali Gonzalez was taken as a child to the larger neighboring island of Mindoro by his father, who was a teacher. There he spent his youth among farmers and fishermen, figures who dominated his fiction. After graduating from the University of the Philippines, then in Manila, he turned to writing a newspaper column, as well as a novel and short tales about the people of Mindoro. He also was one of the Veronicans, a group of young writers striving for stark and striking imagery. The authenticity of his fiction won him national attention just before Japanese Occupation forces landed on Luzon. When English was practically forbidden by the invaders, Gonzalez and others wrote in Tagalog but brought to the native language new techniques, themes, and theories as an alternative to formulas in conventional literature.

Gonzalez's chance for prominence came in 1947, when the Swallow Press in Denver, Colorado, published his prizewinning stories, *Seven Hills Away*. In 1949, a Rockefeller grant allowed him to visit several writing centers in the United States and to attend both Stanford and Bread Loaf workshops. On his return to the Philippines, he was appointed to the faculty of the state university, which had just been constructed in the temporary capital, Quezon City; he taught creative writing and comparative literature there for eighteen years. During Carlos P. Romulo's presidency of the university, Gonzalez served as public relations assistant and speech writer to the former ambassador to the United Nations. Although Gonzalez held no graduate degree, he was tenured on the basis of his distinguished contributions to the national culture as a novelist and short-story writer, as well as editor of the eclectic *Diliman Review* and consultant to Benipayo Press and to Bookmark. Bookmark had risked nonprofit publication of Philippine literature in order to bring recognition and rewards to young writers. In 1964, he wrote in Rome and the Italian Alps on a second Rockefeller grant. In 1968, he held visiting professorships at both the University of Hong Kong and the University of California, Santa Barbara.

Beginning in 1969, Gonzalez was professor of English, particularly developing world literature, at California State University, Hayward. In 1977, he served as visiting professor of Asian American literature at the University of Washington, and in the summer of 1978, after a long absence, he briefly returned to the University of the Philippines as writer-in-residence. One result of that visit was the publication of *Mindoro and Beyond*, a retrospective volume drawn from four decades of his stories, which initiated the Philippine Writers' Series for the University of the Philippines Creative Writing Center. Gonzalez retired from university teaching in 1989. He died in Manila on November 28, 1999.

Analysis

The superiority of N. V. M. Gonzalez's novels lies principally in their ability to provide social realism without submitting to sentimentality, at one extreme, or to any doctrinaire program of violent reform at the other. This same authenticity of character and situation acquits him of the charge of being a mere imitator, even though age-old struggles between peasant and proprietor, between barrio and city values, recur in his work. They do so not because of slavish adherence to literary formulas but because basic social patterns have persisted in Philippine culture for hundreds of years: It is to these patterns that Gonzalez is true, and in response to them that his vision has remained constant.

The Winds of April

Even in his autobiographical first novel, *The Winds of April*, written in his youth, Gonzalez presents attitudes that reappear in his short stories and later novels: an attachment to the array of creatures on land and sea, a respect for the men and women whose lives depend on nature's whims and their own unflagging efforts, and a dream of surmounting these hazards without forgetting them, by moving to cities where opportunities for education and for writing about one's discoveries and their implications abound. At the same time that *The Winds of April* describes the aspirations of the author from birth to young adulthood, it captures the hopes of a whole people on the verge of independence from the United States. Virtually all the copies of that novel, along with hopes for a smooth transition to national sovereignty, were destroyed during World War II.

A Season of Grace

What emerges in *A Season of Grace*, during postwar reconstruction, is a view less naïve but still based on the courage and determination of a people who find in hardship the same promise of life's renewal that the rich volcanic ash of their soil offers their labor. They do not arise abruptly, miraculously, like the phoenix from those ashes, but their right to stand erect is wholly and undeniably earned, if only gradually, painstakingly.

The young married couple, Sabel and Doro, who leave the overworked plots of Tara-Poro and the fishing barrio at Alag to claim interior *kaingins* of their own on Mindoro, are in many ways like adult children. The cadences of Gonzalez's prose resemble rituals of survival, marked by seasons of seedtime, caretaking, and harvest. The action encompasses slightly more than one year's cycle in this couple's efforts to restore a wilderness to its garden state, although Gonzalez knows well that slash-and-burn techniques can destroy more than they cultivate. Petty officials requisition several intricately and meticulously woven mats from them. Their merchant landlord, Epe Ruda, maintains the rule that debts double if they are not repaid in time. Yet after the year covered in the novel, Sabel and Doro are not quite so impoverished as before and they have two male children; they are likely to endure and prevail.

The year has not been one completely filled with favors. Their friend, Blas Marte, once debt-free, has become a sharecropper for a usurious rice merchant. Their own rice sack hangs empty for months, and there are nightmares, premonitions of death and disaster. Multitudes of rats attack their harvest, as greedily bent on taking what is not theirs as are the landlord, the treasurer, and his deputy. Even Sabel and her husband, Doro, come to blows occasionally, as a result of misunderstanding and exhaustion. She is the more resilient, gentle, contemplative, and naturally good-hearted. Doro is sometimes consumed by his own unending chores. When his wife is seriously ill, he is most concerned with how he will survive without her. He can be impatient, jealous without cause, more erratic than Sabel in growth toward maturity.

Yet a contrast clearly is established between these two and their materialistic, childless landlord. The implied emphasis on their compliance rather than on bitter complaint is a sign, from the author, of a resignation nearly religious, an elemental act of faith. At the beginning of a new year, Sabel and Doro begin still another clearing; their infant lies nearby like a seedling, very much part of the stream of the life-force. What seemed a relentless cycle of trial, progress, and frustration has become a slow and painful spiral upward, a combination of change and continuity, of improvement gradual but sure.

The Bamboo Dancers

The true polar opposite to the simple, instinctual peasant such as Doro is not his middle-class landlord but the *ilustrado*, the elitist intellectual portrayed in Gonzalez's *The Bamboo Dancers*. If the wilderness dominates *A Season of Grace*, wasteland imagery permeates the later novel.

Ernie Rama is a sculptor who tries to conceal his lack of creativity by wandering through the world. Such is his nature that, wherever he goes on his study grant in the United States, he keeps a distance between himself and others, in order to avoid facing and confessing his own self-alienation. The stargazer at the Vermont writers' conference waves a message that Ernie avoids; the lonely U.S. Information Service girl in Kyōto whom he planned to meet, disappears; en route to Hiroshima, he is with an interpreter who stays mute; the Japanese switchboard operator and he are mutually unintelligible. Everyone remains a stranger, so quick is Ernie's passage among them, like someone running from an atomic cloudburst. Despite its scenes in Hiroshima, the novel is less about the unspeakable horror of nuclear war than it is about this deliberate detachment, this maintained silence that aggravates differences and helps cause war.

In his travels, Ernie avoids even his own countrymen, especially the elderly, lest they place some claim on his social conscience. He resembles the barren Fisher King from T. S. Eliot's *The Waste Land* (1922), who is doomed to sterility because of his lack of love, his inability to share. What Ernie fathers in an old acquaintance, Helen Reyes, who has turned to him for emotional warmth, is only a miscarriage. He is at best sexually ambivalent, actually preferring no intimacy under any circumstances with anyone. While Helen's American fiancé, Herb Lane, is involved in the accidental death of a Chinese girl in Taipeh, Ernie is characteristically removed from the scene by sickness. When Herb is murdered as a result of that death, Ernie can only offer abstract sympathy. Persuading Helen to escape to Macao, where perhaps she can purchase rare cosmetics, he contaminates her with his own self-indulgence.

Even at the moment of near drowning, while fishing back in the Philippines, when he cries out to be rescued, it is unclear whether he has learned the importance of others except to satisfy his own impulsive needs. To some extent, the people of Hiroshima, who think exclusively of their own suffering but not of those who were their victims in war, represent this same egocentrism, so opposed to the traditional sense of brotherhood among Filipinos.

The great subtlety of this novel lies in the author's strict dependence on a defective narrator, whose self-deception, contradictions, and confusions become evident through a recurring pattern of nonencounters, as well as through certain symbols. The principal symbol employed by Gonzalez is the national dance, the *tinikling*, in which the object is to maintain a rhythm of rapid movement that prevents the feet from ever being touched by the clash of poles. In the Philippines, the caste of "untouchables" is not the impoverished peasant but the elite leadership, on which society depends so much for patronage, but from which the masses more commonly have received indifference, cruelty, and betrayal of purpose.

In *The Bamboo Dancers*, as in his short stories and other novels, Gonzalez's characters are discovered rather than explained. They present themselves without comment from the author. Such subtlety and disciplined self-restraint keep Gonzalez's fiction far from the ordinary literature of protest, which often disregards credibility or complexity of character in order to engage in extensive polemics. Perhaps Gonzalez's constant attentiveness to the manner of speech and even to silence owes much to his culture's reliance, for unobtrusive communication, on courteous consideration of others and on wordless body language. Gonzalez's craft is perfectly expressive of these Asian aspects of Philippine folkways.

Leonard Casper
Updated by L. M. Grow

Other major works

SHORT FICTION: *Seven Hills Away*, 1947; *Children of the Ash-Covered Loam*, 1954; *Look, Stranger, on This Island Now*, 1963; *Mindoro and Beyond*, 1979; *The Bread of Salt, and Other Stories*, 1993; *A Grammar of Dreams, and Other Stories*, 1997.

NONFICTION: *The Father and the Maid: Essays on Filipino Life and Letters*, 1990; *Kalutang: A Filipino in the World*, 1990; *Work on the Mountain*, 1995; *The Novel of Justice: Selected Essays, 1968-1994*, 1996.

Bibliography

Bayuga, Rosy May. "Gonzalez' Sabel: A Brown Madonna." *Philippine Studies* 45, no. 1 (1997): 124-134. This article focuses on the characterization of Sabel, the female protagonist of *The Bamboo Dancers*.

Casper, Leonard. "N. V. M. Gonzalez." In *New Writing from the Philippines: A Critique and Anthology*. Syracuse, N.Y.: Syracuse University Press, 1966. An incisive treatment of Gonzalez's novels is included in this survey by a preeminent critic of Philippine literature in English. Includes a checklist of Philippine literature published in the United States from 1930 until 1965.

Cheung, King-Kok, ed. "Filipino American Literature." In *An Interethnic Companion to Asian American Literature*. New York: Cambridge University Press, 1997. Gonzalez's work is analyzed in this study of literature by North American writers of Asian descent. Includes a bibliography and an index.

De Jesus, Edilberto, Jr. "On This Soil, in This Climate: Growth in the Novels of N. V. M. Gonzalez." In *Brown Heritage: Essays on Philippine Cultural Tradition and Literature*, edited by Antonio G. Manuud. Quezon City, Philippines: Ateneo de Manila, 1967. De Jesus presents a historian's perspective, demonstrating parallels between Philippine society and the society reflected in Gonzalez's novels as subsistence farming became industrialized. Includes a bibliography and an index.

Espiritu, Augusto. "The 'Pre-History' of an 'Asian American' Writer: N. V. M. Gonzalez' Allegory of Decolonization." *Amerasia Journal* 24, no. 3 (1998). A profile of Gonzalez, discussing his personal background, career history, major literary achievements, criticism of his work, and his views on American colonialism in the Philippines. Reprinted in *Recovered Legacies: Authority and Identity in Early Asian American Literature*, edited by Keith Lawrence and Floyd Cheung (Philadelphia: Temple University Press, 2005).

Gonzalez, N. V. M. "Notes on a Method and a Culture." *General Education Journal* 4 (1962): 87-94. An excellent analysis, revealing the author's approach to prose fiction.

Guzman, Richard P. "'As in Myth, the Signs Were All Over': The Fiction of N. V. M. Gonzalez." *Virginia Quarterly Review* 60 (Winter, 1984): 102-118. A lucid explication, particularly of Gonzalez's characterization and style in his fiction.

Tiempo, Edilberto K. "The Fiction of N. V. M. Gonzalez." In *Literary Criticism in the Philippines, and Other Essays*. Manila: De La Salle University Press, 1995. A thorough, extended critique by one of the foremost prose writers of the Philippines. Includes a bibliography and an index.

Zuraek, Maria Elnora C. "N. V. M. Gonzalez' *A Season of Grace*." In *Essays on the Philippine Novel in English*, edited by Joseph A. Galdon. Quezon City, Philippines: Ateneo de Manila, 1979. Zurak comments on the two meanings of grace in the novel: a period of postponement or second chance and regeneration through sanctification by natural forces. Includes a bibliography and an index.

PAUL GOODMAN

Born: New York, New York; September 9, 1911
Died: North Stratford, New Hampshire; August 2, 1972

Principal long fiction

The Grand Piano: Or, The Almanac of Alienation, 1942
The State of Nature, 1946
The Dead of Spring, 1950
Parents' Day, 1951
The Empire City, 1959 (includes *The Grand Piano*, 1942, *The State of Nature*, 1946, *The Dead of Spring*, 1950, and *The Holy Terror*, 1959)
Making Do, 1963

Other literary forms

By any standards, Paul Goodman was a prolific writer. In addition to his novels, he wrote collections of poetry, several of which were privately printed. The most noteworthy are *The Lordly Hudson: Collected Poems* (1962), *Homespun of Oatmeal Gray* (1970), and the *Collected Poems* (1973). He also published ten plays between 1941 and 1970 and three books of literary criticism: *Kafka's Prayer* (1947), *The Structure of Literature* (1954), and *Speaking and Language: Defence of Poetry* (1971). Goodman also wrote a partial autobiography: *Five Years: Thoughts During a Useless Time* (1966). This list, however, represents only a fraction of his oeuvre, which includes more than thirty titles. In addition, he contributed regularly to and served as film-review editor of the *Partisan Review* and as a television critic for *The New Republic*.

Achievements

Paul Goodman more closely approximates the Renaissance man than does perhaps any other twentieth century American of letters. A prolific writer in many genres—novels, poems, essays, dramas, short stories, literary criticism, education, sociology, and community planning—and the author of studies in psychotherapy, Goodman has entries under twenty-one different categories in the catalogs of the New York Public Library. He was not discovered by the reading public until 1960 as a result of his book *Growing Up Absurd* (1960), a spirited attack on the values of midcentury America. Because Goodman wrote in such diverse forms, he is not easily categorized. He shares with many of his colleagues, such as Saul Bellow, Philip Roth, and Bernard Malamud, a perspective that is distinctly Jewish: a feeling for alienation, a skeptical nature that is allied with visionary tendencies, and a penchant for social justice. As a novelist, he is best remembered for *The Empire City*.

Biography

Paul Goodman was born in Greenwich Village, New York City, on September 9, 1911, to a family in financial straits so serious that his father deserted them soon after Paul's birth. Not surprisingly, many of Goodman's books deal with fatherless boys struggling to establish some sort of alliance both with adult males and with society. The lonely boy excelled in school ("he made it difficult for us ordinary geniuses," one classmate remarked).

The years Goodman spent at the College of the City of New York between 1927 and 1931 were formative ones in his intellectual growth. Here he came in contact with the legendary teacher-philosopher Morris Cohen, who found Goodman to be a willing student with an inquiring and skeptical mind. Thereafter, Goodman found outlets for his omnivorous interests, publishing pieces on philosophy, short stories, cinema criticism, and poetry. Though considered a promising writer while still in his twenties, Goodman did not attract a wide audience. During the 1950's, in fact, he grew despondent over his lack of recognition; it was not until shortly before his fiftieth birthday that this reputation burgeoned.

"Too long a sacrifice makes a stone of the heart," remarked William Butler Yeats in a line that is appropriate to Goodman, who was often viewed by contemporaries as arrogant, distant, and hard, yet to his credit was courageous, committed to social good, and helpful to other writers. Complicating his life was his bisexuality, which he explored at length in his fiction. At a time when others were circumspect about such things, Goodman made little effort to conceal his sexuality, being dismissed as a graduate student from the University of Chicago and later from other teaching positions. Very likely, his novel *Parents' Day* chronicles the difficulties related to his sexuality.

In 1942, Goodman published his first novel, *The Grand Piano*. This novel (Goodman referred to this book as an educational romance) focuses on the spiritual growth of a parentless eleven-year-old boy named Horatio Alger, who roams the streets of Manhattan, surviving by his wits and defying all institutions, most notably the educational establishment. He is an "artful dodger" like Goodman himself, who also took pride in his street smarts. Goodman's fascination with psychotherapy—he became a lay analyst for the Gestalt Institute of New York—permeates the later segments of his tetralogy, *The Empire City*. Despite his prolific output, Goodman was for most of his life as unsuccessful financially as his father had been, though he was a good deal more responsible. By his own contention, he lived below the poverty line—until 1960, he both boasted and lamented that he was as poor as any sharecropper.

Goodman's most difficult period occurred during the 1950's, at the height of his creative powers. His marriage was faltering, his daughter was ill, and his submissions were regularly rejected. Very likely, his outspoken views were considered alarming during the McCarthy era. In 1960, the shift in the mood of Americans coincided with the publication of *Growing Up Absurd*, the book that earned Goodman recognition. His success, however, did little to reconcile him to those aspects of American culture he had been deploring; the Vietnam War, so destructive to American morale, ironically established his credentials as a prophet to the young.

Success did not appreciably alter Goodman's lifestyle, though it did make him a sought-after lecturer. The reader who wishes to gain some appreciation of what that lifestyle was like is advised to read *Making Do*, as well as the rare *Parents' Day* and the poetry. In 1967, Goodman's son, Matthew, was killed in a climbing accident, a grievous event that Goodman dealt with extensively in his poetry. Goodman died on August 2, 1972, at the age of sixty, leaving his wife and two daughters.

Analysis

"I have only one subject," wrote Paul Goodman, "the human beings I know in their man-made environments." All of Goodman's novels explore human beings in relation to the institutions that both reflect and shape their values. In Goodman's view, rather than abetting human development, institutions thwart aptitude and foster stupidity. From this base, Goodman argues passionately for a more humane society—one that would offer worthwhile goals, meaningful work, honest public speech, and patriotism and at the same time encourage healthy animal desire. Goodman indicts American culture for being unequal to all these aspirations.

In Goodman's works, society's failure leads individuals to attempt to create their own community—one that is scaled down and decentralized. The author is ab-

Paul Goodman. (Archive Photos)

sorbed with the individual's wresting from the larger social order a more workable and personalized one—a community. In this endeavor, Goodman is not alone: In fact, he is engaged in a quintessentially American occupation, that of creating "a city upon a hill," however different from John Winthrop's ideal. Indeed, Nathaniel Hawthorne manifested a similar interest when he participated in the Brook Farm experiment. In fiction, Mark Twain's Huck Finn flees the larger society to find communion with Jim on the Mississippi. Both Jay Gatsby and Dick Diver among F. Scott Fitzgerald's characters create a community but are ultimately defeated by corrosive contact with the worst aspects of American materialism and illusion. A similar concern for community informs Goodman's writing, though his novels are typically urban; the sole exception, *Parents' Day*, is set in upstate New York. In all of his novels, the protagonist and his friends strive to establish a workable, nourishing community but find themselves in constant danger of engulfment by the debased larger society.

As evidenced by the diversity of his interests, Goodman was an intellectual, keenly aware of his debt to Western traditions. His thought was shaped by Aristotle, Immanuel Kant, Thomas Hobbes, Franz Kafka, Martin Buber, and Wilhelm Reich. From Hobbes and Kant, Goodman derived material for his speculations on the social contract, by means of which people relinquished certain freedoms in order to achieve civilization. In Kafka, Goodman perceived a surrealist and comic spirit as well as the notion that writing was a form of prayer. One critic, Theodore Roszak, has identified a "coarse-grained Hasidic magic" about Goodman's work, presumably a reference to the author's search for transcendence in the mundane. Goodman may well have found Buber's idealized notion of human relations congenial—the effort to transform "I-It" relationships into "I-Thou" ones.

Goodman's work as a lay therapist with the Gestalt Institute of New York no doubt reflected his interest in the psychosexual theories of Reich, which inform all of his writings. One detects this influence in the "therapy" sections of *The Empire City* (especially those in which Horatio woos Rosalind); in *Parents' Day*, where the teacher-narrator uses physical intimacy as an educational tool; and in *Making Do*, where Harold and Terry suffer from sexual deprivation. In all his novels, Goodman argues that personal contact should be communal and psychosexual. It may be disconcerting to the reader to discover that the narrator of *Making Do* is bisexual and that the narrator-teacher of *Parents' Day* is engaged in homosexual liaisons with his adolescent students, but Goodman does not flinch from offering such revelations. Rather, he celebrates his protagonists' (and his own) sexuality—not always to good effect. The reader may well feel distracted when an author insists on toleration for his or her sexuality, may feel annoyed when asked to respond not to the event the artist is rendering but to the artist's challenge.

Though one must be cautious in identifying the narrator with the author, Goodman does not make much effort to conceal the autobiographical nature of much of his fiction. On the contrary, Goodman often addresses the reader in asides that prevent the normal suspension of disbelief. "This is no book/ Who touches this touches a man," boasted Walt Whitman as he artfully concealed himself, yet Goodman does not trouble to disguise himself. The narrators of *Making Do* and *Parents' Day* are interchangeable—both closely resembling the sort of intellectual Goodman was: a man of letters who was also a man of the streets.

At his best, Goodman is imaginative, profound, and witty. *The Empire City*, though uneven, is a neglected masterpiece. At his worst, Goodman becomes hortatory and shrill, as in *The Dead of Spring*, the third work in the tetralogy, or careless in his prose, as in *Making Do*.

THE EMPIRE CITY

The Empire City, Goodman's ambitious tetralogy, follows a cluster of characters who have become alienated from not only society but also themselves. The first novel in the tetralogy, *The Grand Piano*, is subtitled *The Almanac of Alienation*; thus, Goodman announces that he will be exploring what Robert Frost called "inner weather"; he will be attempting a chronicle of the spirit as it unfolds in life. Given this aim, it should not be surprising if some of the book's passages do not yield themselves readily to analysis. Goodman, like his literary forebears, Kafka, André Gide, William Blake, and Rainer Maria Rilke, seems to be charting the ineffable and bidding his reader to follow.

The Grand Piano

The narrator of *The Grand Piano*, hardly distinguishable from Goodman himself, is often obtrusive in the manner of Henry Fielding. By mediating between character and reader, the narrator encourages the reader to regard the protagonists as friends, members of a community of which he or she is a part. These new friends are vital, larger than life, multitalented, heroic. Witness the name of the hero—Horatio Alger—based on the American writer who encouraged boys to lead virtuous lives full of heroic deeds.

The Alger tales dealt with the self-made man who succeeded in that great mecca of success, New York City. Goodman's Alger, however, is a street-smart guttersnipe who, having destroyed all records of his existence, revels in his outcast status. Untouched by social institutions, such as school, he is truly a self-made eleven-year-old youth. In the opening episode, he meets Mynheer Duyck Colijn. The critic Sherman Paul has observed that Mynheer is an exemplar of the cultured man. Like his Dutch forebears, Mynheer is a model of tolerance and civic virtue. If Horatio is alienated, Mynheer is the opposite. In their initial meeting, the cunning, sneering, artful dodger is pitted against the sophisticated, virtuous adult. Reading the latter's name as "Dick Collegian," however, suggests another aspect of his character: his innocence. His rationality and civic pride will be sorely tested by the outbreak of war.

Horatio has no parents but is being reared, as Goodman was, by a brother and sister and, again like Goodman, is searching for a father. He settles on Eliphaz, a sort of Yiddish Daddy Warbucks, but one who combines patriarchal wisdom with financial acumen. In Eliphaz, Goodman achieves the sort of fantastic realism that readers customarily associate with Charles Dickens. Eliphaz's presence creates some of the best scenes in the novel. This merchant prince represents the idealized spirit of early capitalism: He keeps a mysterious ledger containing only an accumulating number of zeros; he practices detachment by selling his own furniture, often while his family is still sitting on it; he idly places a price tag on his own son ("$84.95. $75 cash? Good! Sold!"). He is a man of culture who can spout Johann Wolfgang von Goethe and Baruch Spinoza. Opposed to the anarchistic spirit of the Algers, who subsist on welfare, he impulsively sends them a grand piano, one that is so large that they are forced to sleep under it. Gnomically, he explains his gesture, which proceeds from mixed motives: "It's always worthwhile to hurl large gifts toward your adversary. Where is she going to put such an animal? How is she going to explain it to the relief investigator I'll send around tomorrow?" So wonderful a comic creation is Eliphaz that the reader can only regret his death at the opening of the second novel of the tetralogy. His place in literature has been usurped by the more impersonal Milo Minderbinder of Joseph Heller's *Catch-22* (1961), a similarly restless but more mindless spirit of capitalism.

Other members of the community include Horatio's family, Lothario/Lothair and Laura. Lothair, a follower of the anarchist Prince Petr Kropotkin, is a reformer who is vilified and persecuted by the state. As Sherman Paul comments, he is yet another side of Goodman himself—a reformer and educator. In this respect, he is also reminiscent of the protagonists of *Making Do* and *Parents' Day*. *The Grand Piano* proceeds toward a communal reconciliation that is partial at best; as in Richard Wagner's music, resolution is never far away but never quite arrives. Indeed, the climax of the novel has the characters attending a performance of Wagner's *Die Meistersinger*, which promises "an exulting community spirit," but, as Horatio shrewdly observes, "It's all to be paid for at [Beckmesser's] expense." The survival of the larger society, as it does in fairy tales, hinges on the scapegoating of one of its members, hinges on projecting the dark side of the psyche onto a villain who can then be defeated by a hero.

The novel ends with another musical contest, one involving the grand piano. Embedded in this section are hints of the Arthurian contest to secure the sword Excalibur. Lothair, who is a composer, performs beautifully and by rights should be declared the winner, but he is arrested and transported to jail—presumably a victim of scapegoating by a society preparing itself for war.

The State of Nature

The second novel in the tetralogy, *The State of Nature*, pursues Goodman's interest in the contact point between the organism and its environment. The setting is now 1944. Horatio has grown to young adulthood; his adopted father has died, just like Alfred, Lord Tennyson's King Arthur, leaving behind a world that has grown incomprehensible to him. In this book, the narrator discourses tirelessly (and, at times, tiresomely) on the subject of war, as not only a social reality but also a spiritual phenomenon. Goodman viewed war as a debased form of the spiritual life that requires putting oneself in jeopardy. This novel is weaker than its predecessor, first because Goodman exhorts his reader rather than rendering his material into narrative, and second because the author uses the war as a symbol but does not acknowledge the moral imperatives that made World War II a necessity.

The State of Nature explores the themes of putting oneself in danger and engaging in "a long drawn out losing fight"—both activities in which the social activist Goodman was experienced. In this book, the central figures pass from dissent to alienation. Horatio is shot at by overwrought National Guardsmen. Lothair broods in jail about the paradox that his ardent desire to serve society is unappreciated unless that service takes the form of fighting. Laura, the community planner and wife of Mynheer, has been ordered to undo her work: By means of camouflage, she is to transform a community of her design, a land of milk and honey, back into a desert. Lothair escapes, but, driven mad by social rejection (his name Lothario indicates he is a lover, but of humanity), he executes a plan to release the animals from the zoo. In the pandemonium created, little Gus, incestuous offspring of Arthur and his sister, Emily (both children of Eliphaz), is killed. The zoo's curator happens to be Mynheer, who in contrast to Lothair is permitted to serve humanity but is fated to do so without conviction. He and his wife, Laura, the reader is told, are "alienated from their natures." In his case, the result is that the connection between his intellect and his emotions is severed, rendering him impotent. In a scene reminiscent of Blake's prophetic books, Mynheer (intellect) is paralyzed by Emily's anguished cry (heart) concerning the sight of the tiger destroying little Gus. Lothair then leads Mynheer into the cage vacated by the tiger.

In this chapter, Goodman shifts emphasis from social concerns to psychological ones. Community needs must wait while individuals attempt to restore their shattered equilibrium. Emily, for example, is unable to save her son from the tiger; she is "frozen into inaction by her 'mixed desire.'" The death of her son, however, leads her to a primal cry that enables her to function once again. Her therapeutic experience (this section was conceived at the time of Goodman's developing interest in Gestalt therapy) becomes a paradigmatic model for others who also are experiencing their alienation from self. Social conditions only serve to enforce this alienation, as is revealed in the prophecy of Eliphaz that concludes the novel. In it, the dying capitalist foresees the advent of a consumer economy, mass conformity, and mass education, all resulting in "Asphyxiation"—a state in which the individual is unable to breathe freely or to experience his or her own vital desires. What has replaced human community he scornfully terms "Sociolatry."

The Dead of Spring

The third novel in the tetralogy is *The Dead of Spring*. All must come to grips with the aftermath of war, must fight the long, drawn-out losing fight of the duration, as Eliphaz predicted. Lothair turns inward to his own pain, away from social concerns; Mynheer delivers a valediction on human beings combining elements of Prince Hamlet and Fritz Perls; the marriage between Emily and Lothair proves barren; the community spirit languishes. There is a brief interlude when Horatio meets Laura, but generally this is a gloomy period. Horatio discovers himself to be impotent but is redeemed and taught to love by a young lad, whom Sherman Paul identifies as an aspect of Horatio's own submerged self—the youthful street urchin Horatio had been in the opening novel. As is typical in a romance, the lovers overcome their vicissitudes—though here the impediments are largely of their own devising—and fall in love. As Horatio is about to become a father, however, he is arrested—forced, as it were, by parenthood into recognition of the social contract. Horatio is indicted, not for resisting the state as Lothair had been at the conclusion of *The Grand Piano*, but for refusing to adopt a stand, much like the lost souls in Hell's anteroom of Dante's *Divine Comedy* (c. 1320). Horatio admits to his error but counters it with the information that he is in love; in comic fashion, the conflict is resolved, the charge is dropped.

This lighthearted respite provides comic relief from the chapters that precede it and the event that follows—the suicide of Laura. Her death serves as a sacrificial act, one that will redeem the community. Testaments to its effectiveness are the regenerations of Mynheer, Minetta (the social worker), and Horatio—each of whom begins finding ways to cope with the dilemma that results when one must choose between living within a mad society or the madness of living outside society. The dilemma is expressed, too, in the baseball game that follows, built as it is on a paradox: The participants "played in order to keep the ball alive, nevertheless desperately destroyed the play by bringing nearer the end of the game." Each copes with this paradox in his or her own fashion; each participates as an individual and as a teammate, but nothing can enjoin the game's end. To their common cry "Creator spirit, come," a combination of entreaty and sexual joke, a reply comes in the birth of St. Wayward. He is a restorer, a conservator of humanity's spirit, which has been abused by advancing civilization.

The Holy Terror

In the fourth and final novel of the series, *The Holy Terror*, Goodman promises a "register of reconciliation," and indeed, the principals move toward a harmony, what Blake would call experiencing their "joys and desires." Such chapter titles as "Conversing," "Dancing," "Eating," "Relaxing," and "Wakening" reflect the social nature of their existence. Horatio and Rosalind dance in sexual joy, while Lothair finds fulfillment in his music. They undergo a kind of Gestalt therapy, a form of body mysticism. Each pursues self-awareness: Mynheer experiences primal consciousness by means of the Tao Te Ching; Lothair, the public man, discovers his repressed rage. In a poignant episode, Lothair, overcome by feelings of rage, hope, and love, is slain by his son, Wayward, in a scene rife with Oedipal implications. In killing his father, Wayward achieves adulthood, and his exploits in Ireland, which later cap the book, offer an affirmative ending.

After Lothair's death, Horatio undergoes a form of madness that involves accepting the reality of the world as it is expressed by the now-defunct newspaper *The New York Herald Tribune*. The time is 1952. One symptom of Horatio's insanity is that he wishes to vote for the General—that is, Dwight D. Eisenhower—for president. Although this section is at times amusing, it seems inappropriate, more a symptom of the author's political outrage than a stage in the development of Horatio's personality. No effort is made by the author to imply that Horatio is seriously exploring conservative values; instead, Goodman sacrifices his character's credibility to parody topical theories of politics and education.

Indeed, much of the final book reveals Goodman's flagging imagination. Events are related to one another only thematically rather than as the outgrowth of character. One such example involves the youthful cardplayers who appear as a foil for St. Wayward. The latter transcends and redeems the sordid world of boys, performing miracles in a way that suggests events in the Gospels. The boys, however, are only a convenience for the author, and they disappear from the novel. The Gospel parallel is reinforced in the next chapter, however, which is called "Good News" and deals with the discovery by Lefty Duyvendak, son of Mynheer and Laura, of an edenic community where life is reasonable, joy permissible. As the novel nears its conclusion, the principals meet to reaffirm their sense of community, each announcing the "work that is at hand." The novel ends with a lyrical fantasy of St. Wayward freeing Ireland of its sexual repression. Horatio has the tetralogy's final word, entreating God for more life.

After its publication in 1959, *The Empire City* achieved a kind of cult status. Though at times obscure, it represents Goodman's most ambitious novelistic effort and clearly his best. His reputation as a novelist rests on this often impressive and imaginative work.

Making Do

In *Making Do*, Goodman develops and amplifies themes he had earlier explored in *The Empire City*. "My only literary theme has been the community," he remarked in his journal *Five Years*. Once more, he returns to familiar themes: psychology, education, radical reform, and the efforts of the individual to satisfy natural desire in a repressive environment. *Making Do* is a less hopeful and exuberant novel than its predecessor: As *Communitas* (1947) glosses *The Empire City*, so *Growing Up Absurd* clarifies *Making Do*. The titles of these latter works suggest the more circumscribed possibilities for achievement Goodman perceived in American life. Entitling his earlier work with New York's sobriquet the Empire City does suggest Goodman's hope: his vision of heroism and transcendence that has the capacity to stimulate the protagonists. "Making do," on the other hand, is far less optimistic, a diminished variation of the American credo—"making it"—that spurred an earlier generation of Jewish immigrants (among them Goodman's own father, perhaps). "Making do" implies less a remaking of the environment to render it worthy of its best citizens than an attempt to adjust and find comfort in a framework of truncated possibilities.

Unlike its predecessor, *Making Do* is not a fantasy imbued with the energy and spirit that such a form implies, but is a tale conceived in a realistic-naturalistic vein. As before, the novelist has a dual role as both narrator ("the tired man") and participant (Goodman appears by name in a cameo role). Once again, Goodman presents his characters as special friends, members of a community of which his persona is the guiding spirit. Other members include the saintly Harold, spiritual father to a gang of delinquent Puerto Ricans, and Jason, a graduate student in English with passionate convictions on education. Jason is writing a dissertation on Theodore Dreiser, an author who explored the tragic implications of the American Dream. Another member of the group, Meg, has a generous sexual spirit and guilelessness that render her attractive, however undirected she appears. The narrator's friend, Roger, shares his commitment to their surroundings, as displayed in his eagerness to establish Vanderzee as a haven for artists. Finally, there is Terry, an inarticulate youth full of a kind of puppylike devotion to the community of friends.

The very qualities that make these individuals attractive also prove their undoing. Harold is mocked and abused by his hustler-lover Ramon, who eventually betrays his protector to the police. Jason expresses his rage (and probably Goodman's own) concerning educational textbooks by the impotent gesture of punching a textbook salesman. His dissertation is probably doomed for reasons that make a mockery of the notion of academia as a community of scholars. Meg's tolerant and nurturing sexual practices provide the police with a pretext for attacking the group; her innocence even permits her to cooperate with her persecutors. Terry, like Horatio, though lacking the street smarts and mental discipline to provide him with equilibrium, desperately embraces the notion of community. He is inarticulate, however, a primitive who relies on insight to the exclusion of cognitive thought; hence, he is unable to negotiate in a fallen world and is ultimately institutionalized. Unhappy though he is, the narrator, "the tired man," does cope successfully with the world—in large measure because he is sufficiently detached to achieve at least a modest success, satisfying his needs for love, work, and self-expression. As noted earlier, a character named Paul Goodman appears briefly in the novel, but the lineaments of the author's own life appear most fully in the character of the narrator.

The vicissitudes experienced by the community do not simply result from the larger society's victimization of the group (though that does exist); as in *The Empire City*, they result in large measure from weaknesses within the community. Harold has lost contact with his animal nature, as symbolized both by his impotence with Ramon and by his self-lacerating behavior at the racetrack, where he bets against his own selections. Meg is envious of others' sexual pleasures; Jason is unwilling to act the responsible father; Terry is inarticulate unless he can be physically intimate. Presumably, for Goodman, Terry is the end product of all that is distorted about American culture. The reader, however, may find that Joanna's attraction to him is rather implausible. "She did not see about her any other young man who was worthwhile," the narrator remarks. Hardly a very satisfactory explanation to justify her love affair with a promiscuous, bisexual, drug-addicted dropout on the verge of being institutionalized for schizophrenia. Even the founder of the community, Meg's former husband, Amos, is "insane," and threatens to kill his wife.

The setting of this novel is Vanderzee, a community directly across the river from New York City. For Goodman, everything Dutch has positive connotations (recall Mynheer of *The Empire City* or the collection of poems *The Lordly Hudson*). Vanderzee, however, having betrayed its origins, does not actualize its potential for community; the town is controlled by a venal police force and a narrow-minded mayor, both of whom endorse "community" but mean by it a life-denying, mind-numbing conformity. There is little difference in Goodman's eyes between the self-serving values of the Puerto Rican hustlers and those of the police force (a point Goodman had already made in *Growing Up Absurd*), so that when Ramon is arrested, Judas-like, he betrays the smaller community in order to gain entrance into the larger.

The novel ends on a mixed note. The narrator, "the tired man," has a glimmering vision of a transcendent love of country—an outgrowth, he explains, of erotic love. Harold and Meg find comfort in each other's arms, but Terry is institutionalized, the Puerto Rican youths are arrested, and Amos is left free but homeless.

As a novel, *Making Do* has occasional strengths and glaring weaknesses. Goodman, as ever, is a compelling writer, with trenchant insights into American culture and social life, but this book lacks the exuberant spirit and incandescent invention of *The Empire City*. A serious drawback of the book, as Richard Poirier observes, is that "its actions never [accumulate] the necessity that brings on subsequent actions. . . . The links between the events are largely external." *Making Do* is an interesting book but not a good novel.

Goodman's novels have had a mixed reception. *Parents' Day* is largely forgotten and difficult to find, even in research libraries. (It was reprinted in 1985.) *Making Do*, the most popular of his novels, is marred by serious flaws; it is best remembered for its vivid scenes of communal life in the 1960's. Goodman's reputation as a novelist rests on his tetralogy *The Empire City*, a work that will no doubt endure as a minor classic.

Stan Sulkes

Other major works

SHORT FICTION: *The Facts of Life*, 1945; *The Break-up of Our Camp, and Other Stories*, 1949; *Our Visit to Niagara*, 1960; *Adam and His Works*, 1968; *The Collected Stories and Sketches of Paul Goodman*, 1977-1980 (4 volumes; Taylor Stoehr, editor).

PLAYS: *Jonah*, pb. 1945; *Faustina*, pr. 1949; *The Young Disciple*, pb. 1955; *Tragedy and Comedy: Four Cubist Plays*, pb. 1970.

POETRY: *Stop-light: Five Dance Poems*, 1941; *The Lordly Hudson: Collected Poems*, 1962; *Hawkweed*, 1967; *Homespun of Oatmeal Gray*, 1970; *Collected Poems*, 1973.

NONFICTION: *Communitas*, 1947 (with Percival Goodman); *Kafka's Prayer*, 1947; *Gestalt Therapy: Excitement and Growth in the Human Personality*, 1951 (with Frederick S. Perls and Ralph Hefferline); *The Structure of Literature*, 1954; *Growing Up Absurd*, 1960; *The Community of Scholars*, 1962; *Utopian Essays and Practical Proposals*, 1962; *Compulsory Mis-Education*, 1964; *People or Personnel: Decentralizing and the Mixed System*, 1965; *Five Years: Thoughts During a Useless Time*, 1966; *Like a Conquered Province: The Moral Ambiguity of America*, 1967; *New Reformation: Notes of a Neolithic Conservative*, 1970; *Speaking and Language: Defence of Poetry*, 1971; *Little Prayers and Finite Experience*, 1972; *Creator Spirit Come! The Literary Essays of Paul Goodman*, 1977; *Drawing the Line: The Political Essays of Paul Goodman*, 1977; *Nature Heals: The Psychological Essays of Paul Goodman*, 1977; *Crazy Hope and Finite Experience: Final Essays of Paul Goodman*, 1994.

CHILDREN'S/YOUNG ADULT LITERATURE: *Childish Jokes: Crying Backstage*, 1951.

Bibliography

Fried, Lewis F. *Makers of the City*. Amherst: University of Massachusetts Press, 1990. Fried demonstrates that Goodman's exploration of the ideas of community and of urban culture unites his fiction and nonfiction. Includes detailed notes and a bibliographical essay.

Gilman, Richard. Review of *The Empire City*, by Paul Goodman. *Commonweal* 70 (July 31, 1959): 401-402. This short article examines *The Empire City* as a part of the comic tradition of J. D. Salinger and Saul Bellow. Also cites Goodman's debt to Franz Kafka for his sense of the bizarre. Gilman objects to the sermonizing quality of Goodman's fiction but notes that his characters are intended to teach readers how to live.

Harrington, Michael. "On Paul Goodman." *The Atlantic*, August, 1965. This short article is a general review of Goodman's work and a more intensive examination of his essays *People or Personnel* (1965). Looks at Goodman as an existentialist critic of American life and as a philosopher of the student revolts of the 1960's, finding his belief in the goodness of human nature naïve.

Paul, Sherman. "Paul Goodman's Mourning Labor: *The Empire City*." Review of *The Empire City*, by Paul Goodman. *Southern Review* 4, no. 4 (1968): 894-926. This comprehensive review is a book-by-book analysis of *The Empire City*. Examines its major themes of the education of a young man, looking especially at its themes dealing with war and at its position in the tradition of the philosophical novel.

Sale, Kirkpatrick. "Countercultural Elite." *The Nation*, April 10, 1995. Sale discusses the many facets of Goodman's career, including his writing in many genres, his work as a psychotherapist and cofounder of the American Gestalt movement, and an educator and educational theorist.

Sontag, Susan. *Under the Sign of Saturn*. New York: Farrar, Straus and Giroux, 1980. Contains one of the most sensitive essays on Goodman's life and work. That essay, "On Paul Goodman," treats his fiction seriously and suggests that his reputation suffered because he wrote in so many different genres rather than concentrating on a single form of literature.

Steiner, George. "On Paul Goodman." *Commentary* 36 (August, 1963): 158-163. An important look at Goodman's thinking and writing by a respected literary critic.

Stoehr, Taylor. "Paul Goodman as an Advance-Guard Writer." *Kenyon Review* 25, no. 1 (Winter, 2003): 82-96. Stoehr, Goodman's literary executor, examines Goodman's contributions as a writer, providing an overview of his work. Discusses Goodman's writing strategy and his commitment to a writing career.

NADINE GORDIMER

Born: Springs, Transvaal, South Africa;
November 20, 1923

Principal long fiction

The Lying Days, 1953
A World of Strangers, 1958
Occasion for Loving, 1963
The Late Bourgeois World, 1966
A Guest of Honour, 1970
The Conservationist, 1974
Burger's Daughter, 1979
July's People, 1981
A Sport of Nature, 1987
My Son's Story, 1990
None to Accompany Me, 1994
The House Gun, 1998
The Pickup, 2001
Get a Life, 2005

Other literary forms

Nadine Gordimer (GOHR-dih-muhr) is a prolific writer and one of the twentieth century's greatest writers of short stories. Her first collection of stories, *Face to Face* (1949), was published in Johannesburg by Silver Leaf Books. Her first story published in *The New Yorker*, where most of her stories have initially appeared, was "A Watcher of the Dead" (June 9, 1951). Gordimer's first collection of stories to be published in the United States was *The Soft Voice of the Serpent, and Other Stories* (1952). This collection was followed by many others, including *Six Feet of the Country* (1956), *Friday's Footprint, and Other Stories* (1960), *Not for Publication, and Other Stories* (1965), *A Soldier's Embrace* (1980), *Crimes of Conscience* (1991), *Loot, and Other Stories* (2003), and *Beethoven Was One-Sixteenth Black, and Other Stories* (2007). Gordimer has also written teleplays for three of her stories that were adapted for television ("Country Lovers," "A Chip of Glass Ruby," and "Praise"). She has published numerous literary reviews and other essays and short pieces, usually dealing with literature or with the culture or politics of South Africa. Her collections of essays include *The Black Interpreters: Notes on African Writing* (1973), *The Essential Gesture: Writing, Politics, and Places* (1988; edited by Stephen Clingman), *Writing and Being* (1995), and *Living in Hope and History: Notes from Our Century* (1999). With Lionel Abrahams she edited *South African Writing Today* (1967). Gordimer also contributed to and edited *Telling Tales* (2004), a collection of twenty-one short stories by world-renowned authors; profits from the sale of this volume have been donated to help agencies working to control the spread of human immunodeficiency virus (HIV) and to treat those with HIV and acquired immunodeficiency syndrome (AIDS).

Achievements

Nadine Gordimer won the W. H. Smith Literary Award in 1961 for *Friday's Footprint, and Other Stories*. In 1972, she won the James Tait Black Memorial Prize for her novel *A Guest of Honour*. *The Conservationist* was cowinner of the Booker Prize in 1974. Gordimer also has received the French international literary prize the Grand Aigle d'Or (1975), the Italian Malaparte Prize (1985), and the Nelly Sachs Prize from Germany (1986). She was awarded the Officier de l'Ordre des Arts et des Lettres (1986) and the highest French art and literature decoration, the Commandeur dans l'Ordre des Arts et Lettres (1991). For her 2001 novel *The Pickup*, Gordimer was awarded the 2002 Commonwealth Writers' Prize for the Best Book from Africa. She has been awarded honorary degrees from such American universities as Harvard and Yale (both in 1986) and the New School for Social Research (1987). In the fall of 1994, Gordimer delivered the Charles Eliot Norton Lectures series at Harvard. In 1991, she was honored with the Nobel Prize in Literature.

Nadine Gordimer. (© The Nobel Foundation)

Biography

Nadine Gordimer spent her childhood in a gold-mining town near Johannesburg, South Africa. Her father, Isidore Gordimer, was a watchmaker, a Jew who had immigrated from a Baltic town to Africa when he was thirteen; her mother was born in England. In writing about her childhood, Gordimer has referred to herself as a "bolter." She did not care for the convent school to which she was sent as a day student, and she frequently played hooky. When she did attend, she would sometimes walk out. The pressures of uniformity produced revulsion and rebellion in young Nadine. At eleven, Gordimer was kept home from school by her mother on the pretense of a heart ailment, and she received no formal schooling for about a year; for the next three to four years, she was tutored a few hours a day.

Within Gordimer's environment, a white middle-class girl typically left school at about age fifteen and worked for a few years at a clerical job. Ideally, by her early twenties she would be found by the son of a family like her own and would then be ushered through her season of glory—the engagement party, the linen shower, the marriage, and the birth of the first child. There was no point in such a girl's reading books; that would only impede the inevitable process by which she was readied to fit the mold.

Gordimer, however, was an early reader and an early writer. By the age of nine, she was already writing; at fourteen, she won her first writing prize. She read the stories of Guy de Maupassant, Anton Chekhov, W. Somerset Maugham, D. H. Lawrence, and the Americans O. Henry, Katherine Anne Porter, and Eudora Welty. Reading these great artists of the short story helped Gordimer to refine her own story writing, making her work more sophisticated. She found herself becoming increasingly interested in politics and the plight of black South Africans. Unlike other whites who rejected the white South African way of life, Gordimer did not launch into her writing career as a way to bring change. Already a writer, she could not help "falling, falling through the surface" of white South African life.

In her early twenties, Gordimer was greatly influenced by a young male friend. She has written that he did her the service of telling her how ignorant she was. He jeered at the way she was acquiring knowledge and at her "clumsy battle to chip my way out of shell after shell of readymade concepts." Further, she says, "It was through him, too, that I roused myself sufficiently to insist on going to the university." Since she was twenty-two at the time and still being supported by her father, her family did not appreciate her desire to attend the university.

Continuing to live at home, Gordimer commuted to Johannesburg and the University of the Witwatersrand. While at the university, she met the Afrikaans poet Uys Krige, a man who had broken free of his Afrikaans heritage, lived in France and Spain, and served with the International Brigade in the Spanish Civil War. He had a profound effect on Gordimer. She had bolted from school; she was in the process of bolting from family, class, and the superficial values and culture of white South Africa. Uys Krige gave her a final push. She was free to be committed to honesty alone. When she began sending stories to England and the United States, they were well received. Her course was set.

Despite her contempt for the social system and the economic exploitation that prevailed in South Africa, Gordimer continued to make Johannesburg her home. She gave birth to and reared her children there. She married Reinhold Cassirer, a German-born art dealer, who moved to South Africa in the late 1930's. She and her husband would frequently go abroad, to Europe, to North America, to other African countries. She lectured at leading American universities such as Columbia, Harvard, and Michigan State, but she always returned to Johannesburg. For many years some of her writing was censored or prohibited in South Africa.

Gordimer has remained active in promoting South African culture, particularly writing. A member of Southern African PEN (International Association of Poets, Playwrights, Editors, Essayists, and Novelists) in Johannesburg, she also served as vice president for PEN International. She was a founder and has been an executive member of the Congress of South African Writers (COSAW), a political and cultural organization. She has also worked as a board member under the African National Congress's Department of Arts and Culture for cultural reconstruction in South Africa. In 1990, when the African National Congress again became legal, Gordimer joined and supported the new democracy in South Africa.

Analysis

Until 1991, when the last of South Africa's apartheid laws was repealed, to be personally liberated and to be South African was to be doomed to a continuing struggle between the desire for further freedom and development for oneself and the desire for the liberation of the country's oppressed masses. The question was whether one could pursue both effectually. South Africa was a nation in which a white legislature promulgated laws that made it impossible for the overwhelming majority of nonwhite persons to advance themselves. Apartheid, which in Afrikaans means "apartness," was the law of the land. It became codified after the Nationalists came to power in 1948.

In her novels, Nadine Gordimer is engaged in an ongoing examination of the possible combinations of the private life and the public life. She creates a gallery of characters ranging from pure hedonists concerned only with their own pleasure to those who have committed their lives to bringing liberty, equality, and solidarity to South Africa. Her most interesting characters are those who are wracked and torn by the struggle, those who want to be themselves and yet find it impossible to take personal goals seriously in a society built on the exploitation of blacks.

Some great writers—such as James Joyce and Thomas Mann—believe that to write freely one must live in a free country. During the 1920's, numerous American writers disgusted with American values chose to become expatriates. Other writers, such as the great Russians Fyodor Dostoevski, Leo Tolstoy, and Aleksandr Solzhenitsyn, believe that nothing could be more oppressive to them than to be separated from their fellow citizens, however oppressive the government of their country might be. With some of her books banned, with some charge or other always dangling over her head, with her passport liable to be lifted at any time, Gordimer undoubtedly was tempted to go into exile and live in a free country. She always, however, returned to Johannesburg. To her, the accident of being born in a particular place imposed obligations, and having become a writer with an international reputation imposed special obligations. At the cost of the personal freedom and the very air of freedom that could be hers elsewhere, she remained in South Africa during the apartheid years, living with frustration and danger, a witness to the power of compassion and hope.

The Lying Days

A first novel is often a thinly veiled autobiography of the writer's childhood, adolescence, and coming-of-age. Gordimer's *The Lying Days* is of this type, but it is nevertheless special. Full of innocence, tenderness, courage, and joy, it is an unusually mature celebration of a woman's coming-of-age. It is the story of Helen Shaw's growing up in a mining town not far from Johannesburg, the intoxication of her first love affairs, her days at the university, her immersion in the city's bohemian and radical circles, and finally her drawing back to protect herself from being swamped by values, attitudes, and goals that are not her own.

In her life at home, Helen Shaw is under the thumb of a mother who commands and dominates in the name of all that is conventional and trivial. The motivating force in the mother's life is her desire to guide her family through all the planned stops on the middle-class timetable: tea parties and dances, husband's promotions, the big vacation to Europe, and, most important, the molding of offspring to fit the community's notion of success. To celebrate these achievements and in all else to maintain an unruffled surface—such are the goals of Mrs. Shaw and the placid Mr. Shaw, who, important as he may be to the success of the gold-mining company, is completely submissive at home. As Helen comes to realize, both mother and father, their circle of acquaintances, and those in other similar circles are "insensitive to the real flow of life."

The whites of the mining town have blacks in their midst as servants and are surrounded by "locations" where the black mine workers and their families are housed. Helen chooses a lover, Paul Clark, who has committed his professional and personal life to ameliorating the misery of blacks in the townships on the periphery of Johannesburg, on weekdays through his position in the government office dealing with native housing, on weekends through work for the black African National Congress.

Paul meets with frustration at every turn. His inability to get anything done that will have a lasting impact affects the quality of his relationship with Helen. He torments her in small ways, and she reciprocates. He feels ashamed and she feels ashamed, and they become aware of "a burned-out loneliness in the very center of one's love for the other." Helen, who had come to believe that the only way for a man to fulfill himself in South Africa was "to pit himself against the oppression of the Africans" and who had wanted to live with Paul "in the greatest possible intimacy," is compelled to leave him. His political commitments, which made him so attractive to Helen in the first place, have damaged their love irretrievably.

Helen decides to go to Europe. During the few days she spends at the port city, she meets Joel Aron, with whom she had become good friends in Atherton, the town where they grew up. Joel is off to try to make a life for himself in Israel. At first, Helen is envious of Joel; he is headed for a new life in a new country. She feels homeless. South Africa is like a battleground; she cannot join the whites, and the blacks do not want her. She does not want to end up like Paul, "with a leg and arm nailed to each side." In the course of her conversations with Joel, however, she succeeds in coming to a better understanding of her situation. She is not going to be tempted by exile and a new beginning. She accepts South Africa as home and the place to which she must return.

A World of Strangers

Toby Hood, the protagonist of *A World of Strangers*, has grown up in England in a family quite different from Helen Shaw's. Had Toby been a bolter from school and a rebel against bourgeois values, his parents would have loved him all the more. His parents do not care about what other members of the upper middle class think about them; they care about justice. Through his home goes a constant procession of victims of injustice who have come for aid from the Hoods. Thus, there have been bred into Toby "a horror of the freedom that is freedom only to be free" and a consciousness of the need to make every activity in which one engages an act of conscience. Toby, however, is not persuaded. His parents have not been successful in making him into a reformer and protester like themselves. Abstractions such as justice and socialism do not thrill him. Toby wants to live a life oblivious to the suffering in the world; what he feels most inclined to do is enjoy whatever is left of privilege.

Toby is sent to take over temporarily the management of the South African branch of the family-owned publishing company. Arriving in Johannesburg, he is determined to find his own interests and amusements, and not be channeled by the reformers back in England or distracted by the examples of humanity's cruelty to others that will occur before his eyes. Indeed, it seems to Toby that those who would live private lives have become a hunted species, and he resents being hunted. Toby is confirmed in his desire to avoid being a do-gooder by his discovery of a talented black man who also insists on living his own life, regardless of the condition of his people and his country. Toby marvels at the spirit and vitality of Steven Sitole. Steven refuses to allow the chaos and filth of the black townships and the hovels in which he sleeps either to deaden his spirit or to inflame it to rage. He does what he does, seeking pleasure, satisfaction, or quick delight. He has no time for sorrow, pity, guilt, or even anger. He makes his money running an insurance racket, he gets into debt, he gets drunk, he laughs. He fleeces his own people and outwits whites. He is a new kind of man in the black townships; he is of them and not of them. The blacks who know him love him, and Toby Hood loves him as well.

Toby sees in Steven a brother. Drawn to him as if by a magnet at their first meeting, Toby goes into the townships with Steven, meets Steven's friends, gets drunk with him, and sleeps in the same hovels with him. What Steven can do with his life is so severely limited by white authority that he must live without hope or dignity; his life can only be a succession of gestures. That recognition by Toby illumines his own predicament. Steven was born into a South Africa that would not permit him "to come into his own; and what I believed should have been my own was destroyed before I was born heir to it."

Toby undergoes a transformation in the course of the novel. He has had the unusual experience of being able to enter alternately both black township life and the life of upper-crust Johannesburg. As much as he had thought that the privileged life was his natural base, he finds that life—for all its varied forms of recreation, luxury, freedom, and the outward good health of the rich—an empty, superficial existence. The rich, like Helen Shaw's middle-class mining-town family, are out of touch with "the real flow of life." Toby attempts a love affair with the most beautiful available woman among his circle of rich acquaintances. Primarily because the woman, Cecil Rowe, is incapable of expanding her concerns beyond herself, the affair comes to nothing more than a few perfunctory sexual encounters. On the other hand, Toby's relationship with Anna Louw, who is so different, is no more satisfying. She is a lawyer who is a former Communist and whose professional life is devoted to aiding blacks. Hers is anything but the self-centered life of Steven Sitole or Cecil Rowe; always sober, without embarrassment, she is unresponsive to the lure of euphoria. At the end of the novel, Cecil has accepted the marriage proposal of a wealthy businessman. Anna, too, is to begin a new phase—she has been arrested and is to be tried for treason. Anna is a prototype of the committed woman, the full development of whom in Gordimer's fiction does not occur until twenty years later, in *Burger's Daughter*.

Toby decides to stay in South Africa for a second year. His experiences with Cecil and the rich have made him reassess his conception of himself. As different as Steven and Anna are in character and personality, Toby has been greatly affected by both of them, and the effect has been to make him care about the people of the townships. One of Gordimer's great accomplishments in this novel, as it is in her later work, is her rendering of township life. Toby also undergoes his transformation because of what he has seen of township life on his sojourns with Steven. Life in the townships is more real than life among whites. In the townships, the demands of life cannot be evaded through distractions; reality is right on the surface as well as below: "There is nothing for the frustrated man to do but grumble in the street; there was nothing for the deserted girl to do but sit on the step and wait for her bastard to be born; there was nothing to be done with the drunk but let him lie in the yard until he'd got over it." Among the whites, it is different. Frustrations can be forgotten through golf or horse racing, and trips to Europe take away the pain of broken love affairs.

In *A World of Strangers*, Gordimer attempts to show a young man wholly bent on pursuing private concerns who, in the very process of pursuing those concerns, is changed into someone who cannot remain oblivious to South African injustice and unreason. To the extent that the reader can accept the change in Toby, the novel is successful.

Occasion for Loving

Jessie Stilwell, the protagonist of *Occasion for Loving*, is a well-educated, freethinking socialist of the most enlightened, undogmatic kind. She might well have been arrested and tried for treason, but that would be in a different life from the one that fate has bestowed on her. Her reality is her life as the mother of four children and a helpmate to Tom, a liberal history professor. She could be Helen Shaw fifteen years later, domesticated.

Jessie is content. Her husband, children, and home give continuity to her life; she is in touch with her past, and the future, in five-year blocks at least, seems predictable. She has room to develop; she can pick and choose goals for herself and pursue them to their conclusion. She is a total realist; she knows what is possible and what is not. She is at a point in her life when she will do nothing that is "wild and counter to herself." When someone else in the family causes discord, she will deal with it.

Jessie has a son by a previous marriage who, in his adolescence, has become mildly disruptive. The task she wishes to devote herself to is repairing her relationship with him. Jessie cannot become absorbed in this duty, however, because there are two new presences in her home. Against her better judgment, she has allowed her husband to invite to live with them a colleague and his young wife, Boaz and Ann Cohen. Boaz is a musicologist and is frequently away from Johannesburg to study the music and instruments of tribes. Ann is free to occupy her time as she wishes. What comes to dominate Ann's life is a love affair with a married black man, Gideon Shibalo. The difficulties and dangers of an interracial love affair are such that the lovers necessarily need the help of others; thus the affair between Ann and Gideon, whom Jessie and Tom like, intrudes on the life of the Stilwells, and Jessie resents it.

Even when Jessie goes off with three of her children for a vacation by the sea, she must deal with Ann and Gideon, for they turn up at the remote cottage. Boaz has learned about his wife's affair, and Ann and Gideon decide to be with each other day and night; given South Africa's race laws, that means they must live an underground life. They appeal to Jessie to let them stay. Again, she resents the intrusion, but she yields to their need.

Boaz will not disavow Ann. His freedom to act in response to his wife's adultery is limited by his unwillingness to do anything that would harm a black man. Indeed, the affair itself may owe its birth to its interracial difficulties: "The basis of an exciting sympathy between two people is often some obstacle that lies long submerged in the life of one." After leading Gideon to believe that she was ready to go to Europe or some other African country with him, Ann leaves him and returns to Boaz; the two, reunited, quickly leave South Africa. This action plunges Gideon into alcoholism.

Jessie's meditation on the affair makes clear the meaning Gordimer wants to convey. Race is a force even between lovers; personal lives are affected by society and politics. In South Africa, white privilege is a ubiquitous force; it provides Ann the freedom to go, denying Gideon the same freedom. White privilege is "a silver spoon clamped between your jaws and you might choke on it for all the chance there was of dislodging it." So long as there is no change in South Africa, "nothing could bring integrity to personal relationships." If Jessie were more involved in the plot of the novel or even at the heart of its interest, *Occasion for Loving* would be more satisfying. Jessie, however, remains an objective observer and commentator. It is she with whom the reader identifies, yet not much happens to her; the events belong to Ann and Gideon.

The Late Bourgeois World

Gordimer's fourth novel, *The Late Bourgeois World*, is her least successful. Brief and unconvincing, it is something of a parable, but it does not hit with the impact of the well-told parable. Too much has to be deduced. Without a knowledge of Gordimer's interests from her other works, the reader is hard-pressed to see the meaning and coherence in this work. *The Late Bourgeois World* tells the story, with a great deal of indirection, of a Johannesburg woman whose marriage has broken up and who has responsibility for a teenage son at boarding school. Elizabeth's having to bring her son the news that his father is dead by suicide is what gives the plot its impetus.

Max Van Den Sandt is the scion of one of Johannesburg's best families, but he rejects his heritage and white privilege. He marries Elizabeth, the medical-lab technician whom he has made pregnant. He joins the Communist Party, he participates in marches against the government, and, in the climax to his rebellion, he is arrested on a charge of sabotage. How much of what Max has done is gesture, however, and how much is the result of conviction? After serving fifteen months in prison, Max turns state's evidence and betrays his former colleagues. In return, he is released from prison. Then comes the suicide, which for Elizabeth provides the final answer: Her former husband was a hollow man. It is possible to be a revolutionary without real conviction.

While allowing herself to indulge her contempt for Max, Elizabeth herself turns out to be unwilling to risk very much for the cause. She has the opportunity to respond positively to the plea of a young, handsome black activist for money to help pay for the defense of some of his friends who have been arrested, but Elizabeth equivocates and puts him off. The participation of whites from the middle class in the black revolution, Gordimer seems to suggest, is very unreliable. No matter how strong their sympathies appear to be, for whites the political struggle is not the imperative it is for blacks. The novel's title suggests another, complementary theme. Despite its staunch defense of its own privileges, the bourgeois world is falling apart. Families rupture too easily, and commitments do not count. Elizabeth and Max are case histories.

A Guest of Honour

Set in an invented nation in central Africa for which she provides a detailed history and geography, *A Guest of Honour* is Gordimer's only novel that does not deal with South Africa. Still, the kinds of events depicted in this novel could very well occur in South Africa at some future time. With independence gained and a native government functioning in the place of the former British colonial administration, there are expectations of dramatic changes: Civil rights will be respected, greater care will be taken in the administration of justice, natural resources will be used for the benefit of the people, the standard of living of the masses will improve. President Mweta believes that these legitimate expectations are being fulfilled in an orderly way and at a satisfactory rate. Edward Shinza, without whom independence might not yet have come, is dissatisfied. He believes that the country is no better off than it would have been under colonial rule. He is seeking a way to have an impact on the course of events. He may even be conspiring with the nation across the border. To Mweta, his former comrade Shinza is "a cobra in the house."

The novel's protagonist is Colonel James Bray, an Englishman who has been a district officer in the colonial administration. Bray is likable and loyal, a wholly sympathetic character. During the struggle for independence, he was of significant assistance to Mweta and Shinza. Now Mweta has invited Bray back to be an honored guest at Independence Day celebrations. Much to his chagrin, Bray discovers that while Mweta is covered with glory as the new nation's leader, Shinza, every bit Mweta's equal if not his better, has no role in governing the country and has not been invited to the celebrations; indeed, Shinza is living in obscurity in the bush. To Bray, this is an ominous sign.

President Mweta sends Colonel Bray on a mission to Gala, the district Bray formerly administered. He is to survey the district's educational needs. With Gala, Gordimer gives the first demonstration of her formidable knowledge of the life and people of rural Africa, of which she gives further demonstrations in *July's People* and, to a lesser extent, in *The Conservationist*. With Gala, she has the opportunity to do a canvas of a whole province. She makes Bray pleased to be back in Gala and curious about what has happened in his absence. He knows the language, he likes the people, and he resonates sympathetically with the daily round of life. While in Gala, Bray will track down Shinza and get his viewpoint on the progress of the nation.

Shinza believes Mweta's principal concern is to consolidate his own power. He has no tolerance for dissent and is quite willing to use the police and torture to stifle it. Mweta allows foreign corporations to extract raw materials and export them rather than finding opportunities to make use of the country's natural wealth at home. Mweta will not allow any changes in the country that might give pause to these foreign interests. Shinza believes that Mweta's actions, taken together, make up a pattern of betrayal. While Shinza is trying to reassert himself by becoming a force within the trade-union movement, he also may be gathering a counterrevolutionary army, but his present intention is to attack Mweta through the unions and strikes.

Shinza comes onto center stage for the length of his impassioned speech on the ideals of the revolution at the congress of the People's Independent Party (P.I.P.), which has its factions but is still the only political party. Bray, who attends, cannot help but prefer the ideals of Shinza to the charisma and policies of accommodation of Mweta. In presenting the milieu of the party congress and in revealing the subtleties of motivations, alliances, and positions, Gordimer demonstrates a first-rate political intelligence. She has Shinza make use of his union support as the first phase in his scheme to dislodge Mweta; she has Mweta in turn capitalize on the nationalistic fervor of the youth group within the P.I.P. to get the group to attack strongholds of union supporters. Violence breaks out in Gala, and Bray is an accidental victim.

Bray, Shinza, and Mweta are new characters in Gordimer's gallery. She knows them and their social and political contexts exceedingly well. *A Guest of Honour* shows a prescience and knowledge that carry it to the top rank of political novels.

THE CONSERVATIONIST

With *The Conservationist*, Gordimer turns back to South Africa. Again, she chooses a male protagonist, Mehring, who bears no resemblance to anyone in her previous novels. Although this novel is of far larger scope, it is perhaps most similar to *The Late Bourgeois World*, for in both novels Gordimer attempts to delineate the lifestyle of a particular rung of white Johannesburg society. Mehring is a forty-nine-year-old industrialist and financier; he serves on several boards of directors. Given no other name, Mehring is admired and respected by everyone in his business and social circles, but it is clear that his life is essentially without meaning. He is deeply committed to nothing—not to ideology, country, or class, not to a sport, not to a single human being. He is quite the opposite of Colonel Bray.

Mehring has much more money than he needs. On impulse, he decides to buy a farm, very conveniently located only twenty-five miles from the city. Owning a farm will give him a feeling of being in contact with the land; it is something that is expected of a man of his station and wealth. The farm, however, complicates Mehring's life. He is unable to enjoy simple ownership; he must try to make the farm productive. He will practice conservation; he will see to it that buildings are repaired, fences mended, firebreaks cleared. The farm comes to occupy much more of his time and thought than he had intended. Nothing about the land, the weather, or the black people who live and work on the farm can be taken for granted. Something unexpected and unwanted is always occurring.

A dead man is found on the property. The man is black, and so the white police are not particularly concerned. Mehring expects them to remove the body and conduct an investigation, but they do neither. The unidentified body remains in a shallow, unmarked grave on Mehring's property. The presence of that body in the third pasture is troubling both to Mehring and to his black workers, although Mehring is never moved to do anything about it.

Much of the novel consists of Mehring's stream of consciousness. Along with the black man's body, another frequent presence in Mehring's consciousness is the woman with whom he has been having an affair. An attractive white liberal whose husband is away doing linguistic research in Australia, she has been drawn to Mehring because of his power; she is daring enough to taunt him and make light of that power. She is convinced that the reign of the whites in South Africa is nearing its end, yet she is a dilettante. When she gets into trouble with the authorities because of her associations with blacks, she wants to flee the country. She is humbled into asking Mehring to use his connections so that she can leave, and she sets herself up in London. Mehring, however, continues to think about her long after she has gone.

Mehring's relationship with this woman has been entirely superficial; when she is gone he thinks about her but does not really long for her. His relationships with his colleagues and their families are also superficial. These connections are so meaningless to him that he reaches a point where he does not want either their invitations or their concern. On the few occasions each year when he has the company of his son, he has no real interest in overcoming the barriers between them. His son, like his lover, does not believe that apartheid and white privilege can survive for long. The son is contemptuous of what his father represents. He leaves South Africa to join his mother in New York rather than serve his term in the army. In his self-willed isolation, Mehring spends more of his time at the farm. Despite himself, as he discusses routine farm business with his black foreman, Jacobus, and as they deal with the emergencies caused by drought, fire, and flooding, Mehring finds himself feeling more and more respect for Jacobus.

Mehring spends New Year's Eve alone at the farm. As the new year approaches, he wanders across his moonlit field and settles with his bottle against the wall of a roofless stone storehouse. He carries on a convivial conversation with old Jacobus. They talk about their children, the farm, cattle. They laugh a lot. They get along well. Jacobus, however, is not there. For Mehring, such easy, honest talk with a black man can take place only in fantasy.

In the final chapter of the novel, the unidentified body in the third pasture is brought to the surface by flooding. The black workers, under Jacobus's direction, make a coffin, at last giving the man a proper burial. Mehring, in the meantime, is engaged in another of his faceless sexual encounters. He could be killed. If he is killed, where will he be buried? Who are the real owners of the land to which he has title? Gordimer is suggesting that the unknown black man has more of a claim to the land than Mehring has. Mehring and his kind are going to meet ignoble ends. Their claim to the land of South Africa is so tenuous that their bodies will not even deserve burial.

There is little that is sympathetic about Mehring, which leaves Gordimer with the difficult task of keeping the reader interested in his activities. Once he begins to spend more time on the farm, his activities inevitably involve his black workers. Gordimer seizes the opportunity to render in some detail the life of their community. A few of them become minor characters of substance. Gordimer juxtaposes the flow of vital life in the black community with Mehring's isolation and decadence and thereby saves the novel from being utterly unappealing.

Burger's Daughter

Burger's Daughter is Gordimer's best novel. It is set between 1975 and 1977, as important changes are taking place in southern Africa but not yet in South Africa. The independence movements in Angola and Mozambique have succeeded. The Portuguese are in retreat, their colonial rule to be replaced by native governments. South Africa, however, remains firmly in the grip of the white minority. The white South African government will relinquish nothing.

Rosa Burger, the protagonist, is Gordimer's most fully achieved character. The hero of the novel, however, is Rosa's father, Lionel Burger. Just before he is to be sentenced to life imprisonment, Lionel Burger has the opportunity to address the court. He speaks for almost two hours. He explains why he and the Communist Party, of which he is a leader, have been driven to engage in the acts of sabotage for which he has been on trial. For thirty years, to no avail, he and South African Communists had struggled without resort to violence to gain civil rights and the franchise for the country's black majority. The great mass movement that is the African National Congress has been outlawed. In desperation, selected symbolic targets have been sabotaged. If such symbolic actions fail to move the white ruling class, there will be no further careful consideration of tactics. The only way to a new society will be through massive, cataclysmic violence.

Lionel Burger, in his childhood, was already sensitive to the unjust treatment of blacks. Later, as a medical student and doctor, he found it easier to accustom himself to the physical suffering of patients than to the subjection and humiliation forced upon blacks. He could not be silent and simply accept. He joined the Communist Party because he saw white and black members working side by side; there were people who practiced what they preached; there were white South Africans who did not deny the humanity of black South Africans. As a Communist, Lionel Burger came to accept the Marxist view of the dominance of economic relationships; thus, he perceived the oppression of blacks to be rooted in white South Africans' desire to maintain their economic advantages. Burger made a covenant with the victims.

Rosa Burger is very different from her father. She is also different from her mother, who was familiar with prison and who from young womanhood was known as a "real revolutionary." Both her father and her mother regard the family as totally united in their dedication to the struggle. Rosa, who was named in tribute to Rosa Luxemburg, the German revolutionary Marxist, knows that the family is not united. While her parents are free and active, she has no choice but to be an extension of them. Her mother has died, however, and, after three years of his life term, her father dies. When they are gone, Rosa does not take up their work. She is twenty-seven years old and has been in her parents' revolutionary circle since childhood. She has carried out numerous secret missions. Recently, she has pretended to be the fiancé of a prisoner in order to bring him messages. With the death of her father, she cannot deny that she is tired of such a life. She does not want to have anything more to do with the endangered and the maimed, with conspiracies and fugitives, with courts and prisons.

Much more pointedly, *Burger's Daughter* deals with questions first considered in *A World of Strangers* and *Occasion for Loving*: To what extent must individual lives be governed by the dictates of time and place and circumstances not of the individual's choosing? Can a person ignore the facts and conditions that circumscribe his or her life and still live fully, or must a meaningful life necessarily be one that is integrated with the "real flow of life"? Despite his wealth and station, Mehring leads a dismal life, because it has no such integration. Rosa Burger is not devoid of redeeming qualities, however. She already has given much of herself.

Rosa chooses to escape. At first she escapes within the city of Johannesburg, in the tiny cottage of a rootless young white man, a graduate student of Italian literature who survives by working as a clerk to a bookmaker. Rosa and Conrad start out as lovers; after a while they are more like siblings. Conrad, too, is struggling to be free, not of a revolutionary heritage but of his bourgeois heritage. Even after she is no longer with him, Rosa continues to talk to Conrad, silently.

Rosa decides to leave South Africa, but she cannot get a passport because she is the daughter of Lionel Burger. Brandt Vermeulen is a cosmopolitan Boer, a new Afrikaner of a distinguished old Afrikaner family. He has studied politics at Leyden and Princeton and has spent time in Paris and New York. Vermeulen resembles Mehring, but he is rooted, more cultured, and more committed to the status quo. His solution for South Africa is to create separate nations for whites and blacks. Rosa goes to see him because he has friends in the Ministry of the Interior, which issues passports. Playing on the fact that he and Lionel Burger emerged from very similar backgrounds, Rosa succeeds in persuading him to use his influence to get her a passport.

The second part of this three-part novel takes place in Europe. Rosa goes to the French Riviera and looks up the woman who had been Lionel Burger's wife before he met Rosa's mother. The woman, who used to be known as Katya and now is known as Madame Bagnelli, is delighted that Burger's daughter has come to stay with her. Rosa is welcomed by Madame Bagnelli's circle, which consists of unmarried couples, émigrés, homosexuals, persons formerly prominent in Paris—rootless persons for the most part. On the Riviera, life is easy, difference is distinction. Survival is not an issue. Politics seems a waste of time, revolution a form of craziness.

There is great empathy between Rosa and Madame Bagnelli. As Katya, the latter, years before, found it a relief to give up the role of revolutionary that was required of her as Burger's wife. She had not always been able to put private concerns aside; she had been considered a bourgeois or even a traitor and was subjected to party discipline. She has no regrets about leaving that part of her life. Rosa is encouraged about her own course. She allows herself the luxury of a love affair.

After a summer of love, Rosa and Bernard Chabalier make plans to live together in Paris, where he is a teacher at a lycée. Rosa visits London while Bernard makes arrangements in Paris. She attends a party for South African exiles and is filled with joy at meeting her black "brother," Baasie, who as a child had been taken into the Burger home but whom Rosa has not seen for twenty years. Rosa is shocked by Baasie's attitude; he is hostile and sullen.

That night in London, Rosa's sleep is broken by a phone call from Baasie. He is angry. He wants her to know that he did not have the life Burger's daughter had. He had been pushed back to the mud huts and tin shanties. His father was a revolutionary who also died in prison, driven to hang himself. No one knows of Isaac Vulindlela, but everyone talks about Lionel Burger. He hates hearing about Burger, the great man who suffered for the blacks. He knows plenty of blacks who have done as much as Burger, but they go unknown. He does not want to be her black brother, he tells Rosa.

Rosa goes back to South Africa. She does not want

the soft life Bernard will provide for her in Paris. Defection is not possible. Suffering cannot be evaded. Back in Johannesburg, Rosa takes up the occupation for which she trained, physiotherapy. She also works for the revolution. As the novel ends late in 1977, Rosa is in prison. The authorities have solid evidence that she has committed unlawful acts.

JULY'S PEOPLE

In the brief *July's People* the end has come. Civil war rages; blacks are fighting whites. The whites have discipline, organization, knowledge, and equipment. The blacks have will and numbers. They have the support of the rest of the continent, and the Russians and their Cuban allies are close at hand. Thousands of lives will be lost, but there can be no doubt about the eventual outcome. The artificial society based on apartheid is finished.

Bamford Smales is an architect, an upper-middle-class professional. His wife, Maureen, is, like Jessie Stilwell, an excellent helpmate, a strong, compassionate, intelligent woman. Before the uprisings, Bam and Maureen knew that unless whites, of their own volition, made significant reforms, a conflagration was inevitable. They tried to show the way among their friends and neighbors, treating their male servant, July, with the utmost consideration. They did not, however, go so far as to break their ties with their community. They lived their lives within the pattern they found for their race and their class. Their liberal attitudes had no impact.

When the uprisings begin, the Smaleses flee their Johannesburg suburb. With their three young children, they drive six hundred kilometers in their recreational pickup truck to July's home village. Even though black-white relations are being turned upside down, July is still willing to oblige them; for fifteen years obliging the Smales family has been his life's purpose. Even after their dependence on him is clear, July continues to address Bam Smales as "master." He even moves his mother from her own hut so that the Smales family can settle in it.

When they arrive in the village, the Smaleses are July's people. Over the course of a few weeks, relations change. July has been reunited with his wife and children, whom for fifteen years he has seen only on his vacations every other year. July becomes a presence among the people of his village. *They* become July's people, and his loyalty to the white family is eroded. That erosion occurs slowly through a number of ambiguous situations, for July has no political sensibility. As the relationship between the black servant and the white family loses its structure, July becomes less and less the servant and more and more the master of the family's fate.

When the Smaleses' vehicle, the yellow "bakkie," first pulls in to the village, there is no doubt concerning its ownership, but as July runs errands to the locked bakkie, he comes to be the possessor of the keys to the vehicle. He does not know how to drive, but his young protégé Daniel does. July turns the keys over to Daniel, and they drive off to a store. After this, it is difficult for Bam Smales to claim sole ownership, and it is even more difficult once Daniel has taught July how to drive. Bam Smales has a shotgun. Although he tries to keep its hiding place a secret, the whole village seems to know where the gun is kept. When Bam discovers that the gun is gone, he is beside himself. The loss of the gun emasculates him. On his way to join the freedom fighters, Daniel has helped himself to the gun.

The family's future is completely uncertain. As the villagers begin to break the habit of deference to white skins, the Smaleses become nervous about their safety. They would leave, but they have nowhere to go. The predicament proves too much for Maureen. Sensing an opportunity to save herself, she runs off, frantically, leaving her husband and children. The Smaleses are victims of apartheid. When the tables are turned, as they surely must be, only a miracle will save whites from suffering what they made others suffer.

A SPORT OF NATURE

A Sport of Nature combines elements from several of Gordimer's earlier works. Like Helen in *The Lying Days*, Hillela Capran is a bolter, though not out of obvious rebelliousness. Rather, she is moved by the spirit of the moment in a more unthinking way. The family with whom she lives during her adolescence—her aunt Pauline, uncle Joe, and cousins Sasha and Carole—are similar to the Hoods of *A World of Strangers*, for they also are white liberals, trying ever to be ruled by acts of conscience rather than convenience, as Hillela's Aunt Olga and Uncle Arthur are.

Gordimer's early habit of distancing the reader from her characters is echoed in her treatment of Hillela. The first half of the book has Hillela spoken of mostly in the third person; she does not really come alive until after she meets Whaila Kgomani, a black revolutionary who becomes her first husband and the father of her child. His assassination changes the course of Hillela's life as she inherits his revolution.

Many readers have regarded Hillela's character as amoral and shocking, and even Gordimer has admitted that this creation fascinates her probably as much as anyone else. She does not, however, back down from her portrayal of a revolutionary who accomplishes most of her goals through the use of her feminine wiles. *A Sport of Nature* may not be Gordimer's best book, but it is as thought-provoking as any of her earlier works. Its portrayal of the future, which includes a black African state installed in place of South Africa, has caused some critics to label the work weak and unbelievable.

MY SON'S STORY

Gordimer's novels of the 1990's cover the years from the closing days of apartheid to the new democracy in South Africa. In *My Son's Story* the struggle for freedom is ongoing. Gordimer's recurrent theme of the balance between public and private life is again central. In this novel, the private is sacrificed to the political. Sonny initially seems destined to live under the restrictions of apartheid, but he changes and sacrifices his teaching career to align his life with, and help, those he thinks of as the "real blacks." Sonny moves his family illegally to a white suburb of Johannesburg, one poor enough to ignore the settling of a family of mixed ancestry.

The movement claims first Sonny, then his daughter Baby, and finally his wife Aila. Will, the son named for William Shakespeare, remains aloof from political involvement but chronicles the struggle by narrating the disintegration of his family. Before detention and exile claim the three family members and a bomb destroys their home, the family is already disintegrating from Sonny's liaison with Hannah Plowman, a white human rights worker who visited Sonny the first time he was jailed.

Although Gordimer has used such narrators in her short stories, this is her first novel narrated by a young male character from one of the disenfranchised groups in South Africa. The novel fluctuates between the first-person narration by Will and a seemingly third-person account of information the young Will could not possibly know, such as Sonny's thoughts and the details of his intimacy with Hannah. The last chapter of the novel unites the dual point of view, with Will claiming authorship of the whole. He has created—out of his own frustration, experience, and knowledge of the participants—the scenes and thoughts he could not know firsthand. Thrust by the times and by his family into the role of a writer, Will plans to hone his writing skills by chronicling the struggle for freedom in South Africa.

NONE TO ACCOMPANY ME

None to Accompany Me reveals the life of Vera Stark, a lawyer who heads a foundation that during apartheid works to minimize the removal of blacks to crowded, inferior land and after apartheid works to reclaim for them the land they have lost. With some reluctance, Vera leaves the foundation temporarily to join the commission that is drafting a new constitution for South Africa. The novel emphasizes how all aspects of her personal life—her home, children, and husband—become secondary to her work. True to her name, Vera Stark whittles all excess from her life, striving to find her true center through social responsibility.

THE HOUSE GUN

In *The House Gun*, Claudia and Harald Lindgard, privileged South Africans who neither supported nor demonstrated against apartheid, are thrust out of their private lives into the public sphere. Their twenty-seven-year-old son Duncan has killed a man. The parents keep their pledge, made to Duncan in childhood, that no matter the difficulty, he can always come to them for support. Reconciling themselves to his action is no easy matter, however, and dealing with that truth causes them to question their own attitudes about justice. Suddenly, whether South Africa's new constitution outlaws capital punishment is a vital personal issue.

Duncan's is a personal, not a political, crime, but the novel connects his crime to the violence the country has known and still knows. Both the easy access to a gun and the climate of violence in which Duncan grew up play a part in an appeal for a lenient sentence. Even though the novel makes no overt mention of the country's Truth and Reconciliation Commission, after facing the truth, the

Lindgards must search for reconciliation just as all South Africans are doing the same under the new democracy. Time must determine whether any of the three Lindgards become reconciled to the brutal truth of the murder.

The Pickup

Gordimer's thirteenth novel, *The Pickup*, focuses on the issues of immigration and discrimination. Like her 2005 novel *Get a Life*, *The Pickup* begins in South Africa but moves to other settings, suggesting that the problems faced by individuals in South Africa are of global concern. *The Pickup* opens with reminders of South Africa's apartheid past: Julie Summers has separated herself from her privileged parents' lifestyle. She rents a small cottage apartment, the type inhabited by black workers during apartheid. She begins a relationship with Abdu, a mechanic who works on her car. She soon learns that Abdu is an alias, a name used to shield him from government officials; Ibrahim ibn Musa is an illegal immigrant, a man who has overstayed his permit.

Through the couple's struggle to find a life together, Gordimer reveals that doors that are automatically open to Julie, a white South African, are closed tight to Ibrahim, an Arab immigrant. His university degree in economics provides no practical help, as Ibrahim comes from a country (which remains unnamed) of no prestige, a country rampant with poverty and corruption. Julie wants to abandon what Ibrahim wishes to acquire. Julie's experience in South Africa has taught her that wealth and success are sometimes based on the exploitation of a population; to Ibrahim, wealth and success are a means to live free, to have choices in life.

Forced out of South Africa, Ibrahim marries Julie and takes her to his home village, where they are welcomed by his extended Muslim family. Ibrahim continues his applications to emigrate to some country where he can improve his life; Julie, his opposite in so many ways, surprisingly finds fulfillment in the village. Through meaningful work and the support of a family she respects, she finds a sense of her place in the universe—something she could not have achieved while working in public relations in Johannesburg.

Get a Life

Get a Life centers on a family unit similar to that in *The House Gun*—parents and an adult son. Paul Bannerman is quarantined at his parents' house for a few weeks after having radioactive iodine treatment to combat thyroid cancer. Adrian and Lyndsay Bannerman care for him to protect Paul's wife and young son from possible contamination. Paul's brush with early death and his enforced time in near solitude lead the adults to reevaluate their lives. Paul, a member of an independent research team, spends time thinking about his work as an ecologist and about his marriage to Berenice, a successful advertising executive who at times promotes companies that threaten the South African environment. One of Paul's current concerns, ironically, is to stop the construction of a nuclear reactor.

When Paul returns to his family and research, he has changed internally, but not outwardly. His parents change their lives radically: Adrian, a retired businessman, spends time visiting archaeology sites, an avocation he had let lie dormant as he devoted himself to providing for his family; Lyndsay, a civil rights lawyer, adopts a young orphan who was born HIV-positive. The novel ends optimistically, with projects that Paul's research team viewed as dangerous halted and with a new child born healthy to Berenice and Paul. A haunting suggestion remains, however, that while the child is fine and the projects are halted for now, the future comes with no guarantees.

From her first, somewhat autobiographical novel, *The Lying Days*, Gordimer has probed moral and political questions with honesty and unfailing courage, never being dogmatic or predetermining outcomes, allowing vividly imagined characters and communities lives of their own. Her work does more than shed light on the predicament of South Africa; it deals in depth with the problems of individual identity, commitment and obligation, and justice. Gordimer is a novelist who clearly has a place in the great tradition of George Eliot, Fyodor Dostoevski, Joseph Conrad, and Thomas Mann.

Paul Marx
Updated by Marion Petrillo

Other major works

short fiction: *Face to Face: Short Stories*, 1949; *The Soft Voice of the Serpent, and Other Stories*, 1952; *Six Feet of the Country*, 1956; *Friday's Footprint, and Other Stories*, 1960; *Not for Publication, and Other Stories*, 1965; *Livingstone's Companions: Stories*, 1971;

Selected Stories, 1975; *A Soldier's Embrace*, 1980; *Something Out There*, 1984; *Reflections of South Africa*, 1986; *Crimes of Conscience*, 1991; *Jump, and Other Stories*, 1991; *Why Haven't You Written? Selected Stories, 1950-1972*, 1992; *Loot, and Other Stories*, 2003; *Beethoven Was One-Sixteenth Black, and Other Stories*, 2007.

TELEPLAYS: *A Chip of Glass Ruby*, 1985; *Country Lovers*, 1985; *Oral History*, 1985; *Praise*, 1985.

NONFICTION: *The Black Interpreters: Notes on African Writing*, 1973; *On the Mines*, 1973 (with David Goldblatt); *Lifetimes Under Apartheid*, 1986 (with Goldblatt); *The Essential Gesture: Writing, Politics, and Places*, 1988 (Stephen Clingman, editor); *Conversations with Nadine Gordimer*, 1990 (Nancy Topping Bazin and Marilyn Dallman Seymour, editors); *Three in a Bed: Fiction, Morals, and Politics*, 1991; *Writing and Being*, 1995; *Living in Hope and History: Notes from Our Century*, 1999; *A Writing Life: Celebrating Nadine Gordimer*, 1999 (Andries Walter Oliphant, editor).

EDITED TEXTS: *South African Writing Today*, 1967 (with Lionel Abrahams); *Telling Tales*, 2004.

BIBLIOGRAPHY

Bazin, Nancy Topping, and Marilyn Dallman Seymour, eds. *Conversations with Nadine Gordimer*. Jackson: University Press of Mississippi, 1990. Collection of interviews with Gordimer is invaluable for its scope. Reveals Gordimer's insights and attitudes toward her works and their origins in conversations spanning more than thirty years (1958-1989). Supplemented by bibliography and index.

Clingman, Stephen. *The Novels of Nadine Gordimer: History from the Inside*. 2d ed. Amherst: University of Massachusetts Press, 1992. Interprets Gordimer's novels, through *My Son's Story*, within the context of history in general and the history of South Africa and African literature in particular. A prologue written for this second edition discusses the dismantling of apartheid and Gordimer's Nobel Prize. Includes index.

Ettin, Andre Vogel. *Betrayals of the Body Politic: The Literary Commitments of Nadine Gordimer*. Charlottesville: University Press of Virginia, 1995. Examines all of Gordimer's genres of writing and addresses the recurring themes: betrayal, politics of family, concept of homeland, ethnicity, and feminism.

Head, Dominic. *Nadine Gordimer*. New York: Cambridge University Press, 1994. Provides a comprehensive study of Gordimer's first ten novels. Supplemented by a chronology of Gordimer's career and major South African political events to 1991, a bibliography of works by and about Gordimer, and an index.

King, Bruce, ed. *The Later Fiction of Nadine Gordimer*. New York: St. Martin's Press, 1993. Collection of essays begins with an introduction that surveys the variety in Gordimer's novels from *The Late Bourgeois World* to *My Son's Story*. General essays deal thematically or stylistically with multiple novels; others address one or two novels in depth. Includes index.

Smith, Rowland, ed. *Critical Essays on Nadine Gordimer*. Boston: G. K. Hall, 1990. Excellent selection of sixteen essays, originally published between 1953 and 1988, provides analysis of Gordimer's first ten novels. Includes bibliographical references and index.

Temple-Thurston, Barbara. *Nadine Gordimer Revisited*. New York: Twayne, 1999. Good introductory study of the author and her works. Among the novels discussed are *The Conservationist*, *July's People*, and *The House Gun*. Includes chronology, selected bibliography, and index.

Uledi-Kamanga, Brighton J. *Cracks in the Wall: Nadine Gordimer's Fiction and the Irony of Apartheid*. Trenton, N.J.: Africa World Press, 2002. Presents a generally chronological discussion of Gordimer's works, with emphasis on the novels. Focuses on Gordimer's use of irony and her work in the context of South African politics.

Uraizee, Joya. *This Is No Place for a Woman: Nadine Gordimer, Nayantara Saghal, Buchi Emecheta, and the Politics of Gender*. Trenton, N.J.: Africa World Press, 2000. Places Gordimer and the other two female novelists within the context of postcolonial writers. Thematically organized chapters address in depth the works of each of the writers. Gordimer's novels *The Conservationist*, *A Sport of Nature*, *Burger's Daughter*, and *July's People* receive significant attention.

CAROLINE GORDON

Born: Todd County, Kentucky; October 6, 1895
Died: San Cristóbal de las Casas, Mexico; April 11, 1981
Also known as: Caroline Ferguson Gordon

Principal long fiction

Penhally, 1931
Aleck Maury, Sportsman, 1934
The Garden of Adonis, 1937
None Shall Look Back, 1937
Green Centuries, 1941
The Women on the Porch, 1944
The Strange Children, 1951
The Malefactors, 1956
The Glory of Hera, 1972

Other literary forms

Although Caroline Gordon was primarily a novelist, she wrote a number of superb short stories, several of which have been reprinted in anthologies for use in the classroom; "Old Red" is perhaps the best known, though "The Captive" and "The Last Day in the Field" have also received wide circulation. These and other Gordon stories were published originally in quality journals such as *Scribner's Review*, *Harper's*, *Sewanee Review*, and *Southern Review*, and they have been reprinted in three collections, *The Forest of the South* (1945), *Old Red, and Other Stories* (1963), and *The Collected Stories of Caroline Gordon* (1981), with an introduction by Robert Penn Warren.

Gordon lectured and published commentaries on the fiction of others, but she was not a literary critic in the usual sense; her interest was in setting forth and illustrating her theories about a method of writing fiction. These are contained in two works: *The House of Fiction: An Anthology of the Short Story* (1950, edited with Allen Tate) and *How to Read a Novel* (1957).

Achievements

Caroline Gordon's reputation was firmly established by the publication of her first novel, *Penhally*, particularly after it was reviewed by the English writer Ford Madox Ford in *Bookman*. Ford hailed Gordon as one of the important contemporary novelists writing in the United States. The succession of novels and stories that followed *Penhally*, her marriage to the poet Allen Tate and her association with the Vanderbilt Agrarians, her lectures, and the short-story textbook *The House of Fiction* are all a measure of her significant contribution to the Southern Renaissance.

Gordon has been particularly admired for her craftsmanship, for the skill with which—in the tradition of Henry James, Joseph Conrad, and Ernest Hemingway—she is able to create impressions of life that are at once realistic and symbolic. Following her chief master, James, Gordon was a scholar of the novel, and her fiction emphasizes technique above plot and character, so much so, in fact, that with few exceptions, her books have never had popular appeal. *Aleck Maury, Sportsman* attracted an audience of hunters and anglers, partly because of its subject but also because the hero of the book is an appealing character. *None Shall Look Back* also attracted readers, particularly in the South, because of its evocation of the tragic heroism of the Civil War. *Green Centuries* dealt with material very popular in the 1930's, hardship on the frontier and conflicts between American Indians and white settlers, though it lacks both the sentimentality and moralizing that often made such fiction popular.

The remainder of Gordon's novels are demanding books that require of the reader alertness to symbolic meanings and close attention to the implications of technique. As a consequence of its special kind of excellence, Gordon's fiction appeals primarily to other writers and scholars of narrative craft. Many novelists and short-story writers, including Flannery O'Connor and Walker Percy, have acknowledged a debt to Gordon.

Biography

Caroline Ferguson Gordon was born on a farm in Todd County, Kentucky, on October 6, 1895. Her mother, Nancy Meriwether, was a Kentuckian; her father, James Morris Gordon, was born in Louisa County, Virginia. In the 1880's, he moved west to Kentucky and became tutor to the Meriwether family. Later, he established a classical school for boys in Clarksville, Tennessee, to which his daughter was sent. This was the beginning of her lifelong interest in classical literature, an interest that was deepened during her college years when she studied Greek literature at Bethany College (earning a bachelor of arts degree in 1916). After teaching high school for three years, Gordon took a job as reporter in Chattanooga from 1920 to 1924, an experience she said was of no help to her in learning to write fiction.

In 1924, Gordon married Tate, a poet, essayist, and author of the novel *The Fathers* (1938). She had met Tate through Warren, who lived on a neighboring farm in Kentucky. Her marriage signaled the beginning of an important change not only in her personal life but also in her career as a novelist, for despite Tate being primarily a poet, he also was a perceptive critic of the novel and proved to be one of Gordon's most important early teachers. The Tates moved to New York the year of their marriage, and then, in 1928, went to France on money from Tate's Guggenheim Fellowship. There, a friendship with Ford that had begun in New York was reestablished, and Gordon offered her services to Ford as typist-secretary. The relationship with Ford was most fortunate for Gordon, because it was with Ford's help that she was able to complete her first novel, which later, through his review in *Bookman*, was called to the attention of important readers.

After *Penhally*'s critical success in 1931, Gordon was awarded a Guggenheim Fellowship, and the Tates spent the next year in France. On their return, they settled near Clarksville, Tennessee, and it was there—in a house the Tates called Benfolly—that Gordon wrote her next four novels and a number of short stories. In 1939, the Tates moved to Princeton, New Jersey, and although there were to be protracted stays in other places—Sewanee, Tennessee, and Minneapolis—Princeton was to be Gordon's permanent home for many years. The Tates were divorced in 1959, and thereafter Gordon served as visiting writer at universities in different parts of the United States. In the early 1970's, she founded her own school of writing at the University of Dallas and taught there until shortly before her death. She died in Mexico on April 11, 1981, where she had gone to be near her daughter, Nancy.

One other event in Gordon's life deserves special mention: her conversion in 1947 to Roman Catholicism. That conversion was a significant factor in her artistic as well as her personal life, for it not only influenced her subsequent fiction but also could be seen in retrospect as the logical culmination of a lifelong quest for models of moral perfection.

Analysis

Caroline Gordon's theories of fiction and her debts to the writers who influenced her were spelled out in lectures that she gave at the University of Kansas and later published as *How to Read a Novel*, and in commentaries and appendices to *The House of Fiction*, an anthology of short stories she edited with Tate. In her theory and in her practice, she combined ideas from Aristotle and Dante, Gustave Flaubert, James, Ford, and James Joyce. From the modern masters came the technique of closely rendered scenes, the disappearance of the author from her fiction by means of an impersonal style, and the use of what Gordon called natural symbolism. From Aristotle came certain "constants," particularly his definition of tragedy as an "action of a certain magnitude" and the division of the novel's action into two parts, complication and resolution, with the resolution embedded in the complication. By "action," Gordon understood Aristotle to mean overt action; the hero of a novel, properly understood, was a person who acted, and Gordon went on to add that traditionally the hero always faced the same task: the overcoming of evil so that good might flourish. This is a limited view of the novelistic hero, but for understanding Gordon's fiction it is a useful definition; the heroes of all her novels, from *Penhally* to *The Glory of Hera*, can be understood in this light. The action of her novels invariably involves the facing of evil and an attempt by the hero to overcome it.

Penhally

In Gordon's first novel, *Penhally*, evil is defined from an agrarian perspective, and here one sees Gordon's kinship with the Vanderbilt group, which published Peter Smith's *I'll Take My Stand* in 1930. Penhally is the name of a plantation house in Tennessee, built in 1826 and passed down through the Llewellyn family into modern times. The current master, Nicholas Llewellyn, regards the Penhally lands not as a trust to be handed down but as a commodity to be exploited for his own gain. Nicholas's younger brother, Chance, loves the land but is excluded from ownership and is deeply grieved when Nicholas sells it to a northern woman who turns it into a hunt club for rich strangers. At the opening ceremony of the new club, Chance, taunted by Nicholas for his old-fashioned attitudes, shoots his brother to death. Although this final action is presented in the detached manner of an impartial observer, the irony bitterly underscores the point, as one brother must kill another in a vain attempt to destroy what is evil: the misuse and perversion of the land.

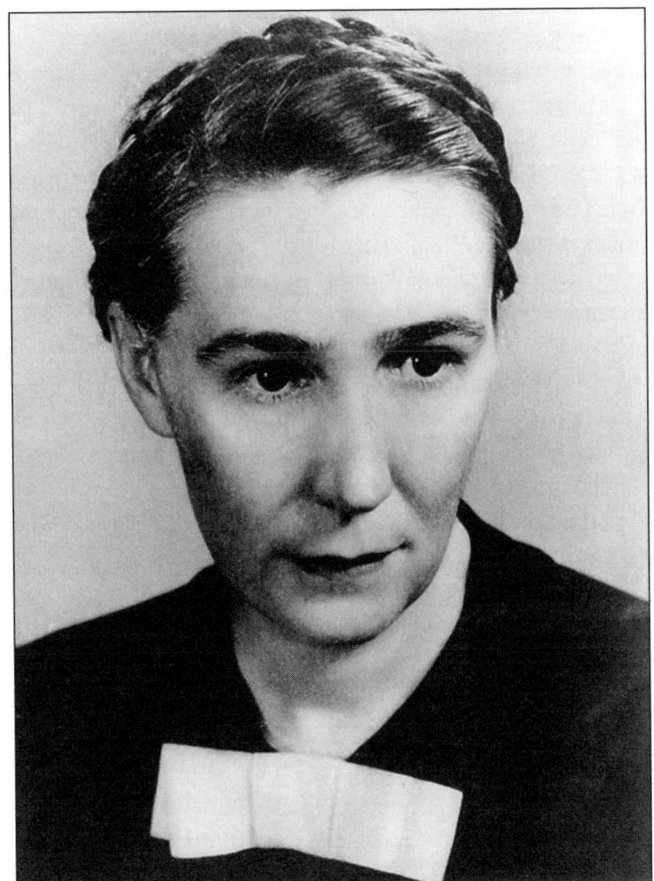

Caroline Gordon. (Library of Congress)

Aleck Maury, Sportsman

Gordon's second novel, influenced to some extent by Siegfried Sassoon's *The Memoirs of a Fox-Hunting Man* (1928), also drew on her memories of her father, the prototype of the novel's hero, Aleck Maury, Gordon's most engaging character. Maury is a hunter and fisherman of remarkable skill and devotion to his sport. Unlike Gordon's other novels, which are written in the third person and in a somewhat detached manner, *Aleck Maury, Sportsman* is told in the first person by Maury himself as he recounts his attempts to escape from the demands of his wife, his teaching duties, and, later, his daughter, so that he can devote himself to the delights of his beloved pastimes. Andrew Lytle has referred to Maury as a man "dislocated" by the economic and cultural ruin of the South after the Civil War, but this is a more solemn view than the novel itself warrants, for Maury is a comic version of the hero: a man who overcomes evil (that is, duty) in order that good (fishing and hunting) might flourish. In this, he is eminently and delightfully successful.

None Shall Look Back

It is not surprising that *Aleck Maury, Sportsman* has been Gordon's most popular novel, for most of her novels present a tragic view of the human condition. Like F. Scott Fitzgerald, Gordon was at heart a traditional moralist, too intelligent to moralize and therefore in search of ways to establish moral values indirectly. Writing in the 1930's and 1940's, periods of disillusionment and rejection of traditional moral and religious beliefs—and herself, at the time, a nonbeliever—she had found in contrasting attitudes toward the land a way of dramatizing the conflict between good and evil.

In *None Shall Look Back*, Gordon located her moral ground on the Civil War battlefields and used actual historical personages, particularly Nathan Bedford Forrest, as exemplars of moral conduct and heroic action in the conflict between good and evil. Forrest, it might be said, represented a model or paradigm of heroic conduct, and by including him (an actual man who did act decisively and selflessly for a cause in which he believed) as a character in *None Shall Look Back*, Gordon could introduce into the novel a standard by which readers could judge the protagonist, Rives Allard, who fights and dies under Forrest's command, and his wife, Lucy, who acts as the point-of-view character through whom the reader experiences the tragic death not only of Rives but also of the whole Southern cause. The distinguished historian of the novel, Walter Allen, complained in *The Modern Novel in Britain and the United States* (1964) that in *None Shall Look Back* Gordon failed to deal with the injustices of slavery. Such criticism misses the point. The novel is meant to be a tragic action, not a tract against slavery or racial prejudice. The Civil War happened, and people gave their lives for a cause in which they believed, a cause that they knew to be doomed. It is this quality of doom and sacrifice that *None Shall Look Back* movingly evokes.

The Garden of Adonis

Because Gordon was neither a rebel against nor a defender of the status quo, but, like William Faulkner, a traditionalist in the modern world, she needed a way of giving authority to traditional values. Agrarianism, as a way of life as well as a philosophy, commanded respect in Nashville and in other pockets of the country, but not in New York or London. What was needed was the kind of mythological underpinning that T. S. Eliot had given his traditional moral vision in *The Waste Land* (1922).

In *The Garden of Adonis*, Gordon was able to provide—and from one of Eliot's sources—that mythological underpinning. The title as well as the general structure of the book came from Sir James G. Frazer's *The Golden Bough* (1922); to be certain that the reader made the connection, Gordon used in an epigraph Frazer's account of how women of ancient Adonis cults would grow and tend newly sprouted plants in baskets (that is, Gardens of Adonis) that, together with images of the dead god, would then be flung into the sea or into springs. Gordon omitted Frazer's description of the more violent practice of sacrificing a living victim in a newly planted field in the belief that his or her death would propitiate the corn spirit and his or her blood would fatten the ears of corn. This omission was probably deliberate, for such descriptions standing at the head of the novel would have revealed too much too soon about the resolution of the action.

In Gordon's handling of the Adonis ritual, the sacrificial victim is a Tennessee planter named Ben Allard. With a young tenant, Allard has planted "on shares" a field of clover that becomes especially valuable when a severe drought ruins Allard's tobacco crop, for the clover survives the drought. The tenant, Ote Mortimer, becomes obsessed with winning the favors of a young woman and, in order to get money to marry her, attempts to harvest the immature clover. Allard plants himself in the way of Ote's team, and Ote strikes him down and kills him. Although Ote is the instrument of Allard's death, it is clear that he is only acting symbolically for the commercial society that hems in and destroys the way of life Allard represents. This is made clear by the contrast between Allard's sense of honor and strict moral code and the promiscuity of his children and their attraction to purely material values. This moral laxness and lust for money, seen not only in Allard's family but also in the woman that Ote wants to marry, is responsible for raising Ote's hand against Allard. Allard's death, viewed in the limited perspective of naturalism, would seem a pointless and ironic sacrifice, but by giving her hero a mythological precursor, Gordon invites the reader to see him not as a hapless victim but rather as the embodiment of timeless values; for whether the world realizes it, Allard is a hero who stands up for what he believes, even gives his life in a heroic, if unprofitable, action.

Green Centuries

Four years elapsed between the publication of *The Garden of Adonis* and *Green Centuries*, Gordon's next novel, and the reason for the delay is quite clear. *The Garden of Adonis* had been written quickly and published the same year as *None Shall Look Back*. It was a novel that came out of the author's direct experience of life in Kentucky and Tennessee in the 1930's. *Green Centuries* is a carefully researched historical novel about southern colonials pushing their way west into the vast new territory of Kentucky and is filled with the kind of detail expected of the best historical fiction: authentic accounts of daily life, travel, husbandry, courting, hunting, and quaint speech ways. One's first impression might be that in electing to write what appears to be another account of hardihood on the frontier, Gordon has abandoned her usual subject in favor of a themeless historical romance.

Still, *Green Centuries* is an exciting book about war and Indian raids and authentic historical characters such as Daniel Boone, the great hunter, and famous Cherokee Indian chiefs Atta Kulla Kulla and Dragging Canoe, and for this the work fully deserved the Pulitzer Prize. (It was considered for the prize, but it did not win.) *Green Centuries* also reflects Gordon's abiding concern for the glory and tragic splendor of heroic action.

The novel has two main heroes: a white hunter, Rion Outlaw, a fictional creation of the author who embodies the qualities to be found in the historical Daniel Boone; and a character based on the Cherokee chief Dragging Canoe. Rion Outlaw, like his namesake Orion, the mythical hunter, leaves the Virginia colony after he participates in a raid on a government powder train and pushes into the west, where eventually he joins forces with settlers who have been attacked by the Cherokee Indians led by Dragging Canoe. When the stockade is attacked by Indians and Rion's beloved wife is killed, he is suddenly made aware both of his loss and of his irrepressible drive to continue westward, losing himself in the turning like the mythical Orion in the heavens.

Dragging Canoe, who led the attack against the settlers, is also heroic, for he has determined against the advice of older and wiser chiefs to fight the settlers rather than give up more Indian lands. Though his cause is doomed—Atta Kulla Kulla has been to London and knows the Indians are no match for the white man's "medicine"—Dragging Canoe dies fighting to preserve his nation and his way of life. Rion Outlaw and Dragging Canoe, though on opposite sides in the struggle over the Kentucky lands, are both presented sympathetically because Gordon is not interested in taking sides in the historical conflict; her interest, as usual, is in the exemplification of heroic virtue wherever it may be found.

The Women on the Porch

There is a sense in which Gordon's return to an earlier and simpler time in American history can be seen as a retreat, for to make her case for heroism, she had to abandon the world of the present that other writers, such as Eliot, Fitzgerald, and Hemingway, seemed to find more conducive to failure and despair than to heroic action. Gordon's next novel, *The Women on the Porch*, is set in the contemporary world, where disillusionment is rife and atrophy of the will is a mark of virtue. Her hero is Jim Chapman, a deracinated intellectual and professor of history at a New York university, whose affair with his assistant, Edith Ross, drives his wife, Catherine, away from the city and back to her ancestral home in Tennessee. For a time, Chapman wallows in uncertainty and moral confusion, but then he follows Catherine west, and after a strange vision in the woods of Swan Quarter, in which Catherine's pioneer forebear appears, Chapman is reunited with his wife. This action, though small when measured against the heroic deeds of the past, is for him deeply meaningful, since it signifies a return to action and a breaking out of the locked-in sensibility that has paralyzed his will.

Between the writing of *The Women on the Porch* and her next novel, *The Strange Children*, Gordon's personal life underwent a profound change; she became a convert to Catholicism. Looking backward from the perspective of this new novel, it is possible to see, if not the inevitability of that conversion, at least the logic of it. For Gordon, the commitment to art and the religious impulse were closely connected; both are, in their different ways, quests for perfection. Prior to her conversion, perfection meant not only perfection of form and style but of moral action as well, but action conceived in secular terms. In *The Strange Children* and in her next two novels, *The Malefactors* and *The Glory of Hera*, heroic action becomes not merely brave and selfless action that ends in an otherwise pointless death but also moral action so that evil might be overcome and good might flourish.

The Strange Children

The protagonist of *The Strange Children* is a girl, Lucy Lewis, whose parents, Stephen and Sarah Lewis, are cultivated intellectuals living at Benfolly, a farm in Tennessee. Stephen Lewis is writing a book about the Civil War, and on the weekend during which the action of the novel takes place, the Lewises are visited by a curious group of people: Kevin Reardon, a very rich, recent convert to Catholicism who has undergone a dramatic religious experience; his pale, beautiful, but mad wife; and a friend, "Uncle" Tubby, who has been having an affair with Reardon's wife. The intrigue between the lovers, a moral crisis in Lucy's life (over a valuable crucifix she took from Reardon's room), and a spiritual crisis through which Lucy's parents are passing are brought together at the end of the novel when the lovers elope, Lucy returns the crucifix, and Stephen Lewis is forced to recognize the desert in which those without religious faith are forced to wander. Reardon knew of Tubby's affair with his wife and had tried to warn him of her madness, but Tubby had only laughed. The good man had acted with the aid of a divine presence, while evil flourished in the elopement of the mad lovers; yet the seeds of understanding are planted in the mind of Stephen Lewis, who at the end of the novel is given to see the barrenness of his past and the terrors of a future devoid of faith.

The Malefactors

Thomas Claiborne, the protagonist of *The Malefactors*, Gordon's second "Catholic" novel, is in much the same state as Lewis at the end of *The Strange Children*, except that Claiborne is unaware of his spiritual emptiness. Like Isabelle Reardon, Claiborne is a poet who is also somewhat mad. He has periods during which he cannot write and hears a voice inside his head that makes critical comments about his conduct and state of mind. Claiborne lives on his wife's farm in Buck's County, Pennsylvania, and Vera Claiborne, a very rich woman, raises prize cattle. Like Tom Chapman of *The Women on the Porch*, Claiborne is a morally paralyzed intellectual, and like Tubby of *The Strange Children*, he becomes enamored of a woman poet, pursues her, and becomes involved in a sordid love affair that eventually drives him to seek guidance from a nun and, later, from a Catholic lay sister who operates a farm for Bowery derelicts.

After a spiritual crisis in which he has frightening dreams and a drunken realization that only his wife truly loves him and that his mistress is interested only in furthering her own career, Claiborne, who had quarreled with his wife, is reunited with her at the upstate farm where she has gone to assist in the work with derelicts. The means by which Claiborne is brought to the threshold of what appears to be a religious conversion is a complicated series of actions involving insights, visions, accounts of miraculous conversions, and revelations about Vera's own early baptism into the Catholic faith. One can see how fully Gordon's own religious conversion made it possible to handle the tangled web of marital infidelity with much more complexity than she had in *The Women on the Porch*. The Church had given her the means to represent the triumph of goodness in a fallen world.

The Glory of Hera

Some time after the publication of *The Malefactors*, Gordon began an ambitious project that she tentatively called *A Narrow Heart: The Portrait of a Woman*, a title that seemed to echo those of two works of which she was very fond: *A Simple Heart* (1877) by Flaubert and *The Portrait of a Lady* (1881) by James. As originally planned, the book was to have had a higher and a lower action, the higher one consisting of tales from Greek mythology, and the lower one, the author's fictionalized autobiography. The plan eventually was abandoned, however, and only the higher action of *A Narrow Heart* was published, under the title *The Glory of Hera*.

In the manner of a realistic novel, *The Glory of Hera* retells the labors of Heracles, which may seem curious in a novelist for whom Christ became the greatest hero and Christian virtue a guide to virtuous living. For Gordon, however, Heracles was a great precursor of Christ, and in retelling the story of his labors—one might say, his miracles—she paid homage to her early and abiding love of Greek mythology by suggesting the Christlike quality of its greatest hero.

When she died in 1981, Gordon was at work on another novel, the fictionalized autobiography that was to have made up the lower action of *A Narrow Heart*. It is not known how close that work was to completion or how it might contribute to her future reputation. There is no doubt about her historical importance; her name always appears in lists of important writers of the Southern Renaissance. As to the literary quality of her fiction, that is a matter to be decided as such matters always are, by the winnowing process of time. Her earliest works—*Penhally*; *Aleck Maury, Sportsman*; *None Shall Look Back*; and *Green Centuries*—seem the best candidates for survival; her later novels, though technically more complex, demand imaginative participation in religious beliefs to which few readers are able or willing to respond.

Gordon wrote against the grain of her time; while the major writers of the period, poets as well as novelists, depicted or implied the collapse of Western civilization and the invalidity of traditional values, she never lost faith in the possibility of redemption by heroic action. To some critics, this was a sign of her attachment to a vanished past and a refusal to confront contemporary realities. Gordon denied that she believed that the southern past, or any past, was superior to the present; what she did believe, however, was that the present was nourished by the best of the past, not because of its pastness, but because it made life richer and more meaningful. Gordon was aware of the misconceptions about her fiction and of the growing indifference of readers to her later work, but she never veered from her belief in the importance of what she was doing. It was her conviction that, if she wrote well, her work would endure and that it would continue to find its own appreciative audience.

W. J. Stuckey

OTHER MAJOR WORKS

SHORT FICTION: *The Forest of the South*, 1945; *Old Red, and Other Stories*, 1963; *The Collected Stories of Caroline Gordon*, 1981.

NONFICTION: *How to Read a Novel*, 1957; *A Good Soldier: A Key to the Novels of Ford Madox Ford*, 1963; *The Southern Mandarins: Letters of Caroline Gordon to Sally Wood, 1924-1937*, 1984; *A Literary Friendship: Correspondence Between Caroline Gordon and Ford Madox Ford*, 1999 (Brita Lindberg-Seyersted, editor).

EDITED TEXT: *The House of Fiction: An Anthology of the Short Story*, 1950 (with Allen Tate).

BIBLIOGRAPHY

Arbery, Virginia L. "'Considerable Emphasis on Decorum': Caroline Gordon and the Abyss." *Modern Age* 36 (Winter, 1994): 157-164. Discusses how Gordon's fiction makes use of American history and examines her depiction of the hero and the pattern of sacred marriage. Argues that critics have inadvertently depreciated the centrality of her often stated claim that women are always on the lookout for heroes.

Boyle, Anne M. *Strange and Lurid Bloom: A Study of the Fiction of Caroline Gordon*. Madison, N.J.: Fairleigh Dickinson University Press, 2002. Boyle discusses Gordon's efforts to attain her own voice and respect as a fiction writer and explores the racial and sexual themes of her works. Includes notes and an index.

Fraistat, Rose A. *Caroline Gordon as Novelist and Woman of Letters*. Baton Rouge: Louisiana State University Press, 1984. A study by a Southern woman of letters. Fraistat examines Gordon's life in terms of her work and places her in historical context.

Makowsky, Veronica A. *Caroline Gordon: A Biography*. New York: Oxford University Press, 1989. Although this work is primarily a biography, it contains extensive analysis of Gordon's fiction, including the novels *Penhally* and *Aleck Maury, Sportsman*. Includes a biography and an index.

Prown, Katherine Hemple. "To Cultivate the Masculine Virtues: Caroline Gordon as Writer, Critic, and Mentor." In *Revising Flannery O'Connor: Southern Literary Culture and the Problem of Female Authorship*. Charlottesville: University Press of Virginia, 2001. Gordon was O'Connor's mentor and played an important role in O'Connor's development as a writer. Prown describes the two writers' relationship and their eventual falling out.

Stuckey, W. J. *Caroline Gordon*. New York: Twayne, 1972. A brief biography and a detailed analysis of Gordon's novels and some of the short stories. One of the volumes in Twayne's United States Authors series.

Trefzer, Annette. "Gendering the Nation: Caroline Gordon's Cherokee Frontier." In *Disturbing Indians: The Archaeology of Southern Fiction*. Tuscaloosa: University of Alabama Press, 2007. Trefzer examines works by Gordon and other Southern Renaissance writers, focusing on their depiction of Native Americans in the colonial South. Includes notes, a bibliography, and an index.

Waldron, Ann. *Close Connections: Caroline Gordon and the Southern Renaissance*. New York: Putnam, 1987. A well-written literary biography that concentrates on Gordon's connections with other writers of the Southern Renaissance and their mutual influence. Includes a bibliography and an index.

MARY GORDON

Born: Far Rockaway, New York; December 8, 1949
Also known as: Mary Catherine Gordon

Principal long fiction

Final Payments, 1978
The Company of Women, 1980
Men and Angels, 1985
The Other Side, 1989
Spending: A Utopian Divertimento, 1998
Pearl, 2005

Other literary forms

Although Mary Gordon has built her literary reputation as a novelist, she has published numerous short stories and essays in such periodicals as *The Atlantic Monthly*, *Harper's*, *Virginia Quarterly Review*, *Southern Review*, *Commonweal*, and *Redbook*. Some of her short stories have been collected in the volumes *Temporary Shelter* (1987) and *The Stories of Mary Gordon* (2006). Among Gordon's works of nonfiction are *Good Boys and Dead Girls, and Other Essays* (1991), a collection of essays about literature and social commentary, and *Seeing Through Places: Reflections on Geography and Identity* (2000), which reveals information about events in Gordon's personal life that have influenced much of her fiction. Her biographical works include *Joan of Arc* (2000) and two biographies of her parents: *The Shadow Man: A Daughter's Search for Her Father* (1996), which chronicles Gordon's search for her father's past; and *Circling My Mother* (2007), the story of her painful and conflicted relationship with her mother. Gordon frequently contributes book reviews to such periodicals as *The Nation* and *The New York Times Book Review*.

Achievements

Mary Gordon's first novel, *Final Payments*, received enthusiastic reviews, and critics hailed Gordon as an important American Catholic writer. She has been compared to her literary idols, Jane Austen and Virginia Woolf, in her precision of perception and her depiction of the reflective and emotional lives of her characters. In 1979 for *Final Payments* and again in 1981 for *The Company of Women*, Gordon won the Janet Heidinger Kafka Prize for Fiction. She has also received the Lila Wallace-Reader's Digest Award and a Guggenheim Fellowship. Her biography *Joan of Arc* earned the O. B. Hardison Award, which is presented by the Massachusetts Center for Renaissance Studies. Gordon's short stories have appeared in several anthologies and have earned numerous prizes, including an O. Henry Award in 1997. She was named a State Author of New York, 2008-2010, by the New York State Writers' Institute.

Biography

Mary Catherine Gordon was born on December 8, 1949, to David and Anna Gagliano Gordon. As Gordon says in *The Shadow Man*, the death of her father when she was seven years old was the most influential event of her life. A convert to an extreme right-wing Catholicism from Judaism, David Gordon had idolized, and been idolized by, his young daughter. "I love you more than God," he told her once, frightening the child with the ambiguity and the cosmic implications of that statement. He regaled her with tales of his days at Harvard and his experiences in Oxford and in Paris with other American expatriates, taught her to read at the age of three, and instructed her in French, German, and Latin. Gordon left his daughter with a paradoxical legacy of lies and a deep intellectual curiosity. Only as an adult, in researching *The Shadow Man*, did Gordon learn the truth about her father: that he was a naturalized American citizen born in Lithuania, not Lorain, Ohio; and that his claim that he attended Harvard and Oxford universities was false—he had never attended college. Although she knew that he had published soft-core pornography as well as poetry and critical analyses of other writers in publications such as *The New Republic*, Gordon did not realize how rabidly anti-Semitic he was until she began her research. In discovering the truth about her father, Gordon was able to separate herself from his influence and accept his loss.

Although Gordon attributes her vocation as a writer to the encouragement of her father, she also credits her mother's side of the family for supplying the rhythms and inflections of her style and the concerns that shape her work. Anna Gordon, who had polio at the age of three and was disabled as a result, worked as a legal secretary to support herself and her daughter after David Gordon's death. She was an excellent letter writer. Anna's Irish Sicilian family members also served as models for many of the characters in Gordon's novels, often to their great displeasure. In *Circling My Mother*, Gordon describes their deeply conflicted relationship; she gained a new understanding of and compassion toward her mother through writing Anna Gordon's story.

Almost as influential on Gordon's life as the death of her father was her decision to turn down a scholarship to Fordham University, a Catholic school, and instead attend Barnard College. In a 1994 interview with Patrick H. Samway, Gordon claimed that her reasons for wanting to attend Barnard were totally shallow; she had read novelist J. D. Salinger and wanted to meet a Seymour Glass. Once she enrolled at Barnard, where she was taught by essayist Elizabeth Hardwick, her life changed.

Mary Gordon. (Eileen Barroso/Columbia University)

She received her B.A. from Barnard in 1971 and her M.A. from Syracuse University in 1973. A brief marriage in 1974 ended in divorce. From 1974 until 1978 Gordon taught at Dutchess Community College in Poughkeepsie, New York. In 1979 she taught at Amherst College and married Arthur Cash, a professor of English in the State University of New York system. They had two children, Anna and David. Since 1988, Gordon has been Millicent McIntosh Professor of Writing at Barnard College in New York City.

Although she has frequently been labeled a Catholic writer, Gordon rejects this definition as far too narrow for the scope of her literary work. Raised as a Catholic, she left the Church for several years but later returned. She reveres Catholicism for its spirituality but criticizes the Church's hierarchy for its dogmatism, especially the refusal to allow women a role equal to that of men in the Church. As a student, Gordon was involved in antiwar and feminist protests, and she continues to be a political activist. She places high value on her work as a teacher and is greatly respected by her students.

Analysis

The literary influences on Gordon's writing are varied and many. She names—in addition to Austen and Woolf—Ford Madox Ford, Charlotte Brontë, Thomas Hardy, and George Eliot. Critics have noted that her writing has something of the pulse of D. H. Lawrence, the ethical concerns of Doris Lessing, and the polish of Flannery O'Connor.

Fathers, whether biological, spiritual, or heavenly, figure strongly in Mary Gordon's fiction. She was deeply affected by the death of her own father when she was young and absorbed the spiritual atmosphere of the patriarchal Catholic Church prior to Vatican II (1961-1963). The tensions of the mother-daughter relationship also constitute a recurring theme in her work. Gordon's novels are reflective, character-driven studies that examine such contrasting topics as sacrifice and self-centeredness, sex and asceticism, art and gaudiness, legalism and spirituality. Praised for her piercing insight and finely patterned writing, Gordon admitted in a 1980 interview that what she likes most about her own writing is that occasionally she writes "really smashing sentences." Although much of her fiction, especially her earlier novels, has been influenced by her spiritual formation as a Catholic, she explores broader philosophical questions in her work, such as the nature of forgiveness and compassion, crises of religious faith, and definitions of moral behavior in the personal and political spheres. Critics have often praised Gordon's meticulous attention to the mastery of her craft, especially her use of metaphor and her finely crafted sentences.

Final Payments

Her first novel, *Final Payments*, garnered Gordon respect and received glowing reviews, perhaps because the work addresses the unfashionable topics of sacrifice and religious devotion. The novel opens with thirty-year-old Isabel Moore reflecting on those who attended her father's funeral. She settles primarily on four people: her two best friends, Eleanor and Liz; her favorite priest, Father Mulcahy; and her former housekeeper, Margaret Casey. Isabel has spent the last eleven years of her life caring for her invalid father, who had a series of debilitating strokes after discovering her in bed with his protégé, David Lowe. In reparation for her sin, she has given over her life to her father. He had been a college professor and an extreme right-wing Catholic; now free of his influence, Isabel turns to her friends Eleanor and Liz for solace and for help in beginning a new life. Her new freedom begins with a trip to the gynecologist for the insertion of an intrauterine device. The reader sees that Isabel's sacrificing her life to her father has been superficial, for once he is gone, she embarks on a course similar to the one that caused the break with her father.

On a visit to the home of Liz and John Ryan, Isabel obtains a job from Ryan, a handsome politician who is totally amoral. Isabel soon falls victim to Ryan's masculinity and sleeps with him, even though she despises him as a person. She does not, however, feel terribly guilty about this act, for she had previously learned that Liz has a lesbian lover. When Isabel falls in love with Hugh Slade, a local veterinarian and also a married man, she begins to question her physical relationship with Ryan. In order to keep her job with Ryan, she continues both affairs until she realizes how her actions are hurting Hugh.

Although she has told herself from the beginning of the affair with Hugh that he would never leave his wife and his children for her, Isabel eventually breaks off her affair with Ryan, risking his anger. Ryan finds the most appropriate way to hurt her: He sets Hugh's angry wife on her. Isabel is stricken and decides she must, once again, sacrifice her life in order to pay for her sins. To do so, she goes to live with Margaret Casey, who had been housekeeper for Isabel and her father until Isabel, at thirteen years of age, discovered that Margaret had designs on her father and threw the woman out of the house. With Margaret, whom Isabel has always despised, she finds, she believes, the perfect sacrifice—to love the unlovable. Isabel tries her best to deal with Margaret until Father Mulcahy convinces her that her sacrifice is without meaning and that she is slowly killing herself. Recognizing the truth in what he says, Isabel "pays" Margaret the twenty thousand dollars she received for the sale of her father's house and returns to her friends Eleanor and Liz to regain her self-respect and renew her life.

Men and Angels

Although Gordon's second novel, *The Company of Women*, deals with many of the Catholic topics present in *Final Payments*, it received mixed reviews upon publication. A series of monologues by Father Cyprian and his female disciples, the novel is primarily the story of the youth and maturing of Felicitas Taylor; in this work, Gordon introduces such issues as abortion and social activism. In her third novel, *Men and Angels*, Gordon moves away from Catholicism to a more general look at moral and religious questions. Anne Foster, a mother with a Harvard Ph.D., has the opportunity to write a catalog for an exhibition by the dead painter Caroline Watson (a character loosely based on several female artists). She must decide whether to accompany her husband to France, where he is to teach for a year, or to pursue her own career as an art historian. She decides to remain in the United States and hires Laura Post to care for her children while she works. Although she instinctively dislikes Laura, Anne is blind to the real danger that Laura, a religious fanatic, presents to her children. Because she desperately needs Laura's help as a caretaker, Anne continues to employ her.

During the year, Anne meets Caroline Watson's daughter-in-law, Jane, for whom Caroline had been a wonderful surrogate mother, despite the fact that she had neglected her own son. Jane, childless herself, takes to Anne from the first and becomes the mother that Anne herself has needed. Laura, whose mother treated her cruelly, had fallen under the influence of charlatan preachers. When Anne begins an extramarital affair, Laura, who has idealized Anne as the perfect mother, decides to save her from her sins by harming the children. The considerable tension that develops in the novel stems from the reader's perception of increasing danger to the children. Anne discovers that Laura, who borders on insanity, has deliberately allowed the children to play on thin ice. She dismisses Laura, who attempts suicide by cutting her wrists in Anne's bathtub.

Men and Angels brings the mother-child relationship into sharp focus, raising questions about the emotional conflicts faced by talented, educated women who attempt to combine careers and motherhood. Feminist critics have praised the novel, Gordon's best-selling work, as a rare exploration of the anguished choices faced by modern women as well as a study of the misery caused by motherhood gone wrong and the dangers of religious fanaticism.

SPENDING

Gordon's fourth novel, *The Other Side*, has not received much critical scrutiny. In many ways her most interesting novel, it tells the story of a day in the life of aged Irish immigrants, Vincent and Ellen MacNamara, through their own interior monologues and those of their family members. Gordon's next work of long fiction, *Spending*, presents a startling change in both style and theme from her previous novels. Artist Monica Szabo's fantasy of sex and money seems at first to be a real departure from Gordon's more overtly moral work. On closer examination, however, this novel—in its pulsing first-person narrative, its interiority, and its concern with art and life and how women combine the two—may be seen more accurately as reflecting a maturing art that no longer has to apologize for its own being.

A successful artist, Monica is delivering a lecture at a gallery owned by a friend when she half-jokingly notes that male artists have always had the benefit of a Muse, the model-inspiration-housekeeper-cook-secretary who also pays the rent. Somewhat wistfully, she wonders where all the male Muses are and is shocked when a gentleman in the audience announces, "Right here." This longtime admirer of Monica's work, whom she refers to only as B, also tells her he is very wealthy and offers to become her patron to enable her to take a sabbatical from her job as a college professor to paint full time. Although she wonders if she is mad, Monica readily agrees.

B, a wealthy and handsome commodities trader, becomes everything that Monica has fantasized about and more. His "spent" (the wordplay is intentional) condition after sex reminds her of paintings of the dead Christ by the old masters. B thus provides the means, the inspiration, and the model for the series of paintings, "Spent Men," that brings Monica her greatest acclaim. In his complete sacrifice of himself and his goods to Monica's needs and desires, B, quite appropriately Jewish, becomes a Christ figure.

Along the way, their relationship metamorphoses as their individual fortunes change. On the heels of Monica's successful show, B loses everything after investing in risky chocolate futures. Luckily, by this time Monica has been befriended by eighty-year-old Peggy Riordan, who had inherited a fortune from her lover of forty years. Peggy becomes Monica's second Muse as well as the more appropriate mother to one of Monica's twins, the conservative Sara. Wanting to divest herself of her assets before she and her current lover have to move into a retirement home, Peggy transfers the bulk of her fortune to Monica. Peggy's resources, along with the savvy of Monica's daughter Rachel (whose Brazilian boyfriend has a genius grandfather who predicts the fate of the coffee crop by examining the bark of the tree), save B's business.

The novel ends with Monica's celebration of B's return to fortune and with her looking forward to beginning her next project, "After Ingres," a series inspired by a trip to the Russian baths, her birthday present to Peggy. Monica has come to a full realization of the joys of love and work. In discussing *Spending*, critics have noted Gordon's ability to write with wit and dark humor about women's sensuality in this work, which is something of a departure from her previous fiction.

PEARL

Gordon's sixth novel, *Pearl*, begins with Maria Meyers, a fiercely overbearing single mother in New York City, receiving an alarming telephone message on Christmas night, 1998. Maria's twenty-year-old daughter Pearl has chained herself to the gates of the American embassy in Dublin, Ireland, and intends to starve herself to death. Pearl, a language student at Trinity College, has taken an Irish lover and is embroiled in the cause of the Irish Republican Army (IRA). She blames herself for the death of a disabled teenage boy, Stevie Donegan, and believes that her own death will be a public statement about the harm human beings cause each other. Joseph Kasperman, lifelong family friend of Maria and a father figure to Pearl, joins Maria in Ireland in the effort to rescue Pearl. The names of Maria and Joseph and the Christmas setting are symbolic. Critics have disagreed about the effectiveness of the unnamed narrator, who frequently challenges the reader by raising philosophical questions about the nature of human existence.

The fraught relationship between mother and daughter creates the tension in the novel; it is entirely possible that Pearl will die. Maria, angry and impetuous, descends on Dublin and the hospital where Pearl has been taken after being removed from her chains and is being fed intravenously against her will. Pearl's physician, Dr. Hazel Morrisey, has little sympathy for Maria and enforces Pearl's wish that her mother not be allowed to see her. Maria, rebelling against her father's extreme Roman Catholic views, has raised Pearl without religious belief. Moreover, Maria is guilty of refusing to forgive her father before he died. She believes that Pearl, unaccountably, seeks martyrdom, while Dr. Morrisey treats her as a suicidal anorexic. Pearl herself believes she must be a public witness to her part in young Stevie's death, an event that the reader understands as a tragic accident. The story is interwoven with the recent history of Ireland, primarily the starvation death of Bobby Sands and other IRA martyrs.

Pearl has refused food for six weeks and is emotionally indifferent, nearing the critical point beyond which death will be inevitable. The narrator asks the reader to make a judgment: Which of the two, Maria or Pearl, is making the morally justified choice? Both are strong-willed. Maria, fighting her daughter's wish to die, believes that "she has failed in the most important thing a mother can do for a child: to give her hope in life." Pearl, equally determined, tears out her feeding tube, an excruciatingly painful act. Pearl is ultimately saved by the Irish doctor's forceful treatment and the life-giving stories told by Tom, the shy medical student assigned to prevent Pearl from harming herself. Joseph, after a mistaken attempt to intervene, leaves Pearl and Maria to their reconciliation in an emotional scene that moves from tears to laughter.

Gordon tackles an astounding range of universal human concerns in this novel, from the need for unconditional forgiveness of those who have wronged us to the tragedy of fanatic idealism that destroys human life. To the ultimate question of the meaning of existence raised by the novel, Maria can only respond with her belief that human beings are meant to live. The narrator has the final word, answering the question of how Maria, Joseph, and Pearl will live out the rest of their lives: "We will hope for the best."

Jaquelyn W. Walsh
Updated by Marjorie Podolsky

Other major works

SHORT FICTION: *Temporary Shelter*, 1987; *The Rest of Life: Three Novellas*, 1993; *The Stories of Mary Gordon*, 2006.

NONFICTION: *Good Boys and Dead Girls, and Other Essays*, 1991; *The Shadow Man: A Daughter's Search for Her Father*, 1996; *Joan of Arc*, 2000; *Seeing Through Places: Reflections on Geography and Identity*, 2000; *Conversations with Mary Gordon*, 2002 (Alma Bennett, editor); *Circling My Mother: A Memoir*, 2007.

Bibliography

Bennett, Alma. *Mary Gordon*. New York: Twayne, 1996. Provides a good critical introduction to Gordon's work as well as biographical information. Includes chronology, bibliography, and index.

_______, ed. *Conversations with Mary Gordon*. Jackson: University Press of Mississippi, 2002. Collection of interviews given by Gordon over the course of her career covers a wide range of topics, including autobiographical elements in her fiction, her own favorite writers, and the influence of her religion on her work. Includes chronology and index.

Ciabarrari, Jane. "Mary Gordon's Novel of Justice and Atonement." Review of *Pearl*, by Mary Gordon. *Chicago Tribune*, February 13, 2005. Examines and praises Gordon's intellectual and emotional understanding of her characters as well as her mastery of language.

Gordon, Mary. "An Interview with Mary Gordon." Interview by Sandy Asirvatham. *Poets and Writers*, July/August, 1997, 50-61. Meaty interview focuses on Gordon's work methods and influences. Includes some brief analysis of her novels and gives detailed attention to the significance of her discoveries about her father.

Lee, Don. "About Mary Gordon." *Ploughshares* 23 (Fall, 1997): 218-226. Detailed biographical essay focuses primarily on the relationship between Gordon's life and her fiction.

Leonard, John. "Martyrs and Daughters." Review of *Pearl*, by Mary Gordon. *The New York Times Book Review*, February 20, 2005. Presents an analysis of Gordon's fiction overall in addition to praising *Pearl* as an intellectually demanding work that "complicates our understanding of the world."

Newman, Judie. "Telling a Woman's Story: Fiction as Biography and Biography as Fiction in Mary Gordon's *Men and Angels* and Alison Lurie's *The Truth About Lorin Jones*." In *Neo-realism in Contemporary American Fiction*, edited by Kristiaan Versluys. Atlanta: Rodopi, 1992. Compares the dilemmas confronting Anne Foster in *Men and Angels* and Lurie's heroine as each explores how best to tell the story of a dead female artist. Particularly interesting is Newman's examination of foremothering, mirroring, and the degree to which women do or do not agree with male fantasies as depicted in Gordon's novel.

Perry, Ruth. "Mary Gordon's Mothers." In *Narrating Mothers: Theorizing Maternal Subjectivities*, edited by Brenda O. Daly and Maureen T. Reddy. Knoxville: University of Tennessee Press, 1991. Discusses *Men and Angels* as an allegory of the dual life of the mother, who is also an intellectual being.

Smiley, Pamela. "The Unspeakable: Mary Gordon and the Angry Mother's Voices." In *Violence, Silence, and Anger: Women's Writing as Transgression*, edited by Deirdre Lashgari. Charlottesville: University Press of Virginia, 1995. Discusses the ideal and flawed mothers in *Men and Angels*, noting that both often exist within the same being in response to different children and environments.

Ward, Susan. "In Search of 'Ordinary Human Happiness': Rebellion and Affirmation in Mary Gordon's Novels." In *Faith of a Woman Writer*, edited by Alice Kessler-Harris and William McBrien. New York: Greenwood Press, 1988. Explores Gordon's theme of rebellion against the patriarchy and the accompanying need for women to establish a new feminine value system based on nature, flexibility, and instinct in order to achieve happiness.

MAXIM GORKY

Born: Nizhny-Novgorod, Russia; March 28, 1868
Died: Gorki, near Moscow, Russia, Soviet Union (now Nizhny Novgorod, Russia); June 18, 1936
Also known as: Aleksey Maksimovich Peshkov; Maksim Gorky; Maxim Gorki

Principal long fiction

Goremyka Pavel, 1894 (novella; *Orphan Paul*, 1946)
Foma Gordeyev, 1899 (English translation, 1901)
Troye, 1901 (*Three of Them*, 1902)
Mat, 1906 (serial), 1907 (book; *Mother*, 1906)
Ispoved, 1908 (*The Confession*, 1909)
Zhizn Matveya Kozhemyakina, 1910 (*The Life of Matvei Kozhemyakin*, 1959)
Delo Artamonovykh, 1925 (*Decadence*, 1927; better known as *The Artamonov Business*, 1948)
Zhizn Klima Samgina, 1927-1936 (*The Life of Klim Samgin*, 1930-1938; includes *The Bystander*, 1930, *The Magnet*, 1931, *Other Fires*, 1933, and *The Specter*, 1938)

Other literary forms

Maxim Gorky (GAWR-kee) wrote a total of fifteen plays, only three of which were staged during his lifetime: *Na dne* (pr., pb. 1902; *The Lower Depths*, 1912), *Vassa Zheleznova* (pb. 1910; English translation, 1945), and *Yegor Bulychov i drugiye* (pr., pb. 1932; *Yegor Bulychov and Others*, 1937). His other plays include *Meshchane* (pr., pb. 1902; *Smug Citizen*, 1906), *Dachniki* (pr., pb. 1904; *Summer Folk*, 1905), *Deti solntsa* (pr., pb. 1905; *Children of the Sun*, 1906), *Varvary* (pr., pb. 1906; *Barbarians*, 1906), *Vragi* (pb. 1906; *Enemies*, 1945), *Chudake* (pr., pb. 1910; *Queer People*, 1945), *Falshivaya moneta* (pr., pb. 1927, wr. 1913; the counterfeit coin), *Zykovy* (pb. 1914; *The Zykovs*, 1945), *Starik* (pr. 1919, wr. 1915; *Old Man*, 1924), and *Dostigayev i drugiye* (pr., pb. 1933; *Dostigayev and Others*, 1937). All are available in Russian in the thirty-volume *Polnoe sobranie sochinenii* (1949-1955; complete works), in the twenty-five-volume *Polnoe sobranie sochinenii* (1968-1976), and in English in *Seven Plays* (1945), *Five Plays* (1956), and *Plays* (1975). The eight-volume *Collected Works of Maxim Gorky* (1979-1981), is also available.

Gorky wrote about three hundred short stories. Among the most important are "Makar Chudra" (1892; English translation, 1901), "Chelkash" (1895; English translation, 1901), "Starukha Izergil" (1895; "The Old Woman Izergil"), "Malva" (1897; English translation), "V stepi" (1897; "In the Steppe"), "Dvadtsat' shest' i odna" (1899; "Twenty-six Men and a Girl," 1902), "Pesnya o burevestnike" (1901; "Song of the Stormy Petrel"), "Pesnya o sokole" (1908; "Song of the Falcon"), and the collections *Po Rusi* (1915; *Through Russia*, 1921) and *Skazki ob Italii* (1911-1913; *Tales of Italy*, 1958?). A three-volume collection of his stories, *Ocherki i rasskazy*, was first published in Russian in 1898-1899. The short stories are available in the collected works; some of the best of them are available in English in *Selected Short Stories* (1959), introduced by Stefan Zweig.

Among Gorky's numerous essays, articles, and nonfiction books, the most important are "O Karamazovshchine" (1913; "On Karamazovism"), "Revolyutsia i kultura" (1917; "Revolution and Culture"), *Vladimir Ilich Lenin* (1924; *V. I. Lenin*, 1931), and "O meshchanstve" (1929; "On the Petty Bourgeois Mentality"). The collection *Untimely Thoughts: Essays on Revolution, Culture, and the Bolsheviks* (1968) includes many of these essays in English translation.

Achievements

Hailed by Soviet critics as a true proletarian writer and the model of Socialist Realism, Maxim Gorky is one of few authors to see their native towns renamed in their honor. Many schools, institutes, universities, and theaters bear his name, as does one of the main streets in Moscow. These honors, says Helen Muchnic, resulted from the fact that Gorky, along with Vladimir Ilich Lenin and Joseph Stalin, "shaped and disseminated the country's official philosophy." Stalin admired Gorky greatly, awarding him the coveted Order of Lenin. As chair of the All-Union Congress of Soviet Writers in 1934, Gorky delivered an address in which he defined Socialist Realism, a doctrine that was to be interpreted in a manner different from what he intended or practiced; the *Soviet Encyclopedia* (1949-1958) calls him "the father of Soviet literature . . . the founder of the literature of Socialist Realism."

Although Gorky's novels are not among the best in Russian literature, they did inaugurate a new type of writing, revealing to the world a new Russia. In contrast to the countless fin de siècle evocations of the tormented Russian soul, with their gallery of superfluous men, Gorky offered a new hero, the proletarian, the revolutionary, such as Pavel Vlassov and his mother, Pelagea Nilovna, in the poorly constructed but ever-popular *Mother*. Indeed, Richard Hare argues that even today *Mother* is the prototype for the socially tendentious novel in the Soviet Union, with its crude but determined effort to look into the dynamism of social change in Russia.

Gorky's highest artistic achievements, however, are his literary portraits; the best, says Muchnic, are those that he drew from life, especially of Leo Tolstoy and Anton Chekhov. Also notable is Gorky's affectionate portrait of his grandmother. Gorky had a strong visual sense, the gift of astute observation, and the ability to translate these insights into sparkling dialogue. He created an entire portrait gallery of vignettes, most of which can be traced to people he met in his endless wanderings through Russia and abroad.

The child of a lower-middle-class family that faced rapid impoverishment, a self-taught student, a young man whose universities were the towns along the Volga and the steamers that made their way along its mighty waters, Gorky was nevertheless sympathetic to culture. He devoured books voraciously and indiscriminately and encouraged others to study. From 1918 to 1921, not wholly in favor with the new regime, he worked tirelessly to save writers and intellectuals from starvation and from censorship. He befriended the Serapion Brothers (a group of young Russian writers formed in 1921) and later Mikhail Sholokhov, always encouraging solid scholarship.

Estimates of Gorky even now depend on political ideology, for he is closely associated with the Russian Revolution. His vision, however, is broader than that of any political movement. He repeats often in his autobiographical works his dismay at the ignorance of people and their lack of desire for a better life, and he felt keenly the injustice done to the innocent. His writing is permeated by the desire to bring people from slavery to freedom, to build a good life; he believed in the power of human beings to change their world. Courageous, generous, and devoted to the public good, Gorky was timid, lacking in self-confidence, and infinitely modest. His commitment to social justice is unquestionable. These qualities may be what Chekhov had in mind when he said that Gorky's works might be forgotten, but that Gorky the man would never be.

Biography

Maxim Gorky, champion of the poor and the downtrodden, was born Aleksey Maksimovich Peshkov in Nizhny-Novgorod (a town that would bear the name Gorki after 1932), on March 28, 1868. His father, who died three years later from cholera, was a joiner-upholsterer and later a shipping agent; his mother's family, the Kashirins, were owners of a dyeing establishment. After his father's death, Gorky's mother left young Gorky to be reared by her parents, with whom he lived until the age of eleven, when his recently remarried mother died. Gorky recounts his childhood experiences in brilliant anecdotes and dialogue in his autobiographical *Detstvo* (1913; *My Childhood*, 1915). The influence of his grandparents was great: His grandfather was a brutal, narrowly religious man, while his grandmother was gentle and pious; her own peculiar version of a benevolent God, sharply in contrast to the harsh religiosity of her husband, marked the impressionable child.

The frequent wanderers in Gorky's works are a reflection of his own experience. In 1879, his grandfather sent him "into the world." He went first to the family of his grandmother's sister's son, Valentin Sergeyev, to whom he was apprenticed as a draftsman. Gorky hated the snobbishness and avarice of this bourgeois family, which became the prototype of the Gordeyevs and the Artamonovs in his fiction. For the next ten years, he filled many other minor posts, from messboy on a Volga steamer to icon painter, reading when and where he could. Other than an idealistic admiration for a neighbor whom he named Queen Margot, there were few bright spots in this period, which he describes in *V lyudyakh* (1916; *In the World*, 1917).

In 1889, after an unsuccessful suicide attempt that left him with a permanently weakened lung, Gorky met the Populist revolutionary Mikhail Romas, who helped him to clarify his confused ideas. At the same time, his acquaintance with the writer Vladimir Korolenko aided his literary development, as Tolstoy and Chekhov were to do in later years. In 1892, Gorky published his first story, "Makar Chudra," assuming at that time the pen name Maxim Gorky, meaning "the bitter one," a reflection of his painful childhood. Gorky wandered through Russia, wrote, and began a series of unsuccessful romantic involvements, first with Olga Kaminskaya, an older woman of some sophistication with whom he lived from 1892 to 1894, and then with Ekaterina Pavlovna Volzhina, a proofreader on the newspaper for which he was working. Gorky married Volzhina in 1896; the couple had two children, Maxim and Ekaterina. Imprisoned several times, Gorky was seldom free of police surveillance. In 1899, he became literary editor of the Marxist newspaper *Zhizn* and directed his attention to the problems of social injustice.

In 1905, Gorky's violent protests of government brutality in suppressing the workers' demonstrations on Bloody Sunday once again brought him imprisonment, this time in the Peter-Paul Fortress. By then, however, Gorky was famous, and celebrities all over Europe and the United States protested the sentence. Upon his release, he once again began to travel, both for political reasons and for his health. He visited New York, which he called "the city of the yellow devil," in 1906, where he attacked the United States for its inequalities and the

United States attacked him for the immorality of his relationship with Maria Fyodorovna Andreyeva, an actor of the celebrated Moscow Art Theater. After six months in the United States, he spent seven years in Italy, settling in Capri, where his Villa Serafina became a center of pilgrimage for all revolutionaries, including Lenin.

Gorky returned to Russia in 1913. When the Revolution broke out in 1917, he was not at first among its wholehearted supporters, although he served on many committees, working especially to safeguard culture. In 1921, for reasons of health, he went to Sorrento, Italy, where he spent his time writing. Although he made periodic visits to his homeland beginning in 1928, it was not until 1932 that he returned to the Soviet Union for good; in that same year, Stalin awarded him the Order of Lenin. In 1934, he was elected chair of the All-Union Congress of Soviet Writers; during this period, he became increasingly active in cultural policy making. Although he continued to write, he produced nothing noteworthy; his four-novel cycle *The Life of Klim Samgin*, the last volume of which he did not live to complete, is an artistic failure. Gorky's death in 1936 was surrounded by mysterious circumstances, although official autopsy reports attribute it to tuberculosis and influenza.

Maxim Gorky. (Library of Congress)

Analysis

Although Soviet critics tend to exalt the realism of Maxim Gorky's works, D. S. Mirsky said that Gorky never wrote a good novel or a good play, while Tolstoy remarked that Gorky's novels are inferior to his stories and that his plays are even worse than his novels. Maintaining that Gorky's "tremendous heroic emotions ring false," Tolstoy criticized Gorky's lack of a sense of proportion, as Chekhov had noted Gorky's lack of restraint. It is obvious that Gorky did not know how to limit his stories, that he piles up details along with extraneous dialogue. His narrative technique consists in recounting the life story of a single protagonist or the saga of a family. His narratives are always linear, often proceeding from birth to death; the main character yearns for a new life and struggles with a stagnant environment, sometimes experiencing flashes of light. Thus, the typical Gorky novel is a tireless and often tiresome documentary on a single theme.

Gorky's weak narrative technique is counterbalanced by excellent characterization. True, he is guilty of oversimplification—his characters are types rather than individuals, figures from a modern morality play—but he introduced into Russian fiction a wide range of figures from many different walks of life rarely or never treated by earlier novelists. Though not highly individualized, Gorky's characterizations are vivid and convincing, imbued with his own energy.

Gorky sees people as social organisms, and therefore he is especially conscious of their role in society. He was particularly familiar with the merchant class or the *meshchane*, because he grew up among them, in the Kashirin and Sergeyev households. They form some of his most successful portraits, representing not only the petty bourgeoisie but also the barge owners, grain dealers, mill owners, and textile manufacturers, the Gordeyevs, Artamonovs, and Kozhemyakins. Gorky represents them as self-centered individualists, characterized by envy, malice, self-righteousness, avarice, and intellectual and spiritual torpor. Their decadence is symbolic of the malady that ravages prerevolutionary Russia.

In contrast to the merchants are the lonely and downtrodden, not always idealized as in the novels of Fyodor Dostoevski but presented, rather, as the ignorant victims of society and its lethargic sycophants. The corrupt and indifferent town of Okurov in *The Life of Matvei Kozhemyakin* symbolizes Russia's decadence, as do the thieves and vagabonds of Kazan, the flophouse of *The Lower Depths*, and the orgies of the theology students in the houses of prostitution. More Dostoevskian are the *bosyaki*, the barefoot tramps, such as Chelkash and Makar Chudra, who are the heralds of the future. Along with them, yet very different in spirit, is the revolutionary intelligentsia, the new heroes created by Gorky. They are Pelagea Nilovna, the "mother"; her son, Pavel; and his friends, Mansurova in *The Life of Matvei Kozhemyakin* and Derenkov and Romas in Gorky's own life. It is for such characters that Gorky is exalted by the Soviets, though to foreign readers they are usually the least attractive.

Gorky's best characters are presented without excessive ideological trappings. They range from his saintly grandmother, Akulina Kashirina, perhaps his most unforgettable character, to Queen Margot, the idol with clay feet. They include Smoury, the cook on the steamer, who first encouraged Gorky to read, and many other simple people whom Gorky was to meet, "kind, solitary, and broken off from life." They also take the form of figures such as the merchant Ignat Gordeyev, the image of the Volga, vital, seething, creative, generous, and resolute.

Most of Gorky's women are victims of violence, beaten by their husbands and unappreciated by their families, such as Natasha Artamonova and the wife of Saveli Kozhemyakin, who is beaten to death by him. Love in Gorky's novels is either accompanied by violence and brutality or idealized, as in Queen Margot or Tanya in the story "Twenty-six Men and a Girl." It ranges from tender devotion in *Mother* to drunken orgies on Foma Gordeyev's Volga steamer. Gorky's own experience of love was unhappy, and he was ill at ease when portraying sexual scenes. Even his coarsely erotic scenes seem to be tinged with a moralizing intent.

Against a background of resplendent nature, the Volga, the sea, or the steppe, Gorky depicts the eruptions of violence and brutality, the orgies and the squalor, the pain and the harshness that, says Muchnic, are at the heart of his work. One has only to read the opening pages of *My Childhood* to feel its force. His own weight of harsh experience impelled him to force others to look at the bestiality that he saw rampant in Russia and to urge them to exterminate it. Ever the champion of social justice, Gorky felt the need to fight ignorance, cruelty, and exploitation.

Foma Gordeyev

Gorky's first and best novel, *Foma Gordeyev*, is set along the banks of the Volga, a region well known to the author. It is the story of the Volga merchants, represented here by the Gordeyev and Mayakin families. Rich, greedy, and passionate, both families represent the iron will and the domination of the merchant class. Gorky's merchants are of peasant origin, unsophisticated and uneducated. In Foma's revolt, Gorky shows the decay of society at the end of the nineteenth century and the impending Revolution, as yet only dimly anticipated.

Foma, the only son of Ignat Gordeyev, a self-made barge owner and one of Gorky's richest character sketches, is brought up by his godfather and his father's business colleague, Yakov Mayakin, whose family has owned the local rope works for generations. Foma shows no talent for or interest in business and, after his father's death, wastes his money on debauchery, drink, and wanton destruction. At first dimly attracted to Lyubov Mayakina, he is unable to conform to her educated tastes, and she, in obedience to her father's wishes, marries the respectable and highly Europeanized Afrikan Smolin. Foma continues his wild rebellion, actually a search for self and meaning, not unlike that of Mikhail Lermontov's Pechorin. Finally institutionalized for apparent insanity, Foma becomes an enlightened vagabond.

Foma Gordeyev follows the story line generally adopted by Gorky: the life story of the hero from birth to a crisis. Although it is weak in plot and characterization, it is readable, especially powerful in its evocation of the Volga, the elemental force that intoxicated the wealthy Ignat. Ignat is a finished portrait of the boisterous, dynamic businessman Gorky knew so well—vital, creative, and resolute. He is one of Gorky's most sympathetic portraits, along with Yakov Mayakin, who shows the characteristic traits of the Russian merchant that go back to the sixteenth century *Domostroy* (a book on social conduct). Foma, though not so well drawn, represents the rift in generations and the universally disturbed mood that pervaded Russia on the eve of the abortive Revolution of 1905. The whole novel attempts to assess the flaws in the capitalistic system and thus is very modern in spirit.

MOTHER

Mother, written while Gorky was in the United States after the 1905 Revolution, reflects his disillusionment with both czarist and capitalistic social structures and his desire "to sustain the failing spirit of opposition to the dark and threatening forces of life." The novel was published first in English, in 1906, by *Appleton's Magazine* in New York, and then in Russian in Berlin. It became the symbol of the revolutionary cause and was widely read and acclaimed, even after the Revolution, as a model of the socialist novel. Translated into many languages, it became the basis for other novels and plays, such as Bertolt Brecht's *Mutter Courage und Ihre Kinder* (1941; *Mother Courage and Her Children*, 1941). As a novel, it is one of Gorky's weakest in characterization and plot, yet its optimistic message and accessible style have assured its continuing popularity.

Written in the third person, through the eyes of the courageous mother, Pelagea Nilovna Vlassova, the novel relates her encounter with the Social Democratic Party, inspired by her son, Pavel. Pelagea suffered mistreatment from her husband and seems destined to continue in the same path with her son until his "conversion" to socialism. Pavel becomes a champion of the proletarian cause, the acknowledged leader of a small group of fellow revolutionaries who study forbidden books and distribute literature among the factory workers in their village. After Pavel's arrest, the illiterate Pelagea continues Pavel's work, stealthily distributing pamphlets and becoming a mother to the other members of the group: Sasha, who is secretly in love with Pavel; the "God-builder" Rybin; Andrei, the charming and humorous *khokhol*; the misanthropic Vesovshchikov; and the open-hearted urban intellectual Nikolai. Pavel's release from prison is immediately followed by his bold leadership in the May Day demonstration, for which he is again imprisoned. The mother's work becomes more daring and widespread as she passes to other villages like the holy wanderers so common in Gorky's early work. After Pavel's condemnation to exile in Siberia, Pelagea herself is arrested as she prepares to distribute the speech her son made prior to his sentence.

The best portrait in this weak novel is that of the mother, the only character to show psychological development. Yet Pelagea passes from one type of religious fervor to another, and her socialist convictions are simply the transferral of her Orthodox beliefs to the kingdom of this world. Even the revolutionaries invoke Christ and compare their work to his. The austere Pavel remains remote and unconvincing, while maternal love is the dominant force in the affectionate and almost mystical Pelagea.

THE ARTAMONOV BUSINESS

Written in 1924 and 1925 while Gorky was living abroad in Sorrento, *The Artamonov Business* is a retrospective novel on the causes of the 1917 Revolution. Encompassing three generations and covering the period from 1863 to 1917, it has a much broader base than most of Gorky's works. Although here, as elsewhere, Gorky fills his narrative with extraneous detail, he draws many convincing portraits of the demoralized merchant class at the turn of the century. Frank M. Borras singles out Gorky's interweaving of the historical theme with the characters' personal destinies as one of the merits of the novel.

Ilya Artamonov is the patriarch of the family, a passionate and dynamic freed serf who establishes a linen factory in the sleepy town of Dryomov. His son, Pyotr, inherits his father's sensuality but not his business skill, and the narrative of his debauchery and indifference to his workers occupies the greater part of the novel. The Artamonov family also includes the more businesslike and adaptable Aleksei and the hunchback Nikita, who becomes a monk though he has lost his faith in God. The women in the novel occupy a secondary and passive role, existing mainly for the sensual gratification of the men, both attracting and repelling them.

Pyotr has two sons and two daughters. The eldest son, Ilya, leaves home to study and, as in Chekhov's stories, becomes an unseen presence, presumably joining the revolutionary Social Democratic Party. Yakov, the second son, is a sensualist, indifferent to business, and is killed by revolutionaries as he escapes in fear of them. Miron, Aleksei's son, though physically weak, shows, like his father, an aptitude for commerce. Yet none is strong enough to save the family's ailing business, weakened by the corruption and indifference of its managers.

Gorky's symbolism is evident in his characterization of Tikhon Vialov (the quiet one), an enigmatic ditchdigger, gardener, and ubiquitous servant of the Artamonov family. It is Tikhon who at the very end of the story proclaims the Revolution, calling for revenge for the injustices that he has suffered at the hands of the Artamonovs. Quite obviously he symbolizes the proletariat, victim of the bourgeoisie. Aside from Tikhon, Gorky emphasizes much less the oppression of the workers than the empty, selfish, and superfluous lives of the factory owners.

Alternating wild episodes of debauchery, cruelty, and murder with scenes of boredom and superfluous dialogue, *The Artamonov Business* is both a modern novel and a return to Dostoevskian melodrama. Gorky had planned to write the novel as early as 1909 but was advised by Lenin to wait for the Revolution, which would be its logical conclusion. This story of the progressive deterioration of a family is also a profound study in the consequences of the failure of human relationships.

Gorky was less a man of ideas and reason than one of instinct and emotion. His best works are based on intuition and observation. His truth and reality are humanistic, not metaphysical; they deal with the useful and the practical. Unlike Honoré de Balzac, whom he admired, Gorky did not succeed in investing the sordid with mystery or the petty with grandeur. He wrote a literature of the moment, "loud but not intense," as Muchnic describes it. It is, however, a literature of the people and for the people, accessible and genuine. Although some of his works are monotonous to today's Western reader, and no doubt to the Russian reader as well, at their best they are honest portrayals of people, inspiring confidence in humanity's power to change the world.

Irma M. Kashuba

Other major works

short fiction: "Makar Chudra" (1892; English translation, 1901); "Chelkash," 1895 (English translation, 1901); "Byvshye lyudi," 1897 ("Creatures That Once Were Men," 1905); *Ocherki i rasskazy*, 1898-1899 (3 volumes); "Dvadtsat' shest' i odna," 1899 ("Twenty-six Men and a Girl," 1902); *Orloff and His Wife: Tales of the Barefoot Brigade*, 1901; *Rasskazy i p'esy*, 1901-1910 (9 volumes); *Skazki ob Italii*, 1911-1913 (*Tales of Italy*, 1958?); *Tales of Two Countries*, 1914; *Chelkash, and Other Stories*, 1915; *Po Rusi*, 1915 (*Through Russia*, 1921); *Stories of the Steppe*, 1918; *Zametki iz dnevnika: Vospominaniia*, 1924 (*Fragments from My Diary*, 1924); *Rasskazy 1922-1924 godov*, 1925; *Selected Short Stories*, 1959; *A Sky-Blue Life, and Selected Stories*, 1964; *The Collected Short Stories of Maxim Gorky*, 1988.

plays: *Meshchane*, pr., pb. 1902 (*Smug Citizen*, 1906); *Na dne*, pr., pb. 1902 (*The Lower Depths*, 1912); *Dachniki*, pr., pb. 1904 (*Summer Folk*, 1905); *Deti solntsa*, pr., pb. 1905 (*Children of the Sun*, 1906); *Varvary*, pr., pb. 1906 (*Barbarians*, 1906); *Vragi*, pb. 1906 (*Enemies*, 1945); *Posledniye*, pr., pb. 1908; *Chudake*, pr., pb. 1910 (*Queer People*, 1945); *Vassa Zheleznova* (first version), pb. 1910 (English translation, 1945); *Zykovy*, pb. 1914 (*The Zykovs*, 1945); *Starik*, pr. 1919 (wr. 1915; *Old Man*, 1924); *Falshivaya moneta*, pr., pb. 1927 (wr. 1913); *Yegor Bulychov i drugiye*, pr., pb. 1932 (*Yegor Bulychov and Others*, 1937); *Dostigayev i drugiye*, pr., pb. 1933 (*Dostigayev and Others*, 1937); *Vassa Zheleznova* (second version), pr., pb. 1935 (English translation, 1975); *Seven Plays*, 1945; *Five Plays*, 1956; *Plays*, 1975.

nonfiction: *Detstvo*, 1913 (*My Childhood*, 1915); *V lyudyakh*, 1916 (*In the World*, 1917); *Vozpominaniya o Lev Nikolayeviche Tolstom*, 1919 (*Reminiscences of Leo Nikolaevich Tolstoy*, 1920); *Moi universitety*, 1923 (*My Universities*, 1923); *Vladimir Ilich Lenin*, 1924 (*V. I. Lenin*, 1931); *Reminiscences of Tolstoy, Chekhov, and Andreyev*, 1949; *Untimely Thoughts: Essays on Revolution, Culture, and the Bolsheviks*, 1968; *Selected Letters*, 1997 (Andrew Barratt and Barry P. Scherr, editors); *Gorky's Tolstoy and Other Reminiscences: Key Writings by and About Maxim Gorky*, 2008 (Donald Fanger, editor).

miscellaneous: *Polnoe sobranie sochinenii*, 1949-1955 (30 volumes); *Polnoe sobranie sochinenii*, 1968-1976 (25 volumes); *Collected Works of Maxim Gorky*, 1979-1981 (8 volumes).

BIBLIOGRAPHY

Borras, F. M. *Maxim Gorky the Writer: An Interpretation*. Oxford, England: Clarendon Press, 1967. One of the more astute interpretations of Gorky's works, especially his novels and plays. Unlike many other books that concentrate on either biography or political issues, Borras's book emphasizes Gorky's artistic achievements.

Hare, Richard. *Maxim Gorky: Romantic Realist and Conservative Revolutionary*. New York: Oxford University Press, 1962. The first substantial study of Gorky in English since Alexander Kaun's 1931 book. Hare combines the political aspects of Gorky's biography with critical analyses of his works, with the latter receiving the short end. Contains some interesting observations obtained from anonymous people who knew Gorky well.

Kaun, Alexander. *Maxim Gorky and His Russia*. New York: Jonathan Cape and Harrison Smith, 1931. The first book on Gorky in English, written while Gorky was still alive and supported by firsthand knowledge about him. Covers literary and nonliterary life in Russia and the atmosphere in Gorky's time. Still one of the best biographies, despite some outdated facts later corrected by history.

Levin, Dan. *Stormy Petrel: The Life and Work of Maxim Gorky*. New York: Schocken Books, 1985. This reprint of the author's 1965 work contains the detailed notes he excised from the original edition. An engrossing biographical and literary interpretation of Gorky's life and work.

Morris, Paul D. *Representation and the Twentieth-Century Novel: Studies in Gorky, Joyce, and Pynchon*. Würzburg, Germany: Königshausen & Neumann, 2005. A critical interpretation of Gorky's *Mother*, as well as James Joyce's *Ulysses* and Thomas Pynchon's *Gravity's Rainbow*, discussing how each novel represents a different literary tradition. Morris views Gorky's book as a paradigm of the Socialist Realist novel. For advanced students.

Scherr, Barry P. *Maxim Gorky*. Boston: Twayne, 1988. Chapters on the writer and revolutionary, his literary beginnings, his career as a young novelist, his plays, his memoirs, and his final achievements. Includes a chronology, detailed notes, and an annotated bibliography. Still the best introductory study.

Troyat, Henri. *Gorky*. Translated by Lowell Bair. New York: Crown, 1989. A translation of a French biography, written by a well-regarded literary biographer, which discusses Gorky's life and works. Includes a bibliography and an index.

Valentino, Russell Scott. *Vicissitudes of Genre in the Russian Novel: Turgenev's "Fathers and Sons," Chernyshevsky's "What Is to Be Done?," Dostoevsky's "Demons," Gorky's "Mother."* New York: Peter Lang, 2001. Analyzes Russian fictional works from the 1860's that are examples of the "tendentious novel" of this period. Describes how these novels influenced twentieth century literature.

Weil, Irwin. *Gorky: His Literary Development and Influence on Soviet Intellectual Life*. New York: Random House, 1966. One of the most scholarly books on Gorky in English, skillfully combining biography with critical analysis. Valuable especially for the discussion of Soviet literary life and Gorky's connections with, and influence on, younger Soviet writers. Contains a select but adequate bibliography.

Yedlin, Tova. *Maxim Gorky: A Political Biography*. Westport, Conn.: Praeger, 1999. Yedlin's biography focuses on Gorky's political and social views and his participation in the political and cultural life of his country. Includes a bibliography and an index.

GÜNTER GRASS

Born: Danzig (now Gdańsk, Poland); October 16, 1927

Also known as: Günter Wilhelm Grass

Principal long fiction

Die Blechtrommel, 1959 (*The Tin Drum*, 1961)
Katz und Maus, 1961 (*Cat and Mouse*, 1963)
Hundejahre, 1963 (*Dog Years*, 1965)
Örtlich betäubt, 1969 (*Local Anaesthetic*, 1969)
Aus dem Tagebuch einer Schnecke, 1972 (*From the Diary of a Snail*, 1973)
Der Butt, 1977 (*The Flounder*, 1978)
Das Treffen in Telgte, 1979 (*The Meeting at Telgte*, 1981)
Danziger Trilogie, 1980 (*Danzig Trilogy*, 1987; includes *The Tin Drum*, *Cat and Mouse*, and *Dog Years*)
Kopfgeburten: Oder, Die Deutschen sterben aus, 1980 (*Headbirths: Or, The Germans Are Dying Out*, 1982)
Die Rättin, 1986 (*The Rat*, 1987)
Unkenrufe, 1992 (*The Call of the Toad*, 1992)
Ein weites Feld, 1995 (*Too Far Afield*, 2000)
Mein Jahrhundert, 1999 (*My Century*, 1999)
Im Krebsgang: Eine Novelle, 2002 (*Crabwalk*, 2003)
Das Danzig-Sextett, 2005 (includes *Die Blechtrommel*, *Katz und Maus*, *Hundejahre*, *Der Butt*, *Unkenrufe*, and *Im Krebsgang*)

Other literary forms

Although Günter Grass achieved fame and critical acclaim as a novelist, he has by no means limited his literary creativity to the genre of prose fiction. In fact, the author first attracted attention—albeit of a limited nature—as a playwright and a poet. In 1958, his one-act play in the absurdist vein *Noch zehn Minuten bis Buffalo* (*Only Ten Minutes to Buffalo*, 1967), was published (it was first staged in 1959), and in 1956, his first collection of poetry, *Die Vorzüge der Windhühner* (the advantages of wind-fowl), was published. There is no exact correspondence between the German editions of Grass's plays and those in English translation. Six plays were collected in *Theaterspiele* (1970; pieces for the theater), including *Only Ten Minutes to Buffalo*, *Hochwasser* (pr. 1957; *Flood*, 1967), *Onkel, Onkel* (pr. 1958; *Mister, Mister*, 1967), and *Die bösen Köche* (pr., pb. 1961; *The Wicked Cooks*, 1967); the English versions of these plays were published in *Four Plays* (1967), whereas *Die Plebejer proben den Aufstand* (pr., pb. 1966; *The Plebeians Rehearse the Uprising*, 1966) and *Davor* (pr., pb. 1969; *Max*, 1972) were published independently in English translations. Complete editions of Grass's plays in the German original are available in Grass's collected works (*Werkausgabe*, 1997).

Grass's collected poems in *Gesammelte Gedichte* (1971) include the previously published volumes *Die Vorzüge der Windhühner*, *Gleisdreieck* (1960; rail interchange), and *Ausgefragt* (1967; *New Poems*, 1968). Selections from the first two collections are available in a bilingual edition under the title *In the Egg, and Other Poems* (1977); *Mariazuehren, Hommageàmarie, Inmarypraise* (1973) was published as a trilingual edition, as the title indicates. The collection titled *Liebe geprüft* (1974; *Love Tested*, 1975) is a bibliophile edition. *Novemberland: Selected Poems, 1956-1993* (1996) is a bilingual edition of Grass's poetry from various collections. Editions of Grass's poetry in the German original may be found in his collected works; selections of Grass's poetry in English translation have also been included in *Cat and Mouse, and Other Writings* (1994) and *The Günter Grass Reader* (2004).

The multitalented Grass, whose poetry gradually evolved from a certain degree of playfulness to a concern with political, social, and environmental problems, has fairly frequently combined prose, poetry, and drawings or graphics in his works. Instructive examples of Grass's art include *Zunge zeigen* (1988; *Show Your Tongue*, 1989), a diary about the author's and his wife's sojourn in Calcutta (now Kolkata), India, in 1986-1987; *Totes Holz* (1990; dead wood), drawings accompanied by text; and the collections of poetry *Novemberland*, *Letzte Tänze* (2003; last dances), *Dummer August* (2007; foolish person). *My Century* is a collection of one hundred linked stories or vignettes—one for each year of the past century—that are accompanied (in the German edition) by Grass's watercolors; the stories seek to recapture the essence of the twentieth century mostly from the perspective of common people.

Grass has also produced a considerable body of writings that originated as a result of his political involvement and, perhaps to a somewhat lesser extent, his commitment to his craft. These speeches, essays, open letters, and other comments have been published in the following major collections: *Über das Selbstverständliche* (1968; partial translation *Speak Out!*, 1969), *Über meinen Lehrer Döblin, und andere Vorträge* (1968; about my teacher Döblin, and other essays), *Der Bürger und seine Stimme* (1974; the citizen and his voice; partially translated in *On Writing and Politics, 1967-1983*), *Denkzettel: Politische Reden und Aufsätze, 1965-76* (1978; lessons to remember: political speeches and essays; partially translated in *On Writing and Politics, 1967-1983*), *Aufsätze zur Literatur* (1980; essays on literature), and *Widerstand lernen: Politische Gegenreden, 1980-1983* (1984; learning how to resist: political rebuttals).

Particularly after the opening of the Berlin Wall on November 9, 1989, and the subsequent German reunification in the following year, Grass voiced his strident and highly controversial views on the new developments in the political realm in a number of speeches, essays, debates, and interviews that were published independently or in small collections, among them *Deutscher Lastenausgleich: Wider das dumpfe Einheitsgebot* (1990; *Two States—One Nation?*, 1990); *Schreiben nach Auschwitz: Frankfurter Poetik-Vorlesung* (1990; "Writing After Auschwitz," in *Two States—One Nation?*), in which he self-righteously postulated that Germans had forfeited the right of self-determination on account of Auschwitz; and *Rede vom Verlust: Über den Niedergang der politischen Kultur im geeinten Deutschland* (1992; "On Loss," in *The Future of German Democracy*, 1993). Grass's stance against German reunification is also reflected in his fiction, especially in the novel *Too Far Afield*. His political and other pronouncements from 1956 to 1986 are included in *Werkausgabe* (1997); the volume *Steine wälzen: Essays und Reden, 1997-2007* (2007; rolling stones) includes his later essays and speeches.

Achievements

Günter Grass has long been acknowledged as a novelist of international stature—a rank he achieved with the publication of *The Tin Drum*, his first novel, the English version of which appeared in 1961 in Great Britain and two years later in the United States. Although Grass continued to publish at a fairly steady pace and to produce works of challenging complexity—notably *The Flounder*—*The Tin Drum* is his most widely acclaimed work. The film version of *The Tin Drum*, with its screenplay by Grass and director Volker Schlöndorff, won the 1979 Academy Award for Best Foreign Language Film and also received several other international prizes.

Grass is generally acknowledged as the "author who put postwar German literature back in the world market" (*Newsweek*, May 24, 1965). His fiction displays a virtuosity of language practically unparalleled in contemporary letters, and he has received numerous domestic (that is, German) as well as foreign literary awards, among them the prestigious prize of Gruppe 47 (1958). In fact, between 1958 and 2005 Grass received more than thirty major European and German literary prizes. The impressive string of the former includes France's Foreign Book Prize (1962), Italy's Mondello Prize (1977), the Viareggio-Versilia Prize (1978), and the Mayakovski Medal of the city of Gdańsk (1978), his former hometown, which also made him an honorary citizen (1993). Among the German awards are the Carl von Ossietzky Medal (1977) and the prestigious Leonhard Frank Ring (1988). In addition, Grass has been awarded five honorary doctorates, including one from Harvard University (1976) and one from the University of Gdańsk (1993). Although ever since the publication of *The Tin Drum* in 1959 Grass had been a serious contender for the Nobel Prize in Literature, it was not until 1999 that he was awarded the coveted prize—without doubt the crowning achievement of his literary career.

Even though Grass's prose fiction from the mid-1980's to the end of the century was faulted by literary critics for its increasingly political polemics and an alleged corresponding diminution of the author's artistic powers, his earlier works of fiction generally continue to be held in high esteem. In addition, Grass's formidable literary stature is acknowledged, if sometimes grudgingly, by most serious students of literature. There are several reasons Grass became the center of public attention. To begin with, Grass aroused topical interest with his chronicling of Germany's Nazi past—if from an idiosyncratic narrative point of view. The surface realism of *The Tin Drum*, for example, is mingled with elements of the fantastic, grotesque, and comical that require readers to reexamine their preconceived notions not only about the period in question but also about the very nature of reality itself. Second, despite Grass's underlying view of history as ultimately meaningless and his perception of human existence as bordering on the absurd, his major works do convey a sense of commitment and responsibility that challenge the reader. Third, Grass has never confined himself to the proverbial ivory tower of the artist—quite the opposite. He has repeatedly stated that his responsibility as both a citizen and a writer demands his active involvement in politics, and he has acted according to his professed belief. Critics who claim to have discerned a diminishing of Grass's creativity as a result of his squandering his energies on time-consuming and exhausting participation in left-wing, grassroots political campaigns have been proved wrong; after each spate of intense political activity, Grass has inevitably returned to literary and other artistic pursuits.

Biography

Günter Wilhelm Grass was born October 16, 1927, in the city of Gdańsk (called Danzig in German), which had formerly been part of the German Empire and in 1920 became a free state according to the stipulations of the Treaty of Versailles. Although Danzig's population was more than 90 percent German, Grass was the offspring of an ethnically mixed marriage; his father was a German, and his mother was of Cassubian or Kashubian—that is, Slavic—origin. Both the ethnic origin of his mother and the social milieu of the lower middle class in which he grew up—Grass's father was a grocer—proved to be lasting influences that inspired particularly his early fiction.

Until the publication of his memoir in 2006, it was generally assumed that Grass, after attending school in Danzig (which at the outbreak of World War II in September, 1939, had been annexed by the Third Reich), had been drafted into the army during the final phase of World War II while he was still a teenager. In 1945, he was wounded and subsequently taken captive by the American forces. After a brief period of imprisonment, he began to work in a potash mine and then became a stonemason's apprentice in Düsseldorf in the Rhineland. From this period of 1946-1947 dates Grass's beginning awareness of Nazi atrocities as well as his first exposure to postwar politics. He was attracted to the pragmatism of the Social Democrats, who tended to prefer the achievement of tangible results in the social and economic realms to blind adherence to ideology.

Although Grass, a self-professed autodidact, eschewed the continuation of his formal education, which had been interrupted by the war, he did enroll at the Düsseldorf and Berlin academies of art (1948-1951 and 1953-1956) to study sculpture under various teachers. In 1954, he married Anna Schwarz, a ballet student from Switzerland, with whom he had three sons and one daughter. The marriage eventually ended in divorce, and Grass married Ute Grunert in 1979.

During the middle and late 1950's, Grass gradually began to attract attention as a writer. In his first phase of literary activity, from approximately 1955 to 1959, he wrote primarily short prose pieces, poetry, and absurdist or poetic plays. In 1955, he was awarded a prize for his lyrics by the Süddeutsche Rundfunk (South German radio network); in the same year, he established contact with Gruppe 47, the most influential association of writers, publishers, and critics in postwar West Germany, and in 1958 he was awarded that group's prestigious prize. Grass's first collection of poetry, *Die Vorzüge der Windhühner*, was published in 1956; meanwhile, he had gone to live in Paris, where he worked on his novel *The Tin Drum*. The publication of *The Tin Drum* in 1959 propelled him to instant fame, or, owing to allegedly obscene and blasphemous passages in the novel, infamy.

The year 1959 thus marks the beginning of the second phase in Grass's career, which was characterized by an outburst of creative energy that the author has perhaps never quite duplicated. In two-year intervals, from 1959 to 1963, the works of what subsequently became known as the *Danzig Trilogy* were published; this trilogy was responsible for establishing Grass as one of the leading contemporary writers of fiction.

Grass's involvement in politics began as early as 1961. In that year, he provided material for the speeches of Social Democrat Willy Brandt, then mayor of West Berlin, who later ran for the office of chancellor of the Federal Republic. Only in 1965, however, did Grass actively campaign on behalf of the Social Democrats by delivering speeches in more than fifty cities. During this third phase of his career, Grass became a public figure whose celebrity, or notoriety, extended far beyond the literary scene. Grass's works from this period reflect his political commitment. The play *The Plebeians Rehearse the Uprising* takes issue with playwright Bertolt Brecht's alleged preference for the aesthetic experience of revolutionary theater when, in 1953, he was faced with a potentially revolutionary situation in East Germany. The novel *Local Anaesthetic* and the play *Max* explore the alternatives to the violent protests and provocative political actions in which radicalized students of the 1968 generation engaged. They opposed the Vietnam War and wanted to revolutionize both the educational system and society at large.

The year 1972 marks the beginning of a fourth phase in Grass's development as a writer. The novel *From the Diary of a Snail*, an account of the author's participation in the 1969 election campaign that ended in Willy Brandt's election as chancellor, harks back to the themes of *Danzig Trilogy* but employs a new narrative perspective. During the early and middle 1970's, Grass refrained from extensive political involvement and devoted his energies to the completion of his great historical novel *The Flounder*, which was followed by two shorter narratives, *The Meeting at Telgte* and *Headbirths: Or, The Germans Are Dying Out*.

Grass's unequivocal and vociferous engagement in the peace movement from 1979, the year of the North Atlantic Treaty Organization (NATO) decision to deploy medium-range nuclear missiles in Western Europe, marks a fifth stage in his development. The author was no longer content to confine himself to grassroots politics in the Federal Republic; on the contrary, owing to his exposure to problems of a global nature—particularly those of developing countries—during his extensive travels, Grass felt compelled to speak out on a host of issues, from the nuclear arms race to the environment. Consequently, Grass's next novel, *The Rat*, envisions a somewhat surreal postnuclear as well as posthuman future with rats as the sole survivors.

In Germany, the fall of the Berlin Wall in 1989 marks the beginning of the sixth stage in Günter Grass's career. Almost alone among German writers, Grass fiercely opposed Germany's reunification in a number of polemical essays and speeches, some of which have been collected in *Two States—One Nation?* Grass's rather unpopular and controversial political stance did not meet with much approval, but it reaffirmed his status as an engaged writer. He continued to state his profound opposition to reunification even after the fact and expressed his severe censure of Chancellor Helmut Kohl, who had seized the chance to reunite the two parts of the divided country, and the policies of his conservative government. Although Grass invested considerable energies in his ultimately futile political interventions, he by no means entirely neglected his craft. In two prose narratives of the 1990's, *The Call of the Toad* and *Too Far Afield*, he conveyed his profound discontent with the new Germany in artistic form. Although *Too Far Afield* in particular met with severe censure when it was published in 1995—the cover of the August 21, 1995, issue of the influential

Günter Grass. (Mottke Weissman/Courtesy, D.C. Public Library)

newsmagazine *Der Spiegel* showed Germany's star critic Marcel Reich-Ranicki literally tearing the book apart—the novel was welcomed by readers and critics in the economically deprived former East Germany, who considered Grass their spokesman and accorded him an enthusiastic welcome when he presented a reading from the novel in the former East Berlin.

Despite the fact that Grass was not impervious to the often ferocious criticism of both his political convictions and his works, he continued to promote unpopular political causes and to provoke conservatives. For example, in 1997, at the presentation of the Peace Prize of the German Book Trade to the Kurdish writer Yashar Kemal, Grass used the occasion to denounce Germany's practice of deporting asylum seekers and delivering arms to Turkey that might be used against the Kurds. After he received the Nobel Prize in Literature in 1999, however, and especially after the 2002 publication of the novella *Crabwalk*, which was well received by critics because it appeared to indicate a shift in Grass's position by depicting Germans as victims rather than perpetrators, the controversies surrounding the author abated for a time.

Grass's unanticipated and shocking confession in his memoir *Beim Häuten der Zwiebel* (2006; *Peeling the Onion*, 2007) that as a teenager he had been a member of the feared Waffen-SS during the waning months of World War II caused an international uproar. In an interview that aired on National Public Radio in August, 2007, Grass's biographer Michael Jürgs, whose biography *Bürger Grass* (2002; Citizen Grass) has not been translated into English, expressed his severe disappointment about Grass's belated revelation of a significant and until then unknown detail of his biography. *The New York Times* devoted several articles to the Grass affair, the citizens of Gdańsk discussed the revocation of Grass's honorary citizenship but decided against it after Grass apologized for his long silence, an Israeli institution of higher learning rescinded its invitation to Grass to receive an honorary degree, and American neoconservative and right-leaning publications accused the writer both of anti-Americanism and of being a Nazi. Although there exists an obvious and somewhat troubling contradiction between the author's perceived status as the political conscience of postwar (West) Germany on one hand and his assumed actions in the service of an evil regime on the other, many critics agreed that, as much as Grass's withholding of an important facet of his biography was to be deplored, ultimately the author's literary reputation would not be damaged irreparably; in all likelihood, his best works will continue to be read as long as people are interested in fiction.

Analysis

Although Günter Grass's novel *The Tin Drum* forms the first part of the *Danzig Trilogy* and shares some characters, events, and themes with *Cat and Mouse* and *Dog Years*, the novel was conceived independently and can be discussed without explicit reference to the other two works. Nevertheless, it should be noted that the title of the trilogy, which was later expanded to a "sextet," reflects the extraordinary significance of Grass's birthplace for his fiction. In fact, this significance has been compared to that of Dublin for James Joyce or Yoknapatawpha County for William Faulkner. Owing to political developments after World War II, Grass was forced to sever his ties with his place of birth forever: Danzig became the Polish Gdańsk, a city that the author was able to visit repeatedly and with which he maintained close ties, but a city that was no longer the predominantly German-speaking Danzig of his youth.

Hence, the very act of narration is an evocation of the past, a resurrection from oblivion. Grass, however, is not concerned either with nostalgic memories or with mourning the lost city; rather, he wants to keep alive in the collective memory the reasons for the loss of Danzig. These reasons are to be sought in history—more specifically, in the Nazi period. In *The Tin Drum*, Grass sets out to elucidate these reasons—albeit from a highly unconventional narrative perspective.

The Tin Drum

Oskar Matzerath, the narrator of *The Tin Drum*, is an inmate in an insane asylum in postwar West Germany—a fact that he freely admits in the very first sentence of the novel. Instead of endeavoring to offer his readers an explanation for his confinement—the reason, his implication in a murder, is only gradually revealed in the course of the novel—Oskar reverses the normal order of things by declaring his hospital bed to be his sanctuary and refuge that protects him from the outside world. Oskar's position as an unapologetic outsider tends to disorient the reader and force him or her to assume a critical attitude.

Oskar's memoirs, written during his confinement, are a record both of his family's history, which began in Danzig around 1900, and of political history. The three books of the novel thus depict the prewar period, World War II, and the postwar period through 1954—the year in which Oskar turns thirty and completes his narration. As aids in his efforts to evoke the past and make history come alive, the narrator uses his tin drum—the instrument that gives the novel its name—and the family photograph album.

Although the novel is realistic in the sense that it provides exact details relating to the topography of Danzig, the speech patterns of various social groups, the milieu of the lower middle class, the chronology of historical events, and so on, fantastic and supernatural elements are by no means absent. In fact, they are introduced, somewhat in the manner of Franz Kafka's *Die Verwandlung* (1915; *The Metamorphosis*, 1936), almost casually. Thus, Oskar claims that his mental faculties were fully developed at birth. Confronted with the unpleasant realization that a return to the safety of his mother's womb is impossible, on his third birthday Oskar opts for the second-best solution—that is, to stop growing. He camouflages this willful act by injuring himself in a way that provides a medical explanation for his retarded physical development.

Without a doubt, Oskar's refusal to grow up is a protest against the world of adults in general and the narrow petit bourgeois sphere of his parents in particular. His diminutive size affords Oskar the possibility of observing the adults in their intimate moments—hence the sexually explicit passages that aroused controversy when the novel was published. Oskar, however, is not a mere voyeur. True, he has a keen eye for the triangular relationship that exists among his mother and his two "presumable" fathers, Matzerath, the German, and Bronski, the Pole, but the outsider Oskar also recognizes clearly the drift toward Nazism in Danzig, with its attendant evils, such as the beginning persecution of the Jews that reaches an early climax during the infamous Kristallnacht (Night of Broken Glass)—an event that robs him of his Jewish toy merchant and supplier of tin drums, who commits suicide.

Even though Oskar is an opponent of Nazism, he rarely uses his supernatural faculties—his evocative, spellbinding drumming and his ability to shatter glass with his voice—for acts of outright opposition. Admittedly, he does disrupt a Nazi rally by magically transforming the martial music of the drums and fifes into waltzes and the Charleston; conversely, Oskar employs his artistic abilities to contribute to the war effort by entertaining the German troops in France on the eve of the invasion of the Allies. Moreover, in some instances, Oskar's shattering of glass seems to be inspired by a desire for wanton destruction rather than by an aroused conscience.

Ultimately, Oskar's role remains somewhat ambivalent. His professed complicity in the deaths of Bronski and Matzerath, for example, appears less heartless when these deaths are viewed as inevitable consequences of his presumable fathers' actions. When the amorous but cowardly Bronski deserts the defenders of the Polish post office in Danzig at the outbreak of World War II, Oskar leads him back to the besieged building; as a consequence, Bronski is executed by the Germans. Amiable Matzerath, who has become a member of the Nazi Party, is killed at the end of World War II by the Soviets, who have invaded Danzig; Oskar contributes to his demise by handing him the party badge that Matzerath has been desperately trying to get rid of.

The fates of Bronski and Matzerath demonstrate that Grass poses the question of the individual's responsibility for his or her actions, regardless of station in life. This question also applies to Oskar himself—who, in fact, seriously ponders it at a decisive juncture in his life that coincides with the historical juncture constituted by the end of World War II. At Matzerath's funeral, Oskar, who in 1945 has turned twenty-one and attained maturity, decides to grow and to assume his proper place in the adult world. Neither Maria, Matzerath's second wife, nor her son Kurth accepts Oskar very enthusiastically as a husband and father substitute, however.

Despite his belated growth, Oskar does not develop into a physically normal adult; he never achieves average height and is disfigured by a hunchback. He thus remains a conspicuous outsider in postwar West German society; his attempts to start afresh and to assume responsibility have essentially failed. Oskar's failure is shared by an entire society that is only too eager to forget the past and savor the blessings of the postwar economic miracle. Although Oskar, who has resumed his artistic drumming, keeps the past alive in the face of the general tendency to suppress it, he must acknowledge his complicity in the evil of the times, his standing aside while others acted. Its parodistic, comical, grotesque, picaresque, and mythical dimensions notwithstanding, in the final analysis the telling of the story, which results in the novel, is the artist Oskar's way of atoning for his failure to conduct himself as a responsible citizen.

Cat and Mouse

The first-person narrator of *Cat and Mouse*, Pilenz, resembles Oskar in that he is compelled by guilt to tell the story of his ambivalent relationship with "the great Mahlke," a youth in wartime Danzig whom he both admires and envies. Mahlke seeks to divert attention from his excessively protuberant Adam's apple by accomplishing astonishing feats—among them an extended masturbation performance—that cannot be matched by his classmates. When Mahlke has become a highly decorated war hero, he gradually begins to realize that his youthful idealism has been misused. As a deserter, he endeavors to hide on a sunken Polish navy vessel, but he perishes in the attempt as a result of Pilenz's lack of support, amounting to a betrayal. Somewhat in the manner of Oskar, Pilenz survives the war in order to be able to tell of his own failure and the martyrdom of Mahlke.

Dog Years

The title of the extraordinarily complex and voluminous novel *Dog Years* alludes to the German shepherd Harras; Harras sired Prince, and Prince became the favorite dog of Adolf Hitler. The period and the localities covered are largely familiar from *The Tin Drum*, although *Dog Years* features three narrators who form an "authors' collective" under the direction of the amazingly versatile and artistically gifted Eduard Amsel. Amsel is of Jewish origin and is motivated in part by a desire to resurrect the past and trace its remnants in the present. He writes the first book, which covers the prewar years in Danzig and environs as well as his miraculous transformation and escape from the Nazis. The second book deals with the war years in Danzig and Berlin and is penned in the form of love letters from Harry Liebenau to his cousin Tulla Pokriefke, perhaps the most memorable female figure in Grass's fiction; she also appears in *Cat and Mouse* and is resurrected in *Crabwalk*. The third book deals with the postwar economic development of West Germany—from the black market to the economic miracle. It is written by Walter Matern, Amsel's erstwhile blood brother, who had turned against him and become a Nazi. In the postwar period, however, Matern directs his aggression at male supporters of the Third Reich; as a punishment, Matern infects their wives and daughters with sexually transmitted diseases. Despite the novel's superabundance of grotesque and surreal elements, *Dog Years* draws attention to the time of World War II as well as the prewar period in order to trace their remnants in postwar society—albeit in a highly idiosyncratic fashion.

Local Anaesthetic

In *Local Anaesthetic* Grass largely abandons the Danzig past and turns to the present in that the narrative takes place in 1967 in the Western part of the divided city of Berlin. The first-person narrator, Starusch, is a teacher of German and history at a secondary school who undergoes a dental treatment. In the first book he projects his thoughts onto the television screen in the dentist's office in an attempt to reconstruct his biography by mingling truth and fiction—a procedure that clearly shows the intertwining of Nazi past and postwar present. The second book, which essentially corresponds to Grass's play *Max*, centers on the plan of Starusch's gifted student Scherbaum, who wants to burn his dog publicly in order to provoke the complacent, dog-loving Berliners who appear to be indifferent to the fate of the Vietnamese who are suffering from the use of napalm by the Americans during the Vietnam War. Among the various options as to how to engage in a meaningful protest with the aim to alter conditions perceived as intolerable, Starusch's unspectacular, gradualist approach ultimately prevails. Scherbaum accepts the position of editor of the school newspaper and will argue for a change of failed policies through persuasive arguments rather than spectacular actions. In the brief third book the dentist reiterates his conviction that hygiene and enlightenment rather than religion and ideology will promote progress—a pragmatic approach that is clearly directed against the radicalism of the leftist student movement in West Germany and West Berlin. Surprisingly, when *Local Anaesthetic* was published, *Time* magazine (April 13, 1970) devoted a cover story to the novel and its author and praised Grass for his attempt to overcome the generation gap by dispassionately discussing the "morality" of the protest movement.

THE FLOUNDER

Grass's rejection of revolutionary, utopian designs is also evident in *From the Diary of a Snail*, a prose text of indistinct genre in which he relates his engagement in the 1969 election campaign on behalf of the Social Democratic Party and uses the snail as the symbol of glacially slow political and social progress. In his next, ambitious project, however, Grass turned to history on a grand scale. In *The Flounder*, and to a somewhat lesser extent in *The Meeting at Telgte* and *Headbirths*, there is a closer correspondence between author and narrator than in the *Danzig Trilogy*. This close correspondence enables Grass to transcend the chronological and spatial boundaries imposed on a single fictional first-person narrator and to give free rein to his exuberant and whimsical imagination. Here, history becomes the raw material to be reshaped and reinvented by the author, who provides alternative versions that challenge presumably established facts. Such imaginative reinterpretation of history is designed to counteract the reader's tendency to regard history as an inevitable and ultimately meaningless process that absolves him or her from the responsibility of participating in it.

The Flounder is a novel set both in Danzig and in postwar Gdańsk, but in comparison to the *Danzig Trilogy* it employs a vastly expanded time frame. Amassing information from the most diverse fields of extant knowledge, Grass uses this encyclopedic material to buttress his plausible account of the antagonistic relationship of the sexes from the Neolithic Age to the 1970's. In particular, Grass follows literary history fairly closely in developing his central conceit—the alleged former existence of a second version of the fairy tale "The Fisherman and His Wife," by the Brothers Grimm. The narrator, who closely resembles the present-day author Grass but who has also assumed the identities of male figures in past centuries, avers that in contrast to the version printed by the Brothers Grimm, the lost second version showed an overweening, prideful male instead of a female falling prey to hubris. Because the predominantly male fairy-tale collectors of the Romantic age, foremost among them the Grimms, perceived the second version to be a potential threat to the patriarchal order, they burned it. Although the narrator was not a participant in the burning, his pervasive guilt as a male who has contributed to the exploitation of women throughout the centuries impels him to reconstruct the alternative version, which depicts women in a favorable light.

While mindful of and sympathetic toward women in general (they are chiefly represented in their vital function as food-providing cooks), the narrator/author warns of the excesses in which the extreme fringe of the women's liberation movement is wont to indulge. On one hand, the women's tribunal puts the mythical, omniscient Flounder of fairy-tale renown, for whom the novel is named, on trial as the embodiment of the male principle; on the other hand, the radical feminists accept the Flounder's help in their efforts to establish their domination over men. In view of the continuing antagonism of the sexes, the novel suggests a synthesis that does not seek to derive the ideological justification for the male or female causes from one version of the fairy tale only; rather, as an old woman had told one of the fairy-tale collectors who had inquired about the "correct" version, both versions taken together would yield a viable solution. Without doubt, the novel represents a major achievement; however, it failed to impress feminist critics, who decried it as misogynistic.

THE MEETING AT TELGTE *and* HEADBIRTHS

The Meeting at Telgte offers another instance of Grass's imaginative re-creation of history and his exploration of alternative possibilities. In this narrative, a fictitious meeting of famous and lesser-known writers takes place in 1647, at the end of the Thirty Years' War. The writers' conference proceeds according to the rituals of Gruppe 47; like their twentieth century colleagues, the seventeenth century poets conceive of themselves as true patriots in a divided country, and they try to resurrect literature from the rubble caused by a devastating war—thereby demonstrating that literature will continue to flourish even in perilous times.

In a similar vein, *Headbirths*, Grass's literary contribution to the election campaign of 1980, is concerned with the place of literature in society, the relationship of art and politics, and the function of the writer. The novel addresses a wide variety of topics; as the title suggests, it also playfully speculates on the possibility of the Germans dying out on account of their low birthrate—thus projecting history into the future. The work's central theme, however, is of a literary nature—that is, how to ensure the survival of literature and, for that matter, life itself, in a world that is threatened by the nuclear arms race and other undesirable results of rampant technological progress. To characterize the magnitude of the task ahead, Grass discards the metaphor of the snail, symbol of slow progress, which he had used in *From the Diary of a Snail*; instead, he employs the myth of Sisyphus as derived from Albert Camus. Only Sisyphean labors, Grass avers, will be able to prevent the advent of the Orwellian state in the 1980's.

The Rat

Although Grass deliberately omitted any genre classification in his next narrative, some critics have tended to view *The Rat* in terms of a conventional novel in order to be able to register their discontent with the imaginative narrative point of view. The rat that lends the narrative its title is both an actual rodent that the first-person narrator receives as a somewhat unusual Christmas present and the imaginary interlocutor with whom the narrator converses in his dreams. The imagined rat categorically proclaims at the very beginning that human history has come to an end as the result of a nuclear holocaust and that the despised and persecuted rats have inherited the earth on account of both their highly developed instincts for survival and their practice of self-effacing solidarity. These qualities, which are lacking in humankind, enabled them to survive both the biblical Flood, during which they were excluded from Noah's Ark, and the atomic catastrophe. Although the narrator seeks to contradict the rat by positing the continuity of human history, in his dreams he sees himself as the sole human survivor, circling the completely devastated planet in a space capsule. When *The Rat* was published in 1986, several critics dismissed Grass's dystopian vision and apocalyptic scenario as mere alarmism; yet the arms race, the major accident in April, 1986, at the nuclear power plant in Chernobyl in the Ukraine, which was then part of the former Soviet Union, and the continued ravaging of the environment provided indications that the doomsday apprehensions that Grass conveyed in his narrative were not entirely far-fetched.

In *The Rat*, Grass returns once more to Danzig/Gdańsk and reintroduces figures known from his previous fiction in several narrative strands that are indicative of the complex structure of the work. Thus Oskar Matzerath, well known from *The Tin Drum*, is now sixty years old. He has abandoned his spellbinding drumming and, somewhat in the manner of science fiction, has become a producer of videos in which the future is anticipated. The feminists who appear in *The Flounder* set out on a voyage in the Baltic—ostensibly to research ecological issues but really in search of Vineta, the Baltic Atlantis. There they hope to establish a matriarchy, but they find the city inhabited by rats. The Brothers Grimm, who also appear in *The Flounder*, fight unsuccessfully against the destruction of the forests; forests need to be preserved as the repository of fairy tales, which provide an important counterbalance to destructive reason, which results in unchecked scientific and technological progress. Ultimately, the tension between the narrator's tentative hope for the survival of a gentler, more peaceful humankind and the rat's categorical denial of such a possibility remains unresolved; Grass leaves it up to the reader to draw his or her own conclusions.

The Call of the Toad

The Call of the Toad, subtitled in the German original *Eine Erzählung* (prose narrative) but without generic classification in the English translation, was the first major literary work that Grass published after German reunification in 1990, the disappearance of the Iron Curtain, and the dissolution of the Soviet Union and the Eastern European bloc in 1991. Grass's well-known opposition to reunification, in conjunction with an unusually intense prepublication publicity campaign on the part of the author's publisher, aroused both readers' and critics' curiosity as to how Grass would manage to convey his political concerns in his fiction.

The very title of the narrative provides an indication of Grass's less-than-optimistic outlook regarding the prospects of future developments in reunited Germany in general and those of German-Polish relations in particular; according to a German proverbial saying, the call of the toad signifies a warning of impending disaster. The narrative begins on a positive note, however, in that it revolves around a not entirely common kind of love story—one involving two elderly people.

As their first names suggest, the male German academic Alexander and the female Polish restorer of art objects Alexandra, who happen to meet in Gdańsk, are destined for each other. Since both of them have suffered from being expelled from the cities of their births as a consequence of World War II—he from Danzig, she from Vilnius (Wilno), the capital of Lithuania—they devise a plan that is designed to promote reconciliation between Germans and Poles by establishing a Gdańsk cemetery association that will allow deceased expellees to be buried in their native soil. The couple's well-intended plan goes awry, however, when a West German entrepreneur takes over the association and ruthlessly pursues the maximization of profits at the expense of fostering understanding between Germans and Poles. The narrative ends on a melancholy note in that both Alexander and Alexandra perish in a car accident; it is left to the virtually anonymous narrator—who is, indeed, a far cry from the highly visible Oskar Matzerath—to write the report of the failed experiment on the basis of Alexander's notes. In general, critics were not very impressed with Grass's first postreunification literary work, but the criticism directed toward *The Call of the Toad* appears muted in comparison to the fierce reactions that his next novel elicited.

TOO FAR AFIELD

In the massive novel *Too Far Afield*, Grass's views on German reunification can be discerned more clearly than in the preceding, comparatively slim narrative *The Call of the Toad*. *Too Far Afield* is mostly set in Berlin, Germany's erstwhile capital since the founding of the German Empire in 1871 until the end of World War II. Although the plot of the novel begins to unfold shortly after the opening of the Berlin Wall in November, 1989, Grass succeeds in presenting a vast historical panorama—primarily through the choice of an unconventional protagonist nicknamed Fonty, for nineteenth century Berlin novelist Theodor Fontane. "Revenant" Fonty identifies with his idol Fontane to such an extent that he quotes incessantly from the latter's entire works, with which he is fully conversant; he also adopts Fontane's habits and even dresses like him. Far from indulging in a mere display of vast literary knowledge, Fonty also cites Fontane's political observations in general and those concerning Otto von Bismarck, the "Iron Chancellor" and chief architect of the 1871 unification, in particular.

Primarily through the views and utterances of Fonty, which are assiduously recorded by members of the Fontane Archives, who form a collective of anonymous narrators, Grass seeks to establish the parallelism between the 1871 unification "with blood and iron" and that of 1990, which Fonty depicts in terms of a colonial takeover of the socialist German Democratic Republic (GDR) by the capitalist Federal Republic. The authority chiefly responsible for this takeover is the "Handover Trust," which was created after reunification in order to dispose of GDR state-owned property and has its headquarters in a Berlin building erected during the Nazi period. Septuagenarian Fonty, who serves the Trust as a low-level employee, has had the opportunity to encounter leading figures of both the Third Reich and the GDR in the building, particularly in its "paternoster," a kind of elevator consisting of a chain of cabins without doors that are in constant motion. This contraption symbolizes the ups and downs—or, rather, circular movement—of German history, which seems to be doomed to repeat past mistakes.

It is not surprising that initial critical reaction to *Too Far Afield* was predominantly negative, owing to the fact that reviewers tended to judge the book in political rather than aesthetic terms. As Marcel Reich-Ranicki, Grass's nemesis among critics, pointed out—not entirely without justification—the author's negative assessment of reunification and the new Germany as well as his tendency to portray the former GDR in a somewhat positive light were not shared by the majority of Germans, even though former GDR citizens inclined toward a more favorable opinion. The debate about *Too Far Afield* reached an intensity that is rarely encountered at the publication of a novel—an indication of Grass's public stature.

CRABWALK

In pronounced contrast to the fairly pervasive drubbing that *Too Far Afield* received, *Crabwalk* elicited almost unmitigated praise when it appeared. For instance, in February, 2002, the prominent newsmagazine *Der Spiegel*, which had mercilessly panned *Too Far Afield*, published a laudatory cover story under the heading

"The German *Titanic*," a reference to the sinking of the *Wilhelm Gustloff* on January 30, 1945, by a Soviet submarine, the central event in *Crabwalk*. The sinking of that ship, which cost the lives of many thousands, among them a great number of children, is a gruesome chapter in the expulsion of Germans from the territories east of the Oder-Neisse line.

A great deal of debate revolved around the question of whether Germans were entitled to claim the status of victims in view of the suffering they had inflicted on others during World War II. The very fact that it took Grass almost fifty years to deal with an issue that was dear to his heart—the ship carried refugees from Danzig and East Prussia who were fleeing the advancing Soviet army—is indicative of the long-lasting reluctance, particularly on the part of the Left, to muddy the waters by blurring the distinction between perpetrators and victims. Grass, however, who appears in the narrative thinly disguised as the "old man" who pressures a journalist into writing the story, evens the score by drawing attention to the potential misuse of the victimhood discourse on the part of the Right: The journalist in question happens to be the son of memorable Tulla Pokriefke, a survivor of the ship's sinking. His son Konrad has been influenced by right-wing Internet propaganda and eventually resorts to violence, killing an adherent of Philo-Semitism who pretends to be Jewish. While in prison, Konrad is elevated to the position of martyr of a right-wing movement—a clear warning that the one-sided emphasis on Germans as victims may have undesirable consequences.

Siegfried Mews

OTHER MAJOR WORKS

PLAYS: *Hochwasser*, pr. 1957 (revised pb. 1963; *Flood*, 1967); *Stoffreste*, pr. 1957 (ballet); *Beritten hin und zurück*, pb. 1958 (*Rocking Back and Forth*, 1967); *Noch zehn Minuten bis Buffalo*, pb. 1958 (*Only Ten Minutes to Buffalo*, 1967); *Onkel, Onkel*, pr. 1958 (revised pb. 1965; *Mister, Mister*, 1967); *Fünf Köche*, pr. 1959 (ballet); *Die bösen Köche*, pr., pb. 1961 (*The Wicked Cooks*, 1967); *Mystisch-barbarisch-gelangweilt*, pr. 1963; *POUM: Oder, Die Vergangenheit fliegt mit*, pb. 1965; *Die Plebejer proben den Aufstand*, pr., pb. 1966 (*The Plebeians Rehearse the Uprising*, 1966); *Four Plays*, 1967 (includes *Only Ten Minutes to Buffalo*, *The Wicked Cooks*, *Flood*, and *Mister, Mister*); *Davor*, pr., pb. 1969 (*Max*, 1972); *Theaterspiele*, 1970 (includes *Noch zehn Minuten bis Buffalo*, *Hochwasser*, *Onkel, Onkel*, and *Die bösen Köche*); *Die Vogelscheuchen*, 1970 (ballet).

POETRY: *Die Vorzüge der Windhühner*, 1956; *Gleisdreieck*, 1960; *Selected Poems*, 1966 (includes poems from *Die Vorzüge der Windhühner* and *Gleisdreieck*); *Ausgefragt*, 1967 (*New Poems*, 1968); *Poems of Günter Grass*, 1969 (includes *Selected Poems* and *New Poems*; also in a bilingual edition as *In the Egg, and Other Poems*, 1977); *Gesammelte Gedichte*, 1971; *Mariazuehren, Hommageàmarie, Inmarypraise*, 1973 (trilingual edition); *Liebe geprüft*, 1974 (*Love Tested*, 1975); *Die Gedichte, 1955-1986*, 1988; *Novemberland: Selected Poems, 1956-1993*, 1996 (bilingual edition); *Letzte Tänze*, 2003; *Dummer August*, 2007.

RADIO PLAYS: *Zweiunddreissig Zähne*, 1959; *Goldmäulchen*, 1963 (staged 1964).

NONFICTION: *Über das Selbstverständliche*, 1968 (partial translation *Speak Out!*, 1969); *Über meinen Lehrer Döblin und andere Vorträge*, 1968; *Der Bürger und seine Stimme*, 1974; *Denkzettel: Politische Reden und Aufsätze, 1965-76*, 1978; *Aufsätze zur Literatur*, 1980; *Widerstand lernen: Politische Gegenreden, 1980-1983*, 1984; *On Writing and Politics, 1967-1983*, 1985; *Zunge zeigen*, 1988 (*Show Your Tongue*, 1989); *Skizzenbuch*, 1989; *Deutscher Lastenausgleich: Wider das dumpfe Einheitsgebot*, 1990 (*Two States—One Nation?*, 1990); *Ein Schnappchen namens DDR: Letzte Reden vorm Glockengelaut*, 1990; *Schreiben nach Auschwitz: Frankfurter Poetik-Vorlesung*, 1990 ("Writing After Auschwitz," in *Two States—One Nation?*, 1990); *Totes Holz: Ein Nachruf*, 1990; *Gegen die verstreichende Zeit: Reden, Aufsätze und Gespräche, 1989-1991*, 1991; *Günter Grass, vier Jahrzehnte*, 1991; *Rede vom Verlust: Über den Niedergang der politischen Kultur im geeinten Deutschland*, 1992 ("On Loss," in *The Future of German Democracy*, 1993); *Angestiftet, Partei zu ergreifen*, 1994; *Die Deutschen und ihre Dichter*, 1995; *Gestern, vor 50 Jahren: Ein deutsch-japanischer Briefwechsel*, 1995; *Fünf Jahrzenhnte: Ein Werkstattbericht*, 2001; *Briefe, 1959-1994*, 2003; *Freiheit nach Börenmass; Geschenkte Freiheit: Zwei Reden zum 8. Mai 1945*,

2005; *Beim Häuten der Zwiebel*, 2006 (*Peeling the Onion*, 2007); *Steine wälzen: Essays and Reden*, 1997-2007, 2007.

MISCELLANEOUS: *Werkausgabe*, 1997 (16 volumes); *Cat and Mouse, and Other Writings*, 1994; *The Günter Grass Reader*, 2004 (Helmut Frielinghaus, editor).

BIBLIOGRAPHY

Brady, Philip, et al., eds. *Günter Grass's "Der Butt": Sexual Politics and the Male Myth of History*. Oxford, England: Clarendon Press, 1990. Collection of wide-ranging critical essays devoted to *The Flounder* focuses on the representation of sexuality, male-female relations, and the use of history in the novel.

Braun, Rebecca, and Frank Brunssen, eds. *Changing the Nation: Günter Grass in International Perspective*. Würzburg, Germany: Königshausen & Neumann, 2008. Collection of essays by Grass scholars from various countries examines his fiction with an emphasis on the international stature of the work.

Hall, Katharina. *Günter Grass's "Danzig Quintet": Explorations in the Memory and History of the Nazi Era from "Die Blechtrommel" to "Im Krebsgang."* New York: Peter Lang, 2007. Presents an interesting examination of Grass's central themes of history and memory. (Hall uses the term "quintet" rather than "sextet" and includes *Local Anaesthetic* rather than *The Flounder* in her discussion.)

Keele, Alan Frank. *Understanding Günter Grass*. Columbia: University of South Carolina Press, 1988. Provides a good introduction to Grass's works for the general reader. Covers the novels through *The Rat*.

Mews, Siegfried. *Günter Grass and His Critics: From "The Tin Drum" to "Crabwalk."* Rochester, N.Y.: Camden House, 2008. Offers a descriptive as well as analytical and evaluative overview of the vast array of the nearly five decades of criticism devoted to Grass's fiction.

O'Neill, Patrick. *Günter Grass Revisited*. New York: Twayne, 1999. Presents a sound overview of Grass's works from *The Tin Drum* to *Too Far Afield*. Includes chronology, select bibliography, and index.

Preece, Julian. *The Life and Works of Günter Grass: Literature, History, Politics*. New York: Palgrave, 2001. Provides biographical information as well as analysis of the author's works up to *Too Far Afield*, with an emphasis on the intertwining of politics and literature.

Shafi, Monika, ed. *Approaches to Teaching Grass's "The Tin Drum."* New York: Modern Language Association, 2008. Collection of essays addresses various aspects of Grass's most famous work. Intended primarily as a tool for teachers, but a valuable resource for any reader wishing to gain access to the novel.

SHIRLEY ANN GRAU

Born: New Orleans, Louisiana; July 8, 1929

PRINCIPAL LONG FICTION

The Hard Blue Sky, 1958
The House on Coliseum Street, 1961
The Keepers of the House, 1964
The Condor Passes, 1971
Evidence of Love, 1977
Roadwalkers, 1994

OTHER LITERARY FORMS

Although Shirley Ann Grau (grow) has written introductions and occasional essays for magazines, two forms—the novel and the short story—have dominated her literary career. The enthusiastic reception that greeted her first collection of short stories, *The Black Prince, and Other Stories* (1955), has assured her reputation in the genre. Scarcely any anthology of American short fiction excludes her work. In spite of her initial success critically, her second collection of stories, *The Wind Shifting West* (1973), was not so warmly received. *Nine Women*, which appeared in 1985, restored Grau's critical acclaim as a short-story writer. Grau also contributed a chapter to *Haunter of the Ruins* (1997), a book on America's foremost surrealist photographer, fellow Louisianian Clarence John Laughlin.

ACHIEVEMENTS

The most obvious testimony to Grau's success is the Pulitzer Prize for fiction that she received in 1965 for *The Keepers of the House*. Significantly enough, the same novel appeared in condensed form in *Ladies' Home Journal*. Thus, one sees evidence of one of the distinguishing characteristics of much of Grau's fiction: the ability to appeal simultaneously to two often opposed audiences, the person looking for the "good read" and the literary sophisticate. Not many contemporary writers have published stories in both *McCall's* and *The New Yorker*. In *Evidence of Love*, Grau seems to have made an attempt to shed any vestige of her image as a "housewife writer" or yet another southern regionalist. While *Evidence of Love* is rather straightforward, even in its effective use of three overlapping narratives, it nevertheless makes few concessions to a reader looking for the conventional melodramatic staples of sex or violence. *Evidence of Love* also silences the critics who, after the disappointment of *The Condor Passes*, sought to dismiss Grau as a one-novel writer. The one recurring criticism of Grau's later work—that her characters seem bloodless—seems less relevant after the success of other novelists with similar ironic visions—Joan Didion, for example.

As is true of all but a handful of contemporary writers, Grau's achievement cannot yet be fully measured. *Evidence of Love* suggests that she has shifted her emphasis away from the engaging plot to the creation of a cool, ironic vision of psychological intensity. While *Roadwalkers* contains all the ironic vision of Grau's earlier novels and emphasizes the psychological, it represents another technical feat for Grau in a reemphasis on and experimentation with plot. Here Grau interweaves the impressionistic tale of Mary Woods with the separate histories of Charles Tucker and Rita Landry but ends the novel with the rather straightforward narrative of Nanda Woods. In the process, she has kept those elements of style—the brilliant sensory images, the directness of language, the complex heroines—that have given vitality to all her work.

BIOGRAPHY

At the age of forty-five, Katherine Grau and her husband, Adolphe, had a baby girl. Although Shirley Ann Grau's parents were well into middle age, she has described her childhood as free of unhappiness or social alienation. Her Protestant family, with roots in both New England and the South, moved back and forth from Montgomery, Alabama, to New Orleans. Grau attended a girls' finishing school in the Alabama capital until her senior year, when she transferred to an accredited high school in New Orleans, the Ursuline Academy—the institution that one of her heroines remembers as a place to knit, chant, and crochet.

Grau's first experiences with writing came while attending Sophie Newcomb College in New Orleans. Her stories appeared in the campus literary magazine, *Carnival*. After she graduated Phi Beta Kappa, Grau lived in the French Quarter of New Orleans and abandoned her graduate studies for a writing career. Success came quickly. In 1955, her volume of short stories, *The Black Prince, and Other Stories*, received exceptionally fine reviews, and her work was compared favorably with that of other southern writers such as Eudora Welty, Flannery O'Connor, and Carson McCullers.

In the same year, Grau married James K. Feibleman, a remarkable professor of philosophy at Tulane University. Many years her senior, Feibleman had become chair of his department even though he himself had attended college for only two months. He had published numerous books and was acquainted with such luminaries as William Faulkner. Grau has described her life as a "conventional upper middle class" one, divided between summers at Martha's Vineyard and school years in New Orleans.

As she reared her children, Grau continued to write. The novels *The Hard Blue Sky* (1958) and *The House on Coliseum Street* (1961) were published. While both works received considerable notice, it seemed as if Grau might be categorized as a regionalist who had mastered local color. Her selection as the Pulitzer Prize winner for fiction in 1965, however, did much to squelch such categorization. *The Keepers of the House*, a novel that attracted attention for its candid treatment of racial themes, brought her national attention; in fact, U.S. president Lyndon B. Johnson appointed her to the Commission on Presidential Scholars in the same year. In spite of this recognition, the rhythm of Grau's life remained largely unchanged, and she did not rush to bring out her next novel. Instead, she taught creative writing at the University of New Orleans, wrote an occasional story, and gave birth to her fourth child. When her next novel, *The Condor Passes*, appeared in 1971, its sales surpassed the combined total of all her previous works. Its critical reception, however, was at best mixed. After that, Grau published only a few more works.

In many ways validating her comment in an interview with John Canfield that writers are "just very inefficient computers," Grau returned to the novel form with *Roadwalkers* in 1994 after an absence of seventeen years. Despite the span of time separating it from Grau's previous novel, *Roadwalkers* received much critical attention, garnering mixed reviews in a rather unique way. Most critics have been extremely favorable to the first half of the novel, which deals primarily with the "feral" child Mary Woods. They have been puzzled by the second half, which centers on her daughter, Nanda, whom they see as bloodless and arrogant, a criticism that has followed Grau's heroines off and on throughout her career.

Grau worked on a piece of nonfiction, *Haunter of the Ruins*, in 1997. Her interest in and perhaps unjustified identification with the southern grotesque made Grau the perfect writer to include in a collection of essays that accompany the photographs of Laughlin, one of America's earliest surrealist photographers. Rather than dealing specifically with Laughlin's photographs, Grau's essay is a set piece that evokes the haunting imagery that pervades his work.

Shirley Ann Grau. (Time & Life Pictures/Getty Images)

Analysis

Shirley Ann Grau shares a fate common to many contemporary writers not yet admitted to the pantheon. They are the object of a handful of critical studies, often short and incomplete, that make only a slight effort to detect what vision, if any, gives continuity to the writers' works. At first glance, Grau's novels do seem to defy any attempt to find even a connecting thread. Until the publication of *Evidence of Love*, the label of "southern regionalist" gave some of Grau's reviewers comfort. Readers familiar only with her last three novels could not avoid the recurrence of semilegendary patriarchs in possession of great wealth.

Revenge at one time or another consumes such heroines as Joan Mitchell in *The House on Coliseum Street* and Abigail Mason Tolliver in *The Keepers of the House*, but an equally strong woman such as Lucy Henley in *Evidence of Love* possesses no such motive. Alwyn Berland (in his essay "The Fiction of Shirley Ann Grau") suggests that Grau's heroines favor the hallucinatory over the real, tend to be passive, and have ambivalent responses to sex. Berland's observation is helpful, but the title of Grau's 1977 novel, *Evidence of Love*, gives the clearest clue to the sometimes elusive vision that informs her fictional world. While most of her male characters mechanically pursue money, sex, power, or ironclad order, the heroines seek some evidence of love. Their failure to find it renders both sexes solitary, and their subsequent sense of futility and despair makes their money and power meaningless. What saves the novels from an almost Jamesian pessimism is the possibility of redemption and rebirth. Both Joan Mitchell and Abigail Tolliver are last seen in literal fetal positions, as if awaiting resurrection. Their possibly temporary withdrawal resembles that of the wives of the fishermen in *The Hard Blue Sky*, who passively await the passing of the hurricane that may or may not destroy them.

In the development of her vision, Grau reveals considerable technical skill. Her sense of place is compelling. Equally convincing are such dissimilar scenes as William Howland's atavistic incursion into Honey Island Swamp and Harold Evans's drift into suicide in his meager and bare house in Princeton. As Paul Schlueter has pointed out, few novelists are as successful as Grau in manipulating sensory images, particularly the olfactory. Most satisfying technically is her ability to treat the melodramatic with a cool, analytical detachment. The embattled house that Abigail defends and keeps is above all else a house, not Tara or Sutpen's Hundred. While Edward Milton Henley in *Evidence of Love* is capable of grandiose, operatic gestures and appetites, Grau's sardonic humor and sense of irony keeps him in the orbit of the real. Grau steadfastly refuses to sentimentalize.

Grau's occasional limitations are perhaps most noticeable in characterization. At times her characters lack emotional depth; the rich are not inherently interesting. In spite of lurid, exotic pasts, characters such as the Old Man in *The Condor Passes* lack the complex humanity necessary to be convincing. Further, her characters' motivations are not always clear. Even the sympathetic reader is not entirely sure, for example, why it is that Abigail so intensely dislikes Margaret's children.

The Hard Blue Sky

Prior to 1964, Grau published two novels that anticipated her technique and vision in *The Keepers of the House*. The first, *The Hard Blue Sky*, revealed her ability to capture the world of southern Louisiana in stunning detail. Her plot consists of two different but connected stories that take place on islands along the Gulf Coast. The first story concerns the youthful Annie Landry's affair with Inky D'Alfonso. When she ultimately marries Inky, Annie is able to leave the islands for what may be a better life in New Orleans. Annie bears little resemblance to Abigail Tolliver: She has neither the wealth, the sense of family tradition, nor the consuming desire for revenge that drives Abigail.

It is the second story that contains the violence and the revenge motif that will appear in *The Keepers of the House*. Rival groups on two different islands attempt to burn one another out after the disappearance of young lovers from the opposing families. Neither story ends with a clear resolution. It is not clear whether Annie's marriage will be a success, nor does one know if the feud will end, especially since both factions are threatened by a hurricane. Thus, in her first novel, Grau struck what became a crucial and familiar note in her fiction: Her characters are left in a state of uncertainty as they face potential harm or destruction.

The House on Coliseum Street

Grau's second novel, *The House on Coliseum Street*, has a much sharper focus than does her first. Joan Mitchell, the protagonist, anticipates Abigail Tolliver in several significant ways. Her relationship with men is disastrous. She is engaged to a businessman named Fred Aleman, whose rather passionless demeanor leaves her vulnerable to a young college professor, Michael Kern; their passionate lovemaking leaves Joan pregnant. After an abortion and Michael's abandonment, a guilt-ridden Joan becomes obsessed with destroying him. She does so by exposing him to his college dean. Like Abigail, Joan brings down her antagonist, but more significantly, she may have destroyed herself emotionally in doing so. That, however, is only a possibility: *The House on Coliseum Street* ends with Joan, having forgotten her key, unable to enter her family house. She is last seen in a fetal position, just as one sees Abigail at the end of *The Keepers of the House*. The possibility of rebirth and redemption is not excluded. Thus, *The House on Coliseum Street*, like *The Hard Blue Sky*, served as a preparation for the greater achievement in *The Keepers of the House*. In both, Grau was able to find sensory images that render the physical world immediate. More important, these early novels introduced Grau's evolving vision of a world with little clear evidence of love or community.

The Keepers of the House

More than forty years after its publication, the reader can see more clearly the truth of Grau's own commentary on *The Keepers of the House*:

> The novel is about the whole human plight of how do you cope with evil? Do you fight back? The people are living in the South but they're just people facing the eternal human problem. I wanted to show the alternation of love and evil, which has always fascinated me. And if there is a moral, it is the self-destructiveness of hatred.

If Grau sees the novel's significance in general moral terms, its popularity nevertheless was rooted in its then explosive characterization of southern racial attitudes.

The novel's narrator, Abigail Tolliver, granddaughter of William Howland, who himself is one of the "keepers of the house," finds herself in almost complete isolation. She and her husband are getting a divorce, two of her children have been forced to go away to school for safety's sake, and she has alienated the citizenry of her hometown, Madison City. Her desolation, mythic in intensity, is tragically linked to the discovery that her grandfather had married his black housekeeper, Margaret Carmichael. While the white community could cavalierly accept a mere sexual liaison, even one that has produced three children, marriage gives legitimacy. Thus, the men of Madison City attempt to burn the Howland estate in retaliation. The discovery of her grandfather's clandestine marriage destroys Abigail's marriage with her amoral, politically ambitious husband. The novel's evil is therefore easy to locate, as is Abigail's vengeful, Medea-like response. She not only burns the cars of the men who come to destroy her house; she also exercises her option to destroy the entire community financially. Yet difficult questions remain when one recalls Grau's own assessment of her work. How convincingly is the love that alternates with evil portrayed? How strongly felt is her "moral"—the self-destructiveness of hate?

Grau will never be accused of sentimentalizing love. Characters rarely, for example, confuse love with sex. When Abigail loses her virginity, she says,

> I found that it wasn't so hard . . . nor painful either. . . . There's only one night like that—ever—where you're filled with wonder and excitement for no other reason but the earth is beautiful and mysterious and your body is young and strong.

Her courtship by and marriage to John Tolliver are presented just as dispassionately. Tolliver, like Stephen Henley in *Evidence of Love* and the Old Man in *The Condor Passes*, subordinates love to ambition. Grau's sexes mate; they rarely love. Neither does there seem to be affection between generations. Abigail bears four children, but they remain abstractions. More mysterious, more horrific is the relation between the black woman, Margaret, and the children she bears William Howland. Half white herself, Margaret sends each child off at the age of eleven to be educated in the North. She refuses to see them thereafter. She is particularly hostile and unyielding toward her oldest daughter, Nina, who returns to the South with her black husband. A certain curiosity exists between these racially mixed children and their mother, but there is no evidence of love.

The possible exception to this bleak vision of human existence is the thirty-year relationship between William Howland and Margaret. After the death of his first wife and the marriage of his daughter, Howland discovers the eighteen-year-old Margaret Carmichael washing clothes at a spring. She comes to him as a housekeeper and ultimately marries him. Both William and Margaret are characterized by Grau in terms larger than life. Howland is heir to the frontier tradition, in which men wrenched a living, indeed an immense fortune, from a hostile environment. Prior to meeting Margaret, he makes a solitary journey into the mystery and danger of Honey Island Swamp, where he at one point strips himself naked and submerges himself into the primordial slime. When he returns to find Margaret at the spring, she appears to him as if she "had folded herself into the earth." Her stride is "a primitive walk, effortless, unassuming, unconscious, old as the earth under her feet." Like gods, apparently, William and Margaret possess the strength and the indifference to violate the most sacrosanct of southern codes. Yet their love, if it exists, is concealed. The only evidence Abigail ever sees of their love is a single embrace.

Until Abigail's epiphany at the novel's end, Margaret is the character most cognizant of evil, particularly the evil inherent in racism. Her own white father abandoned her black mother, who in turn leaves Margaret to search for her missing lover. Margaret further realizes that it is necessary to send her white-appearing children out of the South, a tragic gesture that Abigail alone understands. It is a sacrifice that ends in alienation between parent and child, between white and black.

Grau states that the moral of the novel is the self-destructiveness of hatred. Is she suggesting that the South is destroying itself with its racial hostility? The attack on the Howland farm clearly does not go without destructive retribution. The local bigots have cut their own throats, because Abigail Tolliver owns almost every business in town. Yet her revenge, just as it may be, seems minuscule compared with the sure election of a staunch segregationist as the next governor—the most far-reaching consequence of the exposure of William Howland's marriage.

Of more visceral concern to the reader, however, is the effect of hatred on Abigail. Not only has she decided to destroy Madison City, but she also has chosen to terrorize Margaret's vengeful son, Robert, by threatening to reveal his black origins to his white California wife. Stripped of compassion, devoid of love, Abigail at the conclusion of the novel has not yet taken the step that transcends hate. Her fetal position as she lies weeping in her office offers a possibility of rebirth, but the overriding vision of the novel is one of utter alienation and despair.

The Condor Passes

In the thirteen years between the publication of Grau's novels *The Keepers of the House* and *Evidence of Love*, one other novel appeared. Ironically, *The Condor Passes* received the worst reviews while posting the highest sales of any of Grau's works. The novel, a family chronicle, depicts the ninety-five years of Thomas Henry Oliver, who during his long life has amassed a huge fortune through such nefarious enterprises as prostitution and bootlegging. The novel bears only superficial resemblance to *The Keepers of the House*. As Grau herself has suggested, it is not concerned with the primitive. Survival is no longer a question. Instead, the characters seek to find a sense of identity in the presence of vast wealth. The novel, however, is wedded thematically to Grau's other works in its despairing vision. One senses that the male figures may have gained the whole world but lost their own souls. The Old Man's daughters are more complex, but their attempts to find enduring love are frustrated. They each have one son, but one dies and the other becomes a priest. The family therefore awaits little more than its own extinction.

Evidence of Love

By contrast, *Evidence of Love* is one of Grau's most successful novels. It, too, is a family chronicle, but its construction is still tight and sharply focused. Again the wealthy patriarch appears, but Edward Milton Henley possesses a sense of irony and self-awareness denied to earlier Grau patriarchs. Set outside the South, *Evidence of Love* frees Grau from often invidious comparisons with William Faulkner and allows her to concentrate on what has been one of the central concerns of all her novels, the need for some sign of love.

While the novel traces the lives of four generations of the Henley family, the voices of Edward Henley; his son, Stephen; and his daughter-in-law, Lucy, dominate the narrative. Paul Schlueter maintains that "nowhere is there any 'evidence of love.'" He sees each character "seeking his own form of satisfaction to the exclusion of others." What in fact gives focus to each of the three stories is the pursuit of some apparently reasonable alternative to love. Because he chooses to relate his story in a satiric, ironic mode, it is not always easy to locate in an exact way Edward's feelings. The evidence of paternal love, he tells the reader, is the wealth his father gave him. If his mother, who is both literally and figuratively distant, did not love him, she at least imparted to him a sense of propriety and morality—which Edward chooses to ignore. These parents were, he says, happy. Himself physically and emotionally transient, Edward rather cavalierly dispenses with wives and male lovers. Yet he never indulges in self-pity. "I prefer to see my life as a pageant. Or a processional. Like that wonderful march in *Aida*." Through the elder Henley, Grau presents her paradox. About this old man, who still dreams of recapturing the drug-induced paradise he once experienced in Mexico, there is a considerable vitality. Edward's audacity, his iconoclasm, and his rather mordant humor do not diminish life. His suicide is neither cowardly nor tragic. His life has been long and in its way full—even without the presence of love.

Edward says of his son, "Stephen was quiet and totally self-contained." Stephen is a Gatsby stripped of illusion and romance. As a young man, he makes a detailed plan of his life, a schedule that he unflinchingly follows. His marriage to Lucy Evans is as rational, as free of either anguish or passion, as is his commitment to the ministry without believing in God. Here is a potential monster, but Grau does not ask the reader to see him as such. He does at least have some awareness of his own condition. For Lucy, he says, "I felt a sudden flood of feeling . . . not lust, not love. Something deeper, something older, something asexually human. The sympathy of blood for blood, of aching chalky bone for aching chalky bone. . . . The visceral sympathy of acquired identity." If what Stephen feels for Lucy is only kinship, it perhaps explains why he is confused by the passionate intensity of his youngest son, Paul.

Quite by chance, Paul discovers, he believes, the identity of Stephen's mother, the young Irish woman Edward had paid to bear him a son sixty years earlier. Stephen wonders, "Was the presence of blood so important to him? What strange evidence of love was this?" The inability of yet another generation of Henleys to understand—or love—another is thus assured. Given Stephen's emotional isolation, one senses the inevitability of Stephen dying alone. Even death cannot shake his detachment. There has been no exhilarating pageant. Knowing he is dying, Stephen thinks, "I hardly cared. It didn't matter. Nothing did."

Although they seek refuge in quite opposing activities, both Stephen and his father rather straightforwardly eschew love. With Lucy, Stephen's wife, the case is more ambiguous, more complex. As in her earlier novels, Grau gives her female character a roundness that her males often lack. When Lucy recalls the sexual pleasure and pain she experienced with her first husband, she remarks that "All that was evidence of love." Because Lucy does not indulge in irony, the reader accepts her assessment. Her openness to physical love is reinforced by her enthusiasm for the lushness of Florida, although Lucy has reservations: When Harold makes love to her, she thinks, "I don't like this. . . . I don't like having feelings I can't control." Perhaps the fear of feeling paradoxically allows her to live comfortably for thirty years with Stephen. After his death, she states that "Old women are supposed to quake with an excess of emotion—perhaps love—and start talking to animals and birds and flowers on the windowsill. I didn't."

At times, she seems even more alienated than either her husband or her father-in-law. When her worried son, Paul, phones her, she thinks to herself that "Love between the generations was a burdensome chore." She hopes to be saved from such love. In her way, Lucy proves as evasive to the reader as she does to her son. Ironically, her last appearance in the novel proves in a perverse way to be evidence of love. She hands Edward Henley the Seconal he wants to end a life grown exceedingly tiresome. Lucy's ambiguous complicity in his death is an appropriate action to close Grau's best work. As Edward's voice dies out, it says, "The taste of paradise, the perfect union. It must be here, Here." Grau teases the reader into thought. Paradoxes abound. Indeed, the novel has presented little if any conventional evidence of love, but one senses the value of the lives presented. In its own characteristically ironic way, *Evidence of Love* is just that. The vision is bleak, but here is her most affirmative work.

ROADWALKERS

Roadwalkers once again chronicles a family, but the family here is very nontraditional and certainly not wealthy, at least not until the end of the novel. Mary Woods and her daughter, Nanda, women of color—Mary is black and Nanda's father was from India—exhibit what Susan S. Kissel calls an "inner strength" unknown to Grau's white heroines, a strength that "empowers and enriches their lives." This strength ironically stems in many ways from Mary's early years as a "roadwalker," a child abandoned by her parents and left to roam the countryside of the South during the Depression years, accompanied first by her sister and brother, then by her brother, and finally, alone. In the description of the early years of Mary, or Baby, as she is then called, Grau produces some of her most poetic writing as she recounts the myriad sensations that make up the small child's life: "Her days were like a hoard of bright-colored beads, their connecting thread broken, lying loose, single, jumbled." The early part of the novel is impressionistic, organically written to mimic the experience that Baby is going through where day follows day unconsciously, and growth is measured only by the alternating cycle of heat and cold and the gradual accumulation of life-sustaining skills.

The progress of the novel itself can be gauged in terms of a symbol that many critics previously have noted to be central to Grau's fiction, the house. From homelessness to a shack built of license plates and Coca-

Cola signs to a convent and, finally, to a mansion purchased with the profits of her own talent, Mary Woods's story parallels the rise of displaced African Americans to places of eminence in American society. In her movement from "feral" child to haute-couture designer, Mary encounters hatred, racism, and paternalism, yet somehow comes out of the experience self-assured and happy.

Married at the end of the novel to an alderman who is thinking of running for state representative, Mary spends her days working in her garden, in her own soil, at her own home. The first pages of the novel claim that

> [s]he knew the surface of the earth. Head down, hour after hour, she studied it as she walked. She knew all its forms: dry and blowing with each of her steps; wet and oozing through her toes with a sucking sound. And the grains of the earth: sand fine as sugar; soil black and oily.

At the end, Nanda says of her, "she seems to love the feel of dirt. I've seen her rub light friable soil into dust between her palms and then toss it into the air, solemnly, like a priest dispensing incense." In the meantime the novel recounts the struggle that Mary undergoes to make the world her own from the moment she is ripped from her license-plate shack by the well-meaning Charles Tucker and delivered to the Sister Servants of Mary Home for Children and then focuses on the similarly painful but more typical battle of her own child to excel in a racially charged atmosphere.

Nanda's life resembles her mother's in its struggles. Her struggles are not as much for survival as for acceptance, and they, too, are symbolically mirrored in her places of abode. Unlike the disconnected days of her mother's early life, Nanda recalls her mother's "light high whisper threaded through all my days, linking them tightly together," and her moves are from apartment to apartment and apartment to house rather than on the dusty roads and byways of the roadwalker. "We had passed through a series of lodgings," Nanda says when they move into their first house, "but we had finally gained our castle, the one we had been searching for." She trades this safe haven, however, for a scholarship to the mostly white St. Catherine's and then to college, where she must forge the way for other African Americans. As she returns to her mother's home in the summer, she notices "a change in my mother's world. Black and white were reversing themselves," and she realizes that Mary, a successful clothing designer having "conquered the black kingdom," is now entering "new and dangerous territory on voyages of conquest and discovery." Mary's rise to the top of the fashion world is capped by an article in *Newsweek*, an article that procures their acceptance into the social world.

By the end of the novel the conquest is complete for both Mary and Nanda. Nanda and her husband, Mike, in a happy, if somewhat open, marriage, are free to travel the world at will. Only in the final pages of the book is Nanda settled in a home of her own. Throwing away the basket of toys that had accompanied her through her own nomadic childhood, she says triumphantly, "alone I came into my kingdom. My portion, neither more nor less." The love sought by Grau's previous heroines is found here in mother-child love, in mature husband-wife love, and most significantly and victoriously in Nanda's ability to love herself, thus making *Roadwalkers* the first of Grau's novels to end on an obvious note of triumph and true affirmation.

John K. Saunders
Updated by Jaquelyn W. Walsh

Other major works

SHORT FICTION: *The Black Prince, and Other Stories*, 1955; *The Wind Shifting West*, 1973; *Nine Women*, 1985; *Selected Stories*, 2003.

Bibliography

Kissel, Susan S. *Moving On: The Heroines of Shirley Ann Grau, Anne Tyler, and Gail Godwin*. Bowling Green, Ohio: Bowling Green State University Popular Press, 1996. Kissel examines the female protagonists in the novels of Grau and two other contemporary women writers, demonstrating how these characters show strength and maturity. Includes bibliographical references and an index.

Oleksy, Elzbieta. "The Keepers of the House: Scarlett O'Hara and Abigail Howland." In *Louisiana Women Writers: New Essays and a Comprehensive Bibliography*, edited by Dorothy H. Brown and Barbara C. Ewell. Baton Rouge: Louisiana State University Press, 1992. Although her essay centers on their heroines, Oleksy nonetheless makes a rather complete comparison of Margaret Mitchell's *Gone with the Wind* and Grau's *The Keepers of the House*.

O'Neal, Susan Hines. "Cultural Catholicism in Shirley Ann Grau's *The Hard Blue Sky*." *Louisiana Folklore Miscellany* 10 (1995): 24-36. O'Neal sees the islanders' attitude in the novel not as an example of their indifference to the mutability of life but rather as a ritual acceptance stemming from their Catholicism and its melding with folk philosophy and worldly truths.

Pearson, Ann. "Shirley Ann Grau: 'Nature Is the Vision.'" *Critique: Studies in Modern Fiction* 17, no. 2 (1975): 47-58. This article deals with Grau's use of nature, which seems to permeate her novels and stories. Pearson suggests that Grau's vision of the world lies in her perception of the ever-present closeness of nature.

Perry, Carolyn, and Mary Louise Weaks, eds. *The History of Southern Women's Literature*. Baton Rouge: Louisiana State University Press, 2002. Grau is included in this comprehensive examination of southern women writers. Part 4, "The Contemporary South, 1960-Present," contains an essay on Grau's work.

Richardson, Thomas J. "Roadwalker in the Magic Kingdom: Shirley Ann Grau." In *Literary New Orleans in the Modern World*, edited by Richard S. Kennedy. Baton Rouge: Louisiana State University Press, 1998. This examination of Grau's work is included in a collection of essays that focus on twentieth century literature about New Orleans and analyze how writers have depicted the city's myths as well as its history and other realities.

Schlueter, Paul. *Shirley Ann Grau*. Boston: Twayne, 1981. The first book-length critical study of Grau's work. Excellent use of details, though it is somewhat short on interpretation. Includes an index and a bibliography.

Wagner-Martin, Linda. "Shirley Ann Grau's Wise Fiction." In *Southern Women Writers: The New Generation*, edited by Tonette Bond Inge. Tuscaloosa: University of Alabama Press, 1990. Wagner-Martin argues that Grau's highly stylized manner of narration in many ways resembles the style of the folktale. Contends that one of Grau's most distinctive traits is her interest in ceremony and ritual, and maintains that Grau's best fiction deals with the nonwhite culture's impingement on the patriarchal matrix that dominates southern life.

Yardley, Jonathan. "Shirley Ann Grau's House, on the Street Where You Live." *The Washington Post*, March 8, 2005. Yardley discusses *The House on Coliseum Street*, recounting his attempts to locate the house in New Orleans. One in an occasional series of articles about notable and neglected authors.

ROBERT GRAVES

Born: Wimbledon, Surrey, England; July 24, 1895
Died: Deyá, Majorca, Spain; December 7, 1985
Also known as: Barbara Rich (with Laura Riding); John Doyle

PRINCIPAL LONG FICTION

My Head! My Head!, 1925
No Decency Left, 1932 (as Barbara Rich; with Laura Riding)
Claudius the God and His Wife Messalina, 1934
I, Claudius, 1934
"Antigua, Penny, Puce," 1936 (also known as *The Antigua Stamp*, 1937)
Count Belisarius, 1938
Sergeant Lamb of the Ninth, 1940 (also known as *Sergeant Lamb's America*)
Proceed, Sergeant Lamb, 1941
The Story of Marie Powell, Wife to Mr. Milton, 1943 (also known as *Wife to Mr. Milton, the Story of Marie Powell*)
The Golden Fleece, 1944 (also known as *Hercules, My Shipmate*, 1945)

King Jesus, 1946
The Islands of Unwisdom, 1949 (also known as *The Isles of Unwisdom*)
Watch the North Wind Rise, 1949 (also known as *Seven Days in New Crete*)
Homer's Daughter, 1955
They Hanged My Saintly Billy, 1957

Other literary forms

Robert Graves considered himself primarily a poet. Beginning with *Over the Brazier* (1916) and ending with *New Collected Poems* (1977), he published more than fifty books of poetry. His poems during and for some years after World War I explored themes of fear and guilt, expressive of his experience of trench warfare in France. He later became more objective and philosophical. After he developed his theory of the White Goddess in the 1940's, he wrote love poetry almost exclusively.

Graves also published more than fifty works of nonfiction, including literary criticism, books about writing and language, an autobiography (*Goodbye to All That*, 1929), a biography of T. E. Lawrence (*Lawrence and the Arabs*, 1927), social commentaries, and studies in Greek and Hebrew myths. In addition, he translated the works of such writers as Suetonius, Homer, Hesiod, Lucius Apuleius, and Lucan. He also published a few collections of short fiction.

Achievements

Robert Graves was one of the most versatile writers of the twentieth century, known not only as an excellent poet but also as a mythologist, novelist, translator, lecturer, and persistent intellectual maverick. He has perhaps the clearest claim among twentieth century poets as the inheritor of the Romantic tradition, although he purified his poetry of the kind of flowery elaboration that is often associated with Romanticism. He avoided fads and schools in poetry, perfecting a delicate craftsmanship generally outside the modern trends inspired by T. S. Eliot and Ezra Pound.

For the novel *I, Claudius*, Graves received the Hawthornden Prize, oldest of the famous British literary prizes, and the James Tait Black Memorial Prize, administered through the University of Edinburgh for the year's best novel. Collections of his poetry brought the Loines Award for Poetry (1958), the William Foyle Poetry Prize (1960), the Arts Council Poetry Award (1962), and the Queen's Gold Medal for Poetry (1968).

The White Goddess: A Historical Grammar of Poetic Myth (1948) and Graves's other studies in mythology, particularly *The Greek Myths* (1955), *Hebrew Myths: The Book of Genesis* (1964, with Raphael Patai), and *The Nazarene Gospel Restored* (1953, with Joshua Podro), together with his novels based on myth, have undoubtedly had a subtle and pervasive influence on modern literature. Graves was a prominent spokesman for the view that women and matriarchal values were much more prominent in the ancient world than had previously been realized and that civilization has suffered from the overthrow of women as social and spiritual leaders. The demotion of women from their former prominence, Graves said, is recorded and rationalized in Hebrew texts and classical Greek mythology.

Biography

Robert Graves was born in Wimbledon (outside London) on July 24, 1895, to Alfred Percival Graves and Amalie von Ranke Graves. His father was an inspector of schools, a Gaelic scholar, and a writer of poetry of a conventional sort. His mother was German, descended from Leopold von Ranke, whom Graves has called the first modern historian. Graves had a conventional Victorian home and upbringing, with summer visits to German relatives. These included an aunt, Baronin von Aufsess, who lived in an imposing medieval castle in the Bavarian Alps.

Because his name was listed as R. von R. Graves, his obvious German connections became an embarrassment during his years at Charterhouse, a private boarding school for boys, during the period before World War I, when anti-German sentiment was on the rise in England. He finally earned his classmates' respect, however, by becoming a good boxer. He also became friends with George Mallory, a famous mountaineer who later died on Mount Everest. Mallory interested Edward Marsh, patron of the contemporary Georgian school of poetry, in the poetry Graves was writing. Marsh encouraged Graves in his writing but advised him to modernize his diction, which was forty years behind the times.

When World War I began, Graves joined the Royal Welsh Fusiliers and soon went to France as a nineteen-year-old officer. In his autobiography, written when he was thirty-four, he provides one of the best descriptions of trench warfare to come out of the war—a gritty, objective account of a soldier's daily life. He was badly wounded, however, both physically and mentally, by his war experiences. The autobiography, which followed a long siege of war neurasthenia during which his poetry was haunted by images of horror and guilt, was a conscious attempt to put that part of his life behind him forever. Graves continued to use his gift for narrating war experiences, however, in subsequent novels, such as *Count Belisarius*, the Sergeant Lamb novels, and the Claudius novels.

During the war, Graves married Nancy Nicholson, a young painter, socialist, and vehement feminist. They were in essential agreement about the ruinous effect of male domination in modern society. Graves, along with his wartime friend the famous war poet Siegfried Sassoon, was already thoroughly disillusioned with war and the leaders of society who supported it.

Graves and his wife parted company in 1929 after a shattering domestic crisis involving the American poet Laura Riding. Riding was Graves's companion for the next thirteen years. They established themselves in Deyá, Majorca, Spain, published the critical magazine *Epilogue* through their own Seizin Press, and devoted themselves to writing both poetry and prose. Graves wrote his best historical novels during this period—the Claudius novels and *Count Belisarius*.

After Riding met and married the American poet Schuyler Jackson, Graves—during the Spanish Civil War, when British nationals were evacuated from Majorca—married Beryl Hodge. Graves later returned to Majorca with his new wife, where he stayed until his death in 1985. Graves had eight children, four by Nancy Nicholson and four by his second wife.

During the 1940's, Graves became fascinated with mythology. While he was doing research for his novel about Jason and the Golden Fleece, he became engrossed in the ubiquitous presence of a great goddess associated with the moon, the earth, and the underworld. She was not only the source of life and intuitive wisdom but also, as Muse, the patron of the poets and musicians. She bound humans both to the seasons of nature and to the demands of the spirit. When Graves discovered a similar pattern in Celtic folklore and literature and correlated the findings of such anthropologists as Robert Briffault, Johann Jakob Bachofen, James Frazer, Jane Harrison, and Margaret Murray and some of the recent discoveries in archaeology, he became convinced that the goddess cult once permeated the whole Western world. In this pattern of myth, as explained in *The White Goddess*, Graves found the unified vision he needed to animate his poetry and much of his subsequent prose for the rest of his life. It not only inspired some of the best love poetry of his time but also led to some lively treatments of Greek and Hebrew myth in both fiction and nonfiction.

Robert Graves. (© Washington Post; reprinted by permission of the D.C. Public Library)

Analysis

The novels of Robert Graves are usually a curious combination of detective work in history, legend, or myth and a considerable gift for narration. Graves never claimed any particular ability to invent plots, but he could flesh out imaginatively the skeletal remains of adventures he discovered in the past. Thus, the emperor Claudius lives again as the gossipy information in the works of Suetonius and other Roman chroniclers passes through Graves's shaping imagination. Sometimes, as in *King Jesus*, a traditional tale takes on a startling new dimension through an unconventional combination with other legendary material.

My Head! My Head!

Graves's first attempt at converting ancient history or myth into fiction was a short novel about Elisha and Moses, somewhat inauspiciously titled *My Head! My Head!* It was begun, as most of Graves's subsequent novels were, because the original accounts were somewhat mysterious, leaving much unsaid about what really happened and why. The novel elaborates on the biblical story of Elisha and the Shunamite woman (2 Kings, chapters 8-37) and, secondarily, through Elisha's narration, on the career of Moses.

The novel demonstrates both Graves's tendency to explain miracles in naturalistic terms and his contrary fascination with a certain suprarational possibility for special persons. The writer's curious views on magic are not entirely consistent with his debunking of miracles. The inconsistency is quite noticeable here because of the omniscient point of view. In most of his later novels, Graves wisely used a first-person narrator, which makes seeming inconsistencies the peculiar bias of a persona rather than of the author. *King Jesus* is thus told by a first century narrator who is neither Jewish nor Christian. In such a person, rational skepticism about specific miracles such as the virgin birth might well coexist with a general acceptance of magic.

In spite of its technical shortcomings, *My Head! My Head!* shows Graves's interest in a number of themes that would continue to concern him for the rest of his life: the changing relationships between men and women, the nature of the gods, and the way in which knowledge of the past and of the future must depend on an understanding of the present.

No Decency Left

On those two occasions when Graves did not depend on mythological or historical sources for his fiction, the results were strange, satiric compositions, lucidly told, but somehow disquieting. The first of these, *No Decency Left*, a collaboration with Laura Riding, appeared under the pseudonym "Barbara Rich." It is a satiric potpourri of events, drawing on such discordant elements as the rise of dictators, the man in the iron mask, the miraculous feeding of the multitude in the Bible, and comic-opera romance. The ideas in this fantasy may be attributable more to Riding than to Graves, though the attitudes displayed are quite consistent with Graves's views on the follies of men and the hidden strengths of women.

The action occurs in one day, the twenty-first birthday of Barbara Rich, who decides that on this special day she is going to get everything she wants. She forthwith crashes high society, becomes incredibly rich, marries the heir to the throne, feeds a multitude of hungry unemployed people by invading the zoo and arranging for the slaughter and cooking of zoo animals, captures the Communists who try to take over the country when the old king dies, and becomes a dictator in her own almost-bloodless revolution.

If the tone of this outrageous fable were lighter and its protagonist more lovable, it could be converted into Hollywood farce or Gilbert and Sullivan operetta, but everyone in it is disagreeable. The characters are either uniformly stupid and cowardly or utterly unscrupulous. The book was probably written primarily to make money when Riding and Graves were short of cash. (Graves always claimed that he wrote novels primarily to support himself while he wrote poetry.) It is obviously accidental that the novel, written in 1932, might seem to satirize the blanket powers given to Adolf Hitler by the Reichstag in 1933 or the famous love affair of Great Britain's King Edward with the commoner Wallis Simpson in 1936.

The Antigua Stamp

The view of the human animal, male or female, as vicious, with superior cleverness and ingenuity the mark of the female, also dominates Graves's novel *The Antigua Stamp*. The everlasting battle of the sexes is dramatized here as sibling rivalry that is never outgrown—a controversy over the ownership of an exceedingly valuable stamp. A long-standing, sour feud between brother and sister ends with the latter's victory because she is by far the more clever and conniving of the two. *The Antigua Stamp* and *No Decency Left* are potboilers, though they are interesting for the eccentric attitudes they exhibit toward human character and social affairs. These biases concerning the essential stupidity and greed of men and the intelligence and ruthlessness of women emerge in a somewhat softened form in Graves's better novels.

They Hanged My Saintly Billy

Eight of Graves's novels are based, at least in part, on historical characters and events. The first of these—*I, Claudius*—is the best and also probably the best known because of the sensitive portrayal of Claudius by Derek Jacobi in the 1976 British Broadcasting Corporation (BBC) television miniseries based on the Claudius novels, which first aired in the United States in 1977 on stations of the Public Broadcasting Service (PBS). *Count Belisarius*, about the brilliant general to the Byzantine emperor Justinian, is also a fascinating excursion into an exciting time, even though the character of Belisarius is not so clearly drawn as that of the stuttering Claudius.

Although *Count Belisarius* deserves more attention than it has received, the other historical novels appeal to a rather limited audience. The exception is the last, *They Hanged My Saintly Billy*, which Graves facetiously described in lurid terms: "My novel is full of sex, drink, incest, suicides, dope, horse racing, murder, scandalous legal procedure, cross-examinations, inquests and ends with a good public hanging—attended by 30,000. . . . Nobody can now call me a specialized writer."

The novel is hardly as shocking as this dust-jacket rhetoric implies. The case of Dr. William Palmer, convicted of poisoning his friend John Parsons Cook and executed in 1856, instigated a popular protest against capital punishment in Britain. The notorious case was rife with vague, unsubstantiated suspicions about Dr. Palmer's past and irrelevant disapproval of his taste for gambling and race horses. Moreover, supposed medical experts could never agree about the actual cause of Cook's death.

The novel's best feature is the technique by which Graves preserves the confusion and ambiguity of the case. Most of the novel consists of personal testimony from persons who had known Palmer. Each speaker thus talks from his or her own biases and limited contact, some insisting that "he never had it in him to hurt a fly." Others reveal an incredibly callous schemer who takes out insurance on his brother's life, knowing him to be an alcoholic, then arranges for the brother to drink himself to death. No sure conclusion is ever reached about the justice of the case.

Sergeant Lamb novels

As a member of the Royal Welsh Fusiliers during World War I, Graves became interested in the history of his regiment and discovered the makings of two novels in the career of Roger Lamb, who served in the Ninth Regiment during the American Revolution but joined the Fusiliers after the surrender of General Burgoyne and the incarceration of the Ninth. Graves is more chronicler than novelist in the two books about Roger Lamb, large parts of which are devoted to details of military life and curious anecdotes about the colonists, the Indians, the French Canadians, and the fiascos and triumph of generals.

Graves explains in his foreword to *Sergeant Lamb's America* that this story is not "straight history," though he has invented no main characters. The reader has no way of knowing exactly how accurately he conveys the texture of life in the colonies. "All that readers of an historical novel can fairly ask from the author," Graves writes, "is an assurance that he has nowhere willfully falsified geography, chronology, or character, and that information contained in it is accurate enough to add without discount to their general stock of history." This is a statement to remember, perhaps, in connection with any of Graves's historical novels. Although Graves seemed to have no particular rancor against Americans, the books do reveal a very iconoclastic attitude toward the Founding Fathers. His views of such notables as Benedict Arnold, Major André, and George Washington at least challenge many American readers' preconceptions.

Sergeant Lamb, like Count Belisarius, seems a bit wooden for all his military ingenuity. The protagonist's on-and-off love affair with Kate Harlowe provides only a tenuous thread on which to hang the semblance of a plot. The novels seem to be a scholar's compilation of interesting anecdotes and factual data about the time. Of course, this unimpassioned tone could be defended as exactly appropriate, since the novels are ostensibly the memoirs of a much older Roger Lamb, written when he is a schoolmaster in Dublin. This cool, dispassionate tone is often typical of Graves's style, however, even when he is describing his own experience in warfare in his autobiography, *Goodbye to All That*.

The Islands of Unwisdom

The Islands of Unwisdom celebrates, or rather exposes in its pettiness and greed, an abortive sixteenth century Spanish expedition to colonize the Solomon Islands. The leader of the expedition, Don Alvaro de Mendaña y Castro, had discovered the islands many years before. He called them the Isles of Solomon, thinking perhaps they were the location of the famous gold mines of the biblical King Solomon. The natives adorned themselves with gold. When the king of Spain finally gave permission for the expedition, therefore, a great many avaricious participants joined in the venture, which was ostensibly devoted to Christianizing the heathen.

Though a few devout persons, such as the three priests and the chief pilot, try to maintain the Christian charity of their mission, their feeble efforts are in vain. Practically all the islanders greet the Spaniards with affection and open hospitality, but sooner or later, the senseless slaughter of innocents converts friends into enemies. The combined stupidity and violence of the military and of the three Barretos, Don Alvaro's brothers-in-law, ensure disaster wherever they go. Moreover, Doña Ysabel Barreto, Don Alvaro's beautiful wife, is as proud and cruel as her arrogant brothers. Don Alvaro is devout but indecisive and unable to control the stubborn wills that surround him.

Graves uses the narrator, Don Andrés Serrano, an undersecretary to the general, to propose a theory to account for the superiority of the English over the Spanish in such situations. The English soldier could and often did do a sailor's work when help was needed on shipboard. The more rigid class structure of the Spanish, however, prevented a Spanish soldier from doing anything but fighting. During long and hazardous voyages, the Spanish soldier was idle and bored, while the Spanish sailor was overworked and resentful. When a new land was reached, the Spanish soldier felt impelled to demonstrate his function by killing enemies. If none existed, he soon created them.

Graves was particularly drawn to this sordid bit of history not so much because of the too often repeated folly of bringing civilization to the heathen by murdering them but because of a truly unique feature of this historical event. After the death of her husband, Doña Ysabel achieved the command of a naval vessel—surely an unusual event in any age, and unprecedented in the sixteenth century. Doña Ysabel is not the conventional kind of heroine, to be sure, but a kind that Graves finds most fascinating—beautiful, cruel, and ruthless. This novel was published in the year following *The White Goddess*, and the reader who is familiar with that study may see an uncanny resemblance between Doña Ysabel and the moon goddess in her most sinister phase.

The Story of Marie Powell, Wife to Mr. Milton

The Story of Marie Powell, Wife to Mr. Milton is also rooted in history, yet it echoes Graves's own views of feminine nature as well as his antipathy to John Milton, both as a poet and as a man. That Milton did, indeed, have some marital problems is clear; they were the inspiration for his pamphlet arguing that incompatibility should be sufficient grounds for divorce, which was followed by his brilliant "Areopagitica" against censorship of the press. (Graves notes that in spite of the admitted wisdom of the latter, Milton himself became an official censor under Oliver Cromwell.)

In Graves's treatment, Milton is the epitome of the self-righteous, dominating male, drawn to the poetic, half-pagan rural England from which his young wife emerges but determined in his arid Calvinism to squelch these poetic yearnings in himself and his bride. Milton chooses head over heart, always a mistake in a poet, from Graves's point of view. Though Milton desires love, like any man, he has a preconceived set of rules that would define and coerce love, which can only be given freely. He resolutely divorces sexuality from pleasure, for example, having intercourse with his wife only when trying to impregnate her—in compliance, presumably, with God's orders.

Marie is the weakest of Graves's fictional women, a kind of dethroned queen, a person of independent mind doomed to mental and emotional starvation in Milton's household. T. S. Matthews, in his autobiography *Jacks or Better* (1977), makes the provocative suggestion that

Graves poured his frustration and resentment about the marriage of Laura Riding to Schuyler Jackson into this book. It was written immediately after Graves fled to England, bereft of his longtime companion. Matthews has considerable background for this opinion, since he and his wife were living in the United States with the group (including Riding, Graves, Alan and Beryl Hodge, and Schuyler and Kit Jackson) when the fruit basket was upset. Even though Graves and Riding were not lovers at that time, according to James McKinley in his introduction to Graves's last book, Graves was profoundly shocked at what he may have perceived as Riding's abdication of her proper role. Whether this explanation is valid or not, this novel seems to touch a more personal vein of frustration, resentment, and sadness than do Graves's other historical novels.

Moreover, Graves indulges in a bit of romantic mysticism in this novel, more characteristic of his poetic than his prose style. Marie Milton falls into a three-day swoon during her third pregnancy, at the precise moment that her cousin, her secret "true love," is killed in Ireland. According to her own account, she spends those three days with her beloved. When she awakens she knows that her cousin, with whom she had fallen in love at the age of eleven, is dead. The child she bears thereafter, her first son, looks like her cousin, not Milton, and Marie is more peaceful than she has ever been. Perhaps this touch of fantasy expresses more about Graves than about Marie Powell Milton, but the author is careful to note in the epilogue that when Marie died giving birth to a third daughter, the one son followed her to the grave shortly after.

Readers may find the style of this novel somewhat ponderous, but Graves tries to adjust his diction to the times about which he writes. He deliberately uses some archaic, seventeenth century terms, for which he provides a glossary at the end; most of these words are easily understood in context.

COUNT BELISARIUS

If the pathetic Marie Milton shows the White Goddess in her pitiable decline, one need only return to the powerful women in *Count Belisarius* to see her in her glory. This is true despite the fact that Graves had not yet formulated his theory of the monomyth that he expressed in *The White Goddess*. In retrospect, his fictional women suggest that the goddess haunted his psyche before he knew her name. In *Count Belisarius*, not one but two striking women demonstrate the strength of the female. These are Empress Theodora, wife to Justinian, and Antonina, Belisarius's wife. Both had been carefully educated, pagan courtesans, but they acquired Christianity when it became possible to marry prominent Christians. They inevitably display more good sense than most of the men around them. More than once, Theodora saves Belisarius from the vindictive jealousy of Justinian or convinces the negligent monarch that he should send some relief in troops or supplies to his champion on the frontier. When Belisarius's situation becomes desperate because he is almost always vastly outnumbered on the battlefield and short of supplies as well, Antonina sends a private letter to Empress Theodora, who manages, by flattery or guile, to cajole Justinian into at least some action not altogether disastrous.

Of the two prominent men in the novel, Justinian is the more carefully characterized, even though he is invariably presented in a negative light. After Theodora dies and Belisarius throws Antonina out because of the emperor's campaign to discredit her virtue, nothing remains to protect Belisarius from Justinian's jealousy and fear. Like Samson shorn of his hair, Belisarius is imprisoned and blinded.

Belisarius, the central figure, is the least understandable in psychological terms. Though his exploits against the Persians and against the many tribes that threatened early Christendom are truly remarkable and well told, he himself seems larger than life in moral terms as well as in his undoubted military genius. He is seemingly incorruptible in a world riddled with intrigue and deception, and, as such, almost too good to be true. The jealousy of Justinian is more understandable than Belisarius's unswerving loyalty, devotion, and piety. The reader never knows what preserves Belisarius from the corrupting influence of power and popular adulation.

Ultimately, the effect of the novel is ironic, in spite of the total absence of ambiguity in Belisarius's character. The irony rests in the observation that for all the lifelong efforts of one of history's military geniuses, his accomplishments mattered little, since they were so soon negated by Justinian's bad judgment after the death of his greatest general. All the drama and the pageantry of war cannot compensate for its futility and incredible waste and its glorification of destruction in the name of true religion.

Claudius novels

For his portrait of Claudius, grandchild of Mark Antony and grandnephew of Octavius Augustus, Graves had rich sources of information on which to draw; perhaps that accounts for the greater depth and complexity Claudius seems to exhibit in comparison with Belisarius. Both Tacitus's *Ab excessu divi Augusti* (c. 116; *Annals*, 1598) and Suetonius's *De vita Caesarum* (c. 120; *History of the Twelve Caesars*, 1606), a book that Graves translated from the Latin in 1957 as *The Twelve Caesars*, contain much of the gossipy, possibly slanted history that fills Graves's *I, Claudius* and *Claudius the God and His Wife Messalina*.

I, Claudius is a more successful novel than its sequel. It builds to a natural climax as the protagonist, who calls himself "the cripple, the stammerer, the fool of the family," is proclaimed emperor by riotous Roman soldiers after the assassination of Caligula. Claudius captures the sympathy of the reader in this novel as a survivor of a fifty-year reign of terror in which all the more likely prospects for promotion to emperor are eliminated by Livia, Augustus's wife, to ensure the elevation of her son Tiberius to the throne. Claudius owes his survival mostly to his physical defects, which seemingly preclude his being considered for high office, and to a ready intelligence and wit that protect him somewhat from the cruelties of Caligula, who is the first to give him any role at all in government. The caprice of the troops in choosing the "fool of the family" as emperor is as great a surprise to Claudius as to anyone else. Presumably the terrified Claudius acquiesces to the whim of the military because the only other alternative is assassination along with the rest of Caligula's close relatives.

With *Claudius the God and His Wife Messalina*, the reader can no longer cheer the innocent victim of the vicious intrigues of court life. Claudius now has power and, in some respects, wields it effectively and humanely. He acquires, however, many of the tastes and faults of his class. The man who, as a boy, fainted at bloodshed now has a taste for violent entertainment. The scholar who despised ostentatious show now invades Britain so he may have a glorious triumph on his return. Worse yet, the unassuming person who knew how to survive the formidable machinations of Livia now foolishly succumbs to younger women who are as ruthless as Livia but without her intelligence and executive ability. He dies of poison administered by a faithless wife.

Graves seems to be making a case for the older Claudius as a kind of tragic hero who has come to a realization of his own shortcomings as well as those of his contemporaries. He had once idealistically hoped for the return of the Republic, but in his later years he understands that he has actually made self-government less attractive, simply because his rule has been more benevolent than that of his predecessors, Tiberius and Caligula. He decides that the Republican dream will not arise until the country again suffers under an evil emperor. The government must be worse before it can be better.

Graves attributes to Claudius a rather improbable scheme of secluding his son from the temptations of court life by sending him to Britain, then letting his ambitious second wife secure the throne for her own son, Nero, whose cruelty and decadence Claudius foresees. In the debacle that will occur in the reign of Nero, Claudius hopes his own son can come back as a conquering hero and reestablish the Republic. This rather fanciful scheme misfires because Claudius's son refuses to cooperate, confident that he can deal with his foster brother, Nero, himself. Actually, Claudius's son was assassinated after his father's death, presumably at Nero's orders.

This attempted explanation of Claudius's seeming gullibility in his last days is probably intended to lend dignity to his unfortunate decline into a rather foolish old age. Part of the problem with the second Claudius novel is simply the intractability of historical facts, which do not necessarily make the most effective plots. One of the usual requirements of tragic heroes is that they attain some measure of self-knowledge and that they are partially responsible for their own fall from greatness. Graves tries to retain empathy for a well-intentioned, thoughtful man who foresaw and accepted his fate, to be murdered by his wife, as a means to a greater good. Although this attempt to salvage a fading protagonist is understandable, it is not wholly successful.

Hercules, My Shipmate

As Graves's historical novels depend partially on the intrinsic interest of a historical period, so do his novels based on myth depend on an intrinsic interest in myth interpretation. Quite aside from the familiar story of Jason and the Argonauts, for example, *Hercules, My Shipmate* offers sometimes believable explanations of some of the common ideas found in myth. The centaurs, for example, were not half horse and half man, but a barbaric tribe whose totem animal was the horse. They wore horses' manes and worshiped a mare-headed mother goddess. Many of Jason's shipmates were demigods—that is, the products of matings between humans and gods. This convention has a nonsupernatural explanation as well: Their births were traceable to the ancient custom of attributing the offspring of temple prostitutes or priests to the gods or goddesses under whose auspices they were conceived.

This does not mean that all supernaturalism is rooted out of Graves's treatment of mythic material. Hercules has exaggerated powers analogous to those of the American legendary figure Paul Bunyan, a parody of the Greek ideal of the hero, a man so strong he is dangerous to foe and friend as well. Nor does Graves eliminate all supernaturalism from his *King Jesus*, the most controversial of his novels, which fuses biblical myth with Graves's own ideas about the ancient goddess cult.

KING JESUS

King Jesus creates a new myth about Jesus—a Jesus who is literally the king of the Jews, or at least the proper inheritor of that title. He is inheritor as the grandson of King Herod (through a secret marriage between Mary and Antipater, Herod's son) but also because he is anointed by God's prophet, John the Baptist, which was the traditional Hebrew way of choosing a king. In the latter sense, Herod had less right to the throne than Jesus, since Herod derived his authority from the Romans, not from ancient Hebrew custom. Moreover, Jesus fulfills other expectations built into what Graves presents as ancient Hebrew ritual, such as a marriage to the inheritor of the land. Graves claims that ownership of the land was matrilineal and that in order to become a king, a man had to marry the youngest daughter of the hereditary line, in this case Mary, the sister of Martha and Lazarus. (Graves points out that this matrilineal descent accounts for Egyptian pharaohs marrying their sisters and King David marrying a woman from each of the tribes of Israel in order to unify the tribes.)

Jesus is an ascetic, however, and refuses to cohabit with Mary. Moreover, one of his chief adversaries in the novel is the cult of the goddess, whose chief priestess is yet another Mary, called the Hairdresser—the character known in the Bible as Mary Magdalene. It is no accident that the three vital women who attend Jesus at his crucifixion conveniently represent the Triple Goddess—Mary the mother, Mary the wife, and Mary the crone, who lays out the mythic hero in death. The irony of the situation is that in spite of consciously choosing the pattern of the Suffering Servant, described in the Bible's book of Isaiah, and trying his best to overthrow the cult of the fertility goddess, Jesus nevertheless fulfills the role of the sacrificial hero in the goddess mythology. Though some readers may be offended by the liberties Graves takes with a sacred story, those who are fascinated by the whole of the mythic heritage from the ancient world can appreciate this imaginative retelling.

WATCH THE NORTH WIND RISE

If *King Jesus* is the most serious of Graves's treatments of the goddess mythology, the most lighthearted is *Watch the North Wind Rise*, a futuristic utopian novel in which the great goddess cult has been revived in Crete (its stronghold in the ancient world) as a social experiment. The protagonist is a time traveler, conjured into the future by a witch, in obedience to the goddess. He also serves a Pandora-like function, bringing unrest into a land made dull by continuous peace. Great art, after all, demands conflict, which this ideal land has left behind. The novel is entertaining as a satire of utopian ideas but also provides an interesting exploration of the relationship between an artist (the protagonist) and his muse (the goddess).

HOMER'S DAUGHTER

Graves's last novel on a mythic theme, *Homer's Daughter*, borrows heavily from Homer's *Odyssey* (c. 725 B.C.E.; English translation, 1614) and from Samuel Butler's *The Authoress of the "Odyssey"* (1897), which argues that the *Odyssey* must have been written by a woman. Graves's protagonist is the princess Nausicaa, who in the *Odyssey* befriended the shipwrecked Odysseus. In the novel, it is Nausicaa who endures many rude and insistent suitors, as Penelope does in Homer's epic. A shipwrecked stranger rescues her in a manner attributed to Odysseus, by shooting the unwanted suitors and winning the fair lady for himself. She is the one who composes the *Odyssey*, incorporating her experience into the story.

In spite of the fact that Graves himself dismissed his fiction as a means of providing support for his writing of poetry, his best novels deserve to live on as imaginative treatments of history and myth. While he may not always have captured the "real" past, he helped to make the past important in a time when many people considered it irrelevant. He showed how ancient symbol systems could still capture the imagination of one of the most versatile writers of the twentieth century. He also helped to overthrow the stereotype of women as weak in intelligence and will. This does not mean that Graves was particularly accurate in his perception of women, but his biases do offer a welcome antidote to the more insipid variety of fictional women. Graves's work is also likely partially responsible for renewing interest in mythology and the beginnings of civilization. Part of this is the result of his nonfiction works, such as *The White Goddess*, *The Greek Myths*, and *Hebrew Myths*, but his use of myth in popular novels has probably reached an even wider audience.

Katherine Snipes

Other major works

SHORT FICTION: *The Shout*, 1929; *¡Catacrok! Mostly Stories, Mostly Funny*, 1956; *Collected Short Stories*, 1964.

POETRY: *Goliath and David*, 1916; *Over the Brazier*, 1916; *Fairies and Fusiliers*, 1917; *Treasure Box*, 1919; *Country Sentiment*, 1920; *The Pier-Glass*, 1921; *The Feather Bed*, 1923; *Whipperginny*, 1923; *Mock Beggar Hall*, 1924; *The Marmosite's Miscellany*, 1925 (as John Doyle); *Welchman's Hose*, 1925; *Poems, 1914-1926*, 1927; *Poems, 1914-1927*, 1927; *Poems, 1929*, 1929; *Ten Poems More*, 1930; *Poems, 1926-1930*, 1931; *To Whom Else?*, 1931; *Poems, 1930-1933*, 1933; *Collected Poems*, 1938; *No More Ghosts: Selected Poems*, 1940; *Work in Hand*, 1942 (with others); *Poems, 1938-1945*, 1946; *Collected Poems, 1914-1947*, 1948; *Poems and Satires, 1951*, 1951; *Poems, 1953*, 1953; *Collected Poems, 1955*, 1955; *Poems Selected by Himself*, 1957; *The Poems of Robert Graves Chosen by Himself*, 1958; *Collected Poems, 1959*, 1959; *The Penny Fiddle: Poems for Children*, 1960; *Collected Poems*, 1961; *More Poems, 1961*, 1961; *The More Deserving Cases: Eighteen Old Poems for Reconsideration*, 1962; *New Poems, 1962*, 1962; *Ann at Highwood Hall: Poems for Children*, 1964; *Man Does, Woman Is*, 1964; *Collected Poems, 1965*, 1965; *Love Respelt*, 1965; *Seventeen Poems Missing from "Love Respelt,"* 1966; *Colophon to "Love Respelt,"* 1967; *Poems, 1965-1968*, 1968; *Beyond Giving: Poems*, 1969; *The Crane Bag*, 1969; *Love Respelt Again*, 1969; *Poems About Love*, 1969; *Advice from a Mother*, 1970; *Poems, 1969-1970*, 1970; *Queen-Mother to New Queen*, 1970; *The Green-Sailed Vessel*, 1971; *Poems: Abridged for Dolls and Princes*, 1971; *Poems, 1968-1970*, 1971; *Deyá*, 1972 (with Paul Hogarth); *Poems, 1970-1972*, 1972; *Poems: Selected by Himself*, 1972; *Timeless Meetings: Poems*, 1973; *At the Gate*, 1974; *Collected Poems, 1975*, 1975 (2 volumes); *New Collected Poems*, 1977.

NONFICTION: *On English Poetry*, 1922; *The Meaning of Dreams*, 1924; *Contemporary Techniques of Poetry: A Political Analogy*, 1925; *Poetic Unreason, and Other Studies*, 1925; *Another Future of Poetry*, 1926; *Impenetrability: Or, The Proper Habit of English*, 1926; *The English Ballad: A Short Critical Survey*, 1927; *Lars Porsena: Or, The Future of Swearing and Improper Language*, 1927; *Lawrence and the Arabs*, 1927 (also known as *Lawrence and the Arabian Adventure*, 1928); *A Survey of Modernist Poetry*, 1927 (with Laura Riding); *Mrs. Fisher: Or, The Future of Humour*, 1928; *A Pamphlet Against Anthologies*, 1928 (with Riding; also known as *Against Anthologies*); *Goodbye to All That: An Autobiography*, 1929; *T. E. Lawrence to His Biographer Robert Graves*, 1938; *The Long Week-End: A Social History of Great Britain, 1918-1938*, 1940 (with Alan Hodge); *The Reader over Your Shoulders: A Handbook for Writers of English Prose*, 1943 (with Hodge); *The White Goddess: A Historical Grammar of Poetic Myth*, 1948; *The Common Asphodel: Collected Essays on Poetry, 1922-1949*, 1949; *Occupation: Writer*, 1950; *The Nazarene Gospel Restored*, 1953 (with Joshua Podro); *Adam's Rib and Other Anomalous Elements in the Hebrew Creation Myth: A New View*, 1955; *The Crowning Privilege: The Clark Lectures, 1954-1955*, 1955; *The Greek Myths*, 1955 (2 volumes); *Jesus in Rome: A Historical Conjecture*, 1957 (with Podro); *Five Pens in*

Hand, 1958; *Greek Gods and Heroes*, 1960; *Oxford Addresses on Poetry*, 1962; *Nine Hundred Iron Chariots: The Twelfth Arthur Dehon Little Memorial Lecture*, 1963; *Hebrew Myths: The Book of Genesis*, 1964 (with Raphael Patai); *Majorca Observed*, 1965 (with Paul Hogarty); *Mammon and the Black Goddess*, 1965; *Poetic Craft and Principle*, 1967; *The Crane Bag and Other Disputed Subjects*, 1969; *On Poetry: Collected Talks and Essays*, 1969; *Difficult Questions, Easy Answers*, 1972.

TRANSLATIONS: *Almost Forgotten Germany*, 1936 (with Laura Riding; of Georg Schwarz's memoir); *The Transformation of Lucius, Otherwise Known as "The Golden Ass,"* 1950 (of Lucius Apuleius's novel); *The Cross and the Sword*, 1954 (of Manuel de Jesús Galván's novel); *Pharsalia: Dramatic Episodes of the Civil Wars*, 1956 (of Lucan's epic poem); *Winter in Majorca*, 1956 (of George Sand's memoir); *The Twelve Caesars*, 1957 (of Suetonius's biography); *The Anger of Achilles: Homer's "Iliad,"* 1959; *The Rubáiyát of Omar Khayyám*, 1967 (with Omar Ali-Shah).

CHILDREN'S LITERATURE: *The Big Green Book*, 1962; *The Siege and Fall of Troy*, 1962; *Two Wise Children*, 1966; *The Poor Boy Who Followed His Star*, 1968.

EDITED TEXTS: *Oxford Poetry: 1921*, 1921 (with Alan Porter and Richard Hughes); *John Skelton: Laureate*, 1927; *The Less Familiar Nursery Rhymes*, 1927; *The Comedies of Terence*, 1962; *English and Scottish Ballads*, 1975.

MISCELLANEOUS: *Steps: Stories, Talks, Essays, Poems, Studies in History*, 1958; *Food for Centaurs: Stories, Talks, Critical Studies, Poems*, 1960; *Selected Poetry and Prose*, 1961.

Bibliography

Bloom, Harold, ed. *Robert Graves*. New York: Chelsea House, 1987. Collection of essays presents discussion of *I, Claudius* as well as Graves's other historical novels. Includes chronology and bibliography.

Firla, Ian, ed. *Robert Graves's Historical Novels*. New York: Peter Lang, 2000. Collection of essays focuses on Graves's historical novels, with contributors addressing such topics as the narrative structure of his novels from the 1930's and the cultural relativism of his works. Includes bibliography and index.

Graves, Richard Perceval. *Robert Graves: The Assault Heroic, 1895-1926*. New York: Viking Press, 1986. First volume of a three-volume biography written by Graves's nephew. Though primarily concerned with Graves's life, this volume delineates the conditions that led him to write his autobiography and leave England. The effects of World War I and Graves's rejection of conventional morality play a large role in this study.

_______. *Robert Graves: The Years with Laura, 1926-1940*. New York: Viking Press, 1990. Second volume of Graves's three-volume study. Looking closely at the relationship between Graves and the American poet Laura Riding, this volume provides information concerning the respective contributions of the collaborators. Richard Perceval Graves is concerned with literary matters, though his fascination with the sensational aspects of the years Robert Graves and Riding spent together is evident. Of much interest, as in the first volume, are the notes, which indicate the breadth of the Graves's friendships and the variety of places in which his papers have been placed.

_______. *Robert Graves and the White Goddess, 1940-1985*. London: Weidenfeld & Nicolson, 1995. This concluding volume to Graves's three-volume biography lacks the savor and drama of the second volume because it covers the relatively sedate life of an aged, lionized poet and novelist.

Koelb, Clayton. "The Medium of History: Robert Graves and the Ancient Past." In *Comparative Literary Dimensions: Essays in Honor of Melvin J. Friedman*, edited by Jay L. Halio and Ben Siegel. Newark: University of Delaware Press, 2000. Essay analyzing Graves's work is included in a collection of essays devoted to discussion of the works and thinking of modern and postmodern authors.

Quinn, Patrick J., ed. *New Perspectives on Robert Graves*. Selinsgrove, Pa.: Susquehanna University Press, 1999. Thoughtful volume of essays on the works of Graves provides discussion of the author's contribution to the historical novel in the 1930's. Includes bibliographical references and index.

Seymour, Miranda. *Robert Graves: Life on the Edge*. New York: Henry Holt, 1995. Biographical work divides Graves's life into five parts, describing how in each part an individual woman served as his source of inspiration. Presents previously unavailable information on Graves, with especially interesting details on his experiences in World War I.

Seymour-Smith, Martin. *Robert Graves: His Life and Work*. New York: Paragon House, 1988. Provides an intimate, fascinating glimpse into Graves the man. Seymour-Smith knew Graves since 1943 and wrote extensively about him from 1956 onward. Excellent introduction to Graves's remarkable life and literary career.

ALASDAIR GRAY

Born: Glasgow, Scotland; December 28, 1934
Also known as: Alasdair James Gray

Principal long fiction

Lanark: A Life in Four Books, 1981
1982 Janine, 1984
The Fall of Kelvin Walker: A Fable of the Sixties, 1985
McGrotty and Ludmilla: Or, The Harbinger Report, A Romance of the Eighties, 1989
Something Leather, 1990
Poor Things: Episodes from the Early Life of Archibald McCandless M.D., Scottish Public Health Officer, 1992
A History Maker, 1994
Old Men in Love: John Tunnock's Posthumous Papers, 2007

Other literary forms

In the late 1960's and the 1970's, before he gained recognition as novelist, Alasdair Gray was known as a playwright and had several radio and television plays to his credit. He also wrote for the stage and drew upon these early dramatic works for several later novels. The television and stage play *The Fall of Kelvin Walker* (pr. 1972) and the radio play *McGrotty and Ludmilla* (1976) both became novellas, published individually as books under the same titles.

Gray also has written short stories, which are collected in several volumes. Less frequently he has produced poems and nonfiction, including the notable, and polemical, *Why Scots Should Rule Scotland* (1992). He edited an offbeat contribution to literary history called *The Book of Prefaces: A Short History of Literate Thought in Words by Great Writers of Four Nations from the Seventh to the Twentieth Century* (2000). As readers familiar with his novels might anticipate, *The Book of Prefaces* is typographically and visually adventurous, but also historically rigorous.

Achievements

Alasdair Gray's first novel, *Lanark*, won immediate recognition as a distinctively Scottish creation. It won the Scottish Book of the Year award and the Scottish Arts Council Book Award. A later novel, *Poor Things*, was equally innovative, gaining even more attention. It was awarded the *Guardian* Fiction Prize and the Whitbread Novel Award in 1992. Gray has also won awards for his short fiction, most notably *Unlikely Stories, Mostly* (1983), which was recognized with a Cheltenham Prize in 1983.

Gray's novels were pivotal to the revival of Scottish literature in the 1980's and 1990's, especially by helping to create a literary environment favorable to novels about life in Glasgow, a working-class city long overshadowed by Edinburgh. Glasgow University named him a professor of creative writing, alongside two other leading lights of Scottish literature, James Kelman and Tom Leonard.

Biography

Alasdair James Gray demonstrated literary talent as a young boy, adapting part of Homer's *Odyssey* for a school play. He entered Glasgow Art School in 1952, graduating with a diploma in mural painting and design in 1957. After serving as an art teacher in Lanarkshire and Glasgow, he became a scene painter for Glasgow's Pavilion and Citizen's Theaters in 1961, a position he held for two years. After a period of freelance work, he became an artist recorder for Glasgow's People's Palace Local History Museum in 1976.

Gray's growth as a writer roughly paralleled his development as an artist. Two years into art school, he began writing sections of what became the novel *Lanark* nearly three decades later. The chapter "The War Begins" won a prize in a short-story competition sponsored by *The Observer*. He continued to write short stories. He also painted murals for the Scotland-U.S.S.R. Society and for Greenhead Church of Scotland, in Bridgeton.

Gray's first television and radio plays were broadcast in 1968. In the early 1970's, while he was attending an informal writing group led by Philip Hobsbaum, Gray began his association with Liz Lochhead and Leonard, among other writers. In 1977, Gray was offered the post of writer-in-residence at Glasgow University, a position he held until 1979.

Gray's long years of writing were rewarded in 1981, when *Lanark* was published by Edinburgh's Canongate Press. Because it was an unusually large book for a first novel, Canongate projected only modest sales. Instead, it attracted considerable attention in the United Kingdom and abroad. Gray followed this success with the collection *Unlikely Stories, Mostly* and a second novel, *1982 Janine*. During this period he also worked on a screenplay of *Lanark*, which was not produced.

Gray's later writing received less favorable critical responses. Even though Gray's novels were serious works, concerned with Glasgow life and embodying his interest in democratic socialism, his fictional approach, which often included highly charged sexual scenes, drew charges that his work was pornographic. These charges dampened public reception of novels such as *1982 Janine* and *Something Leather*. Some readers also were disappointed because the highly imaginative *Lanark* was followed by more realistic, and more stridently political, works of fiction.

Poor Things, however, reaffirmed for many readers the promise of *Lanark*. As he did in his first novel, Gray experimented with form and unabashedly embraced elements of science fiction in *Poor Things*. Adventurous and idiosyncratic, with a stated debt to authors including Mary Shelley and Edgar Allan Poe, *Poor Things* proved attractive to both critics and readers, and it became a best seller in the United Kingdom.

The socialist and feminist concerns that animated *Poor Things* also gave energy to Gray's next major work, *A History Maker*. This novel, again, is a highly imaginative tale, set not in the nineteenth century but in the twenty-third century. Gray's next novel, *Old Men in Love*, is experimental in form, too, but it returns to a more realistic mode as well.

Analysis

Without a true, single writing style for his long fiction, Alasdair Gray writes as though speaking from behind a series of masks with different personalities and modes of expression. This has not kept him from having a remarkably distinctive style of his own, however. Once familiar with Gray's works, a reader is likely to pick up a novel or collection of short stories and experience a sense of familiarity. Gray has exerted an unusual control over the visual presentation of his longer fiction, a feature of his style that comes from his background in the graphic arts. In addition to providing cover and interior illustrations, he has enhanced his writing with an array of fonts and type-size variations, and by using a variety of word-spacings.

Gray's writing does not lack the characteristic literary elements, however. Perhaps most significant is his pseudodocumentary approach, in which fictional documents are presented to tell the story. In some novels, these documents take the form of commentaries and glosses that not only provide specious interpretations of events but also give them added depth.

In *Lanark*, these pseudodocumentary glosses appear in small sections parallel to the main text and are reminiscent of those found in *Finnegans Wake* (1939) by James Joyce. In later novels, the pseudodocumentary approach becomes integral to Gray's work as a whole. In *Poor Things*, for instance, Gray assigns his own authorship only to the novel's introduction and endnotes. He presents the rest of the "novel" as a historical document.

Also distinctive are Gray's leading characters, who are typically from working- and lower-class backgrounds.

Alasdair Gray. (Getty Images)

Jock McLeish in *1982 Janine* is an electrician in unhappy circumstances; Archibald McCandless in *Poor Things* is of farm-servant origins, and he must struggle for acceptance among wealthy medical students; John Tunnock in *Old Men in Love* is a retired schoolteacher with unrecognized talents.

Gray has not shied from employing Scotticisms in his fiction, including the words "mibby" for "maybe" and "couldnae" for "couldn't." Some critics also regard Gray's dark humor as distinctively Scottish.

Lanark

Although in some ways a fragmented and willfully distorted narrative, *Lanark* is a remarkably accessible story about two characters, Lanark and Duncan Thaw, who are soon discovered by the reader to be the same person. As the story begins, Lanark and Duncan Thaw are living in separate but related worlds: one a gloomy, imaginary world called Unthank and the other Glasgow in the 1940's and 1950's. Duncan Thaw, in Glasgow, endures fairly mundane, everyday concerns. He decides on a vocation, studies at an art school, moves in and out of relationships, and pursues the beginnings of a career as a muralist.

With a boldness that would become his trademark, Gray chooses to open his novel not in Glasgow but in Unthank, a dimly adumbrated city where people suffer fantastic physical diseases that reflect their psychic states. While living in Unthank, Lanark tries to find friendship, love, and meaning.

Gray's statement on the novel's contents page, "Thaw's story exists within the hull of Lanark's," suggests that even the realistic narrative must be understood in terms of the one that is highly fantastic. Thaw struggles to achieve meaningful goals, and he wants those goals to be understood by the reader. Lanark's struggles, on the other hand, arise from his trying to deal with the puzzling world he is trapped within. Like Thaw, he seeks personal rewards, but in a far more forbidding and restrictive context, one that makes *Lanark* seem at times dystopian.

Poor Things

Poor Things is a striking example of the pseudodocumentary style of Gray's fiction. The novel's subtitle is *Episodes from the Early Life of Archibald McCandless M.D., Scottish Public Health Officer*, and the title page shows Gray as the novel's "editor." Gray admits to writing two parts of the book, the introduction and the section at the end of the novel, "Notes Critical and Historical." In the introduction, Gray states his case for the historical nature of the narrative to follow. He describes the discovery of the manuscript in Glasgow by a Scottish researcher who believes in its authenticity although not its veracity. The main text of the novel then follows, with authorship attributed to the novel's main male character, Archibald McCandless. A letter from McCandless's wife follows, disputing Archibald's account. The book ends with Gray's "Notes Critical and Historical," to which he has signed his own name. The novel also features manuscript facsimiles, portraits of the main characters, medical drawings, and other illustrations.

Gray's patchwork approach is fully appropriate to the story of the novel, a reimagining of Mary Wollstonecraft Shelley's famous novel *Frankenstein: Or, The Modern Prometheus* (1818). Shelley's character, Dr. Victor Frankenstein, uses his medical knowledge to piece together a living man from parts of human corpses. In *Poor Things*, Dr. Godwin Bysshe Baxter performs a similar operation, but he constructs a woman rather than a man. A major theme of the novel is the "making" of people. Chapters include "Making Bella Baxter," "Making Me," and "Making Godwin Baxter."

The name Godwin Bysshe Baxter is a tribute to Shelley's father (William Godwin), her husband (poet Percy Bysshe Shelley), and her friend (William Baxter). The doctor's female creation, Bella Baxter, takes on the married name of Victoria McCandless, which echoes the name of Shelley's fictional doctor, Victor Frankenstein.

In keeping with Gray's other novels, *Poor Things* does not shy away from politics. Whereas Shelley's *Frankenstein* includes Scotland among its locations, *Poor Things* makes Glasgow its most important locale. Scotland's postcolonial difficulties are among the novel's main concerns.

A History Maker

A History Maker takes place in the twenty-third century, in a matriarchal society in which the gender roles are not so much reversed as exaggerated to the point of near absurdity. Sexual freedom is taken for granted on Earth, although traditional marriages prevail in outer-space communities. The common notion that men prefer younger mates is one element reversed in this future society: Men in this world strongly prefer older women, presumably because they hold all the social power.

In this future world, waging war is one of the primary occupations for men. Warfare, now restricted to the use of hand-to-hand weapons, is a game. It is a form of entertainment, recorded by constantly hovering Public Eyes.

Even with vastly improved methods for patching up the wounded and dying, warfare remains a deadly activity. At the beginning of *A History Maker*, one entire warring club, the Ettricks, who have enjoyed fifty years without defeat, are facing not only defeat but utter annihilation; only a few members of the club are still standing. Surrounded by enemy clubs, the Ettrick soldiers opt for a desperate measure that leaves only one soldier, Wat Dryhope, unscathed. The desperate measure was designed in part to win attention, for warfare has now become less interesting and entertaining to both participants and watchers. The ruse works, on several levels: The desperate action attracts global attention, and Dryhope becomes a hero. His becoming a hero, however, threatens the stability of his society.

The story ends only three-quarters of the way through the book. What remains is a glossary that initially performs the simplest of glossary tasks (as in defining the word "neeps" as turnips). The book ends with background information about the story, giving *A History Maker* substantially more weight as a novel.

Mark Rich

Other major works

SHORT FICTION: *Unlikely Stories, Mostly*, 1983 (revised 1997); *Lean Tales*, 1985 (with James Kelman and Agnes Owen); *Ten Tales Tall and True: Social Realism, Sexual Comedy, Science Fiction*, 1993; *The Ends of Our Tethers: Thirteen Sorry Stories*, 2003.

PLAYS: *Dialogue*, pr. 1971; *The Fall of Kelvin Walker*, pr. 1972; *The Loss of the Golden Silence*, pr. 1973; *Tickly Mince*, pr. 1982 (with Tom Leonard and Liz Lochhead); *The Pie of Damocles*, pr. 1983 (with Leonard and Lochhead); *Working Legs: A Two-Act Play for Disabled Performers*, pb. 1997; *Fleck*, pb. 2008.

POETRY: *Old Negatives*, 1989; *Sixteen Occasional Poems, 1990-2000*, 2000.

TELEPLAYS: *The Fall of Kelvin Walker*, 1968; *Dialogue*, 1972; *Triangles*, 1972; *The Man Who Knew About Electricity*, 1973; *Honesty*, 1974; *Today and Yesterday*, 1975 (educational documentary); *Beloved*, 1976; *The Gadfly*, 1977; *The Story of a Recluse*, 1987.

RADIO PLAYS: *Quiet People*, 1968; *The Night Off*, 1969; *Thomas Muir of Huntershill*, 1970; *The Loss of the Golden Silence*, 1974; *McGrotty and Ludmilla*, 1976; *The Vital Witness*, 1979; *Near the Driver*, 1988.

NONFICTION: *Saltire Self-Portrait 4*, 1988 (autobiography); *Why Scots Should Rule Scotland*, 1992.

EDITED TEXTS: *The Anthology of Prefaces*, 1989; *The Book of Prefaces: A Short History of Literate Thought in Words by Great Writers of Four Nations from the Seventh to the Twentieth Century*, 2000.

MISCELLANEOUS: *Mavis Belfrage: A Romantic Novel, with Five Shorter Tales*, 1996.

Bibliography

Bernstein, Stephen. *Alasdair Gray*. Lewisburg, Pa.: Bucknell University Press, 1999. The first comprehensive study of Gray's novels. Emphasizes the coherence of Gray's novels when read as a single body of work. Includes a bibliography.

Bohnke, Dietmar. *Shades of Gray: Science Fiction, History, and the Problem of Postmodernism in the Work of Alasdair Gray*. Leipzig, Germany: Verla, Galda & Wilch, 2004. Examines the contrasting emphases upon the past and future in Gray's novels and his experimental techniques.

Miller, Gavin. *Alasdair Gray: The Fiction of Communion*. New York: Rodopi, 2005. Discusses the ideas found in Gray's novels in the context of Scottish intellectual history, especially ideas in social anthropology and psychiatry.

Moores, Phil, ed. *Alasdair Gray: Critical Appreciations and a Bibliography*. Boston Spa, England: British Library, 2001. Essays on various aspects of Gray's novels. Also features a detailed bibliography and illustrations by Gray.

Petrie, Duncan. *Contemporary Scottish Fictions: Film, Television, and the Novel*. Edinburgh: Edinburgh University Press, 2004. Gray's writings, along with those of James Kelman, receive major attention in this study of the flourishing of Scottish culture in the 1980's and 1990's.

Wallace, Gavin, and Randall Stevenson, eds. *The Scottish Novel Since the Seventies: New Visions, Old Dreams*. 1993. New ed. Edinburgh: Edinburgh University Press, 2005. This study of Gray, James Kelman, and Janice Galloway as experimental novelists places them in the context of other Scottish writers of their time and gives special attention to novels of the city of Glasgow.

HENRY GREEN

Born: Forthampton Court, England; October 29, 1905
Died: London, England; December 13, 1973
Also known as: Henry Vincent Yorke

Principal long fiction

Blindness, 1926
Living, 1929
Party Going, 1939
Caught, 1943
Loving, 1945
Back, 1946
Concluding, 1948
Nothing, 1950
Doting, 1952

Other literary forms

In addition to his novels, Henry Green published an autobiographical book, *Pack My Bag: A Self-Portrait* (1940), and several accounts of his World War II firefighting experiences: "A Rescue," "Mr. Jonas," and "Firefighting." Green's theories regarding writing are expressed in *Pack My Bag* and in his essays "The English Novel of the Future" and "A Novelist to His Readers," which can be found in *Contact* (1950) and *The Listener* (1950, 1951). From time to time, Green wrote book reviews on topics that interested him and personal essays ranging in subject from his friend and editor Edward Garnett to public school life in 1914.

Achievements

For someone who managed both business and literary careers, Henry Green's achievements are remarkable. *Blindness*, published in 1926 when Green was twenty-one years old, announced the arrival of a novelist whose artistic poise was illustrated through narrative daring and an unusual sense of characterization. Successive novels continued to impress critics and reviewers, though some either misunderstood or disliked Green's highly individual technique. "Prose," Green stated in

Pack My Bag, "should be a long intimacy between strangers with no direct appeal to what both may have known." He continued by writing that this intimacy should build slowly and encompass unexpressed feelings that "are not bounded by the associations common to place names or to persons with whom the reader is unexpectedly familiar."

Friends and fellow writers such as Garnett, V. S. Pritchett, W. H. Auden, Evelyn Waugh, Christopher Isherwood, and John Lehman recognized Green's talent. Several have published articles on his work. Although Green is less known in the United States, Terry Southern, Eudora Welty, and John Updike have paid homage to him in interviews and articles. As critical theory has developed to encompass precisely those narrative strategies articulated by Green in 1939, it seems likely that his literary stature, already assured, will increase.

BIOGRAPHY

Henry Green was born Henry Vincent Yorke at Forthampton Court, near Tewkesbury, Gloucestershire, England, on October 29, 1905. He was the third son of a wealthy Midlands industrialist whose business concern, H. Pontifex and Sons, Green was later to manage. Like others of his social class, Green was sent away to school when he was quite young, in his case before he was seven years old. At the age of twelve, he went to Eton and from there to Oxford, where he studied with C. S. Lewis.

While at Eton, Green began writing *Blindness*, whose self-conscious, awkward, dilettantish, yet introspective protagonist, John Haye, is a self-portrait. Like Haye, Green was a member of an art society, an avid reader, and a self-styled aesthete. By the time he arrived at Oxford, however, already somewhat of a celebrity because *Blindness* was about to be published, Green was beginning to question his privileged position and his right to an inherited fortune. This dilemma led him to leave Oxford at the end of his second year without earning a degree. As he reports in *Pack My Bag*, he went to Birmingham "to work in a factory with my wet podgy hands." Far from feeling superior to the laboring class, Green found these working people full of life and humor. His experiences among them inspired *Living*, published in 1929.

That same year, Green married Mary Adelaide Biddulph, with whom he had a son, Sebastian, born in 1934. From 1931 to 1938, Green continued to build his business career and wrote *Party Going*, a reflection of his London social circle. War rumblings in 1939 moved Green to join the Auxiliary Fire Service, in which he served during World War II. The war years proved to be productive for Green; in addition to *Pack My Bag*, a sort of autobiography published in 1940, he wrote three unique war novels, *Caught*, *Loving*, and *Back*.

The war's conclusion returned Green to the directorship of his business and a busy decade of writing (during his lunch hour and after dinner every night). In the 1950's, Green began refining his theories of communication and art, which he published in essay form, delivered in a series of British Broadcasting Corporation broadcasts, and restated in three interviews. While on a cruise to South Africa in 1958, Green decided to retire from business.

No one has been able to account for Green's almost total silence for the remainder of his life. Until his death on December 13, 1973, he published only "An Unfinished Novel" and "Firefighting." His sequel to *Pack My Bag* was unfinished. With increasing deafness, Green withdrew more and more into the privacy of his home and family, leaving behind a literary legacy rich in its suggestiveness.

ANALYSIS

The ambiguous nature of Henry Green's fiction has long piqued and captivated the attention of readers and critics alike, for his individual departures from conventional narrative technique separate him from the literary mainstream. A successful businessman independent of popular success, Green felt free to experiment with the form and theory of the novel. His novels speak directly to the reader with minimal interruption or interpretation; taking on lives of their own, they maintain their own shifting realities and sustain an uncanny sense of the present.

Evident in his novels as early as *Blindness* are characteristics that Green was to polish throughout his writing career: close attention to balance and symmetry, objectivity in character presentation, action developed through juxtaposed scenes, and remarkable re-creation of spoken

English interspersed with lyrical descriptive passages. His singular treatment was given to classical themes. Fascinated by language and the human capacity to interpret, Green dramatized the problems of communication by having his characters misunderstand one another. He further complicated these problems of understanding by creating intentional verbal ambiguity, so that the reader might also be uncertain of the speaker's intent. Often talking at cross purposes, Green's characters, prompted by loneliness, search for love. Although their love objects may at times seem strange, ranging as they do from peacocks and a pig to houses and fantasies, they nevertheless reflect the range of human passion. In an atmosphere suggestive of social dissolution, Green's characters pursue the relative stability of love, which they often discover in unsuspected places.

Most of Green's solipsistic characters are neither intelligent, gifted, nor particularly beautiful. Often vain and fanciful, they reveal themselves to be profoundly human as they engage in conversations revelatory of their own preoccupations. Fascinated by what people communicate through both speech and evasion, Green sought to make dialogue the vehicle for his novels, refining his conversation and decreasing his descriptive passages until, in his last two novels, dialogue carries almost the entire weight. To avoid the static quality of conversation, he created brief scenes, shifting his reader's attention from one group of characters to another. His technique also produces an acute sense of the present, a sense emphasized by the "ing" ending of his novels' titles.

That Green's novels create their own sense of the present is only one of several important factors to be considered when reading his fiction. Above all, Green wanted his work to assume a life of its own, a life differing according to the reader, providing each one with a sense of connection until he or she is drawn into a "community of people." Green accomplishes this primarily by suggesting rather than stating. Time and place, motivation and reaction, action and resolution are often evoked rather than delineated. Behind the slight plots and often silly activities is an unstated social context that tacitly influences action. Green's characters are also created through indirection. By allowing them to inarticulately express their obsessions, fears, anxieties, or confusion, by having them avoid direct responses, by refusing to make authorial judgments, Green populates his novels with lifelike creations. Their humanness is mutely expressed in their search for love. Examining *Blindness*, *Loving*, and *Nothing* with these ideas in mind, the reader can begin to understand Green's elusive art.

Blindness

When Green had a family friend read the manuscript of *Blindness*, he did not receive much praise. He was, however, encouraged to show his work to Garnett, then a publisher's reader, who gave Green sound advice concerning narrative technique and character development. The result is a first novel remarkable primarily for its close attention to structure and its multidimensional characters. While taking a usual avenue for a first novel, Green proceeded to treat his subject with daring. His protagonist, John Haye, a sensitive upper-middle-class schoolboy who aspires to be a writer, is blinded in a freak accident. During the course of the novel, John comes to new terms with himself and his world, awakening in the end to a fresh appreciation of life.

With the theme of growth in mind, Green divided *Blindness* into three sections—"Caterpillar," "Chrysalis," and "Butterfly"—suggesting John's psychological metamorphosis. "Caterpillar," presented as John's diary, reflects his physical response to natural beauty, his passion for literature, and his concentrated ambition to write. Because John derives intense pleasure from visual stimuli, his blindness seems especially cruel. In "Chrysalis," he reconsiders himself. As he lies dormant in layers of a protective cocoon—his bandages, his blindness, his fantasies and self-pity, his stepmother's pity and worry, the physical safety of his inherited estate—his creative life is threatened until he determines to break free of this smothering safety. He emerges in "Butterfly" scarred but acutely aware of the value of life.

The narrative passages of *Blindness* are lush, as exuberant as John's imagination, as soaring as his emotions. Echoing with poetic resonance, Green's descriptive passages in *Blindness* far outweigh the oblique dialogue. Nevertheless, there are signs of Green's later mastery of dialogue: Speech patterns are distinct for each character. The language is spare, with internal monologues reflective of individual character. John's thoughts are full of wonder and pain, his stepmother's are busy with seemingly dissociated concerns. Both characters' thoughts, however, circuitously return to one subject: blindness. Where Green introduces rich visual images through John's eyes in the first portion of the novel, he later confines John's responses to those of touch and sound. Indeed, the novel ends in a cacophony of bells and traffic noises, affirming John's rebirth.

Green seems precocious in his handling of the symbolic value of blindness. This he does by indirectly comparing John's blindness with various metaphorical failures of vision. Mrs. Haye, John's horsey stepmother, is "blind" in a number of respects, lacking all aesthetic response and being completely unintellectual. Two other figures are also introduced to indicate forms of moral blindness: Joan Entwhistle and her father, an unfrocked minister. They epitomize the destructiveness of self-deception, a potential trap awaiting John. Joan, a dirty, dreamy girl who vacillates between romanticizing her situation and luxuriating in its squalor, becomes an unlikely love interest for John, who re-creates her in his imagination and renames her June. Worse still is Joan's father, who wallows in gin and self-pity. Like John, he thinks of himself as a writer, but his only creation is his disastrous life. Ultimately, Reverend Entwhistle has entered a darkness far more profound than John's.

While blindness carries much of the novel's symbolic weight, other images are also alluded to by Green, images that continue to reappear throughout his career, often assuming symbolic value. References to birds, birds' songs, and patterns of birds' flights recur throughout his novels. In *Blindness*, birds provide an oblique comment on human situations. Flowers, particularly roses, are also recurring images in Green's fiction. Their value varying according to the novel, they generally connote love.

While the language and images of *Blindness* are vivid and memorable, it is the characters who are the novel's main strength. Green's impressive talent has created four main characters whose distinct speech and thought patterns and conflicting desires he has woven into a narrative tapestry with perspective, texture, density, and dimension. Arranged in contrasting couples—John and Mrs. Haye, Joan and Reverend Entwhistle—Green plays his characters against one another, in pairs and individually, using this arrangement to illustrate mutual misunderstandings. John and Joan, who have much in common, are first drawn together and then move apart. For purely selfish reasons, each tries to impose a fantasy on the other. John imaginatively re-creates Joan, raising her from a lowly social position. Joan, in turn, sees John as a means of escape, though in the end she prefers her fantasy to reality.

Mrs. Haye and the Reverend Entwhistle are also contrasting figures. The minister, capable of the kind of aesthetic response that John admires, has, however, succumbed to self-delusion. Significantly, the Reverend Entwhistle has scarred Joan. Mrs. Haye, on the other hand, wants to protect John. As guardian of his estate (Barwood), she sees it as her duty to manage his inheritance. When John rejects Barwood, indicating a changing social order, Mrs. Haye reluctantly supports the decision although this means abandoning a comfortable home and secure social role. Rough and tweedy, Mrs. Haye is a triumph of characterization as she awkwardly assumes a maternal role for which she is unfit. She is spared from caricature by Green's ability to portray her confused, rambling feelings through indirection.

Loving

Through three successive novels, Green continued to experiment with narrative technique and character development. In *Loving*, he achieved a balance that has continued to impress readers and critics. Skillfully arranging themes, images, symbols, and characters in the form of a fairy tale and placing them in neutral Ireland during the London Blitz, Green created what is considered to be his finest novel.

Green's setting, "the most celebrated eighteenth-century folly in Eire that had still to be burned down," is ideal for bringing together upper and lower classes and for elaborating favorite themes. Social dissolution, the search for love, and the inability to communicate are intensified by the distant war, which threatens and thus influences all of the characters. Most discomforting is the seeming collapse of the social order. From Raunce the footman's bold takeover of the butler's position to the mingling of the cook's nephew with the owner's granddaughters, the reader is presented with evidence of accelerating social change. Indeed, real power has gravitated to the servants, whose departure would mean disaster for the house and its owners, significantly named Tennant. Far from thinking of leaving, however, most of the servants are intent on pursuing their respective passions, all of which are forms of loving.

Green pays careful attention to balance, transition, and symbol in *Loving* as he encircles the lives of his characters. Beginning and ending with a love moan, having as its center a lost ring, and moving its main characters, Edith and Raunce, in a circular direction, this novel revolves around various love relationships. Thus, *Loving* is rich in extravagant description; only in *Concluding* does Green's language achieve *Loving*'s visual opulence. The color and detail that Green accords his gilded setting underscore its anachronistic existence and lend a sense of high comedy to the human activities taking place. Suggestive images recur throughout the novel, serving as transitional devices and assuming symbolic power. This is especially true of the peacocks and doves that stride and flutter through the action, symbolizing pride and love.

Dialogue in *Loving* is as important as narrative description, with Green seeming at times to be showing off his celebrated ability to create colloquial language. Each of the servants has a particular speech pattern, so peculiar that understanding can be a problem between them. Paddy, the single Irishman employed by the Tennants, speaks so unintelligibly that only Kate, who loves him, can understand what he says. Raunce, who acts as mediator between the servants and the Tennants, uses two different languages. Of course, the Tennants speak in the cultured tones of their class. Not surprisingly, Mrs. Tennant cannot understand what her servants are saying. Indeed, one of the high comic scenes of the novel occurs when she attempts to converse with her cook, who carries on about drains while Mrs. Tennant interrogates her about a ring.

The characters of *Loving* are to a large extent created by their language. Raunce is finely drawn, a complex of contradictory, even mysterious habits. He is a transparent manipulator who rudely asserts his authority over the other servants, and he is, apparently, a dutiful son who faithfully writes to his mother and sends money. A petty thief and would-be blackmailer, Raunce eventually becomes a father figure for a young servant and Edith's trembling lover. While Edith lacks the many facets of Raunce, she is fully realized as the most loving and beloved character in this novel. A dreamy girl believing in the power of love potions, she sheds her fantasies in favor of practical possibilities. Even minor characters achieve distinction in this novel; through wonderfully individualized conversations, Green dramatizes the manifold nature of loving.

Although he had consistently accorded dialogue a prominent role in all of his novels, Green came to believe that pure dialogue, with minimal authorial direction, would constitute the novel of the future. Accordingly, he wrote *Nothing* and *Doting*, which, while bearing familiar Green themes and characters, progress almost entirely through conversation. Again, the unelaborated social background is an important influence. In fact, it may have as much significance in *Nothing* as any other narrative component.

Nothing

While *Nothing* seems to be about very little, involving as it does a love chase among selfish people, it nevertheless implies a great deal. To ignore the subtext of this novel is to miss Green's point, for although he might not have used the term, *Nothing* can be seen as a phenomenological novel, with subjective judgments excluded in order to show reality as it is. Revealed is a protean shield of manners concealing a moral vacuum, the ultimate hollowness of polite society. Green, however, withholds judgment even as he lends a comic ambience to his characters. Thus, whatever judgment is accorded to the themes and characters of this novel will be imposed only by the reader.

The themes of *Nothing* are on a continuum with those of *Blindness*. The social erosion marked by John Haye's departure from his estate is now complete in the almost classless society of the welfare state. Little remains of the upper-middle-class characters' inheritance except memory, and the children of this once privileged class consider themselves lucky to have dull civil service jobs. Aware of the passing of time, Green's characters turn to one another. The result is a comedy of manners involving six characters—John Pomfret and his daughter, Mary; Jane Weatherby and her son, Philip; Liz Jennings, John's mistress; and Dick Abbot, Jane's escort—that provides an opportunity for Green to demonstrate his ability to write ambiguously frothy conversation that reveals the intellectual and emotional shallowness of his characters and the absurdity of their lives.

At the heart of this novel is Jane Weatherby, one of Green's most effective creations, who, having determined to marry John Pomfret, skillfully arranges the lives of other people in order to achieve her ends. A study in calculating graciousness, Jane manages to retain the admiration of friends and verbally dispatch her enemies in the same breath. Though her methods are suspect, they remain undetectable, her intent double-edged. Consequently, Jane wins her man, a prize of dubious value and yet one wholly satisfying to her. The ironic justice of these two characters winding up with each other is not lost on the reader.

While *Nothing* was not Green's last novel, it can be read as a final statement, for he extends his theory of the novel to its logical conclusion. This work exemplifies what Green called the "nonrepresentational novel," a novel "which can live in people who are alive" and "which can die." More than its predecessors, *Nothing* demands the conscious collaboration of its readers. Even with active participation in the novel's present, ambiguities abound. This is just as Green would have wished, because he wanted his novels to evoke a sense of life's texture, a texture he felt was fluctuating constantly. *Nothing*'s moral ambiguity, often cited as its principal flaw, is a significant part of this texture. Creating as it does a palpable sense of life's mutability, *Nothing* perfectly embodies Green's oblique, distinctive approach to the art of fiction.

Karen Carmean

Other major works

NONFICTION: *Pack My Bag: A Self-Portrait*, 1940.

MISCELLANEOUS: *Surviving: The Uncollected Writings of Henry Green*, 1992 (Matthew Yorke, editor).

Bibliography

Bassoff, Bruce. *Toward "Loving": The Poetics of the Novel and the Practice of Henry Green*. Columbia: University of South Carolina Press, 1975. This lengthy study offers a complex, important discussion of Green's theory of "nonrepresentational fiction." His sparse prose, reaching its epitome in *Loving*, requires readers to participate imaginatively in the creation of the fiction. Green's novels show how a postmodernist fiction writer avoids the evaluative, determining narrator at the center of realistic fiction.

Cavaliero, Glen. "A Manner of Speaking: Elizabeth Bowen and Henry Green." In *The Alchemy of Laughter: Comedy in English Fiction*. New York: St. Martin's Press, 2000. Cavaliero includes Green's novels in his examination of comedy in English novels, in which he points out the parody, irony, satire, and other types of humor in these fictional works.

Gorra, Michael Edward. *The English Novel at Mid-Century: From the Leaning Tower*. New York: St. Martin's Press, 1990. Examines the twentieth century novel, with discussions of Green, Anthony Powell, Graham Greene, and Evelyn Waugh. Includes bibliographical references and an index.

Holmesland, Oddvar. *A Critical Introduction to Henry Green's Novels*. New York: St. Martin's Press, 1985. Each of Greene's novels is analyzed in this critical examination of his work. Holmesland defines Green's originality by stressing the similarity of his "dynamic visualization and the effect of film."

Lucas, John. "From Realism to Radicalism: Sylvia Townsend Warner, Patrick Hamilton, and Henry Green in the 1920's." In *Outside Modernism: In Pursuit of the English Novel, 1900-30*, edited by Lynne Hapgood and Nancy L. Paxton. New York: St. Martin's Press, 2000. A reevaluation of Green's works is included in this examination of English novels that were not defined as modernist works when they first appeared. These books are analyzed from the perspectives of postmodern, feminist, Marxist, queer, and cultural theories.

MacKay, Marina. "The Neutrality of Henry Green." *Modernism and World War II*. New York: Cambridge University Press, 2006. MacKay analyzes Green's novels and works by other British authors that appeared during World War II, when modernism was in its decline as an influential literary movement. Pays particular attention to *Caught*, *Loving*, and *Party-Going*.

Mengham, Rod. *The Idiom of Time: The Writings of Henry Green*. New York: Cambridge University Press, 1982. Studies Green's novelistic development from his first novel in 1926, heavily influenced by Gertrude Stein, through his unfinished novel in 1959, which made him stop writing in fear that he was repeating himself.

North, Michael. *Henry Green and the Writing of His Generation*. Charlottesville: University of Virginia Press, 1984. Explores the personal and thematic links between Green and his major literary contemporaries: Evelyn Waugh, Anthony Powell, Stephen Spender, and Christopher Isherwood. The most important tie is a sense of alienation engendered by strong political ideologies, such as fascism and communism. These writers explore the problem of asserting the identity of the individual self in a hostile social environment.

Odom, Keith C. *Henry Green*. Boston: Twayne, 1978. Provides a useful biographical-critical study for the beginning student. After introductions to Green's life, fictional theory, and characteristic style, the book offers insightful reading of each novel, concluding with an estimate of Green's importance and influence.

Russell, John. *Henry Green: Nine Novels and an Unpacked Bag*. New Brunswick, N.J.: Rutgers University Press, 1960. An enthusiastic study of Green. Offers numerous examples of Green's stylistic puzzles, poetry, enigmas, and sleights-of-hand, paying special attention to his autobiography as a source of Green's philosophy of art and life.

Treglown, Jeremy. *Romancing: The Life and Work of Henry Green*. New York: Random House, 2000. A biography that integrates information about Green's life with analysis of his novels and autobiography. Treglown maintains that the author's identity was split between that of Henry Yorke, his real name, and that of Henry Green, his pen name.

JULIEN GREEN

Born: Paris, France; September 6, 1900
Died: Paris, France; August 13, 1998
Also known as: Julien Hartridge Green

Principal long fiction

Mont-Cinère, 1926 (*Avarice House*, 1927)
Adrienne Mesurat, 1927 (*The Closed Garden*, 1928)
Léviathan, 1929 (*The Dark Journey*, 1929)
L'Autre Sommeil, 1931 (*The Other Sleep*, 2001)
Épaves, 1932 (*The Strange River*, 1932)
Le Visionnaire, 1934 (*The Dreamer*, 1934)
Minuit, 1936 (*Midnight*, 1936)
Varouna, 1940 (*Then Shall the Dust Return*, 1941)
Si j'étais vous, 1947 (*If I Were You*, 1949)
Moïra, 1950 (*Moira*, 1951)
Le Malfaiteur, 1955 (*The Transgressor*, 1957)
Chaque homme dans sa nuit, 1960 (*Each in His Darkness*, 1961)
L'Autre, 1971 (*The Other One*, 1973)
Le Mauvais Lieu, 1977
Les Pays lointains, 1987 (*The Distant Lands*, 1990)
Les Étoiles du sud, 1989 (*The Stars of the South*, 1996)
Dixie, 1995

Other literary forms

Julien Green first drew critical attention in the late 1920's as a writer of short fiction (*Le Voyageur sur la terre*, 1930; and *Les Clefs de la mort*, 1927) before attempting the longer narratives that became his forte. Green, however, is almost as well known for his autobiographical works as for his novels. His *Journal*, begun in 1928, has appeared in eighteen volumes published between 1938 and 2006 (partial translations in *Personal Record, 1928-1939*, 1939, and *Diary, 1928-1957*, 1964); a second series, begun in 1963, is more personal and frankly confessional in tone: *Partir avant le jour* (1963; *To Leave Before Dawn*, 1967), *Mille chemins ouverts* (1964; *The War at Sixteen*, 1993), *Terre lointaine* (1966;

Love in America, 1994), and *Jeunesse* (1974; *Restless Youth, 1922-1929*, 1996). An additional volume, *Memories of Happy Days* (1942), was written and published in English during Green's self-imposed wartime exile in the United States.

Encouraged by Louis Jouvet to try his hand at writing plays, Green achieved moderate success as a playwright with *Sud* (pr., pb. 1953; *South*, 1955), *L'Ennemi* (pr., pb. 1954), and *L'Ombre* (pr., pb. 1956), but he soon concluded that his true skills were those of a novelist. In any case, Green's plays are seldom performed and are of interest mainly to readers already familiar with his novels.

Achievements

In 1971, shortly after publication of his novel *The Other One*, Julien Green became, at the age of seventy, the first foreigner ever elected to membership in the French Academy; his election brought sudden and considerable attention to a long, distinguished, but insufficiently appreciated literary career. Green, born in France to American parents, had been writing and publishing novels in French since the age of twenty-five, attracting more critical attention in France than in the United States, despite the availability of his work in English translation. Even in France, however, his novels have not received extensive critical notice, owing in part to his work being difficult to classify.

Encouraged by the success of his earliest writings, Green lost little time in developing a characteristic mode of expression, alternately mystical and sensual, often both at once. Many critics, as if willfully blind to the erotic dimension of Green's work, sought to classify him as a "Catholic" writer in the tradition of Georges Bernanos and François Mauriac. Others, focusing on the oppressive atmosphere pervading many of his novels, sought to place Green closer to the gothic tradition. Neither classification is quite accurate, yet it was not until after Green's autobiography began to appear in 1963 that reassessment of his novels began in earnest.

Using a clear, ornament-free style that has been described as classical, Green quickly involves his readers in the solitary lives of tortured characters obsessed with the need to escape. Often, the compulsion toward escape leads to violence, madness, or death; when it does not, it produces an implied "leap of faith," which is not, however, totally satisfying to those who would see Green as a religious writer in the Catholic tradition. Even in those rare cases in which solutions are offered, it is still the problems that dominate the consciousness of author and reader alike. Endowed with keen powers of observation, Green excels in the portrayal of psychological anguish that any thoughtful reader can understand, even if he or she does not share it.

The publication of Green's autobiography beginning in the 1960's permitted at last a demystification of the novels—in Green's case, more help than hindrance. In the light of Green's frankness, many of the tortures undergone by his characters stood revealed as artistic transpositions of the author's own private anguish as he sought to reconcile his spiritual aspirations with a growing awareness of his homosexuality. Far from detracting from the power of Green's novels, such disclosures shed valuable light on his life in art, allowing critics and casual readers alike to appreciate the true nature of Green's novelistic achievement. Whatever their source, Green's novels remain powerful portraits of alienation and estrangement unmatched in contemporary French or American literature.

Biography

Julien Hartridge Green was born in Paris on September 6, 1900, the youngest of eight children. His father, Edward Moon Green of Virginia, had since 1895 served as European agent of the Southern Cotton Seed Oil Company. Green's mother, Mary Hartridge of Savannah, Georgia, dominated her son's early life with a curious blend of love and Puritan guilt; her death in 1914, instead of liberating the young Green from the tyranny of her moods and ideas, seems rather to have increased her hold upon his developing conscience. Green grew to adulthood torn between a strong, if repressed, sensuality and a mystical desire for sainthood, often equally strong. Converted to Catholicism within a year after his mother's death, he seriously considered entering a monastic order but deferred his plans for the duration of World War I. In 1917, he served as an ambulance driver, first for the American Field Service and later for the Red Cross; the following year, still (as he remained) a U.S. citizen, he obtained a commission in the French army by first enlisting in the Foreign Legion. Demobilized in 1919, he returned to Paris and soon renounced his monastic vocation, a loss that caused him considerable anguish.

Unable to decide on a career, he accepted with some reluctance the offer of a Hartridge uncle to finance his education at the University of Virginia. Enrolled as a "special student," Green read widely in literature, religion, and sociology; in 1921, after two years in residence, he was appointed an assistant professor of French. Still homesick for his native France, more at ease in French than in English, Green returned to Paris in 1922 to study art, gradually discovering instead his vocation as a writer and attracting the attention of such influential literary figures as Jacques de Lacretelle and Gaston Gallimard. By the age of twenty-five, already an established author with a growing reputation, Green had found his lifework.

During his thirties, Green read widely in mysticism and Eastern religions. Returning to the Catholic Church as early as 1939, Green was soon thereafter obliged to leave Paris by the onset of World War II. After the fall of France in 1940, he moved to the United States for the duration, teaching at various colleges and universities before and after brief service as a language instructor in the U.S. Army. Returning to Paris in September, 1945, he remained there, pursuing the life and career of a French man of letters until his death on August 13, 1998.

Julien Green. (Roger Viollet/Getty Images)

Analysis

Educated primarily in the French tradition, Julien Green brought to his novels a distinctly French concern for the presentation and development of character. Whether his novels are set in France, the United States, or elsewhere, his characters are observed and portrayed with the psychological precision that has characterized French fiction from Madame de La Fayette down through Honoré de Balzac and Gustave Flaubert to Marcel Proust. With critical and seemingly pitiless exactitude, Green takes the reader inside his characters to show their thought and motivations, achieving considerable identification even when the characters tend toward violence or madness. On the surface, few of Green's characters would appear to invite identification on the part of the reader; they tend to be misfits of one sort or another, haunted by strange fears and insecurities. It is Green's singular talent, however, to present them and their thoughts in such a way that they seem almost instantly plausible and authentic, and to hold the reader's interest in what will happen to them. Life, as particularized in Green's characters, emerges as both threat and promise, most often as a trap set for the unwary.

Typically, Green's protagonists, often female with one surviving and insensitive parent, find themselves trapped in an existence that they can neither tolerate nor understand; not infrequently, they contribute to their own misfortune through a stubborn refusal to express themselves. Even so, the reader senses that to speak their minds would render them vulnerable to even greater assaults from a hostile environment. Locked within themselves, they suffer all the tortures of an earthly hell from which they yearn to escape. In his autobiography, Green observes that a feeling of imprisonment was a recurring childhood nightmare; in his novels, the theme is enlarged to archetypal proportions, assuming the authority of fable. Green's characters, for all their particularities, emerge as highly convincing exemplars of the human condition.

Escape, for all of its apparent promise, offers no relief to the suffering of Green's characters. Adrienne Mesurat, among the most convincing of Green's early heroines, gradually retreats into madness once she has achieved through an act of violence the freedom for which she has longed; Paul Guéret, the ill-favored viewpoint character of *The Dark Journey*, strikes and disfigures the young woman whose attentions he has sought, thereafter becoming a fugitive. Manuel, the title character of *The Dreamer*, retreats from the undesirable world into a fictional universe of his own making, only to die soon thereafter. Elisabeth, the protagonist of *Midnight*, seeks to escape with her lover, only to be killed with him in a fall. Clearly, the oppressive atmosphere that stifles Green's characters is internal as well as external; like Adrienne Mesurat, they remain imprisoned even when they are free to come and go as they please. Even in the later novels, such as *The Other One*, death is frequently the only means of escape available.

The power of Green's novels derives in no small measure from the author's skill in providing motivation for the behavior of his characters. In the case of Adrienne Mesurat, for example, Green quickly and convincingly shows normal desire stifled by silence until it becomes first an obsession, then true madness. Philippe Cléry, the main viewpoint character of *The Strange River*, passes the age of thirty before being obliged to examine his life; thereafter, he becomes most convincingly self-conscious, questioning his every move in an authentically ineffectual way. Sympathetic or not (and most are not), Green's characters are inescapably human and believable, commanding the reader's identification; although they seem to exist in a world of their own, they are unmistakably drawn from life, the products of Green's keen powers of observation.

It is possible, that, had Green not been reared in a time less tolerant than the twentieth century, his novels might never have come into being. Arguably, Green's expression has responded somewhat to the temper of the times, dealing more and more openly with homosexual attraction in such novels as *The Transgressor*; indeed, by the time Green wrote and published his autobiography in the 1960's, his revelations seemed less scandalous than timely and enlightening. The restraint that helped to shape his earlier works was in a sense no longer necessary. It seems likely, moreover, that the writing of the autobiographical volumes lessened the sense of creative urgency that marks the best of Green's earlier writing. In fact, Green's later novels (*Le Mauvais Lieu* in particular), while still holding the reader's attention, cover little new ground and move perilously close to self-parody.

THE CLOSED GARDEN

Green's second novel, *The Closed Garden*, written and published within a year after the success of *Avarice House*, ranks among his best and is perhaps the most memorable. Refreshingly normal at the start of the novel, eighteen-year-old Adrienne quickly erodes into madness and amnesia as a result of the stifling circumstances of her life. Recently out of school (the time is 1908), she lives in a provincial French town with her retired father and her thirty-five-year-old spinster sister, Germaine. A chronic invalid whose illness their autocratic father refuses even to recognize, Germaine rules over Adrienne with the authority of a mother but with none of the attendant love. As in Green's *Avarice House*, kinship is no guarantee of understanding or even friendship; indeed, the family emerges as perhaps the most inimical and threatening of human institutions. Using heavy irony, Green shows Adrienne's daily interaction with her hostile relatives; the reader, privy to Adrienne's innermost thoughts, looks on with horror as she is repeatedly unable to express them.

At the start of the novel, Adrienne is looking with healthy scorn at a group of family portraits to which she inwardly refers as "the cemetery," concluding with some satisfaction that her own features place her on the "strong" side of the family. Dressed as a servant, she is doing the family housework, exhibiting physical strength by moving heavy furniture with ease. It is precisely such apparent strength that will soon prove to be her undoing, as it turns inward upon herself, accomplishing in several weeks a deterioration that otherwise might take years. Deprived of normal human companionship, Adrienne becomes infatuated with a neighboring physician, Dr. Maurecourt, whom she has seen but once; such adolescent passion, harmless enough at face value, functions rather in Green's universe as an instrument of destruction. Adrienne, unable to confide to her father or sister the relatively innocent causes of her slightly irregular behavior, retreats further and further into her fantasy with each new demand for an explanation.

Steadfastly refusing to name the object of her secret passion, she soon finds herself literally locked up in the house, forbidden to leave but still dreaming of escape. Ironically, it is the nearly bedridden Germaine, rather than the healthy Adrienne, who in fact does manage to escape the father's tyranny, sneaking out of the house with Adrienne's help in order to seek refuge in a convent near Paris. Germaine's departure triggers a rare and violent dispute between Adrienne and her father, who reveals that he, like Germaine, has guessed the identity of Adrienne's lover. Overcome with shame and grief, Adrienne runs toward her father and pushes him downstairs; she is never quite sure whether she intended to kill him. In any case, he dies, and although Adrienne is never formally charged with his murder, she is eventually convicted of the crime by the tribunal of malicious gossip. Indeed, the entire village soon takes on the sinister aspect of Adrienne's now-absent family, hemming her within a circle of watchful and accusing eyes.

A brief attempt at leaving the village finds Adrienne drifting aimlessly from one provincial town to another, beset by nightmares as she sleeps fitfully in seedy hotels, imagining that she is being watched. Returning home to live among her tormentors, she falls physically ill; Dr. Maurecourt is summoned, and at the end of a lengthy and difficult conversation, she blurts out her unrequited love for him. Maurecourt, a frail widower of forty-five, is understandably nonplussed; with genuine compassion, he explains to Adrienne that he is mortally ill, having hardly more than a year left to live, while she, Adrienne, has her whole life ahead of her. For all practical purposes, however, Adrienne's life is as good as over; she again leaves the house, intending to escape but succeeding only in wandering aimlessly about the town until she is found suffering from amnesia.

Like other novels and plays of the period—John O'Hara's *Appointment in Samarra* (1934) and Jean Cocteau's *La Machine infernale* (1934; *The Infernal Machine*, 1936) come readily to mind—*The Closed Garden* is the carefully recorded history of what can happen to a human life and mind when everything possible goes wrong. Subjected to torture such as might be inflicted upon a steel rod in laboratory tests, Adrienne's mind eventually snaps. Until very near the end, however, Adrienne remains painfully lucid, aware of all that is happening to her yet powerless to stop it. Unlike such characters as O'Hara's Julian English and Cocteau's Oedipus, Adrienne seems singularly undeserving of her cruel fate; neither arrogant nor thoughtless, she seems to have been chosen almost at random by unseen forces bent upon destroying her for no good reason.

The Dark Journey

The Dark Journey, Green's third novel, breaks new ground in presenting several viewpoint characters and a number of interlocking subplots. Each of the main characters, reminiscent of Balzac's provincial "monomaniacs," is governed and identified by a ruling passion, much as Adrienne Mesurat is governed by her passion for the helpless Dr. Maurecourt. The main viewpoint character, whose life provides a link among the others, is Paul Guéret, an ill-favored and unhappily married man in his thirties who is obsessed by his passion for the young and attractive Angèle. A typical Green heroine, Angèle has been thrust by circumstances into a thankless and sordid existence from which she longs to escape, presumably in the loving company of a young man her own age. A launderer by day, she moonlights by sleeping with various gentlemen who frequent the restaurant owned and operated by the insatiably curious Madame Londe. In a sense, Angèle is less prostitute than spy, engaged by Madame Londe to supply her with useful information concerning the gentlemen's private lives. Guéret, to his consternation, is excluded from Angèle's regular clientele because he is simply not interesting enough, either as a person or because of his station in life, to warrant Madame Londe's interest. Angèle, meanwhile, is flattered and at least amused by Guéret's awkward attentions, even if she cannot bring herself to return his love in kind.

Guéret, driven nearly to distraction by Angèle's flirtatiousness and inaccessibility, becomes increasingly obsessed with his need to possess the girl, and before long his obsession leads to violence. First, after a long and painful struggle to scale the wall of Angèle's building, he breaks into her room, only to find that she is not there. The next day, unable to tolerate her taunting behavior, he beats her and goes into hiding, leaving her for dead on a riverbank. Angèle survives, although disfigured for life. Guéret, meanwhile, is in fact guilty of murder, having bludgeoned to death an old man who stumbled upon his hiding place. After several months as a fugitive, he is given asylum by the bored and sadistic Eva Grosgeorge, mother of a boy he once tutored. Eventually, Madame Grosgeorge tires of Guéret and denounces him to the police against the protestations of Angèle, still convalescent, who does her best to rescue him. Unsuccessful, Angèle lapses into a dreamlike state and, like Adrienne Mesurat before her, wanders about town in what she thinks is an attempt to escape; delirious, she dies of exposure soon after being brought back to her room. Madame Grosgeorge, meanwhile, having shot herself melodramatically at the moment of Guéret's arrest, is expected to survive.

The Dark Journey differs from Green's earlier novels in both the depth and the scope of its character development. Although both Guéret and Angèle show clear lines of descent from Green's earlier protagonists, such characters as Madame Londe and the Grosgeorge couple bear witness to a broadening of Green's psychological and social observation; Eva Grosgeorge, in particular, is a most convincing grotesque, the bored and self-indulgent younger wife of a rather bovine industrialist. Guéret, the misfit, serves unwittingly as the link between these various social types, whose paths would otherwise be unlikely to cross. As elsewhere in Green's work, interpersonal love is shown to be an unattainable illusion. Guéret's passion for Angèle, among the more normal obsessions portrayed in the book, is doomed by its own intensity. Angèle, meanwhile, is too lost in her own romantic fantasies to see beyond Guéret's ugliness to her own genuine feelings toward him until it is too late for them both.

The Strange River

Less sensational in subject matter and in treatment than *The Closed Garden* or *The Dark Journey*, Green's fifth novel, *The Strange River*, remains one of his least known; nevertheless, it ranks among his best. Nearly devoid of external action or incident, *The Strange River* presents social and psychological analysis of rare accuracy and power, approaching Flaubert's ambition to write a book about "nothing." To a far greater degree than in *The Dark Journey*, Green reveals his seldom-used gifts as a social satirist, here portraying in painful detail the empty existence of the idle rich. *The Strange River* is, moreover, the only one of Green's novels to be set in Paris, where he himself resided.

As in *The Dark Journey*, Green derives considerable effect in *The Strange River* from the presentation of multiple viewpoints, primarily those of Philippe Cléry and his sister-in-law, Eliane, but not excluding that of Philippe's wife, Henriette. Philippe, rich through inheritance, suffers in his own ineffectual way the double torture of being superfluous and knowing it. As titular head of a mining company about which he knows nothing and cares even less, he need only appear (and remain silent) at monthly meetings in order to do all that society expects of him. The rest of the time, he is free to remain in his elegant apartment (he owns the building) or go for long walks dressed as the gentleman he is. At thirty-one, he is aware that his marriage has long since become as meaningless and hollow as his professional title; Henriette goes out on the town without him nearly every evening and has taken a lower-class lover to occupy the rest of her time. Their only child, ten-year-old Robert, spends most of the year out of sight and mind in boarding school; his rare presence during school vacations, when he has nowhere else to go, proves irritating to his parents and aunt, as they have no idea what to say to him. Philippe, meanwhile, unless he is out walking, usually finds himself in the company of Henriette's elder sister, Eliane, who secretly loves Philippe even as she comes to despise him for what he is.

Against such a background of silence and mistrust, Green sketches in the private thoughts and feelings of his characters, expressing the pain of existence in all of its contingency. The plot of *The Strange River*, such as it is, turns upon an incident that Philippe thinks he may have witnessed in the course of one of his long walks: A middle-aged, shabbily dressed couple appeared to be struggling on the banks of the Seine, and the woman may or may not have called out to Philippe for help. In any case, Philippe went on his way, not consulting the police until hours later. As the novel proceeds, the incident often returns to haunt Philippe with its implications.

Anticipating by some twenty-five years the central

incident of Albert Camus's *La Chute* (1956; *The Fall*, 1957), Philippe's experience disrupts the balance of a previously unexamined life; Philippe, however, is already too weak to do much of anything with what he has learned about himself. For months after the incident, he scans the papers for reports of bodies fished from the Seine; at length he finds one, and it is quite likely that he was in fact witness to a murder. In the meantime, another of his nocturnal walks has provided him with further evidence of his own cowardice; accosted by a stranger, he hands over his billfold at the merest threat of violence. Attending a monthly board meeting, he impulsively takes the floor and resigns his post, to the astonishment of his sister-in-law and wife, who fear that he has lost his mind; his life, however, goes on pretty much as before, closely observed by the lovesick spinster Eliane. Like Adrienne Mesurat, Eliane is both powerless and lucid in her unrequited love, increasingly attached to Philippe even as she begins to deduce his guilty secret concerning the couple on the riverbank.

Unlike all but one of Green's other novels (*The Other Sleep*), *The Strange River* is open-ended, leaving the main characters with much of their lives yet before them. The action is not resolved in violence, as in *The Dark Journey*, or in madness, as in the case of Adrienne Mesurat. Philippe, of course, is too weak to do much of anything except worry about himself.

Not until *The Transgressor*, written a quarter of a century later, did Green again try his hand at the sort of social satire so successfully managed in *The Strange River*; despite his skill in such portrayal, it is clear that Greene's true interest lay elsewhere, deep within the conscience of the individual. *The Strange River* is thus in a sense a happy accident; Green, in order to probe the inmost thoughts of a Philippe Cléry, had first to invent Philippe and place him against a social background. The result is a most satisfying work, rather different from Green's other novels but thoroughly successful in accomplishing what it sets out to do.

For a period after *The Strange River*, Green's novels tended increasingly toward fantasy, taking place in a real or fancied dreamworld fashioned by individual characters. It is perhaps no accident that these novels, atypical of Green's work taken as a whole, were written during the time of Green's estrangement from Catholicism, when he was reading extensively in mysticism and Eastern religions. Reconciled with the Church in 1939, Green was soon thereafter to leave France and his career as a novelist for the duration of World War II. *Moira*, the first of Green's true postwar novels, returns to the familiar psychological ground of his earliest work, going even further in its portrayal of the conflict between the mystical and the sensual.

Moira

Returning to the time and setting of his American university experience, Green presents in *Moira* the thoughts and behavior of Joseph Day, a Fundamentalist rustic who is even more of an outsider to the university life than Green himself must have been. Joseph is at odds with the school from the first day of his enrollment, horrified by the license and corruption that he sees all around him. His landlady, Mrs. Dare, smokes cigarettes and wears makeup, and his classmates discuss freely their relations with the opposite sex. His missionary zeal fueled by a truly violent temperament to match his red hair, Joseph seeks to save the souls of those around him; thus inclined, he is quite unable to see either himself or his fellows as human beings. Derisively nicknamed "the avenging angel," he burns with a white heat, quite unaware of the eroticism at its source. Early on, he unwittingly rebuffs the sexual advances of a young, male art student, who later commits suicide as a result; meanwhile, Joseph feels mysteriously drawn to the elegant, aristocratic Praileau, who has made fun of Joseph's red hair. Challenging Praileau to a fight, Joseph is so overcome by an excess of clearly sexual frenzy that he nearly kills the young man, who tells him that he is a potential murderer.

Unable to reconcile his Protestant faith with his increasingly violent feelings and behavior, Joseph confides in a fellow ministerial candidate, David Laird, whose vocation is both stronger and less temperamental than Joseph's own. David, however sympathetic, is quite unprepared to deal with the problems of his tortured friend, who proceeds toward the date with destiny suggested in the book's title. Moira, it seems, is also the name of Mrs. Dare's adopted daughter, a licentious young woman who emerges as almost a caricature of the flapper. Even before he meets the girl, Joseph is scandalized by all that he has heard about her; even so, he is quite unprepared for her taunting, loose-mouthed treatment of him.

Another apparent gay man, Killigrew, tries and fails to get close to Joseph. Joseph does, however, vividly recall Killigrew's description of Moira as a she-monster whenever thoughts of the girl invade his daydreams. At length, Joseph, having changed lodgings, returns to his room to find Moira planted there as part of a prank perpetrated upon the "avenging angel" by his classmates. Moira, of course, is a most willing accessory, her vanity piqued by the one man, Joseph, who has proved resistant to her rather blatant charms. By the time the planned seduction occurs, it is Moira, not Joseph, who believes herself to have fallen in love. In the morning, however, Joseph strangles Moira in a fit of remorse over what they have done. After burying her body without incident, he twice considers the possibility of escape but finally turns himself in to the police, who have sought him for questioning.

Despite a plot almost too tightly rigged to seem quite plausible, *Moira* ranks with the best of Green's earlier novels, showing considerable development in the depth and scope of his literary art. As in *The Dark Journey* and *The Strange River*, Green shows himself to be a shrewd and discerning observer of society and its distinctions. Characteristically, however, he remains concerned primarily with the inner workings of the human mind and emotions, and the variety of characters portrayed in *Moira* affords him ample opportunity to display his talents. Freed from taboos (both internal and external) against the depiction of homosexuality in literature, Green in *Moira* seemed to be moving toward a new, mature frankness of expression. However, the novels that he wrote after *Moira*, though explicit, fail to match that work either in suggestive power or in tightness of construction. The first novel of Green's "mature" period thus remains quite probably that period's best.

David B. Parsell

OTHER MAJOR WORKS

SHORT FICTION: *Le Voyageur sur la terre*, 1930 (*Christine, and Other Stories*, 1930).

PLAYS: *Sud*, pr., pb. 1953 (*South*, 1955); *L'Ennemi*, pr., pb. 1954; *L'Ombre*, pr., pb. 1956.

NONFICTION: *Journal*, 1938-2006 (18 volumes; partial translations in *Personal Record, 1928-1939*, 1939, and *Diary, 1928-1957*, 1964); *Memories of Happy Days*, 1942; *Partir avant le jour*, 1963 (*To Leave Before Dawn*, 1967; also known as *The Green Paradise*); *Mille chemins ouverts*, 1964 (*The War at Sixteen*, 1993); *Terre lointaine*, 1966 (*Love in America*, 1994); *Jeunesse*, 1974 (*Restless Youth, 1922-1929*, 1996); *Memories of Evil Days*, 1976; *Dans la gueule du temps*, 1979; *Une Grande Amitié: Correspondance, 1926-1972*, 1980 (with Jacques Maritain; *The Story of Two Souls: The Correspondence of Jacques Maritain and Julien Green*, 1988); *Frère François*, 1983 (*God's Fool: The Life and Times of Francis of Assisi*, 1985); *Paris*, 1983 (English translation, 1991); *The Apprentice Writer*, 1993; *Jeunesse immortelle*, 1998.

BIBLIOGRAPHY

Armbrecht, Thomas J. D. *At the Periphery of the Center: Sexuality and Literary Genre in the Works of Marguerite Yourcenar and Julien Green*. Amsterdam: Rodopi, 2007. Ambrecht compares the representation of homosexuality in the work of Green and Yourcenar, comparing their depiction of gay characters in their novels and plays. Includes a bibliography.

Burne, Glenn S. *Julian Green*. New York: Twayne, 1972. Provides a comprehensive overview of the first forty-five years of Green's career, culminating in his induction into the French Academy in 1971. Includes a bibliography.

Dunaway, John M. *The Metamorphoses of the Self: The Mystic, the Sensualist, and the Artist in the Works of Julien Green*. Lexington: University Press of Kentucky, 1978. Dunaway's study traces the sources and evolution of Green's narrative art, exploring the biographical genesis of his major fiction. Includes a bibliography and an index.

O'Dwyer, Michael. *Julien Green: A Critical Study*. Portland, Oreg.: Four Courts Press, 1997. O'Dwyer provides a biographical introduction and a critical assessment of Green's novels, short stories, plays, autobiography, journals, and other miscellaneous writings. Highlights the importance of Green's American background for a full appreciation of his work. Includes a foreword by Green.

_______. "Toward a Positive Eschatology: A Study of the Beginning and Ending of Julien Green's *Chaque homme dans sa nuit*." *Renascence* 49, no. 2 (Winter, 1997): 111-119. An analysis of *Each in His Darkness* within the context of Green's ideas about the end of the world. Examines the negative elements of Green's spiritual vision, the identical structure of the first and final chapters, and the echoes, resonances, and parallels between these two chapters.

Peyre, Henri. *French Novelists of Today*. New York: Oxford University Press, 1967. Provides a good overview of Green's career, presenting him as standing outside both the French and the American traditions from which his work derives. Includes useful readings of Green's early and midcareer fiction.

Stokes, Samuel. *Julian Green and the Thorn of Puritanism*. 1955. Reprint. Westport, Conn.: Greenwood Press, 1972. A study of Green's novels, concentrating on the various intellectual influences that help explain the spiritual background of his work. Discusses Green's use of fiction to relate the lives of individuals to the society in which they live.

GRAHAM GREENE

Born: Berkhamsted, Hertfordshire, England; October 2, 1904
Died: Vevey, Switzerland; April 3, 1991
Also known as: Henry Graham Greene

Principal long fiction

The Man Within, 1929
The Name of Action, 1930
Rumour at Nightfall, 1931
Stamboul Train: An Entertainment, 1932 (also known as *Orient Express: An Entertainment*, 1933)
It's a Battlefield, 1934
England Made Me, 1935
A Gun for Sale: An Entertainment, 1936 (also known as *This Gun for Hire: An Entertainment*)
Brighton Rock, 1938
The Confidential Agent, 1939
The Power and the Glory, 1940 (reissued as *The Labyrinthine Ways*)
The Ministry of Fear: An Entertainment, 1943
The Heart of the Matter, 1948
The Third Man: An Entertainment, 1950
"The Third Man" and "The Fallen Idol," 1950
The End of the Affair, 1951
Loser Takes All: An Entertainment, 1955
The Quiet American, 1955
Our Man in Havana: An Entertainment, 1958
A Burnt-Out Case, 1961 (first published in Swedish translation as *Utbränd*, 1960)
The Comedians, 1966
Travels with My Aunt, 1969
The Honorary Consul, 1973
The Human Factor, 1978
Dr. Fischer of Geneva: Or, The Bomb Party, 1980
Monsignor Quixote, 1982
The Tenth Man, 1985
The Captain and the Enemy, 1988
No Man's Land, 2004

Other literary forms

In addition to his novels, Graham Greene published many collections of short stories, including *The Basement Room, and Other Stories* (1935), *Nineteen Stories* (1947), *Twenty-one Stories* (1954; in which two stories from the previous collection were dropped and four added), *A Sense of Reality* (1963), *May We Borrow Your Husband?, and Other Comedies of the Sexual Life* (1967), and *Collected Stories* (1972). He also wrote plays, including *The Living Room* (pr., pb. 1953), *The Potting Shed* (pr., pb. 1957), *The Complaisant Lover* (pr., pb. 1959), *Carving a Statue* (pr., pb. 1964), and *Yes and No* (pr. 1980). With the exception of his first published book, *Babbling April: Poems* (1925), he did not publish poetry except in two private printings, *After Two Years* (1949) and *For Christmas* (1950). He wrote some interesting travel books, two focusing on Africa, *Journey Without Maps: A Travel Book* (1936) and *In Search of a Character: Two African Journals* (1961), and one set in Mexico, *The Lawless Roads: A Mexican Journal* (1939).

Greene published several books of essays and criticism, including *British Dramatists* (1942), *The Lost Childhood, and Other Essays* (1951), *Essais Catholiques* (1953), *Collected Essays* (1969), and *The Pleasure Dome: The Collected Film Criticism, 1935-40, of Graham Greene* (1972), edited by John Russell-Taylor. He also wrote a biography, *Lord Rochester's Monkey: Being the Life of John Wilmot, Second Earl of Rochester* (1974), and two autobiographical works, *A Sort of Life* (1971), carrying the reader up to Greene's first novel, and *Ways of Escape* (1980), bringing the reader up to the time of its writing. A biographical-autobiographical work, *Getting to Know the General: The Story of an Involvement* (1984), spotlights Greene's relationship with General Omar Torrijos Herrera of Panama. Four children's books are also among Greene's works: *The Little Train* (1946), *The Little Fire Engine* (1950), *The Little Horse Bus* (1952), and *The Little Steam Roller: A Story of Mystery and Detection* (1953).

Achievements

Graham Greene's style has often been singled out for praise. He learned economy and precision while working for *The Times* of London. More than anything else, he struggled for precision, "truth" as he called it, in form as well as in substance. *The Power and the Glory* won the Hawthornden Prize in 1941. Additionally, Greene's experience as a film reviewer seems to have given him a feel for cinematic technique.

What Greene's reputation will be a century hence is difficult to predict. Readers will certainly find in him more than a religious writer, more—at least—than a Catholic writer. They will find in him a writer who used for his thematic vehicles all the pressing issues of his era: the Vietnam War, Papa Doc Duvalier's tyranny over Haiti, the struggle between communism and capitalism, apartheid in South Africa, poverty and oppression in Latin America. Will these issues seem too topical for posterity, or will they prove again that only by localizing one's story in the specifics of a time and place can one appeal to readers of another time, another place?

Biography

Henry Graham Greene was born on October 2, 1904, in the town of Berkhamsted, England. The fourth of six children, he was not especially close to his father, perhaps because of his father's position as headmaster of Berkhamsted School, which Greene attended. Some of the boys took sadistic delight in his ambiguous position, and two in particular caused him such humiliation that they created in him an excessive desire to prove himself. Without them, he claimed, he might never have written a book.

Greene made several attempts at suicide during these unhappy years; he later insisted these were efforts to avoid boredom rather than to kill himself. At Oxford, he tried for a while to avoid boredom by drinking alcohol to excess each day of an entire semester. During these Oxford days, Greene met Vivien Dayrell-Browning, a young Catholic woman who had written to him of his error in a film review in referring to Catholic "worship" of the Virgin Mary. He inquired into the "subtle" and "unbelievable theology" out of interest in Vivien and concluded by becoming a Catholic in 1926. Greene married Vivien, and the couple had two children, a boy and a girl. He separated from his parents' family after the wedding and was scrupulous about guarding his own family's privacy.

In 1926, Greene moved from his first, unsalaried, position writing for the *Nottingham Journal* to the position of subeditor for *The Times* of London. There he learned writing technique, pruning the clichés of reporters and condensing their stories without loss of meaning or effect. Moreover, he had mornings free to do his own writing. When, in 1928, Heinemann accepted Greene's first novel, *The Man Within*, for publication, Greene rashly quit *The Times* to make his living as a writer.

Greene's next two novels, *The Name of Action* and *Rumour at Nightfall*, failed, and he later suppressed them. Still, in trying to understand what went wrong with these works, he discovered that he had tried to omit the autobiographical entirely; as a result, the novels lacked life and truth. He would not make that mistake again.

In 1934, Greene took the first of a seemingly endless series of trips to other parts of the world. With his cousin Barbara, he walked without maps across the heart of Liberia. Recorded in his *Journey Without Maps*, this hazardous venture became a turning point in his life. He had once thought death desirable; in the desert, he became a passionate lover of life. He came even to accept the rats in his hut as part of life. Perhaps more important for his writing, he discovered in Liberia the archetypal basis for his earliest nightmares. The frightening creatures of those dreams were not originally evil beings but rather devils in the African sense of beings who control power. Humankind, Greene came to believe, has corrupted these primitive realities and denied the inherited sense of supernatural evil, reducing it to the level of merely human evil. In doing so, humans had forgotten "the finer taste, the finer pleasure, the finer terror on which we might have built." Greene had found the basis for themes that persistently made their way into his novels.

Graham Greene. (Time & Life Pictures/Getty Images)

Greene began his great fiction with *Brighton Rock*, the publication of which, in 1938, followed a trip to Mexico that delighted him much less than the one to Africa. Nevertheless, his observations in Mexico provided the substance of what many consider his finest achievement, *The Power and the Glory*. For the reader interested in a genuine insight into the way Greene moves from fact to fiction, the travel book that emerged from the Mexican journey, *The Lawless Roads*, is very rewarding, showing, for example, how his fictional "whiskey priest" was an amalgam of four real-life priests.

With the outbreak of World War II, Greene was assigned to the Secret Intelligence Service, or MI6, as it was then called. The experience—including his work for the notorious spy Kim Philby—gave him the material for several later works, including *Our Man in Havana* and *The Human Factor*, and nurtured in him that "virtue of disloyalty" that informs his novels.

Greene ceased his writing of explicitly religious novels with *The End of the Affair* in 1951, when people began to treat him as a guru. Although his novels continued to address religious concerns, none—with the possible exception of *A Burnt-Out Case* in 1961—was a religious problem novel. Increasingly, Greene turned to political concerns in novels such as *The Quiet American* and *The Comedians*, but these concerns transcend the topical and speak more enduringly of human involvement.

In his later years, Greene slowed his production somewhat. He continued, however, to write two hundred words every morning, then corrected in great detail in the evening. His practice was to dictate his corrected manuscript into a tape recorder and send the tapes from his home in Antibes, on the French Riviera, to England, where they were typed and then returned. Greene also continued to indulge his taste for travel: He visited dictator Fidel Castro in Cuba, General Omar Torrijos Herrera in Panama, and President Ho Chi Minh in Vietnam. A full catalog of his travels would be virtually endless. Despite the reductive label critics have applied to his settings—"Greeneland"—Greene's novels have more varied settings than those of almost any other novelist, and his settings are authentic. Greene died on April 3, 1991, in Vevey, Switzerland, where he had lived the last years of his life.

Analysis

In an address he called the "Virtue of Disloyalty," which he delivered at the University of Hamburg in 1969, Graham Greene contended that a writer is driven "to be a protestant in a Catholic society, a catholic in a Protestant one," or to be a communist in a capitalist society and a capitalist in a communist one. Whereas loyalty confines a person to accepted opinions, "disloyalty gives the novelist an extra dimension of understanding." Whatever the reader may think of Greene's theory, it is helpful in explaining most of his own novels. From *The Man Within* in 1929, which justified a suicide in the face of Catholic morality's abhorrence for such an act, to *The Human Factor* forty-nine years later, which comes close to justifying treason, Greene practiced this "virtue of disloyalty."

Most of Greene's obsessions originated in his childhood. Where did the desire to be "disloyal," to play devil's advocate, arise? Certainly his serving in MI6 under the authority of Kim Philby was a factor. Greene admired the man in every way except for what appeared to be a personal drive for power. It was this characteristic of Philby that caused Greene finally to resign rather than accept a promotion and become part of Philby's intrigue. Greene later came to see, however, that the man served not himself but a cause, and all his former admiration of Philby returned. Greene continued his friendship even after Philby's treason became known. As he saw it, Philby had found a faith in communism, and he would not discard it because it had been abused by Joseph Stalin, any more than Catholics would discard a faith that had been abused by the Inquisitors or the Roman Curia.

Clearly, however, Greene's "disloyalty" or sympathy for the rebel did not originate here. It too must be traced to his childhood, to his isolation at school, where neither the students nor his headmaster father could treat him unambiguously; it can be traced also to his love of poet Robert Browning, who very early instilled in him an interest in the "dangerous edge of things," in "the honest thief, the tender murderer." It was an influence more lasting, Greene said, than any religious teaching. Religiously, however, Greene's fierce independence manifested itself when, upon conversion to Catholicism, he took the name Thomas, not after the angelic doctor but after the doubter.

Although Greene wrote in many genres, the novel is the form on which his reputation will rest. His strengths in the genre are many. Like all novelists who are more than journeymen, he returns throughout his oeuvre to certain recurring themes. Another strength is his gift for playing the devil's advocate, the dynamics that occur when his character finds himself divided between loyalties. In Greene's first novel, *The Man Within*, that division was handled crudely, externalized in a boy's attraction to two different women; in later novels, the struggle is internalized. Sarah Miles of *The End of the Affair* is torn between her loyalty to God and her loyalty to her lover. Fowler of *The Quiet American* cannot decide whether he wants to eliminate Pyle for the good of Vietnam or to get his woman back from a rival. The characters are shaded in, rendered complex by internal division.

Brighton Rock

Because he was a remarkable self-critic, Greene overcame most of his early weaknesses. He corrected an early tendency to distrust autobiographical material, and he seemed to overcome his difficulty in portraying credible women. In his first twenty-four years as a novelist, he depicted perhaps only two or three complex women: Kate Farrant of *England Made Me*, Sarah Miles of *The End of the Affair*, and possibly Ida Arnold of *Brighton Rock*. His later novels and plays, however, feature a host of well-drawn women, certainly the best of whom is Aunt Augusta of *Travels with My Aunt*. If there is one weakness that mars some of Greene's later novels, it is their prolixity. Too often in his late fiction, characters are merely mouthpieces for ideas.

Brighton Rock was the first of Greene's novels to treat an explicitly religious theme. Moreover, in attempting to play devil's advocate for *Brighton Rock*'s protagonist, Pinkie, the author had chosen one of his most challenging tasks. He made this Catholic protagonist more vicious than he was to make any character in his entire canon, yet Greene demonstrated that Catholic moral law could not condemn Pinkie, could not finally know "the appalling strangeness of the mercy of God."

Pinkie takes over a protection-racket gang from his predecessor, Kite, and must immediately avenge Kite's murder by killing Fred Hale. This murder inspires him to commit a series of other murders necessary to cover his tracks. It also leads to Pinkie's marrying Rose, a potential witness against him, and finally to his attempt to induce Rose to commit suicide. When the police intervene, Pinkie takes his own life.

Vicious as he is, with his sadistic razor slashings, his murders to cover murders, and his cruelty to Rose, Pinkie's guilt is nevertheless extenuated, his amorality rendered somewhat understandable. Pinkie's conscience had not awakened because his imagination had not awakened: "The word 'murder' conveyed no more to him than the word 'box,' 'collar,' 'giraffe.' . . . The imagination hadn't awoken. That was his strength. He couldn't see through other people's eyes, or feel with their nerves."

As with so many of Greene's characters, the explanation for Pinkie's self-destructive character lies in his lost childhood: "In the lost boyhood of Judas, Christ was betrayed." In a parody of William Wordsworth's "Ode: Intimations of Immortality" (1807), Greene said that Pinkie came into the world trailing something other than heavenly clouds of his own glory after him: "Hell lay about him in his infancy." Though Wordsworth might write of the archetypal child that "heaven lay about him in his infancy," Greene saw Pinkie in quite different terms: "Heaven was a word: hell was something he could trust." Pinkie's vivid memory of his father and mother having sexual intercourse in his presence has turned him from all pleasures of the flesh, tempting him for a while with thoughts of the celibate priesthood.

When Pinkie is seventeen, Kite becomes a surrogate father to him. Pinkie's lack of conscience, his unconcern for himself, his sadomasochistic tendencies, which early showed themselves as a substitute for thwarted sexual impulses, stand the youth in good stead for a new vocation that requires unflinching loyalty, razor slashings, and, if necessary, murder. His corruption is almost guaranteed. To say this is not to reduce the novel from a theological level to a sociological one on which environment has determined the boy's character. Rose survives somewhat the same circumstances. Pinkie's guilt is extenuated, never excused.

Pinkie, however, is not the only character in the novel on whose behalf Greene invoked his "virtue of disloyalty." Rose is a prefiguration of the unorthodox "saint" that Greene developed more subtly in his later novels, in the Mexican priest of *The Power and the Glory*, in Sarah Miles of *The End of the Affair*, and to some extent in Scobie of *The Heart of the Matter*. Like Scobie, Rose wills her damnation out of love. She is not so well drawn as Scobie, at times making her naïve goodness less credible than his, but she is motivated by selfless concern for another. When she refuses to reject Pinkie and when she chooses to commit suicide, Rose wants an afterlife with Pinkie. She would rather be damned with him than see him damned alone: Rose will show "them they couldn't pick and choose." This seems unconvincing, until one hears the old priest cite the actual case of Charles Peguy, who would rather have died in a state of sin than have believed that a single soul was damned. In her confession to the old priest, Rose learns of God's mercy and also of the "saintly" Peguy, who, like Rose, preferred to be damned rather than believe that another person had been.

One is asked, then, to be sympathetic both to a character who has willed her own damnation and to one who leads a life of thorough viciousness, to believe that the salvation of both is a real possibility. In asking for this sympathy, for this possibility, Greene is not doctrinaire. As an effective problem novelist, Greene makes no assertions but merely asks questions that enlarge one's understanding. Greene does not equate the Church with Rose's official moral teaching, suggesting that the old priest in this novel and Father Rank in *The Heart of the Matter* are as representative as the teachers of Rose and Pinkie. Still, the moral doctrine provided Greene with the material that he liked to stretch beyond its customary shape.

The Heart of the Matter

In *The Heart of the Matter*, Greene achieved the genuine tragedy that he came close to writing in many of his other novels. His protagonist, Major Scobie, is a virtuous man whose tragic flaw lies in an excess of pity. In Scobie, pity exceeds all bounds and becomes as vicious as Macbeth's ambition. His pity wrecks a marriage he had wanted to save, ruins a lover he had hoped to help, kills his closest friend—his "boy," Ali—and brings about his own moral corruption. Compared to Aristides the Just by one character and to the Old Testament's Daniel by another, Scobie becomes guilty of adultery, smuggling, treason, lies, sacrilege, and murder before he kills himself.

A late edition of the novel restores to the story an early scene between the government spy, Wilson, and Louise Scobie. Greene had written it for the original, then withdrew it since he believed that, told as it was from Wilson's point of view, it broke Scobie's point of view prematurely. When this scene is restored, Louise is seen in a more sympathetic light, and one can no longer see Scobie as hunted to his death by Louise. Though the reader still likes Scobie and is tempted to exonerate him, it is difficult to read the restored text without seeing Scobie's excess of pity for what it is.

The novel's three final, anticlimactic scenes effectively serve to reduce the grandeur of Scobie's act of self-sacrifice, showing the utter waste of his suicide and the fearful pride contained in his act. It is not that the final scenes make Scobie seem a lesser person. On the contrary, his wife and Helen are made to appear more unworthy of him: Louise with her unkind judgments about Scobie's taking money from Yusef when that very money was borrowed to send her to South Africa as she wanted, and Helen giving her body to Bagster immediately after Scobie's death. Nevertheless, the very criticism of these women makes Scobie's suicide more meaningless and even more effectively shows the arrogance of his action.

Scobie's suicide, then, is not meant to be seen as praiseworthy but rather as the result of a tragic flaw—pity. In this respect, it differs from Elizabeth's suicide in *The Man Within*. Still, though his suicide is presented as wrong, the final fault in a good man disintegrating spiritually, the reader is compelled to feel sympathy for Scobie. Louise's insistence on the Church's teaching that he has cut himself off from mercy annoys the reader. One is made to see Scobie through the eyes of Father Rank, who angrily responds to Louise that "the Church knows all the rules. But it doesn't know what goes on in a single human heart." In this novel's complex treatment of suicide, then, Greene does not use the "virtue of disloyalty" to justify Scobie's act but rather "to comprehend sympathetically [a] dissident fellow."

THE HUMAN FACTOR

The epigraph for *The Human Factor* is taken from Joseph Conrad: "I only know that he who forms a tie is lost. The germ of corruption has entered into his soul." Maurice Castle's soul is corrupted because a tie of gratitude exists between him and a Communist friend.

The Human Factor may, in part, have been suggested by Greene's friend and former superior in British Secret Intelligence, Kim Philby, although Greene had written twenty-five thousand words of the novel before Philby's defection. When Philby wrote his story, *My Silent War* (1968), Greene put the novel aside for ten years. In any case, Greene anticipated the novel long before the Philby case in his 1930 story, "I Spy," in which a young boy watches his father being whisked off to Russia after the British have detected his spying.

The Human Factor was Greene's first espionage novel since *Our Man in Havana* in 1958. Greene's protagonist, Maurice Castle, works for the British Secret Service in London and has, the reader learns halfway through the novel, become a double agent. He has agreed to leak information to the Russians to help thwart "Uncle Remus," a plan devised by England, the United States, and South Africa to preserve apartheid, even to use nuclear weapons for the purpose if necessary. Castle has not become a Communist and will not support them in Europe, but he owes a Communist friend a favor for helping his black wife, Sarah, escape from South Africa. Also, he owes his wife's people something better than apartheid.

Castle's spying is eventually discovered, and the Russians remove him from England. They try to make good their promise to have his wife and child follow, but the British Secret Service makes it impossible for Sarah to take the boy when it learns that Sam is not Castle's boy, but the boy of an African who is still alive. The novel ends in bleak fashion when Maurice is permitted to phone from Moscow and learns that his family cannot come. He has escaped into a private prison.

The Human Factor exemplifies again the "virtue of disloyalty," but even more, it demonstrates that Greene does not merely flesh out a story to embody that disloyalty. Though he does everything to enlist the reader's sympathies for Castle, demonstrating his superiority to those for whom he works, Greene ultimately condemns his actions as he condemned Scobie's. As Scobie had been a victim of pity, Castle is a victim of gratitude. In chatting with his wife, Sarah, before she learns that he has been spying, Castle defends his gratitude, and his wife agrees it is a good thing "if it doesn't take you too far." Moreover, as Scobie had an excessive pity even as a boy, Maurice Castle had an exaggerated gratitude. At one point, he asks his mother whether he was a nervous child, and she tells him he always had an "exaggerated sense of gratitude for the least kindness." Once, she tells him, he gave away an expensive pen to a boy who had given him a chocolate bun. At novel's end, when Castle is isolated in Russia, Sarah asks him in a phone conversation how he is, and he recalls his mother's words about the fountain pen: "My mother wasn't far wrong." Like Scobie as well, Castle is the most appealing character in the book, and many a reader will think his defection justified.

THE POWER AND THE GLORY

The novels considered above are perhaps extreme examples of Greene's "virtue of disloyalty," but the same quality can be found in most of his novels. In his well-known *The Power and the Glory*, for example, Greene sets up a metaphorical conflict between the powers of God and the powers of atheism, yet it is his "disloyalty" that prevents the allegory from turning into a medieval morality play. The forces of good and the forces of evil are not so easily separated. Although his unnamed priest acquires a real holiness through suffering, the author depicts him as a much weaker man than his counterpart, the atheistic lieutenant. The latter is not only a strong man but also a good man who is selflessly devoted to the people. His anti-Catholicism has its origins in his boyhood memory of a Church that did not show a similar concern for its people.

Perhaps Greene's fairness to Mexico's dusty rationalism, which he actually despised, is made clearer through a comparison of the novel with its first film version. In the 1947 motion-picture adaptation of *The Power and the Glory* directed by John Ford, which was retitled *The Fugitive*, the viewer is given a hero, the priest, played by Henry Fonda, opposed by a corrupt lieutenant.

THE QUIET AMERICAN

That writer's judgment so firmly founded on "disloyalty" also helped Greene to overcome his tendency to anti-Americanism in *The Quiet American*. While Greene is critical of the naïve and destructive innocence of the young American, Pyle, he is even more critical of the English narrator, Fowler, who is cynically aloof. In the end, Greene's "disloyalty" permits him to show Vietnam suffering at the hands of any and all representatives of the Western world.

Greene's painstaking attempt to see the other side, and to be as "disloyal" as possible to his own, animated his fictional worlds and gave both him and his readers that "extra dimension of understanding."

Henry J. Donaghy

OTHER MAJOR WORKS

SHORT FICTION: *The Basement Room, and Other Stories*, 1935; *The Bear Fell Free*, 1935; *Twenty-four Stories*, 1939 (with James Laver and Sylvia Townsend Warner); *Nineteen Stories*, 1947 (revised as *Twenty-one Stories*, 1954); *A Visit to Morin*, 1959; *A Sense of Reality*, 1963; *May We Borrow Your Husband?, and Other Comedies of the Sexual Life*, 1967; *Collected Stories*, 1972; *How Father Quixote Became a Monsignor*, 1980; *The Last Word, and Other Stories*, 1990.

PLAYS: *The Heart of the Matter*, pr. 1950 (adaptation of his novel; with Basil Dean); *The Living Room*, pr., pb. 1953; *The Potting Shed*, pr., pb. 1957; *The Complaisant Lover*, pr., pb. 1959; *Carving a Statue*, pr., pb. 1964; *The Return of A. J. Raffles: An Edwardian Comedy in Three Acts Based Somewhat Loosely on E. W. Hornung's Characters in "The Amateur Cracksman,"* pr., pb. 1975; *For Whom the Bell Chimes*, pr. 1980; *Yes and No*, pr. 1980; *The Collected Plays of Graham Greene*, 1985.

POETRY: *Babbling April: Poems*, 1925; *After Two Years*, 1949; *For Christmas*, 1950.

SCREENPLAYS: *Twenty-one Days*, 1937; *The New Britain*, 1940; *Brighton Rock*, 1947 (adaptation of his novel; with Terence Rattigan); *The Fallen Idol*, 1948 (adaptation of his novel; with Lesley Storm and William Templeton); *The Third Man*, 1949 (adaptation of his novel; with Carol Reed); *The Stranger's Hand*, 1954 (with Guy Elmes and Giorgino Bassani); *Loser Takes All*, 1956 (adaptation of his novel); *Saint Joan*, 1957 (adaptation of George Bernard Shaw's play); *Our Man in Havana*, 1959 (adaptation of his novel); *The Comedians*, 1967 (adaptation of his novel).

TELEPLAY: *Alas, Poor Maling*, 1975.

RADIO PLAY: *The Great Jowett*, 1939.

NONFICTION: *Journey Without Maps: A Travel Book*, 1936; *The Lawless Roads: A Mexican Journal*, 1939 (reissued as *Another Mexico*); *British Dramatists*, 1942; *Why Do I Write? An Exchange of Views Between Elizabeth Bowen, Graham Greene, and V. S. Pritchett*, 1948; *The Lost Childhood, and Other Essays*, 1951; *Essais Catholiques*, 1953 (Marcelle Sibon, translator); *In Search of a Character: Two African Journals*, 1961; *The Revenge: An Autobiographical Fragment*, 1963; *Victorian Detective Fiction*, 1966; *Collected Essays*, 1969; *A Sort of Life*, 1971; *The Pleasure Dome: The Collected Film Criticism, 1935-40, of Graham Greene*, 1972 (John Russell-Taylor, editor; also known as *The Pleasure-Dome: Graham Greene on Film—Collected Film Criticism, 1935-1940*); *Lord Rochester's Monkey: Being the Life of John Wilmot, Second Earl of Rochester*, 1974; *Ways of Escape*, 1980; *J'accuse: The Dark Side of Nice*, 1982; *Getting to Know the General: The Story of an Involvement*, 1984.

CHILDREN'S LITERATURE: *The Little Train*, 1946; *The Little Fire Engine*, 1950 (also known as *The Little Red Fire Engine*, 1952); *The Little Horse Bus*, 1952; *The Little Steam Roller: A Story of Mystery and Detection*, 1953.

EDITED TEXTS: *The Old School: Essays by Divers Hands*, 1934; *The Best of Saki*, 1950; *The Spy's Bedside Book: An Anthology*, 1957 (with Hugh Greene); *The Bodley Head Ford Madox Ford*, 1962, 1963 (4 volumes); *An Impossible Woman: The Memories of Dottoressa Moor of Capri*, 1975.

MISCELLANEOUS: *The Portable Graham Greene*, 1973 (Philip Stout Ford, editor).

BIBLIOGRAPHY

Bergonzi, Bernard. *A Study in Greene: Graham Greene and the Art of the Novel*. New York: Oxford University Press, 2006. Examines all of Greene's novels, analyzing their language, structure, and recurring motifs. Argues that Greene's earliest work was his best, *Brighton Rock* was his masterpiece, and his novels published after the 1950's showed a marked decline in the author's abilities.

Couto, Maria. *Graham Greene: On the Frontier*. New York: St. Martin's Press, 1988. Well-rounded approach to Greene criticism includes a discussion of the final novels and a retrospective of Greene's career. Contains an insightful interview with Greene and a selection of Greene's letters to the international press from 1953 to 1986.

Falk, Quentin. *Travels in Greeneland: The Complete Cinema of Graham Greene*. 3d ed. New York: Trafalgar Square, 2000. Guide to Greene's association with motion pictures, as a screenwriter and as a reviewer, includes discussion of the numerous adaptations of his novels to film.

Hill, William Thomas. *Graham Greene's Wanderers: The Search for Dwelling—Journeying and Wandering in the Novels of Graham Greene*. San Francisco: International Scholars, 1999. Discusses the themes of dwelling and loss in Greene's fiction, examining how Greene deals with the mother, the father, the nation, and the Catholic Church as the "ground" of dwelling.

Hoskins, Robert. *Graham Greene: An Approach to the Novels*. New York: Garland, 1999. Comprehensive look at Greene's oeuvre features individual chapters providing analysis of fourteen novels, including *Brighton Rock*, *The Quiet American*, and *The End of the Affair*. Also examines the protagonists of Greene's novels in the first and second phases of his career.

Malmet, Elliott. *The World Remade: Graham Greene and the Art of Detection*. New York: Peter Lang, 1998. Focuses on Greene's genre fiction, analyzing the narrative strategies, themes, motifs, and philosophical and theosophical meanings in the author's thrillers and detective novels. Includes bibliography and index.

Miyano, Shoko. *Innocence in Graham Greene's Novels*. New York: Peter Lang, 2006. Addresses innocence as a common theme in Greene's fiction, analyzing the different types of innocence that mark Greene's characters, such as Pinkie Brown in *Brighton Rock*, Harry Lime in *The Third Man*, and Father Quixote in *Monsignor Quixote*.

O'Prey, Paul. *A Reader's Guide to Graham Greene*. New York: Thames and Hudson, 1988. Critical overview of Greene's fiction includes an excellent introduction that serves to familiarize the reader with Greene's major themes. Supplemented by a complete primary bibliography and a brief list of critical works.

Roston, Murray. *Graham Greene's Narrative Strategies: A Study of the Major Novels*. New York: Palgrave Macmillan, 2006. Focuses on seven novels to describe the narrative strategies Greene devised to deflect readers' hostility toward his advocacy of Catholicism and to create heroic characters at a time when the traditional hero was no longer a credible protagonist.

Sheldon, Michael. *Graham Greene: The Enemy Within*. New York: Random House, 1994. Unauthorized biographer Sheldon takes a much more critical view of Greene's life, especially of his politics, than does Norman Sherry, Greene's authorized biographer (cited below). A lively, opinionated narrative. Includes notes and bibliography.

Sherry, Norman. *The Life of Graham Greene*. 3 vols. New York: Viking Press, 1989-2004. Comprehensive, authoritative account of Greene's life was written with complete access to his papers and the full cooperation of Greene's family members, friends, and the novelist himself. Includes a generous collection of photographs, bibliography, and index.

HANS JAKOB CHRISTOFFEL VON GRIMMELSHAUSEN

Born: Gelnhausen (now in Germany); March 17, 1621(?)
Died: Renchen (now in Germany); August 17, 1676
Also known as: Hans Johann Jakob Christoffel von Grimmelshausen; Samuel Greifnson von Hirschfeld

Principal long fiction

Der keusche Joseph, 1666
Der abenteuerliche Simplicissimus, 1669 (*The Adventurous Simplicissimus*, 1912)
Die Continuatio, 1669 (*The Continuation*, 1965; selections)
Dietwald und Amelinde, 1670
Lebensbeschreibung der Ertzbetrügerin und Landstörtzerin Courasche, 1670 (*Courage: The Adventuress*, 1964; also as *The Life of Courage: The Notorious Thief, Whore, and Vagabond*, 2001)
Der seltsame Springinsfeld, 1670 (*The Singular Life Story of Heedless Hopalong*, 1981; also known as *Tearaway*, 2003)
Proximus und Lympida, 1672
Das wunderbarliche Vogelsnest I, 1672
Das wunderbarliche Vogelsnest II, 1675 (*The False Messiah*, 1964)

Other literary forms

Almost everything that Hans Jakob Christoffel von Grimmelshausen (GRIHM-uhls-how-zuhn) wrote falls into the category of narrative fiction. One exception is a series of annual almanacs published between 1671 and 1675. In addition to this series, Grimmelshausen produced a special type of almanac titled *Des Abenteuerlichen Simplicissimi Ewig-währender Calender* (1671; the adventurous Simplicissimus's perpetual calendar). None of the almanacs constitutes a work of major importance, but they remain of interest to literary scholars because they contain a vast amount of information pertaining to the popular culture of the Baroque era. In *Des Abenteuerlichen Simplicissimi Ewig-währender Calender*, moreover, there is an extensive dialogue between an astrologer and the protagonist of *The Adventurous Simplicissimus* that sheds light on certain aspects of the novel's structure.

One may also find Grimmelshausen's views on a variety of mundane and spiritual matters in the twenty discussions in the two volumes of *Der satyrische Pilgram* (1666, 1667; the satiric pilgrim). Although Grimmelshausen wrote but few poems, most of which appear within the context of his novels, his poetry is of a high order, and selections from it are frequently included in anthologies of German verse.

Achievements

Hans Jakob Christoffel von Grimmelshausen's *The Adventurous Simplicissimus* is undoubtedly the greatest German novel of the seventeenth century. The work proved to be an immediate popular success, albeit not a critical one, when it was published in 1669, and Grimmelshausen extended the story by issuing a separately bound continuation in the same year. *The Continuation* was eventually incorporated into later printings of *The Adventurous Simplicissimus*, where it now supplements the five books into which the original novel was divided. Public demand, moreover, led Grimmelshausen to write a number of other sequels over the next few years. Of these continuations, *Courage*, *The Singular Life Story of Heedless Hopalong*, and the two sections of *Das wunderbarliche Vogelsnest* are particularly important. *The Adventurous Simplicissimus* and its sequels are today referred to collectively as the Simplician cycle. What distinguishes these writings from the standard German fiction of that era is that they give the reader a vivid and realistic picture of the devastation caused by the Thirty Years' War and the demoralization of the country in its aftermath. The only other novelist to write anything in a similar vein was Johann Michael Moscherosch, whose *Wunderliche und warhafftige Gesichte Philanders von Sittewald* (1643; the strange and true visions of Philander von Sittewald) contains, as one of its four parts, a section titled "Soldaten Leben" (soldier's life) that foreshadows *The Adventurous Simplicissimus* in presenting a graphic account of the disasters of war.

The literary establishment in Germany during the Baroque period favored the more aristocratic genres, such as the heroic-gallant and historical-political novels, and condemned *The Adventurous Simplicissimus* for its crudity. Eager for critical acclaim, Grimmelshausen attempted to write in the style of courtly literature and produced a pair of tedious novels, *Dietwald und Amelinde* and *Proximus und Lympida*, that embodied this alien aesthetic. These works are, however, of little interest to the modern reader; only the Simplician cycle has survived the test of time. Much of the literary distinction of *The Adventurous Simplicissimus* stems from the ingenious way that Grimmelshausen adapted the form of the picaresque novel to make it serve as a vehicle for religious content. Some critics even go as far as to refer to the novel as antipicaresque. Unlike the usual picaresque novel, there is genuine character development in *The Adventurous Simplicissimus*. Many literary historians, for this reason, regard Grimmelshausen's masterwork as a forerunner of both the bildungsroman (the novel of education) and the *Entwicklungsroman* (the novel of development).

Biography

The author of *The Adventurous Simplicissimus* could trace his descent back to a line of landed nobility that had established itself in Thuringia during the Middle Ages. In the course of the sixteenth century, however, the family gradually became impoverished, to the point that the author's paternal grandfather, Melchior Christoffel, was forced to take up the occupation of baker and innkeeper in Gelnhausen, a predominantly Lutheran town located in Hesse not far from Hanau, and even stopped using his noble surname. It was in Gelnhausen that Hans Johann Jakob Christoffel von Grimmelshausen was born.

On the basis of autobiographical remarks to be found in one of Grimmelshausen's almanacs, the year of his birth appears to be either 1621 or 1622, although subsequent scholarship places the date at or near March 17, 1621. His father, Johannes Christoffel, died a few years later, and his mother, Gertraud, soon moved from Gelnhausen to nearby Frankfurt in order to remarry, leaving her six-year-old son in the care of her father-in-law. The relationship between Melchior and his grandson was full of affection, and the character of the kindly grandfather was later depicted in fictional form in the person of the elderly hermit who plays a key role in the early part of *The Adventurous Simplicissimus*.

For six or seven years, young Grimmelshausen attended the only school in Gelnhausen, receiving, in addition to a thorough indoctrination into the Lutheran faith, extensive instruction in both music and Latin. In 1634, when he was about thirteen years of age, Gelnhausen was sacked by Croatian soldiers serving in the Imperial army. Many of the town's inhabitants, including Grimmelshausen, sought refuge in the city of Hanau for protection by the Swedish garrison stationed there. A month or so later, Grimmelshausen was captured by Croatian soldiers as he was playing outside the walls of Hanau.

His period of captivity under the Croatians was relatively brief; he soon fell into the hands of Protestant units composed of Hessians and was pressed into their service.

What happened to Grimmelshausen while he was with the Hessians is uncertain, but in 1636, at age fifteen, he found himself part of a cavalry unit in the Imperial army that was besieging the Protestant fortress of Magdeburg. He continued to serve as both a light cavalryman and a musketeer in various Catholic armies for the next few years, eventually receiving an appointment as regimental secretary to Count Hans Reinhard von Schauenburg, the commander of the imperial stronghold of Offenburg (a city near the Rhine River to the east of Strasbourg). In 1648, the year in which the Peace of Westphalia was signed, Grimmelshausen left his post with Schauenburg and served with the Bavarian army in some of the final campaigns of the war. He was discharged from military service the following year at about the age of twenty-eight, after having spent some fifteen years at war.

On August 30, 1649, Grimmelshausen married Katharina Henninger, the daughter of an officer who had served in Schauenburg's regiment. That the wedding ceremony was performed by a priest is proof of the bridegroom's formal membership in the Roman Catholic Church at the time of his marriage. Precisely when his conversion to Catholicism occurred, however, remains an unresolved issue. The marital union turned out to be a happy one, and Katharina was to have ten children over the next two decades. A week after the wedding ceremony, Grimmelshausen assumed the duties of a steward on the estate of Count Schauenburg outside the village of Gaisbach near Oberkirch. He left the employ of Schauenburg in 1660 and from 1662 to 1665 worked in a similar position at the summer residence of a Strasbourg physician. After a brief period as the proprietor of an inn in Gelnhausen called The Silver Star, Grimmelshausen accepted an appointment from the bishop of Strasbourg to serve as *Schultheiss* (mayor) in the Black Forest village of Renchen. He continued to occupy that office for the remaining nine years of his life. His last three years proved to be quite trying for him, owing to the warfare between French and Imperial forces that had engulfed the area. At one point in this conflict, he was obliged to resume military service for a time. Grimmelshausen died in Renchen on August 17, 1676, survived by his wife and six of their children.

Hans Jakob Christoffel von Grimmelshausen.

Grimmelshausen's literary career did not begin until he was nearly forty years old. In 1659, he published a German-language version of a French translation of Francis Godwin's *The Man in the Moon: Or, A Discourse of a Voyage Thither by Domingo Gonsales, the Speedy Messenger* (1638). The next year, Grimmelshausen published two satiric dream visions of his own, but his first significant works—*Der satyrische Pilgram I* and *Der keusche Joseph* (the chaste Joseph)—appeared later. It was, however, only after he became mayor of Renchen that Grimmelshausen became truly productive. In addition to publishing *The Adventurous Simplicissimus* and its sequels while at Renchen, he tried his hand at writing aristocratic fiction such as *Dietwald und Amelinde* and *Proximus und Lympida*. Except for these two heroic-gallant novels, which were published under his own name, Grimmelshausen made it a practice to conceal his authorship of fictional works by using pseudonyms that were anagrams of his full name. *The Adventurous Simplicissimus*, for example, was published under the pseudonym Samuel Greifnson von Hirschfeld. He also used eight other pseudonyms. It was not, in fact, until the middle of the nineteenth century, when interest in Baroque literature revived, that German literary scholars were able to establish the identity of the author of *The Adventurous Simplicissimus*.

Analysis

In keeping with the traditional form of the picaresque novel, Hans Jakob Christoffel von Grimmelshausen's *The Adventurous Simplicissimus* is written from the first-person point of view, and the events it relates are presented as autobiography. The protagonist narrates his life history from boyhood to early manhood against the background of the Thirty Years' War and its aftermath. The contents of the novel are highly episodic and often anecdotal in character. Even though supernatural incidents occur with some frequency, most of the narrative is realistic in tone. There is, in fact, much gross physical detail depicting the sexual escapades of the hero as well as the act of brutality committed by combatants serving on both sides of this savage conflict.

Like many other creative spirits of the Baroque era, the author of the Simplician cycle was preoccupied with opposition and contradiction. *The Adventurous Simplicissimus* is frequently described as contrapuntal in its contrast of dualities such as innocence and experience, civilian and military, Catholic and Protestant, and spiritual and mundane. Another prominent feature of the novel is its allegorical character. Although far less didactic than John Bunyan's *The Pilgrim's Progress* (1678, 1684), *The Adventurous Simplicissimus* is likewise an account of the journey of a human soul through the perils of a sinful world in a quest for salvation.

Of the various autobiographical parallels in *The Adventurous Simplicissimus*, the protagonist's conversion to Roman Catholicism is certainly the most controversial. Many scholars suspect that Grimmelshausen's own adherence to this creed was purely a matter of expediency. There is clearly much evidence in the novel to corroborate this opinion. At one point midway through the third book, Simplicius Simplicissimus informs a Protestant clergyman with whom he is debating the merits of competing Christian denominations that the doctrinal differences that separate these sects have nothing to do with the essence of Christianity. When Simplicius does finally convert to Catholicism, moreover, it is out of fear of the Devil rather than from any conviction in the absolute truth of Catholic theology.

In all likelihood, however, Grimmelshausen's impatience with doctrinal disputes manifests itself most emphatically in the visionary exhortations of the madman who believed himself to be the great god Jupiter. In one of the opening chapters of the third book, "Jupiter" prophesies that Germany will one day play host to a national leader who will unify Europe under German hegemony and convene a church council to resolve all theological differences. After that, the prophet goes on to declare, anyone who continues to foster religious dissension will do so only on pain of death. In the light of twentieth century historical experience, the idealism that inspired this utopian vision has too much in common with the goals of the Third Reich to elicit any degree of sympathy from modern readers of *The Adventurous Simplicissimus*.

Grimmelshausen's ardent desire to see religious unity restored to his homeland was a direct response to the horrendous suffering that he witnessed during the course of the Thirty Years' War. This conflict, which lasted from 1618 to 1648, had its origin in the tensions between Catholic and Protestant rulers within the Holy Roman Empire of the German nation. Although the kingdom of Bohemia was traditionally part of the domain of the Habsburg emperors in Vienna, the Bohemian nobility struck a blow for religious freedom by choosing a German prince of the Calvinist faith as their king. Imperial forces soon reestablished Habsburg control over Bohemia, but their subsequent attempt to extend Catholic domination over other areas in Germany provoked a Protestant reaction on both a national and an international level. Before long, Denmark and Sweden sent in troops to aid the beleaguered Protestant states within Germany.

The emperor's chief German ally was Bavaria, but he was also able to draw upon forces from satellite areas such as Croatia. France, despite its formal allegiance to Catholicism, consistently supported the Protestant cause out of fear that a Habsburg victory would pose a threat to its national interests and eventually intervened militarily in order to ensure continued sectarian division among the German states. The religious character of the conflict was thus diluted by political considerations. The German nobility, for its part, was likewise motivated by dynastic and property concerns. Grimmelshausen's own bitterness toward his country's rulers finds full expression in the assertion made by the prophet Jupiter, in which the promised German hero is described as depriving the nobility of its hereditary privileges altogether and instituting a parliamentary government whose membership will be composed of the two wisest men summoned from each town in all of Germany.

The Adventurous Simplicissimus

Grimmelshausen's masterwork begins with a motif that later was popular among the Romantics: The child who comes to be known as Simplicius Simplicissimus is described as having been reared in total isolation from society on a farm in a forest region known as the Spessart. His putative parents are indifferent to his education, and he therefore grows up as a simpleton who spends most of his time tending to the needs of livestock. His greatest joy is to play the bagpipes, the sound of which, he is told, will scare off the wolves that might attack the sheep under his care.

At the age of ten, the boy is forced to flee for safety into a nearby forest in order to escape from a band of marauding soldiers who were plundering the farmstead and who were sure to abduct him if he fell into their hands. To his good fortune, a hermit living in the forest befriends him. It is this hermit who names him Simplicius and attempts to educate him. Among other things, the hermit teaches him to read and write; he also succeeds in transforming the boy into a pious Christian. This tutelage comes to an abrupt end after two years, upon the death of the hermit. Utterly distraught, Simplicius wanders about aimlessly until he is captured by a group of soldiers and taken to the city of Hanau, which at that time was a Protestant stronghold under the control of Swedish forces.

The governor of the fortress is James Ramsay, a Scottish soldier of fortune in the service of the Swedish crown and the sole historical personage to appear in Grimmelshausen's novel. It is soon determined that the hermit who had come to the boy's aid was Ramsay's brother-in-law, an entirely fictional character whose surname is reported to be Sternfels von Fuchshaim and who at one time held the military rank of captain. This nobleman, already sickened by the war, decided to renounce the world altogether after his pregnant wife, Susanna, disappeared amid the turmoil of battle. Much later in the novel, Simplicius, during a visit to a spa near Strasbourg, encounters the peasant who reared him as a child and learns from him that the hermit and Susanna were his true parents. The peasant and his wife had assisted Susanna in the process of childbirth and had decided to adopt the baby after the mother died as a consequence of the dire circumstances surrounding the delivery. Ramsay, of course, has no knowledge of the fact that Simplicius is his nephew, but he takes an immediate liking to the boy and decides to make him his page. This partiality toward Simplicius, the reader is led to believe, may stem from the striking resemblance that the youth bears to his mother, the governor's sister.

Shortly after Simplicius becomes a page, a commissioner representing the Swedish war council comes to inspect the garrison of Hanau. The boy is therefore required to have a family name in order to answer properly during the roll call, and it is the governor himself who proposes that he be called Simplicius Simplicissimus because of his extreme innocence. Totally unfamiliar with the ways of the world, Simplicius is continually appalled by the un-Christian behavior of the men whom he encounters in the garrison. He proves to be so inept as a page, moreover, that the governor finally decides to make him a court jester. A scheme is thereupon concocted to derange the boy's mind in order to render him an even better buffoon than he already is. A clergyman who was a friend of the hermit discovers the plot and forewarns Simplicius of the ordeal that lies ahead. The next night, Simplicius is abducted by four men dressed like devils and is subjected to several unnerving experiences calculated to deprive him of his reason. Following the clergyman's advice, he feigns madness and allows himself to be cast in the role of fool.

Despite the indignity of having to wear a costume that makes him resemble a calf, Simplicius finds the life of a court jester much to his liking; he not only is well fed but also is able to express his unconventional thoughts quite freely. Misfortune, however, soon strikes again. A raiding party composed of Croatian soldiers who were part of the Imperial army captures Simplicius during one of his frequent strolls outside the walls of the fortress and compels him to become a stableboy for their cavalry troop.

Highly dissatisfied with his new masters, Simplicius escapes from the Croatian cavalry unit at the first opportunity and takes to stealing food from peasant homesteads in order to survive. While in a forest, he comes upon a large knapsack containing some provisions and a purse within which is a large sum of gold coins. After consuming the food, he conceals the gold coins by cleverly sewing them into his clothing. Shortly thereafter, he comes upon a witches' Sabbath being held in a wooded area and is obliged to participate. By invoking the Lord's name, however, he manages to cause the entire gathering to disappear and finds himself flying through the air immediately. When he finally descends, Simplicius discovers that he has been supernaturally transported to an open field near Magdeburg, a city that at that time was under siege by Imperial forces.

The colonel in charge of the Imperial camp to which Simplicius is eventually taken decides to keep him on as a fool after hearing the boy's story. Simplicius is, however, provided with a tutor named Ulrich Herzbruder to further his education. The tutor's son, who bears the same name as his father, becomes a steadfast friend of Simplicius. The younger Herzbruder wishes to become the colonel's secretary, a position already held by a villainous character named Olivier. In order to eliminate this threat to his position, Olivier plants evidence to make it appear that the tutor's son has stolen a valuable object from the colonel. The younger Herzbruder, now in total disgrace, would like to be able to purchase an honorable discharge from the Imperial army, and Simplicius comes to the rescue by providing his friend with the necessary sum. A short while after his son's departure, the elder Herzbruder is senselessly killed by an officer who has taken offense at a prophecy concerning his fate that was made by the clairvoyant tutor.

As Simplicius matures, he advances in rank from stableboy to dragoon and finally to elite cavalryman. Simplicius becomes part of a group of horsemen whose task it is to obtain supplies by foraging through the countryside around the Westphalian city of Soest. Military units of that day customarily lived off the land while campaigning. Dressed in the distinctive green attire of a hunter, Simplicius achieves great renown for his courage and resourcefulness and soon acquires the title of Huntsman of Soest. Simplicius considers the rich to be fair game, but he takes great pains never to exploit the poor. It is during this phase of his military career that Simplicius encounters the madman who believes himself to be Jupiter.

Another major episode that occurs at this point involves the entrapment of a villain who, dressed in a habit similar to the one worn by Simplicius, seeks to trade on his reputation as the Huntsman of Soest and has been perpetrating great crimes on the civilian populace under that disguise. The imposter is eventually captured, but when Simplicius sees how terrified the man is, he decides to spare his life. Simplicius's companions, however, insist on forcing the man to perform a degrading act involving animals and scratch up his face before releasing him. Even though there is a bright moon on this particular night, Simplicius inexplicably fails to recognize the culprit as his erstwhile companion, Olivier. Not until he encounters Olivier years later does Simplicius become aware of the identity of the imposter.

While conducting raids, Simplicius usually manages to divert much of the looted treasure to his personal coffer in the hope that this wealth might someday help him achieve his ambition to rise to the rank of officer and perhaps even to be made a member of the nobility itself. After some time, he takes this treasure to Cologne and leaves it with a merchant for safekeeping. Returning from Cologne, Simplicius is captured by Swedish forces and taken to their headquarters in Lippstadt. When the commander learns that his prisoner is the renowned Huntsman of Soest, he proposes to make him an officer in his own battalion. The offer is respectfully declined, but the captive is nevertheless granted complete freedom to move inside and outside the city after pledging not to attempt to escape. During the next six months, Simplicius devotes much time to improving his mastery of firearms and fencing, as well as to reading historical works, heroic fiction, and manuals of love. He also womanizes on a grand scale and is soon the father-to-be of several offspring. His courtship of a retired officer's daughter, however, is a case of true love. When her father catches them in bed together—although a physical union has not been consummated and the entire incident appears to have been calculated to force Simplicius into marriage—Simplicius agrees to marry the girl.

Despite the coercive character of the marriage, Simplicius is so pleased with his new situation that he agrees to become an officer in the Swedish army, and he is permitted to go to Cologne for the purpose of retrieving his fortune. The lovers, however, are destined never to see each other again. Only after the passage of many years is Simplicius able to return to the region and inquire about the fate of his bride of one month. He then learns that his wife died soon after giving birth to a male child and that the boy has been adopted by his sister-in-law and her husband. Simplicius, whose physical appearance has so altered over the years that he is not even recognized, deems it not in the best interests of the child to disrupt this arrangement and therefore decides not to reveal his identity as the child's father.

The journey from Lippstadt to Cologne proves uneventful, but once in the city, Simplicius discovers that he is unable to retrieve his treasure. The merchant to whom he entrusted his money has declared himself bankrupt and left the country. A local attorney, however, volunteers to help Simplicius recover the money. Because the legal process promises to be a protracted one, Simplicius, in order to earn enough wages to meet his living expenses, agrees to drive two noblemen to Paris in the attorney's coach. As soon as the party arrives at its destination, the coach and horses are confiscated by the authorities to settle an outstanding debt owed by the attorney, and Simplicius thus finds himself stranded in the French capital. Forced to live by hook or crook, he eventually becomes a prostitute.

Known locally as Monsieur Beau Alman, Simplicius is in great demand among well-born Parisian ladies and soon accumulates sufficient funds to enable him to return to Germany. On the way back, he suffers from an attack of smallpox that leaves his face permanently disfigured. He is, moreover, robbed of all of his money while undergoing treatment for the affliction and can find no other means of paying for his traveling expenses than to become an itinerant medicine man. Soon after he arrives in his homeland, Simplicius encounters a freebooter who turns out to be Olivier, the nemesis of the younger Herzbruder. Despite his antipathy for Olivier, he enters into a partnership with him and agrees to participate in acts of brigandage. On one of their expeditions, they are attacked by a group of six soldiers. Olivier is slain in the encounter after he kills two of them, and Simplicius is left to dispatch the other four on his own. In this way, the prophecy of the elder Herzbruder, to the effect that Simplicius would avenge the death of Olivier, is fulfilled.

Simplicius soon meets the younger Herzbruder himself and decides to accompany his good friend on a pilgrimage to the shrine of Our Lady of Einsiedeln in Switzerland. There he witnesses an exorcism and becomes so frightened of the Devil that he immediately converts to the Catholic faith. Returning to Germany, Simplicius succeeds, with the assistance of Herzbruder, in obtaining a commission as captain in the Imperial forces. His service in this new rank is, however, a brief one. His company's first engagement with the enemy ends in defeat, and Herzbruder's testicles are shot off as well. Simplicius gives up his commission in order to take care of Herzbruder, who by now is also paralyzed from the waist down. The two friends settle down at a spa near Strasbourg, and while Herzbruder is undergoing treatment, Simplicius visits Cologne and then goes on to Lippstadt.

There he learns of his wife's death and, deeply saddened by the news, returns to the spa in time to witness Herzbruder's death. Before long he runs into his foster father, Melchior, whom he recognizes by the enormous wart in the middle of his forehead, and learns the true identity of his parents. His baptismal name, moreover, proves to have been Melchior Sternfels von Fuchsheim. (This is another anagram of the author's own name.) Simplicius decides to marry a woman that he previously met at the spa, and to make her happy he buys the farm where she was born as their new homestead. His wife, who among other serious shortcomings is guilty of infidelity, gives birth to a baby that looks exactly like one of the hired hands. Both his wife and the child die soon after, from alcohol-related causes.

A widower once again, Simplicius has his foster parents move in with him and turns the management of his estate over to them. In this way, he is free to devote his time to study and meditation. Some local peasants tell him about an unusual body of water called the Mummelsee, located atop one of the highest mountains in the region. His curiosity whetted, Simplicius goes to the lake and makes contact with the water sprites that inhabit it. Their prince takes him on a journey to the center of the earth through the waters of the bottomless lake and endeavors to instruct him in religion and philosophy. After being given a tour of the subterranean realm, Simplicius is returned to the earth's surface, and he once again consecrates himself to his studies.

Swedish forces, however, overrun the region, and their colonel offers to make him a lieutenant colonel under his command. Simplicius accepts and accompanies the colonel to Livonia for the purpose of recruiting a new regiment. The project fails, and the two men go on to Moscow in the hope of obtaining high military positions in the Russian army. After many adventures in Russia and Asia, Simplicius returns to Germany to find that the war has ended; he decides to renounce the world by becoming a hermit and living in a high mountain range that is part of the Black Forest.

Much of what Simplicius learns about life in the course of the novel is foreshadowed in a dream that he has shortly after the death of his hermit mentor. He dreams that all of the trees in the forest in which he dwells are magically transformed into hierarchical symbols of society. At the top of each tree sits a cavalier and below him are branches consisting of groups of soldiers neatly divided according to rank. There is a constant effort among these individuals to rise to higher branches where they would be able to receive greater exposure to rain and sunshine. The roots of the trees are made up of common people—craftsmen and peasants whose labors support the entire social order. At one point in the dream, the forest merges into a single tree on top of which sits the war god, Mars.

In the course of the novel, Simplicius plays several roles in this hierarchy, but at every level the motive forces are lust, greed, and social ambition. Having spent his boyhood in a state of extreme innocence, Simplicius must experience the full measure of the busyness of society before he can bring himself to renounce worldly vanities for a life of piety. When he informs his foster father of his intention to join a community of Hungarian Anabaptists whose simple lifestyle he has come to admire, Melchior cautions Simplicius to remember that there are no honest men. Simplicius thereupon makes his decision to forgo human companionship entirely and to commune with God in the solitude of the forests.

The novel ends with a lengthy adieu to the world that is taken verbatim from a German translation of a work by the Spanish moralist Antonio de Guevara. Grimmelshausen lays the ground for a continuation of Simplicius's story by having his protagonist remark: "Whether I will be able to persevere to the end, as my blessed father did, remains to be seen."

THE CONTINUATION

The Continuation (or book 6 of *The Adventurous Simplicissimus*) begins with Simplicius reporting how his ardor for the life of an anchorite gradually diminished after a few months. He therefore sets out on a pilgrimage to the holy places at Loretto and Rome. After unexpectedly coming into possession of some gold coins, Simplicius persuades himself to go on to Jerusalem as well, but he is captured by robbers in Egypt while en route to Palestine. These robbers exhibit him as a wild man until he is rescued by a party of Europeans. The Middle East has in the meantime become engulfed in war, and Simplicius therefore decides to return to Europe in a large Portuguese galleon via the Cape of Good Hope. Somewhere in the vicinity of Madagascar, the vessel is wrecked in a storm, and only Simplicius and the ship's carpenter manage to reach the shores of a nearby island.

The island proves to be uninhabited but bountiful. Before long, an Abyssinian woman drifts ashore in a box and volunteers to become their cook. She promptly connives with the carpenter to kill Simplicius. The Lord causes her to disappear, however, when Simplicius makes the sign of the cross over his food and asks for divine blessing. The two men are then reconciled, but the carpenter dies an early death as a consequence of his addiction to palm wine. Simplicius resumes the contemplative life of a hermit and finally attains peace of mind. When a Dutch sea captain stops at the island and offers to take Simplicius back to Europe, the offer is declined. Before the captain departs, Simplicius presents him with some palm fronds on which he has recorded his life story; the sea captain later publishes these writings. The memoirs of Simplicius thus come to a formal end.

The Continuation is, for the most part, a worthy supplement to the five books of the original edition of *The Adventurous Simplicissimus*. The effect of the narrative is to intensify the inner struggle experienced by the protagonist in his quest to achieve spiritual salvation. The episode on the island was, incidentally, in no way inspired by Daniel Defoe's *Robinson Crusoe* (1719), a work that first made its appearance fifty years later. An earlier English prototype for Grimmelshausen's "Robinsonade" may, however, be found in the widely translated novel by Henry Nevil titled *The Isle of Pines* (1618).

Courage

The next two sequels to *The Adventurous Simplicissimus* are *Courage* and *The Singular Life Story of Heedless Hopalong*. Both Courage and Springinsfeld are characters who make brief appearances in *The Adventurous Simplicissimus*. Although Grimmelshausen never referred to her by a specific name in the earlier work, Courage turns out to be one of the women of easy virtue with whom Simplicius slept with at the spa in the Black Forest when he was caring for the younger Herzbruder. After Simplicius had married for the second time, Courage left a baby at his doorstep, along with a written message identifying Simplicius as the father of her illegitimate child. In *Courage*, she confesses that the child was not hers at all but that of her maid, who had exchanged sexual favors with an unknown gentleman for a modest sum of money. It is clear that Courage made her allegation against Simplicius out of pure spite for his having jilted her and that her sole intent was to cause problems for her former lover, both with the authorities and with his wife.

Courage's own story begins in 1620, in Bohemia, when she is a thirteen-year-old girl named Libuschka, and ends fifty years later, when she is part of a Gypsy band whose chieftain is her husband. Over this time span, she manages to marry five army officers and a musketeer, as well as to engage in sex for pleasure and profit with a multitude of other men. She acquires the nickname Courage after inadvertently using this term in reference to her genitalia. Modern readers have become familiar with this captivating character through Bertolt Brecht's chronicle play *Mutter Courage und ihre Kinder* (1939; *Mother Courage and Her Children*, 1941). Brecht, however, uses the nickname in its literal sense, to convey the notion of his character's personal tenacity in overcoming adversity.

The episode in Grimmelshausen's novel that serves as the point of departure for Brecht's play occurs when Courage becomes a camp follower who peddles provisions to soldiers. To assist her, Courage enlists the services of a callow youth who is madly in love with her; she promptly calls him Springinsfeld. Best translated as "jump-into-the-field," the name is derived from the opening words of the first command given to him by Courage and is intended to remind him of his subordinate position in both their commercial and their sexual relationships. Under Courage's tutelage, Springinsfeld develops into an accomplished rogue in his own right, but she decides to rid herself of his company after he takes to assaulting her in his sleep, even though he is deeply apologetic once awake. It is after his separation from Courage that Springinsfeld joins Simplicius and his band of marauders in the forests of Soest. Later in life, he encounters an unemployed secretary in the guest room of an inn, to whom he dictates his autobiography. It is this purported narrative that Grimmelshausen published under the title of *The Singular Life Story of Heedless Hopalong*.

The Singular Life Story of Heedless Hopalong

One item of information contained in *The Singular Life Story of Heedless Hopalong* pertains to the identity of the man who fathered the baby boy whom Courage's maid has borne out of wedlock. It comes to light that the unknown gentleman who has made her pregnant is Simplicius himself. By placing this child at his doorstep, Courage has unintentionally done him a great favor, because he would otherwise never have had the pleasure of rearing a child of his own. Her malicious attempt to spite Simplicius, therefore, brings forth the opposite effect. In the final chapters of *The Singular Life Story of Heedless Hopalong*, a magical bird's nest that has the power to render a person invisible comes into the possession of the protagonist and his young wife. The nest soon passes into the hands of a young soldier, who happens to kill Springinsfeld's wife while attempting to arrest her for a series of thefts committed while her spouse was away on military duty. Springinsfeld likewise meets with misfortune, losing a leg in battle. Upon his return from the wars, the penniless widower is granted permission to spend his remaining years on Simplicius's farmstead.

DER WUNDERBARLICHE VOGELSNEST

The further adventures of the young soldier who killed Springinsfeld's wife are related in part 1 of *Das wunderbarliche Vogelsnest* (the magical bird's nest). His ownership of the nest provides him with an unparalleled opportunity to pry into private affairs and to discover the evil that lies behind humankind's facade of civility. The situation is thus remarkably similar to the one depicted in Alain-René Lesage's *Le Diable boiteux* (1707; *The Devil upon Two Sticks*, 1708). Possession of the nest changes hands for a third time after the young soldier attempts to destroy the object that he has come to regard as an instrument of Satan. The new owner is a young merchant whose experiences are described in part 2. Neither part of *Das wunderbarliche Vogelsnest* appears to have any direct connection with the other works in the Simplician cycle. However, in his preface to part 2, which was translated into English as *The False Messiah* (1964), Grimmelshausen insists that both are essential components of the total saga. Regardless of their relationship to the rest of the opus, the two parts of *Der wunderbarliche Vogelsnest* succeed in enlarging our picture of life in seventeenth century Germany. Grimmelshausen, it should never be forgotten, was the only German writer of that century who fully appreciated the literary value of the contemporary scene.

Victor Anthony Rudowski

OTHER MAJOR WORKS

NONFICTION: *Der satyrische Pilgram I*, 1666; *Der satyrische Pilgram II*, 1667; *Des Abenteuerlichen Simplicissimi Ewig-währender Calender*, 1671; *Der Bart-Krieg*, 1673; *Der teutsche Michael*, 1673.

BIBLIOGRAPHY

Anderson, Susan C. *Grass and Grimmelshausen: Günter Grass's "Das Treffen in Telgte" and Rezeptionstheorie*. Columbia, S.C.: Camden House, 1987. A critical study that looks at Grimmelshausen in relation to one of Germany's most famous modern novelists—Günter Grass. Anderson analyzes how Grass's novel *The Meeting in Telgte* was influenced by Grimmelshausen's characters Simplex and Courage.

Aylett, R. P. T. *The Nature of Realism in Grimmelshausen's "Simplicissimus" Cycle of Novels*. Las Vegas, Nev.: Peter Lang, 1982. Aylett reevaluates the novel cycle, analyzing its characters, Grimmelshausen's use of time and space, the integration of real and fictional history, and other common features of the novels. Includes a bibliography.

Bertsch, Janet. "Grimmelshausen's *Der abentheurliche Simplicissimus Teutsch* and *Der seltzame Springinsfeld*." In *Storytelling in the Works of Bunyan, Grimmelshausen, Defoe, and Schnabel*. Rochester, N.Y.: Camden House, 2004. Bertsch examines Grimmelshausen's novels and works by John Bunyan, Daniel Defoe, and J. G. Schnabel. These works were written between 1660 and 1740, a period of transition between intense religiosity and a growing secularization. Bertsch demonstrates how these authors' works reflect this societal change.

Hayens, Kenneth C. *Grimmelshausen*. New York: Oxford University Press, 1932. Remains the only full-length English-language biography of Grimmelshausen.

Horwich, Cara M. *Survival in "Simplicissimus" and "Mutter Courage."* New York: Peter Lang, 1997. A comparison of *Simplicissimus* and Bertolt Brecht's play *Mother Courage and Her Children*, which was based on Grimmelshausen's work. Horwich maintains that the novel and play share a concern with human survival in a dangerous world.

Knight, K. G. "Grimmelshausen's *Simplicissimus*—A Popular Baroque Novel." In *Periods in German Literature*, edited by J. M. Ritchie. Vol. 25. London: O. Wolff, 1970. The Simplicissimus novels are analyzed and compared to other German picaresque novels written in the seventeenth century. Includes bibliographies.

Menhennet, Alan. *Grimmelshausen the Storyteller: A Study of the "Simplician" Novels*. Columbia, S.C.: Camden House, 1997. A detailed examination of Grimmelshausen's novels, in which Menhennet focuses on their common elements. Argues that the novels should not be considered separate books but instead part of a coherent cycle. He also demonstrates how the cycle integrates religious and moral concerns with a more secular curiousness and sense of humor.

Negus, Kenneth. *Grimmelshausen*. New York: Twayne,

1974. Negus recounts the details of Grimmelshausen's life and analyzes all of his fiction—the minor novels as well as the Simplician cycle. Includes a bibliography.

Otto, Karl F., Jr., ed. *A Companion to the Works of Grimmelshausen*. Rochester, N.Y.: Camden House, 2003. A collection of essays analyzing Grimmelshausen's works. The essays examine topics such as Grimmelhausen and the picaresque novel, allegorical and astronomical elements in his works, gender identity in the Simplician cycle, and the non-Simplician novels.

JOHN GRISHAM

Born: Jonesboro, Arkansas; February 8, 1955
Also known as: John Ray Grisham, Jr.

Principal long fiction

A Time to Kill, 1989
The Firm, 1991
The Pelican Brief, 1992
The Client, 1993
The Chamber, 1994
The Rainmaker, 1995
The Runaway Jury, 1996
The Partner, 1997
The Street Lawyer, 1998
The Testament, 1999
The Brethren, 2000
A Painted House, 2001
Skipping Christmas, 2001
The Summons, 2002
Bleachers, 2003
The King of Torts, 2003
The Last Juror, 2004
The Broker, 2005
Playing for Pizza, 2007
The Appeal, 2008

Other literary forms

John Grisham (GRIHSH-uhm) is known primarily for his novels, but in 2006 he published *The Innocent Man: Murder and Injustice in a Small Town*, a nonfiction work that examines the wrongful conviction of a suspect in a 1982 Oklahoma murder case.

Achievements

John Grisham joined novelist-lawyer Scott Turow in establishing and popularizing the genre of legal fiction. Grisham is one of a small group of American novelists whose books are often termed "blockbusters"; so popular are his novels that they are almost guaranteed to lead the best-seller lists from the moment they are published. *Publishers Weekly* called Grisham the "best-selling novelist of the 1990's." Many of his novels have been made into films, including *The Firm* (1993), *The Rainmaker* (1997), and *Runaway Jury* (2003).

Biography

John Ray Grisham, Jr., the second of five children, was born in Jonesboro, Arkansas, and raised in the South. His father was a construction worker, and the family moved frequently during Grisham's childhood. He lived in Arkansas, Louisiana, and Mississippi while he was growing up. Whenever his family moved to a new town, his mother saw that the children received library cards as soon as possible, because, as Grisham has stated, his mother encouraged reading over watching television. He attended high school in Southaven, Mississippi, a small town outside Memphis. He has said that his writing ability grew out of his involvement in a family of readers and storytellers.

Grisham wanted to play professional baseball, and he spent his early college years largely ignoring his studies and concentrating on sports. When he determined that a baseball career was not likely to happen, he turned to accounting as a major, graduating from Mississippi State

University in 1977 with a bachelor's degree. He attended law school at the University of Mississippi, where he received his law degree in 1981. That year he married Renee Jones, with whom he would have two children. They would reside in Charlottesville, Virginia, for half of the year and in Oxford, Mississippi, for the other half. Grisham has said that he writes six months of the year and coaches his son's Little League baseball team the other six months.

From 1981 to 1991, Grisham practiced law in Southaven. He also served in the Mississippi House of Representatives from 1984 to 1990. Although Grisham was a moderately successful lawyer, he said that he found himself becoming rather cynical toward the legal profession, and he became increasingly interested in literature and in writing. He wrote his first novel, *A Time to Kill*, in longhand, rising every morning at 5:00 A.M. and writing for one to two hours each day; he took three years to write that first book. Eventually it was published by a small press, and Grisham personally visited bookstores in numerous locales to try to promote its sales. In spite of his efforts, the book initially sold only about five thousand copies.

The phenomenal success of his writing began with his second novel, *The Firm*, which became a major best seller and was made into a film, the first of many of Grisham's novels to become motion pictures. All of Grisham's novels since *The Firm* have also reached the top of the best-seller lists.

John Grisham. (Courtesy, Doubleday and Co.)

Analysis

John Grisham writes legal thrillers, a type of novel that has virtually become a genre of its own in recent years. Grisham credits writer Scott Turow's *Presumed Innocent* (1987) with beginning the trend, but his own novels have served to define that trend. If, as conventional wisdom holds, Americans do not like lawyers, they have shown that they certainly do like books about lawyers. The reading public has purchased vast numbers of Grisham's books and those of other writers of fiction dealing with the legal profession.

With *The Firm*, Grisham began a pattern (some critics call it a formula) that he has used, with variations, in most of his succeeding books. His plots usually center on protagonists who are young and in some way vulnerable, and who are placed in extraordinary circumstances. They find themselves fighting against overwhelming odds in situations in which they should not be able to prevail. Ultimately they may win out over antagonists of apparently superior strength: the U.S. government, the Mafia, giant insurance companies. Grisham cannot be counted on to give his readers a standard happy ending, however.

Early in Grisham's career, some critics faulted him for shallow character development and for implausible plots; other critics pointed out, however, that popular fiction is virtually defined by such plots. Many observers have noted Grisham's development as a writer over the course of his career. They have praised his ability to, among other things, accurately portray the American South during the early years of racial integration, as southerners attempted to come to grips with the Civil

Rights movement. Grisham himself has said that he writes "to grab readers. This isn't serious literature." Still, some of Grisham's books stand apart from other action thrillers because of the author's genuine interest in, and engrossing presentation of, social concerns affecting modern readers.

Grisham's books are based in the legal profession that he pursued for many years and are usually set in the South, the region in which he grew up and with which he is deeply familiar. Readers familiar with southern settings find few false notes in Grisham's descriptions of his settings in Mississippi, Louisiana, and Tennessee. Readers curious about the internal functioning of the legal world undoubtedly find his books satisfying in their detailed outlining of how the law works in actual practice. Grishham's novels also educate readers about how the American legal system operates and why it functions as it does. In some of his later novels, Grisham has taken on the topic of the influence of politics on the legal system, examining how politics and the law both work together and come into conflict.

A Time to Kill

A Time to Kill, set in Mississippi, begins with the brutal rape of a young black girl by two white men. The child survives, and the men are arrested, but before they can be tried, the girl's father shoots and kills them both. The question of his guilt is not at issue; he has committed the killings in public, in full view of numerous witnesses. The plot centers on whether the jury can be convinced to release a man who has acted to avenge a terrible crime inflicted on his family.

In this novel, Grisham considers the uneasy nature of race relations in modern Mississippi; he spares neither black nor white southerners in his examination of the manipulations for position and media attention related to a highly publicized trial. Some critics have argued that the character development in this novel is richer than in Grisham's subsequent works. The book suffers from faults common to first novels, however; Grisham fails to tie up some of his plot lines in ways that more experienced writers might. Once finished with a character or situation, he tends simply to abandon the person or issue without resolution. Nonetheless, some critics—and Grisham himself—consider this his best book.

The Firm

In *The Firm*, Grisham debuted the formula that would propel his books to the top of the best-seller lists. Protagonist Mitch McDeere is graduating third in his Harvard Law School class. He has several job offers, but the best is from a firm in Memphis, which offers an outstanding salary, an expensive car, an accessible purchase of an expensive home—all sounding too good to be true. Mitch begins to have questions about the firm almost at once: Why has no one ever quit? What about the two people who died a few years back? The law firm has a dirty secret, which would be deadly for Mitch to find out: The firm works for the Mafia. Once Mitch learns this, he must also learn enough to bargain for his life. The plot of *The Firm* is fast-paced and fairly straightforward. The novel has been called simplistic, but in some ways—concerns of popular fiction aside—it also seems more realistic than some of Grisham's later works. That is, one might actually imagine the events of this book happening; in some subsequent Grisham books, one would be hard put to believe that the events portrayed would occur.

The Chamber

The Chamber represents a departure from Grisham's two preceding novels. Dealing as it does with the imposition of the death penalty, the book is the first of Grisham's novels to take on a social issue. Sam Cayhall is scheduled to be executed for murder by the state of Mississippi. He has been convicted of planting a bomb that resulted in the deaths of two Jewish children, and his guilt is not in question. Cayhall has few redeeming qualities: He is an unrepentant racist and a member of the Ku Klux Klan.

His case is taken in the final stage of appeals by young lawyer Adam Hall. He is the grandson of the prisoner, although Cayhall is unaware of this at the beginning of their involvement. Hall realizes that he is facing an uphill fight, but he struggles with the case as if he has a chance to win. The strength of this book lies in the picture it offers of the reality of the death penalty. Grisham does not rail against capital punishment; he simply shows the reader the unattractive truth of it. Even given the horror of Cayhall's crime, one is led to question whether the inhumanity of the death penalty is an appropriate response. The book is flawed by some annoying lapses in editing, but at the time it was published, it received some of Grisham's strongest critical reviews.

THE RUNAWAY JURY

The Runaway Jury is based on an initial premise that may be difficult for some readers to accept: that through skillful positioning and design, one might arrange to become a member of a given jury. This book offers a fascinating look at the inside functions of a jury and at the incredible resources wealthy corporations can bring to bear in attempting to secure verdicts.

In this case, the juror is Nicholas Easter, a member of a jury hearing a lawsuit against a major tobacco company. When the story begins, the tobacco companies have never lost a lawsuit brought because a smoker died of cancer, and they have no intention of losing this one. The lawyers for the tobacco companies have volumes of information on everyone called for jury selection, billions of dollars for defense, and no scruples. What they do not know, however, is that they are up against a person almost as skillful and knowledgeable as they are. Grisham's inside view of the law is, as always, interesting, and the novel's depiction of the jury as it takes shape and reaches its conclusions is particularly fascinating.

THE BROKER

At the opening of *The Broker*, Joel Backman is in jail, serving a sentence of many years. His surprise is genuine when he is suddenly pardoned by a U.S. president leaving office, shipped out of the country, and relocated in Italy. What he doesn't know—though he certainly, and almost immediately, suspects—is that he has been pardoned at the behest of the Central Intelligence Agency (CIA). The CIA wants to set him up to be killed so that the agency can find out who kills him and thus glean information about Backman's affairs. Backman was sent to jail for his work as a lobbyist, dealing with spy satellite equipment that threatened the systems of several nations. Once in Italy, he begins learning the language, trying to fit in, and attempting to make a place for himself. He is not, however, able to do those things. Almost from the first, he is aware that there is more going on than he knows or will ever be told. He decides to take charge of the situation himself.

This book is a good example of Grisham's ability to manipulate legalities, politics, and international ambience in his writing; it also demonstrates his talent for handling multiple plot threads. It is entertaining, though not among Grisham's most popular.

THE APPEAL

Grisham has said that he wrote *The Appeal* to point out the problem inherent in the election of state supreme court justices. When Wes and Mary Grace Payton, spouses and law partners, took on Jeannette Baker's case, they borrowed against everything they had to support her cause. She had lost a husband and a child to cancer caused by chemical contaminants dumped into the Bowmore, Mississippi, water supply by Krane Chemical. The jury found for Baker in the amount of forty-one million dollars. However, Carl Trudeau, multibillionaire and owner of Krane, believes there is a way out of paying the damages. He collaborates with a group that sets out to remove a so-called liberal justice from the Mississippi State Supreme Court, knowing that the court's decisions are frequently split by a vote of five to four. When the handpicked successor is in place, the appeal verdict is virtually assured. This book may be a difficult one for readers who prefer to believe that justice ultimately prevails, and that the courts ultimately make the right decisions.

OTHER NOVELS

On several occasions, Grisham has produced novels that depart from the legal thriller genre. One of these is *Skipping Christmas*, in which a couple whose only daughter is away with the Peace Corps decide to skip the usual holiday amenities and take a cruise instead. They find that it is not that easy, however. Their neighbors are upset that they are not participating in the annual neighborhood decorations, their friends are appalled that they are forgoing the Christmas festivities—and then they hear from their daughter. A film adaptation of the novel, titled *Christmas with the Kranks*, was released in 2004.

A Painted House is another departure from Grisham's legal novels. A farm family in Arkansas in the 1950's is trying to bring in a cotton crop, on which the family survival depends. The story is told through the eyes of a seven-year-old boy, a narrative method reminiscent of Harper Lee's *To Kill a Mockingbird* (1960). Luke Chandler's family is looking to bring in a good cotton crop, though the fact of that is not to be breathed, lest the crop be jinxed. Two groups of cotton pickers have been hired: a white family from the Ozarks and Mexican farmworkers. Conflicts between the groups are inevitable, but some strange alliances also form. This novel seems to provide an authentic picture of farm life in the South during the 1950's; it also depicts a fact of southern life for that period: Farming could not be depended upon to support families as it had in the past. *A Painted House* is a tribute to the passing of the small family farm and, in the end, a bittersweet testimony to their strength and tenacity. The novel was first published in serialized form in the *Oxford American*, a magazine from the Mississippi town of Oxford, and it rescued that journal from extinction.

Bleachers is the story of a group of athletes who are gathering to await the death of their football coach, Eddie Rake. Many of them have had something of a love-hate relationship with Rake; he was both their promoter and their torturer. Neely Crenshaw is especially torn in his feelings. Crenshaw was the quarterback for Rake's outstanding team, and he is not sure whether he loves the man or hates him. As Rake is dying, however, Crenshaw finds out.

In *Playing for Pizza*, Grisham again turns to football, but with a twist: This is American football in Italy. Rick Dockery has managed to snatch defeat from the jaws of victory with the Cleveland Browns. He has cost the team a probable playoff win in an almost impossible way, and he is not being sought by other teams. He does have a chance, however, if he would like to play American football in Italy. If he wants to play, the Parma Panthers are his only shot, and he decides to take it. This is a book about football, about Italy, and about Italians, and Grisham obviously has a love affair with all of them. The book is funny, warm, and a pleasure to read.

June Harris

Other major work

NONFICTION: *The Innocent Man: Murder and Injustice in a Small Town*, 2006.

Bibliography

Bearden, Michelle. "John Grisham: In Six Years He's Gone from Rejection Slips to Mega-Sales." *Publishers Weekly*, February 22, 1993. Discusses Grisham's early career and his rise to the status of best-selling writer.

Cauthen, Cramer R., and Donald G. Alpin III. "The Gift Refused: The Southern Lawyer in *To Kill a Mockingbird*, *The Client*, and *Cape Fear*." *Studies in Popular Culture* 19, no. 2 (October, 1996): 257-275. Comparative scholarly study examines the treatment of the southern lawyer in modern popular fiction, including in Grisham's *The Client*.

Duffy, Martha. "Grisham's Law." *Time*, May 8, 1995. Takes a look at Grisham's life as well as his influence in popular literature at the time of the publication of *The Rainmaker*.

Goodman, Walter. "Legal Thrillers Obey Laws of Commerce." *The New York Times*, February 29, 2000. Discusses five of Grisham's novels, focusing on the author's ability to hold his legion of readers.

Mote, Dave. "John Grisham." In *Contemporary Popular Writers*, edited by Dave Mote. Detroit, Mich.: St. James Press, 1997. Offers a critical look at Grisham's place among popular writers. Discusses the comparative merits of several of the author's books.

Pringle, Mary Beth. *John Grisham: A Critical Companion*. Westport, Conn.: Greenwood Press, 1997. Presents a brief biography of the author as well as critical assessment of all his novels published from 1989 to 1996. Includes bibliography and index.

_______. *Revisiting John Grisham: A Critical Companion*. Westport, Conn.: Greenwood Press, 2007. Continues Pringle's analyses of Grisham's works with examination of the novels published from 1997 onward. Includes bibliography and index.

FREDERICK PHILIP GROVE

Born: Radomno, Prussia (now in Poland); February 14, 1879
Died: Simcoe, Ontario, Canada; August 19, 1948
Also known as: Felix Paul Greve

PRINCIPAL LONG FICTION

Settlers of the Marsh, 1925
A Search for America, 1927
Our Daily Bread, 1928
The Yoke of Life, 1930
Fruits of the Earth, 1933
Two Generations, 1939
The Master of the Mill, 1944
Consider Her Ways, 1947

OTHER LITERARY FORMS

Beyond the novel, Frederick Philip Grove has published travel sketches, represented by his first two published books, *Over Prairie Trails* (1922) and *The Turn of the Year* (1923). Actually narrative essays, the pieces detail Grove's weekly horse-and-carriage journeys between distant points of rural Manitoba. His other essays on a variety of topics appeared in Canadian periodicals and in the collection *It Needs to Be Said* (1929), and a much smaller number of short stories collected and edited by Desmond Pacey appeared under the title *Tales from the Margin: The Selected Short Stories of Frederick Philip Grove* (1971).

In Search of Myself (1946), Grove's fictionalized autobiography, contains a detailed account of his life before he arrived in Canada and of his struggles to achieve recognition as a writer. *Consider Her Ways* (1947), written at the time the autobiography was coming out but conceived much earlier, reflects Grove's long-standing scientific interests, as well as his familiarity with travel literature and with various models of the satiric fable. Grove casts his fable as a narrative communicated to a sympathetic scientist by a tribe of South American ants on an expedition to the north in search of further knowledge about humans. He cleverly satirizes Western civilization not only through the ants' discoveries and observations about the human society they find but also through the behavior of the ants themselves, who engage in the same power struggles and exhibit the same vanity of species they impute to humankind. Although a curiosity in Grove's canon. *Consider Her Ways* displays a tighter structure than most of his more conventional writings as well as many of the same attitudes toward human behavior and history.

ACHIEVEMENTS

Frederick Philip Grove's fiction constitutes Canada's most distinguished contribution to the literature of frontier realism. His work presents an authentic image of pioneer life, particularly in the central Canadian provinces. As an immigrant to Canada, Grove was able to question the North American pioneering effort in a disturbing and often profound manner and to form a perspective unique among the major English realists. Almost all of his fiction in some way scrutinizes the value system of progress behind the frontier movement in Canada and the United States, with implications reaching far beyond the time in which a work was set or written. His portrayal of social change transcends the limits of most frontier realism, often approaching the resonance of Thomas Hardy or Ivan Turgenev.

Grove's writing, however, is not without flaws. Because he acquired English in a purely academic manner, his prose is too often turgid. Also, his plots often lack a logical development, which makes events appear arbitrary. Nevertheless, most of his novels offer a careful delineation of settings and incidents; he also gives his reader many vivid and memorable characters and situations, informed always by a frankness of tone and attitude.

The peculiarly telescoped nature of Canadian literature—whereby the development of basically eighteenth century models into modernism, which occurred more rapidly than in England or the United States—is reflected in the intensity of Grove's writing and vision, an intensity that links him to the later Theodore Dreiser and even to John Steinbeck and that dramatizes the romantic basis of a realism bent on escaping Romanticism. Grove's fiction, and particularly his three strongest novels—*Settlers of the Marsh*, *A Search for America*, and *Fruits of the Earth*—thus carries much interest and value for the literary historian, as well as for the general reader.

Biography

Frederick Philip Grove was born Felix Paul Greve on February 14, 1879, in Radomno, Poland—on what was then the border with Prussia. Grove's most effective fictions were a result of these first thirty years of his life. His parents were middle-class citizens of Hamburg, and he attended the University of Bonn for a few years before dropping out for financial reasons and embarking on a career as a freelance writer and translator. Grove may have known André Gide and others in early twentieth century Paris literary circles, and he certainly did write and publish poetry, fiction, and even drama in addition to his literary criticism and extensive translation.

Grove's migration to North America, in 1909 or 1910, provided for him a new source of subject matter for his fiction. Whether he rode the rails as an itinerant workman, as he often said, is open to question. Most certainly he could have done so for only a year or two, and not for the much longer period suggested in *In Search of America* and reiterated in the autobiography. One can only speculate about his reasons for coming to America and for adopting so elaborate a disguise—of name, of parentage, even of the year of his birth. Perhaps he wished to transcend his modest social station, or to elude the law or creditors—Grove had spent a year in Bonn prison for fraud—or perhaps to escape a constraining marriage.

In 1912, Grove was hired as a public schoolteacher in rural Haskett, Manitoba, Canada, which was the first of several appointments in a rather unhappy career that would last fifteen years. In the summer of 1914, he married Catherine Wiens, a teacher in a school where he had become principal. They had a daughter and a son. The daughter's death in 1927, when she was only eleven years old, climaxed a string of difficulties besetting Grove in the 1920's, difficulties caused by the backward and often intolerant communities in which he found himself employed, by his own ill temper and inflexibility toward the rural mentality, by overwork and chronic financial hardship, and, perhaps most of all, by the erratic and ultimately unencouraging response of publishers and readers to his books.

In the late 1920's, Grove's fortunes turned somewhat as he became championed by a small but loyal and influential group of Canadian writers and academics. Increasing critical recognition of his work led to two lecture tours in 1928, to a brief career in the publishing business from 1929 to 1931, and to Grove's receiving the prestigious Lorne Pierce Medal of the Royal Society of Canada in 1931. Meanwhile, Grove had left teaching and settled with his wife and son on a small farm near Simcoe, Ontario, where he lived until his death. While his writing never made him much money, it won him growing acclaim. He was elected to the Royal Society in 1941, received several honorary degrees, and was given a lifetime grant of one hundred dollars per month by the Canadian Writers Foundation in 1944. A stroke that year left him partly paralyzed. He died in 1948 after a lengthy illness.

Analysis

Among Frederick Philip Grove's primary themes, the foremost is the issue of free will. Through his characters, Grove asks how much freedom anyone has in the face of often accidental but usually overwhelming pressures of instinct and environment. Even as he dramatizes the complexity and frustration wrought by such pressures, Grove seems, paradoxically, to celebrate the determination of his heroic figures to act as if such pressures hardly exist. Of almost equal importance to Grove's vision is the more existential question of where in time one ought to situate objectives. While he can admire the person who plans and looks toward the future, he often exposes the illusions attending such an orientation. His novels also involve themes that develop out of the distinction made between materialism and a more transcendental value system, a distinction that his characters frequently fail to identify. That Grove does not always favor his characters, even as he sympathizes with their search for an authentic New World, suggests the complex viewpoint and dilemma central to much of his writing.

Settlers of the Marsh

After publishing his two books of travel sketches, Grove moved into book-length and explicitly fictional narrative, retaining this critical stance toward the efforts of pioneers to conquer the plains. Although the detailed accounting of nature continues in *Settlers of the Marsh*, Grove's sympathy with nature and his corresponding critique of man-in-nature are found in the novel's characterization and plotting. The pioneering enterprise is questioned through the depiction of Niels Lindstedt, a young Swede who emigrated to escape the perpetual poverty meted him in Europe and to build his own fortune through hard work. Niels outdoes his neighbors and succeeds handsomely: He saves money, clears land, and harvests a bounteous crop. His crowning achievement is the building of a great house, in which he plans to live with Ellen Amundsen. Out of the presumptuousness and naïveté of Niels's scheme, Grove constructs the complications of his novel.

A curiously antiromantic love triangle develops in the novel, which combines elements of Thomas Hardy and D. H. Lawrence with Gustave Flaubert. Niels is cast as impressionable and sexually vulnerable, not unlike Hardy's Jude or the young Paul Morel of *Sons and Lovers* (1913). Just as Paul turns to an older, more aggressive woman when the younger woman of his choice rebuffs his sexuality, so Niels falls prey to the seductiveness of Clara Vogel—whose first name significantly matches that of her counterpart in the Lawrence novel. Grove's Clara, unlike Lawrence's and like Arabella in *Jude the Obscure* (1896), knowingly takes advantage of his ignorance and inexperience in sex. The literary triangle is completed in Ellen's aversion to sex despite her affection for Niels; the complex psychology behind her refusal to marry him recalls the different but equally complex reasoning of Lawrence's Miriam and Sue Bridehead.

To a much greater degree than Hardy or Lawrence, Grove limits sympathy with his central character. Although the reader sees the novel's action almost exclusively from Niels's viewpoint, and although Niels's strengths are reported and his intentions are understandable, each of the two women in his life is given a position of equal validity to his, and Niels's inability, or unwillingness, to appreciate that position constitutes a grave weakness. Ellen's sexual problems stem from her having witnessed the brutal subjugation of her mother by her father—who forced sex on his wife when she was ill and pressured her to seek abortions when she was pregnant—and from having promised her mother she would avoid intimacy with a man. Ellen's telling Niels all of this, even as she insists she admires him and desperately needs his friendship, shocked many of the novel's first readers.

Unfortunately, Niels cannot bring himself to accept a purely friendly relationship with Ellen, or to wait for her to feel differently about him—although subsequent developments suggest waiting might not have gone unrewarded. Instead, he ignores her plea for friendship and largely avoids her. His assumption that he can control his own sexuality backfires in his going to town in search of pleasure, in his succumbing there to Clara, and in—to her astonishment—his remorsefully insisting that they marry.

Despite Clara's promiscuous past, it is mostly Niels's blindness to the dullness of farm life for a city woman and his refusal to free her that lead to Clara's actively seeking other men and to the climactic discovery scene in which Niels murders her. Just as Clara would not idealize sexuality, neither would she denigrate it, or try to compensate for it, as does Niels. His response to the compelling problems of Ellen and Clara reveal him to be more insensitive and more shackled by sex than either of them. Objections to the final reunion of Niels with a now-willing Ellen reflect readers' uneasiness with Niels's ultimately receiving rewards without acknowledging the legitimacy of the two women's claims against him. Aesthetically pleasing injustice in a more or less tragic plot thus gives way to the jarring injustice of a romantic finale.

The problems of the novel's ending are reinforced by Grove's portrayal of prairie women as victims of male stupidity and insensitivity. If Niels's friend Nelson enjoys a happy marriage because, unlike Niels, he pursues a simple, earthy type of woman, Nelson is the exception. Otherwise, Grove surrounds Niels with consistently unhappy marriages, where the blame rests mostly on husbands whose wives are burdened with hard work, too many children, and too little sympathy. Grove finds the problem not to be so much marriage itself but specifically marriage between unequals to which the male pioneer aspires and in which the wife becomes simply another beast of burden subordinate to the husband's selfish ambitions. Grove ironically compounds the human toil of such selfishness in the case of Niels, who has a measure of sensitivity not shared by his fellow settlers. Niels mistakenly acts as if this sensitivity translates into completely good behavior. Having sought a land of freedom, Niels increasingly wonders if he is not, in fact, enslaved. Never does he fully put together the puzzle of his failures, however. Through one of its gentlest members, Grove thus indicts a whole pioneer movement.

A Search for America

A Search for America proved to be much less offensive and much more popular to its first readers than *Settlers in the Marsh*; in fact, it became the most popular of Grove's books. Rather than a narrative of constriction, it offers a story of discovery, of an opening up to the positive possibilities of life in America. In Phil Brandon, the narrator and protagonist, Grove presents his true adventurer, who reveals the moral ambiguities of the feverish activity characterizing North America at the beginning of the twentieth century. Until recently, readers saw the narrative as thinly disguised autobiography; certainly Grove encouraged this notion by inserting parts in *In Search of Myself*. So convincing are many of the novel's scenes and incidents that even now, after the serious inaccuracies in Grove's account of his early years have been exposed, one believes he must have experienced most of the encounters and difficulties Brandon describes.

The literary antecedents of *A Search for America* are, on one hand, *Walden* (1854) and *Adventures of Huckleberry Finn* (1884) and, on the other, a string of later immigrant narratives, from Jacob Riis's affirmative autobiography *The Making of an American* (1901) to the fictional and more skeptical *Rise of David Levinsky* (1917) by Abraham Cahan. How much of this immigrant writing Grove himself had read is unknown; Henry David Thoreau and Mark Twain he cites explicitly. To all of these he adds, as the narrative progresses, strains of Thomas Carlyle and Leo Tolstoy: He takes the injunction from *Sartor Resartus* (1835) about increasing the "fraction of Life" by lessening the denominator as the basis for his turnabout in the middle of his "search," and in the final section compares the magnificent hobo Ivan in *Anna Karenina* (1875-1877).

Phil Brandon is a young man from a wealthy Swedish family whose father's financial crisis drives him to Canada. From Toronto, where he finds work as a waiter, he moves to New York, as a door-to-door book salesman; to the Midwest, as a drifter on the Ohio River; and finally, to the Dakotas, where he works in the great wheat harvest. Although Grove cut his original manuscript in half, the published narrative is frequently rambling and episodic. Nevertheless, it continues to have a legitimate appeal.

The novel features the memorable episodes and characters for which Grove is known, from the cultured young European's encounter with the strange and raw people on his first train trip in the New World, from Montreal to Toronto, to Brandon's being tossed out of a Western town as a radical agitator trying to defend immigrants' property rights. Along the way he meets restaurant employees who cheat in various ways, the rich and the poor on whom publishers try to foist books, a river man so taciturn Brandon mistakes him for a deaf-mute, a village doctor completely trusting of the down-and-out, a millionaire landowner fascinated by radical political talk, and many other notable figures.

In *Frederick Philip Grove* (1973), Margaret R. Stobie points to the dreamlike quality, as well as the double movement, of Brandon's quest. Grove extends his story beyond the limitations of immigrant initiation by moving Brandon from a geographical to a psychological quest, from seeking an America outside himself to finding those "American" values in himself that lead to a vocation. While the result for Brandon is the decision to become a teacher aiding the newly arrived immigrants, the meaning of this decision and the shift of objectives preceding it even speaks to readers solidly established in American society. Grove parallels this shift with the development of the distinction between the superficial America—represented in the novel's first two books by the petty fraud of business—and the "real" America promised in book 3, when Brandon travels the countryside by himself, and in book 4, when he reattaches himself to humanity. He becomes convinced that, his misadventures notwithstanding, there are "real Abe Lincolns" out there, worth seeking and worth cultivating.

Grove's narrator-protagonist comes to devalue "culture" in the European sense, as prefabricated and fragile, and to appreciate the need for developing one's personal culture. Grove's affinity with Thoreau and Twain, as well as with Henri Rousseau, shows especially in Brandon's discovery of a new relationship with nature, responding to the commonplace in nature. Nature suggests to Brandon not only the insignificance of the past—which his flight from European artifice may have already taught him—but also the virtual irrelevance of the future, as he learns to concentrate more on his present situation and less on what it might be. Repeatedly, Brandon wonders at the nature of being, at where he is through no effort or intention. The novel's basic optimism is underlined by the possibility for positive unforeseen events, which softens the determinism of much social thinking in the novel. If the European immigrant's experience in the 1890's seems remote today, Grove's warnings about a culture mired in materialism and separated from its roots in nature still have force.

Fruits of the Earth

Continuing the ideological tendencies of Grove's earlier fiction, *Fruits of the Earth* is not only his most satisfying and moving novel but also arguably one of the two or three finest works to come out of the American frontier tradition. Strictly speaking, it does not concern the frontier so much as the painful transition from pioneer to modern life on the prairie. Abe Spaulding represents one answer to Phil Brandon's search for the authentically Lincolnesque American. Grove describes Spaulding's experiences and development from 1900, when he arrives from Ontario to clear a piece of land near a remote Manitoba village, to the 1920's, when—in his fifties and having achieved patriarchal status among his neighbors—he wrestles with the moral dilemmas posed by community growth, related pressures of mass culture, and his own children's coming-of-age.

Grove divides his novel into two principal sections. The first traces Abe from his start as a young homesteader through his remarkable economic success, which culminates in his building a great house on the site of his beginning. Paralleling this ascent is his rise in the school district and the municipality, where he is respected for his sagacity and honesty and is ultimately elected reeve. Early in the narrative a conflict develops in Abe, by which feelings for his family—to a lesser extent for his wife, who is ill suited for prairie life, and to a greater extent for his son, Charlie, whose sensitivity Abe comes increasingly to value—detract from his sense of external success. Such success is superseded, in Abe's and the reader's minds, by the accidental death of Charlie midway through the novel.

Grove ascribes Spaulding's success largely to the preeminent strengths he brings to the challenge of homesteading. Repeatedly, the secondary characters and events testify to Abe's intelligence and shrewdness, of which his imposing physique is emblematic. He nurses the pioneer ambitions to escape a constricting life, represented by the small family farm he had sold, and to pursue what Grove terms "a clear proposition," unencumbered by complexity. Such a plan rests on the premise that such objectives are inherently good and satisfying, as well as obtainable. Abe soon begins to suspect the fallaciousness of his premise when other values detract from the satisfaction of his success. Grove significantly casts Abe's happiness in the past, so that he rarely experiences it except in memory. His growing property holdings are accompanied by a sense of diminishing economic returns and by a feeling of increasing enslavement by his acquisitions. Even as he builds the magnificent house, Abe feels powerless; house construction, like the prairie itself, is beyond his grasp. Like Hardy and many naturalists, Grove portrays his protagonist in rather unflattering terms against the backdrop of nature. Abe seems never very far ahead of the natural forces he tries to control, and therefore he is unable to enjoy any real repose.

All of these characteristics emerge in the novel's first part. Charlie's death, which coincides with Abe's greatest public triumphs, brings out a latent dissatisfaction with such triumphs. Abe sees in the death an ominous sign of his inability to capture what he has belatedly recognized as more valuable than material or external success. Charlie's death reinforces a depressing sense of fatality, of an irreversible and unmodifiable commitment to decisions made and courses taken many years earlier. Having attended increasingly to Charlie to not only atone but also make up time he had believed he was losing, Abe retreats into himself once Charlie is gone.

The second part of the novel, titled "The District," depicts various changes brought on by the postwar era. Against this background and despite his skepticism regarding "progress"—a skepticism explicitly echoed by Grove—Abe allows unscrupulous political enemies to rob him of power and to proceed to transform the district in the modern commercial spirit he despises. The novel's first part centered on the suspense of when and at what price Abe would realize fully the conflict of values in himself; in the second part, Grove turns the issue to whether, having recognized that conflict, Abe will succumb to a paralysis of will.

Abe, however, ultimately chooses to assert whatever limited influence he may have and to take a stand despite his awareness of his power's limits. Grove indicates that Abe's heroism comes from that awareness rather than from the skills that helped him fashion out his estate or the sensitivity brought out in his relationship to Charlie. Having learned that life's "clear propositions" tend to be elusive and fundamentally unsatisfying, Abe in the end rises from psychological and moral torpor to act with genuine courage.

Grove's artistic successes have helped extend frontier realism beyond the dimensions it is usually accorded. Like his more celebrated American counterparts, Grove marked the ambitions, hopes, and disappointments attending pioneer life around the turn of the century. He also marked the ways in which such universally destructive aspects of human behavior as greed, jealousy, and snobbery found their way into a frontier experience, which had promised escape from them.

Grove's novels came too late to put him in the forefront of frontier realists. Nevertheless, his novels' tardy appearance permitted a perspective of which the other frontier realists were rarely capable. Grove was able to capture not only the futility but also the ultimate immorality of much pioneer venturing. His best fiction records the compromise of simple virtue and pleasure demanded by the misleading complex life on the prairie. This ethical perspective deepens as Grove follows his pioneers beyond World War I and even into the 1930's, where pioneer and modern notions of progress clash openly.

Significantly, Grove shows women and children suffering the consequences of commitments made solely by adult males. Yet, even the hardy pioneers in Grove's world sense the inherent limitations of the economic and social system to which they commit themselves and their families. In depicting their failures, economic and moral, as inevitable, Grove is a pessimist, particularly as he assigns a measure of responsibility to the pioneers themselves. In continuing to insist, however, on the ability of humankind to recognize good and to act on that recognition, Grove avoided naturalistic determinism and offered a measure of hope to the twentieth century.

Bruce K. Martin

Other major works

Short fiction: *Tales from the Margin: The Selected Short Stories of Frederick Philip Grove*, 1971 (Desmond Pacey, editor).

Poetry: *A Dirge for My Daughter*, 2006.

Nonfiction: *Over Prairie Trails*, 1922; *The Turn of the Year*, 1923; *It Needs to Be Said*, 1929; *In Search of Myself*, 1946 (fictionalized autobiography); *The Letters of Frederick Philip Grove*, 1976 (Pacey, editor); *A Stranger to My Time: Essays By and About Frederick Philip Grove*, 1986.

Children's/young adult literature: *The Adventure of Leonard Broadus*, 1983 (in *The Genesis of Grove's "The Adventure of Leonard Broadus": A Text and Commentary*; Mary Rubio, editor).

Bibliography

Hjartarson, Paul, ed. *A Stranger to My Time: Essays by and About Frederick Philip Grove*. Edmonton, Alta.: NeWest Press, 1986. Divided into four sections, each concerned with a Grove persona: the figures of the Other, the Immigrant, Estrangement, and Posterity. Thoroughly updates the evaluation of Grove and his contribution to Canadian literature. Includes an extensive bibliography and an index.

Hjartarson, Paul, and Tracy Kulba, eds. *The Politics of Cultural Mediation: Baroness Elsa von Freytag-Loringhoven and Felix Paul Greve*. Edmonton: University of Alberta Press, 2003. Focuses on Grove's experiences as a German émigré in Canada. Three of the book's essays examine various aspects of his "Canadianization," including one describing the influence of Oscar Wilde on his novel *Settlers of the Marsh*.

Martens, Klaus. *F. P. Grove in Europe and Canada: Translated Lives*. Translated by Paul Morris. Edmonton: University of Alberta Press, 2001. A comprehensive biography, in which Martens recounts Grove's early life in Germany and his new identity in

Canada as a writer and teacher. Martens describes how Grove transmuted his life into his novels and autobiographies.

_______. "Frederick Philip Grove: Reexamining a Prominent Prairie Writer." *Manitoba History* 57 (February, 2008): 50-54. Grove's biographer provides a profile the author, discussing his life and career as a novelist, essayist, translator, and founder of the Centre for Canadian and Anglo American Cultures at Saarland University in Germany. Martens also explains how Grove was among a handful of authors who started their respective careers in Manitoba after World War I.

Pacey, Desmond, ed. *Frederick Philip Grove*. Toronto, Ont.: Ryerson Press, 1970. Contains Pacey's introduction, chronologically arranged critical essays by other authors, book review excerpts about Grove's novels, and a bibliography listing all of Grove's writings. Reflects Pacey's skill at providing a useful overview.

Spettigue, Douglas O. *Frederick Philip Grove*. Toronto, Ont.: Copp Clark, 1969. Spettigue untangles the enigma of Grove's origins and arranges this scholarly, objective book around a consideration of the interdependence between Grove's personality and the themes and heroes of his novels. Notes and a bibliography enhance this important analysis.

Stobie, Margaret R. *Frederick Philip Grove*. New York: Twayne, 1973. Stobie does as much as possible to discover Grove, the man, behind the central theme in his writing: humankind as social and natural beings. Comprises an interwoven analysis of Grove's life and his writing, presenting new insights gleaned from unpublished material and from personal anecdotes of people who knew him. Emphasizes Grove's successes over his failures as a writer. Includes a chronology, a bibliography, and an index.

Sutherland, Ronald, ed. "Thoughts on Five Writers: What Was Frederick Philip Grove?" In *The New Hero: Essays in Comparative Quebec/Canadian Literature*. Toronto, Ont.: Macmillan, 1977. Sutherland considers as "para-literary" this series of interesting linked essays on the individualistic "new" hero emerging from Canadian literature. The section on Grove reflects Sutherland's fascination with that enigmatic personality and praises his writing as that of a literary naturalist, not a social realist. Includes notes and a thorough bibliography.

H

JESSICA HAGEDORN

Born: Manila, Philippines; 1949
Also known as: Jessica Tarahata Hagedorn

Principal long fiction

Dogeaters, 1990
The Gangster of Love, 1997
Dream Jungle, 2003

Other literary forms

Although Jessica Hagedorn's literary reputation rests primarily on her long fiction, she has written poetry, plays, and short fiction and has done editorial work. She also has written review essays and film scripts. Her theater work includes the plays *Chiquita Banana* (pb. 1972), *Mango Tango* (pr. 1978), *Tenement Lover: no palm trees/in new york city* (pr. 1981), *Holy Food* (staged in 1988; pr. 1989 as a radio play), *Dogeaters* (pr. 1998; based on her novel), and *Fe in the Desert* (pr. 2007). Her collaborations include *Where the Mississippi Meets the Amazon* (pr. 1977; with Thulani Davis and Ntozake Shange), *Teenytown* (pr. 1990; with Laurie Carlos and Robbie McCauley), and *Airport Music* (pr. 1994; with Han Ong). She wrote the screenplay for the Shu Lea Cheang film *Fresh Kill* (1994), and with John Woo she created the animated television series *The Pink Palace* (2000).

Hagedorn's literary production includes collections of poems and short fiction: *Dangerous Music* (1975), *Pet Food and Tropical Apparitions* (1981), and *Danger and Beauty* (1993). Two of her published works are anthologies: *Charlie Chan Is Dead: An Anthology of Contemporary Asian American Fiction* (1993) and *Charlie Chan Is Dead II: At Home in the World—An Anthology of Contemporary Asian American Fiction*. Two other works are collaborations: a book of poetry, *Visions of a Daughter, Foretold* (1994), with her daughter Paloma Hagedorn Woo, and a pictorial work, *Burning Heart: A Portrait of the Philippines* (1999), with photographs by Marissa Roth.

Achievements

Jessica Hagedorn won an American Book Award for *Pet Food and Tropical Apparitions* (1981) and a Before Columbus Foundation Award (1983), and she was nominated for a National Book Award in 1991 for *Dogeaters*. She earned MacDowell Colony Fellowships in 1985, 1986, and 1988, and she was nominated for the *Irish Times* International Fiction Prize for *The Gangster of Love* (1996). She also earned a Lucille Lortel Playwrights' Fellowship, a Guggenheim Fiction Fellowship, a Kesserling Prize Honorable Mention, a National Education Association-Theatre Communications Group Playwriting Residency Fellowship, and fellowships with the Sundance Playwrights' Lab and Sundance Screenwriters' Lab. Her first single-author play, *Mango Tango*, was produced by the renowned Shakespearean director Joseph Papp.

Poet Kenneth Rexroth was her mentor, and he edited and wrote the introduction to a book that included her early poems, *Four Young Women: Poems* (1973), by Hagedorn, Alice Karle, Barbara Szerlip, and Carol Tinker. The significance of Hagedorn's body of work is reflected, in part, by the number of poems, short fiction, and plays she has published in anthologies, including *Third World Women* (1972), *Calafia: The California Poetry* (1979), *Networks: An Anthology of San Francisco Bay Area Women Poets* (1979), *The Forbidden Stitch: An Asian American Women's Anthology* (1989), *Sister Stew: Fiction and Poetry by Women* (1991), *Returning a Borrowed Tongue: Poems by Filipino and Filipino American Writers* (1995), and *Tokens? The NYC Asian American Experience on Stage* (1999).

Biography

Jessica Tarahata Hagedorn was born in the Santa Mesa district of Manila in the Philippines. She grew up in an artistic family. Her mother was a painter and her maternal grandfather was a writer. At the age of six, Hagedorn started writing four-page "novels." After she immigrated to the United States in 1963, she studied mime, acting, fencing, martial arts, and tai chi at the American Conservatory Theater in San Francisco, California. Her regimen prepared her for a career as a performance artist. In 1975, she created the West Coast Gangster Choir, renamed the Gangster Choir after she moved to New York City in 1978. The group disbanded in 1985, but from 1988 to 1992, Hagedorn continued working and joined the trio Thought Music. In 1990, Hagedorn became a commentator on National Public Radio's weekly news broadcast *Crossroads*.

Analysis

Jessica Hagedorn's eclecticism is reflected in her prose style and literary devices, which bring together many elements. Multiple narrators, who may contradict one another, and combinations of first-person and third-person perspectives, are the norm, as are discontinuous, nonlinear plots. Interspersed are snippets of historical sources and fictitious news stories, along with transcriptions of real and invented documents. Her narrative stance is established and simultaneously modified by the regular infusion of expressions from three languages—English, Spanish, and Tagalog—and occasional linguistic forays into other languages and dialects. She also introduces profane and obscene street language into her dialogue. The result is kaleidoscopic and, as such, raises and explores two enduring philosophical questions: What is real? and How do we know that what we think is real is actually so?

Hagedorn's themes are the interactions of colony and neocolony; the protean nature of both cultural and personal identity; the complexity of conflict and accommodation of race, class, gender, and geography; and, most prominent, the fascination of the demimonde. Her works include many supporting characters. Though some critics consider this a weakness, a kind of sideshow distraction from plot progression and thematic development and a cause of narrative loose ends, the presence of many characters is congruent with Hagedorn's artistic vision. The many characters in her novels reflect the richness of Philippine cultural life, which is a concatenation of ethnicities, races, social classes, and genders. Her nonlinear plots may indicate her perception of human experience as a staccato, as syncopated, as improvisational, and even as destabilized.

Dogeaters

Dogeaters is Hagedorn's pièce de résistance. The provocative title word "dogeater," which to Filipinos is an ethnic slur, foreshadows literal and symbolic rapacity. The setting of the novel is the dog-eat-dog world of Manila from the 1950's through the 1970's. The novel tells of the relationship of colonizer (the United States) and neocolony (the Philippines).

Jessica Hagedorn. (Nancy Wong)

The novel, not a traditional roman à clef or bildungsroman, has a developmental pattern constructed around two main parts. Part one, "Coconut Palace," is an episodic, tonally varied group of vignettes populated principally by static, one-dimensional function characters. The impression these features create—social stagnation and fragmentation—is bolstered by intercalary chapters, mostly from a real nineteenth century account by Jean Baptiste Mallat, *The Philippines* (1846). The chapter also is supplemented by fictitious news stories from the nonexistent *Metro Manila Daily* newspaper and other sources, the most significant being an address by U.S. president William McKinley in 1898.

Part two, "The Song of Bullets," has a consistent, fast-paced story line. Its momentum is initiated by the assassination of a Senator Avila. The structural integrity of such an imposing array of elements in her fiction has been questioned, but most critics have concluded that the components cohere in a manner similar to mathematical fractals or to mosaic, mural, and collage. Others have argued that a more unitary arrangement would undercut Hagedorn's overarching motifs of protean personal, social, and national identity; gender fixity; and dominant/subaltern political status.

Daisy Avila, the assassinated senator's daughter, begins as an establishment icon—she wins a beauty contest, symbolic, by accepted social norm, of ideal womanhood—and evolves, after her rape and torture by General Nicasio Ledesma, into a guerrilla fighter intent on revolution. This transformation also epitomizes the bifurcation of identity involving the state (the dictatorship) and the nation (the people). In turn, this distinction exposes the dissonance between the officially independent Philippines and the unofficially subservient economic neocolony position of the country, subject to commodification via imported American consumer products.

One particularly consequential imported commodity is the Hollywood film, which by depicting desirable products spurs consumer demand for American goods and strengthens the dependence of the Philippines on the United States. Hollywood films also bring to the fore the question of spectacle as a diversionary strategy, deflecting a focus on pressing social and political matters. Perhaps most significant example of American cultural influence displayed in the novel is the collapse of the hastily constructed edifice to house a film festival. On a popular television show (itself a cultural distraction), the Philippine first lady glosses over the incident with manufactured tears but orders the work on the structure to progress; the bodies of the workmen killed in the accident are covered with cement.

Fluid sex and gender categories constitute another aspect of the dichotomy between appearance and reality. In Western terms, homosexuals (Andreas and Joey), hermaphrodites (Eugenio/Eugenia), and cross-dressers (Perdito) challenge traditional heterosexual and male/female gender stereotyping, reinforced by Hollywood films. In the Philippine context, however, these ambiguities are more pronounced. A smorgasbord of male feminine-gender proclivities ranging from effeminacy to sexual identification and gendered behavior to actual practice, can be encompassed by the Tagalog expression *bakla*. Counterpointing questions of gender are issues involving disrespect for and mistreatment of women. Early in the novel, the issue is brought to the fore when Rio's cousin Pucha, a dull and crude girl whose name is a Tagalog euphemism for *puta* (whore in both Tagalog and Spanish), entices a group of lewd boys to make unseemly remarks. Seemingly harmless, this telltale event leads up to the shocking brutalization of Daisy and is kept in the reader's consciousness by the self-abnegating asceticism of Leonor, General Ledesma's wife, who evidently attempts to atone for her husband's many inhumane transgressions.

Thus, *Dogeaters*, notwithstanding its artistic intricacy, is a novel of searing social criticism. It never names Ferdinand or Imelda Marcos, but its allusions are thin veils over the abuses of the years of martial law.

The Gangster of Love

Hagedorn's second novel, though eliciting mixed reactions from reviewers, broadens the artistic vision of *Dogeaters* and her third novel *Dream Jungle*, both of which are set in the Philippines. *The Gangster of Love* is set, mostly, in the United States. The oxymoronic title, derived from a song by the rhythm-and-blues artist Johnny "Guitar" Watson, establishes the usual Hagedorn polarities (also visible in her book titles *Danger and Beauty* and *Dangerous Music*). For Hagedorn, the aesthetic is not to be found in the ethereal; it is embedded in the sleazy materiality of human existence.

The Gangster of Love opens at the same time that the rock star Jimi Hendrix dies of a drug overdose, emblematic of the intertwining of danger and beauty. Using different narrators, the novel centers on Raquel "Rocky" Rivera, who moves from the Philippines with her mother Milagros and her mentally unstable brother Voltaire. Rocky falls in love with a guitar player named Elvis Chang, with whom she has a child. With Chang and a drummer named Sly, she forms the rock band Gangster of Love.

The Gangster of Love has a comparatively microcosmic focus, revolving around interpersonal rather than social interactions. It may come across as a rendering of late American hippie counterculture, featuring the proverbial sex, drugs, and rock and roll but often carried to the edge of degradation, even perversity. Thus, the story may strike the reader as devoid of the compelling social and political issues and metaphysical and epistemological probings that constitute so much of the intellectual ballast of *Dogeaters*.

Dream Jungle

Dream Jungle, though not generally considered Hagedorn's masterwork, closely approximates *Dogeaters* in terms of artistic merit, setting, thematic development, and narrative stance. Its plot has reverberations, though ironic, of Joseph Conrad's *Lord Jim* (1900), in that it is a movement from civilization to primitivism that raises the question, Which state is really primitive? Even Conrad's famous narrator Marlow is echoed in Hagedorn's character Paz Marlowe; both provide incisive psychological insights. Paz (peace in Spanish) is another ironic element, granted *Dream Jungle*'s allusive texture.

One major story line involves the filming of *Napalm Sunset*, which, as Hagedorn has acknowledged, is her version of *Apocalypse Now* (1979), the epic film about the Vietnam War. The other principal story line centers on the discovery of the Taobo tribe by Zamora López de Legazpi. As Hagedorn has confirmed, the Taobo represent the actual Tasaday people and Legazpi represents the actual Manuel Elizalde, Jr., a Philippine government official. The discovery of a supposedly Stone Age tribe—the Tasaday—in the 1970's raises doubts about historical veracity, and Hagedorn intentionally leaves unresolved the issue of whether the Taobo tribe in her novel is a hoax; the Tasaday and Elizalde's discovery certainly were hoaxes.

Furthermore, the name Legazpi extends the same issue of authenticity to the historical accounts of the colonization of the Philippines, starting with the arrival of Miguel López de Legazpi, the sixteenth century Spanish explorer. The conditions of colonization by the Spanish, the Americans, and the Japanese afforded little real peace internally, and in the 1970's, under dictator Ferdinand Marcos's rule, turmoil, not peace, prevailed. Thus, *Dream Jungle* compels readers to ask, Were the gentle Stone Age people more primitive than the brutal colonizers? Perhaps a "dream jungle" is an idealization like the vision of James Hilton's *Lost Horizon* (1933), an escapist release from tumultuous reality. In any case, it is the direct opposite of the viciousness of the jungle war that will be presented to theatergoers in *Napalm Sunset*, and both the film and the lost tribe may be seen as diversionary spectacles.

L. M. Grow

Other major works

SHORT FICTION: *Two Stories*, 1992.

PLAYS: *Chiquita Banana*, pb. 1972; *Where the Mississippi Meets the Amazon*, pr. 1977 (with Thulani Davis and Ntozake Shange); *Mango Tango*, pr. 1978; *Tenement Lover: no palm trees/in new york city*, pr. 1981; *Holy Food*, pr. 1988 (pr. 1989 as a radio play); *Teenytown*, pr. 1990 (with Laurie Carlos and Robbie McCauley); *Black: Her Story*, pr., pb. 1993; *Airport Music*, pr. 1994 (with Han Ong); *Silent Movie*, pr. 1997 (as part of *The Square*); *Dogeaters*, pr. 1998 (adaptation of her novel); *Fe in the Desert*, pr. 2007.

POETRY: *Four Young Women: Poems*, 1973 (with Alice Karle, Barbara Szerlip, and Carol Tinker); *The Woman Who Thought She Was More than a Samba*, 1978; *Visions of a Daughter, Foretold*, 1994 (with Paloma Hagedorn Woo).

SCREENPLAY: *Fresh Kill*, 1994.

NONFICTION: *Burning Heart: A Portrait of the Philippines*, 1999 (with photographs by Marissa Roth).

EDITED TEXTS: *Charlie Chan Is Dead: An Anthology of Contemporary Asian American Fiction*, 1993; *Charlie Chan Is Dead II: At Home in the World—An Anthology of Contemporary Asian American Fiction*, 2004.

MISCELLANEOUS: *Dangerous Music*, 1975; *Pet Food and Tropical Apparitions*, 1981; *Danger and Beauty*, 1993.

Bibliography

Ancheta, Shirley. Review of *Danger and Beauty*. *Amerasia Journal* 20, no. 1 (Winter, 1994): 197-202. Thoughtful handling of Hagedorn's early prose and poetry by a well-established scholar.

Covi, Giovanna. "Jessica Hagedorn's Decolonialization of Subjectivity: Historical Agency Beyond Gender and Nation." In *Nationalism and Sexuality: Crises of Identity*, edited by Yiorgos Kalogeras and Domna Pastourmatzi. Thessaloniki, Greece: Hellenic Association of American Studies, Aristotle University, 1996. In this collection of articles examining the intersection of national identity and sexuality, Covi presents a thorough treatment of Hagedorn's major work *Dogeaters*, especially with respect to its characterization.

Evangelista, Susan. "Jessica Hagedorn: Pinay Poet." *Philippine Studies* 35, no. 4 (1987): 475-487. Pioneering scholarly study of Hagedorn. Examines all of her works, including her long fiction.

Hau, Caroline S. "*Dogeaters*, Postmodernism, and the 'Worldling' of the Philippines." In *Philippine Post-Colonial Studies: Essays on Language and Literature*, edited by Cristina Hidalgo and Priscelina Patajo-Legasto. Quezon City: University of the Philippines Press, 1993. Erudite exploration of the place that *Dogeaters* occupies in the context of a postcolonial Philippine nation in a postmodern world.

Lowe, Lisa. "Decolonization, Displacement, Disidentification: Asian American 'Novels' and the Question of History." In *Cultural Institutions of the Novel*, edited by Deidre Lynch and William B. Warner. Durham, N.C.: Duke University Press, 1996. Incisive analysis of the role of various forms of cultural discourse, including gossip, in the myriad verbal representations of *Dogeaters*.

Prose, Francine. "Foxy Ladies." *The New York Times Book Review*, September 15, 1996. American novelist Prose provides an exceptionally witty and entertaining review of Hagedorn's *The Gangster of Love*. An accessible review in a major periodical.

San Juan, Epifanio, Jr. *After Postcolonialism: Mapping Philippines-United States Confrontations*. Blue Ridge Summit, Pa.: Rowman & Littlefield, 2000. A meticulous examination of the structure of *Dogeaters* and *The Gangster of Love* in a collection that surveys the place of the Philippines as a nation after colonization.

Upchurch, Michael. "What's Cooking on Mindanao?" *The New York Times Book Review*, October 5, 2003. Unusually penetrating and detailed analysis and assessment of Hagedorn's novel *Dream Jungle*.

RADCLYFFE HALL

Born: Bournemouth, Hampshire, England; August 12, 1880
Died: London, England; October 7, 1943
Also known as: Marguerite Radclyffe Hall

Principal long fiction

The Forge, 1924
The Unlit Lamp, 1924
A Saturday Life, 1925
Adam's Breed, 1926
The Well of Loneliness, 1928
The Master of the House, 1932
The Sixth Beatitude, 1936

Other literary forms

Radclyffe Hall launched her writing career in 1906 with a collection of verse, *'Twixt Earth and Stars*. This well-received collection was followed by four more volumes of Hall's poetry, which were published between 1908 and 1915. In 1907, Hall met Mabel Veronica Batten, an amateur singer and prominent socialite, who helped her set twenty-one of the eighty poems in *'Twixt Earth and Stars* to music. With encouragement from Batten, Hall published *Sheaf of Verses* in 1908. This volume included poems on lesbian sexuality, notably "Ode to Sappho" and "The Scar."

Hall published three more volumes of verse: *Poems*

Radclyffe Hall.

of the Past and Present (1910), *Songs of Three Counties, and Other Poems* (1913), and *The Forgotten Island* (1915). The narrator in *The Forgotten Island* ruminates on her past life on the island of Lesbos and bemoans her fading love for another woman.

Aside from her collections of poetry, Hall published *Miss Ogilvy Finds Herself*, a collection of short stories, in 1934. The five stories in *Miss Ogilvy Finds Herself* mirror some of the author's own inner conflicts. Its critical reception was disappointing. Her letters are collected in *Your John: The Love Letters of Radclyffe Hall* (1997), edited by Joanne Glasgow.

Achievements

Although *The Well of Loneliness* is Radclyffe Hall's best-known novel, she was awarded three prestigious literary prizes for another work, *Adam's Breed*. This perceptive tale portrays Gian-Luca, a food server who becomes so disgusted with watching the gluttonous people he serves stuff themselves with rich food that he eschews food and eventually starves himself.

Adam's Breed brought Hall the Eichelbergher Humane Award in 1926 for the best novel of the year, a prize that was followed in 1927 by the Prix Femina-Vie Heureuse Prize and shortly thereafter by the much-coveted James Tait Black Memorial Prize. Only once before in the history of these awards had a novel—E. M. Forster's *A Passage to India* (1924)—received both awards in the same year.

The celebrity Hall gained through the enthusiastic critical and popular reception of *Adam's Breed* made the reading public clamor for more of her writing. She devoted October and November, 1927, to beginning her next work of long fiction with the working title "Stephen," named for the novel's protagonist. This novel, renamed *The Well of Loneliness*, appeared in 1928. In this book, Hall produced the first piece of long fiction in England to explicitly explore female homosexuality, a topic Hall touched on obliquely in her earlier work. Although most critics do not consider *The Well of Loneliness* Hall's strongest novel, the notoriety that accompanied its publication established its author in feminist and lesbian and gay circles as a social and literary pioneer.

Biography

Marguerite Radclyffe Hall was born on August 12, 1880, to Radclyffe Radclyffe-Hall and Mary Jane Diehl Sager Radclyffe-Hall, an American expatriate from Philadelphia. Hall's father had inherited a sizable legacy from his own father, a savvy businessman who turned his tuberculosis sanitarium into a highly profitable enterprise.

Hall's father, not needing to work, left Mary Jane shortly after his daughter's birth. Mary Jane divorced him and, in 1889, married Alberto Visetti, a voice instructor at the Royal College of Music in London. Mary Jane, hoping that her first child would be a boy, raised her daughter as a boy, often dressing her in male attire and referring to her as John, a name that Hall later adopted. As her writing progressed, Hall dropped her given name and published as Radclyffe Hall.

In her teenage years, Hall inherited a substantial fortune. She entered King's College in London but left after two terms and spent the next year in Dresden, Germany. Returning to England in 1906, she bought a house in Malvern Wells, Worcestershire. In that year she published her first book of verse and met the socially prominent Mabel Veronica Batten, known as Ladye, a woman a generation older than Hall. Batten became her mentor and, in 1908, her lover.

Batten remained a major factor in Hall's life until her death from a stroke in 1916. Hall had became infatuated with Batten's niece, Una Vincenzo Troubridge, and began a sexual relationship with her, causing Batten considerable grief. Her death left Hall and Troubridge feeling terrible guilt, which haunted them until they died.

Hall died in 1943 and was buried beside Batten in Highgate Cemetery. Hall's tombstone bears the following words from Elizabeth Barrett Browning's *Sonnets from the Portuguese* (1850): "And if God Choose I Shall But Love Thee Better After Death," a testimony to the guilt that Hall suffered because of the pain she caused Batten.

Hall's reputation as a poet and novelist increased in the two decades between the publication of her first verse collection and the publication of *Adam's Breed* in 1926. She had verged on revealing her sexuality in much of her earlier writing. In 1927, however, she wrote *The Well of Loneliness*, a lesbian-themed novel in which she argued for the right of people to be different and to marry those they love, even if the "objects" of their love are of the same gender.

Although *The Well of Loneliness* is not prurient, its morality was questioned, and it soon became the subject of much controversy. On August 19, 1927, less than one month after its publication, James Douglas, editor of the *London Sunday Express*, raised questions about the book's morality and insisted that the British home secretary ban it. Hall's publisher, Cape, withdrew the novel but arranged for its re-publication in Paris.

Charges brought under the Obscene Publications Act of 1857 were lodged against the publisher and a bookseller, Leonard Hill, who had sold copies of the novel smuggled from France. Despite court testimony from numerous literary luminaries, the book was banned in England, not to be published there for twenty-two years. A lawsuit to ban the book in the United States found in Hall's favor.

In 1934, Hall became infatuated with a Russian nurse named Evguenia Souline, who was hired to care for the ailing Troubridge. Although Hall entered into an affair with Souline that lasted until shortly before Hall's death, Troubridge, much pained by the relationship, remained loyal to Hall and was at her bedside when Hall succumbed to colon cancer in 1943. In her instructions for distributing her estate, Hall trusted Troubridge to treat Souline equitably.

Analysis

Lesbian sexuality and gender expression were the dominant factors in Radclyffe Hall's life, and the topics pervaded most of her writing directly or indirectly. Hall firmly believed in freedom of choice in human relationships and was ahead of her time in being an advocate for such controversial issues as same-gender marriage.

Society's disdain for homosexuality dominated Hall's thinking, and her opinions about this disdain appear in her long fiction as well as in her early poetry. She was familiar with the studies of sexologists Richard von Krafft-Ebing and Havelock Ellis, who argued that homosexuality is congenital—or genetic—rather than a matter of choice. She felt duty-bound to promote this view in her writing.

Although *The Well of Loneliness* contains Hall's most forthright sentiments regarding female homosexuality, the theme is present in a more subdued form in her first work of long fiction, *The Unlit Lamp*, in which a close relationship, covertly homosexual, exists between Joan Ogden and her governess, Elizabeth Rodney. In Victorian England, the setting of this novel, such relationships were common, but their sexual nature was overlooked in a society that shied away from acknowledging sex, especially between women.

In her next novel, *The Forge*, Hall uses the device of writing about a heterosexual couple in coded language that reveals, to those familiar with that language, that Hilary and Susan Brent are, in actuality, lesbians. The author offers veiled hints throughout the novel of a relationship other than heterosexual.

Hall's finest work of long fiction, as many critics agree, is *Adam's Breed*, in which a fully realized protagonist, Gian-Luca, is Hall's best-realized character. Although this novel does not have the homosexual overtones of much of Hall's work, it explores other important themes, those she addresses in much of her writing: isolation, alienation from family, cruelty to animals, the effects of a troubled childhood upon one's later development, and social persecution.

THE UNLIT LAMP

The Unlit Lamp is Hall's first novel, although it was published after *The Forge*. Hall got the idea to write *The Unlit Lamp* after observing a spinster caring for her demanding mother at a seaside resort. Hall was appalled by how women, especially single women, are drawn into acting gratis as servants to demanding relatives.

As *The Unlit Lamp* begins, the adolescent Joan Ogden wants to become a physician. Her governess, Elizabeth Rodney, plans to help her achieve that end by moving to London with her so that Joan can pursue medical studies. Joan has been trapped in the small town to which her mother retreated following the deaths of Joan's overbearing military father and her younger sister.

Joan and Elizabeth make one last attempt to relocate in London, but Joan's manipulative mother again draws her daughter into her trap. Elizabeth, realizing the futility of trying to fulfill her cherished dream of taking Joan to London, runs away from the small town and is married. In *The Unlit Lamp*, Hall also deals with what one might call a retreat into heterosexuality by having Elizabeth leave Joan and marry a man. Elizabeth seeks the stability and social acceptability of heterosexual marriage over a lesbian relationship.

Joan's mother dies, leaving her without options. She becomes the spinster caregiver for an old man. The frustration, isolation, and futility that pervade this novel lead to thought-provoking questions about a woman's place in society, and they articulate strong feminist sentiments long before such sentiments were common.

ADAM'S BREED

Generally considered Hall's most successful novel, *Adam's Breed* is notable for its psychologically sound character study. The story revolves around the life of Gian-Luca, who feels abandoned and alienated in unique ways. He does not know who his father is until fairly late in his life. His mother dies in childbirth. Gian-Luca's maternal grandmother, who blames him for her daughter's death, raises him.

Isolated and lonely, Gian-Luca eventually becomes headwaiter at the Doric Restaurant and marries a simple young Italian woman. Serving in World War I as a caterer for the military, at war's end he attempts to return to his former life, but the war has changed him. He cannot adjust. Working in the restaurant, he is surrounded by greedy, gluttonous patrons whose excesses disgust him to the point that the sight of food appalls him.

In the restaurant one night, he serves an Italian poet, Ugo Doria, who turns out to be his birth father. Eventually, Gian-Luca leaves his wife and goes to the New Forest to live as a recluse. Realizing that he cannot withdraw from life, he returns to his wife, but he has become so emaciated that he dies of starvation.

In this sensitively told story, Hall pursues many of the themes that interest her most. Isolation and abandonment were major factors in her own life, and she was able in *Adam's Breed* to capture the ways these two forces impinge upon a person's life; in this case, on Gian-Luca's development.

THE WELL OF LONELINESS

Although *The Well of Loneliness* is not Hall's best work of long fiction, it is the novel that reflects her deepest emotions and most pressing concerns. The leading character in the novel is Stephen Gordon, a woman whose aristocratic parents, hoping for a son, gave her a male name and dressed her in masculine clothing. As she matures, she realizes that she is a lesbian. When she receives a marriage proposal from Martin Hallam, she rejects it and then falls in love with Angela Crossby, the wife of a businessman. As Stephen's sexual orientation becomes obvious to many, her mother forces her out of the family home. Stephen goes to London and writes a novel, and even though she spends time with other gays and lesbians, she still suffers inner conflict about her sexuality.

The time is World War I, and Stephen joins the ambulance corps, where she meets and falls in love with Mary Llewellyn, an unsophisticated young woman from Wales. At war's end, the two go to Paris together and rent a house. Mary begins to feel discomfort with Stephen's activities and the people she attracts, and they separate. Stephen generously "gives" Mary to Martin, the man whose marriage proposal Stephen rejected.

The novel ends with the proclamation "Give us also the right to our existence!," a sentiment at the heart of much of Hall's writing. *The Well of Loneliness* remains the work of long fiction for which Hall is remembered. The first novel in England to broach openly the matter of female homosexuality, the book gained sufficient notoriety to ensure its sales both upon publication and after. Two years after its release in 1928, the novel brought Hall sixty thousand dollars in royalties, a princely sum at that time. In the year of Hall's death, 1943, international sales of *The Well of Loneliness* exceeded one hundred thousand copies.

R. Baird Shuman

Other major works

short fiction: *Miss Ogilvy Finds Herself*, 1934.

poetry: *'Twixt Earth and Stars*, 1906; *A Sheaf of Verses*, 1908; *Poems of the Past and Present*, 1910; *Songs of Three Counties, and Other Poems*, 1913; *The Forgotten Island*, 1915.

nonfiction: *Your John: The Love Letters of Radclyffe Hall*, 1997 (Joanne Glasgow, editor).

Bibliography

Castle, Terry. *Noël Coward and Radclyffe Hall: Kindred Spirits*. New York: Columbia University Press, 1996. Castle argues that although they were seeming opposites, British playwright and composer Noël Coward and Hall were friends who contributed directly to each other's work.

Cline, Sally. *Radclyffe Hall: A Woman Called John*. New York: Overlook Press, 1998. This thorough biography of Hall discusses how she assumed essentially a masculine gender identity and chronicles as well her relationships with women, many of those relationships long term.

Dickson, Lovat. *Radclyffe Hall at the Well of Loneliness: A Sapphic Chronicle*. New York: Scribner, 1975. An incisive account of Hall's literary work on the torments of being different in a society with strict gender roles and rules about sexual expression, homosexuality in particular.

Doan, Laura, and Jay Prosser, eds. *Palatable Poison: Critical Perspectives on "The Well of Loneliness."* New York: Columbia University Press, 2001. Twenty-one essays, and a perceptive introductory essay by the editors and an afterword by literary critic Terry Castle, offer excellent analyses of the critical reception of this controversial novel.

Glasgow, Joanne, ed. *Your John: The Love Letters of Radclyffe Hall*. New York: New York University Press, 1997. This collection of 576 letters Hall wrote between 1934 and 1942 to Evguenia Souline, a Russian emigre with whom she was in love, offers keen insights into Hall's character and emotions.

Souhami, Diana. *The Trials of Radclyffe Hall*. New York: Doubleday, 1999. Of particular interest in this critical biography is Souhami's discussion of the triangulated love affair that involved both Una Troubridge, Hall's lover for twenty-eight years, and Evguenia Souline, her paramour for nearly a decade.

Troubridge, Lady Una Vincenzo. *The Life of Radclyffe Hall*. New York: Citadel Press, 1961. A reminiscence by the woman who was Hall's longtime lover. A highly subjective account that is, nonetheless, interesting and informative.

JANE HAMILTON

Born: Oak Park, Illinois; July 13, 1957

Principal long fiction

The Book of Ruth, 1988 (also known as *The Frogs Are Still Singing*, 1989)
A Map of the World, 1994
The Short History of a Prince, 1998
Disobedience, 2000
When Madeline Was Young, 2006

Other literary forms

Jane Hamilton is chiefly a novelist, but she honed her skills writing short fiction. *Harper's* magazine published two of her stories, "Aunt Marji's Happy Ending" and "My Own Earth." Her award-winning *The Book of Ruth* had its origins in a ten-page short story to which the author returned and expanded into a novel.

Achievements

Jane Hamilton achieved early success with the publication of her first novel. In 1989, *The Book of Ruth* received the Great Lakes College Association New Writers Award, the Banta Award, and the Hemingway Foundation/PEN Award for First Fiction. *The Book of Ruth* and *A Map of the World* were selected for Oprah's Book Club, helping them achieve best-seller status worldwide. Both novels were adapted for film, *A Map of the World* for the cinema in 1999 and *The Book of Ruth* for television in 2004. In 1998, *The Short History of a Prince* received the *Chicago Tribune* Heartland Prize and was short-listed for the Orange Prize. *Disobedience* was named to the *School Library Journal*'s list of the best adult books for high school students in 1991.

Biography

Jane Hamilton was born in 1957 in Oak Park, Illinois, the birthplace also of novelist Carol Shields. Hamilton's father was an engineer and her mother was a theater critic. The fifth and last child in a rambunctious brood, Hamilton was the quiet and introspective daughter who, from an early age, preferred the written word over the spoken. Hamilton's mother and grandmother were writers, too, so writing seemed to be her heritage. She once observed that she thought it only natural that she would grow up to become a writer.

In 1979, Hamilton earned her B.A. in English at Carleton College in Minnesota and then headed east to New York, where she had secured a position in the children's fiction division of a publishing house. En route to New York she took a detour. A brief stop at an apple orchard in Wisconsin that belonged to a friend's family became a permanent relocation. Hamilton never made it to New York nor did she regret her lost career in publishing. Instead, she became an apple farmer, laboring in the orchards spring through fall and wintering indoors, where she nurtured her writing skills. She applied for but was denied enrollment in the Iowa Writers' Workshop. Undeterred, she continued to submit her short stories for consideration in several publications, but she received rejections. Seeking more formal training in her craft, she spent time at Ragdale in Illinois, a retreat for writers and artists.

In 1982, Hamilton married Robert Willard, one of the owners of the orchard. In 1983, *Harper's* accepted and published two of her short stories, including "Aunt Marji's Happy Ending," launching Hamilton's career as a writer. The couple had a son, Ben, in 1984, the year Hamilton completed the rough draft of what would become *The Book of Ruth*, a novel about the struggles of a poor rural girl whose life rushes toward catastrophe when she marries an emotionally unstable man. The novel was picked up by Ticknor and Fields in 1987, the same year daughter Hannah was born. Published in 1988, the novel received critical and public favor. The next decade proved to be a successful one for Hamilton; she published more novels, and they, too, were embraced by readers and critics.

Analysis

Critics often compare Jane Hamilton favorably to another midwestern author, Pulitzer Prize winner Jane Smiley, whose novels *A Thousand Acres* and *Moo* are set in farm country and explore human resiliency in the face of great obstacles. Hamilton's novels are set in the Midwest, the area where she spent her childhood, attended college, and lived as a full-time writer. Her fiction is populated by rural and small town family members, mothers and fathers, and sons and daughters, who endure life's tragedies with stoicism and frankness, traits often associated with inhabitants of the heartland; Hamilton, though, does not allow her characters to sink into caricature.

Orchards, fields, farmhouses, and main streets provide the backdrop for events that disrupt the quietude of the country environment. The murder of a mother-in-law in *The Book of Ruth*, allegations of child abuse in *A Map of the World*, the closeted life of a gay man in *The Short History of a Prince*, a mother's extramarital affair in *Disobedience*, and a family secret in *When Madeline Was Young* seem drawn from the tabloids, but Hamilton avoids sensationalism. Instead, the challenges and shocks faced by her characters allow her to explore fundamental human values such as forgiveness, reconciliation, acceptance, and loyalty.

Jane Hamilton. (Time & Life Pictures/Getty Images)

Like its predecessor, *A Map of the World* is set in a rural community, but it shifts its focus to the lives of middle-class transplants who are viewed by the locals with suspicion after an accidental drowning occurs on their property. *The Short History of a Prince* is a departure from the first two novels in its third-person point of view, its focus on a male character, and its lighter tone. *Disobedience* examines the impact of a parent's affair upon a family when discovered by a child. *When Madeline Was Young* presents an intriguing blended family in which the father's first wife, the Madeline of the title, who has suffered brain injury, passes as his daughter in his second marriage.

The Book of Ruth

Hamilton's debut novel was a critical success. The book's title alludes to the Old Testament book of the Bible, and biblical passages appear throughout the novel to form a motif, and they are delivered by a preacher in his sermons and reinterpreted ironically by the disbelieving title character, Ruth. The book, too, is named for the story's protagonist; *The Book of Ruth* is Ruth's book. It is the story of her experiences from childhood through her mid-twenties, and it is narrated from her perspective. Additionally, the story tells of the books that provided Ruth a literary education that was denied her in the public school system. Also, a blind neighbor introduces a young Ruth to audio books.

The classic stories Ruth reads, tales of men and women who endure and survive, run parallel to her own story. The suffering protagonists of Victorian tomes are her particular favorites. At one point, Ruth imagines entering Charles Dickens's *Bleak House* (1852-1853, serial; 1853, book) to assist the novel's heroine, Esther, with the numerous responsibilities she has in the service of others; ironically, Ruth does not recognize that *she* is the one who requires assistance in the form of rescue. When none arrives, she cheats death and rescues herself.

Ruth grows up marginalized by polite society because she is poor, has a plain physique, and has limited knowledge. Her life was punctuated by abuse from her mother and her husband. Ruth is neglected by relatives who otherwise should protect her. She is abandoned first by her father, who skips out on his family, and later by her brother, who leaves home permanently for higher education. She is kept at a distance from the aunt she idealizes. Though separated by only fifty miles, the two communicate solely through letters.

The larger community is also dismissive of Ruth. Despite being the sister of a gifted brother, Ruth is considered average and expendable by teachers at her school. She is on her own when her drug-addled and emotionally uneven husband, in a fit of fury, attempts to kill her and her mother; he succeeds in the latter and leaves Ruth seriously injured. That Ruth has penned her saga as a form of therapy and forgiveness is revealed on the final page of the novel. Ruth notes, "Perhaps I will write a fiction book when I'm through with this," leaving open the possibility of transformation, at least through writing.

A Map of the World

In *A Map of the World*, Alice Godwin is guilty of a lapse in judgment; in the brief minutes during which she takes a breather from the responsibilities of motherhood, a neighbor child in her care drowns in a pond on her property. The tragedy separates Alice, her husband, Howard, and their daughters from the community, and eventually distances wife from husband and mother from children. The community ostracizes Alice further when an accusation of child abuse surfaces at the school where she is employed as a nurse. Eventually she is cleared of the charge, but not before the life she created, a relatively peaceful secluded existence with her family, is altered irrevocably.

Although written from the first-person perspective, the narrative voice is twofold. *A Map of the World* is divided into three parts; Alice narrates the first and third sections, while Howard voices the middle. He relays the story during the time Alice is in jail and cannot speak for herself, including the daily burden of caring for the farm and his daughters as a single parent. The novel explores the process by which a person, ostracized by her community and estranged from her family, works her way back into these folds.

The novel's overarching theme is forgiveness. Alice struggles to forgive those who have transgressed against her, and she can begin to do so only when she forgives herself.

The Short History of a Prince

A coming-of-age story, *The Short History of a Prince* is set in two interwoven decades, the 1970's and the 1990's. In the 1970's, Walter McCloud is a teenage boy whose wish is to be a professional ballet dancer. He is cast as Prince Siegfried in the *Nutcracker* ballet not because he is talented but because he is the sole male dancer in his school old enough for the role. His growing awareness of his limited potential is heightened by adolescent angst, a crush on another boy, and the terminal illness of his older brother.

McCloud in the 1990's is a man recently returned to a small midwestern community to teach English. The interval of the 1980's, during which he worked in New York City in a doll factory, is alluded to but not fully realized. The allusion serves to heighten the contrast between his youthful wishes and his adult responsibilities. A lover of art, music, and books since childhood, McCloud experiences these solaces as a devotee rather than a participant.

Disobedience

Hamilton's fourth novel is about a functioning dysfunctional family, a spying son, and the secrets that family members keep to hold their relationships together. A decade has passed and an older Henry Shaw narrates the events of his senior year of high school, the year of his mother's infidelity. Though troubled by his mother's behavior and his father's apparent ignorance, he imbues his narrative with a sense of humor and compassion. Out of teenage curiosity, he begins to check his mother's e-mail. When he discovers an illicit affair between his mother and a violin maker, his curiosity turns to voyeurism. He begins to feel like an accomplice in the affair because he is the one who set up his mother's e-mail account.

Despite feelings of guilt for snooping, Henry charts the progress of the affair electronically, and wonders how its eventual revelation will impact other family members. His father, a teacher of history, seems blind to events occurring in his own time and in his own family. Henry's sister, Elvira, like her father, prefers past lives, savoring her role as a soldier in Civil War reenactments. Even the mother, in her role as a pianist who performs with a group that plays classics, embraces the past through music. All the members of the Shaw family seem determined to avoid the here and now, even Henry, as he recalls events of ten years prior. The novel's title, *Disobedience*, becomes a reference not only to the mother's betrayal and Henry's invasions of privacy but also to the behavior of an entire family.

Dorothy Dodge Robbins

Bibliography

Charles, Ron. "A Family Quartet Out of Tune with Itself." *Christian Science Monitor*, November 9, 2000. This review considers the characters in *Disobedience* in terms of their uses of technology, in particular the Internet, and their resultant social behaviors. Classifies the novel as a compelling, but troubling, account of infidelity and its impact on a representative American family.

Hutchings, Vicky. "Boy Talk." *New Statesman* 130 (March 12, 2001). A positive appraisal of *Disobedience* that highlights the gender-role reversals of family members in the novel.

Juhasz, Suzanne. "The Prince Is Wearing a Tutu: Queer Identity and Identificatory Reading in Jane Hamilton's *The Short History of a Prince*." *American Imago: Studies in Psychoanalysis and Culture* 61, no. 2 (Summer, 2004): 134-164. Employs principles of psychology and reader response theory to link reader, author, and character in *The Short History of a Prince*. Also examines Hamilton's portrayals of gender, sexuality, and art.

Neville, Maureen. "*When Madeline Was Young*." Review in *Library Journal* 131, no. 12 (July 1, 2006). Positive appraisal of the novel that highlights its blended family of characters, its Chicago setting, and its decades-spanning time frame. Notes that Hamilton uses world events, such as the Vietnam and Iraq Wars, to provide a larger context for familial events in this domestic novel.

Steinberg, Sybil. "Jane Hamilton: A Kinship with Society's Outcasts." *Publishers Weekly*, February 2, 1998. Explores connections between Hamilton's Walter in *The Short History of a Prince* and similar outcast protagonists in her earlier works: the title character in *The Book of Ruth* and Alice in *A Map of the World*.

Strasser, Judith. "Daily Harvest: At Work with Novelist Jane Hamilton." *Poets and Writers* 26, no. 3 (May/June, 1998): 32-45. This interview focuses on Hamilton's family and career, and the effect of each upon the other. *The Book of Ruth* and *Map of the World* are discussed in terms of their origins and public impact.

Taylor, Pegi. "Jane Hamilton: Good Writing Is in the Details." *Writer* 114, no. 1 (January, 2001): 26-31. Taylor interviews Hamilton about her use of metaphorical language and her creation of characters. The relationship of *Disobedience* to earlier works is discussed. In particular, Hamilton explains how young characters in her other novels are precursors to Henry, the son who discovers his mother's affair in *Disobedience*.

DASHIELL HAMMETT

Born: St. Mary's County, Maryland; May 27, 1894
Died: New York, New York; January 10, 1961
Also known as: Samuel Dashiell Hammett

Principal long fiction

$106,000 Blood Money, 1927 (also known as *Blood Money* and *The Big Knockover*)
Red Harvest, 1927-1928 (serial), 1929 (book)
The Dain Curse, 1928-1929 (serial), 1929 (book)
The Maltese Falcon, 1929-1930 (serial), 1930 (book)
The Glass Key, 1930 (serial), 1931 (book)
Woman in the Dark, 1933 (serial), 1951 (book)
The Thin Man, 1934
Complete Novels, 1999

Other literary forms

Dashiell Hammett (HAM-eht) first attracted critical attention as the author of short detective fiction published in *Smart Set* and *Black Mask* magazines as early as 1923. The best of his stories were narratives told in the first person by the nameless "Continental Op," a fat, balding operative working out of the San Francisco office of the Continental Detective Agency. The Continental Op is also the narrator and principal character of Hammett's first two novels, both of which were published in magazines before their appearance in book form. A number of his short stories were anthologized in *The Continental Op* (1945) and, after Hammett's death in 1961, *The Big Knockover: Selected Stories and Short Novels* (1966).

Achievements

Together with his contemporary Raymond Chandler (1888-1959), Dashiell Hammett is credited with defining the form, scope, and tone of the modern detective novel, a distinctly American genre that departs considerably from the earlier tradition inspired by the British. Chandler, although six years Hammett's senior, did not in fact begin publishing detective fiction until 1933 and readily acknowledged the younger writer's prior claim. Together, both authors have exerted considerable influence upon later exponents of the detective genre, notably on Ross Macdonald, their most distinguished successor. Hammett's work in particular has served also as a stylistic model for many novelists working outside the detective genre, among them Ernest Hemingway and John O'Hara.

Unlike his predecessors in the mystery genre, Hammett adopted a starkly realistic, tough-minded tone in his works, sustaining an atmosphere in which questions outnumber answers and no one is to be trusted. Hammett's reputation ultimately rests on his creation of two characters who embody the moral ambiguities of the modern world: Sam Spade (*The Maltese Falcon*) and Nick Charles (*The Thin Man*). Widely popularized through film adaptations of the novels in which they appear, Spade and Charles are among the most famous American detectives, known even to those with little more than marginal interest in the mystery genre. Tough-minded if occasionally softhearted, both characters may be seen as particularized refinements of Hammett's Continental Op, professional detectives who remain true to their personal code of honor and skeptical with regard to everything and everyone else.

Partially because of declining health, Hammett wrote no novels after the age of forty. His reputation, however, was by that time secure; even in the following century, his five novels would remain landmarks of the genre, a model for future novelists and a formidable standard of comparison.

Biography

Samuel Dashiell Hammett was born in St. Mary's County, Maryland, on May 27, 1894, into an old but modest Roman Catholic family. Leaving high school at the age of fourteen after less than a year of attendance, Hammett worked indifferently at a variety of odd jobs before signing on with the Pinkerton Detective Agency around the age of twenty. At last, it seemed he had found work that he enjoyed and could do well, with a dedication later reflected in the character and behavior of the Continental Op. With time out for service in World War I, from which he was demobilized as a sergeant, Hammett continued to serve Pinkerton with distinction until failing health caused him to consider other options.

In 1921, Hammett married Josephine Dolan, a nurse whom he had met during one of his recurring bouts with tuberculosis. The couple moved west to San Francisco, where Hammett returned to work for Pinkerton, only to resign in frustration and disgust after an ironic incident in which his detective talents proved too great for his own good: Assigned by Pinkerton to ship out on an Australian freighter in search of stolen gold believed to be hidden aboard, Hammett managed to find the missing gold in a smokestack during a cursory search just prior to departure and was thus denied the anticipated voyage to Australia.

During such spare time as he could find, Hammett had been trying to prepare himself as a writer; upon leaving Pinkerton, he devoted himself increasingly to writing, eventually leaving his family (which by then included two daughters) and moving to a cheap furnished room where he could live and write. Fearing that he had little time left to live, he wrote at a determined pace; encouraged by his first successes, he gradually developed and refined the writing style that was to make him famous. His first story featuring the Continental Op appeared in October, 1923. Increasingly successful, Hammett soon progressed to the writing of longer stories that were in fact independent sections of novels, eventually published as *Red Harvest* and *The Dain Curse*. Both appeared as hardbound editions in 1929. The following year, Hammett achieved both critical recognition and financial independence with *The Maltese Falcon*, an unquestionably mature and groundbreaking work that sold at once to the film industry; director John Huston's landmark 1941 version of *The Maltese Falcon* was the third Hollywood film to be drawn from a Hammett novel.

In 1930, Hammett made the acquaintance of dramatist Lillian Hellman, eleven years his junior, who was to become the most important and influential woman in his life. Although they never married (each was unhappily married to someone else at the time of their first meeting), Hellman and Hammett remained together in an intense, often turbulent, but intellectually rewarding relationship until Hammett's death some thirty years later at the age of sixty-six. *The Thin Man*, Hammett's next and last published novel (*The Glass Key* having already been written by the time he met Hellman), reflects the author's relationship with Hellman in the portrayal of Nick and Nora Charles, represented in the screen version and its sequels by William Powell and Myrna Loy.

Dashiell Hammett. (Library of Congress)

Following the success of *The Thin Man* both as book and as film, Hammett moved to Hollywood, where he worked as a writer and script doctor on a variety of screen projects. He became increasingly involved in leftist politics and toward the end of the Depression became a member of the Communist Party. Hammett did not, however, consider his politics an impediment to patriotism; soon after the United States entered World War II, he was back in a sergeant's uniform, despite his advanced age and obviously declining health. Attached to the Signal Corps, he served three years in the Aleutian Islands, where his duties included editing a daily newspaper for his fellow servicemen. By the end of the war, however, his health was more precarious than ever, undermined by years of recurrent tuberculosis and heavy drinking. After an alcoholic crisis in 1948, Hammett forswore drinking for the remainder of his life.

At the same time, Hammett's political past was coming back to haunt him; like his fictional characters, however, he remained loyal to his convictions and his friends, declining to testify against his fellow associates in the Communist Party and other political organizations. In 1951, Hammett spent five months in various prisons for contempt of court as a result of his refusal to testify; around the same time, government authorities determined that he was several years behind in the payment of his income tax. Unable to find work in Hollywood because of his political views, Hammett was further impoverished by the attachment of his remaining income for the payment of back taxes. Increasingly infirm, Hammett spent his last years in the care and company of Hellman. He died at Lenox Hill Hospital in New York City on January 10, 1961.

Analysis

Unlike most of their predecessors in the genre, Dashiell Hammett's detectives live and work, as did Hammett himself, in a world populated with actual criminals who violate the law for tangible personal gain. Significantly, Hammett did all of his creative writing during the years of Prohibition, when lawlessness was rampant and organized crime was rapidly gaining a foothold in the American social structure. Prohibition indeed functions prominently in all of Hammett's published work as background, as atmosphere, and frequently as subject. In *Red Harvest*, Hammett's first novel, a loose confederacy of bootleggers, thieves, and hired killers has set up what appears to be a substitute government, replacing law and order with values of their own; the resulting Hobbesian chaos clearly reflects, however indirectly, Hammett's own developing political consciousness. There is little place in such a world for genteel detectives cast in the mold of Dorothy Sayers's Lord Peter Wimsey; accordingly, Hammett presents in the Continental Op and his successors the kind of detective who can deal routinely and effectively with hardened criminals. As Raymond Chandler observed, "Hammett gave murder back to the kind of people who commit it for reasons."

Within such an evil environment, the sleuth often becomes as devious and mendacious as those whom he is pursuing, remaining faithful nevertheless to a highly personal code of honor and justice. Sam Spade, perhaps the most intriguing of Hammett's literary creations, is so well attuned to the criminal mind that he often appears to be a criminal himself; he is known to have been involved romantically with his partner's wife and is thus a likely suspect after the man is murdered. Still, at the end of *The Maltese Falcon*, he persists in turning over to the authorities the thief and murderer Brigid O'Shaughnessy, despite an acknowledged mutual attraction.

Ned Beaumont, the protagonist of *The Glass Key*, remains similarly incorruptible despite outward appearances to the contrary: A detective by temperament, if not by trade, Ned serves as friend and aide to the rising local politician Paul Madvig, involving himself deeply in political deals and trades; still, he persists in revealing a U.S. senator as the murderer of his own son and insists that the senator stand trial rather than commit suicide. The law of the land, however tarnished, remains a strong value in Hammett's novels, suggesting an abiding need for structure against the threat of anarchy.

With *The Thin Man*, Hammett moved in a new direction. For the first time, humor became a significant element in Hammett's fiction, infusing the novel with a lightness of tone that sets it quite apart from the almost documentary seriousness of *Red Harvest* and *The Glass Key*. Its protagonist, Nick Charles, has retired from the detective trade after his marriage to the rich and pretty Nora, some fifteen years his junior. Released from the need to work, he clearly prefers the carefree life of parties, travel, hotels, and round-the-clock drinking, all the while trading jokes and friendly banter with his attractive wife and other boon companions. Still, some habits die hard, and unpredicted events soon bring Nick's well-honed detective instincts back into operation. Moving back and forth between speakeasies and his lavish hotel suite, getting shot at by enraged gangsters, Nick urbanely unravels the mystery until, to no one's real surprise, one of his many casual friends stands revealed as the culprit. It is no secret that Hammett, in his portrayal of the witty Nora and her relationship with Nick, was more than a little influenced by his own developing relationship with Hellman, who returned the favor in her several volumes of memoirs.

Like Nick, Hammett at the time of *The Thin Man* was approaching middle age without the need to work, free at last to indulge his taste for parties and other carefree pursuits. *The Thin Man*, although certainly not planned as Hammett's final novel, is in a sense a fitting valedictory, an exuberant tour de force in which, ironically, the tensions contained in the earlier novels are finally released and perhaps dissipated. An additional irony exists within the book: Nick and Nora Charles may well be Hammett's best-known literary creations, perpetuated by the film version of the novel as well as by several sequels scripted in Hollywood by Hammett himself.

Red Harvest

Hammett's first published novel, *Red Harvest*, originally serialized in *Black Mask*, delivers in ample portion the harsh realism promised in its title. Indeed, the high body count of *Red Harvest* may well have set a kind of record to be met or broken by later efforts in the detective genre. Hammett's intention, however, is not merely to shock the reader; seen in retrospect, *Red Harvest* emerges as a parable of civilization and its possible mutations.

Nowhere in *Red Harvest* are Hammett's intentions more evident than in his choice of location, a mythical Western community called Personville, better known as Poisonville. Some fifty years after the lawless days of the Wild West, Personville/Poisonville has yet to be tamed, even as outlaws have been replaced by gangsters with East Coast accents wearing snap-brim hats instead of Stetsons. The Op, sent to Personville at the request of Donald Willsson, makes an appointment with him only to discover that he has been murdered before the planned meeting can take place. Undaunted, the Op proceeds to investigate Willsson's murder, plunging deeper and deeper into the town's menacing and malevolent atmosphere. Among the more likely suspects is Willsson's father, Elihu, the town boss, who may well have tried to put a stop to his son's muckraking activities as publisher of the local newspaper. Other suspects, however, are present in abundance, at least until they begin to kill off one another during internecine combat partially masterminded by the Op.

The Op, it seems, is particularly skillful in setting the various criminal elements loose upon one another, paving the way for eventual martial law and relative peace, "a sweet-smelling and thornless bed of roses." In the process, however, he frequently faces criminal charges himself; at the same time, the authorities who are pressing the charges may well be as corrupt as the more obvious criminals. In such an environment, the closest thing to a moral imperative is the Op's own case-hardened sense of justice.

The major weakness of *Red Harvest* is a bewildering multiplicity of characters and actions; often, a new character will be introduced and established, only to be killed on the following page. The acts of violence, although symptomatic of social ills and not included for their own sake (as in the work of later hard-boiled mystery writers such as Mickey Spillane), are so numerous as to weary even the least squeamish of readers, although a number of scenes are especially effective; in one, the Op, watching a boxing match that he has helped to "unfix," stands helpless as the unexpected winner falls dead in the ring with a knife at the base of his neck.

The Dain Curse

Later in the same year, 1929, Hammett published *The Dain Curse*, another formerly serialized novel featuring the Op as narrator and main character. Less sophisticated in its presentation than *Red Harvest*, *The Dain Curse* is more severely hampered by a multiplicity of characters and plot twists, all turning around the possibility of a family "curse" brought on by incest. Despite some rather skillful and memorable characterizations, *The Dain Curse* is generally agreed to be Hammett's weakest and least effective novel. Significantly, it is the last of Hammett's novels to feature the Op and the last (until *The Thin Man*, a different sort of novel) to be narrated in the first person.

The Maltese Falcon

Hammett's third novel, *The Maltese Falcon*, narrated dispassionately in the third person, combines the narrative strengths of his earlier works with a far more developed sense of characterization. Its protagonist, Sam Spade, although enough like the Op to be his slightly younger brother, is a more fully realized character caught and portrayed in all his ambiguity. Clearly the "brains" of the Spade and Archer Agency, he is careful to turn over to Miles Archer the case of a young woman client in whose presence he senses trouble. When Archer, blinded by the woman's flattery, goes forth to his death, Spade is hardly surprised, nor does he take many pains to hide his recent affair with the woman who is now Archer's widow. Spade, meanwhile, has grown tired of Iva Archer and her advances. Himself under suspicion for Archer's murder, Spade delves deeper into the case, learning that the young woman has given a number of aliases and cover stories. Her real name, it appears, is Brigid O'Shaughnessy, and it is not long before Spade connects her to a ring of international thieves, each of whom seems to be competing with the others for possession of an ancient and priceless treasure known as the Maltese Falcon. Supposedly, the football-sized sculpted bird, encrusted with precious stones, has been stolen and repossessed numerous times in the four hundred years of its existence, having surfaced most recently in the hands of a Russian general.

Spade's quest eventually brings him in contact with most of the larcenous principals except for the general himself (who at the end of the novel is found to have substituted a worthless leaden counterfeit for the genuine article). Among the thieves are two particularly memorable characters, interpreted in the John Huston film by Sydney Greenstreet and Peter Lorre, respectively: Casper Gutman, an eloquent, grossly fat manipulator and adventurer, keeps trying to maneuver Spade into his confidence; meanwhile, the other, Joel Cairo, openly gay and a member of the international underworld, repeatedly (and most unsuccessfully) tries to intimidate Spade with a handgun that Spade keeps taking away from him. In 1930, Hammett's frank portrayal of a gay man was considered daring in the extreme; by 1941, it was possible for Huston to apply such a characterization to Gutman as well, whose homosexuality in the novel is little more than latent. The book, for example, mentions that Gutman is traveling with a grown daughter, but the daughter is never mentioned in the Huston film.

In both novel and film, Spade's character develops considerably as he attempts to deal simultaneously with the matters at hand and with his growing affection for the obviously perfidious Brigid O'Shaughnessy. In Brigid, it seems, Spade has at last met his proper match, a woman whose deviousness and native intelligence compare favorably with his own. In her presence, it is all too easy for Spade to forget the cloying advances of Iva Archer or even the tomboyish charms of his secretary, Effie Perine; it is less easy, however, for him to forget the tightening web of circumstantial evidence in which he finds Brigid strongly enmeshed. After the coveted falcon has been revealed as a forgery, Spade confronts Brigid with evidence that she, and not her deceased cohort, Floyd Thursby, fired the bullet that killed Miles Archer. For all Archer's weaknesses and Spade's personal contempt for him, Spade remains true to the code that dictates arrest and prosecution for his partner's murderer. Explaining to an incredulous Brigid that he still thinks he loves her but cannot bring himself to trust her, he declares that he is sending her to jail and may or may not be waiting when she is freed. They are locked in an embrace when the police arrive to take her away.

Considerably more thoughtful and resonant than Hammett's earlier novels, *The Maltese Falcon* is his unquestioned masterpiece. The falcon itself, a contested piece of plunder that, in the novel, has occasioned theft and murder throughout recent history and that in its present form turns out to be a fake, is without doubt one of the strongest and best developed images in contemporary American fiction. Another equally effective device, absent from the Huston film, is the Flitcraft parable that Spade tells to Brigid early in their relationship as a way of explaining his behavior.

Early in his career, Spade recalls, he was hired to find a Seattle resident named Flitcraft who had disappeared mysteriously one day during the lunch hour, leaving behind a wife and two children. Spade later learned that, during the lunch break, Flitcraft had glimpsed his own mortality after a narrow escape from a falling beam. "He felt like somebody had taken the lid off his life and let him look at the works." That same day, he abandoned his family, wandering for two years, after which he fashioned for himself in Spokane a professional and family life very much like the one he had left behind in Seattle. "But that's the part of it I always liked," Spade tells Brigid. "He adjusted himself to beams falling, and then no more of them fell, and he adjusted himself to them not falling." Predictably, Spade's narrative has little effect on Brigid; for the reader, however, it does much to explain Hammett's approach to Spade as character and his own developing sense of the novelist's art. During that stage of his career, Hammett moved from "looking at the works" (*Red Harvest*) to a mature sense of contingency in which one's own deeply held convictions are all that matter.

THE GLASS KEY

Acknowledged to have been Hammett's personal favorite among his five published novels, *The Glass Key* is the only one not to feature a trained detective as protagonist. A rather unlikely hero at first glance, Ned Beaumont is tubercular and an avid gambler without a regular job. His principal occupation is that of friend, conscience, and unofficial assistant to Paul Madvig, an amiable politician forty-five years old who, one suspects, without Beaumont's help would have made even more mistakes than he already has. Himself the father of a grown daughter, Madvig is currently unmarried and in love with Janet Henry, daughter of an aristocratic and powerful U.S. senator. Janet has done little to encourage Madvig's attentions, and Beaumont, for his part, is determined to prevent his friend from making a fool of himself. Complications arise with the brutal murder of Taylor Henry, Janet's brother, who may or may not have been in love with Madvig's daughter, Opal. As usual in

Hammett's novels, there is an underworld connection; Taylor, it seems, was deeply in debt to a professional gambler at the time of his death.

As Madvig's loyal friend and aide, Beaumont sets out to discover the truth behind Taylor Henry's murder, displaying detective instincts worthy of Sam Spade or the Continental Op. Amid serious encounters with angry gangsters and corrupt police, Ned perseveres in his efforts to clear Madvig's name of suspicion in the murder, fully aware that he may well be a suspect himself. Meanwhile, to both Madvig's and Beaumont's consternation, Janet Henry appears to be falling in love with Beaumont, if only because he seems to be proof against her charms. As the action proceeds, it becomes increasingly clear to Beaumont that Taylor Henry could only have been killed by the senator, who has somehow prevailed upon Madvig to accept the burden of suspicion. When Beaumont finally confronts the senator with his suspicions, Henry admits to killing his son in a fit of anger and tampering with evidence at the scene of the crime; he asks only that Beaumont give him five minutes alone with his loaded revolver. Predictably, Beaumont refuses: "You'll take what's coming to you." Beaumont decides to leave town permanently, and, in a surprise twist at the end, he agrees to take Janet with him; the relationship awaiting them can only be surmised.

Like *The Maltese Falcon*, *The Glass Key* is a thoughtful and resonant novel, rich in memorable scenes and images. The glass key itself occurs in a dream that Janet has shortly after the start of her problematical relationship with Ned: She dreams that they arrive at a locked house piled high with food that they can see through the windows, yet when they open the door with a key found under the mat the house turns out to be filled with snakes as well. At the end of the novel, Janet reveals that she has not told Ned all of her dream: "The key was glass and shattered in our hands just as we got the door open, because the lock was stiff and we had to force it." Just as the Maltese Falcon dominates the book bearing its name, the glass key comes to symbolize the dangerous fragility of Janet's life and especially of her relationships with men—Paul Madvig, her father, and finally Ned Beaumont. Born to wealth and privilege, Janet is potentially dangerous to herself and others for reasons that Hammett suggests are outside her control; she does not share in her father's venality and is quite possibly a decent person beneath the veneer of her upbringing.

Not easily deceived, Ned Beaumont has been skeptical about the Henrys from the beginning; early in the book, he warns Paul against deeper involvement with either Janet or her father:

> Read about it in the *Post*—one of the few aristocrats left in American politics. And his daughter's an aristocrat. That's why I'm warning you to sew your shirt on when you go to see them, or you'll come away without it, because to them you're a form of lower animal life and none of the rules apply.

To Beaumont, the Henrys are thoughtless and dangerous, much like Tom and Daisy Buchanan as seen by Nick Carraway in F. Scott Fitzgerald's *The Great Gatsby* (1925). Janet, however, develops considerably during the course of the novel, and at the end there is just the barest chance that a change of scenery will allow her to work out a decent life in Ned Beaumont's company.

The Thin Man

Fifth and last of Hammett's novels, *The Thin Man* is the only one to have been written during his acquaintance with Hellman, whose witty presence is reflected throughout the novel. Thanks to the successful film version and various sequels, *The Thin Man* is, next to *The Maltese Falcon*, the most famous of Hammett's novels; it is also the least typical.

The narrator and protagonist of *The Thin Man* is Nick Charles (born Charalambides and proud of his Greek extraction), a former detective in his early forties who has married the rich and beautiful Nora, nearly young enough to be his daughter. Contrary to popular belief, the novel's title refers not to Charles himself but to Clyde Miller Wynant, suspected of various crimes throughout the novel until the end, when he is revealed to have been the real killer's first victim: Wynant, an inventor, is described as being tall and painfully thin; at the end of the novel, his bones are found buried with clothes cut to fit a much larger man. In the filmed sequel, however, the title presumably refers to the dapper detective himself.

Peopled with a cast of café-society characters in addition to the usual underworld types, *The Thin Man* is considerably lighter in tone and texture than Hammett's earlier novels. Nick Charles, although clearly descended from Beaumont, Spade, and the Op, is nearly a playboy by comparison, trading lighthearted jokes and double entendres with his wife and boon companions. Close parallels may be drawn between Charles and the author himself, who by the time of *The Thin Man* had achieved sufficient material success to obviate his need to work. Hellman observed, however, that the actual writing of *The Thin Man* took place during a period of abstemious, almost monastic seclusion that differed sharply from Hammett's usual pattern of behavior during those years, as well as from the carefree life ascribed to Nick and Nora in the novel.

Most of the action of *The Thin Man* turns upon the certifiably eccentric personality of the title character, Clyde Wynant, a former client of Nick during his latter years as a detective. Among the featured characters are Wynant's former wife, son, and daughter, as well as his lawyer, Herbert Macaulay. In particular, the Wynants are memorable, deftly drawn characters, nearly as eccentric in their own ways as the missing paterfamilias. Wynant's son, Gilbert, about eighteen years old, is notable for his voracious reading and morbid curiosity concerning such matters as murder, cannibalism, and abnormal psychology. Dorothy Wynant, a year or two older than Gilbert, keeps trying to parlay a former girlhood crush on Nick into something more serious. Their mother, known as Mimi Jorgensen, is a vain, treacherous woman cut from the same cloth as Brigid O'Shaughnessy of *The Maltese Falcon*; she too makes repeated claims upon Nick's reluctant attentions.

Throughout the novel, Mimi and her children coexist uneasily in a state of armed truce that occasionally erupts into open warfare, providing scenes of conflict between parent and child considered rather daring at the time. Among the featured characters, only Macaulay appears sane or even remotely sympathetic, yet it is he who ultimately stands accused of the financial double-dealing and multiple murders originally attributed to Wynant, not to mention the murder of Wynant himself.

Like Hammett's earlier novels, *The Thin Man* is realistic in its portrayal of urban life during Prohibition, when the criminal element was even more visible and overt in its actions than in later times. Despite the witty urbanity of his characters, Hammett harbors few illusions concerning human nature. When Nora asks Nick at the end of the novel what will become of Mimi and her children, he replies, "Nothing new. They'll go on being Mimi and Dorothy and Gilbert just as you and I will go on being us and the Quinns will go on being the Quinns." The novel ends with Nora telling Nick that his explanation is "pretty unsatisfactory." Perhaps it is, Hammett implies, but that is the nature of life.

Partly because of failing health and the pressures of work in Hollywood, Hammett published no fiction after *The Thin Man*. His reputation thus rests on a small and somewhat uneven body of work, redeemed by frequent flashes of brilliance. Notable for their influence upon the work of Chandler, Macdonald, and a host of lesser-known writers in the mystery genre, Hammett's novels have also exercised an immeasurable influence on novelists and filmmakers outside the genre.

David B. Parsell

Other major works

SHORT FICTION: *Secret Agent X-9*, 1934 (with Alex Raymond); *The Adventures of Sam Spade, and Other Stories*, 1945; *The Continental Op*, 1945; *The Return of the Continental Op*, 1945; *Hammett Homicides*, 1946; *Dead Yellow Women*, 1947; *Nightmare Town*, 1948; *The Creeping Siamese*, 1950; *Woman in the Dark: More Adventures of the Continental Op*, 1951; *A Man Named Thin, and Other Stories*, 1962; *The Big Knockover: Selected Stories and Short Novels*, 1966 (Lillian Hellman, editor); *Nightmare Town: Stories*, 1999 (Kirby McCauley, Martin H. Greenberg, and Ed Gorman, editors); *Crime Stories, and Other Writings*, 2001; *Lost Stories*, 2005.

SCREENPLAYS: *City Streets*, 1931 (with Oliver H. P. Garrett and Max Marcin); *Mister Dynamite*, 1935 (with Doris Malloy and Harry Clork); *After the Thin Man*, 1936 (with Frances Goodrich and Albert Hackett); *Another Thin Man*, 1939 (with Goodrich and Hackett); *Watch on the Rhine*, 1943 (with Hellman).

NONFICTION: *The Battle of the Aleutians*, 1944 (with Robert Colodny); *Selected Letters of Dashiell Hammett, 1921-1960*, 2001 (Richard Layman and Julie M. Rivett, editors).

EDITED TEXT: *Creeps By Night*, 1931 (also known as *Modern Tales of Horror*, *The Red Brain*, and *Breakdown*).

Bibliography

Bruccoli, Matthew J., and Richard Layman, eds. *Hard-boiled Mystery Writers: Raymond Chandler, Dashiell Hammett, Ross Macdonald*. New York: Carroll & Graf, 2002. A handy supplemental reference that includes interviews, letters, and previously published studies. Illustrated.

Gale, Robert L. *A Dashiell Hammett Companion*. Westport, Conn.: Greenwood Press, 2000. An encyclopedia devoted to Hammett, featuring a chronology of the major events in his life and alphabetically arranged entries about his works and characters, his family, and his acquaintances. Includes bibliographical references and an index.

Gregory, Sinda. *Private Investigations: The Novels of Dashiell Hammett*. Carbondale: Southern Illinois University Press, 1985. The first chapter discusses Hammett, his Pinkerton experiences, and the hard-boiled detective genre. Subsequent chapters focus on each of his five major novels. Includes a foreword by Francis M. Nevins, Jr., notes, a bibliography, and an index.

Hammett, Jo. *Dashiell Hammett: A Daughter Remembers*. Edited by Richard Layman, with Julie M. Rivett. New York: Carroll & Graf, 2001. A compelling memoir written by Hammett's daughter, Jo Hammett. Generously illustrated with photographs drawn from family archives.

Johnson, Diane. *Dashiell Hammett: A Life*. New York: Random House, 1983. A comprehensive biography of Hammett. Adds considerable information to the public record of Hammett's life but does not provide much critical analysis of the works. More than half the volume deals with the years after Hammett stopped publishing fiction and during which he devoted most of his time to leftist political activism.

Layman, Richard. *Shadow Man: The Life of Dashiell Hammett*. New York: Harcourt Brace Jovanovich/Bruccoli-Clark, 1981. An academic who earlier produced a descriptive bibliography of Hammett, Layman provides lucid interpretations of the works. While he holds Hammett in high regard as a major figure in twentieth century American fiction, he does not present a totally admiring portrait.

Mellen, Joan. *Hellman and Hammett: The Legendary Passion of Lillian Hellman and Dashiell Hammett*. New York: HarperCollins, 1996. Although primarily a biographical study of the relationship of the two writers, this scrupulously researched work provides insight into the backgrounds of Hammett's fiction. Includes detailed notes and a bibliography.

Metress, Christopher, ed. *The Critical Response to Dashiell Hammett*. Westport, Conn.: Greenwood Press, 1994. A generous compilation of reviews and general studies, written by leading Hammett scholars, as well as pieces by writers Raymond Chandler, Ross Macdonald, Dorothy Parker, James M. Cain, and Rex Stout. Includes a comprehensive introduction, a chronology, and a bibliography.

Nolan, William F. *Hammett: A Life at the Edge*. New York: Congdon and Weed, 1983. Author of the first full-length study of Hammett in 1969, Nolan here builds upon his earlier work and that of others to present a convincing portrait of a singularly private man with a code of honor that paralleled those of his detectives. The discussions of the works are straightforward and sound.

Skenazy, Paul. "The 'Heart's Field': Dashiell Hammett's Anonymous Territory." In *San Francisco in Fiction: Essays in a Regional Literature*, edited by David Fine and Paul Skenazy. Albuquerque: University of New Mexico Press, 1995. A consideration of the importance of history and place in Hammett's fiction. Argues that it is wrong to associate Hammett's concern with expedience, environment, habit, training, and chance with a specifically Wild West tradition.

Wolfe, Peter. *Beams Falling: The Art of Dashiell Hammett*. Bowling Green, Ohio: Bowling Green University Popular Press, 1980. Wolfe surpasses other writers in showing the relationship of each of Hammett's works to the total output. The author of books on other crime-fiction writers (Raymond Chandler, John le Carré, and Ross Macdonald), Wolfe has a knowledge and appreciation of the genre that are apparent in this excellent study.

KNUT HAMSUN

Knut Pedersen

Born: Lom, Norway; August 4, 1859
Died: Nørholm, Norway; February 19, 1952
Also known as: Knut Pedersen

Principal long fiction

Den gådefulde, 1877
Bjørger, 1878
Sult, 1890 (*Hunger*, 1899)
Mysterier, 1892 (*Mysteries*, 1927)
Ny jord, 1893 (*Shallow Soil*, 1914)
Redaktør Lynge, 1893
Pan, 1894 (English translation, 1920)
Victoria, 1898 (English translation, 1929)
Sværmere, 1904 (*Dreamers*, 1921)
Under høststjærnen, 1906 (*Under the Autumn Star*, 1922)
Benoni, 1908 (English translation, 1925)
Rosa, 1908 (English translation, 1926)
En vandrer spiller med sordin, 1909 (*A Wanderer Plays on Muted Strings*, 1922)
Den siste glæde, 1912 (*Look Back on Happiness*, 1940)
Børn av tiden, 1913 (*Children of the Age*, 1924)
Segelfoss by, 1915 (*Segelfoss Town*, 1925)
Markens grøde, 1917 (*Growth of the Soil*, 1920)
Konerne ved vandposten, 1920 (*The Women at the Pump*, 1928)
Wanderers, 1922 (includes *Under the Autumn Star* and *A Wanderer Plays on Muted Strings*)
Siste kapitel, 1923 (*Chapter the Last*, 1929)
Landstrykere, 1927 (*Vagabonds*, 1930; also known as *Wayfarers*)
August, 1930 (English translation, 1931)
Men livet lever, 1933 (*The Road Leads On*, 1934)
Ringen sluttet, 1936 (*The Ring Is Closed*, 1937)

Other literary forms

Although he always considered the novel his strongest genre, Knut Hamsun (HAHM-suhn) also wrote plays, poetry, and expository prose. *Fra det moderne Amerikas aandsliv* (1889; *The Cultural Life of Modern America*, 1969) is an impudent but witty survey of social and cultural conditions in the United States; Hamsun later repudiated it and would not allow it to be reprinted. Some of the poems in *Det vilde kor* (1904; the wild chorus) are among the best written in Norway during the period. Hamsun was a rather weak dramatist, although his trilogy comprising *Vid rigets port* (pb. 1895; at the gate of the kingdom), *Livets spil* (pb. 1896; the game of life), and *Aftenrøde* (pb. 1898; the red of evening) is interesting as a drama of ideas. His memoir *På gjengrodde stier* (1949; *On Overgrown Paths*, 1967), written when he was nearly ninety years old, is one of his finest books.

Achievements

During his long career as a writer, Knut Hamsun was well known and highly regarded not only in his native Norway but also in the rest of Scandinavia, continental Europe, and the English-speaking world. He was one of the first to introduce the modern psychological novel into Scandinavian literature; his *Hunger* is a classic example of the genre. Later, he created works in which analysis of the development of society played an equally important role; one of them, a celebration of agrarian values titled *Growth of the Soil*, earned for him the Nobel Prize in Literature in 1920.

Because he was accused of collaborating with the Germans during World War II, Hamsun suffered a period of neglect in the postwar years. This is no longer the case; both Norwegian and foreign critics now consider him his country's greatest novelist. He appeals both to a general audience and to academic critics; a number of his novels have been reissued in new English translations, and his works are frequently taught in literature courses in both Scandinavia and the United States.

Biography

Knut Hamsun was born Knut Pedersen on August 4, 1859, at the farm Garmotræet in the district of Lom, Norway. His father, Peder Pedersen, was a tailor and small farmer, and Hamsun's mother, Tora, was also of peasant stock. In 1863, Pedersen moved with his family to

Hamarøy in Nordland, Norway, where he settled on his brother-in-law's farm, Hamsund, from which Hamsun later took the name by which he is known.

Hamsun's earliest childhood years were happy ones. The happiness came to an end, however, when at the age of nine he was sent to live with his maternal uncle, a wealthy landowner and merchant. Hamsun's parents were not happy with this arrangement either; it was only when heavy financial pressure was brought to bear on them that they agreed to it. The uncle needed Hamsun's labor, and the boy had many experiences at his uncle's home that later were of use to him in his art, although he was harshly treated.

Hamsun was released from working for his uncle in 1873 and began a long career of odd jobs. He first clerked in several country stores, after which he became an itinerant peddler, then a shoemaker's apprentice, and even a sheriff's deputy. He also worked as a country schoolmaster, a position for which he was qualified by his native intelligence and masterful penmanship.

Knut Hamsun. (Library of Congress)

Hamsun did not read widely during this period of his life, but he had become familiar with the peasant tales of his countryman Bjørnstjerne Bjørnson, and in 1877, when Hamsun was only eighteen years old, he published his first book, a naïve love story titled *Den gådefulde* (the riddle). This youthful work is significant only as the first version of what was to become one of Hamsun's most persistent motifs—namely, a relationship between a lower-class man and an upper-class woman. In the beautiful and lyric novel *Victoria*, this motif became the main theme.

The year 1878 saw the publication of another youthful tale, *Bjørger*. Hamsun's early writings enabled him to obtain the support of a wealthy merchant, and he was able to concentrate fully on the task of becoming a poet of note. To this end, he produced a manuscript and traveled to Copenhagen, Denmark, where he offered it to Scandinavia's best-known publisher, Hegel of Gyldendal. To his dismay, his manuscript was rejected, and he spent a difficult winter in the city of Kristiania (now Oslo), Norway. The experiences of this winter, as well as later, similar ones, provided him with the material for his novel *Hunger*, which in 1890 gave him his breakthrough as a writer.

Prior to the publication of *Hunger*, however, Hamsun spent several years in the United States. During two separate stays, he again worked at a variety of jobs, but in addition he read widely in both European and American literature. He also lectured to Norwegian immigrants on literary and cultural topics. In 1888, after his final return from the United States, he lived in Copenhagen, where he anonymously published the first chapter of *Hunger* in a periodical. This made him a talked-about figure in literary circles even though his identity was known by but a few. The following year, he gave a series of lectures about the United States in Copenhagen's Student Society; these lectures were published as *Fra det moderne Amerikas aandsliv* later in the same year.

After the publication of *Hunger*, a groundbreaking psychological novel, Hamsun wrote an article in 1890 in which he outlined the basic principles employed in its composition. This article, titled "Fra det ubevidste sjæleliv" ("From the Unconscious Life of the Mind"), became the genesis of a series of lectures Hamsun presented in a number of Norwegian cities and towns during the year 1891. In these lectures, Hamsun attacked earlier Norwegian literature for being concerned with social conditions rather than with the mental life of the exceptional individual; he maintained that this made the literature dull.

The 1890's were very productive years for Hamsun, during which he wrote such significant novels as *Mysteries*, *Pan*, and *Victoria*. He enjoyed his growing reputation and traveled extensively in both Scandinavia and Europe. He longed for more stability in his life, however, and hoped that would be the result of his marriage to Bergljot Bech, whom he met in 1897 and married in 1898. The experience of meeting her lies behind the beautiful love story told in his novel *Victoria*, published in the same year. The couple's expectations were not fulfilled, however, and the marriage was dissolved in 1906.

During the years following the divorce, Hamsun wrote a number of works in which the protagonist is a middle-aged wanderer whose experiences and musings on existence constitute the substance of the books. Such novels as *Under the Autumn Star* and *A Wanderer Plays on Muted Strings* are not regarded as among Hamsun's best, but they are important for what they tell about his artistic development. After the author's marriage to the young actor Marie Andersen in 1909, however, his books took a different turn.

In his lectures on literature delivered in 1891, Hamsun had distanced himself from what he considered the dull social literature of his contemporaries, opting for a kind of fiction that would explore the exceptional consciousness. After he entered his second marriage, however, he began to write books that, in a sense, mediate between these opposing standpoints, emphasizing unusual men in their social settings. *Children of the Age* and its sequel, *Segelfoss Town*, are such books; the protagonists are exceptional men, yet, at the same time, the novels analyze the workings of society. In *Segelfoss Town*, for example, the values embodied in the aristocratic Willatz Holmsen give way to those of the modern entrepreneur Tobias Holmengraa, and Hamsun appears to place himself in opposition to all that is new in both intellectual and material culture.

In 1911, Hamsun bought the farm Skogheim in Hamarøy in northern Norway, and for several years he lived there as a farmer and a writer. In 1917, he sold the farm and moved to the southern part of the country; the farm had, however, fulfilled its mission: The year 1917 also saw the publication of Hamsun's best-known book, the novel *Growth of the Soil*, for which he received the Nobel Prize in 1920. This work, which tells the story of a man who goes into the northern Norwegian wilderness, clears land for a farm, and rears a family in close contact with nature, is regarded as a hymn both to agrarian life and to the traditional values that Hamsun espouses in *Children of the Age* and *Segelfoss Town*.

After the publication of *Growth of the Soil*, Hamsun began searching for a new and permanent home. Eventually, he settled at the farm Nørholm, where he lived for the rest of his life. He continued as a combination of writer and farmer, and he improved the farm greatly. During this period, he also published two more novels, *The Women at the Pump* and *Chapter the Last*.

The mid-1920's was a difficult time for Hamsun. He worked hard but feared that his creative powers had begun to fail him. During the winter of 1926, he availed himself of the services of a psychiatrist, and in the fall, he began one of his finest works, the novel *Vagabonds*, which was published the following year. The book is the first volume of a trilogy; the other two volumes are titled *August* and *The Road Leads On*. The trilogy tells about the adventures of August, a dreamer and eccentric, and how his actions influence the lives of people who, were it not for him, could have possessed the stability that he is lacking. The novels continue the investigation of modern society that is so prominent in *Children of the Age* and *Segelfoss Town*. The connection between these earlier books and the trilogy is made obvious by the fact that the action in *The Road Leads On* moves from Polden, the isolated north Norwegian community, which is the setting of the trilogy's first two volumes, to Segelfoss, where characters from *Children of the Age* and *Segelfoss Town* are again encountered. *The Road Leads On* can thus be viewed as the concluding volume of two separate trilogies, both of which treat social conditions during a period of transition.

At the time of the conclusion of his August trilogy, Hamsun was a man well into his seventies. His hearing was failing, and his energies had suffered the decline that normally comes with age. He produced only one more novel, *The Ring Is Closed*, and would probably have remained relatively silent were it not for political developments in both Europe and Norway. Hamsun had always been an admirer of Germany and German culture at the same time that he detested the British. After the German invasion of Norway and the flight to England of King Haakon and his cabinet, Hamsun supported the collaborationist government headed by Vidkun Quisling and encouraged Norwegian soldiers not to fight against the invaders. After the war, he was arrested and charged with treason. In the course of his trial, his mental condition was examined, and he was found not to be senile but to have permanently impaired mental faculties. He was nevertheless convicted of treason and heavily fined, the result of which was that he was left a financially ruined man. After the trial, he published the poignant memoir *On Overgrown Paths*, which abundantly demonstrated that his mental faculties were anything but impaired.

Hamsun's final years were quiet ones. By tacit agreement, no critical attention was paid to his work, and he had nothing further to say. He died on his farm on February 19, 1952.

Analysis

Knut Hamsun the novelist can be viewed as an outsider who writes about outsiders. Originating in a family that by any standard must be considered poor, Hamsun was keenly aware of the difference between himself and those who possessed power and prestige in society. Power and its opposite, powerlessness, are therefore important themes in his work.

Several of Hamsun's early novels, such as *Hunger* and *Pan*, are narrated in the first person, and their first-person protagonists have character traits and experiences that appear to have been modeled on Hamsun's own. The later novels are without exception narrated in the third person, but that does not mean that the autobiographical content is less. In addition, one can always trust the narrators in the later works to represent Hamsun's own views, while unreliability is a feature of some of the early narrators.

The author's interest in the character of the outsider manifests itself in the careful attention paid to individual psychology in the early novels, as well as in Hamsun's interest in the exceptional individual's relation to society and social forces, especially those of social change, which is found in the later works. The early Hamsun hero, who is often an artist or an artistlike figure, attempts to overcome his powerlessness either through his ability to inspire love in a woman of higher social standing or through his art, or both. The typical hero of the later works is either the victim of social change or an embodiment of what is new in modern social and economic life. In the latter case, he is either somewhat of a charlatan, like Tobias Holmengraa in *Segelfoss Town*, or a dreamer and maker of a multitude of stillborn projects, like August of *Vagabonds* and the other two volumes of the August trilogy. Common to all of Hamsun's protagonists is their essential difference from the average person. This difference can be positive or negative, but it always makes for a character whom readers will find interesting.

Hamsun's earliest novel of significance, *Hunger*, has as its setting Kristiania, a city where Hamsun had many unhappy experiences. The greater number of his later novels are set in northern Norway, where the author had lived most of his childhood and youth and where he spent a significant part of his manhood. Most of the action in these novels also takes place in the period of Hamsun's youth, the 1870's and the early 1880's. There is therefore good reason to regard his fiction as fundamentally autobiographical. Hamsun never tired of writing about the experiences of his youth, on which he reflected throughout his long career as a novelist.

Hunger

Hunger, Hamsun's first novel of any importance, was also the first modern psychological novel in Norwegian literature. It is the story of a young writer of exceptional sensibility who, stripped of all of his property and without any secure means of support, is about to succumb to starvation in Norway's capital city of Kristiania. This first-person novel is highly autobiographical; Hamsun had experienced the same degree of destitution on several occasions, most notably in the winter of 1886. Such experiences were surely not unusual among artists at the time; the importance of *Hunger* lies not in its subject matter but rather in the manner in which the author deals with it.

The total narrated time of the novel is two months. The narration is, however, concentrated on four periods during which the narrator suffers greatly from hunger; the author does not appear to be interested in the three periods of time between them when the protagonist seems to live a relatively normal life. The narrator is clearly an individual who earlier was somewhat better off economically, but no reasons for the decline of his fortune are given. Only a few details concerning his identity are mentioned, and these details do not even include his name.

The novel also has but little action in the traditional sense. With the exception of the story of a few attempts made by the narrator to secure employment, as well as the tale of a brief encounter with a lady of the middle class, the text is almost exclusively made up of reports of the narrator's mental life during periods of extreme hunger.

The stream-of-consciousness technique employed by Hamsun is effective in portraying the strange workings of the mind while in an altered state resulting from a lack of nourishment. The reader is given access both to the perceptions, moods, and strange ideas of the narrator and to his reflections on his own state of consciousness. The narrator perceives himself as an artist, and his chief concern is twofold: on one hand, to prevent his hunger from negatively affecting those sensibilities that make him capable of producing art and, on the other hand, to utilize his unpleasant experiences in his art. The narrator's strong tendency toward self-observation can be viewed both as a means of making sure that the demands of his body do not conquer his mental or artistic needs and as part of his artistic project, the gathering of material for the novel presented to the reader.

Hamsun is interested not in the physical effects of starvation per se, but only in its consequences for the mind. This attitude stands in direct opposition to the prevailing trends in Scandinavian literature at the time. A case in point is Arne Garborg's novel *Bondestudentar* (1883; students from the country), in which the protagonist, like the narrator in *Hunger*, suffers from starvation in the city of Kristiania. The difference is that, unlike Hamsun, Garborg portrays only the physical and social consequences of hunger. In contrast, the attitude of Hamsun's narrator toward his hunger could indeed be termed one of experimentation.

It is a question, however, whether Hamsun the artist was as exclusively concerned with the mental side of life as he claimed to be in his 1891 lectures. The narrator's attention to a mysterious young woman of the middle class does not seem to originate in any specific interest in art, but rather in a concern with the social position that can be won by a successful artist or by a young man who has success in any endeavor. The narrator-protagonist in *Hunger*, like his creator Hamsun, can also be regarded as a practical man for whom art is a means of social advancement at least as much as an end in itself.

PAN

In *Hunger*, Hamsun's autobiographical tendencies manifest themselves both in his choice of subject matter and in the location of the action. In *Pan*, the story occurs at a fictional place in northern Norway called Sirilund, but the social milieu is the same as that Hamsun had known so well in his youth. In this novel, the theme of art is subservient to that of love, but the social function of love in *Pan* is similar to that of art in *Hunger*.

Unlike the narrative situation of *Hunger*, that of *Pan* is quite complex. The novel consists of two parts, the main text and a brief epilogue titled "Glahn's Death." Both the text proper and the epilogue are narrated in the first person, but while the main part of the book is narrated by its protagonist, a lieutenant named Thomas Glahn, the epilogue is narrated by his hunting companion and killer, a man whose name is not given.

The main story takes place during the summer months of the year 1855. Lieutenant Glahn is an outsider who has obtained leave from his commission and who is now leading a rather primitive life as a hunter and fisherman in a cabin near the trading post Sirilund. Tired of urban life and incapable of getting along well according to the norms of cultured society, he has immersed himself in nature, attempting to live as part of it. His intermediary position between nature and culture is symbolized by the fact that his cabin is located where the forest meets the fields surrounding Sirilund. In narrating the story, Glahn tells both about the external events of his life in nature and about his reflections on his existence, and from his story, it would appear that he is entirely successful in his attempts to live as an integral part of the natural world. It is clear, however, that he is far too reflective to lay claim to a natural existence entirely unmediated by culture. This and other signs of unreliability are of great significance to any interpretation of the book.

During visits to the trading post at Sirilund, Glahn meets the young Edvarda, the daughter of the post's owner, the trader Mack. Glahn falls in love with Edvarda, who—because of her father's wealth—is his social superior. A love-hate relationship develops between the two, and each tortures the other in turn.

Glahn's love for Edvarda is not an end in itself, however, but rather a means to social advancement. Glahn would simply like to inherit Mack's position of wealth, power, and prestige by marrying his only daughter. Edvarda, on her part, sees in Glahn an opportunity to get away from Sirilund. Glahn's true intentions are revealed by the fact that he has an affair with a young woman named Eva, the wife of a local blacksmith, as soon as he discovers that Mack uses her to satisfy his erotic needs. For Glahn, the affair is little more than a way symbolically to assume Mack's social position, but when the trader discovers it, he punishes them by having Eva killed and by forcing Glahn to leave the place.

Glahn tells the story two years later. The outward reason for his telling the story at this time is that he has just received a message from Edvarda, who is now married to another man. That Glahn writes down the story establishes as a fact, however, something that is at best implied in the text—namely, that Glahn must also be regarded as an artist. It is necessary to be aware of that when the epilogue, "Glahn's Death," is considered.

The epilogue bears the date 1861, which places its narration four years after the telling of the main part of the story. There is, however, no indication of how much time has passed between the events themselves and the telling of them.

The story in the epilogue is about how Glahn causes the unnamed narrator to take his life by making him jealous and taunting him. Glahn apparently wants to die, and this desire has at least in part been brought about by another letter from Edvarda, who cannot forget him. Glahn's killer writes down the story ostensibly in order to make it clear to the dead man's family that there is no longer any need to inquire about his whereabouts through newspaper advertisements. He seems to be unaware that by so doing, he incriminates himself.

The signs of unreliability that can be found in the main portion of the novel, however, together with the curious narrative situation in the epilogue, make it reasonable to suspect that the narrator of the epilogue is indeed Glahn himself, who has simply made up the story of his death as a final attempt to inflict pain on Edvarda. This interpretation is quite reasonable in view of the fact that when Edvarda learns of Glahn's supposed death, as it is told in Hamsun's later novel *Rosa*, it indeed causes her much grief.

Pan is one of Hamsun's most complex novels. Many critics regard it as his finest work from the 1890's, and some claim that it is his masterpiece. It clearly sets forth Hamsun's view of the relationship between power, love, and the artistic temperament.

Segelfoss Town

Published in 1915, *Segelfoss Town* stands in the middle of Hamsun's oeuvre. A continuation of *Children of the Age*, which appeared two years earlier, it is also composed in such a manner that it can be read as a separate work. If its criticism of contemporary society is to be evaluated, however, it is helpful to have some familiarity with the earlier work.

Segelfoss is a small community in northern Norway, consisting mainly of a flour mill and the large estate from which the community has derived its name. For generations, the farm and the mill have been owned by the Holmsen family, which by its inherited wealth and benevolent aristocracy has lent order and stability to the community. In *Children of the Age*, however, it is learned that business has been going poorly for the Holmsens, and when an opportunity to sell the flour mill arises, its owner eagerly accepts.

The new owner is Tobias Holmengraa, a local boy of peasant stock who has accumulated a fortune by means of rather mysterious dealings while abroad. Holmengraa is, within Hamsun's artistic universe, a relation of both the protagonist of *Hunger* and Thomas Glahn, the chief difference being that Holmengraa has both the imagination and the financial wherewithal to attempt to realize his social daydream. Once in the possession of the flour mill, he creates a new age for Segelfoss, which may now rightfully refer to itself as a town. There is an abundance of employment and, consequently, money to be had; a trader, a distant relative of Holmengraa, is asked to come and set up a store; a telegraph station is established; and both a lawyer and a doctor arrive.

Thus, new centers of power are created. The most obvious one is Holmengraa's business, but the store also becomes a means to the accumulation of wealth, especially when Theodor, the son of the original owner, takes over after his father. Through his portrayal of social and economic change, Hamsun analyzes the process by which the old and semifeudal social order vanishes and is replaced by a twentieth century social reality. He strongly voices his distrust of the new, mainly through the character Baardsen, the telegraphist, who is also a musician, something of a philosopher, and a drunkard. A character who is split and divided, he is by far the most interesting figure in the book; in the end, he takes his own life, unable to bear the tension in his existence.

The third-person narrator also allows his voice to be heard directly. What he finds most objectionable in modern life is the absence of respect for authority, especially that of the employer, the new money-based economy, and the fact that talented young people leave the class into which they have been born and through education degenerate into clergymen, doctors, and lawyers. The view that is advanced by the author is thus a totally reactionary one, one that Hamsun later, unfortunately, did not distinguish from the ideology of the Nazi Party and that eventually caused his treason during World War II.

Segelfoss Town, however, is much more than a reactionary tract. If justice is to be done to it as a work of art, it must also be read as a novel about life in all of its variety. In the end, Holmengraa goes bankrupt as a result of his emphasis on the outward show of wealth and his lack of sound business practices, the flour mill is shut down, and the future becomes uncertain for the many workers who have depended on this entrepreneur and charlatan. The disaster is not a victory for Hamsun's reactionary views, however, but rather one for the inhabitants of Segelfoss, who despite economic misfortune find a way to get by. Life itself continues independent of the fates of individuals.

GROWTH OF THE SOIL

Hamsun had used *Segelfoss Town* as a means of voicing his distrust of the development of modern society. In *Growth of the Soil*, he expressed the same norms, but he attempted to prescribe a positive remedy for social ills by giving his public an example worthy of emulation. His rhetorical success is perhaps most clearly indicated by the fact that the novel earned for him the Nobel Prize in 1920.

The protagonist of *Growth of the Soil* is Isak Sellanraa, a man without a past but also without any of the cultural baggage of contemporary life. One day, he is walking through the wilderness somewhere in northern Norway, searching for a place to settle down and make a home for himself, his situation not unlike that of many Norwegian immigrants to the United States. The American immigrant pioneer was a well-known figure in Norway; Hamsun used the comparison in order to point out that breaking new soil in one's own land is better than emigrating.

The first part of the book details the growth of Isak's farm as he clears the land, builds shelter, marries a woman named Inger, and acquires farm animals. The qualitative difference between the man and his wife is indicated by his name, that of an Old Testament patriarch, while her name, Inger, is a common one. Inger is an entirely ordinary person; she casts her lot with the antisocial Isak only because she has a harelip and is therefore unable to find a husband in any other way. Inger is possessed by fear that one of her children will inherit her defect, which indeed happens to her third baby, a girl. Knowing the suffering that is in store for the infant, Inger kills her, later confesses her crime, and is sent to prison for five years.

During this time, she has an operation on her lip, is educated in modern life, and, in Hamsun's view, is spoiled by civilization. When she returns, she is no longer satisfied with the simple life of the farm. This division in Isak's family is then extended to the children; one of his two sons remains a solid young man, while the other is sent to town and is finally fit for nothing but emigration to the United States.

While Isak is struggling to maintain his (and Hamsun's) values in his home, civilization closes in on the farm, both through the arrival of more settlers and through the discovery of copper ore in a nearby mountain, which leads to the establishment of a mine. The catalyst in this development is a curious character named Geissler, who is a carrier of both Hamsun's values and their opposites. Geissler makes *Growth of the Soil* a complex novel whose value system is perhaps not as clear as it has traditionally been thought to be, and this lack of univocality is indicated by his referring to himself as "the fog" in an important monologue at the end of the book.

Growth of the Soil is undoubtedly Hamsun's most widely read novel. Seductive in both rhetoric and style, the novel makes it difficult for the reader to maintain a proper distance from the author's norms. As a work of art, it is splendid; its values, however, like those of *Segelfoss Town*, are some of those that later led Hamsun to embrace the Nazi ideology.

Vagabonds

The first volume of a trilogy and the most significant novel from Hamsun's later years, *Vagabonds* is set mainly in northern Norway. It is centered on a community named Polden, similar to Segelfoss but much smaller. There is, for example, no social or economic leader on the order of a Holmsen or even a Holmengraa. In the novel, the Polden environment is significant as a laboratory for the social change that Hamsun so thoroughly despises, but it is also important as the background for one of Hamsun's most tragic characters and for one of his most comical ones.

The tragic character is Edevart, who as a young boy has one of his decisive experiences in the first few pages of the book. During the wintertime, when all the adult males in the community are away at the Lofoten fisheries, Polden is visited by two foreign-looking confidence men who, by appealing to the inhabitants' need for adventure, succeed in tricking them out of whatever small amounts of money they have. Edevart, who at first is taken in by them but then sees through their sham, thus receives his initiation into the deceit and hollowness of the world. As a result, he loses both some of his innocence and much of that innate faith that, if shielded from the attacks of the world, would have aided him in living a life of happiness and satisfaction. This episode is an important one, for it presents Hamsun's thesis that modern civilization is essentially a similar kind of confidence game, albeit on a grander scale, and that its effects on people are similar to those of the strangers on Edevart.

Edevart has another important experience a few years later, when as a young man he encounters a woman named Lovise Magrete Doppen, with whom he falls deeply in love and who initiates him sexually. Shortly thereafter, Lovise Magrete accompanies her husband, an ex-convict who was in jail when Edevart met her, to the United States. This man, like one of Isak's sons in *Growth of the Soil*, is so depraved that he is fit for nothing but emigration. This experience causes Edevart to lose his trust in the power of love, much as his experience with the confidence men had caused him to lose faith in people. As a result, Edevart becomes a "vagabond in love."

These and similar experiences lead to Edevart's complete demoralization. Dishonesty takes the place of his original honesty, restlessness replaces his sense of belonging in Polden, and dissatisfaction takes the place of his ability to be happy in limited circumstances. The fundamental cause of Edevart's moral decline, however, is not a defect in his personality but the changes that society is undergoing. They include the capitalization of agriculture, the process of industrialization, and the change to a monetary economy, all of which Hamsun opposes. Edevart's development parallels that of society at large.

Hamsun's views, however, are somewhat equivocal. The ambiguity is expressed mainly through the character August, who is one of only two important figures in *Vagabonds* but the clear protagonist of the trilogy of which the novel is the first volume. August has no close relatives; like Tobias Holmengraa in *Segelfoss Town*, he has spent a number of years abroad, and, like Tobias, August is a dreamer. In both *Vagabonds* and the trilogy as a whole, he is an embodiment of the social forces to which Hamsun is opposed. One would, therefore, expect that August should be portrayed as a villain of the highest order, but that is not the case. The author is charmed by him, admires him, and causes the reader to share that admiration. At the same time, Hamsun is critical of what August represents. August therefore expresses Hamsun's ambivalent attitude toward those forces in society that he so soundly condemns. This might be taken as an indication that the author's values are confused, but it could also simply mean that Hamsun, in the final analysis, views life as more complex than any theory or ideology. His tendency to cling to an ideology is, however, present in *Vagabonds* as well as in *Growth of the Soil* and *Segelfoss Town*.

To many present-day readers, Hamsun may seem like a reactionary writer whose values are out of touch with the modern world. There is a fundamental irony in this, as the charge is similar to that which he, in his youth, leveled against his immediate predecessors in Norwegian literature. Even though many of today's critics thus find little to admire in Hamsun's value system, his books nevertheless have the power to charm new generations of readers. Hamsun is a master of his craft, of rhetoric, and of style, and he is therefore a true artist whose books attract readers not because of but in spite of some of the values they express.

Jan Sjåvik

OTHER MAJOR WORKS

SHORT FICTION: *Siesta*, 1897; *Kratskog*, 1903; *Stridende liv*, 1905; *Night Roamers, and Other Stories*, 1992; *Tales of Love and Loss*, 1997 (translation of *Siesta*, *Kratskog*, and *Stridende liv*).

PLAYS: *Vid rigets port*, pb. 1895; *Livets spil*, pb. 1896; *Aftenrøde*, pb. 1898; *Munken Vendt*, pb. 1902; *Dronning Tamara*, pb. 1903; *Livet i vold*, pb. 1910 (*In the Grip of Life*, 1924).

POETRY: *Det vilde kor*, 1904.

NONFICTION: *Fra det moderne Amerikas aandsliv*, 1889 (*The Cultural Life of Modern America*, 1969); *I æventyrland*, 1903; *På gjengrodde stier*, 1949 (memoir; *On Overgrown Paths*, 1967); *Selected Letters of Knut Hamsun*, 1990-1998 (2 volumes); *Knut Hamsuns Brev*, 1994-2000 (letters; 6 volumes).

BIBLIOGRAPHY

Birkerts, Sven. "Love's Wound, Love's Salve: Knut Hamsun's *Pan*." In *Reading Life: Books for the Ages*. Saint Paul, Minn.: Graywolf, 2007. Analysis of *Pan* is part of a larger work in which a literary critic and professor of English at Harvard University revisits and examines in detail books he has enjoyed throughout his life.

Brown, Berit I., ed. *Nordic Experiences: Exploration of Scandinavian Cultures*. Westport, Conn.: Greenwood Press, 1997. Collection of essays includes two pieces about Hamsun: "The Ocean of Consciousness Novel I: *Hunger* by Knut Hamsun—Progenitor of Modernism," and "Knut Hamsun in His Letters."

Ferguson, Robert. *Enigma: The Life of Knut Hamsun*. New York: Farrar, Straus and Giroux, 1987. Illustrated biography provides an excellent, unflinching look at the ambiguities and complexities of Hamsun's life. Divided into three parts: Hamsun's picaresque early life; his middle period, with its back-to-the-earth emphasis; and the later years, including Hamsun's involvement with Adolf Hitler. Includes a bibliography (only a handful of the entries are in English) and a chronological list of Hamsun's works.

Gustafson, Alrik. "Man and the Soil: Knut Hamsun." In *Six Scandinavian Novelists*. Minneapolis: American-Scandinavian Foundation, 1940. Admiring and sentimental essay examines Hamsun's life before World War II, with a generous look at the early years and a novel-by-novel account of Hamsun's greatest works.

Humpál, Martin. *The Roots of Modernist Narrative: Knut Hamsun's Novels "Hunger," "Mysteries," and "Pan."* Oslo: Solum forlag, 1998. Critical study of Hamsun's three modernist novels focuses on the structure of the storytelling, drawing on theories of narratology as well as Humpál's own ideas. Includes bibliography.

Lyngstad, Sverre. *Knut Hamsun, Novelist: A Critical Assessment*. New York: Peter Lang, 2005. Provides in-depth analysis of Hamsun's novels, including consideration of their recurrent themes, narrative techniques, and artistic integrity. Also presents discussion of Hamsun's critical reception, explaining that his support of Nazism, bad translations of his books, and his similarity to Charles Dickens and D. H. Lawrence could explain why Hamsun's works are not more popular in English-speaking countries.

Mazor, Yair. *The Triple Cord: Agnon, Hamsun, Strindberg—Where Scandinavian and Hebrew Literature Meet*. Tel Aviv: Papyrus, 1987. Includes six chapters exploring Hamsun's influence on Hebrew literature, with extensive notes but no bibliography. This work is more wide-ranging than its title suggests; it draws on the best scholarship in both literatures, exploring the fundamental problems of representation in literature and the development of modern fiction.

Næss, Harald S. *Knut Hamsun*. Boston: Twayne, 1984. Good introductory study contains chapters on Hamsun's life and on all of his major novels. Includes chronology, notes, and bibliography.

Sjåvik, Jan. "Two Myths of Artistic Creativity in Knut

Hamsun's *Pan*." In *Reading for the Truth: Rhetorical Constructions in Norwegian Fiction*. Christchurch, New Zealand: Cybereditions, 2004. Analysis of Hamsun's novel is part of a larger discussion of Norwegian fiction from an "intersubjective" perspective. Argues that the meaning of a text has greater validity if two or more readers arrive at the same conclusion than if only a single reader or critic provides an opinion.

Wood, James. "Knut Hamsun's Christian Perversions." In *The Broken Estate: Essays on Literature and Belief*. New York: Random House, 1999. A well-respected literary critic presents his interpretation of the religious aspects of Hamsun's work.

PETER HANDKE

Born: Griffen, Austria; December 6, 1942

Principal long fiction

Die Hornissen, 1966
Der Hausierer, 1967
Die Angst des Tormanns beim Elfmeter, 1970 (*The Goalie's Anxiety at the Penalty Kick*, 1972)
Der kurze Brief zum langen Abschied, 1972 (*Short Letter, Long Farewell*, 1974)
Wunschloses Unglück, 1972 (*A Sorrow Beyond Dreams*, 1974)
Die Stunde der wahren Empfindung, 1975 (*A Moment of True Feeling*, 1977)
Die linkshändige Frau, 1976 (*The Left-Handed Woman*, 1978)
Langsame Heimkehr, 1979 (*The Long Way Around*, 1985)
Die Lehre der Sainte-Victoire, 1980 (*The Lesson of Mont Sainte-Victoire*, 1985)
Kindergeschichte, 1981 (*Child Story*, 1985)
Der Chinese des Schmerzes, 1983 (*Across*, 1986)
Slow Homecoming, 1985 (includes *The Long Way Around*, *The Lesson of Mont Sainte-Victoire*, and *Child Story*)
Die Wiederholung, 1986 (*Repetition*, 1988)
Die Abwesenheit: Ein Märchen, 1987 (*Absence*, 1990)
Nachmittag eines Schriftstellers, 1987 (*The Afternoon of a Writer*, 1989)
Mein Jahr in der Niemandsbucht: Ein Märchen aus den neuen Zeiten, 1994 (*My Year in the No-Man's-Bay*, 1998)
In einer dunklen Nacht ging ich aus meinem stillen Haus, 1997 (*On a Dark Night I Left My Silent House*, 2000)
Der Bildverlust: Oder, Durch die Sierra de Gredos, 2002 (*Crossing the Sierra de Gredos*, 2007)
Don Juan: erzählt von ihn selbst, 2004
Kali: Eine Vorwintergeschichte, 2007

Other literary forms

Peter Handke (HAHNT-kuh) made his debut on the German stage with the drama *Publikumsbeschimpfung* (pr., pb. 1966; *Offending the Audience*, 1969). His subsequent dramatic works include *Hilferufe* (pr. 1967; *Calling for Help*, 1970), *Kaspar* (pr., pb. 1968; English translation, 1969), *Das Mündel will Vormund sein* (pr., pb. 1969; *My Foot My Tutor*, 1970), *Quodlibet* (pr. 1970; English translation, 1976), *Der Ritt über den Bodensee* (pr., pb. 1971; *The Ride Across Lake Constance*, 1972), *Über die Dörfer* (pr., pb. 1982; *Among the Villages*, 1984), *Die Stunde da wir nichts voneinander wussten* (1992; *The Hour We Knew Nothing of Each Other*, 1996), and *Untertagblues: Ein Stationendrama* (pb. 2003).

After publishing several radio plays in the early 1970's, Handke wrote a film script, *Chronik der laufenden Ereignisse* (1971; chronicle of occurring events), which he also produced, and a television script, *Falsche*

Bewegung (1975; wrong move). He has collaborated frequently with film producer and director Wim Wenders and was the screenwriter (with Wenders) for Wenders's 1987 film, *Der Himmel über Berlin* (*Wings of Desire*). An early collection of short stories, *Begrüssung des Aufsichtsrats* (1967; saluting the trustees), should also be noted. Handke's collection of poetry *Die Innenwelt der Aussenwelt der Innenwelt* (1969; *The Innerworld of the Outerworld of the Innerworld*, 1974) gives poetic expression to his recurring concern with language as its phrases, in their description of the outer world, simultaneously reflect the inner world or consciousness of the author and vice versa. Handke has also raised these concerns in several of his critical essays, notably *Ich bin ein Bewohner des Elfenbeinturms* (1972; I am an inhabitant of the ivory tower).

Achievements

With the sudden and unprecedented advent of Peter Handke on the German literary scene in 1966, the era of postwar German literature, which had tried to come to terms with World War II and the Nazi past, reached its conclusion. Handke is the representative of a new generation of German writers for whom the Federal Republic of Germany constitutes the societal reality that furnishes the material and the conflicts that inform their works. Born in Austria, then reared in East Berlin for some years before returning to Austria, Handke regards the new Germany with the eyes of an outsider who nevertheless possesses an insider's intimate knowledge of his subject. Handke's stance as an outsider is reflected in his disregard for social problems, unless they reflect his primary concern for language: In the midst of the student revolts of the late 1960's, he became one of the first writers in West Germany to emphasize that changes in the political realities of the new republic would not come about through protest resolutions or political manifestos but rather through the exact use of the word, the honesty of literary expression, and the truth of fiction (as Manfred Durzak notes). The majority of Handke's fellow West German writers recognized the validity of his claim only after the fall of Willy Brandt as chancellor in 1974.

Handke's outsider's attempts at registering German societal developments and their effects on the individual are in some ways mirrored on a larger and certainly less intellectual scale by frequent media attempts in Germany in which the social and economic ills of that society are blamed on the United States, from which they have supposedly been imported. In contrast, Handke traces the ills that afflict his characters to the larger ills of German society. Under these circumstances, it becomes noteworthy that in two of his novels, *Short Letter, Long Farewell* and *The Long Way Around*, Handke has depicted America's untouched nature as regenerative, offering the possibility of spiritual rebirth for his protagonists. Such a special relationship with America is perhaps connected to the fact that Handke's own birth as an author of prominence took place in the United States rather than in Germany.

In Princeton in early 1966, at the conference of the West German writers' group Gruppe 47, Handke was suddenly pushed into the limelight not so much for his literary production—which was just getting under way—as for his attacks on the production of the German literary establishment at that time. The young outsider Handke had recently had his first novel, *Die Hornissen* (the hornets), accepted by the renowned German publisher Suhrkamp Verlag, under whose auspices he was more or less incidentally invited to participate at the conference. There, he immediately affronted the German literary establishment, proclaiming that their writings were characterized by a sterile descriptive tedium and a total disregard for the dimension most essential to literary realization—namely, language itself. During the next few years, Handke wrote in almost every genre imaginable, while his theme remained always the same. In his prose, his drama, and his poetry, his mission was to question the value of life in a modern age of directed mass communication, whose net of linguistic standards had entangled the individual, leaving no room for self-expression. Literature should, therefore, make the individual conscious of him- or herself again. Handke perceived a metareality beyond the barriers of language, and only the perception of this reality would render the material character of language obvious.

The intensity of Handke's metaphysical search led to his second creative phase, in the early 1970's, when the author's private life began to play an ever-increasing role in his prose. Several critics have termed this "autobiographical" phase Handke's most fruitful and accomplished period; during these years, he wrote his best-known novels, *The Goalie's Anxiety at the Penalty Kick*, *Short Letter, Long Farewell*, and *A Sorrow Beyond Dreams*.

In his later prose and drama, written after the late 1970's, Handke's ego seems to have attained a somewhat inflated stature of "well-practiced narcissism," as one critic has observed. Handke exhibits the visionary zeal of a religious prophet in such novels as *The Long Way Around* and *The Lesson of Mont Sainte-Victoire*. Similar tendencies are obvious in his diary *Das Gewicht der Welt* (1977; *The Weight of the World*, 1984). Handke is quoted as having uttered in this context, "I don't aspire to being a star, but a figure with certain mystical intentions . . . I would not mind that at all." It should be noted that Handke has won most of the prestigious literary awards available to German-language writers.

Biography

Peter Handke's early literary revolt against all repressive systems of rules and social customs and against the experience of daily dependency and dull coercive repetition is certainly linked to his birth and upbringing in a poor working-class environment. His birthplace, Griffen, in the province of Carinthia, Austria, lies about twenty-five miles northeast of Klagenfurt, the only sizable city in the region, and only a few miles from the border with Yugoslavia. Handke's maternal grandfather, of Slovak descent, was a peasant and carpenter; his mother, the fourth of five children, worked as a dishwasher, maid, and cook during World War II and became pregnant with Handke by a German soldier, a bank clerk in civilian life, who was already married. Before Handke's birth, his mother married another German soldier, Bruno Handke, in civilian life a streetcar conductor in Berlin. In 1944, Maria Handke moved to Berlin with her son to await her husband's return from the war. For some time after 1945, Handke's stepfather continued to work as a streetcar conductor in Berlin, until in 1948 he moved his family to Griffen, where he found employment with Maria's father. The stepfather's alcoholism, the cramped quarters—the family, by then numbering six, shared two attic rooms—and the backwardness of the region became increasingly oppressive for the young Handke. After attending the local elementary school, he finally escaped from his hated stepfather and the confines of home by entering a parochial boarding school near Klagenfurt.

At the parochial school, the quiet and serious-minded Handke remained isolated from his fellow pupils. His superior intelligence allowed him to catch up on a year's work in Latin within a short time and to become the best student in class. His German teacher recognized his writing talent and encouraged him to publish his first short stories in the school newspaper. Through this teacher, Handke became acquainted with the works of Thomas Wolfe and William Faulkner, among others. Handke, however, soon felt the pressure of conformity at this school, with its expressed purpose of preparing young men for the priesthood, and he changed schools once more, to attend the *Gymnasium* (college-preparatory secondary school) in Klagenfurt, from which he graduated in 1961. Apparently his former teacher advised Handke upon graduation to enter law school so that the young man might have enough time to pursue his love of writing and reflection. He entered the University of Graz, where he soon came into contact with an avant-garde group of young writers. He was able to publish in their literary magazine, and in 1963 a reading of one of Handke's short stories was broadcast by a regional radio station.

In Graz, Handke met the actor Libgart Schwarz, whom he married soon afterward. Their daughter, Amina, was born in 1969, and in 1972 Handke and his wife separated; Amina continued to live with him. Handke's marriage and divorce and his daughter Amina, respectively, form the autobiographical cores of the novels *Short Letter, Long Farewell* and *Child Story*. In November, 1971, Handke's mother committed suicide. Handke was deeply shaken by her death; it rekindled long-suppressed memories of his own childhood and of his mother's life of constant stricture and monotony, from which she freed herself through voluntary death. Within a few months, Handke wrote *A Sorrow Beyond Dreams*, which several critics consider to be his best work.

Repeated moves and frequent travel characterized Handke's life in the decade after 1965. His spectacular appearance at the 1966 conference of Gruppe 47 had launched his career as a serious and financially independent writer, and he quit law school after having passed several preliminary examinations with distinction. His travels led him to Romania, to Yugoslavia, and, in 1971, on a second trip through the United States. During that decade, he moved several times: In 1966, he left Graz for Düsseldorf; in 1968, he moved to Berlin; in 1969, to Paris; in 1971, to Cologne; in 1972, to Kronberg (outside Frankfurt). In 1975, Handke moved back to Paris, thereafter living in Salzburg, the setting for *Across*.

In 1978-1979 Handke was in United States, and in the late 1980's he went on extended trips and hiking tours in Europe, Alaska, and Japan. His main residence from 1979 to 1991 was in Salzburg, which honored him in 1986 with the City of Salzburg Prize for Literature. In 1987 he received the Great Austrian State Prize. In 1999, Handke moved to Chaville, France, a small town not far from Paris.

Handke is a versatile writer; he is not only a novelist, poet, and playwright but also a literary translator, screenwriter, and film director. He and German director and producer Wim Wenders have collaborated on a number of films, including three adaptations of Handke's novels: *The Goalie's Anxiety at the Penalty Kick* (1971), *The Left-Handed Woman* (1978), and *The Absence* (1993). With Wenders, Handke wrote the screenplay for Wenders's successful film *Wings of Desire* (1987). His account of a trip through war-torn Serbia, *Eine winterliche Reise zu den Flüssen Donau, Save, Morawa and Drina: Oder, Gerechtigkeit für Serbien* (1996; *A Journey to the Rivers: Justice for Serbia*, 1997), unleashed a storm of protest in the European press. Handke's observations are personal and geographical and portray the Serbians as ordinary human beings. His refusal to join in the condemnation of Serbia, and particularly his attendance at the funeral of former Serbian leader Slobodan Milošević in 2006, resulted in a highly adversarial relationship with the media and the literary establishment. After having left the Catholic Church in 1999 in protest against its support of the bombing of Serbia, Handke returned the Büchner Prize (including the prize money) he had been awarded in 1973. When the committee that awarded him the prestigious Heinrich-Heine-Prize in 2006 came under attack from leading German politicians, Handke refused the award and directed that the money from an alternative prize, awarded to him by fellow artists in protest against this political meddling, be given to a war-damaged Serbian village.

Peter Handke. (© Jerry Bauer)

ANALYSIS

"Every story distracts me from my real story. Through its fiction it makes me forget myself and my situation. It makes me forget the world." With this statement from his artistic credo, *Ich bin ein Bewohner des Elfenbeinturms* (I am an inhabitant of the ivory tower), Peter Handke demonstrated not only the intent of his writing but also his relationship to the art of fiction. For the author Handke and for his reader, the familiar fictional methods of describing the world are no longer valid, as their familiarity is evidence that they are not descriptions of the world itself but rather copies of other descriptions. Such copies cannot render any new insights; it is the primary function of genuine literature to break open all seemingly finite concepts of the world. The familiarity with and acceptance of the customary methods of description render society incapable of sensing that it is not the world that is being described but rather the method of description, which finally becomes completely automated in a "trivial realism," in advertising and modern mass communication.

Handke's purpose in writing is to gain clarity about himself, to get to know himself, to learn what he does wrong, what he says without thinking, what he says automatically. His goal is to become more attentive and to make other people so—to become more sensitive, more exact in his communication with other people. Improved communication becomes possible through a close investigation of the vehicle of communication itself—namely, language. Handke's method in his investigation is to observe how he, as an individual, continually grows into a linguistic "adulthood" through an increasing awareness of his encounters with the everyday world, with its commonplaces, its extraordinary situations, its images, and particularly its words.

As the objects of the outside world become, in the true sense of the word, "literal" in the mind, they can be expressed only through the words assigned to them. Their power as signature diminishes, however, as soon as the true reality behind the words is forgotten. Handke's argumentation is indebted to the philosophy of Ludwig Wittgenstein, who postulated that language can never be employed as an instrument in the search for truth, since reality itself is obstructed by the tautological fiction of language.

For Handke it therefore becomes essential to transcend the signature character to reach the real object. This he accomplishes by making the reader conscious of the mere signature character of the word and thereby emphasizing the actual reality behind it. Handke renders the signature character of a given word, phrase, or even story obvious through the conscious—perhaps self-conscious—use of language, syntax, and plot structure. These become the "material" through which the individual gains access to the "real reality" beyond. This "real reality" no longer requires the invention of a fable in the traditional sense; as a matter of fact, such fiction obviously hampers access to it. Handke is concerned with the transmission of experiences, linguistic and nonlinguistic, and for this purpose a conventional story is no longer needed. He concedes that literature might lose some of its "entertainment value" through this method, but through it, the reader gains the "real" aspect of each individual sentence, and the individual word in a sentence, once the obstructive fable is stripped away.

DIE HORNISSEN *and* DER HAUSIERER

Handke's first two novels, *Die Hornissen* and *Der Hausierer* (the peddler), illustrate his theoretical position. They are novels without plots, becoming—in the case of *Die Hornissen*—linguistic exercises that bore the reader to the level of exhaustion, as one critic remarked. *Die Hornissen* represents the creative process of writing a novel rather than the end result of that process. The narrator acts out the perennial dilemma of the writer, who must make choices at all times and who does not—as the reader might imagine from the finished product—have firm control over the action and the characters of the story that unfolds. There is thus no continuity of plot in *Die Hornissen*; instead, there is continuous vacillation between descriptions and explanations, fantasies and dreams. This novel is a writer's confession about the difficulties encountered during his work. Such difficulties can be illustrated only through a plot that the narrator is attempting more or less successfully to construct; thus, there is the trace of a conventional story in *Die Hornissen*. The novel is about two brothers, or perhaps three. One of them has become blind while searching for the second one. A war may have had some influence on his blindness. On a Sunday, much later, the blind brother awakens and is reminded of his absent brother by something that remains rather vague in his mind. The periodic arrival of the local commuter bus seems to be important for the blind man, who shares a house with his father and his father's second wife. The Sunday events are reminiscent of events during the war. Shortly before the end of the novel, there is a hint at a possible connection among all these disjointed elements. The blind narrator thinks of a book, possibly with the title *Die Hornissen*, that he once read. He vaguely remembers some of the events in the book, while he has forgotten particulars. The events still remembered begin to change and become superimposed on events from the present.

Handke had observed that a method of description can be used only once before its repetition becomes the description of the method rather than that of the world, and his second novel, *Der Hausierer*, was an attempt to salvage and revivify a method made moribund by repetition. In it, Handke begins with the perception that the detective story has a plot structure that is always the same, with the same descriptive clichés of murder, death, fear and fright, pursuit and torture. By making his readers conscious of the signature character of these clichés, he attempts to show the true human emotions of fear and pain behind them. *Der Hausierer*, with its barren attempt at making "real reality" perceptible behind a huge inventory of detective-story clichés, has been deemed a monumental failure in novel writing.

The Goalie's Anxiety at the Penalty Kick

Some early critics thought that his failure with *Der Hausierer*, as well as possible difficulties in discovering constantly new descriptive methods, might have forced Handke back into a more conventional narrative stance in his third novel, *The Goalie's Anxiety at the Penalty Kick*. The novel indeed possesses a continuously unfolding plot, clearly defined characters, and a recognizable setting and time frame. Nevertheless, Handke did not abandon his original intention of discovering metaperspectives for himself and his readers. Rather than focusing on language, his investigation this time concentrates on the reliability of psychological causality as it is conventionally depicted in literature. The leitmotif of the novel is the false interpretation of a gesture by the protagonist, Josef Bloch—an "insignificant" event that sets in motion everything that happens thereafter. By describing Bloch's reaction, Handke again questions the validity of a "signature."

A construction worker who was once a well-known soccer goalie, Josef Bloch thinks that he has been fired from his job. Nothing has been said to him to indicate his termination; Bloch has interpreted as a sign of his dismissal the fact that only the foreman looked up from his lunch when Bloch entered the workers' shack, while the other workers continued eating. Out of work, Bloch roams the streets and frequents cheap restaurants and motion-picture houses. He sleeps with a film usherette, Gerda, whom he chokes to death the following morning. He flees to a small border village to hide out with a former acquaintance, Herta, an innkeeper. The police have no leads in the murder case, yet Bloch's reactions and observations of his surroundings are those of a hunted man. He interprets every event in the village—a missing child who accidentally drowned, inquisitive policemen, customs officials on guard—as connected to him alone.

The novel's last scene shows a soccer field where Bloch asks a bystander to observe the game from the perspective of the goalie for a change, rather than from that of the players. Bloch's whole life by now has assumed the typical reactive attitude of a goalie defending against a penalty kick, who must try to anticipate the direction in which the opposing player will kick the ball. A comparison to Franz Kafka's *Die Verwandlung* (1915; *The Metamorphosis*, 1936) seems to offer itself, as Bloch also undergoes an inner metamorphosis and loses contact with his environment. Handke has stated that it was his intention to portray a protagonist for whom the environment proceeded to turn into a "signature" as a consequence of a single event—namely, the murder: "A schizophrenic interprets every event as alluding to himself. This is the principle behind the story, yet the process is not applied to a schizophrenic, but rather to a 'normal' protagonist." *The Goalie's Anxiety at the Penalty Kick* became a best seller in Germany shortly after its publication, and it established Handke's reputation in the United States as one of the foremost modern German-language writers.

Short Letter, Long Farewell

In 1972, Handke published two well-received novels, *Short Letter, Long Farewell* and *A Sorrow Beyond Dreams*. The detective-story cliché of the pursuit, which Handke had used in *The Goalie's Anxiety at the Penalty Kick*, is varied once more in *Short Letter, Long Farewell*. The narrator is at once the victim and the detective-observer of the pursuit. The adoption of first-person narrative in this novel as well as in *A Sorrow Beyond Dreams* is significant. Handke's earlier linguistic experimentation, which he had largely overcome in *The Goalie's Anxiety at the Penalty Kick*, was abandoned altogether to make room for the author-narrator's ego and its relationship to the surrounding world. Destabilizing events in Handke's personal life contributed to this new perspective; in an interview, he stated that these events had led to an expansion of his definition of himself. His mother's death, the birth of his daughter, and the protracted proceedings surrounding his divorce brought on the realization that the automatisms of life itself are as unreliable as the linguistic ones had been found to be.

The autobiographical component would be overstated, however, if one were to assume that these events triggered the writing of the two novels in order simply to free the author from his emotional distress. Handke asserted that he had planned the writing of a bildungsroman, a label frequently applied to *Short Letter, Long Farewell*, for almost ten years prior to its date of publication. Also, the novel does remain a typical Handke product, because, in contrast to the traditional novel of education, it educates its author rather than the protagonist.

The author-narrator, no longer merely Handke's abstract alter ego sifting through possible literary methods and models, has become a concrete and discernible individual in his appeal to himself to know and experience more of the world per se in order to reach his goal of cognition. Handke's former protest against stagnant literary conventions has thus given way to his attempt to find the communicative possibilities inherent in his own earlier models. In *Short Letter, Long Farewell*, Handke has gone forward another step in his quest for truth, now seeking the moral veracity of his own writing. The narrator asserts at the end that "all this has really happened," which is, of course, not true in a factual sense, since Handke never really met the filmmaker John Ford, as depicted in the last scene of the novel. The "real happening" has taken place inside the author-narrator. Repeated statements in the work indicate that Handke had by then separated himself completely from his earlier linguistic experiments as purely evasive maneuvers, in order to come to terms with his literary environment.

The assessment of a nonliterary and very real environment, which Bloch attempts unsuccessfully in *The Goalie's Anxiety at the Penalty Kick*, is taken up by the narrator-author of *Short Letter, Long Farewell*, who has traveled to the United States in search of a new self. The firm ground of his prior existence has begun to sway during the separation from his wife. The fears of his childhood as well as present anxieties and threats must be raised from the subconscious to the level of consciousness. Only then can the narrator, at long last, free himself from them, bid them good-bye, and achieve a new sense of life without fear. The stations of his journey through America become the symbolic backdrop for his gradual liberation. Time and space form a curious congruity in the novel, as the narrator travels from east to west. The geographic east-west progression of the United States in time from infancy to maturity becomes the larger reflection on the narrator's development, as in St. Louis he separates from his traveling companion, Claire, and her daughter, Benedictine. (Their names are certainly symbolic as well.) The child, through her sudden outbreaks of fright, has helped him to comprehend his own childhood fears. A happily married couple in St. Louis serves as a foil in the narrator's assessment of his ended marriage. After these events, he can embark on his journey to the new frontiers of America and his own life.

The novel is divided into two parts, titled "Short Letter" and "Long Farewell," both of which are prefaced by a quotation from a bildungsroman. The first part is prefaced by a passage from *Anton Reiser* (1785-1790), by Karl Philipp Moritz, an eighteenth century writer and companion of Johann Wolfgang von Goethe. The book, written in the form of an autobiographical account, was of great historical importance to the development of psychological fiction, as it entered the innermost depths of the soul and at the same time attempted to be an objective sociocritical and pedagogical account of the age, thereby combining the two prominent currents of Pietism and Enlightenment thought. The relevance of *Anton Reiser* for Handke becomes obvious in its protagonist's disrupted relationship to his environment. He—like Handke's unnamed narrator—draws his sole understanding of his environment from the books he reads during his journey. The loneliness, estrangement, and fear of Anton Reiser are shared by Handke's traveler in the first part. The second part, "Long Farewell," is prefaced by a quotation from the Swiss writer Gottfried Keller's *Der grüne Heinrich* (1854-1855; *Green Henry*, 1960), in which the protagonist does finally achieve the elusive union between himself and his environment, between the inner world and the outer world.

Short Letter, Long Farewell is the story of an unnamed Austrian first-person narrator who is being pursued by his estranged wife, Judith. He has arrived in the United States endowed with sufficient financial means to undertake what might be referred to ironically as the customary nineteenth century *Bildungsreise* (educational journey)—with the typical Handke twist that it is a *Bildungsreise* in reverse, from Europe to America. In Providence, Rhode Island, he receives a letter from

Judith advising him not to look for her, as it "would not be nice" to find her. He travels back to New York, on to Washington, D.C., and then to a small town in Pennsylvania, where he is joined by Claire and Benedictine, with whom he continues to the Midwest. From St. Louis, he sets off by himself to Arizona and finally to Oregon: Pursuer and pursued meet at Oregon's Haystack Rock. Its enormous granite form, standing alone in the midst of the ocean but at the same time in harmonious union with its natural environment, becomes the backdrop for their encounter, as the narrator faces Judith's pointed gun. Together, Judith and the narrator travel on to California to meet John Ford. Ford's film *Young Mr. Lincoln* (1939) had touched the narrator's inner sense of reality, as the people on the screen prefigured those he would soon meet. Like them, he desires to be fully present in body and mind, an equal moving among equals, carried along by their motion yet free to be himself.

A Sorrow Beyond Dreams

A Sorrow Beyond Dreams replaces the utopian hopefulness of America with a provincial Austrian remembrance of the past, dictated by the finality of death. Handke's mother, who, at the age of fifty-one, swallowed a whole prescription of sleeping pills, bore little resemblance to the young and spirited woman of thirty years earlier. Again, quotations preface the novel, this time by Bob Dylan ("He not busy being born is busy dying") and mystery writer Patricia Highsmith ("Dusk was falling quickly. It was just after 7 P.M., and the month was October"). The quotation from Highsmith is meant to evoke the tone of her novels, which are not tied to spectacular events or extraordinary characters and seem to eschew judgmental statements. Handke's often expressed aversion for characterizing, and thereby judging and degrading, the individual prevails in the *Erzählung* (short narrative). Nevertheless, the author seems to reach far beyond the customary emotional detachment from his earlier and also his later protagonists. *A Sorrow Beyond Dreams* may be considered Handke's first work to strike an emotional chord. In it, as June Schlueter has observed, "the intellectual coldness of the earlier novels gives way to a deeply personal retelling of his mother's life and death."

The metalevel of the narrative, as in *Short Letter, Long Farewell*, remains the differentiated investigation of the author-narrator's ability to perceive his environment as well as an analysis of these perceptions themselves. The narrator is thus again the focal point. He explicitly notes the dangerous tendency among abstractions and formulations to grow independent of the person for whose characterization they were created. Consequently, a chain reaction of phrases and sentences sets itself in motion, "as in a dream, a literary ritual in which the life of the individual functions merely as the triggering occasion. Two dangers—the mere realistic retelling of events on the one hand, and the painless disappearance of a person in poetic sentences on the other—these retard my writing." As in his early revolutionary statement at Princeton, Handke thus cautions himself in *A Sorrow Beyond Dreams* against the sterile descriptive tedium of simply retailing a plot, in which he would either permit life itself to tell the story, thereby rendering it without interest to anyone outside his immediate family, or bury the story under an overpowering aesthetic superstructure that would choke it in meaningless poetic formalism.

Handke first had to overcome the stunned perplexity that he felt at reading the obituary notice in the *Kärntner Volkszeitung*. The notice turned his mother's death into a statistic without any further human implication whatsoever. His narration takes its departure from this printed notice: "In the village of A. (G. township), a housewife, aged 51, committed suicide on Friday night by taking an overdose of sleeping pills." Even beyond her death, this woman has thus been denied her existence as an individual. The author-narrator becomes the "remembering and formulating machine" that will restore to his mother what is rightfully hers, at the same time departing, as in *Short Letter, Long Farewell*, on a voyage into his own childhood, which he begins to see in a different light through the description of his mother's life. Two continuous impediments seem to have stifled his mother's attempts at individuation: the socially conditioned, material limitations during her youth, exemplified in the description of the grandfather, and her individually motivated depressions, which she felt as a result of the growing automatisms of her particular life as a woman, for whom a palm reading at the county fair, which was to reveal the future, was nothing but a cruel joke. Handke quotes a rhyme that the girls in her village chanted about the stations in a woman's life: "Tired/ Exhausted/ Sick/ Dying/ Dead."

As the son begins to study at the university, he introduces her to literature: "She read every book as a description of her own life, felt revitalized, learned to speak about herself . . . and so I gradually found out details about her life." Different from those in *Short Letter, Long Farewell*, Maria Handke's visions gleaned from books are only those of the past, making obvious to her the fact that she has no future. Having led his mother to the Tree of Knowledge, the son has become the tempter in the Garden of Eden and therefore is, at least in part, responsible for her death.

A Sorrow Beyond Dreams was Handke's second attempt to "describe the political circumstances as part of an individual story, to connect the individual with the general events." At the same time, the author could reach into himself within a concrete and historically verifiable context instead of his usual private method. This has made *A Sorrow Beyond Dreams* arguably his most lucid and most successful work.

In *A Moment of True Feeling* and *The Left-Handed Woman*, Handke made two renewed attempts at reaching a higher level of feeling beyond the usual literary clichés. In the same measure in which he strove to depict these truer feelings, however, he seems to have missed his mark because of an increasing abandonment of a concretely discernible narrative. *A Moment of True Feeling* has been labeled "an angry act of regression," and *The Left-Handed Woman* "as closed as an oyster, a sign- and signal-labyrinth similar to the universe of a schizophrenic, in which language no longer serves the purpose of communicating, but rather to encode communication."

The diary *The Weight of the World* is the harbinger of Handke's new perception of the world during the 1980's. German critics have been divided in their response to this work; some have seen it as an "inventory of [Handke's] delusions of grandeur," a "trite game of hide-and-go-seek with notes arbitrarily strung together," while others have regarded it as an expansion of Handke's earlier efforts to overcome the shortfalls and deficiencies of language on a higher and more sophisticated level. Peter Pütz has stated that *The Weight of the World* is Handke's most radical attempt "to note, catalogue and thus preserve all appearances, experiences and acts of consciousness" in a preselective state, when their value has not yet been conditioned by human judgments. Everything should be freed from the superfluous value that humans attach to it, permitting a fresh assessment of the world's net weight.

The Long Way Around

Handke widens the focus from singular things, perceptions, and feelings and the intended preservation of their individual weight in his next novel, *The Long Way Around*. There, he strives to uncover the connections between all things as well as their salutary harmony. During his slow homecoming to Europe from the snowy loneliness of Alaska via California and New York, Valentin Sorger, the protagonist of the novel, rediscovers nature as the new essence of reality. In California, Sorger had lost his sense of space under the impact of his return to civilization; in a New York coffee shop, he regains the consciousness of his "earthen form" and subsequently regards his return to Europe as the beginning of a prophetic revelation. There exists an immediate connection between natural things, which fantasy must uncover or—more skeptically—to which Sorger "must apply his own lie." Glimpses of such nature revelations can be found in Handke's earlier novels—for example, in the heaving cypress tree in *Short Letter, Long Farewell* and in the chestnut-tree leaf in *A Moment of True Feeling*. In *The Long Way Around* and *The Lesson of Mont Sainte-Victoire*, these revelations of nature become the essence of reality altogether.

The Lesson of Mont Sainte-Victoire

In *The Lesson of Mont Sainte-Victoire*, a narrative situated somewhere between a short story and an essay, the protagonist of the trilogy has returned to Europe. The narrative perspective has changed from the third to the first person to allow Handke to supply the theoretical supplement for the trilogy that comprises *The Long Way Around*, *The Lesson of Mont Sainte-Victoire*, and the dramatic poem *Über die Dörfer*. Biblical allusions abound, as well as references to Goethe's *Zur Farbenlehre* (1810; *Theory of Colors*, 1840), in which artistic endeavor overcomes the boundaries between writing and painting, poetry and philosophy, and also between present and past, fact and fantasy. Nature, as revealed in art, becomes the author's weapon against the "calcified

Federal Republic which has grown more and more evil" and against the raw brutality of a madly barking dog along the narrator's path.

Mont Sainte-Victoire, near the southern French city of Aix-en-Provence, was painted repeatedly by Paul Cézanne during his most creative years after 1870. In these paintings, the narrator perceives the perfect synthesis between the eternal and the transitory, between nature and human endeavor. As the narrator climbs the mountain for a second time, "the realm of the words" lies suddenly open before him, "with the Great Spirit of The Form." He senses the structure of all things in himself as the ready substance of the works that he will write. His future works will be devoted to the metamorphosis of nature into art and the salvation of those things threatened by the human world.

CHILD STORY

Handke's attempt in *Child Story* to repeat the delicate balance of the inner with the outer world, which he had achieved in *A Sorrow Beyond Dreams*, met with mixed reactions from the critics. The narrator's daughter begins to loosen her bonds with him at the age of ten or eleven, and he reflects on her influence on him and his writing during the decade of their lives together. In the spirit of *The Lesson of Mont Sainte-Victoire*, the novel is Handke's attempt at saving the endangered daughter and eternalizing her. Some critics have noted the "insurmountable ego-stylization" in the novel and have criticized Handke for turning his daughter into a marketable commodity; others interpret the book as Handke's successful redemption from the "almost choking solipsism" that he had displayed in *The Lesson of Mont Sainte-Victoire* and *The Long Way Around*.

ACROSS

Across seems to indicate Handke's return to the messianic stance of those two novels, in this case filtered through the classical restraint of a first-person narrator who is a teacher of Greek and Latin; his name, Loser, might be translated as "the listener." Loser goes further than the protagonists of Handke's earlier novels in his attempts to preserve that which is in danger. He removes language from nature by destroying election posters and slogans that have been attached to trees, and in the second part of the novel, he intervenes decisively by hurling a stone and thereby killing a swastika painter who has desecrated a mountain. "The mountain must remain empty," he triumphs over the murdered man. A circle in Handke's work seems to close with Andreas Loser, a teacher of classical languages and an etymologist whose favorite work is Vergil's *Georgics* (c. 37-29 B.C.E.).

Throughout Handke's novels, the unusually close bond between author and work seems to be both a source of strength and a liability. Handke's early questioning of the automatisms of postwar German literature—and consequently the automatisms of life altogether—required the undetached participation of the author in his works, for Handke, like the schizophrenic whom he mentions in his discussion of *The Goalie's Anxiety at the Penalty Kick*, needed to interpret every event as alluding to him and him alone. Such a schizophrenic stance made Handke the outsider from the start, and it has led almost automatically to some narcissistic excesses in his novels, in which he has begun to regard himself as an isolated seer who can save himself and the world from the forces of these automatisms through an intense, more direct, and somewhat mystical kinship with nature, as it had already been advocated by his nineteenth century compatriot, the Austrian novelist Adalbert Stifter. Such prophetic visions have naturally antagonized some of Handke's critics, who see him as having moved dangerously close to a Nazi *Blut und Boden Romantik* (blood and earth romanticism).

MY YEAR IN THE NO-MAN'S-BAY

Handke wrote *My Year in the No-Man's-Bay* in 1993. It is set ahead in 1997—a technique designed to keep vague any references to world events. The main character, Gregor Keuschnig, is soon to be fifty-six years old. Like Handke, he studied law before becoming a writer; also like Handke, he found himself a single parent after his wife left him. Keuschnig is self-absorbed and goes into great detail about his writing and the landscape in which he feels at home, a place near Paris that he calls the No-Man's-Bay.

As indicated by the novel's subtitle, *A Fairytale from the New Times*, the focus is not on factual events but on personal perceptions. Keuschnig's goal is "to find the way back to the dreamlike, to keep that basic tone and be clear as sunlight." People interest him most as silhouettes. The less he knows about them, the better they fit into his fantasies. For example, he imagines a singer who feels something healing in him that he did not want healed, a painter who loses his relationship to distance, and a priest who has not yet given up the priesthood, but may.

There are strong undercurrents of emotion as Keuschnig acknowledges the importance of others in establishing his own identity. In his solitude he senses the presence of ancestors who dream on in him. Ana, the wife who left him (twice), is present in his thoughts, interrupting his concentration, and appearing to him in others as her double. A midlife situation that could be seen as sad is instead made to seem unconventional by Keuschnig's eccentricities. Handke's subtle use of language and wry humor sustain the sunlight through a long book.

On a Dark Night I Left My Silent House

Handke wrote *On a Dark Night I Left My Silent House* in the summer and fall of 1996. The main character, the pharmacist in the small city of Taxham outside Salzburg, likes to read medieval epics, and Handke works medieval motifs into the story. Like the knights who set out to seek adventure, the pharmacist leaves his house from July to October to work out his problems on a long trip. During that time he is unable to speak and traverses a landscape that bears no resemblance to modern-day Europe. In fact, he wonders at one point if he has ever left the environs of Salzburg.

The trip changes him both outwardly and inwardly for the better. People had previously overlooked him or failed to recognize him outside his pharmacy, but on his return, he seems to have more presence. The pharmacist has come to accept two aspects of his family situation that had previously preyed on his mind. Seeing his son with the Gypsies, the pharmacist no longer "disowns" him, but realizes that the boy must go his own way. Second, he understands that he is not the only man whose wife chooses to live separately from him in other parts of the house. This complex, well-crafted novel supports many levels of interpretation.

Crossing the Sierra de Gredos

Written in 2002 but not translated into English until 2007, the monumental novel *Crossing the Sierra de Gredos* is a comprehensive summation of Handke's view of the decline of Western European culture as well as his most ambitious attempt at including the reader in the creation of a novel, something he first attempted in his 1988 work *Repetition*.

The main thematic focus of the novel, the central importance of images for human existence, is indicated in the German title, *Der Bildverlust: Oder, Durch die Sierra de Gredos*. "Bildverlust" means "loss of images." Indeed, the novel does not deal primarily with an adventurous journey of the protagonist across the Spanish mountain range but with her loss and potential reconstruction of autonomous individual images that she had shored up against the ruins of her personal life.

Thus the American reader expecting a travel-adventure plot will be disappointed. The novel is about a nameless, highly successful female banker of Slavic descent who finds herself confronted with her inner life in tatters, quite in contrast to her public image as it is portrayed in the media. To set the story right she has hired a well-known Spanish writer who lives in the La Mancha region in Spain and has determined to meet him at his home in Spain, after retracing her earlier walking tour from Valladolid to La Mancha across the Sierra the Gredos. She reaches her destination after stopping in several places, most of which cannot be found on a map of Spain but are characterized by an decreasing attachment to contemporary Western material/commercial values and increasing appreciation for the world of the imagination. At the climax of the novel, she suffers a complete breakdown and subsequent break with her former life. When she arrives at the home of the author, she finds that her biography is already finished and she dedicates her future to the images and the world of imagination that had been destroyed by the artificial, manipulative, commercial images propagated by the media.

Crossing the Sierra de Gredos is a complex work of cultural criticism and narratological theory. Handke sees the current era as an "interperiod," a transitory period, characterized by superficiality, lack of imagination, commercialization, and the insinuation of images and the accompanying false values that lead to loss of autonomous images and ideas in the individual. This loss, which began in the late Middle Ages, the time of Cervantes, will eventually lead to a total collapse of Western civilization and, perhaps, a renaissance on the basis of some remembered or imagined fragments of a richer past. *Crossing the Sierra de Gredos* is a "wasteland" novel that holds out the hope of possible redemption and restoration if people are able to recognize where they have gone wrong.

Crossing the Sierra de Gredos thus deals exclusively with travels and adventures of the mind. It deals with an imaginary journey whose plot writes itself as the protagonist travels through her own past and into an uncertain though not entirely hopeless future. Declarative sentences diminish and are replaced by sentences that end in questions or alternative statements and outcomes from which readers are invited to choose, in the process becoming authors themselves. It is a novel that requires much patience and thought from the reader, but it is unquestionably Handke's richest novel to date.

Klaus Hanson; Jean M. Snook
Updated by Franz G. Blaha

Other major works

SHORT FICTION: *Begrüssung des Aufsichtsrats*, 1967.

PLAYS: *Publikumsbeschimpfung*, pr., pb. 1966 (*Offending the Audience*, 1969); *Selbstbezichtigung*, pr., pb. 1966 (*Self-Accusation*, 1969); *Weissagung*, pr., pb. 1966 (*Prophecy*, 1976); *Hilferufe*, pr. 1967 (*Calling for Help*, 1970); *Kaspar*, pr., pb. 1968 (English translation, 1969); *Kaspar, and Other Plays*, 1969; *Das Mündel will Vormund sein*, pr., pb. 1969 (*My Foot My Tutor*, 1970); *Quodlibet*, pr. 1970 (English translation, 1976); *Der Ritt über den Bodensee*, pr., pb. 1971 (*The Ride Across Lake Constance*, 1972); *Die Unvernünftigen sterben aus*, pb. 1973 (*They Are Dying Out*, 1975); *The Ride Across Lake Constance, and Other Plays*, 1976; *Über die Dörfer*, pr., pb. 1982 (*Among the Villages*, 1984); *Das Spiel vom Fragen: Oder, Die Reise zum sonoren Land*, pr., pb. 1989 (*Voyage to the Sonorous Land: Or, The Art of Asking*, 1996); *Die Stunde da wir nichts voneinander wussten*, pr., pb. 1992 (*The Hour We Knew Nothing of Each Other*, 1996); *Zurüstungen zur Unsterblichkeit: Ein Königsdrama*, pr., pb. 1997; *Die Fahrt im Einbaum: Oder, Das Stück zum Film von Krieg*, pr., pb. 1999; *La Cuisine*, pr. 2001 (pb. as *Pourquoi la cuisine?*, 2001; with Mladen Materic); *Untertagblues: Ein Stationendrama*, pb. 2003.

POETRY: *Die Innenwelt der Aussenwelt der Innenwelt*, 1969 (*The Innerworld of the Outerworld of the Innerworld*, 1974); *Gedicht an die Dauer*, 1986.

SCREENPLAYS: *Chronik der laufenden Ereignisse*, 1971; *Der Himmel über Berlin*, 1987 (*Wings of Desire*; with Wim Wenders).

TELEPLAY: *Falsche Bewegung*, 1975.

NONFICTION: *Ich bin ein Bewohner des Elfenbeinturms*, 1972; *Als das Wünschen noch geholfen hat*, 1974; *Das Gewicht der Welt*, 1977 (journal; *The Weight of the World*, 1984); *Das Ende des Flanierens*, 1980; *Die Geschichte des Bleistifts*, 1982 (journal); *Phantasien der Wiederholung*, 1983 (journal); *Aber ich lebe nur von den Zwischenräumen*, 1987; *Versuch über die Müdigkeit*, 1989; *Noch einmal für Thukydides*, 1990 (*Once Again for Thucydides*, 1998); *Versuch über die Jukebox*, 1990; *Versuch über den geglückten Tag*, 1991; *The Jukebox, and Other Essays on Storytelling*, 1994 (translation of *Versuch über die Müdigkeit, Versuch über die Jukebox*, and *Versuch über den geglückten Tag*); *Eine winterliche Reise zu den Flüssen Donau, Save, Morawa und Drina: Oder, Gerechtigkeit für Serbien*, 1996 (*A Journey to the Rivers: Justice for Serbia*, 1997); *Am Felsfenster morgens: Und andere Ortszeiten, 1982-1987*, 1998 (journal); *Rund um das grosse Tribunal*, 2003.

TRANSLATIONS: *Prometheus, gefesselt*, 1986 (of Aeschylus's *Prometheus desmōtēs*); *Das Wintermärchen*, 1991 (of William Shakespeare's *The Winter's Tale*).

Bibliography

Abbot, Scott. "Peter Handke and the Former Yugoslavia: The Rhetoric of War and Peace." *World Literature Today* 75, no. 1 (Winter, 2001): 78-85. Sheds light on Handke's works in support of Serbia and the literary techniques he employs.

Coury, David N., and Frank Pilipp, eds. *The Works of Peter Handke: International Perspectives*. Riverside, Calif.: Ariadne Press, 2005. Collection of fourteen essays offers analyses and interpretations of Handke's writings, including his novels and other prose works.

Demetz, Peter. "Peter Handke: A Fragile Witness." In *After the Fires: Recent Writing in the Germanies, Austria, and Switzerland*. San Diego, Calif.: Harcourt Brace Jovanovich, 1992. Discussion of Handke's work is part of a larger exploration of the postwar literature of several German-language writers.

Firda, Richard Arthur. *Peter Handke*. New York: Twayne, 1993. Provides an excellent introductory overview of Handke's life and work up to 1987, with interpretations of the major works. Includes chronology, annotated bibliography, and index.

Klinkowitz, Jerome, and James Knowlton. *Peter Handke and the Postmodern Transformation: The Goalie's Journey Home*. Columbia: University of Missouri Press, 1983. Well-organized, appreciative study of Handke's works presents a convincing refutation of negative criticism.

Konzett, Matthias. *The Rhetoric of National Dissent in Thomas Bernhard, Peter Handke, and Elfriede Jelinek*. Rochester, N.Y.: Camden House, 2000. Examines the ways in which the three authors expose state-directed consensus and harmonization that impede the development of multicultural awareness in modern-day Europe. Explores how Handke focuses on national suppression of postideological voices in the history telling of marginalized individuals.

Linstead, Michael. "Peter Handke." In *The Modern German Novel*, edited by Keith Bullivant. New York: Berg, 1987. Explains Handke's ideas about forms of description and examines their application in his novels.

Perram, Garvin H. C. *Peter Handke: The Dynamics of the Poetics and the Early Narrative Prose*. New York: Peter Lang, 1992. Examines Handke's early works. Includes bibliographical references.

Turner, Robert L. "Fragmented Narration and Multiple-Path Readings: Towards the Creation of Reader-Driven Texts." *Neophilologus* 89, no. 4 (October, 2005): 495-508. Explains Handke's experiments with making the reader part of the creative process in his later prose fiction. Helpful for an understanding of *Crossing the Sierra de Gredos*.

JAMES HANLEY

Born: Dublin, Ireland; September 3, 1901
Died: London, England; November 11, 1985
Also known as: Patric Shone

Principal long fiction

Drift, 1930
Boy, 1931 (1990, unexpurgated)
Ebb and Flood, 1932
Captain Bottell, 1933
Resurrexit Dominus, 1934
The Furys, 1935
Stoker Bush, 1935
The Secret Journey, 1936
Hollow Sea, 1938
Our Time Is Gone, 1940
The Ocean, 1941
No Directions, 1943
Sailor's Song, 1943
What Farrar Saw, 1946
Emily, 1948
Winter Song, 1950
The House in the Valley, 1951 (as Patric Shone; also known as *Against the Stream*, 1981)
The Closed Harbour, 1952
The Welsh Sonata: Variations on a Theme, 1954
Levine, 1956
An End and a Beginning, 1958
Say Nothing, 1962
Another World, 1972
A Woman in the Sky, 1973
A Dream Journey, 1976
A Kingdom, 1978
Against the Stream, 1981

Other literary forms

James Hanley was one of the most prolific of twentieth century writers. Apart from twenty-six novels and many volumes of short stories, he wrote a considerable number of plays for stage, radio, and television. *Say Nothing* (pr. 1961, broadcast) is a successfully produced play based on his novel by the same name. *Plays One* (1968) includes his famous play "The Inner Journey," which was staged at Lincoln Center, New York, to excellent critical reviews.

Hanley's *Broken Water: An Autobiographical Excursion* (1937) provides insights into his early life at sea and his determined efforts to become a writer. *Grey Children: A Study in Humbug and Misery* (1931), is a compassionate study of unemployment among miners in South Wales. *John Cowper Powys: A Man in the Corner* (1969) is a biographical and critical study of the English novelist whose *A Glastonbury Romance* (1932) was Hanley's favorite novel. In *Herman Melville: A Man in the Customs House* (1971), Hanley's own love for the sea enables him to present Melville from a refreshing new perspective. *Don Quixote Drowned* (1953) is a collection of essays, personal and literary. In one of these essays, Hanley includes a passage that describes himself as a "chunky realist and flounderer in off-Dreiserian prose, naïve and touchy about style." The volume also provides valuable information about some of the sources for Hanley's novels.

Achievements

James Hanley is the neglected giant of modern literature. Around 1940, T. E. Lawrence found in Hanley's novels "a blistering vividness." E. M. Forster called him a novelist of distinction and originality. Henry Green considered him to be superior to Joseph Conrad. Herbert Read commented that Hanley was one of the most vigorous and impressive of contemporary writers. John Cowper Powys called Hanley "a genius." C. P. Snow recognized Hanley's humanity, compassion, and sheer imaginative power. Henry Miller wrote an enthusiastic introduction to the third edition (1946) of Hanley's novel *No Directions*. Yet, in spite of this impressive roster of applause, Hanley has been assessed as "one of the most consistently praised and least-known novelists in the English speaking world."

In the 1930's and early 1940's, Hanley was at the height of his popularity because of his novels about the war and some of the early volumes of the Fury saga. By the 1950's, however, his popularity had declined and his reading public was a small cult group; he was practically unknown in the United States. Hanley is a complex writer who demands from the reader the same undivided attention he devoted to his carefully conceived and crafted novels and plays. Irving Howe points out in his brilliant review of Hanley's *A Dream Journey* that

> Hanley's novels demand to be read slowly, in order to protect oneself from his relentlessness. It's like having your skin rubbed raw by a harsh wind, or like driving yourself to a rare pitch of truth by reflections—honest ones for a change—about the blunders of your life.

Hanley was not unduly concerned about the lack of a wider audience. He pursued his art with dedication and artistic integrity, he was uncompromising and unwilling to change his style to satisfy fluctuating fads and fashions of the literary world, and he survived completely through his writings. Maintaining such an authentic aesthetic individuality over a period of nearly sixty years was in itself a major achievement of James Hanley.

Biography

James Hanley was born on September 3, 1901, in Dublin, Ireland. Early in life, he moved with his family to Liverpool, England, where he grew up. Hanley's father, Edward Hanley, gave up a promising career in law for a life at sea, thereby grievously disappointing his mother; James Hanley was strongly counseled by his grandmother not to go to sea. The advice fell on deaf ears, however, and he left school at age fourteen and went to sea as a ship boy. Some of this experience undoubtedly provided him with the raw material for his novel *Boy*.

During Hanley's first transatlantic voyage, war broke out, and for two years he worked on troopships transporting soldiers across the Mediterranean to Salonika, Greece, and Gallipoli, Turkey. *Hollow Sea* draws upon this phase of his life and portrays the intensity of life on troopships during hazardous missions. At age sixteen, Hanley deserted his ship on a stopover in St. John, New Brunswick, Canada. He lied about his age, took on a name randomly selected from a telephone directory, and joined the Canadian army. After training in Canada and in England, he served in France. When he was discharged from the army and returned to England, he settled down with his parents in Liverpool.

In his autobiography, Hanley writes, "I had finished with the sea. I had finished with the army. I had had practically no education." He had seen the ugly and brutal face of war and survived the trauma. In Liverpool, he came across an old sailor friend to whom he had entrusted a letter to his mother with some money. The friend had taken the money and thrown away the letter, an incident that deeply affected Hanley. He made no more friends, and for the next ten years, he kept to himself like a hermit. He found a new personal meaning in the advice "never trust a friend," from August Strindberg's play *Bränea Tomten* (1907; *After the Fire: Or, The Burned Lot*). He took a job as a storeman on the railway and obsessively started on his self-education. He read voraciously during his spare time, studied French and Russian in evening classes, and indulged in his great passion for music as he struggled to play Bach and Beethoven with his small, rough, workingman's hands.

Hanley also wrote short stories and plays with dogged determination and collected a number of rejection slips. He was determined to write "until he was accepted" and completed a book titled *Soldier's Journal of the War*. He was asked to burn it, however, because, as he put it in his autobiographical *Broken Water*, "it went a bit too far as a picture of the war." He completed his first novel, *Drift*, and, after being rejected by eighteen publishers, it was finally published in 1930, with the support of publisher Eric Partridge. Hanley received five pounds and no royalties in payment.

Hanley's next project was to write "the odyssey of a ship" with no human characters. He abandoned that project and instead wrote the controversial novel *Boy*, which proved to be a major success. Hanley then commenced work on his major achievement, a five-volume saga of the Furys, a Liverpool family. The first volume was published in 1935 and the final volume in 1958. After publishing *Say Nothing* in 1962, Hanley abandoned the novel and wrote plays for the next ten years. In these plays, Hanley shows kinship with playwrights such as Harold Pinter, Samuel Beckett, and Strindberg. "I wrote plays for economic reasons," explained Hanley. "I even wrote under a pseudonym Patric Shone, hoping it might change my luck." In 1972, Hanley returned to the novel form with the publication of *Another World*.

Hanley suffered considerable piracy of his works. Notable examples are *A Passion Before Death* (1930), which was reissued in the United States in a limited edition without any remuneration to Hanley, and the play *Say Nothing*, which ran for two months in New York with Hanley receiving no royalties.

When Hanley wrote, he preferred to be in total isolation. He neither read nor talked with people while creating. "It's like a prisoner being a writer," Hanley said, and Wales provided him with a stimulating kind of solitude. As for the writing of the novel itself, to him it was a "series of blind gropings in a dark tunnel." Character in a novel was the most important feature to him. If after the third chapter, the characters took over the telling of the story, Hanley knew that his novel was going well.

Hanley settled in London but always regretted leaving Wales. His loneliness increased after his wife of more than forty years died in 1980 (they had one son, Liam, an artist). Hanley died in London in 1985.

Analysis

Two themes dominate James Hanley's writings. The first concerns humans at sea in ships. Hanley explored, in each succeeding novel, the strange love-hate relationship that men and women have with the sea. The sea, with its violence and tranquillity, its many mysteries and its hypnotic powers over those who live and die by it, is orchestrated by him and becomes "the central experience of his novels." Hanley views the sea from the sailors' viewpoint, unlike Joseph Conrad, who sees the ship from the vantage point of an officer.

Hanley's second theme—often interrelated with the first—concerns men and women imprisoned in the web of poverty from which they have no desire to escape. They have created a world of deprivation for themselves and are terrified to come out of their self-imprisonment; within this confinement, they revolve and eke out their livelihood. Their despair leads them to weave private dreams, and their reluctance to realize their dreams returns them to despair. His characters, for the most part, are marginal people, the remnants of society, the debris of human life: outcasts, hobos, loners, strangers, broken men, women, and children. Hanley is their compassionate chronicler as he conducts a complex investigation into their lives and discovers poetry and drama in their bleak existence. With deep social concern, Hanley reveals how very much these marginal people matter: "the more insignificant a person is in this whirlpool of industrialized and civilized society, the more important he is for me." In making them touch the readers' wellsprings of compassion, Hanley achieved the hallmark of great literature; he moves readers emotionally.

Boy

The novel *Boy* has become a collector's item. In *Broken Water*, Hanley writes about seeing a boy in a Liverpool slum by the docks dragging a heavy cart "like a mule." The dull, vacant look on that boy's face profoundly touched Hanley and became the creative impulse for *Boy*. Also, in an autobiographical sketch titled "Oddfish," from *Don Quixote Drowned*, Hanley reports his sense of shock when he listened to an episode of a ship boy being thrown overboard because he had developed a contagious disease. The memory of that tale remained with him to become an integral part of *Boy*. Furthermore, in the earlier Hanley story *The German Prisoner* (1930), two mentally unbalanced British soldiers rape and brutalize a beautiful German boy. The passionate outrage against mindless violence coupled with a keen sense of social concern expressed in that story are also echoed in the novel.

Boy, because of its graphic descriptions of brutality, sadism, and homosexuality aboard a ship, was banned upon publication. The work became a cause célèbre, and E. M. Forster came to Hanley's defense. William Faulkner called *Boy* "a damn fine job. It springs up like a purifying cyclone, while most contemporary novels sound as if they were written by weaklings."

Boy is the brutal and tragic story of Arthur Fearon, a Liverpool schoolboy who has dreams of becoming a chemist. His sadistic father has more practical plans of having his son work on the docks to help liquidate family debts. He himself had a brutal job as a boy, and he cannot see a better life for his son. At the age of thirteen, Arthur is initiated into physical horrors by the gang on the dock. Arthur flees home and stows away in the coal bunker on a freighter going to Alexandria.

The boy's humiliating experiences, physical and sexual, on the freighter at the hands of almost everyone on board is the theme of *Boy*. A visit to a brothel in Alexandria, his initiation into manhood, is Arthur's one and only experience with beauty. The beauty of the girl soothes him, and "like a dark tapestry it covered his wounded thought, the spoliation, the degradation, the loneliness, the misery of his existence." From the encounter, he contracts syphilis and is shunned by all on the freighter. The ship's doctor wants Arthur to jump overboard and drown himself. Instead, however, the drunken captain gently invites Arthur to come to him by holding up his great coat, and, when Arthur responds unsuspectingly, the captain smothers him to death. The official report: "Boy was lost overboard."

In spite of all the brutality that Arthur faces, he maintains a boyish idealism to the very end. He remains uncorrupted and thereby heightens the sense of tragedy. The novel's strong connotations of sexual urge and clinical descriptions make it a naturalistic work reminiscent of Stephen Crane's *Maggie: A Girl of the Streets* (1893). The epitome of Hanley's technique and style—the use of letters to keep the flow of narrative, the grinding minutiae of financial details, descriptions that often read like stage directions, the longing for the past and the future because the present is so unbearable, prose rising to poetic eloquence when describing ships and sea—*Boy* is a blueprint of the author's craftsmanship and sets the tone for his later novels.

Fury family chronicle

Comprising 2,295 pages and five volumes, the Fury family chronicle (*The Furys*, *The Secret Journey*, *Our Time Is Gone*, *Winter Song*, and *An End and a Beginning*) is Hanley's magnum opus. Set in Gelton, the fictional counterpart of Liverpool, the sequence of novels chronicles the saga of the Furys, a working-class Liverpool Irish family. Based on references to British and world events, a period of sixteen years from 1911 to 1927 is covered in the novel sequence. In some of the volumes, the period covered is very brief, as in the final volume, *An End and a Beginning*, where the time frame is only three weeks.

Dennis Fury, a seaman, is the main character in the saga. It is his wife, Fanny, however, who is the dominating force in the sequence. One of the most fully realized women in contemporary fiction, she is, as Edward Stokes points out in his study *The Novels of James Hanley* (1964), "both prosaic and legendary, at once middle-aged, dowdy, toil-worn, intensely respectable and bigoted housewife and a creature vital, passionate and a-moral as a heroine of Celtic myth." Fanny Fury holds both the novel and the Fury family together, and Hanley has fused into her something of the obsession of Lady Macbeth. Her son, Peter, whom she wants to be a priest against the wishes of the rest of her family, murders Anna Ragnar, the shrewd moneylender, and so splits the entire Fury family. Fanny uses all her efforts to bring the family together in a semblance of peace. The final novel in the sequence, *An End and a Beginning*, is devoted entirely to Peter Fury, and Hanley skillfully weaves the past and the present to maintain the narrative flow.

In anatomizing the intricacies of the family relationships within the Fury family, Hanley draws upon elements of Lawrentian brutality. Dennis Fury is pitted against his eighty-two-year-old father-in-law, Anthony Mangan, who is incapacitated; Fanny is pitted against her daughter Maureen's husband, John Kilkey, a devout pacifist; the whole family, with the exception of Fanny, is pitted against Peter, who is studying to be a priest at their expense; Fanny and Dennis themselves are locked in ferocious combat concerning a multitude of daily minutiae. Hanley's use of dialogue to reveal these hostilities is crisp, direct, and theatrical in the best sense of the term.

The imagery of a prison dominates the entire saga. To Peter, the seminary is a prison; to Dennis, his home is a prison and the sea is freedom; to Fanny the sea is a steel trap taking away her men, and her very desire to keep the family together imprisons her in her responsibilities; Anthony Mangan, paralyzed and mute, finds that the chair in which he is strapped is his prison, physically and verbally; Peter Fury murders the moneylender and cries out that he is free from debt only to find himself behind prison bars. All the characters in the Fury chronicle are attempting to escape their prisons but find themselves in darker traps for doing so. Hanley has worked out his imagery of frustration, loneliness, and inability to communicate throughout the saga, and an entire study can be made about prison imagery in his novels.

Hanley creates a scene, introduces his characters, gives readers an intense close-up, and reveals his characters through dialogue and intimate conversation. There are always passages of lyrical beauty whenever the sea or a ship is described. Letters, journals, and inner monologues are all used to tell the story and reveal insights into a variety of characters that populate the chronicle. There are a few noteworthy characters among the many found in the novels: John Kilkey, physically repulsive, is a man of deep principles and compassion and a pacifist; Brigid Mangan, Fanny's youngest sister, is a spinster and a devout Catholic strongly feeling her alienation in England and eager to return to her spiritual home, Ireland; Desmond Fury, the eldest son, is ambitious and deeply involved in Labour politics, and his wife, Sheila, has an adulterous affair with Peter Fury; Mrs. Anna Ragner, the sharp moneylender, enjoys having people in her grip and getting rich on poverty; Professor R. H. Titmouse, a self-appointed professor of anthropology, is gay and has a hysterical crush on Peter but acts at times as the voice of sanity when he tells Peter that people are merely sheep ready to be manipulated by politicians. These and a host of other characters give the Fury chronicle a deep richness and diversity of humanity.

The saga of the Furys, however, has not received a great deal of critical attention. It is a work that is original, sustained, and above all, as Edward Stokes maintains, a "compassionate penetration into the dreams and desperations, the illusions and longings of the characters" that move throughout this epic work.

Hollow Sea

The years between 1938 and 1943 were a peak period in Hanley's creativity. He wrote three significant novels about ships and sailors, against the backdrop of war: *Hollow Sea*, *The Ocean*, and *Sailor's Song*. The first novel is set within the time frame of a few weeks and is a story of a troopship. A former liner called *Helicon*, the vessel is painted gray and called *A10* and is involved in a war mission to transport fifteen hundred soldiers to a secret destination. To Captain Dunford, *A10* is "the personification of uncontrollable madness"; to the men in overcrowded holds with shortages of food and water, life aboard the *A10* is nasty, brutish, and uncertain. The ship bristles with tensions, and the voyage becomes "a microcosm of a whole world at war." During the voyage, *A10* gets into a violent and bloody skirmish and is compelled to add another two hundred soldiers to its population. Without adequate hospital facilities, the men die, and the ship's captain refuses to bury them without proper authorization. *A10* becomes "a coffin ship" and pressures intensify. Some men capitalize on the tensions and shortages by carrying on a black market in food; others seek escape in fantasy, letting their minds conjure images of reaching home and reunion with their families.

Hanley characterizes vividly the various men on the ship, from the captain who is "imprisoned by his mission," and hence must be totally authoritative, to boatswain Vesuvius with an "eruption of pimples on his face." There is, however, a poetic quality to the novel that echoes the legend of the Flying Dutchman and the eerie atmosphere evoked by Samuel Taylor Coleridge in *The Rime of the Ancient Mariner* (1798). Edwin Muir felicitously noted this in his review of the novel: "*Hollow Sea*'s great virtue is that it is poetically conceived. We are always conscious that the events that Hanley is describing are part of a large pattern." *Hollow Sea* captures the hustle, the bustle, and the ceaseless throb of life aboard a troopship, and had it not been so long, it would have emerged as a great novel.

THE OCEAN

A tight, short, well-structured novel, *The Ocean* is a powerful study in survival. The entire action takes place in an open boat containing five men: Joseph Curtain, the sailor; Father Michaels, a priest; Gaunt, a middle-aged businessman, who worries about his missing wife, Kay; Stone, a middle-aged teacher; and twenty-year-old Benton. These are the survivors from the torpedoed ship *Aurora*. Hanley has endowed a timeless quality to his story by not giving it a local habitation or a specific time. The reader is constantly made aware of the loneliness and helplessness of these men in the middle of the vast empty sea, which is full of beauty and terror.

Joseph Curtain is the key character in the novel. He knows how to deal with the men and can operate on the whole spectrum of human emotions. There is a lean, spare athletic quality to Hanley's prose in *The Ocean*, an economy of word and style that is reminiscent of the best of Ernest Hemingway. It is remarkable that Hanley, who wrote the long, discursive *Hollow Sea*, could also write *The Ocean*: it is one of his very best.

SAILOR'S SONG

The last of Hanley's sea novels, *Sailor's Song*, is set on a raft and concerns four men. The story, told with biblical simplicity and lyrical beauty, is the story of the delirious sailor, Manion, on the raft. Manion's name is a play on "any man." Carefully, through a series of broken images and shuttling back and forth through the corridors of time, Manion's tale—the sailor's song—is unfolded. Manion is the captive of the sea, hypnotized and held by it. Through his life, Hanley distills the strange umbilical feelings that sailors have for the sea and ships. Delirious, Manion remembers his past, particularly the time when he was without a ship and became restless looking for one, believing in a miracle that would result in his signing on another ship. Hanley was also to use this theme—of a sailor desperately looking for a home, a ship on which to sign—in his novel *The Closed Harbour*. After he has sung his song, told his story, John Manion drifts in his sleep to death. *Sailor's Song* is perhaps Hanley's most moving novel.

THE CLOSED HARBOUR

Continuing to master his primary themes of the sea and entrapment, Hanley's creative talents are not exhausted. *The Closed Harbour*, set in Marseilles, is Hanley's only novel with a non-English setting. It is a powerful and intense study of a French merchant captain, Marius, who is under a cloud of suspicion. He wants to get a ship, but none is available. Hanley relentlessly probes Marius's mind, moving back and forth in a fascinating study of a haunted man. George Painter in reviewing the novel rightly pointed out that Marius "is a figure worthy of Melville, a fallen angel, a monument of man's grandeur in defeat." Felix Levine, of *Levine*, like Marius, is a man without a ship, but Felix is also a man without a country: He is the quintessential displaced person. Felix is a typical Hanley character, who obsessively dreams and weaves fantasies and begins to believe in them so passionately that dreams become his reality. The entire novel itself is a backward dream, and through a series of interior monologues, diaries, and letters, Hanley orchestrates all the subtle nuances that make up the dark despair of loneliness and hunger.

A DREAM JOURNEY

Hanley's 1976 novel, *A Dream Journey*, is the best introduction to Hanley. The story of Clem Stevens, an artist, and his wife, Lena, it is the single novel that distills all of Hanley's themes, styles, concerns, and characterizations. Clem and Lena both appeared earlier in Hanley's short novel *No Directions*. Since Hanley has said that novel writing is a "series of blind gropings in a long dark tunnel," it seems that he looked back at the tunnel where he had left the characters from *No Directions* and found that "they were not so limp" as he had thought they were and so he "gave each character an extra squeeze." In fact, the longest section in *A Dream Journey*, "Yesterday," is the entire text of *No Directions*.

The novel opens in typical Hanley fashion, "a monosyllabic session." The moment a thought appears in the mind of one of the characters, the scene accompanying that thought is conjured in the mind of that character. Everyone is on a dream journey, and dreaming becomes a metaphor for living for both Clem and his wife. They use their dreams to seek tranquillity from the harshness of life by "fondling memories" in their minds.

Clem suffers from depression and has not left his house in more than a year. He has painted a sixty-year-old woman on five canvases, reflecting a whole day in her life, "a whole language of exhaustion." Clem seems to do in painting what Hanley does with words. Yet, Clem is not a successful artist; his paintings sold to the butcher get him "free meat for a month." Lena is his encourager, but the days grind out in sheer monotony, and there is no communication between them. They turn to the past and, in their minds, go on dream journeys. Their small claustrophobic rooms imprison them. Lena thinks of leaving Clem, but "you don't just walk out on a person because he's second rate"; furthermore, "people don't escape from their own illusions, you just live with them." In a way, she enjoys Clem's dependence on her. When the final catastrophe happens—a fire and Clem's death as he attempts to rescue his paintings—it is a logical conclusion based on the characters' "realities." In *A Dream Journey*, Hanley brings to bear the maturity and careful artistry of his talents.

Readers who are familiar with Hanley's works find new meanings and subtle nuances in his writings with each rereading. Those who have the patience to approach and discover his fiction for the first time will be richly rewarded with a satisfying literary and emotional experience. His position as a major literary figure in the twentieth century is firmly established.

K. Bhaskara Rao

Other major works

SHORT FICTION: *The German Prisoner*, 1930; *A Passion Before Death*, 1930; *The Last Voyage*, 1931; *Men in Darkness: Five Stories*, 1931; *Aria and Finale*, 1932; *Stoker Haslett*, 1932; *Quartermaster Clausen*, 1934; *At Bay*, 1935; *Half an Eye: Sea Stories*, 1937; *People Are Curious*, 1938; *At Bay, and Other Stories*, 1944; *Crilley, and Other Stories*, 1945; *Selected Stories*, 1947; *A Walk in the Wilderness*, 1950; *Collected Stories*, 1953; *The Darkness*, 1973; *What Farrar Saw, and Other Stories*, 1984; *The Last Voyage, and Other Stories*, 1997.

PLAYS: *Say Nothing*, pr. 1961 (broadcast); *The Inner Journey*, pb. 1965; *Plays One*, 1968 (collection).

NONFICTION: *Broken Water: An Autobiographical Excursion*, 1937; *Grey Children: A Study in Humbug and Misery*, 1937; *Between the Tides*, 1939; *Don Quixote Drowned*, 1953; *John Cowper Powys: A Man in the Corner*, 1969; *Herman Melville: A Man in the Customs House*, 1971.

Bibliography

Dentith, Simon. "James Hanley's *The Furys*: The Modernist Subject Goes on Strike." *Literature and History* 12, no. 1 (Spring, 2003): 41-56. Dentith analyzes *The Furys*, discussing the influence of modernism on Hanley's writing, the novel's issues of subjectivism, and its depiction of collective life.

Fordham, John. *James Hanley: Modernism and the Working Class*. Cardiff: University of Wales Press, 2002. Fordham examines Hanley's life and writings, concluding that the author's works, which often have been described as "proletarian realism," should be identified more accurately as modernism. He places Hanley's work within a cultural and social context and examines the author's association with Wales, where Hanley lived for more than thirty years.

Harrington, Frank G. *James Hanley: A Bold and Unique Solitary*. Francestown, N.H.: Typographeum, 1989. A good biographical account, written by a friend of Hanley. Includes a list of Hanley's books.

Mathewson, Ruth. "Hanley's Palimpsest." *New Leader*, January 3, 1977. Reviews *A Dream Journey*, noting that it is a good introduction to Hanley's work. Mathewson also briefly discusses Hanley's earlier novels and comments that *A Dream Journey* is a "palimpsest" of his earlier works.

Vinson, James, ed. *St. James Reference Guide to English Literature*. Chicago: St. James Press, 1985. A critical piece by Edward Stokes cites the importance of Hanley's writing, which has been compared to that of Thomas Hardy and Fyodor Dostoevski. Notes, however, that Hanley's work is uneven and his characters lacking in popular appeal.

Wade, Stephen. "James Hanley: A Case for Reassessment." *Contemporary Review* 274 (June, 1999): 307-310. Wade provides a brief, critical overview of Hanley's fiction, arguing that the author remains relevant and deserves to be reread and reconsidered. While he acknowledges that Hanley's output is uneven, he cites six works that are worthy of special attention, including the novels *Boy*, *The Furys*, *No Directions*, and *The Welsh Sonata*.

Williams, Patrick. "'No Struggle but the Home': James Hanley's *The Furys*." In *Recharting the Thirties*, edited by Patrick J. Quinn. Selinsgrove, Pa.: Susquehanna University Press, 1996. William's essay on Hanley's 1935 novel *The Furys* is included in this essay collection that seeks to refamiliarize readers with British authors who have been largely ignored since their major works first appeared in the 1930's. The essay is preceded by a brief biographical sketch of Hanley.

BARRY HANNAH

Born: Meridian, Mississippi; April 23, 1942

Principal long fiction

Geronimo Rex, 1972
Nightwatchmen, 1973
Ray, 1980
The Tennis Handsome, 1983
Hey Jack!, 1987
Boomerang, 1989
Never Die, 1991
Yonder Stands Your Orphan, 2001

Other literary forms

In addition to his novels, Barry Hannah has published short stories in *Esquire* magazine, and some of his short fiction has been collected in *Airships* (1978), *Captain Maximus* (1985), *Bats out of Hell* (1993), and *High Lonesome* (1996).

Achievements

Because his fiction is often set in the contemporary American South and is characterized by violence and gothic humor, Barry Hannah has most often been compared to William Faulkner, Flannery O'Connor, and Carson McCullers, other southern writers who have explored violent and eccentric human behavior in southern settings. Hannah, however, has a style and an energy that set him apart from others as a highly original American writer. His much-acclaimed first novel, *Geronimo Rex*, was awarded the William Faulkner Prize for Fiction and was nominated for a National Book Award, and *Airships*, his first book of short stories, received the Arnold Gingrich Short Fiction Award (Gingrich was founder and editor of *Esquire* magazine). Hannah has received a Bellaman Foundation Award in Fiction (1970), a Bread Loaf Fellowship (1971), and an award for literature from the American Academy of Arts and Letters (1979). He has also been honored with the Robert Penn Warren Lifetime Achievement Award in Fiction and the PEN/Malamud Award, which recognizes excellence in the art of short fiction.

Biography

Barry Hannah was born on April 23, 1942, in Clinton, Mississippi, but he grew up primarily in Meridian. He attended the public schools in Clinton, playing trumpet in the school band, and went on to Mississippi College, where he received his A.B. degree. He continued his education at the University of Arkansas, where he received both an M.A. and an M.F.A. in creative writing. Hannah began writing his first novel, *Geronimo Rex*, while he was working toward his degree in creative writing, and an early version of a chapter from that novel appeared in the first issue of *Intro*, a journal that presented the best work from American university writing programs. Much like Hannah, the protagonist of *Geronimo Rex*, Harry Monroe, is a young man searching for identity in a socially troubled South, and his name, Harry (Barry) Monroe, suggests that the author drew heavily from his own experience. Hannah's other fictional work, such as *Boomerang*, also seems to draw on his personal life: The narrator of *Boomerang* is named Barry, and the novel is set in Clinton and Oxford, where Hannah resides.

Much of Hannah's early fiction was published in *Esquire* magazine, where it received critical acclaim and wide readership. Nine of these stories are among the twenty collected in *Airships*, his finest and best-known collection of short fiction. Hannah is often at his best in short works, and sometimes his novels seem more collections of vignettes and short pieces than expanded unified narratives. Following *Airships* came four novels: *Ray*, *The Tennis Handsome*, *Hey Jack!*, and *Boomerang*. Hannah's three other volumes of short stories—*Captain Maximus*, *Bats out of Hell*, and *High Lonesome*—all received excellent reviews when they appeared; *High Lonesome* was nominated for the Pulitzer Prize in fiction.

Except for a brief period when he lived in California, where he worked on film scripts for director Robert Altman, Hannah has for the most part remained in the South, teaching creative writing and literature at Clemson University in South Carolina, at the University of Alabama, and at the University of Mississippi. He has also taught creative writing at the University of Iowa and the University of Montana and was a writer-in-residence at Middlebury College in Vermont.

Hannah's life and writing have been shaped by many influences, from teachers and musicians to other writers. Music has always been a significant part of Hannah's life (he is often called a "jazz" writer); *Geromimo Rex*, one critic has asserted, has the best description of marching-band music ever written. In interview after interview, Hannah has noted the impact his high school band director had on his life and writing. At the other end of the musical spectrum, rock music legend Jimi Hendrix has had a great impact on Hannah, both for the fury and vision of his music and for the paradoxes of his life and his love of motorcycles. In a more conventional strain, Hannah has mentioned the influence that the poets and professors J. Edgar Simmons and James Whitehead exerted on him during his years at Mississippi College and the University of Arkansas, respectively. Although his style of writing is unique, Hannah cites William Faulkner, James Joyce, and Ernest Hemingway as his literary idols, but he also invokes the names of Henry Miller and John Berryman as kindred spirits. Another spirit, alcohol, however, may have had the most direct bearing on Hannah's writing until he stopped drinking in the early 1990's.

Hannah wrote his eighth novel, *Yonder Stands Your Orphan*, during a bout with cancer, without the benefit of inebriation. Intoxi-

Barry Hannah. (© Miriam Berkley)

cated by word music, Hannah writes with a drunken tilt, uninhibited and energetic, madly in love with what words can do.

ANALYSIS

Barry Hannah's fiction is populated with the Confederate soldiers, redneck idlers, gifted liars, failed intellectuals, desperate women, and violent men that readers of American literature have come to expect from southern writers, but Hannah's comic inventiveness, dazzling prose, and lopsided view of life make them highly original portraits. Hannah writes like a juiced-up Faulkner, and the reader is often swept along by the sheer manic energy of his narratives. While his fiction is often short on plot, it is full of loopy twists and turns, imaginative surprises, and hilarious nonsense.

GERONIMO REX

Hannah's highly acclaimed first novel, *Geronimo Rex*, is a good example. Owing much to the bildungsroman, the novel of experience that chronicles a young person's rise to maturity, and to picaresque tales of adventurous rogues, *Geronimo Rex* is Hannah's portrait of the artist as a young punk. Growing up in a southern mill town during the 1950's, Harry Monroe, the novel's principal character, is a complexity of self-hatred and egotism, sensitivity and self-righteousness, artistry and violence. He sees himself in an old photograph of Apache chieftain Geronimo as a rebel warrior in a wild and savage country; he even starts wearing an American Indian kerchief, boots, and a snakeskin jacket, does war dances on top of parked cars, and carries a gun. What he likes about Geronimo, he muses at one point, is that the Native American had "cheated, lied, stolen, usurped, killed, burned, raped, pillaged, razed, trapped, ripped, mashed," and Harry decides that he "would like to go into that line of work." Unlike other fictional depictions of youth in the 1950's—J. D. Salinger's Holden Caulfield in *The Catcher in the Rye* (1951), for example—Harry is no idealist surrounded by hypocritical adults. Harry *is* the world around him—hypocritical, violent, self-centered, and cynical.

In college, Harry becomes involved with mad racist Peter Lepoyster, whose hatred and sexual obsessions have driven him in and out of Whitfield, the local insane asylum. Harry's college roommate, Bobby Dove Fleece, has stolen from Lepoyster a bundle of erotic love letters written to a woman named Catherine, and Harry and Fleece become as obsessed with Lepoyster as he was with his woman. Lepoyster stalks the streets, spouting racial and anti-Semitic filth, breaking up civil rights demonstrations, and even becoming incensed when a black marching band shows up in a local parade. Harry and Fleece, equally obsessed, stalk Lepoyster and even sneak up on his house one night to take a shot at him, wounding him in the knee. Lepoyster is clearly what Harry himself could become, a comically frightening racist driven out of his mind by sexual desire and hatred, a mad pervert who has succumbed to the irrational drives of death, violence, and despair.

Opposed to Lepoyster, however, is Harley Butte, a black man who once worked in the mattress factory owned by Harry's father. Butte, who worships John Philip Sousa and writes march music of his own, is the director of a high school band modeled on the incredible Dream of Pines Colored High School Band, the best band in the state. If Lepoyster represents southern racial hatred, Butte clearly represents racial harmony, the desire to see both blacks and whites marching to the same music. A musician like Butte, Harry plays the trumpet, but he likes blues and jazz, not Sousa. Harry, it is clear, improvises his own tunes and marches to his own drummer.

It is the pathetic Lepoyster, however, not Harry, who is the true Geronimo, the savage killer in a country not his own. Lepoyster dies violently, shot to death in a gunfight with Fleece, a gentle soul who had never before even fired a gun. By the end of the novel, Harry has married Prissy Lombardo, a young girl who looks like a "pubescent Arab," writes poetry as well as plays the trumpet, and pursues an academic career as an English teacher. Although he is a poet and musician, Harry is still partly Geronimo Rex, the rebel with a streak of violence. Still, the novel, which begins and ends with brilliant descriptions of marching bands (Hannah writes about marching bands better than any other American writer), ends with harmony and hope.

While *Geronimo Rex* may not be a great American novel, it is a very good one, and it is an exceptional first novel for a beginning author. The story is told with a memorably comic and exuberant first-person narrative voice that Hannah skillfully employs in all of his later novels, and it is full of memorable scenes and characters: the death of an old dog and mule that wander into the Monroe yard when Harry is a boy; the rambling, sexually obsessed monologues of Bobby Dove Fleece, Harry's college roommate; and the comic and pathetic Mother Rooney, who runs a boardinghouse where Harry stays.

NIGHTWATCHMEN

Hannah's second novel, *Nightwatchmen*, continues the exploits of Harry Monroe, but he is not the central character. That distinction goes to Thorpe Trove, a striking figure who wears purple prescription glasses perched on his long nose beneath a wild shock of orange hair. In this novel of many voices, Trove is the central narrative voice, and it is he who tape-records the others for the reader. The central plot of *Nightwatchmen*, a kind of surreal mystery thriller, takes place at fictional Southwestern Mississippi University, where an unknown assailant called The Knocker is clubbing graduate students and faculty as they work in their offices late at night. When Conrad, a night watchman, and Spell, a janitor, are not only knocked but also beheaded, it becomes apparent that The Knocker may also be The Killer.

Trove becomes obsessed with finding this mysterious figure (actually, two mysterious figures, as it turns out) and begins tape-recording anyone who might have clues—such as graduate student Harry Monroe. Harry and fellow graduate student Lawrence Head theorize that The Knocker intends only to conk pedants and bores, but when Didi Sweet, a fellow graduate student and an attractive divorcée, is knocked, that theory falls into doubt. The murders of Conrad and Spell, and the later murder of graduate student William Tell, dispel it entirely. Other clues come from part-time plumber Frank Theron Knockre and Douglas David "Dougie" Lotrieux, a film projectionist in a local theater.

Independently wealthy, Trove hires aging private detective Howard Hunter, and together they track down and destroy The Killer during the onslaught of Hurricane Camille. All of this takes place during some memorable scenes of storm and destruction: Dougie being swept along the countryside by 150-mile-per-hour winds, Head's landlady being decapitated by the tin roof of her house, and the bodies from a local graveyard being blown around by the hurricane and found hanging in the trees.

Deciding on corporal punishment for Dougie Lotrieux, who has known all along the identity of The Killer and now wants to die, Trove and his associates bring in Harry Monroe as executioner. Harry is by now completing his Ph.D. in English at Clemson and is about to bring out a second volume of poetry, but he still carries his gun and has wanted throughout the novel to kill something. Harry, who shoots Dougie through the head and buries his body on the beach, remains the divided Harry Monroe of the first novel: a sensitive artist, a judgmental observer of life, and a violent man.

Exactly what issue *Nightwatchmen* is trying to address is unclear. "A nightwatchman," Lawrence Head meditates at one point, "ought to be rather hungry for conversation. He ought to be dying to flood you with talk." The novel is, above all, a flood of talk from lonely and tormented people. Night watchmen keep lonely vigils, like these isolated and lonely night people, and Hurricane Camille seems an appropriate metaphor for the swirling turbulence of emotions within the characters, whose lives also cause death and destruction.

RAY

Hannah's third novel, *Ray*, is a departure from his first two. Condensed from a manuscript that was originally four hundred pages, *Ray* is a book of little more than one hundred pages in sixty-two short sections, some of them consisting of only a sentence or two. Furthermore, the novel is more upbeat than the previous two, for the title is a hearty cheer for life ("Hoo! Ray") as well as the narrator's name. Ray is an Alabama doctor and former fighter pilot who served in the Vietnam War. His fantasies of the American Civil War, in which heat-seeking missiles and phosphorus bombs battle sabers and horsemen, equate one war with another. An alcoholic, Ray administers drugs to addicted patients and practices selective euthanasia on the hurtful and depraved. The divorced father of three children, Ray seeks comfort from Sister, the daughter of the poor and hopeless Hooch family. Sister leaves home to become a prostitute and to model for pornographic photographs and is eventually shot to death by Baptist preacher Maynard Castro; her father is almost killed when his propane lantern explodes.

Ray confronts these tragedies, ministers to the needy, meets a woman with whom he falls in love, and marries her. The victim of life's suffering—"I am infected with every disease I ever tried to cure," he says—Ray survives war, the poverty-ridden South, the loss of friends and lovers, and his own self-pity to become a heroic figure. By the end of the novel, he is plunging forward, saber raised, like the Confederate officers of his Civil War fantasies. A Christ figure—he is thirty-three and, as he states in the opening sentence, "born of religious parents"—Ray suffers so that others may live (old man Hooch survives to become, under Ray's guidance, a gifted poet) and is himself resurrected.

Ray is Hannah's most concise novel, a carryover perhaps from the volume of short stories that constituted the book that preceded it in publication, and in it Hannah comes to grips with the historical past of the Civil War and the grinding poverty of southern families like the Hooches. Ray is in many ways a personification of the United States itself during the 1970's: haunted by war, divided by violent emotions and yearnings for peace, and searching for historical roots. Like his country, Ray lives through the worst of times and survives, perhaps even stronger than ever.

THE TENNIS HANDSOME

The Tennis Handsome, Hannah's fourth novel, first appeared in *Esquire* magazine and was later collected in *Airships*. The wildly improbable tale of a charismatic but brain-damaged tennis professional, his companion, and his high school tennis coach, the novel is a return to Hannah's comic exuberance and expansive style. French Edward, the "tennis handsome" of the title, is a kind of idiot savant, a brilliant tennis player but a vegetable off the court, having survived a plunge from a bridge with only part of his faculties intact.

While in high school, French had come home one afternoon to find his mother in bed with his tennis coach, Jimmy Word, who, previously gay, had apparently rediscovered the joys of heterosexuality. Riddled with Freudian hatred, French had gotten even with Word by challenging the older man to a tennis match; hoping to cause his coach a heart attack, French succeeded only in giving him a stroke, but it was enough to make Word partially blind and to give him a frightful voice ("like that of a man in a cave of wasps"). Such was French's charisma that Word loved him all the more, following him from tournament to tournament, his voice bleating above the crowd, and—"crazed with partisanship"—pinching French with pride after each victory. Even worse, French's mother still loved Word, a fact that drove French to desperation. Grappling with Word above a river, French dropped off the bridge with the old man. Word came out no worse for the experience, but French suffered brain damage.

Now cared for by Dr. Baby Levaster, a former high school tennis teammate and another admirer of tennis handsomes, French wanders the tennis circuit in search of the ineffable. During a match in Boston, lightning strikes his metal racket, turning French "radiant as a silver-plated statue" and somewhat psychic and, for a time, clearing his damaged brain. He even begins to write poetry, though only bawdy doggerel. French continues to seek these crystalline moments. Meanwhile, separated from his wife Cecelia, French finds comfort with a disabled woman named Inez, a Cuban polio victim who becomes pregnant with his child. In spite of being in a wheelchair, Inez also comforts Levaster. In fact, Levaster finds carnal comfort with practically anyone he can, including French's mother, Olive, and a woman named Beth Battrick, who has been having an affair with her nephew, Bobby Smith, a Vietnam veteran haunted by his past.

Smith's story, previously published in both *Esquire* and *Airships* as "Midnight and I'm Not Famous Yet," recounts his capture and subsequent killing of Li Dap, a North Vietnamese general, and the loss of Smith's friend Tubby Wooten. Returned from the war and in love with his aunt, Smith has become entwined in the lives of French and Levaster. The aunt, after nearly being raped by a walrus, runs off with a southern senator. Inez dies in childbirth. Word dies of natural causes in Smith's car, and Smith dumps him off a bridge near Vicksburg. French, looking for the ultimate fix, almost electrocutes himself by clamping onto battery cables. Cecelia, angered at Levaster's refusal to give up French's baby (which has passed from Inez to Smith to Levaster), murders Levaster with a crossbow. Smith, having seen senseless devastation before, somehow survives along with French.

The zaniness of Hannah's narrative—Carson Mc-

Cullers rewritten by Groucho Marx, as one reviewer put it—is entertainment enough, but there may even be message in his madness. The American reverence for athletic prowess, Hannah suggests, is a kind of misplaced religious awe with a dose of sexual longing, as slightly off-center as Bobby Smith's passion for his own aunt. French Edward, a Christ figure in shorts and sneakers, is both saintly and visionary, capable of arousing desire in both sexes, and tennis, like war, is a field of combat where courage, victory, and defeat are exhibited. Like all athletes, French helps the spectator to define himself through the athlete's continual Christlike struggles.

Hey Jack!

Between *The Tennis Handsome* and Hannah's next two novels came his second volume of short stories, *Captain Maximus*. In some of those stories he pays homage to Ernest Hemingway and Richard Hugo, two American authors who confront personal experience directly and write about it with honest sentiment. Hannah attempts to do the same in *Hey Jack!* and *Boomerang*, and both novels are radical departures from his earlier work. Hannah abandons the wildly exuberant comic style of the earlier works for a more measured and direct prose, his narrator seems closer to Hannah himself (the narrator of *Boomerang* is called Barry), and his characters seem drawn more directly from experience than from the imagination.

The Jack of *Hey Jack!* is a seventy-seven-year-old café owner, a former war correspondent, Kentucky sheriff, college professor of criminal science, and Mississippi cattleman. The plot of the novel involves Jack's daughter, a forty-year-old schoolteacher named Alice, who is seeing rock star Ronnie Foot against her father's wishes. Foot, a kind of Elvis Presley from Hell, is a cocaine-snorting egotist who lives in a large mansion with Gramps, an alcoholic redneck who likes to shoot his .22 rifle at the chickens and people outside. Foot, who has a history of using and destroying women, abuses and humiliates Alice, turns her into a drug addict, and kills her with Gramps's .22 while trying to shoot a Coca-Cola bottle off her head. On trial for murder, Foot hangs himself in his cell. The novel is a tribute to men such as Jack and the narrator, Homer, who are like the First Marine Division at Chosin, site of the great Korean War battle in which Homer fought thirty years earlier and which still haunts his dreams: They dig in, attack when they can, bury their dead, and learn to survive.

Boomerang

Boomerang, another novel of survival, again attempts to deal with life's past and present pains. Like the actual boomerang that the narrator finds and learns how to control, past experiences that he has tried to cast away come back to strengthen and instruct the narrator, whose name by this sixth novel has become "Barry." From Harry to Barry, Hannah's voice has been at the center of his narratives, connecting past with present, viewing life's experiences with black humor and irreverence, and involving the reader in his hatreds, loves, failures, and many moods. By this sixth novel, that voice is hard to distinguish from that of the author, for it confronts the reader directly with shared experiences in straightforward, unadorned prose. While Hannah's writing gains strength from the realistic characters and situations, *Boomerang* as a whole lacks the unpredictability and lyric humor of his earlier writings, and the sentiment often teeters into the maudlin.

Never Die

Set in the West in 1910-1913, Hannah's seventh novel, *Never Die*, has had mixed critical reception. Some critics have claimed that although Hannah's characters are usually intentionally undeveloped—although not simple—the characters in *Never Die* are caricatures. Hannah's omnipresent violence has also been targeted for criticism, with some readers finding it too sweeping and too parodic in this novel.

Never Die opens with a flashback to the American Civil War as young Kyle Nitburg turns his mother over to the authorities for spying. It then proceeds to relate events involving the characters who live in the town that bears his name. Aside from Judge Nitburg, who in the past sold one wife into Comanche slavery and then wed a blind dowager, the town is peopled with a wild assortment of characters. Thirty-eight-year-old college-educated gunslinger Fernando Mure, bankrupt and semi-suicidal, has two goals: to burn down the town he has always hated but now detests (it has been overrun by the Chinese) and to build a magnificent coffin factory.

In love with a tubercular whore, Stella, Fernando has his knees broken by Judge Nitburg's thug, the dwarf Smoot, who imagines that he has underground roots and who lusts after the monkey owned by wealthy Navy Remington. Nitburg's daughter is Nandina, a nymphomaniacal schoolteacher with a passion for automobiles. Other characters include Dr. Fingo, who is gay and a supplier of morphine to kill mental or physical pain; Reverend McCorkindale, who believes himself hated by God because of his hairy body and perpetual erection; and Hermit Nermer, a onetime gunslinger. Nermer once killed an Apache child simply because Nermer had a new gun; now he is a penitent mountain man awaiting the judgment of fire that Fernando has promised to inflict on Nitburg.

After Fernando finally sets fire to the courthouse, Nitburg hires assassins to kill him. Forewarned, Fernando goes to his uncle, Navy Remington, for money and ammunition. Events come to a head on the day Fernando returns to Nitburg to await his fate and marry Stella, who, standing in the church door, is mortally wounded by Smoot. Hit man Luther Nix and his assassins storm the town, killing anyone who comes within their sights, including Nandina. Entering the church to face Fernando, Nix decapitates and undresses the corpse of Stella so that he can clothe himself in her rose dress. Even greater chaos erupts; Nix and his band, faced down only momentarily by a lesbian named Tall Jane, seem ready to claim victory when Reverend McCorkindale swoops down in his Sopwith Camel and drops nitroglycerin onto the church. Nix goes into the fire to find Fernando, who shoots him in the stomach. When the smoke clears, there are twelve bodies. Two years later, photographer and voyeur Philip Hine assures Fernando that history will relieve them of their self-hatred. Assured instead of his own villainy, Fernando is buoyed only by the thought that he has another, and better, chance to "make a high mark for good."

YONDER STANDS YOUR ORPHAN

Ten years separate *Never Die* from Hannah's next novel, *Yonder Stands Your Orphan*. The title is taken from a Bob Dylan song, and Hannah surpasses Dylan in his dense, original phrasing. Beneath its surface of dark arabesques, of chaotic and meandering violence, *Yonder Stands Your Orphan* is Hannah's meditation on "age without wisdom." Characters from stories in *Airships* and *Bats out of Hell* return in this work, old men who hang around the dock of Eagle Lake, near Vicksburg. Sidney Farté is still mean, Ulrich sad and a little crazy, Wren a liar. Dr. Harvard is secretly in love with the widow Melanie Wooten, who still makes hearts pound.

Into their midst comes Conway Twitty look-alike Man Mortimer, a successful pimp and loan shark whose emptiness has suddenly become unbearable. Mortimer falls in something like love with Dee Allison and recites his dark autobiography. She is unimpressed. Mortimer discovers that Dee is two-timing him with Frank Booth, a retired military officer, and starts a spree of slashing, stabbing, and decapitation.

The novel is packed with odd characters festooned with elaborate histories and habits. There is Max Raymond, a tortured saxophonist in his Cuban wife's Latin band—he used to be a doctor, until he persuaded Mimi Suarez's abusive husband to follow through on suicidal impulses, leaving him merely brain-damaged, not dead, and bent on revenge. Max is looking for a redeeming vision, but he needs to be near evil—what good is faith if it is not tested? He is glad to be on an extended gig at the casino. Another character is Preacher Egan, an ex-biker with a cross tattooed on his cheek who shoots up holy water during a sermon. His uncle, Carl Bob Feeney, who used to be a priest, now wanders his land with a gun and a pack of abandoned dogs. In rockier days Egan did a little job for Mortimer—drove a car with something heavy in the trunk into a sinkhole on his uncle Feeney's land.

Gene and Penny Ten Hoor react to the death of their young son by nailing fish, cash, and each other to the walls of their lakeside home. Rescued by Dr. Harvard and his cronies, they move across the lake, having recovered enough to find religion and start a camp for orphans—a wild and lawless place they are too addled to manage.

When the sinkhole on Feeney's land drains, the first to notice are Allison's young sons, who find the car Egan hid for Mortimer and the remains of a woman and child in the trunk. The boys talk a young mechanic into wiring the cleaned bones together, then drive the skeletons around for days in a stolen car, smoking, stealing food, and hiding in the woods to watch Mimi Suarez sing naked from her back porch.

As Mortimer slashes his way through Eagle Lake, he shrivels into nothing. Booth, once a Navy Seal, and ex-junkie Peden the junk man fight back, contributing to

Mortimer's physical decline. Many contemplate killing him, but no one does. A few hardened orphans, recently imported, take advantage of the Ten Hoors' madness to start an armed rebellion. When the smoke clears, bodies float in the lake. The scene is hard to untangle, but Mortimer has committed so many crimes that no one questions his guilt.

Hannah remains one of America's most original talents, a southern regionalist whose hilarious, weird, and very human characters shock readers into recognition of themselves. Hannah is a lover of the English language who, as he has said, is always trying to get as much as he can out of words.

Kenneth Seib; Jaquelyn W. Walsh
Updated by Donna Munro

Other major works

SHORT FICTION: *Airships*, 1978; *Captain Maximus*, 1985; *Bats out of Hell*, 1993; *High Lonesome*, 1996.

Bibliography

Bernstein, Richard. "Giving in to the Urge to Do Bad in the South." Review of *Yonder Stands Your Orphan*, by Barry Hannah. *The New York Times*, July 10, 2001. Mixed review praises the novel for "sentences that hum with energy and unexpectedness" but laments its "monotonous eccentricity."

Bone, Martyn, ed. *Perspectives on Barry Hannah*. Jackson: University Press of Mississippi, 2007. Collection of essays examines Hannah's novels, from *Geronimo Rex* to *Yonder Stands Your Orphan*, from a variety of critical perspectives. Includes an interview with Hannah.

Charney, Mark J. *Barry Hannah*. New York: Twayne, 1992. Presents an indispensable guide to all of Hannah's fiction and makes the case that Hannah is one of the South's freshest and most iconoclastic writers. Includes an annotated bibliography.

Hannah, Barry. "At Home with Barry Hannah; Mellowing Out but Unbowed." Interview by Randy Kennedy. *The New York Times*, July 9, 1998. Hannah, interviewed at his home in Oxford, Mississippi, after returning from a stint at the Iowa Writers' Workshop, discusses alcoholism, his recently deceased father, the "homogenization" of American fiction, and his status as a cult figure in France.

_______. "An Interview with Barry Hannah." Interview by Scott Cawelti. *Short Story* 3 (Spring, 1995): 105-116. Intriguing interview includes Hannah's avowal that he himself has never carried a gun as well as his assertion that "it's the absolute act, the act of firing a gun randomly into a crowd—it's the absolute act of art."

_______. "Southern Discomfort." Interview by James Bone. *The Times* (London), September 22, 2001. Hannah discusses his use of characters drawn from his earlier works in *Yonder Stands Your Orphan*, noting, "I wanted to see how the people I had created in my short stories would react to modern evil."

_______. "The Spirits Will Win Through: An Interview with Barry Hannah." Interview by R. Vanarsall. *Southern Review* 19 (Spring, 1983): 314-341. Long, thoughtful interview connects Hannah's own biography with the material in his stories. Discusses topics such as Hannah's alcoholism, his fascination with violence, his work in California as a screenwriter, and his love of the English language.

Madden, David. "Barry Hannah's *Geronimo Rex* in Retrospect." *The Southern Review* 19 (Spring, 1983): 309-316. Madden once found *Geronimo Rex* "the best first novel I've ever reviewed." Considering it again ten years later, he agrees with his original assessment but finds it lacking an intellectual framework and a "conceptualizing imagination."

Weston, Ruth D. *Barry Hannah, Postmodern Romantic*. Baton Rouge: Louisiana State University Press, 1998. Important full-length study discusses Hannah's postmodern style and his ability to express hard truths about the conditions of contemporary life. Provides serious analysis of all of Hannah's long fiction through *Never Die* as well as his short-story collections. Includes bibliography and index.

ELIZABETH HARDWICK

Born: Lexington, Kentucky; July 27, 1916
Died: New York, New York; December 2, 2007
Also known as: Elizabeth Bruce Hardwick

PRINCIPAL LONG FICTION

The Ghostly Lover, 1945
The Simple Truth, 1955
Sleepless Nights, 1979

OTHER LITERARY FORMS

Elizabeth Hardwick's book reviews and literary and cultural criticism have been her most influential work. Her frank, fresh, intellectually audacious, and emotionally engaging comments provided a comprehensive critique of literary and popular culture. Her baroque style and contextual approach, yoking history with art, was formative in developing the particular brand of progressive criticism characteristic of *The New York Review of Books* and in the tradition of the *Partisan Review*, bent upon restoring texture and depth to reviewing. Her most influential essays from 1952 to 1961 were collected from the *Partisan Review*, *Harper's*, *Encounter*, *The New Republic*, and *The New York Times Book Review*, as well as *The New York Review of Books*, in a volume titled *A View of My Own: Essays on Literature and Society* (1962), suggesting in the allusion to Virginia Woolf her intensely personal approach to criticism. Hardwick's long-standing interest in feminist issues is reflected in her second collection of essays, *Seduction and Betrayal: Women and Literature* (1974). A third collection, *Bartleby in Manhattan, and Other Essays*, appeared in 1983.

An important Hardwick essay, "Domestic Manners in a New America," perhaps best illustrates the connections between the public and the private self that she defined as "style," a key concept that informs both her cultural criticism and her fiction. Appearing first in *Daedalus* (Winter, 1978) and later as "Domestic Manners" in *A New America?* (1978)—an anthology of influential articles by social commentators—Hardwick's essay delineates the alterations in contemporary culture brought about by "the power of external forces" and a particular sort of inner change, a new expectation for the private life. The interior perception of life as a long process, one governed by cycles and seasons, is transformed by the deviation and dislocation of contemporary urban life, "the shortened life of the feelings" evidenced in the prevalent failure of will in human relationships, rules, customs, and habits. Hardwick sees in personal "style" the traumatic effects of modernity; for her, as for Jane Austen, style defines moral condition.

ACHIEVEMENTS

Elizabeth Hardwick's criticism engaged not only literary culture but also the wider group of committed intellectuals seeking synthesis between the diverse, apparently dislocated, aspects of contemporary life. Prominent in her critical ideology is the assumption that a substructure of history, biology, and psychology underlies the complex edifice of contemporary culture, a foundation that the critic must show as informing, though not determining, the work. Coupled with this multidisciplinary approach is that process of dynamically yoking together disparate thoughts and feelings in such a way that a new synthesis or a hidden foundation is revealed. This juxtaposition, similar in so many ways to that of the metaphysical poets, has the effect of constantly recombining and transforming experience.

The matter of style seems a crucial point in Hardwick's work, both style as a concept and Hardwick's own yoking of dissimilarities, startling the reader with its expressive, mercurial quality, capturing the play of a mind at work. Her writing frequently has a baroque quality—loose passages coupled with short, pithy statements. Capturing the qualities of supreme thoughtfulness along with engaged feeling, her work creates a sharp effect, combining an almost audacious assertiveness with demure understatement. Her conversational colloquialisms, playful and expressive, appear in Hardwick's conceptual framework as "style," that self-presentation by which the interior, one's relationship to history, is revealed.

The other key concept in Hardwick's thought and practice is that of the "radical," not in the political sense, but meaning a return, often an intellectually jarring return, to the crux of a creative work or a received idea. Certain writers such as Mary McCarthy possessed what Hardwick called a radical vision, always unconventional, often involving a moral stance. Characters become emblems of these root qualities, as in the "radical innocence" of Rudy Peck in *The Simple Truth*. The ability of a writer or a critic to go to the crux of a problem, to perceive something not marked before, to have a genuinely new thought that brings together known facts in surprising ways, was for Hardwick the hallmark of the intellectual and creative life.

Hardwick was the recipient of many awards for creative and critical achievement. She was awarded a Guggenheim Fellowship and presented with the George Jean Nathan Award for drama criticism.

Biography

Elizabeth Bruce Hardwick's own life provides a model of the committed intellectual, demonstrating the dialectic between history and the imagination, thought and feeling, which informs her essays and fiction. Born in Lexington, Kentucky, on July 27, 1916, one of the eleven children of Eugene Allen and Mary Ramsey Hardwick, she attended public schools and then the University of Kentucky. The sense of place so strong in Hardwick appears especially in her early work, the substructure of Kentucky rootedness juxtaposed to the restless, mobile style of middle-class yearnings. The opposite pole is New York, the "Lourdes" of cities, which educates and informs the self.

Although alert to and appreciative of southern literature, Hardwick nevertheless spoke of herself, in a letter of September, 1982, as never having felt drawn to being a southern writer but instead toward "the vague, but somewhat meaningful notion of the 'intellectual.'" In her later work, far from the dreamy southern settings of her first novel, with its matriarchal, mythical grandmother, the interwoven lives of black and white, the cockfights, the wild youth, and, finally, the journey to the wider world of the university and the city itself, Hardwick perhaps epitomizes for many the urban intellectual style.

Hardwick's radical criticism and progressive aesthetic developed from her study of literature and culture, from graduate study at Columbia and the early influence of the *Partisan Review*, an intellectual milieu that she describes as a "combination of radical political ideas of a complicated kind and avant-garde literature." This method was not formalistic or belletristic but always represented the paradoxical product of the progressive politics of the *Partisan Review* and the particular intellectuality and wit of the metaphysical poetry that enjoyed a revival at the time. Hardwick's aesthetic also was influenced by her long teaching career, at Barnard College and at other places, including Columbia Graduate School of the Arts, where she taught creative writing. Many of her essays have the flavor of classroom interchange, a flash of contact between mentor and student, a dynamic oral quality, and a sense of extemporaneous composition, sometimes with inserts and headings like a teacher's lecture notes.

Much of Hardwick's later creative work involved imaginative reconstruction of personal experience, the encounter of the individual with others and the world in modern history. Her marriage to the poet Robert Lowell in July, 1949, exemplified in some ways that special relationship between two creative people that the two of them found in George Eliot and Henry Lewes. Lowell and Hardwick shared not only their intellectual background but also their political commitment, evident in Lowell's indictment for conscientious objection to militarism. In his *Notebook 1967-68* (1969), Lowell writes of Eliot and Lewes, "Writers marry/ their kind still, true and one and clashing," and upon his own twenty-year marriage, "We stand set; two trees, their roots," recalling shared lives, age, friendships, illness, and war, and many cities—Boston, Maine, and New York. "I was then a 'we,'" Hardwick says in *Sleepless Nights*. Her marriage to Lowell ended in divorce in 1972, to be followed by his death in 1977. Of their only child, Harriet Winslow Lowell, Hardwick spoke of feeling a "passion almost criminal." Hardwick died in New York City on December 2, 2007.

Analysis

In her three published novels, Elizabeth Hardwick demonstrates the complex interplay between the buried life of the emotions, "the cemetery of home, education, nerves, heritage, and tics," and the emerging life in which the individual seeks self-definition by her own

Elizabeth Hardwick. (AP/Wide World Photos)

consciousness, her sense of autonomy and transcendence.

THE GHOSTLY LOVER

The protagonist of *The Ghostly Lover*, Hardwick's first novel, is an obviously autobiographical figure. Marian, slowly coming to terms with family and hometown boyfriend, pursues her somewhat foggy destiny far from her southern home in a city university. She has depended on two illusions: that she can only be supported by some outside force, usually a man, and that she must herself support her two rootless parents, who have abandoned her and her brother since childhood. Parents, powerful in the imagination but in life weak and absent, first the "savage's totem" from which "being and power" are derived, are lost in pursuit of the American Dream. Her mother, who has "been in too many places, had lives in too many houses, and been neighbor to too many people," represents in her unformed femininity that immanence of which Simone de Beauvoir speaks, a "guide for the preordained destiny of the daughter" from which Marian must extricate herself at the end, when she is asked to loan the inheritance money on which her journey to the city depends.

Likewise she must reject Bruce, the father-lover of her adolescence who, replacing her own father, pays for her tuition, and then Leo, the city boyfriend, more a peer, but yet representing an escape into marriage and safety. The grandmother, who has reared the children, is an inscrutable matriarch in whom the archaic powers of home and family are located. She personifies that "animal nature," "the hidden violence of union between the two sexes"; her experience, unredeemed by thought and judgment, is found to be not mysterious but simply illiterate.

In a reversal of the traditional scheme, the shy, repressed girl escapes, while the wild, resourceful brother, Albert, is trapped in the family home, conveniently married to a dumpy, unimaginative town girl. Hattie, the black servant girl, is Marian's black double, the frightening other whose stubborn autonomy is at once fearful ("black sinfulness") and attractive. Other women complete her initiation into the underworld of female possibility—neighbor Mary, mother's friend, with her secret abortion; Gertrude, the German library-science student, lost in the anonymous city; another woman friend who attaches herself pathetically to a man. Moving from the deceptive paradise of childhood to the necessary reality of the adult world, she arrives finally at Grand Central again, meeting the objective correlative of her condition, an "icy ray of light," no man to meet her, "separated . . . forever from him [Leo] and his shelter like the forbidden gates of Eden," self-created at last.

THE SIMPLE TRUTH

Published in 1955 and dedicated to her mother, Hardwick's second novel, *The Simple Truth*, concerns moral initiation in a midwestern university town, a location symbolic of American culture and midwestern space and disconnection, marked by psychological introspection and personal anonymity. Rudy Peck, a university student and the son of Finnish immigrants, himself an "anonymous creation" aspiring to selfhood, has murdered his upper-class girlfriend. The girlfriend was an adventurer, self-created in her own uniqueness and style, a quality well noted by Doris Parks, whose Austenesque "true sturdiness" and acute moral sensibility involve her at once as evaluator of the moral landscape in which Rudy, "innocently guilty," is acquitted.

In this variation on the traditional seduction and betrayal motif, Rudy, a serious, thoughtful young man, is, like Theodore Dreiser's Clyde Griffiths, finally not morally accountable. The trial draws the obsessive attention of Doris's husband Joseph, a bumbling, sensitive, aspiring writer of ambiguous possibilities, and Anita Mitchell, a small-town faculty wife seeking escape from her limiting environment of "beefsteak, peas, and whiskey"; both Joseph and Anita see in Rudy an expression of their own unresolved condition. At the close of the novel, Doris, whose perspective has gradually become that of the narrator, recognizes the distinct moral spheres she and Joseph occupy and, with a few tears, accepts her own independence and aloneness, one of the "new women" setting out in the politically and psychologically ambivalent American landscape.

Sleepless Nights

Hardwick's third novel, *Sleepless Nights*, published in 1979, reconstructs personal experience not in the confessional mode associated with Lowell, but as a piece of "transformed and even distorted memory," in a series of communications to a friend, "Mary McC" (Mary McCarthy). From contemplation of her rag rug, "product of a broken old woman in a squalid nursing home," the narrator examines the combination of deprivation and survival, loss and preservation in the histories of the "unfortunate ones"—Juanita the prostitute, bag ladies, spinsters, cleaning women, Billie Holiday, and the new woman Marie—with a mixture of "sympathy and bewilderment" at their shared "fateful fertility" on one hand and, on the other, "the old, profound acceptance of the things of life." In an aura of intimate conversation, they confront broken veins, disease, backbreaking work, self-destruction, divorce, separation, boredom, and perhaps autonomy.

Hardwick's perspective demands connection and sympathy, not the detachment of either irony or sentimentality. Submerged female life, the other side of time-conscious, outer-directed material culture, becomes emblematic, as female weeping becomes the "weeping sores" of the ulcerated legs, the shame and poverty lurking under the intricate surface detail. Hardwick's own childhood, her Columbia homesickness and friends, the life in Maine, Boston, and New York, the "lifetime of worrying and reading," are fused in memory with the paradoxical power and tenacity of the buried life, as the woman, now no longer young, traverses the final sections of the journey into "strange parts of town" fundamental to her creativity and connectedness.

Janet Polansky

Other major works

NONFICTION: *A View of My Own: Essays on Literature and Society*, 1962; *Seduction and Betrayal: Women and Literature*, 1974; *Bartleby in Manhattan, and Other Essays*, 1983; *Sight-Readings: American Fictions*, 1998; *Herman Melville*, 2000.

EDITED TEXTS: *Selected Letters of William James*, 1961; *Rediscovered Fiction by American Women: A Personal Selection*, 1977 (18 volumes); *The Best American Essays, 1986*, 1986.

Bibliography

Als, Hilton. "A Singular Woman." *The New Yorker*, July 13, 1998. This article, published to coincide with the release of *Sight-Readings: American Fiction*, discusses Hardwick's redefinition of the genre of the literary essay; examines her life, writings, and literary career, including her work with *The New York Review of Books*; and presents other writers' comments about her work.

Benbow-Pfalzgraf, Taryn, ed. *American Women Writers: A Critical Reference Guide from Colonial Times to the Present*. 2d ed. 4 vols. Detroit, Mich.: St. James Press, 2000. This reference guide includes an essay on Hardwick containing biographical information, commentary on the thematic content of her principal works, and a bibliography.

Lamont, Rosette C. "The Off-Center Spatiality of Women's Discourse." In *Theory and Practice of Feminist Literary Criticism*, edited by Gabriela Mora and Karen S. Van Hooft. Ypsilanti, Mich.: Bilingual Press, 1982. Lamont analyzes the "off-centeredness" of Hardwick's writing from the perspective of feminist literary theory.

Lehman-Haupt, Christopher. "Elizabeth Hardwick, Critic, Novelist, and Restless Woman of Letters, Is Dead at Ninety-One." *The New York Times*, December 5, 2007. One of the more comprehensive Hardwick obituaries. Recounts Hardwick's life and career, discussing how the "studious Kentucky belle" fulfilled her ambition of becoming a member of the New York literati.

Miller, Jane. "Resisting the Bullies." In *Women Writing About Men*. London: Virago Press, 1986. In this chapter, Miller mentions Hardwick's book *Seduction and Betrayal* and its reference to women who become heroes by gaining mastery over their husbands. In so doing, Miller places Hardwick in the genre of women writers—such as Virginia Woolf—who write about women striving for recognition in their own right.

Nobile, Philip. *Intellectual Skywriting: Literary Politics and "The New York Review of Books."* New York: Charterhouse, 1974. Examines Hardwick's role in the founding of *The New York Review of Books* and her theories about writing as they pertain to the periodical's editorial policies.

Peters, Margaret. "Fiction Under a True Name: Elizabeth Hardwick's *Sleepless Nights*." *Chicago Review* 31, no. 2 (Autumn, 1979): 129-136. Peters provides a feminist analysis emphasizing the autobiographical nature of the novel, and she offers comparisons with *The Ghostly Lover*.

Reynolds, Guy. "Dysfunctional Realism: Ann Petry, Elizabeth Hardwick, Jean Stafford, Jane Bowles." In *Twentieth-Century American Women's Fiction: A Critical Introduction*. New York: St. Martin's Press, 1999. Hardwick's work is analyzed in this history of fiction writing by American women. Reynolds examines the authors' establishment of their identities and recurring themes in their fiction, and places their work within the cultural context of their times.

THOMAS HARDY

Born: Higher Bockhampton, Dorset, England; June 2, 1840

Died: Dorchester, Dorset, England; January 11, 1928

PRINCIPAL LONG FICTION

Desperate Remedies, 1871
Under the Greenwood Tree, 1872
A Pair of Blue Eyes, 1872-1873 (serial), 1873 (book)
Far from the Madding Crowd, 1874
The Hand of Ethelberta, 1875-1876 (serial), 1876 (book)
An Indiscretion in the Life of an Heiress, 1878 (serial), 1934 (book)
The Return of the Native, 1878
The Trumpet-Major, 1880
A Laodicean, 1880-1881 (serial), 1881 (book)
Two on a Tower, 1882
The Mayor of Casterbridge: The Life and Death of a Man of Character, 1886
The Woodlanders, 1886-1887 (serial), 1887 (book)
Tess of the D'Urbervilles: A Pure Woman Faithfully Presented, 1891
Jude the Obscure, 1895
The Well-Beloved, 1897

OTHER LITERARY FORMS

In addition to his novels, Thomas Hardy published four collections of short stories, *Wessex Tales* (1888), *A Group of Noble Dames* (1891), *Life's Little Ironies* (1894), and *A Changed Man, The Waiting Supper, and Other Tales* (1913). In the latter part of his life, after he had stopped writing novels altogether, he published approximately one thousand poems in eight separate volumes, which have since been collected in one volume by his publisher, Macmillan and Company. In addition to this staggering body of work, Hardy also published an epic drama of the Napoleonic wars in three parts between 1903 and 1908 titled *The Dynasts*, a one-act play titled *The Famous Tragedy of the Queen of Cornwall* (pr., pb. 1923), and a series of essays on fiction and other topics that have been collected in individual volumes. All the novels and stories are available in a uniform library edition in eighteen volumes published in the early 1960's by Macmillan. *The Early Life of Thomas Hardy* (1928) and *The Later Years of Thomas Hardy* (1930), although ostensibly a two-volume biography of Hardy by his second wife, Florence Hardy, is generally recognized to be Hardy's own autobiography compiled from his notes in his last few years.

Achievements

Thomas Hardy is second only to Charles Dickens as the most written-about and discussed writer of the Victorian era. Certainly in terms of volume and diversity alone, Hardy is a towering literary figure with two admirable careers—one as novelist and one as poet—to justify his position.

Interest in Hardy's work has followed two basic patterns. The first was philosophical, with many critics discussing metaphysical structures that supposedly underlay his fiction. In the late twentieth century, however, interest shifted to that aspect of Hardy's work most scorned before—his technical facility and generic experimentation. One hundred years after his heyday, what once was termed fictional clumsiness was reevaluated in terms of poetic technique.

Furthermore, Hardy's career as a poet, which has always been under the shadow of his fiction, has been reevaluated. Hardy was a curious blend of the old-fashioned and the modern. With a career that began in the Victorian era and did not end until after World War I, Hardy was contemporary with both Matthew Arnold and T. S. Eliot. Critics, including Babette Deutsch and Vivian de Sola Pinto, have asserted that Hardy bridged the gulf between the Victorian sensibility and the modern era. In his unflinching confrontation with meaninglessness in the universe, Hardy embodied Albert Camus's description of the absurd creator in *Le Mythe de Sisyphe* (1942; *The Myth of Sisyphus*, 1955); he rebelled against the chaos of the world by asserting his own freedom to persist in spite of that meaninglessness.

Hardy was a great existential humanist. His hope for humanity was that people would realize that creeds and conventions that presuppose a god-oriented center of value are baseless. He hoped that humans would loosen themselves from those foolish hopes and creeds and become aware of their freedom to create their own value. If human beings would only realize that all people are equally alone and without hope for divine help, then perhaps they would realize also that it is the height of absurdity for such lost and isolated creatures to fight among themselves.

Biography

Thomas Hardy was born in the small hamlet of Higher Bockhampton in Stinsford parish on June 2, 1840. His father was a master mason, content with his low social status and at home in his rural surroundings. His mother, however, whom Hardy once called "a born bookworm," made Hardy aware of his low social status and encouraged his education. John Hicks, a friend of Hardy's father and a Dorchester architect, took the boy on as a pupil at the age of sixteen. The well-known poet William Barnes had a school next door to Hicks's office, and Hardy developed an influential friendship with the older man that remained with him. Another early influence on the young Hardy was Horace Moule, a classical scholar with a Cambridge education who was an essayist and reviewer. Moule introduced Hardy to intellectual conversation about Greek literature as well as contemporary issues; it was at Moule's suggestion that Hardy read John Stuart Mill as well as the infamous broad-church volume of essays on religion *Essays and Reviews* (1860), both of which contributed to the undermining of Hardy's simple religious faith.

Hardy was twenty-two years old when he went to London to pursue his architectural training. By that time he also entertained literary ambitions and had begun writing poetry. The publication of Algernon Charles Swinburne's *Poems and Ballads* in 1866 so influenced Hardy that he began a two-year period of intensive study and experimentation in writing poetry; none of the many poems he sent out was accepted, however, and he returned to Bockhampton in 1867. It was at this point that Hardy decided to turn to writing fiction. In his old age, he wrote in a letter that he never wanted to write novels at all, but that circumstances compelled him to turn them out.

Hardy's first fictional effort, "The Poor Man and the

Lady," based on the contrast between London and rural life, received some favorable responses from publishers, but after a discussion with George Meredith, Hardy decided not to publish it and instead, on Meredith's advice, wrote *Desperate Remedies* in imitation of the detective style of Wilkie Collins. Later, eager to publish works that would establish his career as a writer, Hardy took the advice of a reader who liked the rural scenes in his unpublished novel and wrote the pastoral idyll *Under the Greenwood Tree*. The book was well received by critics, but sales were poor. One editor advised Hardy to begin writing serials for periodical publication. With the beginning of *A Pair of Blue Eyes*, Hardy said good-bye to architecture as a profession and devoted the rest of his life to writing.

In 1874, Hardy married Emma Lavinia Gifford, a dynamic and socially ambitious young woman who shared his interest in books. In the meantime, *Far from the Madding Crowd* had appeared to many favorable reviews, and editors began asking for Hardy's work. While living with his wife in a cottage at Sturminister Newton, Hardy composed *The Return of the Native* and enjoyed what he later called the happiest years of his life. Hardy and his wife began a social life in London until he became ill and they decided to return to Dorset, where, while writing *The Mayor of Casterbridge*, he had his home, Max Gate, built. For the next several years, Hardy continued his writing, traveled with his wife, and read German philosophy.

His enthusiasm for *Tess of the D'Urbervilles* was dampened when the work was turned down by two editors before being accepted for serial publication by a third. The publication of the work brought hostile reaction and notoriety—a notoriety that increased after the publication of *Jude the Obscure*. Hardy was both puzzled and cynical about these reactions, but he was by then financially secure and decided to return to his first love: After 1897 he wrote no more fiction, instead concentrating solely on poetry. His volumes of poetry were well received, and his experiment with metaphysics in the epic drama *The Dynasts* brought him even more respect, honor, and fame.

The final years of Hardy's life appear to have been spoiled only by the death of his wife in 1912. Within four years following her death, however, he married Florence Dugdale, who had been a friend of the family and had done secretarial work for him. She cared for him for the remainder of his life. Hardy continued to write poetry regularly, and his final volume of poems, *Winter Words in Various Moods and Metres*, was ready to be published when he died on January 11, 1928. His cremated remains were placed in Westminster Abbey.

Analysis

In *The Courage to Be* (1952), Paul Tillich asserts that "the decisive event which underlies the search for meaning and the despair of it in the twentieth century is the loss of God in the nineteenth century." Most critics of the literature of the nineteenth century have accepted this notion and have established a new perspective for studying the period by demonstrating that what is now referred to as the "modern situation" or the "modern artistic dilemma" actually began with the breakup of a value-ordered universe in the Romantic period. Thomas

Thomas Hardy. (Library of Congress)

Hardy, in both philosophical attitude and artistic technique, firmly belongs in this modern tradition.

It is a critical commonplace that at the beginning of his literary career Hardy experienced a loss of belief in a divinely ordered universe. The impact of this loss on Hardy cannot be overestimated. In his childhood recollections he appears as an extremely sensitive boy who attended church so regularly that he knew the service by heart and who firmly believed in a personal and just God who ruled the universe and took cognizance of the situation of humanity. Consequently, when he moved to London in his twenties and was exposed to the concept of a demythologized religion in the *Essays and Reviews* and the valueless nonteleological world of Charles Darwin's *On the Origin of Species by Means of Natural Selection: Or, The Preservation of Favoured Races in the Struggle for Life* (1859), the loss of his childhood god was a traumatic experience.

What is often called Hardy's philosophy can be summed up by one of his earliest notebook entries in 1865: "The world does not despise us; it only neglects us." An interpretation of any of Hardy's novels must begin with this assumption. The difference between Hardy and other nineteenth century artists who experienced similar loss of belief is that while others were able to achieve a measure of faith—William Wordsworth reaffirmed an organic concept of nature and of the creative mind that can penetrate it, and Thomas Carlyle finally came to a similar affirmation of nature as alive and progressive—Hardy never made such an affirmative leap to transcendent value. Hardy was more akin to another romantic figure, Samuel Taylor Coleridge's Ancient Mariner, who, having experienced the nightmarish chaos of a world without meaning or value, can never fully get back into an ordered world again.

Hardy was constantly trying to find a way out of his isolated dilemma, constantly trying to find a value to which he could cling in a world of accident, chance, and meaningless indifference. Since he refused to give in to hope for an external value, however, he refused to submit to illusions of transcendence; the only possibility for him was to find some kind of value in the emptiness itself. Like the Ancient Mariner, all Hardy had was his story of loss and despair, chaos and meaninglessness. If value were to be found at all, it lay in the complete commitment to this story—"facing the worst," and playing it back over and over again, exploring its implications, making others aware of its truth. Consequently, Hardy's art can be seen as a series of variations in form on this one barren theme of loss and chaos—"questionings in the exploration of reality."

While Hardy could imitate popular forms and create popular novels such as *Desperate Remedies*, an imitation of Wilkie Collins's detective novel, or *The Hand of Ethelberta*, an imitation of the social comedy popular at the time, when he wished to write a serious novel, one that would truly express his vision of humanity's situation in the universe, he could find no adequate model in the novels of his contemporaries. He solved this first basic problem in his search for form by returning to the tragic drama of the Greek and Elizabethan ages—a mode with which he was familiar through extensive early reading. Another Greek and Elizabethan mode he used, although he was less conscious of its literary tradition, was the pastoral narrative—a natural choice because of its surface similarity to his own subject matter of isolated country settings and innocent country people.

Hardy's second problem in the search for form arose from the incompatibility between the classical tragic vision and his own uniquely modern view. The classical writers saw humanity within a stable and ordered religious and social context, while Hardy saw humanity isolated, alone, searching for meaning in a world that offered none. Because Hardy denied the static and ordered worldview of the past, he was in turn denied the broad context of myth, symbol, and ritual that stemmed from that view. Lost without a God-ordered mythos, Hardy had to create a modern myth that presupposed the absence of God; he needed a pattern. Hardy's use of the traditional patterns of tragedy and pastoral, combined with his rejection of the old mythos that formerly gave meaning to these patterns, resulted in a peculiar distortion as his novels transcended their original patterns.

Nature in Hardy's "pastoral" novels, *The Woodlanders* and *Far from the Madding Crowd*, is neither benevolent nor divinely ordered. Similarly, the human dilemma in his "tragic" novels, *The Return of the Native* and *The Mayor of Casterbridge*, is completely antithetical to what it was for the dramatists of the past. The Greek hero was tragic because he violated a cosmic order; Hardy's heroes are tragic precisely because there is no such order. For the Greek hero there is a final reconciliation that persuades him to submit to the world. For Hardy's hero there is only the never-ending dialectic between people's nostalgia for value and the empty, indifferent world.

In *Tess of the D'Urbervilles* and *Jude the Obscure*, Hardy rejected the traditional tragic and pastoral patterns and allowed the intrinsic problems of his two protagonists to order the chaotic elements of the works. The structure of these novels can be compared to that of the epic journey of Wordsworth in *The Prelude: Or, The Growth of a Poet's Mind* (1850) and Coleridge in *The Rime of the Ancient Mariner* (1798). As critic Morse Peckham has noted, the task of the nineteenth century artist was no longer to find an external controlling form, but to "symbolize the orientative drive itself, the power of the individual to maintain his identity by creating order which would maintain his gaze at the world as it is, at things as they are." The loss of order is reflected in the structure of *Tess of the D'Urbervilles*, as the young heroine is literally evicted from the familiarity of her world and must endure the nightmarish wandering process of trying to get back inside. The structuring drive of *Jude the Obscure* is Jude's search for an external order that will rid him of the anguish of his own gratuitousness.

Far from the Madding Crowd

Hardy's first important novel, *Far from the Madding Crowd*, was the first in which he successfully adapted a traditional form, the pastoral, to his own purposes, greatly altering it in the process. Hallet Smith has described the pastoral as constituting the ideal of the good life: In the pastoral world, nature is the true home of humankind, and the gods take an active concern in human beings' welfare; the inhabitants of this world are content and self-sufficient. The plot complications of the pastoral usually arise through the intrusion of an aspiring mind from the outside, an antipastoral force that seeks to overthrow the idyllic established order. On the surface, *Far from the Madding Crowd* conforms perfectly to this definition of the pastoral. The story is set in an agricultural community, the main character is a shepherd, and the bulk of the inhabitants are content with their lives. The plot complications arise from the intrusion of the antipastoral Sergeant Troy and the love of three different men for the pastoral maid Bathsheba. To see the novel as a true pastoral, however, is to ignore living form in order to see a preestablished pattern. The pastoral ideal cannot be the vision of this novel because Hardy was struggling with the active tension between human hopes and the world's indifference.

Far from the Madding Crowd begins in a lighthearted mood with the comic situation of Gabriel Oak's unsuccessful attempts to woo the fickle maid Bathsheba, but Gabriel, often called the stabilizing force in the novel, is an ambiguous figure. Although he is described as both a biblical and a classical shepherd, he is unequivocally neither. Moreover, the first section of the novel hovers between tragedy and comedy. Even the "pastoral tragedy," the "murder" of all of Gabriel's sheep by a foolish young dog, is equivocal; the dog is not so much destroyed for his crime as he is executed. Gabriel's character, as well as the entire tone of the novel, shifts after this short prologue. When he next appears he is no longer the contented shepherd with modest ambitions; rather, he has developed the indifference to fate and fortune that, Hardy says, "though it often makes a villain of a man, is the basis of his sublimity when it does not."

The change that takes place in Gabriel is caused by his loss and is more significant than the change in Bathsheba because of her gain of an inheritance. Bathsheba, a typical pastoral coquette in the prologue of the novel, makes an ostensible shift when she inherits a farm of her own, but she is still coquettish and vain enough to be piqued by farmer William Boldwood's indifference to her charms and to send him a valentine saying "Marry Me." Boldwood, "the nearest approach to aristocracy that this remote quarter of the parish could boast of," is a serious, self-sufficient man who sees "no absurd side to the follies of life." The change the valentine causes in him is so extreme as to be comic.

The Bathsheba-Gabriel relationship is complicated by this new wooer. In this section of the novel, until the appearance of Sergeant Troy, there appears a series of scenes in which Gabriel, Boldwood, and Bathsheba are frozen into a tableau with the ever-present sheep in the background. The death and physical suffering of the sheep take on a sinister, grotesque imagery to make an ironic commentary on the absurdity of humanity's ephemeral passions in a world dominated by cruelty and death. The irrationality of physical passion is more evident when Bathsheba is overwhelmed by Troy. Their relationship begins with the feminine frill of her dress being caught in his masculine spur and blossoms with her submission to his dazzling sword exercises. After Boldwood's complete demoralization and the marriage of Bathsheba and Troy, the antipastoral Troy corrupts the innocent harvest festival until it becomes a wild frenzy and then a drunken stupor. The pastoral world of the "good life" is turned upside down as an approaching storm transforms the landscape into something sinister. It is significant that the rustics are asleep during the storm, for they are truly unaware of the sickness of the world and its sinister aspect. Troy, too, is unaware of the storm, as he is always unaware of any incongruity between humanity and the indifferent world. Only Gabriel, Bathsheba, and Boldwood, the involved and suffering characters of the novel, react to this symbolic storm.

Just as the death of the sheep forms the ever-present background to the first two parts of the novel, the death of Fanny Robin dominates the third section. From the time her body begins its journey in Joseph Poorgrass's wagon until the "Gurgoyle" washes Troy's flowers off her grave, death becomes the most important element in the book. By far the most important effect of Fanny Robin's death is on Bathsheba. When she opens the coffin to find out that Fanny was pregnant with Troy's child, the scene is "like an illusion raised by some fiendish incantation." Many critics have asserted that Bathsheba's then running away to seclude herself in the wood is her reconciliation with the natural world of the pastoral, but this view is wholly untenable: Her retreat is on the edge of a swamp of which the "general aspect was malignant." There is no pastoral goodness about the hollow in which she hides. It is a "nursery of pestilences. . . . From its moist and poisonous coat seemed to be exhaled the essences of evil things in the earth." This is one of those grotesque situations in which people become aware of their isolated state, when their need for solace in the natural world is met with only indifference, when they become aware of the absurdity of their demands on a barren and empty world. Bathsheba changes after her experience in this "boundary situation"; she gains the awareness that has characterized Gabriel all along.

After this climactic scene of confrontation with the indifferent world, the book loses its focus. In a diffuse and overlong denouement, Boldwood presses his advantage with Bathsheba until the night of the party, when she is on the point of giving in. Troy's return at this moment and his murder by Boldwood seem forced and melodramatic. Bathsheba's return to marry Gabriel is a concession to the reading public as much as it is to the pastoral pattern of the novel itself. *Far from the Madding Crowd*, a fable of the barrenness and death of the pastoral world and the tragic results of wrong choices through the irrationality of sexual attraction, truly ends with Bathsheba's isolation and painful new awareness in the pestilent swamp.

The Woodlanders

The Woodlanders, although more explicit in its imagistic presentation of the unhealthy natural world and more complex in its conflicts of irrational sexual attraction, manifests much of the same kind of formal distortion as is found in *Far from the Madding Crowd*. The world of Little Hintock, far from being the ideal pastoral world, is even more valueless, more inimical a world than Weatherbury. Instead of the grotesque death of sheep, trees become the symbolic representation of humanity's absurd situation in an empty world. Little Hintock is a wasteland, a world of darkness, isolation, guilt, and human cross-purposes. One's nostrils are always filled with the odor of dead leaves, fermenting cider, and heavy, blossomy perfume. One cannot breathe or stretch out one's arms in this world.

The so-called natural inhabitants of the Wood are dissatisfied with the nature of the world around them. Grace's father, Mr. Melbury, cramped and crippled by his lifetime struggle to make his living from the trees, wants his daughter to be able to escape such a world by marrying an outsider. A conflict is created, however, by the guilt he feels for a wrong he did to Giles Winterborne's father; he tries to atone for it by promising Grace to Giles. John South, Marty's father, on whose life the landholdings of Giles depend, is neurotically afraid of the huge tree in his yard. The tree takes on a symbolic aura as representative of the uncontrollable force of the natural world.

Furthermore, the sophisticated outsiders in the novel are cut off from the world they inhabit and are imaged as "unnatural." Strange unnatural lights can be seen from the house of the young Dr. Fitzpiers, who is said to be in league with the devil. The bored Felice Charmond is so unnatural that she must splice on the luxuriance of natural beauty by having a wig made of Marty South's hair. The isolated and cramped Hintock environment creates a boredom and ennui in these two characters that serve to further the narrative drive of the novel.

Grace, the most equivocal character in the novel, is the active center of its animating conflicts. Her wavering back and forth between the natural world and the antinatural is the central tension that crystallizes the tentative and uncomfortable attitude of all the characters. It is her dilemma of choice that constitutes the major action, just as it is Bathsheba's choice that dominates *Far from the Madding Crowd*. The choices that the characters make to relieve themselves of tension are made through the most irrational emotion, love, in a basically irrational world. Grace marries Fitzpiers in an effort to commit herself to a solid world of value. Fitzpiers sees in Grace the answer to a Shelleyan search for a soul mate. To commit oneself to a line of action that assumes the world is ordered and full of value, to choose a course of action that hopes to lessen the tentativeness of life, to deceive oneself into thinking that solidarity exists—these are the tragic errors that Hardy's characters repeatedly make.

The marriage begins to break up when Fitzpiers, aware that Grace is not the ideal he desired, goes to the lethargic Mrs. Charmond, and when Grace, aware that her hope for solidarity was misdirected, tries to go back to the natural world through the love of Giles. Social conventions—which Hardy views as holdovers from outmoded creeds—interfere, however. Grace is unable to obtain a divorce, for the law makes her irrational first choice inflexible. Despairing of the injustice of natural law as well as of social law, she runs away to Giles, who, too self-effacing to rebel against either code, lets her have his house while he spends the night in an ill-sheltered hut.

At this point, confused and in anguish about what possibility there is left for her, uncertain of the value of any action, Grace confronts the true nature of the world and the absurdity of her past hopes for value in it. The storm that catches Grace alone in the house is a climactic representation for her of the inimical natural world, just as the pestilent swamp is for Bathsheba. "She had never before been so struck with the devilry of a gusty night in the wood, because she had never been so entirely alone in spirit as she was now. She seemed almost to be apart from herself—a vacuous duplicate only." Grace's indecision and absurd hopes have been leading to this bitter moment of realization in which she is made aware of the ephemeral nature of human existence and the absurdity of human hopes in a world without intrinsic value.

Just as in *Far from the Madding Crowd*, the tension of the action collapses after this confrontation. Giles dies, and Fitzpiers returns after having ended his affair with Mrs. Charmond. After a short period of indifference, Grace, still his wife by law, returns to him. In his customary ironic way, however, Hardy does not allow this reconciliation to be completely satisfying, for it is physical only. Grace, having narrowly missed being caught in a mantrap set for Fitzpiers, is enticingly undressed when Fitzpiers rushes to her and asks to be taken back. This physical attraction is the only reason that Fitzpiers desires a reconciliation. Grace is still indifferent to him, but it is now this very indifference that makes their reunion possible. Seeing no one reaction as more valuable than another, she takes the path of least resistance. The rural chorus ends the novel by commenting that they think the union will not last.

THE RETURN OF THE NATIVE

Although many critics have pointed out the formal framework of *The Return of the Native*—the classical five-act division; the unity of time, place, and line of action; and the character similarities to Oedipus and Prometheus—others have struggled with the book's ambiguities and the difficulties involved in seeing it as a classical tragedy. Certainly, the pattern is classical, but the distortion of the pattern becomes the more significant structuring principle. Egdon Heath is the landscape from which God has departed. People in such an empty world will naturally begin to feel an affinity with the wasteland, such as islands, moors, and dunes. Little more needs to be said here about the part the Heath plays in the action, for critics have called it the principal actor in the drama. Indeed, it does dominate the scene, for the actions of all the characters are reactions in some way to the indifference the Heath represents.

As in *Far from the Madding Crowd*, there is a chorus of rustics in *The Return of the Native*. They belong on the

Heath because of their ignorance of the incongruity between human longing for meaning and the intractable indifference of the world. They still maintain a mythical, superstitious belief in a pagan animism and fatalistically accept the nature of things. The Druidical rites of the opening fires, the unimportance of Christian religion, the black mass and Voodoo doll of Susan Nonesuch—all of these characterize the pagan fatalism of the rustics.

The main characters, however, do not belong with the rustics. They make something other than a fatalistic response to the Heath and are characterized by their various reactions to its indifference. Mrs. Yeobright is described as having the very solitude exhaled from the Heath concentrated in her face. Having lived with its desolation longer than any of the others, she can no longer escape, but she is desperate to see that Clym does. Damon Wildeve does not belong to the Heath but has taken over a patch of land a former tenant died in trying to reclaim. Although he is dissatisfied, he is not heroic; he is involved in no search, no vital interaction with the indifferent world. Tomasin Yeobright is characterized in a single image, as she is in the house loft, selecting apples: "The sun shone in a bright yellow patch upon the figure of the maiden as she knelt and plunged her naked arms into the soft brown fern." She aligns herself with the natural world through her innocence and consequently perceives no incongruity. Diggory Venn, the most puzzling figure in the novel, is an outcast. The most typical image of him is by his campfire alone, the red glow reflecting off his own red skin. He simply wanders on the open Heath, minding other people's business and waiting for his chance to marry Tomasin.

These characters, regardless of their conflicts with the irrationality of human choice or the indifference of the Heath, are minor in comparison with the two antithetical attitudes of Eustacia Vye and Clym Yeobright. The most concrete image of Eustacia is of her wandering on the Heath, carrying an hourglass in her hand, gazing aimlessly out over the vast wasteland. Her search for value, her hope for escape from the oppressive indifference of the Heath, lies in being "loved to madness." Clym, however, sees friendliness and geniality written on the Heath. He is the disillusioned intellectual trying to make a return to the mythic simplicity of the natural world. Clym would prefer not to think, not to grapple with the incongruities he has seen. The very disease of thought that forces him to see the "coil of things" makes him desire to teach rather than to think. He is indeed blind, as his mother tells him, in thinking he can instill into the peasants the view that "life is a thing to be put up with," for they have always known it and fatalistically accepted it. Furthermore, he shows his blindness by marrying Eustacia, thinking she will remain with him on the Heath, while Eustacia reveals that she is as misdirected as he is by idealizing him and thinking that he will take her away from the Heath. Both characters search for a meaning and basis for value, but both are trapped by the irrationality of love and vain hopes in an irrational world.

At the beginning of book 4, Clym literally goes blind because of his studying and must actually look at the world through smoked glasses. He welcomes the opportunity to ignore the incongruities of the world by subsuming himself in the Heath and effacing himself in his furze cutting. In his selfish attempt to "not think" about it, he ignores what this means to Eustacia. She can find no meaning at all in such self-effacing indifference; it is the very thing against which she is rebelling. She returns again to her old pagan ways at the village dance and considers the possibility of Wildeve once more.

Mrs. Yeobright's journey across the Heath, a trip colored by grotesque images of the natural world—the tepid, stringy water of nearly dried pools, where "maggoty" shapes cavort; the battered, rude, and wild trees whose limbs are splintered, lopped, and distorted by the weather—is a turning point in the action of the book. In a concatenation of chance events and human misunderstanding, Eustacia turns Mrs. Yeobright away from the door, and the old woman dies as a result. At this point, Eustacia blames some "colossal Prince of the world for framing her situation and ruling her lot."

Clym, still selfish, ignores the problems of the living Eustacia and concentrates on the "riddle of death" of his mother. Had he been able to practice what he professed—human solidarity—he might have saved Eustacia and himself, but instead he bitterly blames her for his mother's death and is the immediate cause of Eustacia's flight. Eustacia's trip across the Heath to her death is similar to Mrs. Yeobright's in that the very natural world seems antagonistic to her. She stumbles over "twisted furze roots, tufts of rushes, or oozing lumps of fleshly fungi, which at this season lay scattered about the Heath like the rotten liver and lungs of some colossal animal." Her leap into the pool is a noble suicide. It is more a rebellion against the indifference of the world around her than it is a submission to its oppressiveness. It is the admission of the absurdity of human hopes by a romantic temperament that refuses to live by such absurdity.

The Mayor of Casterbridge

The tragic pattern of *The Mayor of Casterbridge* has been said by most critics to be more explicit than that of *The Return of the Native*; by the late twentieth century, however, critics were quick to point out that there are serious difficulties involved in seeing *The Mayor of Casterbridge* as an archetypal tragic ritual. Although Henchard is Oedipus-like in his opposition to the rational, Creon-like Farfrae, the plot of the novel, like that of *The Return of the Native*, involves the reactions of a set of characters to the timeless indifference of the world. In this case, the mute and intractable world is imaged in the dead myths and classical legends of Casterbridge.

Secluded as much as Little Hintock, the world of *The Woodlanders*, Casterbridge is "huddled all together, shut in by a square wall of trees like a plot of garden by a box-edging." The town is saturated with the old superstitions and myths of the past. The primary image of the desolate world of the town and its dead and valueless past is the Casterbridge Ring, a relic of an ancient Roman amphitheater. The Ring is a central symbol that embodies the desolation of the old myths of human value. It formerly had been the gallows site, but now it is a place for illicit meetings of all kinds, except, Hardy notes, those of happy lovers. A place of man's inhumanity to man is no place for the celebration of love.

The inhumanity of one person to another and the human need for love play important roles in the action of the novel. While the classical Oedipus is guilty of breaking a cosmic law, Henchard is guilty of breaking a purely human one. By selling his wife, he treats her as a thing, not a human being. He rejects human relationships and violates human interdependence and solidarity. This is the sin that begins to find objectification years later when the blight of the bread agitates the townspeople and when his wife, Susan, returns.

It is not this sin alone that means tragedy for Henchard, just as it is not Oedipus's violation alone that brings his downfall. Henchard's character—his irrational behavior, his perverse clinging to the old order and methods, his rash and impulsive nature—also contributes to his defeat. Henchard is an adherent of the old ways. Though he is ostensibly the mayor, an important man, he is actually closer to the rustic, folk characters than the hero of any other Hardy novel. He is not a rebel against the indifference of the world so much as he is a simple hay stacker, trying desperately to maintain a sense of value in the worn-out codes and superstitions of the past. In the often-quoted "character is Fate" passage in the novel, Hardy makes explicit Henchard's problem. He calls him a Faust-like character, "a vehement, gloomy being who had quitted the ways of vulgar men without light to guide him on a better way." Henchard is thus caught between two worlds, one of them dead and valueless, the other not worthy enough to be a positive replacement. The levelheaded business sense of Farfrae, the social climbing and superficiality of Lucetta, the too-strict rationality of Elizabeth-Jane—all representing the new order of human attitudes—appear anemic and self-deceived in the face of Henchard's dynamic energy.

It often seems that the nature of things is against Henchard, but the nature of things is that events occur that cannot be predicted, and that they often occur just at the time when one does not want them to. Many such unpredicted and ill-timed events accumulate to cause Henchard's tragedy. For example, just when he decides to marry Lucetta, Susan returns; just at the time of Susan's death, he is once more reminded of his obligation to Lucetta; just at the time when he tells Elizabeth-Jane that she is his daughter, he discovers that she is not; and just at the time when he calls on Lucetta to discuss marriage, she has already met and found a better mate in Farfrae.

Many of the events that contribute to Henchard's own downfall are a combination of this "unholy brew" and his impulsive nature. That the weather turned bad during his planned entertainment he could not prevent, but he could have been more prepared for the rain had he not been in such a hurry to best Farfrae. The unpredictable nature of the weather at harvest time was also beyond his control, but again had he not been so intent on ruining Farfrae he might have survived. He begins to wonder if someone is roasting a waxen image of him or stirring an "unholy brew" to confound him. Moreover, the attitudes of other characters accumulate to contribute to Henchard's downfall. Farfrae, as exacting as a machine, rejects Henchard's fatherly love and makes few truly human responses at all. Lucetta, once dependent on Henchard, becomes so infatuated with her new wealth that she no longer needs him. At the beginning of the novel, Susan's simple nature makes her incapable of realizing that Newsom's purchase of her is not valid, and at the end, her daughter, Elizabeth-Jane, is so coldly rational that she can cast Henchard off without possibility of reconciliation. None of these characters faces the anguish of being human as Henchard does.

The ambiguity that arises from the combination of all these forces makes it difficult to attribute Henchard's tragedy to any one of them. His death in the end marks the inevitable disappearance of the old order, but it is also the only conclusion possible for the man who has broken the only possible existing order when a cosmic order is no longer tenable—the human order of man himself. The reader is perhaps made to feel that Henchard has suffered more than he deserved. As a representative of the old order, his fall must be lamented even as the search is carried on for a new foundation of value and order. At the death of the old values in *The Mayor of Casterbridge*, a new order is not available.

Tess of the D'Urbervilles

The form and meaning of *Tess of the D'Urbervilles* springs from Tess's relation to the natural world. At the beginning of the novel she is a true child of nature who, although sensitive to painful incongruities in her experience, is confident that the natural world will provide her with a basis of value and will protect and sustain her. When nature fails her, her perplexity throws her out of the comfortable world of innocence and natural rapport. Tess then begins a journey both inward and outward in search of a stable orientation and a reintegration into a relationship with the natural world.

Tess first appears in her "natural home" in the small hamlet of Marlott, where her innocence is dramatized as she takes part in the May Day dance. There is a sensitivity in Tess that sets her apart from the other inhabitants. Shame for her father's drunken condition makes her volunteer to take the beehives to market, and despair for the laziness of her parents makes her dreamily watch the passing landscape and ignore where she is going. When, as a result, the horse Prince is killed, Tess's sense of duty to her family, now in economic difficulties, overcomes her pride, and she agrees to go to her aristocratic relatives for help. It is her first journey outside the little world of Marlott and her first real encounter with corruption. Alec, her cousin, is a stock figure of the sophisticated, antinatural world. Their first scene together is formalized into an archetypal image of innocence in the grasp of the corrupt.

Just as it is Tess's natural luxuriance and innocence that attracts Alec, it is also her innocence that leads to her fall. When he takes her into the woods, strangely enough she is not afraid of him as before. She feels that she is in her natural element. She so trusts the natural world to protect her that she innocently falls asleep and is seduced by Alec. The antinatural force that began with her father's alleged nobility works together with Tess's own innocence and sensitivity and her naïve trust in the world to make her an outcast. When her illegitimate child dies and the church refuses it a Christian burial, Tess unequivocally denies the validity of organized religion. She probes within herself to try to find some meaning in her despair. Suddenly she becomes quite consciously aware of the abstract reality of death: "Almost at a leap Tess thus changed from simple girl to complex woman." The facing of the idea of death without a firm hope for transcendence is the conclusion of Tess's inward search in this second phase of her experience, when, still maintaining a will to live and enjoy, she has hopes of submerging herself into the natural world again.

The Valley of the Great Dairies where Tess goes next is the natural world magnified, distorted, thrown out of proportion. It is so lush and fertile as to become a symbolic world. As Tess enters the valley, she feels hope for a new reintegration. For the time being, she dismisses the disturbing thought of her doubt in her childhood God and is satisfied to immerse herself within the purely physical world of the farm's lushness. She manages to ignore her moral plight until she meets the morally ambiguous Angel Clare. In contrast to Tess, Angel's moral perplexity arises from intellectual questioning rather than from natural disillusionment. Intellectually convinced that he has lost faith, Angel rebels against the conventions of society and the church and goes to the

Valley of the Great Dairies, where he believes innocence and uncontaminated purity and goodness prevail. For Angel, Tess represents the idealistic goal of natural innocence, but the natural world no more affirms this relationship than it condemned the former one. On the first night of their marriage, Tess confesses to Angel her relationship with Alec. Angel, the idealist, has desired to see a natural perfection in Tess. Doubting that perfection, he rejects her as antinatural. Angel cannot accept the reality of what nature is truly like; he is tied to a conventional orientation more than he realizes.

After Angel leaves her, Tess wanders about the countryside doing farmwork at various places until one morning on the road she awakes to find dead pheasants around her. At this point, Tess becomes aware that in a Darwinistic universe, without teleological possibility and without inherent goodness, violation, injury, and even death are innate realities. Tess realizes that she is not guilty by the laws of such a world. After this realization she can go to the barren world of Chalk-Newton and not feel so much the incongruity of the place. With its "white vacuity of countenance with the lineaments gone," Chalk-Newton represents the wasteland situation of a world without order or value. Tess can remain indifferent to it because of her new realization of its indifference to her.

Cold indifference, however, offers no escape from her moral conflict. Alec D'Urberville comes back into her life, proclaiming that he has accepted Christianity and exhorting her not to "tempt" him again. Ironically, by trying to convince him of her own realization of a world without God and by propounding Angel's uncommitted humanism to him, she only succeeds in reconverting Alec back to his old demoniac nature and thus creates another threat to herself. When her father dies and the family loses its precarious freehold, Tess gives in to Alec's persistent urging once more. When Angel, in the rugged South American mountains, comes to the same realization that Tess experienced on the road, he returns to find that Tess has renounced life and self completely, allowing her body to drift, "like a corpse upon the current, in a direction dissociated from the living will." After the return of Angel, when Tess finds her last hopes dashed, she sees in Alec all the deception and meaninglessness of a world she trusted. When she kills him, she is transformed by her rebellion. Like Percy Bysshe Shelley's Beatrice Cenci, she is aware of no guilt; she transcends any kind of moral judgment. She acknowledges her absolute freedom, and in that fearful moment, she is willing to accept the human penalties for such freedom.

In the last part of the novel, when Angel and Tess wander without any real hope of escape, Tess is already condemned to die. Isolated in the awareness of her own ephemerality in a valueless world, Tess vows that she is "not going to think of anything outside of now." The final scene at Stonehenge is a triumph of symbolic realization of place; the silent, enigmatic stones, mysterious and implacable, resist any attempt at explanation. Tess, in saying that she likes to be there, accepts the indifferent universe. Lying on the altar of a heathen temple, she is the archetypal sacrifice of human rebellion against an empty world. When the carriers of the law of nature and society arrive, Tess, having rebelled against these laws and rejected them, can easily say, "I am ready."

Tess's real tragedy springs from her insistent hope throughout the novel to find external meaning and justification for her life. Only at the end of the novel, when she rebels by killing Alec, does she achieve true awareness. Unlike the classical tragic hero, she is not reconciled to the world through an acceptance of universal justice. Her very salvation, the only kind of salvation in Hardy's world, lies in her denial of such a concept.

JUDE THE OBSCURE

With some significant differences, *Jude the Obscure* is concerned with the same problem that animates *Tess of the D'Urbervilles*—the absurdity and tragedy of human hopes for value in an indifferent universe. As a literary creation, it is a "process" through which Hardy tries to structure the symbolic journey of every person who searches for a foundation, a basis for meaning and value. The problem, however, is that all the symbols that represent meaning to Jude—the colleges, the church, the ethereal freedom of Sue Bridehead, and even the physical beauty of his wife Arabella—are illusory. By contrast, those things that have real symbolic value in the world are the forbidding, sacrosanct walls of the college complex, which Jude cannot enter; the decaying materiality of the churches that he tries to restore; the neurotic irrationality of Sue, which he fails to understand; and his own body, to which he is inextricably tied. It is precisely

Jude's "obscurity," his loss of "at-homeness" in the world, with which the novel is concerned. He is obscure because he is without light, because he tries in every way possible to find an illumination of his relation to the world, but without success.

It is significant that the novel opens with the departure of the schoolmaster Phillotson, for to Jude, orphaned and unwanted by his aunt, the teacher has been the center of the world. His leaving marks the necessity of Jude's finding a new center and a new hope to relieve his loneliness. The first projection of his hopes to find value is naturally toward Christminster, the destination of his teacher. In the first part of the book his dream is seen only as an indefinable glow in the distance that offers all possibilities by its very unknown nature. Although he consciously devotes himself to the Christian framework, one night after having read a classical poem, he kneels and prays to Diana, the goddess of the moon. Both of these value systems—Christian faith and Greek reason—are projected on his vision of Christminster, but both of them are temporarily forgotten when he meets Arabella, "a substantial female animal." Later, when she tells him that she is pregnant, although it destroys all his former plans, he idealizes the marriage state, calls his hopes for Christminster "dreams about books, and degrees and impossible fellowships," and dedicates himself to home, family, and the pedestrian values of Marygreen. His discovery that Arabella has deceived him is only the first reversal in his search for unity and value.

In the second phase of Jude's development, the long-planned journey to Christminster is prompted by the immediacy of seeing a picture of Sue Bridehead; she becomes a concrete symbol of his vision. His first glimpse of Sue has the quality of idealistic wish fulfillment. His growing desire for her expresses a need for an "anchorage" to his thoughts. He goes to the church she attends, and this church, associated with his vision of Sue, temporarily becomes that anchorage. Sue is not, however, representative of Christian values; rather, she is the classical pagan. This dichotomy of values creates a recurring tension in Jude's search throughout the book.

Jude's first major disillusionment at Christminster comes when he is turned down by all five colleges to which he has applied. After this disappointment, he shifts his hopes from the reason and knowledge of the schools to the faith of the church. This religious impulse dominates Jude's hopes in the third phase of his development. He practices the rituals of the church in the hope that he can find a meaning for himself, but Sue, who laughed at his idealistic notions of the intellectual life, tells him that the Church is not the way either. Sue, who changes in Jude's eyes as his goals change, is always important to him as a symbol of his aspirations and ideals. When he loses her to Phillotson, he is struck even more by the "scorn of Nature for man's finer emotions and her lack of interest in his aspirations."

Phase four of Jude's search is a transition section presenting the decay of the values of the past. Jude, studying theology and church ritual with a last weakening hope, is only vaguely aware of the decay and aridity around him. His need for Sue, an ambiguous mixture of desire for the ideal and the physical, begins to take on more importance for him until he decides that he is unfit "to fill the part of a propounder of accredited dogma" and burns all his theology books. Sue, a spiritual creature, cannot live with Phillotson any longer. She goes to Jude, who, having rejected everything else, is ready to project his desires for meaning entirely on an ambiguous union with her as both physical wife and Shelleyan soul mate.

The fifth part of the novel is a phase of movement as Jude and Sue wander from town to town, living as husband and wife in all respects except the sexual. Not until Arabella returns and Sue fears she will lose Jude does she give in to him, but with infinite regret. In the final phase of Jude's development, after the birth of his children, including the mysterious child named Father Time, the family moves back to Christminster. Instead of being optimistic, Jude is merely indifferent. He recognizes himself as an outsider, a stranger to the universe of ideals and hopes of other men. He has undergone a process that has slowly stripped him of such hopes for meaning. He sees the human desire for meaning as absurd in a world that has no concern for humanity, a universe that cannot fulfill dreams of unity or meaning.

The tragedy of Father Time causes Sue to alter her belief that she can live by instinct, abjuring the laws of society. She makes an extreme shift, accepting a supreme deity against whose laws she feels she has transgressed; her self-imposed penance for her "sin" of living with Jude is to go back to Phillotson. After Sue leaves, Jude goes to "a dreary, strange flat scene, where boughs dripped, and coughs and consumption lurked, and where he had never been before." This is a typical Hardy technique for moments of realization: The natural world becomes an inimical reflection of the character's awareness of the absurd. After this, Jude's reaction to the world around him is indifference: He allows himself to be seduced by Arabella again and marries her. Jude's final journey to see Sue is a journey to death and a final rejection of the indifferent universe of which his experiences have made him aware.

In his relentless vision of a world stripped of transcendence, Hardy is a distinctly modern novelist. As Nathan A. Scott has said of him, "not only does he lead us back to that trauma in the nineteenth century out of which the modern existentialist imagination was born, but he also brings us forward to our own time."

Charles E. May

Other major works

SHORT FICTION: *Wessex Tales*, 1888; *A Group of Noble Dames*, 1891; *Life's Little Ironies*, 1894; *A Changed Man, The Waiting Supper, and Other Tales*, 1913; *The Complete Short Stories*, 1989 (Desmond Hawkins, editor).

PLAYS: *The Dynasts: A Drama of the Napoleonic Wars*, pb. 1903, 1906, 1908, 1910 (complete; verse drama; abridged by Harley Granville-Barker); *The Famous Tragedy of the Queen of Cornwall*, pr., pb. 1923 (one act).

POETRY: *Wessex Poems, and Other Verses*, 1898; *Poems of the Past and Present*, 1901; *Time's Laughingstocks, and Other Verses*, 1909; *Satires of Circumstance*, 1914; *Selected Poems of Thomas Hardy*, 1916; *Moments of Vision and Miscellaneous Verses*, 1917; *Late Lyrics and Earlier*, 1922; *Human Shows, Far Phantasies, Songs, and Trifles*, 1925; *Winter Words in Various Moods and Metres*, 1928; *Collected Poems of Thomas Hardy*, 1943; *The Complete Poetical Works*, 1982-1985 (3 volumes; Samuel Hynes, editor).

NONFICTION: *Life and Art*, 1925 (Ernest Brennecke, editor); *The Early Life of Thomas Hardy*, 1928; *The Later Years of Thomas Hardy*, 1930; *Personal Writings*, 1966 (Harold Orel, editor); *The Collected Letters of Thomas Hardy*, 1978-1988 (7 volumes; Richard Little Purdy and Michael Millgate, editors).

Bibliography

Carpenter, Richard C. *Thomas Hardy*. Boston: Twayne, 1964. Examines the characterization, descriptions, plots, and social themes in Hardy's fiction and poetry as well as elements of symbolism, myth, impressionism, and drama in the works. Includes chronology, bibliography, and index.

Chew, Samuel C. *Thomas Hardy: Poet and Novelist*. 1928. Reprint. New York: Russell & Russell, 1964. Although it does not lack sentiment, this volume is still one of the most respected of the traditional analyses of Hardy's work. Examines Hardy's pessimism, his use of coincidence, his conflict of intellect and intuition, and the structural excellence of his Wessex novels, which Chew considers to be a clarification of Victorian technique. Includes bibliography and index.

Daleski, H. M. *Thomas Hardy and Paradoxes of Love*. Columbia: University of Missouri Press, 1997. Reevaluates the treatment of gender in Hardy's novels, defending the author from charges of sexism and maintaining that some of Hardy's female characters are depicted sympathetically.

Gatrell, Simon. *Thomas Hardy and the Proper Study of Mankind*. Charlottesville: University Press of Virginia, 1993. Analyzes Hardy's technique of presenting character in relationship to society. In addition to chapters on individual novels, devotes chapters to Hardy's use of the dance as a folk ritual and to the imperial theme in his fiction.

Guerard, Albert J. *Thomas Hardy: The Novels and Stories*. Cambridge, Mass.: Harvard University Press, 1949. One of the classic critical works on Hardy, examining his poetry and fiction in Victorian and modern contexts. Argues that in relation to Joseph Conrad and André Gide, Hardy is an old-fashioned storyteller, but he anticipates modern elements of antirealism in his conflicting impulses, his symbolic use of coincidence, and his artful technique.

Howe, Irving. *Thomas Hardy*. New York: Macmillan, 1967. One of the earliest book-length studies of Hardy's novels, poetry, and short fiction, tracing his development as a writer and the influences of his background and intellectual environment. The chapter "Let the Day Perish" focuses on Hardy's women characters, especially Tess, who illustrates the transformation and ennobling of a cultural stereotype. Complemented by a primary bibliography and an index.

Kramer, Dale, ed. *The Cambridge Companion to Thomas Hardy*. New York: Cambridge University Press, 1999. Provides an essential introduction and general overview of all Hardy's work and specific demonstrations of Hardy's ideas and literary skills. Individual essays explore Hardy's biography, his aesthetics, and the impact on his work of developments in science, religion, and philosophy in the late nineteenth century. Includes a detailed chronology of Hardy's life.

Millgate, Michael. *Thomas Hardy: A Biography Revisited*. New York: Oxford University Press, 2004. Enhances and replaces Millgate's 1982 biography, considered to be one of the best and most scholarly Hardy biographies available. Includes bibliography and index.

Page, Norman, ed. *Oxford Reader's Companion to Hardy*. New York: Oxford University Press, 2000. Encyclopedic work contains three hundred alphabetically arranged entries examining Hardy's work and discussing his family and friends, important places in his life and work, his influences, critical approaches to his writings, and the history of his works' publication. Also includes a chronology of his life, lists of places and characters in his fiction, a glossary, and a bibliography.

Ray, Martin, ed. *Thomas Hardy Remembered*. London: Ashgate, 2007. Collection of interviews with Hardy and recollections of him by his friends and acquaintances offers readers a fresh perspective on the writer. Also contains observations by Hardy on his writing and his contemporaries' opinions about his life.

Seymour-Smith, Martin. *Hardy*. New York: St. Martin's Press, 1994. Literary biography not only provides detailed information on Hardy's life but also summarizes and critiques previous criticism of Hardy and discusses in a straightforward, nontheoretical way the author's most important works. Includes analysis of the critical reception of Hardy's work and description of critical controversies that have arisen over his fiction and thought.

Tomalin, Claire. *Thomas Hardy*. New York: Penguin Books, 2007. Thorough and finely written biography by a respected Hardy scholar illuminates the novelist's drive to indict the malice, neglect, and ignorance of his fellow human beings. Includes discussion of aspects of Hardy's life that are apparent in his literary works.

WILSON HARRIS

Born: New Amsterdam, British Guiana (now Guyana); March 24, 1921
Also known as: Theodore Wilson Harris; Kona Waruk

Principal long fiction

Palace of the Peacock, 1960
The Far Journey of Oudin, 1961
The Whole Armour, 1962
The Secret Ladder, 1963
Heartland, 1964
The Eye of the Scarecrow, 1965
The Waiting Room, 1967
Tumatumari, 1968
Ascent to Omai, 1970
Black Marsden: A Tabula Rasa Comedy, 1972
Companions of the Day and Night, 1975
Da Silva da Silva's Cultivated Wilderness and Genesis of the Clowns, 1977
The Tree of the Sun, 1978
The Angel at the Gate, 1982
Carnival, 1985

The Guyana Quartet, 1985 (includes *Palace of the Peacock*, *The Far Journey of Oudin*, *The Whole Armour*, and *The Secret Ladder*)
The Infinite Rehearsal, 1987
The Four Banks of the River of Space, 1990
The Carnival Trilogy, 1993 (includes *Carnival*, *The Infinite Rehearsal*, and *The Four Banks of the River of Space*)
Resurrection at Sorrow Hill, 1993
Jonestown, 1996
The Dark Jester, 2001
The Mask of the Beggar, 2003
The Ghost of Memory, 2006

Other literary forms

Wilson Harris's first published novel appeared in 1960, when he was thirty-nine years old. Before that time, his creative efforts were mainly in poetry, which, given the poetic prose of his novels, is not surprising. He published a few volumes of poems, including *Fetish* (1951), issued under the pseudonym Kona Waruk, and *Eternity to Season* (1954). Although the first collection is perceived as apprentice material, the second is generally praised and seen as complementary to Harris's early novels; it anticipates the novels' symbolic use of the Guyanese landscape to explore the various antinomies that shape the artist and the community. Harris has also published two volumes of short stories: *The Sleepers of Roraima* (1970), with three stories; and *The Age of the Rainmakers* (1971), with four. These stories are drawn from the myths and legends of the aborigines of the Guyanese hinterland. Harris does not simply relate the myths and legends; as in his novels, he imbues them with symbolic and allegorical significance.

Conscious of how unconventional and difficult his novels are, Harris has attempted to elucidate his theories of literature in several critical works. His language in these publications, however, is as densely metaphorical as in his novels. Harris's ideas are outlined in *Tradition, the Writer, and Society* (1967), a group of short exploratory essays on the West Indian novel, and *History, Fable, and Myth in the Caribbean and Guianas* (1970), a series of three lectures. These ideas are developed in his later volumes of essays, *Explorations: A Selection of Talks and Articles* (1981) and *The Womb of Space: The Cross-Cultural Imagination* (1983), in which Harris analyzes the works of a wide range of writers, including Ralph Ellison, William Faulkner, Paule Marshall, Christopher Ifekandu Okigbo, Edgar Allan Poe, Raja Rao, Jean Rhys, Derek Walcott, and Patrick White.

Harris's introduction to the 1993 Faber & Faber edition of *The Carnival Trilogy* is a major statement of his principles of concept and technique. Originally an article for the British spiritual journal *Temenos*, the introduction discusses Harris's various debts to Dante, the Faust legend, and modern science. The introduction is valuable not only for explicating the trilogy but also for exposing Harris's pulling together of myth, storytelling, and symbol. *The Radical Imagination: Lectures and Talks*, a book of interviews with Harris, was published in 1992; *Selected Essays of Wilson Harris: The Unfinished Genesis of the Imagination* appeared in 1999. Aside from providing expositions of his own fiction, Harris has addressed issues of conquest and hegemony often assayed by postcolonial critics who desire to revise the cultural arrogance of Western imperialism. Harris, however, draws more or less equally from European and non-European cultures and (as in his essay "Quetzalcoatl and the Smoking Mirror") is more interested in using myth to advance beyond worldly aggression than in addressing specific acts of colonial aggression as such.

Achievements

From the publication of his very first novel, Wilson Harris's work attracted a great deal of attention. Though many readers are puzzled by his innovative techniques and by his mystical ideas, his works have received lavish critical praise. Although firmly established as a major Caribbean novelist, Harris is not seen as simply a regional writer. Critics outside the Caribbean perceive him as one of the most original and significant writers of the second half of the twentieth century and, in trying to come to grips with his ideas and techniques, have compared him with William Blake, Joseph Conrad, William Faulkner, Herman Melville, and William Butler Yeats.

As would be expected of one who eschews the conventional realistic novel, Harris is not without his detractors. Some readers have pounced on his work for being idiosyncratic, obscure, and farraginous. Those who defend him note that Harris's novels demand more of the reader than do more conventional works and that what initially appears to be merely obscure and confused is intended to shock readers and force them to deconstruct habitual perceptions and responses. Harris's importance as a novelist is reflected in the many awards and honors bestowed upon him by cultural and academic institutions: He has received the English Arts Council Award twice (in 1968 and in 1970), and in 1972 he received a Guggenheim Fellowship. He has held many visiting professorships and fellowships at institutions such as Aarhus University (Denmark), Mysore University (India), Newcastle University (Australia), the University of Toronto, the University of the West Indies, the University of Texas, and Yale University. In 1984, he received an honorary doctorate from the University of the West Indies, and subsequently he was awarded the 1987 Guyana Prize for Fiction. In 1992 he won Italy's Mondello Prize for fiction. In 2002, as part of the Guyanese commemoration of Harris's eightieth birthday, he was awarded a special Guyana Prize for Literature in recognition of a lifetime of writing that has explored the implications of Caribbean identity in the postcolonial era.

Biography

Theodore Wilson Harris was born in New Amsterdam, British Guiana (now known as Guyana), on March 24, 1921. From 1934 to 1939, he attended Queen's College, a prestigious high school staffed by English expatriates. He went on to study land surveying and geomorphology and in 1942 became an assistant government surveyor and made the first of many expeditions into the interior of Guyana. Between 1944 and 1953, he led several expeditions into other interior and coastal areas. The interior, with its dense tropical jungles, vast savannahs, and treacherous rivers, and the coastal region, with its mighty estuaries and extensive irrigation system, had a strong effect on Harris, later reflected in his novels. These expeditions also made Harris aware of the life of the Amerindians (indigenous peoples of the region) and of the peoples of Guyana of African, Asian, and European ancestry, who would later populate his novels. While working as a surveyor, he nurtured his artistic talents by writing poems, stories, and short essays for the little magazine *Kyk-over-al*, edited by the poet A. J. Seymour.

In 1950, Harris visited Europe for the first time, touring England and the Continent, and in 1959 he emigrated to Great Britain. That year, he married Margaret Burns, a Scottish writer. (He was married in 1945 to Cecily Carew, but the marriage ended in divorce.) With the publication of his first novel in 1960, Harris became a full-time writer. He settled in London but constantly traveled to take up fellowships and professorships in Europe, Australia, India, the Caribbean, Canada, and the United States. Harris has stated that these travels assisted him in providing some of the global backdrops and cosmic sensibility of his later fictions. His trip to Mexico in 1972, for instance, was especially influential on his use of the Quetzalcoatl legend in *The Carnival Trilogy*.

With tireless devotion to the evolution of his fictional voice and to promoting discussion of the postcolonial culture through numerous prestigious university appointments, Harris continued writing well into his seventies, publishing dense experimental narratives in which he sought in myth what history could not provide: a context for understanding the historical colonial imperative essentially to dismember the Caribbean and Amerindian culture. Perennially short-listed for the Nobel Prize, Harris announced in 2007 through his longtime publisher, Faber & Faber, that *The Ghost of Memory*, his frankest (and most urgent) treatment of the dynamic between myth and history, would be his last novel.

Analysis

Wilson Harris's novels center on his belief that polarization in any community is destructive in any form it takes, whether it is between the imperial and the colonial, the human and the natural, the physical and the spiritual, the historical and the contemporary, the mythic and the scientific, or even the living and the dead. The healthy community should be in a constant state of evolution or metamorphosis, striving to reconcile these static opposites. Artists within such communities must aspire to a unifying perception if they are to be truly creative, and their art must reflect a complementary, reconciling vision. The artist should reject, for example, the rigid conventional demarcation between past and present, corporeal and incorporeal, literal and allegorical. Time past, present, and future should be interlaced. The dead should exist side by side with the living. The literal should be indistinguishable from the metaphorical. In adhering to such ideas of fictional form, Harris produced innovative novels that some see as complex and challenging, others as obscure and idiosyncratic.

This perception of society and the artist and of the form fiction should take informs all of Harris's novels, with gradations in emphasis, scope, and complexity. Some novels, for example, emphasize the polarization rather than the integration of a community. Some accent the allegorical rather than the realistic. Some juxtapose the living with the dead. There are shifts in setting from novel to novel. Harris's artistic psyche is embedded in Guyana, and, though he settled in Great Britain in 1959, in his fiction he constantly returns to his native land, making use of the varied landscape of coastland, estuaries, jungles, waterfalls, mountains, and savannahs. In his later novels, the range of his settings expands to include the Caribbean, Great Britain, and Latin America.

The polarization in the assessment of Harris's work continues. His advocates lavish praise on him, some perceiving him as a candidate for the Nobel Prize. Although an enormous amount of scholarly work has been devoted to Harris's fiction, especially in the 1990's, this Guyanese novelist has not entered into the broad circle of cultured readership that has embraced his Caribbean contemporaries V. S. Naipaul of Trinidad and Gabriel García Márquez of Colombia. Naipaul and García Márquez, both outstanding journalists as well as novelists, create a clear historical context for their fiction. Although a deep level of historical awareness is present in Harris's canon, history is braided with other discourses, such as those of myth, science, and anthropology, as in his use of the Carnival motifs. Perhaps this multilayered quality has inhibited mass reception of Harris's work. Some observers continue to complain that his novels are strange, with, as David Ormerod has observed, "no discernible yardstick for meaning—just a simple bland identification, where X is symbolic of something, perhaps Y or Z, because the author has just this minute decided that such will be the case." Shirley Chew, referring to *The Tree of the Sun*, has stated: "Harris has failed to rise to some of the more common expectations one brings to the reading of a novel." It is possible that such criticism is indicative of an inability to respond to the demands of Harris's challenging innovations; on the other hand, it is perhaps a reminder to Harris of his own rejection of the static polarization in community and creativity, a warning to him to heed the conventional in his pursuit of the innovative.

THE GUYANA QUARTET

Palace of the Peacock, Harris's first novel, is the first of *The Guyana Quartet*, four sequential novels set in different regions of Guyana. The novel is a perfect introduction to Harris's canon: It establishes the ideas and forms that are found in subsequent works. Set in the Guyanese interior, the novel recounts the journey upriver of Donne, an efficient and ruthless captain, and his multiracial crew. They are looking for a settlement where they hope to find the Amerindian laborers who earlier fled Donne's harsh treatment. The account of the journey is provided by a shadowy first-person narrator, Donne's brother, who accompanies them. After an arduous journey, Donne and his crew reach the settlement, only to find that the American Indians have left. They again set out in search of them, and, as they travel farther upriver, several of the crew meet their deaths—some of them accidentally, some not. Eventually, Donne and two members of the crew reach the source of the river, a waterfall, and, abandoning their boat, begin climbing the cliff, only to fall to their deaths. The narrative is quite thin and is not given in as linear and realistic a way as this outline suggests. The novel, for example, begins with Donne being shot and killed before undertaking his journey, then proceeds to tell of the entire crew drowning but coming alive just before they reach the Amerindian settlement, and concludes with Donne falling to his death but reaching the mountaintop where stands the Palace of the Peacock.

The novel clearly is allegorical. Critics agree that Harris employs Donne and his strange crew as representations of antithetical yet complementary aspects of human experience. Their interpretations of what precisely these characters represent are quite diverse, however, and the novel accommodates them all. The novel is seen as examining the brotherhood of invader and invaded, the common destiny of the diverse races of Guyana, and the complementary and interdependent relationship between the material and the spiritual, the historical and the contemporary, and the living and the dead. The novel could be interpreted also as an allegorical study of the growth of the artist in an environment inhospitable to art. Drawing from his own experience in the challenging Guyanese hinterland, where he wrote his early pieces while working as a land surveyor, Harris shows that harsh surroundings put the aspiring artist in a quandary, for he is forced to look to his physical well-being by developing a materialistic, aggressive outlook that works against his contemplative, humane, artistic nature. At the end of the novel, Harris's narrator comes to realize that as an artist he must accept that he is the sum total of all the diverse antithetical experiences and impulses that coexist tensely but creatively in his psyche.

A cursory explication of the novel as such an allegorical bildungsroman will provide an insight into Harris's unconventional artistry. Harris examines his narrator-protagonist's progression toward acceptance of the polarities of his artistic psyche in four broad phases that correspond to the four books of the novel. In book 1, the narrator, aspiring toward artistic and humane goals, suppresses his assertive and dictatorial tendencies. From the opening paragraph, it is evident that the narrator and Donne are alter egos: They represent antithetical aspects of one individual, who could be termed the protagonist. Their oneness is emphasized as much as their polarities. The protagonist's rejection of his Donnean qualities is signified by Donne's death in the novel's opening section and by the awakening of the narrator in a maternity ward, suggestive of a birth. After this scene, the journey upriver begins and Donne is found aboard the boat with his crew, but it is the narrator whose voice is prominent. At the end of book 1, Donne is described as being a shadow of his former self.

In book 2, the protagonist discovers that he cannot totally suppress his Donnean qualities, for to survive as an artist in his harsh environment he must be both the humane, contemplative observer and the assertive, forceful participant. This shift is indicated by the narrator's mellowing attitude toward Donne, who reappears as his former assertive self in book 2. Donne himself, however, mellows toward the narrator, admitting that he is caught up in "material slavery" and that he hates himself for being "a violent taskmaster." Their gradual adjustment to each other is shown in the relationships among the eight members of the crew, who, described by Harris as agents of personality, represent overlapping but distinct impulses of the divided protagonist. Their personalities tend to run the scale from Donne's to the narrator's. They have their own alter egos. In book 3, as Donne and the narrator adjust to each other—that is, as the protagonist tries to resolve the inner conflict between his contemplative and active natures—various pairs of the crew die.

In book 4, the protagonist attains a new conception of himself as an artist—a conception that accommodates his antithetical feelings and attitudes. He now perceives that though as an artist he must resist the qualities of Donne and members of the crew close to him, he cannot deny them, for the artist incorporates all of their characteristics no matter how unrelated to art they may appear to be. The artist must acquire the all-embracing vision. A host of metaphors suggests this complementary conception. The protagonist reaches the Palace of the Peacock, with its panoramic perspective of the savannah, by falling back into the savannah. The Palace of the Peacock is also El Dorado, which Harris describes as "City of Gold, City of God"; it encompasses both material and spiritual riches. The Palace, moreover, has many windows offering an encompassing view of the world below and stands in contrast to Donne's one-windowed prison of the opening chapter. Taken together with the peacock's color spectrum, the many eyes of the peacock's tail, and the harmonious singing that pervades the many palatial rooms, the Palace paradoxically suggests both oneness and multiplicity. Such a perception of the artistic vision offered in this interpretation of *Palace of the Peacock* is not unique; it is found, for example, in the works of Yeats and Blake, whom Harris quotes several times in the novel. The uniqueness of the novel is to be found in the form and setting Harris employs to explore this familiar theme.

The Guyanese hinterland is most evocatively depicted in the novel, though realistic description recedes before the symbolic and allegorical functions of the setting. Although the characters occasionally emerge as living individuals and their conversations have the authentic ring of Guyanese dialect and speech rhythm, they appear primarily not as human figures but as allegorical forms. As a result, the protagonist's conflicts are not dramatized in any particularly credible, realistic situation. (*The Secret Ladder*, the last novel of *The Guyana Quartet*, which describes a similar river journey and a similarly ambivalent, tormented protagonist, provides a slightly more realistic, less allegorical study.)

The Far Journey of Oudin, Harris's second novel, is set in the riparian Abary district of Guyana, which is not too far inland from the Atlantic coast. The setting is as evocatively portrayed as is the Guyanese interior in *Palace of the Peacock*. The inhabitants of this community are East Indian farmers whose forebears came to Guyana as indentured laborers. A few of these farmers have accumulated material wealth and have established a contemporary version of the master-laborer relationship with the less fortunate. *The Far Journey of Oudin* emphasizes the community's greed. It tells of Rajah's conspiring with his cousins to murder their illegitimate half brother, to whom their father left his property. The murderers suffer for their crime: Ram, a powerful, ruthless moneylender, brings about their ruin with the help of Oudin, a drifter, who resembles the murdered half brother. Ram orders Oudin to abduct Rajah's daughter, Beti. Oudin, however, elopes with her. Thirteen years later, when Oudin is dying, Ram seeks to make Oudin and Beti's unborn child his heir.

The narrative in this novel is slightly more substantial than that of *Palace of the Peacock*, but it is similarly submerged beneath Harris's allegorical emphasis. The characters, fluctuating between allegorical and literal functions, do not really come alive. The novel begins with Oudin's death and his vision of the past, which merges with the present and the future. He exists on several levels; he appears, for example, to be the murdered half brother. The novel emphasizes the polarized relationship between Ram, the unscrupulous materialist, and the sensitive, spiritual Oudin, whose unborn child to whom Ram lays claim symbolizes the possibility in the dichotomized community of reintegration—a factor that is underscored by the novel's circular structure and the recurring images of the union of opposites, such as the reference to the marriage of the sun and moon, to the juxtaposition of fire and water, and to the natural cycle of death and rebirth. Oudin, who strives to be an integrated individual, refers to "the dreadful nature in every compassionate alliance one has to break gradually in order to emerge into one's ruling constructive self."

The Whole Armour, the third novel of *The Guyana Quartet*, examines the fragmentation and integration of another Guyanese community, that of the coastal Pomeroon region. While the society of *The Far Journey of Oudin* is disrupted by greedy materialists, whom Harris perceives as the contemporary equivalents of the exploitative colonizers, that of *The Whole Armour* is disturbed by unbridled passion that erupts into violence and murder. Harris does not want to suppress passion, but he believes that it should be counterbalanced by discipline and control. This complementary Dionysian-Apollonian relationship is suggested by a series of betrothal images and particularly by the image of the tiger (the word used for what in the novel is actually a jaguar), which connotes the antithetical but complementary aspects of Blake's tiger.

The plot is difficult to extract because of the virtual inseparability of the actual and the allegorical, the living and the dead, and because of the elusive metaphors, described by Harris as his "fantastication of imagery." The novel, in bare outline, tells of the protagonist Cristo's fleeing the law, having been accused, apparently without justification, of the murder of Sharon's sweetheart. Cristo is sheltered from the law by his mother, Magda, a prostitute, and Abram, who falsely claims to be his father. Cristo and Sharon become lovers and are fugitives together. Eventually they are caught, but they view the future hopefully because of the child Sharon has conceived. Cristo, who is linked with both the tiger and Christ, and the virginal Sharon are set against the passionate older generation. The two constantly yearn for regeneration and perceive themselves as the founders of a new social order. The explicit discussion of this need for a new order has encouraged some critics to see *The Whole Armour* as Harris's most obviously political novel.

The Secret Ladder could be considered a restatement of and a sequel to *Palace of the Peacock*; it has, however, more plausible characterization and straightforward structuring. Like Donne, the protagonist, Fenwick, is in charge of a crew of men who reflect the racial mixture of Guyana. They are on a government hydrographic expedition that is surveying a stretch of the Canje River as the first step in a planned water conservation scheme. Poseidon, the patriarchal head of a primitive community of descendants of runaway slaves, violently resents their intrusion. Fenwick tries, with the help of Bryant, one of his crew, and Catalena, Bryant's mistress, to win him over. There is much misunderstanding and confrontation. In the end, Poseidon is accidentally killed.

Fenwick, like the protagonist of *Palace of the Peacock*, is torn between "imagination and responsibility," between dominating and accommodating. His boat, significantly, is named *Palace of the Peacock*. Evidently, he is aware of the importance of integrating his contrary impulses. He is attempting to live in the world of men with the insight his counterpart, Donne, has gained in thePalace of the Peacock. This attempt leads to inner turmoil and disturbing ambivalence, which the novel underscores with numerous images and metaphors. Fenwick frequently mentions the need to unify the head and the heart. His inner contradiction, like Donne's, is externalized in the relationships among his crew: For example, Weng the hunter is compared with Chiung the hunted; Bryant the thoughtful is juxtaposed with Catalena the emotional. Despite the more conventional plot, characterization, and structure, the novel is clearly Harris's. Its theme is polarization and reconciliation, and it is charged with allegorical and symbolic implications.

Other Guyana novels

Harris's next five novels—*Heartland*, *The Eye of the Scarecrow*, *The Waiting Room*, *Tumatumari*, and *Ascent to Omai*—are also set in Guyana and provide further explorations of community and creativity imperiled by various confrontations and polarizations. In these works, however, Harris places the emphasis on individuals and on deep probing of their consciousness. The protagonists become progressively more internalized. Subtler dichotomies are examined, such as concrete and abstract realities, scientific and mythic truths, fiction reflecting and being reality, and individual and communal aspirations. In *The Waiting Room* and *Tumatumari*, Harris examines for the first time the psyches of female protagonists. He portrays Prudence of *Tumatumari*, for example, as engaged in an imaginative reconstruction of her brutal past, which she metamorphoses into something meaningful to her present. *Ascent to Omai* similarly affirms the possibility of creativity in catastrophe. In these five novels, Harris's audacious experiments with form continue. In *The Eye of the Scarecrow*, which is perhaps the Harris novel that is structurally furthest removed from conventional form, and *The Waiting Room*, he introduces the disjointed diary form.

Middle novels

In his novels published from 1972 to 1982—*Black Marsden*, *Companions of the Day and Night*, *Da Silva da Silva's Cultivated Wilderness and Genesis of the Clowns*, *The Tree of the Sun*, and *The Angel at the Gate*—Harris shifts the emphasis from portraying society's fragmentation, as he did in the early novels, to its possibilities for reintegration. Rebirth and resurrection are common motifs. If the Caribbean's brutal colonial history and its multiracial population provide the ideal context for a heightened consideration of communal disintegration, its "cross-cultural integration" is similarly suited to an exploration of communal integration. These middle novels all feature cross-cultural Caribbean or South American protagonists. In so doing, they are not restrictively regional in scope; they are concerned with the human community at large. This is pointed up by their larger canvases. They are set not simply in the Caribbean and Guyana but in Great Britain, India, and Latin America as well. An increasingly common form of these novels is the employment of narrators as editors and biographers who seek to piece together the protagonists' lives and raise questions about the polarities of art and life and about the literal and representational functions of language itself.

The Carnival Trilogy

The Carnival Trilogy is, after *The Guyana Quartet*, Harris's second great masterwork. Although the three books that compose it do not continue with the same set of characters, they possess common motifs that contribute to a structural unity. *Carnival* is set in London in 1982, though the action stretches back to the town of New Forest in Guyana decades in the past. Everyman Masters, an industrial laborer, who dies in the first chapter of the book, and Jonathan Weyl, a writer, are both Guyanese who have emigrated to Great Britain. Weyl is a generation younger than Masters. This enables Masters to be a surrogate father figure to Weyl and Weyl's guide to the spirit world, conducting him as Vergil conducted Dante in *La divina commedia* (c. 1320; *The Divine Comedy*, 1802).

The killing of the Carnival king by the aggressive

Thomas parallels political upheavals of the twentieth century, in all their grandeur and folly. Weyl's father, Martin, is killed on the day of the Carnival, yet the enactment of the festival keeps his memory alive for his son many years later. Similarly, Amaryllis, the beloved of Weyl, is not just an individual but also an abstract prototype representing several other women in the story: Aunt Alice Bartleby, two women named Jane Fisher, and Aimée, whose name, symbolically, represents love. Masters's descent to the underworld yokes together primitive savagery and modern experience. It provides a crucial act of tutelage not only to Weyl but also to all who live in the modern world. Masters, both ordinary Everyman and Carnival king, encompasses all this experience. He achieves wholeness without self-delusion, a state also represented by the Carnival.

The second book of *The Carnival Trilogy*, *The Infinite Rehearsal*, concentrates memorably around one image: the drowning of a mother, son, and aunt in 1961 a short distance from a South American beach. The most lyrical of the three books, *The Infinite Rehearsal* features a fascinating protagonist, Robin Redbreast Glass. Though he drowns in the book at the age of sixteen, Glass represents all the potential of humanity. Indeed, death is welcome to him, as life is one of the many barriers he tries to transcend. Glass, born in 1945, the year the atomic bombs were dropped, tries to rescue beauty and overcome the horrors of the twentieth century.

There is much that is admirable in his ambition and drive to perfection, but Glass also has liabilities: a naive optimism, of the sort associated with a red-breasted robin, and the fact that, like glass, he is too transparent, his temperament lacking the murky depths of the truly integrated human soul. Appearances by Glass's grandfather, who had written a revisionary treatment of the Faust legend in which Robin is also a character, and the seemingly malevolent Ghost embody the oscillation between dream and reality in Glass's mind. This "infinite rehearsal," which evades any settled definition, helps overcome human aggression and authoritative reality. By the end of the book, the spirit of Robin Redbreast Glass has come to terms with the female, as represented by his cousin Emma, who survives the drama and becomes an archbishop by the year 2025. He has also reconciled with the spirit of death, represented by the Ghost, who ends up redeeming Glass and helping him fulfill his voyage into the future.

The Infinite Rehearsal is a concrete and lyrical novel. *The Four Banks of the River of Space*, however, is far more abstract and discursive. Whereas *The Infinite Rehearsal* is poised on the beach where Glass drowns, in a kind of borderline state between sea and land, *The Four Banks of the River of Space* is set deep within the rain forest of the Guyanese interior. This interior, however, is far from purely physical. Indeed, it represents the totality of the cosmos itself. The main characters in this book are Anselm, an architect and engineer, and Lucius Canaima, a revenge deity. The action begins in 1988; Anselm and Canaima have not met since their youth forty years ago. Anselm's name may allude to the eleventh century Christian writer Anselm of Canterbury, who dealt with the nature of being. Canaima represents the indigenous peoples of South America as well as the entire process of conquest and savagery through history. The river of space transcends time even as it incorporates its terrible, creative beauty. Evil and good change places to a degree, in the manner of Glass and the Ghost in the previous book, as the "good" Anselm is implicated in trends that threaten to destroy the world, and the "evil" Canaima is seen as a spirit of renewal. Like Harris himself, Anselm, in the 1940's, had been a government surveyor among the indigenous Macusi people. Macusi spirituality centers on the waterfall that dominates their territory. The image of the waterfall is converted into the idea of the four banks of the river of space, which all the characters have to traverse to complete their journey toward the future.

The action is complicated by a romantic triangle consisting of Penelope George, modeled on the heroine of Homer's *Odyssey* (c. 725 B.C.E.; English translation, 1614), and her two husbands, Simon and Ross. As is typical of characters in this trilogy, Simon, Ross, and Penelope are all dead in the actual "time" of the novel. The rivalry of Simon and Ross duplicates the antagonism between Canaima and Anselm, who turn out to be complementary, as both evil and good are crucial features of the cosmos. At the end of the book, Anselm and Canaima merge into each other. Anselm becomes genuinely "good," now that he has absorbed the presence and responsibility of evil. The story of Penelope comes to a healing resolution as she brings forth a child, who promises to repair the spiritual and psychological ravages of the past.

Jonestown

In *Jonestown*, Harris takes the event for which Guyana is most known in the outside world, the mass suicide in November, 1978, of the members of the People's Temple cult led by Jim Jones, and links it to a far wider set of associations. Fictionalizing Jim Jones as Jonah Jones, Harris totally invents the rest of his major characters, creating an effect that is the opposite of a journalistic account of the Jonestown massacre. His protagonist, Francisco Bone, is the only survivor of the massacre. He is also heir to the spiritual quest pursued through so many avatars in *The Carnival Trilogy*, as he journeys through past, present, and future in search of a complete understanding of the universe.

The Dark Jester

In *The Dark Jester*, when Harris turns his visionary sense of myth to interrogate a slender moment in Amerindian history when Pizarro, the fifteenth century Spanish conquistador, encountered Atahualpa, the last great Incan king, he avoids the expected polemic that would decry the European/Christian invasion and its barbarity and hypocrisy (Atahualpa, in an attempt to save himself from being burned at the stake, accepts Christianity, but even after his people fill a room full of gold to secure his release, the Peruvian king is nevertheless killed). Rather, Harris engages that historic event through the unsettling medium of a dream: a narrator, known only as Dreamer, conjures a sense of the past, abdicates linear sequence (freely moving about in centuries and even among continents), and resists intrusive commentary on any outrage over the European invasion. Events unfold within a rich symbolic landscape, less a plot than a juxtaposition of dense, freighted imagery (the Bird, the Horse, the Sun, Gold, Fire—the words capitalized to underscore their fabulous dimension), images that suggest the elegiac implications of the irresistible pressure of a vast and mighty culture being eased out of history and into myth.

The prose rewards recitation, Harris drawing on his early grounding in poetry to render the mood of this historic encounter through opulent, even sensuous language. There are few clear narrative moments—generally, the reader follows a dialogue between the conquistador and the Incan king as the gold is brought to the room—but Dreamer, empowered by his contemporary sensibility, recognizes the implications of the events and offers a meditation on the dichotomy of materialism and spirituality. Accompanied by a shadowy figure known only as the Dark Jester, Dreamer opens history into wider dimensions: In the novel's harrowing closing scene, Dreamer encounters along a beach Cortez himself, the very embodiment of the European invasion, on his way, we assume, to begin the grim work of decimating the Aztec empire (within the fluid nonlinearity of the dream, it is in the time before Pizarro). Dreamer has the opportunity to kill Cortez, in essence to interdict the mayhem of colonization; but, of course, he cannot. Nevertheless, Harris refuses to concede to the pull of despair. What intrigues Harris is not the politics of history but rather the construction of it. History cannot be altered, Dreamer cautions—indeed, the Caribbean present is inevitably bound to its colonial past—but history can be reanimated through the interrogation of the pre-Columbian sensibility, with its reverence for the earth and its sense of the spiritual.

History can elevate and lift when it is imbued with the symbolic and the mythic, and that, Harris recognizes, like Blake and Yeats before him, is the especial privilege of the imagination. It alone can regenerate lost cultures through the spell of language and can reanimate through private systems of suggestive symbols the otherwise disturbing record of historic conquest into a visionary argument that extends the promise of immortality within an expansive cosmos that, despite the stubborn argument of the European sensibility, will not accept the limiting parameters of time and place.

The Ghost of Memory

Even without Harris's quiet announcement of his decision to retire after more than four decades of prolific productivity, there is something of a valedictory feel to *The Ghost of Memory*, a kind of summing up that in the work's brevity (barely sixty pages) suggests an urgency to the letting go. Although it opens conventionally, even realistically—a South American man is shot in the back by police, mistaken for a terrorist—the narrative quickly (within a paragraph) gives way to Harris's visionary sensibility: The dead man "falls" through time and into a painting in a gallery that depicts a river journey from the jungle into an Amazonian city. Awakening to his new reality (he is composed of still-wet paint), the ghost/man engages in conversations with other figures in the painting and with visitors to the gallery. He has fallen into a harrowing canvas (titled *Art in the City*) that depicts with apocalyptic Boschian touches of the fabulous and the brutal a disturbing vision of history as a violent and destructive collision between primitive and civilized cultures. The painting thus serves to suggest how art reclaims history, brings such antinomies together through suggestive symbolism, and extends to those victims of such brutality locked in time the regenerative possibility through the agency of the artist. Indeed, the ghost/man morphs into avatars of characters from Greek and Roman myth and Amerindian legend, which transcend the tensions between civilized and primitive, the rational and the subconscious.

The premise becomes less a sustained story and more a philosophical rumination on those questions that have intrigued Harris since his days exploring the Guyanese interior, when he first pondered the implications of a lost culture trying to define a present while struggling with the burden of its complicated history. Here, at the end of his career, Harris clearly pushes toward broader implications, putting the Caribbean postcolonial identity crisis into a wider context. What is History? What is Time? What is the logic of suffering? What is the function of art amid atrocity? Most tellingly, the ghost/man sustains a long (and emotional) discussion with a gallery visitor named Christopher Columbus over a sculpture by Alberto Giacometti. The narrator argues that Giacometti's figure reflects his subconscious ties to a primitive sensibility and that his sculpture creates a vehicle for transcending the stubborn divide between cultures. Columbus, however, is skeptical of such common ground; he embodies the blind arrogance of European imperialism. When the ghost/man suggests that *Art in the City* itself should be developed into a full-dress stage production, that its tableau art should be brought to life, immediate and vivid, Columbus decries the idea and—in a movement freighted with forbidding implications—destroys the painting with a knife.

Harris refuses to concede to such pessimism, however; the novel closes on two minor characters stepping out of the gallery, casting a sweeping glance upward into the night sky, and noting the constellations and their timeless commemoration of myth and legend. That serves as Harris's ultimate celebration of art—like astronomers tracing elaborate pictures in the sky, artists, the ghost figures in contemporary culture, render the forbidding chaos of history into elegant art that transcends time and ultimately death itself.

Victor J. Ramraj; Nicholas Birns
Updated by Joseph Dewey

Other major works

SHORT FICTION: *The Sleepers of Roraima*, 1970; *The Age of the Rainmakers*, 1971.

POETRY: *Fetish*, 1951 (as Kona Waruk); *Eternity to Season*, 1954.

NONFICTION: *Tradition, the Writer, and Society*, 1967; *History, Fable, and Myth in the Caribbean and Guianas*, 1970; *Fossil and Psyche*, 1974; *Explorations: A Selection of Talks and Articles*, 1981; *The Womb of Space: The Cross-Cultural Imagination*, 1983; *The Radical Imagination: Lectures and Talks*, 1992; *Selected Essays of Wilson Harris: The Unfinished Genesis of the Imagination*, 1999.

Bibliography

Adler, Joyce Sparer, ed. *Exploring the Palace of the Peacock: Essays on Wilson Harris*. Kingston: University of West Indies Press, 2003. Collection of essays offers a wide-ranging look at Harris's work, with particular emphasis on *The Guyana Quartet* and its vision of Caribbean identity and the rise and fall of imperialism. Expands on Harris's rejection of realism.

Cribb, Tim. "T. W. Harris, Sworn Surveyor." *Journal of Commonwealth Literature* 28, no. 1 (1993): 33-46. Biographically oriented essay discusses the relevance of Harris's early experience as a surveyor in the Guyanese interior to his fictional oeuvre; especially relevant to *The Four Banks of the River of Space*.

Drake, Sandra. *Wilson Harris and the Modern Tradition: A New Architecture of the World*. Westport, Conn.: Greenwood Press, 1986. Places Harris in the modernist tradition and shows how his fiction constitutes a "Third World modernism," examining four novels—*Palace of the Peacock*, *Tumatumari*, *Ascent to Omai*, and *Genesis of the Clowns*—in this light. Accompanying bibliographical essay provides a valuable survey of the critical response to Harris's work.

Gilkes, Michael, ed. *The Literate Imagination: Essays on the Novels of Wilson Harris*. New York: Macmillan, 1989. Collection of essays, edited by a well-known scholar of Caribbean literature, includes Harris's "Literacy and the Imagination" as well as eleven essays on Wilson's work by international critics.

Maes-Jelinek, Hena. *The Labyrinth of Universality: Wilson Harris's Visionary Art of Fiction*. Atlanta: Rodopi, 2006. One of the most articulate commentators on Harris's work provides exhaustive and compelling readings of all his novels, along with helpful commentary drawn from Harris's nonfiction on his often dense sense of private mythology and symbols.

_______. *Wilson Harris*. Boston: Twayne, 1982. Offers an excellent introduction to Harris's complex body of fiction for the beginning reader of his work. Includes biographical materials and traces the progress of Harris's fiction through detailed analyses of theme and technique. Supplemented with a chronology and extensive primary and secondary bibliographies.

Review of Contemporary Fiction 17, no. 2 (Summer, 1997). Special issue devoted to Harris's writing contains essays and interviews by Harris and literary peers such as Zulfikar Ghose and Kathleen Raine, as well as a selection of critical essays by international contributors, ranging from the analytical to the theoretical.

Riach, Alan, and Mark Williams. "Reading Wilson Harris." In *Wilson Harris: The Uncompromising Imagination*, edited by Hena Maes-Jelinek. Sydney: Dangaroo Press, 1991. Two New Zealand critics provide one of the most insightful practical guides to Harris's work.

Sharrad, Paul. "The Art of Memory and the Liberation of History: Wilson Harris's Witnessing of Time." *Journal of Commonwealth Literature* 27, no. 1 (1992): 110-127. A well-known commentator reflects on whether Harris is a mythical or historical novelist.

Webb, Barbara J. *Myth and History in Caribbean Fiction: Alejo Carpentier, Wilson Harris, and Édouard Glissant*. Amherst: University of Massachusetts Press, 1992. Presents an important reading of Harris within a context of postcolonial Caribbean writing and its grappling with the burden of history and its sense of pre-Columbian mythology.

JIM HARRISON

Born: Grayling, Michigan; December 11, 1937
Also known as: James Thomas Harrison

Principal long fiction

Wolf: A False Memoir, 1971
A Good Day to Die, 1973
Farmer, 1976
Legends of the Fall, 1979 (collection of three novellas: *Revenge*, *The Man Who Gave Up His Name*, and *Legends of the Fall*)
Warlock, 1981
Sundog: The Story of an American Foreman, 1984
Dalva, 1988
The Woman Lit by Fireflies, 1990 (collection of three novellas: *Brown Dog*, *Sunset Limited*, and *The Woman Lit by Fireflies*)
Julip, 1994 (collection of three novellas: *Julip*, *The Seven Ounce Man*, and *The Beige Dolorosa*)
The Road Home, 1998
The Beast God Forgot to Invent, 2000 (collection of three novellas: *The Beast God Forgot to Invent*, *Westward Ho*, and *Forgot to Go to Spain*)
True North, 2004
The Summer He Didn't Die, 2005 (collection of three novellas: *The Summer He Didn't Die*, *Republican Wives*, and *Tracking*)

Returning to Earth, 2007
The English Major, 2008

Other literary forms

To appreciate fully the lyrical voice that dominates Jim Harrison's best novels, it is helpful to bear in mind that he began his career as a poet. His first two volumes of poetry, *Plain Song* (1965), written under the name James Harrison, and *Locations* (1968), received very little attention, and the reviews were mixed. With the publication of *Outlyer and Ghazals* (1971), critics began to give Harrison his due, but his next two volumes, *Letters to Yesenin* (1973) and *Returning to Earth* (1977), both issued by small publishing houses, were again overlooked, even after they were reissued in a single volume in 1979. *Selected and New Poems: 1961-1981* (1982), a volume that included the best of his previous work, demonstrated Harrison's range and complexity and established his as a major voice in American poetry. His collection *The Theory and Practice of Rivers: Poems* (1985) only served to demonstrate more fully both his breadth of interests and his mastery of the poetic form. *The Shape of the Journey: New and Collected Poems* (1998) restores to print lyrics and protest poems of *Plain Song*, the effusive *Letters to Yesenin*, and the Zen-inspired *After Ikkyu, and Other Poems* (1996).

In addition to novels and poetry, Harrison has published numerous essays, predominantly in *Sports Illustrated* and *Esquire*. In many of his essays, Harrison emerges as an amateur naturalist who denounces those who violate fish and game laws, sings the praises of seasoned guides and ardent canoe racers, and laments the passing of the wilderness in the face of urban development. Harrison has also published some food-related nonfiction, including *The Raw and the Cooked: Adventures of a Roving Gourmand* (2001), and the memoir *Off to the Side* (2002).

Achievements

Jim Harrison, a venturesome and talented writer, proved himself an able poet, novelist, and journalist by revitalizing the territories and boundaries explored by others. Along with Nebraska, the territory of Ted Kooser and Willa Cather, both northern Michigan and Key West, the Hemingway provinces, are re-created in Harrison's work. Also present are the subterranean worlds and the connecting roads that the Beats had earmarked, the relatively unsullied outback celebrated by Edward Abbey and Theodore Roethke, and the predominantly masculine worlds explored by writers such as Harrison's friend and fellow hunter Thomas McGuane and Larry McMurtry.

However, it was Denise Levertov who helped Harrison publish his first book of poetry, *Plain Song*. It was not long after that when he received the first of three grants from the National Endowment for the Arts in 1967 and a Guggenheim Fellowship in 1969. These helped him to settle down in the Leelenau Peninsula in northern Michigan and to focus on poetry and finally fiction in the early 1970's. After steadily developing a literary following over two decades, and having his work published in twenty-seven languages, in 1999 Harrison was a finalist for the Los Angeles Times Book Prize, and he was awarded the *Colorado Review*'s Evil Companions Award, along with Michigan State University's College of Arts and Letters Distinguished Alumni Award. In 2000, he received the Spirit of the West Literary Achievement Award and the Michigan State University Distinguished Alumni Award, and in 2007, he was elected to the American Academy of Arts and Letters.

Harrison's greatest achievement, however, might be the fact that he has never changed his approach to theme, style, setting, and characterization to suit anyone but himself, his friends, and his readers. He has held fast to his vision of art as nature, all as real and true as a birch tree or brown trout, and let the scholars and journalists come to him. In fact, the same things for which reviewers criticized him in his first novel, *Wolf*, were the things that reviewers applauded about his 2007 novel *Returning to Earth*. By refusing to limit himself to a single genre and by attending to "audible things, things moving at noon in full raw light," Harrison appeals to a diversified audience and portrays an integrated vision that reflects the subtler nuances of the physical and natural world. While his references are often esoteric, he is a masterful storyteller who easily blends primitive and naturalistic images with arcane literary allusions. The reader is thus able to hear and feel simultaneously the meaning and motion of objects and experiences.

Jim Harrison. (Library of Congress)

BIOGRAPHY

James Thomas Harrison was born December 11, 1937, in Grayling, Michigan; soon after his birth, his family moved to Reed City and then to Haslett, near the Michigan State University (MSU) campus, when Harrison was twelve. While he has repeatedly stated that his childhood was unremarkable, he clearly assimilated the spirit of the land and people found in northern Michigan and was deeply affected by the emotional bonds that held his family together. Perhaps because so much of this land has been ravaged by development, northern Michigan, and certainly its Upper Peninsula, has come to constitute Harrison's version of William Faulkner's fictional Yoknapatawpha County, peopled by figures drawn from his German and Swedish ancestral lines along with the Finns and Chippewa who populate the Upper Peninsula.

After a short period of enrollment at MSU in 1956, Harrison dropped out. Convinced that "you couldn't be an artist in Michigan," he made a number of treks to New York City, San Francisco, and Boston in search of the "right setting" in which to write; not surprisingly, these forays, described in *Wolf*, were unsuccessful. Inevitably, he returned to MSU; he received his B.A. in English in 1960, enrolled in graduate school, and made two key lifelong friendships with writers Thomas McGuane and Dan Gerber. McGuane persuaded Harrison to diversify his work by pursuing long fiction. McGuane also connected him with actor Jack Nicholson, who funded Harrison's writing, after his grant money was spent, in 1978-1979. It was in 1979, with the very successful publication of *Legends of the Fall*, that Harrison began to make a living on his writing alone. Beginning in 1968, Gerber and Harrison coedited the literary journal *Sumac*, in which they published a number of successful poets, such as Diane Wakoski, Charles Simic, Hayden Carruth, Barbara Drake, Adrienne Rich, Gary Snyder, Galway Kinnell, Carl Rokosi, and Denise Levertov.

Tragedy struck Harrison early in life, when he lost sight in one eye after being cut with a broken laboratory beaker. Later, his fourteen-year-old niece died. It was not until after his father and sister were killed in a head-on automobile collision in 1962 that he began to write in earnest. These personal losses, all the greater because they were unexpected, inform several of his novels and poems.

As the allusions that pepper Harrison's writing make clear, he became a prodigious reader early on. Not surprisingly, his graduate work was in comparative literature, and he has called himself an "internationalist" in terms of his literary tastes and influences. An outspoken and somewhat outrageous man, Harrison experienced bouts with severe depression that drove him periodically to the woods of Michigan, where he would write until exhausted, then play, hunt, and wander the beloved fields near his farmhouse near Lake Leelenau, where he lived from 1968 to 2002. In time this setting did not provide enough seclusion, so he purchased a modest cabin on the coast of Lake Superior; this served as a writing retreat until he sold it in 2004, when he finally gave up

Michigan life to spend his time between Livingston, Montana, and Patagonia, Arizona.

An avid outdoorsman, Harrison adopted fishing as a counterweight to his time devoted to writing, being committed to a code of ethics and a way of life that discourage superfluous self-indulgence and encourage husbanding of resources. This earthy, well-read man is known for shunning the literary associations so expected of famed authors, preferring instead a simpler existence of sharing the backwoods with friends when not engaged in verse.

ANALYSIS

What is perhaps most striking about Jim Harrison's novels is the range of emotions they encompass. While in his early fiction he assumes a masculine point of view and revels in violence and debauchery, he is able to capture the romantic spirit that energizes his protagonists. He also avoids the bathetic trap that undermines the artistry of so many novels written from an aggressively male perspective. His central characters, in works such as *Brown Dog*, *Legends of the Fall*, and *Wolf*, though often wantonly callous in their attitudes toward women, are propelled by a youthful wanderlust and are always extremely affable. In his later novels, some of his characters display a type of compassion, love, and generosity that provide readers with a sense of hope in the human spirit. While many writers have described the purpose of literature as exploring the dark side of the human condition, Harrison attempts to provide ways to escape this darkness. There is always a solution in his work if the reader cares to recognize it, and it often parallels the Buddhist path to Nirvana, the Chinese Dao, and the Gospels of the New Testament.

In his novels, Harrison often routinely suspends the narrative sequence and deletes causal explanation. In this way, he constructs a seamless web and traps reader and character alike in a world inhabited by legendary figures who are attuned to primeval nuances and thrive on epic adventure. His penchant for the episodic is complemented by his metaphorical language and lyric sensibilities, which enhance his ability to shift scenes rapidly without sacrificing artistic control or obscuring the qualitative aspects of his various milieus.

Harrison is willing to tackle topics that some other artists may consider too pedestrian. He is willing to experiment and to risk the wrath of his critics. While in terms of his allusions he is very much an artist's artist, he is also very much a people's artist—willing to confront the dilemmas of aging that confront us all and make us look ridiculous on more than one occasion. More important, Harrison is capable of conveying a sense of loss and dispossession as it relates to the wilderness. What saves this sense from overwhelming his writing is his capacity for wonder and his ability to capture the mystery resident in the land and to imagine in life legendary figures whose exploits make life bearable. If one accepts Waldo Frank's definition of a mystic as being one "who *knows* by immediate experience the organic continuity between himself and the cosmos," then Harrison is a mystic. He is a superlative storyteller who is attuned to the rhythms of the earth and a poet whose lyrical voice can be heard on every page.

WOLF

By giving *Wolf* the subtitle *A False Memoir*, Harrison properly alerts the reader to the poetic license that he has taken in reconstructing his biography. Much of what is included is factual, but he has embellished it and transformed it into art. The work is "false" in that it merges time and place in such a way as to convey a gestalt of experiences rather than a sequence of events. It is also "false" because he succumbs to his "constant urge to reorder memory" and indulges himself in "all those oblique forms of mental narcissism." What results is a compelling odyssey of Swanson's impetuous flirtation with decadence and debauchery.

In his relatively obtuse author's note, Harrison provides some biographical data to flesh out the Swanson persona. Also included is an admission that the romance he is about to unfold is somewhat of a self-indulgence that, like his desire to see a wolf in broad daylight, is central to no one but himself. Having thus offered his apologia, he proceeds to enmesh the reader in the tangles of people and places that have affected his narrator, Swanson. When Swanson is introduced, he is on a week-long camping trip in northern Michigan's Huron Mountains. In the course of the novel, he is alternately lost in the woods and lost in his own mental mires as he reflects on the "unbearably convulsive" life he had led between 1956 and 1960.

Swanson's wilderness excursions constitute a correlative for his sallies into the mainstream. When he is in the woods, his hikes produce a configuration resembling a series of concentric circles; he is guided largely by his instincts and his familiarity with certain reference points. Similarly, his treks to Boston, New York City, and San Francisco have a cyclical cadence, and his itineraries are dictated more by his primal emotions than by conscious planning. In both environments, he assumes the stance of a drifter who is searching, against the odds, to discover an ordering principle around which to unscramble his conflicting longings.

A careful reading of *Wolf* reveals that the tension between the freewheeling and nostalgic selves energizes the entire book. By coming to the woods, Swanson is attempting somehow to resolve the dualistic longings that have colored his first thirty-three years, to "weigh the mental scar tissue" acquired during his various rites of passage. While in the woods, he is constantly recalling the head-on crash that killed both his father and his sister; the pain of this memory is undisguised and serves as a counterweight to the bravado with which he depicts his adventuring.

Appropriately, the dominant chord in *Wolf*, as in most of Harrison's work, is a sense of dispossession and loss. Throughout the book, he emphasizes the ways in which greed, technology, and stupidity have led to the despoliation of the wilderness and endangered not only species but ways of life as well. Noting that the "continent was becoming Europe in my own lifetime," Swanson recognizes that the "merest smell of profit would lead us to gut any beauty left." It is this understanding that leads him to depict governments as "azoological beasts," to conceive of the history of the United States in terms of rapine and slaughter, and to indulge himself in fantasies of depredation that come to fruition in *A Good Day to Die*.

When one reaches the end of the novel, however, one senses that Swanson has resolved very little. During his week in the woods, he has not only failed to see the wolf but also failed to illuminate a route "out of the riddle that only leads to another"; even as he labels his urban adventures "small and brutally stupid voyages" and accepts the fact that he longs for the permanence once provided by the remote family homesteads, he acknowledges that he will continue to drift, to "live the life of an animal" and to "transmute my infancies, plural because I always repeat never conquer, a circle rather than a coil or spiral."

A Good Day to Die

A Good Day to Die, as William Crawford Wood observes, constitutes the second part of the song begun in *Wolf*. The novel, which takes its title from a Nez Perce Indian saying regarding war, chronicles the journey of the nameless narrator (who bears a marked resemblance to Swanson) from Key West to northern Arizona and on to Orofino, Idaho. As in *Wolf*, Harrison relies heavily on flashbacks and melds the narrator's memories with ongoing events; the novel is then less a correspondence between two periods than the route by which the narrator comes to accept life's capriciousness as a matter of course.

The nascent urge to avenge nature present in *Wolf* comes to fruition in *A Good Day to Die*. While the narrator, in retreat from his domestic woes, is vacationing and fishing in Key West, he is befriended by Tim, a Vietnam War veteran whose philosophy of life is fatalistic and whose lifestyle is hedonistic. In the midst of an intoxicating evening, the two formulate a vague plan to go west and save the Grand Canyon from damnation. En route, they stop in Valdosta, Georgia, to pick up Sylvia, Tim's childhood sweetheart, who is the epitome of idealized womanhood—beautiful, innocent, and vulnerable—and who, in the course of the journey, unwittingly evokes the basest emotions and reactions from both of her cohorts.

The improbability that such a threesome could long endure is mitigated by Harrison's ability to capture the conflicting urges and needs of all three. While Sylvia may be too homey to be entirely credible, she does assume a very real presence. Throughout the novel, she functions as a counterweight to her companions and serves to underscore the risks inherent in not controlling one's romanticism. While all three have a tendency to delude themselves, she seems the most incapable of grounding herself and perceiving her situation clearly.

Farmer

In *Farmer*, Harrison frees himself from his tendency to write false memoirs in lieu of novels. There are passing references to a nephew who resembles the author, but these serve to underscore Harrison's familiarity with the people and the milieu he is depicting. The portraits are especially sharp and clear in the cases of Joseph, a forty-three-year-old farmer and schoolteacher, and Dr. Evans, a seventy-three-year-old country physician. Equally crystalline is Harrison's portrayal of the northern Michigan environs in which Joseph's long overdue "coming-of-age" occurs.

Against the advice of his twin sister, Arlice, and his best friend, Orin, Joseph has remained on the family homestead in northern Michigan "not wanting to expose himself to the possible cruelties of a new life." Crippled in a farm accident at the age of eight, he has used various pretexts to avoid travel; he has lived through books rather than opening himself to firsthand experience. While his reading has kept him abreast of events in the world, it has done little to sate his hunger for a fuller existence. In fact, his preference for books dealing with the ocean, marine biology, distant wars, and the Orient has contributed to his growing dissatisfaction; he longs to visit the ocean, to partake more fully of the life about which he has only read and dreamed.

Against this backdrop Harrison develops a strain that is present in both of his previous novels: the counterpointing of characters. In this case, the restrained but steadfast Rosealee is set in contrast to the urbanized and impetuous Catherine. Rosealee and Joseph, both reared in the provincial backwaters, have been about to be married for approximately six years. Joseph, who has made love to only a few women in his lifetime, impulsively enters into an affair with Catherine, his seventeen-year-old student, who is attractive, experienced, and willing.

Structurally, the novel moves from June, 1956, back to the events that transpired between October, 1955, and the following June. The affair begins as a self-indulgence, but Joseph becomes increasingly light-headed and childlike, reveling in a swell of sensations and previously unknown emotions; he becomes embroiled in the kind of sexual morass that he had previously associated with the fictional worlds of Henry Miller and D. H. Lawrence. Only in retrospect does he understand the risks he has taken in order to free himself from his spiritual torpor; he has nearly destroyed Rosealee's love.

In the hands of a lesser writer, the story that Harrison unfolds could quickly become melodrama, the tone maudlin. That it does not is a measure of Harrison's talent. *Farmer*, far from lacking ironic distance, as some critics have charged, constitutes a parody of the Romantic novel; throughout the book, Harrison burlesques Joseph's inability to attain "a peace that refused to arrive" and with mock seriousness describes self-pity as "an emotion [Joseph] had never allowed himself." Using Dr. Evans as a foil, Harrison unearths Joseph's buried resentments and fears and concludes the novel in such a way as to confirm the doctor's earlier statement that Catherine "is not even a person yet" and that the dallying has simply served as a diversion for both of them. The fact that Joseph cannot come firmly to this conclusion on his own clearly distinguishes him from the protagonists in *Legends of the Fall*.

LEGENDS OF THE FALL

Legends of the Fall, a collection of three novellas, confirms Harrison's fascination with those elemental and primal emotions that defy logic, are atavistic, and propel one into the "nether reaches of human activity" despite the attendant risks. Cochran in *Revenge*, Nordstrom in *The Man Who Gave up His Name*, and Tristan in *Legends of the Fall* operate in defiance of consensual reality; each builds his own fate, guided more by inner compulsions and a taste for the quintessential mystery of existence than by rational planning.

All three of the main characters are blessed with "supernatural constitutions" and a wariness that allows them to survive against the odds and to perform feats of strength and cunning. Running like a chord through all three of these novellas is Harrison's sense of the gratuitousness of any life plan, his belief that events are "utterly wayward, owning all the design of water in the deepest and furthest reaches of the Pacific." There are countless chance meetings and abrupt turns of plot and any number of catalytic conversions. Whereas in longer works such confluences might strain readers' ability to suspend disbelief, in these novellas one is swept along and becomes a willing coconspirator.

Revenge is, in some respects, the weakest of the three pieces because the reader is asked to believe that Cochran, who spent twenty years in the Navy as a fighter pilot, is so transported by his affair with Miryea that he is blind to the warnings issued by her husband, whose nickname, Tibey, means shark. In the service, Cochran had earned a reputation for being "enviably crazier and bolder than anyone else," but he had also maintained the instinctual mindfulness of the Japanese samurai, insisting on understanding "as completely as possible where he was and why." Once he meets Miryea, however, his circumspection is superseded by his romanticism and his "visionary energy." He conceives of her in terms of an Amedeo Modigliani painting, the quintessence of female beauty and charm; he is plummeted into a "love trance" that "ineluctably peels back his senses." Failing to comprehend the meaning of Tibey's gift of a one-way ticket to Madrid and seven thousand dollars, Cochran sets out heedlessly for a weekend tryst in Agua Prieta, where he and Miryea are beaten unmercifully by Tibey and his henchmen.

Opening with a visage of the badly wounded Cochran lying in the desert, Harrison neatly discounts the pertinence of biographical data and summarily explains how Cochran arrived at his unenviable state. The focus of *Revenge* then comes squarely to rest on Cochran's attempts to avenge himself and recover Miryea. Despite the novella's sparsity, the reader is given sufficient information to comprehend the separate agonies that Cochran, Miryea, and Tibey are experiencing and to understand the emotional flux that resulted in the die being "cast so deeply in blood that none of them would be forgiven by their memories."

The events that transpire, a mix of the comic and the deadly serious, come to a head when Miryea, succumbing to her own agony, becomes comatose—a development that allows Cochran to discover her whereabouts. The denouement follows quickly; Cochran and Tibey journey together to perform what amounts to a deathwatch. The epilogue is deftly understated so as to capture the enormity of Cochran's loss—he mechanically digs a grave "with terrible energy, methodical, inevitable"—and the meaning of the Sicilian adage "Revenge is a dish better served cold" becomes clear and indisputable.

Harrison's ability to write economic and yet sufficiently comprehensive novellas is more fully realized in *The Man Who Gave up His Name*. While again Harrison provides minimal biographical data to explain how Nordstrom, once a prominent Standard Oil executive, has come to be a cook in a modest restaurant in Islamorada, Florida, he focuses the work in such a way as to make Nordstrom's conversion convincing and compelling. Nordstrom, like Joseph in *Farmer*, gradually awakens to his lassitude and, unlike Joseph, decides to do something positive to change his life and to get back in touch with the elemental pleasures that had sustained him when he was growing up in Reinlander, Wisconsin. What enables Nordstrom to make the transition is the fact that he has retained a healthy capacity for wonder. The novella opens with the image of Nordstrom dancing alone so as to recapture the metaphysical edginess that his years of success have denied him. Harrison then provides an overview of the pivotal experiences that have left Nordstrom dissatisfied with himself "for so perfectly living out all of his mediocre assumptions about life." In the course of two short chapters, Harrison introduces Laura, Nordstrom's former wife, and their daughter Sonia, who, when she was sixteen, had jolted Nordstrom out of his lethargy with the observation that he and Laura were both "cold fish." This observation prompted Nordstrom to resign his Standard Oil job and take a less demanding job as vice president of a large book wholesaler and to seek fulfillment through any number of expensive purchases and avocations.

Nordstrom's quest for the "volume and intensity" that had been lacking in his corporate existence is accelerated when his father unexpectedly passes away in October of 1977. As he is grappling with his own sense of loss and "the unthinkable fact of death," he is compelled to question why he has conformed to all the normative expectations that have so little to do with the essence of life. To the amazement and horror of friends and family, he resigns his position and tries to give his money away, even making a contribution of twenty-five thousand dollars to the National Audubon Society, "though he had no special fascination for birds." At the behest of his broker and his ex-wife, he sees a psychiatrist, and it becomes clear that he has exchanged the inessential insanities fostered by the American Dream for the essential insanities that will allow him to free himself from stasis and fulfill personal desires.

The defiance of social expectations that lies at the heart of Nordstrom's transition is even more central to an understanding of Tristan, the main character in *Legends of the Fall*. Unlike Nordstrom, however, Tristan has never paid obeisance to anyone. Having abandoned any sense of cosmic justice at the age of twelve, Tristan has steadfastly made his own rules and run his life according to personal design. He emerges as a legendary voyager, propelled by a seemingly genetic compulsion to wander; spiritually he is the direct descendant of his grandfather, who at the age of eighty-four is still engaged in high-seas adventuring. Like Cochran and Nordstrom, Tristan has chosen to "build his own fate with gestures so personal that no one in the family ever knew what was on his seemingly thankless mind." Accordingly, Tristan is fated to live out certain inevitabilities.

Legends of the Fall is an episodic saga with perimeters that are staggering in their breadth. In the course of eighty-one pages, Harrison manages to imagine into being a multigenerational extended family, recount several complete cycles of events, and examine the ramifications of these sequences as they affect each member. The action spans several decades and several continents, and it is a measure of Harrison's mastery that he can cover this range without sacrificing context or character delineation.

The tale opens in 1914 with the departure of Tristan and his brothers, Alfred and Samuel, from the family homestead in Choteau, Montana; accompanied by One Stab, they travel to Canada to enlist in the war effort. Using several complementary techniques, Harrison economically contrasts the personalities of the three brothers; it quickly becomes clear that Tristan and Alfred are polar opposites and that Samuel, a romantic naturalist in the tradition of Louis Agassiz, is fated to die in World War I.

Just how opposed Tristan and Alfred are becomes a central thread in the novella. After Samuel is killed, Harrison makes a point of underlining the grief and guilt experienced by Tristan and Ludlow, their father; Alfred's response is virtually nonexistent, since "as a child of consensual reality" he alone escaped feelings of guilt. Equally important for understanding the distance between the two is that Tristan's career moves him from the status of horse wrangler to outlaw, while Alfred goes through all the "proper" channels, beginning as an officer and ending as a U.S. senator. Finally, the response of Susannah, who is first married to Tristan and then to Alfred, is telling; her breakdown and ultimate suicide are responses, in part, to the impossibility of ever regaining Tristan's love.

The "legends" that constitute the heart of the novella are Tristan's, but the dominating spirit is One Stab's "Cheyenne sense of fatality." Samuel's death is the first turning point, and, while Ludlow is consumed by his own powerlessness, Tristan is compelled to act. That Samuel's death was the product of the Germans' use of mustard gas serves not only to justify Tristan's revenge—scalping several German soldiers—but also to convey Harrison's antipathy for the grotesqueries justified in the name of modernization.

Tristan's legendary status is enhanced by his joining and then succeeding his grandfather as the pilot of a schooner that traffics in munitions, ivory, and drugs. Rather than dwelling on the specifics of the seven years that Tristan spends at sea, Harrison merely provides a glimpse of the first year and an outline of the next six, noting that the substance of these years is known only to Tristan and his crew. The next leg of Tristan's journey is also neatly understated. It begins when he returns home, "still sunblasted, limping, unconsoled and looking at the world with the world's coldest eye." It soon becomes evident, however, that the wounds that the sea could not assuage are virtually washed away by his marriage to Two, the half-American Indian daughter of Ludlow's foreman, Decker. The seven-year grace period that Tristan experiences is elliptically treated because "there is little to tell of happiness"; Harrison quickly shifts to the coup de grâce that kills Two and leaves Tristan inconsolable, "howling occasionally in a language not known on earth."

With a growing realization that he could never even the score with the world, that his losses have far exceeded his ability to avenge the capriciousness of either Samuel or Two's death, Tristan nevertheless becomes embroiled in a final sequence of death-defying events. Again the denouement is quick, but it involves an unexpected turn as Ludlow assumes the active role. As in the other novellas, the epilogue adds a sense of completeness and juxtaposes the modernized ranch owned by Alfred's heirs with the family graveyard in the canyon where they once had found "the horns of the full curl ram." It comes as no surprise that, "always alone, apart, somehow solitary, Tristan is buried up in Alberta." So ends the legend.

WARLOCK

In his 1981 novel *Warlock*, Harrison melds the tone and techniques of the "false memoir" with those associated with the genre of detective fiction; what initially appears to be a marked unevenness in the pacing of the book is a direct result of this unconventional wedding. The first part of the novel contains minimal action and is used primarily to develop the central characters; the second and third parts, on the other hand, are packed with action and abrupt turns of plot. What unifies the work is Harrison's adept use of several comic devices, including a great deal of what Sigmund Freud called "harmless" wit and humor.

When he is introduced, Warlock, at the age of forty-two, has recently lost his well-paid position as a foundation executive and expends much of his time in self-indulgent reverie and experiments in creative cookery. He is a Keatsian romantic who began his career as an artist "on the tracks of the great Gauguin," finds resonance in the nobility and idealism of works such as Boris Pasternak's *Doctor Zhivago* (1957) and Miguel de Cervantes' *Don Quixote de la Mancha* (1605, 1615), and spends countless hours dreaming of a new beginning. He and Diana have moved north to Michigan's Lake Leelanau Peninsula to maintain "the illusion that one lived in a fairy tale, and everything would work out," a motive that makes him an unlikely candidate for top-secret sleuthing.

Diana, on the other hand, appears to be relatively stable, with a nature almost antithetical to Warlock's. It becomes clear, however, that she is not really any more able to decode the enigmas of reality than he. Although she is repeatedly depicted as a pragmatist, this trait is counterbalanced by her affinity for Asian mysticism and her infatuation with genius. While she is an ardent feminist and an excellent surgical nurse, she is equally drawn to the charades that animate their sexual life and constitute a variant of the living theater in which Warlock later becomes the unwitting star.

It is the dynamic tension between Diana and Warlock that leads him to accept a position as a troubleshooter for Diana's associate, Dr. Rabun; while both acknowledge that Rabun is an eccentric, neither knows the extent of his idiosyncrasies. From the onset, Rabun lets it be known that he does not like to reveal all that he knows; it is his very elusive nature that energizes the last two parts of the novel. How little either Diana or Warlock knows about him becomes clear only after both have been sufficiently beguiled to prostitute themselves and do his bidding.

The initial meeting between Warlock and Rabun and its immediate aftermath resemble slapstick comedy. In addition to the absurdist context into which Harrison implants their clandestine meeting, there is the brusque repartee and the importance each attaches to the inessentials. The contents of a briefcase that Rabun entrusts to Warlock are telling; in addition to two folders outlining Rabun's holdings, there are copies of *Modern Investigative Techniques*, a guide to tax law regulations, and a sensationalized, paperback best seller on business crime. Warlock is given two days to study the material and write a brief reaction to it. Warlock's behavior is no less comic; he arrives home and promptly secretes the briefcase in the refrigerator for safekeeping and deludes himself with grandiose dreams that his life is beginning to merge "with a larger scheme of affairs," a truth that, unknown to him, constitutes a pithy double entendre.

Warlock's father, a top detective in Minneapolis, tries to warn his son away from the position with Rabun and, failing at that, offers a good deal of advice and assistance. Their conversations are peppered throughout and serve to infuse the novel with a droll midwestern humor and to underline Warlock's comic naïveté. Warlock's unpreparedness and vulnerability quickly become a dominant chord; while he conceives of himself as one of the "knights of the surrealistic age," the author makes it clear that, as a knight-errant, he lacks the purity of motive that spurred Don Quixote and the equivalent of a Sancho Panza. Instead, he has only his most unfaithful dog, Hudley, as his "Rozinante though without saddle or snaffle."

Part 2 opens with an image of Warlock setting north on his first mission, completely undaunted despite the fact that he is en route to walk a two-thousand-acre area in the Upper Peninsula in search of lumber poachers. While he has the appropriate sense of adventure for the mission he undertakes, his idealism repeatedly blinds him to clues that should be obvious to the most amateur sleuth. During the third part of the novel, Warlock abruptly discovers that reality is far more evanescent than even the most fleeting of dreams. Sent to Florida to "get the goods" on Rabun's estranged wife and his ostensibly homosexual son, who appear to be cheating

Rabun out of millions of dollars, and on a society dame who has filed a seemingly outrageous suit against Rabun for injuries incurred when one of his health spa machines went wild, Warlock finds himself in a veritable house of mirrors.

The events that transpire during his Florida sally are unexpected and outrageously comedic. Again, Harrison relies on "harmless" humor and evokes compassion for the hapless hero. As a result of Warlock's adventures, Harrison abruptly turns the tables and destroys his preconceptions by unmasking Rabun as a perverted swindler and forcing Warlock to the realization that he has been "played for the fool" by almost everyone, including the charmed Diana.

After recovering a modicum of equilibrium, Warlock takes the offensive; reading only children's books, "to keep his mind cruel and simple," he launches a counterattack that is simultaneously programmatic and impulsive, the former aspects resulting from the work of his father and the latter from Warlock's own primal energies. There is a good deal of mock-heroic action on Warlock's part, but in the end, Rabun is brought to justice and Warlock and Diana are reunited. Like his spiritual heir who returns to La Mancha after having been bested by the Knight of the White Moon, Warlock rejects a job offer to track down a Moonie and returns to his pursuit of Pan.

While *Warlock* is not a "representative" novel, it contains many of the elements that unify Harrison's oeuvre. Warlock, like Swanson in *Wolf* and Joseph in *Farmer*, is a romantic and a dreamer; he is a man ruled by elemental desires who repeatedly becomes embroiled in ill-conceived liaisons and who "belongs" in northern Michigan despite the fact that he has a habit of getting lost in the woods. All of Harrison's central characters seem to have a "capsulated longing for a pre-Adamic earth" and a nostalgia for the unsullied woodlands of their childhoods.

Sundog

With the publication of *Sundog*, Harrison returned to his technique of employing the almost all-too-present narrator. The novel hopscotches between revealing the life of Robert Corvus Strang and chronicling the misadventures of the narrator, who bears a strong resemblance to the persona Harrison created in his earlier works.

The narrator meets Strang during what he describes as a "long voyage back toward Earth," a voyage that would put him in touch with the quintessential American. Strang pursued the American Dream only to be crippled in a fall down a three-hundred-foot dam. His experiences, no less than his persistent refusal to accept defeat, make Strang worth knowing. He is, as Harrison describes him, "a man totally free of the bondage of the appropriate."

It becomes clear that Strang and the narrator are kindred spirits—two sides of a single being. Both have more than average appreciation and respect for the forces of nature, even if the narrator is far less willing to plunge heart, soul, and body into its incomprehensible eddy. Both have unbounded passions and lusts, even if the narrator seems less in control of his anima or animus than Strang and more prone to succumb to melancholy, confusion, and despair. Both harbor a deep need to make sense of their own biographies and to plumb the depths of forgotten events that have unmistakably marked their personalities and approaches toward life. The hint of a biographical connection only strengthens their correspondences.

Robert Corvus Strang, as the reader comes to know him, is a man who has been involved on an international scale, building bridges, dams, and irrigation systems since his debut involvement in the construction of the Mackinac Bridge, despite the fact that he developed epilepsy after he was struck by lightning at the age of seven. His has been a life influenced by the polar personalities of his father, who traveled the revival circuit, and his older brother, Karl, who viewed truth as largely situational. His understanding of mechanical and electrical principles is balanced by his understanding of people, most of whom suffer, in his estimation, "because they live without energy" and can accomplish nothing. Strang, on the other hand, even as he attempts to recover from the side effects of a local remedy for his epilepsy, lives with great energy and maintains his commitment to regain his health and resume his career as a contractor on an upcoming project in New Guinea.

His self-imposed cure requires him to regress to a preadolescent state so as to "repattern his brain and body," the physical corollary to what the narrator asks him to do on a more personal and emotional level. At the novel's conclusion, Strang's attempts to begin again can be seen both as a therapeutic renewal process and as an exorcism through which he conquers the artificial barriers imposed by both modern medicine and those who profess to care for him.

Among the personal dramas of Strang's early life and his current battles, Harrison interweaves a sense of wonder that also serves as a leitmotif in each of his earlier works, again claiming the Upper Peninsula as his own. Against this setting, Harrison offers counterpoints of urban violence, corporate greed and venality, and the unbridled insensitivity and martyrdom of missionaries. The novel's ambiguous denouement only serves to underline Harrison's conviction that life resembles a "crèchelike tableau, a series of three-dimensional photographs of the dominant scenes, the bitterest griefs and the accomplishments." Harrison captures these images in his portrayal of Strang, whose life is keynoted by "love, work, and death . . . held together by wholeness, harmony and radiance."

Dalva

Despite its multiple plot lines, *Dalva* is also held together by a wholeness and a humanitarian spirit. The novel, in some ways, is Harrison's most ambitious undertaking. It is ambitious not only because it seeks to communicate a multigenerational family history but also because two-thirds of the novel is told from a woman's perspective. Harrison's use of Dalva as the primary narrator, no less than his use of Clare as the major force in *The Woman Lit by Fireflies*, demonstrates his capacity to transcend the masculine point of view and enter into a world that, according to the majority of critics, he has never even conceptualized. Dalva, like her mother Naomi, emerges as a woman capable of acting and reacting with equal amounts of certitude.

From the beginning it is clear that, despite caprice and mistreatment, Dalva is not about to "accept life as a brutal approximation." Having lost her only child to adoption, and Duane, the only man she ever loved, to circumstances (and later death), Dalva is caught amid conflicting emotions—knowing what she has to do to earn her own freedom but fearing the consequences and the pain she could cause others. She is also mired in a family matrix that defies easy explanation.

Harrison structures *Dalva* as a three-part novel, centering the first book on Dalva's longings and aspirations, the second on Michael's misbegotten attempts at scholarship, and the third on the events leading up to Dalva's eventual reintegration of the various aspects of her biography. While each of the books has a completeness on a superficial level, the three are ineluctably associated with Dalva's grandfather and his allegiance to the American Indians.

Grandfather's journals allow the reader to comprehend a period of history that has long been whitewashed in American history textbooks, and his sage advice allows Naomi, Dalva, Rachael, and others to make sense out of the tragedies that pepper their lives. His attitude is one born of pragmatism and necessity; having seen the less seemly side of American culture, he fully understands that "each of us must live with a full measure of loneliness that is inescapable and we must not destroy ourselves or our passion to escape this aloneness." It was this same uncanny understanding of the human condition that allowed Grandfather to coexist with the Sioux, who found his ethic toward the land and his rapport with people akin to their own.

The Woman Lit by Fireflies

The ongoing vulnerability of the American Indians is a theme that dominates *Brown Dog*, the first of the three novellas that constitute Harrison's 1990 publication *The Woman Lit by Fireflies*. Harrison's tone, however, is distinctly different. Rather than delving into the historical record, Harrison highlights the insensitivity of modern Americans to Native American traditions and culture and lampoons a legal system that defends the denigrators of history. While his sympathies remain the same as in his earlier works, the approach he takes is more reminiscent of *Warlock* than of *Dalva*.

Because of the seriocomic tone of the work, the book is dominated by characters (both living and dead) who are not entirely believable and who serve, instead, to buttress an assault against the materialism and insensitivity of the modern world. That Harrison casts his story through the filtered lens of Shelly, an aspiring anthropology graduate student, tips his hand from almost the first page. While it is clearly apparent that Brown Dog may well need an editor, Shelly serves as a deflector rather than an editor.

Brown Dog, as a typical Harrison protagonist, is a man trying to cope with middle age. When he finds a three-hundred-pound American Indian chief at the bottom of Lake Superior, he responds with the same degree of maturity that destines Warlock to his misadventures. Like Warlock, he stumbles through life, but unlike Warlock, he lacks an intelligent counterpart. Instead, Brown Dog is teamed with the female equivalent of Dalva's Michael. Shelly is opportunistic and insensitive to the values that make certain areas off-limits to outsiders. She is not unlike Brown Dog, however, as both are comic characters obviously unprepared to deal with the modern world. What she has over Brown Dog is that she comes from a wealthy family and can generally extract the results that she desires.

The ability to buy oneself out of trouble is also a theme that dominates *Sunset Limited*, the second novella in *The Woman Lit by Fireflies*. *Sunset Limited*, unlike *Brown Dog*, reads as a parable in which one is forced to reconsider the parable of the camel and the eye of the needle. It is an abbreviated retrospective akin to Thomas Pynchon's *Vineland* (1989), in which the reader is reacquainted with 1960's radicals and forced to deal with the ways in which their pasts have shaped their presents. Gwen, who seems like an unlikely revolutionary, is teamed with two individuals who have clearly abandoned any insurrectionary thoughts and another who has merely retreated from the fray. That their quest is to gain the freedom of a tired gadfly of a revolutionary who has been hanging on long after his time is both relevant and beside the point. Harrison rather heavy-handedly points out in the final chapter that this is a fable, and, as in most fables, there is a moral that has to do with basic values and the risks of renouncing those values at the expense of the immediate community. Hence, once Billy confesses to his past complicity with the authorities, it comes as no surprise that if a life must be spared, it will be his. Riches, in the elemental world in which Harrison dwells, guarantee very little.

As if to reinforce this point, but from a very different perspective, Harrison closes this set of novellas with *The Woman Lit by Fireflies*, which leaves the reader with no illusions about the protections offered by money. *The Woman Lit by Fireflies* may silence those critics who cannot see Harrison as a universal novelist. His appreciation for the lot of women—their failed expectations, existential angst, and lack of challenge—comes through quite clearly. Clare is a woman wearied from "trying to hold the world together, tired of being the living glue for herself, as if she let go, great pieces of her life would shatter and fall off in a mockery of the apocalypse."

Clare is not an extraordinary character, yet she has the courage to abandon a marriage that has betrayed her expectations decades before. The impetuous escape that she half-consciously orchestrates constitutes a psychic rebirth, a coming to terms with her childhood, adulthood, and future. In relinquishing the creature comforts to which she had always been accustomed, Clare finds new sources of strength as she conquers the dangers of finding shelter, water, and mental balance in a world that is dominated by elemental urges and necessities. Clare is not renouncing money or creature comforts, although along the way she does prove that she can live without them; instead, she is renouncing the predatory ethic of dominance. As she says at one point, "I want to evoke life and [Donald] wants to dominate it."

JULIP

Julip expands Harrison's manly image by leaping past the tradition of maleness to address tender life issues. Like *Legends of the Fall*, *The Woman Lit by Fireflies*, *The Beast God Forgot to Invent*, and *The Summer He Didn't Die*, the book is composed of three novellas. The title story focuses on the stressful attempts by Julip to retrieve her brother Bobby from jail. Surrounded by adversity, an alcoholic father, a cold, calculating mother, a crazy brother, and a nymphomaniac cousin, the tough and resourceful Julip resorts to the gentleness of training dogs and reading Emily Dickinson's poetry to gain solace from the madness surrounding her. Julip attempts to convince her incarcerated sibling to plead insanity as a ploy to be released from his sentence, the result of his killing three men—Julip's past lovers. The ever-continuing conflict between her parents creates a young woman full of doubts and confusion.

In *The Seven Ounce Man*, Harrison renews themes and characters from earlier works. Brown Dog, the epitome of the American existential hero, reminisces of his love for an anthropologist who attempts to desecrate an American Indian burial ground. Somewhat like Harrison, Brown Dog prefers the quiet rhythm of nature to the roaring pace of humanity. He cannot seem to avoid trouble, haphazardly bumbling through incidents, revealing the ridiculous folly that ultimately entangles him with American Indian rights groups.

Harrison selects a fifty-year-old professor accused of having a tryst with a young student as the focus in *The Beige Dolorosa*. Satiated with accusations of impropriety and campus politics, Phillip, the professor, retreats from campus life to the relaxed cadence of the Latino Southwest, where he discovers serenity. Like Julip and Brown Dog, Phillip surrenders to nature as both a form of survival and a restoration of the soul.

The Road Home

The Road Home, a deep, complex, and spiritually oriented work, demonstrates Harrison's maturity. The novel offers five compelling stories told through the multigenerational characters of *Dalva*'s Northridge family. Harrison's strong narrative weaves fantasy with reality and Native American perspectives with midwestern mentality. The novel opens in the 1950's, with the half-Sioux patriarch John remorsefully recounting his youth, his attempts at art, and his final acceptance of a way of life as a horse rancher in Nebraska. Ruthless at times in business, John amasses land, status, and a legacy, but he bemoans not achieving artistic fulfillment. Nelse, Northridge's grandson and Dalva's son, given up at birth for adoption to a wealthy family, portrays himself as a loose wanderer whose passion for birding chips away at his opportunity for a "normal" existence. Nelse targets an abused wife whom he learns to love—and who loves him. Dalva's mother, Naomi, who motivates Nelse into rejoining the family, and Paul, son of Naomi and John, offer rich viewpoints on the intriguing tale from their perspective. Finally, Dalva, the strong, willful one, faces a life-threatening illness and the turmoil of understanding the man who was the baby she gave away at birth.

Harrison uses death as a metaphor for the concept of home, but home also is the Nebraska lands surrounding the Niobara Valley and River, which courses through all the characters in the novel. The author's attention to detail, melding of familiar characters, and masterful storytelling make *The Road Home* a strong sequel to *Dalva*.

True North

True North is set mainly in the city of Marquette of Michigan's Upper Peninsula. It is a first-person narrative told by David Burkett in three parts: the 1960's, the 1970's, and the 1980's. The plot is driven predominantly by David's personal journey to escape the horrible deeds of his ancestors, mainly the lumber barons of his father's family in the middle to late nineteenth century who stole thousands of acres from the Native Americans, raped Michigan's Upper Peninsula, and fostered logging practices that left thousands of men maimed or dead.

David's internal conflict is that he is extremely afraid that he will turn out like his father, and early on there are some similarities between himself and his father. For example, his first two loves, Laurie and Vera, are possibly too young for him and are lusted after by his father as well. Also, there is the hint that David sees the relationship between his sister Cynthia and Donald, the son of the family's gardener, as being in bad taste. On the other hand, his father's inherent problems make David seem very admirable. David's father is a World War II hero turned alcoholic and pedophile who spends his days and nights at the country club when he is not driving to Duluth, Minnesota, to see one of his fifteen-year-old girlfriends or flying to Key West to "fish." One can assume that money is no object on these trips to Key West, as the Burketts have inheritance from both paternal and maternal sides; David's mother comes from a family that became wealthy in the shipping of iron ore from the Upper Peninsula to Gary, Indiana, and Cleveland. As scholar Patrick A. Smith has observed, David's internal conflict is that he is transfixed and possibly doomed by the weight of history.

Typical of a Harrison novel, the protagonist is not a passive victim of circumstance. Consequently, David's external conflict is that he has to create a reality for himself in order to break away from his father's influence and, more important, the type of existence that can only be described as purposeless, living in the doldrums of his ancestors' greed. This manifests itself in many ways. First, the reader learns that David has converted from his parents' Episcopalian faith to the Baptist faith, and he now attends a Baptist church by himself. (He believes that his parents use religion to justify their privileged existence.) He eschews the family tradition of attending Yale by choosing Michigan State University, and he follows that with a stint at seminary school in Chicago. He refuses to socialize with the children of his parents' upper-class friends, preferring to spend his time with

Glenn, a handyman's son. He also accepts the black sheep of the family, his uncle Fred (his mother's brother) as a father figure, if not also the family's live-in accountant, Jesse, and gardener, Clarence. David learns about alternatives to his parents' corrupt version of a Protestant upbringing through Jesse, who is from Mexico; through Clarence, who tends toward the beliefs of his Chippewa ancestors; and through Fred, a religious man who does not believe in organized religion. Most important, instead of killing his father and himself in order to end his bloodline, of which he fantasizes, David decides to write a book about the history of logging in the Upper Peninsula.

Much as Harrison has done in his body of fiction, David aims to put faces, names, and pictures to the people who built the United States and then were left out of the American narrative. The result is that he works on his book for twenty years without much hope for its publication, and, by all accounts, he is unable to balance the quantitative facts with qualitative descriptions. However, his pursuit of this goal and the nontraditional life he leads in the process, mainly in a cabin on the coast of Lake Superior, give him enough knowledge of the past that he is able to throw it away if he pleases. By learning the truth, he is eventually enlightened enough to transcend the past as well as his own futile convictions. Also typical of Harrison's work, David seems to find this truth in nature, where the reality of life, and his place in it, is more apparent.

Returning to Earth

In *Returning to Earth*, a sequel to *True North*, Harrison explores several themes and ideas that are common in his previous novels: nature as the harbinger of truth, the nontraditional family as a positive alternative to a traditional family that breaks itself upon unrealistic expectations, taboo love relationships, and alternate perspectives on reality and the American Dream, along with trying to make sense of the past and one's place in America. In addition, *Returning to Earth* meditates on the multiple ways of coping with death.

The story is told in four parts by four first-person narrators: Donald, Kenneth (much like a young Henry David Thoreau or Jack Kerouac), David Burkett, and David's sister, Cynthia. We learn from Donald in the beginning that he has amyotrophic lateral sclerosis (ALS, or Lou Gehrig's disease) and has only a short time to live. His purpose for writing is to pass along some of his past to his children, Herald and Clare. The fact that he has dyslexia, which probably went completely untreated because he was educated in the 1960's, makes this task a courageous one—it also serves Harrison's artistic need to give a voice to the working class and the working poor. Donald is not a poor man, however; he has been steadily employed as a mason for twenty-five years, and his wife, Cynthia, worked as a teacher on the Bay Mills Indian Reservation right up until he was diagnosed. In fact, Donald and Cynthia could have been wealthy, but she has refused to use her parents' inheritance because her father's money was gained through the actions of his corrupt ancestors.

Donald, like his father, Clarence, in *True North*, is half Finn and half Chippewa. Harrison always uses the parenthetical "(Anishinabe)" after the word "Chippewa." Anishinabe is what the "Chippewa" called themselves; it means the original people. Donald tries his best to give his audience an idea of his family's history, and, in effect, his story conveys some of the humanity that David could not convey in his manuscript on the history of logging in *True North*. Donald's American Dream, at this point, is to die as he pleases. His life, in comparison to that of the Burketts of *True North*, has been ironically profound, but it is the way that he chooses to die and be buried that causes the novel's major conflict.

It is clear that, through *True North* and *Returning to Earth*, Harrison means to compare the lives of the more irresponsible "old money" Americans to those of the working class. The moral is that the honest life of a man and woman who nurture their family, even if their love was once taboo and even if they have to break from traditional expectations, can have a more positive effect on America than a family that allows the deeds of the past to ruin its descendants.

C. Lynn Munro; Craig Gilbert
Updated by Troy Place

Other major works

poetry: *Plain Song*, 1965; *Locations*, 1968; *Outlyer and Ghazals*, 1971; *Letters to Yesenin*, 1973; *Returning to Earth*, 1977; *Selected and New Poems, 1961-1981*, 1982; *Natural World*, 1983 (includes sculpture by Diana

Guest); *The Theory and Practice of Rivers: Poems*, 1985; *The Theory and Practice of Rivers, and New Poems*, 1989; *After Ikkyu, and Other Poems*, 1996; *The Shape of the Journey: New and Collected Poems*, 1998; *Braided Creek: A Conversation in Poetry*, 2003; *Saving Daylight*, 2006.

SCREENPLAYS: *Cold Feet*, 1989 (with Thomas McGuane); *Revenge*, 1989; *Wolf*, 1994 (with Wesley Strick).

NONFICTION: *Just Before Dark: Collected Nonfiction*, 1991; *The Raw and the Cooked: Adventures of a Roving Gourmand*, 2001; *Conversations with Jim Harrison*, 2002 (Robert DeMott, editor); *Off to the Side: A Memoir*, 2002.

CHILDREN'S LITERATURE: *The Boy Who Ran to the Woods*, 2000.

Bibliography

Davis, Todd F., and Kenneth Womack. "Embracing the Fall: Wilderness and Spiritual Transformation in the Novels of Jim Harrison." In *Postmodern Humanism in Contemporary Literature and Culture: Reconciling the Void*. New York: Palgrave Macmillan, 2006. Essay examining Harrison's fiction is part of a larger discussion of contemporary writers' attempts to find meaning and value in a postmodern world. Valuable for an understanding of Harrison's tendency toward resolution.

DeMott, Robert, ed. *Conversations with Jim Harrison*. Jackson: University Press of Mississippi, 2002. Collection of interviews with Harrison spans the years from 1976 to 1999. Includes an informative editor's introduction, chronology, and index.

Harrison, Jim. "The Art of Fiction: Jim Harrison." Interview by Jim Fergus. *The Paris Review* 107 (1988): 53-97. Fergus asks Harrison the right questions about life, literature, and art, and the author's responses are personal and enlightening, giving the reader a variety of interesting insights into the craft of fiction and poetry.

Jones, Allen M. "Six Short Essays About Jim Harrison." *New West*, May 16, 2006. Discusses many topics a Harrison admirer would want to know about the author, including his life in Montana, his friends, and some background stories on his work.

McClintock, James I. "*Dalva*: Jim Harrison's 'Twin Sister.'" *Journal of Men's Studies* (Spring, 1998): 319-331. Examines *Dalva* from a post-Jungian perspective, exploring the feminine side of masculinity as influenced by psychologist James Hillman.

Pichaske, David R. *Rooted: Seven Midwestern Writers of Place*. Iowa City: University of Iowa Press, 2006. In exploring the writing of authors, including Harrison, who have spent their careers expounding on one or two distinct locations, Pichaske provides insight into how geography can shape all facets of fiction and how these writers' works have transcended their respective regions.

Reilly, Edward C. *Jim Harrison*. New York: Twayne, 1996. Provides a good introduction to Harrison's work, discussing, among other topics, the ways in which Harrison uses fiction as a medium for social commentary. Includes brief biographical section and chronology.

Rohrkemper, John. "'Natty Bumppo Wants Tobacco': Jim Harrison's Wilderness." *Great Lakes Review* 8 (1983): 20-28. Suggests that Harrison's poetic treatment of nature is closer to a "dark romantic" view, such as that of Herman Melville, than it is to an Emersonian transcendentalist outlook. Asserts that Harrison's fiction is based on the tradition of his "literary parents and grandparents," the modernists, but with one significant twist: The modernists show the "pristine beauty of nature first, and then nature spoiled," while Harrison shows how nature exists in spite of human influence.

Smith, Patrick A. *"The True Bones of My Life": Essays on the Fiction of Jim Harrison*. East Lansing: Michigan State University Press, 2002. Explores Harrison's fiction in terms of such ideas as the American myth, the American Dream, postmodernism, and the importance of place. Includes several photographs, a critical bibliography, a bibliography of Harrison's work that lists many of his published essays, and an index.

L. P. HARTLEY

Born: Whittlesea, England; December 30, 1895
Died: London, England; December 13, 1972
Also known as: Leslie Poles Hartley

Principal long fiction

Simonetta Perkins, 1925
The Shrimp and the Anemone, 1944
The Sixth Heaven, 1946
Eustace and Hilda, 1947
The Boat, 1949
My Fellow Devils, 1951
The Go-Between, 1953
A Perfect Woman, 1955
The Hireling, 1957
Facial Justice, 1960
The Brickfield, 1964
The Betrayal, 1966
Poor Clare, 1968
The Love-Adept, 1969
My Sisters' Keeper, 1970
The Harness Room, 1971
The Collections, 1972
The Will and the Way, 1973

Other literary forms

L. P. Hartley published, in addition to eighteen novels, six collections of short stories: *Night Fears* (1924), *The Killing Bottle* (1932), *The Traveling Grave* (1948), *The White Wand* (1954), *Two for the River* (1961), and *Mrs. Carteret Receives* (1971). Reprinted in *The Complete Short Stories of L. P. Hartley* (1973), with the exception of ten apprentice pieces from *Night Fears*, the stories reveal Hartley's reliance on the gothic mode. At their least effective, they are workmanlike tales utilizing conventional supernatural machinery. At their best, however, they exhibit a spare symbolic technique used to explore individual human personalities and to analyze the nature of moral evil. The best of Hartley's ghost and horror stories include "A Visitor from Down Under," "Feet Foremost," and "W. S.," the last dealing with an author murdered by a character of his own creation. "Up the Garden Path," "The Pampas Clump," and "The Pylon" reveal a more realistic interest in human psychology, and they deal more directly with the theme central to Hartley's major fiction: the acquisition, on the part of an innocent, even morally naïve, protagonist, of an awareness of the existence of evil.

A frequent lecturer, and a reviewer for such periodicals as *The Observer*, *Saturday Review*, and *Time and Tide* from the early 1920's to the middle 1940's, Hartley published a volume of essays titled *The Novelist's Responsibility: Lectures and Essays* (1967), in which he deplored the twentieth century devaluation of a sense of individual moral responsibility. These essays explain Hartley's fictional preoccupation with identity, moral values, and spiritual insight. His choice of subjects, particularly the works of Jane Austen, Emily Brontë, Nathaniel Hawthorne, and Henry James, suggests the origins of the realistic-symbolic technique he employs in both his short stories and his novels.

Achievements

While L. P. Hartley's novels from *Simonetta Perkins* to *Facial Justice* were published in the United States, they did not enjoy the popularity there that they earned in England. *The Go-Between*, for example, continued to be in print in England since its publication in 1953, and the *Eustace and Hilda* trilogy—comprising *The Shrimp and the Anemone*, *The Sixth Heaven*, and *Eustace and Hilda*—was given a radio dramatization by the British Broadcasting Corporation (BBC). In the course of a literary career of roughly fifty years, Hartley came to be a noted public figure, and his work received favorable attention from Lord David Cecil, Walter Allen, and John Atkins. Only in the United States, however, did his novels receive detailed critical attention. The three full-length studies of his fiction—Peter Bien's *L. P. Hartley* (1963), Anne Mulkeen's *Wild Thyme, Winter Lightning: The Symbolic Novels of L. P. Hartley* (1974), and Edward T. Jones's *L. P. Hartley* (1978)—are all American, as are the notable treatments of Hartley's work by James Hall and Harvey Curtis Webster.

BIOGRAPHY

Born on December 30, 1895, near Whittlesea in Cambridgeshire, Leslie Poles Hartley was named for Sir Leslie Stephen, the father of Virginia Woolf and himself a noted late Victorian literary man. According to Edward T. Jones, whose book *L. P. Hartley* contains the most complete biographical account, Hartley's mother, Mary Elizabeth Thompson, was the daughter of a farmer named William James Thompson of Crawford House, Crowland, Lincolnshire. His father, H. B. Hartley, was a solicitor, justice of the peace, and later director of the successful brickworks founded by the novelist's paternal grandfather. This information figures as part of the background to Hartley's *The Brickfield* and *The Betrayal*.

Hartley was the second of his parents' three children; he had an older sister, Enid, and a younger, Annie Norah. None of the three ever married. Reared at Fletton Tower, near Peterborough, Hartley was educated at Harrow and Balliol College, Oxford, his stay at the latter interrupted by military service as a second lieutenant in the Norfolk Regiment during World War I. He was discharged for medical reasons and did not see action in France. In Oxford after the war, Hartley came into contact with a slightly younger generation of men, among them Anthony Powell, Graham Greene, and Evelyn Waugh. His closest literary friend at this period, however, may have been Lord David Cecil. After leaving Balliol with a second honours degree in 1921, Hartley worked as a reviewer for various periodicals, wrote the stories later collected in *Night Fears* and *The Killing Bottle*, and cultivated friendships with members of both bohemian Bloomsbury and British society. His novella *Simonetta Perkins*, a Jamesian story of a young American woman's inconclusive passion for a Venetian gondolier, was published in 1925.

Hartley made many trips to Venice. From 1933 to 1939, he spent part of each summer and fall there, and he drew on this experience for parts of *Eustace and Hilda*, *The Boat*, and *My Fellow Devils*. Returning to England just before the start of World War II, Hartley started work on the series of novels that earned for him a place in the British literary establishment. Given the James Tait Black Memorial Prize for *Eustace and Hilda* in 1947 and the Heinemann Foundation Prize for *The Go-Between* in 1953, he served as head of the British Association of Poets, Playwrights, Editors, Essayists and Novelists (PEN) and on the management committee of the Society of Authors. In 1956, he was created a Commander of the British Empire by Queen Elizabeth II. In his later years, Hartley gave frequent talks, most notably the Clark lectures delivered at Trinity College, Cambridge, in 1964. Joseph Losey won the Grand Prize at Cannes, France, in 1971 for a film version of *The Go-Between*, for which Harold Pinter wrote the script, and in 1973, Alan Bridges's film of *The Hireling*, from a script by Wolf Mankowitz, won the same prize. Hartley died in London on December 13, 1972.

ANALYSIS

Indebted to Bloomsbury, as shown by a concern with personal conduct and a highly impressionistic style, L. P. Hartley betrays affinities with D. H. Lawrence, Aldous Huxley, and George Orwell in a more fundamental concern with larger social and moral issues. His best books argue for the existence of a spiritual dimension to life and demonstrate that recognition of its motive force, even union of oneself with its will, is a moral imperative. In this emphasis on connection, his novels recall those of E. M. Forster, but unlike his predecessor, Hartley insists that the nature of the motive force is supernatural, even traditionally Christian. In his most successful books, Hartley draws upon elements of both novel and romance, as Richard Chase defines them in *The American Novel and Its Tradition* (1957), and the uniqueness of the resulting hybridization precludes comparisons with the work of most of his contemporaries.

Hartley's moral vision, revealed by the gradual integration of realism and symbolism in his novels, is the most striking characteristic of his long fiction. In a book such as *The Go-Between*, he shows that all people are subject to the power of love, even when they deny it, and that achievement of insight into love's capabilities is a prerequisite of achieving moral responsibility. This pattern of growth at the center of Hartley's novels is conventionally Christian in its outlines. The protagonist of each book, beginning with Eustace Cherrington in the *Eustace and Hilda* trilogy, accepts his status as a "sinner" and experiences, if only briefly and incompletely, a semimystical transcendence of his fallen state.

The epiphanic technique Hartley develops in the trilogy to objectify these moments of insight recurs in various forms in all of his novels, coming in time to be embodied not in symbolism but in the pattern of action in which he casts his plots. Without suggesting that Hartley's fiction is about theology, it is clear that his concern with the subject of morality cannot avoid having religious overtones. Like Nathaniel Hawthorne, he traces the process of spiritual growth in innocent, morally self-assured, and thereby flawed personalities who experience temptation, even commit sins, and eventually attain spiritual kinship with their fellow people. These encounters, in a book such as *Facial Justice*, occur in settings symbolic of traditional religious values, and so while Hartley's novels may be read from psychoanalytic or mythic points of view, they are more fully comprehended from a metaphysical vantage point.

There is a thematic unity to all of Hartley's longer fiction, but after 1960, there is a marked decline in its technical complexity. In one sense, having worked out his thematic viewpoint in the process of fusing realism and symbolism in his earlier books, Hartley no longer feels the need to dramatize the encounter of good and evil and to set it convincingly in a realistic world. His last novels are fables, and in *The Harness Room*, the most successful of them, the lack of realism intensifies his treatment of the psychological and sexual involvement of an adolescent boy and his father's slightly older chauffeur. This book brings Hartley's oeuvre full circle, back to the story of the American spinster and the Venetian gondolier he produced in *Simonetta Perkins* at the start of his career.

EUSTACE AND HILDA TRILOGY

The three novels constituting the *Eustace and Hilda* trilogy—*The Shrimp and the Anemone*, *The Sixth Heaven*, and *Eustace and Hilda*—objectify a process of moral growth and spiritual regeneration to be found in or behind all of Hartley's subsequent fiction. The process is not unlike that which he describes, in the Clark lectures reprinted in *The Novelist's Responsibility*, as characteristic of Hawthorne's treatment of the redeeming experience of sin in *The Marble Faun* (1860). The epiphanic moments Hartley uses to dramatize his protagonist's encounters with Christ the Redeemer reveal truths that can be read on psychological, sociological, and theological levels.

In *The Shrimp and the Anemone*, Hartley depicts the abortive rebellion of Eustace Cherrington, aged nine, against the moral and psychological authority of his thirteen-year-old sister, Hilda. Set in the summers of 1905 and 1906, the novel reveals young Eustace's intimations of a spiritual reality behind the surface of life. Unable to act in terms of these insights, for they are confused with his aesthetic sense, Eustace feeds his romantic inclination to construct an internal fantasy world and refuses to see the moral necessity of action.

In *The Sixth Heaven*, Hartley details Eustace's second effort to achieve his freedom from Hilda, this time by engineering a socially advantageous marriage for her with Dick Staveley, a war hero and rising young member of Parliament. This novel focuses on a visit the Cherringtons make in June, 1920, to the Staveleys, acquaintances who live near their childhood home at Anchorstone. Eustace's adult epiphanic experiences are more insistent. Less tied to his childish aestheticism, they emerge in the context of the novel as hauntingly ambiguous intimations of a moral and spiritual realm that he unconsciously seeks to avoid acknowledging.

In *Eustace and Hilda*, the final novel in the trilogy, Hartley brings his protagonist face-to-face with Christ during the Venetian Feast of the Redeemer, the third Sunday in July, 1920. This encounter leads to Eustace's return to Anchorstone and acceptance of moral responsibility for the emotionally induced paralysis Hilda experienced at the end of her love affair with Dick Staveley. Back in his childhood home, Eustace learns the lesson of self-sacrificial love in Christ's example, and he effects a cure for Hilda by staging a mock accident for her at the edge of Anchorstone Cliff. Because of the strain this involves, he suffers a fatal heart attack, and the novel ends. His death signals the genuineness of the moral growth and spiritual regeneration that had begun in Venice. The interpenetration of realistic narrative and symbolic subtext that occurs by the end of the *Eustace and Hilda* trilogy objectifies Hartley's vision of the world.

THE BOAT

Hartley's equivalent of Ford Madox Ford's and Evelyn Waugh's treatments of men at war, *The Boat* presents the mock-epic struggle of Timothy Casson, a forty-nine-year-old bachelor writer, to gain permission to use his rowing shell on the fishing stream that runs through Upton-on-Swirrell. Timothy, settling back in England in 1940 after an eighteen-year stay in Italy, consciously attempts to isolate himself from the effects of the war in progress in the larger world. He devotes himself to collecting china, to cultivating friends, to raising a dog, and to forcing the village magnates to allow him to row on the Swirrell. In the process, Timothy violates his own self-interest, as well as that of his nation and his class, but he is not the tragicomic figure that Eustace Cherrington becomes in the trilogy. In Hartley's hands, Timothy achieves only a degree of the self-awareness that Eustace does, and this enables the novelist to label him the "common sinner" that all people are, a figure both sinned against and sinning.

Timothy's desire to take his boat out on the river is an assertion of individuality that polarizes the community. His attachment to his boat becomes a measure of his moral and political confusion, for Timothy is torn between the influences of Vera Cross, a Communist secret agent sent to Upton-on-Swirrell to organize unrest among the masses, and Volumnia Purbright, the wife of the Anglican vicar and an unconventional, perhaps mystical, Christian. The emblematic names suggest the comic possibilities Hartley exploits in his treatment of the two, but *The Boat* is a serious novel. Vera represents a social disharmony resultant upon the advocacy of ideology, while Volumnia reflects both social harmony and personal tranquillity resulting from sacrifice of self. Indeed, when Timothy persists in his protest against the prohibition against rowing and sets forth on the flooded Swirrell with two children and his dog as passengers, Volumnia confronts Vera on the riverbank. Vera attacks the vicar's wife, and the two women tumble into the water. When Vera drowns in the Devil's Staircase, Volumnia blames herself for the younger woman's death and subsequently dies from exposure and pneumonia. When at the end of *The Boat* Timothy, who had to be rescued from the river when his boat capsized in the flooded stream, dreams he receives a telephone call from Volumnia inviting him to tea, he hears Vera's voice as well as Volumnia's, and the two women tell him that they are inseparable, as are the moral and ethical positions they represent.

Near the end of the novel, Timothy prepares to leave Upton-on-Swirrell in the company of two old friends, Esther Morwen and Tyrone MacAdam. The two discuss the prospects for Timothy's acceptance of himself as an ordinary human being. At the time of the boating accident, he had managed to rescue one of the children with him, but he needed the fortuitous help of others to rescue the second child and to reach safety himself. Timothy is clearly partially responsible for the deaths of Vera Cross and Volumnia Purbright, and the "true cross" he must bear is an acceptance of moral complexity. Whether he will achieve this insight is an open question at the end of *The Boat*, and Hartley's refusal to make the book a neat statement reinforces its thematic point.

The Go-Between

Hartley's *The Go-Between*, arguably his finest novel, is the only one with a first-person narrator as protagonist. Leo Colston, like the focal characters of the *Eustace and Hilda* trilogy and *The Boat*, frees himself from psychological constraints and achieves a measure of moral insight. Indeed, Leo's story amounts to a rite of passage conforming to the pattern of initiation characteristic of the bildungsroman. More significantly, *The Go-Between* is a study of England on the verge of its second Elizabethan Age, and the patterns of imagery that Hartley uses to reveal the personality of Leo suggest indirectly that the Age of Aquarius will be a golden one.

These linguistic patterns, introduced into the novel by Leo himself, derive from the signs of the zodiac. On one hand, they are a pattern manufactured by Leo as a schoolboy and utilized to explain his conviction that the start of the twentieth century, which he dates incorrectly as January 1, 1900, is the dawn of a second Golden Age. On the other hand, the zodiac motifs, as associated with Leo and other characters in the novel, underscore Hartley's thematic insistence on the power of self-sacrificial love to redeem both individuals and society from error.

At the start of the novel in 1951 or 1952, Leo is an elderly man engaged in sorting through the accumulated memorabilia of a lifetime. Coming upon his diary for the year 1900, inside the cover of which are printed the zodiac signs, he recalls his experiences at Southdown Hill School and his vacation visit to a schoolmate, Marcus Maudsley. In the body of the novel, the account of that nineteen-day visit to Brandham Hall, the narrative voice is split between that of the thirteen-year-old Leo of 1900 and that of the aged man with which the book begins.

Used by Marcus's sister Marian to carry messages to her lover, the tenant farmer Ted Burgess, Leo finds himself faced with the dubious morality of his actions when Marcus tells him that Marian is to marry Viscount Trimingham, the owner of Brandham Hall and a scarred veteran of the Boer War.

In Leo's mind, Marian is the Virgin of the zodiac, Trimingham the Sagittarian archer, and Burgess the Aquarian water-carrier. Determined to break the bond between Marian and Ted and to restore her to Viscount Trimingham, Leo resorts to the schoolboy magic with which he had handled bullies at school. He plans a spell involving the sacrifice of an *atropa belladonna* or deadly nightshade growing in a deserted outbuilding, but the ritual goes awry and he finds himself flat on his back with the plant on top of him. The next day, his thirteenth birthday, Leo is forced to lead Marian's mother to the spot where the girl meets her lover, and they discover the pair engaged in sexual intercourse. For Leo, whose adult sexuality has just begun to develop, this is a significant shock, and he feels that he has been defeated by the beautiful but deadly lady, both the deadly nightshade and Marian herself.

In the epilogue to *The Go-Between*, the elderly Leo Colston returns to Norfolk to find out the consequences of the mutual betrayal. Encountering Marian, now the dowager Lady Trimingham, once more, he undertakes again to be a messenger. This time he goes to her grandson Edward in an effort to reconcile him to the events of the fateful year 1900, to the fact that his father was really the son of Ted Burgess. This action on Leo's part embodies the theme of all of Hartley's fiction: The only evil in life is an unloving heart. At the end of his return journey to Brandham Hall, Leo Colston is a more vital man and a more compassionate one. Having faced the evil both inside and outside himself, he is open to love, and the Age of Aquarius can begin. That it will also be the age of Elizabeth II, given the political and sociological implications of the central action, gives Hartley's *The Go-Between* its particular thematic rightness.

Robert C. Petersen

Other major works

SHORT FICTION: *Night Fears*, 1924; *The Killing Bottle*, 1932; *The Traveling Grave*, 1948; *The White Wand*, 1954; *Two for the River*, 1961; *Mrs. Carteret Receives*, 1971; *The Complete Short Stories of L. P. Hartley*, 1973.

NONFICTION: *The Novelist's Responsibility: Lectures and Essays*, 1967.

Bibliography

Bien, Peter. *L. P. Hartley*. University Park: Pennsylvania State University Press, 1963. The first book on Hartley's fiction, important for its Freudian analysis of his novels; its identification of his indebtedness to Nathaniel Hawthorne, Henry James, and Emily Brontë; and its examination of Hartley's literary criticism. At its best when discussing the novels about the transition from adolescence to adulthood.

Bloomfield, Paul. *L. P. Hartley*. 1962. Rev. ed. Harlow, England: Longman, 1970. Bloomfield, a personal friend of Hartley, focuses on character analysis and thematic concerns, providing a brief discussion of Hartley's novels. Laudatory, perceptive, and very well written.

Fane, Julian. *Best Friends: Memories of Rachel and David Cecil, Cynthia Asquith, L. P. Hartley, and Some Others*. London: Sinclair-Stevenson and St. George's Press, 1990. Fane writes about his friendship with Hartley and others, which helps to situate Hartley's fiction in terms of his sensibility and his time.

Hall, James. *The Tragic Comedians: Seven Modern British Novelists*. Bloomington: Indiana University Press, 1963. Claims that the Hartley protagonist possesses an inadequate emotional pattern that leads inevitably to failure. This neurotic behavior is discussed in his major fiction: *The Boat*, *Eustace and Hilda*, *My Fellow Devils*, and *The Hireling*. In these novels, Hartley demonstrates that confidence is accompanied by a contradictory desire to fail.

Jones, Edward T. *L. P. Hartley*. Boston: Twayne, 1978. An excellent analysis of Hartley's literary work, particularly of his novels, which are conveniently grouped. Also contains a chronology, a biographical introductory chapter, a discussion of Hartley's literary criticism, and an excellent annotated bibliography. Of special interest is Jones's definition of the "Hartleian novel."

Mulkeen, Anne. *Wild Thyme, Winter Lightning: The Symbolic Novels of L. P. Hartley*. Detroit, Mich.:

Wayne State University Press, 1974. Focuses on Hartley's fiction until 1968, stressing the Hawthornian romance elements in his early novels. Particularly concerned with his adaptations of the romance and how his characters are at once themselves and archetypes or symbols.

Webster, Harvey Curtis. *After the Trauma: Representative British Novelists Since 1920*. Lexington: University Press of Kentucky, 1970. The chapter on Hartley, entitled "Diffident Christian," concerns his protagonists' struggles to distinguish between God's orders and society's demands. Discusses *Facial Justice*, *Eustace and Hilda*, *The Boat*, and *The Go-Between* extensively, concluding that Hartley merits more attention than he has been given.

Wright, Adrian. *Foreign Country: The Life of L. P. Hartley*. London: A. Deutsch, 1996. A good biography of Hartley for the beginning student, providing a balanced account of Hartley's life and information about his novels and other works. Includes a bibliography and an index.

York, R. A. " L. P. Hartley: *The Go-Between*." In *The Rules of Time: Time and Rhythm in the Twentieth-Century Novel*. Madison, N.J.: Fairleigh Dickinson University Press, 1999. York's examination of Hartley's book and novels by other authors focuses on the rhythm and pace of reading, maintaining that these elements affect readers' perception of time—a conspicuous presence in all twentieth century fiction.

JAROSLAV HAŠEK

Born: Prague, Bohemia, Austro-Hungarian Empire (now in Czech Republic); April 30, 1883

Died: Lipnice nad Sázavou, Czechoslovakia (now in Czech Republic); January 3, 1923

Principal long fiction

Osudy dobrého vojáka Švejka za světove války, 1921-1923 (4 volumes; *The Good Soldier: Švejk*, 1930; also known as *The Good Soldier Švejk and His Fortunes in the World War*, 1973; better known as *The Good Soldier Švejk*)

Other literary forms

Apart from his single masterpiece, Jaroslav Hašek (HAH-shehk) wrote more than twelve hundred short stories, *feuilletons*, and articles, the best of which were published in a collection translated by Cecil Parrott, *The Red Commissar: Including Further Adventures of the Good Soldier Švejk, and Other Stories* (1981).

Achievements

Jaroslav Hašek was too controversial to be accepted as a great writer in his time. His great unfinished masterpiece, *The Good Soldier Švejk*, sharply divided critics into those who rejected him (most of the literary establishment) and those who understood the originality and comic genius of the novel. Among the latter belonged Max Brod, the biographer of Franz Kafka, and Ivan Olbracht, a noted novelist. Indeed, the biggest spurt toward the worldwide renown of the novel came from Prague's German community following Grete Rainer's German translation in 1926. The novel then established its reputation in Europe as an antimilitarist satire and as a great comic novel. A film version of the novel, *Der brave Soldat Schwejk*, was produced in Germany in 1960 and released in the United States in 1963 as *The Good Soldier Schweik*.

Hašek's main achievement lies in the combination of two kinds of satire: on one hand, topical, historical, political satire of the Austro-Hungarian military machinery; on the other, satire of human nature. This satire is communicated through a unique and sometimes enigmatic character, Josef Švejk, whose stories manifest a distillation of popular wisdom used as a weapon against the inimical environment.

Hašek's influence on the subsequent development of Czech prose has been overwhelming and not always salutary. Hašek's humor at its most subtle is inimitable and wholly his own; superficial adaptations fall flat. Hašek's book does not have a rival in its genre in the twentieth century; the closest equivalent (though distant in time and in its concept of comedy) might be Hans Jakob Christoffel von Grimmelshausen's *Der abenteuerliche Simplicissimus* (1669; *The Adventurous Simplicissimus*, 1912). The appearance of direct descendants of *The Good Soldier Švejk* (as in Bertolt Brecht's play *Schweyk im zweiten Weltkrieg*, pr. 1957) and indirect traces in the works of satirists as diverse as Joseph Heller (in his *Catch-22*, 1961) and Vladimir Voinovich (in his Chonkin books) reveals the enduring influence of Hašek's masterpiece.

Biography

The life and the legend of Jaroslav Hašek are difficult to disentangle. Hašek was a bohemian, a hoaxer, a joker, and a very irresponsible man. His exaggerations, embellishments, and mystifications make the few testimonials by his friends suspect. Even the little that is verifiable about him does not make him look very good: He was by turns an anarchist, a monarchist, and a Communist; he was a bigamist, and, like his father, died as the result of alcoholism.

Hašek was only thirteen when his father died, and, because of the family's poverty, he had to leave school to work in a pharmacist's shop. He later returned to school and was admitted to a commercial academy, where he appears to have acquitted himself very well. On account of his good record, he obtained a position in a bank, but he was unable to keep his job and started to write short *feuilletons*. His journalistic activity fell short of supplying him with steady or sufficient income and only encouraged his bohemian proclivities.

In 1906, Hašek joined the anarchist movement and met Jarmila Mayerová, with whom he fell deeply in love. Jarmila thought that she could influence him to abandon his vagabond life; she had a great willingness to understand him, although her middle-class parents were hoping she would marry a more respectable man. Hašek's involvement with anarchism and his reluctance to lead a different life postponed the wedding until 1910, a good year for his literary production as well: He wrote and published seventy-five stories.

The following year, he published the first stories about the good soldier Švejk. Although the prototype of Švejk in these stories bears some resemblance to the end product, it is but a rough sketch: The humor seems forced, despite the occasional dash of genuine comedy.

After Jarmila bore him a son in 1912, Hašek resumed his bohemian existence, becoming so alienated from society that he refused to register his residence, as was required by law, preferring instead to spend a few days at a time with some of his friends, often disappearing from Prague with common vagabonds. At the same time, he continued to write stories prolifically, living a rather carefree life until 1915, at which time he was drafted into the Austrian army.

World War I was the key experience of Hašek's life, and it would be fair to say that it changed him for the better. Surprisingly, though he was to turn his experience in the Austrian army into a masterpiece of satire that suggests lifelong military involvement, Hašek remained an Austrian soldier for only a few months; he was taken prisoner in September, 1915, by the Russians, after the latter's sudden counterattack. It is rather the larger view of the war as seen from the prisoner-of-war camp that shaped Hašek's thinking. More important still, the most enigmatic part of Hašek's life, his involvement in the Russian Civil War, must also have added to the violent outburst against militarism presented in his masterpiece.

The enigma of Hašek's participation rests in the apparent fact that Hašek managed for the duration of his participation in the Russian Civil War to change himself into a teetotaler and a committed Communist who advanced the cause by, among other activities, disseminating journalistic propaganda among the foreign troops of the Red Army in Ufa and later in Siberia. It is not altogether clear how strong Hašek's commitment was throughout his stay, but after the Communist victory, he returned to Prague with a Russian wife, resuming his irresponsible lifestyle and ignoring Communist Party orders to work as an agitator in a mining district.

Hašek's return was ignominious. He was, after all, a deserter from the Czechoslovak legion that fought the Bolsheviks in the Russian Civil War. He was not prosecuted on account of the amnesty proclaimed after the establishment of the Republic of Czechoslovakia in 1918, and he also was not prosecuted for bigamy, but that still did not change the minds of those who considered him a traitor. He found it very hard to adapt to his new circumstances, but his Russian wife demanded that he try to make money one way or another, and it was then that Hašek decided to attempt to write a long novel; the result was his masterpiece.

Hašek could not find a publisher for the first volume of the projected four and published the work privately. It was a success, and the remaining volumes were eagerly accepted by a publisher. Having started the novel in 1921, Hašek continued writing until his death in 1923. He had bought a modest cottage in Lipnice on the Sázava River, and while it was a good move to go to Lipnice and to concentrate on writing, his health was not improved, for he continued drinking, which aggravated his illness and hastened his death.

The success that Hašek lived to enjoy was only a faint portent of the worldwide fame that came to his masterpiece a few years after his death, yet it is doubtful whether even this would have surprised him.

Analysis: The Good Soldier Švejk

Jaroslav Hašek's *The Good Soldier Švejk* had its genesis in 1911, the time of the publication of the first of his Švejk stories; in a broader sense, his preparation for the work included his whole conscious life. One way to look at his masterpiece is to see it as a compendium of almost three hundred stories told by Švejk and other characters.

The type of story that one finds in the novel is usually likened to a "pub story" (*die Gasthausgeschichte*). It is of anecdotal construction and is often produced as an illustration of some thought, as support for some opinion, or, apologetically, as justification of a certain kind of behavior. There is, however, one important modification in Hašek's story that sets it apart from a common anecdote. A successful anecdote is characterized by a construction in which the "story" moves swiftly toward its "point," with minimal hindrance and no digressions. Not so with Hašek's tale—in this story, it is the digression, the often irrelevant detail, the play on words, the humorous inventiveness that is characteristic.

The fact that the novel is a collection of so many stories has no effect on its unity. Most of the stories come from the main character, Švejk, and they always serve to illustrate a particular point of the main and rather skeletal plot. The plot itself can be summarized briefly: Josef Švejk, who has been making a living by selling dogs whose pedigrees he often forged and who has been certified by the military as an imbecile, is drafted in World War I and transported to the front. Švejk never sees combat, as the writing of the fourth volume, which would have taken him to the front line, was interrupted by Hašek's death. It is to Hašek's credit that he could flesh out this austere plot with vivacity and excitement, mostly derived from humor surrounding Švejk, coming either from the descriptions of Švejk's activities or from the stories Švejk and other characters recount.

Another integrating element of the novel is satire. *The Good Soldier Švejk* is a satiric novel, perhaps the greatest satiric novel written in the twentieth century. The subgenre in which it could be classified is that of antimilitarist satire, though it is mixed with another type of satire: the satire of human nature, or misanthropic satire. The success of the novel can be attributed to the mixture of these two kinds of satire; each type strengthens the other.

Hašek's salvos against the high and mighty are more pronounced and more numerous than his excursions into misanthropic satire, wherein the little guy becomes a target as well. This notwithstanding, it would be a grave mistake to portray Hašek as a champion of the downtrodden—he is far too cynical for that. Nevertheless, that is precisely what the literary establishments in Czechoslovakia and other Communist countries did. They declared Hašek to be an "exemplary novelist of the proletariat, despite occasional ideological errors." Although Hašek's political sympathies might support this view, a close reading of his novel does nothing of the sort. On the contrary, as the famous Czech novelist Milan Kundera has suggested, it is Hašek's "blasphemy"—that is, his misanthropic satire—that is often overlooked and deserves to be studied and noticed more.

The Austro-Hungarian Empire is no more; it was already gone at the time of the writing of the novel. This means that the satiric attacks aimed at the empire, the imperial court, and so on were even then less important to the author than the catalog of stupidity that he found flourishing in the military milieu. It is the atmosphere of the crisis, of the war, of tremendous stress on the individual that reveals best the real qualities of human beings.

The novel also evokes the mood of disillusionment following the terrible clash of the idealistic expectations of the nineteenth century with the reality of mass murder engineered on a gigantic scale in World War I.

One should not forget that the great formative period of Hašek's life was spent in revolutionary Russia, where he witnessed the blood, famine, and pestilence of the new Leviathan. This, too, may have contributed to his doubts about the ability of humans to order their affairs rationally or to bring about true freedom, as he, when he was a young anarchist, once envisioned it.

Hašek was a natural comic; his comic genius is apparent in the many stories that he wrote for the newspapers in his youth. He always found it easy to laugh at the world, to look at the comical side, resolutely rejecting the serious approach to life, refusing the responsibility often asked of him. In addition to this proven natural comic ability, however, it is possible to witness in his fiction the development of a sophisticated artist.

The true value of the art that Hašek's comedy represents can easily be measured through comparison of Hašek's novel with his two previous attempts to write about Švejk. In none of the stories written in 1911 or in 1917 does one encounter the ambiguous and accomplished raconteur and trickster Švejk of the great novel. All of these attempts seem heavy-handed; they lack the highly successful amalgam of two kinds of satires, the political and the misanthropic, achieved only in Hašek's masterpiece.

Although the public success of the novel was immediate, critical acclaim came slowly; when it arrived, however, it elevated Hašek to the first rank of comic geniuses. Critics have acknowledged the ambiguities in Hašek's work and the disturbing question of his misanthropy, but these have been judged of lesser importance when compared with the significance of Hašek's inventiveness, his imagination, and his playful exploitation of language for the purposes of comedy. It is fair to say that, at best, Hašek's comedy transcends the narrowly partisan limits that are suggested in some of his more heavy-handed writing and takes its rightful place next to the works of Miguel de Cervantes and François Rabelais in literature, and those of Molière and Charles Chaplin in the broader area of the art of comedy.

Peter Petro

Other major works

SHORT FICTION: *Dobrý voják Švejk a jiné podivné historky*, 1912; *The Red Commissar: Including Further Adventures of the Good Soldier Švejk, and Other Stories*, 1981; *The Bachura Scandal, and Other Stories and Sketches*, 1991.

POETRY: *Májove výkřiky*, 1903.

Bibliography

Bryant-Bertail, Sarah. "*The Good Soldier Schweik* as Dialectical Theater." In *The Performance of Power: Theatrical Discourse and Politics*, edited by Sue-Ellen Case and Janelle Reinelt. Iowa City: University of Iowa Press, 1991. Interprets the role of Švejk in Hašek's novel as a character in a political play. Part of a collection of articles focusing on "political theater."

Cushman, Jenifer. "Criminal Apprehensions: Prague Minorities and the Habsburg Legal System in Jaroslav Hašek's *The Good Soldier Švejk* and Franz Kafka's *The Trial*." In *Literature and Law*, edited by Michael J. Meyer. Atlanta: Rodopi, 2004. Examination of Hašek's novel focuses on its representation of lawyers and the Austro-Hungarian legal system. Included in a collection of essays that examine legal issues in selected works of literature.

Parrott, Cecil. *The Bad Bohemian: A Life of Jaroslav Hašek*. New York: Cambridge University Press, 1978. Standard biography—one of few such sources available in English—offers a comprehensive account of Hašek's life and complex personality.

_______. *Jaroslav Hašek: A Study of Švejk and the Short Stories*. New York: Cambridge University Press, 1982. Provides a brief biography and extensive background for all Hašek's works. Discusses the major controversy of Hašek's life—his service with the Red Army—and examines its impact on the author's work and reputation.

Pynsent, R. B. "Jaroslav Hašek." In *The Twentieth Century*. Vol. 9 of *European Writers*, edited by George Stade. New York: Charles Scribner's Sons, 1989. Explains Hašek's place in the history of the novel in addition to providing biographical information, analyses of his works, and bibliographies of his writings and of books about him.

Snyder, John. "The Politics and Hermeneutics of Anarchist Satire: Jaroslav Hašek's *The Good Soldier Švejk*." *Literature, Interpretation, Theory* 2, no. 4 (1991): 289-301. Discusses the relationship between Hašek's writing and his lifelong political dissent.

Steiner, Peter. "*Tropos Kynikos: The Good Soldier Švejk* by Jaroslav Hašek." In *The Deserts of Bohemia: Czech Fiction and Its Social Context*. Ithaca, N.Y.: Cornell University Press, 2000. Essay devoted to Hašek's novel is part of a larger work focusing on the political and social ideas expressed in the works of several Czech writers. Argues that in these works, politics cannot be separated from literature.

Weitzman, Erica. "Imperium Stupidum: Švejk, Satire, Sabotage." In *Law and Literature* 18, no. 2 (Summer, 2006): 117-148. Argues that the satire in Hašek's novel "lies less in the irreverence and humor of its content than in its deep structural mechanisms of repetition, delay, and non-resistance pushed to the point of absurdity."

ALFRED HAUGE

Born: Stjernarøy, Norway; October 17, 1915
Died: Stavanger, Norway; October 31, 1986

Principal long fiction

Septemberfrost, 1941
Tuntreet blør, 1942
Storm over Siglarholmen, 1945
Ropet, 1946
Året har ingen vår, 1948
Fossen og bålet, 1949
Vegen til det døde paradiset, 1951
Ingen kjenner dagen, 1955
Kvinner på Galgebakken, 1958
Cleng Peerson, 1961-1965 (includes *Hundevakt*, 1961; *Landkjenning*, 1964; and *Ankerfeste*, 1965; abridged English translation of *Cleng Peerson*, 1975)
Mysterium, 1967
Legenden om Svein og Maria, 1968
Perlemorstrand, 1974
Leviathan, 1979 (includes "Forvandling")

Other literary forms

Although known primarily as a novelist, Alfred Hauge (HOW-geh) also produced works of short prose, poetry, drama, and nonfiction. Much of his short prose and nonfiction originally appeared in the daily newspaper *Stavanger aftenblad*, where he was employed as a cultural correspondent for more than thirty years. In conjunction with the research for his trilogy about Cleng Peerson, the father of Norwegian emigration to the United States, he traced the movement of immigrants across the American continent. Two books, *Gå vest—* (1963; go west) and *Gjennom Amerika i emigrantspor* (1975; through America in the footsteps of the emigrants), resulted from these travels. Later came *Sannferdig saga om Cleng Peerson* (1982; *The True Saga of Cleng Peerson*, 1982), which is a factual presentation of the results of Hauge's research and which was published by the Norwegian Society of Texas on the bicentennial of Peerson's birth on May 17, 1782. Two other important volumes of nonfiction are Hauge's autobiographical *Barndom* (1975; childhood) and *Ungdom* (1977; youth).

Hauge also used the Cleng Peerson material dramatically in his play *Cleng Peerson: Utvandring* (1968; Cleng Peerson: emigration), but on the whole he gave relatively little attention to drama. Poetry was more important to him; his first collection, titled *Skyer i drift over vårgrønt land* (1945; clouds drifting over land green in spring), sold well but was not a critical success. In 1970 came *Det evige sekund* (the eternal second), the third volume in Hauge's hitherto unfinished magnum opus, the Utstein Monastery cycle.

Achievements

Alfred Hauge occupies a singular position in contemporary Norwegian literature. One of its ablest novelists, he was inventive both thematically and formally. It is even more remarkable that he reached his qualitative high at an age when many writers are in decline. His novel *Mysterium* (mystery), the first volume in his Utstein Monastery cycle, is clearly one of the very finest works of post-World War II literature in Norway, and the yet unfinished series to which he contributed *Perlemorstrand* (a shore made of mother-of-pearl) and *Leviathan* may equal it in significance.

Hauge was even better known for his emigrant novels. His trilogy about Peerson was translated into English and published in a two-volume, abridged edition in 1975 as part of the sesquicentennial celebration of Norwegian emigration to the United States. It is Hauge's later novels, however, which stand as his greatest artistic achievement.

Biography

Alfred Hauge was born on October 17, 1915, the oldest child of Kolbein Andersson Hauge and Marianne Rasmusdotter Auglend. His mother's family came from the Jæen district, south of Stavanger, Norway; his father's family lived at Stjernarøy, an island to the northeast, where Hauge grew up. Both sides of the family were farmers. The area is one of the strongholds of popular pietistic religiosity in Norway, and Hauge early accepted the religious ideas that were present in his surroundings.

Having received his basic education in the public schools at home, Hauge traveled to Bryne, Jæen, at the age of fifteen to attend a college-preparatory school for young people of rural origin. He later transferred to a similar school at Voss, east of Bergen, where, in addition to other academic subjects, he was able to receive instruction in Greek. In 1935, he entered the University of Oslo to study theology. In 1937, however, he gave up theology and entered a teacher's college, from which he graduated two years later. He first worked as a teacher at a folk high school, then as a literary consultant for a publishing house, and from 1953 as a cultural correspondent for the daily paper *Stavanger aftenblad*. He married Kirsten Væle on July 27, 1940.

Hauge's literary debut took place in 1941, when he published *Septemberfrost* (the frost of September), a historical novel with a message of encouragement to people in occupied Norway. Then came several novels in which the author drew on his intimate knowledge of life in western Norway; their main value lies in their faithful portrayal of a local community at a time of transition from the old agrarian social order to a twentieth century society. Two novels from this period, *Ropet* (the call) and *Ingen kjenner dagen* (nobody knows the day), also treat the conflict between religious and artistic demands so keenly felt by the author.

Hauge became internationally known for his *Cleng Peerson*, a trilogy based on the life of the man who has been called the father of Norwegian emigration to America. Then came the novel *Mysterium*, the first volume of his unfinished Utstein Monastery cycle, which also includes the poetry collection *Det evige sekund* and the novels *Legenden om Svein og Maria* (the legend of Svein and Maria), *Perlemorstrand*, and *Leviathan*. Hauge died October 31, 1986, in Stavanger, Norway.

Analysis

Alfred Hauge's main concern as a writer was to deepen his understanding of the human soul. The philosophical content in his novels is therefore substantial, but that does not mean that his works are removed from the real world. His early books are firmly anchored in the sociological reality that he knew from his own upbringing. The Cleng Peerson trilogy succeeds admirably in recreating both the Norwegian surroundings of the emigrants and the new world they encountered in America. *Perlemorstrand* and *Leviathan* both draw on the author's intimate knowledge of life in western Norway in the early part of the twentieth century.

The sociological and historical material found in Hauge's books is, however, subordinate to his real concerns. A religious and existential humanist, Hauge asked both the question of how humans should act toward other human beings and how they should relate to the divine. Above all, Hauge considered how humans can achieve the greatest personal growth through full participation in life. His tentative answers were informed both by his nondogmatic Christian faith and by the results of his self-analysis, which is influenced by Jungian thought. Hauge's literary works clearly show that his personal quest for understanding was been a strenuous one.

The personal nature of Hauge's works is reflected in their form. The early novels were written primarily in the third person, but most of his later books were narrated from the first-person point of view. In *Cleng Peerson*, the narrator is the aged Cleng, who relates the story of his life in terms of a never-ending search for understanding of both self and others. In *Mysterium*, *Perlemorstrand*, and *Leviathan*, the narrator is formally identical with the author. It is, however, in the later novels that Hauge's innovative narrative technique most forcefully strikes the reader.

Written during a period of some twenty-five years, the trilogy about Cleng Peerson required considerable research and other formal preparation. Its main theme is the human quest for liberty. Through the story of Cleng's personal search for understanding, Hauge describes the striving for that personal freedom that comes only as a result of a person being at peace with him- or herself through self-knowledge. Through his portrayal of the emigration movement, Hauge describes people's search for religious, political, and economic liberty.

HUNDEVAKT

In the first volume of the trilogy, *Hundevakt* (midwatch), Cleng tells the story of his childhood, youth, and early manhood. The book begins with the young child's attempt to sail to the sun in a small boat. This voyage serves as an illustration of the individual's search for wholeness; according to Jungian thought, the sun is a symbol of both the integrated self and human unity with the divine. The young Cleng is largely unsuccessful in his quest, however, for he is both a scoundrel among others and a sinner before his God. While basically well-meaning, he is unable to distinguish fact from fiction and often tells tall tales, a practice that has a disastrous effect on his associates.

During the Napoleonic wars, Cleng and a number of other Norwegians spend several years on board British prison ships. Some of them become Quakers, and after their return to Norway they are severely persecuted by the civil and religious authorities. One of their options is to emigrate to America, and although not formally a member of the group, Cleng is sent off as a scout. Upon his return, he characteristically exaggerates the virtues of the new land.

LANDKJENNING *and* ANKERFESTE

The second volume of the trilogy, *Landkjenning* (landfall), tells of the trials the emigrants undergo and for which Cleng is to a large extent responsible. This novel and the third one, *Ankerfeste* (anchorage), tell the story of early Norwegian emigration in both broad outline and significant detail. The economic hardships are shown, but Hauge's focus is on the emigrants' striving for religious development. Removed from the authority of the Norwegian State Church, they fall prey to all manner of religious enthusiasms, the most dangerous of which, from Cleng's point of view at least, seems to be Mormonism. The men and women who join the various sects are all searching for spiritual wholeness. So is Cleng, who even goes as far as to seek it by chemical means.

Through a substance derived from mushrooms, he is initiated into an ancient religious mystery by the Indian chief, Shabbona, and the result is that he finally gains a measure of self-knowledge. While in the altered state of consciousness brought on by the drug, he has a vision of himself sitting on a throne like a god, while a figure who looks like both a medieval fool and a rooster (but who, at the same time, is Cleng himself) is dancing around the throne. Cleng thus learns that throughout his life he has worshiped only himself and that his various attempts at charitable acts have been a part of this self-worship. This is a haunting scene that, slightly varied, returns in Hauge's next novel, *Mysterium*.

MYSTERIUM

At the end of the trilogy, Cleng has obtained a modicum of serenity. On the whole, however, his quest for self-knowledge and integration of the personality has failed. Because he did not reach his human potential, he is fundamentally a tragic figure.

Cleng Peerson's development constitutes a partially failed, partially successful process of individuation that is portrayed against the backdrop of the early Norwegian emigration to America. The protagonist in *Mysterium* also undergoes a process of individuation, but in his case the historical and sociological backdrop is almost entirely lacking. *Mysterium* therefore strikes some readers as rather abstract.

When the novel was first published, it was particularly the narrative technique that surprised the reviewers. The first-person narrator, who is formally identical with the author, repeatedly addresses the reader, discusses the novel's characters and their actions "with" him or her, and even invites him or her to finish the work (the last sentence in the book ends with a colon, and the reader is asked to fill in two names). The novel also has little action in the traditional sense. A victim of amnesia named Victor arrives at a place that can be identified as Utstein Monastery in western Norway. There he meets a Greek professor of archaeology named Hermes Oneiropompos. Victor is searching for his lost memory so that he might know where to find his wife and daughter.

The illusion of reality is completely shattered, however, when Victor and the professor begin exploring some tunnels and caverns under the monastery. It soon becomes apparent that their wanderings are actually taking place in the hidden recesses of Victor's unconscious. These experiences are also supplemented by reports of dreams that Victor has between his trips with Oneiropompos. The text thus takes on the appearance of a psychiatrist's journal; Victor is the patient and Oneiropompos (whose name means "he who guides through dreams"), the analyst. Victor finally comes out of the amnesia, remembering that he left his wife and lost his memory at a time when she was in the middle of a sudden attack of pain caused by a malignant brain tumor. He is now ready to return to her and to face the effects that her illness will have on their life together.

In the course of the analysis, it becomes clear that Victor's nervous breakdown with its accompanying amnesia occurred not only because of his inability to tolerate the sight of his wife's suffering but also because her impending death forcefully reminded him that he, too, must die. His awareness of his concern for self in the face of his wife's crisis causes him to feel deeply ashamed. This feeling manifests itself in a series of three dreams that emphasize the tension between appearance and reality, as well as in a scene during the first journey through the subterranean vaults. In this scene, which is reminiscent of a similar one toward the end of *Cleng Peerson*, Victor sees himself sitting on a throne as a god, and a figure that is half himself and half turkey is dancing around the throne.

Throughout *Mysterium*, Hauge encourages readers to compare themselves to Victor and to search their own souls to determine if they possess the human qualities of empathy, tenderness, and the ability to sustain others through suffering that Victor is partly lacking. Victor's process of individuation advances in the course of the novel; through archetypal symbolism, Hauge attempts to engage readers at the level not only of the intellect but also of the unconscious. *Mysterium* thus becomes a kind of Jungian bildungsroman in that it attempts to further the process of individuation in readers by portraying that of its main character.

Hauge's question of how to achieve an integrated self is one that is typical of existential humanism. The answer, which also has strong religious overtones, is to be found in the most important symbol in the novel—namely, a rotating cross to which human beings have been fastened. The cross is a symbol of suffering, but through its rotation it takes on the appearance of a sun, the Jungian symbol of both the unity of the self and the divine, which is also central to *Cleng Peerson*. The author's message is that humans can both achieve unity of the self and move closer to the divine by passing through suffering and by actively identifying with the suffering of others, thus helping them bear their burdens.

PERLEMORSTRAND *and* LEVIATHAN

Mysterium and the two novels that will be dealt with in this section belong to Hauge's Utstein Monastery cycle, a group of thematically related works that stress the need to develop the quintessentially human qualities of empathy, tenderness, and the ability to accompany others through suffering. *Perlemorstrand* and *Leviathan* constitute a subgroup within the cycle, "Århundre" (century). The theme of these two books is similar to that of *Mysterium*, but in the later works, Hauge includes a historical-philosophical dimension that is not present in the earlier book. This philosophy of history informs his choice of narrative technique and is expressed in mythic fashion in a prose poem, "Forvandling" (metamorphosis), which is found both in the author's poetry collection *Det evige sekund* and in *Leviathan*.

"Forvandling" relates the story of a young nobleman and a woman of the people who have a beautiful daughter named Iselin. At the age of five, however, she is suddenly changed into an ugly monster. The parents seek means by which the process can be reversed, but Iselin becomes more monstrous each time another remedy is applied. She finally returns to her normal state, however, and accepts a suitor's proposal of marriage. In the ensuing marriage ceremony, which takes place in church, the groom is called Isidor Saeculum XX, and the bride is called Iselin Saeculum XV. The two are wed but are immediately changed into the fragrance of roses and blood. At the same time, the life processes of their parents are reversed; they gradually become two newborn infants. The priest then christens the father Isidor Saeculum XXI and the mother Iselin Saeculum XVI.

On one level, this prose poem deals with parenthood and the commitment of parents to a child who must pass through much mental and physical suffering. On the historical-philosophical level, however, Hauge allegorically expresses his view that the fifteenth century and the twentieth century are basically similar, in that both can be characterized as periods of fundamental change in social conditions.

The fifteenth century brought about the historical situation in which the Reformation later took place, and the concomitant religious and political upheavals caused people to lose their spiritual bearings. The result was growing fear and superstition; figuratively, because Saeculum XVI was the result of Saeculum XV, the events of Saeculum XXI will be the result of the actions of Saeculum XX, which have caused the present generation to lose the firmer spiritual foundation of the past.

With the exception of the participants in the myth described in "Forvandling," the characters in both *Perlemorstrand* and *Leviathan* are squarely anchored in a historical and social reality, as both novels are set on a small island that appears to have been modeled on the one where Hauge was reared. The main character is Bodvar Staup, and the first-person narrator, who is virtually identical to Hauge, is one of Bodvar's childhood friends. In *Perlemorstrand*, which the author/narrator says was written during the months of September and October, 1973, the narrator primarily tells the story of Bodvar's childhood during the decade of 1920 to 1930. The events of the period are thus seen from the perspective of a contemporary observer who was then a child and who at the time of writing is a man well past the middle of his life. There is an additional temporal level, however, for the narrator also tells about a period that he and Bodvar spent together at Utstein Monastery during the month of June, 1973. At this time, they often talked about the events of their common childhood. The narrator is thus able to give the reader access to Bodvar's own childhood memories, and the author's use of several temporal levels enables the reader to create a panorama of the twentieth century.

The story of Bodvar Staup is brief. He grows up together with his first cousin and foster brother, Mons, and the two are rivals for the love of their common aunt and stepmother. Bodvar, who before his father's remarriage had the upper hand in his relationship with Mons, sees that he is no longer favored and becomes intensely jealous. The narration on the first temporal level ends when Bodvar brings Mons and another of their aunts, Tina, to a drinking bout at the home of a questionable character named Kid Skarvaskjer. The two boys and Tina get drunk, but Bodvar leaves before completely losing control. While both Mons and Tina are in a stupor, Tina is raped by Kid, who then leaves the island. Mons awakens, sees the bloody Tina, believes that he has committed the crime, and takes his own life.

Bodvar, who believes that he is responsible for his brother's death, has a nervous breakdown. He spends some time in a mental institution but continues to feel a desperate need to atone by taking upon himself the suffering of others. The narration on the second temporal level, or the month of June, 1973, ends with one of Bodvar's numerous failures to remove suffering from other people.

In *Leviathan*, Bodvar's story is continued on three temporal levels corresponding to those of the previous novel: a level of remembered experience spanning the years from 1930 to 1970; a second level, when Bodvar and the narrator are together at Utstein Monastery in the summer of 1981 (note that the book was published in 1979); and the time when the story is being written down by the author/narrator, in January, 1979.

The burden of the story is Bodvar's continued search for atonement and his repeated failures, until he recognizes his fundamental megalomania and understands that he cannot free others from suffering, but only assist them in enduring it. Bodvar's path therefore leads from a state of wholeness felt in his earliest childhood, through his fratricidal experience and its attendant schizoid state, then back to a state of inner unity and peace. The mother-of-pearl image, which also refers to the womb, serves as the most important image of wholeness, and the shore made of mother-of-pearl becomes symbolic of the goal of the process of individuation. The sea monster, Leviathan, stands for the forces that prevent humans from reaching their spiritual destination. In *Leviathan*, the monster appears in the shape of a sea serpent, a giant whale that is being trapped and killed, and a shipwrecked oil tanker. The forces that inhibit human spiritual progress can thus be identified as primarily fear and greed. The twentieth century is dominated by the latter.

Both *Perlemorstrand* and *Leviathan* are similar to *Mysterium* in that Hauge frequently addresses the reader directly, much as Cleng Peerson, as narrator of the trilogy, addresses his inscribed reader. Hauge thus breaks down the illusion of reality that he has so skillfully created and is able to communicate with his readers through both their reason and their emotions.

Through his archetypal imagery, he also attempts to reach the reader's unconscious. His sophisticated narrative technique serves as the vehicle for a simple yet important message: Even though humans find themselves in an often-hostile world, they must not neglect the cultivation of the quintessential qualities that define them as human beings. Indeed, the need to develop maturity and wholeness was Hauge's perennial theme.

Jan Sjåvik

Other major works

SHORT FICTION: *Det lyse fastland*, 1965; *Fotspor gjennom årstider*, 1969; *Landskap*, 1972; *Fabelskip*, 1974.

PLAYS: *Cleng Peerson: Utvandring*, pb. 1968; *Morten Kruse*, pb. 1975.

POETRY: *Skyer i drift over vårgrønt land*, 1945; *Det evige sekund*, 1970 (includes "Forvandling"); *Hafrsfjord: Kvad ved fest*, 1975; *Evangelium*, 1977.

NONFICTION: *Gå vest—*, 1963; *Barndom*, 1975; *Gjennom Amerika i emigrantspor*, 1975; *Ungdom*, 1977; *Sannferdig saga om Cleng Peerson*, 1982 (*The True Saga of Cleng Peerson*, 1982); *Manndom*, 1999.

Bibliography

Flatin, Kjetil. "The Rising Sun and the Lark on the Quilt: Quest and Defiance in Alfred Hauge's *Cleng Peerson* Trilogy." *Proceedings of the Pacific Northwest Conference on Foreign Languages* 27 (1976): 133-136. A brief analysis of the themes in the three novels of the Cleng Peerson trilogy.

Sjåvik, Jan. "Alfred Hauge's Utstein Monastery Cycle." *World Literature Today* 56 (1982): 54-57. An examination of Hauge's novels in the Utstein Monastery cycle by a leading scholar of Norwegian literature.

_______. "Norwegian Literature Since 1950." In *A History of Norwegian Literature*, edited by Harald S. Naess. Lincoln: University of Nebraska Press, with the American-Scandinavian Foundation, 1993. This chapter in Naess's comprehensive survey of Norwegian literature devotes some discussion to Hauge's fiction, placing it within the context of Norwegian fiction of the post-World War II period.

JOHN HAWKES

Born: Stamford, Connecticut; August 17, 1925
Died: Providence, Rhode Island; May 15, 1998
Also known as: John Clendennin Burne Hawkes, Jr.

Principal long fiction

The Cannibal, 1949
Charivari, 1949 (novella)
The Beetle Leg, 1951
The Goose on the Grave: Two Short Novels, 1954 (novellas; includes *The Goose on the Grave* and *The Owl*)
The Lime Twig, 1961
Second Skin, 1964
The Blood Oranges, 1971
Death, Sleep, and the Traveler, 1974
Travesty, 1976

The Passion Artist, 1979
Virginie: Her Two Lives, 1982
Adventures in the Alaskan Skin Trade, 1985
Innocence in Extremis, 1985 (novella)
Whistlejacket, 1988
Sweet William: A Memoir of Old Horse, 1993
The Frog, 1996
An Irish Eye, 1997

Other literary forms

In addition to his novels, John Hawkes (hawks) published a collection of four plays (*The Innocent Party: Four Short Plays*, 1966), some poetry (*Fiasco Hall*, 1943—privately printed), volumes of short fiction, and many fragments taken from his longer works and published separately, often while still in progress.

John Hawkes. (Getty Images)

Hawkes gave a number of highly informative interviews during his career, discussing not only past works but also those in progress. Notable conversations may be found in Anthony C. Santore's and Michael Pocalykov's *A John Hawkes Symposium: Design and Debris* (1977). Hawkes also conducted important dialogues with Thomas LeClair (*The New Republic*, November 10, 1979) and with John Barth (*The New York Times Book Review*, April 1, 1979).

Achievements

John Hawkes's lack of a wide readership has always been counterbalanced by a literate and highly vocal following among readers who are professionally interested in contemporary fiction. In fact, perhaps his most accessible and widely read work, *The Blood Oranges*, winner of Le Prix du Meilleur Livre Étranger (France, 1973), is a novel primarily read by college students and professors. Although he belongs to no recognizable school of fiction, many think Hawkes is "feasibly our best writer" of the late twentieth century, as the novelist Thomas McGuane put it. A ruthless poeticizer of fictional terror and aesthetic shock, Hawkes is both a satirist in the tradition of Franz Kafka, Flannery O'Connor, and Nathanael West and an explorer of the interior life in the tradition of Joseph Conrad. His achievement was recognized in 1986 with the awarding of the Prix Medicis Étranger (Paris).

Biography

Born in Stamford, Connecticut, reared in New York City and in Juneau, Alaska, John Clendennin Burne Hawkes, Jr., went to Harvard for his higher education, which was interrupted when World War II broke out. He then joined the American Field Service, driving an ambulance in Italy as Ernest Hemingway and several other American writers did in World War I. After service in Italy, Belgium, and Germany, Hawkes returned to Harvard, took Albert J. Guerard's creative writing class, and stunned classmates and teacher alike with his first major work, *Charivari*, a novella written while Hawkes and his wife were in Montana; *The Cannibal* followed shortly thereafter.

In his own words, Hawkes began life in the late summer or early fall of 1947 when he

> married Sophie, went back to Harvard, met Albert Guerard, and began to write, and through Albert . . . [met] James Laughlin, who became my publisher. So I had a wife, a teacher, and a publisher—all at the age of 22.

Hawkes graduated in 1949 with a bachelor of arts degree from Harvard, where he later held various jobs, including assisting the production manager of Harvard University Press and lecturing in creative writing. In the late 1950's, Hawkes moved to Brown University, eventually becoming a full professor of English. He held a number of visiting professorships and lectureships and lived in Providence, Rhode Island, and in a variety of exotic places in the Caribbean, Greece, and France. He and his wife, formerly Sophie Goode Tazewell, had four children.

Even though many of his works have a nightmarish, violently hallucinatory quality about them, Hawkes himself was hardly an advocate of ugliness in real life. As he said to Thomas LeClair in 1979, "I deplore violence. I want to lead a safe, ordinary life with my wife and children and my friends and students. But ugliness is as essential to fiction as it is to the dream."

Hawkes retired from university teaching in 1988 but continued to make his home in Providence. He died in Providence on May 15, 1998.

Analysis

Essentially a lyric poet operating as a fellow traveler in fiction, John Hawkes writes novels that are finely honed and superbly crafted, whose meaning and coherence arise largely from recurring patterns of imagery, autotelic thematic concerns, and highly unusual and largely unreliable narrative voices. Although the basic unit in the triad of the 1970's (*The Blood Oranges*; *Death, Sleep, and the Traveler*; and *Travesty*) was the relatively short scene arranged in a more or less nonsequential format, Hawkes's novels *The Passion Artist* and *Virginie* represent a return to more linear scenic development, albeit still employing nonsequential flashbacks. Indeed, Hawkes told Barth in 1979 that he no longer subscribed to his earlier, oft-quoted statement that "plot, character, setting, and theme" are the "true enemies" of his fiction, a remark made, he said, when he was very young. Rather, Hawkes's later work combines these linear patterns of development with comically grotesque narrators whose innocence in the face of a horrifying universe only magnifies the tension associated with that horror and with a mode of exposition that relies less heavily on unusual metaphoric connections and more on directed statement; in fact, Hawkes at times quite explicitly and directly tells readers what they are to understand. Nevertheless, even these directed statements are not ordinary referrals to the real world but are, rather, references one can only understand by looking forward or back to something else in Hawkes's mental Yoknapatawpha County.

By creating such unusual and self-contained fictional worlds, Hawkes draws the reader into some rather extraordinary literary experiences: ordinary fragments of conversation refer to highly stylized portrayals of bizarre activities and images of reality that take on nightmarish, hallucinogenic qualities. Explicit literary allusions, when followed up, only point to their own idiosyncratic employment. Narrators tell stories that, from a realistic perspective, could not possibly be told. For example, if there *is* a car crash in *Travesty*, who tells Papa's story? Similarly, how does one know Virginie's impossible story if she, herself, is an impossible child? The genius of Hawkes's writing is that all the possibilities—and perhaps none of them—may be true. One opens each new novel with the expectation of joining the author in creating a fictional world unlike any before known. Straining to make even elementary sense of what is being read, the "ideal" reader finds him- or herself forced to discard most of the more familiar relationships between fictional and real worlds.

As Hawkes himself has reiterated several times, his major themes and interests include the imagination, consciousness, and the nature of women. In the later 1970's and early 1980's, he started discounting—perhaps better stated, demystifying—his interest in women as a crucial subject. For Hawkes, "we live by our imaginations and a sense of strangeness," imaginations that are always "trying to create something from nothing." In addition, paradox is "the second word, after imagination that's most important to [Hawkes], and . . . the word, dignity." Add to these preoccupations an obsession "with such things as horses, dogs, birds, sexual destructiveness, lyricisms, [and] children." All the children in Hawkes's fictions are "maimed, injured, harmed, killed, punished in one way or another because [they] . . . represent the writer himself." Although these sufferings by children and animals may seem cruel, such cruelty "helps to produce a lot of the power of the language."

This cruelty and power, coupled with Hawkes's insistence on the separation of author and narrator, allow him to organize his prose objectively, obtaining the greatest possible tonal dissonance for superb aesthetic effects. Such detachment has led critics to question Hawkes's apparent lack of ethical responsibility. These questions, confusing mimetic and aesthetic ends, are, perhaps, inevitable about someone who says, "I want fiction always to situate us in the psychic and literal spot where life is most difficult, most dangerous, most beautiful."

The Cannibal

Hawkes's best-known early work is *The Cannibal*, a novel that, as Albert Guerard has pointed out, tiptoes on a fine line between the creation of a new universe and the fantastical exploration of the present one. The war-ravaged, degenerating town of Spitzen-on-the-Dein becomes the allegorical microcosmic version of Germany, pre- and postwar, during the twentieth century. Although parts I and II focus on the events of 1945 and following, and part II centers on the militaristic Germany prior to the outbreak of war, the thrust of the novel points toward a time in the future when Teutonic Germany will, for the third time in the twentieth century, rise again from the ashes of total defeat. By extension, such a renewal of nationalistic fervor makes a stable, peaceful world all but impossible.

Zizendorf, the narrator of parts I and III, wants to restore order to the German town (and, by analogy, to the nation). He is convinced that the first step involves killing the Allied representative, the overseer on motorcycle who patrols one-third of the occupied country. Part II details, in both complementary and contrapuntal imagery to the first and last section of the novel, the love affair and subsequent marriage of Madame Stella Snow and her husband, Ernst, which occurs prior to and during World War I. The imagery patterns in all three sections demonstrate how Germany's martial atmosphere made a century of warfare virtually inevitable as the casual, surrealistic horror of life in Spitzen-on-the-Dein suffuses everything, even the newspaper, which is called, comically, the *Crooked Zeitung*.

Stella's sister, Jutta, for example, an innocent girl during World War I, marries and bears two children between the wars, and, after her husband is captured in Russia, she must turn to prostitution to stay alive. One child, a girl, barely tolerated by Zizendorf, sees in the war-torn town a kind of beauty in the fires. Another child, a boy, is chased throughout the novel by a mad duke, who eventually kills, fillets, and cooks the "small fox" in what has to be Hawkes's masterpiece of sustained metaphoric terror. The duke's arrogance and bearing impresses Zizendorf, who thinks of staffing the offices of the new nation with his friends and acquaintances; indeed, thinks Zizendorf, the mad duke "would perhaps make a good Chancellor."

By the end of the novel, the overseer has been killed, the people are informed that once again Germany is "free," and Zizendorf gives one of his first orders to Jutta's child, whom the Commander believes "will have to go" eventually. As many of the citizens of Spitzen-on-the-Dein line up to return to the insane asylum, the girl does "as she was told."

Mere plot summary, however, captures little of the essence of Hawkes's novel; only the experience of reading can fully impart the flavor of the work. In the chase of Jutta's boy by the mad duke, for example, the reader first feels puzzled; he or she marvels how Hawkes has so easily and so well employed the metaphor of the fox hunt yet is vaguely unsettled by the juxtaposition of the hunt and the impact of the novel's title. When Stella's son comes upon them accidentally, one first tends to anticipate some sort of sexual child abuse signified through the chasing of the fox. Most readers, lulled by the son's "uncommon pleasure in the visit of the Duke," are stunned when they realize just how literal the fox hunt has been, as the duke cuts, slices, and finally skins his little "furry animal."

The objectivity and the detachment of the narrative surrounding the boy's dismemberment and the boy's role at the duke's dinner party combine forcefully to demonstrate how skillfully Hawkes is able to write about the most horrible scenes, employing an almost schizophrenic split between description and valuation, between perception and cognition. This ability gives the average reader an experience in what Hawkes calls "true fictive sympathy."

THE BLOOD ORANGES

The problems of consciousness, ethics, the imagination, and sexual love get extensive and unusual treatment in *The Blood Oranges*, a novel set in the mythical kingdom of Illyria, where Cyril and Fiona, a couple who practice sexual extension and multiplicity, meet a second couple, Hugh and Catherine (and their three children), the former a puritanical voyeuristic photographer, the latter a housewife seeking adventure. As Cyril and Fiona encourage Hugh and Catherine to join them in their tapestry of love, momentary acquiescence becomes wholehearted acceptance by Catherine; Hugh cannot purge himself of his former demons and accidentally hangs himself.

For the initial reviewers, the most important question in *The Blood Oranges* seemed to be an ethical one. Many equated the central character, Cyril, "with a studied, self-conscious, and all-pervading aestheticism" that can coldly watch the perpetration of the "greatest of evils," that of a person's apparent suicide. Following this understanding of the plot, critics would then go on to picture Cyril as a latter-day Oscar Wilde, a moral monster whose creator was guilty of either a bankrupt moral vision or a "self-conscious artificiality" so brittle and corrupt that "people have stopped mattering." Later, as the novel went past its sixth printing, various readers came to understand that its lyrical qualities made any naïvely realistic reading of the novel distorted. The reader is not supposed to see the characters as only separate individuals. Instead, in almost Dickensian fashion, the reader must understand that each character represents only part of the issues being raised.

Indeed, *The Blood Oranges* is a wonderfully lyrical and highly moral work of fiction that was influenced not only by William Shakespeare's *Twelfth Night* (1599-1600) and Ford Madox Ford's *The Good Soldier* (1915) but also by selected Platonic dialogues, the Bible, John Milton, Wallace Stevens, and medieval flower symbology. Hawkes's intention seems to be the creation of a new moral order to take the place of Western sexual mores associated with a dying Christian symbolic and ethical tradition. This transposition is done by arranging the story into forty-two nonsequential scenes and scenic fragments arranged imagistically and thematically. Since all of the information comes filtered through Cyril's unusually self-confident voice, the reader must be extremely careful not to make predictions about the "unreality" found in the fictional world without also checking for symbolic patterns, comic utterances, and unusual tonal qualities. Hawkes's vision is so complex, so paradoxical, that to understand any of his fictional patterns, one must be prepared to watch each of them resonate throughout the whole.

As one pieces together the chronology of *The Blood Oranges*, one begins to see that single, apparently simple scenes contain many of the novel's major thematic and character contrasts, contrasts that only later become clear, thus beginning the process of analysis, not ending it. The first major scene starts in a "little medieval church of cold passion" where Cyril and Fiona note that "the little motheaten dress of the infant in Mary's arms," the "thicklettered unreadable injunctions against frivolity and sex," the "effluvium of devotion," and the "comic miracle" of a life-sized wooden arm are enclosed by a "sagging and worm-eaten church door." These images form the first set of oppositions: Christianity as an ethically and aesthetically decaying force. The opposite of the rotting chapel is the composite of Fiona/Cyril, whose sexual and emotional lifestyle counterpoints the images just seen.

As an unusual sort of narrator, Cyril arouses readers' interests in questioning their value choices, their assessments of other people, and, most important, their ability to characterize themselves accurately. In contrast to his unblushing references to his "diligent but unemotional study of sex literature," his living "a life without pain," his role as "a steady, methodical, undesigning lover," Cyril states uncategorically that he is "a man of feeling." Intellectual Cyril and spontaneous Fiona meet Catherine and Hugh in the chapel, a scene that adumbrates the oppositions: the decaying church, the sex-singing couple, and the curious relationships they all share.

After all four meet, one notices that Hugh, with a face like "Saint Peter in stone," has numerous imagistic connections with the church: black clothing and a missing arm that Cyril thinks corresponds to the one over the pulpit. By contrast, the imagistic opposition points obviously to Cyril as exemplar of a joyous sensuality, an aesthetic delight in color, harmony, and sexual extension, and, most important, to an almost religious desire to fertilize the sterility associated with Hugh, the Church, and sexual monogamy. The latter all reflect blackness, decay, repression, and ultimately death. Nevertheless, such pictorial polarities only represent part of Hawkes's master plan, because Cyril, although perceiving himself as gold while Hugh is black, will not be "unduly critical of Hugh."

As the story progresses nonsequentially, the reader senses that not only do Hugh/Cyril form both a set of polarities and of complementarities, but Fiona/Catherine, Christ/Goat-faced man, and sex-singing/child rearing do as well. Neither is complete nor well defined without the opposition/attraction of the other. For example, however seriously the pompous Cyril tries to interest himself in "the possibilities of sex in the domestic landscape," he can never, psychologically speaking, become a parent; Fiona and he are fated only to one cycle. As negative an example as Hugh is, he has created new life with Catherine and will perpetuate the possibility of other beings who may adopt Cyril's values. For Hawkes, the new Jerusalem must be based realistically on the whole of life. Children, family, all life must test the validity of sex-singing and a new moral order.

This type of character dualism is typical of Hawkes's narrators and so becomes a tool with which to read his later novels. One must listen to Cyril, or to Allert (*Death, Sleep, and the Traveler*), or Papa (*Travesty*), or Konrad Vost (*The Passion Artist*), or Virginie (*Virginie*) with an ear for self-delusions, mental mistakes, and misleading self-justifications. Only as readers understand Hawkes's narrative playfulness will they be able to feel the complications arising from the author's paradoxical and fictive imagination.

Travesty

In *Travesty*, Papa is mad and tears down a country road in southern France at "one hundred and forty-nine kilometers per hour . . . in the darkest quarter of the night," hell-bent on killing himself, his daughter, Chantal, and his daughter's lover, Henri (a poet who also happens to be Papa's best friend and the lover of Honorine, Papa's wife). As the car races toward death, the three of them have an hour and forty minutes to discuss why Papa is going to kill them. The only narrative voice, however, is Papa's, a kind of novelistic dramatic monologue sounding like many of Hawkes's other narrators: a voice frighteningly rational, and chillingly single-minded.

As they race along, Papa's calm refutation of Henri's terrified yet suffocating theorizing mesmerizes the reader into what Hawkes has earlier called an intense kind of novelistic sympathy. Readers find themselves shocked yet almost swayed by Papa's self-assurance. He will take them to their "destination"—"Perhaps 'murder' is the proper word, though it offends [his] ear"—not out of cosmic dread, or of hatred for Henri, or jealousy over Honorine or Chantal, and certainly not out of disgust with life. Papa says he wants, above all else, the "purity," the "clarity," the "ecstasy" of an accident in which "invention quite defies interpretation," a matter of "design and debris." Thus, Papa intends to commit the "final and irrevocable act" he so feared in childhood, an act that will elicit this purity, clarity, and perhaps even a "moment of genuine response from Henri." Their death, says Papa, will be "an ironic triumph," signifying "the power to invent the very world we are quitting."

It is through this last statement that Hawkes's larger purposes become clearer; and a formative event in Papa's youth—the "travesty" concerning a car, an elderly poet, and a young girl—points the reader to a greater understanding of the conversation between Papa and Henri. The latter, by ultimately agreeing with Papa's contention that "imagined life is more exhilarating than remembered [real] life," misses his chance to see the light of life and is doomed to die.

Henri and Papa, locked together "like two dancers at arm's length," share mistress, wife, daughter, and near metaphysical bond as well. To read them as if they were merely realistic characters has led some critics to condemn the seemingly moral emptiness of Hawkes's narrators and the author's refusal to provide even minor external clues with which to judge the ethical validity of the storytellers. A realistic reading of *Travesty*, however, may miss half of Hawkes's intentions. It has been argued that no one else but Papa is in the car, that readers are hearing Papa talking only to himself.

Another and more inclusive reading of *Travesty*, one in keeping with Hawkes's artistic intentions and concerns for artists creating art, discounts the stress on arguable realism and focuses instead on the novel as an allegorical playing with Friedrich Nietzsche's fundamental question for the modern world: Suicide or not? If not, philosophy and life continue. If so, then dying with grace and imagination, creating design out of debris, forming debris in order to make possible new design, may be all the control the postmodern human has left over his or her brief life. With this idea in mind, Papa, the other "characters," and the impossible narrative voice all recede into the background, and readers are left with a brilliant but somewhat brittle art object: a work in which the realism is muted, the artifice very obvious, a work that points both to and away from a deadly world made somewhat livable by the imposition of great art between humans and the void.

THE PASSION ARTIST

Moving from the allegories of *Travesty* to the unusual "realism" of *The Passion Artist*, the informed reader can only marvel at the maturity of style and vision Hawkes displays. Although the novel is suffused with influences from Kafka and especially from Rainer Maria Rilke, his voice is still very much his own as he digs deeper into the human condition. Unlike earlier Hawkes protagonists, Konrad Vost is depicted through the filtered yet illuminating light of both his childhood and his mother's. It is a light everyone eventually must face, implies Hawkes, since no one escapes the dragons of childhood.

The Passion Artist concerns the last several days in the life of Konrad Vost, a modern-day Malvolio. Vost spends much of his free time in the café La Violaine (a French portmanteau word, combining the concepts of "rape" and "filth" in a beautiful sounding word—a typical Hawkesian trope), situated across the street from the prison of the same name, waiting for his imprisoned mother, who had murdered his father when Konrad was a small boy. Father burned to death, notorious mother imprisoned for life, young Konrad is sent to a bizarre foster home, the dumping ground for his village's orphans and human refuse, presided over by Anna Kossowski, an older drunken woman with a large body and perverted sexual habits. After his graphic and yet highly lyrical sexual initiation with a horse also named Anna Kossowski and a young but not so innocent girl named Kristol, Konrad runs away, having suffered through those life events that will shape the revolting human encountered at the opening of the novel.

Learning about Konrad's youth in sensuous flashback, the reader opens the novel to Konrad as an adult in his fifties, a psychic cripple unable to finish grieving for his wife, dead for more than five years, unable or unwilling—or both—to recognize that his teenage daughter, like a jinni in a bottle, has escaped his care and become a prostitute. Konrad remains unrequited in his love for his mother, who, in the prison across from La Violaine café, has never written or spoken to him since the murder. After a brief encounter with a child prostitute, who is both friend of and psychic double for his daughter, Konrad Vost volunteers to help put down a prison revolt. Rendered unconscious during the battle for control of the prison, Konrad's unconscious takes command as he dreams of women who describe his personality flaws. Awakening, he believes that his right hand has been axed off, replaced by a silver one encased in a black glove, and vows to conduct a personal search for the escapees. This silver hand is an important image: as a child, Konrad was called "the little trumpeter of the silver hands."

During the search, Konrad frightens an old woman to death and betrays another, a slim young child-woman whom he spies upon, bathing. Konrad, looking for shelter, is seized by two older escapees from La Violaine and is put in the prison, a place where he knew he had wanted to be all along. There, he encounters his mother and a tall, handsome woman with red hair who seduces him and finally shows him a "willed erotic union" and the possibilities of mature sexual expression. Hawkes, however, unwilling to end the novel happily, has Konrad Vost die at the hands of a La Violaine café habitué, possibly the father of a girl Konrad had beaten earlier.

The plot of this novel is detailed in order to show how it represents the skeleton, the outer shell of a highly elaborate work of art. In *The Passion Artist*, Hawkes returns both stylistically and imagistically to the bleak, rotting, rust-filled world of *The Cannibal* and *The Owl*. For example, Konrad Vost thinks of himself as some "military personage" walking "with feigned complacency down a broad avenue awash with urine." La Violaine, the place where his mother is imprisoned, is enclosed by "high narrow rusted gates" and sits in the middle of a city that was "the very domain of the human psyche." As with the earlier novels, the imagistic and metaphoric patterns become the reality of *The Passion Artist*. In looking for a focus, a place with which to begin interpretation, the reader must pay close attention to the repeated visualizations toward which Hawkes continually draws the reader's attention.

In the novel, for example, a pattern of flower references and women is established, and the reader soon realizes the importance of the relationships between Konrad's mental state and the descriptions of landscapes and flowers. To solidify this innocent impression, Hawkes says explicitly, during Konrad's hunt through the swamps, that his inner landscape "had become externalized." There, in the marshes, plants fester "in sockets of ice," reminding the reader that when Konrad's father was killed, the "flowers on the porcelain stove were frozen."

The flower references all point toward an understanding of Konrad's sexuality as locked in cold storage, decaying, unable to flower. Anna Kossowski, wearing a birthmark, a "brown toadstool" on her cheek, and in part responsible for Konrad's problems, becomes a variation of the same basic pattern. Hawkes vividly demonstrates the possibilities of change in Konrad's life by giving the tall, handsome woman with red hair who loves and seduces him at the end of the novel the same image as the prostitute: she too wears a brown rose. With her, however, Konrad Vost learns, after all he has gone through, "the transports of that singular experience which makes every man an artist," a passion artist. In this way, Hawkes uses visual images in place of didactic narrative statement, but he does it so well that information is communicated through an almost completely aesthetic transmission.

Like so many of Hawkes's other narrators, Konrad Vost must never be confused with the author. In the instance of *The Passion Artist*, Konrad Vost's understanding of the world is so clouded, so distorted with his own neuroses, that Hawkes is able to frighten the reader more with what Konrad does not see and feel than he could with a more reasonable or observant narrator. The mental double talk, for example, which so far reflects Konrad's apathetic feelings about killing an old woman, serves only to confirm how despicable a character he really is; and yet, Konrad still remains understandable and even sympathetic to the reader. This attitude is as it should be, as Hawkes has arranged it: readers can sympathize with both victim and victimizer; they can be both murdered and murderer. The simple oppositions Hawkes labors to draw convincingly finally become united in the minds of the readers in what Hawkes has termed "true fictive sympathy."

Thus, Hawkes's lyrically passionate prose style, his wonderfully imaginative, self-contained worlds, his rare ability to make the reader know and understand both victim and victimizer are some of the qualities that make reading the longer fictions of Hawkes one of the most rewarding aesthetic experiences to be found in contemporary American fiction.

John V. Knapp

Other major works

SHORT FICTION: *Lunar Landscapes: Stories and Short Novels, 1949-1963*, 1969.

PLAY: *The Innocent Party: Four Short Plays*, 1966.

POETRY: *Fiasco Hall*, 1943.

MISCELLANEOUS: *Humors of Blood and Skin: A John Hawkes Reader*, 1984.

Bibliography

Berry, Eliot. *A Poetry of Force and Darkness: The Fiction of John Hawkes*. San Bernardino, Calif.: Borgo Press, 1979. Discusses the imaginative art of Hawkes's writing in the context of the romantic novel, likening it to poetry with its rich language and depth. Compares Hawkes to both William Faulkner and Nathaniel Hawthorne.

Bertens, Johannes Willem. *Postmodernism: The Key Figures*. Malden, Mass.: Blackwell, 2002. Hawkes is included in this examination of the major figures of postmodernism in literature, the arts, and other areas.

Bradbury, Malcolm. *The Modern American Novel*. New ed. New York: Penguin Books, 1994. Bradbury places Hawkes in the genre of postmodernism, citing him as a powerfully compelling writer of the "imaginative grotesque" who draws on the tradition of the American gothic. Discusses his novels up to and including

The Passion Artist, noting his increased clarity of technique and greater complexity.

Busch, Frederick. *Hawkes: A Guide to His Fictions*. Syracuse, N.Y.: Syracuse University Press, 1973. Valuable when examining the intricacies of the plots in Hawkes's fiction, but less so when discussing stylistic and thematic concerns. Analyzes image patterns in his novels through *The Blood Oranges*, with a helpful discussion on his use of animal imagery.

Conte, Joseph Mark. "Design and Debris: John Hawkes's *Travesty*, Chaos Theory, and the Swerve." In *Design and Debris: A Chaotics of Postmodern American Fiction*. Tuscaloosa: University of Alabama Press, 2002. Conte explores "orderly disorder," chaos theory, and the relation between science and the writing of postmodern fiction, among other topics, in this book for advanced readers.

Ferrari, Rita. *Innocence, Power, and the Novels of John Hawkes*. Philadelphia: University of Pennsylvania Press, 1996. Ferrari traces Hawkes's development as a novelist, analyzing his experiments with narrative voice and perspective, his representations of gender and identity, and his ideas about language, among other elements of his fiction.

Greiner, Donald J. *Comic Terror: The Novels of John Hawkes*. Memphis, Tenn.: Memphis State University Press, 1978. Greiner cites Hawkes as one of the few "truly gifted writers of the so-called black humor movement." Discusses his later works and shows how they have modified earlier works. Includes a checklist of primary and secondary sources. An important contribution to Hawkes criticism.

Kuehl, John. *John Hawkes and the Craft of Conflict*. New Brunswick, N.J.: Rutgers University Press, 1975. Treats the relationship between Hawkes's central themes and his craft, simultaneously tracing the evolution of both. Explores the Eros/Thanatos conflict in his work and is therefore useful to the Hawkes specialist. Also includes an interview with Hawkes.

Marx, Lesley. *Crystals out of Chaos: John Hawkes and the Shapes of Apocalypse*. Madison, N.J.: Fairleigh Dickinson University Press, 1997. An analysis of Hawkes's novels, focusing on the work published in the late 1980's and early 1990's, including *Adventures in the Alaskan Skin Trade* and *Sweet William: A Memoir of Old Horse*. Marx compares the later novels with Hawkes's earlier works to examine his development as a novelist.

O'Donnell, Patrick. *John Hawkes*. Boston: Twayne, 1982. Provides thorough readings of his works and some biographical information of interest. The purpose of this study is to explain to general readers the difficulties of Hawkes's fiction. Includes a useful selected bibliography.

Whelan, Michaele. *Navigating the Minefield: Hawke's Narratives of Perversion*. New York: Peter Lang, 1998. Whelan analyzes Hawkes's novels from the perspective of psychoanalysis, gender representation, and narrative structure. Among the topics she examines are the dream narrative in *Death, Sleep, and the Traveler* and "autobiography as exhibitionism" in *Adventures in the Skin Trade*.

NATHANIEL HAWTHORNE

Born: Salem, Massachusetts; July 4, 1804
Died: Plymouth, New Hampshire; May 19, 1864
Also known as: Nathaniel Hawthorne, Jr.; Nathaniel Hathorne

PRINCIPAL LONG FICTION

Fanshawe: A Tale, 1828
The Scarlet Letter, 1850
The House of the Seven Gables, 1851
The Blithedale Romance, 1852
The Marble Faun: Or, The Romance of Monte Beni, 1860
Septimius Felton, 1872 (fragment)
The Dolliver Romance, 1876 (fragment)
The Ancestral Footstep, 1883 (fragment)
Doctor Grimshawe's Secret, 1883 (fragment)

Other literary forms

Many of Nathaniel Hawthorne's short stories were originally published anonymously in such magazines as the *Token* and the *New England Magazine* between 1830 and 1837. Several collections appeared during his lifetime, including *Twice-Told Tales* (1837; expanded 1842), *Mosses from an Old Manse* (1846), and *The Snow-Image, and Other Twice-Told Tales* (1851). Houghton Mifflin published the complete works in the Riverside edition (1850-1882) and the Old Manse edition (1900). Hawthorne also wrote stories for children, collected in *Grandfather's Chair* (1841), *Biographical Stories for Children* (1842), *True Stories from History and Biography* (1851), *A Wonder-Book for Boys and Girls* (1852), and *Tanglewood Tales for Boys and Girls* (1853). With the help of his sister, Elizabeth, he edited the *American Magazine of Useful and Entertaining Knowledge* (1836) and *Peter Parley's Universal History* (1837) and, as a favor to would-be president Franklin Pierce, wrote a biography for the presidential campaign. His last completed work was *Our Old Home* (1863), a series of essays about his sojourn in England. At the time of his death, he left four unfinished fragments: *Septimius Felton*, *The Dolliver Romance*, *The Ancestral Footstep*, and *Doctor Grimshawe's Secret*.

Achievements

Few other American authors, with the possible exception of Henry James, have engaged in so deliberate a literary apprenticeship as Nathaniel Hawthorne. After an initial period of anonymity during his so-called solitary years from 1825 to 1837, he achieved an unfaltering reputation as an author of short stories, romances, essays, and children's books. He is remembered for not only furthering the development of the short-story form but also distinguishing between the novel and the romance. The prefaces to his long works elucidate his theory of the "neutral ground"—the junction between the actual and the imaginary—where romance takes place. He is noted for his masterful exploration of the psychology of guilt and sin; his study of the Puritan heritage contributed to the emerging sense of historicity that characterized the American Renaissance of the mid-nineteenth century.

Hawthorne is unrivaled as an allegorist, especially as one whose character typologies and symbols achieve universality through their psychological validity. While he has been faulted for sentimentality, lapses into archaic diction, and gothicism, Hawthorne's works continue to evoke the "truth of the human heart" that is the key to their continuing appeal.

Biography

Nathaniel Hawthorne was born in Salem, Massachusetts, on July 4, 1804. On his father's side, Hawthorne was descended from William Hathorne, who settled in Massachusetts in 1630 and whose son, John, was one of the judges in the 1692 Salem witchcraft trials. Hawthorne's father, a sea captain, married Elizabeth Clarke Manning in 1801. His mother's English ancestors immigrated to the New World in 1679; her brother, Robert, a successful businessman, assumed responsibility for her affairs after Captain Hathorne died of yellow fever in Suriname in 1808.

After his father's death, Hawthorne, his two sisters, Elizabeth Manning and Maria Louisa, and his mother moved into the populous Manning household, a move that on one hand estranged him from his Hathorne relatives and on the other provided him with an attentive family life, albeit an adult one, for the eight aunts and uncles living there were unmarried at that time. Perhaps the adult company accounted in part for his literary tastes, as did his less than regular education. Although he attended a school taught by Joseph Emerson Worcester, a renowned philologist of the time, Hawthorne led a sedentary existence for almost three years after being lamed at the age of nine. During his enforced inactivity, he spent long afternoons reading Edmund Spenser, John Bunyan, and William Shakespeare, his favorite authors.

When Hawthorne was twelve years old, his mother moved the family temporarily to Raymond, Maine, where the Mannings owned a tract of land. The outdoor activity occasioned by nearby Lake Sebago and the surrounding forest land proved beneficial to Hawthorne; quickly recovering his health, he became an able marksman and fisherman. During these years, interrupted by schooling with the Reverend Caleb Bradley, a stern man not to Hawthorne's liking, Hawthorne accumulated Wordsworthian memories of the wilderness and of village life that were to be evoked in his fiction. Recalled to Salem, he began in 1820 to be tutored for college by lawyer Benjamin Lynde Oliver, working, in the meantime, as a bookkeeper for his Uncle Robert, an occupation that foreshadowed his later business ventures. He continued his reading, including such authors as Henry Fielding, Sir Walter Scott, William Godwin, Matthew "Monk" Lewis, and James Hogg, and produced a family newspaper, *The Spectator*, characterized by humorous notices and essays and parodies of sentimental verse.

The first member of his family to attend college, Hawthorne was sent to Bowdoin, where he graduated eighteenth in a class of thirty-eight. Known for his quietness and gentle humor, he disliked declamations, was negligent in many academic requirements, and, indeed, was fined for playing cards. His fellow students at Bowdoin included Henry Wadsworth Longfellow and Franklin Pierce, who later was elected president of the United States.

Nathaniel Hawthorne. (Library of Congress)

Hawthorne had determined early on a career in letters. Returning to Salem upon graduation, he began a self-imposed apprenticeship, the solitary years. During this time, Hawthorne privately published *Fanshawe*, a work that he so thoroughly repudiated that his wife, Sophia, knew nothing of it; he published many short stories anonymously and unsuccessfully attempted to interest publishers in such collections as *Seven Tales of My Native Land*, *Provincial Tales*, and *The Storyteller*. As a means of support he edited the *American Magazine of Useful and Entertaining Knowledge* and compiled *Peter Parley's Universal History*. Not until the publication of *Twice-Told Tales* under the secret financial sponsorship of his friend, Horatio Bridge, did Hawthorne's name become publicly known.

The label "solitary years" is somewhat of a misnomer, for, as his journals indicate, Hawthorne visited with friends, went for long walks and journeys, and, most important, met Sophia Peabody, the daughter of Dr. Nathaniel Peabody. For Hawthorne, Sophia was the key by which he was released from "a life of shadows" to the "truth of the human heart." Four years passed, however, before they could marry—four years in which Hawthorne became measurer in the Boston Custom House, which he called a "grievous thraldom," and then, although not sympathetic to the burgeoning transcendental movement, joined the utopian community Brook Farm (April, 1841), investing one thousand dollars in an attempt to establish a home for himself and Sophia.

After little more than six months, Hawthorne gave up the communal venture and, settling in the Old Manse at Concord, married Sophia on July 19, 1842. His financial difficulties were exacerbated by the birth of Una in 1844; finally, in 1846, when his son, Julian, was born and *Mosses from an Old Manse* was published, he was appointed surveyor of the Salem Custom House, a post he held from 1846 to 1849, when a political upset cost him his job. With more time to write and with the pressure to support a growing family, Hawthorne began a period of intense literary activity; his friendship with Herman Melville dates from that time. *The Scarlet Letter*, whose ending sent Sophia to bed with a grievous headache, was finished in February, 1850. *The House of the Seven Gables* appeared in 1851, the year Hawthorne's daughter, Rose, was born; by the end of the next year, Hawthorne had completed *The Blithedale Romance*, two volumes of children's tales, *The Life of Franklin Pierce*, and a collection of stories, *The Snow-Image, and Other Twice-Told Tales*.

From 1853 to 1857, Hawthorne served as American consul in Liverpool, England, a political appointment under President Pierce. After four years of involvement with the personal and financial problems of stranded Americans, Hawthorne resigned and lived in Rome and Florence from 1857 to 1858, where he acquired ideas for his last romance, *The Marble Faun*. After returning with his family to the United States, Hawthorne worked on four unfinished romances, *Doctor Grimshawe's Secret*, *Septimius Felton*, *The Dolliver Romance*, and *The Ancestral Footstep*, in which two themes are dominant: the search for immortality and the American attempt to establish title to English ancestry. His carefully considered essays on the paucity of American tradition, the depth of British heritage, and the contrast between democracy and entrenched class systems were first published in *The Atlantic Monthly* and then collected as *Our Old Home*. After a lingering illness, he died at Plymouth, New Hampshire, on May 19, 1864, during a trip with Pierce. Hawthorne was buried at Sleepy Hollow Cemetery in Concord, Massachusetts.

Analysis

Central to Nathaniel Hawthorne's romances is his idea of a "neutral territory," described in the Custom House sketch that precedes *The Scarlet Letter* as a place "somewhere between the real world and fairy-land, where the Actual and the Imaginary may meet, and each imbue itself with the nature of the other." A romance, according to Hawthorne, is different from the novel, which maintains a "minute fidelity . . . to the probable and ordinary course of man's experience." In the neutral territory of romance, however, the author may make use of the "marvellous" to heighten atmospheric effects, if he or she also presents "the truth of the human heart." As long as the writer of romance creates characters whose virtues, vices, and sensibilities are distinctly human, he or she may place them in an environment that is out of the ordinary—or that is, in fact, allegorical. Thus, for example, while certain elements—the stigma of the scarlet letter, or Donatello's faun ears—are fantastical in conception, they represent a moral stance that is true to nature. Dimmesdale's guilt at concealing his adultery with Hester Prynne is, indeed, as destructive as the wound on his breast, and Donatello's pagan nature is expressed in the shape of his ears.

A number of recurring thematic patterns and character types appear in Hawthorne's novels and tales, as Randall Stewart suggests in the introduction to *The American Notebooks* (1932). These repetitions show Hawthorne's emphasis on the effects of events on the human heart rather than on the events themselves. One common motif is concern for the past, or, as Hawthorne says in the preface to *The House of the Seven Gables*, his "attempt to connect a bygone time with the very present that is flitting away from us." Hawthorne's interest in the Puritan past was perhaps sparked by his "discovery," as a teenager, of his Hathorne connections; it was certainly influenced by his belief that progress was impeded by inheritance, that "the wrong-doing of one generation lives into the successive ones, and . . . becomes a pure and uncontrollable mischief." For Hawthorne, then, the past must be reckoned with, and then put aside; the eventual decay of aristocratic families is not only inevitable, but desirable.

Hawthorne's understanding of tradition is illustrated in many of his works. In *The Scarlet Letter*, for example, he explores the effect of traditional Puritan social and theological expectations on three kinds of sinners: the adultress (Hester), the hypocrite (Dimmesdale), and the avenger (Chillingworth), only to demonstrate that the punishment they inflict on themselves far outweighs the public castigation. Hester, in fact, inverts the rigidified Puritan system, represented by the scarlet letter, whose meaning she changes from "adultress" to "able." Probably the most specific treatment of the theme, however, is found in *The House of the Seven Gables*, in which the Pyncheon family house and fortune have imprisoned both Hepzibah and Clifford, one in apathy and one in insanity; only Phoebe, the country cousin who cares little for wealth, can lighten the burden, for not only her relatives but also Holgrave, a descendant of the

Maules who invoked the original curse. In *The Marble Faun*, Hawthorne goes to Italy for his "sense of the past," although Hilda and Kenyon are both Americans. The past in this novel is represented not only in the setting but also in Donatello's pagan nature; at the end, both Miriam and the faun figure engage in a purgatorial expiation of the past.

Another recurring theme is that of isolation. Certainly Hawthorne himself felt distanced from normal social converse by his authorial calling. The firsthand descriptions of Hawthorne extant today present him more as an observer than as a participant, a stance over which he himself agonized. In writing to Longfellow about his apprenticeship years, he complained that he was "carried apart from the main current of life" and that "there is no fate in this world so horrible as to have no share in either its joys or sorrows. For the last ten years, I have not lived, but only dreamed about living." For Hawthorne, Sophia was his salvation, his link to human companionship. Perhaps that is why he wrote so evocatively of Hester Prynne's isolation; indeed, Hester's difficult task of rearing the elfin child Pearl without help from Dimmesdale is the obverse of Hawthorne's own happy domestic situation. Almost every character that Hawthorne created experiences some sense of isolation, sometimes from a consciousness of sin, sometimes from innocence itself, or sometimes from a deliberate attempt to remain aloof.

According to Hawthorne, this kind of isolation, most intense when it is self-imposed, frequently comes from a consciousness of sin or from what he calls the "violation of the sanctity of the human heart." For Hawthorne, the "unpardonable sin" is just such a violation, in which one individual becomes subjected to another's intellectual or scientific (rather than emotional) interest. Chillingworth is a good example; as Hester's unacknowledged husband, he lives with Dimmesdale, deliberately intensifying the minister's hidden guilt. In *The Blithedale Romance*, Coverdale's voyeurism (and certainly his name) suggests this kind of violation, as does Westervelt's manipulation of Priscilla and Hollingsworth's of Zenobia. Certainly, Clifford's isolation in insanity is the fault of Judge Pyncheon. There is also the implication that the mysterious model who haunts Miriam in *The Marble Faun* has committed the same sin, thereby isolating both of them. One of the few characters to refuse such violation is Holgrave, who, in *The House of the Seven Gables*, forbears to use his mesmeric powers on Phoebe.

Such a set of recurring themes is bolstered by a pervasive character typology. While literary works such as those by Edmund Spenser, John Milton, William Shakespeare, and John Bunyan form the historical context for many of Hawthorne's characters, many are further developments of his own early character types. *Fanshawe*, for example, introduced the pale, idealistic scholarly hero more fully developed in Dimmesdale. Others, personifications of abstract qualities, seem motivated by purely evil ends. Westervelt is one type; sophisticated and learned in mesmerism, he takes as his victim the innocent Priscilla. Chillingworth, whose literary ancestry can probably be traced to Miltonic devil figures, is old and bent but possesses a compelling intellect that belies his lack of physical strength. Finally, the worldly Judge Pyncheon manifests a practical, unimaginative streak that connects him to Peter Hovenden of Hawthorne's short story "The Artist of the Beautiful." As for Hawthorne's heroines, Hilda and Phoebe embody the domesticity that Hawthorne admired in Sophia; Priscilla, like Alice Pyncheon before her, is frail and easily subjugated; and Hester, Zenobia, and Miriam exhibit an oriental beauty and intellectual pride.

Fanshawe

Three years after Hawthorne graduated from Bowdoin College, he anonymously published the apprenticeship novel *Fanshawe* at his own expense. While he almost immediately repudiated the work, it remains not only a revealing biographical statement but also a testing ground for themes and characters that he later developed with great success.

"No man can be a poet and a bookkeeper at the same time," Hawthorne complained in a letter he wrote while engaged in his Uncle Robert's stagecoach business before college. Just such a dichotomy is illustrated in *Fanshawe*, in which the pale scholar fails to rejoin the course of ordinary life and, in effect, consigns himself to death, while the active individual, Edward Walcott, wins the heroine, Ellen Langton, and so becomes, to use Hawthorne's later words, part of "The magnetic chain of humanity." To be sure, Fanshawe is an overdrawn figure, owing, as Arlin Turner points out, something to Gorham Deane, a Bowdoin schoolmate, and much to Charles

Robert Maturin's gothic novel *Melmoth the Wanderer* (1820), from which Ellen's guardian, Dr. Melmoth, takes his name. In repudiating the book, however, Hawthorne is less repudiating the gothic form than he is an early, faulty conception of a writer's life. Certainly, Hawthorne recognized the tension between the intellectual and the practical lives, as his letters and journals suggest, especially when he was at the Boston and Salem Custom Houses and at the consulate in Liverpool.

Moreover, as Frederick Crews notes, Fanshawe and Walcott are "complementary sides," together fulfilling Hawthorne's twin desire for "self-abnegation" and "heroism and amorous success." Nevertheless, as the pattern of his own life makes clear, Hawthorne did not retire (as did Fanshawe) to an early grave after the solitary apprenticeship years; rather, he married Sophia Peabody (fictionally prefigured in Ellen Langton) and, in becoming involved in the ordinary affairs of life, merged the figures of Fanshawe and Walcott.

The plot of the novel—the abduction of Ellen by the villainous Butler—introduces Hawthorne's later exploration of the misuse of power, while the configuration of characters foreshadows not only the scholar figure but also two other types: the dark villain, whose sexual motivation remains ambiguous, and the innocent, domestic young heroine, later developed as Phoebe and Hilda. That Fanshawe should rescue Ellen, appearing like Milton's Raphael over the thickly wooded valley where Butler has secluded her, suggests that he is able to enter the world of action; but that he should refuse her offer of marriage, saying, "I have no way to prove that I deserve your generosity, but by refusing to take advantage of it," is uncharacteristic in comparison with Hawthorne's later heroes such as Holgrave and Kenyon. It may be that after his marriage to Sophia, Hawthorne could not conceive of a triangle existing when two "soul mates" had found each other, for in similar character configurations in *The House of the Seven Gables* and *The Marble Faun*, both Holgrave and Kenyon have no rivals to fear for Phoebe and Hilda.

In setting, however, *Fanshawe* is a precursor to the later novels, as well as an unformulated precedent for Hawthorne's famous definition of romance. Probably begun while Hawthorne was enrolled at Bowdoin, the novel has as its setting Harley College, a picturesque, secluded institution. Formal classroom tutoring is not the novel's central interest, however, just as it was not in Hawthorne's own life; nor is the novel completely a roman à clef in which actual people and places are thinly disguised. Rather, as is the case in the later novels in which Salem itself, Brook Farm, and Rome are the existing actualities on which Hawthorne draws, so in *Fanshawe* the setting is an excuse for the psychological action. To be sure, the later, sophisticated, symbolic effects are missing, and the interpenetration of the actual by the imaginary is not as successful as in, for instance, *The Scarlet Letter*. Nevertheless, although what later becomes marvelous is here simply melodramatic, the imagination plays a large, if unformulated, role in the novel's success.

The Scarlet Letter

Begun as a tale and completed shortly after Hawthorne's dismissal from the Salem surveyorship, *The Scarlet Letter* is prefaced by an essay titled "The Custom House" in which Hawthorne not only gives an imaginative account of his business experience but also presents a theory of composition. The essay is thus a distillation of the practical and the imaginative. It includes scant praise for the unimaginative William Lee, the antediluvian permanent inspector whose commonplace attitude typified for Hawthorne the customs operation. In writing, however, Hawthorne exorcised his spleen at his political dismissal, which, coupled with charges of malfeasance, was instigated by the Whigs who wanted him replaced; as Arlin Turner comments, "The decapitated surveyor, in becoming a character in a semifictional account, had all but ceased to be Hawthorne." The writer, in short, had made fiction out of his business experiences. He also had speculated about the preconceptions necessary for the creator of romances; such a man, he decided, must be able to perceive the "neutral territory" where the "actual" and the "imaginary" meet. The result of that perception was *The Scarlet Letter*.

In the prefatory essay to the book, Hawthorne establishes the literalism of the scarlet letter, which, he says, he has in his possession as an old, faded, tattered remnant of the past. Just as Hawthorne is said by Terence Martin to contemplate the letter, thus generating the novel, so the reader is forced to direct his or her attention to the primary symbol, not simply of Hester's adultery or of her ability, but of the way in which the restrictions of the Puritan forebears are transcended by the warmth of the human heart. Through this symbol, then, and through its living counterpart, Pearl, the daughter of Hester and Dimmesdale, Hawthorne examines the isolating effects of a sense of sin, using as his psychological setting the Puritan ethos.

With Hester's first public appearance with the infant Pearl and the heavily embroidered scarlet letter on her breast, the child—Hester's "torment" and her "joy"—and the letter become identified. Hester's guilt is a public one; Dimmesdale's is not. To admit to his share in the adultery is to relinquish his standing as the minister of the community, and so, initially too weak to commit himself, he pleads with Hester to confess her partner in the sin. She does not do so, nor does she admit that Chillingworth, the doctor who pursues Dimmesdale, is her husband. Three solitary people, then, are inexorably bound together by the results of the sin but are unable to communicate with one another.

The Puritan intention of bringing the sinner into submission has the opposite effect upon Hester, who, with a pride akin to humility, tenaciously makes a way for herself in the community. As an angel of mercy to the suffering, the sick, and the heavy of heart, she becomes a living model of charity that the townspeople, rigidly enmeshed in their Puritan theology, are unable to emulate. In addition, she exercises a talent for fine embroidery, so that even the bride has her clothing embellished with the sinner's finery. Hester's ostracization hardens her pride until, as she says to Dimmesdale in the forest, their act has a "consecration of its own." The adultery, in short, achieves a validation quite outside the letter of the Puritan law, and Hester finds no reason not to suggest that Dimmesdale run away with her in a repetition of the temptation and the original sin.

In the meantime, Dimmesdale has not had the relief of Hester's public confession. As veiled confessions, his sermons take on an ever growing intensity and apparent sincerity, gaining many converts to the church. Under Chillingworth's scrutiny, however, Dimmesdale's concealed guilt creates a physical manifestation, a scarlet letter inscribed in his flesh. While Hester's letter has yet to work its way inward to repentance, Dimmesdale's is slowly working its way outward. Chillingworth himself, initially a scholar, becomes dedicated to the cause of intensifying the minister's sufferings. Although Chillingworth eventually takes partial responsibility for Hester's sin, admitting that as a scholarly recluse he should not have taken a young wife, he inexorably causes his own spiritual death. He joins a line of scientist-experimenters who deprive their victims of intellectual curiosity, violating "the truth of the human heart" and severing themselves from "the magnetic chain of humanity." He becomes, as Harry Levin notes, the lowest in the hierarchy of sinners, for while Hester and Dimmesdale have at least joined in passion, Chillingworth is isolated in pride.

As Terence Martin suggests, the scaffold scenes are central to the work. For Dimmesdale, public abnegation is the key: Standing as a penitent on the scaffold at midnight is insufficient, for his act is illuminated only by the light of a great comet. His decision to elope with Hester is also insufficient to remove his guilt; what he considers to be the beginning of a "new life" is a reenactment of the original deed. In the end, the scaffold proves the only real escape from the torments devised by Chillingworth, for in facing the community with Hester and Pearl, the minister faces himself and removes the concealment that is a great part of his guilt. His "new life" is, in fact, death, and he offers no hope to Hester that they will meet again, for to do so would be to succumb to temptation again. Only Pearl, who marries a lord, leaves the community permanently; as the innocent victim, she in effect returns to her mother's home to expiate her mother's sin.

Like Fanshawe, then, Dimmesdale causes his own demise, but he is provided with motivation. In Pearl, Hawthorne was influenced perhaps by the antics of Una, his first child, but even her name, which is reminiscent of the medieval Pearl-Poet's "pearl of great price"—his soul—indicates that she is emblematic. Likewise, the minister's name is indicative of the valley of the shadow of death, just as Chillingworth's suggests his cold nature. The successful meshing of the literal and allegorical levels in this tale of the effects of concealed sin and the universality of its theme continue to lend interest to the work.

The House of the Seven Gables

As Hawthorne notes in his preface to *The House of the Seven Gables*, he intends to show the mischief that the past causes when it lives into the present, particularly when coupled with the question of an inheritance. Hawthorne's mood is similar to that of Henry David Thoreau when, in *Walden* (1854), he makes his famous plea to "simplify," evoking the image of Everyman traveling on the road of life, carrying his onerous possessions on his back. The family curse that haunts Hepzibah and Clifford Pyncheon, the hidden property deed, and even Hepzibah's dreams of an unexpected inheritance are so centered on the past that the characters are unable to function in the present. In fact, says Hawthorne, far more worrisome than the missing inheritance is the "moral disease" that is passed from one generation to the next.

This "moral disease" results from the greed of the family progenitor, Colonel Pyncheon, who coveted the small tract of land owned by one Matthew Maule. Maule's curse—"God will give him blood to drink"—comes true on the day the new Pyncheon mansion, built on the site of Maule's hut, is to be consecrated. The Colonel dies, presumably from apoplexy but possibly from foul play, and from that day, Hawthorne says, a throwback to the Colonel appears in each generation—a calculating, practical man, who, as the inheritor, commits again "the great guilt of his ancestor" in not making restoration to the Maule descendants. Clifford, falsely imprisoned for the murder of his uncle, Jaffrey Pyncheon, the one Pyncheon willing to make restitution, is persecuted after his release by Judge Pyncheon, another of Jaffrey's nephews and Jaffrey's real murderer, for his presumed knowledge of the hiding place of the Indian deed giving title to their uncle's property.

In contrast to these forces from the past, Hawthorne poses Phoebe, a Pyncheon country cousin with no pretensions to wealth but with a large fund of domesticity and a warm heart. Almost certainly modeled on Sophia, Phoebe, like Hilda in *The Marble Faun*, possesses an unexpected power, a "homely witchcraft." Symbolically, as Crews suggests, she neutralizes the morbidity in the Pyncheon household and eventually stands as an "ideal parent" to Hepzibah and Clifford. Indeed, Phoebe brings her enfeebled relatives into the circle of humanity.

If Phoebe represents the living present, Holgrave, the daguerreotypist and descendant of the Maules, represents the future. Like Clifford, however, who is saved by his imprisonment from an aesthetic version of the unpardonable sin, Holgrave runs the risk of becoming merely a cold-blooded observer. Like Hawthorne, Holgrave is a writer, boarding at the House of the Seven Gables to observe the drama created as the past spills into the present and turning Pyncheon history into fiction. He is, nevertheless, a reformer. In an echo of Hawthorne's preface, he would have buildings made of impermanent materials, ready to be built anew with each generation; likewise, he would merge old family lines into the stream of humanity. While Holgrave's progressive views become mitigated once he marries Phoebe, he is rescued from becoming a Chillingworth by his integrity, his conscience, and his reverence for the human soul. Although he unintentionally hypnotizes Phoebe by reading her his story of Matthew Maule's mesmerism of Alice Pyncheon, he eschews his power, thereby not only saving himself and her from a Dimmesdale/Chillingworth relationship but also breaking the chain of vengeance that was in his power to perpetuate. The chain of past circumstances is also broken by the death of Judge Pyncheon, who, unlike Holgrave, intended to exercise his psychological power to force Clifford to reveal where the Indian deed is hidden. Stricken by apoplexy (or Maule's curse), however, the Judge is left in solitary possession of the house as Clifford and Hepzibah flee in fear.

Holgrave's integrity and death itself thus prevent a reenactment of the original drama of power and subjection that initiated the curse. As Holgrave learns, the Judge himself murdered his bachelor uncle and destroyed a will that gave the inheritance to Clifford. Although exonerated, Clifford's intellect cannot be recalled to its former state, and so he remains a testimonial to the adverse effects of "violation of the human heart."

During Hepzibah and Clifford's flight from the scene of the Judge's death, Phoebe, representing the present, and Holgrave, the future, pledge their troth, joining the Pyncheon and Maule families. Hawthorne's happy ending, although deliberately prepared, surprised many of his critics, who objected that Holgrave's decision to "plant" a family and to build a stone house were motivated only by the dictates of the plot. F. D. Matthiessen, for example, suggests that Hawthorne's democratic streak blinded him to the implication that Holgrave was simply setting up a new dynasty. On the other hand, for Martin, the decision is foreshadowed; Holgrave's is a compromise position in which he maintains the importance of the structure of society while suggesting that the content be changed, just as a stone house might be redecorated according to its owners' tastes. In marrying Holgrave, Phoebe incorporates Pyncheon blood with the "mass of the people," for the original Maule was a poor man and his son a carpenter.

THE BLITHEDALE ROMANCE

The only one of Hawthorne's romances to be told by a first-person narrator, *The Blithedale Romance* is grounded in Hawthorne's abortive attempt to join the utopian Brook Farm. Like Hawthorne, Miles Coverdale notes the disjunction between a life of labor and a life of poetry; like Hawthorne, he never wholeheartedly participates in the community. In fact, to Crews, the work displays "an inner coherence of self-debate." Coverdale is the isolated man viewed from inside; as a self-conscious observer, he is the most Jamesian of all of Hawthorne's characters. As Martin notes, Hawthorne sacrifices certain aesthetic advantages in allowing Coverdale to tell his own story. Although his name is as evocative as, for example, Chillingworth's, Coverdale loses symbolic intensity because many of his explanations—his noting, for example, that his illness upon arriving at Blithedale is a purgatory preparing him for a new life—sound like figments of an untrustworthy narrator's imagination.

As in his other romances, Hawthorne begins with a preface. While he points out the realistic grounding of the romance, he maintains that the characters are entirely imaginary. He complains that since no convention yet exists for the American romance, the writer must suffer his characters to be compared to real models; hence, says Hawthorne, he has created the Blithedale scenario as a theatrical device to separate the reader from the ordinary course of events (just as the gothic writer did with his medieval trappings). In effect, Coverdale, isolated as he is, serves as the medium who moves between two worlds.

Coverdale's destructive egocentrism is evident throughout the work. His unwillingness to grant a favor to Old Moodie loses him an early acquaintanceship with Priscilla; he cements his position as an outsider by belittling Priscilla and by spying on Zenobia; finally, seeing the intimacy that develops between Priscilla and Hollingsworth after Zenobia's suicide, he retires to enjoy his self-pity. As a minor poet, an urban man who enjoys his cigars and fireplace, he is out of place in the utopian venture; in fact, after his purgatorial illness, he wakes up to death-in-life rather than to reinvigoration. As he moves from Blithedale to the city and back again, his most active participation in the events is his searching for Zenobia's body.

Zenobia herself harks back to Hester, another in the line of Hawthorne's exotic, intellectual women. Like Miriam in *The Marble Faun*, Zenobia has a mysterious past to conceal. She is dogged by Westervelt, her urbane companion whose mesmeric powers become evident in his attempted despoliation of Priscilla. Coverdale imagines her as an orator or an actor; indeed, she is a female reformer whose free and unexpected rhetoric seems to bypass convention. Priscilla, on the other hand, is a frail version of Phoebe and Hilda; she is pliant, domestic, and biddable—hence her susceptibility to Westervelt's powers and her brief tenure as the Veiled Lady. Like Zenobia (whose sister she is revealed to be), she believes in Hollingworth's reformism, but less as a helpmate than as a supporter. In coming to Blithedale, Priscilla really does find the life that is denied to Coverdale, but in falling in love with Hollingsworth, she finds spiritual death.

Hollingsworth is related to Hawthorne's scientist figures. With Holgrave he wants to change society, but his special interest is in criminal reformation. It is Zenobia who, at the end of the novel, realizes that Hollingsworth has identified himself so closely with his plan that he has *become* the plan. Hollingsworth encourages Zenobia's interest in him because of her wealth; he spurns Coverdale's friendship because Coverdale objects to devoting himself entirely to the monomaniacal plan. It is, however, Hollingsworth who rescues Priscilla from Westervelt, exercising the power of affection to break mesmerism, but with him Priscilla simply enters a different kind of subjection.

Indeed, all the main characters suffer real or metaphorical death at the end of the book. Westervelt, like Chillingworth, is frustrated at his victim's escape; Zenobia's suicide has removed her from his power. Priscilla becomes a handmaiden to the ruined ideal of what Hollingsworth might have been, and Hollingsworth becomes a penitent, reforming himself—the criminal responsible for Zenobia's death. Even Coverdale relinquishes a life of feeling; his final secret, that he loves Priscilla, seems only to be fantasizing on the part of the poet who was a master of missed opportunities and who was more comfortable observing his own reactions to a lost love than in pursuing her actively himself.

The Marble Faun

In *The Marble Faun*, the product of a sojourn in Rome, Hawthorne seems to have reversed a progressively narrowing treatment of the effect of the past. In *The Scarlet Letter*, he deals with Puritan theology; in *The House of the Seven Gables*, a family curse; and in *The Blithedale Romance*, the effects of Coverdale's self-created past. In his last completed work, however, he takes the past of all Rome; in short, he copes with a length of time and complexity of events unusual in his writing experience. Hawthorne's reaction to Rome, complicated by his daughter Una's illness, was mixed. While he objected to the poverty, the dirt, and the paradoxical sensuality and spirituality of Rome, he never, as he put it, felt the city "pulling at his heartstrings" as if it were home.

Italy would seem to present to Hawthorne not only the depth of the past he deemed necessary for the flourishing of romance but also a neutral territory, this time completely divorced from his readers' experience. It can be said, however, that while *The Marble Faun* is Hawthorne's attempt to come to terms with the immense variety of the Italian scene, he was not completely successful. In his preface, he once again declares that the story is to be "fanciful" and is to convey a "thoughtful moral" rather than present a novelistic, realistic picture of Italian customs. He inveighs against the "commonplace prosperity" and lack of "antiquity" in the American scene, a lack that satisfies the kind of reforming zeal pictured in Holgrave but militates against the writer of romance.

Hawthorne broadens his canvas in another way as well; instead of presenting one or two main characters, he gives the reader four: Donatello, presumably the living twin of the sculptor Praxiteles' marble faun; Miriam Schaeffer, the mysterious half-Italian painter pursued by the ill-fated Brother Antonio; Kenyon, the American sculptor; and Hilda, the New England copyist. Donatello's double is not found elsewhere in the romances; in fact, he seems to be a male version of both Phoebe and Hilda. Unlike the two women, however, he comes in actual contact with evil and thereby loses his innocence, whereas Hilda's and Phoebe's experiences are vicarious. Perhaps the nearest comparison is Dimmesdale, but the minister is portrayed after he chooses to hide his guilt, not before he has sinned. In Donatello's case, Hawthorne examines the idea of the fortunate fall, demonstrating that Donatello grows in moral understanding after he murders the model, a movement that seems to validate Miriam's secular interpretation of the fall as necessary to the development of a soul more than it validates Hilda's instinctive repudiation of the idea.

For some critics, such as Hyatt Waggoner and Richard Fogle, the *felix culpa*, or fortunate fall, is indeed the theme of *The Marble Faun*; Crews, however, emphasizes Hawthorne's unwillingness to confront the problem, noting that Kenyon is made to accept Hilda's repudiation without question. In the final analysis, Hawthorne does indeed seem reluctant to examine the ramifications of the theme.

Like Zenobia and Hester, Miriam is presented as a large-spirited, speculative woman whose talents are dimmed by a secret past, symbolized by the blood-red jewel she wears. Supposedly, Miriam (unlike Hester), has run away from a marriage with a much older man, but, Hawthorne suggests, her family lineage reveals criminal tendencies. She is followed by Brother Antonio, a wandering devil figure whom she meets in the catacomb of St. Calixtus and whom she employs as a model. The crime that links Miriam to Donatello is not, in this case, adultery, but rather murder. Donatello, who accompanies Miriam everywhere, throws the model from the Tarpeian Rock, the traditional death-place for traitors, saying later that he did what Miriam's eyes asked him to do. Linked in the crime and initially feeling part of the accumulated crimes of centuries, they become alienated from each other and must come separately to an understanding of their own responsibility to other human beings. During this time, Donatello retires to Monte Beni, the family seat, to meditate, and Miriam follows him, disguised.

Just as Miriam and Donatello are linked by their complicity, Kenyon and Hilda are linked by a certain hesitation to share in the other pair's secrets, thereby achieving an isolation that Hawthorne might earlier have seen as a breaking of the magnetic chain of humanity.

Unnoticed as she observes the murder, Hilda nevertheless becomes a vicarious participant. She rejects Miriam's friendship, maintaining that she has been given an unspotted garment of virtue and must keep it pristine, but she does agree to deliver a packet of Miriam's letters to the Palazzo Cenci. For his part, Kenyon compensates for his earlier coldness to Miriam by effecting a reconciliation between her and Donatello. Visiting Monte Beni, he is struck by Donatello's air of sadness and maturity and believes that the pagan "faun," whose power to talk to animals was legendary, has come to an understanding of good and evil and has thereby escaped the possibility of a sensual old age to which the throwback Monte Beni eventually succumbs. Kenyon encourages his friend to work out his penitence in the sphere of human action and reunites him with Miriam under the statue of Pope Julius III in Perugia.

In the meantime, Hilda, suffering the pains of guilt for the murder as if she were the perpetrator, paradoxically gains comfort from confession in St. Peter's. Once she goes to the Palazzo Cenci to deliver Miriam's letters, however, she is incarcerated as a hostage for Miriam. Her disappearance is the novel's analogue to Donatello's self-imposed isolation; her experience in the convent, where she is detained, convinces her of her need for Kenyon. In searching for Hilda, Kenyon undergoes his own purgation, meeting the changed Donatello and Miriam in the Compagna and learning about Miriam's past. On Miriam's advice, he repairs to the Courso in the height of the carnival; it is there that he is reunited with Hilda. Her freedom means the end of Miriam and Donatello's days together, for Donatello is imprisoned for the murder of Brother Antonio. As did Sophia for Hawthorne, Hilda becomes Kenyon's guide to "home"; she is Hawthorne's last full-length evocation of the New England girl on whose moral guidance he wished to rely.

Patricia Marks

Other major works

SHORT FICTION: *Twice-Told Tales*, 1837 (expanded 1842); *Mosses from an Old Manse*, 1846; *The Snow-Image, and Other Twice-Told Tales*, 1851.

NONFICTION: *Life of Franklin Pierce*, 1852; *Our Old Home*, 1863; *The American Notebooks*, 1932; *The French and Italian Notebooks*, 1980; *Letters of Nathaniel Hawthorne*, 1984-1987 (4 volumes); *Selected Letters of Nathaniel Hawthorne*, 2002 (Joel Myerson, editor).

CHILDREN'S LITERATURE: *Grandfather's Chair*, 1841; *Biographical Stories for Children*, 1842; *True Stories from History and Biography*, 1851; *A Wonder-Book for Boys and Girls*, 1852; *Tanglewood Tales for Boys and Girls*, 1853.

EDITED TEXT: *Peter Parley's Universal History*, 1837.

MISCELLANEOUS: *Complete Works*, 1850-1882 (13 volumes); *The Complete Writings of Nathaniel Hawthorne*, 1900 (22 volumes); *The Centenary Edition of the Works of Nathaniel Hawthorne*, 1962-1997 (23 volumes).

Bibliography

Bell, Millicent, ed. *Hawthorne and the Real: Bicentennial Essays*. Columbus: Ohio State University Press, 2005. Commemorates the bicentennial of Hawthorne's birth, exploring the concepts of "the real" and "reality" in his writing. Includes discussions of Hawthorne and politics, slavery, feminism, moral responsibility, and "the problem of American fiction."

Fogle, Richard Harter. *Hawthorne's Fiction: The Light and the Dark*. Rev. ed. Norman: University of Oklahoma Press, 1964. Fogle examines four of Hawthorne's mature novels and eight short stories in detail, concluding that Hawthorne's fiction is both clear ("light") and complex ("dark"). Fogle is particularly adept, although perhaps overly ingenious, in explicating Hawthorne's symbolism.

Mellow, James R. *Nathaniel Hawthorne and His Times*. Boston: Houghton Mifflin, 1980. In this substantial, readable, and illustrated biography, Mellow provides a number of insights into Hawthorne's fiction. Refreshingly, the author presents Sophia Hawthorne as not only the prudish, protective wife of the Hawthorne legend but also a woman with an artistic sensibility and talent of her own. Suitable for students and general readers.

Miller, Edward Havilland. *Salem Is My Dwelling Place: A Life of Nathaniel Hawthorne*. Iowa City: University of Iowa Press, 1991. A large biography of more than six hundred pages, illustrated with more than fifty photographs and drawings. Miller has been able to draw on more manuscripts of family members and

Hawthorne associates than did his predecessors and also developed his subject's family life in more detail.

Millington, Richard H. *The Cambridge Companion to Nathaniel Hawthorne*. New York: Cambridge University Press, 2004. Essays analyze various aspects of Hawthorne's work, including Hawthorne and American masculinity and the question of women. Discusses his major novels.

Moore, Margaret B. *The Salem World of Nathaniel Hawthorne*. Columbia: University of Missouri Press, 1998. Moore explores the relationship between Salem, Massachusetts, and its most famous resident, demonstrating how Hawthorne's association with the city influenced his fiction. She discusses the role of Hawthorne's ancestors in the city's colonial history and examines how the author was affected by Salem's religion and politics.

Pennell, Melissa McFarland. *Student Companion to Nathaniel Hawthorne*. Westport, Conn.: Greenwood Press, 1999. An introductory overview of Hawthorne's life and work designed for high school students and general readers. Includes a discussion of Hawthorne's contribution to American literature, analyses of his four major novels, a bibliography, and an index.

Person, Leland S. *The Cambridge Introduction to Nathaniel Hawthorne*. New York: Cambridge University Press, 2007. An accessible introduction to the author's life and works designed for students and general readers. It includes analysis of Hawthorne's fiction, with separate chapters on the major novels, a brief survey of Hawthorne scholarship, and a bibliography.

Scharnhorst, Gary. *The Critical Response to Hawthorne's "The Scarlet Letter."* New York: Greenwood Press, 1992. Includes chapters on the novel's background and the history of its composition, the contemporary American and early British receptions, the growth of Hawthorne's reputation after his death, modern criticism, and stage and screen adaptations of the novel.

Weldon, Roberta. *Hawthorne, Gender, and Death: Christianity and Its Discontents*. New York: Palgrave Macmillan, 2008. Weldon analyzes how Hawthorne depicts death and his characters' reactions to death in his four major novels and "The Custom House." Includes notes, a bibliography, and an index.

Wineapple, Brenda. *Hawthorne: A Life*. New York: Alfred A. Knopf, 2003. A meticulously researched, even-handed analysis of Hawthorne's often contradictory life that proposes that much of Hawthorne's fiction was autobiographical. Includes more than one hundred pages of notes, a bibliography, and an index.

BESSIE HEAD

Born: Pietermaritzburg, South Africa; July 6, 1937
Died: Serowe, Botswana; April 17, 1986
Also known as: Bessie Amelia Emery

Principal long fiction

When Rain Clouds Gather, 1968
Maru, 1971
A Question of Power, 1973

Other literary forms

Bessie Head first published her writing as a journalist in South Africa. In the early 1960's, she also began writing essays and short stories, some of which appear with later work in two posthumous collections of short pieces, *Tales of Tenderness and Power* (1989) and *A Woman Alone: Autobiographical Writings* (1990). The line between fiction and autobiography was always blurred with Head, and critics disagree about the genre of some pieces. In the 1970's, she began studying the history of the Bamangwato people of Botswana. She interviewed many members of the tribe, and the resulting material informed both an oral history, *Serowe: Village of the Rain Wind* (1981), and a collection of short stories, *The Collector of Treasures, and Other Botswana Village Tales* (1977).

Achievements

In her lifetime, Bessie Head was recognized as one of Africa's greatest writers, although she spent much of her career isolated in Botswana without the papers that would have allowed her to travel and promote her work. She was a featured speaker at the 1976 University of Botswana Writers Workshop, the 1979 Africa Festival in Berlin, and other important events. Her early novel *The Cardinals*, although not published until after her death, is one of the earliest examples of a novel written by an African woman. Her work has been translated into many languages, and *When Rain Clouds Gather* is one of the best-selling volumes in Heinemann's African Writers' series. As a successful writer in Africa in the 1970's and 1980's, she inspired a generation, especially a generation of women.

In 2007, the Bessie Head Heritage Trust and Pentagon Publishers, both in Botswana, announced an annual Bessie Head writing contest to recognize the best creative writing in English by writers in Botswana. That same year, the trust began translating Head's works into Setswana so that they could be used as required readings in Botswana schools.

Biography

Bessie Head was born Bessie Amelia Emery on July 6, 1937, in Pietermaritzburg, South Africa, in the mental hospital where her unmarried white mother, known as Toby, was being treated for schizophrenia. Toby's family had rejected her when they learned that she was pregnant with a mixed-race child. Bessie was placed in foster care, as her father was never identified. At the age of thirteen, she was transferred to an Anglican orphanage in Durban, where she completed high school in 1952 and then studied to become a primary school teacher. After teaching for two years, she moved to Cape Town and then Johannesburg in South Africa, and worked as a journalist for the *Drum* newspapers. In March, 1960, she was briefly arrested, and she attempted suicide in April of that year. In July she met Harold Head, another journalist, and they married that September. She began publishing poetry and short essays in left-wing magazines, using her married name, Bessie Head. Her first novella, *The Cardinals*, was written during this time but was not published until 1993, after her death.

By 1963, Head had a baby son, Howard, but her marriage was over. Her life as a politically aware, biracial woman in white-controlled South Africa was untenable, so she left South Africa for Bechuanaland Protectorate (now Botswana), although she knew she would not be allowed to return to South Africa because of her left-wing political associations. Now an exile, unable to find steady work and unable to obtain a valid passport, she lived with her son in the small village of Serowe and struggled financially until the American publisher Simon and Schuster gave her an eighty-dollar advance to write a novel about the newly independent Botswana. (Editors had read one of her essays, which they liked.) Having depleted the advance, Head wrote what would be her most important work, *When Rain Clouds Gather*, published in 1968. The success of this first novel assured Head's financial stability for a time, but she suffered from periods of mental illness. In 1971, she published *Maru*, her second novel, followed by *A Question of Power* in 1973, an autobiographical novel about a biracial African woman's exile and mental illness.

Since her arrival in Botswana, Head had been studying the history of the Bamanwato tribe, and she produced an oral history and a collection of short stories based on the lives of the people in Serowe. In 1976, she was a featured speaker at the University of Botswana Writers Workshop, and in 1977 and 1978, traveling with documents from the United Nations, she participated in the University of Iowa's International Writing Program. Finally, in 1979, she became a citizen of Botswana, and was free to travel more widely. She gave lectures and readings throughout Africa, Europe, and Australia. In 1984, however, her struggle with mental illness became a struggle with alcohol. Through the last years of her life she was ill and lonely, and she died of hepatitis in 1986 in Serowe at the age of forty-nine. Four of her ten books were published posthumously.

Analysis

Bessie Head's writing occupies a transitional place in African literature between the domestic, village-centered writing of the 1950's and 1960's and the more overtly political and urban writing—much of it written by exiles in Europe and in North America—that came later. Unlike many of her contemporaries who fled South Africa and apartheid, including Es'kia Mphahlele and Lewis Nkosi, Head traveled only as far as Botswana. Her writing focused on life there instead of on the life of problems she had left behind in South Africa.

In addition to village life, Head's great subject was her own life, and the struggle to find a home. She was always "out of place," being a woman in a patriarchal world, a person of mixed race in a racially stratified culture, and a resident of a country that refused to grant her citizenship for fifteen years; she was an exile from a country that would not allow her to return. Her novels and short stories are filled with characters trying to make new homes, trying to fit in, trying to establish community. Frequently, as in *When Rain Clouds Gather*, *Maru*, and shorter works, racism is denounced and harmony is achieved. In addition, she was concerned about the role of capitalism in traditional African agriculture, and a utopian view of communal farming recurs in her work.

Head's fiction, especially *When Rain Clouds Gather* and some of the short stories, is widely read in high school and college classrooms. The qualities that make her work popular with young readers and their teachers—her simple settings and dramatic plots, her optimism, her vivid and sympathetic depictions of African life—have led some critics to call her work immature and naïve. However, her insights into the status of women in African society have made her an important and inspiring early figure in African women's literature.

When Rain Clouds Gather

When Rain Clouds Gather, Head's first and best-known novel, is based in part on the author's own life. It is the story of Makhaya Maseko, a black antiapartheid activist who leaves urban Johannesburg for the small rural village of Golema Mmidi in Botswana in the mid-1960's. Botswana is moving toward independence, and its people are moving toward modern life. Makhaya becomes involved with Gilbert Balfour, a white British agriculturalist, in trying to form a cooperative and teach new farming methods, but they must overcome both the people's hesitation to reject their old ways and the interference of the corrupt subchief Matenge.

Matenge's power is threatened by the egalitarian nature of the project, and he is particularly suspicious of the involvement of women. When he calls out Paulina Sebeso for punishment, the villagers unite against him, and he commits suicide. Makhaya and Paulina marry and begin new lives as nonpolitical farmers in a bucolic village where men and women, blacks and whites, work together for the good of all.

Head's descriptions of the landscape and of the harsh Botswana climate are powerful and beautiful. Later in life, though, Head would remark on the inexperience she demonstrated in *When Rain Clouds Gather*. She came to feel, as have many critics, that the dialogue is stilted, and that the novel's central characters lack complexity—that Makhaya and Matenge are rather two-dimensional representations of good and evil. Still, the novel introduces themes that she would continue to explore throughout her career. The conflict of old and new ways is a common theme in African literature, explored perhaps most famously in Chinua Achebe's *Things Fall Apart* (1958). Head's Matenge, however, is treated much less sympathetically than Achebe's Okonkwo. Makhaya finds peace and hope for the future by settling into a humble rural life—a fate that ultimately evaded Head herself.

A Question of Power

A Question of Power, the most autobiographical of Head's novels, is considered her greatest work. The protagonist is Elizabeth, the child of an unmarried mentally ill white woman and a black man in South Africa under apartheid. With her young son, Elizabeth leaves South Africa for the village of Motabeng in Botswana, but finds no peace there as she tries to adjust to rural living and to find acceptance as an independent-minded woman of mixed race. The only person with whom she shares intellectual interests is Tom, a white American Peace Corps volunteer. Elizabeth suffers from delusions and terrifying dreams and is hospitalized twice with mental breakdowns. Only her responsibility to her son and her tenuous friendship with Tom keep her from falling completely into insanity. Ultimately, she recovers and finds contentment in humble village life.

When she was writing *A Question of Power*, Head was recovering from a mental breakdown that led to her hospitalization. That she was able to create such a powerful and controlled description of mental instability is a testament to her mature skills as a writer and to her strength as a person. The novel revisits several of her recurring themes: the possibility of interracial cooperation; the conflict between old ways and news, especially as played out in agriculture and communal farming; the oppressive power of colonialists and of corrupt Africans; and the values of love, compassion, and generosity. Unlike the more linear *When Rain Clouds Gather*, *A Question of Power* alternates narrative and descriptive passages of village life with vivid scenes from Elizabeth's hallucinations and dreams.

Cynthia A. Bily

Other major works

SHORT FICTION: *The Collector of Treasures, and Other Botswana Village Tales*, 1977; *Tales of Tenderness and Power*, 1989; *The Cardinals, with Meditations and Short Stories*, 1993.

NONFICTION: *Serowe: Village of the Rain Wind*, 1981; *A Bewitched Crossroad: An African Saga*, 1984; *A Woman Alone: Autobiographical Writings*, 1990 (Craig Mackenzie, editor); *A Gesture of Belonging: Letters from Bessie Head, 1965-1979*, 1991 (Randolf Vigne, editor).

Bibliography

Brown, Coreen. *The Creative Vision of Bessie Head.* Madison, N.J.: Fairleigh Dickinson University Press, 2003. Brown examines how Head's fiction arose from her experiences with oppression and mental illness. Includes previously unpublished letters.

Eilersen, Gillian Stead. *Bessie Head: Thunder Behind Her Ears—Her Life and Writing*. Portsmouth, N.H.: Heinemann, 1995. The first full-length biography of the author, this book is both thorough and accessible.

Ibrahim, Huma. *Emerging Perspectives on Bessie Head.* Trenton, N.J.: Africa World Press, 2004. Thirteen essays that include examinations of Head's short stories, her reception outside Africa, and her uses of autobiography.

Johnson, Joyce. *Bessie Head: The Road of Peace of Mind—A Critical Appreciation.* Newark: University of Delaware Press, 2008. Examines how Head's reading, writing, and use of oral literature all informed one another and how they shaped Head's understanding of writing as a political art.

MacKenzie, Craig. *Bessie Head.* New York: Twayne, 1999. Part of the Twayne World Authors series. Includes a critical biography, chronology, and annotated bibliography.

Ola, Virginia Uzoma. *The Life and Works of Bessie Head.* Lewiston, N.Y.: Edwin Mellen Press, 1994. A feminist reading of Head's philosophical approaches to power, racism, love, and exploitation.

Olaussen, Maria. *Forceful Creation in Harsh Terrain: Place and Identity in Three Novels by Bessie Head.* New York: Peter Lang, 1997. Focuses on women's identity in *When Rain Clouds Gather*, *Maru*, and *A Question of Power*.

Sample, Maxine, ed. *Critical Essays on Bessie Head.* Westport, Conn.: Praeger, 2003. Eight essays by female critics examine Head's biography, individual novels, and themes of agriculture, power, and gender in her writings. Includes a bibliographic essay.

ANNE HÉBERT

Born: Sainte-Catherine-de-Fossambault, Quebec, Canada; August 1, 1916
Died: Montreal, Quebec, Canada; January 22, 2000

Principal long fiction

Les Chambres de bois, 1958 (*The Silent Rooms*, 1974)
Kamouraska, 1970 (English translation, 1973)
Les Enfants du sabbat, 1975 (*Children of the Black Sabbath*, 1977)
Héloïse, 1980 (English translation, 1982)
Les Fous de Bassan, 1982 (*In the Shadow of the Wind*, 1983)
Le Premier Jardin, 1988 (*The First Garden*, 1990)
L'Enfant chargé de songes, 1992 (*Burden of Dreams*, 1994)
Aurélien, Clara, Mademoiselle, et le lieutenant anglais, 1995 (*Aurélien, Clara, Mademoiselle, and the English Lieutenant*, 1996)
Est-ce que je te dérange?, 1998 (*Am I Disturbing You?*, 1999)
Un Habit de lumière, 1999 (*A Suit of Light*, 2000)

Other literary forms

In addition to her novels, Anne Hébert (ay-BAYR) explored the forms of poetry, short story, and drama. While the novels, for the most part, are works of her mature years, the poems and stories began appearing simultaneously in magazines and newspapers when the author was in her early twenties. These early poetic works are gathered in *Les Songes en équilibre* (1942), the themes and short-line free verse of which prefigure the more successful *Le Tombeau des rois* (1953; *The Tomb of the Kings*, 1967) and *Le Torrent* (1950, enlarged 1962; *The Torrent: Novellas and Short Stories*, 1973), a short-story collection that, in its final form, includes stories written from 1939 to 1963.

Both *The Torrent* and *Les Songes en équilibre* include juvenilia, but the more finished stories and poems in these collections are beautiful and provocative. The short stories focus on social inequities and the individual suffering they produce. "Un Grand Mariage" ("A Grand Marriage"), "Le Printemps de Catherine" ("Springtime for Catherine"), and "La Mort de Stella" ("The Death of Stella") deal with the effects of material poverty: an ambitious young man who is on the rise from his indigent beginnings to wealth while betraying his true love, a despised drudge who finds freedom in the chaos of war that destroys those with belongings to protect, and the death scene of a tubercular mother of a young family, cast out from society by the guilt of her own suffering. Although some are simplistic in their development of plot and character, all have the intensity that Hébert later brought to her novels, and "The Death of Stella" and "The Torrent" in particular are narratively complex works, drawing characters whose impact on the reader is strong. The shifts of time frame and narrative voice, through change of character speaking or through change in the mental state of a character, prefigure the later development of these devices in the novels.

Eleven years after *Les Songes en équilibre*, Hébert published *The Tomb of the Kings*, which was later reissued with the theoretical essay "Poésie, solitude rompue" ("Poetry, Broken Solitude"), and a new verse collection, *Mystére de la parole* (*Mystery of the Verb*), in *Poémes* (1960; *Poems*, 1975). *The Tomb of the Kings* has been studied extensively as a poetic unit, each individual poem working in harmony to produce a spare, taut, poetic universe, devoid of ornament. The ultimate fears of solitude and death are faced in these verses, in mirrors where deadly shades cling to the reflection ("Vie de Château"; "Château Life"), where hands are planted in the garden, waiting for a flower or the flight of a bird ("Nos Mains au jardin"; "Our Hands in the Garden"), where, in the title poem, the narrator takes her heart on her fist "comme un faucon aveugle" (like a blind falcon) and descends into the tomb of the kings. If the final note of *The Tomb of the Kings* is hope after utter desolation, that hope is expanded in *Mystery of the Verb*, where all aspects of life are offered for celebration in verse lines grown to paragraph length. Hébert's novels often incorporate themes, images, and whole lines from her poems and may be said to put into practice the hope for salvation through words advanced in the verse.

Hébert's drama, collected in *"Le Temps sauvage," "La Mercière assassinée," "Les Invités au procès": Théâtre* (1967), is overburdened thematically and not often performed. All three of her plays are poetically intense at times, albeit unevenly. *Les Invités au procès* is a quasi-religious mystery play, with its introduction of semiallegorical figures and use of characters transformed by death. *La Mercière assassinée* is a curious combination of detective thriller and poetic investigation of solitude and death. The mechanical framework is that of the detective story: A young Canadian journalist on vacation in France stumbles into a local murder mystery, has some farcical exchanges with various local types (the lady innkeeper, the elderly noblewoman, and so on), and eventually solves the mystery. Hébert also includes a character, Achille, who is a sort of poet and prophet, commenting on and predicting the action of the play in necessarily obscure verses. The themes of social injustice, the suffering of a young servant at the hands of jealous young nobles, the roles of time and solitude, and the fear of death are all explored, but the mixing of styles severely hampers the success of the drama.

Le Temps sauvage is Hébert's most consistent play in tone and plot, presenting a family isolated from society by the fierce will of the mother, Agnès, a disappointed woman who seeks her success in her maternity, the only path of development open for her within the terms of Québécois culture. The addition of an orphaned niece to the closed circle leads to its explosion as each individual is catalyzed into examination of his or her own adult hopes and needs, escaping from the enforced perpetual childhood that preserved the mother's triumphant role. Although the Catholic Church is presented as a repressive social force, this play includes the novelty of a priest in a positive role, a rare exception to Hébert's general anticlericalism. Hébert's plays are significant to the readers of her novels chiefly for their development of themes that the novels later treat: death, the return of the dead, isolation from the community, and the struggle of individuals to redeem themselves from the paralyzing force of the past.

ACHIEVEMENTS

Anne Hébert reached a position of eminence among Canadian writers through her work both as a poet and as a novelist. The numerous literary prizes that she won in both roles brought her a modest share of international fame among French-language writers while guaranteeing her place in the foreground of Canadian literary circles as a representative of her native province. Her position as a classic French Canadian writer was guaranteed by her early successes in poetry and the short story. She received the Prix David of the secretariat of Quebec province in 1942 for *Les Songes en équilibre*. It was *Kamouraska*, her second published novel, however, that brought her talents to worldwide attention. A best seller, *Kamouraska* was translated into many languages, winning the prestigious Prix des Libraires de France in 1971.

Anne Hébert. (Ulf Andersen/BOA Editions, Ltd.)

A motion picture based on the novel, directed by Claude Jutra, was released in Canada in 1973.

The subsequent publication of eight more novels confirmed Hébert's commitment to the genre, which she endowed with many of the characteristics of her verse. The novels are painstakingly polished and poetic in their use of language. The emotional atmosphere, as in her poems, is highly charged. Her characteristic choices of theme in both genres are death and the isolation of the individual, embellished by a certain fascination with the supernatural. Hébert's novels are distinguished by an innovative format in which time and states of consciousness are layered and confused, narrators change, and often lurid subject matter is transformed by the novelist's touch. These works appeal to a diverse readership, with their poetic attention to language, their intelligent exploitation of the formal possibilities of the New Novel, and their treatment of themes both romantic enough for a broad audience and controversial enough to win a strong feminist following.

Biography

Anne Hébert was born in the small summer home of her parents in Sainte-Catherine-de-Fossambault, a country village in Quebec province. The eldest of four children, she enjoyed a close relationship with parents who were both intelligent and cultivated. The family's principal residence was in the city of Quebec, where Anne's father, Maurice Hébert, pursued his career as a bureaucrat in the provincial government. Maurice Hébert was also an essayist and poet of some note; he wrote literary criticism of local interest and was a member of the honorific Royal Society of Canada. He is known to have been particularly insistent on correct usage of the French tongue—an issue that assumes particular importance in the population of French Canada.

Both of Hébert's parents were interested in nature, but her mother is said to have been her particular guide to the forest and streams that surrounded their summer home. The summers spent at Sainte-Catherine-de-Fossambault also brought Hébert into close contact with her cousin Hector de Saint-Denys Garneau, four years her senior, who was destined to be a prominent poet, one of the first in his regional tradition to write in modern form and an initiator of the new dynamic of Québécois verse. His illness and premature death from heart disease in 1943, after the cold reception given his innovative verse by the conservative literary establishment in Quebec, made him a symbolic, tragic figure.

Hébert's formal education was largely accomplished at home, under the supervision of her parents, with short stays in several Catholic girls' schools in Quebec. Hébert later said that it was her father's pride in her early poetic production (he copied her poems in a pocket notebook and carried them with him to show to friends) that was the first encouragement she received as a writer. Her verses and short stories began to appear in print in various magazines and newspapers in 1939, and her first collection of poems, *Les Songes en équilibre*, appeared in 1942. This volume, now regarded as a promising bit of juvenilia, won the Prix David and gathered very favorable notice for its graceful treatment in spare, free verse of themes of filial love, religious fervor, and the vocation of the poet. In many ways, the verses are reminiscent of those of Saint-Denys Garneau. Her next major publication, *The Tomb of the Kings*, while also written in short-line free verse, is much more intense and tightly knit and shows a new preoccupation with death, perhaps in part inspired by the deaths of Saint-Denys Garneau and Hébert's own younger sister, Marie, in 1952.

Hébert worked for Radio Canada and the National Film Board from 1950 to 1954, writing scripts for various short features; probably her best-known work in this medium is the lyric text she wrote to accompany a short feature on the life of Saint-Denys Garneau, which did not appear until 1960. In 1954, she received a grant from the Royal Society of Canada, one of the first of a series of awards and stipends that enabled her to devote herself full time to her literary career. She used her newfound independence to leave the close-knit Quebec society and establish herself in Paris. Her subsequent novels and verse were published by the Parisian publishing house Seuil, a significant point for a French Canadian writer, as it indicates not only acceptance by the larger French-speaking community but also the desire to seek such acceptance rather than remain within the familiar circles of Québécois writers and publishers.

In 1958, Seuil published Hébert's first novel, *The Silent Rooms*, a critical success that won for her the Prix France-Canada and the Prix Duvernay of the Société

Saint-Jean-Baptiste in Quebec. In the same year, her murder-mystery drama *La Mercière assassinée* was produced on Canadian television. The year 1960 was marked by her father's death and by the publication of *Poems* by Seuil, the release of *Saint-Denys Garneau* by the National Film Board of Canada, and Hébert's election to membership in the Royal Society of Canada, an honor earlier accorded her father. *Poems* was enthusiastically received and has since inspired many academic critical studies, uniting as it does two very different poetic styles together with the important essay "Poetry, Broken Solitude," a highly personal venture into poetics. *The Tomb of the Kings* explored the kingdoms of solitude and death with surgically spare, short-line free verse. *Mystery of the Verb* is written in *versets*—a poetic form especially associated with Paul Claudel and also with Hébert's fellow Québécois, Rina Lasnier—where the verse line is expanded sometimes to several printed lines, roughly corresponding to the expression of an entire thought or the duration of a breath. In "Poetry, Broken Solitude" and *Mystery of the Verb*, Hébert emphasizes the poet's power to build a new world and the obligation to redeem the old world, in a sense, through words (the *Parole* of the title in French).

In 1961-1962, Hébert received a grant from the Conseil des Arts. The second, augmented edition of *The Torrent* appeared in 1962, published at her own expense; it was later reissued by Seuil in 1965, further evidence of her acceptance in the larger French-speaking world. In 1967, Hébert received the Prix Molson, and the collection of her three plays was published. In her fifties, she had received a great deal of critical praise, attained a position as a major poet in her own country, and attracted a certain amount of attention in the worldwide French community. The publication of *Kamouraska* in 1970 brought her fame as a best-selling novelist. In 1971, she received the Prix des Libraires de France for *Kamouraska*, an event widely reported and celebrated in her native Quebec. Subsequent years saw the publication of *Children of the Black Sabbath*, *Héloïse*, and *In the Shadow of the Wind*, winner of the prestigious Prix Femina. More novels followed, including *The First Garden*, *Burden of Dreams*, and Hébert's final work of long fiction, *A Suit of Light*, published in the year before her death.

Hébert wrote a number of newspaper and journal articles in Quebec on the subject of the role of literature; one cannot ignore the significance of her position as a major French Canadian author during a period when writing in French was considered a political act. Some authors have turned to the Montrealais dialect *joual* and other regional variants of French to emphasize their identification with their homeland, but Hébert chose to write within the impeccable French so prized by her father (although individual characters, in particular the parents in *Children of the Black Sabbath* and the servant girl Amélie Caron in *Kamouraska*, speak in dialect). Her residence in France echoed this rejection of deep politicization of her writing, but her choice of themes and locations important in the literature of Quebec, as well as her continued identification with its literary life, made her a participant in a dynamic, changing world.

As Saint-Denys Garneau became a symbol of the martyrdom of the poet, Anne Hébert became a symbol of hope, of the vibrant life of words beyond suffering and solitude. *The Tomb of the Kings*, in its descent into death at the hands of old kings, ending with a hope of dawn, followed by the exuberant *Mystery of the Verb*, has been interpreted as a call to new life for a province languishing under the tyranny of old traditions and forms. The success of Hébert's later prose work may be seen as the fulfillment of this poetic challenge.

Analysis

The reader of Anne Hébert's poetry and prose will recognize a kinship of theme and language among the different works. *Héloïse* opens with a verse from "En guise de fête" ("A Kind of Feast," from *The Tomb of the Kings*). Its ironic refrain is repeated as the order of the fictional world collapses: "Le monde est en ordre/ Les morts dessous/ Les vivants dessus" ("The world is in order/ The dead below/ The living above"). Olivia de la Haute Mer (Olivia of the High Sea), the ghost of the murdered Olivia Atkins, returns to float with the tides off Griffins Creek in *In the Shadow of the Wind*, quoting another poem from *The Tomb of the Kings:* "Il y a certainement Quelqu'un" ("There is certainly Someone").

More than the practice of direct quotation, however,

the continued exploration of common themes binds the novels to the poems.

The title poem of *The Tomb of the Kings* best outlines one major theme of Hébert's work, that of the child/woman victim or sacrifice. Such a figure is to be found in all of her novels, as either a major or a minor character. Catherine, of *The Silent Rooms*, is brought to the point of death by her husband's pursuit of an aesthetic of immobility and silence. In *Kamouraska*, Élizabeth d'Aulnières leaves the feminine cocoon of her aunts' home to marry a young seigneur, Antoine Tassy, who proves violently abusive, threatening her with death, until he himself is murdered by her lover. In *Children of the Black Sabbath*, the sacrificial figure is Sister Julie, Lady of the Precious Blood, victim and sacrifice for her parents, adepts of the Black Mass, and the later victim of cruelties at the hands of the mother superior and chaplain of her convent. In these three cases, the victim finally escapes from her tormentors and, in fact, may be said to retaliate: Catherine leaves Michel in utter solitude; Antoine Tassy is murdered by his childhood friend, now the lover of his wife; and the nuns of Sister Julie's convent suffer numerous troubles from her malice. In *Héloïse*, however, there is no escape for the young lovers, Bernard and Christine, who are victimized by a pair of vampires, their life and love crushed. Nora and Olivia, the double victims of *In the Shadow of the Wind*, are cousins whose fathers were brothers, their mothers sisters. As they flower into beauty, they absorb the life of the entire community. When they are murdered together at the hands of their cousin, Stevens Brown, their bodies thrown into the sea, their death is the death of the community and their status as victim is doubled with the victimization of other women: an aunt who hangs herself that same summer, never having truly lived; the mother of Olivia, who died of tuberculosis after harvesting the potato crop in freezing weather; the aging cousin abused and abandoned by her young lover.

Yet the toll of victims rises even higher, for the violent Antoine Tassy, Michel, and Stevens Brown, grown men that they are, are all abused children, with the echo of fear ringing in their ears. In *Kamouraska*, Élizabeth d'Aulnières is told by her mother-in-law, the old Madame Tassy, to ignore her husband's drunken rages, that his father had done the same. The lover of Élizabeth, Dr. Nelson, recalls Antoine as a schoolboy, his face always drowned in tears, turning to Nelson as his friend in a solitude otherwise complete.

When Stevens Brown kills Nora, then rapes and kills Olivia, he is convinced that the wild wind of a storm drowns out his victims' screams: The wind is within his mind, the storm his own rage at a childhood of beatings by his father. François, of "The Torrent," is also an abused child, rendered deaf by a beating from his mother, La Grande Claudine. He hears only the roaring of the torrent, as Stevens hears the stormy ocean. Stevens has an idiot brother, an elemental creature named Perceval, who incarnates François's rage and batters La Grande Claudine to death. For both François and Stevens, love of women is poisoned by their tormented boyhood; they can feel desire but do not love. François takes a wandering woman, whom he names Amica, into his home and bed, but she becomes a nightmare presence to him, intruder in his solitude, long before she steals his money and leaves. Stevens seduces and sleeps with his cousin's widow, Maureen, then leaves her with taunts about her age after reawakening her as a sexual being. He brutally murders Nora and Olivia, who consciously and unconsciously returned his desire. Both François and Stevens eventually commit suicide, François in the waters of the torrent, Stevens with pills stolen from a hospital.

It is a petrification that is responsible for the evil in François and Stevens, caught forever by the trauma of their childhood suffering. In *The Silent Rooms*, Michel and Lia, noble-born but abused children grown into abusive adults, are caught in their own rigidity of family heredity and aesthetic preference. So, too, the vampires of *Héloïse* are still clad in the style of their youth, still using the artifacts of the nineteenth century. Héloïse quotes the last line of Charles Baudelaire's sonnet "La Beauté" in acknowledging her need to destroy Bernard to preserve her own immortality, but the first line of the poem, "Je suis belle, ô mortels, comme un rêve de pierre" ("I am beautiful, O mortals, like a dream of stone"), expresses the aesthetic of immobility espoused by Michel, toyed with by Bernard, the hatred of life with its strong odors, colors, and movement.

In both *The Silent Rooms* and *Héloïse*, meals of rice and white fish symbolize the imprisonment of the living by a dead aesthetic, palates too weak to accept the strong savor of life. The near escape of Christine (one cannot ignore the significance of her sacrificial name) and Bernard from the vampires involves a trip to the open marketplace and the preparation of a highly flavored meal of rabbit in mustard sauce. Catherine's decision to break with Michel revolves around a similar trip to the market with her lover, Bruno, and the preparation of a dinner "plein d'odeurs" (full of scents), with "petits citrons amers, des oursins violets, des baies sauvages" (little sour lemons, violet sea urchins, wild bay).

The forces of evil, petrification, and death are shown by Hébert not only on an individual scale but also on the broader scale of institutions and society, within which the individual is a victim of rituals and codes, isolated from self and others. In *Kamouraska*, Élizabeth is presented as vibrantly female, overflowing with sexual energy, pregnant twice within the first year of her first marriage. When this marriage fails, there is no possibility—within the rules of her community—for this energy to be expressed. Her lover is an alien to the society, an American isolated from his own culture by his father's political rigidity (a Royalist who stayed in America after the Revolution), isolated from that of Quebec by his recent arrival, his accented French, the fact that he is a convert to Catholicism. The death of Antoine Tassy, a sacrifice to the demands of society (for Élizabeth must be a widow before she can marry her lover), is a bloody catastrophe in which Dr. Nelson expresses his elemental maleness, his dominance of the other, but utterly fails in all practical aspects of crime, leaving a trail of blood all the way to the American border. Élizabeth, abandoned by her lover, becomes a prisoner of society in a stricter sense; imprisoned, tried, and freed on technical grounds, she redeems her virtue by her exemplary life as wife of the insignificant Jerome Rolland, bearing him eight children to add to her first three. Her maternity is the one expression of her sexuality. Her outer person is a perfect, unchanging shell; her inner self is haunted by the images of her youth, when she was truly alive. It is the recurrence of these memories in her dreams that gives flesh to her story. It is significant that the story is set in Quebec province in the 1840's, a place and period where society's repression of the individual has maximum force.

Children of the Black Sabbath

Children of the Black Sabbath, also set in Quebec province, again invokes the repressive powers of the society in the isolation and sacrifice of the individual. The parents of Julie and Joseph are outcasts from society by choice; they are the witch and her master, practitioners of the Black Mass, but the congregation they gather from the cities and surrounding countryside are the pitiful citizens of a society where dancing is forbidden, where Prohibition reigns, where the Great Depression of the 1930's is in force. The Black Mass frees its celebrants from society's restrictions; they indulge in sexual license, they gorge on the sacrificial pig, they dance and drink moonshine. To this extent, the satanic pair are liberators, but they are also rigidly held within a ritual code, the mother defined by her long lineage of wives and mothers of Satan. The abuse of Julie by her parents is defined within this tradition of evil: She is raped by her father, her body used as the altar on which the Communion bread of the Black Mass is baked.

Later, Julie enters a convent and encounters a parallel ritual, similarly petrified and rigid, and equally evil in its abuse of the individual in the name of the ultimate victim and sacrifice. She undergoes torture at the hands of the mother superior and chaplain, who try the entire surface of her body with a needle in search of a witch's spot that feels no pain. The spot they find is the scar left by burns suffered during the Black Mass. Hébert uses liturgical Latin in *Children of the Black Sabbath* to frame Sister Julie's flight from the "real" world of her convent life to the delirious memories of her childhood, with their increasingly powerful call for her to abandon her amnesia and take up the succession of her mother's race. It is the moral sclerosis of the Church, where women serve the Holy Father as the witches serve Satan, that produces the horrible suffering not only of Sister Julie but also of the other nuns in the convent (exemplified by the nuns dying in the infirmary when the mother superior orders their medication discontinued). The ultimate sin, the killing of a newborn child, is committed not by Sister Julie, who escapes with her shadowy lover, but by the mother superior, anxious to escape a scandal, thus preserving the respectability of her order at the expense of Christian spirit.

In the Shadow of the Wind

As Latin phrases frame the action in *Children of the Black Sabbath*, biblical references introduce the characters of *In the Shadow of the Wind*, characters that are caught in the double isolation of an English-speaking community, exiled like Dr. Nelson through political rigidity following the American Revolution to French-speaking Canada, surviving through the years as a microcosm of a "chosen people" within the body of another "chosen people." The first narrative voice in this novel is given to Pastor Nicholas Jones, speaking in 1982 and recreating two hundred years of his community, only to see it vanish in the recollection of the summer of 1936 when Nora and Olivia Atkins were murdered.

Pastor Nicholas, childless, is a failed patriarch. He longs for sons, yet the only genealogy he can establish is a reversed one; he engenders his own ancestors in framing a history of Griffins Creek. As narrator, he lusts after his nubile nieces, Nora and Olivia, focusing the attention of the reader on them and on their cousin, Stevens Brown, who replaces Nicholas as narrator through letters written to a friend in Florida, the antithesis of Griffins Creek. Stevens has returned only for the summer from a self-imposed exile. At the moment of his return, he takes a panoramic survey of the town: He sees his grandfather as a tree from whose branches all the life of the village springs in the numerous descendants, legitimate and bastard, who people it. Both the pastor and Stevens feel the power of Felicity Brown, mother of the pastor and grandmother of Stevens; she is an enigmatic figure, half sea animal (much is made of the identification *mère/mer*), profoundly female, who dominates her grandchildren.

The sexual tension created by the burgeoning of Nora and Olivia Atkins, within the context of an institutional morality that allows no outlet to sexuality except that of marriage and child rearing, is more than Nicholas or Stevens can bear: Nicholas attempts to molest Nora and is observed by the idiot Perceval, who later screams out at the barn dance when he sees his uncle hover over and leer at the girls. Stevens goes a step further to rape and murder on the last night of the summer. Nicholas's barren wife responds to the unspoken passions of the barn dance with suicide, yet she was never really "alive" and her death has little impact. The death of the Atkins girls destroys the "chosen people" to whom they belonged.

In both *Children of the Black Sabbath* and *In the Shadow of the Wind*, the violence of the individual is part of the violence of the immediate society, which in its turn is framed by the worldwide violence of World War II. Sister Julie's brother Joseph escapes from his family in taking up the uniform of the Canadian armed forces; her supposed psychic violence reaches out to cause his death in battle. Stevens Brown, after being acquitted of murder, also leaves Canada to fight in Europe. He reacts psychotically to combat and spends his postwar life in a psychiatric hospital until his escape allows him to write a final "letter" and give his own account of the night of the murders. The institutionalized murders of wartime trigger unbearable memories of the personal murders of his own past.

Paris novels

If the outer society of the Quebec-based novels acts as an alienating force by the strength of its repressions of the individual, the novels set in Paris show no such repression. *The Silent Rooms* works exclusively on an individual basis—that is, each character is defined and limited within his own history, his own aesthetic choices. In *Héloïse*, the city seems indifferent to the drama of the characters; the throngs that pass through the Métro and down the boulevard Saint Michel simply do not notice that there are vampires in their midst. Bernard, who gives up poetry for the financial promise of law school, is a failed Orpheus, the Parisian Métro the Stygian realm that he must wander. His nemesis, Héloïse, can sit and drink a vial of his blood on the curb of Saint Michel Fountain and pass unremarked among the generation of young drug abusers and social outcasts gathered there. There is no rescue for the beautiful Christine, who, in her dancer's grace, combines body and soul in perfect harmony. Her husband's weakness marks them both as victims of the living dead. While the untouched modern apartment that Christine had longed to live in and make her own can be described in a few words, Hébert devotes pages of lush description to the nineteenth century gem that "waits" for and devours the young couple, a confusion of colors, a profusion of art motifs (including a painting of Orpheus and the animals), crowded to the point of suffocation yet empty, even as the Métro is crowded with people yet empty of humanity.

Quebec novels

The Quebec novels are arguably richer as a group than the Paris novels; they treat the central theme of individual alienation through themes such as the influence of society, the repressive nature of the Church, the impact of World War II on the colony of a principal power, the alienation of the speaker of one language within a society of another tongue—all subjects proper to the French Canadian novel, but with an emotional climate peculiar to Hébert's work. It is in the emotional intensity of her work that Hébert offers her words as an effort at redemption of the very world of evil that she lays before us. In the poem "Le Tombeau des rois" ("The Tomb of the Kings"), the young victim, seven times drunk and crushed by the dead kings, is still a hopeful figure, facing the dawn, "les morts hors de moi, assassinés" ("the dead outside of me, assassinated"). Other poems, especially those of *Mystery of the Verb*, celebrate in detail the poet's power to name and redeem the world, to justify the living and the dead. One of the post-*Poems* verses, "Noël," evokes war and death and the suffering of the innocent in juxtaposition with the Christmas promise of joy, a promise encrusted with the traditions of the centuries. The poet must be the compassionate searcher for knowledge, panning for gold, washing the words "Cœur. Tendresse. Larmes." ("Heart. Tenderness. Tears."), which are "les plus perdus, les plus galvaudés, les plus traînés, les plus trahis" ("the most lost, the most muddled, the most dragged about, the worst betrayed"), in order to renew them and to begin again with nativity and morning. The infant God born of this search is the Word, the beginning of a new world.

Anne Hébert's novels, as they explore the realms of death and terror mapped out in her poems, continue the effort to name the unnamable, to break down the forces of repression and cruelty that freeze the human heart in living death. It is the beauty of her language, the prose poems to be found within the bleakness of a work such as *In the Shadow of the Wind*, that gives hope and purpose to her work, where love and life are so seldom attained and so much desired.

Anne W. Sienkewicz

Other major works

SHORT FICTION: *Le Torrent*, 1950 (enlarged 1962; *The Torrent: Novellas and Short Stories*, 1973).

PLAYS: *Le Temps sauvage*, pr. 1966; *"Le Temps sauvage," "La Mercière assassinée," "Les Invités au procès": Théâtre*, 1967

POETRY: *Les Songes en équilibre*, 1942; *Le Tombeau des rois*, 1953 (*The Tomb of the Kings*, 1967); *Poèmes*, 1960 (*Poems*, 1975); *Anne Hébert: Selected Poems*, 1987; *Le Jour n'a d'égal que la nuit*, 1992 (*Day Has No Equal but Night*, 1994); *Œuvre poètique, 1950-1990*, 1992; *Poèmes pour la main gauche*, 1997.

SCREENPLAY: *Saint-Denys Garneau*, 1960.

NONFICTION: *Dialogue sur la traduction: À propos du "Tombeau des rois,"* 1970 (with Frank R. Scott).

Bibliography

Knight, Kelton W. *Anne Hébert: In Search of the First Garden*. New York: Peter Lang, 1998. Examines how Hébert uses memory in her works, focusing on how memory links the gap between past and present and how this connection is essential to understanding Hébert's characters, her poetics, and her role in the creative process.

Mitchell, Constantina, and Paul Raymond Côté. *Shaping the Novel: Textual Interplay in the Fiction of Malraux, Hébert, and Modiano*. Providence, R.I.: Berghahn Books, 1996. Comparative study of twentieth century French literature focuses on self-referential works by Hébert and other novelists. Includes an analysis of the voice, dreams, and narrative organization of *Burden of Dreams*.

Noble, Peter. "Anne Hébert: *Kamouraska* and *Les Fous de Bassan*." In *Where Are the Voices Coming From? Canadian Culture and the Legacies of History*, edited by Coral Ann Howells. Atlanta: Rodopi, 2004. Analysis of Hébert's novels *Kamouraska* and *In the Shadow of the Wind* is included in a collection of essays that examine how Canadian history and "Canadianness" are depicted in English- and French-language novels and films.

Pallister, Janis L., ed. *The Art and Genius of Anne Hébert: Essays on Her Works—Night and the Day Are One*. Madison, N.J.: Fairleigh Dickinson University Press, 2001. Collection of essays in both English and French pays tribute to Hébert's talents. Among the essays in English are two that examine her novels *Kamouraska* and *The First Garden*.

Paterson, Janet. "Anne Hébert." In *Profiles in Canadian Literature*, edited by Jeffrey M. Heath. Vol. 3. Toronto, Ont.: Dundurn Press, 1980. Provides an overview of Hébert's life and analyzes her work to 1980. Includes a chronology of events in her life and a bibliography of selected criticism.

Russell, Delbert W. *Anne Hébert*. Boston: Twayne, 1983. Excellent in-depth survey discusses Hébert's prose, poetry, and plays to 1980. Includes bibliography and index.

Willging, Jennifer. *Telling Anxiety: Anxious Narration in the Work of Marguerite Duras, Annie Ernaux, Nathalie Sarraute, and Anne Hébert*. Toronto, Ont.: University of Toronto Press, 2007. Analyzes how Hébert and three other women writers represent anxiety in their work, explaining how this depiction reflects postwar skepticism about the ability of language to express the death and destruction of World War II.

URSULA HEGI

Born: Düsseldorf, Germany; May 23, 1946
Also known as: Ursula Johanna Koch

Principal long fiction

Intrusions, 1981
Floating in My Mother's Palm, 1990
Stones from the River, 1994
Salt Dancers, 1995
The Vision of Emma Blau, 2000
Sacred Time, 2003
The Worst Thing I've Done, 2007

Other literary forms

Ursula Hegi (HEHG-ee) is primarily a writer of long fiction but has also written and published short stories. *Unearned Pleasures, and Other Stories* (1988) and *Hotel of the Saints* (2001) are two of her short-story collections. She also has published a children's book, *Trudi and Pia* (2003), about Trudi Montag, the dwarf of her novels, and a circus dwarf named Pia. The book is an adaptation of her novel *Stones from the River*. Hegi's interest in the experience of being an émigré led to her nonfiction work *Tearing the Silence: Being German in America* (1997).

Achievements

Ursula Hegi has received more than thirty grants and awards. In 1988, she won the Indiana Fiction Award. In 1990 and 1994, respectively, her novels *Floating in My Mother's Palm* and *Stones from the River* were selected as *New York Times* Best Books. *Floating in My Mother's Palm* also won the Pacific Northwest Booksellers Award. She was nominated for a PEN/Faulkner Award for *Stones from the River* and for *Floating in My Mother's Palm*. She was awarded a National Endowment for the Arts Fellowship (1990) as well as five PEN Syndicated Fiction Awards. *Stones from the River* was selected for Oprah's Book Club in 1994.

Biography

Ursula Hegi was born Ursula Johanna Koch on May 23, 1946, in Düsseldorf, Germany, to Heinrich and Johanna Koch. She said that she became gradually aware of the world war that had just preceded her birth and even more gradually aware of the war's Nazi regime. She said also that she learned more about that history after she left Germany and emigrated to the United States in 1965. Two years later, in 1967, she married Ernest Hegi, a management consultant. The couple had two sons, Eric and Adam. Hegi became a U.S. citizen in 1970. She and Ernest divorced in 1984.

Hegi earned a bachelor's degree in 1978 and a master's degree in 1979, both at the University of New Hampshire, where she lectured in English from 1978 to 1984. She then became a professor of creative writing at the University of Eastern Washington in Spokane. In 1997, she settled just outside New York City to live with her second husband, Gordon Gagliano.

Much of Hegi's work derives from the pull of the two nations and cultures that has formed so much a part of her life: Germany and the United States. Her ties with Germany have never been broken, yet she has formed a strong bond with her new country. In 1994, she commented on this double allegiance:

> The older I get, the more I realize that we are connected with our country of origin, even if our values are totally different from the values that created that situation. Since I cannot turn my back on my country of origin, I need to try and understand it. For me, it's been a journey of talking about and discovering and dealing with it, instead of leaving it behind.

Analysis

Many of Ursula Hegi's novels deal with Germans or German Americans. The stories often share characters and places. For her German settings, she created the imaginary town Bergdorf, located on the Rhine River near Düsseldorf (the city in which she grew up). The Blau family, the Montag family, and many individual characters come out of that town and emerge in several different novels. Trudi Montag (the *Zwerg*, or dwarf) is certainly the most prominent of these movable characters, appearing first in *Floating in My Mother's Palm*, set in Bergdorf in the 1950's, where she is the town librarian and holder of many of the town's secrets. She is the central character in *Stones from the River* as well, tracing her life from the time of World War I through the rise of the Third Reich and World War II and through 1952. She reappears in *The Vision of Emma Blau*, in which she is the aunt of one of the major characters, Helene Montag, who marries Stefan Blau and moves from Bergdorf to Winnipesaukee, New Hampshire. She also figures prominently in *Trudi and Pia*, a children's story in which she meets and befriends Pia, a circus dwarf.

Hegi's fiction is not focused solely on Germans and German Americans. In *Sacred Time*, for instance, she tells a story of Italian immigrants; *Salt Dancers* is set in Washington State and depicts a struggle to reconcile oneself with the past; and *The Worst Thing I've Done* deals with guilt and recrimination among three friends. Nevertheless, what the novels share is the sense of struggle between the self and the forces that swirl out of place, community, and family—all set against the inexorable passage of time. This sense of struggle perhaps accounts for Hegi's frequent use of water images in the

Ursula Hegi. (Gordon Gagliano)

novels. These images are often literal, as with the currents and eddies of the Rhine or the wide expanse of Lake Winnipesaukee, but they also are figurative, as in the movement of time that catches characters or drags them under, or both. In virtually every novel, Hegi provides a flow of events with their own momentum, carrying the characters into situations they had never expected.

Hegi likes a broad canvas for her novel's backdrops, broad enough to cover a wide sweep of time and include a broad community. In the case of *Stones from the River*, readers come to know many residents of Bergdorf over a span of more than four decades. *The Vision of Emma Blau* covers an even longer time span, 1894 to 1990, during which time readers meet three generations of the Blau family.

Hegi features one stand-out character in each of her fictional works. In the early novels, she uses the device of first-person narrative to give sustained focus to this character. She makes unusual use of the device in her first novel, *Intrusions*. Here, Megan Stone is the central character of a novel in the process of being written, through many interruptions, by the author, who is also central. In *Floating in My Mother's Palm*, Hanna Malter tells her own story of growing up in Bergdorf in the 1950's. Hegi employs a particular technique that helps the reader sustain focus on one character: The character's inner thoughts, dreams, and observations appear in italics in text. This technique is particularly effective in the case of Trudi Montag, who is at the very core of the story in *Stones from the River*. In the novels that follow, Hegi virtually abandoned first-person narrative. The stories are told in the omniscient voice.

Another characteristic of these novels is the gradual isolation of the central character despite all efforts to belong. Community is important in these narratives. It has a force of its own, it dictates terms, it welcomes or rebuffs members, and it can validate one's sense of personal worth. Frequently, community comes in the form of family; even so, the larger world imposes demands and conditions. More often than not, the central character becomes progressively more estranged until she or he is virtually alone. There is a brief exchange between Megan Stone and her friend near the end of *Intrusions* that reflects this progressive isolation of the main character:

> "You know what's overrated?"
> "What, Megan?"
> "Solitude."
> "How can you say that?"
> "Because I am up to my neck in solitude. I feel smothered by solitude."

Isolation is not always negative, though. Trudi Montag ends up isolated but at peace with her past. Hanna Malter hopes to save a life in the Rhine and ends up saving her own. The pattern has the individual set in the middle of family, family in the middle of community, and community in the middle of a national culture. The narratives trace the crosscurrents between them, forcing the characters to exert their energy to control these crosscurrents.

The novels are rich in a language that engages the imagination, not only by conjuring the distinct fictional world but also in reflecting the real world through metaphor and analogy. The result is often compelling and engaging for the reader.

Intrusions

Hegi's earliest novel *Intrusions* is in many ways unique among her other works. One might call it metafiction, or a novel about a novel. The author of the novel in progress faces all sorts of hurdles. She has to put up with intrusions from her children, husband, and the demands of everyday life. To make things worse, her characters, especially Megan Stone, often refuse to cooperate. They become willful and go off on their own, forcing the author to recalculate her story. It is an intriguing creation. No doubt it served as an exploration of the experience of creativity, as if Hegi had to get it out of the way in order to go after the stories so close to her life and concerns.

Floating in My Mother's Palm

Floating in My Mother's Palm, Hegi's second novel, is set in the imaginary town of Bergdorf, Germany, in the 1950's. The story traces the young life of Hanna Malter. In the course of the events that Hanna narrates, the reader becomes acquainted with many of the townspeople: Siegfried Tegern and his seven dogs; Manfred Weiler, whose father accidentally killed himself; Fräulein Mahler, who became Hanna's stepmother; the Hansens and their bake shop; Hanna's friend Karin Baum, who had a baby when she was in the seventh grade; Frau Talmeister, who liked to watch the world from her apartment window; and above all, Trudi Montag, who ran the local pay-library and who knew the secrets of many of the townspeople. It is a fascinating tapestry of interwoven stories, and it is apt preparation for the more ambitious, wide-ranging third novel *Stones from the River*.

Stones from the River

Stones from the River is probably the best known of all Hegi's writings. Some call the novel her masterpiece. In 1986, Hegi returned to Düsseldorf on a travel grant to meet the dwarf she remembered from her childhood. From her she gathered many of the stories and characters that make up both *Stones from the River* and *Floating in My Mother's Palm*. In *Stones from the River*, the dwarf Trudi Montag is the central character. The novel is both an intimate portrayal of the life of Trudi and a panoramic vision of the sweep of German history.

The story begins before the end of World War I and concludes in 1952 to encompass years in which the German nation experienced horrors, reversals, economic pain, vicious oppression, cold and calculated genocide, and finally a ruinous world war. Living through those times, as did Trudi, poses many personal challenges. She has been caught in the storm. She knows her neighbors, sees them suffer, sees some sent to the camps or to war, and sees some bombed out during the raids on the town. She herself is victimized, brought in for interrogation by the Gestapo in the years before World War II. Her own cleverness diverts the authorities from persecuting her, and she survives these horrors and the war that followed. In hindsight, she reconciles herself with the new world.

The novel is a complex, moving portrait that mixes the rush of history with the personal search for dignity and integrity. The contrast of the flowing currents of the Rhine River with the cairns of rocks Trudi assembles is symbolic of the tension so basic to the story.

The Vision of Emma Blau

As with *Stones from the River*, the passing of time and the search for the self are major themes in *The Vision of Emma Blau*, but with a difference. This story sets three generations of a family against time. Stefan Blau, the family patriarch, once had a vision. From a boat at the shore of Lake Winnipesaukee, he envisioned a young girl twirling and dancing in the court of a great stone structure he built and dubbed the Wasserburg (water fortress). The building becomes a microcosm of individuals.

The six-storey apartment house—with six apartments on each floor—weighs on several generations of the Blau family and becomes a heavier and heavier burden, first to Stefan's three wives and then to his children and grandchildren, especially Emma. Emma is the one person Stefan "loved as much as his building," and she, too, becomes obsessed with its permanence.

Sacred Time

Sacred Time is the story of a family's experiences over a relatively long period of time, from the mid-1950's to 2002. The story involves three generations of an Italian American family, the Amedeos, living in the Bronx. This is clearly new territory for Hegi and a departure from her earlier explorations of German American immigrant communities.

The structure of the novel is unusual. It is divided into three books, each with two chapters devoted to a particular family member. The story begins with young Anthony in 1953, followed by a chapter about his mother Leonora in 1955. Part two has two chapters set in the 1970's, one dedicated to Anthony's aunt Floria (his father's sister) in 1975 and the other to his cousin, Floria's daughter Belinda, in 1979. Book three focuses on Floria in 2001 and finally returns to Anthony in 2002.

One event becomes a vortex of the energy over the four decades of the story. The event comes at the end of the first chapter. Anthony's cousin Bianca, twin sister of Belinda, has a fascination with super heroes and has a cape she likes to wear to imitate flying. Anthony tempts her to fly out the window with a vision of her long absent father on an adjacent rooftop. She jumps out the window and falls six floors to her death. The tragedy is kept very much in the background throughout the remainder of the story and yet it colors everything that follows. One curious device that Hegi adopts is to write three of the chapters in the first person: the chapters that belong to Anthony and Belinda. The other chapters are third-person accounts. It is a device that helps maintain the power of Bianca's tragic fall over the whole Amedeo family through the years.

Hegi dedicated the book to her second husband, Gordon Gagliano, and she ends her acknowledgments with these words: "Most of all, thank you to my husband, Gordon Gagliano, who took me to the Bronx and made it magical."

Salt Dancers *and* The Worst Thing I've Done

These two novels share an emphasis on personal relationships involving jealousy, recrimination, and guilt, as characters struggle to reconcile themselves with their past lives. Each novel also focuses on a shared struggle among a small group of people without a sweep of history behind them.

Salt Dancers is set in Washington State and tells the story of a middle-aged woman named Julia as she attempts to make peace with her past, specifically with her abusive father. She does this in the hope of restraining her own tendencies toward cruelty. In the end she discovers more about herself and her family, which makes her capable of reconciliation and recovery.

In *The Worst Thing I've Done*, Hegi provides a collage of the life shared by three characters. Theirs is in some ways a traditional triangle: Mason had married Annie despite his attraction to Jake, who himself is attracted to Annie. At the time of the wedding, Annie's father and pregnant mother had died in an automobile crash but their unborn child was saved. The baby, named Opal, is brought up by the three friends. At the outset of the story, Mason commits suicide in Annie's art studio. This catapults the reader into their shared past and the resultant crosscurrents of guilt and grief. Narrative voice shifts from one character to another. Other characters are called forth in the struggle with what each of them might think of as the "worst thing" he or she has ever done.

Stanley Vincent Longman

OTHER MAJOR WORKS

SHORT FICTION: *Unearned Pleasures, and Other Stories*, 1988; *Hotel of the Saints*, 2001.

NONFICTION: *Tearing the Silence: Being German in America*, 1997.

CHILDREN'S/YOUNG ADULT LITERATURE: *Trudi and Pia*, 2003 (adaptation of her novel *Stones from the River*).

BIBLIOGRAPHY

Cowart, David. *Trailing Clouds: Immigrant Fiction in Contemporary America*. Ithaca, N.Y.: Cornell University Press, 2006. In the chapter "Survival on the Tangled Bank: Hegi's *The Vision of Emma Blau* and Mukherjee's *Jasmine*," Cowart examines, among other topics, Hegi's concerns in her fiction with immigrants obtaining the American Dream.

Elsen, Jon. "What Wasn't Taught in School." *The New York Times Book Review*, March 20, 1994. A brief interview of Hegi as she recounts her discovery of the history of Nazism and the Holocaust only after emigrating from Germany to the United States at the age of eighteen.

Monaghan, Peter. "A Writer Confronts Her German Ghosts." *Chronicle of Higher Education*, December 7, 1994. A portrait of Ursula Hegi following the publication of *Floating in My Mother's Palm* and *Stones from the River*.

Steinberg, Sybil, and Jonathan Bing, eds. *Writing for Your Life*. New York: W. W. Norton, 1997. A collection of interviews about the craft of writing and the methods of publishing. Includes interviews with Hegi and dozens of other writers.

VERNER VON HEIDENSTAM

Born: Olshammar, Sweden; July 6, 1859
Died: Övralid, Sweden; May 20, 1940
Also known as: Carl Gustaf Verner von Heidenstam

PRINCIPAL LONG FICTION

Endymion, 1889
Hans Alienus, 1892
Karolinerna, 1897-1898 (*A King and His Campaigners*, 1902; better known as *The Charles Men*, 1920)
Heliga Birgittas pilgrimsfärd, 1901
Folkungaträdet, 1905-1907 (*The Tree of the Folkungs*, 1925)

OTHER LITERARY FORMS

In addition to his novels, Verner von Heidenstam (HAY-duhn-stahm) published poetry, short stories, and nonfiction works. Among his volumes of poetry are *Vallfart och vandringsår* (1888; pilgrimage and wander years), *Dikter* (1895; poems), and *Nya dikter* (1915; new poems). His two collections of short stories are *Sankt Göran och draken* (1900; Saint George and the dragon) and *Skogen susar* (1904; the woods whisper), and his essays include *Renässans* (1889; Renaissance), *Pepitas bröllop* (1890, with Oscar Levertin; Pepita's wedding), *Modern Barbarism* (1894), *Dagar och händelser* (1909; days and events), and *Vad vilja vi?* (1914; what do we want?). He also wrote an autobiographical work, *Från*

Verner von Heidenstam. (© The Nobel Foundation)

Col di Tenda till Blocksberg (1888; from Col di Tenda to Blocksberg), and a history textbook, *Svenskarna och deras hövdingar* (1908-1910; *The Swedes and Their Chieftains*, 1925). Several volumes of his essays and poetry were published posthumously, including *När kastanjerna blommade* (1941; when the chestnut trees bloomed) and *Sista dikter* (1942; last poems). His collected works have been published in twenty-three volumes by Bonniers.

Achievements

In 1916, Verner von Heidenstam was awarded the Nobel Prize in Literature, which bore the apt inscription "The leader of a new era in our literature." Beginning with his first book of poems, *Vallfart och vandringsår*, in 1888, and continuing until the publication of *Nya dikter* in 1915, Heidenstam challenged the literary trends of his time. He rebelled against the bleak worldview and confining aesthetics of naturalism in his early works and was responsible for ushering in the new poetry of the 1890's. First and foremost a poet, Heidenstam embraced the creative power of the imagination above any attempt in his writing simply to imitate everyday life. His rejection of naturalism did not, however, take him to opposite extremes: Decadence, or art for art's sake, was not an answer for Heidenstam. He tried to blend realism and the inspired creations of the imagination. Disgusted by the pessimism in the writing of his contemporaries, Heidenstam increasingly turned to the past to find a cultural heritage and a set of values powerful enough to launch a new national literature. His three historical novels and *Nya dikter* succeeded in doing so.

The Swedes recognized Heidenstam's important role in revitalizing their national literature. In addition to the Nobel Prize, Heidenstam received several other honors, including membership in the Swedish Academy in 1912 and an honorary doctorate from the Royal Institute of Technology in Stockholm in 1909. It is important to point out, however, that Heidenstam's cultural nationalism does not have at its core a narrow chauvinism. Heidenstam's frame of reference, ultimately, is a classical humanism, based on the love of ideals, beauty, and the creative powers of the human mind.

Biography

Carl Gustaf Verner von Heidenstam was born at the family manor, Olshammar, Sweden, on July 6, 1859. He was the only child of Nils Gustaf von Heidenstam, chief engineer for the Royal Coast Guard, and his wife, Magdalena Charlotta Rütterskiöld. The family lived in Stockholm, where Verner attended the prominent Beskowska School. He spent his summers at Olshammar, where his vivid imagination was nurtured by his grandmother and several other women of the household. During these early years, Heidenstam developed a love for Lake Vättern and the Tiveden landscape, a feeling for the land and its history that he never lost. Because both his health and his academic performance were poor, Heidenstam was taken out of school and sent south to travel. From 1876 to 1878, he toured southern Europe, Egypt, Palestine, Syria, and Greece, recording his impressions in drawings and paintings. These impressions later found expression in the striking vividness and immediacy of the settings in his early works.

In 1879, Heidenstam settled in Rome to become a painter, but he spent an increasing amount of time writing poetry. Against his father's wishes, he married a childhood friend, Emilia Uggla, in 1880, causing a break between father and son. Heidenstam spent the next several years in middle and southern Europe, studying, painting, and writing—striving to find his own artistic form. In 1884, he made contact with Swedish playwright and novelist August Strindberg, at that time living in Switzerland, and the two men began an intense and inspiring series of discussions on all topics, particularly literature and politics. Although Heidenstam presented himself as a radical, his first published volume of poetry, *Vallfart och vandringsår*, with its colorful Eastern exoticism, had little in common with the doctrines of naturalism that Strindberg, at that time, championed.

Heidenstam returned to Sweden in 1887 and was reconciled with his father, who, terminally ill, killed himself the next year. Back in Sweden, the new head of his family, Heidenstam concentrated on his writing. His debut volume of poetry was published in 1888, and in *Renässans* and *Pepitas bröllop*, published in 1889 and 1890, respectively, Heidenstam developed his theories about art, rejecting the naturalism and documentary realism of the 1880's and instead embracing the power of the imagination and love of beauty.

In the late 1890's, Heidenstam wrote increasingly about the issue of cultural nationalism. In both his essays and his creative literature, Heidenstam attempted to define and express the Swedish national character. Mining Swedish history, Heidenstam focused on Charles XII (in *The Charles Men*), Birgitta (in *Heliga Birgittas pilgrimsfärd*), and Folke Filbyter (in *The Tree of the Folkungs*) to explore in historical novels the circumstances and temperament that formed and best expressed the Swedish character. Reacting against the materialism of his day and fearing the influence of foreign countries such as the United States on traditional Swedish social and cultural values, Heidenstam lectured and wrote to raise Swedes' consciousness about their history and cultural heritage. He interrupted a planned series of historical novels to research and write a history textbook, *The Swedes and Their Chieftains*, from 1908 to 1910, a project that exhausted him and apparently drained his creative resources. Although he continued to write essays after completing that text, Heidenstam, with one brilliant exception, *Nya dikter*, was never again able to concentrate his creative powers. Some of his poems, memoirs, and essays were published posthumously, and many were fragments.

While Heidenstam's literary productivity ended in 1915, he lived until 1940. After three failed marriages, to Emilia Uggla (1880-1893), Olga Widberg (1896-1903), and Anna Sjöberg (1903-1906), Heidenstam spent the last decades of his life in a successful relationship with Kate Bang. After 1915, he began another period of travel, revisiting the Riviera, Switzerland, and Italy as well as spending several years in Denmark. In 1925, he retired to Övralid, an estate he built overlooking Lake Vättern. He made occasional public appearances (for example, to speak before the Swedish Academy), but for the most part he lived his last years secluded at Övralid. He died on May 20, 1940, after several years of worsening senility. He is buried at Övralid; his former home has been converted into a museum.

Analysis

Verner von Heidenstam came of age as a writer when he organized and defined his thoughts about literature in *Renässans* and *Pepitas bröllop*. These essays stimulated a new literary and cultural movement in Sweden, one that rejected the doctrines and methodology of naturalism and the philosophical pessimism that Heidenstam saw as its product. Heidenstam called for a new national literature, developing out of and expressing the Swedish national character. Its impulse was to come from Swedish sources, particularly Esaias Tegnér and Victor Rydberg, along with the classical idealism of Johann Wolfgang von Goethe and Friedrich Schiller, and was to unite realism with the "subjective . . . the imagination, the sense of the beautiful." In *Pepitas bröllop*, Heidenstam asks if Mephistopheles and Peer Gynt do not exist with the same intense reality as some of the shadows we talk to on the street corner: "It is not only the purely concrete that comprises reality!"

For Heidenstam, the creative power of the imagination—not the ability to imitate everyday life—was the essence of artistic expression. Heidenstam placed his faith in the insight of the poet; his gifts were more lyric than narrative. His career as a poet began with the publication of *Vallfart och vandringsår*; the work that marks the beginning of Heidenstam's mature period is also a collection of poems, *Dikter;* and *Nya dikter*, perhaps his greatest work, ends his literary production. Between the two volumes of poetry that mark his mature period, however, Heidenstam wrote three historical novels, *The Charles Men*, *Heliga Birgittas pilgrimsfärd*, and *The Tree of the Folkungs*, works that rank Heidenstam among major historical novelists. Historical fiction provided the form Heidenstam needed to express his ideas and offer an alternative to the pessimism and decadence he saw as characteristic of the literature of his time. By writing about the past, Heidenstam believed, he could revitalize traditional values and illustrate aspects of the Swedish national character that he hoped would lead to a humanism based on classical ideals.

Heidenstam's first work, the collection of poems *Vallfart och vandringsår*, added a fresh, vivid, exotic flavor to Swedish poetry. Not only did Heidenstam draw on his travels to provide an exotic setting for many of his poems, but also the lively tone and dynamic, colorful imagery, as well as the themes glorifying youth, beauty, and pleasures of the moment, were a shocking antidote to readers accustomed to the darker settings and themes of naturalism.

Endymion

Heidenstam's first novel, *Endymion*, worked similar ground; the reader enters a world of harems, baths, Bedouin caravans, and bazaars. Although viewed from a foreigner's perspective, the scenes have vitality because they are seen through the eyes of a sensitive, receptive protagonist. Heidenstam depicts the decline of Arabic culture and, with it, the life spirit that had characterized that ancient culture. Although some critics dismissed Heidenstam's first prose work as a travel book disguised as a novel, "a romanticized Baedeker," in this work Heidenstam raised the issues of cultural nationalism and the tragic role of national heroes that he later successfully developed in his major novels.

Hans Alienus

Hans Alienus is a more original book, interesting for its insights into Heidenstam's evolving philosophy, but a chaotic blend of verse and prose—more a book of thoughts than a successfully wrought novel. The protagonist, Hans Alienus, is a stranger in his own time, searching for an ideal image of humanity, a meaning for which he can live. He travels freely through time and space, studying, experiencing, and ultimately rejecting the life philosophies he encounters in places ranging from the Vatican to the court of Sardanapalus to Hades. The last section of the book, strongly autobiographical, finds Hans Alienus in Sweden, reconciled with his father and embracing a belief in beauty and the imagination. The father, however, takes his own life, and the novel ends with Hans Alienus isolated, resigned, and wanting to die.

Despite the novel's obvious autobiographical elements, Heidenstam, fortunately, moved beyond the despair and spiritual bankruptcy that defeat Hans Alienus. In his remaining novels, he turned to the history of the Swedish nation to discover and illustrate those values and beliefs with which to face life and give it meaning.

The Charles Men

In his desire to create a new literature based on Sweden's cultural heritage, Heidenstam looked to the historical past to find subjects capable of infusing a literary national consciousness. In the figure of King Charles XII, Heidenstam found a character whose complexity and stature could express the Swedish national character. Heidenstam read diaries and original documents to gain an accurate sense of the period about which he was writing, but his most important source was Anders Fryxell's history of Charles XII and the men who served under him. Heidenstam's reliance on historical sources, however, was to provide a framework and background for his sketches of the king and of the fates of individual Swedes on campaign during the long war years. Heidenstam depicts these characters, representative of the Swedish people, in revealing anecdotes, which he believed to be the building blocks of historical fiction. The novelist, Heidenstam argued, must select anecdotes of dramatic power and arrange them in an order that most effectively expresses the conception of the novel as a unified whole.

Unity, however, is not easily achieved, as *The Charles Men* demonstrates. Its structure is a series of short stories, much like that of Sherwood Anderson's *Winesburg, Ohio* (1919) or Ernest Hemingway's *In Our Time* (1924, 1925). All three works are complete in themselves but provide composites of central characters—George Willard for Anderson, Nick Adams for Hemingway, and, in Heidenstam's work, Charles XII as well as one other significant composite "character": the Swedish people. Though the stories illuminate the character of Charles XII and provide insight into the moral dilemma he faces, they are not essential parts of an organic whole; they can stand by themselves, and, indeed, some were published several years before they reappeared as chapters in *The Charles Men*. The structure does, however, emphasize Heidenstam's strength as a writer. Instead of a detailed, sweeping historical narrative, Heidenstam gives his readers the individual event, striking and immediate, without rhetorical or interpretive comment. He wastes no words, using the means of the poet to provide meaning—symbol, image, suggestion. Fredrik Böök, coeditor with Kate Bang of Heidenstam's collected works, likened Heidenstam's style to a "monumental fresco," an epic style with limited use of detail whereby even the decorative is simplified and concentrated.

Heidenstam chose to write about a time in history when Sweden was a major power led by a king who gained an international reputation. *The Charles Men*, however, is not a glorification or a romanticized interpretation of Sweden's role in shaping European history. Heidenstam's emphasis is on the defeat of the king and the nation. Charles XII is a complex character, and the reader senses Heidenstam's ambivalent attitude toward his hero. Charles XII is shown as cold and indifferent to other people's suffering; much of the time he is lost in a world of his own thoughts, melancholy and isolated even when surrounded by his men. On the other hand, he is also courageous, leading his soldiers on the battlefield and commanding their loyalty to the bitter end. He is driven by his convictions and willingly sacrifices his men, the country's resources, and ultimately himself in his mission to keep Sweden undivided. Though some of his people question whether the king is not tempting God, a soldier answers, after Charles has been shot: "He believed in the righteousness of his own conduct. Such defiance God forgives. Such defiance even men forgive."

Heidenstam's portrait of Charles XII assumes tragic overtones. The king and his men are doomed to defeat, but, as Heidenstam has written, war can shape brave and stable personalities, "even mold new life in an entire people." The Charles men, hungry, cold, besieged, and imprisoned, are transformed from selfish, weak individuals to self-sacrificing, dutiful men. In Heidenstam's fiction, defeat can be ennobling; greatness can arise out of terrible suffering and self-sacrifice.

Heliga Birgittas pilgrimsfärd

Heidenstam continued his examination of the heroic character under stress in *Heliga Birgittas pilgrimsfärd*, a transitional novel published between his two major prose works. Again the setting is historical, the fourteenth century, and the novel focuses on one of Sweden's most famous figures. The concerns coming under Heidenstam's scrutiny are mainly religious ones, as opposed to the military and political concerns that are primary in *The Charles Men*. In both works, however, Heidenstam is less interested in the broad sweep of historical circumstances than he is in depicting the psychic tensions and pressures they impose on the consciences of his heroes.

For Birgitta, the conflicts are between her "call" and her life as a sexual woman, mother, and wife; between her desire for Christian humility and her selfishness and unyielding pride. Her fanaticism makes her insensitive, even brutal, in her treatment of her children—and herself. She is compared to an octopus, consuming those who come within her reach while "her devilish eyes are directed upward toward the stars." Like Charles, she willingly sacrifices all to follow steadfastly her own will. Heidenstam suggests that an unyielding drive and self-sacrifice are necessary for greatness. *Heliga Birgittas pilgrimsfärd* does delineate, however, as Alrik Gustafson has demonstrated in his study of Heidenstam's works, a new and evolving conception of the tragic hero. Birgitta finds purity and fulfillment in her faith because she transforms her fanaticism through humility and resignation. She discovers that aggressive zealousness can do evil even when she most desires to do good: "So is it Thy meaning that also they who most intensely burn with desire to serve Thy love and righteousness shall do evil." The human condition, she finally recognizes, is both good and evil; resigned to her own imperfections, she can empathize with the feelings of others and become truly humane.

The Tree of the Folkungs

In his last novel, *The Tree of the Folkungs*, Heidenstam returned to the foundation of the Swedish state itself. Part 1 of the novel is set at the end of the Viking period, when Christian worship is slowly replacing heathen beliefs and landowners wield political power. Heidenstam follows the basic history of that period, but because knowledge of the period is sketchy at best, his imagination is given free reign as he transforms names in historical documents into passionate, ambitious human beings. The founder of the Folkungs is Folke Filbyter, a Viking chieftain, who decides to acquire land and domestic animals at home instead of plundering abroad. Folke is a coarse, hulking man, interested in only one thing beyond his physical needs—the accumulation of wealth. He has no regard for social rules or law; in fact, he sends his thralls to rob people on the roads, and he becomes a blood brother with an outlaw. He even kidnaps his neighbor's daughter after his son's request to marry her has been rejected by the neighbor's family. It is on such suspicious beginnings that the Swedish state is founded.

Nevertheless, Heidenstam is able to make Folke sympathetic at the end of part 1. Folke grows to love his grandson; after the boy has been kidnapped by a Christian preacher, the reader can feel Folke's anguish as he scours the country looking for the boy. Decades later, Folke finds him, an earl in the king's service, but the old man is told to keep quiet about the earl's questionable background. Folke, the patriarch, is rejected by his own sons and grandson because he has no culture, no beliefs, no conscience.

In one lifetime, Swedish society has undergone vast changes: Folke's offspring belong to a rising nobility who will establish the central power of the Folkungs. Paganism is being suppressed: The sacred grove of the heathens is burned by young Christian priests in the king's retinue. Weary, displaced, a man left behind by the times, Folke cannot win the love of his sons. Nevertheless, he feels no bitterness; indeed, he is proud of his sons. As the young Folkungs ride off, dreaming of their destiny, Folke assumes a tragic grandeur when he opens his veins and prepares for a house sacrifice, faithful to his own customs and resigned to his fate.

Part 2 takes up the story of the Folkung family two hundred years after Folke Filbyter's death. The Folkungs have consolidated their power. Through the characterizations of two brothers, Valdemar and Magnus, Heidenstam is able to explore what qualities of leadership are necessary to establish effective social and political order. The brothers end up fighting for the crown because Valdemar is indifferent about his duties as a ruler. He seeks the pleasures of the moment, much like the characters in Heidenstam's early fiction, but such irresponsibility is fatal for a leader. His brother Magnus fills the power vacuum.

The state is unified under Magnus's rule. Laws are codified and enforced; ties with the church are strengthened; a state army of knights is trained and mobilized. Despite his success as a temporal leader, however, Magnus is an anguished man, torn by internal conflicts. He feels guilty about imprisoning his brother and usurping Valdemar's power, yet, as a politician and leader, Magnus recognizes the necessity of having done so. He is both selfish and hypocritical, but he is also motivated by a real desire to establish order and justice.

A tortured spirit like Heidenstam's other heroes, Magnus is not able to find happiness. His personal compromises, however, do not overshadow the fact that he has molded a nation striving for peace and a more just society. Heidenstam suggests that his heroes are a mixture of good and evil, possessed of both virtues and vices, and that these heroes reflect the character of the nation as a whole. Though Heidenstam shows Magnus as flawed, one can take heart in the fact that civilization has made great strides from Folke Filbyter's day to Magnus Folkung's: In his last novel, Heidenstam offers the hope of progress.

Christer L. Mossberg

OTHER MAJOR WORKS

SHORT FICTION: *Sankt Göran och draken*, 1900; *Skogen susar*, 1904.

POETRY: *Vallfart och vandringsår*, 1888; *Dikter*, 1895; *Nya dikter*, 1915; *Sweden's Laureate: Selected Poems of Verner von Heidenstam*, 1919; *Sista dikter*, 1942; *Fragment och aforismer*, 1959.

NONFICTION: *Från Col di Tenda till Blocksberg*, 1888; *Renässans*, 1889; *Pepitas bröllop*, 1890 (with Oscar Levertin); *Modern Barbarism*, 1894; *Klassicitet och germanism*, 1898; *Tankar och tekningar*, 1899; *Svenskarna och deras hövdingar*, 1908-1910 (*The Swedes and Their Chieftains*, 1925); *Dagar och händelser*, 1909; *Proletärfilosofiens upplösning och fall*,

1911; *Vad vilja vi?*, 1914; *När kastanjerna blommade*, 1941; *Tankar och utkast*, 1941; *Brev: 1884-1890*, 1999 (letters; Magnus von Platen, editor).

MISCELLANEOUS: *Samlade skrifter*, 1909-1949 (23 volumes).

Bibliography

Blankner, Frederika, ed. *The History of Scandinavian Literatures*. 1938. Reprint. Port Washington, N.Y.: Kennikat Press, 1966. Contains a bibliography of Heidenstam in English translation, along with a brief discussion of the author.

Brantly, Susan. "Heidenstam's *Karolinerna* and the *Fin de Siècle*." In *Fin(s) de Siècle in Scandinavian Perspective*, edited by Faith Ingwersen and Mary Kay Norseng. Columbia, S.C.: Camden House, 1993. Critical study of Heidenstam's novel is included in a collection of essays that examine Scandinavian literature and artistic movements that appeared at the ends of the last four centuries.

_______. "Into the Twentieth Century: 1890-1950." In *A History of Swedish Literature*, edited by Lars G. Warme. Lincoln: University of Nebraska Press, 1996. Heidenstam's work is discussed in the first section of this chapter.

Bredsdorff, Elias, Brita Mortensen, and Ronald Popperwell. *An Introduction to Scandinavian Literature from the Earliest Time to Our Day*. Westport, Conn.: Greenwood Press, 1970. Places Heidenstam in the context of Swedish authors in the period from the 1890's to about 1910.

Gustafson, Alrik. *A History of Swedish Literature*. Minneapolis: University of Minnesota Press, 1961. Survey of Swedish literature includes a discussion of Heidenstam's work.

_______. *Six Scandinavian Novelists: Lie, Jacobsen, Heidenstam, Selma Lagerlöf, Hamsun, Sigrid Undset*. 1940. Reprint. Minneapolis: University of Minnesota Press, 1966. The essay on Heidenstam in this volume is considered one of the best brief critical studies of his work available in English.

Rossel, Sven H. *A History of Scandinavian Literature, 1870-1980*. Translated by Anne C. Ulmer. Minneapolis: University of Minnesota Press, 1982. Survey of Scandinavian literature includes a discussion of Heidenstam's fiction.

ROBERT A. HEINLEIN

Born: Butler, Missouri; July 7, 1907
Died: Carmel, California; May 8, 1988
Also known as: Robert Anson Heinlein; Anson MacDonald; Caleb Saunders; Lyle Monroe; John Riverside

Principal long fiction

Rocket Ship Galileo, 1947
Beyond This Horizon, 1948
Space Cadet, 1948
Red Planet, 1949
Sixth Column, 1949 (also published as *The Day After Tomorrow*, 1951)
Farmer in the Sky, 1950
Between Planets, 1951
The Puppet Masters, 1951
The Rolling Stones, 1952
Starman Jones, 1953
The Star Beast, 1954
Tunnel in the Sky, 1955
Double Star, 1956
Time for the Stars, 1956
Citizen of the Galaxy, 1957
The Door into Summer, 1957
Have Space Suit—Will Travel, 1958
Methuselah's Children, 1958
Starship Troopers, 1959
Stranger in a Strange Land, 1961
Glory Road, 1963
Podkayne of Mars: Her Life and Times, 1963

Farnham's Freehold, 1964
The Moon Is a Harsh Mistress, 1966
I Will Fear No Evil, 1970
Time Enough for Love, 1973
The Notebooks of Lazarus Long, 1978
The Number of the Beast, 1980
Friday, 1982
Job: A Comedy of Justice, 1984
The Cat Who Walks Through Walls, 1985
To Sail Beyond the Sunset, 1987
For Us, the Living, 2004
Variable Star, 2006 (with Spider Robinson)

Other literary forms

Robert A. Heinlein (HIN-lin) was a best-selling writer of science-fiction short stories for ten years before his first novel appeared. Those stories were published in more than one dozen collections, with a great deal of overlap. He cowrote the screenplays for two films, *Destination Moon* (1950) and *Project Moonbase* (1953). He did not publish nonfiction during his lifetime, but his wife, Virginia Heinlein, published his 1946 typescript "How to Be a Politician" as *Take Back Your Government: A Practical Handbook for the Private Citizen Who Wants Democracy to Work* in 1992. His 1953 travelogue *Tramp Royale* was published in 1992.

Heinlein edited *Tomorrow, the Stars* (1952), a collection of short stories by other science-fiction writers. In his introduction to the book, he discusses the terms "science fiction" and "speculative fiction," telling readers that he prefers the term "speculative fiction." His letters, which were published as *Grumbles from the Grave* (1989), were selected and edited by his wife.

Achievements

Known since the 1950's as the dean of science fiction, Robert A. Heinlein was the top-selling author of the golden age of pulp-magazine science fiction (1930's-1940's), the first to sell science fiction to the "slick" magazines (prestigious glossy-paper periodicals such as *The Saturday Evening Post*), and the first major science-fiction author to write for film.

Heinlein's science fiction is of the nuts-and-bolts variety, in which space travel and other future technologies are presented realistically; their engineering is worked out in detail, yet that detail does not intrude on the narrative. Examples of Heinlein's technologies include the space suit, descriptions of which borrow from his own wartime research at the Philadelphia Navy Yard. In fact, his research led to the development of space suits long after he had described them. (Also, he had envisioned and then detailed the water bed.)

Heinlein received the Hugo Award for best science-fiction novel four times, and Science Fiction Writers of America honored him with its first Grand Master award for lifetime achievement. His fiction introduced several words and phrases to the English language, including "free fall" for zero gravity, "waldo" for a mechanical arm (named after a Heinlein character), and his acronym TANSTAAFL (There Ain't No Such Thing As A Free Lunch) for a popular phrase, perhaps borrowed from Rudyard Kipling. The acronym became a byword for libertarians and economists such as Milton Friedman.

Biography

Robert Anson Heinlein was born in Butler, Missouri, and grew up in Kansas City, immersed in what he thought was a Bible Belt culture. His relationship with that culture, as displayed in his fiction, would be partly adversarial.

Heinlein entered the U.S. Naval Academy at Annapolis, from which he emerged as a naval officer in 1929. He served on one of the first aircraft carriers, the USS *Lexington* (1931), and the Wickes-class destroyer, the USS *Roper* (1933-1934). He married Eleanor Curry from his Kansas City hometown, but the marriage lasted only one year. In 1932, he married Leslyn Macdonald. Heinlein's military career was cut short with a diagnosis of tuberculosis, leading to a medical discharge. He dabbled in mining and politics, assisting novelist Upton Sinclair's unsuccessful bid for governor of California in 1934 and running for a seat in the California State assembly in 1938.

In 1939, Heinlein's short story "Life Line" was published in *Astounding Science Fiction*, marking his first publication. A flurry of similar stories in the following years determined his career. In fact, he was so prolific that he began competing with himself: Fan polls in *Astounding Science Fiction* rated him number one, followed by Anson MacDonald—one of his many pseudonyms.

The year 1947 was portentous for Heinlein. First, he broke into the upper echelon of the magazine fiction market with "The Green Hills of Earth" in the February issue of *The Saturday Evening Post*. Second, he began his lucrative and influential series of juvenile novels for Scribner's with *Rocket Ship Galileo*. Third, he divorced his second wife and, the following year, married fellow engineer and naval officer Virginia Gerstenfeld, whom he had met at the Naval Air Experimentation Station in Philadelphia during World War II. Gerstenfeld was the model for many of the celebrated "strong red-headed women" in his fiction.

Heinlein's contract with Scribner's guaranteed him one novel a year, timed for a Christmas release. Scribner's, however, broke the contract in 1959 by rejecting "Starship Troopers." Heinlein sold the manuscript to G. P. Putnam's Sons, which published the book the same year. His next novel, *Stranger in a Strange Land*, created controversy with its frank sexual and religious themes, but it proved that science fiction could be a medium of social criticism. His later novels continued exploring similar controversial themes, while mixing the hard, nuts-and-bolts science fiction with pure fantasy, in a type of magical realism in which the most fantastic events are given scientific plausibility.

Robert A. Heinlein. (Courtesy, Heinlein Centennial Inc.)

Heinlein was a guest commentator for CBS television's coverage of the first U.S. spaceflight to the Moon, and his works were discussed on the Moon by Apollo 15 astronauts in 1971. He almost died from peritonitis in the early 1970's and was ill through most of the decade and unable to write much. In his last decade, however, he wrote five well-regarded novels. He died in his sleep on May 8, 1988, from emphysema and congestive heart failure.

ANALYSIS

The science fiction of Robert A. Heinlein became, by the second half of the twentieth century, the gold standard by which the genre was measured. Along with his friend Isaac Asimov and British author Arthur C. Clarke, Heinlein became one of the "big three" writers of English-language science fiction in the twentieth century.

Heinlein's specialty was twofold: the well-engineered, scientifically plausible exposition of future technologies, and his success at weaving those technologies into his fiction unobtrusively. He also was recognized as one of the pioneers in the integration of the social sciences into science fiction, and many of the major themes of his fiction concern social issues: individual liberty, the nature of authority and civil disobedience, nonconformity, sexual and religious morality, and the role of the military in society. Critics sometimes overstate the importance of sexual, religious, and military themes in Heinlein's fiction, but his conviction was that all three would be impacted by space travel and that speculative fiction—the term Heinlein preferred for the genre in which he wrote—would not give a complete picture of possible futures if it did not take these themes into account.

THE PUPPET MASTERS

One of the marks of this novel's success is that its plot (human bodies being invaded by aliens who control their minds) has become a cliché, particularly in film. *Invasion of the Body Snatchers* (1956, 1978; based on the 1955 novel *The Body Snatchers* by Jack Finney), *I Married a Monster from Outer Space* (1958), and *The Brain Eaters* (1958) are all similar in plot, but Heinlein's

The Puppet Masters preceded them all. In fact, *The Brain Eaters* so clearly "borrowed" from his 1951 novel that Heinlein sued for plagiarism and won an out-of-court settlement. Readers who can get beyond the echoes of later imitators will find a novel of surprising psychological depth that forces its characters to reevaluate the nature of human relationships.

Like most of its imitators, *The Puppet Masters* gains much of its energy from the instinctive horror at the thought of another creature controlling a person completely. That horror is not mitigated by knowing that the alien creatures controlling the humans remove any trace of negative feeling about the experience. The first-person narrator of the novel, Elihu Nivens, is a government agent known by his codename Sam, and he is humanity's last best hope for saving the world from the creatures that attach themselves to the human spinal cord. In the process, Sam's disgust at the prospect (and at one point the reality) of being controlled by another creature forces him to confront the ways in which the human spirit can be dominated without alien interference—through such cultural bulwarks as filial piety (the head of the secret service agency Sam works for turns out to be Sam's father), marriage (Sam's emotional connection with his wife, Mary, also an agent, is used to manipulate him into taking an alien parasite on his back), and religion (Sam wonders if Mary had been a member of a cult known as the Whitmanites).

The book ends with the eradication of the alien puppet masters that are immanent, but more important, the story ends with Sam coming to terms with the imitations of the puppet masters in his social, vocational, and emotional relationships.

Double Star

Heinlein's first Hugo Award winner, *Double Star*, is a science fiction version of Anthony Hope's *Prisoner of Zenda* (1894), in which a look-alike is groomed to stand in for a kidnapped monarch. In *Double Star*, the captured leader, John Joseph Bonforte, is not a monarch (though the solar system is presented in the book as a constitutional monarchy, with an emperor), but the leader of an expansionist coalition. Bonforte's party wants the human government of the solar system to form an alliance with the nonhuman Martians, but there is a great deal of race prejudice against the Martians among Earth's humans (Bonforte's opponents are known as the Humanity Party).

One of the novel's racist humans is the first-person narrator, the egotistical actor Lorenzo Smythe, billed as the Great Lorenzo. Because of his resemblance to Bonforte and because of his acting ability, Smythe is tapped to stand in for Bonforte at a Martian ceremony. Smythe, however, cares little for politics. By projecting the psychology of racism in 1950's America as future prejudice against an alien other, Heinlein took science fiction beyond its literary ghetto and showed that it could engage contemporary social issues—though in this novel the connection was not overt, and certainly not allegorical. The triumph of this novel, however, lies not in any implicit critique of racism but in the development of the character of Smythe.

An egotistical, vain, bigoted aesthete at the beginning of the story, Smythe "modulates" to something nobler. He had expected to play Bonforte only for a single event, but when Bonforte dies in the hands of his captors, Smythe is faced with the prospect of either continuing the charade for the rest of his life or allowing an entire government to collapse. This most selfish of men is poised to sacrifice his entire career for a cause that was not his. This unlikely outcome is possible because of the metamorphosis of Smythe's character from a cad to a hero so likeable that Bonforte's secretary, who hated Smythe from the start, falls in love with him. Fellow science-fiction writer James Blish called Lorenzo Smythe Heinlein's most successful first-person narrator.

Starship Troopers

Reminiscent of the boot-camp films of World War II, this study of the nature of the military mind in an interplanetary future scandalized many readers who considered the novel militaristic and even fascist. Heinlein's editor at Scribner's refused to publish the work, but Putnam's jumped at the chance to publish anything from the popular novelist. The novel led to Heinlein's second Hugo Award.

Starship Troopers posits of a future society in which government service (including, but not limited to, military service) is a prerequisite for citizenship. Some readers chafed at the book's supposed didacticism. It is certainly more discursive than most Heinlein novels: Each difficulty in narrator Juan "Johnny" Rico's training results in a flashback to a lecture in Johnny's high school civics class (a required course designed to prepare students for their government service). The novel's real protagonist might well be the power suit that is the all-purpose soldier's weapon. Heinlein describes the armored suit with the same detail he uses to describe the regular space suit in *Have Space Suit—Will Travel*.

Stranger in a Strange Land

Heinlein's third Hugo-winning novel, *Stranger in a Strange Land*, is probably his best-known and most influential work. The basic premise of the "Martian-eye view" of Earth society had long been a natural narrative device for writers of science fiction. Because the novel's protagonist, Valentine Michael Smith, is biologically human but had been raised by Martians, he arrives as a cultural outsider on Earth. This plot line allows Heinlein to critique his own culture indirectly. While doing so, Heinlein also delves into the science of linguistics by applying the hypotheses of Edward Sapir and Benjamin Whorf.

Indeed, Heinlein's use of linguistic theory in his novels had a major effect on science fiction. The hypothesis is simple: Grammatical categories of a language determine how a speaker of that language views the world. In the novel, Smith has a number of unique abilities, which no other human has. He tries to teach his Earth friends these abilities (telekinesis, voluntary control of autonomic bodily functions, and others) but cannot do so until they learn the Martian language. In the process, Smith creates precedents in international (and interplanetary) law, starts a new religion, and invents unconventional family arrangements, which became actual models for many communes of the 1960's.

John R. Holmes

Other major works

SHORT FICTION: *The Man Who Sold the Moon*, 1950; *Waldo and Magic, Inc.*, 1950; *The Green Hills of Earth*, 1951; *Universe*, 1951 (as *Orphans of the Sky*, 1963); *Assignment in Eternity*, 1953; *Revolt in 2100*, 1953; *The Menace from Earth*, 1959; *The Unpleasant Profession of Jonathan Hoag*, 1959 (as *6 × H*, 1962); *The Worlds of Robert A. Heinlein*, 1966; *The Past Through Tomorrow*, 1967; *Destination Moon*, 1979; *Expanded Universe: The New Worlds of Robert A. Heinlein*, 1980; *Requiem: New Collected Works by Robert A. Heinlein and Tributes to the Grand Master*, 1992; *The Fantasies of Robert A. Heinlein*, 1999; *Off the Main Sequence*, 2005.

SCREENPLAYS: *Destination Moon*, 1950 (with James O'Hanlon and Rip Van Ronkel); *Project Moonbase*, 1953 (with Jack Seaman).

NONFICTION: *Of Worlds Beyond: The Science of Science-Fiction Writing*, 1947 (with others); *The Science Fiction Novel*, 1959 (with others); *Grumbles from the Grave*, 1989 (Virginia Heinlein, editor); *Take Back Your Government: A Practical Handbook for the Private Citizen Who Wants Democracy to Work*, 1992; *Tramp Royale*, 1992 (wr. 1953).

EDITED TEXT: *Tomorrow, the Stars*, 1952.

MISCELLANEOUS: *The Best of Robert A. Heinlein, 1939-1959*, 1973.

Bibliography

Franklin, H. Bruce. *Robert A. Heinlein: America as Science Fiction*. New York: Oxford University Press, 1980. A study of Heinlein's entire corpus, somewhat biased in its Marxist readings. Franklin, unaware of Heinlein's socialist activities in the early 1930's, paints him as a knee-jerk conservative capitalist.

Gifford, James. *Robert A. Heinlein: A Reader's Companion*. Sacramento, Calif.: Nitrosyncretic Press, 2000. Commentary on all known Heinlein works, including each of his short stories. Gifford attempts to balance what he sees as anti-Heinlein rant (Alexei Panshin) and Heinlein chauvinism (Spider Robinson).

Heinlein, Robert A. *Grumbles from the Grave*. Edited by Virginia Heinlein. New York: Del Rey, 1989. Heinlein's letters are helpful not only for biographical background but also critical comment on Heinlein's own fiction.

Olander, Joseph D., and Martin Harry Greenberg. *Robert A. Heinlein*. New York: Taplinger, 1978. This collection includes critical articles that vary in quality. Jack Williamson's article on Heinlein's juvenile articles and Ivor A. Rogers's study of Heinlein's work through the spectrum of folklore are of particular interest.

Panshin, Alexei. *Heinlein in Dimension*. Chicago: Advent, 1968. Now dated, and marred by Panshin's love-hate relationship with Heinlein's fiction, this book-length study of Heinlein's works nevertheless has some value for the perspective of a fellow science-fiction writer (Panshin won a Hugo Award in 1967).

Patterson, William H., Jr., and Andrew Thornton. *The Martian Named Smith: Critical Perspectives on Robert A. Heinlein's "Stranger in a Strange Land."* Sacramento, Calif.: Nitrosyncretic Press, 2001. Criticism of Heinlein's well-known novel, as well as a thorough study of his works overall.

Stover, Leon E. *Robert Heinlein*. Boston: Twayne, 1987. A volume in a standard series of U.S. authors, this is an ideal starting point for most research. Fans have criticized its supposed inaccuracies, but these are all addressed by James Gifford (2000). Includes a helpful annotated bibliography.

JOSEPH HELLER

Born: Brooklyn, New York; May 1, 1923
Died: East Hampton, New York; December 12, 1999

PRINCIPAL LONG FICTION

Catch-22, 1961
Something Happened, 1974
Good as Gold, 1979
God Knows, 1984
Picture This, 1988
Closing Time, 1994
Portrait of an Artist, as an Old Man, 2000

OTHER LITERARY FORMS

Joseph Heller's first published piece was a short story in *Story Magazine* (1945), and in the late 1940's, he placed several other stories with *Esquire* and *The Atlantic Monthly*. Heller's enthusiasm for the theater accounts for the topic of his master's thesis at Columbia University, "The Pulitzer Prize Plays: 1917-1935," and he wrote three plays that deal directly or indirectly with the material he used in *Catch-22*. *We Bombed in New Haven*, a two-act play, was first produced by the Yale School of Drama Repertory Theater in 1967. It later reached Broadway and was published in 1968. *Catch-22: A Dramatization* (1971) was first produced at the John Drew Theater in East Hampton, Long Island, where Heller spent his summers. *Clevinger's Trial*, a dramatization of chapter 8 of *Catch-22*, was produced in London in 1974. Only *We Bombed in New Haven* enjoyed a modicum of critical and commercial success. Heller also contributed to a number of motion-picture and television scripts, the best known of which is *Sex and the Single Girl* (1964), for which he received his only screen credit.

ACHIEVEMENTS

Joseph Heller's reputation rests largely on his first novel, *Catch-22*, the publication of which vaulted him into the front ranks of postwar American novelists. Critics hailed it as "the great representative document of our era" and "probably the finest novel published since World War II." The expression "Catch-22" quickly entered the American lexicon. More than eight million copies of the novel have been printed, and it has been translated into more than a dozen languages. In 1970, Mike Nichols's film adaptation of Heller's tale sparked renewed interest in the novel itself and launched it onto the best-seller lists.

Catch-22 was one of the most widely read and discussed novels of the 1960's and early 1970's; its blend of humor and horror struck a responsive chord, particularly with the young, during the upheavals of the Vietnam era. The critic Josh Greenfield, writing in 1968, claimed that it had "all but become the chapbook of the sixties." Within the context of Vietnam, the novel seemed to be less about World War II than about that Asian war over which Americans were so furiously divided. *Catch-22*, then, remains the classic fictional statement of the antiwar sentiments of its time.

Although some have compared *Catch-22* to Norman Mailer's *The Naked and the Dead* (1948), James Jones's *The Thin Red Line* (1962), and other essentially naturalistic war tales written by Heller's contemporaries, its conception of war in basically absurdist terms and its crazy-quilt structure suggest affinities rather with such works as Kurt Vonnegut's *Slaughterhouse-Five* (1969). Heller's fiction is frequently described as "black comedy." In the tradition of Nathanael West, Günter Grass, Ralph Ellison, and Thomas Pynchon, Heller stretches reality to the point of distortion.

In his novels, as well as in his plays, Heller displays a worldview that shares much with twentieth century existentialist thought: The world is meaningless, it simply exists; humankind by its very nature seeks meaning; the relationship between humanity and its world is thus absurd; when a person recognizes these facts, he or she experiences what Jean-Paul Sartre termed the "nausea" of modern existence. In all of his work, Heller argues for "massive resistance" to routine, regimentation, and authority in whatever form. He affirms, no matter how much that affirmation may be qualified by pain and defeat, the sanctity of the individual. He writes not so much about the life of a soldier (as in *Catch-22*), the life of a businessman (as in *Something Happened*), or the life of a would-be politician (as in *Good as Gold*) as about the threats posed to individual identity by the institutions of modern life.

Biography

Joseph Heller was born in Brooklyn, New York, on May 1, 1923, the son of Russian-Jewish immigrants only recently arrived in the United States. His mother then barely spoke English; his father drove a delivery truck for a bakery until, when Heller was only five years old, he died unexpectedly during a routine ulcer operation. The denial of this death in particular and the bare fact of mortality in general were to color Heller's later life and work. The youngest of three children, Heller spent his boyhood in the Coney Island section of Brooklyn, an enclave of lower-and middle-class Jewish families, in the shadow of the famed amusement park. Both his family and his teachers recognized Heller as a bright but bored student; he tinkered with writing short stories while still in high school.

In 1942, at the age of nineteen, Heller joined the U.S. Army Air Corps. He spent one of the war years flying sixty missions as a wing bombardier in a squadron of B-25's stationed on Corsica in the Mediterranean. This proved to be the crucial year of his life; it provided him with the materials, and the bitterly sardonic attitude, out of which he forged his major work—*Catch-22*—as well as his three plays. Moreover, his sixty missions, many of them brutal and bloody (including the series of raids on Bologna that form the core of *Catch-22*), profoundly affected the attitude toward death that informs all of his work.

Demobilized in 1945, having achieved the rank of first lieutenant, Heller married fellow Brooklynite Shirley Held, with whom he had two children. Heller spent the next seven years within academe. Under the G.I. Bill, he attended college, first at the University of Southern California and then at New York University, where he received his bachelor of arts degree in 1948. Heller then traveled uptown to earn a master's degree at Columbia University before receiving one of the first Fulbright scholarships to study at Oxford. He returned to the United States to teach English at Pennsylvania State University between 1950 and 1952.

During the remainder of the 1950's, Heller was employed in the advertising departments of *Time*, *Look*, and *McCall's* magazines successively. In 1954, he began writing, at night and during odd hours, the manuscript that would be published eight years later as *Catch-22*. Almost forty years old when *Catch-22* finally appeared, Heller ironically referred to himself as an "aging prodigy."

Heller abandoned his successful advertising career during the 1960's and returned to teaching. His position as distinguished professor of English at the City University of New York (CUNY) afforded him both the salary to support his family and the free time to devote to his writing. In these years, he began work on a second novel, wrote several motion-picture and television scripts (usually adaptations of the work of others and often using a pseudonym), and completed his first play, *We Bombed in New Haven*.

Something Happened, Heller's second novel, took thirteen years to complete before appearing in 1974. Never fully at ease with academic life, Heller resigned his chair at CUNY in 1975, and in 1979 he published his third novel, *Good as Gold*. Although he occasionally lectured on the college circuit and served as writer-in-residence at both Yale University and the University of Pennsylvania, Heller was basically a reclusive writer, uncomfortable at literary gatherings and suspicious of the trappings of literary success. His life and work seemed guided by Ralph Waldo Emerson's dictum that "a foolish consistency is the hobgoblin of little minds."

In December, 1981, Heller was diagnosed as having Guillain Barré syndrome, a sometimes fatal condition involving progressive paralysis. He was hospitalized for several months but eventually recovered. The experience resulted in a book, *No Laughing Matter* (1986), written with his friend Speed Vogel, describing Heller's condition and its resolution; the illness also led to his second marriage, to one of his nurses, Valerie Humphries, in 1987.

God Knows returns to the irreverence and defiance of logic that characterized *Catch-22*. Its narrator, the biblical King David, speaks in modern jargon and in his extended version of his life and career displays knowledge of events long after his own time. *Picture This* is a protracted meditation on the ironies of history and of human life, focusing on the Netherlands of Rembrandt's time and the Athens of Aristotle.

In 1994, more than thirty years after the release of *Catch-22*, Heller published *Closing Time*, a sequel to *Catch-22*. Set in the late 1980's, this novel revisits both the characters from Heller's first novel and the experiences of Heller's generation of New York Jews, for whom World War II was a formative experience. In *Closing Time*, both groups come face-to-face with their own mortality and the fate of a world governed by flawed human institutions.

Now and Then: From Coney Island to Here (1998) is an autobiographical account of Heller's life from his boyhood days in Coney Island through the period following the publication of *Catch-22*. Devotees of *Catch-22* may be disappointed to find that Heller spends only part of a chapter on his wartime experience, while much of the early sections of the memoir chart the geography of Coney Island in elaborate detail. Heller would make his home in East Hampton, Long Island, New York. He died there on December 12, 1999.

Joseph Heller. (Mariana Cook)

Analysis

At first glance, Joseph Heller's novels seem quite dissimilar. Heller's manipulation of time and point of view in *Catch-22* is dizzying; it is a hilariously macabre, almost surreal novel. *Something Happened*, on the other hand, is a far more muted book composed of the slow-moving, pessimistic broodings of an American business executive. *Good as Gold* is part remembrance of family life in the impoverished sections of Coney Island and part savage satire of contemporary American political life. Throughout Heller's work, however, all his characters are obsessed with death and passionately searching for some means to deny, or at least stay, their mortality. Heller's characters, like those of Saul Bellow, cry out to assert their individuality, their sense of self, which seems threatened from all sides. For example, Captain John Yossarian in *Catch-22* finds the world in conspiracy to blow him out of the sky. The worlds of *Catch-22*, *Something Happened*, and *Good as Gold* are not so much chaotic as absurdly and illogically routinized. In such an absurd world of callous cruelty, unalloyed ambition, and blithe disregard for human life, Heller maintains, the individual has the right to seek his own survival by any means possible.

Catch-22

While *Catch-22*'s most obvious features are its antiwar theme and its wild, often madhouse humor, the novel itself is exceedingly complex in both meaning and form. In brief, the plot concerns a squadron of American airmen stationed on the fictional Mediterranean island of Pianosa during World War II. More specifically, it concerns the futile attempts of Captain Yossarian, a Syrian American bombardier, to be removed from flying status. Every time he approaches the number of missions necessary to complete a tour of duty, his ambitious commanding officers increase it. Yossarian tries a number of ploys to avoid combat. He malingers, feigns illness, and even poisons the squadron's food with laundry soap to abort one mission. Later, after the gunner Snowden dies in his arms during one particularly lethal mission, Yossarian refuses to fly again, goes naked, and takes to walking backward on the base, all in an attempt to have himself declared insane.

Yossarian is motivated by only one thing—the determination to stay alive. He sees his life threatened not only by the Germans who try to shoot him out of the sky but also by his superior officers, who seem just as intent to kill him off. "The enemy," he concludes at one point, "is anybody who's going to get you killed, no matter which side he's on." When Yossarian attempts to convince the camp's medical officer that his fear of death has driven him over the brink and thus made him unfit to fly, he first learns of the "catch" that will force him to keep flying: "There was only one catch and that was Catch-22, which specified that a concern for one's own safety in the face of dangers that were real and immediate was the process of a rational mind." As Doc Daneeka tells Yossarian, "Anyone who wants to get out of combat duty isn't really crazy."

Most of the large cast of characters surrounding Yossarian are, by any "reasonable" standard, quite mad. They include Colonel Cathcart, who keeps raising the number of missions his troops are required to fly not for the sake of the war effort but for his own personal glory; Major Major Major, who forges Washington Irving's name to official documents and who is pathologically terrified of command; and Milo Minderbinder, the mess officer, a black marketeer who bombs his own base under contract with the Germans. These supporting characters most often fall into one of four categories. The ranking officers—Cathcart, Dreedle, Korn, Black, Cargill, and Scheisskopf—appear more concerned with promotion, neat bombing patterns, and their own petty jealousies than with the war itself or the welfare of their men. A second group, including Doc Daneeka, Minderbinder, and Wintergreen, are also concerned with pursuing the main chance. They are predatory but also extremely comic and very much self-aware. Another group, including Nately, Chief Halfoat, McWatt, Hungry Joe, and Chaplain Tappman, are (like Yossarian himself) outsiders, good men caught within a malevolent system. The dead—Mudd, Snowden, Kraft, and "the soldier in white"—constitute a final group, one that is always present, at least in the background.

It is the military system—which promulgates such absurdly tautological rules as "Catch-22"—that is Yossarian's real enemy. He and the other "good" men of the squadron live in a world that is irrational and inexplicable. As the company's warrant officer explains, "There just doesn't seem to be any logic to their system of rewards and punishments. . . . They have the right to do anything we can't stop them from doing."

As the novel progresses, the victims, increasingly aware of the menace posed by this system, carry their gestures of rebellion to the point of open defiance. Yossarian is the most blatant in this regard: He moans loudly during the briefing for the Avignon mission; he insists that there is a dead man in his tent; he goes naked during the Avignon mission itself and then again during the medal ceremony afterward; he halts the Bologna raid by putting soap in the squadron's food and by moving the bomb-line on the squadron's map; and he requests that he be grounded and eventually refuses to fly. Finally, he deserts, hoping to reach sanctuary in neutral Sweden.

In the world of *Catch-22*, then, the reader is forced to question the very nature of sanity. Sanity is commonly defined as the ability to live within society and to act appropriately according to its rules. If those rules—such as Catch-22—are patently false, however, then adhering to them is in truth an act of insanity, for the end result may be death or the loss of freedom. The world of *Catch-22* is, to Yossarian, a spurious culture, as anthropologists would call it, one that does not meet the basic needs of its members—above all, the need to survive. Authority, duty, and patriotism are all called into question, and Heller demonstrates that when those in authority lack intelligence or respect for life, as is the case with Yossarian's commanding officers, obeying authority can only be self-defeating. Heller thus argues that in an absurd universe, the individual has the right to seek his own survival; he argues that life itself is infinitely more precious than any cause, however just. When Yossarian decides that he has done his part to defeat the Nazis (and after all, he has flown many more missions than most other airmen), his principal duty is to save himself. Yossarian's desertion, then, is a life-affirming act.

As one critic noted, *Catch-22*

> speaks solidly to those who are disaffected, discontented, and disaffiliated, and yet who want to react to life positively. With its occasional affirmations couched in terms of pain and cynical laughter, it makes nihilism seem natural, ordinary, even appealing.

Thus the surface farce of *Catch-22*, when peeled away, reveals a purpose that is literally deadly serious.

If the basic plot of *Catch-22* is fairly simple, its narrative technique and structure most certainly are not. The novel appears to be a chronological jumble, flashing forward and backward from the central event—the death of Snowden—that marks Yossarian's final realization of the mortal threat posed by Catch-22. Time in the novel exists not as clock time but rather as psychological time, and within Yossarian's stream-of-consciousness narrative, events in the present intermingle with cumulative repetitions and gradual clarifications of past actions. For example, in chapter 4, the bare facts of Snowden's death are revealed, that he was killed over Avignon when Dobbs, his copilot, went berserk and grabbed the plane's controls at a crucial moment. Yossarian returns to this incident throughout the novel, but it is not until the penultimate chapter that he reconstructs the story in full. In this fashion, Heller seeks to capture the real ways in which people apprehend the world, incompletely and in fragments.

Catch-22 is intricately structured despite its seeming shapelessness. Until chapter 19, almost everything is told in retrospect while Yossarian is in the hospital; chapter 19 itself begins the movement forward in time leading to Yossarian's desertion. The gradual unfolding of the details of Snowden's death provides another organizing device. Such structural devices as parallelism, doubling, and—most important—repetition, force the reader to share Yossarian's perpetual sense of déjà vu, the illusion of having previously experienced something actually being encountered for the first time. The ultimate effect of such devices is to reinforce the novel's main themes: Yossarian is trapped in a static world, a world in which nothing seems to change and in which events seem to keep repeating themselves. He does not move through his experiences but rather seems condemned to a treadmill existence. The only way to resist this world is to escape it, to desert.

SOMETHING HAPPENED

Heller himself once revealed that he considered Bob Slocum, the protagonist-narrator of his second novel, *Something Happened*, to be "the antithesis of Yossarian—twenty years later." Indeed, the scene shifts dramatically from the dusty, littered airfields of Pianosa to the green, well-kept lawns of suburban Connecticut. In *Something Happened*, Heller details—some say monotonously details—the inner life of an outwardly successful man and, in doing so, seeks to expose the bankruptcy of contemporary middle-class American culture.

Slocum works as a middle-level marketing research manager in a large company. He is middle-aged, married, and the father of three children. Although he is by all appearances successful, Slocum's extended monologue of memories, self-analysis, and carpings at the world reveal that he is anything but happy: "I keep my own counsel and drift speechlessly with my crowd. I float. I float like algae in a colony of green scum, while my wife and I grow old." He sees his life as a series of humiliating failures of nerve, of unfulfilled expectations and missed opportunities. Slocum harks back repeatedly and with regret to his adolescent yearnings for an office girl—later a suicide—with whom he had worked shortly after finishing high school. He now wishes in vain that he could desire someone or something as desperately as he once desired her.

Slocum despises his present job and mistrusts his associates yet politics shamelessly for promotion; he feels bound to his family yet commits numerous adulteries. He is hopelessly at odds with himself and his life. For example, he loves his family in a temporizing kind of way, but he also fears that he has made them all unhappy. His wife, bored and restless, feels isolated in the suburbs and turns to alcohol. His sixteen-year-old daughter is sullen and promiscuous. One son is hopelessly brain-damaged and an insufferable burden to Slocum; the other, Slocum seems truly to want to love, but he cannot help browbeating him. The novel reaches its bleak climax when this latter son is hit by a car and lies bleeding in the street. Slocum cradles the boy in his arms and, at the moment when he feels he can express his love, inadvertently smothers him.

There is no real resolution in *Something Happened*. At novel's end, Slocum has not changed or learned anything of importance. Unlike Yossarian, who is threatened from without, Slocum is his own worst enemy. His sense of alienation, of loss, of failure, is unrelieved.

Critical opinion of *Something Happened* has been mixed. Those who admire the novel most often praise its exact and mercilessly honest replication of the banality and vacuousness of everyday life among the American middle classes, and they argue that Heller, as in *Catch-22*, nicely fuses form and meaning. Others find the novel irritatingly tedious and pessimistic and consider the character of Slocum seriously flawed, unlikable, and unheroic by any standard. Many reviewers could not resist quipping that a more appropriate title for Heller's novel would be *Nothing Happens*.

Good as Gold

Heller's third novel, *Good as Gold*, savagely satirizes the aspirations of the Jewish intellectual community in America. The comic dimension of *Catch-22*, so absent from *Something Happened*, returns. Bruce Gold is a forty-eight-year-old Brooklyn-born English professor who desperately wants to make—or at least have—money. Like Bob Slocum, Gold has problems with his family, which, he knows, considers him a failure because he is not rich. Much of the novel takes place within the Gold family itself, which Gold finds oppressive, if at times amusingly so.

Gold is in most ways a fool—albeit a cynical one—a hypocrite, and a congenital social climber. He is a 1970's version of Budd Schulberg's Sammy Glick. Evidence of this is his engagement to a wealthy WASP socialite with political connections. Gold himself harbors political ambitions. He hungers to replace his alter ego and archnemesis Henry Kissinger as secretary of state and hopes that his fiancé's tycoon father will help him in his quest for political power. Heller savages both Gold and Kissinger, and for precisely the same reason: They represent to him those in the Jewish community who want to escape their heritage while at the same time exploiting it. (To further his financial, academic, and political fortunes, Gold wants to write a "big" book about the Jewish experience in America, about which he knows next to nothing.)

Gold understands his own hypocrisy but promptly dismisses it. Yet, when Gold is eventually offered Kissinger's former cabinet position, he experiences a change of heart. Prompted by the death of his older brother, Gold refuses the post and returns to New York and his family. Like Yossarian, Gold is able to restore his own integrity by deserting.

Heller's work has been compared to that of artists as varied as Eugène Ionesco and the Marx Brothers; *Good as Gold* lies closer to the latter than to the former. Until his decision to renounce his political ambitions, Gold is very much the comic intellectual, pathetically incapable of coping with the difficulties in which he finds himself. The humor of *Good as Gold* is painted with the broadest brush of Heller's career, but its target is his familiar one: the means by which institutions in the modern world coerce the individual and the way in which individuals—such as Slocum and, until his turnabout, Gold—become coconspirators in their own demise.

God Knows

God Knows is Heller's rewriting of a major element of the Old Testament, the story of David. As in all of his fiction, Heller focuses here on the human insistence on repeating earlier mistakes and on the ironies of life. His David is a prototypical wise guy, looking back over his life from his death bed; his language veers from that of the King James version of the Bible to twentieth century slang as he presents his side of various stories, from his encounter with Goliath to his problems with King Saul to his troubles with his children and his various wives.

His first wife—Saul's daughter, Michal—was a shrew to whom he refers as the first Jewish American Princess.

He misses Abigail, his second wife, the only one who loved him completely; she has been dead for many years. Bathsheba, the great passion of his life, has turned into an overweight nag, bored with sex and interested only in trying to convince David to name their son, Solomon, as his successor. Solomon, in David's eyes, is an idiot, a humorless man with no original thoughts who writes down everything his father says and later pretends that they are his ideas. The old king's only solace is the young virgin, Abishag the Shunnamite, who waits on him and worships him.

David complains about his present state, remembers his days of glory, and rationalizes his deeds, avoiding responsibility for any evil that has befallen others but claiming credit for benefits. His knowledge is modern. He maintains, for example, that Michelangelo's famous statue of him is a nice piece of work but it is not "him." His language is laden with quotations from William Shakespeare, Robert Browning, T. S. Eliot, and many others, and he seems to have direct knowledge of most of ancient and modern history.

God Knows is Heller's most engaging fiction since *Catch-22*. Suspense is maintained by David's reluctance to name Solomon as his successor, as he must do, and by the question of whether he will ever hear the voice of God, which he desperately wants. Heller's David is not an admirable man, but he is a fascinating one and an interesting commentator not only on his own life but on human frailty and ambition as well. He is cynical, his faith in God and humanity having left him years before, but even as he complains about the pains of old age, his memory keeps reminding him of the enjoyments of the life he has led.

PICTURE THIS

Picture This is neither conventional fiction nor history but a kind of extended meditation on human weakness. Its inspiration is the famous painting *Aristotle Contemplating the Bust of Homer*, by Dutch painter Rembrandt van Rijn. Heller presents many historical facts, chiefly about the Greece of the time of Aristotle, Plato, and Socrates, as well as the Netherlands of the time of Rembrandt, and he draws frequent parallels between events of those periods and those of the modern age. In discussing the Athenian wars, for example, he makes clear his conviction that the motivations, the mistakes, and the stupidities are parallel to those made by the United States in the years since World War II.

Picture This contains much authentic information, most of which is intended to demonstrate human greed and weakness. Heller seems to be fascinated by the financial aspects of Rembrandt's life, in which great success was frittered away and in which a life of luxury ended with enormous debts; he also writes at length about Rembrandt's marriage and his mistresses. In writing about Greece in the Golden Age, he focuses on the failings of government. The great leader Pericles, in his view, led Athens into self-destructive wars. Pericles was personally noble, but he did his city no good. The tyrant Creon was even worse. Much of what Plato wrote about he could not have observed.

Unlike either *Catch-22* or *God Knows*, *Picture This* fails to provide a leavening of irreverent humor to lighten Heller's dark view of human existence. The only fictional elements in the book are imaginary dialogues between some of the historic figures and the fantasy that Aristotle exists in the painting of him and can observe Rembrandt and his labors; these imaginary flights are only occasionally humorous. Otherwise, the irony in *Picture This* is unrelenting and bitter.

CLOSING TIME

Though *Closing Time* is more humorous, Heller's irony remains bitter, as a World War II generation contemplating the later years of their lives takes the whole world down with them, courtesy of an incompetent U.S. president who, at the novel's conclusion, launches a nuclear strike under the mistaken impression that he is playing a video game. Prior to that apocalyptic finale, readers are reintroduced to Yossarian, who, in the thirty years since the events of *Catch-22*, has been working as an ethics adviser for Milo Minderbinder's multinational corporation. He has been married, had four children, and divorced. As he faces retirement and realizes he is not long for the world, he worries about the future of his children, begins an affair with a younger nurse, and resolves "to live forever, or to die trying."

In terms of genre, *Closing Time* is a difficult book to characterize. As a sequel to *Catch-22*, it takes familiar characters such as Yossarian, Chaplain Tappman, and Milo Minderbinder through an absurdist parody of business, medicine, government, and the military. The addition of two World War II veteran characters (Sammy Singer and Lew Rabinowitz) with only ancillary connections to the main plot brings a nostalgic realism to the novel, more in keeping with Heller's subsequent memoir, *Now and Then*, than with the Yossarian sections of the novel. *Closing Time* also is Heller's most self-consciously postmodern novel, as real-life figures, such as author Kurt Vonnegut, are intertwined with fictional ones; references are made to not only the events of *Catch-22* but also the novel itself and the entry of the term "Catch-22" into the popular lexicon. At its best, this generic combination allows Heller to range widely in his criticism of contemporary society (as in a priceless explanation Yossarian is given of the Freedom of Information Act). Too often, however, these various formats seem at odds with each other, leading to a novel that moves both slowly and in too many directions.

Richard A. Fine
Updated by Jim O'Loughlin

Other major works

PLAYS: *We Bombed in New Haven*, pr. 1967; *Catch-22: A Dramatization*, pr. 1971; *Clevinger's Trial*, pb. 1973.

SCREENPLAYS: *Sex and the Single Girl*, 1964 (with David R. Schwartz); *Casino Royale*, 1967 (with others); *Dirty Dingus Magee*, 1970 (with others).

NONFICTION: *No Laughing Matter*, 1986 (with Speed Vogel); *Now and Then: From Coney Island to Here*, 1998.

Bibliography

Aldridge, John W. *The American Novel and the Way We Live Now*. New York: Oxford University Press, 1983. Aldridge's overview of American fiction after World War II gives Heller's work high marks, praising his skeptical view of modern society and the imaginative qualities of his novels.

Bloom, Harold, ed. *Joseph Heller's "Catch-22."* New ed. New York: Bloom's Literary Criticism, 2008. A collection of critical assessments of the novel, including pieces by respected writers and literary critics, such as Nelson Algren, Christopher Buckley, and Norman Podhoretz, and an introduction by Bloom.

Cacicedo, Alberto. "'You Must Remember This': Trauma and Memory in *Catch-22* and *Slaughterhouse-Five*." *Critique* 46, no. 4 (Summer, 2005): 357-368. A comparison of the novels by Heller and Kurt Vonnegut, focusing on the writers' ability to depict the horrors of World War II while creating a sense of indignation in readers that could result in ethical social action. Critics generally agree that Heller's novel was able to do this, while there is disagreement about the ethical engagement of Vonnegut's novel.

Craig, David M. *Tilting at Mortality: Narrative Strategies in Joseph Heller's Fiction*. Detroit, Mich.: State University Press, 1997. An examination of the ethical dimensions of Heller's work, linking his distinctive stylistic features to his preoccupation with questions of death, meaning, and identity. Includes separate chapters on each of Heller's first six novels.

Klinkowitz, Jerome. *The American 1960's: Imaginative Acts in a Decade of Change*. Ames: Iowa State University Press, 1990. This analysis of American fiction in political terms suggests that Heller's *Catch-22* introduces a distinctively new kind of politics, that of withdrawal from impossible situations, and that in this sense the novel is one of the truly original works of its time.

LeClair, Thomas. "Joseph Heller, *Something Happened*, and the Art of Excess." *Studies in American Fiction* 9 (Autumn, 1981): 245-260. This essay focuses on Heller's second novel, defending its repetitive quality as a stylistic device that is necessary to the portrayal of the dullness and mediocrity of the life of its protagonist and the other characters.

Potts, Stephen W. *From Here to Absurdity: The Moral Battlefields of Joseph Heller*. 2d ed. San Bernardino, Calif.: Borgo Press, 1995. This insightful and accessible overview of Heller's novels and plays emphasizes the continuities throughout Heller's writings, despite the various genres within which he has worked. As a moralist and political cynic, Heller creates characters whose personal crises drive them either to confront or to conform to governing orthodoxy.

Saurian, Adam J. *Conversations with Joseph Heller*. Jackson: University Press of Mississippi, 1993. A collection of interviews conducted during the 1960's,

1970's, and 1980's, in which Heller discusses the themes, structure, and satire in his fiction, the writers who influenced his work, and his political opinions, among other topics. Includes two humorous "anti-interviews" with his friends Mel Brooks and George Mandel.

Seed, David. *The Fiction of Joseph Heller: Against the Grain*. New York: St. Martin's Press, 1989. Analyzes Heller's work published through the late 1980's, demonstrating how the writer's absurdist vision is present in his novels, plays, and essays.

Woodson, Jon. *A Study of Joseph Heller's "Catch-22": Going Around Twice*. New York: Peter Lang, 2001. Uses the New Criticism and mythological criticism that Heller was familiar with to argue that *Catch-22* is in essence a retelling of the epic of Gilgamesh in much the same way that James Joyce's *Ulysses* is a retelling of Homer's *Odyssey*.

MARK HELPRIN

Born: New York, New York; June 28, 1947

Principal long fiction

Refiner's Fire: The Life and Adventures of Marshall Pearl, a Foundling, 1977
Winter's Tale, 1983
A Soldier of the Great War, 1991
Memoir from Antproof Case, 1995
Freddy and Fredericka, 2005

Other literary forms

In addition to his novels, Mark Helprin has published short fiction; his collections include *Ellis Island, and Other Stories* (1981) and *The Pacific, and Other Stories* (2004). He has also published children's books, including *Swan Lake* (1989) and *The Veil of Snows* (1997).

Achievements

Mark Helprin's fiction celebrates the past. Readers who are accustomed to plot-driven fiction within the conventional forms of realism often find his work challenging. Helprin writes long novels (in excess of five hundred pages), and he creates worlds in which anything can and does happen. Among the honors he has received for his work are the Prix de Rome (1982) and a Guggenheim Fellowship (1984). In 1982, he received the National Jewish Book Award for *Ellis Island, and Other Stories*, his second collection of short fiction. *Publishers Weekly* selected *A Soldier of the Great War* as one of its Best Books of 1991. In 2001, Helprin won the Mightier Pen Award from the Center for Security Policy, and in 2006, he received the Peggy V. Helmerich Award from the Tulsa, Oklahoma, City-County Library Foundation.

Biography

Mark Helprin is the only child of Morris Helprin, a journalist who became the president of London Films in California, and Eleanor Lynn (née Lin), a Broadway actor in the 1930's and daughter of Max Lin, a Jew from Sinkiang Province in China. Born in New York City, Helprin spent his early years in Hollywood, California, before his family settled in Ossining, a town along New York's Hudson River known mainly for the prison located there, Sing Sing. Born two months premature, Helprin suffered from problems with his spine and his lungs and was frequently ill as a child.

Helprin earned his B.A. in English from Harvard University, where in 1972 he also earned an M.A. in Middle Eastern studies. He lived in Israel in 1973 and spent the 1982-1983 academic year in Rome after he received the Prix de Rome. He has traced the start of his literary career to the summer of 1964, when on a trip through Europe he wrote a description of the Hagia Sophia church in Istanbul from memory on a blotter in a hotel in Paris. Between 1965 and 1969, he wrote numerous short stories, eventually selling two simultaneously to *The New Yorker*.

In 1989, Helprin signed an unusual multibook publishing contract with the publishing firm Harcourt Brace Jovanovich, which bought the rights to three forthcoming novels and two collections of short stories. His 1995 novel *Memoir from Antproof Case* was the first book published under this arrangement. Since 1999, Helprin has been associated with the Claremont Institute for the Study of Statesmanship and Political Philosophy as an essayist, book reviewer, and senior fellow. He is also a fellow in Middle Eastern studies with the Hudson Institute.

Helprin's personal experiences with illness, his education, and his love of mountain climbing, as well as his service in both the Israeli air force and the British merchant navy, are incorporated into his novels. His closeness to his family is also reflected in the parent-child relationships found in his books. Helprin married the New York tax lawyer and banker Linda Kennedy in 1980, and the couple had two children, Alexandra Morris and Olivia Kennedy. After a few years in Seattle in the 1980's, the Helprins settled in the Hudson River Valley, where Helprin assumed the role of contributing editor to *The Wall Street Journal*. Helprin also writes for *The New York Times*, *Commentary*, *The Atlantic Monthly*, and *The New Yorker*, among other publications. He was former senator Robert Dole's speechwriter at the beginning of Dole's 1996 U.S. presidential campaign, and he rose to prominence again as a political commentator after the terrorist attacks on New York City and Washington, D.C., on September 11, 2001.

Mark Helprin. (© Jerry Bauer)

ANALYSIS

Each of Mark Helprin's novels features a carefully developed, multilayered plot. Helprin pays particular attention to descriptive details and limits the use of literary devices such as symbolism and allusion, yet imagery is key. Most of the stories are narrated in plain language, with flashbacks commonly used to fill in gaps in the characters' lives. Helprin's characters live in a world in which time is told by the seasons; horses, trains, and airplanes are more common than cars; and common standards and values exist among all people. Recurring themes are those of father-son loyalty; the strengths of friendship, especially among men; the beauty of women and children; and the ability to turn weaknesses into strengths. The people in the stories endure series of illnesses and encounters with insanity; many are orphaned or lose their parents at a young age and have to struggle to survive in an adult world. Helprin's characters are robust sorts of heroes whose adventures and the obstacles they overcome reinforce their appreciation for society, one another, and the beauty and power of God and nature.

Helprin often creates opportunities in his stories for elderly characters to say that they are telling their tales to preserve them in the minds of the living, so their pasts will not "die." In 1993, Helprin told an interviewer that he writes "in the service of illumination and memory." On his manner of composing, Helprin has stated that he decides first how the story will end and then develops the plot to focus on those events that will prepare the characters for their fictional fates. Like those of Henry Fielding, Charles Dickens, and Anthony Trollope, Helprin's novels have multiple characters who find themselves in diverse, challenging situations. He is equally at home in creating male and female characters, and his methods of characterization focus on dialogue and description, not on a narrator's analysis. The characters are routinely on quests for justice, identity, or honor, and their actions cause them to intersect with people from all levels of society. Helprin often includes animals in his stories: Many of his characters admire horses greatly for their beauty and strength; in *Memoir from Antproof Case*, two cats play central diversionary roles; in *Freddy and Fredericka*, the falcon's flight marks Freddy's future as the next king of England.

The scope and range of Helprin's novels have troubled some book reviewers, who have faulted Helprin for a lack of control in the complex plots, for arbitrariness in character development, and for the inclusion of extraneous historical or political information that causes unnecessary digression. Such criticisms have not generally been directed toward his 2005 novel *Freddy and Fredericka*, however.

Helprin's plots tend to follow the pattern of the classical drama, supplemented with elements of epic poetry. He uses exposition and rising action to lead to a specific climactic moment from which the action falls and concludes. As in epics, the main character descends into different sorts of underworld experiences, usually involving madness, illness, and physical trials, from which he or she emerges to continue fighting. At times, Helprin employs flashbacks and epilogues to fill out his plots.

Helprin's eye for detail in the settings gives the novels their distinctive quality. He writes of places he has been with the eye of a landscape painter or a photographer. His characters experience the physical world as a source of both pleasure and punishment, and the power of nature is both respected and feared. His narrators concentrate on the actions in which the characters are involved more so than on their inner states of mind.

One of Helprin's chief themes is parents' love for their children. He allows the narrator of *Memoir from Antproof Case*, for example, to state the importance of parental love most succinctly, while other characters, such as Hardesty Marratta in *Winter's Tale*, show it. Helprin avoids ideologies in his fictions, presenting ideas in the debates of the times in which the stories are set. He favors treatment of such universals as the conflicts between good and evil, right and wrong, and justice and injustice. Repeatedly, his characters benefit the most from love of family and friends, and it is from this love and for these people that the characters turn their incapabilities into their capabilities. The novels are only mildly formulaic—in many cases, a primary character is dead at the end, and all the characters are variously abandoned, challenged by evil, loved, or strengthened to perform good works. The works are uniformly positive, and Helprin's reliance on the past for settings enables him to focus on those characteristics that unify, not divide, people.

REFINER'S FIRE

Refiner's Fire, Helprin's first novel, was published in 1977. It is the story of Marshall Pearl, from his birth in 1947 through his late twenties, when he is wounded as an Israeli soldier in the Israel-Syrian War. The novel commences shortly before Marshall is born with the story of his mother Katrina Pearl's escape from Europe in World War II on a ship sailing for Palestine. During a sea battle with the British, who are refusing the refugee ship entry, Katrina is crushed in the hold. The baby is discovered by a child, whose mother gives him to the American captain, Paul Levy, who in turn sends Marshall to French nuns with a note explaining the circumstances of his birth. The sisters send him to a U.S. orphanage, where he is adopted by the Livingstones, a wealthy and childless upstate New York couple. During his first summer-camp experience, Marshall's prowess as a rider earns him the love of Lydia Levy. After some years in New York, Mr. Livingstone moves the family to Jamaica, where Marshall, though a boy, is involved in a territorial war between a local family and Rastafarians. Marshall proves himself an able guerrilla fighter, foreshadowing his future as a soldier.

After enrolling at Harvard, Marshall drops out before he graduates and travels west. He works in a slaughterhouse, spends time with a naturalist in the Rockies, and enlists in the U.S. Navy. He is reunited with Paul Levy, who tells him who he really is, and he learns that Lydia is Paul's younger sister and an heiress. Marshall and Lydia marry and set out to find Marshall's father. This portion of the novel contains the greatest suspense, as Marshall and Lydia are separated as he climbs in the Alps and again when he is drafted into the Israeli army, where he eventually meets his father, Arieh Ben Barak. Helprin tells the story of Marshall's parents' courtship in a flashback.

Fighting against the Syrian tanks, Marshall is severely injured; he becomes comatose and is reported missing. All the members of his family, Paul Levy, the Livingstones, and Lydia, set out separately to find him, finally converging at the hospital. In the final pages, Marshall regains consciousness before he sees anyone, muttering to his faithful nurse, "By God, I'm not down yet. By God, I'm not down yet." Helprin uses a third-person narrator and limited symbolism in the novel, the title of which refers to the purifying power of fire. He also uses flashback, dialogue, suspense, and his own experiences as a soldier in the telling of the story.

Winter's Tale

Winter's Tale is a fantasy that tells the story of New York City in the winters of the nineteenth and twentieth centuries. The parallel main characters are Peter Lake, an Irishman and a thief, and Hardesty Marratta, a San Francisco newspaper writer who moves to New York as a young man. Peter Lake's main companion is a magical white horse, Athansor, while Hardesty's is his wife, another writer, Virginia Gamely. The story is narrated by a third-person omniscient speaker, and Helprin allows both Lake and his horse to fly and to perform feats of great strength and personal endurance.

Lake's life is a series of adventures and misadventures, beginning with his orphanhood and life with the Reverend Mootfowl, who teaches him how to operate complicated nineteenth century machines. After he kills Mootfowl, he joins the Short Tails, a gang led by Pearly Soames. Lake informs on the Short Tails, and for his crime he is pursued for nearly one hundred years in New York City. On the run, he breaks into the home of Isaac Penn. There he sees, then becomes involved with, Penn's beautiful, musical, and terminally ill daughter, Beverly, who becomes his mystical protector after her death. When Lake is later injured, he becomes an amnesiac. On the street he encounters the Marratta family, with their friends, Praeger de Pinto and Jessica Penn, Isaac's granddaughter. They all work for Harry Penn's newspaper, where Lake eventually gets a job operating the old machines, which none of the new mechanics understand. The machines regulate the actions of the city.

When the Marattas' daughter Abby is dying, her father once more encounters Peter Lake, who is now living behind the clock in New York's Grand Central Station. Helprin's knowledge of the city and of the Hudson Valley region are key to the descriptions that drive this book. Lake and Marratta join forces in an effort to travel across the city to his daughter, made difficult because the city's boroughs are at war, thanks to the Short Tails and the sinister Jackson Mead. Lake is wounded by a Short Tail in the journey, and Abby dies.

Lake returns to his job in the machine room at *The Sun* newspaper, where Harry Penn is able to tell him of his identity and his past. He leaves the paper and finds Athansor, who has had a terrible parallel life without Peter, and they go off to their separate ends. In the epilogue, Helprin asks the reader if Lake's death had a purpose and if his attempt to create a city built on justice, with Marratta, was worth the costs. As critic David Rothenberg has observed about the winters of this novel, the cold landscapes are used as positive sources of self-reliance and as images of containment.

A Soldier of the Great War

The protagonist of *A Soldier of the Great War*, Alessandro Giuliani, is the son of a prominent Roman banker and a soldier in Italy's war with Austria (1908). Eschewing a career in the law, Alessandro trains to be a professor of aesthetics, and it is the pursuit of beauty and truth that gives him the greatest personal strength. Once enlisted, he is not at sea but instead on land, serving in the River Guard, a unit that recaptures Italian deserters. One of the deserters kills the captain of this unit, and all the soldiers flee. Alessandro and his friend Guariglia return to Rome. Caught, they are sentenced to death, but Alessandro is saved by orders that his father's former scribe, Orfeo, keeps writing for him at the Ministry of War. Alessandro's life parallels Orfeo's, who is described as the person who is really running the war.

The unit to which Alessandro is assigned is at the front, and while digging trenches there, he is engaged in hand-to-hand combat with Austrian soldiers and is seriously wounded. His beautiful nurse, Ariane, with whom he falls in love, is a French Italian; Alessandro had actually seen her once before, when she was a child. They become lovers and plan to marry; however, the hospital dormitory in which Ariane lives is bombed before Alessandro's eyes by Austrians pursuing an Italian cavalry unit.

As the story is told in a flashback sequence, the reader knows that Ariane is not dead, but it is the perceived loss of her that colors all of Alessandro's actions in his years remaining in the service. For instance, he is taken prisoner while retrieving the body of a college friend, Rafi Foa, to whom his sister was engaged. As a prisoner, Alessandro's adventures include riding with the enemy's hussars, stealing a Lipizzaner stallion to escape, and attempting to kill the German pilot he thought had killed Ariane. Back in Rome, he is reunited with her and their son, Paolo, and the next chapters cover Alessandro's life between 1915 and 1921.

The story is framed by two modern-day chapters in which Alessandro is still demonstrating his sense of justice and his strong will to live. In 1964, he is seventy-four years old and on his way to see his granddaughter on a bus when he gets into an altercation with the bus driver because the driver has failed to stop for a young passenger, Nicolò Sambucco. The bus driver puts the rather frail old man off the bus, and Alessandro and Nicolò, two unlikely companions, decide to walk to their destinations, though this will take several days. As they walk, Alessandro tells the willing Nicolò about the past and provides him with an education the younger man could not have obtained in school.

Helprin has stated that the idea for this novel grew from an experience he had in Italy in 1964. He was stranded at a train station and engaged in a staring match with an elderly, decorated Italian soldier. Helprin believed the incident was an effort on the older man's part to impress his past on the writer's memory and imagination. Although the book is rich in historical and scenic detail, Helprin has clarified that it was not heavily researched and that it is based mostly on his year in Rome and early travels.

MEMOIR FROM ANTPROOF CASE

Memoir from Antproof Case is a humourous satire on social ideas of vice and virtue. In the stream-of-consciousness narrative, a father relates his story for his son; he keeps the pages in an antproof case, so ants cannot destroy the pages. The narrator calls himself Oscar Progresso, which is just one of several aliases he has used in his life. Now in his eighties, he tells a tale of his military heroism as a pilot in the Army Air Force during World War II, of a brilliant robbery, and of his relocation to Nitéroi, Brazil. Once in Brazil, he marries a beautiful bank teller, Marlise, and teaches English to Brazilian naval cadets. He is obsessed with the evil effects of coffee, which he hates because of how it changes the body's action and smell (Helprin humorously dedicates the book to Juan Valdez, the fictitious advertising icon of Colombian coffee).

The narrator is a violent youth who first kills a man on a commuter train in his native New York over an incident involving coffee. He also divorces his first wife, billionaire Constance Lloyd, when she takes up coffee drinking. He is sent as a boy to an asylum in Switzerland, and after his release he works as a runner for the banking firm of Stillman and Chase. He attends Harvard and Oxford, serves as a flying ace in World War II, and rises to partnership as an investment banker in his firm. He offends the senior partner, Edgar B. Edgar, in an incident involving coffee and is sent to stack gold bars in the building's basement. There he sees the foolish overseer throwing out bullion because it does not shine, and he realizes he can steal the gold bars with no trouble.

With a partner who is an engineer and works for the Transit Authority, he devises a successful and elaborate plan that allows them to succeed. His partner settles with his family in luxury in Europe, while Oscar relocates to Brazil. In a flashback chapter, it is revealed that Edgar killed Oscar's parents when they refused to sell their farm for the building of a bridge across the Hudson River in 1914. Oscar kills Edgar before he flees, but on the flight to Brazil he has to make an emergency landing in a river, and he loses the plane and the gold.

The witty and eccentric Oscar places family loyalty above all else in his hierarchy of values. He is even happy to raise the boy Funio, the product of Marlise's affair with another man, as his son. Among the other characters in Helprin's fiction, Oscar is the most physically fit. He is injured only a few times, and his dread of coffee and of alcohol keep him largely in good health. As a first-person narrator, he is engaging, and because he is eighty, his movements in time create variety in the tales he tells. Instead of framing the story with present-time narration at the beginning and the end, Helprin incorporates past and present into most of the chapters, effectively creating time shifts in Oscar's memory. Readers of Helprin's three previous novels will recognize the allusions to the bridge building and a discussion of *La Tempesta* by the Venetian Renaissance painter Giorgione, which is a unifying device in *A Soldier of the Great War*. *Memoir from Antproof Case* ends with Oscar recognizing that it is time to end the writing when he cannot buy a larger antproof case from the son of the stationer in the shop where he bought the first one in 1952.

Freddy and Fredericka

Freddy and Fredericka imagines the Prince and Princess of Wales on a journey through the modern United States in an effort to reclaim the nation for the British crown. Helprin has stated that the story of incognito royalty was suggested to him when, at a restaurant, his children casually asked if a couple washing dishes were Prince Charles and the late Princess Diana. From this germ, Helprin fashioned a hapless and selfish pair who are parachuted into New Jersey in fur bikinis to start their ascent to individuality and ultimately to fitness for the throne of England.

Equipped with false identities, Freddy and Fredericka, who lose their front teeth on impact when dropped from a royal transport plane, must scramble for their lives and learn to work. In the course of their year in the United States, they engage in a variety of trades and occupations, from self-taught dentistry to fire-spotters for the Forest Service, ultimately becoming political advisers to the failed presidential campaign of Senator Dewey Knott. Through all their trials, including various run-ins with the law and time in an asylum, Freddy and Fredericka learn to know themselves, realize the power and intelligence they possess natively, and come to love each other in a way that many of those in arranged marriages may never know.

When they eventually return to England, Freddy has largely lost his penchant for ridiculous antics and malapropisms, and Fredericka has learned that real beauty is not to be found in designer shoes and décolletage. By the novel's end, Freddy has assumed the throne, a wiser and more worldly man; in the course of things, he has lost both Fredericka and his mother, Queen Philippa, to death, and he has become father to Princess Lucia, who was conceived in America.

Critics have rightly noticed the affinity of *Freddy and Fredericka* with the works of Mark Twain, Henry Fielding, and Evelyn Waugh. The novel adheres to Helprin's characteristic themes and interests and contains passages of outlandish humor and deep sincerity, as when Freddy tells Fredericka that one becomes noble "by recognizing the greatness of others and humbly receiving your appointment" or place in the world. Bred to pomposity and a life of frivolity, Freddy and Fredericka develop the mettle to be the monarchs they were destined to be, enhanced by humility and grace.

Beverly Schneller

Other major works

SHORT FICTION: *A Dove of the East, and Other Stories*, 1975; *Ellis Island, and Other Stories*, 1981; "Last Tea with the Armorers," 1995; *The Pacific, and Other Stories*, 2004.

CHILDREN'S LITERATURE: *Swan Lake*, 1989; *A City in Winter: The Queen's Tale*, 1996; *The Veil of Snows*, 1997.

Bibliography

Alexander, Paul. "Big Books, Tall Tales: His Novels Win Critical Acclaim and Hefty Advances, So Why Does Mark Helprin Make Up Stories About Himself?" *The New York Times Magazine*, April 28, 1991. Provides biographical details and discussion of much of Helprin's work (including critical reaction to it) in addition to interview excerpts with Helprin. This article helps to penetrate the mystique with which Helprin has surrounded himself. From stories that his mother was once a slave to others that stretch credulity even further, Helprin has fictionalized his life much as he has his books. Alexander calls Helprin a compulsive storyteller, although Helprin claims that he has learned "to deal in facts—not dreams," especially when talking to journalists.

Butterfield, Isabel. "On Mark Helprin." *Encounter* 72 (January, 1989): 48-52. Argues that Helprin's writings follow in the footsteps of American literary giants such as Mark Twain, William Faulkner, Nathanael West, and Thomas Pynchon.

Goodman, Matthew. "Who Says Which Are Our Greatest Books? The Politics of the Literary Canon." *Utne Reader*, May/June, 1991. Discusses Helprin's introduction to *The Best American Short Stories*, in which he attacks revisionists for desecrating the cause of American literature.

Helprin, Mark. "A Conversation with Mark Helprin." Interview by Mark Johnson. *Image: A Journal of the Arts and Religion* 17 (Fall, 1997): 48-59. Helprin discusses his philosophy of writing, his interest in political and historical writing, and his aesthetics.

_______. Interview by James Linville. *The Paris Review* 35 (Spring, 1993): 160-199. Offers a thorough look at Helprin's ideas on writing, politics, and the reactions he has received to his fiction. Includes holograph pages from his novels and copies of his service records.

Lambert, Craig. "Literary Warrior: Mark Helprin's Fictional Marvels and Political Heterodoxies." *Harvard Magazine*, May/June, 2005. Discusses Helprin's career and his interests as a writer. Includes photographs.

Rothenberg, David. "The Idea of the North: An Iceberg History." In *Wild Ideas*, edited by David Rothenberg. Minneapolis: University of Minnesota Press, 1995. Comments briefly on Helprin's descriptions of winter as compared with the writer's own experiences and other stories set in winter.

Shulevitz, Judith. "Research Kills a Book." *The New York Times Book Review*, May 5, 1991. Brief article provides insight into Helprin's writing priorities, noting that Helprin believes that impersonal facts, or "research," kills the spirit of his writing, and therefore he does not like to place too much importance on historical accuracy.

ERNEST HEMINGWAY

Born: Oak Park, Illinois; July 21, 1899
Died: Ketchum, Idaho; July 2, 1961
Also known as: Ernest Miller Hemingway

Principal long fiction

The Sun Also Rises, 1926
The Torrents of Spring, 1926
A Farewell to Arms, 1929
To Have and Have Not, 1937
For Whom the Bell Tolls, 1940
Across the River and into the Trees, 1950
The Old Man and the Sea, 1952
Islands in the Stream, 1970
The Garden of Eden, 1986
True at First Light, 1999

Other literary forms

Ernest Hemingway will be best remembered for his novels and short stories, though critical debate rages over whether his literary reputation rests more firmly on the former or the latter. In his own time, he was known to popular reading audiences for his newspaper dispatches and for his essays in popular magazines. He wrote, in addition, a treatise on bullfighting (*Death in the Afternoon*, 1932), which is still considered the most authoritative treatment of the subject in English; an account of big-game hunting (*Green Hills of Africa*, 1935); two plays (*Today Is Friday*, pb. 1926, and *The Fifth Column*, pb. 1938); and reminiscences of his experiences in Paris during the 1920's (*A Moveable Feast*, 1964).

Achievements

There is little question that Ernest Hemingway will be remembered as one of the outstanding prose stylists in American literary history, and it was for his contributions in this area that he was awarded the Nobel Prize in Literature in 1954, two years after the publication of *The Old Man and the Sea*. The general reader has often been more intrigued by Hemingway's exploits—hunting, fishing, and living dangerously—than by his virtues as an artist. Ironically, he is often thought of now primarily as the chronicler of the so-called lost generation of the 1920's, a phrase that he heard from Gertrude Stein and incorporated into *The Sun Also Rises* as an epigraph. The

Hemingway "code," which originated as a prescription for living in the post-World War I decade, has become a catchphrase for academicians and general readers alike.

Biography

Ernest Miller Hemingway was the first son of an Oak Park, Illinois, physician, Clarence Edmonds Hemingway, and Grace Hemingway, a Christian Scientist. As a student in the Oak Park public schools, Hemingway received his first journalistic experience writing for the *Trapeze*, a student newspaper. After working as a reporter for the *Kansas City Star* for less than a year, he enlisted as an ambulance driver for the American Red Cross during World War I. He was sent in 1918 to serve on the Italian front, where he received a leg wound. His injury required that he be sent to an American hospital in Milan, and there he met and fell in love with Agnes Von Kurowski, who provided the basis for his characterization of Catherine Barkley in *A Farewell to Arms*. Hemingway was married in 1921 to Hadley Richardson. They moved to the Left Bank of Paris, lived on her income from a trust fund, and became friends of Stein and other Left Bank literary figures.

The Paris years provided Hemingway with material for the autobiographical sketches collected after his death in *A Moveable Feast*. Also in the Paris years, he met the people who would become the major characters in his roman à clef, *The Sun Also Rises*. Hemingway dedicated the novel to Hadley, divorced her (in retrospect, one of the saddest experiences in his life), and married Pauline Pfeiffer in 1927. During the 1930's, Hemingway became attached to the Loyalist cause in Spain, and during the years of the Spanish Civil War, he traveled to that country several times as a war correspondent. His feelings about that war are recorded in *For Whom the Bell Tolls*, which was an enormous popular success. In 1940, he divorced Pauline and married the independent, free-spirited Martha Gellhorn, whom he divorced in 1945, marrying in that same year Mary Welsh, his fourth wife.

The 1952 publication of *The Old Man and the Sea* is usually regarded as evidence that the writing slump that Hemingway had suffered for nearly a decade was ended. The last years of his life were marked by medical problems, resulting to a great extent from injuries that he had sustained in accidents and from years of heavy drinking. In 1961, after being released from the Mayo Clinic, Hemingway returned with Mary to their home in Ketchum, Idaho. He died there on July 2, 1961, of a self-inflicted shotgun wound.

Analysis

"All stories, if continued far enough, end in death, and he is no true story teller who would keep that from you," Ernest Hemingway wrote in *Death in the Afternoon*. He might have added that most of his own stories and novels, if traced back far enough, also begin in death. In *The Sun Also Rises*, death from World War I shadows the actions of most of the main characters; specifically, death has robbed Brett Ashley of the man she loved before she met Jake, and that fact, though only alluded to in the novel, largely accounts for her membership in the lost generation.

A Farewell to Arms begins and ends with death: Catherine Barkley's fiancé was killed before the main events of the novel begin, and her own death at the end will profoundly influence the rest of Frederic Henry's life. The Caporetta retreat scenes, often referred to as the "death chapters" of *A Farewell to Arms*, prompt Frederic Henry to give up the death of war for what he believes to be the life of love. In *For Whom the Bell Tolls*, death is nearby in every scene, a fact suggested first by the image of the bell in the novel's title and epigraph, the bell whose tolling is a death knell. Perhaps most important in *For Whom the Bell Tolls*, Robert Jordan's choice to die as he does comes from his reflections on the heroic death of his grandfather compared with what he sees as the cowardly suicide of his father. Finally, Santiago's memories of his dead wife in *The Old Man and the Sea* play in and out of his mind as he confronts the possibility of his own death in his struggle against the great marlin and the sea.

Indeed, in Hemingway's work, as Nelson Algren observes, it seems "as though a man must earn his death before he could win his life." Yet it would be a mistake to allow what may appear to be Hemingway's preoccupation—or, to some, obsession—with death to obscure the reality that he is, above all, concerned in his fiction with the quality of individual life, even though it must be granted that the quality and intensity of his characters'

Ernest Hemingway. (© The Nobel Foundation)

lives seem to increase in direct proportion to their awareness of the reality of death.

There is a danger, however, in making so general an observation as this. Hemingway's attitudes about life, about living it well and living it courageously in the face of death, changed in the course of his most productive years as a writer, those years between 1926 and 1952, which were marked by the creation of his three best novels and the Nobel Prize-winning novella *The Old Man and the Sea*. During this period, Hemingway shifted away from what many consider the hedonistic value system of Jake, Brett, Frederic, and Catherine, a system often equated with the Hemingway code, to a concern with the collective, almost spiritual value of human life reflected in the actions of Robert Jordan and Santiago. If the constant in Hemingway's works, then, is that "all stories, if continued far enough, end in death," the variable is his subtly changing attitude toward the implications of this fact, no better gauge of which can be found than in the ways his characters choose to live their lives in his major novels.

"Big Two-Hearted River"

The best prologue to Hemingway's novels is a long short story, "Big Two-Hearted River," which has been described as a work in which "nothing happens." By the standards of the traditional, heavily plotted story, very little does happen in "Big Two-Hearted River," but the main reason for this is that so much has happened before the story opens that Nick, Hemingway's autobiographical persona, has been rendered incapable of the kind of action one usually associates with an adventure story. Death has occurred: not literal human death, but the death of the land, and with it the death of Nick's old values. It has been brought about by the burning of once-lush vegetation that covered the soil and surrounded the water of Nick's boyhood hunting and fishing territory. Presented with this scene, Nick must find a way of living in the presence of it, which he does by granting supremacy to his senses, the only guides he can trust. He earns the right to eat his food by carrying the heavy backpack containing it to his campsite; after working with his own hands to provide shelter, he can savor the cooking and eating of the food. He can then catch grasshoppers, which have adapted to the burning of the woods by becoming brown, and use them as natural bait for fishing. Then he can catch fish, clean them, eat them, and return their inedible parts to the earth to help restore its fertility.

It is appropriate that "nothing happens" in this prologue to Hemingway's novels because the dilemma of his main characters is that "nothing" is going to happen unless a modern Perceval removes the plagues of the people and restores fertility to the land. The task for Hemingway's characters, particularly those in his early works, is to establish a code by which they can live in the meantime. Nick, like T. S. Eliot's Fisher King, who sits with his back to an arid plain at the end of *The Waste Land* (1922), is shoring up fragments against his ruins: He is developing a personal system that will enable him to cope with life in the presence of a burned-out, infertile land. Also, like Eliot and many other lost-generation writers, Hemingway suggests that the actual wasteland is a metaphor for the spiritual and psychological impotence of modern humanity, since the state of the land simply mirrors the condition of the postwar human psyche. Like the grasshoppers in "Big Two-Hearted River," who have changed color to adapt outwardly to the changing of the land, Nick must adjust internally to the altered condition of his psyche, whose illusions have been destroyed by the war, just as the land has been destroyed by fire.

The Sun Also Rises

An understanding of the principles set forth in "Big Two-Hearted River" is perhaps essential to an understanding of the life-in-death/death-in-life philosophy that Hemingway presents in his major novels, particularly in *The Sun Also Rises* and *A Farewell to Arms*. Bringing these principles in advance to *The Sun Also Rises* enables a reader to see the mythical substructure that lies beneath the apparent simplicity of the story line.

On the face of it, *The Sun Also Rises* tells the story of Jake Barnes, whose war wound has left him physically incapable of making love, though it has done so without robbing him of sexual desire. Jake has the misfortune to fall in love with the beautiful and, for practical purposes, nymphomaniac Lady Brett Ashley, who loves Jake but must nevertheless make love to other men. Among these men is Robert Cohn, a hopeless romantic who, alone in the novel, believes in the concept of chivalric love. Hemingway explores the frustration of the doomed love affair between Jake and Brett as they wander from Paris and its moral invalids to Pamplona, where Jake and his lost-generation friends participate in the fiesta.

Jake is the only one of the group to have become an *aficionado*, one who is passionate about bullfighting. In the end, however, he betrays his *aficion* by introducing Brett to Pedro Romero, one of the few remaining bullfighters who is true to the spirit of the sport—one who fights honestly and faces death with grace—and this Jake does with full knowledge that Brett will seduce Romero, perhaps corrupting his innocence by infecting him with the jaded philosophy that makes her "lost." Predictably, she does seduce Romero, but less predictably she lets him go, refusing to be "one of these bitches that ruins children." Finally, she and Jake are left where they started, she unrealistically musing that "we could have had such a damned good time together"—presumably if he had not been wounded—and he, perhaps a little wiser, responding, "Yes. . . . Isn't it pretty to think so."

Few will miss the sense of aimless wandering from country to country and bottle to bottle in *The Sun Also Rises*. The reader who approaches Jake's condition as a logical extension, symbolically rendered, of Nick's situation in "Big Two-Hearted River," however, will more fully appreciate Hemingway's design and purpose in the novel. As is the case in "Big Two-Hearted River," the death with which *The Sun Also Rises* begins and ends is less a physical death than it is living or walking death, which, granted, is most acute in Jake's case, but which afflicts all the characters in the novel. They must establish rules for playing a kind of spiritual solitaire, and Jake is the character in the novel who most articulately expresses these rules, perhaps because he is the one who most needs them. "Enjoying living," he says, "was learning to get your money's worth and knowing when you had it." In a literal sense, Jake refers here to the practice of getting what one pays for with actual money, but in another sense, he is talking more abstractly about other kinds of economy—the economy of motion in a good bullfight, for example.

To see how thoroughly Hemingway weaves this idea of economy into the fabric of the novel, one needs only to look at his seemingly offhand joke about writing telegrams. On closer examination, the joke yields a valuable clue for understanding the Hemingway code. When Jake and Bill, his best friend, are fishing in Burguete, they receive a telegram from Cohn, addressed simply, "Barnes, Burguete": "Vengo Jueves Cohn" [I come Thursday]. "What a lousy telegram!" Jake responds. "He could send ten words for the same price." Cohn thinks that he is being clever by writing in Spanish and saving a word, an assumption as naïve as the one that leads him to shorten the name and address to "Barnes, Burguete." The address was free, and Cohn could have included full name and address, thus increasing the probability that Jake would get the message. As a response to Cohn's telegram, Jake and Bill send one equally wasteful: "Arriving to-night." The point is that the price of the telegram includes a laugh at Cohn's expense, and they are willing to pay for it.

After the Burguete scene, there is no direct discussion of the price of telegrams, but through this scene,

Hemingway gives a key for understanding how each character measures up to the standards of the code. Ironically, Bill, with whom Jake has laughed over Cohn's extravagance and whom Jake admires, is as uneconomical as Cohn. From Budapest, he wires Jake, "Back on Monday"; his card from Budapest says, "Jake, Budapest is wonderful." Bill's wastefulness, however, is calculated, and he is quite conscious of his value system. In his attempt to talk Jake into buying a stuffed dog, Bill indicates that, to him, things are equally valueless: Whatever one buys, in essence, will be dead and stuffed. He is a conscious spendthrift who has no intention of conserving emotions or money. He ignores the reality that letters, cards, and telegrams are designed to accommodate messages of different lengths and that one should choose the most appropriate (conservative) form of communication available.

At first, it seems strange that Jake can accept as a true friend one whose value system is so different from his, but just as Frederic Henry in *A Farewell to Arms* will accept the priest, whose code is different, so can Jake accept Bill. Both the priest and Bill are conscious of their value systems. Thus, if Bill's extravagance appears to link him with the wasteful Cohn, the similarity is a superficial one. Like Jake—and unlike Cohn, who still believes in the chivalric code—he has merely chosen extravagance as a way of coping, knowing that whatever he gets will be the equivalent of a stuffed dog. Morally, Bill is less akin to Cohn than he is to Rinaldi in *A Farewell to Arms*, who continues his indiscriminate lovemaking, even though he knows it may result in syphilis. Just as Frederic Henry remains true to Rinaldi, so Jake remains true to Bill.

Standing midway between Bill and Cohn is Brett's fiancé, Michael, whose values, in terms of the code, are sloppy. Like Cohn, Mike sends bad telegrams and letters. His one telegram in the novel is four words long: "Stopped night San Sebastian." His letters are in clipped telegraphese, filled with abbreviations such as "We got here Friday, Brett passed out on the train, so brought her here for 3 days rest with old friends of ours." Michael could have gotten more for his money in the telegram by using the ten allotted words, just as he could have sent a letter without abbreviations for the same price. The telegram and the letter suggest that although he is conscious of the *principle* of economy, he simply has no idea how to be economical. Thus, when Brett says of Michael, "He writes a good letter," there is an irony in her comment that Jake acknowledges: "I know. . . . He wrote me from San Sebastian." In juxtaposing the telegram and the letter, Hemingway shows Michael to be a man without a code, a man who, when asked how he became bankrupt, responds, "Gradually and then suddenly," which is precisely how he is becoming emotionally bankrupt. He sees it coming, but he has no code that will help him deal directly with his "lostness."

Unlike Cohn, Bill, and Mike, both Brett and Jake send ten-word telegrams, thus presumably getting their money's worth. When Brett, in the last chapters of the novel, needs Jake, she wires him: "COULD YOU COME HOTEL MONTANA MADRID AM RATHER IN TROUBLE BRETT"—ten words followed by the signature. This telegram, which had been forwarded from Paris, is immediately followed by another one identical to it, forwarded from Pamplona. In turn, Jake responds with a telegram that also consists of ten words and the signature: "LADY ASHLEY HOTEL MONTANA MADRID ARRIVING SUD EXPRESS TOMORROW LOVE JAKE." Interestingly, he includes the address in the body of the telegram in order to obtain the ten-word limit. The sending of ten-word telegrams indicates that Jake and Brett are bonded by their adherence to the code; since they alone send such telegrams, the reader must see them as members of an exclusive society.

Yet ironically, to Jake and Brett, the code has become a formalized ritual, something superimposed over their emptiness. They have not learned to apply the code to every aspect of their lives, the most striking example of which is Brett's ten-word (excluding the signature) postcard at the beginning of chapter 8: "Darling. Very quiet and healthy. Love to all the chaps. Brett." The postcard has no word limit, except that dictated by the size of one's handwriting. Brett, however, in the absence of clearly labeled values, must fall back on the only form she knows: in this case, that of the ten-word telegram, which is here an empty form, a ritual detached from its meaningful context.

Jake and Brett, then, come back full circle to their initial frustration and mark time with rituals to which they cling for not-so-dear life, looking in the meantime for physical pleasures that will get them through the night. Yet if this seems a low yield for their efforts, one should remember that Hemingway makes no pretense in *The Sun Also Rises* of finding a cure for "lostness." In fact, he heightens the sense of it in his juxtaposition of two epigraphs of the novel: "You are all a lost generation" from Gertrude Stein, and the long quotation from Ecclesiastes that begins "One generation passeth away, and another generation cometh; but the earth abideth forever. . . . The sun also ariseth, and the sun goeth down." As Hemingway maintained, the hero of *The Sun Also Rises* is the abiding earth; the best one can hope for while living on that earth, isolated from one's fellows and cut off from the procreative cycle, is a survival manual. Finally, that is what *The Sun Also Rises* is, and this is the prescription that it offers: One must accept the presence of death in life and face it stoically, one must learn to exhibit grace under pressure, and one must learn to get one's money's worth. In skeleton form, this is the foundation of the Hemingway code—the part of it, at least, that remains constant through all of his novels.

A FAREWELL TO ARMS

Many of the conditions that necessitated the forming of a code for Jake and Brett in *The Sun Also Rises* are still present in *A Farewell to Arms*, and there are obvious similarities between the two novels. Like Jake, Frederic Henry is wounded in the war and falls in love with a woman, Catherine Barkley, whose first love, like Brett's, has been killed before the main events of the novel begin. Yet there has been a subtle change from *The Sun Also Rises* to *A Farewell to Arms* in Hemingway's perception of the human dilemma. The most revealing hint of this change is in the nature of the wound that Frederic receives while serving as an ambulance driver on the Italian front. Unlike Jake's phallic wound, Frederic's is a less debilitating leg wound and, ironically, it is the thing that brings him closer to Catherine, an English nurse who treats him in the field hospital in Milan. Though their relationship begins as a casual one, viewed from the beginning by Frederic as a "chess game" whose object is sexual gratification, it evolves in the course of Catherine's nursing him into a love that is both spiritual and physical. Catherine's pregnancy affirms at least a partial healing of the maimed fisher king and the restoration of fertility to the wasteland that appeared in *The Sun Also Rises*.

With this improved condition, however, come new problems, and with them a need to amend the code practiced by Jake and Brett. Frederic's dilemma at the beginning of the novel, how to find meaning in life when he is surrounded by death, contains clear-cut alternatives: He can seek physical pleasure in the bawdy houses frequented by his fellow soldiers, including his best friend Rinaldi, or he can search for meaning through the religion practiced by the priest from the Abruzzi; he can do either while fulfilling his obligation to the war effort. His choices, simple ones at first, become limited by forces beyond his control.

First, he must discard the possibility of religion, because he cannot believe in it; then, he must reject the life of the bawdy houses, both because it is not fulfilling and because it often brings syphilis. These are choices that even a code novice such as Frederic Henry can make, but his next decision is more difficult. Knowing that Catherine is pregnant and knowing that he loves her, how can he continue to fight, even for a cause to which he feels duty-bound? Catherine, who had earlier lost her fiancé to the war and who had refused to give herself to him completely because of her sense of duty to the abstract virtue of premarital sexual purity, has prepared Frederic for his decision, one forecast by the title *A Farewell to Arms*. Frederic's choice is made easier by the disordered and chaotic scenes that he witnesses during the Caporetta retreat, among them the shooting of his fellow officers by carabinieri. Partly because Catherine has initiated him into the life of love, then, and partly because he needs to escape his own death, Frederic deserts the Italian army in one of the most celebrated baptismal rites in American literature: He dives into the Tagliamento River and washes away his anger "with any obligation," making what he terms a separate peace.

If Hemingway were a different kind of storyteller, the reader could anticipate that Frederic and Catherine would regain paradise, have their child, and live happily ever after. In fact, however, no sooner have they escaped the life-in-death of war in Italy to the neutrality of Switzerland, where the reader could logically expect in a fifth and final chapter of the novel a brief, pleasant postscript, than does the double edge hidden in the title become clear. Catherine has foreseen it all along in her visions of the rain, often a symbol of life but in *A Farewell to Arms* a symbol of death: "Sometimes I see me dead in it," she says. The arms to which Frederic must finally say farewell are those of Catherine, who dies in childbirth. "And this," Frederic observes, "is the price you paid for sleeping together. . . . This was what people get for loving each other."

Some will take this ending and Frederic Henry's observations about love at face value and accuse Hemingway of stacking the odds against Frederic and Catherine, maintaining finally that Hemingway provides a legitimate exit from the wasteland with a code that could work and then barricades it capriciously. There is, however, ample warning. From the beginning of the novel, Hemingway establishes Catherine as one who knows well the dangers of loving, and from the time of her meeting with Frederic, she balances them against the emptiness of not loving. In most ways, Catherine is a model of the code hero-heroine established in *The Sun Also Rises*: She stoically accepts life's difficulties, as evidenced by her acceptance of her fiancé's death; and she exhibits grace under pressure, as shown in her calm acceptance of her own death. In giving herself to Frederic, she adds a dimension to the code by breaking through the isolation and separateness felt by Jake and Brett; finally, even though she does not complete the re-creative cycle by giving birth to a child conceived in love, she at least brings the possibility within reach. The reader must decide whether Frederic will internalize the lessons he has learned through Catherine's life and allow his own initiation into the code, which now contains the possibility of loving, to be accomplished.

There are some tenets of Hemingway's philosophy through the publication of *A Farewell to Arms* about which one is safe in generalizing. The most obvious and most important of these is his belief that the only things in life that one can know about with certainty are those things that can be verified through the senses, as Jake can confirm that he has had good food or good wine and as Frederic can verify that being next to Catherine feels good. Hemingway refuses to judge this belief in the primacy of the senses as moral or immoral, and Jake articulates this refusal with mock uncertainty during a late-night Pamplona monologue on values: "That was morality; things that made you disgusted after. No, that must be immorality." The point is that in referring observations about life to the senses, one relieves oneself of the need to think about abstractions such as love and honor, abstractions that the main characters in the first two novels carefully avoid. Frederic, for example, is "always embarrassed by the words sacred, glorious, and sacrifice and the expression in vain." With such a perspective, the value of life can be rather accurately measured and described in empirical terms. Similarly, death in such a system can be described even more easily, since there is nothing in death to perceive or measure, an idea vividly rendered in Frederic's remarks about his farewell to Catherine: "It was like saying good-by to a statue."

In looking back on Catherine's death, Frederic or the reader may conclude that it had sacrificial value, but until the 1930's, Hemingway was reluctant in his novels to identify death with an abstract virtue such as sacrifice or to write about the value of an individual life in a collective sense. By 1937, however, and the publication of what most critics regard as his weakest novel, *To Have and Have Not*, Hemingway's attitudes toward life and death had changed. Harry Morgan, the "have not" spokesman of the novel, finally with much effort is able to mutter at the end, "One man alone ain't got . . . no chance." After saying this he reflects that "it had taken him a long time to get it out and it had taken him all his life to learn it." The major works to come after *To Have and Have Not*, namely, *For Whom the Bell Tolls* and *The Old Man and the Sea*, amplify Morgan's view and show Hemingway's code characters moving toward a belief in the collective values of their own lives.

For Whom the Bell Tolls

The epigraph of *For Whom the Bell Tolls*, which was taken from a John Donne sermon and gives the novel its title, points clearly to Hemingway's reevaluation of the role of death in life: "No man is an *Iland*, intire of it selfe; every man is a peece of the *Continent*, a part of the *maine*. . . . And therefore never send to know for whom the bell tolls; It tolls for thee." Regardless of the route by which Hemingway came to exchange the "separate peace" idea of *The Sun Also Rises* and *A Farewell to Arms* for the "part of the *maine*" philosophy embraced by Robert Jordan in *For Whom the Bell Tolls*, one can be sure that much of the impetus for his changing came from his strong feelings about Spain's internal strife, particularly as this strife became an all-out conflict during the Spanish Civil War (1936-1939).

This war provides the backdrop for the events of *For Whom the Bell Tolls*, and the novel's main character, like Hemingway, is a passionate supporter of the Loyalist cause. The thing that one immediately notices about Jordan is that he is an idealist, which sets him apart from Jake and Frederic. Also, unlike Jake, who wanders randomly throughout Europe, and unlike Frederic, whose reasons for being in Italy to participate in the war are never clearly defined, Jordan has come to the Sierra de Guadaramas with the specific purpose of blowing up a bridge that would be used to transport ammunition in attacks against the Loyalists. Thrown in with the Loyalist guerrillas of Pablo's band at the beginning of the novel, Jordan is confronted with the near-impossible task of accomplishing the demolition in three days, a task whose difficulty is compounded by Pablo's resistance to the idea and, finally, by increased Fascist activity near the bridge.

Potentially even more threatening to Jordan's mission is his meeting and falling in love with the beautiful and simple Maria, who is in the protection of Pablo's band after having been raped by the Falangists who killed her parents. Again, however, Jordan is not Frederic Henry, which is to say that he has no intention of declaring a separate peace and leaving his duty behind in pursuit of love. He sees no conflict between the two, and to the degree that Hemingway presents him as the rare individual who fulfills his obligations without losing his ability to love, Jordan represents a new version of the code hero: the whole man who respects himself, cares for others, and believes in the cause of individual freedom. Circumstances, however, conspire against Jordan. Seeing that his mission stands little hope of success and that the offensive planned by General Golz is doomed to failure by the presence of more and more Fascists, he attempts to get word through to Golz, but the message arrives too late. Although he manages successfully to demolish the bridge and almost escapes with Maria, his wounded horse falls, rolls over, and crushes Jordan's leg. He remains at the end of the novel in extreme pain, urging the others not to stay and be killed with him, and waiting to shoot the first Fascist officer who comes into range, thus giving Maria and Pablo's group more time to escape.

Jordan is perhaps Hemingway's most ambitious creation, just as *For Whom the Bell Tolls* is his most elaborately conceived novel. Its various strands reflect not only what had become the standard Hemingway subjects of personal death, love, and war but also his growing concern with the broader social implications of individual action. Jordan's consideration of his mission in Spain clearly demonstrates this: "I have fought for what I believe in for a year now," he says. "If we win here we will win everywhere." How well Hemingway has woven together these strands remains a matter of critical debate, but individually the parts are brilliant in conception. One example of the many layers of meaning contained in the novel is the Civil War framework, which leads the reader to not only see the conflict of social forces in Spain but also understand that its analogue is the "civil war" in Jordan's spirit: The reader is reminded periodically of the noble death of Jordan's grandfather in the American Civil War, compared to the "separate peace" suicide of Jordan's father. Jordan debates these alternatives until the last scene, when he decides to opt for an honorable death that gives others a chance to live. This, Hemingway seems finally to say, gives Jordan's life transcendent value.

The Old Man and the Sea

F. Scott Fitzgerald theorized early in his friendship with Hemingway that Hemingway would need a new wife for each "big book." As Scott Donaldson observes, the "theory worked well for his [Hemingway's] first three wives (Hadley: *The Sun Also Rises*; Pauline: *A Farewell to Arms*; Martha: *For Whom the Bell Tolls*) but breaks down in Mary's case" because *The Old Man and the Sea* does not qualify as a "big book." It does qualify, however, as a major epilogue to the "big books," much as "Big Two-Hearted River" qualifies as their prologue. In the prologue, Hemingway outlines the dilemma of modern humanity and establishes the task with which humanity is confronted in a literal and figurative wasteland.

For Nick in the story, Hemingway posits a swamp, which Nick may fish "tomorrow" and which is a symbolic representation of life with all its complexities, including male-female relationships. In the big books,

Hemingway leads the reader through the wasteland, showing first, in *The Sun Also Rises*, the risk of personal isolation and despair in a life cut off from the regenerative cycles of nature. In *A Farewell to Arms*, he dramatizes the vulnerability of the individual even in a life where there is love, and finally, in *For Whom the Bell Tolls*, he presents a "whole man" who recognizes the value of individual sacrifice for the survival of the human race. In the epilogue, *The Old Man and the Sea*, Hemingway carries this principle to its final step and issues, through Santiago, his definitive statement about the role of life in death.

It is no surprise that *The Old Man and the Sea* takes the form of a parable and that its old man takes the form of the archetypal wise man or savior common to most cultures, mythologies, and religions. While others who surround Santiago depend on gadgets to catch their fish, Santiago relies only on his own endurance and courage. He goes eighty-four days before hooking the marlin, against whose strength he will pit his own for nearly two full days, until he is finally able to bring him to the boat and secure him there for the journey from the Gulf Stream.

Numerous critics have noted the similarities between Santiago and Christ. Santiago goes farther out than most men, symbolically taking on a burden for humankind that most men could not or would not take on for themselves. When Santiago returns to land from his ordeal, secures his boat, and heads toward his shack, Hemingway describes his journey explicitly in terms of Christ's ascent to Calvary: "He started to climb again and at the top he fell and lay for some time with the mast across his shoulder." Moreover, Santiago talks with the boy Manolin about those who do not believe in him or his ways in terms that are unmistakably religious: Of the boy's father, who does not want his son to be with the old man, Santiago remarks, "He hasn't much faith." In all of this, Hemingway is leading the reader to see that some, in going out "too far," risk their lives in order to transmit to others the idea that "a man can be destroyed but not defeated." Finally, it is of little importance that sharks have reduced Santiago's great fish to a skeleton by the time he has reached land, because the human spirit that has been tested in his battle with the fish has in the end prevailed; those who are genuinely interested in that spirit are rarely concerned with ocular proof of its existence. Santiago's legacy, which must stand as Hemingway's last major word on the human condition, will go to Manolin and the reader, since, as the old man tells him, "I know you did not leave me because you doubted"; he did not doubt that the human spirit can prevail.

Hemingway, then, traveled a great distance from the nihilistic philosophy and hedonistic code of *The Sun Also Rises* to the affirmative view of humankind expressed in *The Old Man and the Sea*. His four major works, if read chronologically, lead the reader on an odyssey through the seasonal cycle of the human spirit. "All stories, if continued far enough, end in death," and Hemingway never stops reminding the reader of that fact. He does add to it, however, in his later work, the hope of rebirth that waits at the end of the journey, a hope for which nature has historically provided the model. The reader of Hemingway's work may find the idea of metaphorical rebirth less a solace for the individual facing literal death than Hemingway seems to suggest it can be. Few, however, will leave Hemingway's work without feeling that he, at least, speaks in the end with the authority of one who has earned, in Carlos Baker's words, "the proud, quiet knowledge of having fought the fight, of having lasted it out, of having done a great thing to the bitter end of human strength."

Bryant Mangum

Other major works

SHORT FICTION: *Three Stories and Ten Poems*, 1923; *In Our Time*, 1924, 1925; *Men Without Women*, 1927; *Winner Take Nothing*, 1933; *The Fifth Column and the First Forty-nine Stories*, 1938; *The Snows of Kilimanjaro, and Other Stories*, 1961; *The Short Happy Life of Francis Macomber, and Other Stories*, 1963; *The Nick Adams Stories*, 1972; *The Complete Stories of Ernest Hemingway*, 1987.

PLAYS: *Today Is Friday*, pb. 1926; *The Fifth Column*, pb. 1938.

POETRY: *The Collected Poems of Ernest Hemingway*, 1960; *Eighty-eight Poems*, 1979 (enlarged as *Complete Poems*, 1983).

NONFICTION: *Death in the Afternoon*, 1932; *Green Hills of Africa*, 1935; *A Moveable Feast*, 1964; *By-Line: Ernest Hemingway, Selected Articles and Dispatches of*

Four Decades, 1967; *Ernest Hemingway, Cub Reporter: "Kansas City Star" Stories*, 1970 (Matthew J. Bruccoli, editor); *Ernest Hemingway: Selected Letters, 1917-1961*, 1981; *Ernest Hemingway on Writing*, 1984 (Larry W. Phillips, editor); *The Dangerous Summer*, 1985; *Dateline, Toronto: The Complete "Toronto Star" Dispatches, 1920-1924*, 1985; *Conversations with Ernest Hemingway*, 1986 (Bruccoli, editor); *Hemingway at Oak Park High: The High School Writings of Ernest Hemingway, 1916-1917*, 1993; *The Only Thing That Counts: The Ernest Hemingway/Maxwell Perkins Correspondence, 1925-1947*, 1996 (Bruccoli, editor; with Robert W. Trogdon); *Hemingway on Fishing*, 2000 (Nick Lyons, editor); *Hemingway on Hunting*, 2001 (Seán Hemingway, editor); *Hemingway on War*, 2003 (Seán Hemingway, editor); *Dear Papa, Dear Hotch: The Correspondence of Ernest Hemingway and A. E. Hotchner*, 2005 (Albert J. DeFazio III, editor); *Hemingway and the Mechanism of Fame: Statements, Public Letters, Introductions, Forewords, Prefaces, Blurbs, Reviews, and Endorsements*, 2006 (Bruccoli, editor; with Judith S. Baughman); *On Paris*, 2008.

BIBLIOGRAPHY

Berman, Ronald. *Fitzgerald, Hemingway, and the Twenties*. Tuscaloosa: University of Alabama Press, 2001. Berman examines the novels and short stories that both Hemingway and F. Scott Fitzgerald wrote during the 1920's within the context of the decade's intellectual history, philosophy, and popular culture. Includes analysis of *A Farewell to Arms* and *The Sun Also Rises*.

Bloom, Harold, ed. *Ernest Hemingway*. Philadelphia: Chelsea House, 2005. Includes articles analyzing Hemingway's work by a variety of writers, including such eminent literary critics as Edmund Wilson, Robert Penn Warren, and Carlos Baker.

Fantina, Richard. *Ernest Hemingway: Machismo and Masochism*. New York: Palgrave Macmillan, 2005. Focuses on Hemingway's heroes, from Jack Barnes in *The Sun Also Rises* to David Bourne in *The Garden of Eden*. Fantina argues that despite Hemingway's supermasculine image, his male protagonists are "profoundly submissive" and display a "masochistic posture toward women."

Gajdusek, Robert E. *Hemingway in His Own Country*. Notre Dame, Ind.: University of Notre Dame Press, 2002. A collection of essays that interpret Hemingway's works from a wide variety of perspectives. Some of the essays compare the work of Hemingway with that of James Joyce and F. Scott Fitzgerald, discuss Hemingway's representation of women and the androgynous elements in his fiction, and analyze some of his novels.

Hotchner, A. E. *Papa Hemingway: A Personal Memoir*. New ed. New York: Carroll & Graf, 1999. Written by one of Hemingway's close friends as well as an editor, novelist, playwright, and biographer. Considered a definitive biography. Originally published in 1966, this Hemingway Centennial Edition features a new introduction.

Mellow, James R. *Hemingway: A Life Without Consequences*. Boston: Houghton Mifflin, 1992. A well-informed, sensitive handling of the life and work by a seasoned biographer. Particularly good in its discussion of the writers who influenced Hemingway, such as Ezra Pound and Gertrude Stein.

Ott, Mark P. *A Sea of Change: Ernest Hemingway and the Gulf Stream: A Contextual Biography*. Kent, Ohio: Kent State University Press, 2008. Ott examines Hemingway's interest in the effects of the Gulf stream on Florida, arguing that the writer's study of the area moved his fiction from a kind of 1920's Paris modernism to 1950's realism. Includes analysis of *To Have and Have Not* and *The Old Man and the Sea*.

Reynolds, Michael. *The Young Hemingway*. New York: Blackwell, 1986.

_______. *Hemingway: The Paris Years*. New York: Blackwell, 1989.

_______. *Hemingway: The American Homecoming*. New York: W. W. Norton, 1992.

_______. *Hemingway: The 1930's*. New York: W. W. Norton, 1997.

_______. *Hemingway: The Final Years*. New York: W. W. Norton, 1999. Reynolds's multivolume biography chronicles Hemingway's life and his evolution as a writer with meticulous detail and with new material and period documents, creating a sympathetic and comprehensive portrait of the author.

Trogdon, Robert W., ed. *Ernest Hemingway: A Literary Reference*. New York: Carroll & Graf, 2002. A compendium on all-things Hemingway. Includes photographs, letters, interviews, essays, speeches, book reviews, copies of some of his manuscripts-in-process, and his comments about his own work and the work of other writers.

Wagner-Martin, Linda. *Ernest Hemingway: A Literary Life*. New York: Palgrave Macmillan, 2007. Examines Hemingway's life, especially his troubled relationship with his parents. Wagner-Martin makes insightful connections between the author's personal life, his emotions, and his writing.

_______, ed. *Hemingway: Seven Decades of Criticism*. East Lansing: Michigan State University Press, 1998. A collection of essays ranging from Gertrude Stein's 1923 review of Hemingway's stories to contemporary responses to *The Garden of Eden*. Includes essays on *The Sun Also Rises*, *A Farewell to Arms*, and *For Whom the Bell Tolls*.

FRANK HERBERT

Born: Tacoma, Washington; October 8, 1920
Died: Madison, Wisconsin; February 11, 1986
Also known as: Franklin Patrick Herbert, Jr.

Principal long fiction

The Dragon in the Sea, 1956 (also known as *Twenty-first Century Sub* and *Under Pressure*)
Dune, 1965
Destination: Void, 1966 (revised 1978)
The Eyes of Heisenberg, 1966
The Green Brain, 1966
The Heaven Makers, 1968
The Santaroga Barrier, 1968
Dune Messiah, 1969
Whipping Star, 1970
Soul Catcher, 1972
The God Makers, 1972
Hellstrom's Hive, 1973
Children of Dune, 1976
The Dosadi Experiment, 1977
The Jesus Incident, 1979 (with Bill Ransom)
Direct Descent, 1980
God Emperor of Dune, 1981
The White Plague, 1982
The Lazarus Effect, 1983 (with Ransom)
Heretics of Dune, 1984
Chapterhouse: Dune, 1985
Man of Two Worlds, 1986 (with Brian Herbert)
The Ascension Factor, 1988 (with Ransom)
Dune: House Corrino, 2001 (with Kevin J. Anderson)

Other literary forms

Although Frank Herbert is best known for his long fiction, especially the Dune series, he started to write short stories when he was eight years old and was in a hospital working on another story the day he died. He sold more than forty short stories in his lifetime, most of which have been reprinted in book form. He made his first sale to a Western magazine under a pseudonym while he was still in high school. Unfortunately, the pseudonym, the story, and the magazine itself have been lost. His first sale under his own name was the story "The Survival of the Cunning," which he had published in *Esquire* in 1945. In 1952, Herbert sold his first science-fiction story, "Looking for Something," to *Startling Stories*.

Achievements

Dune and its sequels comprise one of the best-selling science-fiction series of all time. *Dune* won the Nebula Award in 1965 and tied as the winner of the Hugo Award in 1966. A 1974 *Locus* poll voted *Dune* the best science-fiction novel of all time. The book is assigned reading for courses in a wide array of fields, including philosophy, psychology, English, and ecology.

Dune has achieved notoriety for several reasons. First, it was one of the first science-fiction novels to apply high literary standards to the genre. Before the 1960's, most of the best science-fiction stories were based on interesting scientific or technological premises and were plot-driven. After the 1960's, writing style and characterization became equally, if not more, important. Second, *Dune* was one of the first great "soft" science-fiction novels. Herbert intentionally minimized the technobabble when he wrote the Dune books so he could concentrate on the characters rather than on their technologies. Third, Herbert created a world with its own unique history, languages, religions, customs, geography, ecology, and economic, social, and political systems, comparable to J. R. R. Tolkien's Middle-earth and C. S. Lewis's Narnia.

Herbert's other writings also won critical acclaim. His only mainstream novel, *Soul Catcher*, was nominated for a National Book Award, and the French edition of *Hellstrom's Hive* won the Prix Apollo.

Biography

Franklin Patrick Herbert, Jr., was born October 8, 1920, to Franklin Patrick Herbert, Sr., and Eileen McCarthy Herbert. His mother's family was descended from Irish political refugees, and he later used this family background in the novel *The White Plague*. Herbert's mother also had eight sisters who were devout Roman Catholics and gave him the idea for the Bene Gesserit, the powerful organization of women dedicated to producing a god, in the Dune books. His paternal grandmother, otherwise illiterate, had an exceptional memory and could calculate large numbers in her head. She was the model for the Mentats, or human computers, in *Dune*.

Herbert learned to read at an early age and could read most of a newspaper when he was five years old. On his eighth birthday, he announced that he wanted to become a writer. When Herbert was thirteen years old, he met a Native American fisherman, upon whom he based the main character in *Soul Catcher*. Herbert graduated from high school in 1939 and got his first newspaper job that fall. He married Flora Parkinson in 1941. They had a daughter, Penny, in 1942, but were divorced in 1945.

Herbert enlisted in the U.S. Navy during World War II but suffered a head injury during a training exercise and was discharged after eight months of service. After the war, he attended the University of Washington on the G.I. Bill. He met Beverly Ann Stuart in a creative writing class. They married in 1946 and had two sons, Brian (b. 1947) and Bruce (b. 1951). Herbert patterned the character of Lady Jessica in the Dune series after his wife.

Herbert left college after one year to return to journalism and to write part time. In 1957, he received an assignment to write a magazine article about the sand dunes in Florence, Oregon. He never finished the article, but he did get the idea that led to *Dune*.

Because of his extensive research, Herbert took six years to write *Dune*. Twice as many pages as the average science-fiction novel of the time, the book first was serialized in *Analog* in eight installments from 1963 to 1965. More than twenty book publishers rejected the novel before Chilton, a small publisher, bought the hardcover rights (Ace bought the paperback rights). *Dune* became a critical success, despite initially modest hardcover sales. Thirty-five hundred initial copies were printed, of which thirteen hundred had to be discarded because of a misprint. The second and third printings came within a few years. By the early 1970's, the paperback edition had become Ace's all-time best seller. By 1973, Herbert's income from his fiction writing finally enabled him to retire from journalism to write full time. In 1976, *Children of Dune* became Herbert's first hardcover best seller.

Beverly Herbert was diagnosed with cancer in 1974 but survived until 1984. The following year, Herbert married Theresa Shackleford. He died in 1986 of a pulmonary embolism while recovering from surgery for pancreatic cancer.

Analysis

Frank Herbert wrote science fiction because the genre allowed him to explore subjects such as philosophy, religion, psychology, and ecology. The issues of human survival and evolution particularly fascinated him. A number of themes recur in Herbert's work.

First, much of his writing is concerned with leadership. (Herbert worked on four unsuccessful political campaigns during the 1950's and once met U.S. president Harry S. Truman.) Although Herbert is usually associated with the political left, he was suspicious of President John F. Kennedy and the media's comparison of his administration to King Arthur's Camelot. He considered charisma an overrated and even dangerous quality. One of the complexities of the Dune books is that the protagonist, Paul Atreides, is a hero in *Dune* and an antihero in *Dune Messiah*. One of the models for Paul was Lawrence of Arabia, and another was Muhammad Ahmad, a late nineteenth century Islamic messianic figure who led an army to victory over the British in Sudan in 1885.

Second, Herbert displays an interest in the intersection of religion, politics, and power. In *The White Plague*, the president of the United States orders the assassination of the Roman Catholic pope when the latter announces a policy at odds with that of the president. In *Dune Messiah*, Paul is both the religious and the political leader of all humans on ten thousand planets. By *God Emperor of Dune*, his son Leto II has taken this position to an even higher level. In *Destination* and *The Jesus Incident*, a self-conscious computer demands to be worshiped as a god.

Third, Herbert was one of the first science-fiction authors to explore ecological ideas in his novels. He believed that people should think in the long term. In *The Dragon in the Sea*, he predicts the worldwide oil shortage. The planet Dune becomes a desert planet because human colonists brought with them an off-world creature that radically changed the planet's ecology. In *The Green Brain*, Herbert postulates a powerful insect intelligence that develops in reaction to insecticides.

Herbert created the Fremen and the Sardaukar in the Dune books and the Dosadi in *The Dosadi Experiment*. These groups became violent peoples because of the harsh living conditions on their home worlds. Herbert modeled the Fremen after the Apaches, a Native American nation whose members live in Mexico and the American Southwest, and the Bedouin nomads of Arabia. The Sardaukar come from the prison planet Salusa Secundus, where only the strong survive. On Dosadi, more than ninety million humans and the alien species Gowachin are crowded into a single habitable valley where they compete for food and the weak go hungry.

Fourth, Herbert also questions human standards of sanity. While some of his characters, such as Piter de Vries in *Dune*, are made into psychopaths, Herbert believed that "normal" and "abnormal" are relative terms and not universally applicable. He preferred to define "sanity" as the ability to adapt to situations, especially life-and-death ones. In *The Dragon in the Sea*, he used the claustrophobic environment of a submarine to explore these issues. *The White Plague* includes a character eventually known as the Madman. At the beginning of the book, he is a socially well-adjusted molecular biologist, but when a terrorist attack kills his wife and two children, he launches an insane plan to kill off all the women in Ireland, England, and Libya, and he nearly succeeds.

Frank Herbert. (Andrew Unangst)

Dune

Dune was one of the first ecological science-fiction novels, written around the time of Rachel Carson's highly successful book *Silent Spring* (1962). *Dune* is set thousands of years in the future, in which most humans live in a vast interstellar empire. Individual planets are ruled by hereditary nobles that in turn swear allegiance to an emperor named Shaddam IV.

Dune tells the story of Paul Atreides, fifteen years old at the beginning of the novel and heir apparent to the leadership of House Atreides. (Atreides was named for a family in Homer's *Iliad.*) Paul's father, the duke Leto, accepts control of the planet Arrakis, the only source of the spice melange, the most important natural substance in the known universe. The longtime inhabitants of the planet are called Fremen, and their name for the planet, Dune, reflects the planetwide desert that is Arrakis. The story takes place on many different levels, including political, religious, ecological, technological, and most important, human. The plot is driven by the desire of different groups and individuals to control Arrakis and its spice.

The name of Paul Atreides' greatest enemy is Vladimir Harkonnen, whose first name is a common Russian one. (The Cold War was at its height when Herbert wrote the book.) Harkonnen drinks the blood of young boys, which makes him a kind of vampire. Emperor Shaddam plays the Atreides and the Harkonnen families against each other, but in the end his schemes backfire when Paul triumphs.

Paul, who shares his first name with a Christian saint, is the product of a secret breeding program established by the Bene Gesserit to produce a superhero capable of ruling the galaxy wisely and justly. His mother Lady Jessica, the duke's concubine and Harkonnen's illegitimate daughter, is a member of the Bene Gesserit. However, she fell in love with Duke Leto and disobeyed her superiors in the order when she gave him a son rather than a daughter.

Herbert's Mentats, the Bene Gesserit, and the Space Guild are just a few examples of what humans could become. The Mentats are human computers in a future in which electronic computers have been outlawed. The Bene Gesserit (the name intentionally rhymes with Jesuit) are themselves the result of generations of breeding and undergo a rigorous training program that provides them acute powers of observation, the ability to control the minds of others through language, and a limited ability to see into the future. All Mentats are males, and all Bene Gesserit are females. The members of the Space Guild are fishlike mutants who use almost pure mathematics to pilot ships between the stars.

Thomas R. Feller

Other major works

SHORT FICTION: *The Worlds of Frank Herbert*, 1970; *The Book of Frank Herbert*, 1973; *The Best of Frank Herbert*, 1975; *The Priests of Psi, and Other Stories*, 1980; *Eye*, 1985.

POETRY: *Songs of Muad'Dib: The Poetry of Frank Herbert*, 1992 (Brian Herbert, editor).

NONFICTION: *Threshold: The Blue Angels Experience*, 1973; *Without Me, You're Nothing*, 1981 (with Max Barnard); *The Maker of Dune*, 1987 (Timothy O'Reilly, editor).

EDITED TEXT: *New World or No World*, 1970.

MISCELLANEOUS: *The Road to Dune*, 2005 (with Brian Herbert and Kevin J. Anderson).

Bibliography

Clarke, Jason. *SparkNotes: Dune, Frank Herbert*. New York: Spark, 2002. Critical study analyzes the characters of Paul Atreides, Lady Jessica, and Baron Harkonnen and the themes of religion, power, and ecology.

Herbert, Brian. *Dreamer of Dune: The Biography of Frank Herbert*. New York: Tor Books, 2003. Personal memoir by Herbert's son, Brian Herbert, who emphasizes his stormy relationship with his father. He interviewed many of his father's friends and had complete access to his father's papers, notes, and unpublished writings.

Herbert, Frank, Brian Herbert, and Kevin J. Anderson. *The Road to Dune*. New York: Tor Books, 2005. Collection of materials related to *Dune*, including an introduction by Herbert's collaborator Bill Ransom, an early (and shorter) draft of the novel, excerpts from Herbert's correspondence, quotations from contemporary reviews, unused chapters from both *Dune* and *Dune Messiah*, and short stories set in the Dune universe.

Leback, Daniel J. H., and Mark Willard. *Dune Master: A Frank Herbert Bibliography*. Westport, Conn.: Meckler, 1988. Annotated bibliography of Herbert's writings that also includes synopses of his writings. Includes several indexes.

McNelley, Willis, ed. *The Dune Encyclopedia*. New York: Berkeley, 1984. Comprehensive guide to the Dune books written through 1983. Approved by Herbert himself. McNelley was a close friend of Herbert.

Miller, David. *Starmont Reader's Guide Five: Frank Herbert*. Mercer Island, Wash.: Starmont, 1980. Brief analysis of Herbert's fiction through 1980, but somewhat dated by later writings and analyses of his work.

Miller, Miriam Y. "Women of *Dune*: Frank Herbert as Social Reactionary?" In *Women Worldwalkers: New Dimensions of Science Fiction and Fantasy*, edited by Jane B. Weedman. Lubbock: Texas Tech Press, 1985. Feminist analysis of Herbert's inclusion of women in the Dune books.

O'Reilly, Timothy. *Frank Herbert*. New York: Frederick Ungar, 1980. Thorough analysis of Herbert's fiction, but also dated by later works. Compares Dune to other science-fiction classics such as Isaac Asimov's Foundation series and to Herbert's other works, and shows how the philosophies of Martin Heidegger and Karl Jaspers influenced Herbert.

Touponce, William F. *Frank Herbert*. Boston: Twayne, 1988. Provides a short biography of Herbert, critical reviews of each Dune book, and synopses of Herbert's other novels.

JOHN HERSEY

Born: Tianjin, China; June 17, 1914
Died: Key West, Florida; March 24, 1993
Also known as: John Richard Hersey

Principal long fiction

A Bell for Adano, 1944
The Wall, 1950
The Marmot Drive, 1953
A Single Pebble, 1956
The War Lover, 1959
The Child Buyer, 1960
White Lotus, 1965
Too Far to Walk, 1966
Under the Eye of the Storm, 1967
The Conspiracy, 1972
My Petition for More Space, 1974
The Walnut Door, 1977
The Call, 1985
Antonietta, 1991

Other literary forms

John Hersey is as well known for his nonfiction as he is for his novels. As a young journalist in World War II, Hersey wrote for *Time* and *Life*, interviewing such figures as Japan's foreign minister Matsuoka, Ambassador Joseph Grew, and Generalissimo Chiang Kai-shek. His first book, *Men on Bataan* (1942), was written in New York from files and clippings; his second, *Into the Valley: A Skirmish of the Marines* (1943), from his own experiences. *Hiroshima* (1946), generally considered to be his most important book, was based on a series of interviews. After *Hiroshima*, he concentrated on writing novels for twenty years, though he often employed the techniques of interviewing and research to establish a factual basis for his novels. *Here to Stay: Studies in Human Tenacity* (1962) reprinted *Hiroshima* and a number of other interviews with people who had survived similar horrors, such as the Warsaw Ghetto. *The Algiers Motel Incident* (1968) was based on research and interviews concerning the Detroit police killing of three African Americans during a period of riots. *Letter to the Alumni* (1970) was a portrait of Yale University during May Day demonstrations, and *The President* (1975) followed President Gerald R. Ford on a typical day. *Life Sketches* (1989) is a book of autobiographical pieces.

Hersey's collections of short stories include *Fling, and Other Stories* (1990). *Blues* (1987), also classified as short fiction, is an idiosyncratic book about bluefishing, cast in the form of a dialogue between a fisherman and a curious stranger and interspersed with poems by Elizabeth Bishop, James Merrill, and others. Hersey also edited *The Writer's Craft* (1974), an anthology of famous writers' comments on the aesthetics and techniques of literary creation.

Achievements

John Hersey's primary achievement was his mastery of the nonfiction novel. Although all the particular techniques of the nonfiction novel have been used for centuries, Hersey can be said to have anticipated the form as it was practiced during the 1960's and 1970's, the era of the New Journalism and of such novels as Gore Vidal's *Burr* (1973) and E. L. Doctorow's *Ragtime* (1975), to cite only two examples. At the beginning of his career as a writer, Hersey was a reporter and based his books on events and people he had observed. Rather than merely recounting his experiences, Hersey molded characters and events to fit a novelistic form, basing, for example, *A Bell for Adano* on what he observed of the U.S. military government at Licata, Sicily. This attention to realistic detail and psychological insight characterizes his best writing and enriches his more imaginative novels, such as *White Lotus*, although these novels were not nearly as well received. Hersey's humanistic perspective is also an important trait of his works and provides a sense of values.

Biography

John Richard Hersey was born in Tianjin, China, on June 17, 1914, to Roscoe and Grace Baird Hersey. His father, a Young Men's Christian Association (YMCA) secretary, and his mother, a missionary, took him on a trip around the world when he was three years old, but most of the first decade of his life was spent in the missionary compound, where, although isolated to an extent from the community, he learned to speak Chinese before he spoke English. From the time he learned to read and write, he amused himself by playing reporter and writing his family news and daily events at the British grammar school and the American school in Tianjin. Despite his early life abroad, Hersey considered his life there "no more exciting than the average child's."

In 1924, Hersey, who knew of the United States only from secondhand accounts and what could be gleaned from books and magazines, was enrolled in the Briarcliff Manor public schools in New York. Three years later, he entered the Hotchkiss School in Lakeville, Connecticut, and graduated in 1932. After receiving his bachelor of arts degree from Yale in 1936, he went on to study eighteenth century English literature on a Mellon Scholarship at Clare College, Cambridge. During this time, he became determined to be a reporter for *Time*, because it seemed "the liveliest enterprise of its type." While waiting for an opening, he became the secretary and driver of Sinclair Lewis in the summer of 1937, the same summer that the Japanese invaded Manchuria. Born in China, Hersey was a natural choice for covering the Sino-Japanese War, and he served as a staff member for *Time* from the fall of 1937 until he was assigned to the Chungking bureau under Theodore White in 1939, where he began the itinerant life he would lead throughout the war.

An enthusiastic, courageous reporter, Hersey often found himself in mortal danger as he covered the war in the South Pacific in 1942, the Sicilian invasion and Mediterranean theater in 1943, and Moscow between 1944 and 1945. Twice, he went down in planes; once he crashed into the Pacific, nearly losing the notes he had taken on Guadalcanal. He was treading water when his notebooks from the sunken plane surfaced only a few feet in front of him. Among other stories that he covered was the first account of PT 109 and its young lieutenant, John F. Kennedy, an account that Kennedy would later use in his campaign for the U.S. Congress. During one trip to the United States from Asia, Hersey married Frances Ann Cannon on April 27, 1940. They had four children (Martin, John, Ann, and Baird) before being divorced in 1958, when he married Barbara Day Addams Kaufman, with whom he had a daughter, Brook.

In 1942, Hersey published his first book, *Men on Bataan*, basically a morale-builder for a United States that had suffered serious setbacks at Pearl Harbor and in the Philippines. Hersey wrote the book only a month after the fall of Corregidor, when most of the men who had actually been on Bataan were imprisoned or assigned to new posts in the Pacific. In New York, he combined *Time-Life* files, letters to the servicemen's families, and a few interviews with reporters and other witnesses to write the book, which had a generally favorable if not overenthusiastic reception. In 1943, he published *Into the Valley*, based on his own experiences with U.S. Marines at the Matanikau River on Guadalcanal. With his experience in actual combat, *Into the Valley* had a substantially different tone from that of *Men on Bataan*, which often tended to jingoism. The extent of Hersey's closeness to combat can be measured by his receiving a letter of commendation from the secretary of the Navy for his work removing wounded during the fighting.

A Bell for Adano, the first book Hersey published as fiction, followed in 1944, and was based on his observations of the U.S. military governance of Licato, Sicily. The novel became a Broadway play and a motion picture. Hersey missed much of the praise because of his continuing assignments as a journalist. During the last year of the war, he observed the evidence of Nazi atrocities in Warsaw and Tallinn that would later lead to his novel *The Wall*. Just as V-E Day occurred, Hersey was awarded the Pulitzer Prize for *A Bell for Adano* and emerged from World War II an extremely successful writer.

During the rest of 1945 and 1946, Hersey was assigned to China and Japan, where he wrote for *Life* and *The New Yorker* and gathered material for what would be his most famous book, *Hiroshima*, the carefully understated story of six people who were in the Japanese city when the first atomic bomb was dropped by the United States. The editor of *The New Yorker*, William Shawn, had intended to run *Hiroshima* as a three-part article; he later changed his mind, however, and decided to print the entire text alone. Nothing else would share the issue with *Hiroshima* except advertising. This dramatic step was kept a secret from the regular staff as Shawn and Hersey sequestered themselves in the office from 10:00 A.M. to 2:00 P.M., Hersey rewriting while the text was fed to a harried makeup man.

Hiroshima became a phenomenon. The Book-of-the-Month Club distributed free copies to its members. It was read aloud in four hourlong radio programs. Physicist Albert Einstein ordered one thousand copies, businessman Bernard Baruch was said to have ordered five hundred, and the mayor of Princeton, New Jersey, sought three thousand reprints. The Belgian chamber of commerce ordered five hundred copies to distribute to officials in Brussels. Three London newspapers requested serial rights. *Hiroshima*, with its concentration on ordinary people trying to cope with the horror of the first atomic blast, made Hersey known worldwide, except in Japan, where the book was banned by the U.S. military government. Hersey donated many of his proceeds from the book to the American Red Cross. Nearly twenty years later, in 1965, when Hersey was invited to the White House Festival of the Arts by President Lyndon B. Johnson, *Hiroshima* was still considered Hersey's most profound work; he read sections of it at the White House gathering in a dramatic protest against the escalation of the war in Vietnam.

The year following *Hiroshima*, Hersey became one of the founders, writers, and editors of *'47—The Magazine of the Year*. It survived only one issue. Hersey became increasingly involved in politics, an involvement that would continue throughout his career. He vigorously supported the United Nations and became a member of such organizations as the Authors' League. During the 1950's, he became a speech writer for politician Adlai Stevenson and actively campaigned for his election by serving as chair of Connecticut Volunteers for Stevenson. Long before the Watergate affair made it fashionable to question the roles of the Federal Bureau of Investigation (FBI) and Central Intelligence Agency (CIA), Hersey was a member of the Committee to End

John Hersey. (AP/Wide World Photos)

Government Secrecy. He also became interested in education, becoming a member of various educational committees and study groups, including the Westport, Connecticut, board of education.

Writing *The Wall* left Hersey little time for journalism in the late 1940's, although he published a few items such as a profile of Harry S. Truman in *The New Yorker*. After extensive research, Hersey published *The Wall* in 1950, repeating the success of *A Bell for Adano* by winning such awards as the Anisfield-Wolf Award, the Daroff Memorial Fiction Award of the Jewish Book Council of America, and the Sidney Hillman Foundation Award. *The Wall*, like *A Bell for Adano*, was later dramatized and then made into a motion picture.

In the early 1950's, Hersey was one of America's most famous writers and was placed in the awkward position of trying to write up to the increasingly higher level expected of him. He began to rely more heavily on his imagination, which tended toward allegorical situations. *The Marmot Drive*, set in Tunxis, a rural New England town, made a political allegory of the town's attempt to rid itself of a threatening colony of woodchucks. A number of Hersey's later books, including *The Child Buyer*, *White Lotus*, *Too Far to Walk*, *Under the Eye of the Storm*, *The Conspiracy*, *My Petition for More Space*, and *The Walnut Door*, have been criticized for their reliance on an underlying allegory or parable to support the plot.

From the 1950's on, Hersey was associated with Yale University's Berkeley College from 1950 to 1965 as a nonteaching fellow, and with Yale's Pierson College from 1965 to 1970 as master. In the latter position, Hersey served as a counselor, confidant, resident administrator, social director, and intellectual mentor for the students, among whom was his son, John, Jr. His closeness to the students allowed him the perceptions he revealed in *Letter to the Alumni*, which was a factual description of the May Day demonstrations of 1969, when Yalies supported the Black Panthers.

After leaving Yale and Connecticut, Hersey lived in Key West, Florida, until his death there in 1993, involving himself in political issues of the day, especially those directly affecting writers. Although he was not a recluse, Hersey generally avoided media attention, only occasionally speaking in public and granting interviews.

ANALYSIS

Critics have generally agreed that John Hersey's greatest strengths as a novelist derive from two sources: the observational skills he developed as a journalist and his belief in the importance of individual human beings in difficult situations. Reviewers throughout his career have praised his attention to realistic detail, which rivals that of William Dean Howells. Hersey gets close to the details of the lives of his characters, so that in his most successful works (both fiction and nonfiction), the reader gets a strong sense of "being there."

When Hersey recaptured his memories of China in the novel *A Single Pebble*, in 1956, he was praised for his acute observations and simple handling of realistic detail, as he would be for nonfictional works such as *Here to Stay*, *The Algiers Motel Incident*, *Letter to the Alumni*, and *The President*. Throughout his career, however, Hersey insisted that he mentally separated and saw a clear difference between the way he wrote fiction and the way he wrote nonfiction. He saw the fiction as his chance to make more profound statements of lasting value—tending to push the works into the allegorical realm—although, ironically, most critics have seen his most profound themes in his more journalistic works, whether fiction or nonfiction, such as *Hiroshima*, *The Wall*, and *A Single Pebble*.

Sometimes, however, Hersey has been criticized for having insufficiently explored his characters in the apparent belief that documentary evidence sufficiently explains them. He has also been charged with cluttering his narratives with excessive detail. Although *A Single Pebble* was generally positively received, one of the criticisms leveled at it was its heavy use of nautical terms that the main character would readily understand but that are confusing to most readers. A similar criticism was leveled at *The War Lover* by a reviewer who asked if Hersey's accounts of twenty-three bombing raids, heavily laden with hour-by-hour details, were really necessary to develop his theme.

Ironically, in his 1949 essay for *The Atlantic Monthly*, "The Novel of Contemporary History," Hersey presented an aesthetic that established the primacy of character over realistic detail. "Palpable facts," he wrote, "are mortal. . . . The things we remember . . . are emotions and impressions and illusions and images and characters: the elements of fiction." He went on to argue that the aim of the novelist of contemporary history was not to illuminate events, but to illuminate the human beings caught up in the events. This concern with the individual gives Hersey great sensitivity to suffering, a sympathy that, combined with his liberal political views, makes his thematic intentions manifest in nearly all of his works, leading to the accusation that Hersey is too allegorical, too moralistic, and too "meaningful" to be taken seriously as a creative artist. Although some critics hoped he would reverse the general trend of antimoralism and experimentalism in the postmodern fiction of the 1950's and 1960's, the more Hersey tried to escape the reportorial style, the less critically successful his novels became, though they continued to sell well.

A Bell for Adano

The genesis of Hersey's first novel, *A Bell for Adano*, was a journalistic assignment in wartime Italy. During the Sicilian campaign, he visited the seaport of Licata, where he observed the workings of the U.S. military government and filed a story for *Life* titled "AMGOT at Work," which was printed on August 23, 1943, along with photographs. The article described a typical day in the life of an anonymous Italian American major from New York as he tried to cope with the problems of governing the newly liberated town. Obviously impressed by the major's common sense, fairness, and accessibility to the locals, Hersey wrote *A Bell for Adano*, based on the article, within six weeks of the *Life* publication.

A comparison of the article with the book provides an interesting insight into Hersey's work methods in those days. He retained every person in the article and expanded several of the problems. The major became Major Victor Joppolo; Licata became Adano. The central problem of the novel is Joppolo's attempt to find a bell to replace the seven-hundred-year-old bell melted down for bullets by the Nazis. Introducing the unsympathetic character of General Marvin, Hersey was clearly making reference to General George Patton, who was known among reporters for his having slapped two shell-shocked soldiers. Because Joppolo disobeys Marvin's orders, he is reassigned to North Africa after getting Adano its bell. Hersey also invented a romantic interest for Joppolo, an invention that later led to a lawsuit by the original major.

With the exception of *Hiroshima*, *A Bell for Adano* is Hersey's most widely read book. Published by Alfred A. Knopf in early 1944, it was a huge success, mostly because of its representation of the ordinary American as good-hearted, sentimental, and rigorously fair. The book reminded the reader that the war was a struggle to preserve democracy, that government was only as good as the people who govern, and that Americans were better than fascists. Despite all the praise, Hersey understood the effect the political situation of the time was having on the evaluation of his work. In 1944, he was in the Soviet Union and wrote an article on the role of Soviet writers in the war effort, saying, "Not a word is written which is not a weapon." One sees, perhaps, in Hersey's ambivalent feelings about his instantaneous success, a motivation for his continual effort to increase the literary merit of his fiction, an effort that, in the estimate of many readers, worked against his best qualities.

Not all reviewers joined the chorus of praise for Hersey's first novel. Malcolm Cowley said that *A Bell for Adano* should be read as a tract and should not be expected to meet the criteria for a novel as well. Diana Trilling ascribed the book's success to its "folk-idealisms and popular assumptions" that surfaced because of the speed of its composition; she saw "very little writing talent" in the novel. These criticisms, though not entirely without justification, did not diminish Hersey's instant reputation as an important novelist.

Shortly after his assignment to Moscow by *Time-Life* in 1945, Hersey and several other reporters were given a tour of the Eastern front by the Red Army. He saw the ruins of the Warsaw Ghetto, interviewed the survivors of the Lodz Ghetto, and saw signs of the atrocities at Tallinn and Rodogoscz. He knew immediately that he would have to write a novel on what he had seen, though his interviews with survivors of Auschwitz convinced him he could never write about the death camps themselves. Later, he wrote, his time spent in Hiroshima "lent urgency to what had been a vague idea." Another possible source of inspiration for *The Wall* may have come from Hersey's childhood friendship with Israel Epstein, who first interested Hersey in the history of the Jews and later became a staunch supporter of the Chinese revolution, editing the English-language magazine *China Reconstructs*.

Hersey went to the survivors in Eastern Europe and

discovered a wealth of diaries, medical records, and other documentary evidence, most of which was untranslated from the original Polish and Yiddish. He hired Mendel Norbermann and L. Danziger to translate directly from the text onto a wire recorder and did further research himself, reading *The Black Book of Polish Jewry* (1943), the works of Sholom Aleichem, the Old Testament, and the Orthodox prayer book, among other sources. Immersed in the moving experience of listening to the tapes, he began writing and soon found the number of characters, themes, and action had grown far too complicated. Four-fifths of his way through the novel, he scrapped what he had written to retell the story through the point of view of Noach Levinson, chronicler of life in the ghetto from November, 1939, to May, 1943, when the last of the buildings was leveled.

The Wall

Hersey observed that "fiction is not afraid of complexity as journalism is. Fiction can deal with confusion." In *The Wall*, Hersey confronted a multiplicity of emotions, attitudes, customs, and events beyond a journalist's interest. The novel derives its power from this confrontation with the ragged edges of reality, and a number of critics consider it to be Hersey's greatest work. Although many reviewers expressed reservations about the length of the book and its numerous characters, most praised Hersey's compassion and argued that the strong feelings that emerged from the sustained reading of it more than made up for the technical faults of the book. Leslie Fiedler, however, said that *The Wall* lacked the strength of inner truth, depending too heavily on statistical, objective material, and he particularly criticized Hersey's themes as unconvincing.

Although Hersey argued in *The Atlantic Monthly* that fiction allowed the writer to deal with confusion and complexity, most of his novels after *The Wall* were criticized for their overly simplistic, message-bearing, allegorical intent. Hersey's works continued to sell very well, but he never earned the esteem of literary critics. Most critics consider Hersey's work to be without sufficient technical expertise. Some defenders of his work, however, compare it to that of John Dos Passos and argue that his humanistic themes are too valuable to ignore.

J. Madison Davis

Other major works

SHORT FICTION: *Blues*, 1987; *Fling, and Other Stories*, 1990; *Key West Tales*, 1994.

NONFICTION: *Men on Bataan*, 1942; *Into the Valley: A Skirmish of the Marines*, 1943; *Hiroshima*, 1946; *Here to Stay: Studies in Human Tenacity*, 1962; *The Algiers Motel Incident*, 1968; *Letter to the Alumni*, 1970; *The President*, 1975; *Aspects of the Presidency: Truman and Ford in Office*, 1980; *Life Sketches*, 1989.

EDITED TEXTS: *Ralph Ellison: A Collection of Critical Essays*, 1974; *The Writer's Craft*, 1974.

Bibliography

Adamson, Lynda G. *Thematic Guide to the American Novel.* Westport, Conn.: Greenwood Press, 2002. Hersey's *A Bell for Adano* is included in this reader's guide to American novels. Discusses related themes among literary works and compares and contrasts those works.

Fiedler, Leslie. "No! in Thunder." In *The Novel: Modern Essays in Criticism*, edited by Robert Murray Davis. Englewood Cliffs, N.J.: Prentice-Hall, 1969. In discussing authors from his point of view that "art is essentially a moral activity," the controversial Fiedler accuses Hersey of being the author of "The Sentimental Liberal Protest Novel" who fights for "slots on the lists of best sellers" with his "ersatz morality." The essay makes for lively reading at best.

Huse, Nancy L. *The Survival Tales of John Hersey.* New York: Whitston, 1983. An eminently readable and informed study that is useful in understanding the scope and development of Hersey as a writer. Explores the relationship between art and moral or political intentions. Includes extensive notes and a bibliography.

Rosen, Alan. "An Entirely Different Culture: English as Translation in John Hersey's *The Wall.*" In *Sounds of Defiance: The Holocaust, Multilingualism, and the Problem of English.* Lincoln: University of Nebraska Press, 2005. Rosen studies Hersey's novel and other English-language writings about the Holocaust that appeared between World War II and the 1990's. Because English was neither the primary language of the Nazis nor of their victims, English-language works have been deemed marginal to the events of the Holocaust. Rosen examines how this marginality affects English-language Holocaust writing and readers' understanding of the tragedy.

Sanders, David. "John Hersey." In *Contemporary Novelists*, edited by James Vinson. New York: St. Martin's Press, 1982. Covers Hersey's work from wartime journalist to novelist. Cites *The Wall* as his greatest novel and considers him the "least biographical of authors." A rather dense study but helpful in quickly establishing themes in Hersey's writings. Includes a chronology and bibliography.

_______. *John Hersey Revisited*. Boston: Twayne, 1991. Begins with Hersey's career as reporter and novelist, while subsequent chapters discuss his major fiction and nonfiction, including his later stories. Includes a chronology, notes, and a bibliography.

"*The Wall*: John Hersey." In *Holocaust Literature*, edited by John K. Roth. Pasadena, Calif.: Salem Press, 2008. A comprehensive reference source for studies of literature on the Holocaust that includes analysis of Hersey's *The Wall*.

HERMANN HESSE

Born: Calw, Germany; July 2, 1877
Died: Montagnola, Switzerland; August 9, 1962

Principal long fiction

Peter Camenzind, 1904 (English translation, 1961)
Unterm Rad, 1906 (*The Prodigy*, 1957; also known as *Beneath the Wheel*, 1968)
Gertrud, 1910 (*Gertrude and I*, 1915; also known as *Gertrude*, 1955)
Rosshalde, 1914 (English translation, 1970)
Knulp: Drei Geschichten aus dem Leben Knulps, 1915 (*Knulp: Three Tales from the Life of Knulp*, 1971)
Demian, 1919 (English translation, 1923)
Klingsors letzter Sommer, 1920 (*Klingsor's Last Summer*, 1970; includes the three novellas *Klein und Wagner*, *Kinderseele*, and *Klingsors letzter Sommer*)
Siddhartha, 1922 (English translation, 1951)
Der Steppenwolf, 1927 (*Steppenwolf*, 1929)
Narziss und Goldmund, 1930 (*Death and the Lover*, 1932; also known as *Narcissus and Goldmund*, 1968)
Die Morgenlandfahrt, 1932 (*The Journey to the East*, 1956)
Das Glasperlenspiel: Versuch einer Lebensbeschreibung des Magister Ludi Josef Knecht samt Knechts hinterlassenen Schriften, 1943 (*Magister Ludi*, 1949; also known as *The Glass Bead Game*, 1969)

Other literary forms

In 1899, Hermann Hesse (HEHS-uh) published a collection of his poems under the title *Romantische Lieder* (romantic songs), and this was to be the first volume of a truly prodigious literary output. In addition to his longer prose works, Hesse wrote several volumes of poems, fairy tales, and short prose pieces. Hesse was also a prolific letter writer and reviewer: In the course of his lifetime, he reviewed more than twenty-five hundred books, and his correspondence fills many volumes. Hesse's essays, which typically express pacifist views or a humanitarian identification with all humankind, have appeared both as separate volumes and as a part of his massive collected works.

Achievements

By the beginning of World War I, Hermann Hesse had become, in the German-speaking countries of Europe, a solid literary success. His poems, prose vignettes, and novels sold well, and he was tantamount to a habit with German readers by 1914. At the outbreak of the war, however, this situation soon changed in Germany, the result primarily of Hesse's outspoken disparagement of militarism and chauvinism. After the war, Hesse once again became a popular author, especially among younger readers, but this popularity lasted only until the advent of National Socialism, and in 1939, Hesse was officially placed on the list of banned authors, having long since been vilified as a "Jew lover" and unpatriotic draft dodger (from 1890 to 1924, Hesse was a German, not a Swiss, citizen). Throughout and despite this ebb and flow of critical celebration, Hesse continued to write.

After World War II, Hesse was once again sought after—personally and as a writer—as one who could offer moral guidance to a spiritually bankrupt and physically crippled Germany. He became, almost overnight, a celebrity, and was awarded a series of literary prizes, including the Goethe Prize and the Nobel Prize in Literature, both in 1946. Although some still voiced doubts about Hesse as a writer and insisted he was not of the stature of a Thomas Mann, a Bertolt Brecht, or a Franz Kafka, Hesse's popularity in Germany lasted until about 1960, when it rapidly declined. It was at that time, paradoxically enough, that an international "Hessemania" took hold, a kind of exuberant reverence that was particularly strong among disaffected young people in countries as disparate as Sweden, Japan, and the United States. In the United States alone, more than ten million copies of Hesse's works were sold between 1960 and 1970 (when the Hesse wave crested), a literary phenomenon without precedent. Whatever reservations one may have about Hesse, it is a fact that he remains the most widely read German author of all time.

Biography

Hermann Hesse was born on July 2, 1877, in Calw, Germany, the son of Johannes Hesse, a Baltic-born Pietist missionary, and Marie Hesse (née Gundert), the eldest daughter of the missionary and scholar of Indic languages Hermann Gundert. From 1881 to 1886, Hesse lived with his parents in Basel, Switzerland, where his father taught at the Basel Mission School, but in 1886, Hesse returned to Calw to attend elementary school. During the academic year 1890-1891, Hesse was a pupil at the Göppingen Latin school, where he prepared to take the rigorous state examinations for entrance to one of Württemberg's four church schools. He passed, and in the fall of 1891 he was sent to the seminary in Maulbronn. There the young Hesse was desperately unhappy, and after seven months, he fled from the institution, resolving to be "either a writer or nothing at all." After a suicide attempt in June of 1892, Hesse was sent for a few months to a home for retarded children in Stetten. Promising better behavior, he was sent in November to the *Gymnasium* (college-preparatory secondary school) in Cannstatt; once again he ran away, however, and this episode concluded Hesse's formal education.

From 1895 to 1898, Hesse worked as an apprentice in a Tübingen bookstore owned by J. J. Heckenhauer, and from 1899 to 1903, he was employed as a stock clerk in a rare-book store in Basel; it was during the latter years that Hesse began to write in earnest. When his articles and reviews began to appear in the *Allgemeine schweizer Zeitung*, he achieved some measure of local success, which was a great source of encouragement to him. Volumes of poems were published in 1899 and 1902, and by the time *Peter Camenzind* was published in 1904, Hesse had "arrived" as a writer. In this same year, Hesse married his first wife, Maria Bernoulli, a member of an old Basel academic family. The couple moved to an idyllic peasant house in Gaienhofen on Lake Constance, where Hesse worked on his novels, painted, and continued his career as a freelance contributor to numerous journals and newspapers. Hesse's sons Bruno, Heiner, and Martin were all born at Gaienhofen between 1905 and 1911. By the latter year, however, Hesse was restless and felt the need to travel to India with his artist friend Hans Sturzenegger; this journey was to have a profound influence on Hesse for the rest of his life.

From the outbreak of World War I through 1919, Hesse's pacifist articles appeared in German, Swiss, and Austrian newspapers. In 1915, Hesse suffered a nervous breakdown and underwent psychotherapy with J. B. Lang, a student of psychologist Carl Jung, in Sonnmatt, near Lucerne. In 1919, he moved to Montagnola, Ticino, in part to escape the memories of Gaienhofen and his first marriage, which ended with his wife's institutionalization. He lived in Montagnola in the Casa Camuzzi until 1931. A writer's block of some eighteen months precipitated therapy once again, this time with Jung himself, in Küsnacht near Zurich. In 1924, Hesse became a Swiss citizen and married Ruth Wenger, the daughter of a writer; at her request, the unhappy union ended in divorce in 1927. In 1931, Hesse married the art historian Ninon Dolbin. The couple moved into a house on the Collina d'Oro with lifetime right of occupancy; this marriage, at last, was a happy one. From 1939 to 1945, Hesse's works were proscribed in Germany, but in 1946, publication of his works was resumed by Suhrkamp, and it was in this year that Hesse received the Goethe Prize and the Nobel Prize. In 1955, Hesse was awarded the Peace Prize of the German Booksellers' Association, and in 1956, a Hermann Hesse Prize was established by the state of Baden-Württemberg. Hesse died at Montagnola on August 9, 1962.

Hermann Hesse. (© The Nobel Foundation)

Analysis

Despite a literary career that, if measured by quantity of literary output or by size of readership, was enormously successful, Hermann Hesse has not been numbered among the luminaries of twentieth century German literature. There are two primary reasons for this critical assessment: First, Hesse's prose is simply too readable and discursive to be considered profound; second, Hesse's limited and recurring themes remain, in their many novelistic permutations, rather juvenile and solipsistic in nature. This may well explain the fact that Hesse's readership has always been primarily a young one.

Hesse was among the first European writers to undergo psychoanalysis, and it was his fascination with the self that, from the beginning to the end of his literary career, was to remain the wellspring of his inspiration. Hesse's interior life became the stuff of his fiction, and it is this "private mythology" (Hesse's term) that is the organizing principle of his novels. It is in this sense that Hesse is a "psychological" writer, and it has often been pointed out in Hesse scholarship that, to a rare degree and perhaps in too facile a manner, the link between personal life and literary work is transparent. As Christopher Middleton has observed, Hesse can be characterized as a literary "acrobat of self-exploration," one who oscillates between self-esteem and self-disgust, often with an implicit moralizing intent. Hesse is an essentially confessional writer, an inveterate and somewhat didactic self-anatomizer.

The narrative scheme of all of Hesse's novels is essentially triadic: A protagonist's character and background are carefully presented; the disillusioned main character chooses to break with his setting and/or former self in search of a new identity or individuation (Hesse's protagonists are invariably males); and the experiment results in a prodigal's return or in a successful forging of deeper inroads into the self, sometimes even in the adoption of an almost new personality.

Demian, published in 1919, was Hesse's sixth novel, but it can be considered his first major one. It was preceded by the following less distinguished works: *Peter Camenzind*, the story of a Swiss village lad who leaves his native surroundings in search of inner peace and who, after much meandering and a variety of experiences, returns to his ailing father and accepts a village way of life; *Beneath the Wheel*, a somewhat stock *Schulroman*, or school novel, which depicts the extreme authoritarianism, inhumanity, and pressures of a typical German secondary school of the time; *Gertrud*, a *Künstlerroman* (a genre that arose in German literature in the late eighteenth century—the term used to designate any novel with an artist as its protagonist) treating the tribulations of a physically handicapped composer; *Rosshalde*, an autobiographical novel reflecting the breakup of Hesse's marriage to Maria Bernoulli, who suffered from a progressive mental illness; and finally *Knulp*, a novel in three parts that marks the culmination of Hesse's Romantic phase and that narrates the picaresque life and death of its central character.

Demian

Demian, Hesse's first postwar novel, incorporates Hesse's reaction to World War I as well as his psychoanalysis during 1916 and 1917. Both of these experiences had led Hesse to a fundamental reassessment of his life, and this reevaluation finds expression in the bildungsroman, which chronicles (in a first-person narrative) the youth of Emil Sinclair. At the outset of the novel, Sinclair becomes acutely conscious of the essential duality of life, a polarity he notes in the disparity between the safe, moral, ordered world of his home and the dynamic, cruel world outside. The latter is represented by the bully Franz Kromer, from whom Sinclair is rescued by a new boy at school, Max Demian. Demian alleviates Sinclair's moral confusion by telling him of the god Abraxas, in whom good and evil are fused and who represents the highest moral order. Demian also emphasizes the decline of European civilization, predicts its impending doom, and anticipates the advent of a regeneration of the world. With the outbreak of war in 1914, Demian's prophecy comes true. Both Demian and Sinclair are called up, and the latter is wounded. He is brought to a field hospital, where he has a final encounter with Demian, who lies dying; Sinclair is then separated from his mentor forever, but he believes himself to be the inheritor of his friend's personality.

Considered as a whole, therefore, the division of the novel is tripartite: Sinclair goes from a state of initial "light," of childhood innocence and security, to a period of "dark," of doubt and inner torment, to a final internal synthesis of the two antipodes. The novel is somewhat fraught with symbols that are intended to underscore the universality of this sequence; one of the book's central dream images is elucidated in a manner that succinctly captures the dynamics of any process of individuation: "The bird fights its way out of the egg. The egg is the world. Who would be born must first destroy a world." Demian is Sinclair's shaman for this process of destruction (Socrates used the word *daimon* to describe the admonishing inner spirit), a process that Hesse imbues with tension by mixing Nietzschean thought, Christian terminology, and a religious, often parable-like tone. At the end of the novel, Sinclair has internalized Demian, much as the Church Fathers and later Christian authors admonished their readers to internalize Christ. Emil Sinclair is, therefore, now a missionary of the new gospel of Demian (read: Hesse)—namely, that one must be willing to suffer the progressive alienation and pain that result from shedding traditional or inherited strictures and definitions, a necessary divestiture that will ultimately make possible a rejuvenation, an authentic sense of self-identity.

Siddhartha

Siddhartha, Hesse's second major novel and arguably his best-known work, took nearly four years to complete. *Siddhartha* is the product both of Hesse's trip to India in 1911 and of his lifelong fascination with that country's philosophy and religion. At the same time, however, it would be an oversimplification to state (as some critics have done) that this novel is a paean to Indic philosophy or Eastern mysticism, since the implicit admonition of the work is that one must seek one's own way in life and not simply adhere to a prescribed system or path.

The plot of *Siddhartha* exhibits the essential tripartite structure of all Hesse's works, two-section and twelve-chapter divisions notwithstanding: The Brahman's son Siddhartha (whose name means "he who has achieved his aim") leaves his paternal home, has the requisite educative experiences of a bildungsroman protagonist, and finally achieves peace. What makes *Siddhartha* such an atypical and successful "novel of education" are its Eastern setting and its complementary stylistic features, the latter signifying a level of technical originality and subtlety Hesse was never again to achieve. Feeling restless, Siddhartha forsakes his home and the teachings of Brahmanism and, with his friend Govinda, becomes a total ascetic. Still unsatisfied, he considers the teachings of Buddha but ultimately departs from him, leaving Govinda behind. As an alternative to his previous existence, Siddhartha seeks a life of the senses; the courtesan Kamala teaches him the art of love, and he acquires a great deal of wealth. After a time, however, he comes to feel that this surfeit of sensual pleasures is robbing him of his soul, and he takes sudden leave of this life and of Kamala, unaware that she is pregnant. In despair and on the verge of suicide, he encounters the wise ferryman Vasudeva, from whom he learns "the secrets of the river," the simultaneity, unity, and timelessness of all that is:

> This stone is stone: it is also animal, it is also God, it is also Buddha. I love and venerate it not because it might someday become this or that—but because it has long been all these things and always will be.

After Siddhartha has spent twelve years at the river, Kamala unexpectedly arrives with their son, whereupon she is bitten by a snake and dies. Siddhartha's son rejects his father's love and teaching—just as Siddhartha himself rejected his father many years earlier—but the protagonist overcomes his anguish and loss with the help of the river. Vasudeva dies, Siddhartha becomes the ferryman in his place, and the narrative concludes with the reunion of Siddhartha and Govinda.

Like *Demian, Siddhartha* is meant to carry universal implications. The protagonists in both novels are stylized figures whose lives and personalities are only episodically sketched, since what was important to Hesse was less their individuality as literary personae than what they embodied. Both stories possess only a modicum of realistic narrative, and both central figures represent the path of individuality that, Hesse was convinced, must be chosen by all self-seekers. Demian's Abraxas and Siddhartha's river are simply narrative means to this end, symbols of the conflux of opposites, the harmony one experiences with self and all existence in a heightened state of self-awareness. As Hesse stated in his diary of 1920, "Nirvana, as I understand it, is the liberating step back behind the *principium individuationis*." Artistically, however, *Demian* and *Siddhartha* are very different. Unlike *Demian*—and indeed, unlike the several major novels of Hesse to follow–*Siddhartha* maintains a stylistic simplicity and an extraordinary harmony of form and substance that Hesse was never again to capture. The book's initial paragraph reveals, even in translation, much of the stylistic genius of *Siddhartha*:

> In the shade of the house, in the sun of the river bank by the boats, in the shade of the Sal forest, in the shade of the fig tree Siddhartha grew up, the handsome son of the Brahman, the young falcon, along with Govinda, his friend, the son of the Brahman.

The paratactic repetitions—incantatory, alliterative, and often threefold in nature—give the work an almost liturgical quality that is consonant with the novel's theme and setting and that exerts a subliminal but obviously well-calculated effect on the reader. Hesse's following work was to be a radical departure in terms of both style and narrative tack.

STEPPENWOLF

Steppenwolf, published in 1927, is certainly Hesse's most unorthodox novel, one that Mann compared to James Joyce's *Ulysses* (1922) and André Gide's *Les Faux-monnayeurs* (1925; *The Counterfeiters*, 1927) in experimental daring. Like these novels, Hesse's work met with a great deal of criticism, a fact that is easily explained in the light of the demands that these narratives place on their readers. Although it is in places essentially surrealistic and is hence somewhat difficult to recapitulate adequately, *Steppenwolf* does evidence Hesse's typical three-part structure: a preliminary or introductory segment, a somewhat realistic central section, and a final part chronicling the protagonist's experiences in a "Magic Theater."

An unnamed and self-described "bourgeois, orderly person" functions as the author of an introduction to the reflections of Harry Haller, whose first-person jottings he is editing. This editor also articulates the two poles of existence, the inner tension of Harry Haller, namely, his fundamental dichotomy as both "wolf" and "bourgeois." The schizophrenic protagonist, a scholarly aesthete and conformist by day but at night an outsider who despises society and its values, describes himself as a living dualism: "I don't know why it is, but I—the homeless Steppenwolf and lonely hater of the petty bourgeois world—I always live in proper middle-class houses." Haller's ruminations on his rootless existence are interrupted, however, by the interjection of a "Tract of the Steppenwolf," a booklet that he has mysteriously acquired while on one of his frequent nocturnal walks. This tract, prefaced by the motto "only for madmen," distinguishes between three levels of existence: that of the Bourgeois, that of the Immortals (the highest plane, which transcends all polarities), and that of the Steppenwolf, a level midway between the first two. In describing a particular Steppenwolf called Harry, the document suggests that he abandon polarity as a life-ordering principle and simply affirm all that is as good, and do so with "a sublime wisdom that can only be realized through humor." Harry Haller is unable to comply, however, and he soon takes up with several sympathizers. Hermine, an oracular prostitute, and Pablo, a drug-using saxophone player, show Haller that there are others of his ilk who choose not to conform to society and yet are happy among themselves. Finally, Harry enters into the "Magic Theater" alluded to in the "Tract" and announced earlier in the novel as well. In this penny arcade of the mind, he sheds the final vestiges of his bourgeois personality by means of a series of surreal, drug-induced experiences. The novel concludes on a note of cautious optimism, with Haller projecting that he will someday "play the game of figures better," that he will someday "learn how to laugh."

As Hesse made obvious by the choice of Harry Haller as his protagonist's name, *Steppenwolf* is a highly autobiographical work. Haller's physiognomy, habits, and tastes are Hesse's, as is his basic psychological dilemma. Hesse at the time of the novel's composition was a fifty-year-old man looking inward and outward with little satisfaction. This accounts for the self-laceration as well as the cultural pessimism of *Steppenwolf*, and such disharmony and negativity reflect an inner relapse on the part of the author of the placid *Siddhartha*. Whether Hesse himself indulged in the erotic and chemical adventures of his protagonist is not known and, ultimately, is of little consequence. Certain, however, is the fact that Hesse suffered a good deal of censure as a result of these elements of the book, a fact that distressed him greatly and caused him to compose and publish in 1928 a poetic postlude to the novel, titled *Krisis*, a candid personal account of his intention in writing *Steppenwolf* and an assessment of the literary realization of this intention.

Like those of many of Hesse's novels, the ending of *Steppenwolf* is abrupt and unsatisfactory. The concept of humor as a tool for rising above inner and outer tensions seems an inadequate solution for Haller's problems, and one senses that this is a very forced conclusion. This feeling is reinforced as well by the amazing formal pendulations of Hesse's novels: *Demian* employs psychological symbolism, *Siddhartha* utilizes psychological exoticism, and *Steppenwolf* uses psychological fantasy and even hallucination in order to delineate the same essential problems (How does one arrive at any true self-definition? How is one to reconcile inner polarities, the flesh and the spirit? What is the artist's place in society?) via a variety of expressive modes. If the endings are often truncated or lacking in aesthetic closure, it is because these individual "fragments of a long confession" (Hesse's phrase) represent only one phase, one segment of a process that was to continue. It is no surprise, therefore, that Hesse chose in his next novel yet another narrative format with which to allegorize his dualistic dilemmas.

NARCISSUS AND GOLDMUND

Much like *Siddhartha, Narcissus and Goldmund* can be viewed as a lull following a storm. Hesse himself described *Narcissus and Goldmund* as an essentially escapist tale, and it is the novel about which his critics are most divided. Joseph Mileck, for example, considers it Hesse's finest work, whereas Theodore Ziolkowski flatly states that it is his "most imperfect" work; many critics find the story cloying and regard the novel as a whole as highbrow kitsch.

The names of the two protagonists are symbolic: Narcissus represents the world of the spirit—in this case, the medieval monastery—and is a prototype of the introverted, reflective, self-preoccupied individual; Goldmund (golden mouth) is an artistic extrovert who personifies the world of nature, of the flesh. Hesse once again presents the reader with types rather than with flesh-and-blood characters. Narcissus is the mentor of Goldmund in a monastic school called Mariabronn, but it soon becomes evident that the latter is rather unsuited for a celibate life. He leaves the monastery and leads a life replete with varied experiences and love affairs, all of which lead him closer to his artistic crystallization of the "pole of nature," exemplified in his mind by the image of his mother and eventually by Eve, the "primal mother."

Related to these love-thematics is the stark reality and insuperable dominance of death, which Goldmund seeks to conquer by love. Both protagonists discuss the topic of death and confront it, each in his own manner: Narcissus seeks to exist in a timeless realm of the spirit that in itself is a preparation for death, while Goldmund, hearing in his heart but dreading "the wild song of death," abandons himself to life and love. Sensing this to be an unsatisfactory modus vivendi in the light of the transitory nature of everything human, yet unable to accept Narcissus's way as his own, Goldmund eventually discovers in art his answer to death: "When, as artists, we create images or, as thinkers, seek laws and formulate thoughts, we do so in order to save something from the Great Dance of Death, to establish something that has a longer duration than we ourselves." Goldmund dies in peace, having returned to the monastery not as an ascetic, but as an artist.

The underlying idea or conception of art personified in Goldmund is Hesse's own, at least in that it represents his personal ideal. That this ideal is in essence a Romantic one is clear if one outlines the narrative trellis on which the Goldmund character is strung: He represents the vital vagrant who, by dint of a wealth of contacts and experiences, is impelled (if only temporarily) to recede from the din of life in order to internalize, incubate, and finally express what he has encountered in the Orphic creation of a new and timeless work of art. It is in a certain sense true, therefore, that the Hesse who published from 1898 to 1930 never went beyond Romanticism, beyond this conception of the self as the font of meaning and progenitor of all art. This explains as well why realistic fiction was of little importance to Hesse; if literary art is conceived of as an array of self-reflecting mirrors, then exterior reality can be of only secondary or even tertiary significance. It is to Hesse's credit that he came to see that such self-preoccupation was tantamount to irresponsible self-paralysis, and that this *l'art pour l'art* approach was abandoned in his final novel.

Shortly after Hesse's *Narcissus and Goldmund*, his *The Journey to the East* appeared, in 1932. The novel is another experiment in narrative technique and setting and is perhaps the most esoteric of Hesse's works. In many ways, this story of "H. H."—of his acceptance into an Order, his participation in a "journey to the East," and his defection and eventual return to the fold—prefigures the dynamics and thematics of Hesse's final novel, *The Glass Bead Game*, published in 1943. The latter took eleven years to compose and is considered by many critics to be Hesse's most substantive novel, his magnum opus, which recapitulates but also modifies all that preceded it.

The Glass Bead Game

The Glass Bead Game is a modified bildungsroman about Josef Knecht, whose surname means "servant," and is seen by some critics as Hesse's response to the quintessential German novels of education, Johann Wolfgang von Goethe's Wilhelm Meister novels (the surname meaning "master"). Hesse's novel contains three chief divisions: an introduction describing the history of the "glass bead game," characterized as "the quintessence of intellectuality and art, the sublime cult, the *unio mystica* of all separate members of the *universitas litterarum*"; the middle section, which outlines the life of Josef Knecht; and finally an appendix, consisting of some of Knecht's supposed posthumous papers.

The novel is set in the twenty-fourth century in a "pedagogical province" called Castalia, in which, in at least quasi-monastic fashion, an elite group dedicates itself to the life of the spirit and the highly developed glass bead game. The latter has evolved in the course of time from a relatively simple game played on an abacus frame into a complex interdisciplinary exercise combining quantitative and theoretical knowledge from various disciplines with symbology and meditation. Knecht becomes a master game-player, the *magister ludi* and head of the Order. Gradually, however, inspired partly by his conversations with a brilliant Benedictine monk by the name of Pater Jakobus and partly by his own nagging feelings of responsibility to the world at large, Knecht's reservations about Castalia and its life of utter aestheticism grow to the point that he resigns his post and leaves the rarefied realm he seemed destined from his very youth to lead. Three days after doing so, however, he drowns by accident in an icy mountain lake.

Hesse's final novel is many interesting things, not the

least of which is a very clever roman à clef, the name games and onomastics of which can occupy one inclined to puzzle over them for some time. More significantly, however, the work represents a personal breakthrough for Hesse, since in Knecht one is at last presented with a Hessean protagonist who attempts to overcome his paralytic self-enclosure and accept some notion of social responsibility. Theodore Ziolkowski has suggested that this gesture, represented clearly by Knecht's decision to leave Castalia and commit himself to something practical, was not Hesse's original intention, but that the imminent outbreak of war forced Hesse to abandon his initial literary and aesthetic ideal while writing the second section of the novel. This is more than plausible, and it would explain as well the book's narrative shift regarding the depiction of Castalia.

A stylistic comparison of *The Glass Bead Game* with Hesse's earlier works reveals that language has been given less attention in this final novel, the result in part of the work's heavy freight of theoretical and philosophical ideas (ranging from a theory of music to intellectual concerns of various kinds). Indeed, Josef Knecht is even less a flesh-and-blood persona than are Hesse's customary protagonists.

As to the glass bead game itself—described in length but always in somewhat nebulous terms—it appears clear that it symbolizes the attempt on the part of some to achieve an integrated synthesis of what is good or salvageable from the fragmented debris of modern civilization. In this respect, Hesse's last novel marks a fitting conclusion to a lifelong quest for spiritual wholeness.

N. J. Meyerhofer

Other major works

SHORT FICTION: *Eine Stunde hinter Mitternacht*, 1899; *Hinterlassene Schriften und Gedichte von Hermann Lauscher*, 1901; *Diesseits: Erzählungen*, 1907; *Nachbarn: Erzählungen*, 1908; *Umwege: Erzählungen*, 1912; *Aus Indien*, 1913; *Am Weg*, 1915; *Schön ist die Jugend*, 1916; *Märchen*, 1919 (*Strange News from Another Star, and Other Tales*, 1972); *Piktors Verwandlungen: Ein Märchen*, 1925; *Die Nürnberger Reise*, 1927; *Weg nach Innen*, 1931; *Kleine Welt: Erzählungen*, 1933; *Stunden im Garten: Eine Idylle*, 1936; *Traumfährte: Neue Erzählungen und Märchen*, 1945 (*The War Goes On*, 1971); *Späte Prosa*, 1951; *Beschwörungen*, 1955; *Gesammelte Schriften*, 1957; *Stories of Five Decades*, 1972.

POETRY: *Romantische Lieder*, 1899; *Unterwegs: Gedichte*, 1911; *Musik des Einsamen: Neue Gedichte*, 1915; *Gedichte des Malers*, 1920; *Ausgewählte Gedichte*, 1921; *Krisis*, 1928; *Trost der Nacht: Neue Gedichte*, 1929; *Vom Baum des Lebens*, 1934; *Neue Gedichte*, 1937; *Die Gedichte*, 1942; *Späte Gedichte*, 1946; *Poems*, 1970.

NONFICTION: *Boccaccio*, 1904; *Franz von Assisi*, 1904; *Zarathustras Wiederkehr: Ein Wort an die deutsche Jugend von einem Deutschen*, 1919; *Blick ins Chaos*, 1920 (*In Sight of Chaos*, 1923); *Betrachtungen*, 1928; *Kleine Betrachtungen*, 1941; *Krieg und Frieden: Betrachtungen zu Krieg und Politik seit dem Jahr 1914*, 1946 (revised 1949; *If the War Goes On . . . Reflections on War and Politics*, 1971); *Hermann Hesse: Essays*, 1970; *Autobiographical Writings*, 1972; *My Belief: Essays on Life and Art*, 1974; *Reflections*, 1974.

MISCELLANEOUS: *Gesammelte Dichtungen*, 1952 (6 volumes).

Bibliography

Bloom, Harold, ed. *Hermann Hesse*. Philadelphia: Chelsea House, 2003. Collection of essays provides interpretations of Hesse's works, including the novels *Steppenwolf*, *The Glass Bead Game*, and *Narcissus and Goldmund*. Thomas Mann's introduction to *Demian* is also reprinted in this volume.

Boulby, Mark. *Hermann Hesse: His Mind and Art*. Ithaca, N.Y.: Cornell University Press, 1967. Presents an extensive examination of Hesse's novels from the perspective that definable, basic, and yet complex structural patterns are revealed in a survey of all the longer works. Underlying the examination is the assertion that the pivotal point of Hesse's work is his universalization of a personal conflict in artistic from. Provides in-depth analysis of each of the major novels, including the earlier *Peter Camenzind* and *Beneath the Wheel*.

Brink, Andrew. "Hermann Hesse and Bisexuality." In *Obsession and Culture: A Study of Sexual Obsession in Modern Fiction*. Madison, N.J.: Fairleigh Dickinson University Press, 1996. Chapter on Hesse's work is part of a larger study of twentieth century authors that focuses on the argument that male sexual obsession is a primary driving cultural force.

Field, George Wallis. *Hermann Hesse*. New York: Twayne, 1970. Concentrates on Hesse's novels, integrating the works' themes with biographical information and outlining some of the historical and literary influences on the author, such as the tradition of the bildungsroman.

Mileck, Joseph. *Hermann Hesse: Life and Art*. Berkeley: University of California Press, 1978. Comprehensive biography emphasizes the reflective aspects of Hesse's life and art while delineating the nature of his creative impetus and process. Presents extensive background on Hesse's many novels, tales, fantasies, essays, and works in other genres. Includes a German/English index of Hesse's works.

Richards, David G. *Exploring the Divided Self: Hermann Hesse's "Steppenwolf" and Its Critics*. Columbia, S.C.: Camden House, 1996. Traces the critical writing about *Steppenwolf* from the book's initial publication through the 1990's; the novel was a disappointment to many when it first appeared, but it later came to be considered one of Hesse's finest achievements. Includes bibliographical references and index.

_______. *The Hero's Quest for the Self: An Archetypal Approach to Hesse's "Demian" and Other Novels*. Lanham, Md.: University Press of America, 1987. Applies the theories of Carl Jung to a discussion of Hesse's novels. Asserts that Hesse anticipated Jung and that his works serve as "poeticized" models of Jungian concepts. Explores issues central to Hesse's work, the conflicts in which deal primarily with German dualism and the need for self-integration.

Robertson, Ritchie. "Gender Anxiety and the Shaping of the Self in Some Modernist Writers: Musil, Hesse, Hoffmannsthal, Jahnn." In *The Cambridge Companion to the Modern German Novel*, edited by Graham Bartram. New York: Cambridge University Press, 2004. Hesse's novels are among the works examined in this introductory survey of German-language novels from the late nineteenth and early twentieth centuries. Includes chronology and bibliography.

Rose, Ernst. *Faith from the Abyss: Hermann Hesse's Way from Romanticism to Modernity*. New York: New York University Press, 1965. Takes a biographical approach to Hesse's works, contending that many of them "read almost like a spiritual autobiography" and that they illustrate "the reality of an existential problem" raised by Hesse in his artistic response to Romanticism. This problem—the nature of reality—emphasizes Hesse's concern with a means by which to resolve polarities into a coherent worldview.

Tusken, Lewis W. *Understanding Hermann Hesse: The Man, His Myth, His Metaphor*. Columbia: University of South Carolina Press, 1998. Presents analysis of Hesse's work aimed at students and general readers. Focuses on Hesse's novels, discussing their common themes and metaphors, and provides biographical information in order to describe the confessional nature of Hesse's work.

Ziolkowski, Theodore, ed. *Hesse: A Collection of Critical Essays*. Englewood Cliffs, N.J.: Prentice-Hall, 1973. Collection of essays on Hesse's work includes an introduction that discusses the phenomenon of "Hessemania," the cultlike response to Hesse's works, and the crossing-over of Hesse's icons to the popular culture. Provides an overview of the critical reactions to Hesse's works while outlining major reasons for their popularity. Includes ten essays by renowned writers such as Martin Buber and Thomas Mann.

Zipes, Jack. "Hermann Hesse's Fairy Tales and the Pursuit of Home." In *When Dreams Came True: Classical Fairy Tales and their Tradition*. 2d ed. New York: Routledge, 2007. Examines how Hesse used the form of the fairy tale in his writing and discusses some of the fantasy-like elements in Hesse's fiction.

PATRICIA HIGHSMITH

Born: Fort Worth, Texas; January 19, 1921
Died: Locarno, Switzerland; February 4, 1995
Also known as: Mary Patricia Plangman; Claire Morgan

Principal long fiction

Strangers on a Train, 1950
The Price of Salt, 1952 (as Claire Morgan; also published as *Carol*)
The Blunderer, 1954 (also known as *Lament for a Lover*, 1956)
The Talented Mr. Ripley, 1955
Deep Water, 1957
A Game for the Living, 1958
This Sweet Sickness, 1960
The Cry of the Owl, 1962
The Glass Cell, 1964
The Two Faces of January, 1964
The Story-Teller, 1965 (also known as *A Suspension of Mercy*, 2001)
Those Who Walk Away, 1967
The Tremor of Forgery, 1969
Ripley Under Ground, 1970
A Dog's Ransom, 1972
Ripley's Game, 1974
Edith's Diary, 1977
The Boy Who Followed Ripley, 1980
People Who Knock on the Door, 1983
The Mysterious Mr. Ripley, 1985 (includes *The Talented Mr. Ripley*, *Ripley Under Ground*, and *Ripley's Game*)
Found in the Street, 1986
Ripley Under Water, 1991
Small g: A Summer Idyll, 1995
The Complete Ripley Novels, 2008

Other literary forms

In addition to her novels, Patricia Highsmith wrote several collections of short stories, including *The Snail-Watcher, and Other Stories* (1970), *The Animal-Lover's Book of Beastly Murder* (1975), *Slowly, Slowly in the Wind* (1979), *The Black House* (1981), *Mermaids on the Golf Course, and Other Stories* (1985), and *Tales of Natural and Unnatural Catastrophes* (1987). In 1966, she published a how-to book, *Plotting and Writing Suspense Fiction* (reprinted and expanded three times by the author), which provides a good introduction to her work. She also wrote one children's book, *Miranda the Panda Is on the Veranda* (1958), in collaboration with a friend, Doris Sanders. Although Highsmith wrote prizewinning short stories, she is best known for her novels, especially the Ripley series.

Achievements

Patricia Highsmith was honored several times. For her first published story, "The Heroine," which was written while she was a student at Barnard College, she was included in the *O. Henry Prize Stories of 1946*. The novel *The Talented Mr. Ripley* was awarded the Grand Prix de Littérature Policière in 1957 and the Edgar Allan Poe Scroll from the Mystery Writers of America. For *The Two Faces of January* she received the Award of the Crime Writers Association of Great Britain.

Biography

Patricia Highsmith's mother, father, and stepfather were all commercial artists. She was born Mary Patricia Plangman a few months after her mother, Mary Coates, and father, Jay Bernard Plangman, were divorced, and she lived the first six years of her life with her grandmother in the house where she was born, in Fort Worth, Texas.

At the age of six, she went to New York City to join her mother and stepfather in a small apartment in Greenwich Village. She later went to high school in New York and on to Barnard College. Life with quarreling parents made her unhappy, but she did inherit from them a love of painting, and she considered it as a vocation. She ultimately decided to be a writer because she could explore moral and intellectual questions in more depth by writing novels than by painting. Highsmith enjoyed early success with a short story she wrote in college that was later published in *Harper's Bazaar* and included in the *O. Henry Prize Stories of 1946*.

Attracted to travel early, Highsmith set out for Mexico in 1943 to write a book. With only part of it written, she ran out of money and returned to New York, where she continued living with her parents and writing comics in the day and fiction at night and on the weekends to save enough money for a trip to Europe. She left for Europe in 1949, after finishing her first novel, *Strangers on a Train*, which was bought and made into a film by Alfred Hitchcock.

The next few years saw Highsmith traveling between Europe and New York and writing novels and short stories that found publishers in New York and throughout Europe. After several visits, she moved permanently to Europe, first to England for four years, then to France (to a small town near Fontainebleau, which became the setting for later Ripley stories), and finally to Switzerland in 1982. When she died in a hospital in Locarno in 1995, she left an estate of more than five million dollars. Highsmith was a solitary figure, shunning reporters and publicity. She lived alone with her favorite cat, Charlotte, working in her garden and painting. She revisited the United States but never returned to live.

Analysis

Patricia Highsmith remains less a household name than other, more traditional crime novelists largely because she wrote about good men who turn bad and bad men who escape punishment. A moral compass is missing in her work, and guilt is hard to assign. She is better known and more interesting to critics in Europe, especially in England and Germany, than in her own country, which she left permanently in 1963. In a final tribute at the time of her death in 1995, critic Michael Tolkin wrote that the Hitchcock adaptation of her first published novel, *Strangers on a Train*, in which only the psychopath is permitted to kill, "is a perfect example of the kind of American cultural repression that I like to imagine as one of the reasons she left."

In Europe, too, her heroes who "kill not without feeling," says critic Susannah Clapp in *London Review of Books*, "but without fear of reprisal" have brought cries of disapproval. In a 1965 review of *The Glass Cell*, one critic declared, "There are not many nastier fiction worlds than Patricia Highsmith's and soon they sicken." Margharita Laski wrote in *The Listener*, "I used to be the only person I knew who loathed Patricia Highsmith's work for its inhumanity to man, but our numbers are growing." On the other hand, a number of respected crime writers, including Julian Symons, consider her among the best crime writers and at least one of her novels a work of true literature. American novelist and critic Gore Vidal wrote, "She is one of our greatest modernist writers."

Highsmith's killers or near killers are middle class and intelligent; they are usually artists or professionals, and they often have sophisticated tastes. In a 1980 interview with Diana Cooper-Clark, Highsmith explained why this is so. Since she believed that most criminals are not particularly intelligent, they do not interest her very much. She chose middle-class characters because she thought writers can write successfully only about their own social milieus. Since "standards of morality come from the society around," pleasant, well-mannered men often commit murder in her fictional world: "The contrast between respectability and murderous thoughts is bound to turn up in most of my books." The five novels

Patricia Highsmith. (© Hope Curtis)

about Tom Ripley focus on an otherwise nice young man who gets away with murder. Critics have analyzed this unlikely killer in considerable detail.

The 1980's and 1990's saw a renewed interest in Highsmith as a lesbian writer. In most of her novels women are not the active center; they do not commit murder. When asked about this, she explained that she found men more violent by nature than women. Women seemed passive to her, less likely to create action. Her women characters are among her least admirable. They often seem present only as decor or as a means of furthering the actions of the male characters. There are three novels that represent a degree of exception to this pattern. *The Price of Salt* (later published as *Carol*) is the story of two women who fall in love, and the novel—"a very up-beat, pro-lesbian book," according to its editor, Barbara Grier—has a relatively happy ending. *Edith's Diary*, the only other Highsmith novel with a woman at the center, was viewed more as a commentary of American political and social life in the 1960's than as a suspense novel. Her last book, *Small g: A Summer Idyll*, about gays, lesbians, and the human immunodeficiency virus (HIV), could not find an American publisher and was published in England to mixed reviews. Feminists find little support in Highsmith's work. Feminist critic Odette L'Henry Evans observed in a 1990 essay that the women are not loving wives and mothers, and it is often the father who loves and cares for the child.

If Highsmith has a philosophy, it could best be described as a negative one, difficult to identify except as a rebellion against the moral status quo. In spite of the disturbing and pessimistic conclusion that readers must draw from her work—that justice is seldom truly important in human affairs, that it is a "manmade conceit," in the words of critic Brooks Peters—she is recognized as a crime writer who has important things to say about human nature and who says them uncommonly well.

Russell Harrison, in the first full-length study of Highsmith, categorized most of the best known of her novels. The early novels may generally be considered stories of American domestic life: *Deep Water*, *This Sweet Sickness*, and *The Cry of the Owl*. In the 1960's, according to Harrison, Highsmith began to examine U.S. foreign relations and political and social issues in *The Tremor of Forgery*, *A Dog's Ransom*, and *Edith's Diary*. Finally, he examines the gay and lesbian novels, *The Price of Salt* and *Small g: A Summer Idyll*. Two important novels he does not discuss are *The Glass Cell* and *The Two Faces of January*, which might be grouped with the social-issue novels.

The Talented Mr. Ripley

The Talented Mr. Ripley was the Highsmith's favorite book, and Tom Ripley is her most popular character. Highsmith once said that writing fiction was a game to her and that she had to be amused to keep writing. The game here is keeping Ripley out of the hands of the police, and much of the fun lies in allowing him to live high on his ill-gotten gains. "I've always had a lurking liking for those who flout the law," Highsmith once admitted. Critic Tolkin described Ripley aptly as "a small-time American crook who moves to Europe and kills his way to happiness." Highsmith was at odds with herself about Ripley's true value. He stands in sharp contrast to stereotypical morality, which is often hypocritical, but he also has almost no conscience and so is, in Highsmith's words, "a little bit sick in the head."

Dickie Greenleaf, a rich young man who has left home and his disapproving parents to become a painter in Italy, is Ripley's first victim. Ripley arrives on the scene, sent by the father to persuade Dickie to return. Ripley decides that he would rather stay and share Dickie's lazy expatriate life. When Dickie becomes angry about Ripley's imitation of him, Ripley decides to eliminate the real Dickie and take his place. Ripley's real talent is this imitation—he once thought of becoming an actor—and he succeeds in deceiving everyone until Freddie, an old friend of Dickie, becomes suspicious. It is necessary for Ripley to murder again in order not to be unmasked. Freddie is killed, but the police suspect Tom/Dickie of the crime. So Dickie is twice murdered, and Tom Ripley is reborn—along with a fake will in which Dickie leaves him everything. One critic finds this protean man a very contemporary type, one often found in serious literature. Ripley is indeed a classic of his kind, and while Highsmith's touch is almost playful, some readers shudder at Ripley's indifference to his own ghastly crimes. As the Ripley stories multiplied, some readers and critics alike worried that Highsmith had grown too fond of her talented but diabolical hero who is in some ways a monster.

The Glass Cell

The dreariness of the style of *The Glass Cell* is the dreariness of its prison atmosphere. There is very little relief from the monotony of wrongfully convicted Philip Carter's life in prison, and there are no scenes of the high life to enjoy. In *Plotting and Writing Suspense Fiction*, Highsmith provides a case history of how three versions of this novel came to be written.

The idea came from a true story, but the story changed as Philip Carter became a Highsmith protagonist. To be interesting, he had to become more active as the novel evolved, and so he kills not once but three times. The alibi he concocts for the murders is coldly calculated; prison has made a ruthless man of him. Highsmith says that she wanted Carter to go free after he commits two postprison murders because he had suffered so much in prison. He had been strung up by his thumbs by a sadistic guard, and he suffers continual physical pain in his hands. The police suspect him of murder but can prove nothing, and Carter and his wife and son are free to go on with their lives together. Highsmith delivers her own kind of justice to a once-innocent man unjustly punished by the courts.

Lucy Golsan

Other major works

SHORT FICTION: *The Snail-Watcher, and Other Stories*, 1970 (also known as *Eleven*); *Kleine Geschichten für Weiberfeinde*, 1974 (*Little Tales of Misogyny*, 1977); *The Animal-Lover's Book of Beastly Murder*, 1975; *Slowly, Slowly in the Wind*, 1979; *The Black House*, 1981; *Mermaids on the Golf Course, and Other Stories*, 1985; *Tales of Natural and Unnatural Catastrophes*, 1987; *The Selected Stories of Patricia Highsmith*, 2001; *Nothing that Meets the Eye: The Uncollected Stories of Patricia Highsmith*, 2002.

NONFICTION: *Plotting and Writing Suspense Fiction*, 1966.

CHILDREN'S LITERATURE: *Miranda the Panda Is on the Veranda*, 1958 (with Doris Sanders).

Bibliography

Bloom, Harold, ed. *Lesbian and Bisexual Fiction Writers*. Philadelphia: Chelsea House, 1997. Highsmith is one of the writers included in this overview of lesbian, gay, and bisexual fiction writers. Contains a brief biography, excerpts from reviews and criticism, and a bibliography.

Brophy, Brigid. "Highsmith." In *Don't Never Forget: Collected Views and Reviews*. New York: Henry Holt, 1966. Brophy compares Highsmith's artistic achievements to those of Georges Simenon to argue that Highsmith's crime novels, with their moral ambiguity, "transcend the limits of the genre while staying strictly inside its rules."

Cochran, David. "'Some Torture That Perversely Eased': Patricia Highsmith and the Everyday Schizophrenia of American Life." In *America Noir: Underground Writers and Filmmakers of the Postwar Era*. Washington, D.C.: Smithsonian Institution Press, 2000. In his study of underground writers and filmmakers, Cochran describes how Highsmith's amoral Mr. Ripley and other aspects of her fiction challenged the pieties of the 1950's.

Dupont, Joan. "Criminal Pursuits." *The New York Times Magazine*, June 12, 1988. Notes that although Highsmith is a celebrity in the rest of the world, she is relatively unknown in her native United States; suggests that because Highsmith has lived abroad and has never been in the United States to promote her books, she has never developed a strong link with publishers or readers. Others believe it is because her books are not clearly classifiable as thrillers, mysteries, or literature.

Harrison, Russell. *Patricia Highsmith*. New York: Twayne, 1997. This first book-length study of Highsmith in English explores the aesthetic, philosophical, and sociopolitical dimensions of her writing. Harrison focuses on Highsmith's novels, including her gay- and lesbian-focused novels.

Highsmith, Patricia. "Not Thinking with the Dishes." *Writer's Digest* 62 (October, 1983). Highsmith says she follows no set rules for story writing; she begins with a theme, an unusual circumstance or a situation of surprise or coincidence, and creates the narrative around it. Her focus is on what is happening in the minds of her protagonists, and her settings are always ones she knows personally.

Mawer, Noel. *A Critical Study of the Fiction of Patricia Highsmith—From the Psychological to the Political.*

Lewiston, N.Y.: Edwin Mellen Press, 2004. An examination of Highsmith's fiction, including the Ripley novels, *The Glass Cell*, and *A Game for the Living*. Although some of Highsmith's novels can be categorized as mystery and detective fiction, Mawer argues that many of her novels explore "the mystery of character," or, how people create their own identities by interacting with others in particular situations.

Summers, Claude J., ed. *Gay and Lesbian Literary Heritage: A Reader's Companion to the Writers and Their Works, from Antiquity to the Present*. Rev. ed. New York: Routledge, 2002. This expanded edition of a book originally published in 1995 includes an excellent essay by Gina Macdonald on Highsmith's life and work to the time of her death in 1995.

Symons, Julian. *Mortal Consequences: A History from the Detective Story to the Crime Novel*. New York: Harper & Row, 1972. Symons calls Highsmith "the most important crime novelist" of her time, a fine writer whose tricky plot devices are merely starting points "for profound and subtle character studies," particularly of likable figures attracted by crime and violence. Highsmith's imaginative power gives her criminal heroes a "terrifying reality" amid carefully chosen settings, and she is at her best describing subtle, deadly games of pursuit.

Tolkin, Michael. "In Memory of Patricia Highsmith." *Los Angeles Times Book Review*, February 12, 1995. A tribute to Highsmith as "our best expatriate writer since Henry James" and an excellent analysis of why her heroes, especially Ripley, are not appreciated in the United States.

Wilson, Andrew. *Beautiful Shadow: A Life of Patricia Highsmith*. New York: Bloomsbury, 2004. The first biography of Highsmith, chronicling the author's troubled life and tracing the roots of her fiction to the works of Edgar Allan Poe, noir, and existentialism. Winner of the 2004 Edgar Award for Best Critical/Biographical Work.

JAMAKE HIGHWATER

Born: Place unknown; 1930's(?)
Died: Los Angeles, California; June 3, 2001
Also known as: J. Marks; Jay Marks; Jack Marks

Principal long fiction

Anpao: An American Indian Odyssey, 1977
Journey to the Sky, 1978
The Sun, He Dies, 1980
Legend Days, 1984
The Ceremony of Innocence, 1985
Eyes of Darkness, 1985
I Wear the Morning Star, 1986
Kill Hole, 1992
Dark Legend, 1994
The Ghost Horse Cycle, 1997 (includes *Legend Days*, *The Ceremony of Innocence*, and *I Wear the Morning Star*)

Other literary forms

Published under the name J. Marks, the early works of Jamake Highwater include *Rock and Other Four Letter Words* (1968) and *Mick Jagger: The Singer, Not the Song* (1973). *Moonsong Lullaby* (1981), relating the importance of the moon in American Indian culture, is a tale for young children. Highwater also published books on Native American painting, artists, and history through art as well as on Native American dance and ceremonies. Other book-length publications include five editions of *Europe Under Twenty-five: A Young Person's Guide* (1971) and *Indian America: A Cultural and Travel Guide* (1975). This latter book, the first Fodor's guide on American Indians, is important as not only a guide for tourists but also a study of the history and cultures of American Indians. Highwater also wrote short fiction, magazine articles, and scripts for television shows.

Highwater published the nonfiction work *The Language of Vision: Meditations on Myth and Metaphor* in 1994. *Songs for the Seasons* (1995) is a children's book in which Highwater tells a tale of two red-tailed hawks. He interprets the lifestyle changes facing the hawks during different seasons. Illustrations in the book are by Sandra Speidel. *The Mythology of Transgression: Homosexuality as Metaphor* (1997) is a weighty essay focused on the homophobia of Western culture.

ACHIEVEMENTS

Jamake Highwater was recognized for a variety of talents. Novelist John Gardner said of Highwater that "he is one of the purest writers at work—a clean, clear voice." In addition to writing books and articles, Highwater hosted, wrote, and narrated *Songs of the Thunderbird* (1979) for the Public Broadcasting Service. In the field of music, Highwater's interests were diverse and included rock, American Indian, and classical music; he was a contributing editor of *Stereo Review* and classical music editor of the *Soho Weekly News*.

Highwater was called "a writer of exceptional vision and power" by Anaïs Nin. He was named a consultant to the New York State Council on the Arts, and at one time he served on the art task panel of the President's Commission on Mental Health. He also was named an honorary citizen of Oklahoma.

Among the honors that Highwater received, one of the most important to him personally was awarded at the Blackfeet Reserve in Alberta, Canada. Ed Calf Robe, elder of the Blood Reserve of Blackfeet, gave Highwater the name Piitai Sahkomaapii, which means Eagle Son. This honor, Calf Robe stated, was given because Highwater "soars highest and catches many truths which he carries to many lands." In spite of Highwater's genuine talents and achievements, after the mid-1980's he was viewed less favorably by some critics because his longstanding claim of American Indian ancestry was found to be essentially insupportable.

BIOGRAPHY

Portions of the biography of Jamake Highwater are open to question. Until the mid-1980's, Highwater maintained that he was born in Glacier County, Montana, on February 14, 1942, and that his mother, Amana Bonneville, was of the Blackfeet Nation (or was part Blackfoot and part French Canadian) and his father, Jamie, was a Cherokee. His early years, he said, were spent on the Blackfeet Indian Reservation in Montana and in Alberta, Canada, where the Blackfeet people held their summer encampments. At the age of eight, Highwater went to Hollywood with his father, a founding member of the American Indian Rodeo Association and a stunt man in Western films. Highwater said he lived in an orphanage after his father was killed in an automobile accident until his mother remarried. His stepfather, Alexander Marks, a white man, adopted him.

In the mid-1980's, this version of Highwater's life story was called into question by journalists and scholars. Highwater himself eventually intimated that he had invented some of the details. As a result, a new effort was made to construct his biography. The following represents a general consensus.

Highwater was born probably between 1930 and 1933. The place and date of his birth are unknown because he was given up for adoption by his mother. He was adopted when he was about five years old and lived most of his childhood in the San Fernando Valley in Los Angeles. He was known as Jay or Jack Marks, Marks being the last name of his adoptive parents. In the 1950's, he was inspired to continue to pursue a writing career by a correspondence with writer Nin. He also became interested in modern dance. He moved to San Francisco, where, with others, he formed a dance company called the San Francisco Contemporary Dancers. Highwater moved to New York in 1967.

Events such as the 1969 takeover of Alcatraz Island by American Indian activists bolstered his already strong interest in Native American issues and culture. Highwater said that in the mid-1970's his adoptive mother and foster sister told him they believed he had at least some "Indian blood." Around 1974 he changed his name to Jamake Highwater. In the 1970's and 1980's, Highwater lived primarily in the Soho section of Manhattan. He founded the Native Land Foundation to promote world folk art and its influence on the modern visual and performing arts.

In the 1980's, Highwater's American Indian identity was publicly called into question, and some Indian activists and writers, among them Vine DeLoria, Jr., stated their belief that he was not Native American. Highwater was undoubtedly disappointed in a lack of support from his associates regarding his claim to Indian ancestry. In 1992, he moved back to Los Angeles and relocated the Native Land Foundation there. His writing generally began to move away from specifically Native American topics.

Analysis

In much of his fiction and nonfiction, Jamake Highwater attempts to convey basic American Indian beliefs and presuppositions. When he emphasizes the differences between contemporary American values and those of American Indians, he stresses that there is more than one reality and that one is not necessarily more valid than another. Each reality has its own truths. By expressing the truths of various Indian cultures as he understands them, Highwater attempts to foster the understanding that must precede peaceful coexistence.

Anpao

Anpao, a Newbery Honor Book in 1978, has perhaps received less attention than it deserves. Recognition as an outstanding book for children suggests to some critics that a book is intended only for a young audience. Like Mark Twain's *Adventures of Huckleberry Finn* (1884), however, *Anpao* may be enjoyed by those of all ages. As an odyssey of the American Indian, *Anpao* is a compilation of legends, an oral history of Indian tribes. Highwater chooses a number of versions from recorded accounts of these legends, giving credit to his sources. The book's hero, Anpao, is his own creation.

The novel begins with Anpao's falling in love with the beautiful Ko-ko-mik-e-is, who agrees to marry him if he will journey to the Sun and get the Sun's permission for her to marry. The quest begins; Anpao, also called Scarface, sets forth. On his journey, he learns that Anpao means "the Dawn" and that his father is the Sun. Anpao's mother was a human who went to the World-Above-the-World without dying. After the birth of her son, Anpao, she becomes homesick and attempts an escape with her son, but she manages to get only part way to Earth because the rope that she has woven from sinew is not long enough. When the Sun is taunted by his jealous first wife, the Moon, he becomes angry. He follows the footsteps of his human wife to a hole in the sky. Seeing her dangling just above the trees on Earth, he makes a hoop from the branch of a willow tree and orders the hoop to kill the woman but to spare the child. The Sun is not quick enough to snatch the rope when the root that holds the rope in the World-Above-the-World sags because of pity for the dead mother of Anpao. When the child falls onto the dead body of his mother, blood from her body causes a scar to appear on his face. The child, Anpao, lives on Earth, and his journey toward the Sun involves the learning of basic truths of American Indian culture. The legends that he learns on his travels are imparted primarily through traditional storytelling, a mode of teaching used not only by Native Americans but also by ancient Greeks and Romans.

Like Homer in the *Iliad* (c. 750 B.C.E.; English translation, 1611) and the *Odyssey* (c. 725 B.C.E.; English translation, 1614), Highwater states his theme in the short opening chapter and then moves to the story in medias res. Anpao and his twin brother (created when Anpao disobeyed the warning of the Spider Woman, with whom he lived, not to throw his hoop into the air) are poor youths who arrive in the village where the beautiful young girl Ko-ko-mik-e-is lives. After Anpao sets forth on his journey to the Sun, he meets an old woman who tells him the story of the beginning of the world, of the death of the creator Napi, and of his own birth. Then the creation of Oapna, the contrary twin brother of Anpao, is accounted for, and his death is also told. The Clown/Contrary is a familiar figure in American Indian legends.

In another typical Indian legend, Anpao meets with a sorceress, a meeting that invites comparison with Odysseus's meeting with Circe. One of the most important obstacles that Anpao has to overcome is the intense dislike of the Moon, who, as the first wife of the Sun, despises the child born to the human responsible for the Sun's misalliance. Anpao, however, earns the love of the Moon when he saves her son, Morning Star, from death; thus, Anpao becomes the first person to have the power of the Sun, Moon, and Earth.

As a result of his journey to the Sun, Anpao has the ugly scar removed from his face, thus enabling him to prove to Ko-ko-mik-e-is that he did indeed make the journey. The marriage of Anpao (the Dawn and the son of the Sun) and Ko-ko-mik-e-is (Night-red-light, which is related to the Moon) takes place, and Anpao begs the people of Ko-ko-mik-e-is's village to follow the couple as they leave to escape the death, sickness, and greed that are coming to their world. The people will not follow; instead they laugh at Anpao. (This action suggests the lack of unity among American Indians, a lack that may have been crucial to the course of Indian history.) Undaunted, Anpao, taking his beautiful bride with him, goes to the village beneath the water. Ko-ko-mik-e-is is assured by Anpao that what is happening will not be the end, because they and their people are the rivers, the land, the prairies, the rocks—all of nature. This unity with nature is fundamental to American Indian culture.

Most of the legends in *Anpao* belong to times long ago, but Highwater also has included some more modern tales that tell of the arrival of whites with their horses, weapons, and diseases. The legends selected by Highwater are, as American Indian writer N. Scott Momaday says, "truly reflective of the oral tradition and rich heritage of Native American story-telling." The legends, old and new, are the cornerstone of Indian culture.

JOURNEY TO THE SKY

After writing *Anpao*, essentially a mythical journey, Highwater turned to recorded events for material for his next novel, *Journey to the Sky*. This journey is a fictionalized account of the actual explorations of two white men, John Lloyd Stephens, a New York attorney, and Frederick Catherwood, a British artist and architect. Stephens and Catherwood began their first trip in search of the lost cities of the Mayan kingdom in October, 1839. The men made two extended trips to the kingdom of the Mayan peoples, but Highwater confines his tale to the first exploration, which ended late in July, 1840.

Journey to the Sky is a suspense-filled adventure story that displays Highwater's writing talents more effectively than does his first novel. Although the narrative is interrupted occasionally by Highwater's accounts of later archaeological findings, the suspense and excitement of the journey are sustained throughout. Particularly impressive is Highwater's narrative skill in selecting highlights from the historical account of the Stephens-Catherwood expedition (Stephens did the writing, while Catherwood provided illustrations). Like a number of novels that appeared in the 1970's, including E. L. Doctorow's *Ragtime* (1975) and Aleksandr Solzhenitsyn's *Lennin v Tsyurikhe* (1975; *Lenin in Zurich*, 1976), *Journey to the Sky* is a new kind of historical fiction.

Having been appointed by President Martin Van Buren as U.S. diplomatic agent to the Central American Confederacy, Stephens fulfills his public duties as a diplomat, but his true interest is in the search for ruins. He meets with leaders of various colonies in Central America, paying courtesy calls and extending greetings from the U.S. government. Although Stephens finds the performance of his official duties pleasurable, he is in a hurry to begin explorations.

Early in the trip, while in Belize, the two explorers hire a young cutthroat, Augustin, as their servant. Although they seriously doubt that he will serve them well, by the end of the journey, they realize the rightness of their choice; he proves to be a loyal and valuable servant and friend. They also hire men to help transport their belongings, which include tools, food (including live chickens), and clothing. From time to time, and for differing reasons, new employees must be found.

The trip over Mico Mountain is extremely hazardous because of jungle, rocks, mud, and treacherous gullies. The rough terrain is only one of many natural hazards that they encounter during their explorations in Central America. Insects, climate, earthquakes, and malaria are some of the other forces of nature that they encounter. In addition, they meet such varied characters as the double-dealing Colonel Archibald MacDonald, superintendent of the English colonies in Central America, the petty tyrant Don Gregorio in Copan, good and bad padres, and hospitable and inhospitable people. The explorers are imprisoned, threatened with murder, and surrounded by an active rebellion in Central America.

Highwater captures the enthusiasm of Stephens and Catherwood as they discover the "lost city" just outside Copan. They are the first white men to see these tumbling pyramids and idols, evidence of the religion of the Mayas. Stephens and two helpers begin removing the foliage from rock piles that the people of Copan have been ignoring as piles of rubbish, and Catherwood sets to work documenting their discovery by making drawings of each of the fallen figures. To Stephens, this desolate city with its many magnificent works of art is evidence that the Mayas were master craftspersons.

Having located and documented the ruins at Copan, Stephens and Catherwood move to other sites, where they find further evidence of the Mayan culture. Even illness cannot deter them. From one site to another, the explorers continue their amazing trip. Although warned not to go to Palenque because of the danger to whites as a result of political upheaval, they go. There they find ruins that are quite different from those in Copan. After documenting the Palenque ruins, they go to Uxmal. Many times during the journey in Central America, the New York attorney and the British artist are warned about the hostile Indians, yet the Indians are often more hospitable than the white people they encounter. Stephens and Catherwood's discoveries of a Mayan civilization that rose and fell prior to the Spanish invasion corroborate a basic thesis of Highwater's—that American Indian cultures are meaningful and remarkable.

The Sun, He Dies

In *The Sun, He Dies*, Highwater once again turned to recorded history to provide a firm base for his story. The conquering of Montezuma II, ruler of the Aztec nation, by the Spaniard Hernando Cortés with a small contingent of men is perplexing to some historians, who sometimes credit Cortés with an unusual amount of tactical knowledge and ability. Highwater, on the other hand, looks carefully at the character of Montezuma and the religious beliefs of this powerful figure and concludes that these elements were the basic causes of his downfall.

Although the downfall of Montezuma is the backdrop for *The Sun, He Dies*, the novel is also an initiation story, a history of an important Aztec ruler, a history of the Aztec people, and an immersion into Native American culture. Highwater creates a narrator, Nanautzin, to tell the story: This narrative voice unifies the episodic material drawn from the oral traditions of American Indian peoples.

Beginning with "Call me Nanautzin," echoing the opening sentence of Herman Melville's *Moby Dick* (1851), *The Sun, He Dies* unfolds in chronological order. In the epic tradition, Nanautzin, the outcast woodcutter, despised by his people, announces his intention to sing of the great Aztec nation. Like Ishmael in *Moby Dick*, he alone is left to tell the story of all that happened.

Nanautzin briefly tells of his early life in his native village, where he is taunted by the children, cast away by his father, and loved by his mother. The ugly scars that signal the beginning of the unhappy life of the narrator are created by his fall, as a small child, into a cooking fire. The resultant deformities cause his father to abandon him and the villagers to name him the Ugly One. Unlike Oedipus, Nanautzin is not physically cast away; he is given an ax, called a woodcutter, and forgotten. He grows up lonely and friendless.

Nanautzin goes to Tenochtitlan for the installation of Montezuma II as the Great Speaker, even though the people of his village, Tlaxcala, loathe the lord of the greatest city in Mexico. Although Nanautzin feels honor for this great man, the trip does nothing to win for him honor or friends among his people. Because of his physical appearance, he remains the Ugly One, despised and rejected.

Eventually, Nanautzin wanders into a marvelous forest, where, although he knows he should not, he begins to chop firewood. Soon a man appears and questions him, demanding to know why he is cutting wood in the forest. The young man blurts out that, since Montezuma has become ruler, the people of Tlaxcala have not been permitted to cut dead wood wherever they wish and life has become very difficult for his people. Instead of being punished on the spot, Nanautzin is ordered to appear at the Palace of Tenochtitlan on the following day.

Fearing for his life, yet obedient, Nanautzin goes to the palace, where he discovers that the stranger he met in the forest is the Great Speaker himself. Instead of receiving punishment for his honest reply to Montezuma on the preceding day, Nanautzin is transformed into the Chief Orator because of his honesty. Then he is taken to the ruins at Tula, the once great city of the ancient Toltecs, where he, along with young boys, is taught by the priests and where he learns that here the greatest of all men once lived. This experience at Tula is both an initiation and a religious experience.

After his experience at Tula, Nanautzin becomes the confidant of Montezuma, who tells him the many legends of his people. Montezuma also confides that, according to his horoscope, his life is balanced between the war god, Huitzilopochtli, who fills the body of Montezuma with power, and the gentle god, Quetzalcoatl, who fills Montezuma's body with love. The Toltecs were the wise people created by the gentle Quetzalcoatl, who, like the Norse god Odin, was a benefactor to his people. Evil people loathed Quetzalcoatl, the tall, noble, holy white god who would not permit his people to be sacrificed. The evil men managed to trick this loving god with a mirror; drunk with pulque, Quetzalcoatl, who had seen his body in the mirror, became passionate and slept with a forbidden priestess. Evil came into the land and Quetzalcoatl went into exile in the land of Yucatan, but promised to return in the year One Reed, at which time he would recapture his throne and bring peace forevermore. Montezuma believes that Quetzalcoatl will return.

Although believing in the return of Quetzalcoatl, Montezuma also believes the horoscope, thus making him susceptible to doubt about himself: Is he one of the evil ones who destroyed this great god or one of the faithful who follow him? On one hand, he demands tributes and sacrifices from the people, ruling much of the time by force, thus acceding to Huitzilopochtli and alienating many of the tribes. On the other hand, he honors the gentle Quetzalcoatl and longs for his return.

During his early years as Chief Orator, Nanautzin learns the beliefs of this mighty leader and the history of the people. He recognizes the goodness in the Great Speaker of Tenochtitlan. Even though Montezuma appears to be a ruthless ruler, he has been kind to Nanautzin, he admires honesty, and he has great faith in the prediction that Quetzalcoatl will return. Montezuma's faith in the promise of this great and good god indicates the Aztec ruler's devotion to his religion.

From the favorable signs that appear in the year One Reed, Montezuma draws great confidence, but a time comes when the signs change. Montezuma is no longer the almost divine figure that Nanautzin has observed. Instead, the Great Speaker can no longer make up his own mind, which has become so divided that one part is contrary to the other part. Montezuma, like Ahab in *Moby Dick*, becomes obsessed. When he learns of the white men who have arrived at Chalco, the Great Speaker concludes that Quetzalcoatl's prediction is about to come true. Although the priests, the soothsayers, the noblemen, and the warriors warn Montezuma that these mysterious men are not Quetzalcoatl and his court, the Great Speaker is not to be shaken in his belief. Because Montezuma has alienated many of the neighboring tribes, he is hated; it is, therefore, easy for Cortés and his troops to enlist the aid of the alienated tribes, including the people of Tlazcala, in the march against Tenochtitlan.

Instead of trying to defend his city, Montezuma makes offerings to Cortés, whom he believes to be the gentle god Quetzalcoatl. It becomes an easy matter for Cortés to enter the realm of Montezuma and then, with the help of the alienated tribes, wreak havoc not only on the Great Speaker but also on the people of Tenochtitlan.

The narrative structure of *The Sun, He Dies* is strong, and the development of the character of Montezuma makes believable the idea that Tenochtitlan falls not because of the tactical superiority of Cortés but because of Montezuma's religious beliefs and obsessions. In addition to the recounting of history, the novel is a collection of tales that are an integral part of the beliefs of the Aztec nation. The Ugly One who becomes the Chief Orator for Montezuma II, although he comes full circle from being a lonely figure in Tlaxcala to being the figure left alone, is far wiser than the ignorant woodcutter Nanautzin who wanders into the forest owned by the Great Speaker. Nevertheless, the once powerful Aztec nation is destroyed and Nanautzin can only sing of what has been.

"What has been" is pertinent to many of Highwater's novels. Based on oral and recorded history, *Anpao, Journey to the Sky*, and *The Sun, He Dies*, for example, convey truths of three important American Indian cultures. The Indian respect for and allegiance to the forces of nature determined their actions. The significance of religion in the fall of Montezuma, in the ruins of Yucatan, and in the lives of Native Americans adds another dimension to recorded history.

THE GHOST HORSE CYCLE

Using his knowledge of Native American myth and his own techniques of storytelling, Highwater applied his enthusiasm for the retelling of history to his trilogy, collectively referred to as *The Ghost Horse Cycle*. In the first book, *Legend Days*, the story begins as a mythic chronicle of the character Amana, a young girl of the Blood tribe of the northern Plains, who lived in the late nineteenth century. Her people have contracted smallpox from the white traders and are dying in large numbers. Her sister, SoodaWa, sends Amana away; in a strange, dreamlike sequence, Amana is captured by the evil owls, rescued by the kindly foxes, and protected from harm by sleeping in a cave for a year. During that time, she receives a vision in which she becomes a man, a warrior, and hunts with other men. She is given a set of warrior's clothes by her spirit helper, which she must never reveal until the proper time. She returns to her village only to find two old women left, all the rest having died or fled.

Eventually Amana is reunited with her sister and her sister's husband, Far Away Son, who have been living with Big Belly, a chief of the Gros Ventres tribe. Amana marries Far Away Son, as is the custom among the Bloods—orphaned girls marry their sister's husbands. She tries to be a good wife, but secretly her vision makes her long to be a warrior. The story rehearses the agonizing plight of the northern Plains tribes as the extensive hunting of buffalo dwindled the supply of food, disease ravaged the population, and the whites' influence, such as whiskey, paralyzed Native American culture.

Legend Days—a book written as a myth and centered in recorded history—reads very much like other Highwater narratives, but *The Ghost Horse Cycle* trilogy is more personal than most Highwater works. Continuing with *Eyes of Darkness* and then with *I Wear the Morning Star*, it becomes evident that the myth only begins the story. Amana eventually weds a French trader named Jean-Pierre Bonneville and has a daughter, Jemina Bonneville, who in turn weds Jamie Ghost Horse, a Native American working as a Hollywood stuntman. They have two children, Reno and Sitko. The focus of the novels turns from the rather hazy myth of *Legend Days* to the concrete story of one family's efforts to survive the onslaught of the modern world in their lives.

Eyes of Darkness chronicles the marriage of Amana and Jean-Pierre, as well as Amana's introduction into white society, a transition that for her is never really successful. Her daughter Jemina's stormy marriage to Jamie Ghost Horse shows Native Americans confronting newly acquired economic realities, newly acquired problems such as alcoholism, and newly acquired stigmas, such as discrimination and racism.

I Wear the Morning Star focuses on Jemina's two children, Reno, who seeks to deny his American Indian heritage, and Sitko, who listens attentively to his grandmother's stories and longs for the old ways. Jemina is forced by circumstance and poverty to place the boys in an orphanage until she remarries a white man named Alexander Miller, and the boys return to her household only to aggravate further the number of underlying problems each is having. For the grandchildren of Amana, life has become too complex; they live in a world that is neither American Indian nor white, not knowing whether to follow the ways of the whites or to listen to the compelling stories of their grandmother. The need to adopt white customs and practices is apparent, but Sitko especially learns that Grandmother Amana offers something that the whites cannot: "[F]rom Grandmother Amana I learned how to dream myself into existence." Sitko becomes an artist and begins to explore his heritage through his art.

Kill Hole

In *Kill Hole*, Highwater leads Sitko Ghost Horse, his artist-hero, through life experiences that appear as nightmarish sequences. They bring to light the idea that imagination is the only human identity of consequence. Sitko, an adopted child who has been renamed Seymour Miller by his father, suffers the indignities of this abusive parent who erases Sitko's North American Indian identity. Sitko's grandmother inspires the youth with her tribal stories, compelling him to seek his lost culture. Discovering art as his medium of expression, Sitko makes the visionary connection between his ancestral past of harmony with nature and the present marked by environmental calamities, a plague reminiscent of acquired immunodeficiency syndrome (AIDS), and a breakdown of human connections in a society that exhibits a hatred of art and a fear of the unknown.

In a Kafkaesque desert village, Sitko is tried for being an interloper; unless he can prove that he is a bona fide Indian, he will be put to death. Imprisoned, he comes in contact with a brutish dwarf who instills his hatred of the arts on the villagers he rules. Patu, Sitko's sympathetic supporter, overcomes her fear of art to nurture her compassion for him. Sitko survives prison by recounting his past and bringing truth and art together in picture stories. Highwater concludes his complicated story by affirming the power of artistic imagination over social antagonism. A number of commentators have noted that to some extent the tale represents Highwater's response to the assertions he is not Native American.

Dark Legend

Dark Legend provides Highwater a forum for introducing European concepts to non-European settings. The novel is based on the story of Richard Wagner's Ring cycle (1874; *Der Ring des Nibelungen*). It adapts the operatic story to mythic pre-Columbian America. The book teems with gods, goddesses, giants, and other supernatural beings. Magical maidens bathe in a gold-blessed river that loses its precious metal to Caru, a greedy dwarf. In short duration, the thief is captured and the gold is recovered, now forged into a ring and magic crown. Lord Kuwai and his consort Amaru remain worried; the recovered treasure no longer shines. Kuwai's avarice spreads disaster. His zeal for the treasure causes his son's death and estrangement from his only daughter. The valiant warrior Washi collects the gold, falls in love with the daughter, Idera, and returns the metal to the river. Earth becomes balanced again.

Virginia A. Duck
Updated by Craig Gilbert

Other major works

NONFICTION: *Rock and Other Four Letter Words*, 1968 (as J. Marks); *Europe Under Twenty-five: A Young Person's Guide*, 1971; *Mick Jagger: The Singer, Not the Song*, 1973 (as J. Marks); *Fodor's Indian America*, 1975; *Indian America: A Cultural and Travel Guide*, 1975; *Song from the Earth: American Indian Painting*, 1976; *Ritual of the Wind: North American Indian Dances and Music*, 1977; *Dance: Rituals of Experience*, 1978; *Many Smokes, Many Moons: A Chronology of American Indian History Through Indian Art*, 1978; *The Sweet Grass Lives On: Fifty Contemporary North American Indian Artists*, 1980; *The Primal Mind: Vision and Reality in Indian America*, 1981; *Arts of the Indian Americas: Leaves from the Sacred Tree*, 1983; *Native Land: Sagas of the Indian Americas*, 1986; *Shadow Show: An Autobiographical Insinuation*, 1986; *Myth and Sexuality*, 1990; *The Language of Vision: Meditations on Myth and Metaphor*, 1994; *The Mythology of Transgression: Homosexuality as Metaphor*, 1997.

CHILDREN'S LITERATURE: *Moonsong Lullaby*, 1981; *Rama: A Legend*, 1994 (adaptation of *The Ramayana*); *Songs for the Seasons*, 1995 (Sandra Speidel, illustrator).

EDITED TEXT: *Words in the Blood: Contemporary Indian Literature of North and South America*, 1984.

Bibliography

Churchill, Ward. *Fantasies of the Master Race: Literature, Cinema, and the Colonization of the American Indians*. Monroe, Maine: Common Courage Press, 1992. An intriguing exposé of the practice of pretending to be American Indian. Highwater receives ample attention in the book, and Churchill disputes Highwater's claim of North American Indian heritage.

Grimes, Ronald L. "To Hear the Eagles Cry: Contemporary Themes in Native American Spirituality." *American Indian Quarterly* 20 (June 22, 1996): 433-451. This lengthy multiparticipant discussion focuses on educating American Indians in religious precepts. Highwater serves as a source for several of the concepts discussed in the debate.

Katz, Jane, ed. *This Song Remembers: Self-Portraits of Native Americans in the Arts*. Boston: Houghton Mifflin, 1980. Katz's work includes essays from many different American Indian artists who are active in the visual arts, poetry, literature, and dance. Highwater's self-portrait centers on the importance of myth and Indian culture to his life and art.

Kutzer, M. Daphne, ed. *Writers of Multicultural Fiction for Young Adults: A Bio-Critical Sourcebook*. Westport, Conn.: Greenwood Press, 1996. Highwater is one of the writers of fiction for young adults included in this reference book; the fourteen-page entry about him features a biography, criticism, and a bibliography.

Shanley, Kathryn W. "The Indians America Loves to Love and Read: American Indian Identity and Cultural Appropriation." *American Indian Quarterly* 21, no. 4 (Fall, 1997). After recounting the controversy over Highwater's Indian heritage, Shanley addresses what she describes as the "primary issue" regarding the author: "His romanticized version of American Indian identity" and his assumption of "a place for himself as the primary spokesperson for Indians . . . with an arrogance that belies a disrespect for American Indian communities."

Stott, Jon C. "Narrative Expectations and Textual Misreadings: Jamake Highwater's *Anpao* Analyzed and Reanalyzed." *Studies in the Literary Imagination* 18, no. 2 (Fall, 1985): 93-105. Highwater's award-winning book *Anpao* is given a thorough critical analysis. Stott describes how his initial expectations of the book were based on his belief that Highwater was a "Native writer," and how these conceptions were challenged after revelations that Highwater was not of Blackfoot/Cherokee heritage.

OSCAR HIJUELOS

Born: New York, New York; August 24, 1951

Principal long fiction

Our House in the Last World, 1983
The Mambo Kings Play Songs of Love, 1989
The Fourteen Sisters of Emilio Montez O'Brien, 1993
Mr. Ives' Christmas, 1995
Empress of the Splendid Season, 1999
A Simple Habana Melody (from When the World Was Good), 2002
Dark Dude, 2008

Other literary forms

Although he has produced several short stories and poems, Oscar Hijuelos (ee-HWAY-lohs) gained wide readership for long fiction after publication of his first novel, *Our House in the Last World*, which he developed from a story line written on scraps of paper as he worked as a clerk for an advertising agency.

Achievements

Oscar Hijuelos attained a large audience after he was awarded the Pulitzer Prize in 1990 for his novel *The Mambo Kings Play Songs of Love*. Although Latino authors are often neglected by mainstream publishers and other media, Hijuelos broke through ethnic barriers with his persistence, his style, and his Pulitzer Prize. On the strength of his first novel, Hijuelos received several grants from the National Endowment for the Arts, and the American Academy of Arts and Letters Rome Prize provided him with a stipend that allowed him to live in Italy for a year of composition and reflection.

Through Hijuelos's observations, dark memories, and radiant storytelling, readers can appreciate Cuban immigrant culture. *The Mambo Kings Play Songs of Love* demonstrates the acceptance of Hispanic literature beyond the previous limited scope of small Latino presses. Critics labeled the book a breakthrough for Latino writers. A motion-picture adaptation of the novel, titled *The Mambo Kings*, was released in 1992. The work was also adapted as a stage musical and was slated to open on Broadway in the summer of 2005, but plans for the Broadway opening were dropped after a lackluster response to the show in San Francisco. In 2008, Hijuelos expanded his audience to include young adults with *Dark Dude*, a novel about an adolescent.

Biography

Oscar Hijuelos's family hailed from the Oriente province of Cuba, home of entertainer Desi Arnaz and Cuban dictators Fulgencio Batista y Zaldívar and Fidel Castro—wild roots for the New York-born, iconoclastic author. At age four, Oscar and his mother Magdalena visited Cuba, and upon their return he developed nephritis, a critical-stage kidney inflammation. Bedridden, Oscar lingered in a children's hospital for two long years. This separation from family and language removed Oscar from Hispanic connections; the theme of separation would later saturate his novels.

Oscar's father Pascual drank heavily, leaving Magdalena to raise her children in a rough, lower-class neighborhood of New York. Hijuelos has expressed sadness about his youth, in which most fathers he knew were drunk, limousines came only for funerals, and "the working class hate[d] everyone else." The area where he played was caught between the affluence of the Columbia University campus and the habitat of muggers, thieves, and junkies of Morningside Park. Hijuelos hid from this hell by reading, watching television, and observing the traits of his family, as a partially sober father arose to go to his job as a cook at the Biltmore Hotel each day. Affection flooded the household, even with the dysfunction of poverty and neighborhood chaos. Forced to speak English outside his home, Hijuelos easily abandoned his Cuban tongue, although his parents expected Spanish discourse in the home. Thereby alienated, Hijuelos neglected thoughtful conversations with either parent, a theme that would later recur in his work.

Frederick Tuten, director of the City University of New York's creative writing program, has remarked that this "intense writer" does not "create books from nothing; he's lived." Attending college while working, Hijuelos created his style and honed his skill by writing long responses to assignments, exaggerating the length to fulfill his personal need for expression. After receiving his M.A. in 1976 from the City University of New York, he moved just a few blocks away from his humble childhood home to begin life as an author, supported by work as an inventory controller in an advertising agency.

Hijuelos is a mystery to some Latino writers because he has chosen to distance himself from their coterie. Hispanic writers must meet two differing sets of standards: acceptance from the American reading public and acceptance from their Latin American counterparts. With his works mostly devoid of political motives, Hijuelos has drawn criticism for not drawing sufficient attention to his Latin roots. Even with this controversy, Hijuelos has been adopted by many as the voice of Latinos, the symbol of their culture in the United States.

Analysis

Oscar Hijuelos represents a new generation of Cuban American writers. His Latino roots enrich his chronicles of the immigrant experience. Latino writers often face quandaries when choosing the language for their literary expression (Spanish or English), when committing to traditions of their descendants, and when chronicling immigrant life in their new world. Hijuelos balances the sensitivities of the American reader and the expectations of the Latino reader by presenting characters who, removed from the security of their Cuban homeland, are tossed into the diversity and adversity of big-city life; they survive and still bring grace to their daily existence. Hijuelos's two shorter novels, *Our House in the Last World*, his autobiographical debut, and *Mr. Ives' Christmas*, an exploration of spirituality, provide balance to his long works. Proud of his heritage, yet choosing to explore themes beyond issues of immigration and assimilation, Hijuelos places his characters in situations that reflect universal themes as well as particular historical events and communities.

Our House in the Last World

Our House in the Last World explores the questions of identity and perspective through the travails of the members of the Santinio family, who are seeking their fortune by moving from Cuba to New York City. The father, Alejo, expects the younger son, Héctor, to live a macho existence and to be "Cuban," while the mother, Mercedes, smothers Héctor with her anxieties, limiting his ability to develop as a normal boy in the neighborhood. Hijuelos offers two views of innocence: that of the wonder and confusion of a family facing a new life in an unknown world and that of their children's bewilderment in a harsh environment.

The novel begins in the ticket office of a movie theater in Holguín, Cuba. Mercedes, twenty-seven, almost past the age of marriage, meets Alejo, who woos her, marries her, and moves her to New York, where they share an apartment with other Cubans who come and go. Some attain status and wealth, while the Santinios remain impoverished. Alejo becomes a sot, a gluttonous man who allows his sister to wage a harsh campaign against his wife. Mercedes transfers the memory of her father onto Alejo, and it is only after Alejo's death near the end of the novel that she is free to realize her dreams as her own.

Oscar Hijuelos. (Roberto Koch)

The older son, Horatio, epitomizes the image of the man he thinks his mother demands. A womanizer and philanderer, he finally adopts a military lifestyle as an escape from fear of failure. Héctor contracts a near-fatal disease while on holiday in Cuba, and the months of hospitalization that follow embitter him toward the culture of his homeland and all things Cuban. Mercedes becomes unbearably overprotective, and Héctor's anxieties prevent him from reacting to the drunken excesses of his father and the hysteria of his mother. Castro has taken over Cuba during this time, and Mercedes and Alejo are disengaged from the lost world of their youth; New York will hold them until death.

Hijuelos embraces these characters with pure affection and gentleness, as he allows the relatives to flow through the Santinios' life. He describes their downward slide from hope to resignation, from effort to insanity, and from love to harassment. Love does not conquer all, but it does provide a basis for life. The Santinios are a tribute to perseverance.

The Mambo Kings Play Songs of Love

Hijuelos's life in the advertising agency had little to do with his passion for writing. When he first began thinking of the story that would become *The Mambo Kings Play Songs of Love*, he knew that an uncle and an elevator operator would be his models. The uncle, a musician with the band led by Xavier Cugat in the 1930's, and a building superintendent, patterned after an elevator operator and musician, merge to become Cesar Castillo, the Mambo King. Cesar's brother, Néstor, laconic, retrospective, lamenting the loss of a Latina lover he left behind in Cuba, writes a song in her memory that draws the attention of Desi Arnaz, who will change their lives.

As the book opens, Cesar rots with his half-empty whiskey glass tipped at the television beaming old reruns; he seeks the *I Love Lucy* episode that features him and Néstor as the Mambo Kings. Néstor has tragically died. Cesar pathetically reveals his aging process, the cirrhosis, the loss of flamboyant times. Cesar's old, scratchy records, black, brittle, and warped, resurrect his music stardom. He laments his brother's death by leafing through fading pictures.

In *The Mambo Kings Play Songs of Love*, Hijuelos presents pre-Castro Cubans who, after World War II, streamed in torrents to New York, their experiences creating a historical perspective for future developing-world immigration. All communities may strive for the American Dream, but in Latino quarters, music, the mainstream of a culture, sought to free the oppressed. The Castillo brothers become, for a moment, cultural icons with their appearance on *I Love Lucy*. The fame short-lived, Cesar comforts his ego with debauchery, and Néstor dies ungracefully and suddenly. The ironically named Hotel Splendour is where Cesar commits suicide—in Cuban culture, a respectable ending to life. Latino culture encourages the machismo of men such as Cesar, and Hijuelos, through the story's narrator, Eugenio, nephew of the Castillo brothers, may be asking his countrymen to review that attitude.

The Fourteen Sisters of Emilio Montez O'Brien

The Fourteen Sisters of Emilio Montez O'Brien again paints Hijuelos's theme of immigrant life in the United States, this time on the canvas of a small rural town. Family traditions pass down, hopes spring eternal, and sadness and attempts to assimilate fade as the book's characters meet disappointments and victories to varying degrees. Nelson O'Brien leaves Ireland, sister in tow, for the better life promised in America. Weakened by the journey and her general frailty, the sister dies, leaving Nelson to wander aimlessly until he retreats to Cuba to take pictures of the Spanish-American War. He meets the sixteen-year-old Mariela Montez and courts her every Sunday for seven weeks. Seducing her with stories of his Pennsylvania farm and with her first sexual experiences, Nelson convinces her to marry and move to the farm, offering a telescope as a token of their future.

The Montez O'Brien household is fertile, and fourteen magnetic sisters charge the home with a feminine aura. Finally, the lone son, Emilio, is born. Mostly told through the eldest daughter's eyes, the story portrays the ferocity of Nelson's ambition and character through the overbearing feminine mystique that surrounds his life, his decisions, and his focus on the future. Emilio, on the other hand, becomes a gentle soul who adores and is adored by his sisters. The sisters grow, many without mates, into expected positions in the world—entertainers, homemakers, expectant mothers, recluses, gluttons—carrying the name and bravado of their father with them. Emilio attracts women and suffers the vanity of his charm and good looks, eventually becoming an actor in B-pictures. His drunken tendencies and a sordid affair with a pregnant teen turn his life sour, and he turns to a reclusive existence until he finds his soul mate in an improbable café in an Alaskan fishing village. She dies before the novel's end, breaking Emilio's heart but allowing the sisters to provide him with solace. Hijuelos finishes the novel succinctly, with both tragedies and dreams having been realized.

Mr. Ives' Christmas

In *Mr. Ives' Christmas*, Hijuelos somberly presents Mr. Edward Ives, a character unlike the romanticized Cesar, the macho Mambo King. Mr. Ives sensitively and sanely goes through his life with no malice toward fellow man or woman. He seeks those rewards he has become accustomed to earning.

Mr. Ives's life is oddly shaped by the Christmas season, a time he loves. One Christmas season when he is a boy, a widowed printmaker visits him, a Cuban child, in a New York City orphanage, adopts him and names him Edward Ives. The adoptive father idyllically rears his dark-skinned son, inspires him to pursue his love for drawing, and eventually guides him to the Arts Student League, where, one Christmas Eve, he meets his future wife. The picture-postcard family image is grotesquely distorted years later when, on another Christmas Eve, the Iveses' seventeen-year-old son is gunned down as he leaves church choir practice. A fourteen-year-old Puerto Rican gunman has killed the boy for ten dollars. Mr. Ives proceeds to devote his life to obsessive attempts to rehabilitate the murderer.

Mr. Ives's favorite book is a signed copy of Charles Dickens's *A Christmas Carol* (1843). Hijuelos relies strongly on this book to link the two tales. He emulates Dickens's populous canvases and uses Dickens's love of coincidence and contrivance as a metaphor for God's mysterious workings. The temperance of Mr. Ives engenders his longing for grace, a gift for contemplation, and a world curiosity.

In this novel, Hijuelos draws heavily on images from his New York neighborhood, his coterie of friends, and the milieu of gangs, muggers, and drug addicts at the end of his street. *Mr. Ives' Christmas* speaks of faith—a faith that mysteriously probes emotions, tested by death and the opportunity of forgiveness.

Empress of the Splendid Season

In *Empress of the Splendid Season*, Lydia Espana is banished from her Cuban home by her father, a small-town alcalde, because she overstayed her allowed time at a dance with a young man. Disheartened, she makes her way to New York and in time marries and gains employment as a cleaning lady. In near poverty, she and her chronically ill husband, a waiter, attempt to maintain respectability and keep food on the table for their two children. Lydia resorts to fantasy as a coping mechanism, envisioning herself as the "Empress of the Splendid Season," a poetic term of endearment used by her husband during the early days of their romance.

Hijuelos describes Lydia's passage from privileged girlhood to a widowed old age through her relationships with family, friends, and employers. A wealthy employer sends Lydia's son to a prestigious university. He becomes a successful psychologist, but he is unhappy and feels disconnected from the world. Lydia's daughter grows into a rebellious young woman who later marries an Anglo and moves to the suburbs. She chooses to rear Lydia's grandchildren far from her Cuban roots. Hijuelos again digs beneath the core of tenement life, bringing a magical mystique into his characters' lives through rich text and powerful prose.

A Simple Habana Melody

The protagonist of *A Simple Habana Melody* is Oscar Levis, a renowned Cuban composer and musician. As the novel opens, Levis returns to Cuba, after many years abroad, as an exhausted man and frail version of his former corpulent, expansive self. Having sought to escape the restrictive and politically tumultuous life in Cuba in the late 1930's, he made a home in Paris, where, to his shock and dismay, he—who had grown up Catholic—was identified in 1943 as a Jew. He was forced to wear a yellow star and was shipped to a detention camp after the Nazi occupation of Paris. His return to Cuba provokes his recollection of his life and fame, his loves, and his happy participation in a community of musicians and artists.

In this novel Hijuelos revisits themes explored in his earlier works, particularly in *The Mambo Kings Play Songs of Love*. Like Néstor Castillo, Oscar Levis creates for a woman he loves—and who remains forever out of reach for him—a song that propels him to fame and fortune. Like the Castillo brother, Levis too inhabits the musical community of the mambo era. His experiences and popularity illustrate the influence of Cuban musicians and music in the Americas and Europe. Similar to Néstor Castillo, Levis epitomizes the longing for love and the essential loneliness of all humankind. His experiences describe the milieu of artistry in Havana and Paris as well as the horror of the Holocaust.

Dark Dude

In *Dark Dude*, a novel aimed at young adults, Hijuelos depicts the challenges faced by a young light-skinned boy of Cuban heritage as he grows up in Harlem and tries to find his place in the world. Hijuelos defines "dark dude" as a colloquial term used by persons of color in Harlem between the years of 1965 and 1970 to refer derisively to a person of light skin, a person lacking street smarts, an outsider. Dark dude defines the social position of Rico Fuentes, a blond Hispanic who does not speak Spanish well.

Rico's difficulties begin when he reaches high school age and can no longer attend the Catholic school where he spent his elementary years. He does not fit in with any crowd at the local high school, and when his parents decide to send him to a military school in Florida, Rico runs away to be with an older friend who, having just won the lottery, has escaped from the gritty streets to rural Wisconsin, where he has started college. Rico adapts to his life in Wisconsin, but after a year of being away from home, he misses the warm affection of his parents and feels guilty for the pain he caused them with his departure. He decides to go back and face the challenges of his neighborhood, recognizing that he cannot turn his back on his family and his life. Here, as in his other novels, Hijuelos explores some of the many struggles that individuals face as they grow up or grow into their lives while coming to terms with personal strengths and limitations and the joys and sorrows of human existence.

Craig Gilbert
Updated by Bernadette Flynn Low

Bibliography

Barbato, Joseph. "Latino Writers in the American Market." *Publishers Weekly*, February 1, 1991. Presents an accurate summary of the place of Latino writers, including Hijuelos, in the American literary marketplace.

Chávez, Lydia. "Cuban Riffs: Songs of Love." *Los Angeles Times Magazine*, April 18, 1993. Provides an in-depth look at Hijuelos as a man and as a writer in a readable, conversational style. Includes serious revelations by this thought-provoking author.

"A Cubano Huck Finn." *Publishers Weekly*, September 1, 2008. Brief review cogently describes the abundance of themes and adventures packed into this novel for young people.

Hijuelos, Oscar. "Lunch at the Biltmore." *The New Yorker*, January 17, 2005. Through his own description of himself as a child on an outing with his father, Hijuelos shows some of the persons and circumstances that have become inspirations for many of his novels.

Kevane, Bridget. "The Fiction of Oscar Hijuelos: *The Mambo Kings Play Songs of Love* (1989)." In *Latino Literature in America: Literature as Windows to World Cultures*. Westport, Conn.: Greenwood Press, 2003. Discusses how Hijuelos's work shows that Latino literature does not necessarily focus solely on the immigrant experience; rather, it often expresses broader human themes and depicts particular historical or artistic eras.

Patteson, Richard F. "Oscar Hijuelos: 'Eternal Homesickness' and the Music of Memory." *Critique* 44, no. 1 (2002): 38-48. Analyzes the themes of music and memory in *The Mambo Kings Play Songs of Love*.

Pérez-Firmat, Gustavo. *Life on the Hyphen: The Cuban-American Way*. Austin: University of Texas Press, 1994. Scholarly study examines the work of Hijuelos and other Cuban American writers and performers who have become cultural figures.

Socolovsky, Maya. "The Homelessness of Immigrant American Ghosts: Hauntings and Photographic Narrative in Oscar Hijuelos's *The Fourteen Sisters of Emilio Montez O'Brien*." *Proceedings of the Modern Language Association* 117, no. 2 (2002): 252-264. Uses theories of photography to analyze Hijuelos's depiction of photography and immigrant experience in his novel.

CHESTER HIMES

Born: Jefferson City, Missouri; July 29, 1909
Died: Moraira, Spain; November 12, 1984
Also known as: Chester Bomar Himes

Principal long fiction

If He Hollers Let Him Go, 1945
Lonely Crusade, 1947
Cast the First Stone, 1952 (unexpurgated edition, *Yesterday Will Make You Cry*, 1998)
The Third Generation, 1954
The Primitive, 1955 (unexpurgated edition, *The End of a Primitive*, 1997)
For Love of Imabelle, 1957 (revised as *A Rage in Harlem*, 1965)
Il pluet des coups durs, 1958 (*The Real Cool Killers*, 1959)
Couché dans le pain, 1959 (*The Crazy Kill*, 1959)
Dare-dare, 1959 (*Run Man Run*, 1966)
Tout pour plaire, 1959 (*The Big Gold Dream*, 1960)
Imbroglio negro, 1960 (*All Shot Up*, 1960)
Ne nous énervons pas!, 1961 (*The Heat's On*, 1966; also known as *Come Back Charleston Blue*, 1974)
Pinktoes, 1961
Une affaire de viol, 1963 (*A Case of Rape*, 1980)
Retour en Afrique, 1964 (*Cotton Comes to Harlem*, 1965)
Blind Man with a Pistol, 1969 (also known as *Hot Day, Hot Night*, 1970)
Plan B, 1983 (English translation, 1993)

Other literary forms

Chester Himes was primarily a writer of long fiction, but near the end of his life he published a revealing two-volume autobiography, which, if not wholly accurate about his life, nevertheless is engaging as a testament of survival of a black artist struggling to make his voice heard. Like many writers of his generation, Himes began publishing short fiction in the many periodicals of the time. As his life and career progressed—and the number of publishers declined—Himes worked less in the field. A posthumous collection of his short fiction was published in 1990. Finally, Himes also turned his hand to dramatic writing, both plays and film scripts, the most accessible of which is "Baby Sister," which was published in his book of miscellaneous writings, *Black on Black: "Baby Sister" and Selected Writings* (1973).

Achievements

As the title of a biography of Chester Himes suggests, Himes led several lives during the seventy-five years of his troublesome career. He was the youngest son in a rising African American family, who worked his way into the middle class only to fall back again. Himes learned the craft of writing as an inmate in the Ohio correctional system, and after his release from prison he was a writer of angry and violent protest novels, which earned him a reputation as one of the more celebrated black writers in the United States.

Beginning in the mid-1950's, Himes expatriated and became a tangential member of the community of black artists, which included Richard Wright and James Baldwin, who fled American racism to settle in Europe during the period after World War II. In his later years, he wrote a two-volume autobiography and a series of masterful crime novels, the "Harlem domestic" books. The second of the series, *The Real Cool Killers*, won in 1958 the prestigious Grand Prix de la Littérature Policiére for best crime novel published in France. In all of his "lives," Himes struggled to come to grips with the racist American society into which he was born and to realize his place in that society as a black man and as an artist.

From the publication of his first novel, *If He Hollers Let Him Go*, Himes confounded the critics, and they rarely understood his work. Was his fiction too violent or was it merely revealing the realities of American racism? Was Himes sexist or just reflecting the tensions inherent in a community where African American males were desperately searching for a sense of self? Did he compromise his art for the publishing world dominated by white editors when he wrote his Harlem domestic series, or were these hard-hitting yet more mainstream crime novels an extension of his more "artistic" but less popular protest novels? Was his autobiography merely a self-serving complaint against the slights against him or an uncompromising portrait of one black man's struggle for survival?

Perhaps it is because of the contradictions of his life that Himes remains fascinating, and it is through the mixed, often confused, responses to his work that he achieved his measure of importance, not just as a black writer but as an American writer, one who captured something of the truth of America and of its literature.

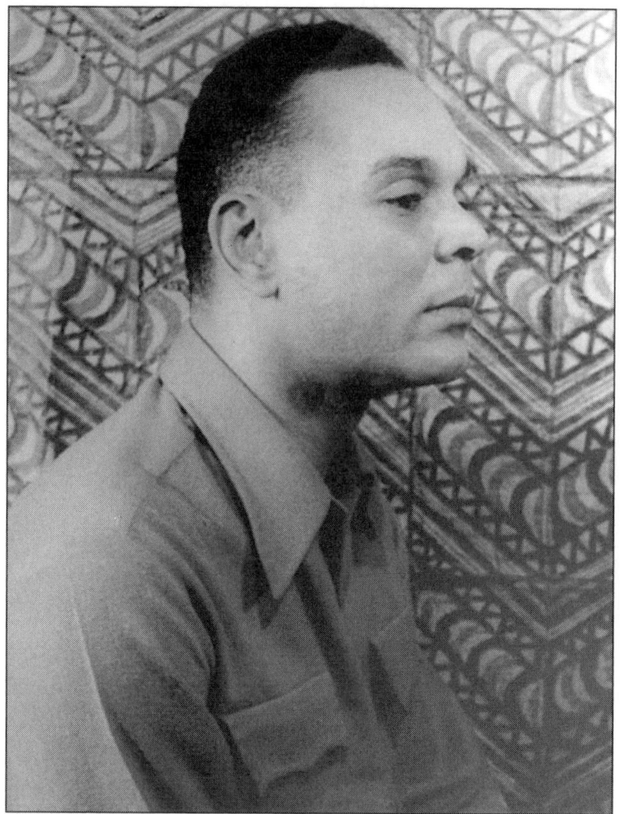

Chester Himes. (Library of Congress)

Biography

Chester Bomar Himes was the youngest of three sons of Joseph Sandy Himes and Estelle Bomar Himes. His father was a teacher of industrial arts and spent the years of Himes's youth as a faculty member at several black institutions predominantly in the South. By the time Himes was in his teens the family had settled in Cleveland, and after his graduation from Glenville High School he entered Ohio State University in the fall of 1926. However, his university career was short-lived, and at the end of the spring quarter, 1927, he was asked to leave because of poor grades and his participation in a speakeasy fight.

Back in Cleveland, Himes slipped into a life on the edges of the city's crime world. After several run-ins with the law he was caught for robbery, convicted, and sentenced to a lengthy term in the Ohio State Penitentiary. For the next seven-and-a-half years Himes served time, and in the enforced discipline of prison life he began to write fiction. His first publication, "His Last Day," appeared in *Abbott's Monthly* in November, 1932. Himes was paroled on April 1, 1936, and the next year he married Jean Johnson. After his prison experience Himes worked at a number of menial jobs while continuing to write.

On April 3, 1953, Himes embarked for Europe, and, except for several brief trips to the United States, he remained an exile for the rest of his life. During these years Himes's writing was devoted mainly to his Harlem detective series featuring Grave Digger Jones and Coffin Ed Johnson. Throughout his years in Europe, Himes traveled extensively, finally settling in Alicante, Spain, with his second wife, Leslie Packard. In 1963, Himes suffered a stroke and in his later years experienced various health problems. He died on November 12, 1984, in Moraira, Spain.

Analysis

In his review of *Lonely Crusade*, James Baldwin hit on the central theme of Chester Himes's work: creating individual black characters who were many faceted and reflected the ambivalence of living in an American society full of contradictions and insecurities. Unfortunately, Baldwin's grasp of the essence of Himes's fiction was not shared by all. Many of the reviewers of Himes's early "protest" fiction either criticized the violence of the books, apologized for it, or merely complained about what they saw as his awkwardness of style. Most reviews simply dismissed the books. Some acknowledged that Himes's portrait of American racism was accurate but deplored his lack of any constructive suggestions for its amelioration. Even when Himes received a certain measure of fame through the republication of his detective novels in the United States, the critical notices, with few exceptions, remained slight. After Himes's death, however, this changed. Himes's literary reputation in France undoubtedly affected his reception in the United States.

Himes once believed that in American letters there was room at the top for only one African American writer at a time, and therefore black writers were always competing against one another for that coveted spot. He felt that he always came in second, initially behind Richard Wright and then behind Baldwin. Certainly this is no longer true (if it ever was). The proliferation of novels, drama, and poetry by such authors as Toni Morrison, Ernest J. Gaines, Gloria Naylor, Derek Walcott, Maya Angelou, Alice Walker, and other black writers suggests that whatever constraints Himes felt as an exiled black writer seem to be loosening. Himes is now being accorded a place beside Wright, Baldwin, and Ralph Ellison, the novelists of his generation who opened the doors for African American writers to be accepted as full-fledged American writers, a part of the native grain.

If He Hollers Let Him Go

In *If He Hollers Let Him Go* the central character, Bob Jones, is a black Everyman—as his name would suggest—who comes to represent the experience of all black males who find themselves thwarted while trying to live out their dreams. Jones is an African American who has moved to California to work in the defense plants during World War II. Here he experiences American racism in all its ugly insidiousness and spends the five days covered by the novel's narrative trying to escape the oppressions and humiliations society tries to impose on him.

As an articulate man, with a few years of college, Jones is both better educated and more perceptive than the working-class whites he works with in the aircraft plants. When he is elevated to the position of supervisor at work, he brings out the racism of his coworkers, who are jealous of his success. An altercation on the job, tensions with his white girlfriend, and finally the accusation of rape by a woman at work whose overtures he has rejected, convince Jones that his hopes and dreams will not come true even in Los Angeles, where he thought he would be rid of the racist attitudes of his native South. After his arrest a judge strips him of his military deferment, and as the novel ends he is being sent off to join the U.S. Army.

Himes's first published novel provides the basic themes he would pursue not only in his protest books but also in his crime fiction. In the course of the novel Himes explores the issues of race, class, and sexual positioning and demonstrates how Jones, despite his best efforts, remains trapped within a historically determined social role as a black man trying simply to earn a living, gain some personal respect, and find love. At every turn he finds himself prevented from fulfilling the most basic of American rights and aspirations.

The Primitive

The narrative of *The Primitive* focuses on writer Jesse Robinson and his relationship with his white girlfriend, Kriss Cummings. Again in this novel Himes uses a contained time scheme, covering only a few days in the lives of his central characters. After a chance meeting with an old acquaintance, Kriss, Jesse experiences a rapidly accelerating series of seriocomic episodes, which propel him to the novel's conclusion: In an alcoholic fog he stabs Kriss to death in her Gramercy Park apartment. The novel alternates between following Kriss's life and Jesse's thoughts as he tries, in vain, to examine his feelings about his relationship with a white woman and what she stands for in his world, as well as his growing sense of himself as a writer trying to come to grips with his experience as an African American living in a racist culture that will give him recognition as neither an artist nor a man.

The Primitive is often described as one of Himes's "confessional" novels, fiction in which he examines themes that had plagued him since the publication of *If He Hollers Let Him Go*: the rejection he felt as a writer and the obsession with white women often experienced by black men. As critics have pointed out, obsession with white women is a constant theme in Himes's writing and represents attraction, repulsion, and, because of the taboo of miscegenation, long a central anxiety of white Americans, the fear of death and social rejection. Rather than merely striking out against white society, Jesse murders Kriss out of self-hatred for his own desires to join that society, moving the murder beyond the blind killing of Bigger Thomas in Wright's *Native Son* (1940). In the end, Jesse, although still a rejected author, discovers that he has the skills of a fine writer who can put into words his feelings about the conditions of his life.

COTTON COMES TO HARLEM

Cotton Comes to Harlem begins in Harlem at a "back to Africa" rally sponsored by the Reverend Deke O'Malley, who is fraudulently bilking his gullible followers. The rally is interrupted by a gang of thieves who steal the raised money and hide it in a bale of cotton, which they lose on their escape. Into this plot come two African American detectives, Grave Digger Jones and Coffin Ed Johnson, two of the toughest police officers in New York. The rest of the novel involves their attempts to recover the loot, expose the fraud, and make amends to the local residents. The ending of the novel provides an ironic twist, as a poor, old man who found the bale does go to Africa to live out the dream promised by the Reverend O'Malley at the novel's opening.

Cotton Comes to Harlem is one a series of crime novels set in New York's Harlem and featuring two African American detectives, a series Himes called his Harlem domestic books. The series began when his French publisher Marcel Duhamel contracted him to write a novel for Gallimard's La Série Noire, a notable series of crime fiction published in France. In these novels, Himes concentrates as much on the social, political, and economic conditions of the people of Harlem as he does on the solving of crimes. As Himes carefully explores the racism inherent in American culture, he chronicles the world of his characters sympathetically, and without becoming didactic he demonstrates the harmful effects of almost four hundred years of oppression and exploitation of African Americans.

Charles L. P. Silet

OTHER MAJOR WORKS

SHORT FICTION: *The Collected Stories of Chester Himes*, 1990.

NONFICTION: *The Quality of Hurt: The Autobiography of Chester Himes, Volume I*, 1972; *My Life of Absurdity: The Autobiography of Chester Himes, Volume II*, 1976; *Conversations with Chester Himes*, 1995 (Michel Fabre and Robert E. Skinner, editors); *Dear Chester, Dear John: Letters Between Chester Himes and John A. Williams* (John A. Williams and Lori Williams, compilers and editors).

MISCELLANEOUS: *Black on Black: "Baby Sister" and Selected Writings*, 1973.

BIBLIOGRAPHY

Fabre, Michael, and Robert Skinner, eds. *Conversations with Chester Himes*. Jackson: University Press of Mississippi, 1995. A collection of interviews in which Himes speaks candidly about his work, the work of other black writers, racial politics in the United States, the African American community in Harlem, and other topics.

Himes, Chester. *Dear Chester, Dear John: Letters Between Chester Himes and John A. Williams*, compiled and edited by John A. Williams and Lori Williams. Detroit, Mich.: Wayne State University Press, 2008. Himes met Williams, a novice African American writer sixteen years his junior, in 1961, and the two became friends who corresponded for almost thirty years. The letters reveal Himes's personality and his experiences as a black writer. Includes an interview with Himes.

Lundquist, James. *Chester Himes*. New York: Frederick Ungar, 1976. An introductory volume to Himes's life and works, with chapters on the war novels, confessional novels, and detective novels. The first chapter, "November, 1928," describes the armed robbery for which Himes was arrested and the subsequent arrest and trial, in detail. Chronology, notes, bibliography of primary and secondary sources, index.

Margolies, Edward. "Race and Sex: The Novels of Chester Himes." In *Native Sons: A Critical Study of Twentieth-Century Negro American Authors*. Philadelphia: J. B. Lippincott, 1968. A discussion of Himes's major novels. The author sees Himes as considerably different than the group of protest writers following Richard Wright and believes that his European sojourn weakened his writings about the United States. Includes a bibliography and an index.

Margolies, Edward, and Michel Fabre. *The Several Lives of Chester Himes*. Jackson: University Press of Mississippi, 1997. This full-length biography of Himes, written by two people who knew him during the last twenty years of his life, is indispensable for information about his life.

Muller, Gilbert. *Chester Himes*. Boston: Twayne, 1989. An excellent introduction to Himes's life and works. Traces the evolution of his writing, describing how he expressed his grotesque, revolutionary view of life for African Americans in the United States in several literary modes, culminating in his detective fiction. Includes chronology, appendix, index, and annotated bibliographies of primary and secondary works.

Sallis, James. *Chester Himes: A Life*. New York: Walker, 2001. Sallis, a novelist and poet, draws on updated information to provide this detailed recounting of the events of Himes's life and how this life related to his writings.

Silet, Charles L. P., ed. *The Critical Response to Chester Himes*. Westport, Conn.: Greenwood Press, 1999. Reviews and essays analyzing Himes's novels, detective fiction, use of the doppelganger, his anti-Semitism, and his hard-boiled detective tradition. Includes bibliography and index.

Skinner, Robert E. *Two Guns from Harlem: The Detective Fiction of Chester Himes*. Bowling Green, Ohio: Bowling Green State University Popular Press, 1989. Skinner's study presents a comprehensive examination of Himes's mystery and detective novels. He describes how Himes's creation of Coffin Ed Johnson and Grave Digger Jones, two African American police officers, led other writers to create hard-boiled ethnic and female detectives.

Walters, Wendy W. "Harlem on My Mind: Exile and Community in Chester Himes's Detective Fiction." In *At Home in Diaspora: Black International Writing*. Minneapolis: University of Minnesota Press, 2005. Walters describes how Himes's sense of homesickness during his self-imposed exile in Paris led him to write detective novels set in Harlem, even though he never lived there. Himes's Harlem is an imaginary home that reflects both his nostalgia for an African American community and a critique of American racism.

ROLANDO HINOJOSA

Born: Mercedes, Texas; January 21, 1929
Also known as: Rolando Hinojosa-Smith

PRINCIPAL LONG FICTION

Estampas del valle, y otras obras/Sketches of the Valley, and Other Works, 1973 (English revision, *The Valley*, 1983)
Klail City y sus alrededores, 1976 (*Klail City: A Novel*, 1987)
Mi querido Rafa, 1981 (*Dear Rafe*, 1985)
Rites and Witnesses, 1982
Partners in Crime: A Rafe Buenrostro Mystery, 1985
Claros varones de Belken, 1986 (*Fair Gentlemen of Belken County*, 1986)
Becky and Her Friends, 1990
The Useless Servants, 1993
Ask a Policeman, 1998
We Happy Few, 2006

OTHER LITERARY FORMS

Rolando Hinojosa (ee-noh-HOH-sah) is known primarily for his long fiction in both English and Spanish. He has also written a verse novel, *Korean Love Songs from Klail City Death Trip* (1978; printed 1980). Hinojosa produced the book *Agricultural Workers of the Rio Grande and Rio Bravo Valleys* in 1984.

ACHIEVEMENTS

After the death of Tomás Rivera in 1984, Rolando Hinojosa became considered the dean of Mexican American belles lettres and selflessly advanced Mexican American literature throughout the United States, Latin America, and Europe. His works have been translated into German, French, Italian, English, and Spanish, and they have been anthologized by numerous presses. He has received many accolades and awards, including the Premio Quinto Sol in 1972, the Casa de las Américas Prize in 1976, and the Lon Tinkle Award for Lifetime Achievement from the Texas Institute of Letters in 1998. In 2007, Hinojosa, along with Dagoberto Gilb, received the prestigious Bookends Award at the Texas Book Festival in Austin, Texas, in recognition of his lifetime literary achievement. He has lectured and read from his works widely, and scholars—both in the United States and abroad, particularly in Europe—continue to write Ph.D. dissertations and master's theses about his works.

Hinojosa's distinctively concise literary style, in English and Spanish (or a combination of the two), is marked by irony, satire, stark realism, and an extraordinary cutting wit. While his works are often quite experimental, Hinojosa has masterfully incorporated various genres into his novels, including sketches, reportage, epistles, poetry, journal entries, and murder mysteries. Among all Mexican American authors, he is without question the most accomplished and versatile.

Biography

Rolando Hinojosa-Smith was born in Mercedes, Texas, in the Lower Rio Grande Valley of South Texas, to parents who came from mixed ethnic backgrounds—his father, Manuel Guzmán Hinojosa, was a Texas Mexican, and his mother, Carrie Effie Smith, was a Texas Anglo. On his father's side, he is descended from the first Spanish Mexican land-grant settlers who colonized the region in 1749. On his mother's side were Anglo-Texan settlers who arrived in South Texas in 1887. He studied English and Spanish in Texan and Mexican schools, and he was reared to be both bilingual and bicultural in a family that fostered a rich reading environment, with literature from both sides of the U.S.-Mexican border and both sides of the Atlantic. This family background influenced his future literary and cultural interests.

At seventeen, Hinojosa enlisted in the U.S. Army, and after serving his time he entered the University of Texas at Austin under the G.I. Bill. His education was interrupted by the Korean War, but after his tour of duty in Korea, he returned to Austin and in 1953 received his B.S. degree in Spanish literature. He then married, had a son, taught high school, and worked at several other jobs; he and his wife later divorced. After completing an M.A. in Spanish literature at New Mexico Highlands University in 1962, he remarried and entered a doctoral program in 1963 at the University of Illinois, Urbana. There he received a Ph.D. in Spanish literature in 1969 after writing a dissertation on the Spanish writer Benito Pérez Galdós. By this point in his academic career, Hinojosa was the father of two daughters from his second marriage as well as a son from his previous marriage.

Hinojosa then began his college teaching career at Trinity University in San Antonio, Texas. In 1970, he taught Spanish at Texas A&I University in Kingsville, Texas, where he would later serve as chair of the Spanish Department, dean of the College of Arts and Sciences in 1974, and vice president of academic affairs in 1976. His wife's decision to enter law school caused the family to move to the University of Minnesota, where Hinojosa chaired a Chicano studies program and taught creative writing as an English professor. In 1981 he returned to the University of Texas at Austin as a professor of English, teaching Mexican American literature, literature of the Southwest, and creative writing. In 1986 he became Ellen Clayton Garwood Chair of the English Department, a position he continues to hold. His second wife divorced him in 1988 after rearing two daughters with him.

Analysis

In 1970, Rolando Hinojosa began publishing fiction, nonfiction, and poetry, primarily in small Mexican American presses and journals. His major work comprises a series of short novels that he entitled the Klail City Death Trip series after publishing *Korean Love Songs from Klail City Death Trip*, which he has referred to as a novel in verse form. The Klail City Death Trip series is distinguished by the fact that it includes several novels published in both Spanish and English, but the different language renditions do not always represent exactly the same narrative. Significant differences between the two versions or renditions of a given novel exist in the narrative sequence of chapters, with some chapters deleted, others added, and others rearranged. One should thus read both language editions of any of the novels to gain a comprehensive and fully accurate understanding of the Klail City Death Trip series. Some of the novels, moreover, suffer from egregious publishing errors, owing to the failure of Arte Público Press to submit the texts to copyediting before going to press; in some cases large passages are repeated and in others significant passages are completely left out. The most conspicuous of these errors occurred when the publisher omitted the climactic chapter at the end of *The Useless Servants*.

The works in the series were not published in strict chronological order. *Fair Gentlemen of Belken County*, the fourth serial entry of the Klail City Death Trip series, for instance, was written prior to *Dear Rafe* but was published after it.

The Valley

With *The Valley*, Hinojosa begins his serial project by introducing a host of characters, some of whom are extensively developed in succeeding novels. This novel is made up of four loosely connected sections of sketches that give readers a wide sense of the character of the Mexican Texan people inhabiting the fictional Belken County in "the Valley," the area north of the Mexican border in South Texas. Here, the people of various towns are shown at home, in their communities, carrying on with their daily lives. Two cousins, Jehá Malacara and Rafe Buenrostro, are introduced for the first time; the lives of these characters are examined in greater detail in later novels. Both are orphans, with Jehú being raised by various people unrelated to him while Rafe and his brothers are raised by their uncle Julian.

Klail City

Klail City continues with the same format and purpose as *The Valley*, with three sections of sketches. Hinojosa continues to develop his two main characters' lives, but with this novel, he develops a theme that permeates the entire series: the historical conflict between Anglo-Texans and Mexican Texans over the land and the laws governing their lives. In this novel, readers are informed of the cause of Rafe's father's death, murder by a member of a rival Mexican American clan, the Leguizamóns. While Jesús Buenrostro's murder is avenged by his brother Julian, the clans' animosity toward each other remains undiminished as the Klail City Death Trip series progresses. Also introduced in this

Rolando Hinojosa. (Courtesy, University of Texas at Austin)

novel is a greater conflict, the Korean War, which will later affect the main characters' lives, especially Rafe's.

The Useless Servants

The Useless Servants, in prose, extensively shows Rafe's day-to-day life in the war. The masterfully written realism of the battlefield makes both *Korean Love Songs from Klail City Death Trip* and *The Useless Servants* extraordinary testaments to the horror and senselessness of war. One fact that does not escape Rafe and other Mexican Texan soldiers in Korea, however, is that even while defending their country, they are still subjected to racism by their Anglo-American counterparts.

Dear Rafe

Dear Rafe jumps ahead in the serial narrative and portrays Jehú as a principal, though elliptical, character. Incorporating the epistolary and reportage genres, Hinojosa provides multiple perspectives from which readers see the financial, real estate, and political maneuvers enhancing the Anglo-American power structure, as represented by the Klail, Blanchard, Cook (KBC) clan. Employed as a loan officer in a Klail City bank owned by the most powerful Anglo-Texan family in the Valley, Jehú apprentices under bank president Noddy Perkins. Through liaisons Jehú has with three women, he works the system to his clan's advantage by covertly acquiring lands that would otherwise fall into the hands of the rival Leguizamón clan or the KBC clan.

In the first half of the novel, readers gain an understanding of the events by reading a series of letters written by Jehú to Rafe, who is interned in a veterans' hospital for problems arising from wounds suffered in Korea. In the second half, readers are shown a series of interviews conducted with more than a dozen primary and secondary characters by P. Galindo, who has access to Jehú's letters. The novel's main action involves Noddy backing a Mexican Texan, Ira Escobar, against an Anglo-Texan for county commissioner, something the Anglo-Amerian power structure had never done before. As the action progresses, Jehú comes to understand that Ira has been backed for political office because he is an easily manipulated puppet. More important, Noddy brings Ira's Anglo-Texan opponent, Roger Terry, to his knees to control him, through a political ruse, as the Valley's new U.S. congressman, which was Noddy's intention all along. Jehú, however, leaves the bank, disgusted with the state of local politics, and this apparently causes P. Galindo to conduct his interviews. Jehú returns to the bank three years later, as is revealed in *Partners in Crime*.

Rites and Witnesses

This novel's action precedes that of *Dear Rafe* and fills in gaps in the lives of both Rafe and Jehú, incorporating reportage, letters, and sketches, with chapters alternating between action in Korea and events foreshadowing *Dear Rafe*. Noddy Perkins approaches Jehú to run for county commissioner, but Jehú is wise enough to refuse the offer, causing Noddy to recruit Ira Escobar later.

Partners in Crime

With *Partners in Crime* Hinojosa changes direction by writing a murder mystery. A lieutenant in Belken County's homicide squad, Rafe, with his squad, investigates and solves gangland killings related to drug trafficking in the Valley. No longer a place where adverse race relations dominate, the Valley has become corrupted by the economic influence of Mexican drug dealers' laundered money. The cooperation of law-enforcement agencies on both sides of the border becomes the focus of the Klail City Death Trip series. In this novel the head of the Mexican law-enforcement agency, Lisandro Solís, is responsible for the killings and the drug trafficking. In the end he escapes persecution, but he reappears in *Ask a Policeman*.

Fair Gentlemen of Belken County

Written before *Dear Rafe* but not published until 1986, this novel of longer sketches continues filling gaps in Rafe and Jehú's lives after their return from Korea. Hinojosa brilliantly depicts the texture of the Valley's Mexican Texan culture in this novel. While the life of the prominent Mexican Texan elder, Esteban Echevarría, ends, his legacy and wisdom are preserved and honored by Rafe and Jehú.

Becky and Her Friends

Using reportage, like the second half of *Dear Rafe*, *Becky and Her Friends* provides more than two dozen interviews with various people associated with Becky Escobar, who, by her marriage to Ira, is kin to the rival Leguizamón clan. At the beginning of the novel, Becky throws Ira out of their home and asks him for a divorce. They divorce, and as the interviews progress, readers learn the circumstances surrounding her astounding transformation from an utterly anglicized and naïve Mexican Texan to a Mexicanized and independent woman. She is then employed as a business manager by Viola Barragán, a wealthy and successful Mexican Texan businesswoman who figures prominently in previous novels. Under Viola's guidance, Becky asserts her independence and marries Jehú, with whom she had an affair during the political campaigns in *Dear Rafe*. Readers also learn that Rafe has married Noddy Perkins's daughter Sammie Jo, thus cementing, through these two marriages, a resolution between formerly rivaling clans. More important, lands formerly split by these clans are reunited.

Ask a Policeman

In *Ask a Policeman*, another murder mystery, Rafe has been promoted to chief inspector of the Belken County homicide squad. He and his squad again solve drug-related gangland killings, including the murder of Lisandro Solís, who escaped prosecution for his part in the drug running and killings depicted in *Partners in Crime*. This time, the chief law-enforcement officer on the Mexican side, María Luisa (Lu) Cetina, contributes to the successful apprehension of the guilty parties, who include Lisandro's brother and Lisandro's twin sons as well as Canadian and Central American assassins.

WE HAPPY FEW

The action in *We Happy Few* revolves around university politics, including the politicized process of selecting a new president for Belken State University (BSU) in Klail City. After the current university president, Nick Crowder, is diagnosed with terminal cancer, the process of selecting and interviewing candidates to fill this important post ends with the selection of an experienced unmarried Anglo woman, Merle Malone. Her selection sets a gender precedent for the university and goes against what many key players would prefer, as many believe a Mexican American should be selected to fill the BSU presidency, given that BSU is a minority university.

Although the novel's central characters are Anglo administrators, also featured are Mexican American faculty and influential members of the board of regents. Through sparse dialogue, Hinojosa shows how the members of the university's faculty and the administrators appraise each other, sometimes scathingly. The characters also debate the affirmative action hiring policies the president uses to increase the number of minority faculty members. In the end, the rationale for judging, selecting, and appointing both faculty and administrators, including the university president, is guided by what is best for the students and the community. Hinojosa is unsparingly realistic in his judgment of the state of academic affairs in minority universities like BSU, as he covers both the corruption and the integrity of the university administration.

Jaime Armin Mejía

OTHER MAJOR WORKS

POETRY: *Korean Love Songs from Klail City Death Trip*, 1978 (printed 1980, includes some prose).

EDITED TEXT: *Tomás Rivera, 1935-1984: The Man and His Work*, 1988 (with Gary D. Keller and Vernon E. Lattin).

MISCELLANEOUS: *Generaciones, Notas, y Brechas/ Generations, Notes, and Trails*, 1978; *Agricultural Workers of the Rio Grande and Rio Bravo Valleys*, 1984.

BIBLIOGRAPHY

Hernandez, Guillermo E. *Chicano Satire: A Study in Literary Culture*. Austin: University of Texas Press, 1991. Explores how satire is employed in the works of three Chicano authors: Luis Miguel Valdez, José Montoya, and Rolando Hinojosa. Provides insights into some of the volumes of Hinojosa's Klail City Death Trip series.

Karem, Jeff. "The Permeable Borders of Rolando Hinojosa's Valley." In *The Romance of Authenticity: The Cultural Politics of Regional and Ethnic Literatures*. Charlottesville: University of Virginia Press, 2004. Shows how Hinojosa consistently evades limiting categories of ethnic authenticity by placing characters on opposite sides of where they are expected to be. Part of a larger work that analyzes how authors William Faulkner, Richard Wright, Ernest Gaines, Leslie Marmon Silko, and Hinojosa embrace or elude categories of cultural authenticity.

Lee, Joyce Glover. *Rolando Hinojosa and the American Dream*. Denton: University of North Texas Press, 1997. Provides a good examination of Hinojosa's works and attempts to bring biographical and psychological analysis to the Klail City Death Trip series.

Saldívar, José David, ed. *The Rolando Hinojosa Reader: Essays Historical and Critical*. Houston: Arte Público Press, 1985. Collection of essays includes contributions by a small number of scholars who discuss Hinojosa's works as well as by Hinojosa himself. Shows how the Klail City Death Trip series was approached in early critical analyses.

Saldívar, Ramón. "Rolando Hinojosa's *Korean Love Songs* and the *Klail City Death Trip*: A Border Ballad and Its Heroes." In *Chicano Narrative: The Dialectics of Difference*. Madison: University of Wisconsin Press, 1990. Chapter examining the Klail City Death Trip series is part of one of the most important works of Chicano literary criticism published to date.

Zilles, Klaus. *Rolando Hinojosa: A Reader's Guide*. Albuquerque: University of New Mexico Press, 2001. Guide provides information on Hinojosa's Valley and its inhabitants, focusing on the theme of oral history represented in the series.

S. E. HINTON

Born: Tulsa, Oklahoma; July 22, 1948
Also known as: Susan Eloise Hinton

Principal long fiction

The Outsiders, 1967
That Was Then, This Is Now, 1971
Rumble Fish, 1975
Tex, 1979
Taming the Star Runner, 1988
Hawkes Harbor, 2004

Other literary forms

Although known primarily for her long fiction, S. E. Hinton has also written two children's books, the humorous picture book *Big David, Little David* (1995) and the elementary-age chapter book *The Puppy Sister* (1995), both loosely inspired by her own son. In 2007, Hinton published *Some of Tim's Stories*, a collection of linked short stories that also contains several interviews not published elsewhere. She received credit with Francis Ford Coppola for the 1983 screenplay adaptation of her novel *Rumble Fish* and served as an adviser and played cameo roles in the film adaptations of *Tex* (1982) and *The Outsiders* (1983).

Achievements

S. E. Hinton's novels have collectively sold more than ten million copies and have been translated into more than twenty languages. Her first four books were cited by the American Library Association as Best Books for Young Adults. In 1988, shortly before the publication of her fifth novel, Hinton became the first recipient of the Margaret A. Edwards Award, a lifetime achievement award given by the young adult division of the American Library Association and *School Library Journal*. In 1997, Hinton received the Arrell Gibson Lifetime Achievement Award from the Oklahoma Center for the Book. Her first four novels were adapted into films that helped launch the careers of several notable actors, including Matt Dillon, Patrick Swayze, and Tom Cruise. *The Outsiders* also was adapted as a short-lived television series in the 1990's. Hinton is widely recognized by scholars as having helped create the contemporary form of young adult literature, and she has made a long-lasting and undeniable impact on the field.

Biography

Susan Eloise Hinton was born in Tulsa, Oklahoma, in 1948. As a teenager, she was shy and did not like to draw attention to herself, yet she did not conform to the expected pursuits of a teenage girl at that time. She was a tomboy who loved horses, and although she generally did not suffer directly from the social tension that existed between the socioeconomic classes in her town, she felt keenly the effects that such tension had on those around her.

While Hinton was in high school, her father was diagnosed with a brain tumor and was hospitalized for extended periods of time. In response, Hinton threw herself into the novel she had begun writing in order to create the type of realistic fiction she herself craved as a reader. She completed the first draft during her junior year, around the same time her father died. She then polished the work in subsequent drafts but did not consider submitting it for publication until a writer acquaintance advised her to send it to her own agent. The book was quickly accepted, and during the editorial process, Hinton graduated from high school and began attending the University of Tulsa, initially majoring in journalism and later switching to education. It was during this time that Hinton's publisher encouraged her to use the gender-neutral initials for her byline, fearing that reviewers might dismiss a male-oriented book written by a female author.

Although it was not technically an overnight sensation, benefiting instead by word of mouth among its target audience and eventually teachers, *The Outsiders* received enough attention that Hinton's life changed drastically. Her inherent shyness made interviewing difficult, and her study of other writers negatively impacted her confidence in her own abilities. Hinton developed a severe case of writer's block that persisted until her boyfriend David Inhofe convinced her to sit down and write two pages per day before allowing herself to go anywhere. Hinton graduated in 1970 with a degree in education; in that same year, she married Inhofe and sent off her second book, *That Was Then, This Is Now*, which was published the following year.

Hinton continued to keep a relatively low profile for a successful author. Her third book, *Rumble Fish*, was published in 1975, and her fourth, *Tex*, was published in 1979. Both novels continued to explore the theme of teenage boys trying to find their place in a sometimes heartless world, often with little or no parental support. In the early 1980's, Hinton's comfortable routine was shaken up when Disney purchased the rights to turn *Tex* into a film. Hinton was closely involved in the making of the film, even convincing the producers to use her own horse in the film and teaching the young star, Matt Dillon, how to ride. Hinton also gave birth to her son, Nicholas, in 1983.

As Hinton concentrated on her family life, her writing pace slowed further. A fifth young adult novel, *Taming the Star Runner*, was published in 1988 to generally positive reviews. Then, after the largest gap since she had begun publishing, *Hawkes Harbor*, an unusual vampire novel for adults, appeared in 2004, generating confused reactions from reviewers.

Analysis

S. E. Hinton's novels are fine examples of young adult literature, and *The Outsiders* in particular is credited with igniting the trend toward realistically based young adult fiction. Her uncanny ability to write about issues that concern young people, such as finding their place in a cruel and unfair world, has resulted in enduring popularity among new generations of young adults over the years. Hinton creates effective, memorable characters who stand out as individuals even though they are often quite similar to one another, and her use of male protagonists with introspective sensibilities helps her reach a broad audience of both male and female readers. Hinton's fans also delight in the subtle connections between her novels, with major characters from earlier books sometimes appearing in small but significant roles in later books.

As a whole, Hinton's body of work shows the developments that have taken place not only in her writing but also her personal life and the world around her. Her earliest work focuses primarily on the tensions between socioeconomic classes and lack of parental support, whether through death or abandonment. Gradually, however, she began incorporating into her fiction the growing threat of drug abuse and the development of hippie culture, as well as her personal love of horses. The long-enduring popularity of her books has given her the freedom to experiment outside the genre for which she is known.

The Outsiders

Hinton's first novel, *The Outsiders*, remains her best-known book. It is a staple on high school reading lists, but is also regularly challenged because of its controversial subject matter. Written from the first-person perspective of a fourteen-year-old boy, *The Outsiders* is not autobiographical but rather based on amalgams of the people and situations that Hinton observed around her, thus contributing to its realism. The narrator, Ponyboy Curtis, reflects on his life as a greaser, or kid from the wrong side of the tracks, a life that has become more dif-

S. E. Hinton. (David Inhofe)

ficult since a car accident claimed his parents' lives. Ponyboy and his two older brothers must fend for themselves, yet they are far better off than many of the greasers who make up their extended family, including Johnny Cade, who is alternately beaten and ignored by his parents, and Dallas "Dally" Winston, who in spite of his young age has already done jail time.

Ponyboy's life rapidly spirals out of control when he and Johnny are attacked by a drunken group of Sociables, or Socs (pronounced SOHSH-ehz), the well-off teens from the other side of town. Fearing for their lives, Johnny stabs and kills one of the attackers, and the two friends must go on the run. They eventually decide to turn themselves in but are diverted by a fire, in which Johnny is critically injured while trying to save some children. When Johnny dies from his injuries, Dally is devastated and deliberately creates a situation that will cause the police to shoot him. The three deaths in rapid succession shock the town, and Ponyboy tries to pick up the pieces of his life, starting with writing about the events for a school assignment.

Because of its sharp contrast with the more superficial books that were popular at the time, *The Outsiders* shocked many adults with its frank descriptions of parental abuse, underage drinking, violent fights, and other delinquent behavior. Young readers found the realism refreshing, however, and Hinton received mail from countless readers thanking her for writing the book. While critics pointed out that the story was perhaps overly sentimental and the writing undisciplined, many of them recognized the raw emotional power that Hinton had harnessed.

THAT WAS THEN, THIS IS NOW

That Was Then, This Is Now, Hinton's second novel, takes place in the same setting as *The Outsiders* and even features Ponyboy Curtis in a small role, but the work is not considered a sequel. In this story, Bryon has been friends with Mark from early childhood; in fact, Mark has lived with Bryon and his mother ever since his own parents killed each other in a drunken argument. Byron's mother, although loving, has medical problems that prevent her from monitoring the boys' activities, and they have grown up drinking, smoking, hustling pool, and getting in fights on a regular basis. Bryon considers his life normal, but his world is turned upside down when a friend, Charlie, is killed trying to protect Bryon and Mark from some angry thugs they have hustled. Then, just after witnessing the possibly irreversible effects of an LSD overdose on a young boy named M&M, Bryon learns that Mark is dealing drugs. The timing of this discovery causes Bryon to turn Mark in to the police, irrevocably ending their friendship as well as ending Bryon's ability to relate to the people around him.

Although some critics believe *That Was Then, This Is Now* did not live up to *The Outsiders* in terms of raw emotional power, others found the book to be more mature and therefore equally effective. In addition, the book incorporated a powerful message about the devastating effects of drugs, a theme Hinton revisits in later works.

RUMBLE FISH

In *Rumble Fish*, Rusty James aspires to be like his older brother, Motorcycle Boy, who is feared and respected for his calm, tough demeanor. The days of organized gang fighting have waned, however, and both Rusty and Motorcycle Boy are having trouble finding their place in this changed environment. Motorcycle Boy takes off for extended intervals, while Rusty tries to hang on to the life he knows, with only their kind but mostly absent alcoholic father for company. After a long trip, Motorcycle Boy reveals that he has had contact with the boys' mother, who had left them many years before. This encounter seems to hasten his feelings of desperation, and much like Dallas Winston in *The Outsiders*, Motorcycle Boy deliberately sets up a situation in which the police will inevitably shoot and kill him, leaving Rusty to wander aimlessly. Through flashback, the reader learns that Rusty's memory has become sporadic and he has served some jail time.

Critical reactions to *Rumble Fish* varied widely. Some felt that the book was a mere rehashing of Hinton's earlier work, while others found that Rusty's inarticulate and confused narrative and the book's moody atmosphere were extremely effective. In working with Hinton to translate the story to film, Coppola shot in black and white and utilized short, choppy sequences heavy with imagery to retain what he interpreted as Hinton's raw emotional power.

TEX

In *Tex*, Texas "Tex" McCormick is devastated when his older brother Mason sells Tex's beloved horse to pay the bills. Their mother had died years earlier from pneumonia and their father leaves for months at a time to follow the rodeo circuit, often forgetting to send the boys money. In addition, Tex must deal with his first love, his brother's anxiety over trying to make ends meet, and being kidnapped by a hitchhiker who has escaped from prison (Mark from *That Was Then, This Is Now*). Just as things seem to be improving, Tex learns that he was actually fathered by someone else while the man he thinks of as his father was in prison. Reeling from this discovery, Tex unthinkingly gets caught up in a bad drug deal and is shot. He survives, but it is clear that he will have to rethink and rebuild his entire world.

Most reviewers remarked upon the novel's new level of maturity and its consistent voice. In addition, Tex's love for his horse gives the story an extra layer of poignancy, and in spite of the somewhat melodramatic events, the novel ends with more hope than Hinton's previous work.

TAMING THE STAR RUNNER

In many ways, *Taming the Star Runner* is the most autobiographical of Hinton's novels, even though the main character, Travis Harris, is male. Employing third-person narration for the first time, the story begins when Travis goes to live with his uncle after a violent altercation with his stepfather. His uncle is going through a divorce and initially treats Travis like a stranger, but the two gradually get to know each other in one of the most interesting and positive teen-adult relationships in any of Hinton's books.

Although a mediocre student at best, Travis has been seriously writing for some time and is stunned when he sells his first novel while still in high school. During publishing negotiations, Travis's editor advises him to start writing a new book right away to avoid writer's block. The reader cannot help but wonder if Hinton wishes she could give the same advice to her younger self.

In the meantime, Travis has become fascinated with Casey, a feisty young woman who runs a riding school and is attempting to tame a wild horse named Star Runner. Travis observes those around him with a writer's insight and thus is the only one who understands Casey's motivations in continuing to work with the dangerous horse. The growing romantic potential between them is quenched when Star Runner is tragically killed by lightning, but their friendship remains, and the reader has the impression that Travis has taken his first steps toward meaningful adult relationships.

Although some critics believed that the detailed descriptions of stables and riding competition would put off Hinton's regular audience, others felt it added yet another new layer of realism and emotion to her work. In addition, some felt the addition of a subplot, in which one of Travis's friends from back home gets tangled up in a murder case, was overly dramatic and emphasized that Travis benefited more from luck than his own efforts. Other reviewers, however, found the message about luck and timing to be effective and realistic and that *Taming the Star Runner* offered more of a genuine glimpse into the author's mind than her previous work.

Amy Sisson

OTHER MAJOR WORKS

SHORT FICTION: *Some of Tim's Stories*, 2007.

SCREENPLAY: *Rumble Fish*, 1983 (adaptation of her novel; with Francis Ford Coppola).

CHILDREN'S LITERATURE: *Big David, Little David*, 1995; *The Puppy Sister*, 1995.

BIBLIOGRAPHY

Abrams, Dennis. *S. E. Hinton*. New York: Chelsea House, 2009. Introductory book on Hinton's life and fiction written especially for younger readers. Part of the Who Wrote That? series. Includes a chronology, a bibliography, photographs, and an index.

Daly, Jay. *Presenting S. E. Hinton*. Boston: Twayne, 1987. This examination of Hinton's first four novels includes extensive coverage of reviewers' reactions to each title, background information on the development of each story, and details about Hinton's involvement in the filmed adaptations.

Hinton, S. E. *Some of Tim's Stories*. Norman: University of Oklahoma Press, 2007. Although the first half of this book consists of short stories, the second half contains interviews of the author not published elsewhere, offering retrospective insights into the author's early writing years.

Kjelle, Marylou Morano. *S. E. Hinton: Author of "The Outsiders."* Berkeley Heights, N.J.: Enslow, 2008.

This biography intersperses analysis of Hinton's work, especially *The Outsiders*, with facts about her life. Includes transcripts of speeches, interviews, and some photographs.

Wilson, Antoine. *S. E. Hinton*. New York: Rosen Central, 2003. This biography discusses Hinton's young adult novels, her life, and her writing style and philosophy.

EDWARD HOAGLAND

Born: New York, New York; December 21, 1932

PRINCIPAL LONG FICTION

Cat Man, 1956
The Circle Home, 1960
The Peacock's Tail, 1965
Seven Rivers West, 1986

OTHER LITERARY FORMS

Edward Hoagland is known primarily not for his novels but for his essays and travel books. As an essayist and reviewer, he has been published in such periodicals as *Harper's*, *The Village Voice*, *Sports Illustrated*, *Commentary*, and *The Atlantic Monthly*; several anthologies of his essays remain in print. His travel narratives include *Notes from the Century Before: A Journal from British Columbia* (1969) and *African Calliope: A Journey to the Sudan* (1979). During the 1960's, he also wrote short stories, which appeared in publications such as *Esquire*, *The New Yorker*, *New American Review*, and *The Paris Review*; three of his short stories have been republished in *City Tales* (1986). A collection of three of his short stories, *The Final Fate of the Alligators: Stories from the City* (1992), received favorable reviews. Hoagland also edited the twenty-nine-volume Penguin Nature Library, and he also writes book reviews and nature-based editorials for *The New York Times*.

ACHIEVEMENTS

With the publication of his first novel, *Cat Man*, in 1956, Edward Hoagland received much favorable attention from the critics. The book won for Hoagland a Houghton Mifflin Literary Fellowship, and critics saw in him the makings of a first-rate novelist. They particularly praised his ability to capture a milieu—in this case, the seamy world of circus roustabouts, a world he presents with knowledgeable and detailed frankness. His second novel, *The Circle Home*, confirmed his potential. Once again, he succeeded in vividly re-creating a colorful environment, the sweaty world of a boxing gymnasium. He received several honors during this period as well, including a Longview Foundation Award in 1961, an American Academy of Arts and Letters Traveling Fellowship in 1964, and a Guggenheim Fellowship in 1964.

Hoagland received another Guggenheim in 1975 and was a nominee for the 1979 National Book Critics Circle Award for the travel book *African Calliope*. In 1971, he received an O. Henry Award and in 1972 a literary citation from the Brandeis University Creative Arts Awards Commission. He received the Harold D. Vursell Award of the American Academy of Arts and Letters in 1981, and he was elected to membership in the academy in 1982.

With the publication of *The Peacock's Tail* in 1965, Hoagland's fiction career suffered a setback. In both the critics' and his own opinion, this book was a failure, and Hoagland, whose novels had never won for him a wide audience, turned away from long fiction. For the next twenty years, he worked primarily in nonfiction, producing essays and travel narratives to considerable acclaim. In 1986, he made a triumphal return to the novel. *Seven Rivers West* was well received, combining as it does Hoagland's ability to re-create a sense of place—here, the North American wilderness—with his impressive knowledge of the natural world.

Biography

Edward Hoagland was born on December 21, 1932, in New York City. His father was a financial lawyer whose employers included Standard Oil of New Jersey and the U.S. Defense and State departments. When he was eight years old, his family moved to New Canaan, Connecticut, a fashionable community of country estates and exclusive clubs. He was sent off to boarding school at Deerfield Academy, where, because of his bookishness, he was assigned to a special corridor known as the Zoo, which was reserved for those whom the school deemed incorrigible misfits. Hoagland did have great difficulty fitting in as a child. In large part this was because of his stutter. Understandably, he shunned potentially embarrassing social situations, developing a love of solitude and wildlife instead. Indeed, from the age of ten onward, he became very close to nature and kept a variety of pets ranging from dogs to alligators.

Hoagland went to Harvard, where he was strongly drawn to writing, a medium in which he could speak unhampered by his stutter. He studied literature under such notables as Alfred Kazin, Archibald MacLeish, and John Berryman; encouraged by his professors, he set to work on his first novel. In his spare time he read Socialist publications and attended meetings of a Trotskyite cell in the theater district of Boston. He graduated from Harvard cum laude in 1954 with his first novel already accepted by Houghton Mifflin.

Hoagland had to put his literary career on hold, however, when he was drafted. He served in the U.S. Army from 1955 to 1957, working in the medical laboratory and looking after the morgue at Valley Forge Army Hospital in Pennsylvania. Following his discharge, Hoagland returned to New York City. Financially, times were very difficult. His father, who disapproved of his decision to become a writer, had cut him off. In fact, his father was so opposed to his son's career that he wrote to Houghton Mifflin's lawyer to try to stop publication of his first novel. Hoagland's annual income over the next fifteen years averaged three thousand dollars.

In 1960, Hoagland's second novel was published and he married Amy Ferrara, from whom he was divorced in 1964. At about this time he also became active politically, marching in civil rights and peace demonstrations and mailing his draft card to President Lyndon B. Johnson. To supplement his income, he began accepting academic posts as well, teaching at such schools as Rutgers, Sarah Lawrence, Iowa, and Columbia. In 1968, he married Marion Magid, the managing editor of *Commentary*, with whom he had a daughter, Molly.

For many years Hoagland lived in New York City but spent several months of each year in upper Vermont. He also traveled to diverse areas such as Yemen and the Alaskan and Canadian wilderness. He and Magid were divorced in 1993. Hoagland began teaching at Bennington College and dividing his time between Bennington and Barton, Vermont, where he lived several months of the year in an eight-room farmhouse, without electricity or telephone lines. The property adjoins an eight-thousand-acre state forest to which Hoagland willed most of his land. Hoagland suffered blindness in the late 1990's but had his sight restored through surgery; however, it was feared that the condition might recur. Although Hoagland was essentially disinherited by his father, he was able to make a living from writing and teaching.

Analysis

Edward Hoagland's novels are marked by a keen eye for detail and a remarkable sense of place. They masterfully re-create unusual and often male-dominated environments, such as that of the circus or a boxing gym. His protagonists tend to be isolated and lonely men, cut off through their own actions from those they love, men who generally have failed in their relationships with women. They are misfits, drifters, or dreamers, and the novels are often organized around their journeys, which may be merely flight, as in *The Circle Home*, or a clearly focused quest, as in *Seven Rivers West*. Because of this episodic structure, the books have a looseness that can approach the discursive at times, with flashbacks and digressions slowing the pace.

Cat Man

Many of these traits are already apparent in Hoagland's first work, *Cat Man*. Drawn from his own experience working in a circus, *Cat Man* offers a graphic and harrowing portrayal of the life of the low-paid circus roustabouts, most of whom are derelicts or social outcasts. With his usual attraction to the eccentric and offbeat, Hoagland creates a human menagerie, a gallery of

Edward Hoagland. (© Nancy Crampton)

grotesques such as Dogwash, who will not touch water and cleans himself by wiping his whole body as hard as he can with paper. The novel presents a brutal world in which violence threatens constantly from both the workers and the animals. In fact, the book begins with an attempted murder and ends with a lion attack. It is also a world of rampant racism, a world in which the insane are to be laughed at and women sexually used and abandoned. As sordid and disturbing as all this is, Hoagland conveys it with remarkable vividness and attention to detail. Indeed, it is the searing portrayal of this world that is the novel's great strength.

Fiddler, the main character, is a classic Hoagland protagonist. A youth who has been with the circus only seven weeks, he has been cut off from his family by his alcoholism and is very much an alienated man. Suffering from low self-esteem, he develops a foolhardy and almost obsessive fascination with the beauty and grace of his charges, the lions and tigers that it is his job, as a cat man, to tend. Hoagland's own interest in and knowledge of animals is quite evident, as he endows the cats with as much individuality as the humans. Yet while Hoagland is clearly as fascinated as Fiddler with the animals, he never sentimentalizes them. The cats may be magnificent but they can also be uncaring and deadly, a lesson that Fiddler finally and fatally learns.

Also typical of Hoagland's novels is the fact that *Cat Man* has a loose structure. Ostensibly, it is the story of one tragic day in Council Bluffs, but interspersed throughout the narrative are the events of other days in other places as Fiddler travels cross-country with the circus. Many of these episodes could stand on their own as quite good short stories, but inserted as they are within the novel's main narrative they interrupt the momentum and slow the book's flow.

The Circle Home

Hoagland's second novel, *The Circle Home*, once again features a main character who is a lonely misfit. In this work, the protagonist is an over-the-hill boxer who rightly fears that he is doomed to become a derelict like his father. Again, too, he is a man who, through his own actions, is alienated from his family. Denny Kelly, however, is a less sympathetic figure than Fiddler. He has been so abusive toward his wife, Patsy, that she has repeatedly thrown him out. In fact, Denny seems incapable of committing himself to another person and simply takes advantage of women such as his wife or Margaret, an older woman whom he exploits for whatever material and sexual comforts she can supply.

Essentially, Denny is an immature child (indeed, he is strongly attracted to children), with all the selfishness and irresponsibility that that implies. Moreover, he avoids serious introspection whenever possible and actively fights any inclination toward thought by drowning himself in sensual pleasures. If Hoagland presents animals with considerable understanding in *Cat Man*, in *The Circle Home* he focuses on an individual who exists on little more than an animal level. Denny is incapable of expressing his feelings or organizing his life, and he responds simply to the need for food, shelter, and sex.

If Fiddler clung to the cats in an attempt to give his life meaning, the one element in Denny's life that gives him a sense of achievement is boxing. The novel examines his fate once that is lost to him. Completely demoralized by being brutally beaten in a training bout, Denny abandons the ring and takes to the road, drifting closer and closer to his feared future as a derelict. While the ending of *Cat Man* was utterly bleak, *The Circle Home* offers some hope: In hitting rock bottom, Denny gains some degree of self-awareness. Although his future is far from certain, Denny does at least attempt to overcome his irresponsibility and selfishness as he tries to reconcile with his wife. He has made "the circle home," returning via a long and circuitous route of self-discovery.

Critics were generally enthusiastic about *The Circle Home*, praising in particular its convincing portrayal of the grimy world of the Better Champions' Gym. If *Cat Man* showed Hoagland's detailed knowledge of the circus, this novel shows his thorough familiarity with boxing, as he digresses on such subjects as types of fighters and gym equipment. The book's structure, however, is again quite loose, with repeated shifts in time and place and the use of an episodic journey as an organizing principle.

The Peacock's Tail

In Hoagland's third novel, however, the problems are more than simply structural. Regarded by the critics as his weakest piece of long fiction, *The Peacock's Tail* is the rambling story of Ben Pringle, a prejudiced and maladjusted white, Anglo-Saxon, Protestant, or WASP, who has taken up residence in a seedy New York City hotel. As usual, Hoagland's main character is a misfit isolated from those he loves. Like Denny, Ben has difficulty maintaining a lasting relationship with a woman and has just been rejected by his lover, an experience that has left him with a badly damaged ego. Indeed, like the earlier protagonists, Ben in his troubled state needs stability and support. While Fiddler clung to his cats and Denny to boxing to retain some sense of pride and avoid a total collapse, Ben turns to children, becoming a storyteller and pied piper to the hordes of youngsters who inhabit his hotel.

If Denny was attracted to children, who mirrored his own arrested development, Ben seems to turn to them out of an inability to deal with adults, using their approval to boost his crumbling sense of self-worth. Powerless and out of control with his peers, he derives a sense of power and control from the adulation of the young. Hoagland apparently intends for the reader to believe that Ben finds happiness and fulfillment leading hundreds of children through the streets of New York to the strains of his newly acquired harmonica. Yet Ben's newfound role as pied piper seems less a solution to his problems than a frenzied attempt to escape them.

Once one doubts the validity of Ben's solution, however, one is also forced to question the reality of the novel's setting. While the faithful depiction of milieu was the great strength of Hoagland's earlier novels, *The Peacock's Tail* takes place in an Upper West Side welfare hotel, which is presented as if it were one large amusement park. The hotel is inhabited by vibrant, lusty blacks and Hispanics who exude an earthiness and enthusiasm that is apparently meant to balance Ben's Waspish reserve and alienation. The earlier novels portrayed their environments with a hard-edged and knowledgeable use of detail. Here the portrait is sentimentalized, a musical-comedy version of a welfare hotel.

Seven Rivers West

The artistic and critical failure of *The Peacock's Tail* represented a setback for Hoagland's promising novelistic career, and he followed it with a twenty-year hiatus from long fiction. With his fourth novel, however, Hoagland fully redeemed himself. *Seven Rivers West* is an entertaining and dazzlingly inventive tale. Set in the North American West of the 1880's, it features the most likable incarnation of the Hoagland protagonist: Cecil Roop. Another man isolated from his loved ones, he, like Denny, has abandoned his family and is now on a journey. Yet while Denny drifted aimlessly, Cecil is on a quest: He wants to capture a grizzly bear. At least, that is his goal until he learns of the existence of Bigfoot, which then becomes his obsession. Like Fiddler's obsession with cats, however, Cecil's fascination with this mysterious creature ultimately proves tragic.

If this sounds like a tall tale, Hoagland grounds it in an utterly convincing reality, presented with documentary exactness. In fact, the novel includes a wealth of information about nature. Yet this information emerges spontaneously as the characters seek to understand their magnificent and overwhelming environment; the pace never slows as the book vigorously follows the characters' picaresque and perilous journey. Moreover, the novel includes Hoagland's most colorful assortment of eccentrics, ranging from Cecil's companion who specializes in jumping forty feet into a tub of water to a trader celebrated for his prowess in bladder-voiding competitions.

Probably the book's greatest achievement, however, as in Hoagland's first two novels, is its stunning and detailed sense of place. The unsentimental portrayal of the unspoiled West is at times rhapsodic as Hoagland presents a world that can chill with its beauty. Hoagland depicts not only the full glory but also the full fury of nature. He offers the reader a world that is as casually violent as that of *Cat Man*, a world where creatures can almost without warning be swept away in torrents or mauled by savage beasts. With its energy, its imaginativeness, and its sheer grandeur, *Seven Rivers West* is Hoagland at his best.

Hoagland's novels, published over a period of thirty years, have a number of traits in common. One is their focus on and sympathy for the downcast and outcast, for the social misfit who finds himself alone as he journeys through a hostile and dangerous world in which his mere survival is tenuous. Isolation is a constant theme, with the protagonists having great difficulty maintaining relationships with women. Yet as harsh and as lonely as these environments are, Hoagland's ability to describe them with honesty and fidelity gives his books a vividness and immediacy that leaves a lasting impact.

Charles Trainor
Updated by Margaret A. Dodson

Other major works

SHORT FICTION: *City Tales*, 1986; *The Final Fate of the Alligators: Stories from the City*, 1992.

NONFICTION: *Notes from the Century Before: A Journal from British Columbia*, 1969; *The Courage of Turtles: Fifteen Essays About Compassion, Pain, and Love*, 1970; *Walking the Dead Diamond River*, 1973; *The Moose on the Wall: Field Notes from the Vermont Wilderness*, 1974; *Red Wolves and Black Bears*, 1976; *The Edward Hoagland Reader*, 1976; *African Calliope: A Journey to the Sudan*, 1979; *The Tugman's Passage*, 1982; *Heart's Desire: The Best of Edward Hoagland—Essays From Twenty Years*, 1988; *Balancing Acts: Essays*, 1992; *Tigers and Ice: Essays on Life and Nature*, 1999; *Compass Points: How I Lived*, 2001; *Hoagland on Nature: Essays*, 2003; *Early In the Season: A British Columbia Journal*, 2008.

EDITED TEXT: *The Best American Essays, 1999*, 1999.

Bibliography

Baker, John F. "Frank Memoir by a Hopeful Traveler." *Publishers Weekly*, March 19, 2001. A profile of Hoagland that explores his background and writing career. This article appeared after the publication of Hoagland's 2001 memoir *Compass Points: How I Lived.* Hoagland says in the article that he is beginning to believe that he "perhaps can't quite make the necessary imaginative leap" that would enable him to publish another novel.

Ehrlich, Gretel. "An Essayist's Search for Bedrock." *Los Angeles Times Book Review*, April 30, 1995. A review of Hoagland's *African Calliope*, *The Tugman's Passage*, and *Red Wolves and Black Bears*. Discusses the lasting quality of Hoagland's personal perspective and style in his essays.

Hicks, Granville. "The Many Faces of Failure." *Saturday Review* 48 (August 14, 1965): 21-22. Discusses Hoagland's depiction of misfits in his fiction, particularly in his novel *The Peacock's Tail.*

Johnson, Ronald L. Review of *Seven Rivers West*, by Edward Hoagland. *Western American Literature* 22 (November, 1987): 227-228. Johnson contrasts the novel's lavish description of the Canadian landscape with what he believes is a less than compelling plot.

"Member Profile." *Wilderness* (December, 2006/2007): 46. Hoagland, a member of the Wilderness Society, is profiled in the organization's journal. He recollects his struggles with childhood stuttering, his work at a zoo, and the publication of *Cat Man*, which is based on his circus experiences. Hoagland eventually concentrated on writing essays instead of novels because, he tells the interviewer, "I didn't have the genes for it. Novelists need stronger memories and imaginations."

Mills, Nicolaus. "A Rural Life Style." *Yale Review* 60 (June, 1971): 609-613. Looks at *The Courage of Turtles* as an expression of the rural movement in American writing. Hoagland notices what others miss about rural life: that it can be uncomfortable, angry, and in need of political organization. He also shows that it is ironically inaccessible to the very people who need it the most—those who have had to move from the country to the city because they could not afford their rural lifestyle.

Sagalyn, Raphael. Review of *The Edward Hoagland Reader* and *African Calliope*, by Edward Hoagland. *The New Republic*, December 19, 1979. A review of two of Hoagland's nonfiction works that contrasts his personal essays with his fiction. *African Calliope* is described as an apparently disjointed travel book which becomes clearer as its people come alive and discoveries are made while journeying through the Sudan.

Updike, John. "Back to Nature." *The New Yorker*, March 30, 1987. Focuses on the novel *Seven Rivers West*, which Updike praises for its detailed information about frontier life. While there is much visual material, Updike says there is less sound and feeling in the novel, and the heroes' motives are not as exciting as those of the hero in *Cat Man*. In the pursuit of Bigfoot, Updike finds an invitation to compare it with the quest for Moby Dick, and pronounces Hoagland significant in the company of the American nineteenth century Transcendentalists.

_______. "Journeyers." *The New Yorker*, March 10, 1980. Updike examines *The Edward Hoagland Reader* in the context of its preceding novel, *Cat Man*, and compares the reader with other travel books of the time.

ALICE HOFFMAN

Born: New York, New York; March 16, 1952

Principal long fiction

Property Of, 1977
The Drowning Season, 1979
Angel Landing, 1980
White Horses, 1982
Fortune's Daughter, 1985
Illumination Night, 1987
At Risk, 1988
Seventh Heaven, 1990
Turtle Moon, 1992
Second Nature, 1994
Practical Magic, 1995
Here on Earth, 1997
Local Girls, 1999
The River King, 2000
Blue Diary, 2001
The Probable Future, 2003
The Ice Queen, 2005
Skylight Confessions, 2007
The Third Angel, 2008

Other literary forms

Alice Hoffman's short stories and nonfiction have appeared in such notable publications as *The New York Times*, *Boston Globe* magazine, *Kenyon Review*, *Boulevard*, *Architectural Digest*, *Gourmet*, *Premier*, *Self*, *Southwestern Review*, and *Redbook*. Her work also has been published in the anthologies *Family*, *Thirty-Three Things Every Girl Should Know*, and *Cape Cod Stories*. In addition, she has written novels for young adults as well as children's books.

Achievements

Alice Hoffman's novels have been recognized as notable books of the year by *The New York Times*, the *Los Angeles Times*, *Library Journal*, and *People* magazine. In 2007, her teen novel *Incantation* won the Massachusetts Book Award. A number of her works have been adapted for film, and she was the original screenwriter for the film *Independence Day* (1983). Her 1997 novel *Here on Earth* was selected for Oprah Winfrey's Book Club, which helped her gain more readers as well as international acclaim. Her books have been translated into more than twenty languages. Her 1988 novel *At Risk* is included as required reading on many academic reading lists. After successful treatment for breast cancer in 1998, she established the Hoffman Breast Center at Mount Auburn Hospital in Cambridge, Massachusetts.

Biography

Alice Hoffman was born in New York City on March 16, 1952, and grew up on Long Island. Her mother was a teacher and social worker, and her father was a real estate agent. Though her parents divorced when she was eight years old, her father remained a constant in her life because he had left her his vast collection of fantasy and science-fiction magazines and novels, including the works of Robert A. Heinlein and Ray Bradbury. She became an insatiable reader. She loved fairy tales and myths, which she later deemed the inspiration for all literature to follow. The dark, scary tales by the Grimm brothers appealed to her more than the lighter offerings of Mother Goose and Hans Christian Andersen.

After graduating from high school, Hoffman entered the workforce, but a single morning in the factory of Doubleday convinced her that she was not suited for supervised eight-hour days and restroom passes; she quit that job at noon. Though she had not considered herself college material, she enrolled at Adelphi University, graduating with a degree in English and anthropology in 1973. She was awarded a Mirrellees Fellowship and studied at Stanford University, earning her master of arts degree in 1975.

Hoffman attributes her motivation to become a writer to her mentor and professor, Albert J. Guerard, and to Maclin Bocock Guerard, both accomplished authors who encouraged her to publish her first short story. Her first novel, *Property Of*, was published in 1977. From then on, aside from establishing a home and raising two children with husband Ted Martin, writing has been her life.

Neither her breast-cancer diagnosis in 1998 nor the yearlong radiation treatments could interfere with Hoffman's will to keep writing. She has said that when she was too sick to sit at her desk, she would move to her office futon, switching from one to the other throughout the day while she explored plot ideas and characters. Hoffman has said that she is not always comfortable in the world, often feeling horrified and adrift, like an outsider looking in, a state that helps her powers of observation when studying people as potential characters. Having struggled with phobias, panic attacks, a lingering fear of bridge crossings, as well as a natural cynicism and fatalism, she has always considered writing a means of healing. She believes that in giving life to inner terrors, she can help readers recognize the truth of emotional illness.

Analysis

Alice Hoffman writes for a wide audience of adults, teenagers, and children. Her works grow from her belief that the greatest reality is in fiction, that all lives contain elements of fantasy. She finds the stuff of fairy tales in everyday life. Monsters and compassionate people live side by side. The woods hold mysteries, if only of the mind. Some dwellings might as well be palaces, in their distancing of ordinary folks. Animals have distinct personalities and can communicate with humans. Children are abused by wicked adults and sometimes rescued by forces of good. Partners and loved ones are abandoned, and people die. Dreams and other images can be haunting, and sounds and smells can evoke memories that seem otherworldly.

Hoffman bases some of her works on fairy tales because she appreciates their emotional truths; the lessons they teach about human nature, love, and hatred. Though a witch may not wait before an open fire for Hansel and Gretel, there are purveyors of evil in the world and sometimes a long-toothed slathering wolf will drape himself in the coat of a kindly sheep.

Hoffman often lulls readers by beginning her stories simply, with characters seeming to live perfect lives; but the asp is in the garden, ready to change things. Children, the most vulnerable of creatures, die or are kidnapped; old people wither into death; people divorce, drink, philander, take drugs, commit suicide, abuse the less powerful, murder, engage in incest, and succumb to mental illness. Women give in to their attractions to bad men. They suffer. Some evolve, some never recover. Many need to sink to the depths of darkness before they can emerge into the light.

Hoffman's method of introducing otherworldly themes in her narrative is so subtle, so natural, that even readers who prefer straight-on fiction often overlook what they would otherwise consider lapses. Her stories are true psychologically. Who, on occasion, has not sensed the identity of the caller on a ringing phone or had a dream become a life event?

Hoffman uses recurring themes that follow familiar patterns, mainly because, she notes, there are just so many variations on what can happen to people. The key, she says, is in the voice, how the writer makes basic plots seem new and exciting. One of her favorite devices is having a mysterious stranger enter the scene, upsetting the lives of otherwise unremarkable people in their undistinguished towns. Readers recognize and appreciate these elements of her fiction because of the familiarity, and then they wait to find the twists or new ways of expressing old truths.

In many of Hoffman's novels, nature has magic properties, casting a spell that makes it almost another character. Growing things seem to respond to human actions. In one novel, a garden begins producing poisonous blooms with evil names, such as black nightshade, hemlock, and thorn apple.

Hoffman notes that all of her characters contain a bit of herself, that she writes emotional autobiography rather than using actual events in her life. Her depiction of a woman whose simmering sense of dread leads to full-fledged panic attacks, brain-chemistry disorders that strike randomly, will ring true to readers who suffer the same condition. The "Force," as Hoffman labels it, may lead a character to narrow her realm of experience until she is no longer able to leave the house (the disorder is called agoraphobia).

Hoffman's novels always include outsiders, people who do not fit easily into the greater world: the lonely, the frightened, and the socially inept; sometimes the scar-faced, leather-jacketed hoods; girls of easy virtue; junkies; and scholastic achievers who must downplay their intelligence to fit in. Hoffman's love of folk tales has led her to create such characters as an eight-foot-tall man, a child of possible stunted growth, and assorted women trapped like princesses in towers, who also have to rescue themselves.

Alice Hoffman. (Deborah Feingold/Courtesy, Goldberg McDuffie)

AT RISK

At Risk details the impact of AIDS on a family of four, and on the people of the town in which they live. Eleven-year-old Amanda, an accomplished gymnast and possible Olympics contender, is infected with the virus that causes the disease after getting a blood transfusion. The blamelessness of the child and the waste of a life would make this novel unbearably sad were it not for the greater story of people of indomitable spirit who adjust to a situation that can only be endured. Hoffman also brings to light an alternate reality: the anger people have at the disease, and also at the victim, the all-too-real feeling of blaming the one who is afflicted.

Amanda is not simply a sweet, curly-haired cherub. Eleven-year-olds, including Amanda, can be willful, manipulative, nasty, unthinking, demanding, and bratty. Her mother understands this, but is constrained by her adored daughter's impending death and becomes tired of always putting the situation in its proper perspective.

What difference does it make if Amanda snaps at her, given that one day she will not be there to snap? Her mother is wracked with guilt and sapped by her impatience.

Eight-year-old Charlie can be a typical bratty younger brother, but he loves his sister. Now he is hateful, resentful, and jealous of the attention she is getting. There is much self-recrimination in the novel, with characters appalled at their thoughts, attempting to deny their uncharitable feelings. Added to this situation are the fears of the community that lead to the family's isolation.

HERE ON EARTH

Here on Earth has many of the elements of one of Hoffman's favorite authors, Emily Brontë, and of her novel *Wuthering Heights* (1847). *Here on Earth* is similar with its dramatic landscape and clearly defined characters. The location is a small town outside Boston, where nature looms as a constant backdrop with stygian nights and exploding August heat.

The heroine, March Murray, returns to her childhood home after twenty years to attend the funeral of Judith Dale, her beloved housekeeper. She brings her snarly daughter Gwen and leaves behind the man she had married when Hollis, the boy she loved as a youth, had abandoned her. A foundling, Hollis is now wealthy and in the process of buying up the whole town. He, too, had married, but his wife died under mysterious circumstances. He is determined to claim March. His allure is so great that she allows her world to be subverted, her friends hurt. Hoffman uses this plot angle frequently to show the ramifications of following the heart instead of the head and to portray women who find the strength to rise from the depths of destructive obsessions.

As the plot unfolds, March learns a great deal about her past. Her brother became an incapacitated alcoholic who now lives in a shack deep in the woods. Hollis was a hired horse killer who helped owners collect insurance money on their prize winners by making the deaths seem natural or necessary. Judith Dale has her own secrets.

March soon moves in with Hollis, and Gwen develops a fondness for both Hollis's farm help, Jody, and his nearly wild horse. The horse responds to her soft words. Gwen's powers seem magical. Jody is torn between his allegiance to the man who gave him a job and a place to live and the woman he has come to love. Hoffman's common plot elements are here: deception, mental and physical abuse, dysfunctional relationships, alcoholism, obsession, mental illness, people unwise in love, alienation, and despair.

ILLUMINATION NIGHT

Illumination Night takes place in Martha's Vineyard, where once a year the townspeople gather in the town square, which has been illuminated with candles. The central characters, Andre and Vonny, are worried about their four-year-old son Simon because he is short in stature. He is often mistaken for a much younger child and refuses to celebrate another birthday until he grows more. The elderly woman next door, in a literal flight of fancy, flaps her arms out of an upper-story window, leading her sixteen-year-old granddaughter Jody to monitor her behavior. Jody finds her neighbors fascinating and begins babysitting for Simon and flirting with Andre. Emotional conflicts and hostility arise, as do resolution, love, and acceptance.

Jody and her grandmother have always found themselves outside the realm of ordinary interactions, Andre has always been too close-lipped to attract serious friends, and Vonny has fallen into a pattern of agoraphobia that threatens her own existence, her ability to even walk out her front door in comfort.

Add to this mix Ed, the giant of a man who lives just outside the town, mostly isolated from those who fear him. The reader sees seemingly ordinary people experiencing self-doubt, isolation, deception, guilt, and terror, a whole range of common human emotions.

Gay Pitman Zieger

OTHER MAJOR WORKS

SHORT FICTION: *Blackbird House*, 2004.

SCREENPLAY: *Independence Day*, 1983.

CHILDREN'S/YOUNG ADULT LITERATURE: *Fireflies*, 1997; *Horsefly*, 2000; *Aquamarine*, 2001; *Indigo*, 2002; *Green Angel*, 2003; *The Foretelling*, 2005; *Incantation*, 2006.

BIBLIOGRAPHY

Aguiar, Sarah Appleton. *The Bitch Is Back: Wicked Women in Literature*. Carbondale: Southern Illinois University Press, 2001. Examination of the presence of the archetypal "bitch" character in modern fiction includes brief discussion of Hoffman's novel *Here on Earth*.

Brown-Davidson, Terri. "'To Build Is to Dwell': The Beautiful, Strange Architectures of Alice Hoffman's Novels." *Hollins Critic* 33, no. 5 (December, 1996). Provides an extensive literary critique of Hoffman's work. Brown-Davidson tends to incorporate her own rather vast awareness of literature, sometimes filling her prose with references that may be obscure to general readers.

Hoffman, Alice. "At Home with Alice Hoffman: A Writer Set Free by Magic." Interview by Ruth Reichl. *The New York Times*, February 10, 1994. Hoffman answers penetrating questions, dealing frankly with her life and work.

E. T. A. HOFFMANN

Born: Königsberg, East Prussia (now Kaliningrad, Russia); January 24, 1776

Died: Berlin, Prussia (now in Germany); June 25, 1822

Also known as: Ernst Theodor Wilhelm Hoffmann

Principal long fiction

Die Elixiere des Teufels: Nachgelassene Papiere des Bruders Medardus, eines Kapuziners, 1815-1816 (*The Devil's Elixirs: From the Posthumous Papers of Brother Medardus, a Capuchin Friar*, 1824)

Lebensansichten des Katers Murr, nebst fragmentarischer Biographie des Kapellmeisters Johannes Kreisler in zufälligen Makulaturblättern, 1819-1821 (*The Life and Opinions of Kater Murr, with the Fragmentary Biography of Kapellmeister Johannes Kreisler on Random Sheets of Scrap Paper*, 1969; also known as *The Educated Cat*)

Other literary forms

For most of his life, E. T. A. Hoffmann (HAWF-mahn) cherished the hope that he would one day be remembered as a composer, and it was only late in his career as an artist that literary preoccupations began to outweigh his interest in music. By the time of his death, Hoffmann had nevertheless produced a considerable literary oeuvre that included two novels and more than seventy tales. Hoffmann gathered most of the tales into three collections. He published the first under the title *Fantasiestücke in Callots Manier* (1814-1815; *Fantasy Pieces in Callot's Manner*, 1996). Included in this collection are Hoffmann's important first story, "Ritter Gluck: Eine Erinnerung aus dem Jahr 1809" ("Ritter Gluck"), as well as his most famous fairy tale, "Der goldene Topf: Ein Märchen aus der neuen Zeit" ("The Golden Flower Pot"). Hoffmann's second collection, *Nachtstücke* (1817; night pieces), contains his most ghostly, even ghoulish, creations. Its opening story, "Der Sandmann" ("The Sandman"), still served Sigmund Freud in 1919 as a case study of the human sense of the uncanny. Into the four volumes of *Die Serapionsbrüder* (1819-1821; *The Serapion Brethren*, 1886-1892) Hoffmann incorporated "Rat Krespel" ("Councillor Krespel"), "Die Bergwerke zu Falun" ("The Mines of Falun"), and—immortalized by Peter Ilich Tchaikovsky in 1892 as *The Nutcracker Suite*—the fairy tale "Nussknacker und Mausekönig" ("Nutcracker and the King of Mice"). The first detective story in European literature and Hoffmann's most popular tale during his lifetime, "Das Fräulein von Scudéri" ("Mademoiselle de Scudéri"), also appeared in *The Serapion Brethren*.

During the last three years of his life, Hoffmann wrote three lengthy, complex tales in which he tried to achieve a unique blend of fairy tale, social satire, and aesthetic speculation: *Klein Zaches, genannt Zinnober* (1819; *Little Zaches, Surnamed Zinnober*, 1971), *Prinzessin Brambilla: Ein Capriccio nach Jakob Callot*

(1821; *Princess Brambilla: A "Capriccio" in the Style of Jacques Callot*, 1971), and *Meister Floh: Ein Märchen in sieben Abenteuern zweier Freunde* (1822; *Master Flea: A Fairy Tale in Seven Adventures of Two Friends*, 1826). Hoffmann's letters and diaries were published in the four-volume *Tagebücher* in 1971, and a volume of his letters was published in English in 1977.

ACHIEVEMENTS

In his own day, E. T. A. Hoffmann became a successful writer in a remarkably short time. His ghost and horror stories were received with favor by critics and with enthusiasm by the general reading public. Still, few would have considered Hoffmann to be more than an admittedly original and masterful entertainer. With his mixture of the miraculous, the fantastic, and the horrible, he clearly catered to his generation's fascination with the occult and his readers' thirst for the thrill of a spine-chilling story.

After Hoffmann's death, his reputation as a writer diminished rapidly and was finally destroyed by a formidable opponent from abroad. In 1827, Sir Walter Scott published in *Foreign Quarterly Review* a scathing attack against the excessive employment of supernatural elements in fiction titled "On the Supernatural in Fictitious Composition; and Particularly on the Works of Ernest Theodore William Hoffmann." Using the works of Hoffmann to make his point, Scott concluded that only an opium-inflamed mind could have conceived such frightful chimeras. Scott's assault on Hoffmann's reputation proved fatal, because Johann Wolfgang von Goethe then made it his personal mission to recommend Scott's indictment of the unsavory Hoffmann to the sane sensibilities of his German compatriots.

That Hoffmann's writings survived this Olympian disapproval is largely the result of their success in France. Though none of Hoffmann's works had been translated into a foreign language during his life, French translations of several of his tales appeared shortly after his death and were quickly followed by a veritable Hoffmann vogue among France's most distinguished writers. Honoré de Balzac and Charles Baudelaire showed themselves to be greatly impressed, and in 1836, Gérard de Nerval summarized the French conception of Germany's literary pantheon by speaking of Germany as the land of Friedrich Schiller, Goethe, and Hoffmann. Stimulated by the French reception, enthusiasm for Hoffmann caught fire in Russia as well. Indeed, no major Russian writer of the nineteenth century—from Alexander Pushkin and Nikolai Gogol to Fyodor Dostoevski and Leo Tolstoy—failed to acknowledge Hoffmann's impact on his work.

In the Anglo-Saxon world, by contrast, Scott's article squelched whatever interest there might have been in the achievements of Hoffmann. Still, as if by an ironic twist, it is in that world that Hoffmann doubtless found his most congenial successor, Edgar Allan Poe. The precise nature and extent of Hoffmann's influence on Poe, however, remains a much-debated and apparently elusive issue among literary historians.

Hoffmann would certainly have derived special gratification from the fact that, while his own musical compositions did not bring him fame, composers throughout the nineteenth century set his literary inspirations to music. Thus, for a wide and international audience, Hoffmann's name is often linked, if not identified, with the names of his greatest musical admirers. Robert Schumann's *Kreisleriana* (1838; eight fantasies for keyboard devoted to Kreisler, the hero of Hoffmann's second novel), Jacques Offenbach's opera *Les Contes d'Hoffmann* (1881; *The Tales of Hoffmann*), and Tchaikovsky's ballet *The Nutcracker Suite* are only the best known of many musical offerings to the genius of Hoffmann.

In the twentieth century, Hoffmann finally emerged, even in Germany, as one of that country's most brilliant writers of fiction. He became especially valued as a fearless explorer of the labyrinthine qualities of the human psyche in its desperate search for inner order in the face of instinctual lust and aggression. Hoffmann's works definitely began to cast their spell again, although more than ever before readers often found themselves feeling ambivalent about what is charm and what is curse within that spell's obsessive power.

BIOGRAPHY

Ernst Theodor Wilhelm Hoffmann—who in later life replaced his third baptismal name with Amadeus, in honor of Wolfgang Amadeus Mozart—was born in Königsberg, then the capital of East Prussia, now a Russian city known as Kaliningrad. The disastrous marriage between his father, an alcoholic lawyer, and his mother, a mentally unstable recluse, was dissolved when Hoffmann was only three years old. He subsequently grew up under the pedantic tutelage of a bachelor uncle. The precocious boy spent a loveless and lonely childhood from which only his instructions in music and painting provided some much-needed relief.

At the age of sixteen, Hoffmann enrolled as a student of law at the University of Königsberg. Three years later, he passed his examinations with great distinction. He then joined the legal branch of Prussia's civil service and was employed in various capacities in Glogau (1796-1798), Berlin (1798-1800), Posen (1800-1802), Plock (1802-1804), and Warsaw (1804-1806). All through these years, Hoffmann combined a punctilious execution of his official duties with an increasing interest in music as well as a wild bachelor existence in which the consumption of alcohol played an increasingly significant part. Hoffmann's marriage in 1802 to Michalina Rohrer, the daughter of a minor Polish civil servant, was entered into almost casually and seems to have been of little consequence to Hoffmann for the rest of his life.

It was in Warsaw that Hoffmann seriously started to cultivate a second career as composer and conductor. When, in 1806, the collapse of Prussia's Polish empire under the Napoleonic onslaught deprived him of his position and livelihood in Warsaw, he decided to embark on a musical career. For more than a year, he tried to establish himself in Berlin—an impossible task, as it turned out, in the defeated and impoverished capital of Prussia. He finally accepted a position as music director at the theater and opera house of Bamberg, a small town in northeastern Bavaria.

Hoffmann began his career in music with great expectations and, in spite of an almost immediate disenchantment with the new occupation, remained in Bamberg for four and a half years, supplementing his frequently uncertain income by giving music lessons to members of patrician families in town. His hopeless passion for the gifted vocal student Julia Marc was to become the most embittering experience of his stay. In 1813, Hoffmann joined an opera company that traveled between Leipzig and Dresden, yet this change only caused his professional frustrations to reach new heights. When an influential friend, Theodor Gottlieb von Hippel, managed to have him reinstated in Prussia's legal service in 1814, Hoffmann eagerly jumped at the chance. He returned to his beloved Berlin, where he was to reside until his death in 1822.

In 1814, Hoffmann was thirty-eight years old. Until that time, little in his life suggested that during the eight years left to him he was to become one of the most prominent writers of his age. In the preceding ten years, he had made a concerted effort to establish himself as a composer. By 1814, the list of his compositions included several operas, two masses, and one symphony as well as a considerable quantity of vocal and instrumental music, yet it was only with the publication of his first collection

E. T. A. Hoffmann. (Library of Congress)

of tales, during the same year, that Hoffmann finally gained the recognition that had eluded him in all of his musical productivity. Obviously exhilarated by the experience of success, Hoffmann set out to write with single-minded fervor. Publishers sought him out, and so did the literary salons of Berlin. The publishers Hoffmann tried to satisfy; the literary salons, however, he more and more regularly exchanged for the wine cellar of Lutter and Wegener, where he and his alter ego, the famous actor Ludwig Devrient, drank themselves into states of fantastic exaltation.

In spite of his private excesses, Hoffmann's professional career—he was to become vice president of the Supreme Court of Prussia—and literary career proceeded with unimpeded speed until his body gave way under the triple strain. In 1821, Hoffmann began to suffer from a rapidly advancing paralysis, perhaps the result of a syphilitic infection. Writing—finally dictating—at a feverish pace, Hoffmann died several months later, at the age of forty-six.

Analysis

E. T. A. Hoffmann's literary work constitutes a compelling and insightful expression of the prevailing anxieties of a deeply unsettled age. The rational improvement of the private self and the enforced stability of the social self were severely shaken by the upheavals of the French Revolution and the rise of Napoleon I's will to power. The heroes of this restless time revealed to the perceptive observer unexpectedly atavistic passions compared to which all existing social and ethical norms proved exceedingly insubstantial. People came to the realization that they had hardly known themselves to that point and that it was critical for them to learn more about what was asserting itself so menacingly in their lives. Interest in marginal, even pathological, states of the mind—in hypnosis, telepathy, magnetism, somnambulism, dreams, and trances—became a widespread obsession. In the wake of this trend, there arose the specter of a human existence threatened from within by chaotic instincts and threatened from without by capricious turns of events.

Probably more than any other writer of his time, Hoffmann delved into the vicissitudes that the defenseless psyche undergoes as it finds itself in the grip of conflicting demands that it can neither adjudicate nor deny. To introduce the reader to the torture chambers of the mind, Hoffmann employed an arsenal of literary devices that his audience knew well from gothic horror stories. Madness, witchery, cloak-and-dagger intrigues, secret passageways, mysterious doubles, incest, rape, and human sacrifice follow one another with baffling speed in mystifying plots that disorient readers until they can no longer tell what is real and what is imagined, what is mere wish and what is accomplished fact.

The Devil's Elixirs

In *The Devil's Elixirs*, the plot of which was clearly inspired by Matthew Gregory Lewis's gothic novel *The Monk: A Romance* (1796; also known as *Ambrosio: Or, The Monk*), the Capuchin friar Medardus recounts the story of his rebellious flight from the monastery and his repentant return to it. Medardus is born within the precincts of a monastery, grows up in the vicinity of a nunnery, and promptly resolves to live a religious life himself. After having become an extraordinarily successful preacher at his monastery, he suddenly experiences a breakdown of his rhetorical abilities and is desperate for a cure from the mysterious ailment. He knows that among the monastery's sacred relics is preserved a flask filled with a potent elixir that the Devil had once offered to the hermit Saint Anthony during his temptations in the desert. Medardus takes a drink from the flask and finds his powers restored, but he also senses new and ominous passions rushing through his veins. Medardus's superior, concerned about the peace of the monastic community, soon finds himself forced to send the agitated and arrogant monk on a mission to Rome.

From the moment Medardus leaves the monastery, the reader is hard put to assess the actual nature of the monk's frenzied adventures. Torn between contradictory desires, Medardus's personality repeatedly breaks apart, integral elements battling one another as life-size enemies. Presented with a chance to assume another identity—which in fact appeals to everything he has suppressed during his years as a monk—Medardus wantonly enters an adulterous affair with a baroness while, at the same time, falling in love with her angelic stepdaughter, Aurelie. The resulting emotional turmoil culminates in a scene of horror in which Medardus poisons the baroness and tries to rape Aurelie. Momentarily exorcised from his evil self by the enormity of the crime, he hurries away in frantic fear of his own passions.

After further wanderings, Medardus meets Aurelie again. This time, he is determined to court her with genuine love and devotion, yet the demoniac compulsion to subjugate and destroy the love he awakens never completely leaves him. On their wedding day, the indomitable strain in Medardus's soul flares up with renewed ferocity. As he sees his alter ego carted off to execution, he refuses to let it die, rejects Aurelie and everything noble in himself, and runs off, his satanic double on his back, until rage and frustration deprive him of his senses. Several months later, Medardus revives, finding himself in an Italian insane asylum. He proceeds to submit his body to a rigorous course of penance, and, after many additional adventures, he returns to the monastery from which he had set out. He arrives the day before Aurelie is to take her religious vows in a nearby convent. Overwhelmed by the coincidence, Medardus feels rent apart again. He claims Aurelie for himself and slays her on the steps of the altar. Having thus destroyed the object of his passion, Medardus is at last free to reject the call of instinct and to reenter the tranquillity of monastic life.

The Devil's Elixirs can be read on at least two levels. Late in the novel, the reader is told that the main characters are, unbeknown to themselves, members of one family that for several generations has lived under a curse resulting from a sacrilege committed by an ancestor. That curse can be laid to rest only if the remaining members of the family renounce earthly love and thus mark the family for extinction. Medardus and Aurelie, the last of the unholy clan, embrace the necessary self-denial and break the chain of sin and guilt. The notion of an inherited curse was the stock-in-trade of the gothic novel. The introduction of supernatural agencies allowed authors to explain the many otherwise inexplicable coincidences needed to sustain the suspense of their stories. The real impact of *The Devil's Elixirs*, therefore, does not arise from Hoffmann's belated revelations about Medardus's guilt-ridden family but rather from his relentless depiction of a man's fearful struggle with instincts that lie, in stubborn and hostile cynicism, beyond the reach of his moral self.

Medardus, of course, does put an end to the curse, not only for his family but also for his own troubled self. *The Devil's Elixirs*, after all, is his autobiography; it contains his retrospective creation of a continuous self and signals a significant victory over his chaotic past. The success with which Medardus has managed to construct—from the fragmented impulses of his psyche—the notion of a responsible personality shows that he has established for himself a basis for moral behavior. Still, he has stabilized his personality at a high price: the exclusion of all instinct, the truncating of his very life. Secure as Medardus's self now might be, a unified self it is not, and no amount of Catholic pageantry can disguise the pessimism of that conclusion.

The Life and Opinions of Kater Murr

Hoffmann's second novel, *The Life and Opinions of Kater Murr*, remained a fragment, a fact that—considering the less-than-convincing end of *The Devil's Elixirs*—rather enhances its effectiveness. In contrast to *The Devil's Elixirs*, which in spite of its confusing plot follows the traditional technique of a chronological narration, *The Life and Opinions of Kater Murr* surprises the reader with one of the most amusingly original structures in German literature. The novel is composed of two distinct narratives bewilderingly conflated: the autobiography of a tomcat (Murr) and the biography of a musician (Kreisler). Murr, so the editor apologizes, had, while writing his memoirs, torn up the biography of Kreisler in order to use its pages as writing pad and blotting paper. When Murr had his work published, the printer mistakenly thought the sheets from Kreisler's life to be part of the tomcat's autobiography, so that in the finished product two very dissimilar stories interrupt each other with maddening regularity.

In Murr's account, Hoffmann parodies the educational novel, the bildungsroman, of his day. Murr, a smugly egotistical tomcat, pompously details the stages by which he planned to advance himself in the world. With all the naïveté of his inflated ego, he tells how he first embarked on an academic career, then felt free to pursue romantic love, became involved in the political arena, and finally aspired to be recognized as a true gentleman. At the end, the reader is informed that the splendid cat has unfortunately died, a fate common to those who achieve too much at too early an age.

That Murr's penmanship at least left much to be desired might be gathered from the fact that about two-thirds of all pages in the book were apparently needed as blotting paper. These pages tell of the life of Johannes Kreisler. The story opens at the small court of Sieghartsweiler, where for some time now the former mistress of Prince Irenäus has spun an intrigue that is to lead to a marriage between Irenäus's half-witted son Ignaz and her own daughter, the beautiful and sensitive Julia.

The plot gets under way as the eccentric musician Kreisler joins the tedious life at the miniature court. He soon is asked to give Julia and Hedwiga, Prince Irenäus's only daughter, music lessons, and the two girls are quickly attracted to Kreisler by the strange powers that his curiously extravagant behavior reveals. Their idyllic association is destroyed by the news that Hedwiga is to marry the handsome but unscrupulous Prince Hektor. Hektor, assured that in time he will possess Hedwiga, promptly sets out to seduce Julia. For a while, Kreisler manages to foil Hektor's plans, until an attempt on Kreisler's life forces the musician to flee from court. He takes up residence in a nearby Benedictine abbey and there resumes work as composer and music director. Unfortunately, Kreisler has barely achieved peace in his new surroundings when an urgent letter from Sieghartsweiler implores him to return to court, where a double wedding joining Hektor and Hedwiga as well as Ignaz and Julia is about to take place. Whether Kreisler was able to prevent this impending misfortune remains unclear, as the novel breaks off in the middle of a sentence.

Throughout the story, evidence accumulates suggesting that Kreisler, whose identity is the central mystery of the plot, may well be the victim of a long-standing court intrigue. The attraction that Kreisler's character exerts, however, seems to depend even less on the unraveling of a web of fateful family relations than does the account of the friar Medardus. What the torn-out pages of Kreisler's biography tell about the torn-up life of its hero, no clandestine schemes could possibly bind together. Kreisler's existential rootlessness is ultimately the result not of clever machinations from without but of his own self-lacerating quest for human perfection in a petty environment. Sheltering a highly idealistic and highly vulnerable personality behind masks of cynicism and eccentricity, Kreisler is plagued by the sudden shifts of an artistic vision that shows the trivial to be sublime as often as it shows the sublime to be trivial. Thus barred from any consistent perspective on world or self, he is forced to vacillate between ecstatic joy and despondent frustration: ecstatic joy at the world's grandeur, despondent frustration at its inevitable depreciation at the hands of unresponsive men. In contrast to Medardus, who could still reconstruct his divided will from the secure vision of an undisputed faith, Kreisler's divided perception finds no such security; even his monastic retreat offers him hardly more than a brief respite from his self-tormented life.

It would be inaccurate, however, to think of *The Life and Opinions of Kater Murr* as a thoroughly pessimistic novel. It must not be forgotten that Hoffmann chained Kreisler's volatile idealism to the pedestrian common sense of the tomcat Murr. If the musician unmasks the cat's vain shallowness, Murr, too, provides a mocking mirror for Kreisler's pursuit of perfection at the Lilliputian court of Sieghartsweiler. How serious Hoffmann was about seeing the perspectives of the conformist animal and of the nonconformist artist as complementary becomes clear when Murr ends his memoirs with the remark that henceforth he will live with a new master, the concertmaster Kreisler.

Murr's death, of course, leaves it to the reader to imagine what the unlikely companions could have meant to each other. For Hoffmann, the outcome of their partnership cannot be in doubt. Whenever people admit to being part self-serving cat and part self-effacing idealist, self-irony—the tolerant smile at one's own incongruous personality—will turn the menace of a divided ego into the promise of a healthily deflated, less commanding but also less aggressive self. Although Hoffmann's creatures have not yet attained their creator's humorous wisdom, the reader understands and is invited to rise to its challenge.

Joachim Scholz

Other major works

SHORT FICTION: *Fantasiestücke in Callots Manier*, 1814-1815 (*Fantasy Pieces in Callot's Manner*, 1996); *Nachtstücke*, 1817; *Klein Zaches, genannt Zinnober*, 1819 (*Little Zaches, Surnamed Zinnober*, 1971); *Die Serapionsbrüder*, 1819-1821 (4 volumes; *The Serapion Brethren*, 1886-1892); *Prinzessin Brambilla: Ein Ca-*

priccio nach Jakob Callot, 1821 (*Princess Brambilla: A "Capriccio" in the Style of Jacques Callot*, 1971); *Meister Floh: Ein Märchen in sieben Abenteuern zweier Freunde*, 1822 (*Master Flea: A Fairy Tale in Seven Adventures of Two Friends*, 1826); *Four Tales*, 1962; *The Best Tales of Hoffmann*, 1967; *Selected Writings of E. T. A. Hoffmann*, 1969 (2 volumes); *The Golden Pot, and Other Tales*, 1992.

NONFICTION: *Briefwechsel*, 1967-1969 (3 volumes; correspondence); *Tagebücher*, 1971 (4 volumes; diaries); *Selected Letters*, 1977.

MUSICAL COMPOSITIONS: *Liebe und Eifersucht: Oper*, 1807; *Trois Canzonettes*, 1808; *Arlequinn: Ballett*, 1811; *Undine*, 1816; *Musikalische Werke*, 1922-1927.

BIBLIOGRAPHY

Chantler, Abigail. *E. T. A. Hoffmann's Musical Aesthetics*. Burlington, Vt.: Ashgate, 2006. Hoffmann was a music critic and composer as well as a writer, and this book describes his aesthetic ideas about music, placing them within the context of late eighteenth and early nineteenth century philosophy. Also discusses the significance of Hoffmann's literary works.

Daemmrich, Horst S. *The Shattered Self: E. T. A. Hoffmann's Tragic Vision*. Detroit, Mich.: Wayne State University Press, 1973. Important study of Hoffmann's literary work begins with an introduction that places Hoffmann in historical context and outlines critical appraisals of his work. Analysis of Hoffmann's major themes and motifs finds in the author's work a portrayal of "the disintegration of the individual in a world of uncontrolled forces." Includes extensive notes, bibliography, and index.

Hewett-Thayer, Harvey W. *Hoffmann: Author of the Tales*. Princeton, N.J.: Princeton University Press, 1938. Classic work, intended as an introduction for both students and general readers, that provides a comprehensive biography of Hoffmann and discussion of his works, with very readable story analyses. Informative footnotes include suggestions for further reading as well as the original German for many passages when these appear in English translation in the main text. Supplemented by a listing of Hoffmann's literary works with dates of publication, a bibliography, and an index of names and works.

Kohlenbach, Margarete. "Women and Artists: E. T. A. Hoffmann's Implicit Critique of Early Romanticism." *Modern Language Review* 89, no. 3 (July, 1994): 659-673. Examines the Romantic philosophy of love in the novel *The Life and Opinions of Kater Murr* and in Hoffmann's other works. Argues that the character Johannes Kreisler expresses ideas about love that are at variance with Hoffmann's writings as a whole and explains the significance of this divergence.

McGlathery, James M. *E. T. A. Hoffmann*. New York: Twayne, 1997. Interesting introduction to Hoffmann's life and work analyzes his major works of fiction and also discusses the critical reception of Hoffmann's writings and Hoffmann's own works of criticism.

Negus, Kenneth. *E. T. A. Hoffmann's Other World: The Romantic Author and His "New Mythology."* Philadelphia: University of Pennsylvania Press, 1965. Very readable monograph focuses on Hoffmann's development of a coherent body of myth in his fantasy world—a "new mythology" founded on an inner spiritual (or psychological) world but extending to form a "cosmic myth." Examines all of Hoffmann's major literary works as well as many of his minor works with a view to laying a critical foundation for his narrative art. Includes select bibliography and index.

Riou, Jeanne. *Imagination in German Romanticism: Rethinking the Self and Its Environment*. New York: Peter Lang, 2004. Examines the works of Hoffmann and other German writers and philosophers to explore the Romantic concept of the imagination and the imagination's critique of reason.

PAUL HORGAN

Born: Buffalo, New York; August 1, 1903
Died: Middletown, Connecticut; March 8, 1995
Also known as: Paul George Vincent O'Shaughnessy Horgan

Principal long fiction

The Fault of Angels, 1933
No Quarter Given, 1935
Main Line West, 1936
A Lamp on the Plains, 1937
Far from Cibola, 1938
The Habit of Empire, 1938
The Common Heart, 1942
The Devil in the Desert: A Legend of Life and Death in the Rio Grande, 1952
The Saintmaker's Christmas Eve, 1955
Give Me Possession, 1957
A Distant Trumpet, 1960
Mountain Standard Time, 1962 (includes *Main Line West*, *Far from Cibola*, and *The Common Heart*)
Things as They Are, 1964
Memories of the Future, 1966
Everything to Live For, 1968
Whitewater, 1970
The Thin Mountain Air, 1977
Mexico Bay, 1982

Other literary forms

Throughout his long and meritorious career, Paul Horgan was known as widely for his short fiction and nonfiction as for his novels. Most of his short fiction is found in three collections, but the best of his stories appear in *The Peach Stone: Stories from Four Decades* (1967). Like his fiction, Horgan's histories and biographies revolve around events and people of the American Southwest. His most prestigious history is *Great River: The Rio Grande in North American History* (1954), but *The Centuries of Santa Fe* (1956) and *Conquistadors in North American History* (1963) are also important works. His biographies, most notably *Lamy of Santa Fé: His Life and Times* (1975) and *Josiah Gregg and His Visions of the Early West* (1979), vividly chronicle the struggle of individuals and the clash of Spanish and American Indian cultures on the southwestern frontier. Horgan's work in drama includes the play *Yours, A. Lincoln* (pr. 1942) and the libretto to *A Tree on the Plains: A Music Play for Americans* (pb. 1943), an American folk opera with music by Ernst Bacon. His *Approaches to Writing* (1973) is composed of three long essays explaining his craft. Horgan's novel *A Distant Trumpet* was filmed in 1964; *Things as They Are* was filmed in 1970.

Achievements

As a novelist as well as a distinguished writer of nonfiction, Paul Horgan devoted his career to the American Southwest. Although he is regarded as a regionalist, some critics have rightly pointed out that he uses regional figures and settings essentially as vehicles for universal themes, much as William Faulkner used regional materials. Horgan's work should not be identified with the popular, formulaic Western writing of such authors as Zane Grey, Louis L'Amour, and Max Brand; rather, he should be seen as a significant figure in the tradition of literary Western fiction that has attracted the attention of critics and readers since the early 1960's.

Recognition for Horgan's writing came in many forms. He won seventy-five hundred dollars in the Harper Prize Novel Contest for *The Fault of Angels* in 1933. He was awarded two Guggenheim fellowships (1945 and 1958) to work on his nonfiction. For *Great River*, Horgan won the Pulitzer Prize in history and the Bancroft Prize of Columbia University. In 1957, the Campion Award for eminent service to Catholic letters was presented to him. The Western Literature Association paid tribute to Horgan with its distinguished Achievement Award (1973), and the Western Writers of America cited him with their Silver Spur Award (1976). He was twice honored by the Texas Institute of Letters (1954 and 1971).

Just as important as these awards, and an indication of the wide range of Horgan's interests and abilities, are the ways in which he served his community and country.

Horgan served as president of the board of the Santa Fe Opera (1958-1962) and the Roswell Museum (1946-1952). He became director of the Wesleyan Center for Advanced Studies in 1962 and remained so until 1967. President Lyndon B. Johnson made Horgan one of his first appointees to the Council of the National Endowment for the Humanities. In addition to being visiting scholar and writer-in-residence at a number of colleges and universities, Horgan served on the board of the Aspen Institute and the Book-of-the-Month Club.

Although some of his novels have sold in the millions and despite his long career, Horgan was not as well known as many of his contemporaries. Those who are familiar with his work, however, see him as a prescient figure, a writer whose concern with the complex, multicultural history of the Southwest anticipated the challenging revisionism of the 1970's and the 1980's, when scholars and fiction writers alike offered a new, critical look at the West.

Paul Horgan. (National Archives)

BIOGRAPHY

Paul George Vincent O'Shaughnessy Horgan was born in Buffalo, New York, on August 1, 1903. He moved to Albuquerque, New Mexico, with his parents in 1915 and attended the New Mexico Military Institute in Roswell until 1921, when he left to be at home when his father was dying. After working for a year at the *Albuquerque Morning Journal*, he moved to the East Coast in 1923 to study at the Eastman School of Music in Rochester, New York. He returned to Roswell in 1926 and accepted the job of librarian at the New Mexico Military Institute. He remained in Roswell until 1942 and wrote his first five novels. Horgan spent World War II in Washington, D.C., as chief of the U.S. Army Information Branch of the Information and Education Division of the War Department, where he supervised all the information that was sent to American troops all over the world. Horgan returned to New Mexico after the war and worked on his nonfiction, but after 1960 he became associated with Wesleyan University in different capacities, living and writing on the Wesleyan campus. He died in Middletown, Connecticut, in March of 1995.

ANALYSIS

Paul Horgan's fiction is dominated on one level by a skillful, aesthetic evocation of the southwestern landscape and climate and a sensitive delineation of character. His novels are exceptionally well written, with sharp detail and imagery often matched by a lyrical tone perfectly suited to the basic goodness of his protagonists. Yet to dwell on this strong sense of place is to miss a basic theme in his works and to misjudge the appeal of his writing. The strength of Horgan's fiction lies in the reader's immediate and sympathetic identification with the protagonists. Curiosity is perhaps humankind's most distinguishing feature. This is true not only in an academic sense but in a personal way as well: To varying degrees, people take an interest in their ancestry and family histories. They want to know who they are and whence they come. It is both a peculiarity and a trademark of Horgan's fiction that this kind of knowing is its constant concern. The dramatic center in Horgan's books revolves around people learning the truth about themselves and their lives.

Horgan employs two main narrative strategies to accomplish his end. In books such as *Far from Cibola* and *A Distant Trumpet*, individuals must deal with an unexpected event upsetting the routine of everyday life and, as a result, are challenged to define their own lives more clearly. On the other hand, in novels such as *Things as They Are* and *Whitewater*, his protagonists conduct a more conscious search for an understanding of who they are and make a deliberate attempt to come to terms with their own pasts.

Far from Cibola

Often in Horgan's fiction, discovering the truth about oneself occurs after some startling event disrupts the ordinary flow of life. Such is the case in *Far from Cibola*, which many critics regard as Horgan's best novel. This short work, set in and around a small town in New Mexico during the early years of the Great Depression, records what happens to a dozen of the local inhabitants during a day in which they are all briefly brought together as part of a large crowd protesting economic conditions. After the crowd threatens to turn into an unruly mob, the sheriff fires a warning shot above their heads into some trees and accidentally kills a teenager who had climbed up the tree to watch the excitement. The crowd disperses after the gunfire, and the remaining chapters describe what happens to the dozen characters the rest of the day. Although these figures span a broad band of the socioeconomic spectrum of the New Mexican (and American) landscape of the 1930's, *Far from Cibola* is not simply another proletarian novel of that decade. Economic problems and hardships are uppermost in the minds of almost everyone in the story, but the fate of each character hinges on his or her ability to recognize and accept reality as it suddenly appears.

The opening chapter provides a good example of what happens to all the characters in the novel. It begins with serene, pastoral images: Mountains are shimmering in the morning haze, and smoke from breakfast fires rises straight into the clear April sky. In Ellen Rood's kitchen, there is a springlike feeling of peace and well-being. As she lays wood for her own stove, Ellen listens to the sounds of her two small children out in the farmyard. Her son, Donald, is chopping at some wood with an ax that is too big for his hands, and her daughter, Lena, is washing her face from a tin dish sitting on the edge of the well. Without warning, however, smoke rolls back into her eyes and sparks sting her arms when Ellen attempts to start the fire. At about the same time, Ellen realizes that her children are strangely quiet. When she investigates, she discovers a huge rattlesnake nearby; she quickly hacks it to death before it can harm her children. There are many scenes such as this one in *Far from Cibola*, in which people suddenly have an idyllic world overturned by a more sober, often harsher reality. How they react is a good measure of their character. Not everyone can prevail as Ellen does.

The incident in the courthouse provides a social context for what happens to the novel's individuals. Until the crowd becomes violent, everything is fairly calm and orderly. There may be hunger and economic desperation in the community, but people have not yet fully faced the fact that there are no hidden food supplies and the government cannot help them. The killing underscores this bleak reality, and society as a whole must deal with this truth, as Ellen had to face the rattlesnake outside her kitchen door.

A Distant Trumpet

A Distant Trumpet, written more than two decades later, shows thematic concerns similar to those of *Far from Cibola*, but Horgan achieves them in a slightly different manner. The novel's primary setting is Fort Delivery, a frontier outpost near the Mexican border in the Arizona Territory during the late 1880's. Although there are a number of characters, the story centers on a young U.S. Army lieutenant named Matthew Hazard and an Apache scout called Joe Dummy. Deftly and incisively, Horgan dramatizes Hazard's and Joe Dummy's roles in helping to make peace with a rebellious band of American Indians who had escaped into Mexico, and the novel ends with Hazard, bitter and disillusioned, resigning from the Army when Joe Dummy is treated no better than the Indians he helped to defeat.

Rather than using startling and often violent images, as in *Far from Cibola*, Horgan makes extensive use of flashbacks to the American Civil War period and earlier as a useful device for pulling down and digging out illusion and sham and seeing the truth clearly. That Matthew Hazard is Horgan's vehicle for showing the necessity not only of recognizing but also of maintaining self-knowledge is brought out in a very short section titled

"Scenes from Early Times." Consisting of a series of short questions and answers between Hazard and an unknown person, the conversation reveals the earliest and most important knowledge Matthew can recall: that he was his father's child. Indeed, it is no accident that this book often reads like a biography. To be one's father's child in *A Distant Trumpet* means being able to acknowledge the less well-known aspects of self as well as the more openly accepted parts. Tragedy occurs when individuals cannot or will not see that darker side.

One of the more striking scenes in the novel occurs when Matthew, on his way to Fort Delivery for the first time, meets White Horn. Sergeant Blickner, who has come to take Matthew to the fort, refuses to take an Indian along in his wagon, and Matthew must give him a direct order to do so. Even after this, Blickner baits White Horn on the way back and calls him Joe Dummy, a nickname picked up later by soldiers at the fort. In previous sections, however, White Horn's courageous and often heroic life has been described at length, so that he has become an individual to the reader. Thus, readers share the narrator's feeling of outrage and indignation that no one at the fort can see Joe Dummy as anything but another "grimy" Indian. Horgan laments bitterly the failure of these people to see clearly and suggests that they will be lost until they somehow discover the truth about themselves and their social structure. In this sense, Fort Delivery becomes an ironic name for an individual's self-imprisonment. Horgan's flashbacks in *A Distant Trumpet* force his readers to look beyond appearance and not accept the false and commonplace, in much the same way the rattlesnake and courthouse incident in *Far from Cibola* made people confront the unpleasant realities in their lives. *A Distant Trumpet* poignantly reveals what happens when individuals (and society) are unable to see worlds other than their own.

Things as They Are

In *Things as They Are*, perhaps the most autobiographical of all of his works, Horgan approaches the question of knowing oneself more directly. The novel is narrated by Richard, an adult writer who recounts certain events in his early childhood to help him understand the way he is now. Horgan continues Richard's story in two later novels: *Everything to Live For* and *The Thin Mountain Air*. *Things as They Are*, then, is a bildungsroman, a story of growth and awakening, and through this format, Richard articulates his need to understand himself and others more clearly.

Like most stories about growing up, the boy Richard undergoes a variety of experiences that the adult Richard must then interpret if he is to make some sense of his life. Although he describes a close family life and happy summer trips to the mountains, Richard also discloses certain important conflicts and tensions for the young boy: an uncle who commits suicide, an autocratic grandfather, a well-meaning but overly protective mother, a father who is not quite strong enough. The novel's structure in its simplest terms is a delicate balancing act between Richard's honestly depicting these family tensions and then explaining both what they meant to him and how they resulted in his seeing things as they are.

Whitewater

Things as They Are may be regarded as a prelude to *Whitewater*, which is also about a young man, Phillipson Durham, growing up. Set in the West Texas town of Belvedere during the years 1948-1949, the novel describes what happens to Phillipson and two high school classmates (Billy Breedlove and Marilee Underwood) during his senior year. Within this framework, the novel is essentially one long flashback by a much older Phillipson, who has written it, as the last chapter makes clear, for much the same reason Richard told his story in *Things as They Are*. Phillipson is probing for clues in his past that will allow him to understand the events of his senior year and what has happened to him since. Phillipson's search is less successful than Richard's and his conclusions more tentative.

Phillipson's quest for self-knowledge is marked by three central images in the novel: Lake Whitewater, Victoria Cochran's house, and the town's water tower. Lake Whitewater is a large, human-made lake formed when Whitewater Dam went into operation. What intrigues Phillipson is that deep under the lake's surface lies an abandoned town complete with houses, yards, and street lamps. Billy informs Phillipson that when the lake is calm, the town can still be seen. The lake and submerged town thus become a metaphor for Phillipson's own lost knowledge about himself. Like the town, his past is still there, waiting to be viewed and understood if only he can see it clearly. Linked with this image is Crystal Wells, the home of Victoria Cochran, an elderly widow who befriends Phillipson and becomes his mentor. At Crystal Wells, Phillipson escapes the dreary provincialism of Belvedere and explores his own ideas and beliefs. It becomes an intellectual oasis where he can begin to define his own life.

Opposed to this image is that of Belvedere's water tower, which Horgan unmistakably identifies with unthinking and impulsive behavior. Caught up in the excitement of springtime and the end of his senior year, Billy Breedlove climbs to the top of the tower to paint the words "Beat Orpha City" on its side. He loses his footing, however, and falls ninety feet to the ground below. Billy's death and Marilee's subsequent suicide are warnings to Phillipson that impulse and feeling by themselves threaten understanding and growth. Phillipson overcomes his grief at Crystal Wells and recognizes that his own education is only beginning. As the last section of *Whitewater* suggests, however, Phillipson years later is still growing, still trying to understand those events and himself, quite aware that there are things that he cannot and perhaps will never know completely. Nevertheless, as Richard does in *Things as They Are*, Phillipson focuses on maintaining moments of wakeful insight.

In understanding Horgan's novels, it is important to recognize that the protagonists are driven by a need to know themselves and their pasts. Given this theme, Horgan uses two main narrative techniques. On one hand, as in *Far from Cibola* and *A Distant Trumpet*, his characters are confronted with events that suddenly disrupt their lives and their normal sense of things. In novels such as *Things as They Are* and *Whitewater*, on the other hand, his protagonists deliberately set about exploring their pasts to learn about themselves. Horgan's message is the same in both cases: Individuals must pursue the truth about themselves, no matter what the cost. Anything else is escapism, a kind of vicarious participation in life.

Terry L. Hansen

Other major works

SHORT FICTION: *The Return of the Weed*, 1936; *Figures in a Landscape*, 1940; *The Peach Stone: Stories from Four Decades*, 1967.

PLAYS: *Yours, A. Lincoln*, pr. 1942; *A Tree on the Plains: A Music Play for Americans*, pb. 1943 (libretto; music by Ernst Bacon).

POETRY: *Lamb of God*, 1927; *Songs After Lincoln*, 1965; *The Clerihews of Paul Horgan*, 1985.

NONFICTION: *New Mexico's Own Chronicle*, 1937 (with Maurice G. Fulton); *Great River: The Rio Grande in North American History*, 1954; *The Centuries of Santa Fe*, 1956; *Rome Eternal*, 1959; *A Citizen of New Salem*, 1961; *Conquistadors in North American History*, 1963; *Peter Hurd: A Portrait Sketch from Life*, 1965; *The Heroic Triad: Essays in the Social Energies of Three Southwestern Cultures*, 1970; *Encounters with Stravinsky: A Personal Record*, 1972; *Approaches to Writing*, 1973; *Lamy of Santa Fé: His Life and Times*, 1975; *Josiah Gregg and His Visions of the Early West*, 1979; *Of America East and West: Selections from the Writings of Paul Horgan*, 1984; *A Certain Climate: Essays on History, Arts, and Letters*, 1988; *A Writer's Eye: Field Notes and Watercolors*, 1988; *Tracings: A Book of Partial Portraits*, 1993; *Henriette Wyeth: The Artifice of Blue Light*, 1994.

CHILDREN'S LITERATURE: *Men of Arms*, 1931.

Bibliography

Erisman, Fred. "Western Regional Writers and the Uses of Place." *Journal of the West* 19 (1980): 36-44. Reprinted in *The American Literary West*, edited by Richard W. Etulain. Manhattan, Kans.: Sunflower University Press, 1980. Placing Horgan in the company of Willa Cather, John Steinbeck, and John Graves, this article presents Horgan's writings as among those who meet the challenge of Ralph Waldo Emerson for artists to use the most American of materials—the experience of the West.

Gish, Robert. *Nueva Granada: Paul Horgan and the Southwest*. College Station: Texas A&M University Press, 1995. Contains a lengthy and previously unpublished interview with Horgan, as well as selected essays and articles about his life and Southwestern writings. Gish demonstrates how Horgan's work transcends Western regionalism and how it recognizes a "new West" of geographic, ethnic, and cultural diversity.

_______. *Paul Horgan*. Boston: Twayne, 1983. Gish argues that Horgan's writing is not merely regionalist, but moves from East to West and back again; he covers Horgan as novelist, short-story writer, historian, and essayist. Includes a chronology, notes and references, a selected, annotated bibliography, and an index.

_______. "Paul Horgan." In *A Literary History of the American West*. Fort Worth: Texas Christian University Press, 1987. Horgan receives a chapter in this important book of literary scholarship that assesses his place in American literary history as a writer of Southwest regionalism. Includes a selected bibliography of primary and secondary sources.

Labrie, Ross. "Paul Horgan (1903-1995)." In *The Catholic Imagination in American Literature*. Columbia: University of Missouri Press, 1997. Labrie analyzes representative works by Horgan and other Catholic writers and poets to describe how these works express each writer's particular interpretation of Catholic teaching.

McInerny, Ralph. "Paul Horgan." In *Some Catholic Writers*. South Bend, Ind.: St. Augustine's Press, 2007. This collection of brief articles about American and European writers whose work was in some way influenced by Catholicism includes an article on Horgan.

Pilkington, William T. "Paul Horgan." In *My Blood's Country: Studies in Southwestern Literature*. Fort Worth: Texas Christian University Press, 1973. Although Horgan was a prolific writer in a variety of forms, Pilkington argues that his best work reveals an understanding of human desires and disappointments as expressed in the concrete details of lived experience. Besides Christian values, Horgan's writing expresses features of Ralph Waldo Emerson's transcendental philosophy.

NICK HORNBY

Born: Redhill, Surrey, England; April 17, 1957

Principal long fiction

High Fidelity, 1995
About a Boy, 1998
How to Be Good, 2001
A Long Way Down, 2005
Not a Star, 2006

Other literary forms

Nick Hornby emerged at the literary forefront with the publication of *Fever Pitch*, his 1992 memoir that focuses on his life as a fan of British football, or soccer, specifically the Arsenal Football Club. Organized as a series of short essays, each connects a theme to a specific football match between 1968 and 1992. One essay, for example, is titled "A Male Fantasy: Arsenal v Charlton Athletic, 18.11.86."

Hornby's first young adult novel, *Slam* (2007), is narrated by the teenager Sam Jones, an avid skateboarder. Sam's hero is famous skateboarder Tony Hawk, whose poster he talks to and from whom he receives advice as he recites passages from his autobiography in Sam's imagination. When Sam's girlfriend Alicia informs him she is pregnant with his child, he must come to terms with pending fatherhood.

Essays that address topics also found in his fiction appear in several of Hornby's anthologies. In *Thirty-one Songs* (2003; also known as *Songbook*), he discusses various songs, musicians, and specific aspects of music such as the emotions it inspires in him and how it has influenced his life and work. His collections *The Polysyllabic Spree* (2004) and *Housekeeping vs. the Dirt* (2006) are compilations of essays about books, some of which appeared in the book review column "Stuff I've Been Reading," which Hornby has written for *The Believer*. In these books, he lists for specific months the books he has bought and those he has read. *My Favourite Year: A Collection of New Football Writing* (1993) and *The Picador Book of Sportswriting* (1996), coedited with Nick Cole-

Nick Hornby. (AP/Wide World Photos)

man, gather essays about sports. Additionally, Hornby edited *Contemporary American Fiction* (1992), a collection of essays about American minimalist writers, and *Speaking with the Angel* (2000), a collection of short fiction.

Achievements

In 1999, Nick Hornby was awarded the E. M. Forster Award by the American Academy of Arts and Letters. In 2003, he was presented with the Writer's Writer Award at the Orange Word International Writers Festival, an honor chosen by fellow writers. *Fever Pitch* received the William Hill Sports Book of the Year Award. *How to Be Good* was long-listed for the Booker Prize and was chosen by the public as the United Kingdom's favorite fictional work at the W. H. Smith Fiction Awards. *Thirty-one Songs* was a finalist for the 2003 National Book Critics Circle Award. *A Long Way Down* was short-listed for the Whitbread Novel Award, the Commonwealth Writers Prize, and the *Los Angeles Times* Book Prize for Fiction. *High Fidelity*, *Fever Pitch*, and *About a Boy* have been adapted into successful films.

Biography

Nick Hornby was raised in Maidenhead, England, where he attended Maidenhead Grammar School. During his adolescence, his parents divorced, and Hornby spent weekends with his father watching Arsenal football games. He later attended Jesus College in Cambridge and studied English. He spent a few years teaching, but the tediousness of the job prompted him to pursue a full-time writing career. While working for Samsung, where he taught Korean employees, he remained in journalism and published articles in distinguished periodicals such as *The Sunday Times*, *Esquire*, *Vogue*, *GQ*, *Time*, and *The Independent*. The commercial success of *Fever Pitch* provided him with the means to focus exclusively on his writing career.

As it is in his novels, music is important in Hornby's personal life. He frequently collaborates with the rock band Marah and has toured with the band, sometimes appearing on stage to read essays he has written about music.

Analysis

Nick Hornby is considered a major writer of "lad lit," a contemporary genre that critics refer to as the male equivalent of "chick lit." Representative of lad lit, his novels generally take place in urban settings and feature characters who are most often single and in their thirties. They are forever seeking romantic relationships with women while maintaining a stereotypically masculine appreciation for sports and drinking. His characters struggle with identity issues as well as concerns with romance, and they usually display comical characteristics that border on neurosis. Frequently, they are obsessive and engage in self-reflection. They fret over self-image and are fashion conscious and concerned with portraying themselves as hip.

As critic Mikko Keskinen points out, Hornby's first novel, *High Fidelity*,

> epitomizes the British author's oeuvre, which is populated by male monomaniacs, perennial bachelors, or early middle-age adolescents. The football enthusiast in *Fever Pitch*, the commitment-avoiding womanizer in *About a Boy*, and the seemingly saintly men in *How to Be Good* can be read as versions of Rob Fleming, the protagonist and narrator of *High Fidelity*.

Hornby's novels reflect the bildungsroman tradition, as they can be classified as coming-of-age novels. Even though the protagonists of *High Fidelity* and *About a Boy* are in their mid-thirties, they have yet to cross the threshold from adolescence to adulthood in terms of emotional maturity. They develop from characters who meander around without goals and drift from one personal relationship to another, and from those characters who move into adulthood by discovering a sense of self and finding a more focused view of life.

Throughout his works, Hornby frequently alludes to popular culture, especially music and sports but also political figures, local establishments, and brand names. He describes avid fans such as the protagonist of *Slam*, who idolizes skateboarder Tony Hawk, and he portrays his own personal obsession with football in his memoir *Fever Pitch*.

In an interesting twist, just as popular culture has influenced Hornby's works, Hornby's works have influenced popular culture. The popularity of *Fever Pitch* has been credited with helping raise public opinion about football, making it more fashionable in English culture, especially in political and literary circles. After the book was published, English political leaders began to announce teams they rooted for and other authors began to write about the game and voice support for particular teams.

Hornby also is a comic writer whose humorous style is comparable to Martin Amis, Tony Parsons, and Julian Barnes. In addition to one-liners, he teases his characters by making light of their insecurities, obsessions, and failed attempts to reach manhood. However, his wit often expresses a character's epiphany or sparks a human truth. For example, his novel *A Long Way Down* uses black humor to illustrate the plight of four characters who contemplate suicide.

High Fidelity

High Fidelity, Hornby's first novel, remains his most significant fictional work. The novel concerns thirty-five-year-old Rob Fleming, who owns Championship Vinyl, a record store in London. Rob's girlfriend Laura has left him, which leads him to make a list of his five most memorable breakups. This list establishes a pattern that recurs throughout the novel, in which Rob lists things such as his top five jobs, top five films, and his favorite records. These lists reflect Rob's obsessive tendencies, also revealed through his desire for Laura and his record collection. As critic Barry Faulk notes:

> Rob's internal monologue summarizes and evaluates his past. His constant exhumation of his romantic biography cannot be separated from his connoisseurship of rock. Rob's experiences, both erotic and audio, social and private, become filtered and ordered through a grid familiar to the pop fanatic: the top-five list.

Rob recalls that he first arranged the records chronologically; when Laura was in his life, he arranged them alphabetically. He now decides to organize them in the order in which he purchased them. Arranging the records exemplifies Rob's attempt to create order from his chaotic, unpredictable life. Suggesting that his record collection parallels his personal history, he says that arranging the records according to date of purchase is the way he hopes to write his autobiography. The new filing system for his record collection gives him a false sense of security because he thinks he can organize his life into similar predictable patterns.

Rob spends his days at the record store with his employees Dick and Barry, who are likewise obsessive and become his sidekicks. The three of them remain trapped in an adolescent mindset, and the humor that comes from their conversations and adventures is colorful. They become straight men for each other in both the adventures they share and the one-liners they spin.

The three men wonder whether they will be able to maintain romantic relationships and massive record collections at the same time. Although the novel does not provide a definitive answer, the rationale behind the question defines their thought processes. An answer is implied at the end of the novel, when Rob and Laura reunite and Rob begins to consider making a compilation tape for her that represents songs she is familiar with and wants to listen to.

About a Boy

About a Boy concerns the plight of thirty-six-year-old Will Freeman who, much like Rob, remains frozen in a state of adolescence. Because his sole source of income are royalties from "Santa's Super Sleigh," a Christmas song written by his father, he is able to escape adult responsibilities such as having a job. Although Will despises the song, he understands that the profits enable him to meander aimlessly through life, where his primary goal is his passion for women. After his affair with Angie, the beautiful single mother who Will thinks would be out of his reach if not for her status as a single woman, he joins the single-parent organization SPAT (Single Parents—Alone Together). In search of single mothers, he pretends he has a son, and ironically, through attending the meetings, he becomes a surrogate father to twelve-year-old Marcus, whose suicidal mother is a member of SPAT.

About a Boy addresses ways the fashion-savvy and wanna-be-cool Will helps Marcus overcome his image as a nerd. He teaches him about Kurt Cobain and Nirvana, buys him stylish tennis shoes and clothes, and gets him a fashionable haircut. While mentoring Marcus, it turns out, Will learns much from the boy. Marcus teaches Will to accept adult responsibility, to commit, and to focus on goals. Will's insights do not come easily, for when he concocted the plan to join SPAT and formed an imaginary son, Ned, he had envisioned a life with innocent, playful children, not ones who might show up at his house and become part of his life (like Marcus). As he says, "He had imagined entering their world, but he hadn't foreseen that they might be able to penetrate his. He was one of life's visitors; he didn't want to be visited."

How to Be Good

How to Be Good marks a departure in Hornby's fiction. Here, he writes from a woman's point of view and portrays the story of a family. The novel opens with protagonist Katie Carr's bold announcement to her husband David Grant that she does not want to be married to him anymore. The fact that she has done so over a cellular phone prompts her to examine her personal ethics because she did not think herself the type of person to make such an announcement over the phone.

David, the writer of the "Angriest Man in Holloway" column, is engaging in self-assessment as well. When he meets DJ GoodNews, who quickly becomes his spiritual mentor, he abruptly stops writing his novel and his column. With DJ GoodNews, he sets out to become a socially conscious pillar of the community. David attempts to become the model Good Samaritan, donating his son's computer, giving large sums of money to homeless people on the streets, and urging his neighbors to take in homeless people.

Throughout *How to Be Good*, Kate vacillates between feelings of moral inadequacy to feelings of being a victim of David's self-righteousness. She questions not only whether she is a "good person" but also the very notion of what defines a good person. Although, in the end, David sees his attempts as fruitless and makes plans for a new novel with the appropriate working title *How to Be Good*, the search for spiritual goodness has taught him many lessons about himself, his wife, and life in general. David's search also inspires the reluctant Kate to perform more in-depth soul searching of her own, and like David's journey, the search for spiritual fulfillment teaches Kate similar insights. She concludes that she wants to try to make her marriage to David work.

A Long Way Down

A Long Way Down illustrates four uniquely developed characters and switches between each of their points of view throughout the novel. The characters are Martin, a television talk-show host whose affair with a teenage girl has ruined his career; JJ, a failed rock musician; Jess, a drug-abusing teenager; and Maureen, a single mother taking care of her disabled son.

The characters meet on New Year's Eve night atop Toppers' House, a London building infamous as a place from which people jump to commit suicide. As the four contemplate suicide, they befriend each other. Instead of jumping to their deaths, they leave the building together. They remain friends as they struggle to continue their lives and establish new goals for themselves.

Jess's epiphany, which comes from a conversation she has with a minor character, Nodog, illustrates the sort of profound truths Hornby often illustrates with his wit:

Oh, I'm always trying to top myself. And I was like, Well, you can't be much good at it, and he went, That's not the idea, though is it? And I was like, Isn't it? And he said that the idea was to, like constantly offer yourself up to the gods of Life and Death. . . . And if the god of Life wanted you, then you lived, and if the god of Death wanted you, you didn't. So he reckoned that on New Year's Eve I'd been chosen by the god of Life, and that's why I never jumped.

Laurie Champion

Other major works

SCREENPLAY: *Fever Pitch*, 1997 (adaptation of his memoir).

NONFICTION: *Contemporary American Fiction*, 1992; *Fever Pitch*, 1992 (memoir); *My Favourite Year: A Collection of New Football Writing*, 1993; *The Picador Book of Sportswriting*, 1996 (with Nick Coleman); *Songbook*, 2002; *The Polysyllabic Spree*, 2004; *Housekeeping vs. the Dirt*, 2006.

YOUNG ADULT LITERATURE: *Slam*, 2007.

EDITED TEXTS: *Speaking with the Angel*, 2000; *Thirty-one Songs*, 2003 (also known as *Songbook*).

Bibliography

Faulk, Barry J. "Love and Lists in Nick Hornby's *High Fidelity*." *Cultural Critique* 66, no. 1 (2007): 153-176. Insightful scholarly essay in which Faulk analyzes the obsession with lists and listing in Hornby's novel *High Fidelity*.

Keskinen, Mikko. "Single, Long-Playing, and Compilation: The Formats of Audio and Amorousness in Nick Hornby's *High Fidelity*." *Critique* 47 (Fall, 2005): 3-21. Keskinen examines the ways in which various formats of audio technology relate to the patterns of love and relationships in *High Fidelity*.

Kiesow, Holger. *Literature as a Mirror of Society the Representation of Masculinity in Contemporary British Fiction*. Saarbrücken, Germany: Müller 2007. Contrasts the lad lit that predominated in British fiction through the twentieth century with a literature seeking a new story about masculinity and manhood. Includes discussion of Hornby's *About a Boy*.

Knowles, Joanne. *Nick Hornby's "High Fidelity": A Reader's Guide*. New York: Continuum, 2002. Brief but thorough analysis of Hornby's famous novel. A good source for critical commentary and reviews on the book.

KHALED HOSSEINI

Born: Kabul, Afghanistan; March 4, 1965

Principal long fiction

The Kite Runner, 2003
A Thousand Splendid Suns, 2007

Other literary forms

While Khaled Hosseini (hoh-SAY-nee) is best known for his long fiction, he has written articles for national publications including *The Wall Street Journal* and *Newsweek*. His editorial in defense of Sayed Perwiz Kambakhsh, an Afghan journalism student sentenced to death for distributing information that questions Islamic laws, is the most notable of his writings in nonfiction.

Achievements

Published in more than forty languages, Khaled Hosseini's *The Kite Runner* has received widespread acclaim from critics and the general public. Awards for the book include the *San Francisco Chronicle* Best Book of the Year for 2003, the American Library Association's Notable Book Award in 2004, and the American Place Theatre's Literature to Life Award in 2005. The novel was adapted for the cinema and released in 2007. *A Thousand Splendid Suns* appeared on many best-seller lists, won a Galaxy British Book Awards—the Richard & Judy Award for Best Read of the Year—and a Book Sense Book of the Year Award in 2008 from the American Booksellers Association.

Hosseini has been honored both for his writing and humanitarian work. In 2006, the United Nations Office of the High Commissioner for Refugees named him its humanitarian of the year. In addition, *Time* magazine included Hosseini in its 2008 list of the most influential people. Former American first lady Laura Bush, an advocate for Afghan women, wrote the *Time* entry about Hosseini and his work.

Biography

Khaled Hosseini was born March 4, 1965, in Kabul, Afghanistan, and spent his boyhood there with his siblings and parents: his mother, a high school teacher, and his father, a diplomat. During that time, the family enjoyed prosperity in a peaceful Afghanistan. In 1976, Hosseini and his family moved to Paris, France, where his father received a new post at the Afghan embassy. The family expected to remain in Paris for only four years, the duration of his father's assignment, and then to return to Afghanistan. However, they found that returning to their country would be too dangerous after it was invaded by the Soviet Union in 1979. Thus, the family applied for and was granted political asylum by the United States. In 1980, they moved to San Jose, California.

After graduating from Santa Clara University with a degree in biology, Hosseini studied medicine at the University of California, San Diego. He graduated in 1993 with a specialization in internal medicine. He was a practicing physician until 2004, shortly after *The Kite Runner* was published.

Analysis

The Kite Runner and *A Thousand Splendid Suns* explore the themes of exile, displacement, immigration, and a person's relationship to one's nation, themes commonly associated with postcolonial literature. Many nations, such as India, Jamaica, and Afghanistan, were once colonies of more powerful countries, including Great Britain, the Netherlands, France, and the United States, seeking to expand their wealth and territories. As the once colonized areas gained independence, they created new national identities, most visibly through art and literature. Theorists have categorized as postcolonial the literature and art that explores the relationships between colonized and colonizer.

Afghanistan has struggled for independence from various invading nations throughout its history; in the twentieth and twenty-first centuries alone, England, the former Soviet Union, and United Nations peacekeeping forces, primarily consisting of U.S. soldiers, have occupied the country. As a result, many Afghans have migrated either by force or by choice to different countries. Both *The Kite Runner* and *A Thousand Splendid Suns* describe the lives of characters who have left their homelands—either to another country or a safer part of their own country—as a result of war.

While far from a direct representation of his childhood in Kabul and young adulthood in California, to which Hosseini's family migrated, the characters in *The Kite Runner* were nevertheless inspired by Hosseini's friends and family. Hosseini acknowledges that his own father inspired the magnanimity of the character Baba, and the mother of another character, Amir, is a professor of Farsi and history, much like Hosseini's own mother, who taught the same subjects in high school. Hosseini said that one of his own family's servants in Kabul, Hossein Khan, and the relationship he had with him, inspired the characterization of Hassan and his friendship with Amir.

One of the most salient ways in which Hosseini examines the tension between selfhood and nationality is through intertextuality—drawing on other literary works to illuminate a novel or poem. In *The Kite Runner*, Amir and Hassan enjoy reading the story of Rostam and Sohrab, which comes from Persian poet Firdusi's *Shahnamah* (c. 1010), the poetic epic of Iran, Afghanistan, and other Persian-speaking countries. Much like the mythologized history of the Greco-Roman world found in classic works of poetry by Homer, the *Shahnamah* poetically narrates the creation of the Persian Empire, of which Afghanistan was once a part. Rostam, a proud and successful warrior, and Sohrab, a champion in his own right, are father and son but have never met. Fighting to protect their country from invaders, they destroy each other and save the nation. Hosseini depicts how the relationships between fathers and sons and the secrets they keep from one another have the potential to determine individual and national characters.

A Thousand Splendid Suns borrows its title from a poem by Sā'ib, a seventeenth century Persian poet. A translation of the poem's most pertinent lines reads as follows: "One could not count the moons that shimmer on her roofs/ And the thousand splendid suns that hide behind her walls."

In contrast to the main characters in *The Kite Runner*, Mariam and Laila, protagonists in *A Thousand Splendid Suns*, remain in Afghanistan throughout several invasions. Laila and her father cite the lines of this poem when thinking of the Kabul they knew before the wars. The poem conveys a strong love for the city and nation, but it also serves as a haunting lament for how Afghanistan's troubled history has impacted its peoples.

THE KITE RUNNER

In *The Kite Runner*, Hosseini employs the genre called bildungsroman, or the coming-of-age story, to follow the development of Amir, the protagonist and narrator, from his youth in Kabul through his adulthood in the area of San Francisco, California. Foils and father-son relationships unify the sprawling, yet symmetrical narrative.

As a little boy and preteen, Amir lives with his father Baba; his best friend and servant Hassan; and Hassan's father Ali, also a servant. Amir and Hassan play in Kabul's streets, watch American Westerns at the cinema, run kites together, and live, in many ways, as brothers. Similarly, Baba, a child of the upper class, grew up in the same household with Ali acting as his servant, friend, and brother figure. However, the idyllic surroundings in which Amir matures are troubled by these relationships. Amir desperately seeks Baba's attention, whereas Hassan, despite Baba not claiming him as his son, receives the praise and affection that Amir desires. At once, Amir admires Hassan's goodness, loyalty, bravery, and his relationship with Baba, but he is jealous of him. This creates tension between the two boys, as Amir often resorts to cruelty toward Hassan when he feels inadequate.

While Amir and Hassan are described throughout the novel as "milk brothers," boys who suckled from the same woman as infants, their closeness is frowned upon. Amir is a Pashtun, the majority ethnic group in Afghanistan; Hassan is a Hazara and, as a result, relegated to the servant class in Kabul. Despite their intimacy, the two boys are not supposed to be friends according to cultural beliefs. The tension in their friendship parallels national conflicts between the majority and minority ethnic groups in Afghanistan that have engendered division and war in that country.

After Amir wins a citywide kite-flying tournament, Hassan retrieves the kite for him and encounters a gang who has threatened the two boys before. The gang leader, Assef, physically and sexually assaults Hassan while Amir watches. This act of betrayal affects Amir in myriad ways: He gains Baba's affection, albeit temporarily, by having won the tournament, yet his guilt for failing to protect his best friend Hassan destroys his friendship with Hassan and plagues Amir into adulthood.

Baba and Amir are forced to leave Kabul, escaping to Pakistan and then to the United States as a result of the Soviet invasion. Settling in Northern California, they live relatively tranquil lives in spite of diminished economic circumstances and become members of a vibrant

Khaled Hosseini. (Courtesy, Penguin)

Afghan immigrant culture. After a decade, Baba dies, and Amir, a newly published author, creates a life with his wife Soraya. When Amir receives a telephone call from Baba's best friend from Kabul, Rahim Khan, telling him that "there is a way to be good again," Amir finds that he must return to Kabul. Rahim Khan reveals to Amir that Hassan is his biological half-brother, the son of Baba and Ali's servant wife. He then asks Amir to retrieve Hassan's son Sohrab from one of the underfunded and failing orphanages in Kabul.

Amir's journey to rescue Sohrab acts as a physical and moral journey to redeem himself from guilt and from the cowardice that he and his father shared. Ultimately, he stands up to the men who have brutalized Sohrab and brings him to California. Critics have argued that the symmetrical plot and moralistic theme undercut the novel's realism. In addition, some have claimed that the narrative, if viewed as an allegory of Afghanistan's national crisis and its "redemption" by the West, reads as too simplistic and patronizing. However, it is important to remember that Amir's quest does not paint him as a savior of anyone or any nation. Any fairy-tale endings for Amir, Sohrab, or Afghanistan are quickly dismissed when one takes into account the continuing struggles of survivors and refugees.

A Thousand Splendid Suns

Hosseini's second novel has been heralded for its realistic portrayal of Afghanistan during its occupation by the Soviets, the mujahideen—Islamic guerrilla fighters—the Taliban, and U.N. peacekeeping forces. In contrast to *The Kite Runner*, *A Thousand Splendid Suns* examines relationships between women as they are influenced by customs and class.

Spanning a period of nearly thirty years, the novel describes the intertwining lives of Mariam and Laila. Mariam, the daughter of Jalil, a wealthy businessman, and his servant Nana, is raised by her mother in a hut outside Herat, one of Afghanistan's most beautiful cities. Nana, having been ousted by Jalil and disowned by her family, cultivates a pristine bitterness that she tries to pass on to Mariam. Life treated Nana cruelly, and she believes it her job to steal Mariam from the shattered hopes that she will encounter because she is a woman and a *harami*, or illegitimate child.

Despite her mother's admonishments, Mariam relishes the weekly visits Jalil makes to her home. During their time together, Jalil gives Mariam gifts, tells her she's beautiful, and listens to her in a way that Nana cannot. The intimacy between father and daughter, however, is tempered by Jalil having legitimate children and wives in Herat; thus, he cannot publicly accept Mariam as his child—the only gift that Mariam really wants from her father. When she is fifteen years old, Mariam decides to visit Jalil in the city, much to Nana's dismay, and finds that Jalil will not accept her into his home. Still angry from the shame of being forced to sleep on the street in front of her father's house, Mariam returns to her home outside Herat, only to find that Nana has committed suicide. This puts Mariam in extremely precarious circumstances: She is an illegitimate female orphan without a male protector in a culture that values the honor and chastity of women. To rectify the situation, Jalil arranges her marriage to Rasheed, a shoemaker in Kabul who is nearly twice her age.

The early days of their marriage are filled with excitement for Mariam. On the surface, it appears that her life has improved, now that she lives in a house instead of a shack and receives frequent kindnesses from her husband. Rasheed, however, forces her to wear a burka, a garment designed to cover women from head to foot. He also forbids her to leave the house without him. After Mariam miscarries several times, Rasheed begins to beat her consistently. Without a male heir to carry on the family name, he finds Mariam useless. Verses from the Qur{hamza}{amacr}n taught by her friend and village mullah, or teacher of Islam, keep Mariam from sinking into despair.

Nearly two decades Mariam's junior, Laila was raised as the daughter of liberal parents in a middle-class household. Her childhood lies in stark contrast to that of Mariam, as she lived in relative freedom and luxury and aspired as a youth to attend the university. However, war infiltrates Kabul and she is left the only survivor of her family. As an act of "mercy," the now-middle-age Rasheed agrees to take adolescent Laila as his second wife. While the relationship between Laila and Mariam is strained at first, the two begin to love one another. The birth of Aziza and the mother-daughter-grandmother relationships that the women share brings purpose and meaning to their otherwise painful existence.

As conditions in Kabul worsen with the Taliban's occupation and as the family increases in size, they suffer from a privation so desperate that Rasheed forces Aziza to live in one of the city's many orphanages while his and Laila's son, Zalmai, continues to live at home. Rasheed continues to abuse Mariam; and, the Taliban, on the lookout for women unaccompanied by male protectors, beats Laila as she makes her way to the orphanage to visit her daughter. When Tariq, Laila's first love and Aziza's birth father, returns to Kabul, the women hope to escape, but it becomes clear that Rasheed will never let them do so. In an act of self-sacrifice, Mariam kills Rasheed and accepts the Taliban's sentence—death by execution—so that Laila, Tariq, Aziza, and Zalmai can live in a loving home. After peacekeeping forces control the Taliban in Kabul, Laila returns to the city and becomes a teacher in an orphanage to honor Mariam's memory and contribute to her country's recovery.

The beauty and sorrow of *A Thousand Splendid Suns* can be seen in the relationship between Mariam and Laila—two women born into vastly different circumstances who find themselves with the same abusive husband. Hosseini presents traditional customs regarding women in a relatively balanced fashion, offering in the novel that some woman accept veiling and the protection it provides. However, the contrast between Mariam's and Laila's expected fates highlights several undeniable issues, most saliently that women and children survivors are the true victims of war and that education and employment are fundamental to individual survival and national redevelopment.

DaRelle M. Rollins

Bibliography

Ahmed-Gosh, Huma. "A History of Women in Afghanistan: Lessons Learnt for the Future." *Journal of International Women's Studies* 4, no. 3 (2003): 1-14. Study of the history of women in Afghanistan in the late twentieth century that also suggests ways for a freer future.

Bloom, Harold, ed. *Khalid Hosseini's "The Kite Runner."* New York: Bloom's Literary Criticism, 2009. Comprehensive study guide on *The Kite Runner* with essays written especially for students in grades 9 through 12. Part of the Bloom's Guides series of analyses of classic works of literature.

Katsoulis, Melissa. "Kites of Passage: New Fiction." *The Times* (London), August 30, 2003. Brief review of Hosseini's novel *The Kite Runner* in a renowned British periodical.

Lemar-Aftaab. June, 2004. Special issue of this Web-based magazine devoted to Khaled Hosseini and his works. Two articles explore themes in *The Kite Runner*. Also features an interview with Hosseini. Available at http://afghanmagazine.com/2004_06/.

WILLIAM DEAN HOWELLS

Born: Martinsville (now Martins Ferry), Ohio; March 1, 1837

Died: New York, New York; May 11, 1920

Principal long fiction

Their Wedding Journey, 1872
A Chance Acquaintance, 1873
A Foregone Conclusion, 1875
The Lady of the Aroostook, 1879
The Undiscovered Country, 1880
Doctor Breen's Practice, 1881
A Modern Instance, 1882
A Woman's Reason, 1883
The Rise of Silas Lapham, 1885
Indian Summer, 1886
April Hopes, 1887
The Minister's Charge: Or, The Apprenticeship of Lemuel Barker, 1887
Annie Kilburn, 1888
A Hazard of New Fortunes, 1889
The Shadow of a Dream, 1890
An Imperative Duty, 1891

The Quality of Mercy, 1892
The Coast of Bohemia, 1893
The World of Chance, 1893
A Traveler from Altruria, 1894
The Day of Their Wedding, 1896
A Parting and a Meeting, 1896
The Landlord at Lion's Head, 1897
An Open-Eyed Conspiracy: An Idyl of Saratoga, 1897
The Story of a Play, 1898
Ragged Lady, 1899
Their Silver Wedding Journey, 1899
The Kentons, 1902
The Son of Royal Langbirth, 1904
Miss Bellard's Inspiration, 1905
Through the Eye of the Needle, 1907
Fennel and Rue, 1908
New Leaf Mills, 1913
The Leatherwood God, 1916
The Vacation of the Kelwyns, 1920
Mrs. Farrell, 1921

Other literary forms

William Dean Howells was unquestionably one of the most versatile and productive writers of the late nineteenth and early twentieth centuries. In addition to approximately forty novels, Howells produced several volumes of short fiction, among them *A Fearful Responsibility, and Other Stories* (1881) and *Christmas Every Day, and Other Stories Told for Children* (1893). He also wrote more than thirty dramas, including *The Parlor Car* (pb. 1876), *The Mouse-Trap, and Other Farces* (pb. 1889), and *Parting Friends* (pb. 1911), which generally were designed to be read aloud rather than performed.

In addition, one of Howells's earliest and most enduring passions was the writing of poetry. His first published collection was *Poems of Two Friends* (1860, with John J. Piatt); nearly fifty years later, he published *The Mother and the Father* (1909). The genre that first brought him to public attention was travel literature, including *Venetian Life* (1866) and *Italian Journeys* (1867); other volumes continued to appear throughout his career. Howells also is renowned as a perceptive critic and literary historian. Still of literary value are *Criticism and Fiction* (1891), *My Literary Passions* (1895), *Literature and Life* (1902), and *My Mark Twain* (1910). In addition, a substantial number of Howells's critical essays appeared in *Harper's* magazine from 1886 to 1892, and between 1900 until his death in 1920. Finally, Howells wrote biographies such as *Lives and Speeches of Abraham Lincoln and Hannibal Hamlin* (1860), as well as several autobiographical works, including *My Year in a Log Cabin* (1893) and *Years of My Youth* (1916).

Achievements

William Dean Howells is remembered today as an important early exponent of realism in fiction. Reacting against the highly "sentimental' novels of his day, Howells—both in his own fiction and in his criticism—advocated less reliance on love-oriented stories with formulaic plots and characters, and more interest in emphasizing real people, situations, and behavior. This is not to say that Howells shared the naturalists' interest in sex, low-life, and violence, for in fact he was quite reserved in his dealings with these aspects of life. He did, however, acknowledge their existence, and in so doing paved the way for Theodore Dreiser, Stephen Crane, and the modern realistic novel.

Inspired by his reading of European literature (notably Leo Tolstoy), Howells also argued that fiction could be a tool for social reform. Finally, in his influential positions at *The Atlantic Monthly* and *Harper's*, Howells was able to offer help and encouragement to rising young American authors, including Crane and Henry James.

Howells's later years were full of recognition: He received an honorary doctorate from Yale University (1901), as well as from Oxford (1904) and Columbia (1905). He received a doctorate in humane letters from Princeton in 1912. He was elected first president of the American Academy of Arts and Letters in 1908, and seven years later he received the academy's gold medal for fiction.

Biography

Although early in his career he was accepted into the charmed literary circles of Boston and New York, William Dean Howells was born and reared in the Midwest, and he never fully lost touch with his midwestern background. He was born on March 1, 1837, in Martin's Ferry (then Martinsville), Ohio, the second of eight children. His early life was singularly unstable: Because his father was something of a political radical whose principles jeopardized the prosperity of every newspaper with which he was associated, the family was periodically compelled to move away from one conservative Ohio village after another. Despite such instability, Howells found the variety of experiences enriching and was able to make the most of the spotty formal education he received.

Howells's exposure to the written word came at an early age: When Howells was only three, his father moved the little family to Hamilton, Ohio, where he had acquired a local newspaper, the *Intelligencer*; by the age of six, the precocious Howells was setting type in his father's printing office, and not long after that he began to compose poems and brief sketches. In 1850, the family made one of their more fortunate moves by establishing themselves in a one-room log cabin in the utopian community at Eureka Mills near Xenia, Ohio. It was a welcome interlude in the family's struggle to find a political, economic, and social niche that would satisfy the father, and Howells would remember it fondly much later in *My Year in a Log Cabin*. The next move was to Columbus, where young Howells acquired a position as a compositor on the *Ohio State Journal*. Already beginning to diversify his literary endeavors, the fourteen-year-old Howells was also writing poetry in the manner of Alexander Pope.

In 1852, Howells's father bought a share in the *Ashtabula Sentinel* and moved it to Jefferson, Ohio. For once, his principles did not clash with those of the community: The little newspaper was a success, and it was to remain in the Howells family for forty years. While living in Jefferson, a community composed largely of well-educated, transplanted New Englanders, the teenage Howells embarked on a plan of intensive self-education that included studies of Pope, Oliver Goldsmith, Oliver Wendell Holmes, Edgar Allan Poe, and Heinrich Heine. As much as this program compromised his social life, Howells derived enormous intellectual benefits from it, and several of the townspeople of Jefferson even offered to help finance a Harvard education for this gifted lad; his father declined the offer, however, and Howells remained at Jefferson, publishing his stories pseudonymously beginning in 1853.

As his father gradually rose in Ohio state politics (he was elected clerk of the state House of Representatives in 1855), Howells rose with him, and in 1857 he was offered a permanent position as a correspondent on the *Cincinnati Gazette*. Howells, not yet twenty years old, was too emotionally dependent upon his family and too much of a hypochondriac to stay more than a few weeks at the *Cincinnati Gazette*, but when, in the following year, he received another opportunity in journalism, this time from the *Ohio State Journal*, he was able to accept the offer from his previous employer and to succeed. In

William Dean Howells. (Library of Congress)

addition to his duties as a reporter and editor, Howells found time to write sketches and verse, and some of his writings appeared in *The Atlantic Monthly*, the prestigious Boston-based journal-magazine of which he was to become editor in chief many years later.

The year 1860 was the most significant one of Howells's life: He met Elinor Mead of Brattleboro, Vermont, whom he would marry two years later in Paris; he published his first book, *Poems of Two Friends*, coauthored with John J. Piatt; and—at the urging of the volume's Cincinnati publisher, Frank Foster—Howells prepared a campaign biography of Abraham Lincoln. Although assembled out of information Howells had gleaned from printed sources rather than from Lincoln himself, and written in only a few weeks, the book proved to be a moving and inspiring account of his fellow midwesterner. With its royalties, the resourceful and ambitious Howells financed a trip to two literary meccas, Boston and New York, where he arranged to meet some of the most important writers and editors of the day, and he returned to Ohio confirmed in his desire to pursue a career in literature.

Following the outbreak of the American Civil War, Howells—temperamentally ill suited to military life—decided to seek a foreign diplomatic post. Cashing in on the success of his popular Lincoln biography, the twenty-four-year-old Howells managed to be appointed as the U.S. consul at Venice, a pleasant and remunerative position he held for four years. Howells was able to draw on his Italian experiences in a series of travel essays that were collected in book form as *Venetian Life* and *Italian Journeys*. When he returned to the United States in the summer of 1865, he was sufficiently established as a writer to be able to embark on a freelance writing career in New York. After a brief stint at the newly founded magazine *The Nation*, Howells was lured to Boston and a subeditorship at *The Atlantic Monthly* under James T. Fields; after five years Howells became editor in chief (1871-1881). By the age of thirty, Howells was already a prominent member of Boston's literati. He received an honorary master's degree from Harvard in 1867 and was forging friendships with such literary figures as Henry James (whom he had met in 1866) and Samuel Clemens (Mark Twain), destined to become a lifelong friend.

At about that time (the late 1860's) Howells came to accept that there was no market for his poetry; so, while he continued to write travel literature, he began to prepare descriptive sketches that would evolve rapidly into the literary form to which he was particularly well suited: the novel. The first product of this transitional period was *Their Wedding Journey*, which was serialized in *The Atlantic Monthly* in 1871 and published in book form in 1872. *Their Wedding Journey*, which manages to straddle both travel literature and fiction, features Basil and Isabel March (based on William and Elinor Howells), characters who would recur throughout Howells's fiction, most notably in *A Hazard of New Fortunes*. After *Their Wedding Journey*, Howells produced novels with almost machinelike speed and regularity. *A Chance Acquaintance* is a psychological romance that served to demythologize the idea of the "proper Bostonian" that Howells had so admired in his youth. *A Foregone Conclusion*, in which a young American girl clashes with traditional European society, anticipates James's *Daisy Miller* by three years. Two "international novels" that contrast American and Italian values and lifestyles are *The Lady of Aroostook* and *A Fearful Responsibility, and Other Stories*. *The Undiscovered Country* probes spiritualism and the Shakers, while *Doctor Breen's Practice* is the social and psychological study of a woman physician.

In 1881, Howells found himself caught in the dissolution of his publisher's partnership, Osgood and Houghton, so he left *The Atlantic Monthly* and began to serialize stories in *Century* magazine. During this period, Howells began to focus increasingly on ethical problems, and in the 1880's he produced in rapid succession the novels that are generally held to be his greatest achievements in fiction. In 1882 appeared *A Modern Instance*, the so-called divorce novel that is now regarded as Howells's first major work in long fiction. During its composition, he suffered a breakdown, in part the result of the worsening health of his daughter, Winny, who died only a few years later at the age of twenty-six. An extended trip to Italy proved disappointing, but it enabled Howells to recover sufficiently to write another major novel, *The Rise of Silas Lapham*, followed immediately by the book he enjoyed writing most, *Indian Summer*. As a comedy of manners set in Italy, *Indian*

Summer was a reversion to Howells's earliest fictional style and subject matter as well as a welcome change from the intense social realism that characterized his fiction in the 1880's.

By that time, Howells was living permanently in New York and was a member of the editorial staff of *Harper's*. In January, 1886, he began a regular feature in *Harper's* called the "Editor's Study," which continued until 1892 and served as the organ through which he campaigned for realism and a greater social consciousness in fiction. Howells had so reoriented himself away from Boston, the cynosure of his youth, that he turned down a professorship at Harvard and wrote his first novel set in New York, *A Hazard of New Fortunes*, regarded as one of his finest works.

Howells's novels in the 1890's were even more insistently illustrative of his strong social consciousness than those of the previous decade. *The Quality of Mercy* is the study of a crime (embezzlement) that is to be blamed less on the individual who committed it than on the society that created that person. *An Imperative Duty* deals with miscegenation, and *A Traveler from Altruria* and its belated sequel, *Through the Eye of the Needle*, were written within the literary tradition of the utopian novel. Late in his career, Howells tended to resurrect and rework earlier material (the March family of *Their Wedding Journey*, Howells's earliest novel, reappeared in *Their Silver Wedding Journey*). One of his finest character studies is that of Jeff Durgin in the late novel *The Landlord at Lion's Head*, the only work by Howells that clearly shows the influence of naturalism.

After a lecture tour through the West, Howells, in 1900, began to write a regular column, the "The Editor's Easy Chair," for *Harper's*, and continued to do so until his death in 1920. His last major works were *My Mark Twain*, an appreciative account of his friend published in 1910 (the year of the deaths of Clemens and Howells's wife), and the posthumous *The Vacation of the Kelwyns*, published in 1920.

Howells died in New York City on May 11, 1920, still productive until his death. Although he realized that his creative powers had long since dimmed, he nevertheless had managed to maintain over much of his extraordinary life his well-deserved position as the dean of American letters.

ANALYSIS

Throughout his career as a fiction writer, William Dean Howells worked against the sentimentality and idealization that pervaded popular American literature in the nineteenth century. He pleaded for characters, situations, behavior, values, settings, and even speech patterns that were true to life. While twentieth century readers came to take such elements for granted, the fact remains that in Howells's day he was regarded as something of a literary radical. One indication of his radicalism was his preference for character over plot in his fiction: He was far less interested in telling a good story (albeit his stories are good) than in presenting flesh-and-blood characters who think, feel, make mistakes, and are products of genetic, social, and economic conditions—in other words, who are as imperfect (and as interesting) as real people. Howells did not indulge in meticulous psychological analyses of his characters, as did his friend Henry James, and his plots tend to be far more linear and straightforward than are the convoluted and carefully patterned ones of James. Nevertheless, Howells was an innovative and influential writer who changed the quality of American fiction.

A MODERN INSTANCE

A hallmark of Howells's advocacy of realism was his interest in topics that were taboo in Victorian times. Such a topic was divorce, which in the nineteenth century was still regarded by much of society as scandalous and shameful, and which Howells utilized as the resolution of his first major novel, *A Modern Instance*. This was not a "divorce novel" per se, as was maintained by several of Howells's shocked contemporaries, but in an era when "they married and lived happily ever after" was a fictional norm, the divorce of Bartley and Marcia Hubbard was quite unpalatable. Given the situation of the characters, however, the breakup was inevitable—in a word, realistic. As William M. Gibson explains in his excellent introduction to the Riverside edition of *A Modern Instance* (1957), the story apparently germinated when Howells saw an impressive performance of Euripides' *Medea* in Boston in the spring of 1875, and in fact the working title of the novel was *The New Medea*. The novel's genesis and working title are significant, for the story's female protagonist harbors a passion that is both overpowering and destructive.

Marcia Gaylord, the only child of Squire Gaylord and his self-effacing wife, Miranda, grows up in Equity, Maine, in an era when the state's once-impressive commercial prominence has all but decayed. Her domineering but indulgent father and her ineffectual mother have failed to mold Marcia's personality in a positive way, and this lack of a strong character, interacting with an environment caught in economic, cultural, political, and spiritual decline, compels Marcia to leave Equity while rendering her utterly unequipped to deal with the outside world. Not surprisingly, she becomes enamored of the first attractive young man to happen her way: Bartley Hubbard, editor of the newspaper of Equity. Superficially, Hubbard has all the earmarks of the hero of a romantic novel: Orphaned young, he is intelligent enough to have succeeded at a country college, and with his education, charm, and diligence, he seems well on his way to a career in law. There, however, the Lincolnesque qualities end. Ambitious, manipulative, shrewd, unscrupulous, and self-centered, Bartley is the worst possible husband for the shallow Marcia, and after a courtship rife with spats, jealousy, and misunderstandings (even the short-lived engagement is the result of misinterpreted behavior), the ill-matched pair elope and settle in Boston.

The remainder of the novel is an analysis of the characters of Marcia and Bartley as they are revealed by the social, professional, and economic pressures of Boston, and a concomitant study of the deterioration of their marriage. Marcia is motivated by her sexual passion for Bartley and her deep emotional attachment to her father—an attachment so intense that she names her daughter after him and attempts to force Bartley into following in his footsteps as a lawyer. Locked into the roles of wife and daughter, Marcia has no separate identity, no concrete values, no sense of purpose. As Marcia struggles with her disordered personality, Bartley's becomes only too clear: His success as a newspaperman is the direct result of his being both shrewd in his estimation of the low level of popular taste, and unscrupulous in finding material and assuming (or disavowing) responsibility for it.

Bartley's foil is a native Bostonian and former classmate, Ben Halleck. A wealthy man without being spoiled, a trained attorney too moralistic to practice law, and a good judge of character who refuses to use that talent for ignoble ends, Halleck is all that Bartley Hubbard could have been under more favorable circumstances. Even so, Ben does not fit into the world of nineteenth century America: As is graphically symbolized by his being disabled, Ben cannot find a satisfying occupation, a meaningful religion, or a warm relationship with a woman. In fact, it is Howells's trenchant indictment of the social, economic, and spiritual problems of nineteenth century America that not a single character in *A Modern Instance* is psychically whole. To further compound his difficulties, Ben loves Marcia, having adored her for years after noticing her from afar as a school girl in Maine. In his efforts to aid her by lending money to Bartley and pressuring her to stand by her husband, Ben unwittingly contributes to Bartley's abandonment of Marcia, to her resultant emotional crisis, and to the devastating divorce in Indiana.

Carefully avoiding the traditional happy ending, Howells completes his story with a scene of human wreckage: Bartley, unscrupulous newspaperman to the end, is shot to death by a disgruntled reader in Arizona; Squire Gaylord, emotionally destroyed by defending his daughter in the divorce suit, dies a broken man; Ben, unsuccessful as a schoolteacher in Uruguay, flees to backwoods Maine to preach; and Marcia returns to the narrow world of Equity, her beauty and spirit long vanished. Interesting, complex, and bitter, *A Modern Instance* so strained Howells's emotional and physical well-being that he suffered a breakdown while writing it. The "falling off" of energy and style in the second part of the novel, noted by many commentators, may be attributed to the breakdown as well as to the related stress engendered by the serious psychosomatic illness of his beloved daughter, Winny. It should be borne in mind, however, that the novel's singularly unhappy ending cannot be attributed to either crisis; the book's conclusion, planned from the story's inception, was itself meant to be a commentary on a nation buffeted by spiritual, social, and economic change.

The Rise of Silas Lapham

On a level with *A Modern Instance* is Howells's best-known novel, *The Rise of Silas Lapham*. Serialized in *Century* magazine from November, 1884, to August, 1885, and published in book form in the late summer of

1885, *The Rise of Silas Lapham* takes a realistic look at the upheavals in late nineteenth century America by focusing on the archetypal self-made man. Colonel Silas Lapham of Lumberville, Vermont, has made a fortune in the paint business by virtue of hard work, honest dealings, and the help and guidance of a good woman, his wife, Persis. The sentimental portrait of the self-made American captain of industry is significantly compromised, however, by the fact that Lapham owes much of his success to simple luck (his father accidentally found a superb paint mine on his farm) and to an early partner's capital (Rogers, a shadowy and rather demoniac figure whom Lapham "squeezed out" once his paint business began to thrive). Even more compromising is that Lapham's great wealth and success cannot compensate for his personality and background: Boastful, oafish (his hands are "hairy fists"), and devoid of any aesthetic sensibility, Lapham seeks to buy his way into proper Boston society by building a fabulous mansion on the Back Bay and encouraging a romance between his daughter and Tom Corey, a Harvard graduate with "old" Boston money.

The Coreys are, in fact, foils of the Laphams: Tom's father, Bromfield Corey, is also indirectly associated with paint (he has a talent for portraiture), but having inherited substantial wealth, he has never worked, preferring instead to live off the labors of his ancestors. Ultimately, neither man is acceptable to Howells: Lapham, for all his substantial new wealth, is vulgar and ambitious; Bromfield Corey, for all his old money and polish, is lethargic and ineffectual. The wives do not fare much better. Persis Lapham is burdened with a Puritan reserve that at vital moments renders her incapable of giving her husband emotional support, and Anna Corey, despite her fine manners, is stuffy and judgmental.

The most admirable characters in the novel are two of the five children. Penelope Lapham is a quick-witted, plain girl with a passion for reading George Eliot, while Tom Corey is an educated, enterprising young man who sincerely wants an active business career. Although clearly Pen and Tom are ideally suited to each other, their relationship almost fails to materialize because virtually everyone in the novel—and the reader as well—naturally assumes Tom to be attracted to young Irene Lapham, who is strikingly pretty, beautifully attired, and considerably less intellectually endowed than her sister. In his campaign for realism in literature, Howells intentionally blurs the distinctions between the world of reality (where people like Pen and Tom fall in love) and the world of sentiment (where beautiful, empty-headed Irene is the ideal girl). The blurring is so complete that the Laphams, brainwashed by the romanticized standards of nineteenth century American life, almost deliberately scuttle Pen's relationship with Tom simply because pretty Irene had a crush on him first. The level-headed Reverend Sewell, with his realistic belief in the "economy of pain," is needed to convince the parties involved that they were acting out of "the shallowest sentimentality" rather than common sense in promoting Irene's match with Tom.

As part of his questioning of nineteenth century sentimentality, Howells specifically attacks one of its most graphic manifestations, the self-made man. In the heyday of the Horatio Alger stories, Howells presents a protagonist who to many Americans was the ultimate role model: a Vermont farm lad who became a Boston millionaire. Howells's undermining of Lapham is, however, so meticulous and so complete—he even opens the novel with Lapham being interviewed by sardonic Bartley Hubbard (of *A Modern Instance*) for the "Solid Men of Boston" series in a local pulp newspaper—that the reader is left uncertain whether to admire Lapham for his sound character and business achievements, or to laugh at him for his personality flaws and social blunders. This uncertainty is attributable to the unclear tone of the novel, as George Arms points out in his excellent introduction to *The Rise of Silas Lapham* (1949). The tone is, in fact, a major flaw in the novel, as are some episodes of dubious worth (such as the ostensible affair between Lapham and his typist) and Howells's disinclination to develop some potentially vital characters (such as Tom Corey's uncle and Lapham's financial adviser, James Bellingham).

A more fundamental problem is Howells's refusal to face squarely the matter of morality: He never fully resolves the complex relationship between Lapham and his former partner, Rogers, a relationship that raises such questions as whether good intentions can serve evil ends, and to what extent one has moral obligations toward business associates, friends, and even strangers.

Not surprisingly, the end of the novel is less than satisfying: Tom Corey marries Pen Lapham and they move to Mexico, where presumably the disparity in their backgrounds will be less glaring; the financially ruined Laphams return to the old Vermont farm, where ostensibly they are far happier than they were as wealthy Bostonians; and pretty young Irene endures spinsterhood. Despite these problems and an overreliance on dialogue (at times the novel reads like a play), *The Rise of Silas Lapham* is indeed, as Arms remarks, "a work of competence and illumination" that rightly deserves its status as an outstanding example of late nineteenth century realistic fiction.

A Hazard of New Fortunes

Four years after *The Rise of Silas Lapham*, Howells published the novel that he personally felt to be his best and "most vital" book: *A Hazard of New Fortunes*. A long novel (more than five hundred pages), it features a rather unwieldy number of characters who all know one another professionally or socially (indeed, the "it's a small world" motif is rather strained at times), who possess widely varying degrees of social consciousness, and who come from a number of geographic, economic, and intellectual backgrounds. This cross section of humanity resides in New York City, and the interaction among the remarkably diverse characters occurs as a result of three catalysts: a new magazine titled *Every Other Week*, a boardinghouse run by the Leightons, and a period of labor unrest among the city's streetcar workers.

The magazine subplot nicely illustrates Howells's extraordinary ability to interweave characters, plot, and themes around a controlling element. *Every Other Week* is a new magazine to be published under the general editorship of a person named Fulkerson. As its literary editor, he hires Basil March, a transplanted middle-class Indianian who has left his position as an insurance agent in Boston to begin a new life at the age of fifty in New York. As the magazine's art editor, there is young Angus Beaton, a shallow ladies' man and dilettante who cannot escape his humble background in Syracuse. The translator is Berthold Lindau, an elderly, well-read German who had befriended March as a boy and who had lost a hand in the Civil War. The financial "angel" of the magazine is Jacob Dryfoos, an uncultured midwestern farmer who has made a fortune through the natural gas wells on his land, and who forces his Christlike son, Conrad, to handle the financial aspects of the magazine as a way of learning about business. The magazine's cover artist is Alma Leighton, a feminist whom Beaton loves, and a frequent contributor of articles is Colonel Woodburn, a ruined Virginian who boards with the Leightons and whose daughter marries Fulkerson.

Each individual associated with *Every Other Week* perceives the magazine in a different light; each is attracted to it (or repulsed by it) for a different reason. As *Every Other Week* becomes a success, Howells allows it to drift out of the focus of the novel, leaving the reader to observe the interactions (usually clashes) of the various characters' personalities, interests, and motives. Lindau, whose social consciousness calls for unions and socialism, is in essential agreement with Conrad Dryfoos, although the latter disdains the German's advocacy of violence; both men clash with Jacob Dryfoos, who, no longer in touch with the earthy Indiana lifestyle of his early years, believes that pro-union workers should be shot. The artist, Beaton—who loves the feline quality of Conrad's sister Christine as much as he loves the independence of Alma Leighton and the goodness of socialite worker Margaret Vance—does not care about economic and social matters one way or another, while Colonel Woodburn advocates slavery.

The character whose attitudes most closely parallel those of Howells himself is Basil March, whose social consciousness grows in the course of the novel as he witnesses the poverty of the New York slums, the senseless deaths of Lindau and Conrad, and the pathetic, belated efforts of Jacob Dryfoos to correct his mistakes through the lavish spending of money. In many respects, March is a projection of Howells's attitudes and experiences, and his tendency at the end of the novel to make speeches to his wife about labor, religion, and injustice is a reflection of Howells's reading of Tolstoy. Even so, it would be incorrect to perceive March as the story's main character. That distinction most properly belongs to Jacob Dryfoos, a sort of Pennsylvania Dutch version of Silas Lapham whose values, home, lifestyle, and attitude have been undermined forever by the finding of gas deposits on his farm.

Although much of Howells's fiction deals with social and personal upheaval in late nineteenth century America, nowhere is it more poignantly depicted than in *A Hazard of New Fortunes*. In the light of this poignancy, it is to Howells's credit that the novel does not turn into a cold social tract: The characters are flesh-and-blood rather than caricatures. The novel contains considerable humor, most notably in the early chapters dealing with the Marches house-hunting in New York. There is also a surprising emphasis on feminism and a concomitant questioning of marriage and the false behavioral ideals propagated by sentimental fiction. In addition, Howells provides psychological probing (particularly in the form of fantasizing) such as one would expect of James more readily than Howells, and above all there is the aforementioned interweaving of characters, incidents, and themes.

Of Howells's approximately forty novels written during his long career, at least half a dozen—including *A Modern Instance*, *The Rise of Silas Lapham*, and *A Hazard of New Fortunes*—have endured, a testament to not only their brilliant, realistic evocation of life in late nineteenth century America but also the distinctive skills, interests, and sensibility of the dean of American letters.

Alice Hall Petry

Other major works

SHORT FICTION: *A Fearful Responsibility, and Other Stories*, 1881; *Selected Short Stories of William Dean Howells*, 1997.

PLAYS: *The Parlor Car*, pb. 1876; *A Counterfeit Presentment*, pb. 1877; *Out of the Question*, pb. 1877; *The Register*, pb. 1884; *A Sea-Change*, pb. 1887; *The Mouse-Trap, and Other Farces*, pb. 1889; *The Albany Depot*, pb. 1892; *A Letter of Introduction*, pb. 1892; *The Unexpected Guests*, pb. 1893; *A Previous Engagement*, pb. 1897; *An Indian Giver*, pb. 1900; *Room Forty-five*, pb. 1900; *The Smoking Car*, pb. 1900; *Parting Friends*, pb. 1911; *The Complete Plays of W. D. Howells*, 1960 (Walter J. Meserve, editor).

POETRY: *Poems of Two Friends*, 1860 (with John J. Piatt); *Poems*, 1873; *Samson*, 1874; *Priscilla: A Comedy*, 1882; *A Sea Change: Or, Love's Stowaway*, 1884; *Stops of Various Quills*, 1895; *The Mother and the Father*, 1909; *Pebbles, Monochromes, and Other Modern Poems, 1891-1916*, 2000 (Edwin H. Cady, editor).

NONFICTION: *Lives and Speeches of Abraham Lincoln and Hannibal Hamlin*, 1860 (with others); *Venetian Life*, 1866; *Italian Journeys*, 1867; *Tuscan Cities*, 1885; *Modern Italian Poets*, 1887; *A Boy's Town*, 1890; *Criticism and Fiction*, 1891; *My Year in a Log Cabin*, 1893; *My Literary Passions*, 1895; *Impressions and Experiences*, 1896; *Stories of Ohio*, 1897; *Literary Friends and Acquaintances*, 1900; *Heroines of Fiction*, 1901; *Literature and Life*, 1902; *Letters Home*, 1903; *London Films*, 1905; *Certain Delightful English Towns*, 1906; *Roman Holidays*, 1908; *Seven English Cities*, 1909; *Imaginary Interviews*, 1910; *My Mark Twain*, 1910; *Familiar Spanish Travels*, 1913; *New Leaf Mills*, 1913; *Years of My Youth*, 1916; *Eighty Years and After*, 1921; *The Life and Letters of William Dean Howells*, 1928 (M. Howells, editor); *A Realist in the American Theatre: Selected Drama Criticism of William Dean Howells*, 1992 (Brenda Murphy, editor); *Selected Literary Criticism*, 1993 (3 volumes); *Letters, Fictions, Lives: Henry James and William Dean Howells*, 1997 (Michael Anesko, editor).

CHILDREN'S LITERATURE: *Christmas Every Day, and Other Stories Told for Children*, 1893.

Bibliography

Abeln, Paul. *William Dean Howells and the Ends of Realism*. New York: Routledge, 2004. Abeln analyzes Howells's fiction, providing a close look at his late works, to demonstrate that Howells's work is as significant in the American literary tradition as that of his better-regarded contemporaries Henry James and Mark Twain.

Cady, Edwin H. *The Road to Realism: The Early Years, 1837-1885, of William Dean Howells*. Syracuse, N.Y.: Syracuse University Press, 1956.

_______. *The Realist at War: The Mature Years, 1885-1920, of William Dean Howells*. Syracuse, N.Y.: Syracuse University Press, 1958. These two volumes are useful studies of Howell's life and the development of his literary theories, as well as analyses of his novels.

Crowley, John W. *The Dean of American Letters: The Late Career of William Dean Howells*. Amherst: University of Massachusetts Press, 1999. A biography by a noted Howells scholar. Crowley looks at

Howells's career after 1890, when he had become a cultural icon, and analyzes how Howells responded to his celebrity and to increasing competition in the publishing industry.

_______. *The Mask of Fiction: Essays on W. D. Howells*. Amherst: University of Massachusetts Press, 1989. Examines Howells's unconscious in his writings, incorporating both the "probing psychologism" of the works published in the 1890's and the deeper psychic integration of his later light fiction. An important contribution to critical studies on Howells.

Eble, Kenneth E. *William Dean Howells*. 2d ed. Boston: Twayne, 1982. An excellent introduction to Howells in the Twayne United States Authors series, devoted almost entirely to the major novels. Includes a bibliography and an index.

Goodman, Susan, and Carl Dawson. *William Dean Howells: A Writer's Life*. Berkeley: University of California Press, 2005. This broad and compelling biography of the literary giant is an important resource for the study of Howells's life and work. Among other topics, the biographers discuss Howells's friendships with and support of contemporary writers and his significance in American letters. Includes illustrations and a bibliography.

Mielke, Robert. *"The Riddle of the Painful Earth": Suffering and Society in W. D. Howells' Major Writings of the Early 1890's*. Kirksville, Mo.: Thomas Jefferson University Press at Northeast Missouri State University, 1994. Treats Howells's literary profession as a form of social activism.

Nettels, Elsa. *Language and Gender in American Fiction: Howells, James, Wharton, and Cather*. Charlottesville: University Press of Virginia, 1997. Nettels examines the work of Howells and three other nineteenth century American writers, analyzing how they represent gender and distinguish male and female conversation in their writings.

Olsen, Rodney D. *Dancing in Chains: The Youth of William Dean Howells*. New York: New York University Press, 1991. Olsen provides a careful study of the middle-class roots of Howells's fiction, showing how his society shaped him and how his fiction not only appealed to that society but also was an expression of it. Includes very detailed notes.

Stratman, Gregory J. *Speaking for Howells: Charting the Dean's Career Through the Language of His Characters*. Lanham, Md.: University Press of America, 2001. Analyzes Howells's interest in language, focusing on the language of his characters and his use of literary dialect. Argues that Howells's use of and writing about language demonstrates how his career moved in a circular path from Romanticism to realism and back to Romanticism.

W. H. HUDSON

Born: Quilmes, Argentina; August 4, 1841
Died: London, England; August 18, 1922
Also known as: William Henry Hudson; Henry Harford

Principal long fiction

The Purple Land, 1885 (originally pb. as *The Purple Land That England Lost*)
A Crystal Age, 1887
Fan: The Story of a Young Girl's Life, 1892 (as Henry Harford)
El Ombú, 1902 (reissued as *South American Sketches*, 1909; also known as *Tales of the Pampas*, 1916)
Green Mansions, 1904
A Little Boy Lost, 1905

Other literary forms

W. H. Hudson was most prolific as an essayist; most of his essays record his observations as a field naturalist. He was particularly fascinated by bird life; between 1888 and 1889 he compiled and published, with the aid of Philip Lutley Sclater, *Argentine Ornithology*, which was later revised as *Birds of La Plata* (1920). He followed this with books titled *Birds in a Village* (1893) and *British Birds* (1895). More general reflections on nature can be found in such of his books as *Idle Days in Patagonia* (1893) and *Nature in Downland* (1900). Although Hudson was primarily an observer and not a theorist, his last book of this type, *A Hind in Richmond Park* (1922), is a much more philosophical work, occasionally tending to the mystical, discussing the nature of sensory experience in animals and humans and linking this analysis to aesthetic theory and the "spiritualizing" of humans. He also wrote an autobiography, *Far Away and Long Ago* (1918), a lyrical work recalling his childhood in South America; it deals only with his early life and refers to no incidents after 1859.

Achievements

W. H. Hudson is almost a forgotten writer today, remembered primarily for *Green Mansions*. He was equally unappreciated for most of his own lifetime—he lived in poverty and was virtually ignored by the literary public until *Green Mansions* became a best seller in the United States, by which time he was well into his sixties. He seems to have had mixed feelings about this late success—it is significant that he refrained from writing any further romances, though his juvenile novel *A Little Boy Lost* appeared the following year. Hudson wanted to be known as a naturalist, and he considered his essays on nature his most important works. These books did, indeed, attract a small coterie of admirers, and for a few years before and immediately after his death they received due attention. He is commemorated by a bird sanctuary in Hyde Park, where there is a Jacob Epstein statue representing Rima, the enigmatic nature-spirit from *Green Mansions*. In 1924, J. M. Dent and Sons reissued his complete works in twenty-four volumes and his friend Morley Roberts published an appreciative memoir of him.

Hudson's nonfiction is generally more interesting and more valuable than his fiction. His essays on nature provide an unusual combination of patient and scrupulous observation with occasional speculative rhapsodies of a metaphysical character. In his visionary moments, Hudson held a view of the living world akin to that of philosopher Henri Bergson, author of *Creative Evolution* (1907), but this aspect of his work is of historical and psychological interest only. His careful and minute observations are of more enduring value, especially when he turned his attention—as he often did—from birds to people. His accounts of human life from the detached viewpoint of the field naturalist are always fascinating, and his documentation of the life of a small rural village in *A Shepherd's Life* (1910) is a rare glimpse of a world that has passed almost without record.

Hudson's fiction enjoys what reputation it has because of its combination of the same contrasting traits that are to be found in his nonfiction: His descriptions of the natural world in his South American romances are delicate and scrupulous, and the same is true of his observations of the life of the inhabitants of the Banda Oriental (now Uruguay) in *The Purple Land* or the savages in *Green Mansions*. At the same time, however, the best of these stories has an imaginative component so ambitious that it permits the reader to see the world—and other possible and impossible worlds too—through new eyes. There is a sense in which his visions of a quasi-supernatural ecological harmony fit in better with ideas that are current in the early twenty-first century than they did with the zeitgeist of Hudson's own age, and it is therefore surprising that his work does not get more attention. It is possible that he is ripe for rediscovery, and that a new assessment of his achievement may yet be made.

Biography

William Henry Hudson was born on August 4, 1841, on an estancia about ten miles outside Buenos Aires, Argentina. His parents were both American, but he had British grandparents on both sides of the family. His parents seem to have been very devoted to their children, and Hudson apparently enjoyed an idyllic childhood on the pampas; his memories of it recorded in *Far Away and Long Ago* were fond in the extreme. During his adolescence, however, he developed solitary tendencies, drifting away from the company of his siblings. During these years, he gave himself over to the patient and lonely study of nature.

Very little is known of Hudson's later years in South America; his autobiography has nothing to say of his life

W. H. Hudson. (E. P. Dutton & Co., 1918)

after he reached adolescence, and Morley Roberts, who wrote a book about Hudson's later life, did not meet him until 1880. By the time Hudson went to England in 1869, his parents were dead and the family had dispersed. Apparently, he had spent a good deal of the previous few years wandering aimlessly in South America; it is tempting to associate certain incidents described in *The Purple Land* with experiences he may have had during these years, but to do so would be mere conjecture.

Hudson's early days in England are also undocumented. He apparently had various odd jobs, including researching genealogies for Americans, but did not settle down or make much of a living. In 1876, he met and married Emily Wingrave, who was some twenty years older than he. While he wrote, she gave singing lessons, but neither activity brought in much money, and the two had to run a boardinghouse in Bayswater for some years. Even after the publication of *The Purple Land* (which was received with indifference), they were close to desperation, but Emily inherited a large house in Bayswater that they turned into flats, retaining two rooms for themselves and living off the rents from the remainder. Though Hudson frequently went on long excursions into the country, and in later life took to wintering in Penzance, the couple stayed in Bayswater until their deaths, Emily's in 1921 and Hudson's in 1922. Hudson was naturalized in 1900, by which time he was just beginning to attract favorable attention through his essays. Sir Edward Grey procured for him a state pension in 1901, a few years before the commercial success of *Green Mansions* freed him from financial worry.

Hudson's acquaintances seem to have formed very different impressions of him. Robert Hamilton quotes summaries of his character offered by half a dozen different people that are anything but unanimous—some are flatly contradictory. If an overall impression can be gained, it is that he was usually friendly and courteous but rather reserved. More than one acquaintance suspected that he was secretly lonely and unhappy, and women seem to have formed a distinctly poorer opinion of him than men, suggesting that he was uneasy in their company. The autobiography that ceases so early in his life may provide the best insight into his character, as much by what it omits as by what it says. Hudson seems to have emerged from childhood reluctantly and with great regret; he apparently never tried particularly hard to adapt himself to the adult world, where he always felt himself to be an outsider. Although he did not marry until he was in his mid-thirties, the woman he selected as a wife probably served as a mother-substitute whose age precluded any possibility of parenthood. These details are highly significant in the consideration of his novels, especially *A Crystal Age*.

Analysis

The majority of W. H. Hudson's fictions are categorized as "South American romances"—at one time a collection was issued under that title. Included under this label are the novels *The Purple Land* and *Green Mansions* and various shorter pieces from Hudson's short-story collection *El Ombú*; the most important of these shorter pieces are the novellas "El Ombú" and "Marta Riquelme." All of these works make constructive use of the author's autobiographical background.

The Purple Land

The Purple Land is a documentary novel containing no plot, an imaginary travelogue set in the Banda Oriental. Its protagonist, Richard Lamb, has been forced to flee to Montevideo after eloping with the daughter of a powerful Argentinean family. The story concerns Lamb's wanderings in connection with an abortive attempt to find a job managing an inland plantation. At one point, he becomes entangled in the affairs of the rebel general Santa Coloma and fights with him in an ill-fated revolution. He also attracts the attention of several women, including two very beautiful girls who mistake him for a single man and are bitterly disappointed when he informs them belatedly of his unavailability. One of these women, however, he rescues from an awkward predicament and smuggles her back to Argentina in spite of the risk to himself (the reader has already been told in the first chapter that these wanderings preceded a long spell in jail, an event that was instigated by his vengeful father-in-law and broke his wife's heart).

The attractive features of this novel are the local color and the attention to anthropological detail. It offers a convincing picture of the life of the country, and one can easily believe that some of the episodes are based on experience, and that Hudson actually heard some of the tall stories that are told to Lamb by Santa Coloma's rebel gauchos. The amorous encounters, however, fail to convince, and there is a certain perversity in hearing the protagonist's overheated expressions of devotion to a wife from whom he is willingly separated, and whom he is destined to lose. In contrast to the bleak note on which the novel begins and ends, the protestations of love are melodramatic.

"El Ombú" *and* "Marta Riquelme"

There is no trace of this fault in the two novellas set in the same region. "El Ombú" is a chronicle of unremitting cruelty and misfortune, detailing the sufferings of a family through the memories of an old man who loves to sit and reminisce in the shadow of an ombú tree. "Marta Riquelme," which Hudson thought the best of his stories, is even more ruthless, and it makes use of a legend connected with a species of bird called the Kakué fowl, into which men and women who experience unendurable suffering were said to change. The story is narrated by a Jesuit priest, who describes the tragic career of Marta, captured by Indians, robbed of her child, and so mutilated that when she returns to her own people they will not accept her and drive her out to find her fate.

These stories were called "romances" because their subject matter was exotic to an English audience; in fact, however, they are examples of determined narrative realism (unless one accepts the Jesuit priest's dubious allegation that Marta Riquelme really does turn into a Kakué fowl). They present a view of life in South America that is very different from that of *The Purple Land*, a book that glosses over the plight of the common people and the cruelties visited upon them. They bear witness to the fact that Hudson, once emerged from the cocoon of his ideal childhood and initiated into the ways of the world, was deeply affected by what he discovered. He carried away from South America much fonder memories of the birds than of the people, the grotesqueness of whose lives appalled him even though he tried with all his might to sympathize with them.

A Crystal Age

In between *The Purple Land* and "El Ombú," Hudson wrote two other novels. One, the pseudonymous *Fan*, appears to have been an attempt to write a conventional three-decker novel of domestic life. The book has little to recommend it, being an entirely artificial product with little of Hudson in it, appearing when the day of the three-decker was already past. The other novel, *A Crystal Age*, also appeared without Hudson's name on it, being issued anonymously, but Hudson acknowledged authorship when it was reprinted in the wake of the success of *Green Mansions*.

A Crystal Age is a difficult work to classify: It is a vision of an earthly paradise, but it is Arcadian rather than utopian in character and is by no means polemical. It carries no political message and might best be regarded as a fatalist parable lamenting the imperfections of nineteenth century humankind.

The narrator of the story tells the reader nothing about himself except that he is an Englishman named Smith. He is precipitated into a distant future where human beings live in perfect ecological harmony with their environment. Each community is a single family, based in a House that is organized around its Mother. The Mother of the House that takes Smith in is secluded because of illness, and it is some time before Smith realizes that she is an actual person rather than an imaginary goddess. When he repairs the most damaging of his many breaches of etiquette by making himself known to her, she treats him harshly but later forgives him and awards him a special place in her affections.

Smith never fully understands this peculiar world. He is passionately in love with a daughter of the House, Yoletta, whom he believes to be about seventeen years of age. Even when she tells him how old she really is, he cannot see the truth: that these people are so long-lived, and live so free from danger, that their reproductive rate has to be very slow. The Mother is revered because she really is *the* mother of the household: the only reproductive individual. When Smith tries desperately to woo Yoletta, she genuinely cannot understand him. Nor can Smith see, though the reader can, that the Mother holds him in special esteem because she plans to be followed in her role by Yoletta and is grooming him for the role of the Father. He remains lost in an anguish of uncertainty until he finds a bottle whose label promises a cure for misery. He immediately believes that it is the means by which his hosts suppress their sexual feelings, and he drinks to drown his own passion. He discovers too late that it is actually the means by which those in mortal agony achieve a merciful release.

In a sense, the world of *A Crystal Age* is the opposite of the world described in "El Ombú": It is a heaven constructed by reacting against the hellish aspects of the life of the South American peasantry. It is a world where humans and nature peacefully coexist and where human society enjoys the harmonious organization of the beehive without the loss of individual identity that has made the beehive a horrific stereotype in stories of hypothetical societies. Nevertheless, *A Crystal Age* is just as misanthropic as "El Ombú," in that Smith—the book's Everyman figure—is mercilessly pilloried for being too brutal and stupid to adapt himself to the perfect world.

A Little Boy Lost

In view of Hudson's personal history, it is difficult to doubt that the matricentric nature of the imaginary society, and Smith's own peculiar relationship with the Mother, are of some psychological significance. The same seems to be true of *A Little Boy Lost*, whose protagonist, Martin, runs away from home to follow a mirage. When he becomes homesick, it is not to his real parents that he returns (there had been a quaintly unconvincing suggestion earlier that his real father was a bird—a martin) but to a surrogate mother called the Lady of the Hills. She smothers him with affection, but he eventually leaves her, too, attracted to the distant seashore beyond the reach of her powers. When he falls into danger there, he longs for this surrogate mother rather than the real one, but there is no going back of any kind; in the end, he is picked up by a ship that seems to be sailing to the England that his parents left before he was born. Some of Martin's other adventures—especially his encounter with savage Indians—recall elements in Hudson's other works, and it is a rather baleful world from which the Lady of the Hills temporarily rescues him. If all of this could be analyzed in the light of a more detailed knowledge of Hudson's thoughts and feelings, it might well turn out to reveal some interesting symbolic patterns.

Green Mansions

Hudson's idea of perfection, which is displayed as a whole world in *A Crystal Age*, is embodied in *Green Mansions* in a single person. In a sense, *Green Mansions* is *A Crystal Age* in reverse: It features a visitor from the imaginary world of ecological harmony cast adrift in the familiar world. Rima, the delicate refugee, can no more survive here than Smith could in the Mother's House: She is brutally murdered by savages who believe that she is an evil spirit ruining their hunting.

The story is told by a placid and gentle old man named Mr. Abel, recalling his youth when he was forced to flee from his native Venezuela because of his complicity in an abortive coup. After wandering for some time, the young Abel rests for a while in an Indian village somewhere in the remoter regions of the Orinoco River basin. In a forested area nearby, which the Indians are reluctant to enter, he hears a voice that seems to be part birdsong and part human, and he eventually discovers Rima, a tiny and somewhat ethereal girl who can communicate with birds and animals. She lives there with her adopted grandfather, Nuflo, and takes Abel in after he is bitten by a snake.

Rima is desperate to return to her half-forgotten place of origin, but Nuflo will not take her. Abel mentions a mountain chain called Riolama, and she recognizes the name, insisting that they go there. The journey is fruitless—the remote valley where Rima's people lived has been destroyed, and Abel realizes that her mother must have been the last survivor of the catastrophe. Rima decides to settle in her forest haven with Abel, but even this scheme is thwarted by the Indians, who have reclaimed the wood during Rima's absence and who destroy her by trapping her in the branches of a solitary tree and burning it. Abel, sick and hallucinating, sets off on a phantasmagoric trip through the rain forest, back to civilization. On the way, imagined encounters with Rima's ghost instill in him the capacity to rebuild his life; he becomes convinced that he can be reunited with her after death if he accepts his situation and learns patience.

Green Mansions is a magnificently lush tragedy, and it is not difficult to understand why it captured the public imagination—at least in America—firmly enough to become established as a kind of classic. The passionate yearning that drives Abel is something with which almost everyone can identify: the yearning for an imaginary golden age of love and tranquillity that somehow seems to be located equally in the personal and prehistoric past. What Abel is chasing is a fantasy that cannot be brought down to earth, and he is bound to fail, but in his failing there is a kind of disappointment that is common to all people.

Hudson's version of this particular myth is remarkable in two ways. First of all, he was able to exploit, as he had in *The Purple Land*, "El Ombú," and "Marta Riquelme," a realism that seemed to his readers to be romanticism. This encompasses both his descriptions of the various landscapes of the story (especially the forests of Abel's last delirious journey) and his description of the way of life of the savage Indians. These are no Rousseau-esque examples of a wild nobility, but of brutish individuals who are no better integrated into their environment than is Abel. (Indeed, Abel is the wiser, for he at least can appreciate, thanks to his intellect and imagination, the *possibility* of living in harmony with nature.) Second, the novel is remarkable for its characterization of the bird-girl Rima. Although not particularly convincing as a character, she is so close to the author's personal notion of perfection that his regard for her infects the novel and gives her the same status in the reader's eyes as she has in Abel's.

Again, one is tempted to look below the surface of *Green Mansions* for some psychological significance that will cast light on Hudson's enigmatic personality. It is easy enough to connect Rima with the Lady of the Hills and to observe that, in common with all the other desirable women in Hudson's fiction, she has an essential inaccessibility. Monica, Mercedes, and Demetria in *The Purple Land* are all unavailable to the hero because he is married; Yoletta in *A Crystal Age* is forbidden to Smith by social convention and cannot respond to his passion because she has no sexuality of her own; Rima is a member of a different race, more nature-spirit than human, and though there seems no obvious reason why, it is always clear that she and Abel can never be united. One "explanation" for the dearth of successful amatory ventures in Hudson's work might be found in the suggestion that all these love objects really ought to be interpreted as mother figures rather than suitable brides, but the truth is probably more complicated. For Hudson's male characters, all feelings of sexual attraction are—or ought to be—guilt-ridden, forbidden by taboos of which they are sometimes only half aware. The possibility that Hudson suffered from a mother fixation may help to account for this but is hardly likely to be the whole story—especially when one remembers that the Lady of the Hills, in *A Little Boy Lost*, is specifically declared to be a substitute mother who displaces the real one in the child-hero's affections.

Why Hudson wrote no more significant fiction after 1905 is not altogether clear, especially as he had only just made a name for himself. He was well into his sixties, but his creative powers showed no sign of diminution. His three best books—*A Shepherd's Life*, *Far Away and Long Ago*, and *A Hind in Richmond Park*—were still to be written, the last when he was in his eighties. Perhaps, with the death of Rima, he laid aside his dream of a supernaturally harmonized creation—the dream that provided the imaginative fuel for *A Crystal Age* and *Green Mansions*. In *A Little Boy Lost*, that same dream is displayed as a childish illusion—even on the story's own terms it is difficult to decide exactly how much takes place inside Martin's head.

The new introduction that Hudson wrote for *A Crystal Age* when it was reissued in 1906 supports this view. This brief essay is full of disillusionment, informing the reader that romances of the future are always interesting even though none of them is really any good. Hudson disparages *A Crystal Age* for being a product of its own era, and he regrets that it cannot possibly induce belief because "the ending of passion and strife is the beginning of decay." This remark echoes Hudson's ambivalent feelings about Darwinism—he was resistant to the ideas of the struggle for existence and the survival of the fittest. For Hudson it was the human world, not the world of nature, that was red in tooth and claw. Despite his reluctance, however, he could not help but accept much of the Darwinian argument and was forced thereby to acknowledge the hopelessness of his own ideals. This special disenchantment is something that lurks below the surface of almost all his work; whether or not it is the cognitive reflection of a much more personal disenchantment must remain an unanswered question.

Brian Stableford

Other major works

SHORT FICTION: *"Dead Man's Plack" and "An Old Thorn,"* 1920.

NONFICTION: *Argentine Ornithology*, 1888-1889 (with Philip Lutley Sclater); *The Naturalist in La Plata*, 1892; *Birds in a Village*, 1893; *Idle Days in Patagonia*, 1893; *British Birds*, 1895; *Nature in Downland*, 1900; *Birds and Man*, 1901; *Hampshire Days*, 1903; *The Land's End*, 1908; *Afoot in England*, 1909; *A Shepherd's Life*, 1910; *Adventures Among Birds*, 1913; *Far Away and Long Ago*, 1918; *The Book of a Naturalist*, 1919; *Birds of La Plata*, 1920; *A Traveller in Little Things*, 1921; *A Hind in Richmond Park*, 1922; *One Hundred Fifty-three Letters from W. H. Hudson*, 1923 (with Edward Garnett, editor); *Men, Books, and Birds*, 1925; *Birds of a Feather: Unpublished Letters of W. H. Hudson*, 1981 (Dennis Shrubsall, editor).

Bibliography

Arocena, Felipe. *William Henry Hudson: Life, Literature, and Science*. Translated by Richard Manning. Jefferson, N.C.: McFarland, 2003. Previously published in Spanish, this book examines *The Purple Land* and some of Hudson's other writings. Arocena argues that Hudson's works were primarily about traveling across frontiers, including the frontiers of different countries and cultures.

Frederick, John T. *William Henry Hudson*. New York: Twayne, 1972. A standard biography, with literary analysis, from Twayne's English Authors series. Includes a bibliography and an index.

Haymaker, Richard E. *From Pampas to Hedgerows and Downs: A Study of W. H. Hudson*. New York: Bookman, 1954. Although dated, this work is a thorough full-length study of Hudson. A must-read for serious scholars of this writer. Includes a bibliography.

Miller, David. *W. H. Hudson and the Elusive Paradise*. New York: St. Martin's Press, 1990. Contains chapters on all of Hudson's major prose fiction, exploring such themes as the supernatural, the imagination, symbolic meaning, immortality, and ideology. Includes detailed notes and a bibliography.

Parrinder, Patrick. "Entering Dystopia, Entering Erewhon." *Critical Survey* 17, no. 1 (2005): 6-21. Parrinder describes the characteristics of dystopian romances written in the late Victorian era, focusing on the representations of dystopia in Hudson's *A Crystal Age* and Samuel Butler's *Erewon*.

Roberts, Morley. *W. H. Hudson: A Portrait*. New York: E. P. Dutton, 1924. A personal, intimate account of Hudson from the perspective of Roberts's long-term relationship with this writer and naturalist. Dated but remains useful.

Ronner, Amy D. *W. H. Hudson: The Man, the Novelist, the Naturalist*. New York: AMS Press, 1986. A much-needed addition to critical studies on Hudson, examining Hudson's work in relationship to his contemporaries, his immigration to England, and his development as a naturalist and writer. Concludes with an interesting account of Charles Darwin's influence on Hudson and consequently on his writing.

Shrubsall, Dennis. *W. H. Hudson: Writer and Naturalist*. Tisbury, England: Compton Press, 1978. Provides much useful background on Hudson's early years in Argentina and traces his development as a naturalist and his integrity as a writer on nature.

Tomalin, Ruth. *W. H. Hudson: A Biography*. London: Faber & Faber, 1982. A lively biography that has been thoroughly and painstakingly researched. Highly recommended for any serious study of Hudson. Contains excerpts of the letter that Hudson wrote in an attack on Charles Darwin and of Darwin's response.

VICTOR HUGO

Born: Besançon, France; February 26, 1802
Died: Paris, France; May 22, 1885
Also known as: Victor-Marie Hugo

Principal long fiction

Han d'Islande, 1823 (*Hans of Iceland*, 1845)
Bug-Jargal, 1826 (*The Noble Rival*, 1845)
Le Dernier Jour d'un condamné, 1829 (*The Last Day of a Condemned*, 1840)
Notre-Dame de Paris, 1831 (*The Hunchback of Notre Dame*, 1833)
Claude Gueux, 1834
Les Misérables, 1862 (English translation, 1862)
Les Travailleurs de la mer, 1866 (*The Toilers of the Sea*, 1866)
L'Homme qui rit, 1869 (*The Man Who Laughs*, 1869)
Quatre-vingt-treize, 1874 (*Ninety-Three*, 1874)

Other literary forms

Victor Hugo (YEW-goh) dominates nineteenth century literature in France both by the length of his writing career and by the diversity of his work. Indeed, it is difficult to think of a literary form Hugo did not employ. Lyric, satiric, and epic poetry; drama in verse and prose; political polemic and social criticism—all are found in his oeuvre. His early plays and poetry made him a leader of the Romantic movement. His political writing included the publication of a newspaper, *L'Événement*, in 1851, which contributed to his exile from the Second Empire. During his exile, he wrote vehement criticism of Napoleon III as well as visionary works of poetry. His poetic genius ranged from light verse to profound epics; his prose works include accounts of his travels and literary criticism as well as fiction.

Achievements

The complete works of Victor Hugo constitute more nearly a legend than an achievement. In poetry, Hugo had become a national institution by the end of his life. He was a member of the Académie Française, an officer of the Légion d'Honneur, and a Peer of France under the monarchy of Louis-Philippe. When he died, he was accorded the singular honor of lying in state beneath Paris's Arc de Triomphe before his burial in the Panthéon.

During his lifetime, Hugo's novels accounted for much of his popularity with the public. Both sentimental and dramatic, they were excellent vehicles for spreading his humanitarian ideas among large numbers of people. His two most famous novels are *The Hunchback of Notre Dame* and *Les Misérables*. The former is an example of dramatic historical romance, inspired in France by the novels of Sir Walter Scott. It is said to have created interest in and ensured the architectural preservation of the Notre Dame cathedral in Paris. It is also a study in Romanticism, with its evocation of the dark force of fate and the intricate intertwining of the grotesque and the sublime.

Les Misérables testifies to Hugo's optimistic faith in humanitarian principles and social progress. The intricate and elaborate plot confronts both social injustice and indifference. It is typical of many nineteenth century attitudes in its emphasis on education, charity, and love as powerful forces in saving the unfortunate creatures of the lower classes from becoming hardened criminals. *Les Misérables* is a novel on an epic scale both in its historical tableaux and as the story of a human soul. Thus, even though Hugo's achievements in the novel are of a lesser scale than his poetry and drama, they are enduring and worthy monuments to the author and to his century.

Biography

Victor-Marie Hugo was born in Besançon, France, in 1802, the third son of Joseph-Léopold-Sigisbert Hugo and Sophie-Françoise Trébuchet. His father had been born in Nancy and his mother in Nantes. They met in the Vendée, where Léopold Hugo was serving in the Napoleonic army. His military career kept the family on the move, and it was during Major Hugo's tour of duty with the Army of the Rhine that Victor-Marie was born in Besançon.

Léopold and Sophie did not have a happy marriage, and after the birth of their third son, they were frequently separated. By 1808, Léopold had been promoted to general and was made a count in Napoleon I's empire. During one reunion of Hugo's parents, Victor and his brothers joined General Hugo in Spain, a land that fascinated Victor and left its mark on his poetic imagination.

In spite of their father's desire that they should study for entrance to the École Polytechnique, Victor and his next older brother, Eugène, spent their free time writing poetry, hoping to emulate their master, François-René de Chateaubriand. In 1817, Victor earned the first official recognition of his talent by winning an honorable mention in a poetry competition sponsored by the Académie Française. Because he was only fifteen, the secretary of the Académie asked to meet him, and the press displayed an interest in the young poet.

Eugène and Victor received permission from their father to study law in 1818 and left their boarding school to live with their mother in Paris. Sophie encouraged them in their ambition to become writers and never insisted that they attend lectures or study for examinations. Victor continued to receive recognition for his poems, and the brothers founded a review, *Le Conservateur littéraire*, in 1819. Unfortunately, the two brothers also shared a passion for the same young woman, Adèle Foucher. In love as well as in poetry, Eugène took second place to his younger brother. Adèle and Victor were betrothed after the death of Madame Hugo, who had opposed the marriage. The wedding took place in 1822. At the wedding feast, Eugène went insane; he spent nearly all the rest of his life in institutions.

Hugo's early publications were favorably received by the avant-garde of Romanticism, and by 1824, Hugo was a dominant personality in Charles Nodier's Cénacle, a group of Romantic poets united in their struggle against the rules of French classicism. The year 1824 also marked the birth of Léopoldine, the Hugos' second child and the first to survive infancy. She was always to have a special place in her father's heart. In 1827, the Hugos had another child, Charles.

The Hugos were acquainted with many of those writers and artists who are now considered major figures in the Romantic movement, among them Alexandre Dumas, *père*, Alfred de Vigny, and Eugène Delacroix. The sculptor David d'Angers recorded Hugo's youthful appearance on a medallion. (Decades later, sculptor Auguste Rodin would also preserve his impression of the aged poet.) The influential critic Charles-Augustin Sainte-Beuve also became a frequent visitor to the Hugos' apartment.

Momentum was building for the Romantic movement, and in December, 1827, Hugo published a play, *Cromwell* (English translation, 1896), the preface to which became the manifesto of the young Romantics. Two years later, his verse drama *Hernani* (pr., pb. 1830; English translation, 1830) would provide the battleground between Romanticism and classicism. In the meantime, General Hugo had died in 1828, and a son, François-Victor, had been born to Victor and Adèle.

The famous "battle of *Hernani*" at the work's premiere on January 10, 1830, was an outcry against outmoded conventions in every form of art. Artists sympathetic to Romanticism had been recruited from the Latin Quarter in support of Hugo's play, which breaks the rules of versification as well as the three unities of classical drama (time, place, and action). They engaged in a battle for modern artistic freedom against the "authorities" of the past. *Hernani* therefore had political significance as well: The restoration of the Bourbons was in its final months.

Stormy performances continued at the Théâtre-Français for several months, and, by the end, the tyranny of classicism had been demolished. In addition to artistic freedom for all, *Hernani* brought financial well-being to the Hugos. It also brought Sainte-Beuve increasingly into their family circle, where he kept Adèle company while Hugo was distracted by the *Hernani* affair.

In July of 1830, Victor and Adèle's last child, Adèle, came into the world to the sound of the shots of the July Revolution, which deposed Charles X, the last Bourbon "king of France." The new monarch was Louis-Philippe of the Orléans branch of the royal family, who called himself "king of the French." There was now a deep attachment between Madame Hugo and Sainte-Beuve. Although Adèle and Victor were never to separate, their marriage had become a platonic companionship.

In 1832, the Hugos moved to the Place Royale (now called the Place des Vosges), to the home that would later become the Victor Hugo museum in Paris. Scarcely a year passed without a publication by Hugo. By that time, he was able to command enormous sums for his work in comparison with other authors of his day. He was already becoming a legend, with disciples rather than friends. His ambition had always been fierce, and he was beginning to portray himself as a bard, a seer with powers to guide all France. Only in his family life was he suffering from less than complete success.

At the time, *Lucrèce Borgia* (pr., pb. 1833; *Lucretia Borgia*, 1842) was in rehearsal, and among the cast was a lovely young actor, Juliette Drouet. Soon after opening night, she and Hugo became lovers, and they remained so for many years. Juliette had not been a brilliant actor, but she abandoned what might have been a moderately successful career to live the rest of her life in seclusion and devotion to Hugo. In *Les Chants du crépuscule* (1835; *Songs of Twilight*, 1836), Hugo included thirteen poems to Juliette and three to Adèle, expressing the deep affection he still felt for his wife.

Critics were beginning to snipe at Hugo for what seemed to be shallow emotions and facile expressions. (Sainte-Beuve deplored Hugo's lack of taste, but Sainte-Beuve was hardly a disinterested critic.) The fashion for Hugo seemed to be somewhat on the wane, although adverse criticism did not inhibit the flow of his writing. The publication of *Les Rayons et les ombres* (1840) marked the end of one phase of Hugo's poetry. The splendor of the language and the music in his verse as well as the visual imagery were richer than ever, but Hugo was still criticized for lacking genuine emotion. He had by this time decided, however, to devote himself to his political ambitions.

He was determined to become a Peer of France, having been made an officer of the Légion d'Honneur several years before. In order to obtain a peerage, a man of letters had to be a member of the Académie Française. After presenting himself for the fifth time, he was elected to the Académie in 1841, and in the spring of 1845 he was named a Peer of France, a status that protected him from arrest the following summer, when police found him in flagrante delicto with the wife of Auguste Biard. Léonie Biard was sent to the Saint-Lazare prison, but Hugo's cordial relations with King Louis-Philippe helped calm the scandal, and Léonie retired to a convent for a short while before resuming her affair with Hugo.

An event of much deeper emotional impact had occurred in 1843, when Hugo's eldest daughter, Léopoldine, had married Charles Vacquerie. Hugo had found it difficult to be separated from his child, who went to live in Le Havre. That summer, in July, he paid a brief visit to the young couple before leaving on a journey with Juliette. In early September, while traveling, Hugo read in a newspaper that Léopoldine and Charles had been drowned in a boating accident several days before. Grief-stricken, Hugo was also beset by guilt at having left his family for a trip with his mistress. He published nothing more for nine years.

Victor Hugo. (Library of Congress)

Eventually, the political events of 1848 eclipsed Hugo's complex relationship with his wife and two mistresses. During the Revolution of 1848, Louis-Philippe was forced to abdicate. The monarchy was rejected outright by the provisional government under the leadership of the Romantic poet Alphonse de Lamartine. The peerage was also abolished, and although Hugo sought political office, he was generally considered to be too dramatic and rhetorical to be of practical use in government. More than a few of his contemporary politicians viewed him as a self-interested opportunist. He seems to have longed for the glory of being a statesman without the necessary political sense.

On June 24, 1848, militant insurgents had occupied the Hugo apartment on the Place Royal. The family had fled, and Adèle had refused to live there again. One of the first visitors to their new apartment was Louis-Napoleon Bonaparte, nephew of Napoleon I. He was seeking Hugo's support of his candidacy for president of the new republic. Thereafter, Louis-Napoleon was endorsed in Hugo's newspaper, *L'Événement*, which he had founded that summer and which was edited and published by his sons.

Louis-Napoleon became president in December of 1848, but he did not long remain on good terms with Hugo. Hugo and *L'Événement* increasingly took leftist political positions as the new government was moving toward the Right. Freedom of the press was increasingly limited, and, in 1851, both of Hugo's sons were imprisoned for violating restrictions on the press and for showing disrespect to the government.

It was in this year that Juliette and Léonie attempted to force Hugo to choose between them. In the end, politics resolved the conflict. On December 2, 1851, Louis-Napoleon dissolved the National Assembly and declared himself prince-president for ten years. When Hugo learned of the coup d'état, he attempted to organize some resistance. There was shooting in the streets of Paris. Juliette is given credit for saving him from violence. She hid him successfully while a false passport was prepared, and on December 11, he took the train to Brussels in disguise and under a false name. Juliette followed him into exile.

From exile, the pen was Hugo's only political weapon, and he wrote *Napoléon le petit* (1852; *Napoleon the Little*, 1852) and *Histoire d'un crime* (1877; *The History of a Crime*, 1877-1878). Having been authorized to stay in Belgium for only three months, Hugo made plans to move to Jersey, one of the Channel Islands. His family joined him, and Juliette took rooms nearby. He began work on *Les Châtiments* (1853), poems inspired by anger and pride. France remained his preoccupation while he was in exile. Indeed, it has been said that exile renewed Hugo's career. Certainly, his fame suffered neither from his banishment nor from the tone of righteous indignation with which he could thus proclaim his contempt for the empire of Napoleon III.

There was a group of militant exiles on the island, and when, in 1855, they attacked Queen Victoria in their newspaper for visiting Napoleon III, Jersey officials informed them that they would have to leave. The Hugos moved to Guernsey, where they eventually purchased Hauteville House. At about the same time, in the spring of 1856, *Les Contemplations* was published, marking Hugo's reappearance as a lyric poet. Juliette moved to a nearby house that she called Hauteville-Féerie, where the lawn was inscribed with flowers forming a bright "V H." Although Hugo's prestige benefited immensely from his exile, his family suffered from their isolation, especially his daughter Adèle, who was in her early twenties. Eventually, she followed an army officer, Albert Pinson, to Canada, convinced that they would marry. After nine years of erratic, senseless wandering, she was brought home to end her life in a mental institution.

For her father, exile was a time to write. The first two volumes of *La Légende des siècles* (1859-1883; *The Legend of the Centuries*, 1894) was followed by *The Toilers of the Sea* and *The Man Who Laughs*, among other works. In 1859, Napoleon III offered amnesty of Republican exiles, but Hugo refused to accept it, preferring the grandeur of defiance and martyrdom on his rocky island.

After Adèle's flight, the island became intolerable for Madame Hugo. In 1865, she left for Brussels with the younger son, François-Victor, and spent most of her time there during the remainder of Hugo's exile. In his isolation, Hugo continued his work.

On the occasion of the Paris International Exposition in 1867, the imperial censors permitted a revival of *Hernani* at the Théâtre-Français. Adèle traveled to Paris to witness the great success of the play and the adulation of her husband. Another visitor to the Paris Exposition would be instrumental in ending Hugo's self-imposed banishment. Future German Chancellor Otto von Bismarck came to Paris ostensibly on a state visit from Prussia but secretly taking the measure of French armaments. Adèle died in Brussels the following year. Her sons accompanied her body to its grave in France; Hugo stopped at the French border and soon returned to Guernsey with Juliette.

One of Hugo's dreams had always been a United States of Europe, and in Lausanne in 1869, he presided over the congress of the International League for Peace and Freedom. Early in 1870, he was honored by the Second Empire with a revival of *Lucretia Borgia* and a recitation of his poetry before the emperor by Sarah Bernhardt. On July 14 of that year, the poet planted an acorn at Hauteville House. The future tree was dedicated to "the United States of Europe." By the following day, France and Prussia were at war.

The Franco-Prussian War brought an end to the Second Empire and to Hugo's nineteen years of exile. He returned in time to participate in the siege of Paris and to witness the cataclysmic events of the Commune. His own politics, however, although idealistically liberal and Republican, did not mesh with any political group in a practical way. He refused several minor offices that were offered to him by the new government and resigned after only a month as an elected deputy for Paris to the new National Assembly.

The following years were marked by family sorrows. Soon following Hugo's resignation from active politics, his elder son, Charles, died of an apoplectic stroke. Hugo was to remain devoted to his son's widow, Alice, and to his grandchildren, Jeanne and Georges. In 1872, Adèle was brought home from Barbados, insane. The following year, his younger son, François-Victor, died of tuberculosis. Only the faithful Juliette remained as a companion to Hugo in his old age.

He continued to write unceasingly in Paris, but in 1878 he suffered a stroke. This virtually brought his writing to an end, although works he had written earlier continued to be published. On his birthday in 1881, the Republic organized elaborate festivities in his honor, including a procession of admirers who passed beneath his window for hours. In May, the main part of the avenue d'Eylau was rechristened the avenue Victor-Hugo.

Juliette died in May of 1883. On his birthday in 1885, Hugo received tributes from all quarters as a venerated symbol of the French spirit. He became seriously ill in May, suffering from a lesion of the heart and congestion of the lungs. He died on May 22, 1885. Hugo's funeral was a national ceremony, the coffin lying in state beneath the Arc de Triomphe. He was the only Frenchman to be so honored before the Unknown Soldier after World War I. While Napoleon III lay buried in exile, the remains of Victor Hugo were ceremoniously interred in the Panthéon, France's shrine to her great men of letters.

Analysis

The earliest published full-length fiction by Victor Hugo was *Hans of Iceland*, begun when he was eighteen years old, although not published until three years later. In part a tribute to Adèle Foucher, who was to become his wife, it is a convoluted gothic romance in which it is not clear where the author is being serious and where he is deliberately creating a parody of the popular gothic genre. It is worthwhile to begin with this youthful work, however, because it contains many themes and images that were to remain important in Hugo's work throughout his life.

Hans of Iceland

The characters in *Hans of Iceland* are archetypes rather than psychologically realistic figures. In a sense, it is unfair to criticize Hugo for a lack of complexity in his characterizations, because he is a creator of myths and legends—his genius does not lie in the realm of the realistic novel. This is the reason his talent as a novelist is eclipsed by the other great novelists of his century, Stendhal, Honoré de Balzac, Gustave Flaubert, and Émile Zola. Hugo's last novels were written after Flaubert's *Madame Bovary* (1857; English translation, 1886) and after Zola's first naturalistic novels, yet Hugo's late books remain closer in tone to *Hans of Iceland* than to any contemporary novel.

It is thus more useful to consider *Hans of Iceland* as a romance, following the patterns of myths and legends, rather than as a novel with claims to psychological and historical realism. Although tenuously based on historical fact, set in seventeenth century Norway, the plot of

Hans of Iceland closely resembles that of the traditional quest. The hero, Ordener Guldenlew (Golden Lion), disguises his noble birth and sets out to rescue his beloved, the pure maiden Ethel, from the evil forces that imprison her with her father, Jean Schumaker, Count Griffenfeld. Ordener's adventures take him through dark and fearsome settings where he must overcome the monster Hans of Iceland, a mysterious being who, although a man, possesses demoniac powers and beastly desires.

As in traditional romance, the characters in *Hans of Iceland* are all good or evil, like black and white pieces in a chess game. Ethel's father is the good former grand chancellor who has been imprisoned for some years after having been unjustly accused of treason. His counterpart is the wicked Count d'Ahlefeld, who, with the treacherous countess, is responsible for Schumaker's downfall. Their son Frédéric is Ordener's rival for Ethel's love. The most treacherous villain is the count's adviser, Musdoemon, who turns out to be Frédéric's real father. Opposed to everyone, good or evil, is the man-demon Hans of Iceland, who haunts the land by dark of night, leaving the marks of his clawlike nails on his victims.

Ordener's quest begins in the morgue, where he seeks a box that had been in the possession of a military officer killed by Hans. The box contains documents proving Schumaker's innocence. Believing it to be in Hans's possession, Ordener sets off through storms and danger to recover the box.

As the adventure progresses, Hugo begins to reveal his personal preoccupations and thus to depart from the traditional romance. Hans's ambiguous nature, grotesque as he is, has some unsettling sympathetic qualities. One begins to feel, as the story progresses and as the social villains become more devious and nefarious, that Hans, the social outcast, is morally superior in spite of his diabolically glowing eyes and his tendency to crunch human bones. Hugo appears to suggest the Romantic noble savage beneath a diabolic exterior. Because Ordener is a strangely passive hero, who fails to slay Hans or even to find the box, the reader's interest is transferred to Hans. In this monster with redeeming human qualities, it is not difficult to see the prefiguration of later grotesques such as Quasimodo in *The Hunchback of Notre Dame*.

The social commentary that is constant in Hugo's narratives has its beginning here in the figure of Musdoemon, the true evil figure of the work. This adviser to the aristocracy, whose name reveals that he has the soul of a rat, betrays everyone until he is at last himself betrayed and hanged. The executioner turns out to be his brother, delighted to have revenge for Musdoemon's treachery toward him years before.

At one point, Musdoemon tricks a group of miners (the good common people) into rebelling against the king in Schumaker's name. Ordener finds himself in the midst of the angry mob as they battle the king's troops. Hans attacks both sides, increasing the confusion and slaughter. Later, at the trial of the rebels on charges of treason, Ordener takes full responsibility, thus diverting blame from Schumaker. Given the choice of execution or marriage to the daughter of the wicked d'Ahlefeld, he chooses death. He and Ethel are married in his cell and are saved by the chance discovery of the documents. Hans gives himself up and dies by his own hand.

By comparing *Hans of Iceland* with another early novel, *The Noble Rival*, the reader can trace the preoccupations that led to *The Hunchback of Notre Dame* and *Les Misérables*. *The Noble Rival* is the story of a slave revolt in Santo Domingo, Dominican Republic. The hero of the title is a slave as well as the spiritually noble leader of his people. The Romantic hero is Léopold, a Frenchman visiting his uncle's plantation. Like Ordener, Léopold is pure but essentially passive. The heroic energy belongs to the outcast from society, Bug-Jargal. In both novels, Hugo's sympathy for the "people" is apparent. The miners and the slaves point directly to the commoners of Paris in *The Hunchback of Notre Dame*.

The Hunchback of Notre Dame

At the center of *The Hunchback of Notre Dame* is the theme of fatality, a word that the author imagines to have been inscribed on the wall of one of the cathedral towers as the Greek *anankè*. The cathedral is the focus of the novel, as it was the heart of medieval Paris. It is a spiritual center with an ambiguous demoniac-grotesque spirit within. Claude Frollo, the priest, is consumed by lust for a Gypsy girl, Esmeralda. Quasimodo, the bell ringer, a hunchback frighteningly deformed, is elevated by his pure love for Esmeralda, whom he attempts to save from the pernicious Frollo. In an image central to the novel and to Hugo's entire work, Frollo watches a spider and a fly caught in its web. The web, however, stretches across a pane of glass so that even if the fly should manage to escape, it will only hurl itself against the invisible barrier in its flight toward the sun. The priest will be the spider to Esmeralda but also the fly, caught in the trap of his own consuming desire. All the characters risk entrapment in the web prepared for them by fate. Even if they somehow break free of the web, the glass will block escape until death releases them from earthly concerns.

Esmeralda believes she can "fly to the sun" in the person of the handsome military captain Phoebus, but he is interested in her only in an earthly way. Frollo's destructive passion leads him to set a trap for Esmeralda. For a fee, Phoebus agrees to hide Frollo where he can watch a rendezvous between Phoebus and Esmeralda. Unable to contain himself, the priest leaves his hiding place, stabs Phoebus, and leaves. Esmeralda is, of course, accused of the crime.

Quasimodo saves her from execution and gives her sanctuary in the cathedral, but she is betrayed again by Frollo, who orders her to choose between him and the gallows. Like the fly, Esmeralda tears herself away from the priest to collapse at the foot of the gibbet. Phoebus, who did not die of his wound, remains indifferent to her plight, but Quasimodo pushes Frollo to his death from the tower of Notre Dame as the priest gloats over Esmeralda's execution. Quasimodo, the grotesque, gains in moral stature throughout the novel, just as Frollo falls from grace. Two years later, a deformed skeleton is found in a burial vault beside that of the virtuous Esmeralda.

The Hunchback of Notre Dame and *Les Misérables* are justly Hugo's most famous novels because they combine the exposition of his social ideas with an aesthetically unified structure. By contrast, *The Last Day of a Condemned*, written in 1829, is basically a social treatise on the horrors of prison life. In the same way, *Claude Gueux*, a short work of 1834, protests against the death penalty. In both works, the writer speaks out against society's injustice to man, but it was with *Les Misérables* that the reformer's voice spoke most effectively.

Les Misérables

Les Misérables tells of the spiritual journey of Jean Valjean, a poor but honorable man, driven in desperation to steal a loaf of bread to feed his widowed sister and her children. Sent to prison, he becomes an embittered, morally deformed creature, until he is redeemed by his love for the orphan girl Cosette. The plot of the novel is quite complex, as Jean rises to respectability and descends again several times. This is true because, as a convict, he must live under an assumed name. His spiritual voyage will not end until he can stand once more as Jean Valjean. His name suggests the French verb *valoir*, "to be worth." Jean must become worthy of Jean; he cannot have value under a counterfeit name.

His first reappearance as a respectable bourgeois is as Monsieur Madeleine, Mayor of Montreuil-sur-Mer. He is soon called upon, however, to reveal his true identity in order to save another from life imprisonment for having been identified as Jean Valjean, parole breaker. He descends into society's underworld, eluding capture by his nemesis, the policeman Javert. In Hugo's works, the way down is always the way up to salvation. Just as Ordener descended into the mines, Jean must now pass through a valley (*Val*) in order to save Jean. Here, as in *The Hunchback of Notre Dame*, moral superiority is to be found among the lowly.

In order to save himself, Jean must be the savior of others. He begins by rescuing Cosette from her wicked foster parents. Later, he will save Javert from insurrectionists. His greatest test, however, will be that of saving Marius, the man Cosette loves and who will separate Jean from the girl who is his paradise. This episode is the famous flight through the sewers of Paris, a true descent into the underworld, whence Jean Valjean is reborn, his soul transfigured, clear, and serene. He still has one more trial to endure, that of regaining his own name, which, through a misunderstanding, brings a painful estrangement from Cosette and Marius. He begins to die but is reconciled with his children at the last moment and leaves this life with a soul radiantly transformed.

The Toilers of the Sea

Les Misérables was written partly in exile, and certain episodes begin to show a preference for images of water. *The Toilers of the Sea*, written on Guernsey in 1864 and 1865, is a novel dominated by the sea. The text originally included an introductory section titled "L'Archipel de la Manche" ("The Archipelago of the English Channel"), which Hugo's editor persuaded him to publish separately at a later date (1883). The two parts reveal that Hugo has separated sociology from fiction. It would seem that, at odds with the predominant novelistic style of his time, Hugo preferred not to communicate his social philosophy through the imagery and structure of his novels. Thus, the prologue contains Hugo's doctrine of social progress and his analysis of the geology, customs, and language of the Channel Islands. The larger section that became the published novel is once again the story of a solitary quest.

The hero, Gilliatt, is a fisherman who lives a simple, rather ordinary life with his elderly mother on the island of Guernsey. In their house, they keep a marriage chest containing a trousseau for Gilliatt's future bride. Gilliatt loves Déruchette, niece of Mess Lethierry, inventor of the steamboat *Durande*, with which he has made his fortune in commerce. When the villain, Clubin, steals Lethierry's money and wrecks his steamer, Gilliatt's adventures begin.

Like the king of myth or legend, Lethierry offers his niece's hand in marriage to whomever can salvage the *Durande*. Gilliatt sets out upon the sea. Ominously missing are the magical beasts or mysterious beings who normally appear to assist the hero as he sets off. Even Ordener, for example, had a guide, Benignus Spiagudry, at the beginning of his quest. It is entirely unaided that Gilliatt leaves shore.

He now faces nature and the unknown, completely cut off from human society. He survives a titanic struggle for the ship against the hurricane forces of nature, but he must still descend into an underwater grotto, where he is seized by a hideous octopus. Gilliatt is, in Hugo's words, "the fly of that spider." The language of the passage makes it clear that in freeing himself from the octopus, Gilliatt frees himself from evil.

Exhausted, Gilliatt prays, then sleeps. When he wakes, the sea is calm. He returns to land a savior, bringing the engine of the ship as well as the stolen money. When he learns that Déruchette wishes to marry another, he gives her his own marriage chest and leaves to die in the rising tide. *The Toilers of the Sea* is considered by many to be the finest and purest expression of Hugo's mythic vision.

The Man Who Laughs

Almost immediately after *The Toilers of the Sea*, Hugo turned his attention back to history. In 1866, he began work on the first novel of what he intended to be a trilogy focusing in turn on aristocracy, monarchy, and democracy. The first, *The Man Who Laughs*, is set in England after 1688; the second would have taken place in prerevolutionary France; and the third is *Ninety-three*, a vision of France after 1789. The role of fate is diminished in these last two novels because Hugo wished to emphasize man's conscience and free will in a social and political context.

In *The Man Who Laughs*, the disfigured hero, Gwynplaine, chooses to leave his humble earthly paradise when he learns that he had been born to the aristocracy. Predictably, the way up leads to Gwynplaine's downfall. Noble society is a hellish labyrinth (another type of web) from which Gwynplaine barely manages to escape. A wolf named Homo helps him find his lost love again, a blind girl named Déa. When she dies, Gwynplaine finds salvation by letting himself sink beneath the water of the Thames.

Ninety-three

Hugo's vivid portrayal of a demoniac aristocratic society justified the cause of the French Revolution in 1789, preparing the way for his vision of an egalitarian future as described in his last novel, *Ninety-three*. By choosing to write about 1793 instead of the fall of the Bastille, Hugo was attempting to deal with the Terror, which he considered to have deformed the original ideals of the Revolution.

Rather than the familiar love interest, Hugo places the characters Michelle Fléchard and her three children at the center of the novel. In Hugo's works, kindness to children can redeem almost any amount of wickedness. The monstrous Hans of Iceland, for example, is partially excused because he was avenging the death of his son. It is therefore not surprising to find in *Ninety-three* that each faction in the Revolution is tested and judged according to its treatment of Michelle and her children.

The extreme positions in the violent political clash are represented by the Marquis de Lantenac, the Royalist leader, and his counterpart, Cimourdain, a former priest and fanatic revolutionary. Both men are inflexible and coldly logical in their courageous devotion to their beliefs. The violent excesses of both sides are depicted as demoniac no matter how noble the cause. Human charity and benign moderation are represented in Gauvain, a general in the revolutionary army. He is Lantenac's nephew and the former pupil of Cimourdain. He is clearly also the spokesman for Hugo's point of view.

In the course of events, Lantenac redeems his inhumanity by rescuing Michelle's children from a burning tower. He is now Gauvain's prisoner and should be sent to the guillotine. Gauvain's humanity, however, responds to Lantenac's act of self-sacrifice, and Gauvain arranges for him to escape. It is now Cimourdain's turn, but he remains loyal to his principles, condemning to death his beloved disciple. Before his execution, Gauvain expounds his (Hugo's) idealistic social philosophy in a dialogue with Cimourdin's pragmatic view of a disciplined society based on strict justice.

In this final novel, Hugo's desire to express his visionary ideology overwhelms his talents as a novelist. At the age of seventy, he had become the prophet of a transfigured social order of the future. He would create no more of his compelling fictional worlds. It was time for Hugo the creator of legends to assume the legendary stature of his final decade.

Jan St. Martin

Other major works

PLAYS: *Cromwell*, pb. 1827 (verse drama; English translation, 1896); *Amy Robsart*, pr. 1828 (English translation, 1895); *Hernani*, pr., pb. 1830 (verse drama; English translation, 1830); *Marion de Lorme*, pr., pb. 1831 (verse drama; English translation, 1895); *Le Roi s'amuse*, pr., pb. 1832 (verse drama; *The King's Fool*, 1842; also known as *The King Amuses Himself*, 1964); *Lucrèce Borgia*, pr., pb. 1833 (*Lucretia Borgia*, 1842); *Marie Tudor*, pr., pb. 1833 (English translation, 1895); *Angelo, tyran de Padoue*, pr., pb. 1835 (*Angelo, Tyrant of Padua*, 1880); *Ruy Blas*, pr., pb. 1838 (verse drama; English translation, 1890); *Les Burgraves*, pr., pb. 1843 (*The Burgraves*, 1896); *Inez de Castro*, pb. 1863 (wr. c. 1818; verse drama); *La Grand-mère*, pb. 1865; *Mille Francs de Recompense*, pb. 1866; *Les Deux Trouvailles de Gallus*, pb. 1881; *Torquemada*, pb. 1882 (wr. 1869; English translation, 1896); *Théâtre en liberté*, pb. 1886 (includes *Mangeront-ils?*); *The Dramatic Works*, 1887; *The Dramatic Works of Victor Hugo*, 1895-1896 (4 volumes); *Irtamène*, pb. 1934 (wr. 1816; verse drama).

POETRY: *Odes et poésies diverses*, 1822, 1823; *Nouvelles Odes*, 1824; *Odes et ballades*, 1826; *Les Orientales*, 1829 (*Les Orientales: Or, Eastern Lyrics*, 1879); *Les Feuilles d'automne*, 1831; *Les Chants du crépuscule*, 1835 (*Songs of Twilight*, 1836); *Les Voix intérieures*, 1837; *Les Rayons et les ombres*, 1840; *Les Châtiments*, 1853; *Les Contemplations*, 1856; *La Légende des siècles*, 1859-1883 (5 volumes; *The Legend of the Centuries*, 1894); *Les Chansons des rues et des bois*, 1865; *L'Année terrible*, 1872; *L'Art d'être grand-père*, 1877; *Le Pape*, 1878; *La Pitié suprême*, 1879; *L'Âne*, 1880; *Les Quatre vents de l'esprit*, 1881; *The Literary Life and Poetical Works of Victor Hugo*, 1883; *La Fin de Satan*, 1886; *Toute la lyre*, 1888; *Dieu*, 1891; *Les Années funestes*, 1896; *Poems from Victor Hugo*, 1901; *Dernière Gerbe*, 1902; *Poems*, 1902; *The Poems of Victor Hugo*, 1906; *Océan*, 1942.

NONFICTION: *La Préface de Cromwell*, 1827 (English translation, 1896); *Littérature et philosophie mêlées*, 1834; *Le Rhin*, 1842 (*The Rhine*, 1843); *Napoléon le petit*, 1852 (*Napoleon the Little*, 1852); *William Shakespeare*, 1864 (English translation, 1864); *Actes et paroles*, 1875-1876; *Histoire d'un crime*, 1877 (*The History of a Crime*, 1877-1878); *Religions et religion*, 1880; *Le Théâtre en liberté*, 1886; *Choses vues*, 1887 (*Things Seen*, 1887); *En voyage: Alpes et Pyrénées*, 1890 (*The Alps and Pyrenees*, 1898); *France et Belgique*, 1892; *Correspondance*, 1896-1898.

MISCELLANEOUS: *Œuvres complètes*, 1880-1892 (57 volumes); *Victor Hugo's Works*, 1892 (30 volumes); *Works*, 1907 (10 volumes).

Bibliography

Bloom, Harold, ed. *Victor Hugo*. New York: Chelsea House, 1988. Collection of twelve essays discusses all aspects of Hugo's career. Two essays are devoted to analysis of *Les Misérables*. Includes introduction, chronology, and bibliography.

Brombert, Victor. *Victor Hugo and the Visionary Novel*. Cambridge, Mass.: Harvard University Press, 1984. Study by one of the most distinguished scholars of modern French literature includes an especially informative chapter on *Les Misérables*. Provides detailed notes and bibliography.

Frey, John Andrew. *A Victor Hugo Encyclopedia*. Westport, Conn.: Greenwood Press, 1999. Comprehensive guide to the works of Hugo includes introductory and biographical material. Addresses Hugo as a leading poet, novelist, artist, and religious and revolutionary thinker of France. The balance of the volume contains alphabetically arranged entries discussing his works, characters, and themes as well as relevant historical persons and places. Includes a general bibliography.

Grossman, Kathryn M. *"Les Misérables": Conversion, Revolution, Redemption.* New York: Twayne, 1996. Examination of the novel, aimed at students and general readers, recounts the historical events leading up to the novel's publication, discusses the importance of the book, describes how Hugo's political and philosophical ideas are expressed in the work, and analyzes the character of protagonist Jean Valjean. Includes bibliographical references and index.

Maurois, André. *Olympio: The Life of Victor Hugo.* Translated by Gerard Hopkins. New York: Harper & Row, 1956. This work, originally published in French in 1954, is probably as close an approach as possible to an ideal one-volume biography dealing with both the life and the work of a monumental figure such as Hugo. Of the sparse illustrations, several are superb; the bibliography, principally of sources in French, provides a sense of Hugo's celebrity and influence, which persisted well into the twentieth century.

_______. *Victor Hugo and His World.* London: Thames and Hudson, 1966. The 1956 English translation of Maurois's text noted above was edited to conform to the format of a series of illustrated books. The result is interesting and intelligible, but rather schematic. In compensation for the vast cuts in text, a chronology and dozens of well-annotated illustrations have been added.

Porter, Laurence M. *Victor Hugo.* New York: Twayne, 1999. Study of Hugo and his works provides a biography, separate chapters analyzing *The Hunchback of Notre Dame* and *Les Misérables*, and discussions of Hugo's plays and poetry. Includes bibliography and index.

Raser, Timothy. *The Simplest of Signs: Victor Hugo and the Language of Images in France, 1850-1950.* Newark: University of Delaware Press, 2004. Analyzes the relationship of Hugo's works to French architecture and other visual arts, examining how Hugo used language to describe time, place, and visual details, his aesthetics and politics, and the language and methods of French art criticism.

Richardson, Joanna. *Victor Hugo.* New York: St. Martin's Press, 1976. Well-written, scholarly biography of Hugo is divided into three sections: "The Man," "The Prophet," and "The Legend." Includes detailed notes, extensive bibliography, and index.

Robb, Graham. *Victor Hugo.* New York: W. W. Norton, 1998. Thorough biography reveals many previously unknown aspects of Hugo's long life and literary career. Robb's introduction discusses earlier biographies. Includes detailed notes and bibliography.

Vargas Llosa, Mario. *The Temptation of the Impossible: Victor Hugo and "Les Misérables."* Princeton, N.J.: Princeton University Press, 2007. Provides a fascinating look at Hugo's writing of *Les Misérables*, including an examination of the work's structure and narration. Includes comparisons to modern novels and critics' reactions to the novel in Hugo's day.

ZORA NEALE HURSTON

Born: Notasulga, Alabama; January 7, 1891
Died: Fort Pierce, Florida; January 28, 1960

PRINCIPAL LONG FICTION

Jonah's Gourd Vine, 1934
Their Eyes Were Watching God, 1937
Moses, Man of the Mountain, 1939
Seraph on the Suwanee, 1948

OTHER LITERARY FORMS

In addition to her four novels, Zora Neale Hurston produced two collections of folklore, *Mules and Men* (1935) and *Tell My Horse* (1938), and an autobiography, *Dust Tracks on a Road* (1942). Hurston also published plays, short stories, and essays in anthologies and in magazines as diverse as *Opportunity*, *Journal of Negro History*, *The Saturday Evening Post*, *Journal of American Folklore*, and *American Legion Magazine*. Finally, she wrote several articles and reviews for such newspapers as the *New York Herald Tribune* and the *Pittsburgh Courier*. Hurston's major works were only reissued in the late twentieth century. Some of her essays and stories have also been collected and reprinted. Although the anthologies *I Love Myself When I Am Laughing* . . . (1979) and *The Sanctified Church* (1981) helped to bring her writing back into critical focus, some of her works ceased to be readily available, and her numerous unpublished manuscripts can be seen only at university archives and the Library of Congress.

ACHIEVEMENTS

Zora Neale Hurston was the best and most prolific African American woman writer of the 1930's. Her novels were highly praised. Even so, Hurston never made more than one thousand dollars in royalties on even her most successful works, and when she died in 1960 in Florida, she was nearly penniless and forgotten. Hurston's career testifies to the difficulties of a black woman writing for a mainstream white audience whose appreciation was usually superficial and for a black audience whose responses to her work were, of necessity, politicized.

Hurston achieved recognition at a time when, as Langston Hughes declared, "the Negro was in vogue." The Harlem Renaissance, the black literary and cultural movement of the 1920's, created an interracial audience for her stories and plays. Enthusiasm for her work extended through the 1930's, although that decade also marked the beginning of critical attacks. Hurston did not portray blacks as victims stunted by a racist society. Such a view, she believed, implies that black life is only a defensive reaction to white racism. Black and left-wing critics, however, complained that her unwillingness to represent the oppression of blacks and her focus, instead, on an autonomous, unresentful black folk culture served to perpetuate minstrel stereotypes and thus fueled white racism.

The radical, racial protest literature of Richard Wright, one of Hurston's strongest critics, became the model for black literature in the 1940's, and publishers on the lookout for protest works showed less and less interest in Hurston's manuscripts. Yet, when she did speak out against American racism and imperialism, her work was often censored. Her autobiography, published in 1942, as well as a number of her stories and articles were tailored by editors to please white audiences. Caught between the attacks of black critics and the censorship of the white publishing industry, Hurston floundered, struggling through the 1940's and 1950's to find other subjects. She largely dropped out of public view in the 1950's, though she continued to publish magazine and newspaper articles.

The African American and feminist political and cultural movements of the 1960's and 1970's provided the impetus for Hurston's rediscovery. The publication of Robert Hemenway's excellent book *Zora Neale Hurston: A Literary Biography* (1977) and the reissue of Hurston's novels, her autobiography, and her folklore collections seem to promise the sustained critical recognition Hurston deserves.

BIOGRAPHY

Zora Neale Hurston was born on January 7, 1891, in Alabama. Later, her family lived in the all-black Florida town of Eatonville in an eight-room house with a five-acre garden. Her father, the Reverend John Hurston, mayor of Eatonville for three terms and moderator of the South Florida Baptist Association, wanted to temper his daughter's high spirits, but her intelligent and forceful mother, Lucy Potts Hurston, encouraged her to "jump at de sun." When Hurston was about nine years old, her mother died. That event and her father's rapid remarriage to a woman his daughter did not like prematurely ended Hurston's childhood. In the next few years, she lived only intermittently at home, spending some time at a school in Jacksonville and some time with relatives. Her father withdrew all financial support during this period, forcing her to commence what was to be a lifelong struggle to make her own living.

When Hurston was fourteen years old, she took a job as a wardrobe girl to a repertory company touring the South. Hurston left the troupe in Baltimore eighteen months later and finished high school there at Morgan Academy. She went on to study part-time at Howard University in 1918, taking jobs as a manicurist, a waitress, and a maid in order to support herself. At Howard, her literary talents began to emerge. She was admitted to a campus literary club, formed by Alain Locke, a Howard professor and one of the forces behind the Harlem Renaissance. Locke brought Hurston to the attention of Charles S. Johnson, another key promoter of the Harlem Renaissance. Editor of *Opportunity: A Journal of Negro Life*, he published one of her stories and encouraged her to enter the literary contest sponsored by his magazine.

With several manuscripts but little money, Hurston moved to New York City in 1925, hoping to make a career of her writing. Her success in that year's *Opportunity* contest—she received prizes for a play and a story—won her the patronage of Fanny Hurst and a scholarship to complete her education at Barnard College. She studied anthropology there under Franz Boas, leading a seemingly schizophrenic life in the next two years as an eccentric, iconoclastic artist of the Harlem Renaissance on one hand and a budding, scholarly social scientist on the other.

The common ground linking these seemingly disparate parts of Hurston's life was her interest in black folk culture. Beginning in 1927 and extending through the 1930's, she made several trips to collect black folklore in the South and in the Bahamas, Haiti, and Jamaica. Collecting trips were costly, however, as was the time to write up their results. Charlotte Osgood Mason, a wealthy, domineering white patron to a number of African American artists, supported some of that work, as did the Association for the Study of Negro Life and History and the Guggenheim Foundation. Hurston also worked intermittently during the 1930's as a drama teacher at Bethune Cookman College in Florida and at North Carolina College, as a drama coach for the WPA Federal Theatre Project in New York, and as an editor for the Federal Writers' Project in Florida.

Mules and Men and several scholarly and popular articles on folklore were the products of Hurston's collecting trips in the late 1920's and early 1930's. In 1938, she published *Tell My Horse*, the result of trips to Haiti and Jamaica to study hoodoo. As a creative writer, Hurston devised other outlets for her folk materials. Her plays, short stories, and three of her novels—*Jonah's Gourd Vine*, *Their Eyes Were Watching God*, and *Moses, Man of the Mountain*—make use of folklore. She also presented folk materials in theatrical revues, but even though the productions were enthusiastically received, she could never generate enough backing to finance commercially successful long-term showings.

Hurston's intense interest in black folklore prevented her from sustaining either of her two marriages. She could not reconcile the competing claims of love and work. She married Herbert Sheen, a medical student, in 1927 but separated from him a few months later. They were divorced in 1931. She married Albert Price III in 1939, and they too parted less than one year later. Other romantic relationships ended for the same reason.

In the 1940's, Hurston lost her enthusiasm for writing about black folk culture. She wrote her autobiography and in 1948 published her last novel, *Seraph on the Suwanee*, a work that turns away from black folk culture entirely. The last decade of her life took a downward turn. Falsely accused of committing sodomy with a young boy, Hurston, depressed, dropped out of public view. Through the 1950's, she lived in Florida, struggling for economic survival. She barely managed to support herself by writing newspaper and magazine articles, many of which expressed her increasing political conservatism, and by working as a maid, a substitute teacher, and a librarian. In 1959, she suffered a stroke. Too ill to nurse herself, she was forced to enter a welfare home. She died there on January 28, 1960.

ANALYSIS

For much of her career, Zora Neale Hurston was dedicated to the presentation of black folk culture. She introduced readers to hoodoo, folktales, lying contests, spirituals, the blues, sermons, children's games, riddles, playing the dozens, and, in general, a highly metaphoric folk idiom. Although she represented black folk culture in several genres, Hurston was drawn to the novel form because it could convey folklore as communal behavior. Hurston knew that much of the unconscious artistry of folklore appears in the gestures and tones in which it is expressed and that it gains much of its meaning in performance. Even *Mules and Men*, the folklore collection she completed just before embarking on her first novel (although it was published after *Jonah's Gourd Vine*), "novelizes" what could have been an anthology of disconnected folk materials. By inventing a narrator who witnesses, even participates in, the performance of folk traditions, she combated the inevitable distortion of an oral culture by its textual documentation.

Zora Neale Hurston. (Library of Congress)

Hurston's motives for presenting black folklore were, in part, political. She wanted to refute contemporary claims that African Americans lacked a distinct culture of their own. Her novels depict the unconscious creativity of the African American proletariat or folk. They represent community members participating in a highly expressive communication system that taught them to survive racial oppression and, moreover, to respect themselves and their community. At the beginning of Hurston's second novel, for example, the community's members are sitting on porches. "Mules and other brutes had occupied their skins" all day, but now it is night, work is over, and they can talk and feel "powerful and human" again: "They became lords of sounds and lesser things. They passed nations through their mouths. They sat in judgment." By showing the richness and the healthy influence of black folk culture, Hurston hoped not only to defeat racist attitudes but also to encourage racial pride among blacks. Why should African Americans wish to imitate a white bourgeoisie? The "Negro lowest down" had a richer culture.

Hurston also had a psychological motive for presenting black folk culture. She drew the folk materials for her novels from the rural, southern black life she knew as a child and subsequently recorded in folklore-collecting trips in the late 1920's and 1930's. She had fond memories of her childhood in the all-black town of Eatonville, where she did not experience poverty or racism. In her autobiographical writings, she suggests that she did not even know that she was "black" until she left Eatonville. Finally, in Eatonville, she had a close relationship with and a strong advocate in her mother. In representing the rich culture of black rural southerners, she was also evoking a happier personal past.

Although the novel's witnessing narrator provided Hurston with the means to dramatize folklore, she also needed meaningful fictional contexts for its presentation. Her novels are a series of attempts to develop such contexts. Initially, she maintained the southern rural setting for black folk traditions. In her first novel, *Jonah's Gourd Vine*, she re-created Eatonville and neighboring Florida towns. Hurston also loosely re-created her parents' lives with the central characters, John and Lucy Pearson. Though Hurston claimed that an unhappy love affair she had had with a man she met in New York was the catalyst for her second novel, *Their Eyes Were Watching God*, the feeling rather than the details of that affair appear in the novel. The work takes the reader back to Eatonville again and to the porch-sitting storytellers Hurston knew as a child.

Moses, Man of the Mountain

With her third novel, *Moses, Man of the Mountain*, however, Hurston turned in a new direction, leaving the Eatonville milieu behind. The novel retells the biblical story of Moses via the folk idiom and traditions of southern rural blacks. Hurston leaves much of the plot of the biblical story intact—Moses does lead the Hebrews out of Egypt—but, for example, she shows Moses to be a great hoodoo doctor as well as a leader and lawgiver. In effect, Hurston simulated the creative processes of folk culture, transforming the story of Moses for modern African Americans just as slaves had adapted biblical stories in spirituals. Hurston may have reenacted an oral and communal process as a solitary writer, but she gave an imaginative rendering of the cultural process all the same.

Seraph on the Suwanee

Seraph on the Suwanee, Hurston's last novel, marks another dramatic shift in her writing. With this novel, however, she did not create a new context for the representation of folk culture. Rather, she turned away from the effort to present black folklore. *Seraph on the Suwanee* is set in the rural South, but its central characters are white. Hurston apparently wanted to prove that she could write about whites as well as blacks, a desire that surfaced, no doubt, in response to the criticism and disinterest her work increasingly faced in the 1940's. Yet, even when writing of upwardly mobile southern "crackers," Hurston could not entirely leave her previous mission behind. Her white characters, perhaps unintentionally, often use the black folk idiom.

Although Hurston's novels, with the exception of the last, create contexts or develop other strategies for the presentation of folklore, they are not simply showcases for folk traditions; black folk culture defines the novels' themes. The most interesting of these thematic renderings appear in Hurston's first two novels. Hurston knew that black folk culture was composed of brilliant adaptations of African culture to American life. She admired the ingenuity of these adaptations but worried about their preservation. Would a sterile, materialistic white world ultimately absorb blacks, destroying the folk culture they had developed? Her first two novels demonstrate the disturbing influence of white America on black folkways.

Jonah's Gourd Vine

Jonah's Gourd Vine, Hurston's first novel, portrays the tragic experience of a black preacher caught between black cultural values and the values imposed by his white-influenced church. The novel charts the life of John Pearson, laborer, foreman, and carpenter, who discovers that he has an extraordinary talent for preaching. With his linguistic skills and his wife Lucy's wise counsel, he becomes pastor of the large church Zion Hope and ultimately moderator of a Florida Baptist convention. His sexual promiscuity, however, eventually destroys his marriage and his career.

Though his verbal skills make him a success while his promiscuity ruins him, the novel shows that both his linguistic gifts and his sexual vitality are part of the same cultural heritage. His sexual conduct is pagan and so is his preaching. In praying, according to the narrator, it was as if he "rolled his African drum up to the altar, and called his Congo Gods by Christian names." Both aspects of his cultural heritage speak through him. Indeed, they speak through all members of the African American community, if most intensely through John. A key moment early in the novel, when John crosses over Big Creek, marks the symbolic beginning of his life and shows the double cultural heritage he brings to it. John heads down to the Creek, "singing a new song and stomping the beats." He makes up "some words to go with the drums of the Creek," with the animal noises in the woods, and with the hound dog's cry. He begins to think about the girls living on the other side of Big Creek: "John almost trumpeted exultantly at the new sun. He breathed lustily. He stripped and carried his clothes across, then recrossed and plunged into the swift water and breasted strongly over."

To understand why two expressions of the same heritage have such different effects on John's life, one has to turn to the community to which he belongs. Members of his congregation subscribe to differing views of the spiritual life. The view most often endorsed by the novel emerges from the folk culture. As Larry Neal, one of Hurston's best critics, explains in his introduction to the 1971 reprint of the novel, that view belongs to "a formerly enslaved communal society, non-Christian in background," which does not strictly dichotomize body and soul. The other view comes out of a white culture. It is "more rigid, being a blend of Puritan concepts and the fire-and-brimstone imagery of the white evangelical tradition." That view insists that John, as a preacher, exercise self-restraint. The cultural conflict over spirituality pervades his congregation. While the deacons, whom Hurston often portrays satirically, pressure him to stop preaching, he still has some loyal supporters among his parishioners.

White America's cultural styles and perceptions invade Pearson's community in other ways as well. By means of a kind of preaching competition, the deacons attempt to replace Pearson with the pompous Reverend Felton Cozy, whose preaching style is white. Cozy's style, however, fails to captivate most members of the congregation. Pearson is a great preacher in the folk tradition, moving his congregation to a frenzy with "barbaric thunder-poems." By contrast, Cozy, as one of the parishioners complains, does not give a sermon; he lectures. In an essay Hurston wrote on "The Sanctified Church," she explains this reaction: "The real, singing Negro derides the Negro who adopts the white man's religious ways. . . . They say of that type of preacher, 'Why he don't preach at all. He just lectures.'"

If Pearson triumphs over Cozy, he nevertheless ultimately falls. His sexual conduct destroys his marriage and leads to an unhappy remarriage with one of his mistresses, Hattie Tyson. He is finally forced to stop preaching at Zion Hope. Divorced from Hattie, he moves to another town, where he meets and marries Sally Lovelace, a woman much like Lucy. With her support, he returns to preaching. On a visit to a friend, however, he is tempted by a young prostitute and, to his dismay, succumbs. Although he has wanted to be faithful to his new wife, he will always be a pagan preacher, spirit and flesh. Fleeing back to Sally, he is killed when a train strikes his car.

In its presentation of folklore and its complex representation of cultural conflict, *Jonah's Gourd Vine* is a brilliant first novel, although Hurston does not always make her argument sufficiently clear. The novel lacks a consistent point of view. Though she endorses Pearson's African heritage and ridicules representatives of white cultural views, she also creates an admirable and very sympathetic character in Lucy Pearson, who is ruined by her husband's pagan behavior. Nor did Hurston seem to know how to resolve the cultural conflict she portrayed—hence, the deus ex machina ending. It was not until she wrote her next novel, *Their Eyes Were Watching God*, that Hurston learned to control point of view and presented a solution to the problem of white influences on black culture.

THEIR EYES WERE WATCHING GOD

The life of Janie Crawford, the heroine of *Their Eyes Were Watching God*, is shaped by bourgeois values—white in origin. She finds love and self-identity only by rejecting that life and becoming a wholehearted participant in black folk culture. Her grandmother directs Janie's entrance into adulthood. Born into slavery, the older woman hopes to find protection and materialistic comforts for Janie in a marriage to the property-owning Logan Killicks. Janie, who has grown up in a different generation, does not share her grandmother's values. When she finds she cannot love her husband, she runs off with Jody Stark, who is on his way to Eatonville, where he hopes to become a "big voice," an appropriate phrase for life in a community that highly values verbal ability. Jody becomes that "big voice" as mayor of the town, owner of the general store, and head of the post office. He lives both a bourgeois and a folk life in Eatonville. He constructs a big house—the kind white people have—but he wanders out to the porch of the general store whenever he wants to enjoy the perpetual storytelling that takes place there. Even though Janie has demonstrated a talent for oratory, however, he will not let her join these sessions or participate in the mock funeral for a mule that has become a popular character in the townspeople's stories. "He didn't," the narrator suggests, "want her talking after such trashy people." As Janie tells a friend years later, Jody "classed me off." He does so by silencing her.

For several years, Janie has no voice in the community or in her private life. Her life begins to seem unreal: "She sat and watched the shadow of herself going about tending store and prostrating itself before Jody." One day, after Stark insults her in front of customers in the store, however, she speaks out and, playing the dozens, insults his manhood. The insult causes an irreconcilable break between them.

After Jody's death, Janie is courted by Tea Cake Woods, a laborer with little money. Though many of her neighbors disapprove of the match, Janie marries him. "Dis ain't no business proposition," she tells her friend Pheoby, "and no race after property and titles. Dis is uh love game. Ah done lived Grandma's way, now Ah means tuh live mine." Marriage to Tea Cake lowers her social status but frees her from her submissive female role, from her shadow existence. Refusing to use her money, Tea Cake takes her down to the Everglades, where they become migrant workers. She picks beans with him in the fields, and he helps her prepare their dinners. With Tea Cake, she also enters into the folk culture of the Everglades, and that more than anything else enables her to shed her former submissive identity. Workers show up at their house every night to sing, dance, gamble, and, above all, to talk, like the folks in Eatonville on the front porch of the general store. Janie learns how to tell "big stories" from listening to the others, and she is encouraged to do so.

This happy phase of Janie's life ends tragically as she and Tea Cake attempt to escape a hurricane and the ensuing flood. Tea Cake saves Janie from drowning but, in the process, is bitten by a rabid dog. Sick and crazed, he tries to shoot Janie. She is forced to kill him in self-defense. Not everything she has gained during her relationship with Tea Cake, however, dies with him. The strong self-identity she has achieved while living in the Everglades enables her to withstand the unjust resentment of their black friends as well as her trial for murder in a white court. Most important, she is able to endure her own loss and returns to Eatonville, self-reliant and wise. Tea Cake, she knows, will live on in her thoughts and feelings—and in her words. She tells her story to her friend Pheoby—that storytelling event frames the novel—and allows Pheoby to bring it to the other members of the community. As the story enters the community's oral culture, it will influence it. Indeed, as the novel closes, Janie's story has already affected Pheoby. "Ah done growed ten feet higher from jus' listenin' tuh you," she tells Janie. "Ah ain't satisfied wid mahself no mo'."

In her novels, Hurston did not represent the oppression of blacks because she refused to view African American life as impoverished. If she would not focus on white racism, however, her novels do oppose white culture. In *Their Eyes Were Watching God*, Janie does not find happiness until she gives up a life governed by white values and enters into the verbal ceremonies of black folk culture. Loving celebrations of a separate black folk life were Hurston's effective political weapon; racial pride was one of her great gifts to American literature. "Sometimes, I feel discriminated against," she once told her readers, "but it does not make me angry. It merely astonishes me. How *can* any deny themselves the pleasure of my company? It's beyond me."

Deborah Kaplan

Other major works

SHORT FICTION: *Spunk: The Selected Short Stories of Zora Neale Hurston*, 1985; *The Complete Stories*, 1995.

PLAYS: *Color Struck*, pb. 1926; *The First One*, pb. 1927; *Mule Bone*, pb. 1931 (with Langston Hughes); *Polk County*, pb. 1944.

NONFICTION: *Mules and Men*, 1935; *Tell My Horse*, 1938; *Dust Tracks on a Road*, 1942; *The Sanctified Church*, 1981; *Folklore, Memoirs, and Other Writings*, 1995; *Go Gator and Muddy the Water: Writings*, 1999 (Pamela Bordelon, editor); *Every Tongue Got to Confess: Negro Folk-tales from the Gulf States*, 2001 (Carla Kaplan, editor); *Zora Neale Hurston: A Life in Letters*, 2002 (Kaplan, editor).

MISCELLANEOUS: *I Love Myself When I Am Laughing . . . and Then Again When I Am Looking Mean and Impressive: A Zora Neale Hurston Reader*, 1979 (Alice Walker, editor).

BIBLIOGRAPHY

Boyd, Valerie. *Wrapped in Rainbows: The Life of Zora Neale Hurston*. New York: Scribner, 2002. A comprehensive, meticulously researched account of Hurston the woman and the writer, based in part on information available after the early 1980's. Includes a discussion of the Hurston "resurrection," a list of her published works, a select bibliography, and an index.

Campbell, Josie P. *Student Companion to Zora Neale Hurston*. Westport, Conn.: Greenwood Press, 2001. Designed for students and general readers, this book includes a brief biography, an overview of Hurston's fiction, and separate chapters discussing each of her four novels.

Cooper, Jan. "Zora Neale Hurston Was Always a Southerner Too." In *The Female Tradition in Southern Literature*, edited by Carol S. Manning. Urbana: University of Illinois Press, 1993. Examines the hitherto neglected role that Hurston played in the Southern Renaissance between 1920 and 1950. Argues that Hurston's fiction is informed by a modern southern agrarian sense of community. Suggests that the Southern Renaissance was a "transracial," cross-cultural product of the South.

Cronin, Gloria L., ed. *Critical Essays on Zora Neale Hurston*. New York: G. K. Hall, 1998. A useful collection, featuring contemporary reviews of Hurston's four novels, feminist interpretations and other analyses of her works, and a discussion of Hurston and the Harlem Renaissance. Includes bibliographical references and an index.

Donlon, Jocelyn Hazelwood. "Porches: Stories: Power: Spatial and Racial Intersections in Faulkner and Hurston." *Journal of American Culture* 19 (Winter, 1996): 95-110. Comments on the role of the porch in Faulkner and Hurston's fiction as a transitional space between the public and the private where the individual can negotiate an identity through telling stories.

Glassman, Steve, and Kathryn Lee Siedel, eds. *Zora in Florida*. Orlando: University of Central Florida Press, 1991. This collection of essays by seventeen Hurston scholars explores the overall presence and influence of Florida in and on the works of Hurston. This collection grew out of a Hurston symposium held in Daytona Beach, Florida, in 1989, and includes an excellent introduction to the importance of Florida in the study of Hurston.

Hill, Lynda Marion. *Social Rituals and the Verbal Art of Zora Neale Hurston*. Washington, D.C.: Howard University Press, 1996. Features chapters on Hurston's treatment of everyday life, science and humanism, folklore, color, race, and class. Hill also considers dramatic reenactments of Hurston's writing. Includes notes, bibliography, and an appendix on "characteristics of Negro expression."

Howard, Lillie P. *Zora Neale Hurston*. Boston: Twayne, 1980. A good general introduction to the life and works of Hurston. Contains valuable plot summaries and commentaries on Hurston's works. Supplemented by a chronology and a bibliography.

Hurston, Lucy Anne. *Speak, So You Can Speak Again: The Life of Zora Neale Hurston*. New York: Doubleday, 2004. A brief biography written by Hurston's niece. Most notable for the inclusion of rare photographs, writings, and other multimedia personal artifacts. Also contains an audio compact disc of Hurston reading and singing.

Lyons, Mary E. *Sorrow's Kitchen: The Life and Folklore of Zora Neale Hurston*. New York: Charles Scribner's Sons, 1990. A straightforward biography of Hurston, written for younger readers. Especially useful for those who need a primer on Hurston's background in all-black Eatonville.

Plant, Deborah G. *Zora Neale Hurston: A Biography of the Spirit*. Westport, Conn.: Praeger, 2007. Portrays Hurston's strength and tenacity of spirit. Her literary achievements, including her novel *Their Eyes Were Watching God*, are also discussed here. This work draws on Hurston's 1942 autobiography *Dust Tracks on the Road* as well as newly discovered sources.

West, Margaret Genevieve. *Zora Neale Hurston and American Literary Culture*. Gainesville: University Press of Florida, 2005. A chronicle of Hurston's literary career, describing how her work was marketed and reviewed during her lifetime and why her writing did not gain popularity until long after her death.

ALDOUS HUXLEY

Born: Laleham, near Godalming, Surrey, England; July 26, 1894
Died: Los Angeles, California; November 22, 1963
Also known as: Aldous Leonard Huxley

Principal long fiction

Crome Yellow, 1921
Antic Hay, 1923
Those Barren Leaves, 1925
Point Counter Point, 1928
Brave New World, 1932
Eyeless in Gaza, 1936
After Many a Summer Dies the Swan, 1939
Time Must Have a Stop, 1944
Ape and Essence, 1948
The Genius and the Goddess, 1955
Island, 1962

Other literary forms

In addition to the novel, Aldous Huxley wrote in every other major literary form. He published several volumes of essays and won universal acclaim as a first-rate essayist. He also wrote poetry, plays, short stories, biographies, and travelogues.

Achievements

Aldous Huxley achieved fame as a satiric novelist and essayist in the decade following World War I. In his article "Aldous Huxley: The Ultra-modern Satirist," published in *The Nation* in 1926, Edwin Muir observed, "No other writer of our time has built up a serious reputation so rapidly and so surely; compared with his rise to acceptance that of Mr. Lawrence or Mr. Eliot has been gradual, almost painful." In the 1920's and the early 1930's, Huxley became so popular that the first London editions of his books were, within a decade of their publication, held at a premium by dealers and collectors. Huxley's early readers, whose sensibilities had been hardened by the war, found his wit, his iconoclasm, and his cynicism to their taste. They were also impressed by his prophetic gifts. Bertrand Russell said, "What Huxley thinks today, England thinks tomorrow." Believing that all available knowledge should be absorbed if humanity is to survive, Huxley assimilated ideas from a wide range of fields and allowed them to find their way into his novels, which came to be variously identified as "novels of ideas," "discussion novels," or "conversation novels." His increasing store of knowledge did not, however, help him overcome his pessimistic and cynical outlook on life.

Huxley's reputation as a novelist suffered a sharp decline in his later years. In his 1939 work *The Novel and the Modern World*, literary critic David Daiches took a highly critical view of Huxley's novels, and since then, many other critics have joined him. It is often asserted that Huxley was essentially an essayist whose novels frequently turn into intellectual tracts. It has also been held that his plots lack dramatic interest and his characters are devoid of real substance. Attempts were made in the late twentieth century, however, to rehabilitate Huxley as an important novelist. In any case, no serious discussion of twentieth century fiction can afford to ignore Huxley's novels.

Biography

Aldous Leonard Huxley was born at Laleham, near Godalming, Surrey, on July 26, 1894. His father, Leonard Huxley, a biographer and historian, was the son of Thomas Henry Huxley, the great Darwinist, and his mother, Julia, was the niece of poet Matthew Arnold. Julian Huxley, Aldous's older brother, would grow up to become a famous biologist. With this intellectual and literary family background, Huxley entered Eton at the age of fourteen. He had to withdraw from school within two years, however, owing to an attack of *keratitis punctata* that caused blindness. This event left a permanent mark on his character that was evident in his reflective temperament and detached manner. He learned to read Braille and continued his studies under tutors. As soon as he was able to read with the help of a magnifying glass, he went to Balliol College, Oxford, where he studied English literature and philosophy.

Huxley started his career as a journalist on the editorial staff of *The Athenaeum* under J. Middleton Murry.

He relinquished his journalistic career when he could support himself by his writing. By 1920, he had three volumes of verse and a collection of short stories to his credit. He had also become acquainted with a number of writers, including D. H. Lawrence. While in Italy in the 1920's, he met Lawrence again, and the two became close friends. Lawrence exercised a profound influence on Huxley, particularly in his distrust of intellect against his faith in blood consciousness. Later, Huxley became a disciple of Gerald Heard and took an active part in Heard's pacifist movement. In 1937, he moved to California, where he came into contact with the Ramakrishna Mission in Hollywood. In Hinduism and Buddhism, Huxley found the means of liberation from human bondage to the ego, a problem that had concerned him for a long time. To see if the mystical experience could be chemically induced, Huxley took hallucinogenic drugs in 1953, and his subsequent writings concerning such drugs helped to popularize their use.

Huxley married Maria Nys in 1919. After her death in 1955, he married Laura Archera in 1956. On November 22, 1963, Huxley died in Los Angeles, where his body was cremated the same day. There was no funeral, but friends in London held a memorial service the next month.

Analysis

Aldous Huxley's novels present, on the whole, a bitterly satiric and cynical picture of contemporary society. Recurring themes in these works are the egocentricity of the people of the twentieth century, their ignorance of any reality transcending the self, their loneliness and despair, and their pointless and sordid existence. Devoid of any sense of ultimate purpose, the world often appears to Huxley as a wilderness of apes, baboons, monkeys, and maggots, a veritable inferno, presided over by the demon Belial himself. The dominant negativism in the novelist's outlook on life is pointedly and powerfully revealed by Will Farnaby, a character in Huxley's book *Island*, who is fond of saying that he will not take yes for an answer.

Although Huxley finds the contemporary world largely hopeless, he reveals the possibility of redemption. Little oases of humanity, islands of decency, and atolls of liberated souls generally appear in his fictional worlds. A good number of his characters transcend their egos, achieve completeness of being, recognize the higher spiritual goals of life, and even dedicate their lives to the service of an indifferent humanity. Even Will Farnaby, who will not take yes for an answer, finally casts his lot with the islanders against the corrupt and the corrupting world. It is true that these liberated individuals are not, in Huxley's novels, a force strong enough to resist the onward march of civilization toward self-destruction, but they are nevertheless a testimony to the author's faith in the possibilities of sanity even in the most difficult of times. No one who agrees with Huxley's assessment of the modern world will ask for a stronger affirmation of faith in human redemption.

Huxley believed that humankind's redemption lies in the attainment of "wholeness" and integrity. His concept of wholeness did not, however, remain the same from

Aldous Huxley. (Library of Congress)

the beginning to the end of his career. As he matured as a novelist, Huxley's sense of wholeness achieved greater depth and clarity. Under the influence of D. H. Lawrence, Huxley viewed wholeness in terms of the harmonious blending of all human faculties. Writing under the influence of Gerald Heard, he expanded his idea of wholeness to include a mystical awareness of the unity of humanity with nature. Influenced by the Eastern religions, especially Hinduism and Buddhism, Huxley gave his concept of wholeness further spiritual and metaphysical depth.

Crome Yellow

In *Crome Yellow*, his first novel, Huxley exposes the egocentricity of modern human beings, their inability to relate to others or to recognize any reality, social or spiritual, outside themselves, and the utter pointlessness of their lives. Jenny Mullion, a minor character in the novel, symbolically represents the situation that prevails in the modern world by the almost impenetrable barriers of her deafness. It is difficult for anyone to carry on an intelligent conversation with her. Once, early in the book, when Denis Stone, a poet, inquires of Jenny if she slept well, she speaks to him, in reply, about thunderstorms. Following this ineffectual conversation, Denis reflects on the nature of Jenny Mullion:

> Parallel straight lines . . . meet only at infinity. He might talk for ever of care-charmer sleep and she of meteorology till the end of time. Did one ever establish contact with anyone? We are all parallel straight lines. Jenny was only a little more parallel than most.

Almost every character in the novel is set fast in a world that he or she has made and cannot come out of that world to establish contact with others. Henry even declaims, "How gay and delightful life would be if one could get rid of all the human contacts!" He is of the view that "the proper study of mankind is books." He obviously undertook his history of his family, which took him twenty-five years to write and four years to print, in order to escape human contacts. If Henry is occupied with the history of Crome (his family home), Priscilla, his wife, spends her time cultivating a rather ill-defined malady, placing bets, reading horoscopes, and studying Barbecue-Smith's books on spiritualism. Barbecue-Smith busies himself with infinity. Bodiham, the village priest, is obsessed with the Second Coming. Having read somewhere about the dangers of sexual repression, Mary Bracegirdle hunts for a lover who will provide her with an outlet for her repressed instincts. Denis broods constantly over his failure as a writer, as a lover, and as a man. Scogan, disdainful of life, people, and the arts, finds consolation only in reason and ideas and dreams about a scientifically controlled Rational State where babies are produced in test tubes and artists are sent to a lethal chamber.

Although a good deal of interaction occurs among the guests at Crome, no real meetings of minds or hearts take place among them; this failure to connect is best illustrated by the numerous hopeless love affairs described in the novel. Denis, for example, loves Anne, but his repeated attempts to convey his love for her fail. Anne, who is four years older than Denis, talks to him as if he were a child and does not know that he is courting her. Mary falls in love with Denis only to be rebuffed. She then makes advances to Gombauld, the painter, with no better result. Next, she pursues Ivor, the man of many gifts and talents, and is brokenhearted to learn that she means nothing to him. She is finally seen in the embrace of a young farmer of heroic proportions, and it is anybody's guess what comes of this affair. Even the relationship between Anne and Gombauld, which showed every promise of maturation into one of lasting love, meets, at the end, the same fate as the others.

Thumbing through Jenny's red notebook of cartoons, Denis suddenly becomes conscious of points of view other than his own. He learns that there are others who are "in their way as elaborate and complete as he is in his." Denis's appreciation of the world outside himself comes, however, too late in the novel. Though he would like to abandon the plan of his intended departure from Crome, particularly when he sees that it makes Anne feel wretched, he is too proud to change his mind and stay to try again with her. The characters in *Crome Yellow* thus remain self-absorbed, separated from one another, and hardly concerned with the ultimate ends of life. Scogan betrays himself and others when he says, "We all know that there's no ultimate point."

Antic Hay

Antic Hay, Huxley's second novel, presents, like *Crome Yellow*, an inferno-like picture of contemporary society. The novel is dominated by egocentric characters living in total isolation from society and suffering extreme loneliness, boredom, and despair. Evidence of self-preoccupation and isolation is abundant. Gumbril Junior continually dwells on his failings and on his prospects of getting rich. He retires every now and then to his private rooms at Great Russell Street, where he enjoys his stay, away from people. Lypiatt, a painter, poet, and musician, is without a sympathetic audience. "I find myself alone, spiritually alone," he complains. Shearwater, the scientist, has no interest in anything or anyone except the study of the regulative function of the kidneys. Mercaptan is a writer whose theme is "the pettiness, the simian limitations, the insignificance and the absurd pretentiousness of *Homo* soi-disant *Sapiens*."

The men and women in *Antic Hay*, each living in his or her private universe, are unable to establish any true and meaningful relationships with one another. Myra Viveash is cold and callous toward men who come to her and offer their love: Gumbril Junior, Lypiatt, Shearwater, and others. She contemptuously lends herself to them. Lypiatt, hopelessly in love with her, finally takes his life. Gumbril, deserted by Myra, feels vengeful; in turn, he is cruelly cynical in his treatment of Mrs. Rosie Shearwater. Because of his carelessness, he loses Emily, who might have brought some happiness and meaning into his life. Engaged in his scientific research, Shearwater completely ignores his wife, with the result that she gives herself to other men. These men and women can easily find sexual partners, but that does not close the distances between them: They remain as distant as ever.

On the eve of Gumbril's intended departure from London for the Continent, Gumbril and Myra ride in a taxi the entire length and breadth of the West End to meet friends and invite them to a dinner that night. Their friends are, significantly enough, engaged in one way or another and shut up in their rooms—Lypiatt writing his life for Myra, Coleman sleeping with Rosie, and Shearwater cycling in a hot box in his laboratory. Despite the lovely moon above on the summer night and the poignant sorrow in their hearts, Gumbril and Myra make no attempt to take advantage of their last ride together and come closer. Instead, they travel aimlessly from place to place.

Those Barren Leaves

Huxley's next novel, *Those Barren Leaves*, shows how people who might be expected to be more enlightened are as self-centered as the mass of humanity. The setting of the novel, which deals with a circle of British intellectuals in Italy, immediately and powerfully reinforces the fact of the characters' social isolation.

Mrs. Lilian Aldwinkle, a patroness of the arts and a votary of love, wants to believe that the whole world revolves around her. As usual, she is possessive of her guests, who have assembled at her newly bought palace of Cybo Malaspina in the village of Vezza in Italy, and she wants them to do as she commands. She is unable, however, to hold them completely under her control. In spite of all her efforts, she fails to win the love of Calamy, and later of Francis Chelifer; Chelifer remains unmoved even when she goes down on her knees and begs for his love. She sinks into real despair when her niece escapes her smothering possessiveness and falls in love with Lord Hovenden. Well past her youth, Mrs. Aldwinkle finds herself left alone with nobody to blame but herself for her plight.

Miss Mary Thriplow and Francis Chelifer are both egocentric writers who are cut off from the world of real human beings. Miss Thriplow is obsessed with her suffering and pain, which are mostly self-induced. Her mind is constantly busy, spinning stories on gossamer passions she experiences while moving, talking, and loving. Conscious of the unreality of the life of upper-class society, Chelifer gives up poetry and also the opportunity of receiving a fellowship at Oxford in favor of a job as editor of *The Rabbit Fanciers' Gazette* in London. The squalor, the repulsiveness, and the stupidity of modern life constitute, in Chelifer's opinion, reality. Because it is the artist's duty to live amid reality, he lives among an assorted group of eccentrics in a boardinghouse in Gog's court, which he describes as "the navel of reality." If Miss Thriplow is lost in her world of imagination and art, Chelifer is lost in "the navel of reality"—equidistant from the heart of reality.

Through the character of Calamy, Huxley suggests a way to overcome the perverse modern world. Rich, handsome, and hedonistic, Calamy was once a part of that world, but he no longer enjoys running after women, wasting his time in futile intercourse, and pursuing pleasure. Rather, he spends his time reading, satisfying his curiosity about things, and thinking. He withdraws to a mountain retreat, hoping that his meditation will ultimately lead him into the mysteries of existence, the relationship between human beings, and that between humanity and the external world.

Calamy's withdrawal to a mountain retreat is, no doubt, an unsatisfactory solution, particularly in view of the problem of egocentricity and isolation of the individual from society raised in *Those Barren Leaves* and Huxley's two preceding novels. It may be noted, however, that Calamy's isolation is not a result of his egocentricity: He recognizes that there are spheres of reality beyond the self.

Point Counter Point

Many critics regard *Point Counter Point*, Huxley's first mature novel, as his masterpiece, a major work of twentieth century fiction. By introducing similar characters facing different situations and different characters facing a similar situation, a technique analogous to the musical device of counterpoint, Huxley presents a comprehensive and penetrating picture of the sordidness of contemporary society.

Mark Rampion, a character modeled on D. H. Lawrence, sees the problem of modern man as one of lopsided development. Instead of achieving a harmonious development of all human faculties—reason, intellect, emotion, instinct, and body—modern man allows one faculty to develop at the expense of the others. "It's time," Rampion says, "there was a revolt in favor of life and wholeness."

Huxley makes a penetrating analysis of the failure of his characters to achieve love and understanding. Particularly acute is his analysis of Philip Quarles, a critical self-portrait of the author. Since a childhood accident that left him slightly lame in one leg, Philip has shunned society and has developed a reflective and intellectual temperament. As a result of his constant preoccupation with ideas, the emotional side of his character atrophies, and he is unable to love even his wife with any degree of warmth. In the ordinary daily world of human contacts, he is curiously like a foreigner, not at home with his fellows, finding it difficult or impossible to enter into communication with any but those who can speak his native intellectual language of ideas. He knows his weakness, and he tries unsuccessfully to transform a detached intellectual skepticism into a way of harmonious living. It is no wonder that his wife, Lilian, feels exasperated with his coldness and unresponsiveness and feels that she could as well love a bookcase.

Philip, however, is not as hopeless a case of lopsided development as are the rest of the characters who crowd the world of *Point Counter Point*. Lord Edward Tantamount, a forty-year-old scientist, is in all but intellect a child. He is engaged in research involving the transplantation of the tail of a newt onto the stump of its amputated foreleg to find out if the tail will grow into a leg or continue incongruously to grow as a tail. He shuts himself up in his laboratory most of the day and a good part of the night, avoiding all human contact. Lady Edward, his wife, and Lucy Tantamount, his daughter, live for sexual excitement. Spandril, who prides himself on being a sensualist, actually hates women. Suffering from a sense of betrayal by his mother when she remarries, he attracts women only to torture them. Burlap wears a mask of spirituality, but he is a materialist to the core. Molly, pretty and plump, makes herself desirable to men but lacks genuine emotional interest. The novel contains an assortment of barbarians (to use the language of Rampion) of the intellect, of the body, and of the spirit, suffering from "Newton's disease," "Henry Ford's disease," "Jesus' disease," and so on—various forms of imbalance in which one human faculty is emphasized at the expense of the others.

Point Counter Point presents an extremely divided world. None of the numerous marriages, except that of the Rampions, turns out well, nor do the extramarital relationships. Both Lilian Quarles and her brother, Walter Bidlake, have problems with their spouses. Lilian plans to leave her husband, Philip, and go to Everard Webley, a political leader, who has been courting her, but the plan is terminated with Webley's murder. After leaving his wife, Walter lives with Marjorie Carling, but within two years he finds her dull and unexciting. Ignoring Marjorie, who is pregnant with his child, Walter begins to court Lucy Tantamount, a professional siren, who, after keeping him for a long time in a state of uncertainty, turns him away. John Bidlake, the father of Lilian and Walter, has been married three times and has had a number of love affairs. Sidney Quarles, the father of Philip, has had many secret affairs. Disharmony thus marks the marital world presented in the novel, effectively dramatized by means of parallel, contrapuntal plots.

Mark and Mary Rampion serve as a counterpoint to the gallery of barbarians and lopsided characters in the novel. Although Mary comes from an aristocratic family and Mark belongs to the working class, they do not suffer from the usual class prejudices. Transcending their origins, they have also transcended the common run of egocentric and self-divided personalities. They have achieved wholeness and integrity in personality and outlook. There is no dichotomy between what they say and what they do. Mark's art is a product of lived experience, and his concern for it is inseparable from his concern for life.

Though the dominant mood of Huxley's early novels is one of negativism and despair, the Rampions exemplify the author's faith in the possibility of achieving individual wholeness and loving human relationships. The Rampions may not be able to change the state of affairs in the modern world, but their presence itself is inspiring; what is more, they are, unlike Calamy of *Those Barren Leaves*, easily accessible to all those who want to meet them.

BRAVE NEW WORLD

Brave New World, Huxley's best-known work, describes a centrally administered and scientifically controlled future society in A.F. 632 (A.F. standing for After Ford), around six hundred years after the twentieth century. It is difficult to recognize the people of Huxley's future World State as human beings. Decanted from test tubes in laboratories, the population of the "brave new world" comes in five standardized varieties: Alphas, Betas, Gammas, Deltas, and Epsilons. The members of each group are genetically conditioned to carry out particular tasks. By various methods of psychological conditioning, they are trained to live in total identification with society and to shun all activities that threaten the stability of the community. The State takes full care of them, including the emotional side of their life. All their desires are satisfied; they do not want what they cannot get. With substitutes and surrogates such as the Pregnancy Substitute and the Violent Passion Surrogate, life is made happy and comfortable for everyone. Although people have nothing of which to complain, they seem to suffer pain continually. Relief from pain is, however, readily available to them in the drug *soma*, which is distributed by the State every day.

Sentiments, ideas, and practices that liberate the human spirit find no place in Huxley's scientific utopia and are, in fact, put down as harmful to the stability of the community. Parentage, family, and home become obsolete. Sex is denuded of all its mystery and significance: Small children are encouraged to indulge in erotic play so that they learn to take a strictly matter-of-fact view of sex, and men and women indulge in copulation to fill idle hours. Loyalty in sex and love is regarded as abnormal behavior. Love of nature and the desire for solitude and meditation are looked upon as serious maladies requiring urgent medical attention. Art, science, and religion are all considered threatening. Patience, courage, self-denial, beauty, nobility, and truth become irrelevant to a society that believes in consumerism, comfort, and happiness.

Huxley shows how some people in the "brave new world," despite every care taken by the State to ensure their place in the social order, do not fall into line. Bernard Marx yearns for Lenina Crowne and wants to take her on long walks in lonely places. Helmholtz Watson's creative impulses demand poetic expression. Even Mustapha Mond, the Resident Controller of Western Europe, is somewhat regretful over his abandonment of scientific research in favor of his present position. People who stubbornly refuse to conform to the social order are removed promptly by the State to an island, where they can live freely according to their wishes.

It is through the character of John, the Savage, from the Reservation that Huxley clearly exposes the vulgarity and horror of the brave new world. Attracted to civilization on seeing Lenina, the Savage soon comes to recoil from it. In a long conversation with Mustapha Mond, the Savage expresses his preference for the natural world of disease, unhappiness, and death over the mechanical world of swarming indistinguishable sameness. Unable to get out of it, he retires to a lonely place where he undertakes his purification by taking mustard and warm water, doing hard labor, and resorting to self-flagellation.

In *Brave New World*, Huxley presents a world in which wholeness becomes an object of a hopeless quest.

Later, looking back at the novel, he observed that this is the most serious defect in the story. In a foreword written in 1946, he said that if he were to rewrite the book, he would offer the Savage a third alternative: Between the utopian and the primitive horns of his dilemma would lie the possibility of sanity—a possibility already actualized, to some extent, in a community of exiles and refugees from the brave new world living within the borders of the Reservation.

Eyeless in Gaza

In *Eyeless in Gaza*, Huxley returns to the subject of egocentric modern man deeply buried in intellectual preoccupations, sensuality, ideology, and fanaticism. Sensualists abound in *Eyeless in Gaza*. The most notorious among them are Mrs. Mary Amberley and her daughter, Helen Ledwidge, both mistresses at different times to Anthony Beavis, the central character in the novel. Believing in "sharp, short, and exciting" affairs, Mary keeps changing lovers until she is prematurely old, spent, and poor. When nobody wants to have her anymore, she takes to morphine to forget her misery. Helen marries Hugh Ledwidge but soon realizes that he is incapable of taking an interest in anything except his books. To compensate for her unhappy married life, she goes from man to man in search of emotional satisfaction. Indeed, sensuality marks the lives of most of the members of the upper-class society presented in the novel.

In addition to sensualists, various other types of single-minded characters share the world of *Eyeless in Gaza*. Brian, one of Anthony's classmates and friends, suffers from a maniacal concern for chastity, and his mother shows a great possessiveness toward him. Mark, another of Anthony's classmates, becomes a cynical revolutionary. John Beavis, Anthony's father, makes philology the sole interest of his life. There are also Communists, Fascists, Fabians, and other fanatics, all fighting for their different causes.

Anthony Beavis is estranged early in his life from men and society after the death of his mother. He grows into manhood cold and indifferent to people. He finds it a disagreeable and laborious task to establish contacts; even with his own father, he maintains a distance. He does not give himself away to his friends or to the women he loves. *Elements of Sociology*, a book Beavis is engaged in writing, assumes the highest priority in his life, and he is careful to avoid the "non-job," personal relations and emotional entanglements that might interfere with his work's progress. As he matures, however, Beavis aspires to achieve a sense of completeness above the self: "I value completeness. I think it's one's duty to develop all one's potentialities—*all* of them." At this stage, he believes in knowledge, acquired by means of intellect rather than by Laurentian intuition. He is interested only in knowing about truth, not experiencing it like a saint: "I'm quite content with only *knowing* about the way of perfection." He thinks that experience is not worth the price, for it costs one's liberty. Gradually, he realizes that knowledge is a means to an end, rather than an end in itself, a means to achieve freedom from the self. After being so enlightened, he feels genuine love for Helen, who remains unmoved, however, because of her past experiences with him. From Dr. Miller, the anthropologist, Beavis learns how to obliterate the self and achieve wholeness through love and selfless service. He has a mystic experience of the unity of all life and becomes a pacifist to serve humankind.

After Many a Summer Dies the Swan

In *After Many a Summer Dies the Swan*, his first novel after his move to California, Huxley satirized the frenzied attempts made by people of the twentieth century to enrich their lives, stressing that the peace that comes with transcendence can bring an enduring joy. Huxley illustrates the vacuity of modern life through the character of Mr. Stoyte, an old California oil magnate living amid every conceivable luxury and comfort. With endless opportunities before him to make more money and enjoy life (he keeps a young mistress of twenty-two), Stoyte wants to live as long as he can. He finances Dr. Obispo's research on longevity in the hope that he will be able to benefit from the results of the doctor's experiments. He acquires the valuable Haubert Papers, relating to the history of an old English family, in order to discover the secret of the long life of the Fifth Earl, and he hires Jeremy Pordage, an English scholar, to arrange the papers. Dr. Obispo and his assistant, Pete, are basically no different from Mr. Stoyte in their outlooks. They believe that they will be rendering a great service to humanity by extending the life span, little realizing that growing up, as they conceive it, is really growing back into the kind of apelike existence represented by the life of the Fifth Earl. Jeremy Pordage has no real interest in anything except literature, and he too betrays a narrowness of outlook.

Propter exemplifies Huxley's dedicated search for more-than-personal consciousness. Retired from his university job, he spends his time helping poor migrant workers, trying to find ways of being self-reliant, and thinking about the timeless good. He argues that nothing good can be achieved at the human level, which is the level of "time and craving," the two aspects of evil. He disapproves most of what goes on in the name of patriotism, idealism, and spiritualism because he thinks that they are marks of humankind's greed and covetousness. One should, in his view, aim for the highest ideal: the liberation from personality, time, and craving into eternity.

Time Must Have a Stop

Bruno Rontini, the mystic saint in *Time Must Have a Stop*, observes that only one out of every ten thousand herrings manages to break out of his carapace completely, and few of those that break out become full-sized fish. He adds that the odds against a human being's spiritual maturation today are even greater. Most people remain, according to him, spiritual children.

Time Must Have a Stop presents the obstacles that Sebastian Barnack has to face before he can reach full spiritual maturation. If egocentricity and single-mindedness are the main hurdles for Philip Quarles and Anthony Beavis, Sebastian's problems are created by his weak personality, shaped by his puritanical and idealistic father. Sebastian possesses fine poetic and intellectual endowments, but he is disappointed with his own immature appearance. Even though he is aware of his superior gifts, he looks "like a child" at seventeen. Naturally, his relatives and friends take an adoptive attitude toward him and try to influence him in different ways. Eustace, his rich and self-indulgent uncle, teaches him how to live and let live and enjoy life. Mrs. Thwale helps him to overcome his shyness in a most outrageous manner. Many others also try to mold Sebastian's destiny and prevent him from achieving true self-realization.

Huxley offers further insights into Propter's mystical faith through the character of Bruno Rontini, under whose guidance Sebastian finally receives enlightenment. Bruno believes that there is only one corner of the universe that one can be certain of improving, and that is one's own self. He says that a person has to begin there, not outside, not on other people, for an individual has to *be* good before he or she can *do* good. Bruno believes that only by taking the fact of eternity into account can one free one's enslaved thoughts: "And it is only by deliberately paying our attention and our primary allegiance to eternity that we can prevent time from turning our lives into a pointless or diabolic foolery." Under the guidance of Bruno, Sebastian becomes aware of a timeless and infinite presence. After his spiritual liberation, he begins to work for world peace. He thinks that one of the indispensable conditions for peace is "a shared theology." He evolves a "Minimum Working Hypothesis" to which all men of all countries and religions can subscribe.

Ape and Essence

Huxley's increasing faith in the possibility of man's liberation in this world did not, at any time, blind him to man's immense capacity for evil. *Ape and Essence* describes how man's apelike instincts bring about the destruction of the world through a nuclear World War III. New Zealand escapes the holocaust, and in 2108 C.E., about one hundred years after the war, the country's Re-Discovery Expedition to North America reaches the coast of Southern California, at a place about twenty miles west of Los Angeles, where Dr. Poole, the Chief Botanist of the party, is taken prisoner by descendants of people who survived the war. Though some Californians have survived the war, the effects of radioactivity still show in the birth of deformed babies, who are liquidated one day of the year in the name of the Purification of the Race. Men and women are allowed free sexual intercourse only two weeks a year following the Purification ceremony so that all the deformed babies that are born in the year are taken care of at one time. Women wear shirts and trousers embroidered with the word "no" on their breasts and seats, and people who indulge in sex during any other part of the year, "Hots" as they are called, are buried alive or castrated and forced to join the priesthood, unless they are able to escape into the community of "Hots" in the north. The California survivors dig up graves to relieve the dead bodies of their clothes and other valuable items, roast bread over fires fueled by books from the Public Library, and worship Belial.

Introducing the film script of *Ape and Essence*, Huxley suggested that present society, even under normal conditions, is not basically different from the society of the survivors depicted in the novel. Gandhi's assassination, he says, had very little impact on most people, who remained preoccupied with their own petty personal problems. Under normal conditions, this unspiritual society would grow into the kind of society represented by Dr. Poole and his team. Dr. Poole is portrayed as a middle-aged child, full of inhibitions and suppressed desires, suffering under the dominance of his puritanical mother.

Ironically, Dr. Poole experiences a sense of wholeness in the satanic postatomic world, as he sheds his inhibitions and finds a free outlet for his suppressed desires during the sexual orgies following the Purification ceremony. Declining the invitation of the Arch Vicar to join his order, Dr. Poole escapes with Loola, the girl who has effected his awakening, into the land of the "Hots." Through the episode of Dr. Poole, Huxley suggests that self-transcendence is possible even in the worst of times.

THE GENIUS AND THE GODDESS

The Genius and the Goddess describes how Rivers, brought up like Dr. Poole of *Apes and Essence* in a puritanical family, undergoes a series of disturbing experiences in the household of Henry and Katy Maartens, which apparently lead him into a spiritual awakening in the end. Rivers joins the Maartens household to assist Henry, the "genius," in his scientific research. He is shocked when Katy, the "goddess," climbs into his bed and shocked again when he sees Katy, rejuvenated by her adultery, performing her wifely devotions with all earnestness, as if nothing had happened. To his further bewilderment and shock, he discovers that he is sought by the daughter as well. The mother outwits the daughter, but Katy and Rivers face the danger of being exposed before Henry. Rivers is, however, saved from disgrace when the mother and daughter both are killed in a car accident. Rivers is an old man as he narrates the story of his progress toward awareness. Though his final awakening is not described, one can safely infer from his attitude toward his past experiences that he has risen above Katy's passion and Henry's intellect to a level outside and above time and has achieved a sense of wholeness. There is, indeed, no way of telling how grace comes.

ISLAND

As previously noted, Huxley creates in almost every novel an island of decency to illustrate the possibility of achieving liberation from bondage to the ego and to time even amid the chaos of modern life. This island is generally represented by an individual or a group of individuals, or it is simply stated to be located in some remote corner of the world. In his last novel, *Island*, Huxley offers a picture of a whole society that has evolved a set of operations, such as yoga, *dhyana* (meditation), *maithuna* (yoga of love), and Zen, to achieve self-transcendence and realize the Vedantic truth, *tat tvam asi*, "thou art That."

On Huxley's island of Pala, the chief concern underlying child care, education, religion, and government is to ensure among the citizens a harmonious development of all human faculties and an achievement of a sense of completeness. To save their children from crippling influences, the parents of Pala bring up one another's children on a basis of mutual exchange. In school, children are taught the important aspects of life from biology to ecology, from sex to religion. They are taken to maternity hospitals so that they can see how children are born; they are even shown how people die. No one subject or area is given exclusive importance. The credo is that "nothing short of everything will really do." When they come of age, boys and girls freely engage in sex. Suppressed feelings and emotions are given an outlet in a vigorous type of dance. An admixture of Hinduism and Buddhism is the religion of the people, but there is no orthodoxy about it. "Karuna," or compassion, and an attention to "here and now," to what is happening at any given moment, are the basic tenets of their way of life. Moksha medicines are freely available to those who want to extend their awareness and get a glimpse of the Clear Light and a knowledge of the Divine Ground. As people know how to live gracefully, they also know how to die gracefully when the time for death comes. The country has followed a benevolent monarchy for one hundred years. The nation is aligned neither with the capitalist countries nor with the communists. It is opposed to industrialization and militarization. It has rich oil resources but has refused to grant licenses to the numerous oil companies that are vying to exploit Pala. Will Farnaby, the journalist who has managed to sneak ashore on the forbidden island, is so greatly impressed by the imaginative and creative Palanese way of life that he abandons the mission for which he went to the island, which was to obtain, by any means possible, a license for the South East-Asia Petroleum Company to drill for oil on the island.

Huxley fully recognizes the extreme vulnerability of the ideal of integrity and wholeness in the modern world. The state of Pala has, for example, incurred the displeasure of both the capitalist and Communist countries through its policy of nonalignment. Many big companies are resorting to bribery in an effort to get a foothold on the island. Colonel Dipa, the military dictator of the neighboring state of Randang-Lobo, has expansionist ambitions. While Pala is thus threatened by the outside world, corruption has also set in from within. Dowager Rani and Murugan, her son, disapprove of the isolationist policies of the island and want their country to march along with the rest of the world. On the day Murugan is sworn king, he invites the army from Randang-Lobo to enter the island and massacre the people who have been opposed to his progressive outlook.

Huxley's novels not only present the horrors of the modern world but also show ways of achieving spiritual liberation and wholeness. Huxley is among the few writers of the twentieth century who fought a brave and relentless battle against life-destroying forces. Untiringly, he sought ways of enriching life by cleansing the doors of perception in his attempt to awaken his readers to the vital spiritual side of their beings.

S. Krishnamoorthy Aithal

Other major works

SHORT FICTION: *Limbo*, 1920; *Mortal Coils*, 1922; *Little Mexican, and Other Stories*, 1924 (also known as *Young Archimedes, and Other Stories*); *Two or Three Graces, and Other Stories*, 1926; *Brief Candles: Stories*, 1930; *The Gioconda Smile*, 1938 (first published in *Mortal Coils*); *Twice Seven: Fourteen Selected Stories*, 1944; *Collected Short Stories*, 1957.

PLAYS: *Happy Families*, pb. 1919; *Permutations Among the Nightingales*, pb. 1920; *Albert, Prince Consort*, pb. 1923; *The Discovery*, pb. 1924; *The World of Light*, pb. 1931; *The Gioconda Smile*, pr., pb. 1948; *Now More Than Ever*, pb. 2000.

POETRY: *The Burning Wheel*, 1916; *Jonah*, 1917; *The Defeat of Youth*, 1918; *Leda*, 1920; *Selected Poems*, 1925; *Arabia Infelix*, 1929; *The Cicadas, and Other Poems*, 1931.

NONFICTION: *On the Margin: Notes and Essays*, 1923; *Along the Road: Notes and Essays of a Tourist*, 1925; *Essays New and Old*, 1926; *Jesting Pilate*, 1926; *Proper Studies*, 1927; *Do What You Will*, 1929; *Holy Face, and Other Essays*, 1929; *Vulgarity in Literature*, 1930; *Music at Night*, 1931; *Texts and Pretexts*, 1932; *Beyond the Mexique Bay*, 1934; *The Olive Tree*, 1936; *Ends and Means*, 1937; *Grey Eminence*, 1941; *The Art of Seeing*, 1942; *The Perennial Philosophy*, 1945; *Themes and Variations*, 1950; *The Devils of Loudun*, 1952; *The Doors of Perception*, 1954; *Heaven and Hell*, 1956; *Tomorrow and Tomorrow and Tomorrow*, 1956 (also known as *Adonis and the Alphabet, and Other Essays*); *Brave New World Revisited*, 1958; *Collected Essays*, 1959; *Literature and Science*, 1963; *Huxley and God: Essays*, 1992 (Jacqueline Hazard Bridgeman, editor); *Between the Wars: Essays and Lectures*, 1994 (David Bradshaw, editor); *The Hidden Huxley: Contempt and Compassion for the Masses, 1920-36*, 1994 (Bradshaw, editor); *Complete Essays*, 2000 (4 volumes); *Selected Letters of Aldous Huxley*, 2007 (James Sexton, editor).

MISCELLANEOUS: *Rotunda: A Selection from the Works of Aldous Huxley*, 1932; *Retrospect: An Omnibus of Aldous Huxley's Books*, 1933; *Stories, Essays, and Poems*, 1937; *The World of Aldous Huxley: An Omnibus of His Fiction and Non-fiction over Three Decades*, 1947.

Bibliography

Baker, Robert S. *The Dark Historic Page: Social Satire and Historicism in the Novels of Aldous Huxley, 1921-1939*. Madison: University of Wisconsin Press, 1982. Interesting study of Huxley's work focuses on the history and satire in *Eyeless in Gaza*, *Brave New World*, and other novels. Includes bibliography and index.

Barfoot, C. C., ed. *Aldous Huxley: Between East and West*. Atlanta: Rodopi, 2001. Collection of essays includes analysis of such topics as the themes of science and modernity in Huxley's interwar novels, utopian themes in his work, his views of nature, and his use of psychedelic drugs and mescaline. Two of the essays examine the novels *Crome Yellow* and *Island*.

Bloom, Harold, ed. *Aldous Huxley's "Brave New World."* Philadelphia: Chelsea House, 2003. Collection of essays by Huxley scholars examines the novel as both utopian and dystopian fiction and discusses its representations of technology, gender, psychology, and the world state.

Brander, Laurence. *Aldous Huxley: A Critical Study*. Lewisburg, Pa.: Bucknell University Press, 1970. One of the few resources available that addresses all of Huxley's major works—the short stories, essays, and travelogues as well as the novels. Includes a bibliography.

Deery, June. *Aldous Huxley and the Mysticism of Science*. New York: St. Martin's Press, 1996. Examines Huxley's attempts to reconcile science and religion, describing his knowledge of science, his use of science in his fiction and nonfiction, and his influence on the New Age movement and other popular philosophies of the late twentieth century.

Holmes, Charles M. *Aldous Huxley and the Way to Reality*. Bloomington: Indiana University Press, 1970. Surveys the autobiographical meanings and development in Huxley's works, focusing on the novels, including *Antic Hay*, *Crome Yellow*, *Brave New World*, and *Ape and Essence*.

Meckier, Jerome, ed. *Critical Essays on Aldous Huxley*. New York: G. K. Hall, 1996. Collection of thoughtful essays on Huxley's oeuvre presents discussion of topics such as Huxley's response to James Joyce, Huxley's *Point Counter Point* and Thomas Mann's *The Magic Mountain* as novels of ideas, and time in Huxley's novels. Includes bibliography and index.

Murray, Nicholas. *Aldous Huxley: A Biography*. New York: St. Martin's Press, 2003. Combination biography and intellectual history presents a wide-ranging survey of Huxley's writing and his social, personal, and political life. Stretches from Huxley's early satirical writing to his peace activism and from his close relations and friendships with Hollywood filmmakers and other intellectuals to his fascination with spirituality and mysticism. Includes illustrations, bibliography, and index.

Nance, Guinevera A. *Aldous Huxley*. New York: Continuum, 1988. Nance's introductory biographical chapter reflects this volume's emphasis on Huxley's "novels of ideas." Divides Huxley's novels, which , with the utopian novels included in the second group. Includes detailed chronology and fairly extensive bibliography.

Woodcock, George. *Dawn and the Darkest Hour: A Study of Aldous Huxley*. 1972. Reprint. Montreal: Black Rose Press, 2007. Biography traces Huxley's development as a writer, viewing his works as the stages of "a spiritual pilgrimage" and arguing that Huxley created a unified oeuvre that attempted to bring "movement out of darkness toward light."